Strategic Brand Management

Building, Measuring, and Managing Brand Equity

Strategic Brand Management

Building, Measuring, and Managing Brand Equity

4e

Kevin Lane Keller
Tuck School of Business
Dartmouth College

PEARSON

Boston Columbus Indianapolis New York San Francisco Upper Saddle River
Amsterdam Cape Town Dubai London Madrid Milan Munich Paris Montreal Toronto
Delhi Mexico City São Paulo Sydney Hong Kong Seoul Singapore Taipei Tokyo

Editor in Chief: Stephanie Wall
Senior Acquisitions Editor: Erin Gardner
Senior Editorial Project Manager: Kierra Bloom
Editorial Assistant: Jacob Garber
Director of Marketing: Maggie Moylan
Executive Marketing Manager: Anne Fahlgren
Senior Managing Editor: Judy Leale
Senior Production Project Manager: Ann Pulido
Senior Operations Supervisor: Arnold Vila
Operation Specialist: Cathleen Petersen
Creative Art Director: Blair Brown

Senior Art Director: Janet Slowik
Interior and Cover Designer: Karen Quigley
Cover Image: George Abe c/o theispot.com
Media Project Manager, Editorial: Denise Vaughn
Media Project Manager, Production: Lisa Rinaldi
Composition/Full-Service Project Management:
   PreMediaGlobal
Printer/Binder: Courier/Kendallville
Cover Printer: Lehigh-Phoenix Color/Hagerstown
Text Font: Times LT Std

Library of Congress Cataloging-in-Publication Data

Keller, Kevin Lane, 1956-
Strategic brand management : building, measuring, and managing brand equity /
   Kevin Lane Keller.—4th ed.
   p. cm.
ISBN 978-0-13-266425-7 (hbk.)
1. Brand name products—Management. I. Title.

HD69.B7K45 2013
658.8'27—dc23

2012024141

10 9 8 7 6 5 4 3   V011

ISBN 10: 0-13-266425-9
ISBN 13: 978-0-13-266425-7

Dedication

This book is dedicated to
my mother and the memory of my father
with much love, respect, and admiration.

Brief Contents

Contents

Prologue: Branding Is Not Rocket Science

Although the challenges in branding can be immense and difficult, branding is not necessarily rocket science. I should know. I am not a rocket scientist—but my dad was. He was a physicist in the Air Force for 20 years, working on various rocket fuels. Always interested in what I did, he once asked what the book was all about. I explained the concept of brand equity and how the book addressed how to build, measure, and manage it. He listened, paused, and remarked, "That's very interesting but, uh, that's not *exactly* rocket science."

He's right. Branding is not rocket science. In fact, it is an art and a science. There's always a creativity and originality component involved with marketing. Even if someone were to follow all the guidelines in this book—and all the guidelines were properly specified—the success or failure of a brand strategy would still depend largely on how, exactly, this strategy would be implemented.

Nevertheless, good marketing is all about improving the odds for success. My hope is that this book adds to the scientific aspect of branding, illuminating the subject and providing guidance to those who make brand-related decisions.

Preface

Let me answer a few questions as to what this book is about, how it's different from other books about branding, what's new with this fourth edition, who should read it, how it's organized, and how you can get the most out of it.

WHAT IS THE BOOK ABOUT?

This book deals with brands—why they are important, what they represent to consumers, and what firms should do to manage them properly. As many business executives correctly recognize, perhaps one of the most valuable assets a firm has are the brands it has invested in and developed over time. Although competitors can often duplicate manufacturing processes and factory designs, it's not so easy to reproduce strongly held beliefs and attitudes established in the minds of consumers. The difficulty and expense of introducing new products, however, puts more pressure than ever on firms to skillfully launch their new products as well as manage their existing brands.

Although brands may represent invaluable intangible assets, creating and nurturing a strong brand poses considerable challenges. Fortunately, the concept of *brand equity*—the main focus of this book—can provide marketers with valuable perspective and a common denominator to interpret the potential effects and trade-offs of various strategies and tactics for their brands. Think of brand equity as the marketing effects uniquely attributable to the brand. In a practical sense, brand equity is the added value a product accrues as a result of past investments in the marketing activity for the brand. It's the bridge between what happened to the brand in the past and what should happen to it in the future.

The chief purpose of this book is to provide a comprehensive and up-to-date treatment of the subjects of brands, brand equity, and *strategic brand management*—the design and implementation of marketing programs and activities to build, measure, and manage brand equity. One of the book's important goals is to provide managers with concepts and techniques to improve the long-term profitability of their brand strategies. We'll incorporate current thinking and developments on these topics from both academics and industry participants, and combine a comprehensive theoretical foundation with enough practical insights to assist managers in their day-to-day and long-term brand decisions. And we'll draw on illustrative examples and case studies of brands marketed in the United States and all over the world.

Specifically, we'll provide insights into how to create profitable brand strategies by building, measuring, and managing brand equity. We address three important questions:

1. How can we create brand equity?
2. How can we measure brand equity?
3. How can we sustain brand equity to expand business opportunities?

Readers will learn:

- The role of brands, the concept of brand equity, and the advantages of creating strong brands
- The three main ways to build brand equity by properly choosing brand elements, designing marketing programs and activities, and leveraging secondary associations
- Different approaches to measuring brand equity, and how to implement a brand equity measurement system
- Alternative branding strategies and how to design a brand architecture strategy and devise brand hierarchies and brand portfolios

- The role of corporate brands, family brands, individual brands, modifiers, and how to combine them into sub-brands
- How to adjust branding strategies over time and across geographic boundaries to maximize brand equity

WHAT'S DIFFERENT ABOUT THIS BOOK?

My objective in writing this book was to satisfy three key criteria by which any marketing text should be judged:

- *Depth:* The material in the book had to be presented in the context of conceptual frameworks that were comprehensive, internally consistent and cohesive, and well grounded in the academic and practitioner literature.
- *Breadth:* The book had to cover all those topics that practicing managers and students of brand management found intriguing and/or important.
- *Relevance:* Finally, the book had to be well grounded in practice and easily related to past and present marketing activities, events, and case studies.

Although a number of excellent books have been written about brands, no book has really maximized those three dimensions to the greatest possible extent. This book sets out to fill that gap by accomplishing three things.

First, we develop our main framework that provides a definition of brand equity, identifies sources and outcomes of brand equity, and provides tactical guidelines about how to build, measure, and manage brand equity. Recognizing the general importance of consumers and customers to marketing—understanding and satisfying their needs and wants—this broad framework approaches branding from the perspective of the consumer; it is called *customer-based brand equity.* We then introduce a number of more specific frameworks to provide more detailed guidance.

Second, besides these broad, fundamentally important branding topics, for completeness, numerous Science of Branding boxes provide in-depth treatment of cutting-edge ideas and concepts, and each chapter contains a Brand Focus appendix that delves into detail on specific, related branding topics, such as brand audits, legal issues, brand crises, and private labels.

Finally, to maximize relevance, numerous in-text examples illuminate the discussion of virtually every topic, and a series of Branding Brief boxes provide more in-depth examinations of selected topics or brands.

Thus, this book can help readers understand the important issues in planning and evaluating brand strategies, as well as providing appropriate concepts, theories, and other tools to make better branding decisions. We identify successful and unsuccessful brand marketers—and why they have been so—to offer readers a greater appreciation of the range of issues in branding, as well as a means to organize their own thoughts about those issues.

WHO SHOULD READ THE BOOK?

A wide range of people can benefit from reading this book:

- Students interested in increasing both their understanding of basic branding principles and their exposure to classic and contemporary branding applications and case studies
- Managers and analysts concerned with the effects of their day-to-day marketing decisions on brand performance
- Senior executives concerned with the longer-term prosperity of their brand franchises and product or service portfolios
- All marketers interested in new ideas with implications for marketing strategies and tactics

The perspective we adopt is relevant to any type of organization (public or private, large or small), and the examples cover a wide range of industries and geographies. To illuminate branding concepts across different settings, we review specific applications to online, industrial, high-tech, service, retailer, and small business in Chapters 1 and 15.

HOW IS THE BOOK ORGANIZED?

The book is divided into six major parts, adhering to the "three-exposure opportunity" approach to learning new material. Part I introduces branding concepts; Parts II, III, IV, and V provide all the specific details of those concepts; and Part VI summarizes and applies the concepts in various contexts. The specific chapters for each part and their contents are as follows.

Part I sets the stage by providing the "big picture" of what strategic brand management is all about and provides a blueprint for the rest of the book. The goal is to provide a sense for the content and context of strategic brand management by identifying key branding decisions and suggesting some of the important considerations for those decisions. Specifically, Chapter 1 introduces some basic notions about brands, and the role they've played and continue to play in marketing strategies. It defines what a brand is, why brands matter, and how anything can be branded, and provides an overview of the strategic brand management process.

Part II addresses the topic of brand equity and introduces three models critical for brand planning. Chapter 2 introduces the concept of customer-based brand equity, outlines the customer-based brand equity framework, and provides detailed guidelines for the critically important topic of brand positioning. Chapter 3 describes the brand resonance and brand value chain models that assist marketers in developing profitable marketing programs for their brand and creating much customer loyalty.

Part III examines the three major ways to build customer-based brand equity, taking a single product–single brand perspective. Chapter 4 addresses the first way to build customer-based brand equity and how to choose brand elements (brand names, logos, symbols, slogans), and the role they play in contributing to brand equity. Chapters 5 and 6 outline the second way to build brand equity and how to optimize the marketing mix to create customer-based brand equity. Chapter 5 covers product, pricing, and distribution strategies; Chapter 6 is devoted to creating integrated marketing communication programs to build brand equity. Although most readers are probably familiar with these "4 P's" of marketing, it's illuminating to consider them from the standpoint of brand equity and the effects of brand knowledge on consumer response to marketing mix activity and vice versa. Finally, Chapter 7 examines the third major way to build brand equity—by leveraging secondary associations from other entities like a company, geographical region, person, or other brand.

Part IV looks at how to measure customer-based brand equity. These chapters take a detailed look at what consumers know about brands, what marketers want them to know, and how marketers can develop measurement procedures to assess how well they're doing. Chapter 8 provides a big-picture perspective of these topics, specifically examining how to develop and implement an efficient and effective brand equity measurement system. Chapter 9 examines approaches to measuring customers' brand knowledge structures, in order to identify and quantify potential sources of brand equity. Chapter 10 looks at measuring potential outcomes of brand equity in terms of the major benefits a firm accrues from these sources of brand equity as well as how to measure the overall value of a brand.

Part V addresses how to manage brand equity, taking a broader, multiple product–multiple brand perspective as well as a longer-term, multiple-market view of brands. Chapter 11 considers issues related to brand architecture strategies—which brand elements a firm chooses to apply across its various products—and how to maximize brand equity across all the different brands and products that a firm might sell. It also describes two important tools to help formulate branding strategies—brand portfolios and the brand hierarchies. Chapter 12 outlines the pros and cons of brand extensions and develops guidelines for introducing and naming new products and brand extensions. Chapter 13 considers how to reinforce, revitalize, and retire brands, examining a number of specific topics in managing brands over time. Chapter 14 examines the implications of differences in consumer behavior and different types of market segments for managing brand equity. We pay particular attention to international issues and global branding strategies.

Finally, Part VI considers some implications and applications of the customer-based brand equity framework. Chapter 15 highlights managerial guidelines and key themes that emerged in earlier chapters of the book. This chapter also summarizes success factors for branding and applies the customer-based brand equity framework to address specific strategic brand management issues for different types of products (online, industrial goods, high-tech products, services, retailers, and small businesses).

REVISION STRATEGY FOR FOURTH EDITION

The overarching goal of the revision of *Strategic Brand Management* was to preserve the aspects of the text that worked well, but to improve it as much as possible by updating and adding new material as needed. We deliberately avoided change for change's sake. Our driving concern was to create the best possible textbook for readers willing to invest their time and energy at mastering the subject of branding.

We retained the customer-based brand equity framework that was the centerpiece of the third edition, and the three dimensions of depth, breadth, and relevance. Given all the academic research progress that has been made in recent years, however, as well as all the new market developments and events, the book required—and got—some important updates.

1. *New and updated Branding Briefs and in-text examples:* Many new Branding Briefs and numerous in-text examples have been added. The goal was to blend classic and contemporary examples, so many still-relevant and illuminating examples remain.

2. *Additional academic references:* As noted, the branding area continues to receive concerted academic research attention. Accordingly, each chapter incorporates new references and sources for additional study.

3. *Tighter chapters:* Chapters have been trimmed and large boxed material carefully screened to provide a snappier, more concise read.

4. *Stronger visuals:* The text includes numerous engaging photos and graphics. These visuals highlight many of the important and interesting concepts and examples from the chapters.

5. *Updated and new original cases:* To provide broader, more relevant coverage, four new cases have been added to the *Best Practices in Branding* casebook—PRODUCT (RED), King Arthur Flour, ESPN X Games, and Target. Each of the 14 other cases has been significantly updated. All of the cases are considerably shorter and tighter. Collectively, these cases provide insights into the thinking and activities of some of the world's best marketers while also highlighting the many challenges they still face.

In terms of content, the book continues to incorporate material to address the changing technological, cultural, global, and economic environment that brands face. Some of the specific new topics reviewed in depth in the fourth edition include:

• Marketing in a recession	• Brand communities
• Luxury branding	• Brand characters
• Brand personas	• Brand makeovers
• Shopper marketing	• Person branding
• Social currency	• Brand potential
• Brand extension scorecard	• Culture and branding
• Brand flashbacks	• Future brand priorities

Some of the many brands and companies receiving greater attention include:

• Converse	• L'Oréal	• X Games
• SNICKERS	• Michelin	• Liz Claiborne
• W Hotels	• MTV	• Gatorade
• HBO	• Macy's	• TOMS
• Tupperware	• Johnnie Walker	• Chobani
• Groupon	• Old Spice	• Kindle
• Blue Moon	• Gannett	• Coldplay
• Netflix	• Subway	• Febreze
• L.L. Bean	• M&M's	• Oreo
• Boloco	• Ford Fiesta	• DHL

Some of the more major chapter changes from the third edition include the following:

- Chapters 2 and 3 have been reorganized and updated to show how the brand positioning, brand resonance, and brand value chain models are linked, providing a comprehensive set of tools to help readers understand how brand equity can be created and tracked.
- Chapter 6 has been reorganized and updated around four major marketing communication options: (1) Advertising and promotion; (2) Interactive marketing; (3) Events and experiences; and (4) Mobile marketing. Guidelines and examples are provided for each of the four options. Special attention is paid to the role of social media.
- Chapters 9 and 10 have been updated to include much new material on industry models of brand equity and financial and valuation perspectives on branding.
- Chapters 11 and 12 have been reorganized and updated to provide an in-depth three-step model of how to develop a brand architecture strategy. As part of these changes, a detailed brand extension scorecard is presented.
- Chapter 14 has been updated to include much new material on developing markets.
- Chapter 15 has been updated to include much new material on future brand priorities.

HOW CAN YOU GET THE MOST OUT OF THE BOOK?

Branding is a fascinating topic that receives much attention in the popular press. The ideas presented in the book will help you interpret current branding developments. One good way to better understand branding and the customer-based brand equity framework is to apply the concepts and ideas presented in the book to current events, or to any of the more detailed branding issues or case studies presented in the Branding Briefs. The Discussion Questions at the end of the chapters often ask you to pick a brand and apply one or more concepts from that chapter. Focusing on one brand across all the questions—perhaps as part of a class project—permits some cumulative and integrated learning and is an excellent way to become more comfortable with and fluent in the material in the book.

This book truly belongs to you, the reader. Like most marketing, branding doesn't offer "right" or "wrong" answers, and you should question things you don't understand or don't believe. The book is designed to facilitate your understanding of strategic brand management and present some "best practice" guidelines. At the end of the day, however, what you get out of it will be what you put into it, and how you blend the ideas contained in these pages with what you already know or believe.

FACULTY RESOURCES

Instructors can access a variety of print, media, and presentation resources through www.pearsonhighered.com/kevinlanekeller.

Acknowledgments

I have been gratified by the acceptance of the first three editions of *Strategic Brand Management*. It has been translated and adapted in numerous languages and countries, adopted by many top universities, and used by scores of marketing executives around the world. The success of the text is in large part due to the help and support of others whom I would like to acknowledge and thank.

The Prentice Hall team on the fourth edition was a huge help in the revision—many thanks to Stephanie Wall, Erin Gardner, Kierra Bloom, Ann Pulido, and Stacy Greene. Elisa Adams superbly edited the text with a very keen and helpful eye. Keri Miksza tracked down permissions and provided an impressive array of ads and photos from which to choose. Katie Dougherty, Duncan Hall, and Alex Tarnoff offered much research assistance and support for the text. Lowey Sichol has joined me as co-author of the *Best Practices in Branding* casebook and has applied her marketing experience and wisdom to craft a set of informative, intriguing cases. John Lin has been a steady long-time contributor about what is happening in the tech world. Alison Pearson provided her usual superb administrative assistance in a number of areas.

I have learned much about branding in my work with industry participants, who have unique perspectives on what is working and not working (and why) in the marketplace. Our discussions have enriched my appreciation for the challenges in building, measuring, and managing brand equity and the factors affecting the success and failure of brand strategies.

I have benefited from the wisdom of my colleagues at the institutions where I have held academic positions: Dartmouth College, Duke University, the University of California at Berkeley, Stanford University, the Australian Graduate School of Management, and the University of North Carolina at Chapel Hill.

Over the years, the doctoral students I advised have helped in my branding pursuits in a variety of useful ways, including Sheri Bridges, Christie Brown, Jennifer Aaker, Meg Campbell, and Sanjay Sood. I have also learned much from my research partners and from the marketing field as a whole that has recognized the importance of branding in their research studies and programs. Their work provides much insight and inspiration.

Finally, special thanks go to my wife, Punam Anand Keller, and two daughters, Carolyn and Allison, for their never-ending patience, understanding, and support.

About the Author

Kevin Lane Keller is the E. B. Osborn Professor of Marketing at the Tuck School of Business at Dartmouth College. Professor Keller has degrees from Cornell, Carnegie-Mellon, and Duke universities. At Dartmouth, he teaches MBA courses on marketing management and strategic brand management and lectures in executive programs on those topics.

Previously, Professor Keller was on the faculty at Stanford University, where he also served as the head of the marketing group. Additionally, he has been on the faculty at the University of California at Berkeley and the University of North Carolina at Chapel Hill, been a visiting professor at Duke University and the Australian Graduate School of Management, and has two years of industry experience as Marketing Consultant for Bank of America.

Professor Keller's general area of expertise lies in marketing strategy and planning, and branding. His specific research interest is in how understanding theories and concepts related to consumer behavior can improve marketing and branding strategies. His research has been published in three of the major marketing journals—the *Journal of Marketing*, the *Journal of Marketing Research*, and the *Journal of Consumer Research*. He also has served on the Editorial Review Boards of those journals. With over 90 published papers, his research has been widely cited and has received numerous awards.

Actively involved with industry, he has worked on a host of different types of marketing projects. He has served as a consultant and advisor to marketers for some of the world's most successful brands, including Accenture, American Express, Disney, Ford, Intel, Levi Strauss, Procter & Gamble, and Samsung. Additional brand consulting activities have been with other top companies such as Allstate, Beiersdorf (Nivea), BlueCross BlueShield, Campbell, Colgate, Eli Lilly, ExxonMobil, General Mills, GfK, Goodyear, Hasbro, Intuit, Johnson & Johnson, Kodak, L.L. Bean, Mayo Clinic, MTV, Nordstrom, Ocean Spray, Red Hat, SAB Miller, Shell Oil, Starbucks, Unilever, and Young & Rubicam. He has also served as an academic trustee for the Marketing Science Institute.

A popular and highly sought-after speaker, he has made speeches and conducted marketing seminars to top executives in a variety of forums. Some of his senior management and marketing training clients include such diverse business organizations as Cisco, Coca-Cola, Deutsche Telekom, GE, Google, IBM, Macy's, Microsoft, Nestle, Novartis, Pepsico, and Wyeth. He has lectured all over the world, from Seoul to Johannesburg, from Sydney to Stockholm, and from Sao Paulo to Mumbai. He has served as keynote speaker at conferences with hundreds to thousands of participants.

Professor Keller is currently conducting a variety of studies that address strategies to build, measure, and manage brand equity. In addition to *Strategic Brand Management*, in its 3rd edition, which has been heralded as the "bible of branding," he is also the co-author with Philip Kotler of the all-time best-selling introductory marketing textbook, *Marketing Management*, now in its 14th edition.

An avid sports, music, and film enthusiast, in his so-called spare time, he has helped to manage and market, as well as serve as executive producer, for one of Australia's great rock and roll treasures, The Church, as well as American power-pop legends Tommy Keene and Dwight Twilley. Additionally, he is the Principal Investor and Marketing Advisor for Second Motion Records. He also serves on the Board of Directors for The Doug Flutie, Jr. Foundation for Autism and the Montshire Museum of Science. Professor Keller lives in Etna, NH with his wife, Punam (also a Tuck marketing professor), and his two daughters, Carolyn and Allison.

Brands and Brand Management

1

Learning Objectives

After reading this chapter, you should be able to

1. Define "brand," state how brand differs from a product, and explain what brand equity is.
2. Summarize why brands are important.
3. Explain how branding applies to virtually everything.
4. Describe the main branding challenges and opportunities.
5. Identify the steps in the strategic brand management process.

A brand can be a person, place, firm, or organization

Sources: Pictorial Press Ltd / Alamy; Damian P. Gadal/Alamy; somchaij/Shutterstock; Jason Lindsey/Alamy

Preview

Ever more firms and other organizations have come to the realization that one of their most valuable assets is the brand names associated with their products or services. In our increasingly complex world, all of us, as individuals and as business managers, face more choices with less time to make them. Thus a strong brand's ability to simplify decision making, reduce risk, and set expectations is invaluable. Creating strong brands that deliver on that promise, and maintaining and enhancing the strength of those brands over time, is a management imperative.

This text will help you reach a deeper understanding of how to achieve those branding goals. Its basic objectives are

1. To explore the important issues in planning, implementing, and evaluating brand strategies.
2. To provide appropriate concepts, theories, models, and other tools to make better branding decisions.

We place particular emphasis on understanding psychological principles at the individual or organizational level in order to make better decisions about brands. Our objective is to be relevant for any type of organization regardless of its size, nature of business, or profit orientation.[1]

With these goals in mind, this first chapter defines what a brand is. We consider the functions of a brand from the perspective of both consumers and firms and discuss why brands are important to both. We look at what can and cannot be branded and identify some strong brands. The chapter concludes with an introduction to the concept of brand equity and the strategic brand management process. Brand Focus 1.0 at the end of the chapter traces some of the historical origins of branding.

WHAT IS A BRAND?

Branding has been around for centuries as a means to distinguish the goods of one producer from those of another. In fact, the word *brand* is derived from the Old Norse word *brandr,* which means "to burn," as brands were and still are the means by which owners of livestock mark their animals to identify them.[2]

According to the American Marketing Association (AMA), a **brand** is a "name, term, sign, symbol, or design, or a combination of them, intended to identify the goods and services of one seller or group of sellers and to differentiate them from those of competition." Technically speaking, then, whenever a marketer creates a new name, logo, or symbol for a new product, he or she has created a brand.

In fact, however, many practicing managers refer to a brand as more than that—as something that has actually created a certain amount of awareness, reputation, prominence, and so on in the marketplace. Thus we can make a distinction between the AMA definition of a "brand" with a small *b* and the industry's concept of a "Brand" with a big *B*. The difference is important for us because disagreements about branding principles or guidelines often revolve around what we mean by the term.

Brand Elements

Thus, the key to creating a brand, according to the AMA definition, is to be able to choose a name, logo, symbol, package design, or other characteristic that identifies a product and distinguishes it from others. These different components of a brand that identify and differentiate it are **brand elements.** We'll see in Chapter 4 that brand elements come in many different forms.

For example, consider the variety of brand name strategies. Some companies, like General Electric and Samsung, use their names for essentially all their products. Other manufacturers assign new products individual brand names that are unrelated to the company name, like Procter & Gamble's Tide, Pampers, and Pantene product brands. Retailers create their own brands based on their store name or some other means; for example, Macy's has its own Alfani, INC, Charter Club, and Club Room brands.

Brand names themselves come in many different forms.[3] There are brand names based on people's names, like Estée Lauder cosmetics, Porsche automobiles, and Orville Reden-bacher popcorn; names based on places, like Sante Fe cologne, Chevrolet Tahoe SUV, and

British Airways; and names based on animals or birds, like Mustang automobiles, Dove soap, and Greyhound buses. In the category of "other," we find Apple computers, Shell gasoline, and Carnation evaporated milk.

Some brand names use words with inherent product meaning, like Lean Cuisine, Ocean Spray 100% Juice Blends, and Ticketron, or suggesting important attributes or benefits, like DieHard auto batteries, Mop & Glo floor cleaner, and Beautyrest mattresses. Other names are made up and include prefixes and suffixes that sound scientific, natural, or prestigious, like Lexus automobiles, Pentium microprocessors, and Visteon auto supplies.

Not just names but other brand elements like logos and symbols also can be based on people, places, things, and abstract images. In creating a brand, marketers have many choices about the number and nature of the brand elements they use to identify their products.

Brands versus Products

How do we contrast a brand and a product? A *product* is anything we can offer to a market for attention, acquisition, use, or consumption that might satisfy a need or want. Thus, a product may be a physical good like a cereal, tennis racquet, or automobile; a service such as an airline, bank, or insurance company; a retail outlet like a department store, specialty store, or supermarket; a person such as a political figure, entertainer, or professional athlete; an organization like a nonprofit, trade organization, or arts group; a place including a city, state, or country; or even an idea like a political or social cause. This very broad definition of product is the one we adopt in the book. We'll discuss the role of brands in some of these different categories in more detail later in this chapter and in Chapter 15.

We can define five levels of meaning for a product:[4]

1. The *core benefit level* is the fundamental need or want that consumers satisfy by consuming the product or service.
2. The *generic product level* is a basic version of the product containing only those attributes or characteristics absolutely necessary for its functioning but with no distinguishing features. This is basically a stripped-down, no-frills version of the product that adequately performs the product function.
3. The *expected product level* is a set of attributes or characteristics that buyers normally expect and agree to when they purchase a product.
4. The *augmented product level* includes additional product attributes, benefits, or related services that distinguish the product from competitors.
5. The *potential product level* includes all the augmentations and transformations that a product might ultimately undergo in the future.

Figure 1-1 illustrates these different levels in the context of an air conditioner. In many markets most competition takes place at the product augmentation level, because most firms can successfully build satisfactory products at the expected product level. Harvard's Ted Levitt argued that "the new competition is not between what companies produce in their factories but between what they add to their factory output in the form of packaging, services, advertising, customer advice, financing, delivery arrangements, warehousing, and other things that people value."[5]

A brand is therefore more than a product, because it can have dimensions that differentiate it in some way from other products designed to satisfy the same need. These differences may be rational and tangible—related to product performance of the brand—or more symbolic, emotional, and intangible—related to what the brand represents.

Extending our previous example, a branded product may be a physical good like Kellogg's Corn Flakes cereal, Prince tennis racquets, or Ford Mustang automobiles; a service such as Delta Airlines, Bank of America, or Allstate insurance; a store like Bloomingdale's department store, Body Shop specialty store, or Safeway supermarket; a person such as Warren Buffett, Mariah Carey, or George Clooney; a place like the city of London, state of California, or country of Australia; an organization such as the Red Cross, American Automobile Association, or the Rolling Stones; or an idea like corporate responsibility, free trade, or freedom of speech.

Some brands create competitive advantages with product performance. For example, brands such as Gillette, Merck, and others have been leaders in their product categories for decades, due, in part, to continual innovation. Steady investments in research and development have produced leading-edge products, and sophisticated mass marketing practices have ensured rapid adoption of new technologies in the consumer market. A number of media organizations rank firms on their ability to innovate. Figure 1-2 lists 10 innovative companies that showed up on many of those lists in 2011.

Other brands create competitive advantages through non-product-related means. For example, Coca-Cola, Chanel No. 5, and others have been leaders in their product categories for decades by understanding consumer motivations and desires and creating relevant and appealing images surrounding their products. Often these intangible image associations may be the only way to distinguish different brands in a product category.

Brands, especially strong ones, carry a number of different types of associations, and marketers must account for all of them in making marketing decisions. The marketers behind some brands have learned this lesson the hard way. Branding Brief 1-1 describes the problems

BRANDING BRIEF 1-1

Coca-Cola's Branding Lesson

One of the classic marketing mistakes occurred in April 1985 when Coca-Cola replaced its flagship cola brand with a new formula. The motivation behind the change was primarily a competitive one. Pepsi-Cola's "Pepsi Challenge" promotion had posed a strong challenge to Coke's supremacy over the cola market. Starting initially just in Texas, the promotion involved advertising and in-store sampling showcasing consumer blind taste tests between Coca-Cola and Pepsi-Cola. Invariably, Pepsi won these tests. Fearful that the promotion, if expanded nationally, could take a big bite out of Coca-Cola's sales, especially among younger cola drinkers, Coca-Cola felt compelled to act.

Coca-Cola's strategy was to change the formulation of Coke to more closely match the slightly sweeter taste of Pepsi. To arrive at a new formulation, Coke conducted taste tests with an astounding number of consumers—190,000! The findings from this research clearly indicated that consumers "overwhelmingly" preferred the taste of the new formulation to the old one. Brimming with confidence, Coca-Cola announced the formulation change with much fanfare.

Consumer reaction was swift but, unfortunately for Coca-Cola, negative. In Seattle, retired real estate investor Gay Mullins founded the "Old Cola Drinkers of America" and set up a hotline for angry consumers. A Beverly Hills wine merchant bought 500 cases of "Vintage Coke" and sold them at a premium. Meanwhile, back at Coca-Cola headquarters, roughly 1,500 calls a day and literally truckloads of mail poured in, virtually all condemning the company's actions. Finally, after several months of slumping sales, Coca-Cola announced that the old formulation would return as "Coca-Cola Classic" and join "New" Coke in the marketplace (see the accompanying photo).

The New Coke debacle taught Coca-Cola a very important, albeit painful and public, lesson about its brand. Coke clearly is not just seen as a beverage or thirst-quenching refreshment by consumers. Rather, it seems to be viewed as more of an American icon, and much of its appeal lies not only in its ingredients but also in what it represents in terms of Americana, nostalgia, and its heritage and relationship with consumers. Coke's brand image certainly has emotional components, and consumers have a great deal of strong feelings for the brand.

The epic failure of New Coke taught Coca-Cola a valuable lesson about branding.

Source: Al Freni/Time & Life Pictures/Getty Images

Although Coca-Cola made a number of other mistakes in introducing New Coke (both its advertising and its packaging probably failed to clearly differentiate the brand and communicate its sweeter quality), its biggest slip was losing sight of what the brand meant to consumers in its totality. The *psychological* response to a brand can be as important as the *physiological* response to the product. At the same time, American consumers also learned a lesson—just how much the Coke brand really meant to them. As a result of Coke's marketing fiasco, it is doubtful that either side will take the other for granted from now on.

Sources: Patricia Winters, "For New Coke, 'What Price Success?'" *Advertising Age*, 20 March 1989, S1–S2; Jeremiah McWilliams, "Twenty-Five Years Since Coca-Cola's Big Blunder," *Atlanta Business News*, 26 April 2010; Abbey Klaassen, "New Coke: One of Marketing's Biggest Blunders Turns 25," 23 April 2010, www.adage.com.

Coca-Cola encountered in the introduction of "New Coke" when it failed to account for all the different aspects of the Coca-Cola brand image.

Not only are there many different types of associations to link to the brand, but there are many different means to create them—the entire marketing program can contribute to consumers' understanding of the brand and how they value it as well as other factors outside the control of the marketer.

By creating perceived differences among products through branding and by developing a loyal consumer franchise, marketers create value that can translate to financial profits for the firm. The reality is that the most valuable assets many firms have may not be tangible ones, such as plants, equipment, and real estate, but *intangible* assets such as management skills, marketing, financial and operations expertise, and, most important, the brands themselves. This value was recognized

Level	Air Conditioner
1. Core Benefit	Cooling and comfort.
2. Generic Product	Sufficient cooling capacity (Btu per hour), an acceptable energy efficiency rating, adequate air intakes and exhausts, and so on.
3. Expected Product	*Consumer Reports* states that for a typical large air conditioner, consumers should expect at least two cooling speeds, expandable plastic side panels, adjustable louvers, removable air filter, vent for exhausting air, environmentally friendly R-410A refrigerant, power cord at least 60 inches long, one year parts-and-labor warranty on the entire unit, and a five-year parts-and-labor warranty on the refrigeration system.
4. Augmented Product	Optional features might include electric touch-pad controls, a display to show indoor and outdoor temperatures and the thermostat setting, an automatic mode to adjust fan speed based on the thermostat setting and room temperature, a toll-free 800 number for customer service, and so on.
5. Potential Product	Silently running, completely balanced throughout the room, and completely energy self-sufficient.

FIGURE 1-1
Examples of Different Product Levels

1. Apple
2. Amazon
3. Facebook
4. General Electric
5. Google
6. Groupon
7. Intel
8. Microsoft
9. Twitter
10. Zynga

FIGURE 1-2
Ten Firms Rated Highly on Innovation

Sources: Based on "The 50 Most Innovative Companies," *Bloomberg BusinessWeek,* 25 April 2010; "The World's Most Innovative Companies," *Forbes,* 4 March 2011; "The World's 50 Most Innovative Companies," *Fast Company,* March 2011; "The 50 Most Innovative Companies 2011," *Technology Review,* March 2011.

by John Stuart, CEO of Quaker Oats from 1922 to 1956, who famously said, "If this company were to split up I would give you the property, plant and equipment and I would take the brands and the trademarks and I would fare better than you."[6] Let's see why brands are so valuable.

WHY DO BRANDS MATTER?

An obvious question is, why are brands important? What functions do they perform that make them so valuable to marketers? We can take a couple of perspectives to uncover the value of brands to both customers and firms themselves. Figure 1-3 provides an overview of the different roles that brands play for these two parties. We'll talk about consumers first.

Consumers

As with the term *product*, this book uses the term **consumer** broadly to encompass all types of customers, including individuals as well as organizations. To consumers, brands provide important functions. Brands identify the source or maker of a product and allow consumers to assign responsibility to a particular manufacturer or distributor. Most important, brands take on special meaning to consumers. Because of past experiences with the product and its marketing program over the years, consumers find out which brands satisfy their needs and which ones do not. As a result, brands provide a shorthand device or means of simplification for their product decisions.[7]

If consumers recognize a brand and have some knowledge about it, then they do not have to engage in a lot of additional thought or processing of information to make a product decision. Thus, from an economic perspective, brands allow consumers to lower the search costs for products both internally (in terms of how much they have to think) and externally (in terms of how much they have to look around). Based on what they already know about the brand—its quality, product characteristics, and so forth—consumers can make assumptions and form reasonable expectations about what they may *not* know about the brand.

The meaning imbued in brands can be quite profound, allowing us to think of the relationship between a brand and the consumer as a type of bond or pact. Consumers offer their trust and loyalty with the implicit understanding that the brand will behave in certain ways and provide them utility through consistent product performance and appropriate pricing, promotion, and distribution programs and actions. To the extent that consumers realize advantages and benefits from purchasing the brand, and as long as they derive satisfaction from product consumption, they are likely to continue to buy it.

These benefits may not be purely functional in nature. Brands can serve as symbolic devices, allowing consumers to project their self-image. Certain brands are associated with certain types of people and thus reflect different values or traits. Consuming such products is a means by which consumers can communicate to others—or even to themselves—the type of person they are or would like to be.[8]

Some branding experts believe that for some people, certain brands even play a religious role of sorts and substitute for religious practices and help reinforce self-worth.[9] The cultural influence of brands is profound and much interest has been generated in recent years in understanding the interplay between consumer culture and brands.[10]

Consumers
Identification of source of product
Assignment of responsibility to product maker
Risk reducer
Search cost reducer
Promise, bond, or pact with maker of product
Symbolic device
Signal of quality

Manufacturers
Means of identification to simplify handling or tracing
Means of legally protecting unique features
Signal of quality level to satisfied customers
Means of endowing products with unique associations
Source of competitive advantage
Source of financial returns

FIGURE 1-3

Roles That Brands Play

Brands can also play a significant role in signaling certain product characteristics to consumers. Researchers have classified products and their associated attributes or benefits into three major categories: search goods, experience goods, and credence goods.[11]

- For *search goods* like grocery produce, consumers can evaluate product attributes like sturdiness, size, color, style, design, weight, and ingredient composition by visual inspection.
- For *experience goods* like automobile tires, consumers cannot assess product attributes like durability, service quality, safety, and ease of handling or use so easily by inspection, and actual product trial and experience is necessary.
- For *credence goods* like insurance coverage, consumers may rarely learn product attributes.

Given the difficulty of assessing and interpreting product attributes and benefits for experience and credence goods, brands may be particularly important signals of quality and other characteristics to consumers for these types of products.[12]

Brands can reduce the risks in product decisions. Consumers may perceive many different types of risks in buying and consuming a product:[13]

- *Functional risk:* The product does not perform up to expectations.
- *Physical risk:* The product poses a threat to the physical well-being or health of the user or others.
- *Financial risk:* The product is not worth the price paid.
- *Social risk:* The product results in embarrassment from others.
- *Psychological risk:* The product affects the mental well-being of the user.
- *Time risk:* The failure of the product results in an opportunity cost of finding another satisfactory product.

Consumers can certainly handle these risks in a number of ways, but one way is obviously to buy well-known brands, especially those with which consumers have had favorable past experiences. Thus, brands can be a very important risk-handling device, especially in business-to-business settings where risks can sometimes have quite profound implications.

In summary, to consumers, the special meaning that brands take on can change their perceptions and experiences with a product. The identical product may be evaluated differently depending on the brand identification or attribution it carries. Brands take on unique, personal meanings to consumers that facilitate their day-to-day activities and enrich their lives. As consumers' lives become more complicated, rushed, and time starved, the ability of a brand to simplify decision making and reduce risk is invaluable.

Firms

Brands also provide a number of valuable functions to their firms.[14] Fundamentally, they serve an identification purpose, to simplify product handling or tracing. Operationally, brands help organize inventory and accounting records. A brand also offers the firm legal protection for unique features or aspects of the product. A brand can retain intellectual property rights, giving legal title to the brand owner.[15] The brand name can be protected through registered trademarks; manufacturing processes can be protected through patents; and packaging can be protected through copyrights and designs. These intellectual property rights ensure that the firm can safely invest in the brand and reap the benefits of a valuable asset.

We've seen that these investments in the brand can endow a product with unique associations and meanings that differentiate it from other products. Brands can signal a certain level of quality so that satisfied buyers can easily choose the product again.[16] This brand loyalty provides predictability and security of demand for the firm and creates barriers of entry that make it difficult for other firms to enter the market.

Although manufacturing processes and product designs may be easily duplicated, lasting impressions in the minds of individuals and organizations from years of marketing activity and product experience may not be so easily reproduced. One advantage that brands such as Colgate toothpaste, Cheerios cereal, and Levi's jeans have is that consumers have literally grown up with them. In this sense, branding can be seen as a powerful means to secure a competitive advantage.

In short, to firms, brands represent enormously valuable pieces of legal property, capable of influencing consumer behavior, being bought and sold, and providing the security of sustained future revenues.[17] For these reasons, huge sums, often representing large multiples of a brand's earnings, have been paid for brands in mergers or acquisitions, starting with the boom years of

Brand	Brand Value ($MM)	Market Cap ($MM)	% of Market Cap
Coca-Cola	70,452	146,730	48%
IBM	64,727	200,290	32%
Microsoft	60,895	226,530	27%
Google	43,557	199,690	22%
General Electric	42,808	228,250	19%
McDonald's	33,578	80,450	42%
Intel	32,015	119,130	27%
Nokia	29,495	33,640	88%
Disney	28,731	81,590	35%
Hewlett-Packard	26,867	105,120	26%

FIGURE 1-4

Brand Value as a Percentage of Market Capitalization (2010)

Sources: Based on Interbrand. "Best Global Brands 2010." Yahoo! Finance, February, 2011.

the mid-1980s. The merger and acquisition frenzy during this time led Wall Street financiers to seek out undervalued companies from which to make investment or takeover profits. One of the primary undervalued assets of such firms was their brands, given that they were off-balance-sheet items. Implicit in Wall Street's interest was a belief that strong brands result in better earnings and profit performance for firms, which, in turn, creates greater value for shareholders.

The price premium paid for many companies is clearly justified by the opportunity to earn and sustain extra profits from their brands, as well as by the tremendous difficulty and expense of creating similar brands from scratch. For a typical fast-moving consumer goods company, net tangible assets may be as little as 10 percent of the total value (see Figure 1-4). Most of the value lies in intangible assets and goodwill, and as much as 70 percent of intangible assets can be supplied by brands.

CAN ANYTHING BE BRANDED?

Brands clearly provide important benefits to both consumers and firms. An obvious question, then, is, how are brands created? How do you "brand" a product? Although firms provide the impetus for brand creation through their marketing programs and other activities, ultimately *a brand is something that resides in the minds of consumers*. A brand is a perceptual entity rooted in reality, but it is more than that—it reflects the perceptions and perhaps even the idiosyncrasies of consumers.

To brand a product it is necessary to teach consumers "who" the product is—by giving it a name and using other brand elements to help identify it—as well as what the product does and why consumers should care. In other words, marketers must give consumers a *label* for the product ("here's how you can identify the product") and provide *meaning* for the brand ("here's what this particular product can do for you, and why it's special and different from other brand name products").

Branding creates mental structures and helps consumers organize their knowledge about products and services in a way that clarifies their decision making and, in the process, provides value to the firm. *The key to branding is that consumers perceive differences among brands in a product category*. These differences can be related to attributes or benefits of the product or service itself, or they may be related to more intangible image considerations.

Whenever and wherever consumers are deciding between alternatives, brands can play an important decision-making role. *Accordingly, marketers can benefit from branding whenever consumers are in a choice situation*. Given the myriad choices consumers make each and every day—commercial and otherwise—it is no surprise how pervasive branding has become. Consider these two very diverse applications of branding:[18]

1. Bonnaroo Music and Arts Festival (Bonnaroo means "good times" in Creole), a 100-band jamboree with an eclectic mix of A-list musical stars, has been the top-grossing music

Bonnaroo Music and Arts Festival has become a strong brand by creating a unique musical experience with broad appeal.

Source: ZUMA Press/ Newscom

festival in North America for years. Multiple revenue sources are generated through ticket sales (from $250 general admission to $18,500 luxury packages), 16 profit centers on-site (from concessions and merchandise to paid showers), licensing, media deals, and the Web. With all its success, festival organizers are exploring expanding the brand's "curatorial voice" to nonfestival settings such as television programming and mobile phone apps.

2. Halloween night in Madison, Wisconsin, home of the University of Wisconsin–Madison, had become frightening—literally—for local businesses due to out-of-control partying. As one participant put it, "The main objective on Halloween in Madison was not to get blackout drunk . . . it was to incite enough of a ruckus that riot police had to show up on horseback with tear gas and pepper spray." The success of that strategy was evident in 2005 when more than 450 people were arrested and $350,000 was spent by the town government on enforcement. The next year, the mayor of Madison tried a marketing solution instead. He branded the event "Freakfest," installing floodlights in a gated stretch of a main street and providing concert entertainment for 50,000 partygoers. The number of arrests and the amount of vandalism were dramatically lower. One town official observed, "Since we rebranded the event, it's become something we are proud of."

As another example, Branding Brief 1-2 considers how even one-time commodities have been branded.

We can recognize the universality of branding by looking at some different product applications in the categories we defined previously—physical goods, services, retail stores, online businesses, people, organizations, places, and ideas. For each of these different types of products, we will review some basic considerations and look at examples. (We consider some of these special cases in more detail in Chapter 15.)

Physical Goods

Physical goods are what are traditionally associated with brands and include many of the best-known and highly regarded consumer products, like Mercedes-Benz, Nescafé, and Sony. More and more companies selling industrial products or durable goods to other companies are recognizing the benefits of developing strong brands. Brands have begun to emerge among certain types of physical goods that never supported brands before. Let us consider the role of branding in industrial "business-to-business" products and technologically intensive "high-tech" products.

Business-to-business products.   The business-to-business (B2B) market makes up a huge percentage of the global economy. Some of the world's most accomplished and respected brands belong to business marketers, such as ABB, Caterpillar, DuPont, FedEx, GE, Hewlett-Packard, IBM, Intel, Microsoft, Oracle, SAP, and Siemens.

Business-to-business branding creates a positive image and reputation for the company as a whole. Creating such goodwill with business customers is thought to lead to greater selling

BRANDING BRIEF 1-2

Branding Commodities

A *commodity* is a product so basic that it cannot be physically differentiated from competitors in the minds of consumers. Over the years, a number of products that at one time were seen as essentially commodities have become highly differentiated as strong brands have emerged in the category. Some notable examples are coffee (Maxwell House), bath soap (Ivory), flour (Gold Medal), beer (Budweiser), salt (Morton), oatmeal (Quaker), pickles (Vlasic), bananas (Chiquita), chickens (Perdue), pineapples (Dole), and even water (Perrier).

These products became branded in various ways. The key success factor in each case, however, was that consumers became convinced that all the product offerings in the category were not the same and that meaningful differences existed. In some instances, such as with produce, marketers convinced consumers that a product was *not* a commodity and could actually vary appreciably in quality. In these cases, the brand was seen as ensuring uniformly high quality in the product category on which consumers could depend. In other cases, like Perrier bottled mineral water, because product differences were virtually nonexistent, brands have been created by image or other non-product-related considerations.

One of the best examples of branding a commodity in this fashion is diamonds. De Beers Group added the phrase

"A Diamond Is Forever" as the tagline in its ongoing ad campaign in 1948. The diamond supplier, which was founded in 1888 and sells about 60 percent of the world's rough diamonds, wanted to attach more emotion and symbolic meaning to the purchase of diamond jewelry. "A Diamond Is Forever" became one of the most recognized slogans in advertising and helped fuel a diamond jewelry industry that's now worth nearly $25 billion per year in the United States alone.

After years of successful campaigns that helped generate buzz for the overall diamond industry, De Beers began to focus on its proprietary brands. Its 2009 campaign highlighted its new Everlon line. Partly in reaction to the recession, De Beers's marketing also began to focus on the long-term value and staying power of diamonds; new campaigns included the slogans "Fewer Better Things" and "Here Today, Here Tomorrow."

Sources: Theodore Levitt, "Marketing Success Through Differentiation— of Anything," *Harvard Business Review* (January–February 1980): 83–91; Sandra O'Loughlin, "Sparkler on the Other Hand," *Brandweek*, 19 April 2004; Blythe Yee, "Ads Remind Women They Have *Two* Hands," *Wall Street Journal*, 14 August 2003; Lauren Weber, "De Beers to Open First U.S. Retail Store," *Newsday*, 22 June 2005; "De Beers Will Double Ad Spending," *MediaPost*, 17 November 2008.

opportunities and more profitable relationships. A strong brand can provide valuable reassurance and clarity to business customers who may be putting their company's fate—and perhaps their own careers!—on the line. A strong business-to-business brand can thus provide a strong competitive advantage.

Some B2B firms, however, carry the attitude that purchasers of their products are so well-informed and professional that brands don't matter. Savvy business marketers reject that reasoning and are recognizing the importance of their brand and how they must execute well in a number of areas to gain marketplace success.

Boeing, which makes everything from commercial airplanes to satellites, implemented the "One Firm" brand strategy to unify all its different operations with a one-brand culture. The strategy was based in part on a "triple helix" representation: 1) Enterprising Spirit (*why* Boeing does what it does), 2) Precision Performance (*how* Boeing gets things done), and 3) Defining the Future (*what* Boeing achieves as a firm).[19] The Science of Branding 1-1 describes some particularly important guidelines for business-to-business branding. Here is how Cisco approaches brand differentiation.

CISCO

Cisco, the network communications equipment manufacturer that leads the market in supplying the switches and routers that direct traffic on the Internet, sought growth by directing considerable research and marketing resources at an underserved market: small- and medium-sized business (SMB) customers, which the company defined as those with fewer than 250 employees. To better understand buyer behavior, Cisco conducted customer research that segmented the overall SMB market into four tiers by networking expenditure and purchase patterns. Tier 1 and tier 2 companies, which view networking as the core of their business, make up 30 percent of the SMB space but account for 75 percent of total networking expenditures. Tier 3 and tier 4 companies make up 70 percent of the market but are hesitant to invest heavily in networking technology.

Based on this understanding of the market, Cisco was able to target these segments with products and services designed specifically for them. It developed a program called the "Smart Business Roadmap" that matched common business issues faced by SMB customer types with long-term technology solutions. One of these solutions was Linksys One, a hosted communications service offering telephone, video, data, and Internet networking on one high-speed connection that debuted back in 2005. Overall, Cisco raised its R&D budget for the SMB market to $2 billion and directed 40 percent of its total marketing expenditure toward this market. The program generated 22 percent growth in Cisco's business with SMBs.[20]

High-tech Products.   Many technology companies have struggled with branding. Managed by technologists, these firms often lack any kind of brand strategy and sometimes see branding as simply naming their products. In many of their markets, however, financial success is no longer driven by product innovation alone, or by the latest and greatest product specifications and features. Marketing skills are playing an increasingly important role in the adoption and success of high-tech products.

INTUIT

Intuit has introduced several highly successful software packages. In discussing the origins of his company, Intuit's founder Scott Cook comments: "We started with the belief that it is a consumer market, not a technology market. We'd run it like Procter & Gamble." Applying classic package-goods marketing techniques, Intuit first conducted extensive research with consumers and then designed a product to satisfy the unmet needs and wants of the market. Because research revealed that most consumers did not like doing financial management and found it a necessary evil, Intuit designed the Quicken personal-finance software to offer two key benefits—ease of use and speed—that were not then offered by other products in the market.

Through the years, Intuit has been expanding its services and products as well as its customer base, acquiring Mint.com, a free personal money management site, in 2009 for $170 million. In 2010, Intuit focused on its TurboTax tax software, creating a campaign—with a fully coordinated digital component—that kicked off tax season alongside the Super Bowl. Intuit has extended its consumer-centric strategy by expanding into social media. With TurboTax, the company has created the "Friends Like You" program, which allows users of the software to share reviews via social networking sites. With its QuickBooks business accounting software, the company has created a community where its diehard fans can pose questions to each other and exchange helpful tips.[21]

Intuit applies the latest consumer marketing strategies, such as the creation of an on-line community for its successful Quickbooks brand.

Source: Screen shots © Intuit Inc. All rights reserved.

THE SCIENCE OF BRANDING 1-1

Understanding Business-to-Business Branding

Because business-to-business purchase decisions are complex and often high risk, branding plays an important role in B2B markets. Six specific guidelines—developed in greater detail in later chapters—can be defined for marketers of B2B brands.

1. ***Ensure the entire organization understands and supports branding and brand management***. Employees at all levels and in all departments must have a complete, up-to-date understanding of the vision for the brand and their role in supporting it. A particularly crucial area is the sales force; personal selling is often the profit driver of a business-to-business organization. The sales force must be properly aligned so that the department can more effectively leverage and reinforce the brand promise. If branding is done right, the sales force can ensure that target customers recognize the brand's benefits sufficiently to pay a price commensurate with the brand's potential value.

2. ***Adopt a corporate branding strategy if possible and create a well-defined brand hierarchy***. Because of the breadth and complexity of the product or service mix, companies selling business-to-business are more likely to emphasize corporate brands (such as Hewlett-Packard, ABB, or BASF). Ideally, they will also create straightforward sub-brands that combine the corporate brand name with descriptive product modifiers, such as with EMC or GE. If a company has a distinctive line of business, however, a more clearly differentiated sub-brand may need to be developed, like Praxair's Medipure brand of medical oxygen, DuPont's Teflon coating, and Intel's Centrino mobile technology.

3. ***Frame value perceptions.*** Given the highly competitive nature of business-to-business markets, marketers must ensure that customers fully appreciate how their offerings are different. *Framing* occurs when customers are given a perspective or point of view that allows the brand to "put its best foot forward." Framing can be as simple as making sure customers realize all the benefits or cost savings offered by the brand, or becoming more active in shaping how customers view the economics of purchasing, owning, using and disposing of the brand in a different way. Framing requires understanding how customers currently think of brands and choose among products and services, and then determining how they *should* ideally think and choose.

4. ***Link relevant non-product-related brand associations***. In a business-to-business setting, a brand may be differentiated on the basis of factors beyond product performance, such as having superior customer service or well-respected customers or clients. Other relevant brand imagery might relate to the size or type of firm. For example, Microsoft and Oracle might be seen as "aggressive" companies, whereas 3M and Apple might be seen as "innovative." Imagery may also be a function of the other organizations to which the firm sells. For example, customers may believe that a company with many customers is established and a market leader.

5. ***Find relevant emotional associations for the brand***. B2B marketers too often overlook the power of emotions in their branding. Emotional associations related to a sense of security, social or peer approval, and self-respect can also be linked to the brand and serve as key sources of brand equity. That is, reducing risk to improve customers' sense of security can be a powerful driver of many decisions and thus an important source of brand equity; being seen as someone who works with other top firms may inspire peer approval and personal recognition within the organization; and, beyond respect and admiration from others, a business decision-maker may just feel more satisfied by working with top organizations and brands.

6. ***Segment customers carefully both within and across companies***. Finally, in a business-to-business setting, different customer segments may exist both within and across organizations. Within organizations, different people may assume the various roles in the purchase decision process: Initiator, user, influencer, decider, approver, buyer and gatekeeper. Across organizations, businesses can vary according to industry and company size, technologies used and other capabilities, purchasing policies, and even risk and loyalty profiles. Brand building must take these different segmentation perspectives in mind in building tailored marketing programs.

Sources: James C. Anderson and James A. Narus, *Business Market Management: Understanding, Creating, and Delivering Value*, 3rd ed. (Upper Saddle River, NJ: Prentice Hall, 2009); Kevin Lane Keller and Frederick E. Webster, Jr., "A Roadmap for Branding in Industrial Markets," *Journal of Brand Management*, 11 (May 2004): 388–40; Philip Kotler and Waldemar Pfoertsch, *B2B Brand Management* (Berlin-Heidelberg, Germany: Springer, 2006); Kevin Lane Keller, "Building a Strong Business-to-Business Brand," in *Business-to-Business Brand Management: Theory, Research, and Executive Case Study Exercises*, in *Advances in Business Marketing & Purchasing* series, Volume 15, ed. Arch Woodside (Bingley, UK: Emerald Group Publishing Limited, 2009), 11-31; Kevin Lane Keller and Philip Kotler, "Branding in Business-to-Business Firms," in *Business to Business Marketing Handbook*, eds. Gary L. Lilien and Rajdeep Grewal (Northampton, MA: Edward Elgar Publishing, 2012).

The speed and brevity of technology product life cycles create unique branding challenges. Trust is critical, and customers often buy into companies as much as products. Marketing budgets may be small, although high-tech firms' adoption of classic consumer marketing techniques has increased expenditures on marketing communications. The Science of Branding 1-2 provides a set of guidelines for marketing managers at high-tech companies.

THE SCIENCE OF BRANDING 1-2

Understanding High-Tech Branding

Marketers operating in technologically intensive markets face a number of unique challenges. Here are 10 guidelines that managers for high-tech companies can use to improve their company's brand strategy.

1. *It is important to have a brand strategy that provides a roadmap for the future*. Technology companies too often rely on the faulty assumption that the best product based on the best technology will sell itself. As the market failure of the Sony Betamax illustrates, the company with the best technology does not always win.

2. *Understand your brand hierarchy and manage it appropriately over time.* A strong corporate brand is vital in the technology industry to provide stability and help establish a presence on Wall Street. Since product innovations provide the growth drivers for technology companies, however, brand equity is sometimes built in the product name to the detriment of corporate brand equity.

3. *Know who your customer is and build an appropriate brand strategy*. Many technology companies understand that when corporate customers purchase business-to-business products or services, they are typically committing to a long-term relationship. For this reason, it is advisable for technology companies to establish a strong corporate brand that will endure over time.

4. *Realize that building brand equity and selling products are two different exercises*. Too often, the emphasis on developing products leads to an overemphasis on branding them. When a company applies distinct brand names to too many products in rapid succession, the brand portfolio becomes cluttered and consumers may lose perspective on the brand hierarchy. Rather than branding each new innovation separately, a better approach is to plan for future innovations by developing an extendable branding strategy.

5. *Brands are owned by customers, not engineers*. In many high-tech firms, CEOs work their way up the ladder through the engineering divisions. Although engineers have an intimate knowledge of products and technology, they may lack the big-picture brand view. Compounding this problem is the fact that technology companies typically spend less on consumer research compared with other types of companies. As a result of these factors, tech companies often do not invest in building strong brands.

6. *Brand strategies need to account for the attributes of the CEO and adjust accordingly*. Many of the world's top technology companies have highly visible CEOs, especially compared with other industries. Some notable high-tech CEOs with prominent public personas include Oracle's Larry Ellison, Cisco's John Chambers, Dell's Michael Dell, and (until 2011), Apple's Steve Jobs. In each case, the CEO's identity and persona are inextricably woven into the fabric of the brand.

7. *Brand building on a small budget necessitates leveraging every possible positive association.* Technology companies typically prioritize their marketing mix as follows (in order from most important to least important): industry analyst relations, public relations, trade shows, seminars, direct mail, and advertising. Often, direct mail and advertising are discretionary items in a company's marketing budget and may in fact receive no outlay.

8. *Technology categories are created by customers and external forces, not by companies themselves.* In their quest for product differentiation, new technology companies have a tendency to reinvent the wheel and claim they have created a new category. Yet only two groups can truly create categories: analysts and customers. For this reason, it is important for technology companies to manage their relationships with analysts in order to attract consumers.

9. *The rapidly changing environment demands that you stay in tune with your internal and external environment.* The rapid pace of innovation in the technology sector dictates that marketers closely observe the market conditions in which their brands do business. Trends in brand strategy change almost as rapidly as the technology.

10. *Invest the time to understand the technology and value proposition and do not be afraid to ask questions.* It is important for technology marketers to ask questions in order to educate themselves and build credibility with the company's engineering corps and with customers. To build trust among engineers and customers, marketers must strive to learn as much as they can about the technology.

Sources: Patrick Tickle, Kevin Lane Keller, and Keith Richey, "Branding in High-Technology Markets," *Market Leader* 22 (Autumn 2003): 21–26; Jakki Mohr, Sanjit Sengupta, and Stanley Slater, *Marketing of High-Technology Products and Innovations*, 3rd ed. (Upper Saddle River, NJ: Pearson Prentice Hall, 2010); Eloise Coupey, *Digital Business: Concepts and Strategies*, 2nd ed. (Upper Saddle River, NJ: Pearson Prentice Hall, 2005).

Services

Although strong service brands like American Express, British Airways, Ritz-Carlton, Merrill Lynch, and Federal Express have existed for years, the pervasiveness of service branding and its sophistication have accelerated in the past decade.

Role of Branding with Services.   One of the challenges in marketing services is that they are less tangible than products and more likely to vary in quality, depending on the particular person or people providing them. For that reason, branding can be particularly important to service firms as a way to address intangibility and variability problems. Brand symbols may also be especially important, because they help make the abstract nature of services more concrete. Brands can help identify and provide meaning to the different services provided by a firm. For example, branding has become especially important in financial services to help organize and label the myriad new offerings in a manner that consumers can understand.

Branding a service can also be an effective way to signal to consumers that the firm has designed a particular service offering that is special and deserving of its name. For example, British Airways not only brands its premium business class service as "Club World"; it also brands its regular coach service as "World Traveler," a clever way to communicate to the airline's regular passengers that they are also special in some way and that their patronage is not taken for granted. Branding has clearly become a competitive weapon for services.

Professional Services.   Professional services firm such as Accenture (consulting), Goldman Sachs (investment banking), Ernst & Young (accounting), and Baker Botts (law) offer specialized expertise and support to other businesses and organizations. Professional services branding is an interesting combination of B2B branding and traditional consumer services branding.

Corporate credibility is key in terms of expertise, trustworthiness, and likability. Variability is more of an issue with professional services because it is harder to standardize the services of a consulting firm than those of a typical consumer services firm (like Mayflower movers or Orkin pest control). Long-term relationships are crucial too; losing one customer can be disastrous if it is a big enough account.

One big difference in professional services is that individual employees have a lot more of their own equity in the firm and are often brands in their own right! The challenge is therefore to ensure that their words and actions help build the corporate brand and not just their

For a service firm like Mayflower, dependable, high-quality service is critical.

Source: Mayflower Transit, LLC

own. Ensuring that the organization retain at least some of the equity that employees (especially senior ones) build is thus crucial in case any of them leave.

Referrals and testimonials can be powerful when the services offered are highly intangible and subjective. Emotions also play a big role in terms of sense of security and social approval. Switching costs can be significant and pose barriers to entry for competitors, but clients do have the opportunity to bargain and will often do so to acquire more customized solutions.

Retailers and Distributors

To retailers and other channel members distributing products, brands provide a number of important functions. Brands can generate consumer interest, patronage, and loyalty in a store, as consumers learn to expect certain brands and products. To the extent "you are what you sell," brands help retailers create an image and establish positioning. Retailers can also create their own brand image by attaching unique associations to the quality of their service, their product assortment and merchandising, and their pricing and credit policy. Finally, the appeal and attraction of brands, whether manufacturers' brands or the retailers' own brands, can yield higher price margins, increased sales volumes, and greater profits.

Retailers can introduce their own brands by using their store name, creating new names, or some combination of the two. Many distributors, especially in Europe, have actually introduced their own brands, which they sell in addition to—or sometimes even instead of—manufacturers' brands. Products bearing these *store brands* or *private label* brands offer another way for retailers to increase customer loyalty and generate higher margins and profits.

By mid-July 2009, private labels accounted for 17 percent of grocery purchases in food, drug, and mass merchandisers in North America.[22] In Britain, five or six grocery chains selling their own brands account for roughly half the country's food and packaged-goods sales, led by Sainsbury and Tesco. Another top British retailer, Marks & Spencer, sells only its own-brand goods, under the label of St. Michael. Several U.S. retailers also emphasize their own brands. (Chapter 5 considers store brands and private labels in greater detail.)

The Internet has transformed retailing in recent years as retailers have adopted a "bricks and clicks" approach to their business or, in many cases, become pure-play online retailers, operating only on the Web. Regardless of the exact form, to be competitive online, many retailers have had to improve their online service by making customer service agents available in real time, shipping products promptly, providing tracking updates, and adopting liberal return policies.

Online Products and Services

Some of the strongest brands in recent years have been born online. Google, Facebook, and Twitter are three notable examples. That wasn't always the case. At the onset of the Internet, many online marketers made serious—and sometimes fatal—mistakes. Some oversimplified the branding process, equating flashy or unusual advertising with building a brand. Although such marketing efforts sometimes caught consumers' attention, more often than not they failed to create awareness of what products or services the brand represented, why those products or services were unique or different, and most important, why consumers should visit their Web site.

Online marketers now realize the realities of brand building. First, as for any brand, it is critical to create unique aspects of the brand on some dimension that is important to consumers, such as convenience, price, or variety. At the same time, the brand needs to perform satisfactorily in other areas, such as customer service, credibility, and personality. For instance, customers increasingly began to demand higher levels of service both during and after their Web site visits.

Successful online brands have been well positioned and have found unique ways to satisfy consumers' unmet needs. By offering unique features and services to consumers, the best online brands are able to avoid extensive advertising or lavish marketing campaigns, relying more on word-of-mouth and publicity.

- Hulu enables consumers to watch videos of their past and present favorite TV programs at their own convenience.

- Pandora allows customers to customize online radio stations with bands and genres they enjoy, while learning about other music they might also like.
- Online encyclopedia Wikipedia provides consumers with extensive, constantly updated, user-generated information about practically everything.

Google is perhaps the classic example of how to build a successful online brand.

GOOGLE

Founded in 1998 by two Stanford University Ph.D. students, Google takes its name from a play on the word *googol*—the number 1 followed by 100 zeroes—a reference to the huge amount of data online. Google's stated mission is "To organize the world's information and make it universally accessible and useful." The company has become the market leader in the search engine industry through its business focus and constant innovation. Its home page focuses on searches but also allows users to employ many other Google services. By focusing on plain text, avoiding pop-up ads, and using sophisticated search algorithms, Google provides fast and reliable service. Google's revenue traditionally was driven by search ads, text-based boxes that advertisers pay for only when users click on them. Increasingly, Google is seeking additional sources of revenue from new services and acquisitions.[23]

Google's classic application of branding principles has helped to made it an industry powerhouse.
Source: TassPhotos/Newscom

Online brands also learned the importance of off-line activities to draw customers to Web sites. Home page Web addresses, or URLs, began to appear on all collateral and marketing material. Partnerships became critical as online brands developed networks of online partners and links. They also began to target specific customer groups—often geographically widely dispersed—for which the brand could offer unique value propositions. As we will describe more in Chapter 6, Web site designs have finally begun to maximize the benefits of interactivity, customization, and timeliness and the advantages of being able to inform, persuade, and sell all at the same time.

People and Organizations

When the product category is people or organizations, the naming aspect of branding, at least, is generally straightforward. These often have well-defined images that are easily understood and liked (or disliked) by others. That's particularly true for public figures such as politicians, entertainers, and professional athletes. All these compete in some sense for public approval and acceptance, and all benefit from conveying a strong and desirable image.

RACHAEL RAY

Rachael Ray's brand is an accessible one. Her "can-do" personality aligns well with her no-fuss cooking approach, and her likeability led her to be named one of *Forbes* magazine's "Ten Most Trusted Celebrities" and one of *Time* magazine's "100 Most Influential People in 2006." Ray's magazine—launched in 2005—has a circulation of 1.8 million. Her brand, which started with her *Food Network* show, has been expanded to include product endorsements (such as Dunkin' Donuts and Kraft's Nabisco) and cookbooks. In 2010, Ray launched her own iPod app that includes recipes, cooking tips, and a function that helps food shoppers calculate ingredients and amounts. Ray's initial success was built around her ability to recognize consumer needs in the culinary market; specifically, she identified that consumers need recipes and cooking tools to teach them how to cook quickly and easily. Ray herself has identified her talent as being "good at trying to understand what [my] customer wants and needs, and giving it to them."[24]

Rachel Ray's multimedia brand is based on her down-to-earth attitude and understanding of consumer needs.

Source: MCMULLAN CO/SIPA/Newscom

That's not to say that only the well-known or famous can be thought of as a brand. Certainly, one key for a successful career in almost any area is that co-workers, superiors, or even important people outside your company or organization know who you are and recognize your skills, talents, attitude, and so forth. By building up a name and reputation in a business context, you are essentially creating your own brand.[25] The right awareness and image can be invaluable in shaping the way people treat you and interpret your words, actions, and deeds.[26]

Similarly, organizations often take on meanings through their programs, activities, and products. Nonprofit organizations such as the Sierra Club, the American Red Cross, and Amnesty International have increasingly emphasized marketing. The children's advocate nonprofit UNICEF has initiated a number of marketing activities and programs through the years.

UNICEF

UNICEF launched its "Tap Project" campaign in 2007, which asked diners to pay $1 for a glass of New York City tap water in restaurants, with the funds going to support the organization's clean water programs. That was the first time UNICEF had run a consumer campaign in over 50 years. The UNICEF logo was featured on the Barcelona soccer team's jersey from 2006 to 2011 under an arrangement in which the team donated $2 million annually to the organization. UNICEF launched another consumer campaign in the UK in February 2010. This five-year "Put it Right" campaign features celebrity ambassadors for the organization and aims to protect the rights of children. One of UNICEF's most successful corporate relationships has been with IKEA. The partnership, which also emphasizes children's rights, was established in 2000 and encompasses direct donations from IKEA and an annual toy campaign, the sales from which directly benefit UNICEF programs.[27]

Nonprofit organizations like UNICEF need strong brands and modern marketing practices to help them fundraise and satisfy their organizational goals and mission.

Source: Picture Contact BV/Alamy

Sports, Arts, and Entertainment

A special case of marketing people and organizations as brands exists in the sports, arts, and entertainment industries. Sports marketing has become highly sophisticated in recent years, employing traditional packaged-goods techniques. No longer content to allow win–loss records to dictate attendance levels and financial fortunes, many sports teams are marketing themselves through a creative combination of advertising, promotions, sponsorship, direct mail, digital, and other forms of communication. By building awareness, image, and loyalty, these sports franchises are able to meet ticket sales targets regardless of what their team's actual performance might turn out to be. Brand symbols and logos in particular have become an important financial contributor to professional sports through licensing agreements.

Branding plays an especially valuable function in the arts and entertainment industries that bring us movies, television, music, and books. These offerings are good examples of experience goods: prospective buyers cannot judge quality by inspection and must use cues such as the particular people involved, the concept or rationale behind the project, and word-of-mouth and critical reviews.

Think of a movie as a product whose "ingredients" are the plot, actors, and director.[28] Certain movie franchises such as *Spider Man*, *James Bond*, and *Twilight* have established themselves as strong brands by combining all these ingredients into a formula that appeals to consumers and allows the studios to release sequels (essentially brand extensions) that rely on the title's initial popularity. For years, some of the most valuable movie franchises have featured recurring characters or ongoing stories, and many successful recent films have been sequels. Their success is due to the fact that moviegoers know from the title and the actors, producers, directors, and other contributors that they can expect a certain experience—a classic application of branding.

HARRY POTTER

With its ability to transcend its original format—books—the *Harry Potter* film series has been likened to the *Star Wars* franchise. All seven of the popular novels have been turned into blockbuster movies, generating over $7.7 billion worldwide by the end of 2011. In the first year it launched Harry Potter toys, Mattel saw $160 million in sales. And in 2010, Universal Studios opened a Florida theme park based on the Harry Potter stories. The Harry Potter empire has been praised for its attention to core marketing techniques—a good product, emotional involvement of its consumers, word-of-mouth promotion, "tease" marketing, and brand consistency. Several estimates have pegged the Harry Potter brand to be worth $15 billion, which, beyond the movies and the books, included more than $1 billion in DVD sales, nearly $12 million in licensing, and $13 million in music sales related to the films.[29]

Few brands have generated as much worldwide consumer loyalty—and profits—as *Harry Potter.*
Source: WARNER BROS. PICTURES/Album/Newscom

A strong brand is valuable in the entertainment industry because of the fervent feelings that names generate as a result of pleasurable past experiences. A new album release from Neil Finn would probably not cause much of a ripple in the marketplace, even if it were marketed as coming from a founding member of the band Crowded House. If it were to actually be released and marketed under the Crowded House name, however, greater media attention and higher sales would be virtually guaranteed.

BRANDING BRIEF 1-3

Place Branding

Branding is not limited to vacation destinations. Countries, states, and cities large and small are beginning to brand their respective images as they try to draw visitors or encourage relocation. Some notable early examples of place branding include "Virginia Is for Lovers" and "Shrimp on the Barbie" (Australia). Now virtually every physical location, area, or region considers place branding. More recent examples include Santa Rosa's new slogan "Place of Plenty" and the "Cleveland Plus" campaign. The San Diego Convention and Visitors Bureau ran an integrated campaign, titled "Happy Happens," in 2009.

Las Vegas ran its hugely successful "What Happens Here, Stays Here" campaign beginning in 2003. The ads were meant to sell Las Vegas as an experience. In 2008, the city took a different route, selling Vegas differently and in more practical terms in light of the economy. The "What Happens Here" ads returned in 2009, however, when marketing research showed that consumers missed them. In 2010, the Las Vegas Convention and Visitors Authority had an $86 million advertising campaign budget, larger than the city's top competitors' budgets combined.

Branding countries to increase appeal to tourists is also a growing phenomenon. Some recent success stories include Spain's use of a logo designed by Spanish artist Joan Miró, the "Incredible India" campaign, and New Zealand's marketing of itself in relation to the *Lord of the Rings* movie franchise. Some other tourist slogans include "No Artificial Ingredients" for Costa Rica and "Mother Nature's Best-Kept Secret" for Belize. Future Brand, a brand consultancy and research company, ranks countries on the strengths of their respective brands. In 2010, it deemed the top five country brands to be Canada, Australia, New Zealand, the United States, and Switzerland.

Sources: Roger Yu, "Cities Use Destination Branding to Lure Tourists," *USA Today*, 12 February 2010; Yana Polikarpov, "Visitors Bureau Lures Tourists to 'Happy' San Diego," *Brandweek*, 23 April 2009; Liz Benston, "Will Vegas Advertising That Worked Before, Work Again?," *Las Vegas Sun*, 27 September 2009; Sean O'Neill, "Careful with Those Tourist Slogans," *Budget Travel*, 24 September 2009; John Cook, "Packaging a Nation," *Travel + Leisure*, January 2007.

Geographic Locations

Increased mobility of both people and businesses and growth in the tourism industry have contributed to the rise of place marketing. Cities, states, regions, and countries are now actively promoted through advertising, direct mail, and other communication tools. These campaigns aim to create awareness and a favorable image of a location that will entice temporary visits or permanent moves from individuals and businesses alike. Although the brand name is usually preordained by the name of the location, there are a number of different considerations in building a place brand, some of which are considered in Branding Brief 1-3.

Ideas and Causes

Finally, numerous ideas and causes have been branded, especially by nonprofit organizations. They may be captured in a phrase or slogan and even be represented by a symbol, such as AIDS ribbons. By making ideas and causes more visible and concrete, branding can provide much value. As Chapter 11 describes, cause marketing increasingly relies on sophisticated marketing practices to inform or persuade consumers about the issues surrounding a cause.

WHAT ARE THE STRONGEST BRANDS?

It's clear from these examples that virtually anything can be and has been branded. Which brands are the strongest, that is, the best known or most highly regarded? Figure 1-5 reveals Interbrand's ranking of the world's 25 most valuable brands in 2011 based on its brand valuation methodology (see Chapter 10), as published in its annual "Best Global Brands" report.[30]

We can easily find some of the best-known brands by simply walking down a supermarket aisle. It's also easy to identify a number of other brands with amazing staying power that have been market leaders in their categories for decades. According to research by marketing consultant Jack Trout, in 25 popular product categories, 20 of the leading brands in 1923 were still leading brands over 80 years later—only five have lost their leadership position.[31]

2011 Rank	Brand	2011 Brand Value	2010 Brand Value	2011–2010 Percent Change	Country of Ownership
1	Coca-Cola	71,861	70,452	2%	United States
2	IBM	69,905	64,727	8%	United States
3	Microsoft	59,087	60,895	−3%	United States
4	Google	55,317	43,557	27%	United States
5	GE	42,808	42,808	0%	United States
6	McDonald's	35,593	33,578	6%	United States
7	Intel	35,217	32,015	10%	United States
8	Apple	33,492	21,143	58%	United States
9	Disney	29,018	28,731	1%	United States
10	Hewlett-Packard	28,479	26,867	6%	United States
11	Toyota	27,764	26,192	6%	Japan
12	Mercedes-Benz	27,445	25,179	9%	Germany
13	Cisco	25,309	23,219	9%	United States
14	Nokia	25,071	29,495	−15%	Finland
15	BMW	24,554	22,322	10%	Germany
16	Gillette	23,997	23,298	3%	United States
17	Samsung	23,430	19,491	20%	South Korea
18	Louis Vuitton	23,172	21,860	6%	France
19	Honda	19,431	18,506	5%	Japan
20	Oracle	17,262	14,881	16%	United States
21	H&M	16,459	16,136	2%	Sweden
22	Pepsi	14,590	14,061	4%	United States
23	American Express	14,572	13,944	5%	United States
24	SAP	14,542	12,756	14%	Germany
25	Nike	14,528	13,706	6%	United States

FIGURE 1-5

Twenty-Five Most Valuable Global Brands

Sources: Based on Interbrand. "The 100 Most Valuable Global Brands 2011," pp. 17–43. Interbrand. "Best Global Brands 2010," p. 14.

Similarly, many brands that were number one in the United Kingdom in 1933 remain strong today: Hovis bread, Stork margarine, Kellogg's Corn Flakes, Cadbury's chocolates, Gillette razors, Schweppes mixers, Brooke Bond tea, Colgate toothpaste, and Hoover vacuum cleaners. Many of these brands have evolved over the years, however, and made a number of changes. Most of them barely resemble their original forms.

At the same time, some seemingly invincible brands, including Levi-Strauss, General Motors, Montgomery Ward, Polaroid, and Xerox, have run into difficulties and seen their market preeminence challenged or even lost. Although some of these failures are related to factors beyond the control of the firm, such as technological advances or shifting consumer preferences, in other cases the blame could probably be placed on the action or inaction of the marketers behind the brands. Some failed to account for changing market conditions and continued to operate with a "business as usual" attitude or, perhaps even worse, recognized that changes were necessary but reacted inadequately or inappropriately. The Science of Branding 1-3 provides some academic insights into factors affecting market leadership.

The bottom line is that any brand—no matter how strong at one point in time—is vulnerable and susceptible to poor brand management. The next section discusses why it is so difficult to

THE SCIENCE OF BRANDING 1-3

Understanding Market Leadership

The extent of the enduring nature of market leadership has been the source of much debate. According to a study by Dartmouth's Tuck School of Business Professor Peter Golder, leading brands are more likely to *lose* their leadership position over time than retain it. Golder evaluated more than 650 products in 100 categories and compared the category leaders from 1923 with the category leaders in 1997 (see Figure 1-6). His study found that

Category	1923 Leaders	1997 Leaders
Cleansers	Old Dutch	Comet Soft Scrub Ajax
Chewing gum	Wrigley Adams	Wrigley's Bubble Yum Bubblicious
Motorcycles	Indian Harley-Davidson	Harley-Davidson Honda Kawasaki
Five cent mint candies	Life Savers	Breath-Savers Tic Tac Certs
Peanut butter	Beech-Nut Heinz	Jif Skippy Peter Pan
Razors	Gillette Gem Ever ready	Gillette Bic Schick
Soft drinks	Coca-Cola Cliquot Club Bevo	Coca-Cola Pepsi Dr. Pepper/Cadbury
Coffee	Arbuckle's Yuban White House Hotel Astor	Folger's Maxwell House Hills Bros.
Laundry soap	Fels Naptha Octagon Kirkman	Tide Cheer Wisk
Cigarettes	Camel Fatima Pall Mall	Marlboro Winston Newport
Shoes	Douglas Walkover	Nike Reebok
Candy	Huyler's Loft Page & Shaw	Hershey M&M/Mars Nestlé
Jelly or jam	Heinz	Smucker's Welch's Kraft

FIGURE 1-6

Brands Then and Now

Source: Reprinted with permission from *Journal of Marketing Research,* published by the American Marketing Association, May 2000, pp. 156–172.

only 23 of the top brands in the 100 categories remained market leaders in 1997, and 28 percent of the leading brands had failed by 1997. The clothing and fashion category experienced the greatest percentage of failures (67 percent) and had no brands that remained leaders in 1997. Leaders in the food and beverage category fared better, with 39 percent of brands maintaining leadership while only 21 percent failed.

One 1923 leader that did not maintain leadership was Underwood typewriters. Underwood's primary mistake was lack of innovation. Rather than invest in research and development, Underwood followed a harvesting strategy that sought the highest margin possible for its products. By 1950, several competitors had already invested in computer technology, whereas Underwood acquired a small computer firm only in 1952. Subsequent developments in the market further damaged Underwood's position. Between 1956 and 1961, lower-priced foreign competitors more than doubled their share of manual typewriter sales. Sales of electric typewriters, which Underwood did not make, overtook sales of manual typewriters in the early 1960s. Olivetti acquired Underwood in the mid-1960s, and the brand name was dropped in the 1980s.

Golder uses Wrigley, which has dominated the chewing gum market for nine decades, as an example of a long-term leader. According to Golder, Wrigley's success is based on three factors: "maintaining and building strong brands, focusing on a single product, and being in a category that has not changed much." Wrigley has consistently marketed its brand with high-profile sponsorship and advertising. It also used subsidiaries to extend into new product categories like sugarless gum and bubblegum, so as not to dilute the brand. Wrigley's sole focus on chewing gum enables the company to achieve maximum results in what is considered a mature category. During the 1990s, sales of Wrigley's products grew almost 10 percent annually. Finally, the chewing gum market is historically stable and uncomplicated. Still, Wrigley's makes considerable investments in product and packaging improvement to maintain its edge.

Golder and his co-author Gerard Tellis argue that dedication to the brand is vital for sustained brand leadership, elucidating five factors for enduring market leadership (see Figure 1-7). They comment:

The real causes of enduring market leadership are vision and will. Enduring market leaders have a revolutionary and inspiring vision of the mass market, and they exhibit an indomitable will to realize that vision. They persist under adversity, innovate relentlessly, commit financial resources and leverage assets to realize their vision.

By failing to innovate beyond manual typewriters, Underwood was left behind when consumers moved on to electric typewriters.

Source: Peter Carroll/Alamy

Follow-up research by Golder and his colleagues of brand leaders in 126 categories over a span from 1921 to 2005 found the following:

- Leading brands are more likely to persist during economic slowdowns and when inflation is high, and less likely to persist during economic expansion and when inflation is low.

- Half the leading brands in the sample lost their leadership over periods ranging from 12 to 39 years.

- The rate of brand leadership persistence has been substantially lower in recent eras than in earlier eras.

- Once brand leadership is lost, it is rarely regained.

- Category types with above-average rates of brand leadership persistence are food and household supplies; category types with below-average rates of brand leadership persistence are durables and clothing.

Sources: Peter N. Golder, Julie R. Irwin, Debanjan Mitra, "Will You Still Try Me, Will You Still Buy Me, When I'm 64? How Economic Conditions Affect Long-Term Brand Leadership Persistence," working paper, Tuck School of Business at Dartmouth College, 2011; Peter N. Golder, "Historical Method in Marketing Research with New Evidence on Long-Term Market Share Stability," *Journal of Marketing Research*, 37 (May 2000): 156–172; Peter N. Golder and Gerard J. Tellis, "Growing, Growing, Gone: Cascades, Diffusion, and Turning Points in the Product Life Cycle," *Marketing Science*, 23 (Spring 2004): 207–218; Laurie Freeman, "Study: Leading Brands Aren't Always Enduring," *Advertising Age*, 28 February 2000; Gerald J. Tellis and Peter N. Golder, "First to Market, First to Fail? Real Causes of Enduring Market Leadership," *MIT Sloan Management Review*, 1 January 1996.

THE SCIENCE OF BRANDING 1-3   *(continued)*

FIGURE 1-7

Factors Determining
Enduring Leadership

Source: Gerard J. Tellis and
Peter N. Golder, "First to
Market, First to Fail? Real
Causes of Enduring Market
Leadership," *MIT Sloan
Management Review,*
1 January 1996. Used by
permission of the publisher.
Copyright © 2007 by
Massachusetts Institute
of Technology. All rights
reserved.

Tellis and Golder identify the following five factors and rationale as the keys to enduring brand leadership.

Vision of the Mass Market
Companies with a keen eye for mass market tastes are more likely to build a broad and sustainable customer base. Although Pampers was not the market leader in the disposable diaper category during its first several years, it spent significantly on research and development in order to design an affordable and effective disposable diaper. Pampers quickly became the market leader.

Managerial Persistence
The "breakthrough" technology that can drive market leadership often requires the commitment of company resources over long periods of time. For example, JVC spent 21 years researching the VHS video recorder before launching it in 1976 and becoming a market leader.

Financial Commitment
The cost of maintaining leadership is high because of the demands for research and development and marketing. Companies that aim for short-term profitability rather than long-term leadership, as Rheingold Brewery did when it curtailed support of its Gablinger's light beer a year after the 1967 introduction of the product, are unlikely to enjoy enduring leadership.

Relentless Innovation
Due to changes in consumer tastes and competition from other firms, companies that wish to maintain leadership positions must continually innovate. Gillette, both a long-term leader and historically an innovator, typically has at least 20 shaving products on the drawing board at any given time.

Asset Leverage
Companies can become leaders in some categories if they hold a leadership position in a related category. For instance, Coca-Cola leveraged its success and experience with cola (Coke) and diet cola (Tab) to introduce Diet Coke in 1982. Within one year of its introduction, Diet Coke became the market leader.

manage brands in today's environment. Figure 1-8 displays an analysis of fast-growing "breakaway brands" by leading marketing consultant firm Landor. Brand Focus 1.0 at the end of the chapter describes some of the historical origins of branding and brand management.

BRANDING CHALLENGES AND OPPORTUNITIES

Although brands may be as important as ever to consumers, in reality *brand management may be more difficult than ever*. Let's look at some recent developments that have significantly complicated marketing practices and pose challenges for brand managers (see Figure 1-9).[32]

Savvy Customers

Increasingly, consumers and businesses have become more experienced with marketing, more knowledgeable about how it works, and more demanding. A well-developed media market pays increased attention to companies' marketing actions and motivations. Consumer information and support exists in the form of consumer guides (*Consumer Reports*), Web sites (Epinions .com), influential blogs, and so on.

Brand	Growth in Brand Strength 2007–2010
Facebook	195%
Skype	79%
YouTube	78%
Netflix	72%
Samsung	66%
Apple	51%
iTunes	50%
Amazon.com	44%
Reese's	42%
National Guard	35%

FIGURE 1-8

Landor Breakaway Brands (2011)

The Breakaway Brands survey, conducted by Landor Associates using Young & Rubicam's BrandAsset Valuator database, identifies those brands that exhibited the greatest increases in Brand Strength from 2007–2010. Growth in brand strength indicates how much the brand's raw strength score has risen over the past three years, expressed in percentage terms (www.landor.com).

Savvy customers
More complex brand families and portfolios
Maturing markets
More sophisticated and increasing competition
Difficulty in differentiating
Decreasing brand loyalty in many categories
Growth of private labels
Increasing trade power
Fragmenting media coverage
Eroding traditional media effectiveness
Emerging new communication options
Increasing promotional expenditures
Decreasing advertising expenditures
Increasing cost of product introduction and support
Short-term performance orientation
Increasing job turnover
Pronounced economic cycles

FIGURE 1-9

Challenges to Brand Builders

Friends/peers	81%
Fashion magazines	68%
Ads	58%
Company Web sites	44%
Consumer Reviews	36%
Celebrities	33%
Parents/adults	25%
Bloggers	14%

FIGURE 1-10

Example of Multiple Consumer Information Sources
(Percentage of teen girls, ages 13–18, who identify a source of information they typically use when trying to learn about the latest trends)

Source: Varsity Brands/ Ketchum Global Research Network, as cited in "Teen Girls as Avid Shoppers," *ADWEEK MEDIA*, 15 November 2010.

One of the key challenges in today's marketing environment is the vast number of sources of information consumers may consult. Figure 1-10 displays some of the ways teenage girls collect information. For these and other reasons, many believe that it is more difficult to persuade consumers with traditional communications than it used to be. An empowered consumer may play a more active role in a brand's fortune, as has been the case with Converse.

CONVERSE

CMO Geoff Cottrill maintains that an important priority at Converse is "to shut up and listen." With a small budget, marketing for the brand has focused on digital and social media. The Web site is chock full of consumer-generated content. On Facebook, the brand went from 6 to 9 million fans as consumers chose to take pictures of their shoes, draw on them, and post about them. Cottrill notes that although there are places where the company tells stories about its shoes—in stores and on the Web site—"for the most part we let the conversation go … it's those creative people that are really pushing the brand." The brand has also functioned as a curator of sorts for new music, art, and entertainment. Converse has built a studio called Rubber Tracks in New York City to support new, emerging bands by allowing them to record there for free.[33]

Converse has reinvigorated its brand by getting consumers actively involved in its marketing.

Source: Kristoffer Tripplaar/Alamy

Economic Downturns

A severe recession that commenced in 2008 threatened the fortunes of many brands. One research study of consumers at the end of 2009 found the following sobering facts:

- 18 percent of consumers reported that they had bought lower-priced brands of consumer packaged goods in the past two years.
- 46 percent of the switchers to less expensive products said "they found better performance than they expected," with the vast majority saying performance was actually *much* better than expected.
- 34 percent of the switchers said "they no longer preferred higher-priced products."

As the economy appeared to move out of the recession, the question was whether attitudes and behaviors that did change would revert back to their pre-recession norms. Regardless, there will always be economic cycles and ups and downs, and The Science of Branding 1-4 offers some guidelines for marketing brands during economic downturns.

Brand Proliferation

Another important change in the branding environment is the proliferation of new brands and products, in part spurred by the rise in line and brand extensions. As a result, a brand name may now be identified with a number of different products with varying degrees of similarity. Marketers of brands such as Coke, Nivea, Dove, and Virgin have added a host of new products under their brand umbrellas in recent years. There are few single (or "mono") product brands around, which complicates the decisions that marketers have to make.

THE SCIENCE OF BRANDING 1-4

Marketing Brands in a Recession

Tough times present opportunities as well as challenges, as was the case with the most recent recession. Although many marketers face reduced funding and intense pressure to justify marketing programs as cost-effective, there are tactics that can help marketers survive—or even thrive—in a recession, both in the short run *and* over the long haul. Here are five guidelines to improve the odds for success during this time.

Explore the Upside of Actually Increasing Investment

Does it pay to invest during a recession? Forty years of evidence from past recessions suggest that firms willing to capitalize on a marketing opportunity by investing during a recession have, on average, improved their fortunes compared with firms that chose to cut back.

Now, More Than Ever, Get Closer to Your Consumer

In tough times, consumers may change what they want and can afford, where and how they shop, even what they want to see and hear from a firm. A downturn is an opportunity for marketers to learn even more about what consumers are thinking, feeling, and doing, especially the loyal customer base that is the source of so much of a brand's profitability. Any changes must be identified and characterized as temporary adjustments versus permanent shifts.

Rethink How You Spend Your Money

Budget allocations can be sticky and not change enough to reflect a fluid marketing environment. A recession provides an opportunity for marketers to closely review how much and in what ways they are spending their money. Budget reallocations can allow marketers to try new, promising options and eliminate sacred-cow approaches that no longer provide sufficient revenue benefits.

Put Forth the Most Compelling Value Proposition

It's a mistake in a recession to be overly focused on price reductions and discounts that can harm long-term brand equity and price integrity. Marketers should focus on increasing—and clearly communicating—the value their brands offer consumers, making sure consumers appreciate all the financial, logistical, and psychological benefits compared with the competition.

Fine-Tune Your Brand and Product Offerings

Marketers must make sure they have the right products to sell to the right consumers in the right places and times. They should carefully review their product portfolios and brand architecture to ensure that brands and sub-brands are clearly differentiated and targeted, and that optimal support is given to brands and sub-brands based on their prospects. Because certain brands or sub-brands appeal to different economic segments, those that target the lower end of the socioeconomic spectrum may be particularly important during a recession. Bad times also are an opportunity to prune brands or products that have diminished prospects.

With so many brands engaged in expansion, channels of distribution have become clogged, and many brand battles are waged just to get products on the shelf. The average supermarket now holds 30,000 different brands, three times the number 30 years ago.[35]

Media Transformation

Another important change in the marketing environment is the erosion or fragmentation of traditional advertising media and the emergence of interactive and nontraditional media, promotion, and other communication alternatives. For several reasons related to media cost, clutter, and fragmentation—as outlined in Chapter 6—marketers have become disenchanted with traditional advertising media, especially network television.

Thus the percentage of the communication budget devoted to advertising has shrunk over the years. In its place, marketers are spending more on nontraditional forms of communication and on new and emerging forms of communication such as interactive digital media; sports and event sponsorship; in-store advertising; mini-billboards in transit vehicles, parking meters, and other locations; and product placement in movies.

Consider how Procter & Gamble (P&G) has dramatically changed its marketing communications in recent years. The one-time queen of daytime TV soap operas—the company produced the shows and ran ads during the broadcasts—P&G has dramatically overhauled the way it markets its brands. It no longer airs any soap operas and puts more emphasis on social media instead. The company sells Pampers diapers on Facebook, offers an iPhone application for Always feminine products that allows women to track menstrual cycles and ask questions, and uses social media to sell its traditionally male-targeted Old Spice personal care products.[36]

OLD SPICE

Old Spice's "Smell Like a Man, Man" campaign became a viral and pop culture sensation in 2010. The tongue-in-cheek ad featured rugged ex-NFL football player Isaiah Mustafa as "The Man Your Man Could Smell Like." In one seamless take, Mustafa confidently strikes a variety of romantic poses while taking a shower in a bathroom, then standing on a boat, then riding a white horse. Old Spice's Facebook page included a Web application called "My Perpetual Love," which featured Mustafa offering men the opportunity to be "more like him" by e-mailing and tweeting their sweethearts virtual love notes. The campaign's effectiveness is evident in the staggering number of responses it received: 1.8 billion impressions (people who saw, read, or heard about the commercials); over 140 million YouTube views; and a 2700 percent increase in Twitter followers.[37]

Increased Competition

One reason marketers have been forced to use so many financial incentives or discounts is that the marketplace has become more competitive. Both demand-side and supply-side factors have contributed to the increase in competitive intensity. On the demand side, consumption for many products and services has flattened and hit the maturity stage, or even the decline stage, of the product life cycle. As a result, marketers can achieve sales growth for brands only by taking away competitors' market share. On the supply side, new competitors have emerged due to a number of factors, such as the following:

- *Globalization:* Although firms have embraced globalization as a means to open new markets and potential sources of revenue, it has also increased the number of competitors in existing markets, threatening current sources of revenue.
- *Low-priced competitors:* Market penetration by generics, private labels, and low-priced "clones" imitating product leaders has increased on a worldwide-basis. Retailers have gained power and often dictate what happens within the store. Their chief marketing weapon is price, and they have introduced and pushed their own brands and demanded greater compensation from trade promotions to stock and display national brands.
- *Brand extensions:* We've noted that many companies have taken their existing brands and launched products with the same name into new categories. Many of these brands provide formidable opposition to market leaders.
- *Deregulation:* Certain industries like telecommunications, financial services, health care, and transportation have become deregulated, leading to increased competition from outside traditionally defined product-market boundaries.

Increased Costs

At the same time that competition is increasing, the cost of introducing a new product or supporting an existing product has increased rapidly, making it difficult to match the investment and level of support that brands were able to receive in previous years. In 2008, about 123,000 new consumer products were introduced in the United States, but with a failure rate estimated at over 90 percent. Given the millions of dollars spent on developing and marketing a new product, the total failure cost was conservatively estimated by one group to exceed billions of dollars.[38]

Greater Accountability

Finally, marketers often find themselves responsible for meeting ambitious short-term profit targets because of financial market pressures and senior management imperatives. Stock analysts value strong and consistent earnings reports as an indication of the long-term financial health of a firm. As a result, marketing managers may find themselves in the dilemma of having to make decisions with short-term benefits but long-term costs (such as cutting advertising expenditures). Moreover, many of these same managers have experienced rapid job turnover and promotions and may not anticipate being in their current positions for very long. One study found that the average tenure of a CMO is about three and a half years, suggesting they have little time to make an impact.[39] These different organizational pressures may encourage quick-fix solutions with perhaps adverse long-run consequences.

THE BRAND EQUITY CONCEPT

Marketers clearly face a number of competitive challenges, and some critics feel the response of many has been ineffective or, worse, has further aggravated the problem. In the rest of this book, we'll present theories, models, and frameworks that accommodate and reflect marketing's new challenges in order to provide useful managerial guidelines and suggest promising new directions for future thought and research. We'll introduce a "common denominator" or unified conceptual framework, based on the concept of brand equity, as a tool to interpret the potential effects of various brand strategies.

One of the most popular and potentially important marketing concepts to arise in the 1980s was *brand equity.* Its emergence, however, has meant both good news and bad news to marketers. The good news is that brand equity has elevated the importance of the brand in marketing strategy and provided focus for managerial interest and research activity. The bad news is that, confusingly, the concept has been defined a number of different ways for a number of different purposes. No common viewpoint has emerged about how to conceptualize and measure brand equity.

Fundamentally, branding is all about endowing products and services with the power of brand equity. Despite the many different views, most observers agree that brand equity consists of the marketing effects uniquely attributable to a brand. That is, brand equity explains why different outcomes result from the marketing of a branded product or service than if it were not branded. That is the view we take in this book. As a stark example of the transformational power of branding, consider the auctions sales in Figure 1-11. Without such celebrity associations, it is doubtful that any of these items would cost more than a few hundred dollars at a flea market.[40]

Branding is all about creating differences. Most marketing observers also agree with the following basic principles of branding and brand equity:

- Differences in outcomes arise from the "added value" endowed to a product as a result of past marketing activity for the brand.
- This value can be created for a brand in many different ways.
- Brand equity provides a common denominator for interpreting marketing strategies and assessing the value of a brand.
- There are many different ways in which the value of a brand can be manifested or exploited to benefit the firm (in terms of greater proceeds or lower costs or both).

Fundamentally, the brand equity concept reinforces how important the brand is in marketing strategies. Chapters 2 and 3 in Part II of the book provide an overview of brand equity and a blueprint for the rest of the book. The remainder of the book addresses in much greater depth

- A glove Michael Jackson wore on tour sold for $330,000 in 2010.

- A '29 Duesenberg Model J Dual Cowl Phaeton driven by Elvis Presley in the 1966 movie *Spinout* sold for $1.2 million in 2011.

- A dog collar owned by Charles Dickens sold for nearly $12,000 in 2009.

- The Supergirl costume made for the movie in 1984 sold for over $11,000 in a Christie's 2010 auction.

- A T-shirt worn by The Who's Keith Moon sold for $3,550 at another Christie's auction in 2010.

- A dress worn by Audrey Hepburn in *Funny Face* sold for $56,250, a sweater worn by Marilyn Monroe sold for $11,875, and a pair of earrings worn by Kate Winslet in *Titanic* fetched $25,000 at an auction in 2010.

FIGURE 1-11

Notable Recent Auction Sales

A sweater is just a sweater, unless it was worn or owned by Marilyn Monroe, in which case it could be worth thousands of dollars.

Source: Album/Newscom

how to build brand equity (Chapters 4–7 in Part III), measure brand equity (Chapters 8–10 in Part IV), and manage brand equity (Chapters 11–14 in Part V). The concluding Chapter 15 in Part VI provides some additional applications and perspective.

The remainder of this chapter provides an overview of the strategic brand management process that helps pull all these various concepts together.

STRATEGIC BRAND MANAGEMENT PROCESS

Strategic brand management involves the design and implementation of marketing programs and activities to build, measure, and manage brand equity. In this text, we define the *strategic brand management process* as having four main steps (see Figure 1-12):

1. Identifying and developing brand plans
2. Designing and implementing brand marketing programs
3. Measuring and interpreting brand performance
4. Growing and sustaining brand equity

Let's briefly highlight each of these four steps.[41]

Identifying and Developing Brand Plans

The strategic brand management process starts with a clear understanding of what the brand is to represent and how it should be positioned with respect to competitors.[42] Brand planning, as described in Chapters 2 and 3, uses the following three interlocking models.

- The *brand positioning model* describes how to guide integrated marketing to maximize competitive advantages.
- The *brand resonance model* describes how to create intense, activity loyalty relationships with customers.
- The *brand value chain* is a means to trace the value creation process for brands, to better understand the financial impact of brand marketing expenditures and investments.

Designing and Implementing Brand Marketing Programs

As Chapter 2 outlines, building brand equity requires properly positioning the brand in the minds of customers and achieving as much brand resonance as possible. In general, this knowledge-building process will depend on three factors:

1. The initial choices of the brand elements making up the brand and how they are mixed and matched;

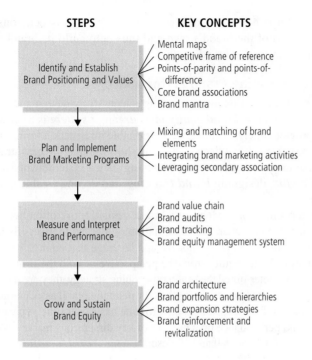

STEPS

KEY CONCEPTS

Identify and Establish Brand Positioning and Values
- Mental maps
- Competitive frame of reference
- Points-of-parity and points-of-difference
- Core brand associations
- Brand mantra

Plan and Implement Brand Marketing Programs
- Mixing and matching of brand elements
- Integrating brand marketing activities
- Leveraging secondary association

Measure and Interpret Brand Performance
- Brand value chain
- Brand audits
- Brand tracking
- Brand equity management system

Grow and Sustain Brand Equity
- Brand architecture
- Brand portfolios and hierarchies
- Brand expansion strategies
- Brand reinforcement and revitalization

FIGURE 1-12
Strategic Brand Management Process

2. The marketing activities and supporting marketing programs and the way the brand is integrated into them; and

3. Other associations indirectly transferred to or leveraged by the brand as a result of linking it to some other entity (such as the company, country of origin, channel of distribution, or another brand).

Some important considerations of each of these three factors are as follows.

Choosing Brand Elements. The most common brand elements are brand names, URLs, logos, symbols, characters, packaging, and slogans. The best test of the brand-building contribution of a brand element is what consumers would think about the product or service if they knew only its brand name or its associated logo or other element. Because different elements have different advantages, marketing managers often use a subset of all the possible brand elements or even all of them. Chapter 4 examines in detail the means by which the choice and design of brand elements can help to build brand equity.

Integrating the Brand into Marketing Activities and the Supporting Marketing Program. Although the judicious choice of brand elements can make some contribution to building brand equity, the biggest contribution comes from marketing activities related to the brand. This text highlights only some particularly important marketing program considerations for building brand equity. Chapter 5 addresses new developments in designing marketing programs as well as issues in product strategy, pricing strategy, and channels strategy. Chapter 6 addresses issues in communications strategy.

Leveraging Secondary Associations. The third and final way to build brand equity is to leverage secondary associations. Brand associations may themselves be linked to other entities that have their own associations, creating these secondary associations. For example, the brand may be linked to certain source factors, such as the company (through branding strategies), countries or other geographical regions (through identification of product origin), and channels of distribution (through channel strategy), as well as to other brands (through ingredients or co-branding), characters (through licensing), spokespeople (through endorsements), sporting or cultural events (through sponsorship), or some other third-party sources (through awards or reviews).

Because the brand becomes identified with another entity, even though this entity may not directly relate to the product or service performance, consumers may *infer* that the brand shares associations with that entity, thus producing indirect or secondary associations for the brand.

In essence, the marketer is borrowing or leveraging some other associations for the brand to create some associations of the brand's own and thus help build its brand equity. Chapter 7 describes the means of leveraging brand equity.

Measuring and Interpreting Brand Performance

To manage their brands profitably, managers must successfully design and implement a brand equity measurement system. A *brand equity measurement system* is a set of research procedures designed to provide timely, accurate, and actionable information for marketers so that they can make the best possible tactical decisions in the short run and the best strategic decisions in the long run. As described in Chapter 8, implementing such a system involves three key steps—conducting *brand audits*, designing *brand tracking* studies, and establishing a *brand equity management system*.

The task of determining or evaluating a brand's positioning often benefits from a brand audit. A *brand audit* is a comprehensive examination of a brand to assess its health, uncover its sources of equity, and suggest ways to improve and leverage that equity. A brand audit requires understanding sources of brand equity from the perspective of both the firm and the consumer.

Once marketers have determined the brand positioning strategy, they are ready to put into place the actual marketing program to create, strengthen, or maintain brand associations. *Brand tracking studies* collect information from consumers on a routine basis over time, typically through quantitative measures of brand performance on a number of key dimensions marketers can identify in the brand audit or other means. Chapters 9 and 10 describe a number of measures to operationalize it.

A *brand equity management system* is a set of organizational processes designed to improve the understanding and use of the brand equity concept within a firm. Three major steps help implement a brand equity management system: creating brand equity charters, assembling brand equity reports, and defining brand equity responsibilities.

Growing and Sustaining Brand Equity

Maintaining and expanding on brand equity can be quite challenging. Brand equity management activities take a broader and more diverse perspective of the brand's equity—understanding how branding strategies should reflect corporate concerns and be adjusted, if at all, over time or over geographical boundaries or multiple market segments.

Defining Brand Architecture.   The firm's brand architecture provides general guidelines about its branding strategy and which brand elements to apply across all the different products sold by the firm. Two key concepts in defining brand architecture are brand portfolios and the brand hierarchy. The *brand portfolio* is the set of different brands that a particular firm offers for sale to buyers in a particular category. The *brand hierarchy* displays the number and nature of common and distinctive brand components across the firm's set of brands. Chapter 11 reviews a three-step approach to brand architecture and how to devise brand portfolios and hierarchies. Chapter 12 concentrates on the topic of brand extensions in which an existing brand is used to launch a product into a different category or sub-category.

Managing Brand Equity over Time.   Effective brand management also requires taking a long-term view of marketing decisions. A long-term perspective of brand management recognizes that any changes in the supporting marketing program for a brand may, by changing consumer knowledge, affect the success of future marketing programs. A long-term view also produces proactive strategies designed to maintain and enhance customer-based brand equity over time and reactive strategies to revitalize a brand that encounters some difficulties or problems. Chapter 13 outlines issues related to managing brand equity over time.

Managing Brand Equity over Geographic Boundaries, Cultures, and Market Segments.   Another important consideration in managing brand equity is recognizing and accounting for different types of consumers in developing branding and marketing programs. International factors and global branding strategies are particularly important in these decisions. In expanding a brand overseas, managers need to build equity by relying on specific knowledge about the experience and behaviors of those market segments. Chapter 14 examines issues related to broadening of brand equity across market segments.

REVIEW

This chapter began by defining a brand as a name, term, sign, symbol, or design, or some combination of these elements, intended to identify the goods and services of one seller or group of sellers and to differentiate them from those of competitors. The different components of a brand (brand names, logos, symbols, package designs, and so forth) are brand elements. Brand elements come in many different forms. A brand is distinguished from a product, which is defined as anything that can be offered to a market for attention, acquisition, use, or consumption that might satisfy a need or want. A product may be a physical good, service, retail store, person, organization, place, or idea.

A brand is a product, but one that adds other dimensions that differentiate it in some way from other products designed to satisfy the same need. These differences may be rational and tangible—related to product performance of the brand—or more symbolic, emotional, or intangible—related to what the brand represents. Brands themselves are valuable intangible assets that need to be managed carefully. Brands offer a number of benefits to customers and the firms.

The key to branding is that consumers perceive differences among brands in a product category. Marketers can brand virtually any type of product by giving the product a name and attaching meaning to it in terms of what it has to offer and how it differs from competitors. A number of branding challenges and opportunities faced by present-day marketing managers were outlined related to changes in customer attitudes and behavior, competitive forces, marketing efficiency and effectiveness, and internal company dynamics.

The strategic brand management process has four steps:

1. Identifying and developing brand plans
2. Designing and implementing brand marketing programs
3. Measuring and interpreting brand performance
4. Growing and sustaining brand equity

The remainder of the book outlines these steps in detail.

DISCUSSION QUESTIONS

1. What do brands mean to you? What are your favorite brands and why? Check to see how your perceptions of brands might differ from those of others.
2. Who do you think has the strongest brands? Why? What do you think of the Interbrand list of the 25 strongest brands in Figure 1-5? Do you agree with the rankings? Why or why not?
3. Can you think of anything that cannot be branded? Pick an example that was not discussed in each of the categories provided (services; retailers and distributors; people and organizations; sports, arts, and entertainment) and describe how each is a brand.
4. Can you think of yourself as a brand? What do you do to "brand" yourself?
5. What do you think of the new branding challenges and opportunities that were listed in the chapter? Can you think of any other issues?

BRAND FOCUS 1.0

History of Branding

This appendix traces the history of branding and brand management, dividing the development into six distinct phases.

Early Origins: Before 1860

Branding, in one form or another, has been around for centuries. The original motivation for branding was for craftsmen and others to identify the fruits of their labors so that customers could easily recognize them. Branding, or at least trademarks, can be traced back to ancient pottery and stonemason's marks, which were applied to handcrafted goods to identify their source.

Pottery and clay lamps were sometimes sold far from the shops where they were made, and buyers looked for the stamps of reliable potters as a guide to quality. Marks have been found on early Chinese porcelain, on pottery jars from ancient Greece and Rome, and on goods from India dating back to about 1300 B.C.

In medieval times, potters' marks were joined by printers' marks, watermarks on paper, bread marks, and the marks of various craft guilds. In some cases, these were used to attract buyers loyal to particular makers, but the marks were also used to police infringers of the guild monopolies and to single out the makers of inferior goods. An English law passed in 1266 required bakers to put their mark on every loaf of bread sold, "to the end that if any bread bu faultie in weight, it may bee then knowne in whom the fault is." Goldsmiths and silversmiths were also required to mark their goods, both with their signature or personal symbol and with a sign of the quality of the metal. In 1597, two goldsmiths convicted of putting false marks on their wares were nailed to the pillory by their ears. Similarly harsh punishments were decreed for those who counterfeited other artisans' marks.

When Europeans began to settle in North America, they brought the convention and practice of branding with them. The makers of patent medicines and tobacco manufacturers were early U.S. branding pioneers. Medicine potions such as Swaim's Panacea, Fahnestock's Vermifuge, and Perry Davis' Vegetable Pain Killer became well known to the public prior to the American Civil War. Patent medicines were packaged in small bottles and, because they were not seen as a necessity, were vigorously promoted. To further influence consumer choices in stores, manufacturers of these medicines printed elaborate and distinctive labels, often with their own portrait featured in the center.

Tobacco manufacturers had been exporting their crop since the early 1600s. By the early 1800s, manufacturers had packed bales of tobacco under labels such as Smith's Plug and Brown and Black's Twist. During the 1850s, many tobacco manufacturers recognized that more creative names—such as Cantaloupe, Rock Candy, Wedding Cake, and Lone Jack—were helpful in selling their tobacco products. In the 1860s, tobacco manufacturers began to sell their wares in small bags directly to consumers. Attractive-looking packages were seen as important, and picture labels, decorations, and symbols were designed as a result.

Emergence of National Manufacturer Brands: 1860 to 1914

In the United States after the American Civil War, a number of forces combined to make widely distributed, manufacturer-branded products a profitable venture:

- Improvements in transportation (e.g., railroads) and communication (e.g., telegraph and telephone) made regional and even national distribution increasingly easy.

- Improvements in production processes made it possible to produce large quantities of high-quality products inexpensively.

- Improvements in packaging made individual (as opposed to bulk) packages that could be identified with the manufacturer's trademark increasingly viable.

- Changes in U.S. trademark law in 1879, the 1880s, and 1906 made it easier to protect brand identities.

- Advertising became perceived as a more credible option, and newspapers and magazines eagerly sought out advertising revenues.

- Retail institutions such as department and variety stores and national mail order houses served as effective middlemen and encouraged consumer spending.

- The population increased due to liberal immigration policies.

- Increasing industrialization and urbanization raised the standard of living and aspirations of Americans, although many products on the market still were of uneven quality.

- Literacy rose as the percentage of illiterate Americans dropped from 20 percent in 1870 to 10 percent in 1900.

All these factors facilitated the development of consistent-quality consumer products that could be efficiently sold to consumers through mass market advertising campaigns. In this fertile branding environment, mass-produced merchandise in packages largely replaced locally produced merchandise sold from bulk containers. This change brought about the widespread use of trademarks. For example, Procter & Gamble made candles in Cincinnati and shipped them to merchants in other cities along the Ohio and Mississippi rivers. In 1851, wharf hands began to brand crates of Procter & Gamble candles with a crude star. The firm soon noticed that buyers downriver relied on the star as a mark of quality, and merchants refused the candles if the crates arrived without the mark. As a result, the candles were marked with a more formal star label on all packages, branded as "Star," and began to develop a loyal following.

The development and management of these brands was largely driven by the owners of the firm and their top-level management. For example, the first president of National Biscuit was involved heavily in the introduction in 1898 of Uneeda Biscuits, the first nationally branded biscuit. One of their first decisions was to create a pictorial symbol for the brand, the Uneeda biscuit slicker boy, who appeared in the supporting ad campaigns. H. J. Heinz built up the Heinz brand name through production innovations and spectacular promotions. Coca-Cola became a national powerhouse due to the efforts of Asa Candler, who actively oversaw the growth of the extensive distribution channel.

National manufacturers sometimes had to overcome resistance from consumers, retailers, wholesalers, and even employees from within their own company. To do so, these firms employed sustained "push" and "pull" efforts to keep both consumers and retailers happy and accepting of national brands. Consumers were attracted through the use of sampling, premiums, product education brochures, and heavy advertising. Retailers were lured by in-store sampling and promotional programs and shelf maintenance assistance.

As the use of brand names and trademarks spread, so did the practice of imitation and counterfeiting. Although the laws were somewhat unclear, more and more firms sought protection by sending their trademarks and labels to district courts for registration. Congress finally separated the registration of trademarks and labels in 1870 with the enactment of the country's first federal trademark law. Under the law, registrants were required to send a facsimile of their mark with a description of the type of goods on which it was used to the Patent Office in Washington along with a $25 fee. One of the first marks submitted to the Patent Office under the new law was the Underwood Devil, which was registered to William Underwood & Company of Boston on November 29, 1870 for use on "Deviled Entremets." By 1890, most countries had trademark acts, establishing brand names, labels, and designs as legally protectable assets.

Dominance of Mass Marketed Brands: 1915 to 1929

By 1915, manufacturer brands had become well established in the United States on both a regional and national basis. The next 15 years saw increasing acceptance and even admiration of manufacturer brands by consumers. The marketing of brands became more specialized under the guidance of functional experts in charge of production, promotion, personal selling, and other areas. This greater specialization led to more advanced marketing techniques. Design professionals were enlisted to assist in the process of trademark selection. Personal selling became more sophisticated as salesmen were carefully selected and trained to systematically handle accounts and seek out new businesses. Advertising combined more powerful creativity with more persuasive copy and slogans. Government and industry regulation came into place to reduce deceptive advertising. Marketing research became more important and influential in supporting marketing decisions.

Although functional management of brands had these virtues, it also presented problems. Because responsibility for any one brand was divided among two or more functional managers—as well as advertising specialists—poor coordination was always a potential problem. For example, the introduction of Wheaties cereal by General Mills was nearly sabotaged by the company's salesmen, who were reluctant to take on new duties to support the brand. Three years after the cereal's introduction and on the verge of its being dropped, a manager from the advertising department at General Mills decided to become a product champion for Wheaties, and the brand went on to great success in the following decades.

Challenges to Manufacturer Brands: 1930 to 1945

The onset of the Great Depression in 1929 posed new challenges to manufacturer brands. Greater price sensitivity swung the pendulum of power in the favor of retailers who pushed their own brands and dropped nonperforming manufacturer brands. Advertising came under fire as manipulative, deceptive, and tasteless and was increasingly being ignored by certain segments of the population. In 1938, the Wheeler Amendment gave power to the Federal Trade Commission (FTC) to regulate advertising practices. In response to these trends, manufacturers' advertising went beyond slogans and jingles to give consumers specific reasons why they should buy advertised products.

There were few dramatic changes in marketing of brands during this time. As a notable exception, Procter & Gamble put the first brand management system into place, whereby each of their brands had a manager assigned only to that brand who was responsible for its financial success. Other firms were slow to follow, however, and relied more on their long-standing reputation for good quality—and a lack of competition—to sustain sales. During World War II, manufacturer brands became relatively scarce as resources were diverted to the war effort. Nevertheless, many brands continued to advertise and helped bolster consumer demand during these tough times.

The Lanham Act of 1946 permitted federal registration of service marks (marks used to designate services rather than products) and collective marks such as union labels and club emblems.

Establishment of Brand Management Standards: 1946 to 1985

After World War II, the pent-up demand for high-quality brands led to an explosion of sales. Personal income grew as the economy took off, and market demand intensified as the rate of population growth exploded. Demand for national brands soared, fueled by a burst of new products and a receptive and growing middle class. Firm after firm during this time period adopted the brand management system.

In the brand management system, a brand manager took "ownership" of a brand. A brand manager was responsible for developing and implementing the annual marketing plan for his or her brand, as well as identifying new business opportunities.

The brand manager might be assisted, internally, by representatives from manufacturing, the sales force, marketing research, financial planning, research and development, personnel, legal, and public relations and, externally, by representatives from advertising agencies, research suppliers, and public relations agencies.

Then, as now, a successful brand manager had to be a versatile jack-of-all-trades. The skills that began to be required then have only become more important now, including:

- Marketing fundamentals
- Cultural insights to understand the diversity of consumers
- IT and Web skills to guide digital activities
- Technical sophistication to appreciate new research methods and models
- Design fluency to work with design techniques and designers
- Creativity to devise holistic solutions

Branding Becomes More Pervasive: 1986 to Now

The merger and acquisitions boom of the mid-1980s raised the interest of top executives and other board members as to the financial value of brands. With this realization came an appreciation of the importance of managing brands as valuable intangible assets. At the same time, more different types of firms began to see the advantages of having a strong brand and the corresponding disadvantages of having a weak brand.

The last 25 years have seen an explosion in the interest and application of branding as more firms have embraced the concept. As more and more different kinds of products are sold or promoted directly to consumers, the adoption of modern marketing practices and branding has spread further. Consider the pharmaceutical industry.

THE PHARMACEUTICAL INDUSTRY

In the United States, prescription drugs are increasingly being branded and sold to consumers with traditional marketing tactics such as advertising and promotion. Direct-to-consumer advertising for prescription drugs also grew from $242 million in 1994 to $4.2 billion in 2010. In 2009, Pfizer spent over $1 billion in direct-to-consumer advertising. Much of this effort is focused on what we might call "disease branding," in which marketers shape public impressions of a medical malady to make treating it more attractive to potential patients. Panic disorder, reflux disease, erectile dysfunction, and restless legs syndrome were all relatively obscure to the public until they were given a specific name and meaning by drug companies. By highlighting and destigmatizing medical conditions, disease branding increases demand for the drugs being sold for treatment. When Pharmacia launched Detrol, it labeled what physicians had been calling "urge incontinence" as an "overactive bladder," a much more vigorous-sounding condition. Millions of prescriptions followed. Some pharmaceutical companies, however, are cutting back on direct-to-consumer advertising in light of the lower number of new-drug introductions and increasing government scrutiny of the practice. They are selective in deciding which brands to market directly to consumers; of over 2,000 drugs recently studied, only 100 were targeted via advertising to consumers.[44]

Branding has become part of the everyday vernacular and it is not uncommon to hear people of all walks of life talk about branding and branding concepts. Although the interest in branding has many positive consequences, people don't always seem to understand how branding works or apply branding concepts correctly. For branding success, an appreciation of and aptitude for using appropriate branding concepts—a focus of this book—is critical.

Notes

1. For general background and in-depth research on a number of branding issues, consult the *Journal of Brand Management* and *Journal of Brand Strategy*, Henry Stewart publications.

2. Interbrand Group, *World's Greatest Brands: An International Review* (New York: John Wiley, 1992).

3. Adrian Room, *Dictionary of Trade Greatest Brands: An International Review* (New York: John Wiley, 1992); Adrian Room, *Dictionary of Trade Name Origins* (London: Routledge & Kegan Paul, 1982).

4. The second through fifth levels are based on a conceptualization in Theodore Levitt, "Marketing Success Through Differentiation—of Anything," *Harvard Business Review* (January–February 1980): 83–91.

5. Theodore Levitt, "Marketing Myopia," *Harvard Business Review* (July–August 1960): 45–56.

6. Thomas J. Madden, Frank Fehle, and Susan M. Fournier, "Brands Matter: An Empirical Demonstration of the Creation of Shareholder Value through Brands," *Journal of the Academy of Marketing Science* 34, no. 2 (2006): 224–235; Frank Fehle, Susan M. Fournier, Thomas J. Madden, and David G. Shrider, "Brand Value and Asset Pricing," *Quarterly Journal of Finance & Accounting* 47, no. 1 (2008): 59–82.

7. Jacob Jacoby, Jerry C. Olson, and Rafael Haddock, "Price, Brand Name, and Product Composition Characteristics as Determinants of Perceived Quality," *Journal of Consumer Research* 3, no. 4 (1971): 209–216; Jacob Jacoby, George Syzbillo, and Jacqueline Busato-Sehach, "Information Acquisition Behavior in Brand Choice Situations," *Journal of Marketing Research* 11 (1977): 63–69.

8. Susan Fournier, "Consumers and Their Brands: Developing Relationship Theory in Consumer Research," *Journal of Consumer Research* 24, no. 3 (1997): 343–373.

9. Susan Fournier, "Consumers and Their Brands: Developing Relationship Theory in Consumer Research," *Journal of Consumer Research* 24, no. 3 (1997): 343–373; Aric Rindfleisch, Nancy Wong, and James E. Burroughs, "God and Mammon: The Influence of Religiosity on Brand Connections," in *The Connected Customer: The Changing Nature of Consumer and Business Markets*, eds. Stefan H. K. Wuyts, Marnik G. Dekimpe, Els Gijsbrechts, and Rik Pieters (Mahwah, NJ: Lawrence Erlbaum, 2010), 163–201; Ron Shachar, Tülin Erdem, Keisha M. Cutright, and Gavan J. Fitzsimons, "Brands: The Opiate of the Nonreligious Masses?," *Marketing Science* 30 (January–February 2011): 92–110.

10. For an excellent example of the work being done on culture and branding, consult the following: Grant McCracken, *Culture and Consumption II: Markets, Meaning and Brand Management* (Bloomington, IN: Indiana University Press, 2005) and Grant McCracken, *Chief Culture Officer: How to Create a Living, Breathing Corporation* (New York: Basic Books, 2009). For a broader discussion of culture and consumer behavior, see Eric J. Arnould and Craig J. Thompson, "Consumer Culture Theory (CCT): Twenty Years of Research," *Journal of Consumer Research* 31(March 2005): 868–882.

11. Philip Nelson, "Information and Consumer Behavior," *Journal of Political Economy* 78 (1970): 311–329; and Michael R. Darby and Edi Karni, "Free Competition and the Optimal Amount of Fraud," *Journal of Law and Economics* 16 (April 1974): 67–88.

12. Allan D. Shocker and Richard Chay, "How Marketing Researchers Can Harness the Power of Brand Equity." Presentation to New Zealand Marketing Research Society, August 1992.

13. Ted Roselius, "Consumer Ranking of Risk Reduction Methods," *Journal of Marketing* 35 (January 1971): 56–61.

14. Leslie de Chernatony and Gil McWilliam, "The Varying Nature of Brands as Assets," *International Journal of Advertising* 8 (1989): 339–349.

15. Constance E. Bagley and Diane W. Savage, *Managers and the Legal Environment: Strategies for the 21st Century*, 6th ed. (Mason, OH: Southwestern-Cengage Learning, 2010).

16. Tülin Erdem and Joffre Swait, "Brand Equity as a Signaling Phenomenon," *Journal of Consumer Psychology* 7, no. 2 (1998): 131–157.

17. Charles Bymer, "Valuing Your Brands: Lessons from Wall Street and the Impact on Marketers," ARF Third Annual Advertising and Promotion Workshop, February 5–6, 1991.

18. Josh Eells, "Who Says the Music Industry is Kaput?" *Bloomberg BusinessWeek*, May 31–June 6, 2010, 77–79; Aimee Groth, "Mayhem! Sponsored by …," *Bloomberg BusinessWeek*, 7 November, 2010, 84–85.

19. Elisabeth Sullivan, "Building a Better Brand," *Marketing News*, 15 (September 2009): 14–17.

20. Kevin Lane Keller, "Building a Strong Business-to-Business Brand," in *Business-to-Business Brand Management: Theory, Research, and Executive Case Study Exercises,* in *Advances in Business Marketing & Purchasing* series, Volume 15, ed. Arch Woodside (Bingley, UK: Emerald Group Publishing Limited, 2009): 11–31; Luc Halstead, "Cisco's Race for the

SMB Market," www.crn.com, 21 July 2004; Paolo Del Nibletto, "Cisco to Drill Deeper Into the SMB Market," www.itbusiness.ca, 4 April 2007; Anita Campbell, "Segmenting 'Small Business' for IT Needs," www.smallbiztrends.com, 14 October 2004.

21. Todd Wasserman, "Intuit Program Combines Reviews and Social Networking," *Brandweek*, 14 February 2010; "Intuit: The 'Turbo' Tron," www.OMMA.com, 1 September 2010.

22. "As Consumers Seek Savings, Private Label Sales Up 7.4 Percent," *NielsenWire*, 13 August 2009.

23. Brad Stone, "I'll Take It from Here," *Bloomberg BusinessWeek*, 6 February 2011, 50–56; Michael V. Copeland, "Google: The Search Party Is Over," *Fortune*, 16 August 2010, 58–67; Helen Walters, "How Google Got Its New Look," *Bloomberg BusinessWeek*, 5 May 2010; Andrei Hagiu and David B. Yoffie, "What's Your Google Strategy?," *Harvard Business Review* (April 2009).

24. Jenna Goodreau, "Dishing with Rachael Ray," www.forbes.com, 3 February 2010; "6 Celebrity Chef-Preneurs," www.money.cnn.com, 7 June 2011; www.rachaelray.com.

25. David Lidsky, "Me Inc.: the Rethink," *Fast Company*, March 2005, 16.

26. University professors are certainly aware of the power of the name as a brand. In fact, one reason many professors choose to have students identify themselves on exams by numbers of some type instead of by name is so they will not be biased in grading by their knowledge of which student's exam they are reading. Otherwise, it may be too easy to give higher grades to those students the professor likes or, for whatever reason, expects to have done well on the exam.

27. www.unicef.org; Ariel Schwartz, "The UNICEF TAP Project Charges Cash for Tap Water to Raise Funds, Awareness," *Fast Company*, 22 March 2011; "UNICEF Aims to 'Put It Right' with a Five-Year Plan to Raise £55m," *Mail Media Centre*, 6 February 2010; Rosie Baker, "UNICEF Brings Campaign to London Streets," *Marketing Week*, 15 February 2010; www.ikea.com.

28. Joel Hochberg, "Package Goods Marketing vs. Hollywood," *Advertising Age*, 20 January 1992.

29. "Harry Potter and the Endless Cash Saga," www.news.sky.com, 7 July 2011; "The Harry Potter Economy," *The Economist*, 17 December 2009; Susan Gunelius, "The Marketing Magic Behind Harry Potter," *Entrepreneur*, 22 November 2010; Beth Snyder Bulik, "Harry Potter: The $15 Billion Man," *Advertising Age*, 16 July 2007; "*Harry Potter* Casts the Superpowerful Moneymaking Spell," *Entertainment Weekly*, December 23/30, 2011, 26.

30. For an illuminating analysis of top brands, see Francis J. Kelley III and Barry Silverstein, *The Breakaway Brand: How Great Brands Stand Out* (New York, McGraw-Hill, 2005).

31. Jack Trout, "Branding Can't Exist Without Positioning," *Advertising Age*, 14 March 2005, 28.

32. Allan D. Shocker, Rajendra Srivastava, and Robert Ruekert, "Challenges and Opportunities Facing Brand Management: An Introduction to the Special Issue," *Journal of Marketing Research* 31 (May 1994): 149–158.

33. Ben Sisario, "Looking to a Sneaker for a Band's Big Break," *New York Times*, 6 October 2010; Rebecca Cullers, "Stepping Up," *Brandweek*, 13 September 2010; Eleftheria Parpis, "Converse Turns Up the Noise," *Adweek*, 14 July 2008; Erin Ailworth, "Pros and Cons," *Boston Globe*, 2 March 2008.

34. Betsy Bohlen, Steve Carlotti, and Liz Mihas, "How the Recession Has Changed U.S. Consumer Behavior," *McKinsey Quarterly*, December 2009.

35. John Gerzema and Ed Lebar, *The Brand Bubble* (San Francisco, CA: Jossey-Bass, 2008).

36. Dan Sewell, "Procter & Gamble Moves from Soap Operas to Social Media," *USA TODAY*, December 11, 2010.

37. Dan Sewall, "Old Spice Rolls Out New Ads," *Associated Press*, July 1, 2010; Adam Tschorn, "Old Spice Ad Connects Women to Male Brand with a Wink," *Los Angeles Times*, 6 March 2010; Mary Elizabeth Williams, "Take That, Super Bowl," www.salon.com, 22 February 2010.

38. www.bases.com/news/news03052001.html; "New Products Generate $21 Billion in Sales in 2008," *NielsenWire*, 30 January 2009.

39. Frederick E. Allen, "CMOs Are Staying on the Job Longer Than Ever," *Forbes*, 24 March 2011.

40. Jem Aswad, "Single Michael Jackson Glove Sold for over $300K," *Rolling Stone*, 6 December 2010; Jerry Garrett, "Putting a Price on Star Power," *New York Times*, 28 January 2011; www.christies.com. For an academic treatment of the topic, see George E. Newman, Gil Diesendruck, and Paul Bloom, "Celebrity Contagion and the Value of Objects," *Journal of Consumer Research*, 38 (August 2011): 215–228.

41. For discussion of some other approaches to branding, see David A. Aaker, *Managing Brand Equity* (New York: Free Press, 1991); David A. Aaker, *Building Strong Brands* (New York: Free Press, 1996); David A. Aaker and Erich Joachimsthaler, *Brand Leadership* (New York: Free Press, 2000); Jean-Noel Kapferer, *Strategic Brand Management*, 2nd ed. (New York: Free Press, 2005); Scott M. Davis, *Brand Asset Management* (New York: Free Press, 2000); Giep Franzen and Sandra Moriarty, *The Science and Art of Branding* (Armonk, NY: M. E. Sharpe, 2009). For an overview of current research findings, see *Brands and Brand Management: Contemporary Research Perspectives*, eds. Barbara Loken, Rohini Ahluwalia, and Michael J. Houston (New York: Taylor and Francis, 2010) and *Kellogg on Branding*, eds. Alice M. Tybout and Tim Calkins (Hoboken, NJ: John Wiley & Sons, 2005).

42. For a very practical brand building guide, see David Taylor and David Nichols, *The Brand Gym*, 2nd ed. (West Sussex, UK: John Wiley & Sons, 2010).

43. Much of this section is adapted in part from an excellent article by George S. Low and Ronald A. Fullerton, "Brands, Brand Management, and the Brand Manager System: A Critical-Historical Evaluation," *Journal of*

Marketing Research 31 (May 1994): 173–190; and an excellent book by Hal Morgan, *Symbols of America* (Steam Press, 1986).

44. Carl Elliott, "How to Brand a Disease—and Sell a Cure," www.cnn.com, 11 October 2010; Keith J. Winstein and Suzanne Vranica, "Drug Firms' Spending on Consumer Ads Fell 8% in '08, a Rare Marketing Pullback," *Wall Street Journal*, 16 April 2009; Matthew Arnold, "Flat Is the New Up," *Medical Marketing & Media* (April 2010); Yumiko Ono, "Prescription-Drug Makers Heighten Hard-Sell Tactics," *Wall Street Journal*, 29 August 1994, B-1

Customer-Based Brand Equity and Brand Positioning

2

Learning Objectives

After reading this chapter, you should be able to

1. Define customer-based brand equity.

2. Outline the sources and outcomes of customer-based brand equity.

3. Identify the four components of brand positioning.

4. Describe the guidelines in developing a good brand positioning.

5. Explain brand mantra and how it should be developed.

Starbucks' unique brand positioning helped to fuel its phenomenal growth.
Source: AP Photo/Ted S. Warren

Preview

Chapter 1 introduced some basic notions about brands, particularly brand equity, and the roles they have played and are playing in marketing strategies. Part II of the text explores how to develop brand strategies. Great brands are not accidents. They are a result of thoughtful and imaginative planning. Anyone building or managing a brand must carefully develop and implement creative brand strategies.

To aid in that planning, three tools or models are helpful. Like the famous Russian nesting *matryoshka* dolls, the three models are interconnected and in turn become larger in scope: the first model is a component in the second model; the second model, in turn, is a component in the third. Combined, the three models provide crucial micro and macro perspectives on successful brand building. These are the three models:

1. *Brand positioning model* describes how to establish competitive advantages in the minds of customers in the marketplace;
2. *Brand resonance model* describes how to take these competitive advantages and create intense, active loyalty relationships with customers for brands; and
3. *Brand value chain model* describes how to trace the value creation process to better understand the financial impact of marketing expenditures and investments to create loyal customers and strong brands.

Collectively, these three models help marketers devise branding strategies and tactics to maximize profits and long-term brand equity and track their progress along the way. Chapter 2 develops the brand positioning model; Chapter 3 reviews the brand resonance and brand value chain models.

This chapter begins, however, by more formally examining the brand equity concept, introducing one particular view—the concept of customer-based brand equity—that will serve as a useful organizing framework for the rest of the book.[1] We'll consider the sources of customer-based brand equity to provide the groundwork for our discussion of brand positioning.

Positioning requires defining our desired or ideal brand knowledge structures and establishing points-of-parity and points-of-difference to establish the right brand identity and brand image. Unique, meaningful *points-of-difference (PODs)* provide a competitive advantage and the "reason why" consumers should buy the brand. On the other hand, some brand associations can be roughly as favorable as those of competing brands, so they function as *points-of-parity (POPs)* in consumers' minds—and negate potential points-of-difference for competitors. In other words, these associations are designed to provide "no reason why not" for consumers to choose the brand.

The chapter then reviews how to identify and establish brand positioning and create a brand mantra, a shorthand expression of the positioning.[2] We conclude with Brand Focus 2.0 and an examination of the many benefits of creating a strong brand.

CUSTOMER-BASED BRAND EQUITY

Two questions often arise in brand marketing: What makes a brand strong? and How do you build a strong brand? To help answer both, we introduce the concept of customer-based brand equity (CBBE). Although a number of useful perspectives concerning brand equity have been put forth, the CBBE concept provides a unique point of view on what brand equity is and how it should best be built, measured, and managed.

Defining Customer-Based Brand Equity

The CBBE concept approaches brand equity from the perspective of the consumer—whether the consumer is an individual or an organization or an existing or prospective customer. Understanding the needs and wants of consumers and organizations and devising products and programs to satisfy them are at the heart of successful marketing. In particular, marketers face two fundamentally important questions: What do different brands mean to consumers? and How does the brand knowledge of consumers affect their response to marketing activity?

The basic premise of the CBBE concept is that the power of a brand lies in what customers have learned, felt, seen, and heard about the brand as a result of their experiences over time. In other words, *the power of a brand lies in what resides in the minds and hearts of customers.* The challenge for marketers in building a strong brand is ensuring that customers have the right type of experiences with products and services and their accompanying marketing programs so that the desired thoughts, feelings, images, beliefs, perceptions, opinions, and experiences become linked to the brand.

We formally define **customer-based brand equity** as the differential effect that brand knowledge has on consumer response to the marketing of that brand. A brand has positive customer-based brand equity when consumers react more favorably to a product and the way it is marketed when the brand is identified than when it is not (say, when the product is attributed to a fictitious name or is unnamed). Thus, customers might be more accepting of a new brand extension for a brand with positive customer-based brand equity, less sensitive to price increases and withdrawal of advertising support, or more willing to seek the brand in a new distribution channel. On the other hand, a brand has *negative* customer-based brand equity if consumers react less favorably to marketing activity for the brand compared with an unnamed or fictitiously named version of the product.

Let's look at the three key ingredients to this definition: (1) "differential effect," (2) "brand knowledge," and (3) "consumer response to marketing." First, brand equity arises from differences in consumer response. If no differences occur, then the brand-name product can essentially be classified as a commodity or a generic version of the product. Competition, most likely, would then just be based on price. Second, these differences in response are a result of consumers' knowledge about the brand, that is, what they have learned, felt, seen, and heard about the brand as a result of their experiences over time. Thus, although strongly influenced by the marketing activity of the firm, brand equity ultimately depends on what resides in the minds and hearts of consumers. Third, customers' differential responses, which make up brand equity, are reflected in perceptions, preferences, and behavior related to all aspects of brand marketing, for example, including choice of a brand, recall of copy points from an ad, response to a sales promotion, and evaluations of a proposed brand extension. Brand Focus 2.0 provides a detailed account of these advantages, as summarized in Figure 2-1.

The simplest way to illustrate what we mean by customer-based brand equity is to consider one of the typical results of product sampling or comparison tests. In blind taste tests, two groups of consumers sample a product: one group knows which brand it is, the other doesn't. Invariably, the two groups have different opinions despite consuming the same product.

These branding effects occur in the marketplace too. For example, at one time, Hitachi and General Electric (GE) jointly owned a factory in England that made identical televisions for the two companies. The only difference was the brand name on the television. Nevertheless, the Hitachi televisions sold for a $75 premium over the GE televisions. Moreover, Hitachi sold twice as many sets as GE despite the higher price.[3]

> Improved perceptions of product performance
> Greater loyalty
> Less vulnerability to competitive marketing actions
> Less vulnerability to marketing crises
> Larger margins
> More inelastic consumer response to price increases
> More elastic consumer response to price decreases
> Greater trade cooperation and support
> Increased marketing communication effectiveness
> Possible licensing opportunities
> Additional brand extension opportunities

FIGURE 2-1

Marketing Advantages
of Strong Brands

Consumers may be willing to pay more for the exact same television set if the right brand name is on it.

Source: Tomohiro Ohsumi/ Bloomberg via Getty Images

When consumers report different opinions about branded and unbranded versions of identical products—which almost invariably happens—it must be the case that knowledge about the brand, created by whatever means (past experiences, marketing activity for the brand, or word of mouth), has somehow changed customers' product perceptions. This result has occurred with virtually every type of product—conclusive evidence that consumers' perceptions of product performance are highly dependent on their impressions of the brand that goes along with it. In other words, clothes may seem to fit better, a car may seem to drive more smoothly, and the wait in a bank line may seem shorter, depending on the particular brand involved.

Brand Equity as a Bridge

Thus, according to the customer-based brand equity concept, consumer knowledge drives the differences that manifest themselves in terms of brand equity. This realization has important managerial implications. For one thing, brand equity provides marketers with a vital strategic bridge from their past to their future.

Brands as a Reflection of the Past.   Marketers should consider all the dollars spent on manufacturing and marketing products each year not so much as "expenses" but as "investments" in what consumers saw, heard, learned, felt, and experienced about the brand. If not properly designed and implemented, these expenditures may not be good investments, in that they may not have created the right knowledge structures in consumers' minds, but we should consider them investments nonetheless. Thus, the *quality* of the investment in brand building is the most critical factor, not the *quantity* beyond some minimal threshold amount. In fact, it is possible to "overspend" on brand building if money is not being spent wisely. Conversely, as we'll see throughout the book, some brands are considerably outspent but amass a great deal of brand equity through marketing activities that create valuable, enduring memory traces in the minds of consumers, as has been the case with Snickers.

SNICKERS® Brand

Creatively marketed, Mars Chocolate North America's best-selling SNICKERS® bar has long been advertised as the candy bar that "satisfies" as a filling snack or means to stave off hunger before a meal. One recent ad campaign centered on a make-believe language, "Snacklish," that puts a SNICKERS® spin on everyday words and phrases. Taxi, bus-stop, and subway posters and a variety of online postings featured catchy phrases like "Pledge your nutlegience," "Snaxi" and "Nougetaboutit." To reinforce its branding, the phrases all appeared in the typeface and colors of the SNICKERS® bar logo.[4]

SNICKERS® created its own brand-centric language to help promote its
well-positioned candy bar.

Source: SNICKERS® is a registered trademark of Mars, Incorporated and its affiliates. This
trademark is used with permission. Mars, Incorporated is not associated with Pearson
Education, Inc. The SNICKERS® advertisement is printed with permission of Mars, Incorporated.

Brands as a Direction for the Future. The brand knowledge that marketers create over
time dictates appropriate and inappropriate future directions for the brand. Consumers will
decide, based on their brand knowledge, where they think the brand should go and grant permission (or not) to any marketing action or program. Thus, at the end of the day, the true value and
future prospects of a brand rest with consumers and their knowledge about the brand.

No matter how we define brand equity, though, its value to marketers as a concept ultimately
depends on how they use it. Brand equity can offer focus and guidance, providing a means to interpret past marketing performance and design future marketing programs. Everything the firm
does can help enhance or detract from brand equity. Those marketers who build strong brands
have embraced the concept and use it to its fullest as a means of clarifying, communicating, and
implementing their marketing actions.

DISCOVERY CHANNEL

The Discovery Channel was launched with the motto "Explore Your World" and well-defined brand values
of adventure, exploration, science, and curiosity. After a detour to reality programming featuring crime and
forensics shows and biker and car content, the channel returned to its mission of producing high-quality work
that the company could be proud of and that was beneficial for people. Today, Discovery's 13 U.S. channels
cumulatively reach 745 million subscribing households, and its 120 overseas channels in 180 countries reach
969 million homes. One hundred fifty thousand hours of content supplied by Discovery Education is used by
more than 1 million teachers in half of all schools in the United States. Discovery's Web sites attract 24 million
unique visitors every month. The company also launched *Discovery Channel Magazine* in Asia.[5]

Other factors can influence brand success, and brand equity has meaning for other constituents
besides customers, such as employees, suppliers, channel members, media, and the government.[6]
Nevertheless, success with customers is often crucial for success for the firm, so the next section
considers brand knowledge and CBBE in more detail. The process of creating such brand power
is not without its critics, however, as described in The Science of Branding 2-1.

MAKING A BRAND STRONG: BRAND KNOWLEDGE

From the perspective of the CBBE concept, brand knowledge is the key to creating brand equity,
because it creates the differential effect that drives brand equity. What marketers need, then, is
an insightful way to represent how brand knowledge exists in consumer memory. An influential
model of memory developed by psychologists is helpful for this purpose.[7]

The ***associative network memory model*** views memory as a network of nodes and connecting links, in which nodes represent stored information or concepts, and links represent

THE SCIENCE OF BRANDING 2-1

Brand Critics

In her book *No Logo,* Naomi Klein details the aspects of global corporate growth that have led to consumer backlash against brands. She explains the subject of her book as follows:

> The title *No Logo* is not meant to be read as a literal slogan (as in No More Logos!), or a post-logo logo (there is already a No Logo clothing line, I'm told). Rather, it is an attempt to capture an anti-corporate attitude I see emerging among many young activists. This book is hinged on a simple hypothesis: that as more people discover the brand-name secrets of the global logo web, their outrage will fuel the next big political movement, a vast wave of opposition squarely targeting those with very high name-brand recognition.

Klein cites marketing campaigns that exist within schools and universities, among other examples of advertising encroaching on traditionally ad-free space. She asserts that as marketers compete for "eyeballs" using unconventional and unexpected means, fewer ad-free spaces remain, and consumer resentment builds. Klein then argues that the vast number of mergers and acquisitions in the past two decades, and the increasing number of brand extensions, have severely limited consumer choice and engendered additional consumer resentment. She cautions that an inherent danger of building a strong brand is that the public will be all the more eager to see the brand tarnished once unseemly facts surface.

Klein also details the numerous movements that have arisen to protest the growing power of corporations and the proliferation of branded space that accompanies this growth. The author highlights such anticorporate practices as "culture jamming" and "ad-busting," which serve to subvert and undermine corporate marketing by attacking the marketers on their own terms.

She also discusses the formation of labor activist organizations such as Essential Action and the International Labour Organization, which perform labor monitoring and hold companies accountable for the treatment of their labor forces.

Klein observes that the issues of corporate conduct are now highly politicized. As a result, she notes, "Political rallies, which once wound their predicable course in front of government buildings and consulates, are now just as likely to take place in front of the stores of the corporate giants." Ten years after the fact, Klein revisited her book *No Logo* and actually did apply the concepts to politics in an update.

Klein is certainly not the only critic. In his book *Branding Only Works on Cattle,* brand consultant Jonathan Baskin argues that branding is no longer effective because it relies on the status quo and is not keeping up with consumers' needs. He faults current brand techniques. In 2007, British writer Neil Boorman started a blog and then published a book called *Bonfire of the Brands* that detailed the breaking of his brand obsession. Boorman refers to himself as a member of "a generation that has been sold to from the day it was born" and calls brands "nothing but an expensive con."

Sources: Naomi Klein, *No Logo: Taking Aim at the Brand Bullies* (10th anniversary edition) (New York: Picador, 2000); Naomi Klein, *Fences and Windows: Dispatches from the Front Lines of the Globalization Debate* (New York: Picador, 2002); Review, *Publishers Weekly,* 2002. "Naomi Klein on How Corporate Branding Has Taken over America," *The Guardian,* 16 January 2010; Andrew Potter, "The Revenge of the Brands," *Reason,* May 2010; Jonathan Salem Baskin, *Branding Only Works on Cattle* (New York: Business Plus, 2008); Neil Boorman, *Bonfire of the Brands: How I Learned to Live Without Labels* (London: Canongate Books Ltd, 2007); Neil Boorman, "Name Dropper," The *Guardian,* 25 August 2007.

the strength of association between the nodes. Any type of information—whether it's verbal, abstract, or contextual—can be stored in the memory network.

Using the associative network memory model, let's think of brand knowledge as consisting of a brand node in memory with a variety of associations linked to it. We can consider brand knowledge as having two components: brand awareness and brand image. **Brand awareness** is related to the strength of the brand node or trace in memory, which we can measure as the consumer's ability to identify the brand under different conditions.[8] It is a necessary, but not always a sufficient, step in building brand equity. Other considerations, such as the image of the brand, often come into play.

Brand image has long been recognized as an important concept in marketing.[9] Although marketers have not always agreed about how to measure it, one generally accepted view is that, consistent with our associative network memory model, **brand image** is consumers' perceptions about a brand, as reflected by the brand associations held in consumer memory.[10] In other words, brand associations are the other informational nodes linked to the brand node in memory and contain the meaning of the brand for consumers. Associations come in all forms and may reflect characteristics of the product or aspects independent of the product.

For example, if someone asked you what came to mind when you thought of Apple computers, what would you say? You might reply with associations such as "well-designed," "easy to use," "leading-edge technology," and so forth. Figure 2-2 displays some commonly mentioned associations for Apple that consumers have expressed in the past.[11] The associations that came to *your* mind make up your brand image for Apple. Through breakthrough products and skillful marketing, Apple has been able to achieve a rich brand image made up of a host of

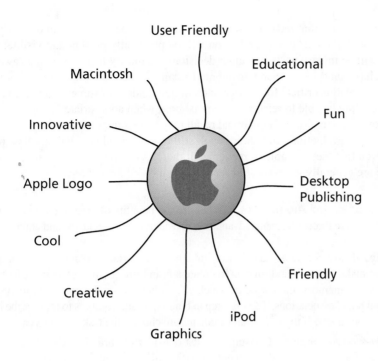

User Friendly
Educational
Macintosh
Fun
Innovative
Apple Logo
Desktop Publishing
Cool
Friendly
Creative
iPod
Graphics

FIGURE 2-2
Possible Apple
Computer Associations
Source: KRT/Newscom

brand associations. Many are likely to be shared by a majority of consumers, so we can refer to "the" brand image of Apple, but at the same time, we recognize that this image varies, perhaps even considerably, depending on the consumer or market segment.

Other brands, of course, carry a different set of associations. For example, McDonald's marketing program attempts to create brand associations in consumers' minds between its products and "quality," "service," "cleanliness," and "value." McDonald's rich brand image probably also includes strong associations to "Ronald McDonald," "golden arches," "for kids," and "convenient" as well as perhaps potentially negative associations such as "fast food." Whereas Mercedes-Benz has achieved strong associations to "performance" and "status," Volvo has created a strong association to "safety." We'll return in later chapters to the different types of associations and how to measure their strength.

SOURCES OF BRAND EQUITY

What causes brand equity to exist? How do marketers create it? *Customer-based brand equity occurs when the consumer has a high level of awareness and familiarity with the brand and holds some strong, favorable, and unique brand associations in memory.* In some cases, brand awareness alone is enough to create favorable consumer response; for example, in low-involvement decisions when consumers are willing to base their choices on mere familiarity. In most other cases, however, the strength, favorability, and uniqueness of brand associations play a critical role in determining the differential response that makes up brand equity. If customers perceive the brand as only representative of the product or service category, then they'll respond as if the offering were unbranded.

Thus marketers must also convince consumers that there are meaningful differences among brands. Consumers must not think all brands in the category are the same. Establishing a positive brand image in consumer memory—strong, favorable, and unique brand associations—goes hand-in-hand with creating brand awareness to build customer-based brand equity. Let's look at both these sources of brand equity.

Brand Awareness

Brand awareness consists of brand recognition and brand recall performance:

- *Brand recognition* is consumers' ability to confirm prior exposure to the brand when given the brand as a cue. In other words, when they go to the store, will they be able to recognize the brand as one to which they have already been exposed?
- *Brand recall* is consumers' ability to retrieve the brand from memory when given the product category, the needs fulfilled by the category, or a purchase or usage situation as a cue. In other words, consumers' recall of Kellogg's Corn Flakes will depend on their ability to retrieve the brand when they think of the cereal category or of what they should eat for breakfast or a snack, whether at the store when making a purchase or at home when deciding what to eat.

If research reveals that many consumer decisions are made at the point of purchase, where the brand name, logo, packaging, and so on will be physically present and visible, then brand recognition will be important. If consumer decisions are mostly made in settings away from the point of purchase, on the other hand, then brand recall will be more important.[12] For this reason, creating brand recall is critical for service and online brands: Consumers must actively seek the brand and therefore be able to retrieve it from memory when appropriate.

Note, however, that even though brand recall may be less important at the point of purchase, consumers' brand evaluations and choices will still often depend on what else they recall about the brand given that they are able to recognize it there. As is the case with most information in memory, we are generally more adept at recognizing a brand than at recalling it.

Advantages of Brand Awareness.   What are the benefits of creating a high level of brand awareness? There are three—learning advantages, consideration advantages, and choice advantages.

Learning Advantages: Brand awareness influences the formation and strength of the associations that make up the brand image. To create a brand image, marketers must first establish a brand node in memory, the nature of which affects how easily the consumer learns and stores additional brand associations. The first step in building brand equity is to register the brand in the minds of consumers. If the right brand elements are chosen, the task becomes easier.

Consideration Advantages: Consumers must consider the brand whenever they are making a purchase for which it could be acceptable or fulfilling a need it could satisfy. Raising brand awareness increases the likelihood that the brand will be a member of the **consideration set,** the handful of brands that receive serious consideration for purchase.[13] Much research has shown that consumers are rarely loyal to only one brand but instead have a set of brands they would consider buying and another—possibly smaller—set of brands they actually buy on a regular basis. Because consumers typically consider only a few brands for purchase, making sure that the brand is in the consideration set also makes other brands less likely to be considered or recalled.[14]

Choice Advantages: The third advantage of creating a high level of brand awareness is that it can affect choices among brands in the consideration set, even if there are essentially no other associations to those brands.[15] For example, consumers have been shown to adopt a decision rule in some cases to buy only more familiar, well-established brands.[16] Thus, in low-involvement decision settings, a minimum level of brand awareness may be sufficient for product choice, even in the absence of a well-formed attitude.[17]

One influential model of attitude change and persuasion, the elaboration-likelihood model, is consistent with the notion that consumers may make choices based on brand awareness considerations when they have low involvement. Low involvement results when consumers lack either purchase motivation (they don't care about the product or service) or purchase ability (they don't know anything else about the brands in a category).[18]

1. *Consumer purchase motivation:* Although products and brands may be critically important to marketers, choosing a brand in many categories is not a life-or-death decision for most consumers. For example, despite millions of dollars spent in TV advertising over the years to persuade consumers of product differences, 40 percent of consumers in one survey believed all brands of gasoline were about the same or did not know which brand was best. A lack of perceived differences among brands in a category is likely to leave consumers unmotivated about the choice process.
2. *Consumer purchase ability:* Consumers in some product categories just do not have the necessary knowledge or experience to judge product quality even if they so desired. The obvious examples are products with a high degree of technical sophistication, like telecommunications equipment with state-of-the-art features. But consumers may be unable to judge quality even in low-tech categories. Consider the college student who has not really had to cook or clean before, shopping the supermarket aisles in earnest for the first time, or a new manager forced to make an expensive capital purchase for the first time. The reality is that product quality is often highly ambiguous and difficult to judge without a great deal of prior experience and expertise. In such cases, consumers will use whatever shortcut or **heuristic** they can come up with to make their decisions in the best manner possible. Sometimes they simply choose the brand with which they are most familiar and aware.

Establishing Brand Awareness.   How do you create brand awareness? In the abstract, creating brand awareness means increasing the familiarity of the brand through repeated exposure, although this is generally more effective for brand recognition than for brand recall. That is, the more a consumer "experiences" the brand by seeing it, hearing it, or thinking about it, the more likely he or she is to strongly register the brand in memory.

Thus, anything that causes consumers to experience one of a brand's element—its name, symbol, logo, character, packaging, or slogan, including advertising and promotion, sponsorship and event marketing, publicity and public relations, and outdoor advertising—can increase familiarity and awareness of that brand element. And the more elements marketers can reinforce, usually the better. For instance, in addition to its name, Intel uses the "Intel Inside" logo and its distinctive symbol as well as its famous four-note jingle in TV ads to enhance awareness.

Repetition increases recognizability, but improving brand recall also requires linkages in memory to appropriate product categories or other purchase or consumption cues. A slogan or jingle creatively pairs the brand and the appropriate cues (and, ideally, the brand positioning as well, helping build a positive brand image). Other brand elements like logos, symbols, characters, and packaging can also aid recall.

The way marketers pair the brand and its product category, such as with an advertising slogan, helps determine the strength of product category links. For brands with strong category associations, like Ford cars, the distinction between brand recognition and recall may not matter much—consumers thinking of the category are likely to think of the brand. In competitive markets or when the brand is new to the category, it is more important to emphasize category links in the marketing program. Strong links between the brand and the category or other relevant cues may become especially important over time if the product meaning of the brand changes through brand extensions, mergers, or acquisitions.

GANNETT

In March 2011, Gannett launched its first nationwide branding and advertising campaign, themed "It's All Within Reach." The company traces its origins to a small newspaper in Elmira, NY, in 1906 and over the decades has grown into a leading international media and marketing solutions company. Gannett's media properties include USA TODAY; 81 U.S. community newspapers (such as the *Arizona Republic, Indianapolis Star,* and *Detroit Free Press*); 23 broadcasting stations; over 100 digital properties; Point Roll, an industry leader in rich media advertising solutions; Career Builder, the nation's top employment site; and Captivate, a digital programming and advertising network with nearly 10,000 elevator and lobby screens in about 1,000 buildings. Then-Chairman and CEO Craig Dubow explained the campaign as, "Today, Gannett offers consumers and businesses everything they need to connect and engage with what matters most to them—anywhere, anytime and on every platform. It's important for our brand to reflect and promote our company as it is today and the tremendous value we bring."[19]

As part of its media expansion beyond newspapers, Gannett now offers lobby and elevator advertising via its Captivate service.

Source: Captivate Network

Many marketers have attempted to create brand awareness through so-called shock advertising, using bizarre themes. For example, at the height of the dot-com boom, online retailer Outpost.com used ads featuring gerbils shot from cannons, wolverines attacking marching bands, and preschoolers having the brand name tattooed on their foreheads. The problem with such approaches is that they invariably fail to create strong category links because the product is just not prominent enough in the ad. They also can generate a fair amount of ill will. Often coming across as desperate measures, they rarely provide a foundation for long-term brand equity. In the case of Outpost.com, most potential customers did not have a clue what the company was about.

Brand Image

Creating brand awareness by increasing the familiarity of the brand through repeated exposure (for brand recognition) and forging strong associations with the appropriate product category or other relevant purchase or consumption cues (for brand recall) is an important first step in building brand equity. Once a sufficient level of brand awareness is created, marketers can put more emphasis on crafting a brand image.

ALLY FINANCIAL

In re-branding GMAC Financial as Ally Financial, the firm initially ran a campaign featuring a smarmy man, who represented the typical bank, being mean to unsuspecting, trusting children, who represented typical bank customers. After about a year, the firm switched to a new campaign profiling the "wacky ways" customers showed how much they loved their bank. As Ally's CMO put it, the first campaign "did a nice job of successfully informing customers we're a different bank. But now that we established that, the idea is to focus more on what Ally offers, like innovative products, no hidden fees, and being able to talk to an actual person."[20]

Ally has evolved its advertising and communications from creating brand awareness to building brand image.

Source: Ally Bank

Creating a positive brand image takes marketing programs that link strong, favorable, and unique associations to the brand in memory. Brand associations may be either brand attributes or benefits. *Brand attributes* are those descriptive features that characterize a product or service. *Brand benefits* are the personal value and meaning that consumers attach to the product or service attributes.

Consumers form beliefs about brand attributes and benefits in different ways. The definition of customer-based brand equity, however, does not distinguish between the source of brand associations and the manner in which they are formed; all that matters is their strength, favorability, and uniqueness. This means that consumers can form brand associations in a variety of ways other than marketing activities: from direct experience; online surfing; through information from other commercial or nonpartisan sources such as *Consumer Reports* or other media vehicles; from word of mouth; and by assumptions or inferences consumers make about the brand itself, its name, logo, or identification with a company, country, channel of distribution, or person, place, or event.

Marketers should recognize the influence of these other sources of information by both managing them as well as possible and by adequately accounting for them in designing communication strategies. Consider how The Body Shop originally built its brand equity.

THE BODY SHOP

The Body Shop successfully created a global brand image without using conventional advertising. Its strong associations to personal care and environmental concern occurred through its products (natural ingredients only, never tested on animals), packaging (simple, refillable, recyclable), merchandising (detailed point-of-sale posters, brochures, and displays), staff (encouraged to be enthusiastic and informative concerning environmental issues), sourcing policies (using small local producers from around the world), social action program (requiring each franchisee to run a local community program), and public relations programs and activities (taking visible and sometimes outspoken stands on various issues).[21]

Body Shop built a strong brand without extensive use of advertising.
Source: Convery flowers/Alamy

In short, to create the differential response that leads to customer-based brand equity, marketers need to make sure that some strongly held brand associations are not only favorable but also unique and not shared with competing brands. Unique associations help consumers choose the brand. To choose which favorable and unique associations to strongly link to the brand, marketers carefully analyze the consumer and the competition to determine the best positioning for the brand. Let's consider some factors that, in general, affect the strength, favorability, and uniqueness of brand associations.

Strength of Brand Associations.   The more deeply a person thinks about product information and relates it to existing brand knowledge, the stronger the resulting brand associations will be. Two factors that strengthen association to any piece of information are its personal relevance and the consistency with which it is presented over time. The particular associations we recall and their salience will depend not only on the strength of association, but also on the retrieval cues present and the context in which we consider the brand.

In general, direct experiences create the strongest brand attribute and benefit associations and are particularly influential in consumers' decisions when they accurately interpret them. Word-of-mouth is likely to be particularly important for restaurants, entertainment, banking, and personal services. Starbucks, Google, Red Bull, and Amazon are all classic examples of companies that created amazingly rich brand images without the benefit of intensive advertising programs. Mike's Hard Lemonade sold its first 10 million cases without any advertising because it was a "discovery" brand fueled by word-of-mouth.[22]

On the other hand, company-influenced sources of information, such as advertising, are often likely to create the weakest associations and thus may be the most easily changed. To overcome this hurdle, marketing communication programs use creative communications that cause consumers to elaborate on brand-related information and relate it appropriately to existing knowledge. They expose consumers to communications repeatedly over time, and ensure that many retrieval cues are present as reminders.

Favorability of Brand Associations.   Marketers create favorable brand associations by convincing consumers that the brand possesses relevant attributes and benefits that satisfy their needs and wants, such that they form positive overall brand judgments. Consumers will not hold all brand associations to be equally important, nor will they view them all favorably or value them all equally across different purchase or consumption situations. Brand associations may be situation- or context-dependent and vary according to what consumers want to achieve in that purchase or consumption decision.[23] An association may thus be valued in one situation but not another.[24]

For example, the associations that come to mind when consumers think of FedEx may be "fast," "reliable," and "convenient," with "purple and orange packages." The color of the packaging may matter little to most consumers when actually choosing an overnight delivery service, although it may perhaps play an important brand awareness function. Fast, reliable, and convenient service may be more important, but even then only under certain situations. A consumer who needs delivery only "as soon as possible" may consider less expensive options, like USPS Priority Mail, which may take one to two days.

Uniqueness of Brand Associations.   The essence of brand positioning is that the brand has a sustainable competitive advantage or "unique selling proposition" that gives consumers a compelling reason why they should buy it.[25] Marketers can make this unique difference explicit through direct comparisons with competitors, or they may highlight it implicitly. They may base it on performance-related or non-performance-related attributes or benefits.

Although unique associations are critical to a brand's success, unless the brand faces no competition, it will most likely share some associations with other brands. One function of shared associations is to establish category membership and define the scope of competition with other products and services.[26]

A product or service category can also share a set of associations that include specific beliefs about any member in the category, as well as overall attitudes toward all members in the category. These beliefs might include many of the relevant performance-related attributes for brands in the category, as well as more descriptive attributes that do not necessarily relate to product or service performance, like the color of a product, such as red for ketchup.

Consumers may consider certain attributes or benefits prototypical and essential to all brands in the category, and a specific brand an exemplar and most representative.[27] For example, they might expect a running shoe to provide support and comfort and to be built well enough to withstand repeated wearings, and they may believe that Asics, New Balance, or some other leading brand best represents a running shoe. Similarly, consumers might expect an online retailer to offer easy navigation, a variety of offerings, reasonable shipping options, secure purchase procedures, responsive customer service, and strict privacy guidelines, and they may consider L.L. Bean or some other market leader to be the best example of an online retailer.

Because the brand is linked to the product category, some category associations may also become linked to the brand, either specific beliefs or overall attitudes. Product category attitudes can be a particularly important determinant of consumer response. For example, if a consumer thinks that all brokerage houses are basically greedy and that brokers are in it for themselves, then he or she probably will have similarly unfavorable beliefs about and negative attitudes toward any particular brokerage house, simply by virtue of its membership in the category.

Thus, in almost all cases, some product category associations will be shared with all brands in the category. Note that the strength of the brand associations to the product category is an important determinant of brand awareness.[28]

IDENTIFYING AND ESTABLISHING BRAND POSITIONING

Having developed the CBBE concept in some detail as background, we next outline how marketers should approach brand positioning.

Basic Concepts

Brand positioning is at the heart of marketing strategy. It is the "act of designing the company's offer and image so that it occupies a distinct and valued place in the target customer's minds."[29] As the name implies, positioning means finding the proper "location" in the minds of a group of consumers or market segment, so that they think about a product or service in the "right" or desired way to maximize potential benefit to the firm. Good brand positioning helps guide marketing strategy by clarifying what a brand is all about, how it is unique and how it is similar to competitive brands, and why consumers should purchase and use it.

Deciding on a positioning requires determining a frame of reference (by identifying the target market and the nature of competition) and the optimal points-of-parity and points-of-difference brand associations. In other words, marketers need to know (1) who the target consumer is, (2) who the main competitors are, (3) how the brand is similar to these competitors, and (4) how the brand is different from them. We'll talk about each of these.

Target Market

Identifying the consumer target is important because different consumers may have different brand knowledge structures and thus different perceptions and preferences for the brand. Without this understanding, it may be difficult for marketers to say which brand associations should be strongly held, favorable, and unique. Let's look at defining and segmenting a market and choosing target market segments.

A *market* is the set of all actual and potential buyers who have sufficient interest in, income for, and access to a product. *Market segmentation* divides the market into distinct groups of homogeneous consumers who have similar needs and consumer behavior, and who thus require similar marketing mixes. Market segmentation requires making trade-offs between costs and benefits. The more finely segmented the market, the more likely that the firm will be able to implement marketing programs that meet the needs of consumers in any one segment. That advantage, however, can be offset by the greater costs of reduced standardization.

Segmentation Bases.   Figures 2-3 and 2-4 display some possible segmentation bases for consumer and business-to-business markets, respectively. We can classify these bases as descriptive or customer-oriented (related to what kind of person or organization the customer is), or as behavioral or product-oriented (related to how the customer thinks of or uses the brand or product).

Behavioral segmentation bases are often most valuable in understanding branding issues because they have clearer strategic implications. For example, defining a benefit segment makes it clear what should be the ideal point-of-difference or desired benefit with which to establish the positioning. Take the toothpaste market. One research study uncovered four main segments:[30]

1. *The sensory segment:* Seeking flavor and product appearance
2. *The sociables:* Seeking brightness of teeth
3. *The worriers:* Seeking decay prevention
4. *The independent segment:* Seeking low price

Behavioral
User status
Usage rate
Usage occasion
Brand loyalty
Benefits sought

Demographic
Income
Age
Sex
Race
Family

Psychographic
Values, opinions, and attitudes
Activities and lifestyle

Geographic
International
Regional

FIGURE 2-3

Consumer Segmentation Bases

FIGURE 2-4

Business-to-Business Segmentation Bases

Nature of Good
Kind
Where used
Type of buy

Buying Condition
Purchase location
Who buys
Type of buy

Demographic
SIC code
Number of employees
Number of production workers
Annual sales volume
Number of establishments

Given this market segmentation scheme, marketing programs could be put into place to attract one or more segments. For example, Close-Up initially targeted the first two segments, whereas Crest primarily concentrated on the third. Taking no chances, Aquafresh was introduced to go after all three segments, designing its toothpaste with three stripes to dramatize each of the three product benefits. With the success of multipurpose toothpastes such as Colgate Total, virtually all brands now offer products that emphasize multiple performance benefits.

Other segmentation approaches build on brand loyalty in some way. The classic "funnel" model traces consumer behavior in terms of initial awareness through brand-most-often-used. Figure 2-5 shows a hypothetical pattern of results. For the purposes of brand building, marketers want to understand both (1) the percentage of target market that is present at each stage and (2) factors facilitating or inhibiting the transition from one stage to the next. In the hypothetical example, a key bottleneck appears to be converting those consumers who have ever tried the brand to those who recently tried, as less than half (46 percent) "convert." To convince more consumers to consider trying the brand again, marketers may need to raise brand salience or make the brand more acceptable in the target consumer's repertoire.

Marketers often segment consumers by their behavior. For example, a firm may target a certain age group, but the underlying reason is that they are particularly heavy users of the product, are unusually brand loyal, or are most likely to seek the benefit the product is best able to deliver. Nestlé's Yorkie chocolate is boldly marketed in the U.K. as "It is Not For Girls" because the chunky bar is thought to appeal more to men.

In some cases, however, broad demographic descriptors may mask important underlying differences.[31] A fairly specific target market of "women aged 40 to 49" may contain a number of very different segments who require totally different marketing mixes (think Celine Dion vs. Courtney Love). Baby boomers are difficult to segment based on the size of the generation and individual views on aging. Age Wave, a consulting firm, created four segments for post-retirement consumers: "ageless explorers," "comfortably contents," "live for todays," and "sick and tireds."[32]

The main advantage of demographic segmentation bases is that the demographics of traditional media vehicles are generally well known from consumer research; as a result, it has been easier to buy media on that basis. With the growing importance of digital and nontraditional media and other forms of communication as well as the capability to build databases to profile customers on a behavioral and media usage basis, however, this advantage has become less important. For example, online Web sites can now target such previously hard-to-reach markets as African Americans (BlackPlanet.com), Hispanics (Quepasa.com), Asian Americans (AsianAvenue.com), college students (teen.com), and gays (gay.com).

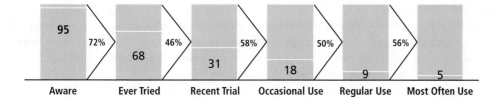

FIGURE 2-5
Hypothetical Examples
of Funnel Stages and
Transitions

Criteria.   A number of criteria have been offered to guide segmentation and target market decisions, such as the following:[33]

- *Identifiability:* Can we easily identify the segment?
- *Size:* Is there adequate sales potential in the segment?
- *Accessibility:* Are specialized distribution outlets and communication media available to reach the segment?
- *Responsiveness:* How favorably will the segment respond to a tailored marketing program?

The obvious overriding consideration in defining market segments is profitability. In many cases, profitability can be related to behavioral considerations. Developing a segmentation scheme with direct customer lifetime value perspectives can be highly advantageous. To improve the long-term profitability of their customer base, drugstore chain CVS considered the role of beauty products for its customers at three distinct stages of life, producing the following hypothetical profiles or personas:[34]

- *Caroline*, a single 20-something, is relatively new to her career and still has an active social life. She is an extremely important beauty customer who visits the chain once a week. Her favorite part of shopping is getting new beauty products, and she looks to CVS to help her cultivate her look at a price she can afford.
- Caroline will grow into *Vanessa*, the soccer mom with three children; she may not be as consumed with fashion as she once was, but preserving her youthful appearance is definitely still a major priority. She squeezes in trips to the store en route to or from work or school, and convenient features such as drive-through pharmacies are paramount for Vanessa.
- Vanessa becomes *Sophie*. Sophie isn't much of a beauty customer, but she is CVS's most profitable demographic—a regular pharmacy customer who actively shops the front of the store for key OTC items.

Nature of Competition

At least implicitly, deciding to target a certain type of consumer often defines the nature of competition, because other firms have also decided to target that segment in the past or plan to do so in the future, or because consumers in that segment already may look to other brands in their purchase decisions. Competition takes place on other bases, of course, such as channels of distribution. Competitive analysis considers a whole host of factors—including the resources, capabilities, and likely intentions of various other firms—in order for marketers to choose markets where consumers can be profitably served.[35]

A specific demographic such as "women aged 40–49" would include such diverse personalities as Celine Dion and Courtney Love.

Source: GABRIEL BOUYS/AFP/Getty Images/Newscom   *Source:* ZUMA Press/Newscom

Indirect Competition.   One lesson stressed by many marketing strategists is not to define competition too narrowly. Research on noncomparable alternatives suggests that even if a brand does not face direct competition in its product category, and thus does not share performance-related attributes with other brands, it can still share more abstract associations and face indirect competition in a more broadly defined product category.[36]

Competition often occurs at the benefit level rather than the attribute level. Thus, a luxury good with a strong hedonic benefit like stereo equipment may compete as much with a vacation as with other durable goods like furniture. A maker of educational software products may be implicitly competing with all other forms of education and entertainment, such as books, videos, television, and magazines. For these reasons, branding principles are now being used to market a number of different categories as a whole—for example, banks, furniture, carpets, bowling, and trains, to name just a few.

Unfortunately, many firms narrowly define competition and fail to recognize the most compelling threats and opportunities. For example, sales in the apparel industry often have been stagnant in recent years as consumers have decided to spend on home furnishings, electronics, and other products that better suit their lifestyle.[37] Leading clothing makers may be better off considering the points-of-differences of their offerings not so much against other clothing labels as against other discretionary purchases.

As Chapter 3 outlines, products are often organized in consumers' minds in a hierarchical fashion, meaning that marketers can define competition at a number of different levels. Take Fresca, a grapefruit-flavored soft drink, as an example: At the product type level, it competes with non-cola-flavored soft drinks; at the product category level, it competes with all soft drinks; and at the product class level, it competes with all beverages.

Multiple Frames of Reference.   It is not uncommon for a brand to identify more than one frame of reference. This may be the result of broader category competition or the intended future growth of a brand, or it can occur when the same function can be performed by different types of products. For example, Canon EOS Rebel digital cameras compete with digital cameras from Nikon, Kodak, and others, but also with photo-taking cell phones. Their advantages against cell phones—such as easy photo sharing on social networks like Facebook or the ability to shoot high-definition video for sharing—would not necessarily be an advantage at all against other digital camera brands.[38]

As another example, Starbucks can define very distinct sets of competitors, which would suggest very different POPs and PODs as a result:

1. *Quick-serve restaurants and convenience shops (McDonald's and Dunkin' Donuts).* Intended PODs might be quality, image, experience, and variety; intended POPs might be convenience and value.
2. *Supermarket brands for home consumption (Nescafé and Folger's).* Intended PODs might be quality, image, experience, variety, and freshness; intended POPs might be convenience and value.
3. *Local cafés.* Intended PODs might be convenience and service quality; intended POPs might be quality, variety, price, and community.

Note that some POPs and PODs are shared across competitors; others are unique to a particular competitor. Under such circumstances, marketers have to decide what to do. There are two main options. Ideally, a robust positioning could be developed that would be effective across the multiple frames somehow. If not, then it is necessary to prioritize and choose the most relevant set of competitors to serve as the competitive frame. One thing that is crucial though is to be careful to not try to be all things to all people—that typically leads to ineffective "lowest common denominator" positioning.

Finally, note that if there are many competitors in different categories or subcategories, it may be useful to either develop the positioning at the categorical level for all relevant categories ("quick-serve restaurants" or "supermarket take-home coffee" for Starbucks) or with an exemplar from each category (McDonald's or Nescafé for Starbucks).

Points-of-Parity and Points-of-Difference

The target and competitive frame of reference chosen will dictate the breadth of brand awareness and the situations and types of cues that should become closely related to the brand. Once marketers have fixed the appropriate competitive frame of reference for positioning by defining the customer target market and the nature of competition, they can define the basis of the positioning itself. Arriving at the proper positioning requires establishing the correct points-of-difference and points-of-parity associations.

Points-of-Difference Associations. *Points-of-difference* (PODs) are formally defined as attributes or benefits that consumers strongly associate with a brand, positively evaluate, and believe that they could not find to the same extent with a competitive brand.[39] Although myriad different types of brand associations are possible, we can classify candidates as either functional, performance-related considerations or as abstract, imagery-related considerations.

Consumers' actual brand choices often depend on the perceived uniqueness of brand associations. Swedish retailer Ikea took a luxury product—home furnishings and furniture—and made it a reasonably priced alternative for the mass market. Ikea supports its low prices by having customers serve themselves and deliver and assemble their own purchases. Ikea also gains a point-of-difference through its product offerings. As one commentator noted, "Ikea built their reputation on the notion that Sweden produces good, safe, well-built things for the masses. They have some of the most innovative designs at the lowest cost out there."[40] As another example, consider Subaru.

SUBARU

By 1993, Subaru was selling only 104,000 cars annually in the United States, down 60 percent from its earlier peak. Cumulative U.S. losses approached $1 billion. Advertised as "Inexpensive and Built to Stay That Way," Subaru was seen as a me-too car that was undifferentiated from Toyota, Honda, and all their followers. To provide a clear, distinct image, Subaru decided to sell only all-wheel-drive in its passenger cars. After upgrading its luxury image—and increasing its price—Subaru sold over 187,000 cars by 2004. Even more recently, the company launched its "Share the Love" ad campaign, which focused on the fun, adventure, and experiences the vehicles afford and the strong passion and loyalty its customers have for the brand. With its "Share the Love Event," Subaru created a cause program in which it donates to one of five charities a customer can designate when he or she leases or buys a new car. Subaru's unique emotional play for relatively upscale buyers who value freedom and frugality paid off in the 2008–2010 recession, when it bucked the industry tide to experience record sales.[41]

Once Subaru clarified its positioning as a rugged luxury car that drivers loved, sales took off.
Source: Subaru of America, Inc.

Points-of-difference may rely on performance attributes (Hyundai provides six front and back seat "side curtain" airbags as standard equipment on all its models for increased safety) or performance benefits (Magnavox's electronic products have "consumer-friendly" technological features, such as television sets with "Smart Sound" to keep volume levels constant while flipping through channels and commercial breaks, and "Smart Picture" to automatically adjust picture settings to optimal levels). In other cases, PODs come from imagery associations (the luxury and status imagery of Louis Vuitton or the fact that British Airways is advertised as the "world's favourite airline"). Many top brands attempt to create a point-of-difference on "overall superior quality," whereas other firms become the "low-cost provider" of a product or service.

Thus, a host of different types of PODs are possible. PODs are generally defined in terms of consumer benefits. These benefits often have important underlying "proof points" or *reasons to believe* (RTBs). These proof points can come in many forms: functional design concerns (a unique shaving system technology, leading to the benefit of a "closer electric shave"); key attributes (a unique tread design, leading to the benefit of "safer tires"); key ingredients (contains fluoride, leading to the benefit of "prevents dental cavities"); or key endorsements (recommended by more audio engineers, leading to the benefit of "superior music fidelity").[42] Having compelling proof points and RTBs are often critical to the deliverability aspect of a POD.

Points-of-Parity Associations.   *Points-of-parity associations* (POPs), on the other hand, are not necessarily unique to the brand but may in fact be shared with other brands. There are three types: category, competitive, and correlational.

Category points-of-parity represent necessary—but not necessarily sufficient—conditions for brand choice. They exist minimally at the generic product level and are most likely at the expected product level. Thus, consumers might not consider a bank truly a "bank" unless it offered a range of checking and savings plans; provided safety deposit boxes, traveler's checks, and other such services; and had convenient hours and automated teller machines. Category POPs may change over time because of technological advances, legal developments, and consumer trends, but these attributes and benefits are like "greens fees" to play the marketing game.

Competitive points-of-parity are those associations designed to negate competitors' points-of-difference. In other words, if a brand can "break even" in those areas where its competitors are trying to find an advantage and can achieve its own advantages in some other areas, the brand should be in a strong—and perhaps unbeatable—competitive position.

Correlational points-of-parity are those potentially negative associations that arise from the existence of other, more positive associations for the brand. One challenge for marketers is that many of the attributes or benefits that make up their POPs or PODs are inversely related. In other words, in the minds of consumers, if your brand is good at one thing, it can't be seen as also good on something else. For example, consumers might find it hard to believe a brand is "inexpensive" and at the same time "of the highest quality." Figure 2-6 displays some other examples of negatively correlated attributes and benefits.

Moreover, individual attributes and benefits often have both positive and negative aspects. A long heritage could be seen as a positive attribute because it can suggest experience, wisdom, and expertise. On the other hand, it could be a negative attribute because it might imply being old-fashioned and not contemporary and up-to-date. Below, we consider strategies to address these trade-offs.

Points-of-Parity versus Points-of-Difference.   POPs are important because they can undermine PODs: unless certain POPs can be achieved to overcome potential weaknesses, PODs may not even matter. For the brand to achieve a point-of-parity on a particular attribute or benefit, a sufficient number of consumers must believe that the brand is "good enough" on that dimension.

There is a "zone" or "range of tolerance or acceptance" with POPs. The brand does not have to be seen as *literally* equal to competitors, but consumers must feel that it does sufficiently well on that particular attribute or benefit so that they do not consider it to be a negative or a problem. Assuming consumers feel that way, they may then be willing to base their evaluations and decisions on other factors potentially more favorable to the brand.

FIGURE 2-6

Examples of Negatively Correlated Attributes and Benefits

Low price vs. high quality
Taste vs. low calories
Nutritious vs. good tasting
Efficacious vs. mild
Powerful vs. safe
Strong vs. refined
Ubiquitous vs. exclusive
Varied vs. simple

Points-of-parity are thus easier to achieve than points-of-difference, where the brand must demonstrate clear superiority. Often, the key to positioning is not so much achieving a POD as achieving necessary, competitive and correlational POPs.

POSITIONING GUIDELINES

The concepts of points-of-difference and points-of-parity can be invaluable tools to guide positioning. Two key issues in arriving at the optimal competitive brand positioning are (1) defining and communicating the competitive frame of reference and (2) choosing and establishing points-of-parity and points-of-difference.[43]

Defining and Communicating the Competitive Frame of Reference

A starting point in defining a competitive frame of reference for a brand positioning is to determine category membership. With which products or sets of products does the brand compete? As noted above, choosing to compete in different categories often results in different competitive frames of reference and thus different POPs and PODs.

The product's category membership tells consumers about the goals they might achieve by using a product or service. For highly established products and services, category membership is not a focal issue. Customers are aware that Coca-Cola is a leading brand of soft drink, Kellogg's Corn Flakes is a leading brand of cereal, McKinsey is a leading strategy consulting firm, and so on.

There are many situations, however, in which it is important to inform consumers of a brand's category membership. Perhaps the most obvious is the introduction of new products, where the category membership is not always apparent.

FREELINE SKATES

The challenge for Ryan Farrelly, inventor of Freeline skates, is to convey how the product fits in with existing products. Dubbed "The Next Ride," Freeline skates are a blend of skates and skateboards: a small square skateboard with two wheels apiece, each smaller than the rider's foot, to be ridden sideways. Although Freelines are more nimble than a traditional skateboard, the skateboarding community has taken a dim view of them, seeing them as akin to in-line skates, which they disdain. Farrelly might be encouraged by the experiences of Jake Burton, one of the early snowboarding pioneers. When Burton began his business, the ski, skate, and surf shops weren't interested in selling his product, forcing the company to initially sell by mail order. After catching fire with consumers, the category experienced rapid growth, but even after 30 years in the business, Burton still owns almost 60 percent of the market.[44]

Positioning a new-to-the-world product like Freeline skates—a hybrid of skates and skateboards—presents a unique marketing challenge.

Source: Freeline Skates

Sometimes consumers know a brand's category membership but may not be convinced the brand is a true, valid member of the category. For example, consumers may be aware that Sony produces computers, but they may not be certain whether Sony Vaio computers are in the same "class" as Dell, HP, and Lenovo. In this instance, it might be useful to reinforce category membership.

Brands are sometimes affiliated with categories in which they do not hold membership rather than with the one in which they do. This approach is a viable way to highlight a brand's point-of-difference from competitors, provided that consumers know the brand's actual membership. For example, Bristol-Myers Squibb ran commercials at one time for its Excedrin aspirin acknowledging Tylenol's perceived consumer acceptance for aches and pains, but touting the Excedrin brand as "the Headache Medicine." With this approach, however, it is important that consumers understand what the brand is, and not just what it is *not*.

The preferred approach to positioning is to inform consumers of a brand's membership before stating its point-of-difference in relationship to other category members. Presumably, consumers need to know what a product is and what function it serves before they can decide whether it dominates the brands against which it competes. For new products, separate marketing programs are generally needed to inform consumers of membership and to educate them about a brand's point-of-difference. For brands with limited resources, this implies the development of a marketing strategy that establishes category membership prior to one that states a point-of-difference. Brands with greater resources can develop concurrent marketing programs, one of which features membership and the other the point-of-difference. Efforts to inform consumers of membership and points-of-difference in the same ad, however, are often not effective.

There are three main ways to convey a brand's category membership: communicating category benefits, comparing to exemplars, and relying on a product descriptor.

Communicating Category Benefits.

To reassure consumers that a brand will deliver on the fundamental reason for using a category, marketers frequently use benefits to announce category membership. Thus, industrial motors might claim to have power, and analgesics might announce their efficacy. These benefits are presented in a manner that does not imply brand superiority but merely notes that the brand possesses them as a means to establish category POPs. Performance and imagery associations can provide supporting evidence. A cake mix might attain membership in the cake category by claiming the benefit of great taste and might support this benefit claim by possessing high-quality ingredients (performance) or by showing users delighting in its consumption (imagery).

Exemplars.

Well-known, noteworthy brands in a category can also be used as exemplars to specify a brand's category membership. When Tommy Hilfiger was an unknown designer, advertising announced his membership as a great American designer by associating him with Geoffrey Beene, Stanley Blacker, Calvin Klein, and Perry Ellis, who were recognized members of that category at that time. The National Pork Board successfully advertised for over two decades that pork was "the Other White Meat," riding the coattails of the popularity of chicken in the process.[45]

Product Descriptor.

The product descriptor that follows the brand name is often a very compact means of conveying category origin. For example, USAir changed its name to US Airways, according to CEO Stephen Wolf, as part of the airline's attempted transformation from a regional carrier with a poor reputation to a strong national or even international brand. The argument was that other major airlines had the word *airlines* or *airways* in their names rather than *air*, which was felt to be typically associated with smaller, regional carriers.[46] Consider these two examples:

Although carrots were a primary ingredient, the marketers of V8 Splash deliberately avoided invoking the vegetable in the brand name, given its sometimes negative connotations.

Source: Campbell Soup Company

- When Campbell's launched its V-8 Splash beverage line, it deliberately avoided including the word "carrot" in the brand name despite the fact that carrot was the main ingredient. The name was chosen to convey healthful benefits but to avoid the negative perception of carrots.[47]
- California's prune growers and marketers have attempted to establish an alternative name for their product, "dried plums," because prunes were seen by the target market of 35- to 50-year-old women as "a laxative for old people."[48]

Establishing a brand's category membership is usually not sufficient for effective brand positioning. If many firms engage in category-building tactics, the result may even be consumer confusion. For example, at the peak of the dot-com boom, Ameritrade, E*TRADE, Datek, and others advertised lower commission rates on stock trades than conventional brokerage firms.

A sound positioning strategy requires marketers to specify not only the category but also how the brand dominates other members of its category. Developing compelling points-of-difference is thus critical to effective brand positioning.[49]

Choosing Points-of-Difference

A brand must offer a compelling and credible reason for choosing it over the other options. In determining whether an attribute or benefit for a brand can serve as point-of-difference, there are three key considerations. The brand association must be seen as desirable, deliverable, and differentiating. These three considerations for developing an optimal positioning align with the three perspectives on which any brand must be evaluated, namely the consumer, the company, and the competition. *Desirability* is determined from the consumer's point of view, *deliverability* is based on a company's inherent capabilities, and *differentiation* is determined relative to the competitors.

To function as a POD, consumers ideally would see the attribute or benefit as highly important, feel confident that the firm has the capabilities to deliver it, and be convinced that no other brand could offer it to the same extent. If these three criteria are satisfied, the brand association should have sufficient strength, favorability, and uniqueness to be an effective POD. Each of these three criteria has a number of considerations, which we look at next.

Desirability Criteria.   Target consumers must find the POD personally relevant and important. Brands that tap into growing trends with consumers often find compelling PODs. For example, Apple & Eve's pure, natural fruit juices have ridden the wave of the natural foods movement to find success in an increasingly health-minded beverage market.[50]

Just being different is not enough—the differences must matter to consumers. For example, at one time a number of brands in different product categories (colas, dishwashing soaps, beer, deodorants, gasoline) introduced clear versions of their products to better differentiate themselves. The "clear" association has not seemed to be of enduring value or to be sustainable as a point-of-difference. In most cases, these brands experienced declining market share or disappeared altogether.

Deliverability Criteria.   The deliverability of an attribute or benefit brand association depends on both a company's actual ability to make the product or service (feasibility) as well as their effectiveness in convincing consumers of their ability to do so (communicability), as follows:[51]

- *Feasibility:* Can the firm actually supply the benefit underlying the POD? The product and marketing must be designed in a way to support the desired association. It is obviously easier to convince consumers of some fact about the brand that they were unaware of or may have overlooked than to make changes in the product and convince consumers of the value of these changes. As noted above, perhaps the simplest and most effective approach is to point to a unique attribute of the product as a proof point or reason-to-believe. Thus, Mountain Dew may argue that it is more energizing than other soft drinks and support this claim by noting that it has a higher level of caffeine. On the other hand, when the point-of-difference is abstract or image based, support for the claim may reside in more general associations to the company that have been developed over time. Thus, Chanel No. 5 perfume may claim to be the quintessential elegant, French perfume and support this claim by noting the long association between Chanel and haute couture.
- *Communicability:* The key issue in communicability is consumers' perceptions of the brand and the resulting brand associations. It is very difficult to create an association that is not consistent with existing consumer knowledge, or that consumers, for whatever reason, have trouble believing in. What factual, verifiable evidence or "proof points" can marketers communicate as support, so that consumers will actually believe in the brand and its desired associations? These "reasons-to-believe" are critical for consumer acceptance of a potential POD. Any claims must pass legal scrutiny too. The makers of category leader POM Wonderful 100% Pomegranate Juice have battled with the Federal Trade Commission over what the FTC deems as "false and unsubstantiated claims" about treating or preventing heart disease, prostate cancer, and erectile dysfunction.[52]

Differentiation Criteria.   Finally, target consumers must find the POD distinctive and superior. When marketers are entering a category in which there are established brands, the challenge is to find a viable, long-term basis for differentiation. Is the positioning preemptive, defensible, and difficult to attack? Can the brand association be reinforced and strengthened over time? If these are the case, the positioning is likely to last for years.

Sustainability depends on internal commitment and use of resources as well as external market forces. Before encountering tough economic times, Applebee's strategy for leadership in the casual dining restaurant business, in part, was to enter smaller markets where a second major competitor might be unlikely to enter—hello Hays, Kansas! Although there are downsides to such a strategy—potentially smaller volume and lethal word-of-mouth from any service snafus—competitive threats are minimal.[53]

Establishing Points-of-Parity *and* Points-of-Difference

The key to branding success is to establish both points-of-parity *and* points-of-difference. Branding Brief 2-1 describes how the two major U.S. political parties have applied basic branding and positioning principles in their pursuit of elected office.

In creating both POPs and PODs, one of the challenges in positioning is the inverse relationships that may exist in the minds of many consumers. Unfortunately, as noted above, consumers typically want to maximize both the negatively correlated attributes and benefits. To make things worse, competitors often are trying to achieve their point-of-difference on an attribute that is negatively correlated with the point-of-difference of the target brand.

Much of the art and science of marketing is knowing how to deal with trade-offs, and positioning is no different. The best approach clearly is to develop a product or service that performs well on both dimensions. Gore-Tex, for example, was able to overcome the seemingly conflicting product image of "breathable" and "waterproof" through technological advances.

Several additional ways exist to address the problem of negatively correlated POPs and PODs. The following three approaches are listed in increasing order of effectiveness—but also increasing order of difficulty.

Separate the Attributes. An expensive but sometimes effective approach is to launch two different marketing campaigns, each devoted to a different brand attribute or benefit. These campaigns may run concurrently or sequentially. For example, Head & Shoulders met success in Europe with a dual campaign in which one ad emphasized its dandruff removal efficacy while another ad emphasized the appearance and beauty of hair after its use. The hope is that consumers will be less critical when judging the POP and POD benefits in isolation, because the negative correlation might be less apparent. The downside is that two strong campaigns have to be developed—not just one. Moreover, if the marketer does not address the negative correlation head-on, consumers may not develop as positive an association as desired.

Leverage Equity of Another Entity. Brands can link themselves to any kind of entity that possesses the right kind of equity—a person, other brand, event, and so forth—as a means to establish an attribute or benefit as a POP or POD. Self-branded ingredients may also lend some credibility to a questionable attribute in consumers' minds.

The introduction of Miller Lite beer is a classic example of a brand "borrowing" or leveraging the equity of well-known and well-liked celebrities to lend credibility to one of the negatively correlated benefits.

MILLER LITE

When Philip Morris bought Miller Brewing, its flagship High Life brand was not competing particularly well, leading the company to decide to introduce a light beer. The initial advertising strategy for Miller Lite was to ensure parity with a necessary and important consideration in the category by stating that it "tastes great," while at the same time creating a point-of-difference with the fact that it contained one-third fewer calories (96 calories versus 150 calories for conventional 12-ounce full-strength beer) and was thus "less filling." The point-of-parity and point-of-difference were somewhat conflicting, as consumers tend to equate taste with calories. To overcome potential consumer resistance to this notion, Miller employed credible spokespeople, primarily popular former professional athletes who would presumably not drink a beer unless it tasted good. These ex-jocks were placed in amusing situations in ads where they debated which of the two product benefits—"tastes great" or "less filling"—was more descriptive of the beer, creating valuable points-of-parity and points-of-difference. The ads ended with the clever tag line "Everything You've Always Wanted in a Beer . . . and Less."

Borrowing equity, however, is neither costless nor riskless. Chapter 7 reviews these considerations in detail and outlines the pros and cons of leveraging equity.

BRANDING BRIEF 2-1

Positioning Politicians

The importance of marketing has not been lost on politicians, and, although there are a number of different ways to interpret their words and actions, one way to interpret campaign strategies is from a branding perspective. For example, consultants to political candidates stress the importance of having "high name ID" or, in other words, a high level of brand awareness. In major races, at least 90 percent awareness is desired. Consultants also emphasize "positives–negatives"—voters' responses when asked whether they think positively or negatively of a candidate. A 3:1 ratio is desired (and 4:1 is even better). This measure corresponds to brand attitude in marketing terms.

The last three decades of presidential campaigns are revealing about the importance of properly positioning a politician. George H. W. Bush ran a textbook presidential campaign in 1988. The objective was to move the candidate to the center of the political spectrum and make him a "safe" choice, and to move his Democratic opponent, Massachusetts governor Michael Dukakis, to the left and make him seem more liberal and a "risky" choice. Specific goals were to create a point-of-difference on traditional Republican issues such as defense, the economy (and taxes), and crime and to create a point-of-parity—thus negating the opponent's point-of-difference—on traditional Democratic issues such as the environment, education, and abortion rights. Having successfully achieved these points-of-parity and points-of-difference in the minds of the voters, Bush won in a landslide.

Although the Republicans ran a nearly flawless campaign in 1988, that was not the case in 1992. The new Democratic candidate, Bill Clinton, was a fierce campaigner who ran a focused effort to create a key point-of-difference on one main issue—the economy. Rather than attempting to achieve a point-of-parity on this issue, Bush, who was running for reelection, campaigned on other issues such as family values. By conceding a key point-of-difference to the Democrats and failing to create a compelling one of their own, Bush and the Republicans were defeated handily.

Failing to learn from their mistakes, the Republicans ran a meandering campaign in 1996 that failed to achieve either points-of-parity or points-of-difference. Not surprisingly, their presidential candidate, Bob Dole, lost decisively to the incumbent Bill Clinton. The closeness of the 2000 election between Al Gore and George W. Bush reflected the failure of either candidate to create a strong point-of-difference with the electorate. There was a similarly tight election in 2004 because neither

Barack Obama's 2008 presidential campaign was a textbook classic of modern marketing with a heavy dose of social media.
Source: Christopher Fitzgerald/CandidatePhotos/Newscom

George W. Bush nor John Kerry was successful at carving out a strong position in voters' minds.

The 2008 presidential election, however, was another textbook application of branding as Barack Obama ran a very sophisticated and modern marketing campaign. Republican candidate John McCain attempted to create a point-of-difference on experience and traditional Republican values; Obama sought to create a point-of-difference on new ideas and hope. Their vice presidential choices helped shore up their needed points-of-parity: Joe Biden for Obama offered trusted seniority; Sarah Palin for McCain, albeit controversial, offered a younger, fresher voice.

The Obama campaign team effectively hammered home his message. Multimedia tactics combined offline and online media as well as free and paid media. In addition to traditional print, broadcast, and outdoor ads, social media like Facebook, Meetup, YouTube, and Twitter and long-form videos were employed so people could learn more about Obama and the passion others had about the candidate. Even Obama's slogans ("Yes We Can" and "Change We Can Believe In") and campaign posters (the popular stencil portrait of Obama in solid red, white, and pastel and dark shades of blue with the word "PROGRESS," "HOPE," or "CHANGE" prominently below) became iconic symbols, and Obama breezed to victory.

Sources: "Gore and Bush Are Like Classic Brands," *New York Times*, 25 July 2000, B8; Michael Learmonth, "Social Media Paves Way to White House," *Advertising Age*, 30 March 2009, 16; Noreen O'Leary, "GMBB," *AdweekMedia*, 15 June 2009, 2; John Quelch, "The Marketing of a President," *Harvard Business School Working Knowledge*, 12 November 2008.

Redefine the Relationship. Finally, another potentially powerful but often difficult way to address the negative relationship between attributes and benefits in the minds of consumers is to convince them that in fact the relationship is positive. Marketers can achieve this by providing consumers with a different perspective and suggesting that they may be overlooking or ignoring certain factors or other considerations. Apple offers another classic example.

APPLE

When Apple launched the Macintosh computer in the 1980s—back in the early days of personal computing—its key point-of-difference was "user friendly." Many consumers valued ease of use—especially those who bought personal computers for the home—because in a pre-Windows world, the DOS PC operating system was complex and clumsy. One drawback with that association for Apple, however, was that customers who bought personal computers for business applications inferred that if a personal computer was easy to use, then it also must not be very powerful—and power was a key choice consideration in the business market. Recognizing this potential problem, Apple ran a clever ad campaign with the tag line "The Power to Be Your Best," in an attempt to redefine what being a powerful computer meant. The message behind the ads was that because Apple was easy to use, people in fact did just that—they used them!—a simple but important indication of "power." In other words, the most powerful computers were ones that people actually used.

Apple has worked hard through the years to convince consumers that its computer products are powerful and easy to use.
Source: pcruciatti/Alamy

Although difficult to achieve, such a strategy can be powerful because the two associations can become mutually reinforcing. The challenge is to develop a credible story with which consumers can agree.

Straddle Positions

Occasionally, a company will be able to straddle two frames of reference with one set of points-of-difference and points-of-parity. In these cases, the points-of-difference in one category become points-of-parity in the other and vice-versa for points-of-parity. For example, Accenture defines itself as the company that combines (1) strategic insight, vision, and thought leadership and (2) information technology expertise in developing client solutions. This strategy permits points-of-parity with its two main competitors, McKinsey and IBM, while simultaneously achieving points-of-difference. Specifically, Accenture has a point-of-difference on technology and execution with respect to McKinsey and a point-of-parity on strategy and vision. The reverse is true with respect to IBM: technology and execution are points-of-parity, but strategy and vision are points-of-difference. Another brand that has successfully employed a straddle positioning is BMW.

BMW

When BMW first made a strong competitive push into the U.S. market in the early 1980s, it positioned the brand as being the only automobile that offered both luxury *and* performance. At that time, U.S. luxury cars like Cadillac were seen by many as lacking performance, and U.S. performance cars like the Chevy Corvette were seen as lacking luxury. By relying on the design of its cars, its German heritage, and other aspects of a well-designed marketing program, BMW was able to simultaneously achieve (1) a point-of-difference on performance and a point-of-parity on luxury with respect to luxury cars and (2) a point-of-difference on luxury and a point-of-parity on performance with respect to performance cars. The clever slogan, "The Ultimate Driving Machine," effectively captured the newly created umbrella category—luxury performance cars.

BMW's "Ultimate Driving Machine" slogan nicely captures the brand's dual features of luxury and performance.
Source: BMW AG

While a straddle positioning often is attractive as a means of reconciling potentially conflicting consumer goals and creating a "best-of-both-worlds" solution, it also carries an extra burden. If the points-of-parity and points-of-difference with respect to both categories are not credible, consumers may not view the brand as a legitimate player in *either* category. Many early PDAs that unsuccessfully tried to straddle categories ranging from pagers to laptop computers provide a vivid illustration of this risk.

Updating Positioning over Time

The previous section described some positioning guidelines that are especially useful for launching a new brand. With an established brand, an important question is how often to update its positioning. As a general rule, positioning should be fundamentally changed very infrequently, and only when circumstances significantly reduce the effectiveness of existing POPs and PODs.

Positioning, however, will evolve over time to better reflect market opportunities or challenges. A point-of-difference or point-of-parity may be refined, added, or dropped as situations dictate. One common market opportunity that often arises is the need to deepen the meaning of the brand to permit further expansion—*laddering*. One common market challenge is how to respond to competitive actions that threaten an existing positioning—*reacting*. We consider the positioning implications of each in turn.

Laddering.   Although identifying PODs to dominate competition on benefits that are important to consumers provides a sound way to build an initial position, once the target market attains a basic understanding of how the brand relates to alternatives in the same category, it may be necessary to deepen the meanings associated with the brand positioning. It is often useful to explore underlying consumer motivations in a product category to uncover the relevant associations. For example, Maslow's hierarchy maintains that consumers have different priorities and levels of needs.[54]

From lowest to highest priority, they are as follows:

1. Physiological needs (food, water, air, shelter, sex)
2. Safety and security needs (protection, order, stability)
3. Social needs (affection, friendship, belonging)
4. Ego needs (prestige, status, self-respect)
5. Self-actualization (self-fulfillment)

According to Maslow, higher-level needs become relevant once lower-level needs have been satisfied.

Marketers have also recognized the importance of higher-level needs. For example, *means-end chains* have been devised as a way of understanding higher-level meanings of brand characteristics. A means-end chain takes the following structure: attributes (descriptive features that characterize a product) lead to benefits (the personal value and meaning attached to product attributes), which, in turn, lead to values (stable and enduring personal goals or motivations).[55]

In other words, a consumer chooses a product that delivers an attribute (A) that provides benefits or has certain consequences (B/C) that satisfy values (V). For example, in a study of salty snacks, one respondent noted that a flavored chip (A) with a strong taste (A) would mean that she would eat less (B/C), not get fat (B/C), and have a better figure (B/C), all of which would enhance her self-esteem (V).

Laddering thus progresses from attributes to benefits to more abstract values or motivations. In effect, laddering repeatedly asks what the implication of an attribute or benefit is for the consumer. Failure to move up the ladder may reduce the strategic alternatives available to a brand.[56] For example, P&G introduced low-sudsing Dash detergent to attract consumers who used front-loading washing machines. Many years of advertising Dash in this manner made this position impenetrable by other brands. Dash was so associated with front-loaders, however, that when this type of machine went out of fashion, so did Dash, despite the fact that it was among P&G's most effective detergents, and despite significant efforts to reposition the brand.

Some attributes and benefits may lend themselves to laddering more easily than others. For example, the Betty Crocker brand appears on a number of different baking products and is characterized by the physical warmth associated with baking. Such an association makes it relatively easy to talk about emotional warmth and the joy of baking or the good feelings that might arise from baking for others across a wide range of baking-related products.

Thus, some of the strongest brands deepen their points-of-difference to create benefit and value associations, for example, Volvo and Michelin (safety and peace of mind), Intel (performance and compatibility), Marlboro (western imagery), Coke (Americana and refreshment), Disney (fun, magic, family entertainment), Nike (innovative products and peak athletic performance), and BMW (styling and driving performance).

As a brand becomes associated with more and more products and moves up the product hierarchy, the brand's meaning will become more abstract. At the same time, it is important that the proper category membership and POPs and PODs exist in the minds of consumers for any particular products sold under the brand name, as discussed in Chapter 11.

Reacting.   Competitive actions are often directed at eliminating points-of-difference to make them points-of-parity or to strengthen or establish new points-of-difference. Often competitive advantages exist for only a short period of time before competitors attempt to match them. For example, when Goodyear introduced RunOnFlat tires (which allowed tires to keep going for up to 50 miles at a speed of 55 mph after a tire puncture or blowout), Michelin quickly responded with the Zero Pressure tire, which offered the same consumer benefit.

When a competitor challenges an existing POD or attempts to overcome a POP, there are essentially three main options for the target brand—from no reaction to moderate to significant reactions.

- *Do nothing.* If the competitive actions seem unlikely to recapture a POD or create a new POD, then the best reaction is probably to just stay the course and continue brand-building efforts.
- *Go on the defensive.* If the competitive actions appear to have the potential to disrupt the market some, then it may be necessary to take a defensive stance. One way to defend the positioning is to add some reassurance in the product or advertising to strengthen POPs and PODs.
- *Go on the offensive.* If the competitive actions seem potentially quite damaging, then it might be necessary to take a more aggressive stance and reposition the brand to address the threat. One approach might be to launch a product extension or ad campaign that fundamentally changes the meaning of the brand.

A brand audit can help marketers assess the severity of the competitive threat and the appropriate competitive stance, as described in Chapter 8.

Developing a Good Positioning

A few final comments are useful to help guide positioning efforts. First, a good positioning has a "foot in the present" and a "foot in the future." It needs to be somewhat aspirational so that the brand has room to grow and improve. Positioning on the basis of the current state of the market is not forward-looking enough; but, at the same time, the positioning cannot be so removed from the current reality that it is essentially unobtainable. The real trick in positioning is to strike just the right balance between what the brand is and what it could be.

Second, a good positioning is careful to identify all relevant points-of-parity. Too often marketers overlook or ignore crucial areas where the brand is potentially disadvantaged to concentrate on areas of strength. Both are obviously necessary as points-of-difference will not matter without the requisite points-of-parity. One good way to uncover key competitive points-of-parity is to role play competitor's positioning and infer their intended points-of-difference. Competitor's PODs will, in turn, become the brand's POPs. Consumer research into the trade-offs in decision-making that exist in the minds of consumers can also be informative.

Third, a good positioning should reflect a consumer point of view in terms of the benefits that consumers derive from the brand. It is not enough to advertise that you are the "biggest selling gasoline in the world"—as Shell Oil did once. An effective POD should make clear *why* that it so desirable to consumers. In other words, what benefits would a consumer get from that unique attribute? Does that mean Shell Oil is more convenient due to more locations, or perhaps able to charge lower prices due to economies of scale? Those benefits, if evident, should become the basis for the positioning, with the proof point or RTB being the attribute of "biggest selling gasoline."

Finally, as we will develop in greater detail with the brand resonance model in the next chapter, it is important that a duality exists in the positioning of a brand such that there are rational and emotional components. In other words, a good positioning contains points-of-difference and points-of-parity that appeal both to the "head" and the "heart."

DEFINING A BRAND MANTRA

Brand positioning describes how a brand can effectively compete against a specified set of competitors in a particular market. In many cases, however, brands span multiple product categories and therefore may have multiple distinct—yet related—positionings. As brands evolve and expand across categories, marketers will want to craft a brand mantra that reflects the essential "heart and soul" of the brand.

Brand Mantras

To better establish what a brand represents, marketers will often define a brand mantra.[57] A *brand mantra* is a short, three- to five-word phrase that captures the irrefutable essence or spirit of the brand positioning. It's similar to "brand essence" or "core brand promise," and its purpose is to ensure that all employees and external marketing partners understand what the brand most fundamentally is to represent to consumers so they can adjust their actions accordingly. For example, McDonald's brand philosophy of "Food, Folks, and Fun" nicely captures its brand essence and core brand promise.

Brand mantras are powerful devices. They can provide guidance about what products to introduce under the brand, what ad campaigns to run, and where and how the brand should be sold. They may even guide the most seemingly unrelated or mundane decisions, such as the look of a reception area and the way employees answer the phone. In effect, brand mantras create a mental filter to screen out brand-inappropriate marketing activities or actions of any type that may have a negative bearing on customers' impressions of a brand.

Brand mantras help the brand present a consistent image. Any time a consumer or customer encounters a brand—in any way, shape, or form—his or her knowledge about that brand may change and affect the equity of the brand. Given that a vast number of employees come into contact with consumers, either directly or indirectly, their words and actions should consistently reinforce and support the brand meaning. Marketing partners like ad agency members may not even recognize their role in influencing equity. The brand mantra signals its meaning and importance to the firm, as well as the crucial role of employees and marketing partners in its management. It also provides memorable shorthand as to what are the crucial considerations of the brand that should be kept most salient and top-of-mind.

Designing a Brand Mantra.   What makes a good brand mantra? Two high-profile and successful examples of brand mantras come from two powerful brands, Nike and Disney, as described in Branding Briefs 2-2 and 2-3. Brand mantras must economically communicate what the brand is and what it is *not*. The Nike and Disney examples show the power and utility of a well-designed brand mantra. They also help suggest what might characterize a good brand mantra. Both examples are essentially structured the same way, with three terms, as follows:

	Emotional Modifier	**Descriptive Modifier**	**Brand Function**
Nike	Authentic	Athletic	Performance
Disney	Fun	Family	Entertainment

BRANDING BRIEF 2-2

Nike Brand Mantra

A brand with a keen sense of what it represents to consumers is Nike. Nike has a rich set of associations with consumers, revolving around such considerations as its innovative product designs, its sponsorships of top athletes, its award-winning advertising, its competitive drive, and its irreverent attitude. Internally, Nike marketers adopted a three-word brand mantra of "authentic athletic performance" to guide their marketing efforts. Thus, in Nike's eyes, its entire marketing program—its products and how they are sold—must reflect the key brand values conveyed by the brand mantra.

Nike's brand mantra has had profound implications for its marketing. In the words of ex-Nike marketing gurus Scott Bedbury and Jerome Conlon, the brand mantra provided the "intellectual guard rails" to keep the brand moving in the right direction and to make sure it did not get off track somehow. Nike's brand mantra has even affected product development. Over the years, Nike has expanded its brand meaning from "running shoes" to "athletic shoes" to "athletic shoes and apparel" to "all things associated with athletics (including equipment)."

Each step of the way, however, it has been guided by its "authentic athletic performance" brand mantra. For example, as Nike rolled out its successful apparel line, one important hurdle for the products was that they should be innovative enough through material, cut, or design to truly benefit top athletes. The revolutionary moisture-wicking technology of their Dri-Fit apparel line left athletes drier and more comfortable as they sweat. At the same time, the company has been careful to avoid using the Nike name to brand products that did not fit with the brand mantra, like casual "brown" shoes.

When Nike has experienced problems with its marketing program, they have often been a result of its failure to figure out how to translate its brand mantra to the marketing challenge at hand. For example, in going to Europe, Nike experienced several false starts until realizing that "authentic athletic performance" has a different meaning over there and, in particular, has to involve soccer in a major way. Similarly, Nike

Nike's brand mantra of "authentic athletic performance" is exemplified by athletes such as Roger Federer.
Source: Jean Catuffe, PacificCoastNews/Newscom

stumbled in developing its All Conditions Gear (ACG) outdoors shoes and clothing sub-brand, which attempted to translate its brand mantra into a less competitive arena.

BRANDING BRIEF 2-3

Disney Brand Mantra

Disney developed its brand mantra in response to its incredible growth through licensing and product development during the mid-1980s. In the late 1980s, Disney became concerned that some of its characters, like Mickey Mouse and Donald Duck, were being used inappropriately and becoming overexposed. To investigate the severity of the problem, Disney undertook an extensive brand audit. As part of a brand inventory, it first compiled a list of all Disney products that were available (licensed and company manufactured) and all third-party promotions (complete with point-of-purchase displays and relevant merchandising) from stores across the country and all over the world. At the same time, Disney launched a major consumer research study—a brand exploratory—to investigate how consumers felt about the Disney brand.

Disney's brand mantra of "fun family entertainment" gave marketers "guard rails" to help avoid brand-inconsistent actions.
Source: ZHANG JUN/Xinhua/Photoshot/Newscom

The results of the brand inventory revealed some potentially serious problems: the Disney characters were on so many products and marketed in so many ways that in some cases it was difficult to discern the rationale behind the deal to start with. The consumer study only heightened Disney's concerns. Because of the broad exposure of the characters in the marketplace, many consumers had begun to feel that Disney was exploiting its name. In some cases, consumers felt that the characters added little value to products and, worse yet, involved children in purchase decisions that they would typically ignore.

Because of its aggressive marketing efforts, Disney had written contracts with many of the "park participants" for copromotions or licensing arrangements. Disney characters were selling everything from diapers to cars to McDonald's hamburgers. Disney learned in the consumer study, however, that consumers did not differentiate between all the product endorsements. "Disney was Disney" to consumers, whether they saw the characters in films, records, theme parks, or consumer products. Consequently, *all* products and services that used the Disney name or characters had an impact on Disney's brand equity. Consumers reported that they resented some of these endorsements because they felt that they had a special,

personal relationship with the characters and with Disney that should not be handled so carelessly.

As a result of the brand audit, Disney moved quickly to establish a brand equity team to better manage the brand franchise and more carefully evaluate licensing and other third-party promotional opportunities. One of the mandates of this team was to ensure that a consistent image for Disney—reinforcing its key brand associations—was conveyed by all third-party products and services. To facilitate this supervision, Disney adopted an internal brand mantra of "fun family entertainment" to serve as a screening device for proposed ventures.

Opportunities that were not consistent with the brand mantra—no matter how appealing—were rejected. For example, Disney was approached to cobrand a mutual fund in Europe that was designed as a way for parents to save for the college expenses of their children. The opportunity was declined despite the consistent "family" association, because Disney believed that a connection with the financial community or banking suggested other associations that were inconsistent with its brand image (mutual funds are rarely intended to be entertaining!).

The ***brand functions*** term describes the nature of the product or service or the type of experiences or benefits the brand provides. It can range from concrete language that reflects the product category itself, to more abstract notions (like Nike's and Disney's), where the term relates to higher-order experiences or benefits that a variety of different products could deliver. The ***descriptive modifier*** further clarifies its nature. Thus, Nike's performance is not just any kind (not artistic performance, for instance) but only *athletic* performance; Disney's entertainment is not just any kind (not adult-oriented) but only *family* entertainment (and arguably an additional modifier, "magical," could add even more distinctiveness). Combined, the brand function term and descriptive modifier help delineate the brand boundaries. Finally, the *emotional modifier* provides another qualifier—how exactly does the brand provide benefits and in what ways?

Brand mantras don't necessarily have to follow this exact structure, but they should clearly delineate what the brand is supposed to represent and therefore, at least implicitly, what it is not. Several additional points are worth noting.

1. Brand mantras derive their power and usefulness from their collective meaning. Other brands may be strong on one, or perhaps even a few, of the brand associations making up the brand mantra. For the brand mantra to be effective, no other brand should singularly excel on all dimensions. Part of the key to both Nike's and Disney's success is that for years, no other competitor could really deliver on the promise suggested by their brand mantras as well as they did.

2. Brand mantras typically are designed to capture the brand's points-of-difference, that is, what is unique about the brand. Other aspects of the brand positioning—especially the brand's points-of-parity—may also be important and may need to be reinforced in other ways.

3. For brands facing rapid growth, a brand functions term can provide critical guidance as to appropriate and inappropriate categories into which to extend. For brands in more stable categories, the brand mantra may focus more on points-of-difference as expressed by the functional and emotional modifiers, perhaps not even including a brand functions term.

Implementing a Brand Mantra. Brand mantras should be developed at the same time as the brand positioning. As we've seen, brand positioning typically is a result of an in-depth examination of the brand through some form of brand audit or other activities. Brand mantras may benefit from the learning gained from those activities but, at the same time, require more internal examination and involve input from a wider range of company employees and marketing staff. Part of this internal exercise is actually to determine the different means by which each and every employee currently affects brand equity, and how he or she can contribute in a positive way to a brand's destiny. The importance of internal branding is reinforced in The Science of Branding 2-2.

Marketers can often summarize the brand positioning in a few sentences or a short paragraph that suggests the ideal core brand associations consumers should hold. Based on these core brand associations, a brainstorming session can attempt to identify PODs, POPs, and different brand mantra candidates. In the final brand mantra, the following considerations should come into play:

- *Communicate:* A good brand mantra should both define the category (or categories) of the business to set the brand boundaries and clarify what is unique about the brand.
- *Simplify:* An effective brand mantra should be memorable. That means it should be short, crisp, and vivid. A three-word mantra is ideal because it is the most economical way to convey the brand positioning.
- *Inspire:* Ideally, the brand mantra should also stake out ground that is personally meaningful and relevant to as many employees as possible. Brand mantras can do more than inform and guide; they can also inspire, if the brand values tap into higher-level meaning with employees as well as consumers.

Regardless of how many words make up the mantra, however, *there will always be a level of meaning beneath the brand mantra itself that will need to be articulated.* Virtually any word may have many interpretations. For example, the words *fun, family,* and *entertainment* in Disney's brand mantra can each take on multiple meanings, leading Disney to drill deeper to provide a stronger foundation for the mantra. Two or three short phrases were therefore added later to clarify each of the three words.

THE SCIENCE OF BRANDING 2-2

Branding Inside the Organization

Brand mantras point out the importance of *internal branding*—making sure that members of the organization are properly aligned with the brand and what it represents. Much of the branding literature has taken an *external* perspective, focusing on strategies and tactics that firms should take to build or manage brand equity with customers. Without question, at the heart of all marketing activity is the positioning of a brand and the essence of its meaning with consumers.

Equally important, however, is positioning the brand *internally*.[58] For service companies especially, it's critical that all employees have an up-to-date and deep understanding of the brand. Recently, a number of companies have put forth initiatives to improve their internal branding.

One of the fastest growing and most successful restaurant chains in the United States, Panda Express, devotes significant resources to internal training and development for employees. Besides services training, privately owned Panda Express supports the personal improvement efforts of its staff—controlling weight, working on communications skills, jogging, and attending seminars—in the belief that healthier, happier employees increase sales and profitability.

Singapore Airlines also invests heavily in employee training: new recruits receive four months of training, twice as long as the industry average. The company also spends about $70 million a year on retraining each of its 14,500 existing employees. Training focuses on deportment, etiquette, wine appreciation, and cultural sensitivity. Cabin crew learn how to interact differently with Japanese, Chinese, and U.S. passengers as well as the importance of communicating at eye level and not "looking down" at passengers.

Companies need to engage in continual open dialogue with their employees. Branding should be perceived as participatory. Some firms have pushed B2E (business-to-employee) programs through corporate intranets and other means. Disney is seen as so successful at internal branding that its Disney Institute holds seminars on the "Disney Style" of creativity, service, and loyalty for employees from other companies.

In short, for both motivating employees and attracting external customers, internal branding is a critical management priority.

Sources: Karl Taro Greenfeld, "The Sharin' Huggin' Lovin' Carin' Chinese Food Money Machine," *Bloomberg Businessweek*, 28 November 2010, 98–103; Loizos Heracleous and Joachen Wirtz, "Singapore Airlines' Balancing Act," *Harvard Business Review*, July–August 2010, 145–149; James Wallace, "Singapore Airlines Raises the Bar for Luxury Flying," www.seattlepi.com, 16 January 2007. For some seminal writings in the area, see Hamish Pringle and William Gordon, *Brand Manners: How to Create the Self-Confident Organization to Live the Brand* (New York: John Wiley & Sons, 2001); Thomas Gad, *4-D Branding: Cracking the Corporate Code of the Network Economy* (London: Financial Times Prentice Hall, 2000); Nicholas Ind, *Living the Brand: How to Transform Every Member of Your Organization into a Brand Champion*, 2nd ed. (London, UK: Kogan Page, 2004); Scott M. Davis and Kenneth Dunn, *Building the Brand-Driven Business: Operationalize Your Brand to Drive Profitable Growth* (San Francisco: Jossey-Bass, 2002); Mary Jo Hatch and Make Schultz, *Taking Brand Initiative: How Companies Can Align Strategy, Culture, and Identity Through Corporate Branding* (San Francisco, CA: Jossey-Bass, 2008); Andy Bird and Mhairi McEwan, *The Growth Drivers: The Definitive Guide to Transforming Marketing Capabilities* (West Sussex, UK: John Wiley & Sons, 2012).

REVIEW

Customer-based brand equity is the differential effect that brand knowledge has on consumer response to the marketing of that brand. A brand has positive customer-based brand equity when customers react more favorably to a product and the way it is marketed when the brand is identified than when it is not.

We can define brand knowledge in terms of an associative network memory model, as a network of nodes and links wherein the brand node in memory has a variety of associations linked to it. We can characterize brand knowledge in terms of two components: brand awareness and brand image. Brand awareness is related to the strength of the brand node or trace in memory, as reflected by consumers' ability to recall or recognize the brand under different conditions. It has both depth and breadth. The depth of brand awareness measures the likelihood that consumers can recognize or recall the brand. The breadth of brand awareness measures the variety of purchase and consumption situations in which the brand comes to mind. Brand image is consumer perceptions of a brand as reflected by the brand associations held in consumers' memory.

Customer-based brand equity occurs when the consumer has a high level of awareness and familiarity with the brand and holds some strong, favorable, and unique brand associations in memory. In some cases, brand awareness alone is sufficient to result in more favorable consumer response—for example, in low-involvement decision settings where consumers are willing to base their choices merely on familiar brands. In other cases, the strength, favorability, and uniqueness of the brand associations play a critical role in determining the differential response making up the brand equity.

Deciding on a positioning requires determining a frame of reference (by identifying the target market and the nature of competition), the optimal points-of-parity and points-of-difference brand associations, and an overall brand mantra as a summary. First, marketers need to understand consumer behavior and the consideration sets that consumers adopt in making brand choices. After establishing this frame of reference, they can then turn to identifying the best possible points-of-parity and points-of-difference.

Points-of-difference are those associations that are unique to the brand, strongly held, and favorably evaluated by consumers. Marketers should find points-of-difference associations that are strong, favorable, and unique based on desirability, deliverability, and differentiation considerations, as well as the resulting anticipated levels of sales and costs that might be expected with achieving those points-of-difference.

Points-of-parity, on the other hand, are those associations that are not necessarily unique to the brand but may in fact be shared with other brands. Category points-of-parity associations are necessary to being a legitimate and credible product offering within a certain category. Competitive points-of-parity associations negate competitors' points-of-differences. Correlational points-of-parity negate any possible disadvantages or negatives that might also arise from a point-of-difference.

Finally, a brand mantra is an articulation of the "heart and soul" of the brand, a three- to five-word phrase that captures the irrefutable essence or spirit of the brand positioning and brand values. Its purpose is to ensure that all employees and all external marketing partners understand what the brand is, most fundamentally, in order to represent it with consumers.

The choice of these four ingredients determines the brand positioning and the desired brand knowledge structures.

DISCUSSION QUESTIONS

1. Apply the categorization model to a product category other than beverages. How do consumers make decisions whether or not to buy the product, and how do they arrive at their final brand decision? What are the implications for brand equity management for the brands in the category? How does it affect positioning, for example?
2. Pick a category basically dominated by two main brands. Evaluate the positioning of each brand. Who are their target markets? What are their main points-of-parity and points-of-difference? Have they defined their positioning correctly? How might it be improved?
3. Consider a book store in your area. What competitive frames of reference does it face? What are the implications of those frames of reference for its positioning?
4. Can you think of any negatively correlated attributes and benefits other than those listed in Figure 2-6? Can you think of any other strategies to deal with negatively correlated attributes and benefits?
5. What do you think of Naomi Klein's positions as espoused in *No Logos?* How would you respond to her propositions? Do you agree or disagree about her beliefs on the growth of corporate power?

BRAND FOCUS 2.0

The Marketing Advantages of Strong Brands

Customer-based brand equity occurs when consumer response to marketing activity differs when consumers know the brand and when they do not. How that response differs will depend on the level of brand awareness and how favorably and uniquely consumers evaluate brand associations, as well as the particular marketing activity under consideration.

A number of benefits can result from a strong brand, both in terms of greater revenue and lower costs.[59] For example, one marketing expert categorizes the factors creating financial value for strong brands into two categories: factors related to growth (a brand's ability to attract new customers, resist competitive activity, introduce line extensions, and cross international borders) and factors related to profitability (brand loyalty, premium pricing, lower price elasticity, lower advertising/sales ratios, and trade leverage).[60]

This appendix considers in detail some of the benefits to the firm of having brands with a high level of awareness and a positive brand image.[61]

Greater Loyalty and Less Vulnerability to Competitive Marketing Actions and Crises

Research shows that different types of brand associations—if favorable—can affect consumer product evaluations, perceptions of quality, and purchase rates.[62] This influence may be especially apparent with difficult-to-assess "experience" goods[63] and as the uniqueness of brand associations increases.[64] In addition, familiarity with a brand has been shown to increase consumer confidence, attitude toward the brand, and purchase intention,[65] and to mitigate the negative impact of a poor trial experience.[66]

For these and other reasons, one characteristic of brands with a great deal of equity is that consumers feel great loyalty to them. Some top brands have been market leaders for years despite significant changes in both consumer attitudes and competitive activity over time. Through it all, consumers have valued these brands enough to stick with them and reject the overtures of competitors, creating a steady stream of revenues for the firm. Research also shows that brands with large market shares are more likely to have more loyal customers than brands with small market shares, a phenomenon called *double jeopardy*.[67] One study found that brand equity was strongly correlated (.75) with subsequent market share and profitability.[68]

A brand with a positive brand image also is more likely to successfully weather a brand crisis or downturn in the brand's fortunes.[69] Perhaps the most compelling example is Johnson & Johnson's (J&J) Tylenol brand. Brand Focus 11.0 describes how J&J contended with a tragic product-tampering episode in the early 1980s. Despite seeing its market share drop from 37 percent to almost zero overnight and fearing Tylenol would be written off as a brand with no future, J&J was able to regain virtually all lost market share for the brand through its skillful handling of the crisis and a good deal of brand equity.

The lesson is that effective handling of a marketing crisis requires swift and sincere action, an immediate admission that something has gone wrong, and assurance that an effective remedy will be put in place. The greater the brand equity, the more likely that these statements will be credible enough to keep customers understanding and patient as the firm sets out to solve the crisis. Without some underlying brand equity, however, even the best-laid plans for recovery may fall short with a suspicious or uninformed public.[70] Finally, even absent a crisis, a strong brand offers protection in a marketing downturn or when the brand's fortunes fall.

Larger Margins

Brands with positive customer-based brand equity can command a price premium.[71] Moreover, consumers should also have a fairly inelastic response to price increases and elastic responses to price decreases or discounts for the brand over time.[72] Consistent with this reasoning, research has shown that consumers loyal to a brand are less likely to switch in the face of price increases and more likely to increase the quantity of the brand purchased in the face of price decreases.[73] In a competitive sense, brand leaders draw a disproportionate amount of share from smaller-share competitors.[74] At the same time,

market leaders are relatively immune to price competition from these small-share brands.[75]

In a classic early study, Intelliquest explored the role of brand name and price in the decision purchase of business computer buyers.[76] Survey respondents were asked, "What is the incremental dollar value you would be willing to pay over a 'no-name' clone computer brand?" IBM commanded the greatest price premium, followed by Compaq and Hewlett-Packard. Some brands had negative brand equity; they actually received negative numbers. Clearly, according to this study, brands had specific meaning in the personal computer market that consumers valued and were willing to pay for.

Greater Trade Cooperation and Support

Wholesalers, retailers, and other middlemen in the distribution channel play an important role in the selling of many products. Their activities can thus facilitate or inhibit the success of the brand. If a brand has a positive image, retailers and other middlemen are more likely to respond to the wishes of consumers and actively promote and sell the brand.[77] Channel members are also less likely to require any marketing push from the manufacturer and will be more receptive to manufacturers' suggestions to stock, reorder, and display the brand,[78] as well as to pass through trade promotions, demand smaller slotting allowances, give more favorable shelf space or position, and so on. Given that many consumer decisions are made in the store, the possibility of additional marketing push by retailers is important.

Increased Marketing Communication Effectiveness

A host of advertising and communication benefits may result from creating awareness of and a positive image for a brand. One well-established view of consumer response to marketing communications is the hierarchy of effects models. These models assume that consumers move through a series of stages or mental states on the basis of marketing communications—for example, exposure to, attention to, comprehension of, yielding to, retention of, and behaving on the basis of a marketing communication.

A brand with a great deal of equity already has created some knowledge structures in consumers' minds, increasing the likelihood that consumers will pass through various stages of the hierarchy. For example, consider the effects of a positive brand image on the persuasive ability of advertising: Consumers may be more likely to notice an ad, may more easily learn about the brand and form favorable opinions, and may retain and act on these beliefs over time.

Familiar, well-liked brands are less susceptible to "interference" and confusion from competitive ads,[79] are more responsive to creative strategies such as humor appeals,[80] and are less vulnerable to negative reactions due to concentrated repetition schedules.[81] In addition, panel diary members who were highly loyal to a brand increased purchases when advertising for the brand increased.[82] Other advantages associated with more advertising include increased likelihood of being the focus of attention and increased "brand interest."[83]

Because strong brand associations exist, lower levels of repetition may be necessary. For example, in a classic study of advertising weights, Anheuser-Busch ran a carefully conducted field experiment in which it varied the amount of Budweiser advertising shown to consumers in different matched test markets.[84] Seven different advertising expenditure levels were tested, representing increases and decreases from the previous advertising expenditure levels: minus 100 percent (no advertising), minus 50 percent, 0 percent (same level), plus 50 percent, plus 100 percent (double the level of advertising), plus 150 percent, and plus 200 percent. These expenditure levels were run for one year and revealed that the "no advertising" level resulted in the same amount of sales as the current program. In fact, the 50 percent cut in advertising expenditures actually resulted in an increase in sales, consistent with the notion that strong brands such as Budweiser do not require the same advertising levels, at least over a short period of time, as a less well-known or well-liked brand.[85]

Similarly, because of existing brand knowledge structures, consumers may be more likely to notice sales promotions, direct mail offerings, or other sales-oriented marketing communications and respond favorably. For example, several studies have shown that promotion effectiveness is asymmetric in favor of a higher-quality brand.[86]

Possible Licensing and Brand Extension Opportunities

A strong brand often has associations that may be desirable in other product categories. To capitalize on this value, as discussed in Chapter 7, a firm may choose to license its name, logo, or other trademark item to another company for use on its products and merchandise. The rationale for the licensee (the company obtaining the rights to use the trademark) is that consumers will pay more for a product because of the recognition and image lent by the trademark. One marketing research study showed that consumers would pay $60 for cookware licensed under the Julia Child name as opposed to only $40 for identical cookware bearing the Sears name.[87]

As will be outlined in Chapter 11, a **brand extension** occurs when a firm uses an established brand name to enter a new market. A **line extension** uses a current brand name to enter a new market segment in the existing product class, say with new varieties, new flavors, or new sizes.

Academic research has shown that well-known and well-regarded brands can extend more successfully and into more diverse categories than other brands.[88] In addition, the amount of brand equity has been shown to be correlated with the highest- or lowest-quality member in the product line for vertical product extensions.[89] Research has also shown that positive symbolic associations may be the basis of these evaluations, even if overall brand attitude itself is not necessarily high.[90]

Brands with varied product category associations through past extensions have been shown to be especially extendable.[91] As a result, introductory marketing programs for extensions from an established brand may be more efficient than others.[92] Several studies have indicated that extension activity has aided (or at least did not dilute) brand equity for the parent brand. For instance, brand extensions strengthened parent brand associations, and "flagship brands" were highly resistant to dilution or other potential negative effects caused by negative experiences with an extension.[93] Research has also found evidence of an ownership effect, whereby current owners generally had more favorable responses to brand line extensions.[94] Finally, extensions of brands that have both high familiarity and positive attitudes have been shown to receive higher initial stock market reactions than other brands.[95]

Other Benefits

Brands with positive customer-based brand equity may provide other advantages to the firm not directly related to the products themselves, such as helping the firm to attract or motivate better employees, generate greater interest from investors, and garner more support from shareholders.[96] In terms of the latter, several research studies have shown that brand equity can be directly related to corporate stock price.[97]

Notes

1. Kevin Lane Keller, "Conceptualizing, Measuring, and Managing Customer-Based Brand Equity," *Journal of Marketing* (January 1993): 1–29.
2. Much of this chapter is based on Kevin Lane Keller, Brian Sternthal, and Alice Tybout, "Three Questions You Need to Ask About Your Brand," *Harvard Business Review* 80, no. 9 (September 2002): 80–89.
3. Norman Berry, "Revitalizing Brands," *Journal of Consumer Marketing* 5, no. 3 (1988): 15–20.
4. Elaine Wong, "Top 10 Most Popular Campaigns of 2009," *Brandweek*, 30 December 2009; Stuart Elliott, "The Vocabulary of Snacking, Lightly Sweetened," *New York Times*, 3 March 2009; Michael Bush, "As 2011 Super Bowl Faded, Doritos and Snickers Proved Lasting Winners," *Advertising Age*, 16 February 2011.
5. "Discovery Channel Looks to Bring New Energy, Focus to Brand Identity," *Art & Business in Motion*, www.dennytu.wordpress.com, 26 August 2011; Dan Butcher, "Discovery Channel Launches Cross-Network Ad Campaign with Microsoft," *Mobile Marketer*, 26 April 2009; www.dsc.discovery.com.
6. Richard Jones, "Finding Sources of Brand Value: Developing a Stakeholder Model of Brand Equity," *Journal of Brand Management*, 13, no. 1 (October 2005): 10–32.
7. John R. Anderson, *The Architecture of Cognition* (Cambridge, MA: Harvard University Press, 1983); Robert S. Wyer, Jr. and Thomas K. Srull, "Person Memory and Judgment," *Psychological Review* 96, no. 1 (1989): 58–83.
8. John R. Rossiter and Larry Percy, *Advertising and Promotion Management* (New York: McGraw-Hill, 1987).
9. Burleigh B. Gardner and Sidney J. Levy, "The Product and the Brand," *Harvard Business Review* (March–April 1955): 33–39.
10. H. Herzog, "Behavioral Science Concepts for Analyzing the Consumer," in *Marketing and the Behavioral Sciences*, ed. Perry Bliss (Boston: Allyn & Bacon, 1963), 76–86; Joseph W. Newman, "New Insight, New Progress for Marketing," *Harvard Business Review* (November–December, 1957): 95–102.
11. Jim Joseph, "How Do I Love Thee, Apple? Let Me Count the Ways," *Brandweek*, 24 May 2010; Michael

Learmonth, "Can the Apple Brand Survive Without Steve Jobs?," *Advertising Age*, 14 January 2009; Miguel Helft and Ashlee Vance, "Apple Passes Microsoft as No. 1 in Tech," *New York Times*, 26 May 2010.

12. James R. Bettman, *An Information Processing Theory of Consumer Choice* (Reading, MA: Addison-Wesley, 1979); Rossiter and Percy, *Advertising and Promotion Management*.

13. William Baker, J. Wesley Hutchinson, Danny Moore, and Prakash Nedungadi, "Brand Familiarity and Advertising: Effects on the Evoked Set and Brand Preference," in *Advances in Consumer Research*, Vol. 13, ed. Richard J. Lutz (Provo, UT: Association for Consumer Research, 1986), 637–642; Prakash Nedungadi, "Recall and Consumer Consideration Sets: Influencing Choice without Altering Brand Evaluations," *Journal of Consumer Research* 17 (December 1990): 263–276.

14. For seminal supporting memory research, see Henry L. Roediger, "Inhibition in Recall from Cuing with Recall Targets," *Journal of Verbal Learning and Verbal Behavior* 12 (1973): 644–657; and Raymond S. Nickerson, "Retrieval Inhibition from Part-Set Cuing: A Persisting Enigma in Memory Research," *Memory and Cognition* 12 (November 1984): 531–552.

15. Rashmi Adaval, "How Good Gets Better and Bad Gets Worse: Understanding the Impact of Affect on Evaluations of Known Brands," *Journal of Consumer Research* 30 (December 2003): 352–367.

16. Jacob Jacoby, George J. Syzabillo, and Jacqeline Busato-Schach, "Information Acquisition Behavior in Brand Choice Situations," *Journal of Consumer Research* 3 (1977): 209–216; Ted Roselius, "Consumer Ranking of Risk Reduction Methods," *Journal of Marketing* 35 (January 1977): 56–61.

17. James R. Bettman and C. Whan Park, "Effects of Prior Knowledge and Experience and Phase of the Choice Process on Consumer Decision Processes: A Protocol Analysis," *Journal of Consumer Research* 7 (December 1980): 234–248; Wayne D. Hoyer and Steven P. Brown, "Effects of Brand Awareness on Choice for a Common, Repeat-Purchase Product," *Journal of Consumer Research* 17 (September 1990): 141–148; C. W. Park and V. Parker Lessig, "Familiarity and Its Impact on Consumer Biases and Heuristics," *Journal of Consumer Research* 8 (September 1981): 223–230.

18. Richard E. Petty and John T. Cacioppo, *Attitudes and Persuasion: Classic and Contemporary Approaches.* (Boulder, CO: Westview, 1996).

19. "Gannett Launches Branding, Ad Campaign," *The Clarion-Ledger*, 7 March 2011; Nat Worden, "Gannett Reaches Out With a New Slogan," *Wall Street Journal*, 7 March 2011; "Gannett Launches New 'It's All Within Reach' National Brand Campaign," *Business Wire*, 7 March 2011; "First Mover: Maryam Banikarim," *Adweek*, 19 September 2011.

20. Stuart Elliott, "Bank Leaves Child's Play Behind," *New York Times*, 17 September 2010; Dakin Campbell, "Ally's New Campaign Replaces Ads That Showed Bankers as Cheaters," *Bloomberg Business Week*, 20 September 2010; "If Advertising Doesn't Work, Then Why

Is 'Ally' a Household Word?," www.thefinancialbrand .com, 12 November 2010.

21. Stuart Elliott, "Body Shop Begins a Campaign Against Sex Trafficking," *New York Times*, 17 March 2010; Elaine Wong, "The Body Shop Finds New Ways to Beauty," *Brandweek*, 26 August 2008.

22. Heather Landi, "When Life Gives You Lemons," *Beverage World*, November 2010, 18–22.

23. George S. Day, Allan D. Shocker, and Rajendra K. Srivastava, "Customer-Oriented Approaches to Identifying Products-Markets," *Journal of Marketing* 43 (Fall 1979): 8–19.

24. K. E. Miller and J. L. Ginter, "An Investigation of Situational Variation in Brand Choice Behavior and Attitude," *Journal of Marketing Research* 16 (February 1979): 111–123.

25. David A. Aaker, "Positioning Your Brand," *Business Horizons* 25 (May/June 1982): 56–62; Al Ries and Jack Trout, *Positioning: The Battle for Your Mind* (New York: McGraw-Hill, 1979); Yoram Wind, *Product Policy: Concepts, Methods, and Strategy* (Reading, MA: Addison-Wesley, 1982).

26. Dipankar Chakravarti, Deborah J. MacInnis, and Kent Nakamoto, "Product Category Perceptions, Elaborative Processing and Brand Name Extension Strategies," in *Advances in Consumer Research* 17, eds. M. Goldberg, G. Gorn, and R. Pollay (Ann Arbor, MI: Association for Consumer Research, 1990): 910–916; Mita Sujan and James R. Bettman, "The Effects of Brand Positioning Strategies on Consumers' Brand and Category Perceptions: Some Insights from Schema Research," *Journal of Marketing Research* 26 (November 1989): 454–467.

27. Joel B. Cohen and Kanul Basu, "Alternative Models of Categorization: Towards a Contingent Processing Framework," *Journal of Consumer Research* 13 (March 1987): 455–472; Prakash Nedungadi and J. Wesley Hutchinson, "The Prototypicality of Brands: Relationships with Brand Awareness, Preference, and Usage," in *Advances in Consumer Research*, Vol. 12, eds. Elizabeth C. Hirschman and Morris B. Holbrook (Provo, UT: Association for Consumer Research, 1985), 489–503; Eleanor Rosch and Carolyn B. Mervis, "Family Resemblance: Studies in the Internal Structure of Categories," *Cognitive Psychology* 7 (October 1975): 573–605; James Ward and Barbara Loken, "The Quintessential Snack Food: Measurement of Prototypes," in *Advances in Consumer Research*, Vol. 13, ed. Richard J. Lutz (Provo, UT: Association for Consumer Research, 1986), 126–131.

28. Nedungadi and Hutchinson, "The Prototypicality of Brands"; Ward and Loken, "The Quintessential Snack Food."

29. Phillip Kotler and Kevin Lane Keller, *Marketing Management*, 14th ed. (Upper Saddle River, NJ: Prentice Hall, 2012).

30. Russell I. Haley, "Benefit Segmentation: A Decision-Oriented Research Tool," *Journal of Marketing* 32 (July 1968): 30–35.

31. Also, it may be the case that the actual demographic specifications given do not fully reflect consumers' underlying perceptions. For example, when the Ford Mustang

was introduced, the intended market segment was much younger than the ages of the customers who actually bought the car. Evidently, these consumers felt or wanted to feel younger psychologically than they really were.

32. Jerry Shereshewsky, "Why Baby Boomers Can't Be Put in One Box," *Advertising Age*, 2 March 2010; Charles Duhigg, "Six Decades at the Center of Attention, and Counting," *New York Times*, 6 January 2008.

33. Ronald Frank, William Massey, and Yoram Wind, *Market Segmentation* (Englewood Cliffs, NJ: Prentice Hall, 1972); Malcolm McDonald and Ian Dunbar, *Market Segmentation: How to Do It, How to Profit from It* (Oxford, UK: Elsevier Butterworth-Heinemann, 2004).

34. "CVS' Goal: Attract Customers for Life," *DSN Retailing Today*, 23 May 2005; "Women Making a Difference at CVS," *Chain Drug Review*, 18 April 2005.

35. A complete treatment of this material is beyond the scope of this chapter. Useful reviews can be found in any good marketing strategy text. For example, see David A. Aaker, *Strategic Market Management*, 9th ed. (New York: John Wiley & Sons, 2011) or Donald R. Lehmann and Russell S. Winer, *Product Management*, 4th ed. (New York: McGraw-Hill/Irwin, 2005).

36. James R. Bettman and Mita Sujan, "Effects of Framing on Evaluation of Comparable and Noncomparable Alternatives by Expert and Novice Consumers," *Journal of Consumer Research* 14 (September 1987): 141–154; Michael D. Johnson, "Consumer Choice Strategies for Comparing Noncomparable Alternatives,"*Journal of Consumer Research* 11 (December 1984): 741–753; C. Whan Park and Daniel C. Smith, "Product Level Choice: A Top-Down or Bottom-Up Process?" *Journal of Consumer Research* 16 (December 1989): 289–299.

37. Teri Agins, "As Consumers Find Other Ways to Splurge, Apparel Hits a Snag," *Wall Street Journal*, 4 February 2005, A1, A6.

38. Isaac Arnsdorf, "The Best Shot: Cell or Camera?," *Wall Street Journal*, 23 June 2010.

39. Patrick Barwise and Sean Meehan, *Simply Better: Winning and Keeping Customers by Delivering What Matters Most* (Cambridge, MA: Harvard Business School Press, 2004).

40. Richard Heller, "Folk Fortune," *Forbes*, September 4, 2000, 66–69; Lauren Collins, "House Perfect," *New Yorker*, 3 October 2011.

41. Jeff Green and Alan Ohnsman, "At Subaru, Sharing the Love Is a Market Strategy," *Bloomberg BusinessWeek*, 24–30 May 2010, 18–20; Jean Halliday, "Subaru of America: An America's Hottest Brands Case Study," *Advertising Age*, 16 November 2009; "Love Guru: How Tim Mahoney Got Subaru Back on Track," *Brandweek*, 13 September 2010; "Subaru Announces Third Annual Share the Love Event," *PR Newswire*, 8 November 2010.

42. Personal correspondence, Leonora Polansky, 16 June 2011.

43. Interestingly, when Miller Lite was first introduced, the assumption was that the relevant motivation underlying the benefit of "less filling" for consumers was that they could drink more beer. Consequently, Miller targeted heavy users of beer with a sizable introductory ad campaign concentrated on mass-market sports programs. As it turned out, the initial research showed that the market segment they attracted was more the moderate user—older and upscale. Why? The brand promise of "less filling" is actually fairly ambiguous. To this group of consumers, "less filling" meant that they could drink beer and stay mentally and physically agile (sin with no penalty!). From Miller's standpoint, attracting this target market was an unexpected but happy outcome because it meant that there would be less cannibalization with their more mass-market High Life brand. To better match the motivations of this group, there were some changes in the types of athletes in the ads, such as using ex-bullfighters to better represent mental and physical agility.

44. Chris Woodyard, "Wheeling Its Way to the Future," *USA TODAY*, 27 December 2010, 3B; Dinah Eng, "Jake Burton: My Life As a Pioneer," *Fortune*, 6 December 2010, 72.

45. Robert Klara, "'The Other White Meat' Finally Cedes Its Place in the Pen," *Brandweek*, 4 March 2011.

46. Richard A. Melcher, "Why Zima Faded So Fast," *Business Week*, 10 March 1997, 110–114.

47. Keith Naughton, "Ford's 'Perfect Storm,'" *Newsweek*, 17 September 2001, 48–50.

48. Elizabeth Jensen, "Campbell's Juice Scheme: Stealth Health," *Wall Street Journal*, 18 April 1997, B6.

49. David A. Aaker, *Brand Relevance: Making Competitors Irrelevant* (San Francisco: John Wiley & Sons, 2011).

50. Heather Landi, "Good to the Core," *Beverage World*, August 2010, 35–42.

51. For a thorough examination of how an organization can improve its marketing capabilities, see Andy Bird and Mhairi McEwan, *The Growth Drivers: The Definitive Guide to Transforming Marketing Capabilities* (West Sussex, UK: John Wiley & Sons, 2012).

52. "POM Battles FTC Over Health Claims," *Beverage World*, October 2010, 14.

53. Steven Gray, "How Applebee's Is Making It Big in Small Towns," *Wall Street Journal*, 2 August 2004, B1, B4; Douglas Quenqua, "Polishing Up the Apple in Applebee's, *New York Times*, 25 October 2007; Kenneth Hein, "Applebee's Plan to Emulate IHOP, *Brandweek*, 8 July 2008.

54. Abraham Maslow, *Motivation and Personality*, 2nd ed. (New York: Harper & Row, 1970).

55. Thomas J. Reynolds and Jonathan Gutman, "Laddering Theory: Method, Analysis, and Interpretation," *Journal of Advertising Research* (February/March 1988): 11–31. Thomas J. Reynolds and David B. Whitlark, "Applying Laddering Data to Communications Strategy and Advertising Practice," *Journal of Advertising Research* (July/August 1995): 9–17.

56. Brian Wansink, "Using Laddering to Understand and Leverage a Brand's Equity," *Qualitative Market Research* 6, no. 2 (2003): 111–118.

57. Marco Vriens and Frenkel Ter Hofstede, "Linking Attributes, Benefits, and Consumer Values," *Marketing Research* (Fall 2000): 3–8.

58. Kevin Lane Keller, "Brand Mantras: Rationale, Criteria, and Examples," *Journal of Marketing Management* 15 (1999): 43–51.

59. Brand Focus 2.0 is based in part on Steven Hoeffler and Kevin Lane Keller, "The Marketing Advantages of Strong Brands," *Journal of Brand Management* 10 (August 2003): 421–445.

60. Ian M. Lewis, "Brand Equity or Why the Board of Directors Needs Marketing Research," paper presented at the ARF Fifth Annual Advertising and Promotion Workshop, 1 February 1993.

61. The following sections review seminal research in each of the areas. For more recent research on these topics, see Philip Kotler and Kevin Lane Keller, *Marketing Management*, 14th ed. (Upper Saddle River, NJ: Prentice Hall, 2012).

62. Peter A. Dacin and Daniel C. Smith, "The Effect of Brand Portfolio Characteristics on Consumer Evaluations of Brand Extensions," *Journal of Marketing Research* 31 (May 1994): 229–242; George S. Day and Terry Deutscher, "Attitudinal Predictions of Choices of Major Appliance Brands," *Journal of Marketing Research* 19 (May 1982), 192–198; W. B. Dodds, K. B. Monroe, and D. Grewal, "Effects of Price, Brand, and Store Information on Buyers' Product Evaluations," *Journal of Marketing Research* 28 (August 1991): 307–319; France Leclerc, Bernd H. Schmitt, and Laurette Dube, "Foreign Branding and Its Effects on Product Perceptions and Attitudes," *Journal of Marketing Research* 31, no. 5 (1994): 263–270; Akshay R. Rao and K. B. Monroe, "The Effects of Price, Brand Name, and Store Name on Buyers' Perceptions of Product Quality: An Integrative Review," *Journal of Marketing Research* 26 (August 1989): 351–357.

63. B. Wernerfelt, "Umbrella Branding as a Signal of New Product Quality: An Example of Signaling by Posting a Bond," *Rand Journal of Economics* 19, no. 3 (1988): 458–466; Tullin Erdem, "An Empirical Analysis of Umbrella Branding," *Journal of Marketing Research* 35, no. 8 (1998): 339–351.

64. Fred M. Feinberg, Barbara E. Kahn, and Leigh McAllister, "Market Share Response When Consumers Seek Variety," *Journal of Marketing Research* 29 (May 1992): 227–237.

65. Michel Laroche, Chankon Kim, and Lianxi Zhou, "Brand Familiarity and Confidence as Determinants of Purchase Intention: An Empirical Test in a Multiple Brand Context," *Journal of Business Research* 37 (1996): 115–120.

66. Robert E. Smith, "Integrating Information from Advertising and Trial," *Journal of Marketing Research* 30 (May 1993): 204–219.

67. Andrew S. C. Ehrenberg, Gerard J. Goodhardt, and Patrick T. Barwise, "Double Jeopardy Revisited," *Journal of Marketing* 54 (July 1990): 82–91.

68. Ipsos-ASI, January 30, 2003.

69. Rohini Ahluwalia, Robert E. Burnkrant, and H. Rao Unnava, "Consumer Response to Negative Publicity: The Moderating Role of Commitment," *Journal of Marketing Research* 37 (May 2000): 203–214; Narij Dawar and Madam M. Pillutla, "Impact of Product-Harm Crises on Brand Equity: The Moderating Role of Consumer Expectations," *Journal of Marketing Research* 37 (May 2000): 215–226.

70. Susan Caminit, "The Payoff from a Good Corporate Reputation," *Fortune*, 10 February 1992, 74–77.

71. Deepak Agrawal, "Effects of Brand Loyalty on Advertising and Trade Promotions: A Game Theoretic Analysis with Empirical Evidence," *Marketing Science* 15, no. 1 (1996): 86–108; Chan Su Park and V. Srinivasan, "A Survey-Based Method for Measuring and Understanding Brand Equity and Its Extendability," *Journal of Marketing Research* 31 (May 1994): 271–288; Raj Sethuraman, "A Model of How Discounting High-Priced Brands Affects the Sales of Low-Priced Brands," *Journal of Marketing Research* 33 (November 1996): 399–409.

72. Hermann Simon, "Dynamics of Price Elasticity and Brand Life Cycles: An Empirical Study," *Journal of Marketing Research* 16 (November 1979): 439–452; K. Sivakumar and S. P. Raj, "Quality Tier Competition: How Price Change Influences Brand Choice and Category Choice," *Journal of Marketing* 61 (July 1997): 71–84.

73. Lakshman Krishnamurthi and S. P. Raj, "An Empirical Analysis of the Relationship Between Brand Loyalty and Consumer Price Elasticity," *Marketing Science* 10, no. 2 (Spring 1991): 172–183. See also, Garrett Sonnier and Andrew Ainsle, "Estimating the Value of Brand-Image Associations: The Role of General and Specific Brand Image," *Journal of Marketing Research*, 48 (June 2011): 518–531; William Boulding, Eunkyu Lee, and Richard Staelin, "Mastering the Mix: Do Advertising, Promotion, and Sales Force Activities Lead to Differentiation?" *Journal of Marketing Research* 31 (May 1994): 159–172. See also Vinay Kanetkar, Charles B. Weinberg, and Doyle L. Weiss, "Price Sensitivity and Television Advertising Exposures: Some Empirical Findings," *Marketing Science* 11 (Fall 1992): 359–371.

74. Greg M. Allenby and Peter E. Rossi, "Quality Perceptions and Asymmetric Switching Between Brands," *Marketing Science* 10 (Summer 1991): 185–204; Rajiv Grover and V. Srinivasan, "Evaluating the Multiple Effects of Retail Promotions on Brand Loyal and Brand Switching Segments," *Journal of Marketing Research* 29 (February 1992): 76–89; Gary J. Russell and Wagner A. Kamakura, "Understanding Brand Competition Using Micro and Macro Scanner Data," *Journal of Marketing Research* 31 (May 1994): 289–303.

75. Albert C. Bemmaor and Dominique Mouchoux, "Measuring the Short-Term Effect of In-Store Promotion and Retail Advertising on Brand Sales: A Factorial Experiment," *Journal of Marketing Research* 28 (May 1991): 202–214; Robert C. Blattberg and Kenneth J. Wisniewski, "Price-Induced Patterns of Competition," *Marketing Science* 8 (Fall 1989): 291–309; Randolph E. Bucklin, Sunil Gupta, and Sangman Han, "A Brand's Eye View of Response Segmentation in Consumer Brand Choice Behavior," *Journal of Marketing*

Research 32 (February 1995): 66–74; Sivakumar and Raj, "Quality Tier Competition."

76. Kyle Pope, "Computers: They're No Commodity," *Wall Street Journal*, 15 October 1993, B1.

77. Peter S. Fader and David C. Schmittlein, "Excess Behavioral Loyalty for High-Share Brands: Deviations from the Dirichlet Model for Repeat Purchasing," *Journal of Marketing Research* 30, no. 11 (1993): 478–493; Rajiv Lal and Chakravarthi Narasimhan, "The Inverse Relationship Between Manufacturer and Retailer Margins: A Theory," *Marketing Science* 15, no. 2 (1996): 132–151; Mark S. Glynn, "The Moderating Effect of Brand Strength in Manufacturer-Reseller Relationships," *Industrial Marketing Management* 39, no. 8 (2010): 1226–1233.

78. David B. Montgomery, "New Product Distribution: An Analysis of Supermarket Buyer Decisions," *Journal of Marketing Research* 12, no. 3 (1978): 255–264.

79. Robert J. Kent and Chris T. Allen, "Competitive Interference Effects in Consumer Memory for Advertising: The Role of Brand Familiarity," *Journal of Marketing* 58 (July 1994): 97–105.

80. Amitava Chattopadyay and Kunal Basu, "Humor in Advertising: The Moderating Role of Prior Brand Evaluation," *Journal of Marketing Research* 27 (November 1990): 466–476; D. W. Stewart and David H. Furse, *Effective Television Advertising: A Study of 1000 Commercials* (Lexington, MA: D.C. Heath, 1986); M. G. Weinburger and C. Gulas, "The Impact of Humor in Advertising: A Review," *Journal of Advertising* 21, no. 4 (1992): 35–60.

81. Margaret Campbell and Kevin Lane Keller, "Brand Familiarity and Ad Repetition Effects," *Journal of Consumer Research* 30, no. 2 (September 2003), 292–304.

82. S. P. Raj, "The Effects of Advertising on High and Low Loyalty Consumer Segments," *Journal of Consumer Research* 9 (June 1982): 77–89.

83. Ravi Dhar and Itamar Simonson, "The Effect of the Focus of Comparison on Consumer Preferences," *Journal of Marketing Research* 29 (November 1992): 430–440; Karen A. Machleit, Chris T. Allen, and Thomas J. Madden, "The Mature Brand and Brand Interest: An Alternative Consequence of Ad-Evoked Affect," *Journal of Marketing* 57 (October 1993): 72–82; Itamar Simonson, Joel Huber, and John Payne, "The Relationship Between Prior Brand Knowledge and Information Acquisition Order," *Journal of Consumer Research* 14 (March 1988): 566–578.

84. Russell L. Ackoff and James R. Emshoff, "Advertising Research at Anheuser-Busch, Inc. (1963–1968)," *Sloan Management Review* (Winter 1975): 1–15.

85. These results should be interpreted carefully, however, as they do not suggest that large advertising expenditures did not play an important role in creating equity for the brand in the past, or that advertising expenditures could be cut severely without some adverse sales consequences at some point in the future.

86. See Robert C. Blattberg, Richard Briesch, and Edward J. Fox, "How Promotions Work," *Marketing Science* 14 (1995): G122–G132. See also Bart J. Bronnenberg and Luc Wathieu, "Asymmetric Promotion Effects and Brand Positioning," *Marketing Science* 15, no. 4 (1996): 379–394. This study shows how the relative promotion effectiveness of high- and low-quality brands depends on their positioning along both price and quality dimensions.

87. Frank E. James, "I'll Wear the Coke Pants Tonight; They Go Well with My Harley-Davidson Ring," *Wall Street Journal*, 6 June 1985.

88. David A. Aaker and Kevin Lane Keller, "Consumer Evaluations of Brand Extensions," *Journal of Marketing* 54, no. 1 (1990): 27–41; Kevin Lane Keller and David A. Aaker, "The Effects of Sequential Introduction of Brand Extensions," *Journal of Marketing Research* 29 (February 1992): 35–50; A. Rangaswamy, R. R. Burke, and T. A. Oliva, "Brand Equity and the Extendibility of Brand Names," *International Journal of Research in Marketing* 10, no. 3 (1993): 61–75.

89. Taylor Randall, Karl Ulrich, and David Reibstein, "Brand Equity and Vertical Product Line Extent," *Marketing Science* 17, no. 4 (1998): 356–379.

90. Srinivas K. Reddy, Susan Holak, and Subodh Bhat, "To Extend or Not to Extend: Success Determinants of Line Extensions," *Journal of Marketing Research* 31, no. 5 (1994): 243–262; C. Whan Park, Sandra Milberg, and Robert Lawson, "Evaluation of Brand Extensions: The Role of Product Feature Similarity and Brand Concept Consistency," *Journal of Consumer Research* 18, no. 9 (1991): 185–193; Susan M. Broniarcysyk and Joseph W. Alba, "The Importance of the Brand in Brand Extension," *Journal of Marketing Research* 31, no. 5 (1994): 214–228.

91. Peter A. Dacin and Daniel C. Smith, "The Effect of Brand Portfolio Characteristics on Consumer Evaluations of Brand Extensions," *Journal of Marketing Research* 31 (May 1994): 229–242; Keller and Aaker, "The Effects of Sequential Introduction of Brand Extensions"; Daniel A. Sheinin and Bernd H. Schmitt, "Extending Brands with New Product Concepts: The Role of Category Attribute Congruity, Brand Affect, and Brand Breadth," *Journal of Business Research* 31 (1994): 1–10.

92. Roger A. Kerin, Gurumurthy Kalyanaram, and Daniel J. Howard, "Product Hierarchy and Brand Strategy Influences on the Order of Entry Effect for Consumer Packaged Goods," *Journal of Product Innovation Management* 13 (1996): 21–34.

93. Maureen Morrin, "The Impact of Brand Extensions on Parent Brand Memory Structures and Retrieval Processes," *Journal of Marketing Research* 36 (November 1999): 517–525; John Roedder, Barbara Loken, and Christopher Joiner, "The Negative Impact of Extensions: Can Flagship Products Be Diluted?" *Journal of Marketing* 62 (January 1998): 19–32; Daniel A. Sheinin, "The Effects of Experience with Brand

Extensions on Parent Brand Knowledge," *Journal of Business Research* 49 (2000): 47–55.

94. Amna Kirmani, Sanjay Sood, and Sheri Bridges, "The Ownership Effect in Consumer Responses to Brand Line Stretches," *Journal of Marketing* 63 (January 1999): 88–101.

95. Vicki R. Lane and Robert Jacobson, "Stock Market Reactions to Brand Extension Announcements: The Effects of Brand Attitude and Familiarity," *Journal of Marketing* 59, no. 1 (1995): 63–77.

96. Douglas E. Hughes and Michael Ahearne, "Energizing the Reseller's Sales Force: The Power of Brand Identification," *Journal of Marketing* 74 (July 2010): 81–96;

V. Kumar and Denish Shah, "Can Marketing Lift Stock Prices?," *MIT Sloan Management Review*, 52 (Summer 2011): 24–26.

97. David A. Aaker and Robert Jacobson, "The Financial Information Content of Perceived Quality," *Journal of Marketing Research* 31, no. 5 (1994): 191–201; David A. Aaker and Robert Jacobson, "The Value Relevance of Brand Attitude in High-Technology Markets," *Journal of Marketing Research* 38 (November 2001): 485–493; M. E. Barth, M. Clement, G. Foster, and R. Kasznik, "Brand Values and Capital Market Valuation," *Review of Accounting Studies* 3 (1998): 41–68.

3 Brand Resonance and the Brand Value Chain

Learning Objectives

After reading this chapter, you should be able to

1. Define brand resonance.
2. Describe the steps in building brand resonance.
3. Define the brand value chain.
4. Identify the stages in the brand value chain.
5. Contrast brand equity and customer equity.

Corona used its strong brand imagery of "beach in a bottle" to become the leading U.S. import beer.

Source: AP Photo/Amy Sancetta

Preview

Chapter 2 outlined in detail the concept of customer-based brand equity and introduced a brand positioning model based on the concepts of points-of-parity and points-of-difference. We next broaden our discussion to consider the two other interlinking models, which all together make up the brand planning system.

We first present the *brand resonance model*, which describes how to create intense, active loyalty relationships with customers. The model considers how brand positioning affects what consumers think, feel, and do and the degree to which they resonate or connect with a brand. After discussing some of the main implications of that model, we consider how brand resonance and these loyalty relationships, in turn, create brand equity or value.

The *brand value chain model* is a means by which marketers can trace the value creation process for their brands to better understand the financial impact of their marketing expenditures and investments. Based in part on the customer-based brand equity (CBBE) concept developed in Chapter 2, it offers a holistic, integrated approach to understanding how brands create value.

Brand Focus 3.0 at the end of the chapter provides a detailed overview of the topic of customer equity.

BUILDING A STRONG BRAND: THE FOUR STEPS OF BRAND BUILDING

The brand resonance model looks at building a brand as a sequence of steps, each of which is contingent on successfully achieving the objectives of the previous one. The steps are as follows:

1. Ensure identification of the brand with customers and an association of the brand in customers' minds with a specific product class, product benefit, or customer need.
2. Firmly establish the totality of brand meaning in the minds of customers by strategically linking a host of tangible and intangible brand associations.
3. Elicit the proper customer responses to the brand.
4. Convert brand responses to create brand resonance and an intense, active loyalty relationship between customers and the brand.

These four steps represent a set of fundamental questions that customers invariably ask about brands—at least implicitly. The four questions (with corresponding brand steps in parentheses) are:

1. Who are you? (brand identity)
2. What are you? (brand meaning)
3. What about you? What do I think or feel about you? (brand responses)
4. What about you and me? What kind of association and how much of a connection would I like to have with you? (brand relationships)

Notice the ordering of the steps in this *branding ladder*, from identity to meaning to responses to relationships. That is, we cannot establish meaning unless we have created identity; responses cannot occur unless we have developed the right meaning; and we cannot forge a relationship unless we have elicited the proper responses.

To provide some structure, let us think of establishing six *brand building blocks* with customers that we can assemble in a pyramid, with significant brand equity only resulting if brands reach the top of the pyramid. This brand-building process is illustrated in Figures 3-1 and 3-2. We'll look at each of these steps and corresponding brand building blocks and their subdimensions in the following sections. As will become apparent, building blocks up the left side of the pyramid represent a more "rational route" to brand building, whereas building blocks up the right side of the pyramid represent a more "emotional route." Most strong brands are built by going up both sides of the pyramid.

Brand Salience

Achieving the right brand identity means creating brand salience with customers. *Brand salience* measures various aspects of the awareness of the brand and how easily and often the brand is evoked under various situations or circumstances. To what extent is the brand top-of-mind and easily

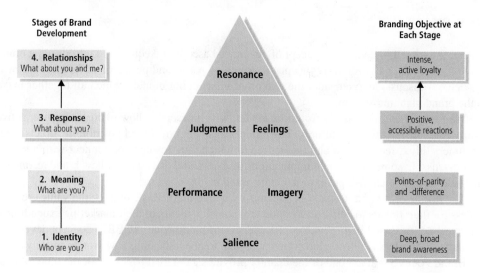

FIGURE 3-1

Brand Resonance
Pyramid

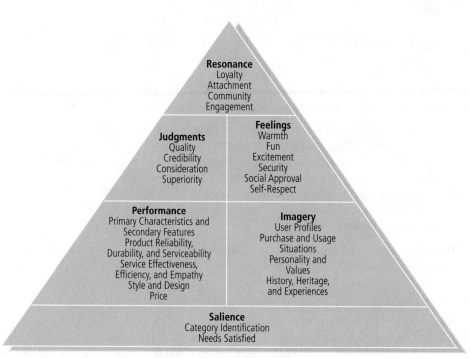

FIGURE 3-2

Subdimensions of Brand
Building Blocks

recalled or recognized? What types of cues or reminders are necessary? How pervasive is this brand awareness?

We've said that brand awareness refers to customers' ability to recall and recognize the brand under different conditions and to link the brand name, logo, symbol, and so forth to certain associations in memory. In particular, building brand awareness helps customers understand the product or service category in which the brand competes and what products or services are sold under the brand name. It also ensures that customers know which of their "needs" the brand—through these products—is designed to satisfy. In other words, what basic functions does the brand provide to customers?

Breadth and Depth of Awareness. Brand awareness thus gives the product an identity by linking brand elements to a product category and associated purchase and consumption or usage situations. The *depth* of brand awareness measures how likely it is for a brand element to come to mind, and the ease with which it does so. A brand we easily recall has a deeper level of brand awareness than one that we recognize only when we see it. The *breadth* of brand awareness measures the range of purchase and usage situations in which the brand element comes to mind and depends to a large extent on the organization of brand and product knowledge in memory.[1] To see how this works, consider the breadth and depth of brand awareness for Tropicana orange juice.

TROPICANA

Consumers should at least recognize the Tropicana brand when it is presented to them. Beyond that, consumers should think of Tropicana whenever they think of orange juice, particularly when they are considering buying orange juice. Ideally, consumers would think of Tropicana whenever they were deciding which type of beverage to drink, especially when seeking a "tasty but healthy" beverage. Thus, consumers must think of Tropicana as satisfying a certain set of needs whenever those needs arise. One of the challenges for any provider of orange juice is to link the product to usage situations beyond the traditional one of breakfast—hence the industry campaign to boost consumption of Florida orange juice that used the slogan "It's Not Just for Breakfast Anymore."

For Tropicana, it's important that consumers think of the brand in other consumption situations beyond breakfast.

Source: Keri Miksza

Product Category Structure. As the Tropicana example suggests, to fully understand brand recall, we need to appreciate ***product category structure***, or how product categories are organized in memory. Typically, marketers assume that products are grouped at varying levels of specificity and can be organized in a hierarchical fashion.[2] Thus, in consumers' minds, a product hierarchy often exists, with product class information at the highest level, product category information at the second-highest level, product type information at the next level, and brand information at the lowest level.

The beverage market provides a good setting to examine issues in category structure and the effects of brand awareness on brand equity. Figure 3-3 illustrates one hierarchy that might exist in consumers' minds. According to this representation, consumers first distinguish between flavored and nonflavored beverages (water). Next, they distinguish between nonalcoholic and alcoholic flavored beverages. They further distinguish nonalcoholic beverages into hot drinks like coffee or tea, and cold drinks like milk, juices, and soft drinks. Alcoholic beverages are distinguished by whether they are wine, beer, or distilled spirits. We can make even further distinctions. For example, we can divide the beer category into no-alcohol, low-alcohol (or "light"), and full-strength beers, and divide full-strength beers by variety (ale or lager), by brewing method (draft, ice, or dry), by price and quality (discount, premium, or super-premium), and so on.

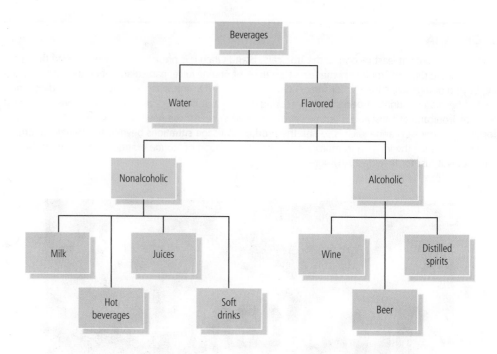

FIGURE 3-3

Beverage Category
Hierarchy

The organization of the product category hierarchy that generally prevails in memory will play an important role in brand awareness, brand consideration, and consumer decision making. For example, consumers often make decisions in a top-down fashion, first deciding whether to have water or some type of flavored beverage. If the consumer chooses a flavored drink, the next decision would be whether to have an alcoholic or a nonalcoholic drink, and so on. Finally, consumers might then choose a particular brand within the product category in which they are interested.

The depth of brand awareness will influence the likelihood that the brand comes to mind, whereas the breadth of brand awareness describes the different types of situations in which the brand might come to mind. In general, soft drinks have great breadth of awareness in that they come to mind in a variety of different consumption situations. A consumer may consider drinking one of the different varieties of Coke virtually any time, anywhere. Other beverages, such as alcoholic beverages, milk, and juices, have much more limited perceived consumption situations.

Strategic Implications. The product hierarchy shows us that not only the depth of awareness matters but also the breadth. In other words, the brand must not only be top-of-mind and have sufficient "mind share," but it must also do so at the right times and places.

Breadth is an oft-neglected consideration, even for brands that are category leaders. For many brands, the key question is not *whether* consumers can recall the brand but *where* they think of it, *when* they think of it, and how *easily* and how *often* they think of it. Many brands and products are ignored or forgotten during possible usage situations. For those brands, the best route for improving sales may be not to try to improve consumer attitudes but, instead, increasing brand salience and the breadth of brand awareness and situations in which consumers would consider using the brand to drive consumption and increase sales volume.

Tax preparer H&R Block makes a concerted effort to make sure its brand is top-of-mind at all times, reminding consumers that tax-pertinent events happen all year round, such as when taking clients out to dinner, buying a new laptop computer, or looking for a new job.[3] Consider the brand salience challenges for Campbell's soup.

CAMPBELL'S SOUP

Ads for Campbell's soup through the years have sometimes emphasized taste, with its long-time advertising slogan "Mmm, Mmm, Good," or nutrition, with "Never Underestimate the Power of Soup." Part of Campbell's challenge in increasing sales may lie not so much in the consumer attitudes these slogans address as with memory considerations and the fact that people do not think of using or eating soup as often as they should for certain meal occasions. In 2010, Campbell launched a new ad campaign, "It's

Amazing What Soup Can Do," showcasing the soup as an indispensible food for any occasion—paired with a variety of foods; poured over meat, pasta, or rice as a sauce; or used as an ingredient in a recipe. Creating a communication program for those consumers who already have a favorable attitude toward the brand that will help them remember it in more varied consumption settings may be the most profitable way to grow the Campbell's soup franchise.[4]

Campbell Soup's best growth prospect might be just to remind consumers of more situations in which they could eat the soup.

Source: Campbell Soup Company

In other words, it may be harder to try to *change* existing brand attitudes than to *remind* people of their existing attitudes toward a brand in additional, but appropriate, consumption situations.

Summary.   A highly salient brand is one that has both depth and breadth of brand awareness, such that customers always make sufficient purchases as well as always think of the brand across a variety of settings in which it could possibly be employed or consumed. Brand salience is an important first step in building brand equity, but is usually not sufficient. For many customers in many situations, other considerations, such as the meaning or image of the brand, also come into play.

Creating brand meaning includes establishing a brand image—what the brand is characterized by and should stand for in the minds of customers. Brand meaning is made up of two major categories of brand associations related to performance and imagery. These associations can be formed directly, from a customer's own experiences and contact with the brand, or indirectly, through advertising or by some other source of information, such as word of mouth.

The next section describes the two main types of brand meaning—brand performance and brand imagery—and the subcategories within each of those two building blocks.

Brand Performance

The product itself is at the heart of brand equity, because it is the primary influence on what consumers experience with a brand, what they hear about a brand from others, and what the firm can tell customers about the brand in their communications. Designing and delivering a product that fully satisfies consumer needs and wants is a prerequisite for successful marketing, regardless of whether the product is a tangible good, service, organization, or person. To create brand loyalty and resonance, marketers must ensure that consumers' experiences with the product at least meet, if not actually surpass, their expectations. As Chapter 1 noted, numerous studies have shown that high-quality brands tend to perform better financially and yield higher returns on investment.

Brand performance describes how well the product or service meets customers' more functional needs. How well does the brand rate on objective assessments of quality? To what extent does the brand satisfy utilitarian, aesthetic, and economic customer needs and wants in the product or service category?

SUBWAY

Subway has zoomed to the top as the biggest-selling quick-serve restaurant through a clever positioning of offering healthy, good-tasting sandwiches. This straddle positioning allows the brand to create a POP on taste and a POD on health with respect to quick-serve restaurants such as McDonald's and Burger King but, at the same time, a POP on health and a POD on taste with respect to health food restaurants and cafés. One of Subway's highly successful product launches was the $5 footlong sandwich. Dreamed up by a franchise operator in Miami, the idea quickly took hold and was the perfect solution for hungry, cash-starved consumers during the recession. This strong performance and value message has allowed Subway to significantly expand its market coverage and potential customer base.[5]

By combining taste, health, and convenience, Subway has become a leader in the quick-serve restaurant business.
Source: TRIPPLAAR KRISTOFFER/SIPA/Newscom

Brand performance transcends the product's ingredients and features to include dimensions that differentiate the brand. Often, the strongest brand positioning relies on performance advantages of some kind, and it is rare that a brand can overcome severe performance deficiencies. Five important types of attributes and benefits often underlie brand performance, as follows:[6]

1. *Primary ingredients and supplementary features.* Customers often have beliefs about the levels at which the primary ingredients of the product operate (low, medium, high, or very high), and about special, perhaps even patented, features or secondary elements that complement these primary ingredients. Some attributes are essential ingredients necessary for a product to work, whereas others are supplementary features that allow for customization and more versatile, personalized usage. Of course these vary by product or service category.

2. *Product reliability, durability, and serviceability. Reliability* measures the consistency of performance over time and from purchase to purchase. *Durability* is the expected economic life of the product, and *serviceability,* the ease of repairing the product if needed. Thus, perceptions of product performance are affected by factors such as the speed, accuracy, and care of product delivery and installation; the promptness, courtesy, and helpfulness of customer service and training; and the quality of repair service and the time involved.

3. *Service effectiveness, efficiency, and empathy.* Customers often have performance-related associations with service. *Service effectiveness* measures how well the brand satisfies customers' service requirements. *Service efficiency* describes the speed and responsiveness of service. Finally, *service empathy* is the extent to which service providers are seen as trusting, caring, and having the customer's interests in mind.

4. *Style and design.* Design has a functional aspect in terms of how a product works that affects performance associations. Consumers also may have associations with the product that go beyond its functional aspects to more aesthetic considerations such as its size, shape, materials, and color involved. Thus, performance may also depend on sensory aspects such as how a product looks and feels, and perhaps even what it sounds or smells like.

5. *Price.* The pricing policy for the brand can create associations in consumers' minds about how relatively expensive (or inexpensive) the brand is, and whether it is frequently or substantially discounted. Price is a particularly important performance association because consumers may organize their product category knowledge in terms of the price tiers of different brands.[7]

Brand Imagery

The other main type of brand meaning is brand imagery. Brand imagery depends on the extrinsic properties of the product or service, including the ways in which the brand attempts to meet customers' psychological or social needs. It is the way people think about a brand abstractly, rather than what they think the brand actually does. Thus, imagery refers to more intangible aspects of the brand, and consumers can form imagery associations directly from their own experience or indirectly through advertising or by some other source of information, such as word of mouth. Many kinds of intangibles can be linked to a brand, but four main ones are:

1. User profiles
2. Purchase and usage situations
3. Personality and values
4. History, heritage, and experiences

For example, take a brand with rich brand imagery such as Nivea in Europe, makers of many different skin care and personal care products. Some of its more notable intangible associations include: (1) family/shared experiences/maternal, (2) multipurpose, (3) classic/timeless, and (4) childhood memories. Luxury brands often rely a great deal on brand intangibles, as described in The Science of Branding 3-1.

User Imagery.   One set of brand imagery associations is about the type of person or organization who uses the brand. This imagery may result in customers' mental image of actual users or more aspirational, idealized users. Consumers may base associations of a typical or idealized

THE SCIENCE OF BRANDING 3-1

Luxury Branding

Luxury brands are perhaps one of the purest examples of branding, because the brand and its image are often key competitive advantages. A number of characteristics define luxury branding and suggest strategic and tactical guidelines. Here are some of those guidelines, each of which merits further thought and discussion.

- Maintaining a premium, prestige image with luxury branding is crucial; controlling that image is thus a priority. Ideally the image will be designed to be globally relevant.

- Luxury branding often relies on an aspirational image that benefits from a "trickle-down" effect to a broader audience via PR and word-of-mouth, but there must be a good balance between accessibility and exclusivity.

- Marketers of luxury brands must control all aspects of the marketing program to ensure quality products and services and pleasurable purchase and consumption experiences.

- Distribution for luxury brands should be carefully controlled via a selective distribution strategy that may include company stores.

- Luxury brands are enhanced by a premium pricing strategy with strong quality cues and few discounts or markdowns.

- Brand architecture for luxury brands must be managed very carefully with only selective, strategic licensing and extensions (especially vertically). Brand hierarchies and portfolios must be employed, with appropriate sub-brands to minimize cannibalization and optimize equity flows.

- Luxury brands can sometimes benefit from secondary associations with linked personalities, events, countries, and so on.

- Brand elements besides brand names—such as logos and packaging—can be important drivers of brand equity for luxury brands.

- Competition may need to be defined broadly, because luxury brands can compete with luxury brands from other categories for discretionary consumer dollars.

- Luxury brands must legally protect all trademarks and aggressively combat counterfeits.

Sources: Kevin Lane Keller, "Managing the Growth Tradeoff: Challenges and Opportunities in Luxury Branding" in special issue, "Luxury Branding," of *Journal of Brand Management* 16 (March–May 2009): 290–301; Uche Okonkwo, *Luxury Fashion Branding: Trends, Tactics, and Techniques* (New York, NY: Palgrave MacMillan, 2007); Michael J. Silverstein and Neil Fiske, *Trading Up: The New American Luxury* (New York, NY: Penguin Group, 2003); Jean-Noël Kapferer and Vincent Basten, "The Specificity of Luxury Management: Turning Marketing Upside Down," *Journal of Brand Management* 16, nos. 5/6 (2009): 311–322.

brand user on descriptive demographic factors or more abstract psychographic factors. Demographic factors might include the following:

- *Gender.* Venus razors and Secret deodorant have "feminine" associations, whereas Gillette razors and Axe deodorant have more "masculine" associations.[8]
- *Age.* Pepsi Cola, Powerade energy sports drink, and Under Armour performance clothing, shoes and accessories have positioned themselves as fresher and younger in spirit than Coke, Gatorade, and Nike, respectively.
- *Race.* Goya foods and the Univision television network have a strong identification with the Hispanic market.
- *Income.* Sperry Topsider shoes, Polo shirts, and BMW automobiles became associated with "yuppies"—young, affluent, urban professionals.

Psychographic factors might include attitudes toward life, careers, possessions, social issues, or political institutions; for example, a brand user might be seen as iconoclastic or as more traditional and conservative.

In a business-to-business setting, user imagery might relate to the size or type of organization. For example, buyers might see Microsoft as an "aggressive" company and L. L. Bean as a "caring" company. User imagery may focus on more than characteristics of just one type of individual and center on broader issues in terms of perceptions of a group as a whole. For example, customers may believe that a brand is used by many people and therefore view the brand as "popular" or a "market leader."

Purchase and Usage Imagery. A second set of associations tells consumers under what conditions or situations they can or should buy and use the brand. Associations can relate to type of channel, such as department stores, specialty stores, or the Internet; to specific stores such as Macy's, Foot Locker, or Bluefly; and to ease of purchase and associated rewards (if any).

Associations to a typical usage situation can relate to the time of day, week, month, or year to use the brand; location—for instance, inside or outside the home; and type of activity during which to use the brand—formal or informal. For a long time, pizza chain restaurants had strong associations to their channels of distribution and the manner by which customers would purchase and eat the pizza—Domino's was known for delivery, Little Caesar for takeout, and Pizza Hut for dine-in service—although in recent years each of these major competitors has made inroads in the traditional markets of the others.

Brand Personality and Values.   Through consumer experience or marketing activities, brands may take on personality traits or human values and, like a person, appear to be "modern," "old-fashioned," "lively," or "exotic."[9] Five dimensions of brand personality (with corresponding subdimensions) are sincerity (down-to-earth, honest, wholesome, and cheerful), excitement (daring, spirited, imaginative, and up-to-date), competence (reliable, intelligent, successful), sophistication (upper class and charming), and ruggedness (outdoorsy and tough).[10]

How does brand personality get formed? Any aspect of a brand may be used by consumers to infer brand personality. One research study found that consumers perceived nonprofit companies as being "warmer" than for-profit companies but as less competent. Further, consumers were less willing to buy a product made by a nonprofit than a for-profit company because of their perception that the firm lacked competence, but those purchasing misgivings disappeared when perceptions of the competency of the nonprofit were improved, for example, by a credible endorsement such as from the *Wall Street Journal*.[11]

Although any aspect of the marketing program may affect brand personality, marketing communications and advertising may be especially influential because of the inferences consumers make about the underlying user or usage situation depicted or reflected in an ad. For example, advertisers may imbue a brand with personality traits through anthropomorphization and product animation techniques; through personification and the use of brand characters; and through user imagery, such as the preppy look of Abercrombie & Fitch models.[12] More generally, the actors in an ad, the tone or style of the creative strategy, and the emotions or feelings evoked by the ad can affect brand personality. Once brands develop a personality, it can be difficult for consumers to accept information they see as inconsistent with that personality.[13]

Still, user imagery and brand personality may not always be in agreement. When performance-related attributes are central to consumer decisions, as they are for food products, for example, brand personality and user imagery may be less closely related. Differences between personality and imagery may arise for other reasons too. For example, early in its U.S. brand development, Perrier's brand personality was "sophisticated" and "stylish," whereas its actual user imagery was not as flattering or subdued but "flashy" and "trendy."

When user and usage imagery are important to consumer decisions, however, brand personality and imagery are more likely to be related, as they are for cars, beer, liquor, cigarettes, and cosmetics. Thus, consumers often choose and use brands that have a brand personality consistent with their own self-concept, although in some cases the match may be based on consumers' desired rather than their actual image.[14] These effects may also be more pronounced for publicly consumed products than for privately consumed goods because the signaling aspect of a brand may be more important under those conditions.[15] Consumers who are high "self-monitors" and sensitive to how others see them are more likely to choose brands whose personalities fit the consumption situation.[16]

User and usage imagery is often an issue in the highly competitive automotive category. One company looking to sharpen its brand personality and imagery is Chrysler.

CHRYSLER

After a disastrous corporate marriage to Germany's Daimler had been dissolved, Chrysler's new partner Fiat set out to revitalize the brand, in part by injecting some Italian style and sex appeal. Determined to attract younger, hipper, and wealthier customers, Fiat developed new car designs similar to the quirky little cars most likely found in Rome. Fiat is not planning to walk away, however, from some of the equity in its existing brands such as the Dodge Ram pickup truck and Town & Country minivan. For the relatively new Chrysler 300, a $1 billion model makeover retained the powerful German-engineered transmission but added an elegant look and attitude. A two-minute, $9 million TV ad run during the Super Bowl used controversial rapper Eminem to boldly proclaim that the car was "Imported from Detroit."[17]

To create more brand imagery, Chrysler 300 is boldly marketed as "Imported from Detroit."
Source: Courtesy of Chrysler Group LLC

Brand History, Heritage, and Experiences.   Finally, brands may take on associations to their past and certain noteworthy events in the brand's history. These types of associations may recall distinctly personal experiences and episodes or past behaviors and experiences of friends, family, or others. They can be highly personal and individual, or more well-known and shared by many people. For example, there may be associations to aspects of the brand's marketing program, the color of the product or look of its package, the company or person that makes the product and the country in which it is made, the type of store in which it is sold, the events for which the brand is a sponsor, and the people who endorse the brand.

These types of associations can help create strong points-of-difference. In the midst of the recent major recession, Northern Trust used the fact that it was over 120 years old and had weathered many financial downturns through the years to reinforce trust and stability to its wealthy clientele.[18] In any case, associations to history, heritage, and experiences draw upon more specific, concrete examples that transcend the generalizations that make up the usage imagery. In the extreme case, brands become iconic by combining all these types of associations into what is in effect a myth, tapping into enduring consumer hopes and dreams.[19]

Summary.   A number of different types of associations related to either performance or imagery may become linked to the brand. We can characterize the brand associations making up the brand image and meaning according to three important dimensions—strength, favorability, and uniqueness—that provide the key to building brand equity. Successful results on these three dimensions produce the most positive brand responses, the underpinning of intense and active brand loyalty.

Creating strong, favorable, and unique associations is a real challenge to marketers, but essential to building customer-based brand equity. Strong brands typically have firmly established favorable and unique brand associations with consumers. Brand meaning is what helps produce **brand responses**, or what customers think or feel about the brand. We can distinguish brand responses as either brand judgments or brand feelings, that is, in terms of whether they arise from the "head" or from the "heart," as the following sections describe.

Brand Judgments

Brand judgments are customers' personal opinions about and evaluations of the brand, which consumers form by putting together all the different brand performance and imagery associations. Customers may make all types of judgments with respect to a brand, but four types are particularly important: judgments about quality, credibility, consideration, and superiority.

Brand Quality.   Brand attitudes are consumers' overall evaluations of a brand and often form the basis for brand choice.[20] Brand attitudes generally depend on specific attributes and benefits of the brand. For example, consider Hilton hotels. A consumer's attitude toward Hilton depends on how much he or she believes the brand is characterized by certain associations that matter to the consumer for a hotel chain, like location; room comfort, design, and appearance; service quality of staff; recreational facilities; food service; security; prices; and so on.

Consumers can hold a host of attitudes toward a brand, but the most important relate to its perceived quality and to customer value and satisfaction. Perceived quality measures are inherent in many approaches to brand equity. In the annual EquiTrend study by Harris Interactive, 20,000 consumers aged 15 or older rate a random selection of 60 brands from a total of 1,200 brands across 46 categories on several dimensions: Equity, Consumer Connection, Commitment, Brand Behavior, Brand Advocacy, and Trust. An Equity score is determined by a calculation of measures of Familiarity, Quality, and Purchase Consideration.[21]

Brand Credibility.   Customers may also form judgments about the company or organization behind the brand. *Brand credibility* describes the extent to which customers see the brand as credible in terms of three dimensions: perceived expertise, trustworthiness, and likability. Is the brand seen as (1) competent, innovative, and a market leader (*brand expertise*); (2) dependable and keeping customer interests in mind (*brand trustworthiness*); and (3) fun, interesting, and worth spending time with (*brand likability*)? In other words, credibility measures whether consumers see the company or organization behind the brand as good at what it does, concerned about its customers, and just plain likable.[22]

FEDEX

From its earliest advertising, "When It Absolutely, Positively Has to Be There Overnight," FedEx has stressed its speed, skill, and dependability in shipping and delivery. Its most recent brand campaign, "We Understand," reinforces that FedEx is "the perfect enabler and facilitator of great service and partnership." Internationally, its "FedEx Delivers to a Changing World" ad campaign reinforces that "one of the constants in the world is FedEx." The company wants customers to think of it as a trusted partner, with a commitment to reliable but cost-effective shipping all over the world. Its advertising, however, often uses humor and high production values. FedEx ads that run during the Super Bowl are often rated among the most enjoyable by consumers. Through its flawless service delivery and creative marketing communications, FedEx is able to establish all three dimensions of credibility: expertise, trustworthiness, and likability.[23]

A brand like Fedex is seen as highly credible due to its expertise, trustworthiness, and likability.

Source: Adam Slinger/Alamy

Brand Consideration. Favorable brand attitudes and perceptions of credibility are important, but not important enough if customers don't actually *consider* the brand for possible purchase or use. As Chapter 2 introduced, consideration depends in part on how personally relevant customers find the brand and is a crucial filter in terms of building brand equity. No matter how highly they regard the brand or how credible they find it, unless they also give it serious consideration and deem it relevant, customers will keep a brand at a distance and never closely embrace it. Brand consideration depends in large part on the extent to which strong and favorable brand associations can be created as part of the brand image.

Brand Superiority. Superiority measures the extent to which customers view the brand as unique and better than other brands. Do customers believe it offers advantages that other brands cannot? Superiority is absolutely critical to building intense and active relationships with customers and depends to a great degree on the number and nature of unique brand associations that make up the brand image.

Brand Feelings

Brand feelings are customers' emotional responses and reactions to the brand. Brand feelings also relate to the social currency evoked by the brand. What feelings are evoked by the marketing program for the brand or by other means? How does the brand affect customers' feelings about themselves and their relationship with others? These feelings can be mild or intense and can be positive or negative.

For example, Kevin Roberts of Saatchi & Saatchi argues that companies must transcend brands to create "trustmarks"—a name or symbol that emotionally binds a company with the desires and aspirations of its customers—and ultimately "lovemarks." He argues that it is not enough for a brand to be just respected.

> Pretty much everything today can be seen in relation to a love-respect axis. You can plot any relationship—with a person, with a brand—by whether it's based on love or based on respect. It used to be that a high respect rating would win. But these days, a high love rating wins. If I don't love what you're offering me, I'm not even interested.[24]

A passionate believer in the concept, Roberts reinforces the point that trustmarks truly belong to the people who offer the love to the brand, and that an emotional connection is critical.[25]

The emotions evoked by a brand can become so strongly associated that they are accessible during product consumption or use. Researchers have defined ***transformational advertising*** as advertising designed to change consumers' perceptions of the actual usage experience with the product.[26] Corona Extra overtook Heineken as the leading imported beer in the United States via its "beach in a bottle" advertising. With a tagline "Miles Away from Ordinary," the campaign was designed to transform drinkers—at least mentally—to sunny, tranquil beaches.[27]

A brand that successfully injected some emotion into an industry is W hotels.

W HOTELS

Launched in the early era of boutique hotels, the Starwood-owned W hotel chain quickly gained a reputation as being the cool place for hipsters to visit, either as hotel guests or just as local residents looking for a fun night out. In a 2009 press release, Starwood described W Hotels as:

"An innovative luxury lifestyle brand and the hotel category buster with 26 properties in the most vibrant destinations around the world. Inspiring, iconic, innovative and influential, W Hotels provides the ultimate in insider access to a world of 'Wow.' Each hotel offers a unique mix of innovative design and passions around design, architecture, fashion, music, entertainment, pop culture, and everything in between. W Hotels are unique and individual expressions of modern living, reflected in the brand's sensibility to a holistic lifestyle experience with cutting-edge design, contemporary restaurant concepts, glamorous nightlife experiences, and signature spas."

During Media Summit and Investor Day events held in 2006, Starwood management revealed that they positioned W as follows: "From San Diego to Seoul . . . and soon Hoboken to Hong Kong, W's flirty, insider, escape offers guests unique experiences around the warmth of cool." Clearly W Hotels are every bit as much about the emotions and experiences they create as they are about getting a comfortable night's rest.[28]

W Hotels pioneered the "lifestyle luxury hotel" category through its unique design elements and guest experiences.

Source: Starwood Hotels & Resorts Worldwide, Inc.

More and more firms are attempting to tap into more consumer emotions with their brands. The following are six important types of brand-building feelings:[29]

1. *Warmth:* The brand evokes soothing types of feelings and makes consumers feel a sense of calm or peacefulness. Consumers may feel sentimental, warmhearted, or affectionate about the brand. Many heritage brands such as Welch's jelly, Quaker oatmeal, and Aunt Jemima pancake mix and syrup tap into feelings of warmth.

2. *Fun:* Upbeat types of feelings make consumers feel amused, lighthearted, joyous, playful, cheerful, and so on. With its iconic characters and theme park rides, Disney is a brand often associated with fun.

3. *Excitement:* The brand makes consumers feel energized and that they are experiencing something special. Brands that evoke excitement may generate a sense of elation, of "being alive," or being cool, sexy, etc. MTV is a brand seen by many teens and young adults as exciting.

4. *Security:* The brand produces a feeling of safety, comfort, and self-assurance. As a result of the brand, consumers do not experience worry or concerns that they might have otherwise felt. Allstate Insurance and its "Good Hands" symbol and State Farm and its "Like a Good Neighbor" slogan are brands that communicate security to many.

5. *Social approval:* The brand gives consumers a belief that others look favorably on their appearance, behavior, and so on. This approval may be a result of direct acknowledgment of the consumer's use of the brand by others or may be less overt and a result of attribution of product use to consumers. To an older generation of consumers, Cadillac is a brand that historically has been a signal of social approval.

6. *Self-respect:* The brand makes consumers feel better about themselves; consumers feel a sense of pride, accomplishment, or fulfillment. A brand like Tide laundry detergent is able to link its brand to "doing the best things for the family" to many homemakers.

These six feelings can be divided into two broad categories: The first three types of feelings are experiential and immediate, increasing in level of intensity; the latter three types of feelings are private and enduring, increasing in level of gravity.

Summary.   Although all types of customer responses are possible—driven from both the head and heart—ultimately what matters is how positive they are. Responses must also be accessible and come to mind when consumers think of the brand. Brand judgments and feelings can favorably affect consumer behavior only if consumers internalize or think of positive responses in their various encounters with the brand.

Brand Resonance

The final step of the model focuses on the ultimate relationship and level of identification that the customer has with the brand.[30] *Brand resonance* describes the nature of this relationship and the extent to which customers feel that they are "in sync" with the brand. Examples of brands with historically high resonance include Harley-Davidson, Apple, and eBay.

Resonance is characterized in terms of *intensity*, or the depth of the psychological bond that customers have with the brand, as well as the level of *activity* engendered by this loyalty (repeat purchase rates and the extent to which customers seek out brand information, events, and other loyal customers). We can break down these two dimensions of brand resonance into four categories:

1. Behavioral loyalty
2. Attitudinal attachment
3. Sense of community
4. Active engagement

Behavioral Loyalty.   We can gauge *behavioral loyalty* in terms of repeat purchases and the amount or share of category volume attributed to the brand, that is, the "share of category requirements." In other words, how often do customers purchase a brand and how much do they purchase? For bottom-line profit results, the brand must generate sufficient purchase frequencies and volumes.

The lifetime value of behaviorally loyal consumers can be enormous.[31] For example, a loyal General Motors customer could be worth $276,000 over his or her lifetime (assuming 11 or more vehicles bought and word-of-mouth endorsement that makes friends and relatives more likely to consider GM products). Or consider new parents. By spending $100 a month on diapers and wipes for 24–30 months, they can create lifetime value of as much as $3,000 for just one baby.

Attitudinal Attachment.   Behavioral loyalty is necessary but not sufficient for resonance to occur.[32] Some customers may buy out of necessity—because the brand is the only product stocked or readily accessible, the only one they can afford, or other reasons. Resonance, however, requires a strong personal *attachment*. Customers should go beyond having a positive attitude to viewing the brand as something special in a broader context. For example, customers with a great deal of attitudinal attachment to a brand may state that they "love" the brand, describe it as one of their favorite possessions, or view it as a "little pleasure" that they look forward to.

Prior research has shown that mere satisfaction may not be enough.[33] Xerox found that when customer satisfaction was ranked on a scale of 1 (completely dissatisfied) to 5 (completely satisfied), customers who rated Xerox products and services as "4"—and thus were satisfied—were six times more likely to defect to competitors than those customers who provided ratings of "5."[34]

Similarly, loyalty guru Frederick Reichheld points out that although more than 90 percent of car buyers are satisfied or very satisfied when they drive away from the dealer's showroom, fewer than half buy the same brand of automobile the next time.[35] Creating greater loyalty requires creating deeper attitudinal attachment, through marketing programs and products and services that fully satisfy consumer needs.

Sense of Community.   The brand may also take on broader meaning to the customer by conveying a sense of *community*.[36] Identification with a brand community may reflect an important social phenomenon in which customers feel a kinship or affiliation with other people associated with the brand, whether fellow brand users or customers, or employees or representatives of the company. A brand community can exist online or off-line.[37] Branding Brief 3-1 profiles three company-initiated programs to help build brand communities. A stronger sense of community among loyal users can engender favorable brand attitudes and intentions.[38]

Active Engagement.   Finally, perhaps the strongest affirmation of brand loyalty occurs when customers are *engaged*, or willing to invest time, energy, money, or other resources in the brand beyond those expended during purchase or consumption of the brand.[39] For example, customers may choose to join a club centered on a brand, receive updates, and exchange correspondence with other brand users or formal or informal representatives of the brand itself. Companies are making it increasingly easy for customers to buy a range of branded merchandise so they can literally express their loyalty.

BMW

BMW's lifestyle business was started 15 years ago as a marketing initiative whose objectives were to broaden the brand's presence and strengthen loyalty. The lifestyle division focuses primarily on selling mobility products, including bicycles and skateboards for kids, and aims for a profit margin (7%) similar to what BMW generates from sales of its cars. More than 2,000 products are sold, from €39 ($52) Mini rain boots to the highly regarded €2750 ($3,620) lightweight M Carbon Racer bike from BMW's M performance unit. These are not your run-of-the-mill products, though. BMW's €79 ($105) Snow Racer sled has replaceable metal runners, a suspension-system in the red steering ski, and a horn to warn inattentive passersby. The battery-powered Baby Racer, designed internally by BMW Designworks, comes in three different models and

BMW has a highly successful licensing business—exemplified by this popular Baby Racer for kids—to help customers find more ways to experience the brand.
Source: BMW AG

costs €79 ($106). Winner of several design prizes and featured in the MOMA in New York, it sells 60,000 units a year. In China, which is now its third-largest market for car sales, BMW opened a store selling merchandise a year before it began assembling cars in the country and had more than 50 BMW stores there by the end of 2012.[40]

Customers may choose to visit brand-related Web sites, participate in chat rooms, or post to discussions. In this case, customers themselves became brand evangelists and ambassadors and help communicate about the brand and strengthen the brand ties of others. Strong attitudinal attachment or social identity or both are typically necessary, however, for active engagement with the brand to occur.

BRANDING BRIEF 3-1

Building Brand Communities

Apple

Apple encourages owners of its computers to form local Apple user groups. Over 800 groups exist worldwide, ranging in size from fewer than 25 members to over 1,000 members. Many groups offer monthly meetings, an informative newsletter, member discounts, special interest groups, classes, and one-on-one support. Larger groups offer extensive training programs, computer labs, and resource libraries. The user groups provide Apple owners with opportunities to learn more about their computers, share ideas, friendships with fellow Apple users, as well as sponsor special activities and events and perform community service. A visit to Apple's Web site helps customers find nearby user groups.

With 1.2 million members, Harley Owners Group is the quintessential example of a brand community.

Source: culture-images GmbH/Alamy

Harley-Davidson

The world-famous motorcycle company sponsors the Harley Owners Group (HOG), which by 2011 had 1,200,000 members in chapter groups all over the world sharing a very simple mission, "To Ride and Have Fun." The first-time buyer of a Harley-Davidson motorcycle gets a free one-year membership. HOG benefits include a magazine called *Hog Tales*, a touring handbook, emergency road service, a specially designed insurance program, theft reward service, discount hotel rates, and a Fly & Ride program enabling members to rent Harleys while on vacation. The company also maintains an extensive Web site devoted to HOG, which includes information about club chapters and events and features a special members-only section.

Jeep

In addition to joining the hundreds of local Jeep enthusiast clubs throughout the world, Jeep owners can convene with their vehicles in wilderness areas across the United States as part of the company's official Jeep Jamborees and Jeep Rocks and Road. A tradition since 1953, Jeep Jamborees bring Jeep owners and their families together for two-day off-road adventures in 30 different locations throughout the United States from spring through autumn each year. Trails and obstacles are rated on a 1–10 scale in terms of difficulty. Promising to be "every bit as muddy," the 2010 Jeep Rocks and Road tour hit 11 different venues across the country to allow existing and prospective Jeep owners to put the 2011 vehicle lineup through their paces on and off road.

Sources: www.apple.com, www.harley-davidson.com, and www.jeep.com; accessed 9 December 2011.

Summary. In short, brand resonance and the relationships consumers have with brands have two dimensions: ***intensity*** and ***activity***. Intensity measures the strength of the attitudinal attachment and sense of community. Activity tells us how frequently the consumer buys and uses the brand, as well as engages in other activities not related to purchase and consumption.

Brand-Building Implications

The brand resonance model provides a road map and guidance for brand building, a yardstick by which brands can assess their progress in their brand-building efforts as well as a guide for marketing research initiatives. With respect to the latter, one model application aids in brand tracking and providing quantitative measures of the success of brand-building efforts (see Chapter 8). Figure 3-4 contains a set of candidate measures for the six brand building blocks.

The brand resonance model also reinforces a number of important branding tenets, five of which are particularly noteworthy. We discuss them in the following sections.

I. **Salience**

What brands of product or service category can you think of?
   (using increasingly specific product category cues)
Have you ever heard of these brands?
Which brands might you be likely to use under the following
   situations . . . ?
How frequently do you think of this brand?

II. **Performance**

Compared with other brands in the category, how well does this brand
   provide the basic functions of the product or service category?
Compared with other brands in the category, how well does this brand
   satisfy the basic needs of the product or service category?
To what extent does this brand have special features?
How reliable is this brand?
How durable is this brand?
How easily serviced is this brand?
How effective is this brand's service? Does it completely satisfy your
   requirements?
How efficient is this brand's service in terms of speed, responsiveness, and
   so forth?
How courteous and helpful are the providers of this brand's service?
How stylish do you find this brand?
How much do you like the look, feel, and other design aspects of
   this brand?
Compared with other brands in the category with which it competes, are
   this brand's prices generally higher, lower, or about the same?
Compared with other brands in the category with which it competes, do
   this brand's prices change more frequently, less frequently, or about the
   same amount?

III. **Imagery**

To what extent do people you admire and respect use this brand?
How much do you like people who use this brand?
How well do the following words describe this brand: down-to-earth,
   honest, daring, up-to-date, reliable, successful, upper class, charming,
   outdoorsy?
What places are appropriate to buy this brand?
How appropriate are the following situations to use this brand?
Can you buy this brand in a lot of places?
Is this a brand that you can use in a lot of different situations?
To what extent does thinking of the brand bring back pleasant memories?
To what extent do you feel you grew up with the brand?

IV. **Judgments**

Quality
What is your overall opinion of this brand?
What is your assessment of the product quality of this brand?
To what extent does this brand fully satisfy your product needs?
How good a value is this brand?

Credibility
How knowledgeable are the makers of this brand?
How innovative are the makers of this brand?
How much do you trust the makers of this brand?
To what extent do the makers of this brand understand your needs?
To what extent do the makers of this brand care about your opinions?
To what extent do the makers of this brand have your interests in mind?

(Continued)

FIGURE 3-4

Possible Measures of
Brand Building Blocks

Credibility (cont.)

How much do you like this brand?

How much do you admire this brand?

How much do you respect this brand?

Consideration

How likely would you be to recommend this brand to others?

Which are your favorite products in this brand category?

How personally relevant is this brand to you?

Superiority

How unique is this brand?

To what extent does this brand offer advantages that other brands cannot?

How superior is this brand to others in the category?

V. **Feelings**

Does this brand give you a feeling of warmth?

Does this brand give you a feeling of fun?

Does this brand give you a feeling of excitement?

Does this brand give you a feeling of security?

Does this brand give you a feeling of social approval?

Does this brand give you a feeling of self-respect?

VI. **Resonance**

Loyalty

I consider myself loyal to this brand.

I buy this brand whenever I can.

I buy as much of this brand as I can.

I feel this is the only brand of this product I need.

This is the one brand I would prefer to buy/use.

If this brand were not available, it would make little difference to me if I had to use another brand.

I would go out of my way to use this brand.

Attachment

I really love this brand.

I would really miss this brand if it went away.

This brand is special to me.

This brand is more than a product to me.

Community

I really identify with people who use this brand.

I feel as if I almost belong to a club with other users of this brand.

This is a brand used by people like me.

I feel a deep connection with others who use this brand.

Engagement

I really like to talk about this brand to others.

I am always interested in learning more about this brand.

I would be interested in merchandise with this brand's name on it.

I am proud to have others know I use this brand.

I like to visit the Web site for this brand.

Compared with other people, I follow news about this brand closely.

It should be recognized that the core brand values at the bottom two levels of the pyramid—brand salience, performance, and imagery—are typically more idiosyncratic and unique to a product and service category than other brand values.

Customers Own the Brands.   The basic premise of the brand resonance model is that the true measure of the strength of a brand is the way consumers think, feel, and act with respect to that brand. The strongest brands will be those to which consumers become so attached and passionate that they, in effect, become evangelists or missionaries and attempt to share their beliefs and spread the word about the brand. *The power of the brand and its ultimate value to the firm reside with customers.*

It is through learning about and experiencing a brand that customers end up thinking, feeling, and acting in a way that allows the firm to reap the benefits of brand equity. Although marketers must take responsibility for designing and implementing the most effective and efficient brand-building marketing programs possible, the success of those marketing efforts ultimately depends on how consumers respond and the actions they take. This response, in turn, depends on the knowledge that has been created in their minds and hearts for those brands. The Science of Branding 3-2 describes some criteria to determine whether a company is truly consumer-centric.

Don't Take Shortcuts with Brands.   The brand resonance model reinforces the fact that there are no shortcuts in building a brand. A great brand is not built by accident but is the product of carefully accomplishing—either explicitly or implicitly—a series of logically linked steps with consumers. The more explicitly marketers recognize the steps and define them as concrete goals, the more likely they will give them the proper attention and fully realize them so they can provide the greatest contribution to brand building. *The length of time to build a strong brand will therefore be directly proportional to the amount of time it takes to create sufficient awareness and understanding so that firmly held and felt beliefs and attitudes about the brand are formed that can serve as the foundation for brand equity.*

The brand-building steps may not be equally difficult. Creating brand awareness is a step that an effectively designed marketing program often can accomplish in a relatively short period of time. Unfortunately, this step is the one that many brand marketers tend to skip in their mistaken haste to quickly establish an image for the brand. It is difficult for consumers to appreciate the advantages and uniqueness of a brand unless they have some sort of frame of reference for what the brand is supposed to do and with whom or what it is supposed to compete. Similarly, consumers cannot have highly positive responses without a reasonably complete understanding of the brand's dimensions and characteristics.

Even if, due to circumstances in the marketplace, consumers actually start a repeated-purchase or behavioral loyalty relationship with a brand without much underlying feeling, judgment, or associations, these other brand-building blocks will have to come into place at some point to create true resonance. That is, although the start point may differ, the same steps in brand building eventually must occur to create a truly strong brand.

Brands Should Have a Duality.   One important point reinforced by the model is that a strong brand has a duality—it appeals to both the head and the heart. Thus, although there may be two different ways to build loyalty and resonance—going up the left-hand and right-hand sides of the pyramid—strong brands often do both. *Strong brands blend product performance and imagery to create a rich, varied, but complementary set of consumer responses to the brand.*

By appealing to both rational and emotional concerns, a strong brand provides consumers with multiple access points while reducing competitive vulnerability. Rational concerns can satisfy utilitarian needs, whereas emotional concerns can satisfy psychological or emotional needs. Combining the two allows brands to create a formidable brand position. Consistent with this reasoning, a McKinsey study of 51 corporate brands found that having distinctive physical *and* emotional benefits drove greater shareholder value, especially when the two were linked.[41]

MASTERCARD

MasterCard is an example of a brand with much duality, because it emphasizes both the rational advantages of the credit card—its acceptance at establishments worldwide—as well as the emotional advantages—expressed in the award-winning "Priceless" advertising campaign. Ads depict people buying items to achieve both a very practical goal and a more important emotional goal. The first ad, for example, showed a father taking his son to a baseball game. As they made purchases on the way to their seats, superimposed on the screen and in a voiceover came the words:

"Two tickets . . . $46,
"Two hotdogs, two popcorns, two sodas . . . $27,
"One autographed baseball . . . $50,
"Real conversation with 11-year-old son . . . priceless."

THE SCIENCE OF BRANDING 3-2

Putting Customers First

At most companies, employees don't have any idea what their firm's return on invested capital is, let alone the returns on specific customer segments—and even if they knew, they'd be powerless to do anything about it. But according to authors Larry Selden and Geoffrey Colvin, a few companies, such as Dell, Best Buy, and Royal Bank of Canada, have been solid stocks for shareholders through the years because of their customer-centric approach.

According to these authors, **customer-centricity** means that all employees understand how their actions affect share price. Selden and Colvin maintain that customer-centric companies are a good bet for investors because they hold an advantage that can lead to a jump in share price. To determine whether a company is truly customer-focused, Selden and Colvin suggest asking the following five questions:

7-Eleven Japan solicits employee input to devise new ways to better satisfy customers.
Source: REUTERS/Kim Kyung Hoon

1. ***Is the company looking for ways to take care of you?*** Only a few companies identify customer needs first, and then create ways to meet them. Too many companies try to make customers buy the products and services they already offer. Royal Bank of Canada is an example of a company that found a customer segment with unique needs and met those needs. Many of the bank's customers were Canadians who spent winters in Florida or Arizona. Those customers, who tended to be affluent, wanted to borrow money in the United States for homes and get a U.S. credit rating that reflected their Canadian record. They also wanted to be served by employees who knew the United States as well as Canada. To serve those customers, the bank opened a branch in Florida through its U.S. subsidiary. The results were exceptional: customers signed up in droves, and the new branch was profitable in months rather than the typical years. Opening new branches aimed at specific customer segments represented a growth opportunity for the bank's shareholders.

2. ***Does the company know its customers well enough to differentiate between them?*** True differentiation means knowing who your various customer segments are, what each group wants, where the groups are shopping, and how to serve the customers individually. For example, Best Buy configures some stores to serve its "soccer-mom" customer segment and others to entice a segment of affluent entertainment lovers with stores that have home-theater demo rooms.

3. ***Is someone accountable for customers?*** At most companies, various departments own pieces of customer segments, but no one owns any specific one. At companies with customer-centric approaches, however, things are different. At Best Buy, for example, one manager is accountable for the "soccer-mom" segment across multiple stores.

4. ***Is the company managed for shareholder value?*** If a company is managed for shareholder value, employees know about earning a return on invested capital that exceeds the cost of capital, plus investing increasing amounts of capital at that positive spread and maintaining that spread for as long as possible. Customer-centric companies apply those criteria to customer segments. They know how much capital they've invested in a segment and how much return they earn on it. They maintain the positive spread by creating and reinventing enduring customer relationships.

5. ***Is the company testing new customer offers and learning from the results?*** Constant learning about what customers want and a formal process for sharing it are critical to customer-centricity. 7-Eleven Japan has done this well. Every week, employees from all over Japan would meet to discuss hypotheses tested and verified in the stores. Ideas such as changing the lunch menu for the next day based on the predicted weather (like serving hot noodles on a cool day) were heard throughout the company.

Sources: Larry Selden and Geoffrey Colvin, "5 Rules for Finding the Next Dell," *Fortune*, 12 July 2004; Larry Selden and Geoffrey Colvin, *Angel Customers and Demon Customers: Discover Which Is Which and Turbo-Charge Your Stock* (New York: Portfolio, 2003).

The ad ended with the tagline, "There Are Some Things Money Can't Buy; For Everything Else There's MasterCard" and "Accepted At Ballparks Coast-to-Coast." The ads reinforced the notion that the ultimate goal of MasterCard—a feeling, an accomplishment, or other intangible—was truly "priceless." The campaign has been so successful that it has run around the world, with appropriate cultural adaptation. The baseball spot, for example, was redone as a cricket ad for Australia. The campaign has received many awards, including four EFFIES from the American Marketing Association for effectiveness.[42]

Brands Should Have Richness. The level of detail in the brand resonance model highlights the number of possible ways to create meaning with consumers and the range of possible avenues to elicit consumer responses. Collectively, these various aspects of brand meaning and the resulting responses produce strong consumer bonds to the brand. The various associations making up the brand image may be reinforcing, helping strengthen or increase the favorability of other brand associations, or they may be unique, helping add distinctiveness or offset some potential deficiencies. Strong brands thus have both breadth (in terms of duality) *and* depth (in terms of richness).

At the same time, brands should not necessarily be expected to score highly on all the various dimensions and categories making up each core brand value. Building blocks can have hierarchies in their own right. For example, with respect to brand awareness, typically marketers should first establish category identification in some way before considering strategies to expand brand breadth via needs satisfied or benefits offered. With brand performance, they may wish to first link primary characteristics and related features before attempting to link additional, more peripheral associations.

Similarly, brand imagery often begins with a fairly concrete initial articulation of user and usage imagery that, over time, leads to broader, more abstract brand associations of personality, value, history, heritage, and experience. Brand judgments usually begin with positive quality and credibility perceptions that can lead to brand consideration and then perhaps ultimately to assessments of brand superiority. Brand feelings usually start with either experiential ones (warmth, fun, and excitement) or inward ones (security, social approval, and self-respect.) Finally, resonance again has a clear ordering, whereby behavioral loyalty is a starting point, but attitudinal attachment or a sense of community is almost always needed for active engagement to occur.

Brand Resonance Provides Important Focus. As Figure 3-1 shows, brand resonance is the pinnacle of the brand resonance model and provides important focus and priority for decision making about marketing. Marketers building brands should use brand resonance as a goal and a means to interpret their brand-related marketing activities. The question to ask is, To what extent is marketing activity affecting the key dimensions of brand resonance—consumer loyalty, attachment, community, or engagement with the brand? Is marketing activity creating brand performance and imagery associations and consumer judgments and feelings that will support these brand resonance dimensions?

SHUTTERFLY

A brand that has explicitly considered how to build brand resonance is Shutterfly. Although known in particular for its online photographic services, Shutterfly defines itself more broadly as an "Internet-based social expression and personal publishing service" that "provides high-quality products and world-class services that make it easy, convenient and fun for consumers to preserve their digital photos in a creative and thoughtful manner." In a highly competitive marketplace, Shutterfly's flagship product, Photo Book, allows customers to create custom photo books in professionally bound coffee table form. The company's brand objective is to be a "Trusted Partner." To further that goal and to help create a strong personal connection with its users, brand marketing emphasizes social influence and being smart and fun. Shutterfly also offers social media services that allow users to share photos uploaded on their site with blogs and social networks like Facebook and Twitter.[43]

It is virtually impossible, however, for consumers to experience an intense, active loyalty relationship with *all* the brands they purchase and consume. Thus, some brands will be more meaningful to consumers than others, because of the nature of their associated product or service, the characteristics of the consumer, and so on. Some brands have more resonance potential than others. When it is difficult to create a varied set of feelings and imagery associations, marketers might not be able to obtain the deeper aspects of brand resonance like active engagement. Nevertheless, by taking a broader view of brand loyalty, they may be able to gain a more holistic appreciation for their brand and how it connects to consumers. And by defining the proper role for the brand, they should be able to obtain higher levels of brand resonance.

THE BRAND VALUE CHAIN

Developing a strong positioning and building brand resonance are crucial marketing goals. To better understand the ROI of marketing investments, however, another tool is necessary. The ***brand value chain*** is a structured approach to assessing the sources and outcomes of brand equity and the manner by which marketing activities create brand value.[44] It recognizes that many different people within an organization can affect brand equity and need to be aware of relevant branding effects. The brand value chain thus provides insights to support brand managers, chief marketing officers, managing directors, and chief executive officers, all of whom may need different types of information.

The brand value chain has several basic premises. Consistent with the brand resonance model, it assumes that the value of a brand ultimately resides with customers. Based on this insight, the model next assumes that the brand value creation process begins when the firm invests in a marketing program targeting actual or potential customers (stage 1). The associated marketing activity then affects the customer mind-set—what customers know and feel about the brand—as reflected by the brand resonance model (stage 2). This mind-set, across a broad group of customers, produces the brand's performance in the marketplace—how much and when customers purchase, the price that they pay, and so forth (stage 3). Finally, the investment community considers this market performance—and other factors such as replacement cost and purchase price in acquisitions—to arrive at an assessment of shareholder value in general and a value of the brand in particular (stage 4).

The model also assumes that a number of linking factors intervene between these stages. These linking factors determine the extent to which value created at one stage transfers or "multiplies" to the next stage. Three sets of multipliers moderate the transfer between the marketing program and the three value stages: the program quality multiplier, the marketplace conditions multiplier, and the investor sentiment multiplier. The brand value chain model is summarized in Figure 3-5. Next we describe the value stages and multiplying factors in more detail and look at examples of both positive and negative multiplier effects.

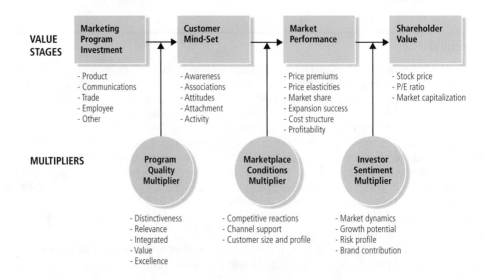

FIGURE 3-5

Brand Value Chain

Value Stages

Brand value creation begins with marketing activity by the firm.

Marketing Program Investment.   Any marketing program investment that can contribute to brand value development, intentionally or not, falls into this first value stage. Chapters 4–7 outline many such marketing activities, like product research, development, and design; trade or intermediary support; marketing communications including advertising, promotion, sponsorship, direct and interactive marketing, personal selling, publicity, and public relations; and employee training. A big investment of course does not guarantee success. The ability of a marketing program investment to transfer or multiply farther down the chain depends on *qualitative* aspects of the marketing program and the program quality multiplier.

Program Quality Multiplier.   The ability of the marketing program to affect the customer mind-set will depend on its quality. Throughout the book, we review a number of different means to judge the quality of a marketing program. One handy way to remember some key considerations is through the acronym DRIVE, as follows:

1. *Distinctiveness:* How unique is the marketing program? How creative or differentiating is it?
2. *Relevance:* How meaningful is the marketing program to customers? Do consumers feel the brand is one they should seriously consider?
3. *Integrated:* How well integrated is the marketing program at one point in time and over time? Do all aspects combine to create the biggest impact with customers as possible? Does the marketing program relate effectively to past marketing programs and properly balance continuity and change, evolving the brand in the right direction?
4. *Value:* How much short-run and long-run value does the marketing program create? Will it profitably drive sales in the short run? Will it build brand equity in the long run?
5. *Excellence:* Is the individual marketing activity designed to satisfy the highest standards? Does it reflect state-of-the art thinking and corporate wisdom as success factors for that particular type of marketing activity?

Not surprisingly, a well-integrated marketing program, carefully designed and implemented to be highly relevant and unique, is likely to achieve a greater return on investment from marketing program expenditures. For example, despite being outspent by such beverage brand giants as Coca-Cola, Pepsi, and Budweiser, the California Milk Processor Board was able to reverse a decades-long decline in consumption of milk in California through the well-designed and executed "Got Milk?" campaign.

On the other hand, numerous marketers have found that expensive marketing programs do not necessarily produce sales unless they are well conceived. For example, through the years, brands such as Michelob, Minute Maid, 7UP, and others have seen their sales slide despite sizable marketing expenditures because of poorly targeted and delivered marketing campaigns.

Customer Mind-Set.   In what ways have customers been changed as a result of the marketing program? How have those changes manifested themselves in the customer mind-set?

Remember, the customer mind-set includes everything that exists in the minds of customers with respect to a brand: thoughts, feelings, experiences, images, perceptions, beliefs, and attitudes. In its totality, the brand resonance model captures a wide range of aspects of the customer mind-set. To provide a concise summary, a shorter "5 As" list can highlight important measures of the customer mind-set as suggested by the resonance model:

1. *Brand Awareness:* The extent and ease with which customers recall and recognize the brand and can identify the products and services with which it is associated.
2. *Brand Associations:* The strength, favorability, and uniqueness of perceived attributes and benefits for the brand. Brand associations often represent key sources of brand value, because they are the means by which consumers feel brands satisfy their needs.
3. *Brand Attitudes:* Overall evaluations of the brand in terms of its quality and the satisfaction it generates.

4. *Brand Attachment:* The degree of loyalty the customer feels toward the brand. A strong form of attachment, *adherence*, is the consumer's resistance to change and the ability of a brand to withstand bad news like a product or service failure. In the extreme, attachment can even become *addiction.*

5. *Brand Activity:* The extent to which customers use the brand, talk to others about the brand, seek out brand information, promotions, and events, and so on.

These five dimensions can be easily related to the brand resonance model (awareness relates to salience, associations relate to performance and imagery, attitudes relate to judgments and feelings, and attachment and activity relate to resonance). As in the resonance model, an obvious hierarchy exists in the dimensions of value: awareness supports associations, which drive attitudes that lead to attachment and activity. Brand value is created at this stage when customers have (1) deep, broad brand awareness; (2) appropriately strong, favorable, and unique points-of-parity and points-of-difference; (3) positive brand judgments and feelings; (4) intense brand attachment and loyalty; and (5) a high degree of brand activity.

Creating the right customer mind-set can be critical in terms of building brand equity and value. AMD and Cyrix found that achieving performance parity with Intel's microprocessors did not return benefits in 1998, when original equipment manufacturers were reluctant to adopt the new chips because of their lack of a strong brand image with consumers. Moreover, success with consumers may not translate to success in the marketplace unless other conditions also prevail. The ability of this customer mind-set to create value at the next stage depends on external factors we call the marketplace conditions multiplier, as follows.

Marketplace Conditions Multiplier.   The extent to which value created in the minds of customers affects market performance depends on factors beyond the individual customer. Three such factors are:

1. *Competitive superiority:* How effective are the marketing investments of competing brands?
2. *Channel and other intermediary support:* How much brand reinforcement and selling effort is being put forth by various marketing partners?
3. *Customer size and profile:* How many and what types of customers are attracted to the brand? Are they profitable?

The value created in the minds of customers will translate to favorable market performance when competitors fail to provide a significant threat, when channel members and other intermediaries provide strong support, and when a sizable number of profitable customers are attracted to the brand.

The competitive context faced by a brand can have a profound effect on its fortunes. For example, Nike and McDonald's have benefited in the past from the prolonged marketing woes of their main rivals, Reebok and Burger King, which both have suffered from numerous repositionings and management changes. On the other hand, MasterCard has had to contend for the past decade with two strong, well-marketed brands in Visa and American Express and consequently has faced an uphill battle gaining market share despite its well-received "Priceless" ad campaign, as described earlier in this chapter.

Market Performance.   We saw in Chapter 2 that the customer mind-set affects how customers react in the marketplace in six main ways. The first two relate to price premiums and price elasticities. How much extra are customers willing to pay for a comparable product because of its brand? And how much does their demand increase or decrease when the price rises or falls? A third outcome is market share, which measures the success of the marketing program in driving brand sales. Taken together, the first three outcomes determine the direct revenue stream attributable to the brand over time. Brand value is created with higher market shares, greater price premiums, and more elastic responses to price decreases and inelastic responses to price increases.

The fourth outcome is brand expansion, the success of the brand in supporting line and category extensions and new-product launches into related categories. This dimension captures the brand's ability to add enhancements to the revenue stream. The fifth outcome is cost structure or, more specifically, reduced marketing program expenditures thanks to the prevailing customer mind-set. When customers already have favorable opinions and knowledge about a brand, any aspect of the marketing program is likely to be more effective for the same expenditure level;

alternatively, the same level of effectiveness can be achieved at a lower cost because ads are more memorable, sales calls more productive, and so on. When combined, these five outcomes lead to brand profitability, the sixth outcome.

The ability of the brand value created at this stage to reach the final stage in terms of stock market valuation again depends on external factors, this time according to the investor sentiment multiplier.

Investor Sentiment Multiplier.   Financial analysts and investors consider a host of factors in arriving at their brand valuations and investment decisions. Among them are the following:

- *Market dynamics:* What are the dynamics of the financial markets as a whole (interest rates, investor sentiment, supply of capital)?
- *Growth potential:* What is the growth potential or prospects for the brand and the industry in which it operates? For example, how helpful are the facilitating factors and how inhibiting are the hindering external factors that make up the firm's economic, social, physical, and legal environment?
- *Risk profile:* What is the risk profile for the brand? How vulnerable is the brand to those facilitating and inhibiting factors?
- *Brand contribution:* How important is the brand to the firm's brand portfolio?

The value the brand creates in the marketplace is most likely fully reflected in shareholder value when the firm is operating in a healthy industry without serious environmental hindrances or barriers, and when the brand contributes a significant portion of the firm's revenues and appears to have bright prospects.

The obvious examples of brands that benefited from a strong market multiplier—at least for a while—were the numerous dot-com brands at the turn of the century, such as Pets.com, eToys, Boo.com, and Webvan. The huge premium placed on their (actually negative) market performance, however, quickly disappeared—and in some cases so did the whole company!

On the other hand, many firms have lamented what they perceive as undervaluation by the market. For example, repositioned companies such as Corning have found it difficult to realize what they viewed as their true market value due to lingering investor perceptions from their past. Corning's heritage was in dishes and cookware; its more recent emphasis is on telecommunications, flat panel displays, and the environmental, life sciences, and semiconductor industries.

Shareholder Value.   Based on all available current and forecasted information about a brand, as well as many other considerations, the financial marketplace formulates opinions and assessments that have very direct financial implications for the brand value. Three particularly important indicators are the stock price, the price/earnings multiple, and overall market capitalization for the firm. Research has shown that not only can strong brands deliver greater returns to stockholders, they can do so with less risk.[45]

Implications

According to the brand value chain, marketers create value first by making shrewd investments in their marketing program and then by maximizing, as much as possible, the program, customer, and market multipliers that translate that investment into bottom-line financial benefits. The brand value chain thus provides a structured means for managers to understand where and how value is created and where to look to improve that process. Certain stages will be of greater interest to different members of the organization.

Brand and category marketing managers are likely to be interested in the customer mind-set and the impact of the marketing program on customers. Chief marketing officers (CMOs), on the other hand, are likely to be more interested in market performance and the impact of customer mind-set on actual market behaviors. Finally, a managing director or CEO is likely to focus on shareholder value and the impact of market performance on investment decisions.

The brand value chain has a number of implications. First, value creation begins with the marketing program investment. Therefore, a necessary—but not sufficient—condition for value creation is a well-funded, well-designed, and well-implemented marketing program. It is rare that marketers can get something for nothing.

Second, value creation requires more than the initial marketing investment. Each of the three multipliers can increase or decrease market value as it moves from stage to stage. In other words, value creation also means ensuring that value transfers from stage to stage. Unfortunately, many factors that can inhibit value creation may be largely out of the marketer's hands, like investors' industry sentiment. Recognizing the uncontrollable nature of these factors is important to help put in perspective the relative success or failure of a marketing program to create brand value. Just as sports coaches cannot be held accountable for unforeseen circumstances such as injuries to key players and financial constraints that make it difficult to attract top talent, so marketers cannot necessarily be held accountable for certain market forces and dynamics.

Third, as we'll outline in Chapters 8–10, the brand value chain provides a detailed road map for tracking value creation that can make marketing research and intelligence efforts easier. Each of the stages and multipliers has a set of measures by which we can assess it. In general, there are three main sources of information, and each taps into one value stage and one multiplier. The first stage, the marketing program investment, is straightforward and can come from the marketing plan and budget. We can assess both customer mind-set and the program quality multiplier with quantitative and qualitative customer research. Market performance and the marketplace conditions multiplier appear in market scans and internal accounting records. Finally, we can estimate shareholder value and the investor sentiment multiplier through investor analysis and interviews.

Modifications to the brand value chain can expand its relevance and applicability. First, there are a number of feedback loops. For example, stock prices can have an important effect on employee morale and motivation. Second, in some cases, the value creation may not occur sequentially. For example, stock analysts may react to an ad campaign for the brand—either personally or in recognition of public acceptance—and factor those reactions directly into their investment assessments. Third, some marketing activities may have only very diffuse effects that manifest over the long term. For example, cause-related or social responsibility marketing activity might affect customer or investor sentiment slowly over time. Fourth, both the mean and the variance of some brand value chain measures could matter. For example, a niche brand may receive very high marks but only across a very narrow range of customers.

REVIEW

Brand planning is aided by three interlocking models that can both qualitatively guide and interpret possible marketing actions as well as quantitatively measure marketing effects (see Figure 3-6). Chapter 2 introduced the brand positioning model. This chapter described in detail the second and third brand planning tools—the brand resonance and brand value chain models.

The brand resonance model lists a series of steps for building a strong brand: (1) establishing the proper brand identity, (2) creating the appropriate brand meaning, (3) eliciting the right brand responses, and (4) forging appropriate brand relationships with customers. Specifically, according to this model, building a strong brand requires establishing breadth and depth of brand awareness; creating strong, favorable, and unique brand associations; eliciting positive, accessible brand responses; and forging intense, active brand relationships. Achieving these four steps, in turn, means establishing six brand building blocks: brand salience, brand performance, brand imagery, brand judgments, brand feelings, and brand resonance.

The strongest brands excel on all six of these dimensions and thus fully execute all four steps of building a brand. In the brand resonance model, the most valuable brand building block, brand resonance, occurs when all the other core brand values are completely "in sync" with respect to customers' needs, wants, and desires. In other words, brand resonance reflects a completely harmonious relationship between customers and the brand. With true brand resonance, customers have a high degree of loyalty marked by a close relationship with the brand and actively seek means to interact with the brand and share their experiences with others. Firms that are able to achieve resonance and affinity with their customers should reap a host of valuable benefits, such as greater price premiums and more efficient and effective marketing programs.

Thus, the basic premise of the brand resonance model is that the true measure of the strength of a brand depends on how consumers think, feel, and act with respect to that brand. Achieving brand resonance requires eliciting the proper cognitive appraisals and emotional reactions to the brand from customers. That, in turn, necessitates establishing brand identity

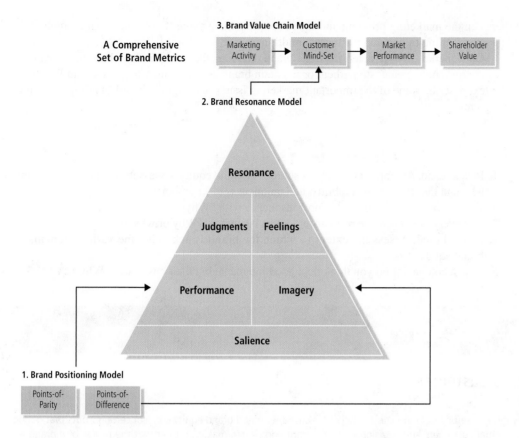

FIGURE 3-6

The Brand Planning Models

and creating the right meaning in terms of brand performance and brand imagery associations. A brand with the right identity and meaning can make a customer believe it is relevant and "my kind of product." The strongest brands will be those to which consumers become so attached and passionate that they, in effect, become evangelists or missionaries and attempt to share their beliefs and spread the word about the brand.

The brand value chain is a means to trace the value creation process for brands to better understand the financial impact of brand marketing expenditures and investments. Taking the customer's perspective of the value of a brand, the brand value chain assumes that the brand value creation process begins when the firm invests in a marketing program targeting actual or potential customers. Any marketing program investment that potentially can be attributed to brand value development falls into this category, for example, product research, development, and design; trade or intermediary support; and marketing communications.

The marketing activity associated with the program then affects the customer mind-set with respect to the brand—what customers know and feel about the brand. The customer mind-set includes everything that exists in the minds of customers with respect to a brand: thoughts, feelings, experiences, images, perceptions, beliefs, attitudes, and so forth. Consistent with the brand resonance model, five key dimensions that are particularly important measures of the customer mind-set are brand awareness, brand associations, brand attitudes, brand attachment, and brand activity or experience.

The customer mind-set affects how customers react or respond in the marketplace in a variety of ways. Six key outcomes of that response are price premiums, price elasticities, market share, brand expansion, cost structure, and brand profitability. Based on a thorough understanding of the brand's past, current and future prospects, as well as other factors, the financial marketplace then formulates opinions and makes various assessments that have direct financial implications for the value of the brand. Three particularly important indicators are the stock price, the price/earnings multiple, and overall market capitalization for the firm.

The model also assumes that a number of linking factors intervene between these stages. These linking factors determine the extent to which value created at one stage transfers or "multiplies" to the next stage. Thus, there are three sets of multipliers that moderate the transfer between the marketing program and the subsequent three value stages: the program multiplier, the customer multiplier, and the market multiplier.

Once marketers have determined the brand planning, they can put into place the actual marketing program to create, strengthen, or maintain brand associations. Chapters 4–7 in Part III of the text describe some of the important marketing issues in designing brand-building marketing programs.

DISCUSSION QUESTIONS

1. Pick a brand. Attempt to identify its sources of brand equity. Assess its level of brand awareness and the strength, favorability, and uniqueness of its associations.
2. Which brands do you have the most resonance with? Why?
3. Can every brand achieve resonance with its customers? Why or why not?
4. Pick a brand. Assess the extent to which the brand is achieving the various benefits of brand equity.
5. Which companies do you think do a good job managing their customers? Why?

BRAND FOCUS 3.0

Creating Customer Value

Many firms are now more carefully defining the financial value of prospective and actual customers and devising marketing programs to optimize that value. Customer–brand relationships are the foundation of brand resonance and building a strong brand. Marketers have long recognized the importance of adopting a strong consumer and customer orientation. The customer-based brand equity concept certainly puts that notion front and center, making it clear that the power of a brand resides in the minds of consumers and customers.

Too many firms, however, still find themselves paying the price for lacking a customer focus. Even the biggest firms can stumble.

VOLKSWAGEN

After a remarkable revival in the 1990s when it enjoyed 50 percent growth for seven straight years, Volkswagen AG did not fare well around the turn of the century. By 2005, the company was experiencing stagnant sales and losing money in its critical U.S. market. The culprit? According to VW CEO Bernd Pischetsrieder, "The biggest failure in Volkswagen is too little customer focus." In his view, the company was paying too much attention to technology and features that he felt customers didn't necessarily want to pay for. According to Pischetsrieder, "The first question is, how does it help the customer and will the customer pay for it? When we have a test drive, the question is not whether I like it. It's will the customer pay for it? Or will the customer not even notice it?" As an example of its new reemphasis on the consumer, VW changed the design of the 2011 Jetta it sold in the United States to better reflect U.S. preferences (and bigger bodies). Greater leg and trunk room and larger cup holders were added and costs savings were found to make it more affordable versus its Japanese import competitors.[46]

Volkswagen is not alone in recognizing the financial value of customer experiences. Many firms are now more carefully defining the financial value of prospective and actual customers and devising marketing programs to optimize that value.

Customer Equity

Many firms have introduced customer relationship marketing programs to improve customer interactions. Some marketing observers encourage firms to formally define and manage the value of their customers. The concept of customer equity can be useful in that regard. Although we can define customer equity in different ways, one definition calls it "the sum of lifetime values of all customers."[47] Customer lifetime value (CLV) is affected by revenue and by the cost of customer acquisition, retention, and cross-selling. Several different concepts and approaches have been put forth that are relevant to the topic of customer equity. Let's look at a few.

Blattberg and Colleagues. Blattberg and Deighton have defined customer equity as the optimal balance between what marketers spend on customer acquisition and what they spend on customer retention.[48] They calculated customer equity as follows:

> We first measure each customer's expected contribution toward offsetting the company's fixed costs over the expected life of that customer. Then we discount the expected contributions to a net present value at the company's target rate of return for marketing investments. Finally, we add together the discounted, expected contributions of all current contributions.

The authors offer the following observation:

> Ultimately, we contend that the appropriate question for judging new products, new programs, and new customer-service initiatives should not be, Will it attract new customers? or, Will it increase our retention rates? but rather, Will it grow our customer equity? The goal of maximizing customer equity by balancing acquisition and retention efforts properly should serve as the star by which a company steers its entire marketing program.

Blattberg and Deighton offer eight guidelines as a means of maximizing customer equity:

1. Invest in highest-value customers first.
2. Transform product management into customer management.
3. Consider how add-on sales and cross-selling can increase customer equity.
4. Look for ways to reduce acquisition costs.
5. Track customer equity gains and losses against marketing programs.
6. Relate branding to customer equity.
7. Monitor the intrinsic retainability of your customers.
8. Consider writing separate marketing plans—or even building two marketing organizations—for acquisition and retention efforts.

Rust, Zeithaml, and Lemon. Rust, Zeithaml, and Lemon define customer equity as the discounted lifetime values of a firm's customer base.[49] According to their view, customer equity is made up of three components and key drivers:

- *Value equity:* Customers' objective assessment of the utility of a brand based on perceptions of what is given up for what is received. Three drivers of value equity are quality, price, and convenience.
- *Brand equity:* Customers' subjective and intangible assessment of the brand, above and beyond its objectively perceived value. Three key drivers of brand equity are customer brand awareness, customer brand attitudes, and customer perception of brand ethics.
- *Relationship equity:* Customers' tendency to stick with the brand, above and beyond objective and subjective assessments of the brand. Four key drivers of relationship equity are loyalty programs, special recognition and treatment programs, community-building programs, and knowledge-building programs.

Note that this definition of brand equity differs from the customer-based brand equity definition proposed in this text, which puts the focus on the beneficial differential response to marketing activity that strong brands produce.

These authors propose that the three components of customer equity vary in importance by company and industry. For example, they suggest that brand equity will matter more with low-involvement purchases involving simple decision processes (like facial tissues), when the product is highly visible to others, when experiences associated with the product can be passed from one individual or generation to the next, or when it is difficult to evaluate the quality of a product or service prior to consumption. On the other hand, value equity will be more important in business-to-business settings, whereas retention equity will be more important for companies that sell a variety of products and services to the same customer.

Rust and colleagues advocate customer-centered brand management to firms with the following directives that, they maintain, go against current management convention:

1. Make brand decisions subservient to decisions about customer relationships.
2. Build brands around customer segments, not the other way around.
3. Make your brands as narrow as possible.
4. Plan brand extensions based on customer needs, not component similarities.
5. Develop the capability and the mind-set to hand off customers to other brands in the company.
6. Take no heroic measures to try to save ineffective brands.
7. Change how you measure brand equity to make individual-level calculations.

Kumar and Colleagues.   In a series of studies, Kumar and his colleagues explore a number of questions concerning customer lifetime value and how firms should allocate their marketing spending to customer acquisition and retention efforts.[50] The authors show that marketing contacts across various channels influence CLV nonlinearly. Customers who are selected on the basis of their lifetime value provide higher profits in future periods than do customers selected on the basis of several other customer-based metrics. Kumar and his colleagues show how each customer varies in his or her lifetime value to a firm, and how customer lifetime value computations require different approaches depending on the business application. They also demonstrate how their framework, which incorporates projected profitability of customers in the computation of lifetime duration, can be superior to traditional methods such as the recency, frequency, and monetary value framework and past customer value.

Relationship of Customer Equity to Brand Equity.   Brand equity management can be related to customer equity management in different ways. One way to reconcile the two points of view is to think of a matrix where all the brands and sub-brands and variants that a company offers are rows, and all the different customer segments or individual customers that purchase those brands are columns (see Figure 3-7). Effective brand and customer management would necessarily take into account both the rows and the columns to arrive at optimal marketing solutions.

Differences Between the Two Points of View.   As they have been developed conceptually and put into practice, however, the two perspectives tend to emphasize different aspects (see Figure 3-8). The customer equity perspective puts much focus on the bottom-line financial value created by customers. Its clear benefit is the quantifiable measures of financial performance it provides. In its calculations, however, the customer equity perspective largely ignores some of the important advantages of creating a strong brand, such as the ability of a strong brand to attract higher quality employees, elicit stronger support from channel and supply chain partners, create growth opportunities through line and category extensions and licensing, and so on.

The customer equity perspective also tends to be less prescriptive about specific marketing activities beyond general recommendations toward customer acquisition, retention, and cross-selling. The customer equity perspective does not always fully account for competitive response

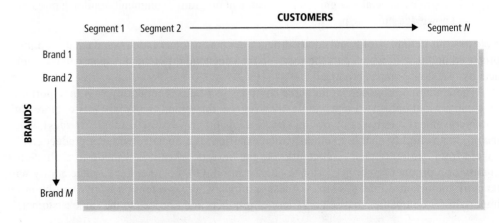

FIGURE 3-7

Brand and Customer Management

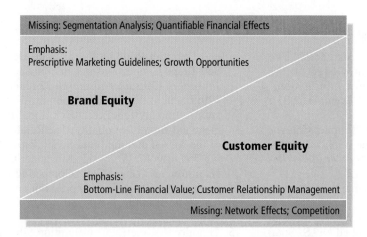

Missing: Segmentation Analysis; Quantifiable Financial Effects

Emphasis:
Prescriptive Marketing Guidelines; Growth Opportunities

Brand Equity

Customer Equity

Emphasis:
Bottom-Line Financial Value; Customer Relationship Management

Missing: Network Effects; Competition

FIGURE 3-8

Brand Equity vs.
Customer Equity

and the resulting moves and countermoves, nor does it fully account for social network effects, word of mouth, and customer-to-customer recommendations.

Thus, customer equity approaches can overlook the "option value" of brands and their potential impact on revenues and costs beyond the current marketing environment. Brand equity, on the other hand, tends to put more emphasis on strategic issues in managing brands and how marketing programs can be designed to create and leverage brand awareness and image with customers. It provides much practical guidance for specific marketing activities.

With a focus on brands, however, managers do not always develop detailed customer analyses in terms of the brand equity they achieve with specific consumers or groups of consumers and the resulting long-term profitability that is created. Brand equity approaches could benefit from sharper segmentation schemes.

Reconciling the Two Points of View. There is no question that customer equity and brand equity are related. In theory, both approaches can be expanded to incorporate the other point of view and they are clearly inextricably linked. Customers drive the success of brands, but brands are the necessary touchpoint that firms have to connect with their customers. Customer-based brand equity maintains that brands create value by eliciting differential customer response to marketing activities. The higher price premiums and increased levels of loyalty engendered by brands generate incremental cash flows.

Many of the actions that will increase brand equity will increase customer equity and vice versa. In practice, customer equity and brand equity are complementary notions in that they tend to emphasize different considerations. Brand equity tends to put more emphasis on the "front end" of marketing programs and intangible value potentially created by marketing programs; customer equity tends to put more emphasis on the "back end" of marketing programs and the realized value of marketing activities in terms of revenue.

The two concepts go hand in hand: customers need and value brands, but a brand ultimately is only as good as the customers it attracts. As evidence of this duality, consider the role of the retailer as "middleman" between firms and consumers. Retailers clearly recognize the importance of both brands and customers. A retailer chooses to sell those brands that are the best "bait" for those customers it wants to attract. Retailers essentially assemble brand portfolios to establish a profitable customer portfolio. Manufacturers make similar decisions, developing brand portfolios and hierarchies to maximize their customer franchises.

But effective brand management is critical, and it is a mistake to ignore its important role in developing long-term profit streams for firms. Some marketing observers have perhaps minimized the challenge and value of strong brands to overly emphasize the customer equity perspective, for example, maintaining that "our attitude should be that brands come and go—but customers . . . must remain."[51] Yet, that statement can easily be taken to the logical, but opposite, conclusion: "Through the years, customers may come and go, but strong brands will endure." Perhaps the main point is that both are really crucial, and the two perspectives can help improve the marketing success of a firm. The customer-based brand equity concept is an attempt to do just that.

Notes

1. Elizabeth Cowley and Andrew A. Mitchell, "The Moderating Effect of Product Knowledge on the Learning and Organization of Product Information," *Journal of Consumer Research* 30 (December 2003): 443–454.

2. Mita Sujan and Christine Dekleva, "Product Categorization and Inference Making: Some Implications for Comparative Advertising," *Journal of Consumer Research* 14 (December 1987): 372–378.

3. "For H&R Block's CMO, It's Tax Time Year-Round," *Brandweek*, 23 August 2009.

4. "Campbell Launches 'It's Amazing What Soup Can Do' Ad Campaign to Promote Campbell's U.S. Soup Brands," *Business Wire*, 7 September 2010; Al Lewis, "Soup's Suffering Sales," *Wall Street Journal*, 12 September 2010; Elaine Wong, "Campbell Gets Happy in 100 Mil. Push," *Brandweek*, 7 September 2010.

5. Chip Heath and Dan Heath, *Made to Stick: Why Some Ideas Survive and Others Die* (New York: Random House, 2007); Matthew Boyle, "The Accidental Hero," *Businessweek*, 16 November 2009, 58–61.

6. David Garvin, "Product Quality: An Important Strategic Weapon," *Business Horizons* 27 (May–June 1984): 40–43; Philip Kotler and Kevin Lane Keller, *Marketing Management*, 14th ed. (Upper Saddle River, NJ: Prentice Hall, 2012).

7. Robert C. Blattberg and Kenneth J. Wisniewski, "Price-Induced Patterns of Competition," *Marketing Science* 8 (Fall 1989): 291–309; Raj Sethuraman and V. Srinivasan, "The Asymmetric Share Effect: An Empirical Generalization on Cross-Price Effects," *Journal of Marketing Research* 39 (August 2002): 379–386.

8. Bianca Grohmann, "Gender Dimensions of Brand Personality," *Journal of Marketing Research* 46 (February 2009): 105–119.

9. Joseph T. Plummer, "How Personality Makes a Difference," *Journal of Advertising Research* 24 (December 1984/January 1985): 27–31.

10. See Jennifer Aaker, "Dimensions of Brand Personality," *Journal of Marketing Research* 34 (August 1997): 347–357.

11. Jennifer Aaker, Kathleen Vohs, and Cassie Mogilner, "Nonprofits Are Seen as Warm and For-Profits as Competent: Firm Stereotypes Matter," *Journal of Consumer Research* 37 (August 2010): 277–291.

12. Aaker, "Dimensions of Brand Personality"; Susan Fournier, "Consumers and Their Brands: Developing Relationship Theory in Consumer Research," *Journal of Consumer Research* 24, no. 3 (1997): 343–373.

13. Gita Venkataramani Johar, Jaideep Sengupta, and Jennifer L. Aaker, "Two Roads to Updating Brand Personality Impressions: Trait Versus Evaluative Inferencing," *Journal of Marketing Research* 42 (November 2005): 458–469; see also Alokparna Basu Monga and Loraine Lau-Gesk, "Blending Cobrand Personalities: An Examination of the Complex Self," *Journal of Marketing Research* 44 (August 2007): 389–400.

14. M. Joseph Sirgy, "Self Concept in Consumer Behavior: A Critical Review," *Journal of Consumer Research* 9 (December 1982): 287–300; Lan Nguyen Chaplin and Deborah Roedder John, "The Development of Self-Brand Connections in Children and Adolescents," *Journal of Consumer Research* 32 (June 2005): 119–129; Lucia Malär, Harley Krohmer, Wayne D. Hoyer, and Bettina Nyffenegger, "Emotional Brand Attachment and Brand Personality: The Relative Importance of the Actual and the Ideal Self," *Journal of Marketing* 75 (July 2011): 35–52; Alexander Chernev, Ryan Hamilton, and David Gal, "Competing for Consumer Identity: Limits to Self-Expression and the Perils of Lifestyle Branding," *Journal of Marketing* 75 (May 2011): 66–82.

15. Timothy R. Graeff, "Consumption Situations and the Effects of Brand Image on Consumers' Brand Evaluations," *Psychology & Marketing* 14, no. 1 (1997): 49–70; Timothy R. Graeff, "Image Congruence Effects on Product Evaluations: The Role of Self-Monitoring and Public/Private Consumption," *Psychology & Marketing* 13, no. 5 (1996): 481–499. See also, Ji Kyung Park and Deborah Roedder John, "Got to Get You into My Life: Do Brand Personalities Rub Off on Consumers?," *Journal of Consumer Research* 37 (December 2010): 655–669.

16. Jennifer L. Aaker, "The Malleable Self: The Role of Self-Expression in Persuasion," *Journal of Marketing Research* 36, no. 2 (1999): 45–57. See also, Vanitha Swaminathan, Karen Stilley, and Rohini Ahluwalia, "When Brand Personality Matters: The Moderating Role of Attachment Styles," *Journal of Consumer Research* 35 (April 2009): 985–1002.

17. David Kiley, "How Chrysler Chief Olivier Francois Is Selling Detroit," *Advertising Age*, 21 February 2011; Bill Vlasic, "A Resurgent Chrysler Says It Is Here to Stay," *New York Times*, 10 January 2011; David Welch, "Can Sex and Saucy Ads Sell Chryslers?," *Bloomberg Businessweek*, 15 March 2010, 56–57; Doron Levin, "The 300: Can Chrysler Really Steal Bimmer and Caddy Buyers?," www.cnnmoney.com, 4 February 2011; Joann Muller, "Can Fiat's First Lady Make It in America?," *Forbes*, 28 February 2011, 84–87.

18. Northern Trust, "Top Performers: World's Most Admired Companies," *Fortune*, 16 August 2010, 16.

19. Douglas B. Holt, *How Brands Become Icons* (Cambridge, MA: Harvard Business School Press, 2004). Holt has a number of other thought-provoking pieces, including "Why Do Brands Cause Trouble? A Dialectical Theory of Consumer Culture and Branding," *Journal of Consumer Research* 29 (June 2002): 70–90; Douglas B. Holt and Craig J. Thompson, "Man-of-Action Heroes: The Pursuit of Heroic Masculinity in Everyday Consumption," *Journal of Consumer Research* 31 (September 2004): 425–440.

20. William L. Wilkie, *Consumer Behavior*, 3rd ed. (New York: John Wiley & Sons, 1994).

21. http://www.harrisinteractive.com/Products/EquiTrend.aspx, accessed December 9, 2011.

22. For an insightful examination of credibility and the related concept of truth, see Lynn Upshaw, *Truth: The New Rules for Marketing in a Skeptical World* (New York: AMACOM, 2007).

23. Elaine Wong, "FedEx Rolls with Changes in Global Campaign," *Brandweek*, 29 October 2009; "CPG Brands Top Most Trusted List," *Brandweek*, 22 February 2010.

24. Alan M. Webber, "Trust in the Future," *Fast Company*, September 2000, 210–220.

25. Kevin Roberts, *Lovemarks: The Future Beyond Brands* (New York: Powerhouse Books, 2004).

26. For seminal research, see William D. Wells, "How Advertising Works," unpublished paper, 1980; Christopher P. Puto and William D. Wells, "Informational and Transformational Advertising: The Differential Effects of Time," in *Advances in Consumer Research*, Vol. 11, ed. Thomas C. Kinnear (Ann Arbor, MI: Association for Consumer Research, 1983), 638–643; Stephen J. Hoch and John Deighton, "Managing What Consumers Learn from Experience," *Journal of Marketing* 53 (April 1989): 1–20; for a current application, see also Gillian Naylor, Susan Bardi Kleiser, Julie Baker, and Eric Yorkston, "Using Transformational Appeals to Enhance the Retail Experience," *Journal of Retailing* 84 (April 2008): 49–57.

27. Elizabeth Olson, "Corona Light Sets Sights on a Younger Party Crowd," *New York Times*, 1 August 2010.

28. "Eva Zeigler Assumes Top Role for W Hotels," *Business Wire*, 13 February 2009; Belinda Lanks, "W Hotels Goes Local," *Metropolis Magazine*, April 2010; "Starwood Hotels & Resorts Presents Strategy, Brand Positioning and Outlook to Media and Investors," *Business Wire*, 16 May 2006.

29. Lynn R. Kahle, Basil Poulos, and Ajay Sukhdial, "Changes in Social Values in the United States During the Past Decade," *Journal of Advertising Research* (February/March 1988): 35–41.

30. For a stimulating and comprehensive set of readings, see Deborah J. MacInnis, C. Whan Park, Joseph R. Priester, eds. *Handbook of Brand Relationships* (Armonk, NY: M. E. Sharpe, 2009).

31. Greg Farrell, "Marketers Put a Price on Your Life," *USA Today*, 7 July 1999, 3B.

32. Arjun Chaudhuri and Morris B. Holbrook, "The Chain of Effects from Brand Trust and Brand Affect to Brand Performance: The Role of Brand Loyalty," *Journal of Marketing* 65 (April 2001): 81–93.

33. Thomas A. Stewart, "A Satisfied Customer Is Not Enough," *Fortune*, 21 July 1997, 112–113.

34. Thomas O. Jones and W. Earl Sasser Jr. "Why Satisfied Customers Defect," *Harvard Business Review* (November–December 1995): 88–99.

35. Fredrick Reichheld, *The Loyalty Effect: The Hidden Force Behind Growth, Profits, and Lasting Value* (Boston: Harvard Business School Press, 1996).

36. James H. McAlexander, John W. Schouten, and Harold F. Koenig, "Building Brand Community," *Journal of Marketing* 66 (January 2002): 38–54; Albert Muniz and Thomas O'Guinn, "Brand Community," *Journal of Consumer Research* 27 (March 2001): 412–432.

37. Gil McWilliam, "Building Stronger Brands Through Online Communities," *MIT Sloan Management Review* 41, no. 3 (Spring 2000): 43–54.

38. Rene Algesheimer, Utpal M. Dholakia, and Andreas Hermann, "The Social Influence of Brand Community: Evidence from European Car Clubs," *Journal of Marketing* 69 (July 2005): 19–34.

39. Rob Walker, *Buying In* (New York: Random House, 2008).

40. Chris Reiter, "For Luxury Automakers, Selling Toys Is No Game," *Bloomberg Businessweek*, 29 November–5 December 2010, 26–28; Markus Seidel, "BMW Uses Lifestyle Products as a Strategic Differentiating Factor in the Automotive Industry," *PDMA Visions*, July 2004, 24–25; http://www.shopbmwusa.com.

41. Nikki Hopewell, "Generating Brand Passion," *Marketing News*, 15 May 2005, 10.

42. "Creative: Inside Priceless MasterCard Moments," *Adweek*, 12 April 1999; Marc De Swaan Arons, "MasterCard—Finding a Compelling Global Positioning, www.allaboutbranding.com, 6 August 2005; www.effie.org.

43. "Shutterfly Learns How to Build a More Powerful Connection Between Its Online Brand and Consumers," KN Case Study, www.knowledgenetworks.com, Fall/Winter 2010; Mansi Dutta and S. John Tilak, "Embracing Social Media, Photo Sites Stay in the Game," Thomson Reuters, 3 September 2009; www.shutterfly.com; Andrew Murr, "Shutterfly: It's Picture Perfect," *Newsweek*, 23 May 2008.

44. Kevin Lane Keller and Don Lehmann, "How Do Brands Create Value?" *Marketing Management* (May/June 2003): 26–31. See also R. K. Srivastava, T. A. Shervani, and L. Fahey, "Market-Based Assets and Shareholder Value," *Journal of Marketing* 62, no. 1 (1998): 2–18; and M. J. Epstein and R. A. Westbrook, "Linking Actions to Profits in Strategic Decision Making," *MIT Sloan Management Review* (Spring 2001): 39–49. In terms of related empirical insights, see Manoj K. Agrawal and Vithala Rao, "An Empirical Comparison of Consumer-Based Measures of Brand Equity," *Marketing Letters* 7, no. 3 (1996): 237–247; and Walfried Lassar, Banwari Mittal, and Arun Sharma, "Measuring Customer-Based Brand Equity," *Journal of Consumer Marketing* 12, no. 4 (1995): 11–19.

45. Thomas J. Madden, Frank Fehle, and Susan Fournier, "Brands Matter: An Empirical Demonstration of the Creation of Shareholder Value Through Branding" *Journal of the Academy of Marketing Science, 2006.*

46. Joseph B. White and Stephen Power, "VW Chief Confronts Corporate Culture," *Wall Street Journal*, 19 September 2005, B2; Vanessa Fuhrmans, "Volkswagen Aims at Fast Lane in U.S.," *Wall Street Journal*, October 5, 2010; David Kiley, "Is VW Ready to Retake America?," *AOL Autos*, 12 August 2010.

47. Roland T. Rust, Valarie A. Zeithamal, and Katherine Lemon, "Customer-Centered Brand Management," *Harvard Business Review* (September 2004), 110–118.

48. Robert C. Blattberg and John Deighton, "Manage Marketing by the Customer Equity Test," *Harvard Business Review* (July–August 1996). See also Robert C. Blattberg, Gary Getz, and Jacquelyn S. Thomas, *Customer Equity: Building and Managing Relationships as Valuable Assets* (Boston, MA: Harvard Business School Press, 2001); Robert Blattberg and Jacquelyn

Thomas, "Valuing, Analyzing, and Managing the Marketing Function Using Customer Equity Principles," in *Kellogg on Marketing*, ed. Dawn Iacobucci (New York, John Wiley & Sons, 2001).

49. Roland T. Rust, Valarie A. Zeithaml, and Katherine Lemon, *Driving Customer Equity* (New York: Free Press, 2000); Roland T. Rust, Valarie A. Zeithaml, and Katherine Lemon, "Customer-Centered Brand Management," *Harvard Business Review* (September 2004), 110–118.

50. W. Reinartz, J. Thomas, and V. Kumar, "Balancing Acquisition and Retention Resources to Maximize Profitability," *Journal of Marketing* 69 (January 2005): 63–79; R. Venkatesan and V. Kumar, "A Customer Lifetime Value Framework for Customer Selections and Resource Allocation Strategy," *Journal of Marketing* 68, no. 4 (October 2004): 106–125; V. Kumar, G. Ramani, and T. Bohling, "Customer Lifetime Value Approaches and Best Practice Applications," *Journal of Interactive Marketing* 18, no. 3 (Summer 2004): 60–72; J. Thomas, W. Reinartz, and V. Kumar, "Getting the Most Out of All Your Customers," *Harvard Business Review* (July–August 2004): 116–123; W. Reinartz and V. Kumar, "The Impact of Customer Relationship Characteristics on Profitable Lifetime Duration," *Journal of Marketing* 67, no. 1 (2003): 77–99.

51. Roland T. Rust, Valarie A. Zeithamal, and Katherine Lemon, "Customer-Centered Brand Management," *Harvard Business Review* (September 2004), 110–118.

Choosing Brand Elements to Build Brand Equity

Learning Objectives

After reading this chapter, you should be able to

1. Identify the different types of brand elements.
2. List the general criteria for choosing brand elements.
3. Describe key tactics in choosing different brand elements.
4. Explain the rationale for "mixing and matching" brand elements.
5. Highlight some of the legal issues surrounding brand elements.

A brand symbol like the Energizer Bunny can reinforce key brand associations and be used in a variety of different communication applications.

Source: Paul Martinka/ Polaris/Newscom

Preview

Brand elements, sometimes called brand identities, are those trademarkable devices that serve to identify and differentiate the brand. The main ones are brand names, URLs, logos, symbols, characters, spokespeople, slogans, jingles, packages, and signage. The customer-based brand equity model suggests that marketers should choose brand elements to enhance brand awareness; facilitate the formation of strong, favorable, and unique brand associations; or elicit positive brand judgments and feelings. The test of the brand-building ability of a brand element is what consumers would think or feel about the product *if they knew only that particular brand element* and not anything else about the product and how else it would be branded or marketed. A brand element that provides a positive contribution to brand equity conveys or implies certain valued associations or responses.

This chapter considers how marketers choose brand elements to build brand equity. After describing the general criteria for choosing brand elements, we consider specific tactical issues for each of the different types of brand elements and finish by discussing how to choose the best brand elements to build brand equity. Brand Focus 4.0 at the end of the chapter highlights some legal issues for branding.

CRITERIA FOR CHOOSING BRAND ELEMENTS

In general, there are six criteria for brand elements (with more specific subchoices for each, as shown in Figure 4-1):

1. Memorable
2. Meaningful
3. Likable
4. Transferable
5. Adaptable
6. Protectable

1. **Memorable**
   Easily recognized
   Easily recalled

2. **Meaningful**
   Descriptive
   Persuasive

3. **Likable**
   Fun and interesting
   Rich visual and verbal imagery
   Aesthetically pleasing

4. **Transferable**
   Within and across product categories
   Across geographic boundaries and cultures

5. **Adaptable**
   Flexible
   Updatable

6. **Protectable**
   Legally
   Competitively

FIGURE 4-1

Criteria for Choosing
Brand Elements

The first three criteria—memorability, meaningfulness, and likability—are the marketer's offensive strategy and build brand equity. The latter three, however, play a defensive role for leveraging and maintaining brand equity in the face of different opportunities and constraints. Let's consider each of these general criteria.

Memorability

A necessary condition for building brand equity is achieving a high level of brand awareness. Brand elements that promote that goal are inherently memorable and attention-getting and therefore facilitate recall or recognition in purchase or consumption settings. For example, a brand of propane gas cylinders named Blue Rhino featuring a powder-blue animal mascot with a distinctive yellow flame is likely to stick in the minds of consumers.

Meaningfulness

Brand elements may take on all kinds of meaning, with either descriptive or persuasive content. We saw in Chapter 1 that brand names can be based on people, places, animals or birds, or other things or objects. Two particularly important criteria are how well the brand element conveys the following:

- *General information about the function of the product or service:* Does the brand element have descriptive meaning and suggest something about the product category, the needs satisfied or benefits supplied? How likely is it that a consumer could correctly identify the product category for the brand based on any one brand element? Does the brand element seem credible in the product category?
- *Specific information about particular attributes and benefits of the brand:* Does the brand element have persuasive meaning and suggest something about the particular kind of product, or its key points-of-difference attributes or benefits? Does it suggest something about some aspect of the product performance or the type of person who might use the brand?

The first dimension is an important determinant of brand awareness and salience; the second, of brand image and positioning.

Likability

Independent of its memorability and meaningfulness, do customers find the brand element aesthetically appealing?[1] Is it likable visually, verbally, and in other ways? Brand elements can be rich in imagery and inherently fun and interesting, even if not always directly related to the product.

A memorable, meaningful, and likable set of brand elements offers many advantages because consumers often do not examine much information in making product decisions. Descriptive and persuasive elements reduce the burden on marketing communications to build awareness and link brand associations and equity, especially when few other product-related associations exist. Often, the less concrete the possible product benefits are, the more important is the creative potential of the brand name and other brand elements to capture intangible characteristics of a brand.

M&M'S® BRAND CHOCOLATE CANDIES

A classic example of developing a powerful set of brand elements is Hershey's candy-colored chocolate, M&M'S®. One the most famous slogans of all time—"Melts in Your Mouth, Not in Your Hand"—reveals the key product benefit. Mars introduced its first "spokes-character," Red, in 1954, 13 years after the candy-coated chocolates debuted, followed by Yellow, a nut-filled mascot, when the company launched M&M'S® Peanut Candies later that year. Over the last 50-plus years, M&M'S® has introduced three more spokes-candies to represent new flavors, colors, and themes, each with a distinct personality. Green, introduced in 1997, is the company's first female spokes-candy. Recognizing that MM means 2000 in Roman numerals, in early 1998, the M&M'S® characters proclaimed themselves the "Official Spokescandies of the New Millennium." In late 1997, Mars opened "M&M'S® World"—the brand's own colorful retail store on the Las Vegas strip, featuring one-of-a-kind branded merchandise ranging from T-shirts and designer jackets to designer dresses, jewelry, and furniture.[2]

The hugely popular M&M® "spokes-characters" have given the brand valuable personality and imagery.

Source: M&M'S® and the M&M'S® Characters are registered trademarks of Mars, Incorporated and its affiliates. This trademarks are used with permission. Mars, Incorporated is not associated with Pearson Education, Inc. The M&M'S® advertisement is printed with permission of Mars, Incorporated.

Transferability

Transferability measures the extent to which the brand element adds to the brand equity for new products or in new markets for the brand. There are several aspects to this criterion.

First, how useful is the brand element for line or category extensions? In general, the less specific the name, the more easily it can be transferred across categories. For example, Amazon connotes a massive South American river and therefore as a brand can be appropriate for a variety of different types of products. Books "R" Us obviously would not have afforded the same flexibility if Amazon had chosen that name to describe its original line of business.

Second, to what extent does the brand element add to brand equity across geographic boundaries and market segments? To a large extent this depends on the cultural content and linguistic qualities of the brand element. One of the main advantages of nonmeaningful, synthetic names like Exxon is that they transfer well into other languages.

The difficulties or mistakes that even top marketers have encountered in translating their brand names, slogans, and packages into other languages and cultures over the years have become legendary. As an example, Microsoft was challenged when launching its Vista operating system in Latvia, because the name means "chicken" or "frumpy woman" in the local language.[3] Figure 4-2 includes some of the more notorious mishaps.[4] To avoid such complications, companies must review all their brand elements for cultural meaning before introducing the brand into a new market.

Adaptability

The fifth consideration for brand elements is their adaptability over time. Because of changes in consumer values and opinions, or simply because of a need to remain contemporary, most brand elements must be updated. The more adaptable and flexible the brand element, the easier it is to update it. For example, logos and characters can be given a new look or a new design to make them appear more modern and relevant.

Although it can be difficult to judge the accuracy of some reports of past marketing failures, here are some of the more widely cited global branding failures reported over the years.

1. When Braniff translated a slogan touting its upholstery, "Fly in leather," it came out in Spanish as "Fly naked."

2. Coors put its slogan, "Turn it loose," into Spanish, where it was read as "Suffer from diarrhea."

3. Chicken magnate Frank Perdue's line, "It takes a tough man to make a tender chicken," sounds much more interesting in Spanish: "It takes a sexually stimulated man to make a chicken affectionate."

4. When Pepsi started marketing its products in China, it translated the slogan "Pepsi Brings You Back to Life" pretty literally. In Chinese it really meant, "Pepsi Brings Your Ancestors Back from the Grave."

5. Clairol introduced the "Mist Stick," a curling iron, into Germany only to find out that mist is slang for manure in German.

6. Japan's Mitsubishi Motors had to rename its Pajero model in Spanish-speaking countries because the term related to masturbation.

7. Toyota Motor's MR2 model dropped the number in France because the combination sounded like a French swearword.

FIGURE 4-2
Global Branding Mishaps

MICHELIN MAN

Michelin recently launched a newer, slimmer version of its famous tubby Michelin Man (whose real name is Bibendum) to mark his 100th year. A company press release notes, "Thinner and smiling, Bibendum will look like the leader he is, with an open and reassuring manner." Michelin has used the character to promote its brand values of research, safety, and environmentalism through the years. In 2000, Bibendum was voted the "greatest logo in history" in a competition sponsored by the *Financial Times*. In a 2009 global campaign that featured the character as a hero, the Michelin Man—which has been the exclusive focus of Michelin advertising since 2001—moved from a "more passive endorser to a more active problem solver." Reinforced by the slogan "The Right Tire Changes Everything," the new ad campaign emphasized the role tires play people's everyday lives.[5]

The Michelin Man—whose actual name is Bibendum—has served as the centerpiece of the tire brand's advertising for years.
Source: Michelin, North America

THE SCIENCE OF BRANDING 4-1

Counterfeit Business Is Booming

From Calloway golf clubs to Louis Vuitton handbags, counterfeit versions of well-known brands are everywhere. The current size of the counterfeit market is estimated to be $600 billion, representing costs of $200–$250 billion annually to U.S. businesses. The fakes are soaking up profits faster than multinationals can squash counterfeiting operations, and they're getting tougher and tougher to distinguish from the real thing. The difference can be as subtle as lesser-quality leather in a purse or fake batteries inside a cell phone. And counterfeiters can produce fakes cheaply by cutting corners on safety and quality, as well as by avoiding paying for marketing, R&D, or advertising.

It's not just luxury items and consumer electronics that are being copied. The World Health Organization says up to 10 percent of medicines worldwide are counterfeited. Those drugs not only purloin pharmaceutical industry profits but also present a danger to anyone who takes them because they are manufactured under inadequate safety controls.

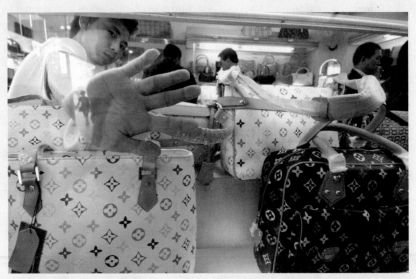

A popular target for counterfeiters who turn out fakes like these, Louis Vuitton uses legal means to vigorously defend its trademarks.
Source: Iain Masterton/Alamy

Counterfeiting has become increasingly sophisticated and pervasive. To avoid being detected, counterfeiters are knocking off smaller brands that don't have the resources to fight back, focusing on fewer high-end brands given the recent economic downturn, and increasing prices on fake goods sold over the Web to counter consumer suspicions.

The U.S. Trade Representative's office now publishes an annual "notorious markets" list of the worst sites—physical and online—for piracy and counterfeiting. These days, 81 percent of counterfeit goods in the United States come from China. Other sources are Russia, Ukraine, Pakistan, India, Mexico, and several countries in Southeast Asia (Philippines, Thailand, and Indonesia) and Latin America (Ecuador, Paraguay, and Argentina).

The operations are financed by such varied sources as Middle East businessmen who invest in facilities in Asian countries for export, local Chinese entrepreneurs, and criminal networks. Online auction retailers such as eBay and China's Baidu have become unintentional middleman in the market and have been successfully sued for millions by luxury makers such as LVMH (which makes Louis Vuitton, among other brands).

The replication process has also speeded up as counterfeiters have honed their engineering skills and increased their speed. Chinese factories can now copy a new model of a golf club in less than a week. And executives at a variety of companies say counterfeiters have no trouble copying holograms and other security devices intended to distinguish real products from fakes.

Producing counterfeit goods is as profitable as trading in illegal drugs but does not carry the same risk. In many countries, convicted counterfeiters get off with a fine of a few thousand dollars. Chinese authorities have ignored the problem for years, mostly because it did not hurt Chinese industries. But as the country's corporate interests grow and Chinese companies start getting hurt by the counterfeit industry, experts say the Chinese government will be more cooperative. They believe China is the key to stemming the counterfeit trade.

Some companies have decided to target the end users of knockoff products, hoping manufacturers will eventually be forced to get a license and pay royalties. And some patent holders are beginning to get creative and target anyone on the supply chain who knowingly ignores counterfeit businesses. Louis Vuitton has partnered with New York City landlords to prevent the sale of counterfeit Louis Vuitton goods by tenants on notorious knockoff hot spot Canal Street. But because the business of counterfeiting thrives on globalization, experts say all many companies can do for now is hope to slow, not stop, the counterfeiters.

Interestingly, some provocative academic research shows that fake products are not uniformly bad for companies. Although some consumers may initially feel pleased at buying a fake handbag, for example, many ultimately realize the fake cannot replace the genuine item. While some who cannot afford to buy genuine luxury items may always buy fakes, other consumers will find that buying a counterfeit motivates them to later buy the real thing.

Sources: Julia Boorstin, "Louis Vuitton Tests a New Way to Fight the Faux," *Fortune*, 16 May 2005; Robert Klara, "The Fight Against Fakes," *Brandweek*, 27 June 2009; Stephanie Clifford, "Economic Indicator: Even Cheaper Knockoffs," *New York Times*, 31 July 2010; "U.S. Calls China's Baidu 'Notorious Market'," *Reuters*, 28 February 2011; Renée Richardson Gosline, "Rethinking Brand Contamination: How Consumers Maintain Distinction When Symbolic Boundaries Are Breached," working paper, MIT Sloan School of Management, 2009; Keith Wilcox, Hyeong Min Kim, and Sankar Sen, "Why Do Consumers Buy Counterfeit Luxury Brands?," *Journal of Marketing Research*, 46 (April 2009): 247–259; Young Jee Han, Joseph C Nunes, and Xavier Drèze, "Signaling Status with Luxury Goods: The Role of Brand Prominence," *Journal of Marketing* 74 (July 2010): 15–30; Katherine White and Jennifer J. Argo, "When Imitation Doesn't Flatter: The Role of Consumer Distinctiveness in Responses to Mimicry," *Journal of Consumer Research* 38 (December 2011): 667–680.

Protectability

The sixth and final general consideration is the extent to which the brand element is protectable—both in a legal and a competitive sense. Marketers should (1) choose brand elements that can be legally protected internationally, (2) formally register them with the appropriate legal bodies, and (3) vigorously defend trademarks from unauthorized competitive infringement. The necessity of legally protecting the brand is dramatized by the billions of dollars in losses in the United States alone from unauthorized use of patents, trademarks, and copyrights, as described in The Science of Branding 4-1.

Another consideration is whether the brand is competitively protectable. If a name, package, or other attribute is too easily copied, much of the uniqueness of the brand may disappear. For example, consider the once red-hot ice-beer category. Although Molson Ice was one of the early entries in the category, it quickly lost its pioneering advantage when Miller Ice and what later became Bud Ice were introduced. Marketers need to reduce the likelihood that competitors can create a derivative based on the product's own elements.

OPTIONS AND TACTICS FOR BRAND ELEMENTS

Consider the advantages of "Apple" as the name of a personal computer. Apple was a simple but well-known word that was distinctive in the product category—which helped develop brand awareness. The meaning of the name also gave the company a "friendly shine" and warm brand personality. It could also be reinforced visually with a logo that would transfer easily across geographic and cultural boundaries. Finally, the name could serve as a platform for sub-brands like the Macintosh, aiding the introduction of brand extensions. As Apple illustrates, a well-chosen brand name can make an appreciable contribution to the creation of brand equity.

What would an ideal brand element be like? Consider brand names—perhaps the most central of all brand elements. Ideally, a brand name would be easily remembered, highly suggestive of both the product class and the particular benefits that served as the basis of its positioning, inherently fun or interesting, rich with creative potential, transferable to a wide variety of product and geographic settings, enduring in meaning and relevant over time, and strongly protectable both legally and competitively.

Unfortunately, it is difficult to choose a brand name—or any brand element, for that matter—that satisfies all these criteria. The more meaningful the brand name, for example, the more difficult it may be to transfer it to new product categories or translate it to other cultures. This is one reason why it's preferable to have multiple brand elements. Let's look at the major considerations for each type of brand element.

Brand Names

The brand name is a fundamentally important choice because it often captures the central theme or key associations of a product in a very compact and economical fashion. Brand names can be an extremely effective shorthand means of communication.[6] Whereas an advertisement lasts half a minute and a sales call could run to hours, customers can notice the brand name and register its meaning or activate it in memory in just a few seconds.

Because it is so closely tied to the product in the minds of consumers, however, the brand name is also the most difficult element for marketers to change. So they systematically research them before making a choice. The days when Henry Ford II could name his new automobile the "Edsel" after the name of a family member seem to be long gone.

Is it difficult to come up with a brand name? Ira Bachrach, a well-known branding consultant, has noted that although there are 140,000 words in the English vocabulary, the average U.S. adult recognizes only 20,000; Bachrach's consulting company, NameLab, sticks to the 7,000 words that make up the vocabulary of most TV programs and commercials.

Although that may seem to allow a lot of choices, each year tens of thousands of new brands are registered as legal trademarks. In fact, arriving at a satisfactory brand name for a new product can be a painfully difficult and prolonged process. After realizing that most of the desirable brand names are already legally registered, many a frustrated executive has lamented that "all the good ones are taken."

In some ways, this difficulty should not be surprising. Any parent can probably sympathize with how hard it can be to choose a name for a child, as evidenced by the thousands of babies born without names each year because their parents have not decided on—or perhaps not agreed upon—a name yet. It is rare that naming a product can be as easy as it was for Ford when it introduced the Taurus automobile.

"Taurus" was the code name given to the car during its design stage because the chief engineer's and product manager's wives were both born under that astrological sign. As luck would have it, upon closer examination, the name turned out to have a number of desirable characteristics. When it was chosen as the actual name for the car, Ford saved thousands and thousands of dollars in additional research and consulting expenses.

Naming Guidelines.   Selecting a brand name for a new product is certainly an art and a science. Figure 4-3 displays the different types of possible brand names according to brand identity experts Lippincott. Like any brand element, brand names must be chosen with the six general criteria of memorability, meaningfulness, likability, transferability, adaptability, and protectability in mind.

Brand Awareness   Brand names that are simple and easy to pronounce or spell, familiar and meaningful, and different, distinctive, and unusual can obviously improve brand awareness.[7]

Simplicity and Ease of Pronunciation and Spelling.   Simplicity reduces the effort consumers have to make to comprehend and process the brand name. Short names often facilitate recall because they are easy to encode and store in memory—consider Aim toothpaste, Raid pest spray, Bold laundry detergent, Suave shampoo, Off insect repellent, Jif peanut butter, Ban deodorant, and Bic pens. Marketers can shorten longer names to make them easier to recall. For example, over the years Chevrolet cars have also become known as "Chevy," Budweiser beer has become "Bud," and Coca-Cola is also "Coke."[8]

Surname
   Dell, Siemens, Gillette

Descriptive
   American Online, Pizza Hut, General Motors

Invented
   Häagen-Dazs, Kodak, Xerox

Connotative
   Duracell, Humana, Infiniti

Bridge
   Westin, DaimlerChrysler, ExxonMobil

Arbitrary
   Apple, Yahoo!, Infiniti

FIGURE 4-3

Lippincott Brand Name Taxonomy

Source: http://www.lippincott.com/

To encourage word-of-mouth exposure that helps build strong memory links, marketers should also make brand names easy to pronounce. Also keep in mind that rather than risk the embarrassment of mispronouncing a difficult name like Hyundai automobiles, Shiseido cosmetics, or Façonnable clothing, consumers may just avoid pronouncing it altogether.

Brands with difficult-to-pronounce names have an uphill battle because the firm has to devote so much of its initial marketing effort to teaching consumers how to pronounce the name. Polish vodka Wyborowa (pronounced VEE-ba-ro-va) was supported by a print ad to help consumers pronounce the brand name—a key factor for success in the distilled spirits category, where little self-service exists and consumers usually need to ask for the brand in the store.[9]

Ideally, the brand name should have a clear, understandable, and unambiguous pronunciation and meaning. However, the way a brand is pronounced can affect its meaning, so consumers may take away different perceptions if ambiguous pronunciation results in different meanings. One research study showed that certain hypothetical products with brand names that were acceptable in both English and French, such as Vaner, Randal, and Massin, were perceived as more "hedonic" (providing pleasure) and were better liked when pronounced in French than in English.[10]

Pronunciation problems may arise from not conforming to linguistic rules. Although Honda chose the name "Acura" because it was associated with words connoting precision in several languages, it initially had some trouble with consumer pronunciation of the name (AK-yur-a) in the U.S. market, perhaps in part because the company chose not to use the phonetically simpler English spelling of Accura (with a double *c*).

To improve pronounceability and recallability, many marketers seek a desirable cadence and pleasant sound in their brand names.[11] For example, brand names may use alliteration (repetition of consonants, such as in Coleco), assonance (repetition of vowel sounds, such as in Ramada Inn), consonance (repetition of consonants with intervening vowel change, such as in Hamburger Helper), or rhythm (repetition of pattern of syllable stress, such as in Better Business Bureau). Some words employ onomatopoeia—words composed of syllables that when pronounced generate a sound strongly suggestive of the word's meaning, like Sizzler restaurants, Cap'n Crunch cereal, Ping golf clubs, and Schweppes carbonated beverages.

Familiarity and Meaningfulness.   The brand name should be familiar and meaningful so it can tap into existing knowledge structures. It can be concrete or abstract in meaning. Because the names of people, objects, birds, animals, and inanimate objects already exist in memory, consumers have to do less learning to understand their meanings as brand names.[12] Links form more easily, increasing memorability.[13] Thus, when a consumer sees an ad for the first time for a car called "Fiesta," the fact that the consumer already has the word stored in memory should make it easier to encode the product name and thus improve its recallability.

To help create strong brand-category links and aid brand recall, the brand name may also suggest the product or service category, as do JuicyJuice 100 percent fruit juices, Ticketron ticket selling service, and *Newsweek* weekly news magazine. Brand elements that are highly descriptive of the product category or its attribute and benefits can be quite restrictive, however.[14] For example, it may be difficult to introduce a soft drink extension for a brand called JuicyJuice!

Differentiated, Distinctive, and Unique.   Although choosing a simple, easy-to-pronounce, familiar, and meaningful brand name can improve recallability, to improve brand recognition, on the other hand, brand names should be different, distinctive, and unusual. As Chapter 2 noted, recognition depends on consumers' ability to discriminate between brands, and more complex brand names are more easily distinguished. Distinctive brand names can also make it easier for consumers to learn intrinsic product information.[15]

A brand name can be distinctive because it is inherently unique, or because it is unique in the context of other brands in the category.[16] Distinctive words may be seldom-used or atypical words for the product category, like Apple computers; unusual combinations of real words, like Toys"R"Us; or completely made-up words, like Cognos or Luxottica. Even made-up brand names, however, have to satisfy prevailing linguistic rules and conventions—for example, try to pronounce names without vowels such as Blfft, Xgpr, or Msdy!

FIGURE 4-4

Sample Suggestive
Brand Names

> ColorStay lipsticks
> Head & Shoulders shampoo
> Close-Up toothpaste
> SnackWell reduced fat snacks
> DieHard auto batteries
> Mop & Glo floor wax
> Lean Cuisine low-calorie frozen entrees
> Shake'n Bake chicken seasoning
> Sub-Zero refrigerators and freezers
> Cling-Free static buildup remover

Here too there are trade-offs. Even if a distinctive brand name is advantageous for brand recognition, it also has to be credible and desirable in the product category. A notable exception is Smuckers jelly, which has tried to turn the handicap of its distinctive—but potentially dislikable—name into a positive through its slogan, "With a Name Like Smucker's, It Has to Be Good!"

Brand Associations Because the brand name is a compact form of communication, the explicit and implicit meanings consumers extract from it are important. In naming a new peer-to-peer communication technology, the founders landed on the descriptive "Sky peer-to-peer" which they decided to shorten to Skyper. When the corresponding Web address Skyper.com was not available, they shortened it again to the much more user-friendly Skype.[17]

The brand name can be chosen to reinforce an important attribute or benefit association that makes up its product positioning (see Figure 4-4). Besides performance-related considerations, brand names can also communicate more abstract considerations as do names like Joy dishwashing liquid, Caress soap, and Obsession perfume. Consider the reasoning behind the name of Colgate's new mini toothbrush.

COLGATE WISP

Famed brand-identity firm Lexicon has developed some wildly successful brand names, such as BlackBerry, Dasani, Febreze, OnStar, Pentium, Scion, and Swiffer. To develop a name for a new disposable mini toothbrush from Colgate, the firm went through a careful development process. The center of the disposable toothbrush held a dab of special toothpaste that made rinsing unnecessary and brushing on the go possible. Deciding to focus on the lightness, softness, and gentleness of the product, Lexicon's global network of 70 linguists in 50 countries brainstormed metaphors and sounds that conveyed lightness. One name—Wisp—jumped out at company founder David Placek. Subsequent consumer research validated its positive connotations, and a new name was born.[18]

Colgate decided to call its new disposable mini-toothbrush Wisp because the name had positive connotations of lightness.

Source: Colgate-Palmolive Company

A descriptive brand name should make it easier to link the reinforced attribute or benefit.[19] Consumers will find it easier to believe that a laundry detergent "adds fresh scent" to clothes if it has a name like "Blossom" than if it's called something neutral like "Circle."[20] However, brand names that reinforce the initial positioning of a brand may make it harder to link new associations to the brand if it later has to be repositioned.[21] For example, if a laundry detergent named Blossom is positioned as "adding fresh scent," it may be more difficult to later reposition the product, if necessary, and add a new brand association that it "fights tough stains." Consumers may find it more difficult to accept or just too easy to forget the new positioning when the brand name continues to remind them of other product considerations.

With sufficient time and the proper marketing programs, however, this difficulty can sometimes be overcome. Southwest Airlines no longer stands for airline service just in Texas and the southwestern United States; and RadioShack doesn't just provide equipment for ham radio operators and now sells a wide variety of consumer electronics. Such marketing maneuvers can be a long and expensive process, however. Imagine the difficulty of repositioning brands such as "I Can't Believe It's Not Butter!" or "Gee, Your Hair Smells Terrific!" Thus, it is important when choosing a meaningful name to consider the possibility of later repositioning and the necessity of linking other associations.

Meaningful names are not restricted to real words. Consumers can extract meaning, if they so desire, even from made-up or fanciful brand names. For example, one study of computer-generated brand names containing random combinations of syllables found that "whumies" and "quax" reminded consumers of a breakfast cereal and that "dehax" reminded them of a laundry detergent.[22] Thus, consumers were able to extract at least some product meaning from these essentially arbitrary names when instructed to do so. Nevertheless, consumers are likely to extract meaning from highly abstract names only when they are sufficiently motivated.

Marketers generally devise made-up brand names systematically, basing words on combinations of morphemes. A *morpheme* is the smallest linguistic unit having meaning. There are 7,000 morphemes in the English language, including real words like "man" and prefixes, suffixes, or roots. For example, Nissan's Sentra automobile is a combination of two morphemes suggesting "central" and "sentry."[23] By combining carefully chosen morphemes, marketers can construct brand names that actually have some relatively easily inferred or implicit meaning.

Brand names raise a number of interesting linguistic issues.[24] Figure 4-5 contains an overview of different categories of linguistic characteristics, with definitions and examples. Even individual letters can contain meaning that may be useful in developing a new brand name. The letter *X* became popular (e.g., ESPN's X Games and Nissan's Xterra SUV) because *X* represents "extreme," "on the edge," and "youth."[25] Research has shown that in some instances, consumers prefer products with brand names bearing some of the letters from their own name (Jonathan may exhibit a greater-than-expected preference for a product named Jonoki).[26]

The sounds of letters can take on meaning as well.[27] For example, some words begin with phonemic elements called *plosives,* like the letters *b, c, d, g, k, p,* and *t,* whereas others use *sibilants,* which are sounds like *s* and soft *c.* Plosives escape from the mouth more quickly than sibilants and are harsher and more direct. Consequently, they are thought to make names more specific and less abstract, and to be more easily recognized and recalled.[28] On the other hand, because sibilants have a softer sound, they tend to conjure up romantic, serene images and are often found in the names of products such as perfumes—think of Chanel, Ciara (by Revlon), and Shalimar and Samsara (Guerlin).[29]

One study found a relationship between certain characteristics of the letters of brand names and product features: As consonant hardness and vowel pitch increased in hypothetical brand names for toilet paper and household cleansers, consumer perception of the harshness of the product also increased.[30] The actual font or logotype used to express the brand name may also change consumer impressions.[31]

Brands are not restricted to letters alone.[32] Alphanumeric names may include a mixture of letters and digits (WD-40), a mixture of words and digits (Formula 409), or mixtures of letters or words and numbers in written form (Saks Fifth Avenue). They can also designate generations or relationships in a product line like BMW's 3, 5, and 7 series.

Characteristics	Definitions and/or Examples
Phonetic Devices	
Alliteration	Consonant repetition (Coca-Cola)
Assonance	Vowel repetition (Kal Kan)
Consonance	Consonant repetition with intervening vowel changes (Weight Watchers)
Masculine rhyme	Rhyme with end-of-syllable stress (Max Pax)
Feminine rhyme	Unaccented syllable followed by accented syllable (American Airlines)
Weak/imperfect/slant rhyme	Vowels differ or consonants similar, not identical (Black & Decker)
Onomatopoeia	Use of syllable phonetics to resemble the object itself (Wisk)
Clipping	Product names attenuated (Chevy)
Blending	Morphemic combination, usually with elision (Aspergum, Duracell)
Initial plosives	/b/, /c-hard/, /d/, /g-hard/, /k/, /p/, /q/, /t/ (Bic)
Orthographic Devices	
Unusual or incorrect spellings	Kool-Aid
Abbreviations	7 UP for Seven Up
Acronyms	Amoco
Morphologic Devices	
Affixation	Jell-O
Compounding	Janitor-in-a-Drum
Semantic Devices	
Metaphor	Representing something as if it were something else (Arrid); simile is included with metaphor when a name describes a likeness and not an equality (AquaFresh)
Metonymy	Application of one object or quality for another (Midas)
Synecdoche	Substitution of a part for the whole (Red Lobster)
Personification/pathetic fallacy	Humanizing the nonhuman, or ascription of human emotions to the inanimate (Betty Crocker)
Oxymoron	Conjunction of opposites (Easy-Off)
Paranomasia	Pun and word plays (Hawaiian Punch)
Semantic appositeness	Fit of name with object (Bufferin)

FIGURE 4-5

Brand Name Linguistic Characteristics

Naming Procedures.   A number of different procedures or systems have been suggested for naming new products. Most adopt a procedure something along the following lines. Figure 4-6 displays some common naming mistakes according to leading marketing and branding consultancy Lippincott.[33]

1. *Define objectives.* First, define the branding objectives in terms of the six general criteria we noted earlier, and in particular define the ideal meaning the brand should convey. Recognize the role of the brand within the corporate branding hierarchy and how it should relate to other brands and products (we'll discuss this in Chapter 11). In many cases, existing brand names may serve, at least in part. Finally, understand the role of the brand within the entire marketing program and the target market.

1	**Using cliched words such as "Innovation" or "Solution" in a name.**	In most industry situations these kinds of words are so overused, they no longer have meaning.
2	**Insisting on a name that can be found in an English dictionary.**	Not only are such names scarce, they also may cause translation or other linguistic problems.
3	**Taking the easy way out and settling on initials.**	Initials may be easier to trademark, but an enormous budget is typically required to give them meaning.
4	**Using terms like "Extra," "Plus," or "New" to communicate next generation products or improved line extensions.**	Three more examples of words that have lost their meaning through overuse.
5	**Adopting license-plate shorthand.**	A name that customers have to work too hard to figure out is a turnoff—and a wasted opportunity.
6	**Seeing how many names can be combined to make a confusing brand**	Most that initially started in this direction have truncated to simpler shorter alternatives.
7	**Asking for suggestions from friends and other uninformed sources.**	The results that come from this approach seldom relate to or express a company's business startegy.

FIGURE 4-6

Seven Crucial Naming Mistakes

Source: http://www. lippincott.com/

2. *Generate names.* With the branding strategy in place, next generate as many names and concepts as possible. Any potential sources of names are valid: company management and employees; existing or potential customers (including retailers or suppliers if relevant); ad agencies, professional name consultants, and specialized computer-based naming companies. Tens, hundreds, or even thousands of names may result from this step.

3. *Screen initial candidates.* Screen all the names against the branding objectives and marketing considerations identified in step 1 and apply the test of common sense to produce a more manageable list. For example, General Mills starts by eliminating the following:

   • Names that have unintentional double meaning
   • Names that are unpronounceable, already in use, or too close to an existing name
   • Names that have obvious legal complications
   • Names that represent an obvious contradiction of the positioning

   Next General Mills runs in-depth evaluation sessions with management personnel and marketing partners to narrow the list to a handful of names, often conducting a quick-and-dirty legal search to help screen out possible problems.

4. *Study candidate names.* Collect more extensive information about each of the final 5–10 names. Before spending large amounts of money on consumer research, it is usually advisable to do an extensive international legal search. Because this step is expensive, marketers often search on a sequential basis, testing in each country only those names that survived the legal screening from the previous country.

5. *Research the final candidates.* Next, conduct consumer research to confirm management expectations about the memorability and meaningfulness of the remaining names. Consumer testing can take all forms. Many firms attempt to simulate the actual marketing program and consumers' likely purchase experiences as much as possible.[34] Thus, they may show consumers the product and its packaging, price, or promotion so that they understand the rationale for the brand name and how it will be used. Other aids in this kind of research are realistic three-dimensional packages and concept boards or low-cost animatic advertising using digital techniques. Marketers may survey many consumers to capture differences in

regional or ethnic appeal. They should also factor in the effects of repeated exposure to the brand name and what happens when the name is spoken versus written.

6. *Select the final name.* Based on all the information collected from the previous step, management should choose the name that maximizes the firm's branding and marketing objectives and then formally register it.

Some segment of consumers or another will always have at least some potentially negative associations with a new brand name. In most cases, however, assuming they are not severe, these associations will disappear after the initial marketing launch. Some consumers will dislike a new brand name because it's unfamiliar or represents a deviation from the norm. Marketers should remember to separate these temporal considerations from more enduring effects. Here is how a new airline arrived at its name.[35]

JETBLUE

Traditionally, airlines use descriptive names that evoke specific geographic origins, like American, or broad geographic reach, like United. In launching a new airline with a fresh concept—stylish travel for the budget-minded flier—JetBlue decided it needed an evocative name, but not one that sounded like an airline. Working with its ad agency, Merkley & Partners, and brand consultant, Landor, the company generated a list of candidate names—Fresh Air, Taxi, Egg, and It. The name Blue, suggesting peaceful clear skies, quickly became a favorite, but trademark lawyers noted that it would be impossible to protect the name without a distinctive qualifier. The first candidate, TrueBlue, went by the wayside when it was found to also be the name of a car rental agency. JetBlue emerged as the best substitute and the brand was born. JetBlue has also leveraged the "jet" portion of its brand name with its optimistic "jetting" campaign, which occurred during the economic downturn and was a response to difficult times in the airline industry. The ads served to distinguish JetBlue and its "maverick" approach to service. Its "TrueBlue" loyalty program cleverly leverages the second half of its name.[36]

Jet Blue has used evocative brand imagery and a strong customer focus to build its brand.

Source: JetBlue Airways

URLs

URLs (uniform resource locators) specify locations of pages on the Web and are also commonly referred to as *domain names.* Anyone wishing to own a specific URL must register and pay for the name. As companies clamored for space on the Web, the number of registered URLs increased dramatically. Every three-letter combination and virtually all words in a typical English dictionary have been registered. The sheer volume of registered URLs often makes it necessary for companies to use coined words for new brands if they wish to have a Web site for the brand. For example, when Andersen Consulting selected its new name, it chose the coined word "Accenture" in part because the URL www.accenture.com had not been registered.

Another issue facing companies with regard to URLs is protecting their brands from unauthorized use in other domain names.[37] A company can sue the current owner of the URL for copyright infringement, buy the name from the current owner, or register all conceivable variations of its brand as domain names ahead of time.

In 2010, cybersquatting cases reached record levels. *Cybersquatting* or *domain squatting,* as defined by government law, is registering, trafficking in, or using a domain name with bad-faith intent to profit from the goodwill of a trademark belonging to someone else. The cybersquatter then offers to sell the domain to the person or company who owns a trademark contained within the name at an inflated price. Under such cases, trademark holders sue for infringement of their domain names through the WIPO (an agency of the UN).[38]

The top five areas of legal activity initiated by companies are in the retail, banking and finance, biotechnology and pharmaceuticals, Internet and IT, and fashion industries. In 2009, Citibank successfully filed suit against Shui of China under the Anticybersquatting and Consumer Protection Act by showing that (1) Shui had a bad-faith intent to profit from using the domain name citybank.org; and (2) that the name was confusingly similar to, or dilutive of, Citibank's distinctive or famous mark. Shui was forced to pay Citibank $100,000 and its legal fees.[39]

Many sources list the current total of registered domain names at or close to the 200 million mark. As the domain name market has exploded, ICANN—a nonprofit that governs the industry—announced it would begin accepting applications to register customized and unlimited URLs. This decision could have a significant impact for companies, which can now register brand URLs. Canon and Hitachi were among the first brands to apply to register their brand names under the new top-level domain policy.

Brand recall is critical for URLs because it increases the likelihood that consumers easily remember the URL to get to the site. At the peak of the Internet boom, investors paid $7.5 million for Business.com, $2.2 million for Autos.com, and $1.1 million for Bingo.com. Many of these "common noun" sites failed, however, and were criticized, among other things, for having names that were too generic. Many firms adopted names that started with a lowercase *e* or *i* and ended in "net," "systems," or, especially, "com." Most of these names became liabilities after the Internet bubble burst, forcing firms such as Internet.com to revert to a more conventional name, INTMedia Group.

Yahoo!, however, was able to create a memorable brand and URL. Jerry Yang and David Filo named their Internet portal (created as a Stanford University thesis project) "Yahoo!" after thumbing through the dictionary for words that began with "ya," the universal computing acronym for "yet another." Filo stumbled upon *yahoo,* which brought back fond childhood memories of his father calling him "little yahoo." Liking the name, they created a more complete acronym: "Yet another hierarchical officious oracle."[40]

Typically, for an existing brand, the main URL is a straightforward and maybe even literal translation of the brand name, like www.shell.com, although there are some exceptions and variations, such as www.purplepill.com for the Nexium acid-reflux medication Web site.

Logos and Symbols

Although the brand name typically is the central element of the brand, visual elements also play a critical role in building brand equity and especially brand awareness. *Logos* have a long history as a means to indicate origin, ownership, or association. For example, families and countries have used logos for centuries to visually represent their names (think of the Hapsburg eagle of the Austro-Hungarian Empire).

Logos range from corporate names or trademarks (word marks with text only) written in a distinctive form, to entirely abstract designs that may be completely unrelated to the word mark, corporate name, or corporate activities.[41] Examples of brands with strong word marks and no accompanying logo separate from the name include Coca-Cola, Dunhill, and Kit Kat. Examples of abstract logos include the Mercedes star, Rolex crown, CBS eye, Nike swoosh, and Olympic rings. These non–word mark logos are also often called *symbols.*

Many logos fall between these two extremes. Some are literal representations of the brand name, enhancing brand meaning and awareness, such as the Arm and Hammer, American Red Cross, and Apple logos. Logos can be quite concrete or pictorial in nature like the American Express centurion, the Land o' Lakes Native American, the Morton salt girl with umbrella, and Ralph Lauren's polo player. Certain physical elements of the product or company can become a symbol, as did the Goodyear blimp, McDonald's golden arches, and the Playboy bunny ears.

Like names, abstract logos can be quite distinctive and thus recognizable. Nevertheless, because abstract logos may lack the inherent meaning present with a more concrete logo, one danger is that consumers may not understand what the logo is intended to represent without a significant marketing initiative to explain its meaning. Consumers can evaluate even fairly abstract logos differently depending on the shape.

Benefits. Logos and symbols are often easily recognized and can be a valuable way to identify products, although consumers may recognize them but be unable to link them to any specific product or brand. Many insurance firms use symbols of strength (the Rock of Gibraltar for Prudential and the stag for Hartford) or security (the "good hands" of Allstate, the hard hat of Fireman's Fund, and the red umbrella of Travelers).

Another branding advantage of logos is their versatility: Because they are often nonverbal, logos transfer well across cultures and over a range of product categories. For example, corporate brands often develop logos in order to confer their identity on a wide range of products and to endorse different sub-brands. Marketers must think carefully, however, as to how prominent the brand name and logo should be on any product, especially more luxury ones.[42]

Abstract logos offer advantages when the full brand name is difficult to use for any reason. In the United Kingdom, for example, National Westminster Bank created a triangular device as a logo because the name itself was long and cumbersome and the logo could more easily appear as an identification device on checkbooks, literature, signage, and promotional material. The logo also uses the shortened version of the company name, NatWest.[43]

Finally, unlike brand names, logos can be easily adapted over time to achieve a more contemporary look. For example, in 2000, John Deere revamped its deer trademark for the first time in 32 years, making the animal appear to be leaping up rather than landing. The change was intended to "convey a message of strength and agility with a technology edge."[44]

In updating, however, marketers should make gradual changes and not lose sight of the inherent advantages of the logo. In the 1980s, the trend for many firms was to create more abstract, stylized versions of their logos. In the process, some of the meaning residing in these logos, and thus some equity, was lost. Recognizing the logo's potential contribution to brand equity, some firms in the 1990s reverted to a more traditional look for their symbols.

Prudential's Rock of Gibraltar logo was changed back from black-and-white slanted lines introduced in 1984 to a more faithful rendition. To harken back to its historic past and reflect its engineering and design prowess, Chrysler used a winged badge to replace the Pentastar five-pointed star design as a symbol of the brand. The wings, intended to symbolize freedom and flying, were found on the first Chrysler manufactured in 1924.

Regardless of the reason for doing it, changing a logo is not cheap. According to branding experts, engaging a firm for four to six months to create a symbol or remaking an old one for a big brand "usually costs $1 million."[45]

Characters

Characters represent a special type of brand symbol—one that takes on human or real-life characteristics. Brand characters typically are introduced through advertising and can play a central role in ad campaigns and package designs. Some are animated characters like the Pillsbury Doughboy, Peter Pan peanut butter, and numerous cereal characters such as Tony the Tiger and Snap, Crackle & Pop. Others are live-action figures like Juan Valdez (Colombian coffee) and Ronald McDonald. One character has been both in its lifetime.

GREEN GIANT

One of the most powerful brand characters ever introduced is General Mills's Jolly Green Giant. His origin can be traced back to the 1920s, when the Minnesota Valley Canning Company placed a green giant on the label of a new variety of sweet, large English peas as a means to circumvent trademark laws that prevented the firm from naming the product "Green Giant." Ad Agency Leo Burnett used the Jolly Green Giant character in print ads beginning in 1930 and in TV ads beginning in the early 1960s. At first, TV ads featured an actor wearing green body makeup and a suit of leaves. Later, the ads moved to full animation. Creatively, the ads have been very consistent. The Green Giant is always in the background, with his features obscure, and he says only "Ho Ho Ho!" He moves very little, doesn't walk, and never leaves the valley. The Green Giant has been introduced into international markets, following the same basic set of rules. The Little Sprout character was introduced in 1973 to bring a new look to the brand and allow for more flexibility. Unlike the Green Giant, the Little Sprout is a chatterbox, often imparting valuable product information. The Green Giant brand has enormous equity to General Mills, and using the name and character on a new product has been an effective signal to consumers that the product is "wholesome" and "healthy." Not surprisingly, the company has tied many of their recent green initiatives on sustainability to the Green Giant.[46]

One of the most enduring—and most powerful—brand characters ever devised is the Jolly Green Giant.
Source: General Mills, Inc.

Benefits.   Because they are often colorful and rich in imagery, brand characters tend to be attention getting and quite useful for creating brand awareness. Brand characters can help brands break through marketplace clutter as well as help communicate a key product benefit. For example, Maytag's Lonely Repairman has helped reinforce the company's key "reliability" product association.

The human element of brand characters can enhance likeability and help create perceptions of the brand as fun and interesting.[47] A consumer may more easily form a relationship with a brand when the brand literally has a human or other character presence. Characters avoid many of the problems that plague human spokespeople—they don't grow old, demand pay raises, or cheat on their wives. An interesting exception occurred, however, when Aflac fired the human voice to its famed duck character, comedian Gilbert Gottfried, after he posted some controversial remarks on Twitter that made light of the fallout from the earthquake and tsunami in Japan.[48]

Finally, because brand characters do not typically have direct product meaning, they may also be transferred relatively easily across product categories. For example, Aaker notes that "the Keebler's elf identity (which combines a sense of home-style baking with a touch of magic and fun) gives the brand latitude to extend into other baked goods—and perhaps even into other types of food where homemade magic and fun might be perceived as a benefit."[49] Popular characters also often become valuable licensing properties, providing direct revenue and additional brand exposure.

Cautions.   There are some cautions and drawbacks to using brand characters. Brand characters can be so attention getting and well liked that they dominate other brand elements and actually *dampen* brand awareness.

EVEREADY

When Ralston Purina introduced its drumming pink bunny that "kept going . . . and going . . . and going" in ads for the Eveready Energizer battery, many consumers were so captivated by the character that they paid little attention to the name of the advertised brand. As a result, they often mistakenly believed that the ad was for Eveready's chief competitor, Duracell. Eveready had to add the pink bunny to its packages, promotions, and other marketing communications to create stronger brand links. Through its concerted marketing efforts through the years, however, the Energizer Bunny has now achieved iconic status. Many marketing experts view the character as the "ultimate product demo" because of how effectively it showcases the product's unique selling proposition—long-lived batteries—in an inventive, fresh way. As the company's CEO noted, "The message of the Energizer Bunny has remained consistent over the last two decades; he speaks to longevity, determination and perseverance." The bunny celebrated its 20th anniversary in 2009, having achieved several milestones, including 95 percent awareness among consumers and an entry in the Oxford English Dictionary. Perhaps the greatest compliment, however, is how often everyone from politicians to sport stars have used the Energizer Bunny to describe their own staying power.[50]

Characters often must be updated over time so that their image and personality remain relevant to the target market. Japan's famous Hello Kitty character, which became a multibillion dollar product and license powerhouse, found its sales shrinking over the last decade, a victim in part of overexposure and a failure to make the character modern and appealing across multiple media.[51]

In general, the more realistic the brand character, the more important it is to keep it up-to-date. One advantage of fictitious or animated characters is that their appeal can be more enduring and timeless than that of real people. Branding Brief 4-1 describes the efforts by General Mills to evolve the Betty Crocker character over time. Finally, some characters are so culturally specific that they do not travel well to other countries. The Science of Branding 4-2 describes some guidelines from a leading consultant.

Slogans

Slogans are short phrases that communicate descriptive or persuasive information about the brand. They often appear in advertising but can play an important role on packaging and in other aspects of the marketing program. When Snickers advertised, "Hungry? Grab a Snickers," the slogan also appeared on the candy bar wrapper itself.

Slogans are powerful branding devices because, like brand names, they are an extremely efficient, shorthand means to build brand equity. They can function as useful "hooks" or "handles" to help consumers grasp the meaning of a brand—what it is and what makes it special.[52] They are an indispensable means of summarizing and translating the intent of a marketing program in a few short words or phrases. For example, State Farm Insurance's "Like a Good Neighbor, State Farm Is There" has been used for decades to represent the brand's dependability and aura of friendship.

Benefits.   Some slogans help build brand awareness by playing off the brand name in some way, as in "The Citi Never Sleeps." Others build brand awareness even more explicitly by making strong links between the brand and the corresponding product category, like when Lifetime would advertise that it was "Television for Women." Most important, slogans can help reinforce the brand positioning as in "Staples. That Was Easy." For HBO, a slogan was critical to conveying its unique positioning.

BRANDING BRIEF 4-1

Updating Betty Crocker

In 1921, Washburn Crosby Company, makers of Gold Medal flour, launched a picture puzzle contest. The contest was a huge success—the company received 30,000 entries—and several hundred contestants sent along requests for recipes and advice about baking. To handle those requests, the company decided to create a spokesperson. Managers chose the name Betty Crocker because "Betty" was a popular, friendly sounding name and "Crocker" was a reference to William G. Crocker, a well-liked, recently retired executive. The company merged with General Mills in 1928, and the newly merged company introduced the *Betty Crocker Cooking School of the Air* as a national radio program. During this time, Betty was given a voice and her signature began to appear on nearly every product the company produced.

In 1936, the Betty Crocker portrait was drawn by artist Neysa McMein as a composite of some of the home economists at the company. Prim and proper, Betty was shown with pursed lips, a hard stare, and graying hair. Her appearance has been updated a number of times over the years (see the accompanying figure) and has become more friendly, although she has never lost her reserved look.

One advantage of characters—they can be timeless. Although Betty Crocker is over 75 years old, she still looks 35!

Source: AP Photo/General Mills

Prior to a makeover in 1986, Betty Crocker was seen as honest and dependable, friendly and concerned about customers, and a specialist in baked goods, but also out-of-date, old and traditional, a manufacturer of "old standby products," and not particularly contemporary or innovative. The challenge was to give Betty a look that would attract younger consumers but not alienate older ones who remembered her as the stern homemaker of the past. There needed to be a certain fashionableness about her—not too dowdy and not too trendy, since the new look would need to last for 5 to 10 years. Her look also needed to be relevant to working women. Finally, for the first time, Betty Crocker's look was also designed to appeal to men, given the results of a General Mills study that showed that 30 percent of U.S. men at the time sometimes cooked for themselves.

A few years later, Betty Crocker received another update. This ultramodern model, the current one, was the work of a committee that selected images of 75 women of many different races to create a computerized composite. This seventh makeover seemed to have taken—although Betty Crocker was now close to 75, she didn't look a day over 35! Although the Betty Crocker name is on 200 or so products, her visual image has been largely replaced by the red spoon symbol and signature on package fronts, and she appears only on cookbooks, advertising, and online, where she has over 1.5 million Facebook friends, a Twitter account, and a mobile app downloaded by millions.

Sources: Charles Panati, *Panati's Extraordinary Origins of Everyday Things* (New York: Harper & Row, 1989); Milton Moskowitz, Robert Levering, and Michael Katz, *Everybody's Business: A Field Guide to the 400 Leading Companies in America* (New York: Doubleday/Currency, 1990); "FYI Have You Seen This Person?," *Minneapolis–St. Paul Star Tribune*, 11 October 2000; Susan Marks, *Finding Betty Crocker: The Secret Life of America's First Lady of Food* (New York: Simon & Schuster, 2005); "Betty Crocker Celebrates 90th Birthday," www.marketwatch.com, 18 November 2011.

THE SCIENCE OF BRANDING 4-2

Balance Creative and Strategic Thinking to Create Great Characters

Great characters, the Pillsbury Doughboy, for example, can embody a brand's story and spark enthusiasm for it. But bringing a character to life through advertising requires navigating a host of pitfalls. Character, a company based in Portland, Oregon, helps create new corporate brand characters and revitalize old ones.

During three-day "Character" camps, a team from a client company learns to flesh out a new or current brand character through improvisational acting, discussion, and reflection. According to Character president David Altschul, brand characters are unique in that they straddle the worlds of marketing and entertainment. Their function is to represent a brand, but they compete for attention with other characters to which consumers are exposed through television, movies, video games, and novels. Altschul emphasizes maintaining consistency across all communications and familiarizing all employees with the story behind the brand. The results of Character Camps are intended to equip creative directors with background and insights into the company's character that can spur new ideas and approaches.

These are some tips for brand characters presented at Character Camps.

1. ***Don't be a shill.*** Human traits are appealing. M&M's were successful in giving the brand more appeal once the M&M characters were given more human traits.

2. ***Create a life.*** Create a full backstory to fill out the character. This ensures that the character can evolve over time and continue to connect with consumers.

3. ***Make characters vulnerable.*** Even superheroes have flaws. Maytag launched a new character, the Apprentice, to complement its famous lonely repairman.

4. ***Imagine the long run.*** Characters like General Mills's Jolly Green Giant have been around for decades. Don't get rid of older characters just to make room for new ones. Consumers can get very attached to longtime characters.

5. ***Don't ask too much.*** Characters with a simple task or purpose work best. Using characters for new lines or other purposes can dilute their effectiveness.

To be truly effective, brand characters have to be engaging in their own right while staying true to the brand. Most characters though, are conceived as short-term solutions to solve specific problems. If the audience likes a character, companies face the challenge of turning it into an asset. At this point, some companies try to freeze all the character's attributes and preserve them. But Altschul cautions against this strategy, saying static characters can lose their appeal and fail to emotionally connect with consumers. On the other hand, characters that are mass-marketed too heavily can also crash and burn. The California Raisins met such a fate when their licensing program pushed them into every possible type of paraphernalia without much thought about their backstory.

Altschul maintains that viewers connect with characters whose struggles are familiar. He says the way to ensure that a brand character adds value for the long run is to address strategic questions such as: "What is this story about?" "What are the flaws, vulnerabilities, and sources of conflict that connect the character to the brand in a deep, intrinsic way?" "What human truth is revealed through the story that audiences can relate to?"

Altschul's company helps clients find this intersection between story and marketing by defining the essence of a brand and the character and then clarifying the connection between the two. The brand character is profiled to bring out the personality traits, behavior, and mission that may be used for future storylines. And the participants talk about how the character should look, act, and interact with others to most effectively communicate the essence of the brand. The goal is to create guidelines for how the character may evolve and suggests ways the character could be used beyond traditional advertising media. Altschul suggests that companies also establish principles for the brand to stay "in character," including ways the character can serve as conscience for the brand when making decisions such as line extensions, alliances, and competitive responses.

Sources: Fara Warner, "Brands with Character," *Fast Company*, May 2004; David Altschul, "The Balancing Act of Building Character," *Advertising Age*, 4 July 2005; Carlye Adler, "Mascot Makeover: How The Pillsbury Doughboy Explains Consumer Behavior," *Fortune Small Business*, October 2006, 30–40; www.characterweb.com.

HBO

As a pay TV channel, HBO has always needed to convince viewers it was worth paying extra money for. More than just a pay movie channel, HBO had a tradition of broadcasting original, edgy programming such as *Sex and the City*, *The Sopranos*, and *Entourage* that would not be found on free channels. To highlight its most compelling point-of-difference and brand essence, HBO developed a clever slogan in 1996: "It's Not TV, It's HBO." Externally, the slogan gave viewers a point of reference to understand and categorize the brand. Internally, the slogan gave employees a clear vision and goal to keep in mind: No matter what they did, it should never look like ordinary TV.[53]

The clever slogan "It's Not TV, It's HBO" reinforces how the cable network with shows like *Entourage* is different from other networks.

Source: AF archive/Alamy

Slogans often become closely tied to advertising campaigns and serve as tag lines to summarize the descriptive or persuasive information conveyed in the ads. DeBeers's "A Diamond Is Forever" tag line communicates that diamonds bring eternal love and romance and never lose value. Slogans can be more expansive and more enduring than just ad tag lines, though campaign-specific tag lines may help reinforce the message of a particular campaign instead of the brand slogan for a certain period of time.

For example, through the years, Nike has used tag lines specific to ad campaigns for events or sports such as "Prepare for Battle" and "Quick Can't Be Caught" (basketball); "Write the Future," (World Cup); "My Better Is Better" (multisport); and "Here I Am" (women) instead of the well-known brand slogan, "Just Do It." Such substitutions can emphasize that the ad campaign represents a departure of some kind from the message conveyed by the brand slogan, or just a means to give the brand slogan a rest so that it remains fresh.

Designing Slogans.   Some of the most powerful slogans contribute to brand equity in multiple ways.[54] They can play off the brand name to build both awareness *and* image, such as "Be Certain with Certs" for Certs breath mints; "Maybe She's Born with It, Maybe It's Maybelline" for Maybelline cosmetics; or "The Big Q Stands for Quality" for Quaker State motor oil.

Slogans also can contain product-related messages and other meanings. Consider the historical Champion sportswear slogan, "It Takes a Little More to Make a Champion." The slogan could be interpreted in terms of product performance, meaning that Champion sportswear is made with a little extra care or with extra-special materials, but it could mean that Champion sportswear is associated with top athletes. This combination of superior product performance and aspirational user imagery is a powerful platform on which to build brand image and equity.

Benetton has had an equally strong slogan on which to build brand equity ("United Colors of Benetton"), but as Branding Brief 4-2 describes, the company has not always taken full advantage of it.

Updating Slogans.   Some slogans become so strongly linked to the brand that it becomes difficult to introduce new ones (take the famous slogan quiz in Figure 4-7 and check the accompanying footnote to see how many slogans you can correctly identify). Marketers of 7UP tried a number of different successors to the popular "Uncola" slogan—including "Freedom of Choice," "Crisp and Clean and No Caffeine," "Don't You Feel Good About 7UP," and "Feels So Good Coming Down," and for over five years the somewhat edgy "Make 7UP Yours." A new ad in 2011 featuring hip-hop singer–songwriter Cee Lo Green beatboxing used yet another tag line, "Be Yourself. Be Refreshing. Be 7UP."

BRANDING BRIEF 4-2

Benetton's Brand Equity Management

One of the world's top clothing manufacturers (with global sales of $2.4 billion), Benetton has experienced some ups and downs in managing its brand equity. Benetton built a powerful brand by creating a broad range of basic and colorful clothes that appealed to a wide range of consumers. Their corporate slogan, "United Colors of Benetton," would seem to almost perfectly capture their desired image and positioning. It embraces both product considerations (the colorful character of the clothes) and user considerations (the diversity of the people who wore the clothes), providing a strong platform for the brand. Benetton's ad campaigns reinforced this positioning by showing people from a variety of different racial backgrounds wearing a range of different-colored clothes and products.

Benetton's ad campaigns switched directions, however, in the 1980s by addressing controversial social issues.

Bennetton has never been afraid to court controversy with its advertising, although it has sometimes been to the detriment of the brand.
Source: Newscom

Created in-house by famed designer Oliviero Toscani, Benetton print ads and posters featured such unusual and sometimes disturbing images as a white child wearing angel's wings alongside a black child sporting devil's horns; a priest kissing a nun; an AIDS patient and his family in the hospital moments before his death; and, in an ad run only once, 56 close-up photos of male and female genitalia. In 1994, Benetton launched a $15 million ad campaign in newspapers and billboards in 110 countries featuring the torn and bloodied uniform of a dead Bosnian soldier. In 2000, a campaign titled "We, on Death Row" showcased U.S. death row inmates with pictures of the prisoners and details about their crimes and length of incarceration.

Critics labeled these various campaigns gimmicky "shock" advertising and accused Benetton of exploiting sensitive social issues to sell sweaters. One fact is evident. Although the campaigns may have succeeded with a certain market segment, they were certainly more "exclusive" in nature—distancing the brand from many other consumers—than the early Benetton ad campaigns, which were strikingly inviting to consumers and "inclusive" in nature. Not surprisingly, the new ads were not always well received by its retailers and franchise owners.

The ad displaying the dead Bosnian soldier received an especially hostile reaction throughout Europe. In the United States, some of Benetton's more controversial ads were rejected by the media, and Benetton's U.S. retailers commissioned their own campaign from TBWA/Chiat/Day ad agency in an attempt to create a more sophisticated image for the brand. After the

death row ads debuted, Sears pulled the brand from shelves of its 400 stores. Response from U.S. consumers was equally negative: U.S. sales of Benetton products shrank by 50 percent to $52 million between 1993 and 2000. By 2001, the number of Benetton stores in the United States dropped to 150 from 600 in 1987.

Since 2001, Benetton's advertisements have featured more conventional images—teenagers in colorful Benetton clothing. Benetton maintained that the company would maintain its "socially responsible" status by focusing on noncontroversial themes like racial discrimination, poverty, child labor, AIDS awareness, and so forth. Accordingly, a variety of campaigns were introduced in the ensuing decade, such as "Food for Life" and "Microcredit Africa Works." The first decade in the new millennium, however, saw the emergence of fierce competition from Zara, H&M, and others. Lacking the same vertical integration and "fast fashion" business practices and having lost brand momentum, Benetton found itself surpassed by its more nimbler, popular rivals.

Sources: Leigh Gallagher, "About Face," *Forbes*, 19 March 2001; Michael McCarthy, "Benetton in Spotlight," *USA Today*, 16 February 2002, B3; George E. Belch and Michael A. Belch, "Benetton Group: Evolution of Communication Strategy," *Advertising & Promotion: An Integrated Marketing Communications Perspective*, 7th ed. (Boston: McGraw-Hill, 2007); Armoral Kenna, "Benetton: A Must-Have Becomes a Has-Been," *Bloomberg BusinessWeek*, 10 March 2011.

1._____ Reach Out and Touch Someone

2._____ Have It Your Way

3._____ Just Do It

4._____ When It Absolutely, Positively Has to Be
There Overnight

5._____ Drivers Wanted

6._____ Don't Leave Home Without It

7._____ Like a Rock

8._____ Because I'm Worth It

9._____ The Ultimate Driving Machine

10._____ When You Care Enough to Send the Very Best

11._____ Capitalist Tool

12._____ The Wonder Drug That Works Wonders

13._____ No More Tears

14._____ Melts in Your Mouth, Not in Your Hands

15._____ We Try Harder

16._____ The Antidote for Civilization

17._____ Where Do You Want to Go Today?

18._____ Let Your Fingers Do the Walking

19._____ Breakfast of Champions

20._____ Fly the Friendly Skies

Answers: (1) Bell Telephone; (2) Burger King; (3) Nike; (4) Federal Express; (5) Volkswagen; (6) American Express; (7) Chevrolet; (8) L'Oreal; (9) BMW; (10) Hallmark; (11) Forbes magazine; (12) Bayer aspirin; (13) Johnson's Baby Shampoo; (14) M&M's; (15) Avis; (16) Club Med; (17) Microsoft; (18) Yellow Pages; (19) Wheaties; and (20) United Airlines.

FIGURE 4-7
Famous Slogans Quiz

A slogan that becomes so strongly identified with a brand can box it in. Or successful slogans can take on lives of their own and become public catch phrases (like Wendy's "Where's the Beef?" in the 1980s, MasterCard's "Priceless" in the 1990s, and the "Got Milk?" spoofs in the 2000s), but there can also be a down side to this kind of success: the slogan can quickly become overexposed and lose specific brand or product meaning.

Once a slogan achieves such a high level of recognition and acceptance, it may still contribute to brand equity, but probably as more of a reminder of the brand. Consumers are unlikely to consider what the slogan means in a thoughtful way after seeing or hearing it too many times. At the same time, a potential difficulty arises if the slogan continues to convey some product meaning that the brand no longer needs to reinforce. In this case, by not facilitating the linkage of new, desired brand associations, the slogan can become restrictive and fail to allow the brand to be updated as much as desired or necessary.

Because slogans are perhaps the easiest brand element to change over time, marketers have more flexibility in managing them. In changing slogans, however, they must do the following:

1. Recognize how the slogan is contributing to brand equity, if at all, through enhanced awareness or image.

2. Decide how much of this equity enhancement, if any, is still needed.
3. Retain the needed or desired equities still residing in the slogan as much as possible while providing whatever new twists of meaning are necessary to contribute to equity in other ways.

Sometimes modifying an existing slogan is more fruitful than introducing a new slogan with a completely new set of meanings. For example, Dockers switched its slogan from the well-received "Nice Pants" to "One Leg at a Time" in the late 1990s before reverting to the previous slogan when recognizing it had given up too much built-up equity.

Jingles

Jingles are musical messages written around the brand. Typically composed by professional songwriters, they often have enough catchy hooks and choruses to become almost permanently registered in the minds of listeners—sometimes whether they want them to or not! During the first half of the twentieth century, when broadcast advertising was confined primarily to radio, jingles were important branding devices.

We can think of jingles as extended musical slogans, and in that sense classify them as a brand element. Because of their musical nature, however, jingles are not nearly as transferable as other brand elements. They can communicate brand benefits, but they often convey product meaning in a nondirect and fairly abstract fashion. Thus the potential associations they might create for the brand are most likely to relate to feelings and personality and other intangibles.

Jingles are perhaps most valuable in enhancing brand awareness. Often, they repeat the brand name in clever and amusing ways that allow consumers multiple encoding opportunities. Consumers are also likely to mentally rehearse or repeat catchy jingles after the ad is over, providing even more encoding opportunities and increasing memorability.

A well-known jingle can serve as an advertising foundation for years. The familiar "Give Me a Break" jingle for Kit Kat candy bars has been sung in ads since 1988 and has helped make the brand the sixth best-selling chocolate candy bar in the United States.[55] There was an uproar when, after two decades, the U.S. Army switched from its familiar "Be All That You Can Be" to "Army of One." Finally, the distinctive four-note signature to Intel's ads echoes the company's slogan "In-tel In-side." Although the jingle seems simple, the first note alone is a mix of 16 sounds, including a tambourine and a hammer striking a brass pipe.[56]

Packaging

Packaging is the activities of designing and producing containers or wrappers for a product. Like other brand elements, packages have a long history. Early humans used leaves and animal skin to cover and carry food and water. Glass containers first appeared in Egypt as early as 2000 B.C. Later, the French emperor Napoleon awarded 12,000 francs to the winner of a contest to find a better way to preserve food, leading to the first crude method of vacuum packing.[57]

From the perspective of both the firm and consumers, packaging must achieve a number of objectives:[58]

- Identify the brand.
- Convey descriptive and persuasive information.
- Facilitate product transportation and protection.
- Assist in at-home storage.
- Aid product consumption.

Marketers must choose the aesthetic and functional components of packaging correctly to achieve marketing objectives and meet consumers' needs. Aesthetic considerations govern a package's size and shape, material, color, text, and graphics. Innovations in printing processes now permit eye-catching and appealing graphics that convey elaborate and colorful messages on the package at the "moment of truth"—the point of purchase.[59]

Functionally, structural design is crucial. For example, innovations over the years have resulted in food packages that are resealable, tamperproof, and more convenient to use—easy to hold, easy to open, or squeezable. Consider these recent General Mills packaging innovations: Yoplait Go-Gurt's yogurt in a tube packaging concept was a huge hit with kids and their parents; packaging for Betty Crocker Warm Delights showcased a microwavable (two minutes), convenient, single-serve dessert treat; and Green Giant Valley Fresh Steamers uses materials that withstand microwave cooking temperatures to offer steamable vegetables with sauce.[60]

Benefits.   Often, one of the strongest associations consumers have with a brand is inspired by the look of its packaging. For example, if you ask the average consumer what comes to mind when he or she thinks of Heineken beer, a common response is a "green bottle." The package can become an important means of brand recognition and convey or imply information to build or reinforce valuable brand associations. Molson's beer sales increased by 40 percent in the United States after the company modified the bottle's back labels to include cheeky "ice-breakers" for bar patrons such as "On the Rebound," "Sure, You Can Have My Number," and "Fairly Intimidated by Your Beauty." Buoyed by that success, they later introduced "Answer Honestly" bottle back labels that gave drinkers challenging choices to mull over.[61]

Structural packaging innovations can create a point-of-difference that permits a higher margin. New packages can also expand a market and capture new market segments. Packaging changes can have immediate impact on customer shopping behavior and sales: a redesign of Häagen-Dazs packaging increased flavor shoppability by 21 percent; General Mills saw an increase in sales of 80 percent after redesigning Bisquick Shake n' Pour package to improve its ergonomics and by creating a "smooth, curvy form that reinforces the brand equity"; and a redesign on the packaging for Jimmy Dean's Biscuit Sandwiches lead to an increase of 13 percent in household penetration.[62]

One of the major packaging trends of recent years is to make both bigger and smaller packaged versions of products (as well as portions) to appeal to new market segments.[63] Jumbo sizes have been successfully introduced for hot dogs, pizzas, English muffins, frozen dinners, and beer. Pillsbury's Grands! biscuits—40 percent larger than existing offerings—were the most successful new product in the company's 126-year history when introduced. But sometimes smaller has proven to be successful too.

100-CALORIE PACKS

By 2007, a few years after their introduction by Kraft, 100-calorie snack packs of crackers, chips, cookies, and candy had passed the $200-million mark. Truly a consumer-driven packaging innovation, they had an appeal that was plain and simple—portion control made easy. The products were identical to those in larger packages but conveniently placed in handy 100-calorie packs for which calorie-conscious consumers were willing to pay a premium. With sales of the packs growing at almost 30 percent a year by 2007, most top food manufacturers—including Kraft's Nabisco, Hershey, PepsiCo's Frito-Lay and Quaker Oats, and Campbell's Pepperidge Farm—introduced their own versions. In the years that followed, however, the 100-calorie snack pack market began to slow down. A number of factors contributed to the cooling off, such as market saturation (190 products were introduced in 2008 and at least 68 in 2009) and customer concerns about their actual effectiveness in controlling caloric intake, their relatively high price, and the amount of wasteful packaging.[64]

Though they were a very successful packaging innovation, 100-calorie snack packs did find it hard to sustain their sales growth over time.

Source: Keri Miksza

Packaging at the Point of Purchase.   The right packaging can create strong appeal on the store shelf and help products stand out from the clutter, critical when you realize that the average supermarket shopper can be exposed to 20,000 or more products in a shopping visit that may last less than 30 minutes and include many unplanned purchases. Many consumers may first encounter a new brand on the supermarket shelf or in the store. Because few product differences exist in some categories, packaging innovations can provide at least a temporary edge on competition.

For these reasons, packaging is a particularly cost-effective way to build brand equity.[65] It is sometimes called the "last five seconds of marketing" as well as "permanent media" or "the last salesman." Walmart looks at packaging critically and tests whether consumers understand the brand promise behind the package within three seconds and up to 15 feet from the shelf. Note that consumer exposure to packaging is not restricted to the point of purchase and moments of consumption, because brand packages often can play a starring role in advertising.

Packaging Innovations.   Packaging innovations can both lower costs and/or improve demand. One important supply-side goal for many firms is to redesign packages and employ more recyclable materials to lower the use of paper and plastic. Toward that goal, U.S. food, beverage, and consumer product manufacturers reported that they had eliminated 1.5 billion pounds of packaging between 2005 and 2011 with another 2.5 billion pounds expected to be avoided by 2020, representing an overall reduction of 19 percent in total average U.S. packaging weight.[66]

On the demand side, in mature markets especially, package innovations can provide a short-term sales boost. The beverage industry in general has been characterized by a number of packaging innovations. For example, following the lead of Snapple's wide-mouth glass bottle, Arizona iced teas and fruit drinks in oversize (24-ounce), pastel-colored cans with a southwestern motif became a $300 million brand in a few years with no marketing support beyond point-of-purchase and rudimentary outdoor ads, designed in-house.[67]

Package Design.   An integral part of product development and launch, package design has become a more sophisticated process. In the past, it was often an afterthought, and colors, materials, and so forth were often chosen fairly arbitrarily. For example, legend has it that Campbell's famous soup is red and white because one executive at the company liked the uniforms of Cornell University's football team!

These days, specialized package designers bring artistic techniques and scientific skills to package design in an attempt to meet the marketing objectives for a brand. These consultants conduct detailed analyses to break down the package into a number of different elements.[68] They decide on the optimal look and content of each element and choose which elements should be dominant in any one package—whether the brand name, illustration, or some other graphical element—and how the elements should relate to each other. Designers can also decide which elements should be shared across packages and which should differ (and how).

Designers often refer to the "shelf impact" of a package—the visual effect the package has at the point of the purchase when consumers see it in the context of other packages in the category. For example, "bigger and brighter" packages are not always better when competitors' packages are also factored in.[69] Given enough shelf space, however, manufacturers can create billboard effects with their brand to raise their prominence and impact. General Mill deliberately "tiled" graphical elements of their packaging so that some of their mega-brands with multiple varieties such as Cheerios, Nature Valley Granola Bars, and Progresso Soup would stand out.[70]

Although packaging is subject to some legal requirements, such as nutrition information on food products, there is plenty of scope for improving brand awareness and forming brand associations. Perhaps one of the most important visual design elements for a package is its color.[71] Some package designers believe that consumers have a "color vocabulary" when it comes to products and expect certain types of products to have a particular look.

For example, it would be difficult to sell milk in anything but a white carton, club soda in anything but a blue package, and so forth. At the same time, certain brands are thought to have "color ownership" such that it would be difficult for other brands to use a similar look. Here is how some experts see the brand color palette:[72]

Red: Ritz crackers, Folgers coffee, Colgate toothpaste, Target retailer, and Coca-Cola soft drinks

Orange: Tide laundry detergent, Wheaties cereal, Home Depot retailer, and Stouffer's frozen dinners

Yellow: Kodak film, Juicy Fruit chewing gum, McDonald's restaurants, IKEA retailers, Cheerios cereal, Lipton tea, and Bisquick biscuit mix

Green: Del Monte canned vegetables, Green Giant frozen vegetables, Walmart retailers, Starbucks coffee, BP retail gasoline, and 7UP lemon-lime soft drink

Blue: IBM technology and services, Ford automobiles, Windex cleaner, Downy fabric softener, and Pepsi-Cola soft drinks

Packaging color can affect consumers' perceptions of the product itself.[73] For example, the darker the orange shade of a can or bottle, the sweeter consumers believe the drink inside to be. Color is thus a critical element of packaging. Like other packaging design elements, color should be consistent with information conveyed by other aspects of the marketing program.

Packaging Changes. Although packaging changes can be expensive, they can be cost-effective compared with other marketing communication costs. Firms change their packaging for a number of reasons:[74]

- *To signal a higher price, or to more effectively sell products through new or shifting distribution channels.* For instance, Kendall Oil redid its package to make it more appealing to do-it-yourselfers when it found more of its sales coming from supermarkets and hardware stores rather than service stations.
- *When a significant product line expansion would benefit from a common look,* as with Planter's nuts, Weight Watchers foods, and Stouffer's frozen foods.
- *To accompany a new product innovation to signal changes to consumers.* To emphasize the brand's "green" heritage, Stevia redesigned the packaging on its SweetLeaf product, changing the look and the size and promoting the 100 percent recycled materials used in its manufacture.[75]
- *When the old package just looks outdated.* Kraft updated its Macaroni & Cheese packaging in 2010—the first time in more than 10 years—to better underscore the brand's core equities (happiness, smiles, and joy) through a "noodle smile" symbol as well as to unify its three sub-brands.[76]

Packaging changes have accelerated in recent years as marketers have sought to gain an advantage wherever possible. As one Coca-Cola ad executive noted, "There's no question the crowded marketplace has inspired companies to change their boxes more often, and there's greater use of promotional packages to give the appearance that things are changing."

In making a packaging change, marketers need to recognize its effect on the original or current customer franchise for the brand.[77] Under these circumstances, marketers must not lose the key package equities that have been built up. Branding Brief 4-3 describes some setbacks marketers have faced updating packaging and other brand elements in recent years.

To identify or confirm key package equities, consumer research is usually helpful (see Branding Brief 4-3). If packaging recognition is a critical consumer success factor for the brand, however, marketers must be especially careful. It would be a mistake to change the packaging so significantly that consumers don't recognize it in the store. Retailers' opinions can also be important too.

Some marketing observers consider packaging important enough to be the "fifth P" of the marketing mix. Packaging can play an important role in building brand equity directly, through points-of-difference created by functional or aesthetic elements of the packaging, or indirectly through the reinforcement of brand awareness and image. The Science of Branding 4-3 reviews some insightful academic research.[78]

PUTTING IT ALL TOGETHER

Each brand element can play a different role in building brand equity, so marketers "mix and match" to maximize brand equity.[79] For example, meaningful brand names that are visually represented through logos are easier to remember with than without such reinforcement.[80]

The entire set of brand elements makes up the ***brand identity,*** the contribution of all brand elements to awareness and image. The cohesiveness of the brand identity depends on the extent to which the brand elements are consistent. Ideally, marketers choose each element to support the others, and all can be easily incorporated into other aspects of the brand and the marketing program.

BRANDING BRIEF 4-3

Do-Overs with Brand Makeovers

With more markets characterized by intense competition, rapidly changing products, and increasingly fickle customers, many marketers are looking at makeovers to breathe new life into their brands. Logos, symbols, packaging, and even brand names are being updated to create greater meaning, relevance, differentiation. Unfortunately, in an increasingly networked world, consumer reaction to changes to any brand element—both pro and con—can be quickly spread. Here are some high-profile examples and the challenges and difficulties their brand makeovers encountered.

Tropicana. In February 2009, Pepsi introduced a dramatic overhaul to its category-leading orange juice. Gone was the visual image of an orange with a straw protruding from it (designed to evoke freshness); in its place was a close-up image of a glass of orange juice and the phrase "100% Orange." Consumer reaction was swift and largely negative. Customers complained about being unable to differentiate between the company's pulp-free, traditional, and other juice varieties. Even worse, customers also felt the look was too generic. Facing online fury and with the words "ugly," "stupid," and "bargain brand" ringing in their ears, Pepsi capitulated. Announcing that it had "underestimated the deep emotional bond" consumers had with the original packaging, the company reverted to the old versions after only six weeks.

The Gap. Another brand walking into a digital brand-makeover firestorm, The Gap actually asked for it. After unexpectedly un-veiling a new logo (the word *Gap* in a basic black Helvetica font with a small blue square over the upper-right hand portion of the p), the company asked consumers on its Facebook page for comments and further logo ideas. Feedback was far from kind, and after enduring a long week of criticism, Gap management announced that "We've heard loud and clear that you don't like the new logo" and reverted to its iconic white text logo and unique brand font.

Gatorade & Pepsi. Around the same time as the Tropicana makeover, Pepsi also completely overhauled its Gatorade brand as well as its classic Pepsi-cola product lineup. Gatorade's make-over included introducing a whole new system of thirst quench-ers and fluid restoration for before (Prime 01), during (Perform 02), and after (Recover 03) exercise. The new brand goal was

to reach athletes in a wide range of sports and experience lev-els while positioning itself as the one-stop source for hydration and other needs before, during, and after their workouts. Pepsi's makeover included a new logo—a white band in the middle of the Pepsi circle that appeared to loosely form a smile. Both brand makeovers received some negative feedback and the products experienced sluggish sales afterwards, although several factors may have contributed, including the severe recession.

Lessons. When changing a well-received or even iconic brand element—a character, logo, or packaging—two issues are key. One, the new brand element must be inherently highly regarded. Part of the problems some brands have run into is that their new logos or packaging are just not that appealing to consumers, leading the consumer to wonder why a change needed to be made. Two, regardless of the inherent appeal of a new brand element, changes are hard for consumers and should be handled carefully and patiently.

No wonder Starbucks went to great pains in 2010 to care-fully explain the rationale of its logo makeover, its fourth since the brand was created in 1971. The change was prompted by the company's fortieth anniversary and the new directions it was considering, which would take the brand outside the coffee cat-egory. Founder Howard Schultz explained that the iconic green Siren in the center of the logo was made more prominent—by dropping the words "Starbucks Coffee"—to reflect new business lines and new international markets. Like many brand makeovers, it initially met mixed public reaction.

Sources: Linda Tischler, "Never Mind!" Pepsi Pulls Much-Loathed Tropicana Packaging," *Fast Company*, 23 February 2009; Stuart Elliott, "Tropicana Discovers Some Buyers Are Passionate About Packaging," *New York Times*, 23 February 2009; "Tropicana to Abandon Much-Maligned Juice Carton," *Wall Street Journal*, 24 February 2011; Tim Nudd, "People Not Falling in Love with New Gap Logo," *Adweek*, 6 October 2010; Christine Birkner, "Minding the Gap: Retailer Caught in Logo Fiasco," *Marketing News*, 21 October 2010; Natalie Zmuda, What Went into the Update Pepsi Logo," *Advertising Age*, 27 October 2008; Jeremiah Williams," PepsiCo Revamps Formidable Gatorade Franchise After Rocky 2009," *Atlanta Journal-Constitution*, 23 March 2010; Valarie Bauerlein "Gatorade's 'Mission': Sell More Drinks," *Wall Street Journal*, 13 September 2010; Julie Jargon, "Starbucks Drops Cof-fee from Logo," *Wall Street Journal*, 6 January 2011; Sarah Skidmore, "Starbucks Gives Logo a New Look," *Associated Press*, 5 January 2011.

Some strong brands have a number of valuable brand elements that directly reinforce each other. For example, consider Charmin toilet tissue. Phonetically, the name itself conveys softness. The brand character, Mr. Whipple, and the brand slogan, "Please Don't Squeeze the Charmin," also help reinforce the key point-of-difference for the brand of "softness."

Brand names characterized by rich, concrete visual imagery often can yield powerful logos or symbols. Wells Fargo, a large California-based bank, has a brand name rich in Western heritage that can be exploited throughout its marketing program. Wells Fargo has adopted

THE SCIENCE OF BRANDING 4-3

The Psychology of Packaging

Cornell University's Brian Wansink has conducted a series of research studies into the consumer psychology of packaging. His basic premise is as follows: "Many managers think the package's main purpose is to encourage purchase. For many consumer packaged goods, the package keeps on marketing the brand and influencing consumers long after it is purchased. After it is home it can influence how a person perceives its taste and value, how much a person uses at a time, and even how he or she uses it." Here are four of his fascinating findings.

Packaging Can Influence Taste
Our sense of taste and touch is very suggestible, and what we see on a package can lead us to taste what we think we are going to taste. In one study, 181 people were sent home with nutrition bars that claimed to contain either "10 grams of protein" or "10 grams of soy protein." In reality, both nutrition bars were identical, and neither contained any soy. Nevertheless, because many people believe soy to have an unappetizing taste, they rated the bars with "soy" on the package as "grainy," "unappealing," and "tasteless." The right words and image on a package can have a big influence on these expectations.

Packaging Can Influence Value
Long after we have bought a product, a package can still lead us to believe we bought it for a good value. First, most people believe the bigger the package, the better the price per ounce. Yet even the shape of a package can influence what we think. One study found that people believe tall, narrow packages hold more of a product than short, wide packages.

Packaging Can Influence Consumption
Studies of 48 different types of foods and personal care products have shown that people pour and consume 18–32 percent more of a product as the size of the container doubles. A big part of the reason is that larger sizes subtly suggest a higher "consumption norm." One study gave Chicago moviegoers free medium-size or large-size popcorn buckets and showed that those given the larger buckets ate 45 percent more! Even when the popcorn was 14 days old, people still ate 32 percent more, though they said they hated it. The same thing happens at parties. MBA students at a Champaign, IL, Super Bowl party were offered Chex Mix from either huge gallon-size bowls or from twice as many half-gallon bowls. Those dishing from the gallon-size bowls took and ate 53 percent more. Shapes affect drinking too: people pour an average of 34 percent more into short wide glasses than tall narrow ones.

Packaging Can Influence How a Person Uses a Product
One strategy to increase use of mature products has been to encourage people to use the brand in new situations, like soup for breakfast, or for new uses, like baking soda as a refrigerator deodorizer. An analysis of 26 products and 402 consumers showed that twice as many people learned about the new use from the package than from television ads. Part of the reason such on-package suggestions are effective is that they are guaranteed to reach a person who is already favorable to the brand.

Sources: Brian Wansink and Se-Bum Park, "Sensory Suggestiveness and Labeling: Do Soy Labels Bias Taste?" *Journal of Sensory Studies* 17 (November 2002): 483–491; Brian Wansink, "Can Package Size Accelerate Usage Volume?" *Journal of Marketing* 60 (July 1996): 1–14; Brian Wansink, "Environmental Factors That Increase the Food Intake and Consumption Volume of Unknowing Consumers," *Annual Review of Nutrition* 24 (2004): 455–479; Brian Wansink and Se-Bum Park, "At the Movies: How External Cues and Perceived Taste Impact Consumption Volume," *Food Quality and Preference* 12, no. 1 (January 2001): 69–74; Brian Wansink and Junyong Kim, "Bad Popcorn in Big Buckets: Portion Size Can Influence Intake as Much as Taste," *Journal of Nutrition Education and Behavior* 37 (Sept–Oct 2005): 242–245; Brian Wansink and Matthew M. Cheney, "Super Bowls: Serving Bowl Size and Food Consumption," *Journal of the American Medical Association* 293, no. 14 (2005): 1727–1728; Brian Wansink and Jennifer M. Gilmore, "New Uses That Revitalize Old Brands," *Journal of Advertising Research* 39 (April/May 1999): 90–98; Brian Wansink, *Mindless Eating* (New York: Bantam Books, 2006).

a stagecoach as a symbol and has named individual services to be thematically consistent, for example, creating investment funds under the Stagecoach Funds brand umbrella.

Although the actual product or service itself is critical in building a strong brand, the right brand elements can be invaluable in developing brand equity. Method Products is a prime example of the payoffs from getting both correct.

METHOD

Celebrating its tenth anniversary in 2011 and still one of the fastest-growing companies in the United States, Method Products is the brainchild of former high school buddies Eric Ryan and Adam Lowry. The company took a big supermarket category—cleaning and household products—and literally and figuratively turned things upside down by taking a completely fresh approach. Ryan and Lowry designed a sleek, uncluttered dish soap container that also had a functional advantage—the bottle, shaped like a chess piece, was built to let soap flow out the bottom, so users would never have to turn it upside down. This signature product, with its pleasant fragrance, was designed by award-winning industrial designer Karim Rashid. By creating a line of nontoxic, biodegradable household cleaning products with bright colors and sleek designs totally unique to the category, Method has surpassed $100 million in annual revenues. Although it is available in such desirable retail outlets as Target and Lowe's, the company believes its marketing must work harder to express the brand positioning given its limited advertising budget. In addition to its attractive packaging, the company is capitalizing on growing interest in green products by emphasizing its nontoxic, nonpolluting ingredients. It is also developing a strong brand personality as hip, modern, and somewhat irreverent as reflected by its slogan, "People Against Dirty."[81]

Method built a highly successful line of cleaning products by paying attention to what was inside the bottle as well as outside.
Source: Christopher Schall/Impact Photo

REVIEW

Brand elements are those trademarkable devices that identify and differentiate the brand. The main ones are brand names, URLs, logos, symbols, characters, slogans, jingles, and packages. Brand elements can both enhance brand awareness and facilitate the formation of strong, favorable, and unique brand associations.

Six criteria are particularly important. First, brand elements should be inherently memorable, easy to recognize, and easy to recall. Second, they should be inherently meaningful to convey information about the nature of the product category, the particular attributes and benefits of a brand, or both. The brand element may even reflect brand personality, user or usage imagery, or feelings for the brand. Third, the information conveyed by brand elements does not necessarily have to relate to the product alone and may simply be inherently appealing or likable. Fourth, brand elements can be transferable within and across product categories to support line and brand extensions, and across geographic and cultural boundaries and market segments. Fifth, brand elements should be adaptable and flexible over time. Finally, they should be legally protectable and, as much as possible, competitively defensible. Brand Focus 4.0 outlines some of the key legal considerations in protecting the brand.

	Brand Element				
Criterion	Brand Names and URLs	Logos and Symbols	Characters	Slogans and Jingles	Packaging and Signage
Memorability	Can be chosen to enhance brand recall and recognition	Generally more useful for brand recognition	Generally more useful for brand recognition	Can be chosen to enhance brand recall and recognition	Generally more useful for brand recognition
Meaningfulness	Can reinforce almost any type of association, although sometimes only indirectly	Can reinforce almost any type of association, although sometimes only indirectly	Generally more useful for non-product-related imagery and brand personality	Can convey almost any type of association explicitly	Can convey almost any type of association explicitly
Likability	Can evoke much verbal imagery	Can provoke visual appeal	Can generate human qualities	Can evoke much verbal imagery	Can combine visual and verbal appeal
Transferability	Can be somewhat limited	Excellent	Can be somewhat limited	Can be somewhat limited	Good
Adaptability	Difficult	Can typically be redesigned	Can sometimes be redesigned	Can be modified	Can typically be redesigned
Protectability	Generally good, but with limits	Excellent	Excellent	Excellent	Can be closely copied

FIGURE 4-8

Critique of Brand Element Options

Because different brand elements have different strengths and weaknesses, marketers "mix and match" to maximize their collective contribution to brand equity. Figure 4-8 offers a critique of different brand elements according to the six key criteria.

DISCUSSION QUESTIONS

1. Pick a brand. Identify all its brand elements and assess their ability to contribute to brand equity according to the choice criteria identified in this chapter.
2. What are your favorite brand characters? Do you think they contribute to brand equity in any way? How? Can you relate their effects to the customer-based brand equity model?
3. What are some other examples of slogans not listed in the chapter that make strong contributions to brand equity? Why? Can you think of any "bad" slogans? Why do you consider them to be so?
4. Choose a package of any supermarket product. Assess its contribution to brand equity. Justify your decisions.
5. Can you think of some general guidelines to help marketers mix and match brand elements? Can you ever have "too many" brand elements? Which brand do you think does the best job of mixing and matching brand elements?

BRAND FOCUS 4.0

Legal Branding Considerations

According to Dorothy Cohen, under common law, "a 'technical' trademark is defined as any fanciful arbitrary, distinctive, and nondescriptive mark, word, letter, number, design, or picture that denominates and is affixed to goods; it is an inherently distinctive trade symbol that identifies a product."[82] She maintains that **trademark strategy** involves proper trademark planning, implementation, and control, as follows:

• **Trademark planning** requires selecting a valid trademark, adopting and using the trademark, and engaging in search and clearance processes.

• **Trademark implementation** requires effectively using the trademark in enacting marketing decisions, especially with respect to promotional and distributional strategies.

• **Trademark control** requires a program of aggressive policing of a trademark to ensure its efficient usage in marketing activities, including efforts to reduce trademark counterfeiting and to prevent the trademark from becoming generic, as well as instituting suits for infringement of the trademark.

This appendix highlights a few key legal branding considerations. For more comprehensive treatments, it is necessary to consider other sources.[83]

Counterfeit and Imitator Brands

Why is trademark protection of brand elements such as brand names, logos, and symbols such an important brand management priority? As noted above, virtually any product is fair game for illegal counterfeiting or questionable copycat mimicking—from Nike apparel to Windows software, and from Similac baby formula to ACDelco auto parts.[84]

In addition, some products attempt to gain market share by imitating successful brands. These copycat brands may mimic any one of the possible brand elements, such as brand names or packaging. For example, Calvin Klein's popular Obsession perfume and cologne has had to withstand imitators such as Compulsion, Enamoured, and Confess, whose package slogan proclaimed, "If you like Obsession, you'll love Confess."

Many copycat brands are put forth by retailers as store brands, putting national brands in the dilemma of protecting their trade dress by cracking down on some of their best customers. Complicating matters is the fact that if challenged, many private labels contend, with some justification, that they should be permitted to continue labeling and packaging practices that have come to identify entire categories of products rather than a single national brand.[85] In other words, certain packaging looks may become a necessary point-of-parity in a product category. A common victim of brand cloning, Contac cold medication underwent its first packaging overhaul in 33 years to better prevent knockoffs as well as update its image.

Many national brand manufacturers are also responding through legal action. For national brands, the key is proving that brand clones are misleading consumers, who may think that they are buying national brands. The burden of proof is to establish that an appreciable number of reasonably acting consumers are confused and mistaken in their purchases.[86] In such cases, many factors might be considered by courts in determining likelihood of confusion, such as the strength of the national brand's mark, the relatedness of the national brand and brand clone products, the similarity of the marks, evidence of actual confusion, the similarity of marketing channels used, the likely degree of buyer care, the brand clone's intent in selecting the mark, and the likelihood of expansion of the product lines.

Simonson provides an in-depth discussion of these issues and methods to assess the likelihood of confusion and "genericness" of a trademark. He stresses the importance of recognizing that consumers may vary in their level or degree of confusion and that it is difficult as a result to identify a precise threshold level above which confusion occurs. He also notes how survey research methods must accurately reflect the consumers' state of mind when engaged in marketplace activities.[87]

Historical and Legal Precedence

Simonson and Holbrook have made some provocative observations about and connections between appropriation and dilution, making the following points.[88] They begin by noting that legally, a brand name is a "conditional-type property"—protected only after it has been used in commerce to identify products (goods or services) and only in relation to those products or to closely related offerings. To preserve a brand name's role in identifying products, the authors note, federal law protects brands from actions of others that may tend to cause confusion concerning proper source identification.

By contrast with the case of confusion, Simonson and Holbrook identify **trademark appropriation** as a developing area of state law that can severely curtail even those brand strategies that do not "confuse" consumers. They define appropriation in terms of enhancing the image of a new offering via the use of some property aspect of an existing brand. That is, appropriation resembles theft of an intangible property right. They note that the typical argument to prevent imitations is that even in the absence of confusion, a weaker brand will tend to benefit by imitating an existing brand name. Jerre Swann similarly argues that "the owner of a strong, unique brand should thus be entitled, incipiently, to prevent impairment of the brand's communicative clarity by its substantial association with another brand, particularly where there is an element of misappropriation."[89]

Simonson and Holbrook also summarize the legal concept of **trademark dilution**:

> Protection from "dilution"—a weakening or reduction in the ability of a mark to clearly and unmistakably distinguish the source—arose in 1927 when a legal ruling declared that "once a mark has come to indicate to the public a constant and uniform source of satisfaction, its owner should be allowed the broadest scope possible for the 'natural expansion of his trade' to other lines or fields of enterprise."

They observe that two brand-related rights followed: (1) the right to preempt and preserve areas for brand extensions and (2) the right to stop the introduction of similar or identical brand names even in the absence of consumer confusion so as to protect a brand's image and distinctiveness from being diluted.

Dilution can occur in three ways: blurring, tarnishment, and cybersquatting.[90] **Blurring** happens when the use of an existing mark by a different company in a different category alters the "unique and distinctive significance" of that mark. **Tarnishment** is when a different company employs the mark in order to degrade its quality, such as in the context of a parody or satire. **Cybersquatting** occurs when an unaffiliated party purchases an Internet "domain name consisting of the mark or name of a company for the purpose of relinquishing the right to that domain name to the legitimate owner for a price."[91]

New American laws register trademarks for only 10 years (instead of 20); to renew trademarks, firms must prove they are using the name and not just holding it in reserve. The Trademark Law Revision Act of 1988 allowed entities to apply for a trademark based on their "intent to use" it within 36 months, eliminating the need to have an actual product in the works. To determine legal status, marketers must search trademark registrations, brand name directories, phone books, trade journals and advertisements, and so forth. As a result, the pool of potentially available trademarks has shrunk.[92]

The remainder of this appendix describes some of the particular issues involved with two important brand elements: brand names and packaging.

Trademark Issues Concerning Names

Without adequate trademark protection, brand names can become legally declared generic, as was the case with *vaseline, victrola, cellophane, escalator,* and *thermos.* For example, when Bayer set out to trademark the "wonder drug" acetylsalicylic acid, they failed to provide a "generic" term or common descriptor for the product and provided only a trademark, Aspirin. Without any other option available in the language, the trademark became the common name for the product. In 1921, a U.S. district court ruled that Bayer had lost all its rights in the trademark. Other brand names have struggled to retain their legal trademark status, for example, Band-Aids, Kleenex, Scotch Tape, Q-Tips, and Jello. Xerox spends $100,000 a year explaining that you don't "Xerox" a document, you photocopy it.[93]

Legally, the courts have created a hierarchy for determining eligibility for registration. In descending order of protection, these categories are as follows (with concepts and examples in parentheses):

1. Fanciful (made-up word with no inherent meaning, e.g., Kodak)
2. Arbitrary (actual word but not associated with product, e.g., Camel)
3. Suggestive (actual word evocative of product feature or benefit, e.g., Eveready)
4. Descriptive (common word protected only with secondary meaning, e.g., Ivory)
5. Generic (word synonymous with the product category, e.g., Aspirin)

Thus, fanciful names are the most easily protected, but at the same time are less suggestive or descriptive of the product itself, suggesting the type of trade-off involved in choosing brand elements. Generic terms are never protectable. Marks that are difficult to protect include those that are surnames, descriptive terms, or geographic names or those that relate to a functional product feature. Marks that are not inherently distinctive and thus are not immediately protectable may attain trademark protection if they acquire secondary meaning.

Secondary meaning refers to a mark gaining a meaning other than the older (primary) meaning. The secondary meaning must be the meaning the public usually attaches to the mark and that indicates the association between the mark and goods from a single source. Secondary meaning is usually proven through extensive advertising, distribution, availability, sales volume, length and manner of use, and market share.[94] Secondary meaning is necessary to establish trademark protection for descriptive marks, geographic terms, and personal names.

Trademark Issues Concerning Packaging

In general, names and graphic designs are more legally defensible than shapes and colors. The issue of legal protection of the color of packaging for a brand is a complicated one. One federal appeals court in San Francisco ruled that companies cannot get trademark protection for a product's color alone.[95] The court ruled against a small Chicago manufacturer that makes green-gold padding used by dry cleaners and garment makers on machines that press clothes; the manufacturer had filed suit against a competitor that had started selling padding of the same hue. In rejecting protection for the color alone, the court said manufacturers with distinctively colored products can rely on existing law that protects "trade dress" related to the overall appearance of the product: "Adequate protection is available when color is combined in distinctive patterns or designs or combined in distinctive logos."

Color is one factor, but not a determinative one, under a trade dress analysis. This ruling differed from a landmark ruling in 1985 arising from a suit by Owens-Corning Fiberglas Corporation, which sought to protect the pink color of its insulation. A Washington court ruled in the corporation's favor. Other courts have made similar rulings, but at least two other appeals courts in other regions of the country have subsequently ruled that colors cannot be trademarked. Note that these trademark rulings apply only when color is not an integral part of the product. However, given the lack of uniform trademark protection across the United States, companies planning a national campaign may have to rely on the harder-to-prove trade dress arguments.

Notes

1. Bernd H. Schmitt and Alex Simonson, *Marketing Aesthetics: The Strategic Management of Brands, Identity, and Image* (New York: Free Press, 1997).
2. "In Pictures: America's Best-Loved Spokescreatures," www.forbes.com, 18 March 2010; www.m-ms.com/us/about/characters; Bernadette Casey, "A New Message from Your Mars," *License Global*, October 2009.
3. Nick Farrell, "Latvians Laugh at Vista," *The Inquirer*, 8 September 2006.
4. For some provocative discussion, see Matt Haig, *Brand Failures* (London: Kogan Page, 2003) and www.snopes.com
5. Eleftheria Parpis, "Michelin Gets Pumped Up," *Brandweek*, 6 October 2009; Roger Parloff, "Michelin Man: The Inside Story," *Fortune*, 19 September 2005; Brent Marcus, "Brand Icons Get an Online Facelift," www.imediaconnection.com, 30 May 2007.
6. For a stimulating treatment of brand naming, see Alex Frankel, *Word Craft* (New York: Crown, 2004).
7. An excellent overview of the topic, some of which this section draws on, can be found in Kim R. Robertson, "Strategically Desirable Brand Name Characteristics," *Journal of Consumer Marketing* 6, no. 4 (1989): 61–71.
8. Interestingly, GM sent a memo to its headquarter Chevrolet employees in June 2010 telling them, for the sake of brand consistency, to stop using the Chevy nickname, a move many branding experts criticized for not reflecting consumer desires. Richard S. Chang, "GM Wants to Kick Popular Nickname 'Chevy' to the Curb," *New York Times*, 10 June 2010.
9. Later, after meeting with some success in the UK, Wyborowa launched an ad campaign based again on its name. Themed "There is No V in Wodka," it was based on the fact that in Poland, where vodka originated, the spirit is called wodka! "Wyborowa Campaigns for No V in Wodka," *Harpers Wine & Spirits Trades Review*, 6 June 2008.
10. Frances Leclerc, Bernd H. Schmitt, and Laurette Dube, "Foreign Branding and Its Effects on Product Perceptions and Attitudes," *Journal of Marketing Research* 31 (May 1994): 263–270. See also M. V. Thakor and B. G. Pacheco, "Foreign Branding and Its Effect on Product Perceptions and Attitudes: A Replication and Extension in a Multicultural Setting," *Journal of Marketing Theory and Practice* (Winter 1997): 15–30.

11. Eric Yorkston and Geeta Menon, "A Sound Idea: Phonetic Effects of Brand Names on Consumer Judgments," *Journal of Consumer Research* 31 (June 2004): 43–51; Richard R. Klink, "Creating Brand Names with Meaning: The Use of Sound Symbolism," *Marketing Letters* 11, no. 1 (2000): 5–20.

12. Kim R. Robertson, "Recall and Recognition Effects of Brand Name Imagery," *Psychology and Marketing* 4 (1987): 3–15.

13. Robert N. Kanungo, "Effects of Fittingness, Meaningfulness, and Product Utility," *Journal of Applied Psychology* 52 (1968): 290–295.

14. Kevin Lane Keller, Susan Heckler, and Michael J. Houston, "The Effects of Brand Name Suggestiveness on Advertising Recall," *Journal of Marketing* 62 (January 1998): 48–57.

15. Luk Warlop, S. Ratneshwar, and Stijn M. J. van Osselaer, "Distinctive Brand Cues and Memory for Product Consumption Experiences," *International Journal of Research in Marketing* 22 (2005): 27–44.

16. Daniel J. Howard, Roger A. Kerin, and Charles Gengler, "The Effects of Brand Name Similarity on Brand Source Confusion: Implications for Trademark Infringement," *Journal of Public Policy & Marketing* 19 (Fall 2000): 250–264.

17. Rob Lammle, "How Etsy, eBay, Reddit Got Their Names," www.cnn.com, 22 April 2001.

18. Dan Heath and Chip Heath, "The Quest for the Perfect Name," *Fast Company*, December 2010/January 2011, 72–73; www.lexiconbranding.com; www.ciulla-assoc.com; "Colgate's Portable Wisp Targets Young, On-the-Go Consumers," www.launchpr.com, 21 April 2009.

19. William L. Moore and Donald R. Lehmann, "Effects of Usage and Name on Perceptions of New Products," *Marketing Science* 1, no. 4 (1982): 351–370.

20. Yih Hwai Lee and Kim Soon Ang, "Brand Name Suggestiveness: A Chinese Language Perspective," *International Journal of Research in Marketing*, 20 (December 2003): 323–335.

21. Keller, Heckler, and Houston, "Effects of Brand Name Suggestiveness on Advertising Recall."

22. Robert A. Peterson and Ivan Ross, "How to Name New Brands," *Journal of Advertising Research* 12, no. 6 (December 1972): 29–34.

23. Robert A. Mamis, "Name Calling," *Inc.,* July 1984.

24. Tina M. Lowrey, L. J. Shrum, and Tony M. Dubitsky, "The Relationship Between Brand-Name Linguistic Characteristics and Brand-Name Memory," *Journal of Advertising* 32, no. 3 (2003): 7–17; Tina M. Lowrey and L. J. Shrum, "Phonetic Symbolism and Brand Name Preference," *Journal of Consumer Research* 34 (October 2007): 406–414.

25. Michael McCarthy, "Xterra Discovers Extra Success," *USA Today*, 26 February 2001, 4B.

26. C. Miguel Brendl, Amitava Chattopadyhay, Brett W. Pelham, and Mauricio Carvallo, "Name Letter Branding: Valence Transfers When Product Specific Needs Are Active," *Journal of Consumer Research* 32 (December 2005): 405–415.

27. Jennifer J. Argo, Monica Popa, and Malcolm C. Smith, "The Sound of Brands," *Journal of Marketing* 74 (July 2010): 97–109.

28. Bruce G. Vanden Bergh, Janay Collins, Myrna Schultz, and Keith Adler, "Sound Advice on Brand Names," *Journalism Quarterly* 61, no. 4 (1984): 835–840; Bruce G. Vanden Bergh, Keith E. Adler, and Lauren Oliver, "Use of Linguistic Characteristics with Various Brand-Name Styles," *Journalism Quarterly* 65 (1987): 464–468.

29. Daniel L. Doeden, "How to Select a Brand Name," *Marketing Communications* (November 1981): 58–61.

30. Timothy B. Heath, Subimal Chatterjee, and Karen Russo, "Using the Phonemes of Brand Names to Symbolize Brand Attributes," in *The AMA Educator's Proceedings: Enhancing Knowledge Development in Marketing*, eds. William Bearden and A. Parasuraman (Chicago: American Marketing Association, August 1990).

31. John R. Doyle and Paul A. Bottomley, "Dressed for the Occasion: Font-Product Congruity in the Perception of Logotype," *Journal of Consumer Psychology* 16, no. 2, 2006: 112–123. See also Pamela W. Henderson, Joan L. Giese, and Joseph A. Cote, "Impression Management Using Typeface Design," *Journal of Marketing* 68 (October 2004): 60–72; Terry L. Childers and Jeffrey Jass, "All Dressed Up with Something to Say: Effects of Typeface Semantic Associations on Brand Perceptions and Consumer Memory," *Journal of Consumer Psychology* 12, no. 2 (2002): 93–106.

32. Much of this passage is based on Teresa M. Paiva and Janeen Arnold Costa, "The Winning Number: Consumer Perceptions of Alpha-Numeric Brand Names," *Journal of Marketing* 57 (July 1993): 85–98. See also, Kunter Gunasti and William T. Ross Jr., "How and When Alphanumeric Brand Names Affect Consumer Preferences," *Journal of Marketing Research* 48 (December 2010): 1177–1192.

33. Beth Snyder Bulik, "Tech Sector Ponders: What's in a Name?" *Advertising Age*, 9 May 2005, 24.

34. John Murphy, *Brand Strateg*y (Upper Saddle River, NJ: Prentice Hall, 1990), 79.

35. Alex Frankel, "The New Science of Naming," *Business 2.0*, December 2004, 53–55; Chuck Slater, "Project Runway," *Fast Company*, October 2010, 170–174.

36. Brett Snyder, "How JetBlue Tends to Its Brand, www.bnet.com, 14 July 2010; Cliff Medney, "Flying Sucks. They Know," *Brandweek*, 16 June 2008; Rupal Parekh, "How JetBlue Became One of the Hottest Brands in America, *Advertising Age*, 6 July 2010; www.jetblue.com.

37. Matt Hicks, "Order Out of Chaos," *eWeek*, 1 July 2001.

38. Anticybersquatting Consumer Protection Act (ACPA), November 29, 1999; "Cybersquatting Hits Record Level, WIPO Center Rolls Out New Services," www.wpio.int, 31 March 2011; Evan Brown and Brian Beckham, "Internet Law in the Courts," *Journal of Internet Law* (May 2009): 24–26.

39. ACPA; "Cybersquatting Hits Record Level"; Brown and Beckham, *Journal of Internet Law*.

40. Rachel Konrad, "Companies Resurrect Abandoned Names, Ditch '.com,'" www.CNET News.com, 13 November 2000.

41. Murphy, *Brand Strategy*.

42. Young Jee Han, Joseph C. Nunes, and Xavier Drèze, "Signaling Status with Luxury Goods: The Role of

Brand Prominence," *Journal of Marketing* 74 (July 2010): 15–30.

43. Murphy, *Brand Strategy*.

44. Michael McCarthy, "More Firms Flash New Badge," *USA Today*, 4 October 2000, B3.

45. McCarthy, "More Firms Flash New Badge"; Natalie Zmuda, "What Went into the Updated Pepsi Logo," *Advertising Age*, October 27, 2008.

46. www.generalmills.com; Cyndee Miller, "The Green Giant: An Enduring Figure Lives Happily Ever After," *Marketing News*, 15 April 1991, 2; "The Jolly Green Giant Is Back!," *Business Wire*, 10 November 2005.

47. Dorothy Pomerantz and Lacey Rose, "America's Most Loved Spokescreatures," www.forbes.com, 18 March 2010.

48. Andrew Ross Sorkin, "The Aflac Duck Will Quack Again," *New York Times*, 22 March 2011.

49. David A. Aaker, *Building Strong Brands* (New York: Free Press, 1996), 203.

50. "Still Going and Going: Energizer Bunny Enters His 20th Year," *Associated Press*, 29 November 2008; www.energizer.com; "The Energizer Bunny," Ad Age Advertising Century: Icons, www.adage.com, 1999.

51. Hiroko Tabuchi, "In Search of Adorable, as Hello Kitty Gets Closer to Goodbye," *New York Times*, 14 May 2010, B1.

52. Claudiu V. Dimotfe, "Consumer Response to Polysemous Brand Slogans," *Journal of Consumer Research* 33 (March 2007): 515–522.

53. Allen Adamson, *BrandSimple* (New York: Palgrave Macmillan, 2007); Melissa Grego, "It's Not Just Any Network Executive," *Broadcasting & Cable*, February 2010.

54. Claudiu V. Dimofte and Richard F. Yalch, "Consumer Response to Polysemous Brand Slogans," *Journal of Consumer Research*, 33 (March 2007): 515–522.

55. The classic lyrics are:

Gimme a break,
Gimme a break,
Break me off a piece o' that
Kit Kat bar

That chocolatey taste is gonna make your day,
Everywhere you go you hear the people say

Gimme a break,
Gimme a break,
Break me off a piece o' that
Kit Kat bar

56. Dirk Smillie, "Now Hear This," *Forbes*, 25 December 2000, 234.

57. Nancy Croft, "Wrapping Up Sales," *Nation's Business* (October 1985): 41–42.

58. Susan B. Bassin, "Value-Added Packaging Cuts Through Store Clutter," *Marketing News*, 26 September 1988, 21.

59. Raymond Serafin, "Packaging Becomes an Art," *Advertising Age*, 12 August 1985, 66.

60. Pan Demetrakakes, "Packaging Innovator of the Decade," *Food and Beverage Packaging*, 1 April 2009.

61. Nate Nickerson, "How About This Beer Label: 'I'm in Advertising!,'" *Fast Company*, March 2004, 43; "Coors Brewing Company Reveals 2008 Advertising," *Business Wire*, 8 April 2008.

62. Stephanie Hildebrandt, "A Taste-full Redesign," *Brand Packaging*, July/August 2010; Pan Demetrakakes, "Packaging Innovator of the Decade," *Food and Beverage Packaging*, 1 April 2009; Elaine Wong, "IRI Summit: How Sara Lee Beefed Up Jimmy Dean Brand," *Brandweek*, 23 March 2010.

63. Eben Shapiro, "Portions and Packages Grow Bigger and Bigger," *Wall Street Journal*, 12 October 1993, B1.

64. Melanie Warner, "Goodies in Small Packages Prove to Be a Big Hit," *New York Times*, 30 May 2005; Jeremy W. Peters, "In Small Packages, Fewer Calories and More Profit," *New York Times*, 7 July 2007; Elaine Wong, "100-Calorie Packs Pack It In," *Brandweek*, 26 May 2009.

65. Alecia Swasy, "Sales Lost Their Vim? Try Repackaging," *Wall Street Journal*, 11 October 1989, B1.

66. "CPGs Cutting 4 Billion Pounds of Packaging," *Supermarket News*, 17 March 2011.

67. Gerry Khermouch, "John Ferolito, Don Vultaggio," *Brandweek*, 14 November 1995, 57.

68. For some academic perspectives on package design, see Ulrich R. Orth and Keven Malkewitz, "Holistic Package Design and Consumer Brand Impressions," *Journal of Marketing* 72 (May 2008): 64–81.

69. For interesting discussion, see Margaret C. Campbell and Ronald C. Goodstein, "The Moderating Effect of Perceived Risk on Consumers' Evaluations of Product Incongruity: Preference for the Norm," *Journal of Consumer Research* 28 (December 2001): 439–449.

70. Pan Demetrakakes, "Packaging Innovator of the Decade," *Food and Beverage Packaging*, 1 April 2009.

71. For an interesting application of color to brand names, see Elizabeth G. Miller and Barbara E. Kahn, "Shades of Meaning: The Effect of Color and Flavor Names on Consumer Choice," *Journal of Consumer Research* 32 (June 2005): 86–92.

72. Michael Purvis, president of Sidjakov, Berman, and Gomez, as quoted in Carla Marinucci, "Advertising on the Store Shelves," *San Francisco Examiner*, 20 October 1986, C1–C2; Angela Bright, "Why Color Matters," *Beneath the Brand*, 13 December 2010.

73. Lawrence L. Garber Jr., Raymond R. Burke, and J. Morgan Jones, "The Role of Package Color in Consumer Purchase Consideration and Choice," MSI Report 00–104 (Cambridge, MA: Marketing Science Institute, 2000); Ronald Alsop, "Color Grows More Important in Catching Consumers' Eyes," *Wall Street Journal*, 29 November 1984, 37.

74. Bill Abrams and David P. Garino, "Package Design Gains Stature as Visual Competition Grows," *Wall Street Journal*, 14 March 1979, 48.

75. Ann Marie Mohan, "Established Stevia Brand Refreshes Packaging for Greater Green Mileage," *Packaging World*, October 2010.

76. Jim George, "Kraft Says 'Smile' With Updated Macaroni & Cheese," *Shelf Impact!*, 17 February 2011.

77. Garber, Burke, and Jones, "Role of Package Color."

78. See also Peter H. Bloch, "Seeking the Ideal Form—Product Design and Consumer Response," *Journal of Marketing* 59, no. 3 (1995): 16–29; Peter H. Bloch, Frederick F. Brunel, and T. J. Arnold, "Individual Differences in the Centrality of Visual Product

Aesthetics: Concept and Measurement," *Journal of Consumer Research* 29, no. 4 (2003): 551–565; Priya Raghubir and Aradna Krishna, "Vital Dimensions in Volume Perception: Can the Eye Fool the Stomach?" *Journal of Marketing Research* 36 (August 1999): 313–326; Valerie Folkes, Ingrid Martin, and Kamal Gupta, "When to Say When: Effects of Supply on Usage," *Journal of Consumer Research* 20 (December 1993): 467–477; Valerie Folkes and Shashi Matta, "The Effects of Package Shape on Consumers' Judgment of Product Volume: Attention as Mental Containment," *Journal of Consumer Research* 31 (September 2004): 390–401.

79. Alina Wheeler, *Designing Brand Identity: An Essential Guide for the Whole Branding Team*, 3rd ed. (Hoboken, NJ: John Wiley & Sons, 2009).

80. Terry L. Childers and Michael J. Houston, "Conditions for a Picture Superiority Effect on Consumer Memory," *Journal of Consumer Research* 11 (September 1984): 551–563; Kathy A. Lutz and Richard J. Lutz, "Effects of Interactive Imagery on Learning: Application to Advertising," *Journal of Applied Psychology* 62, no. 4 (1977): 493–498.

81. Jessica Shambora, "David vs. Goliath: Method vs. Clorox," *Fortune*, 15 November 2010; Stuart Elliott, "A Clean Break with Staid Detergent Ads," *New York Times*, 3 February 2010; Ilana DeBare, "Cleaning Up without Dot-Coms," *San Francisco Chronicle*, 8 October 2006; "Marketers of the Next Generation," *Brandweek*, 17 April 2006, 30.

82. Dorothy Cohen, "Trademark Strategy," *Journal of Marketing* 50 (January 1986): 61–74; Dorothy Cohen, "Trademark Strategy Revisited," *Journal of Marketing* 55 (July 1991): 46–59.

83. For example, see Judy Zaichkowsky, *Defending Your Brand Against Imitation* (Westpoint, CO: Quorom Books, 1995); Judy Zaichkowsky, *The Psychology Behind Trademark Infringement and Counterfeiting* (Mahwah, NJ: Lawrence Erlbaum Associates, 2006); Jerre B. Swann, Sr., David Aaker, and Matt Reback, "Trademarks and Marketing," *The Trademark Reporter* 91 (July–August 2001): 787; and a series of articles by Ross D. Petty in the *Journal of Brand Management*, e.g., "Naming Names: Part Three—Safeguarding Brand Equity in the United States by Developing a Family of Trademarks," *Journal of Brand Management* 17 (2010): 561–567.

84. David Stipp, "Farewell, My Logo," *Fortune*, 27 May 1996, 128–140.

85. Paul F. Kilmer, "Tips for Protecting Brand from Private Label Lawyer," *Advertising Age*, 5 December 1994, 29.

86. Greg Erickson, "Seeing Double," *Brandweek*, 17 October 1994, 31–35.

87. Itamar Simonson, "Trademark Infringement from the Buyer Perspective: Conceptual Analysis and Measurement Implications," *Journal of Public Policy & Marketing* 13, no. 2 (Fall 1994): 181–199.

88. Alex Simonson and Morris Holbrook, "Evaluating the Impact of Brand-Name Replications on Product Evaluations," working paper, Marketing Department, Seton Hall University, 1994.

89. Jerre B. Swann, "Dilution Redefined for the Year 2000," *Houston Law Review* 37 (2000): 729.

90. For a detailed discussion of dilution, see Jerre B. Swann, "Dilution Redefined for the Year 2002," *The Trademark Reporter* 92 (May/June 2002): 585–613. See also Maureen Morrin and Jacob Jacoby, "Trademark Dilution: Empirical Measures for an Elusive Concept," *Journal of Public Policy & Marketing* 19, no. 2 (Fall 2000): 265–276; Maureen Morrin, Jonathan Lee, and Greg M. Allenby, "Determinants of Trademark Dilution," *Journal of Consumer Research* 33 (September 2006): 248–257; and Chris Pullig, Carolyn J. Simmons, and Richard G. Netemeyer, "Brand Dilution: When Do New Brands Hurt Existing Brands?" *Journal of Marketing* 70 (April 2006): 52–66.

91. J. Thomas McCarthy, *McCarthy on Trademarks and Unfair Competition*, 4th ed. (Deerfield, IL: Clark Boardman Callaghan, 1996).

92. Alex Frankel, "Name-o-rama," *Wired*, June 1997, 94.

93. Constance E. Bagley, *Managers and the Legal Environment: Strategies for the 21st Century*, 2nd ed. (Minneapolis, MN: West, 1995).

94. Garry Schuman, "Trademark Protection of Container and Package Configurations—A Primer," *Chicago Kent Law Review* 59 (1982): 779–815.

95. Junda Woo, "Product's Color Alone Can't Get Trademark Protection," *Wall Street Journal*, 5 January 1994, B8.

Designing Marketing Programs to Build Brand Equity

5

Learning Objectives

After reading this chapter, you should be able to

1. Identify some of the new perspectives and developments in marketing.
2. Describe how marketers enhance product experience.
3. Explain the rationale for value pricing.
4. List some of the direct and indirect channel options.
5. Summarize the reasons for the growth in private labels.

Part of John Deere's success is its well-conceived and executed product, pricing, and channel strategies.

Source: Eric Schlegel/The New York Times/Redux Pictures

Preview

This chapter considers how marketing activities in general—and product, pricing, and distribution strategies in particular—build brand equity. How can marketers integrate these activities to enhance brand awareness, improve the brand image, elicit positive brand responses, and increase brand resonance?

Our focus is on designing marketing activities from a branding perspective. We'll consider how the brand itself can be effectively integrated into the marketing program to create brand equity. Of necessity, we leave a broader perspective on marketing activities to basic marketing management texts.[1] We begin by considering some key developments in designing marketing programs. After reviewing product, pricing, and channel strategies, we conclude by considering private labels in Brand Focus 5.0.

NEW PERSPECTIVES ON MARKETING

The strategy and tactics behind marketing programs have changed dramatically in recent years as firms have dealt with enormous shifts in their external marketing environments. As outlined in Chapter 1, changes in the economic, technological, political–legal, sociocultural, and competitive environments have forced marketers to embrace new approaches and philosophies. Some of these changes include:[2]

- Rapid technological developments
- Greater customer empowerment
- Fragmentation of traditional media
- Growth of interactive and mobile marketing options
- Channel transformation and disintermediation
- Increased competition and industry convergence
- Globalization and growth of developing markets
- Heightened environmental, community, and social concerns
- Severe economic recession

These changes, and others such as privatization and regulation, have combined to give customers and companies new capabilities with a number of implications for the practice of brand management (see Figure 5-1). Marketers are increasingly abandoning the mass-market strategies that built brand powerhouses in the twentieth century to implement new approaches for a new marketing era. Even marketers in staid, traditional categories and industries are rethinking their practices and not doing business as usual.

Consumers

Can wield substantially more customer power.

Can purchase a greater variety of available goods and services.

Can obtain a great amount of information about practically anything.

Can more easily interact with marketers in placing and receiving orders.

Can interact with other consumers and compare notes on products and services.

Companies

Can operate a powerful new information and sales channel with augmented geographic reach to inform and promote their company and its products.

Can collect fuller and richer information about their markets, customers, prospects, and competitors.

Can facilitate two-way communication with their customers and prospects, and facilitate transaction efficiency.

Can send ads, coupons, promotion, and information by e-mail to customers and prospects who give them permission.

Can customize their offerings and services to individual customers.

Can improve their purchasing, recruiting, training, and internal and external communication.

FIGURE 5-1

The New Capabilities of
the New Economy

CLIF BAR

Started in 1990 by avid cyclist Gary Erickson and named to honor his father, CLIF® Bar set out to offer a better-tasting energy bar with wholesome ingredients. With very little advertising support, it grew in popularity through the years via word-of-mouth and PR. The CLIF Bar product line also grew to include dozens of flavors and varieties, some formulated especially for kids and women, and for energy, healthy snacking, and sports nutrition. Behind CLIF Bar products is a strong socially and environmentally responsible corporate message. The company is active in its local community and known for its passionate employees, who are allowed to do volunteer work on company time. It uses extensive organic ingredients, relies on biodiesel-powered vehicles, and supports the constructions of farmer- and Native American–owned wind farm through carbon offsets. Its nontraditional marketing activities focus on athletic sponsorships and public events. To broaden its appeal, it launched its "Meet the Moment™"campaign in the summer of 2011, in which participants provided stories and photos of inspirational athletic adventures. The integrated marketing campaign featured a fully interactive Web site and mobile applications for iPhone and Android systems. All these marketing efforts have paid off: CLIF Bar was the number one breakaway brand in a survey by *Forbes* magazine and Landor Associates measuring brand momentum from 2006 to 2009.

CLIF Bar has adopted modern marketing practices to build a highly successful twenty-first-century brand.
Source: Clif Bar & Company

The new marketing environment of the twenty-first century has forced marketers to fundamentally change the way they develop their marketing programs. Integration and personalization, in particular, have become increasingly crucial factors in building and maintaining strong brands, as companies strive to use a broad set of tightly focused, personally meaningful marketing activities to win customers.

INTEGRATING MARKETING

In today's marketplace, there are many different means by which products and services and their corresponding marketing programs can build brand equity. Channel strategies, communication strategies, pricing strategies, and other marketing activities can all enhance or detract from brand equity. The customer-based brand equity model provides some useful guidance to interpret these effects. One implication of the conceptualization of customer-based brand equity is that the *manner* in which brand associations are formed does not matter—only the resulting awareness and strength, favorability, and uniqueness of brand associations.

In other words, if a consumer has an equally strong and favorable brand association from Rolaids antacids to the concept "relief," whether it's based on past product experiences, a *Consumer Reports* article, exposure to a "problem-solution" television ad that concludes with the tag line "R-O-L-A-I-D-S spells relief," *or* knowledge that Rolaids has sponsored the "Rolaids Relief Man of the Year" award to the best relief pitchers in major league baseball since 1976, the impact in terms of customer-based brand equity should be identical unless additional associations such as "advertised on television" are created, or existing associations such as "speed or potency of effects" are affected in some way.[3]

Thus, marketers should evaluate *all* possible means to create knowledge, considering not just efficiency and cost but also effectiveness. At the center of all brand-building efforts is the actual product or service. Marketing activities surrounding that product, however, can be critical, as is the way marketers integrate the brand into them.

Consistent with this view, Schultz, Tannenbaum, and Lauterborn conceptualize one aspect of integrated marketing, integrated marketing communications, in terms of contacts.[4] They define a ***contact*** as any information-bearing experience that a customer or prospect has with the brand, the product category, or the market that relates to the marketer's product or service. According to these authors, a person can come in contact with a brand in numerous ways:

> For example, a contact can include friends' and neighbors' comments, packaging, newspaper, magazine, and television information, ways the customer or prospect is treated in the retail store, where the product is shelved in the store, and the type of signage that appears in retail establishments. And the contacts do not stop with the purchase. Contacts also consist of what friends, relatives, and bosses say about a person who is using the product. Contacts include the type of customer service given with returns or inquiries, or even the types of letters the company writes to resolve problems or to solicit additional business. All of these are customer contacts with the brand. These bits and pieces of information, experiences, and relationships, created over time, influence the potential relationship among the customer, the brand, and the marketer.

In a similar vein, Chattopadhyay and Laborie develop a methodology for managing brand experience contact points.[5]

The bottom line is that there are many different ways to build brand equity. Unfortunately, there are also many different firms attempting to build their brand equity in the marketplace. Creative and original thinking is necessary to create fresh new marketing programs that break through the noise in the marketplace to connect with customers. Marketers are increasingly trying a host of unconventional means of building brand equity.

MOOSEJAW MOUNTAINEERING

Targeting a young college-age demographic, offbeat outdoor apparel and gear retailer Moosejaw Mountaineering has found success with a marketing strategy it calls "Love the Madness." Founded by two former wilderness guides, the company has adopted the motto, "We sell the best outdoor gear in the world and have the most fun doing it." Selling most major brands of snowboarding, rock climbing, hiking, and camping products—as well as its own private label—through nine stores in Michigan, Illinois, Colorado, and Massachusetts as well as a catalog and Web site, the retailer succeeds because of the *way* it sells. Virtually any consumer touchpoint with Moosejaw has an irreverent side. As co-founder Robert Wolfe says, "We have the great product, but then we put some stupid little twist to it that makes us stand out from everybody else." In Moosejaw's "Operation Sale," store customers were invited to play the old electronic board game at checkout. Picking up the charley horse without setting off the buzzer brought the customer 20 percent off! The company launched a "Break-Up Service" in which it volunteered to make the difficult call to help customers seeking to end relationships. Text messages from the store offer discounts for replies. One text challenged customers to a digital version of the popular "Rock, Paper, Scissors" game with a 20 percent discount for winners. When the company added a single line to its catalog asking readers to send their best illustration of "crying tomatoes," 300 people replied. All these different efforts have had a payoff: company market research shows that the 40 percent of customers who can be classified as "highly engaged" with the brand place at least four orders with the company, more than the norm.[6]

Moosejaw Mountaineering's unconventional branding approach has created much engagement and loyalty with customers.

Source: Moosejaw Mountaineering

Creativity must not sacrifice a brand-building goal, however, and marketers must orchestrate programs to provide seamlessly integrated solutions and personalized experiences for customers that create awareness, spur demand, and cultivate loyalty.

Personalizing Marketing

The rapid expansion of the Internet and continued fragmentation of mass media have brought the need for personalized marketing into sharp focus. Many maintain that the modern economy celebrates the power of the individual consumer. To adapt to the increased consumer desire for personalization, marketers have embraced concepts such as experiential marketing and relationship marketing.

Experiential Marketing. *Experiential marketing* promotes a product by not only communicating a product's features and benefits but also connecting it with unique and interesting consumer experiences. One marketing commentator describes experiential marketing this way: "The idea is not to sell something, but to demonstrate how a brand can enrich a customer's life."[7]

Pine and Gilmore, pioneers on the topic, argued over a decade ago that we are on the threshold of the "Experience Economy," a new economic era in which all businesses must orchestrate memorable events for their customers.[8] They made the following assertions:

- If you charge for stuff, then you are in the *commodity business.*
- If you charge for tangible things, then you are in the *goods business.*
- If you charge for the activities you perform, then you are in the *service business.*
- If you charge for the time customers spend with you, then and only then are you in the *experience business.*

Citing a range of examples from Disney to AOL, they maintain that saleable experiences come in four varieties: entertainment, education, aesthetic, and escapist.

Columbia University's Bernd Schmitt, another pioneering expert on the subject, notes that "experiential marketing is usually broadly defined as any form of customer-focused marketing activity, at various touchpoints, that creates a sensory-emotional connection to customers."[9] Schmitt details five different types of marketing experiences that are becoming increasingly vital to consumers' perceptions of brands:

- *Sense marketing* appeals to consumers' senses (sight, sound, touch, taste, and smell).
- *Feel marketing* appeals to customers' inner feelings and emotions, ranging from mildly positive moods linked to a brand (e.g., for a noninvolving, nondurable grocery brand or service or industrial product) to strong emotions of joy and pride (e.g., for a consumer durable, technology, or social marketing campaign).
- *Think marketing* appeals to the intellect in order to deliver cognitive, problem-solving experiences that engage customers creatively.
- *Act marketing* targets physical behaviors, lifestyles, and interactions.
- *Relate marketing* creates experiences by taking into account individuals' desires to be part of a social context (e.g., to their self-esteem, being part of a subculture, or a brand community).

He also describes how various "experience providers" (such as communications, visual/verbal identity and signage, product presence, co-branding, spatial environments, electronic media, and salespeople) can become part of a marketing campaign to create these experiences. In describing the increasingly more demanding consumer, Schmitt writes, "Customers want to be entertained, stimulated, emotionally affected and creatively challenged."

Figure 5-2 displays a scale developed by Schmitt and his colleagues to measure experiences and its dimensions. Their study respondents rated LEGO, Victoria's Secret, iPod, and Starbucks as the most experiential brands.[10]

Meyer and Schwager describe a customer experience management (CEM) process that involves monitoring three different patterns: past patterns (evaluating completed transactions), present patterns (tracking current relationships), and potential patterns (conducting inquiries in the hope of unveiling future opportunities).[11] The Science of Branding 5-1 describes how some marketers are thinking more carefully about one particularly interesting aspect of brand experiences—brand scents!

Relationship Marketing. Marketing strategies must transcend the actual product or service to create stronger bonds with consumers and maximize brand resonance. This broader set of activities is sometimes called ***relationship marketing*** and is based on the premise that current customers are the key to long-term brand success.[12] Relationship marketing attempts to provide a more holistic, personalized brand experience to create stronger consumer ties. It expands both the depth and the breadth of brand-building marketing programs.

Victoria's Secret has been praised for its success in creating an experiential brand.

Source: Louis Johnny/SIPA/Newscom

FIGURE 5-2

Brand Experience Scale

Source: Based on J. Joško Brakus, Bernd H. Schmitt, and Lia Zarantonello, "Brand Experience: What Is It? How Is It Measured? Does It Affect Loyalty?," *Journal of Marketing* 73 (May 2009): 52–68.

SENSORY	This brand makes a strong impression on my visual sense or other senses.
	I find this brand interesting in a sensory way.
	This brand does not appeal to my senses.
AFFECTIVE	This brand induces feelings and sentiments.
	I do not have strong emotions for this brand.
	This brand is an emotional brand.
BEHAVIORAL	I engage in physical actions and behaviors when I use this brand.
	This brand results in bodily experiences.
	This brand is not action oriented.
INTELLECTUAL	I engage in a lot of thinking when I encounter this brand.
	This brand does not make me think.
	This brand stimulates my curiosity and problem solving.

THE SCIENCE OF BRANDING 5-1

Making Sense Out of Brand Scents

The smell of a new car is distinctive. When Rolls-Royce customers complained in the 1990s that the new cars weren't as good as the old models, researchers tracked the problem to a surprising source: the car's smell. The company then recreated the aroma of a 1965 Rolls and now sprays it in all the new models. So can scent be used to entice customers or to make a place a little more memorable?

Las Vegas casinos have long infused scents into gaming areas to encourage gamblers to stay a little longer. Now the connection between scent and shopping experience is being explored in more venues than ever. More and more companies looking for an edge are tinkering with scent as a way to distinguish their brand or store. The ever-growing barrage of advertising consumers take in is heavily weighted toward visuals. Although distinctive ring tones and other sounds are used to build brand awareness, most communication appeals to only one of the five human senses: sight.

Retailers are looking to capitalize on scent as a way to lure customers into their stores and into lingering longer than they otherwise might. Victoria's Secret has long used vanilla scents in its stores, but now retailers like the Samsung Experience concept store are starting to get in on the action as a way to distinguish themselves from competitors. But experts caution that scents aren't guaranteed to boost sales. The best scents are unobtrusive. Anything overwhelming can be a negative. And smells should appeal to the same gender the product is trying to appeal to.

Scents that are appropriate or consistent with a product can influence brand evaluations and judgments. Westin Hotels carefully developed a new fragrance, White Tea, to infuse into the hotels' public spaces. The scent is designed to have international appeal and contribute to a subtle, relaxing vibe in the lobbies. Travelers also encounter a unique scent on Singapore Airlines through the scented towels handed out during all flights. The theory is that passengers will associate the subtle scent with a positive, relaxing experience.

Some brands have a built-in sensory marketing advantage. Crayola Crayons were not originally designed to have a signature scent, but the manufacturing process left them with a recognizable odor. Many adults connect the smell of Crayons with childhood, leaving Crayola with an incidental brand element that can be very valuable. When Crayola's parent company was recently considering ways to stand out among the generic competition in new markets, it decided to trademark the smell. Scents have actually been shown to improve product memory across a range of product attributes.

Of course, some products are all about scent. Procter & Gamble built a $1 billion brand with Febreze air freshener. From its origins as a fabric treatment to freshen up coats, drapes, and mattresses, the brand's product line grew to include specific sprays for cars, sportswear, pets, carpets, and allergen reduction, as well as decorative candles, scented reed diffusers, and flameless scented luminaries. Scents are available for those looking to solve a problem (such as pet odor) or to create an ambiance around the house.

Sources: Linda Tischler, "Smells Like Brand Spirit," *Fast Company*, August 2005; Martin Lindstrom, "Smelling a Branding Opportunity," *Brandweek*, 14 March 2005; Lucas Conley, "Brand Sense," *Fast Company*, March 2005; Maureen Morrin and S. Ratneshwar, "Does It Make Sense to Use Scents to Enhance Brand Memory?," *Journal of Marketing Research* 40 (February 2003): 10–25; Anick Bosmans, "Scents and Sensibility: When Do (In)congruent Ambient Scents Influence Product Evaluations?," *Journal of Marketing* 70 (July 2006): 32–43; Aradhna Krishna, A., Ryan S. Elder, and Cindy Caldara, "Feminine to Smell but Masculine to Touch? Multisensory Congruence and Its Effects on the Aesthetic Experience," *Journal of Consumer Psychology* 20, no. 4 (2010): 410–418; Aradhna Krishna, May Lwin, and Maureen Morrin, "Product Scent and Memory," *Journal of Consumer Research* 37 (June 2010): 57–67; Ellen Byron, "Febreze Joins P&G's $1 Billion Club," *Wall Street Journal*, 9 March 2011; Joann Peck and Terry L. Childers, "Effect of Sensory Factors on Consumer Behavior," in *Handbook of Consumer Psychology*, eds. Curtis T. Haugtvedt, Paul M. Herr, and Frank R. Kardes (New York: Taylor & Francis, 2008), 193–220.

Here are just a few of the basic benefits relationship marketing provides:[13]

- Acquiring new customers can cost five times as much as satisfying and retaining current customers.
- The average company loses 10 percent of its customers each year.
- A 5 percent reduction in the customer defection rate can increase profits by 25–85 percent, depending on the industry.
- The customer profit rate tends to increase over the life of the retained customer.

We next review three concepts that can be helpful with relationship marketing: mass customization, one-to-one marketing, and permission marketing.

Mass Customization. The concept behind mass customization, namely making products to fit the customer's exact specifications, is an old one, but the advent of digital-age technology enables companies to offer customized products on a previously unheard-of scale. Going online, customers can communicate their preferences directly to the manufacturer, which, by using advanced production methods, can assemble the product for a price comparable to that of a noncustomized item.

In an age defined by the pervasiveness of mass-market goods, mass customization enables consumers to distinguish themselves with even basic purchases. The online jeweler Blue Nile lets customers design their own rings. Custom messenger-bag maker Rickshaw Bagworks lets customers design their own bags before they are made to order. Sportswear vendor Shorto-matic lets customers upload their own images and overlay them on a pair of custom-designed shorts. Land's End also allows customization of certain styles of pants and shirts on its Web site to allow for a better fit.[14]

Mass customization is not restricted to products. Many service organizations such as banks are developing customer-specific services and trying to improve the personal nature of their service experience with more service options, more customer-contact personnel, and longer service hours.[15]

Mass customization can offer supply-side benefits too. Retailers can reduce inventory, saving warehouse space and the expense of keeping track of everything and discounting leftover merchandise.[16] Mass customization has its limitations, however, because not every product is easily customized and not every product demands customization. Returns are also more problematic for a customized product that may not have broader appeal.

With the advent of social media, customers can now share with others what they have co-created with firms. For example, Nike enables customers to put their own personalized message on a pair of shoes with the NIKEiD program. At the NIKEiD Web site, visitors can make a customized shoe by selecting the size, width, and color scheme and affixing an eight-character personal ID to their creation. Then they can share it with others for them to admire.[17]

One-to-One Marketing.   Don Peppers and Martha Rogers popularized the concept of one-to-one marketing, an influential perspective on relationship marketing.[18] The basic rationale is that consumers help add value by providing information to marketers; marketers add value, in turn, by taking that information and generating rewarding experiences for consumers. The firm is then able to create switching costs, reduce transaction costs, and maximize utility for consumers, all of which help build strong, profitable relationships.

One-to-one marketing is thus based on several fundamental strategies:

- Focus on individual consumers through consumer databases—"We single out consumers."
- Respond to consumer dialogue via interactivity—"The consumer talks to us."
- Customize products and services—"We make something unique for him or her."

Another tenet of one-to-one marketing is treating different consumers differently because of their different needs, and their different current and future value to the firm. In particular, Peppers and Rogers stress the importance of devoting more marketing effort to the most valuable consumers.

With NIKEiD, customers can customize their shoes and share their creations with others online.

Source: Getty Images/Getty Images for Nike

Peppers and Rogers identified several examples of brands that have practiced one-to-one marketing through the years, such as Avon, Owens-Corning, and Nike.[19] They note how Ritz-Carlton hotels use databases to store consumer preferences, so that if a customer makes a special request in one of its hotels, it is already known when he or she stays in another.

Peppers and Rogers also provide an example of a localized version of one-to-one marketing. After having ordered flowers at a local florist for his or her mother, a customer might receive a post-card "reminding him that he had sent roses and star lilies last year and that a phone call would put a beautiful arrangement on her doorstep again for her birthday this year." Although such online or offline reminders can be helpful, marketers must not assume that customers always want to repeat their behaviors. For example, what if the flowers were a doomed, last-chance attempt to salvage a failing relationship? Then a reminder under such circumstances may not be exactly welcome!

An example of a highly successful relationship marketing program comes from Tesco, the United Kingdom's largest grocer.

TESCO

Celebrating its fifteenth anniversary in 2010, Tesco Clubcard is one of the world's most successful retail loyalty schemes. Each of the 10 million members in the program has a unique "DNA profile" based on the products he or she buys. Products themselves are classified on up to 40 dimensions—such as package size, healthy, own label, ecofriendly, ready-to-eat, and so on—to facilitate this customer categorization. In exchange for providing their purchase information and basic demographic information, members receive a variety of purchase benefits across a wide range of products and services beyond what is sold in their stores. Tracking customers' purchases in the program, in turn, helps Tesco uncover price elasticities, offer targeted promotions, and improve marketing efficiency. By also strengthening customer loyalty, the Clubcard program has been estimated to generate cumulative savings to Tesco of over £350 million. The range of products, the nature of merchandising, and even the location of Tesco's convenience stores all benefit from the use of this customer data to develop tailored solutions. Tesco has introduced a number of Clubcard program innovations through the years, including key fobs and newly designed cards issued in 2008.[20]

Tesco's Clubcard is the centerpiece of one of the world's most successful retail loyalty programs.

Source: Tesco Stores Ltd.

Permission Marketing. *Permission marketing,* the practice of marketing to consumers only after gaining their express permission, was another influential perspective on how companies can break through the clutter and build customer loyalty. A pioneer on the topic, Seth Godin, has noted that marketers can no longer employ "interruption marketing" or mass media campaigns featuring magazines, direct mail, billboards, radio and television commercials, and the like, because consumers have come to expect—but not necessarily appreciate—these interruptions.[21] By contrast, Godin asserts, consumers appreciate receiving marketing messages they gave permission for: "The worse the clutter gets, the more profitable your permission marketing efforts become."

Given the large number of marketing communications that bombard consumers every day, Godin argues that if marketers want to attract a consumer's attention, they first need to get his or her permission with some kind of inducement—a free sample, a sales promotion or discount, a contest, and so on. By eliciting consumer cooperation in this manner, marketers *might* develop stronger relationships with consumers so that they desire to receive further communications in the future. Those relationships will only develop, however, if marketers respect consumers' wishes, and if consumers express a willingness to become more involved with the brand.[22]

With the help of large databases and advanced software, companies can store gigabytes of customer data and process this information in order to send targeted, personalized marketing e-mail messages to customers. Godin identifies five steps to effective permission marketing:

1. Offer the prospect an incentive to volunteer.
2. Offer the interested prospect a curriculum over time, teaching the consumer about the product or service being marketed.
3. Reinforce the incentive to guarantee that the prospect maintains his or her permission.
4. Offer additional incentives to get more permission from the consumer.
5. Over time, leverage the permission to change consumer behavior toward profits.

In Godin's view, effective permission marketing works because it is "anticipated, personal, and relevant." A recent consumer research study provides some support: 87 percent of respondents agreed that e-mail "is a great way for me to hear about new products available from retail companies"; 88 percent of respondents said a retailer's e-mail has prompted them to download/print out a coupon; 75 percent said it has led them to buy a product online; 67 percent said it has prompted an offline purchase; and 60 percent have been moved to "try a new product for the first time."[23] Amazon.com has successfully applied permission marketing on the Web for years.[24]

AMAZON

With customer permission, online retailer Amazon uses database software to track its customers' purchase habits and send them personalized marketing messages. Each time a customer purchases something from Amazon.com, he or she can receive a follow-up e-mail containing information about other products that might interest him or her based on that purchase. For example, if a customer buys a book, Amazon might send an e-mail containing a list of titles by the same author, or of titles also purchased by customers who bought the original title. With just one click, the customer can get more detailed information. Amazon also sends periodic e-mails to customers informing them of new products, special offers, and sales. Each message is tailored to the individual customer based on past purchases and specified preferences, according to customer wishes. Amazon keeps an exhaustive list of past purchases for each customer and makes extensive recommendations.

Permission marketing is a way of developing the "consumer dialogue" component of one-to-one marketing in more detail. One drawback to permission marketing, however, is that it presumes that consumers have some sense of what they want. In many cases, consumers have undefined, ambiguous, or conflicting preferences that might be difficult for them to express. Thus, marketers must recognize that consumers may need to be given guidance and assistance in forming and conveying their preferences. In that regard, *participation marketing* may be a more appropriate term and concept to employ, because marketers and consumers need to work together to find out how the firm can best satisfy consumer goals.[25]

Reconciling the Different Marketing Approaches

These and other different approaches to personalization help reinforce a number of important marketing concepts and techniques. From a branding point of view, they are particularly useful means of both eliciting positive brand responses and creating brand resonance to build customer-based brand equity. Mass customization and one-to-one and permission marketing are all potentially effective means of getting consumers more actively engaged with a brand.

According to the customer-based brand equity (CBBE) model, however, these different approaches emphasize different aspects of brand equity. For example, mass customization and one-to-one and permission marketing might be particularly effective at creating greater relevance, stronger behavioral loyalty, and attitudinal attachment. Experiential marketing, on the other hand, would seem to be particularly effective at establishing brand imagery and tapping into a variety of different feelings as well as helping build brand communities. Despite potentially different areas of emphasis, all four approaches can build stronger consumer–brand bonds.

One implication of these new approaches is that the traditional "marketing mix" concept and the notion of the "4 Ps" of marketing—product, price, place (or distribution), and promotion (or marketing communications)—may not fully describe modern marketing programs, or the many activities, such as loyalty programs or pop-up stores, that may not necessarily fit neatly into one of those designations. Nevertheless, firms still have to make decisions about what exactly they are going to sell, how (and where) they are going to sell it, and at what price. In other words, firms must still devise product, pricing, and distribution strategies as part of their marketing programs.

The specifics of how they set those strategies, however, have changed considerably. We turn next to these topics and highlight a key development in each area, recognizing that there are many other important areas beyond the scope of this text. With product strategy, we emphasize the role of extrinsic factors; with pricing strategy, we focus on value pricing; and with channel strategy, we concentrate on channel integration.

PRODUCT STRATEGY

The product itself is the primary influence on what consumers experience with a brand, what they hear about a brand from others, and what the firm can tell customers about the brand. At the heart of a great brand is invariably a great product.

Designing and delivering a product or service that fully satisfies consumer needs and wants is a prerequisite for successful marketing, regardless of whether the product is a tangible good, service, or organization. For brand loyalty to exist, consumers' experiences with the product must at least meet, if not actually surpass, their expectations.

After considering how consumers form their opinions of the quality and value of a product, we consider how marketers can go beyond the actual product to enhance product experiences and add additional value before, during, and after product use.

Perceived Quality

Perceived quality is customers' perception of the overall quality or superiority of a product or service compared to alternatives and with respect to its intended purpose. Achieving a satisfactory level of perceived quality has become more difficult as continual product improvements over the years have led to heightened consumer expectations.[26]

Much research has tried to understand how consumers form their opinions about quality. The specific attributes of product quality can vary from category to category. Nevertheless, consistent with the brand resonance model from Chapter 3, research has identified the following general dimensions: primary ingredients and supplementary features; product reliability, durability and serviceability; and style and design.[27] Consumer beliefs about these characteristics often define quality and, in turn, influence attitudes and behavior toward a brand.

Product quality depends not only on functional product performance but on broader performance considerations as well, like speed, accuracy, and care of product delivery and installation; the promptness, courtesy, and helpfulness of customer service and training; and the quality of repair service.

Brand attitudes may also depend on more abstract product imagery, such as the symbolism or personality reflected in the brand. These "augmented" aspects of a product are often crucial to its equity. Finally, consumer evaluations may not correspond to the perceived quality of the product and may be formed by less thoughtful decision making, such as simple heuristics and decision rules based on brand reputation or product characteristics such as color or scent.

Aftermarketing

To achieve the desired brand image, product strategies should focus on both purchase *and* consumption. Much marketing activity is devoted to finding ways to encourage trial and repeat purchases by consumers. Perhaps the strongest and potentially most favorable associations, however, result from actual product experience—what Procter & Gamble calls the "second moment of truth" (the "first moment of truth" occurs at purchase).

Unfortunately, too little marketing attention is devoted to finding new ways for consumers to truly appreciate the advantages and capabilities of products. Perhaps in response to this oversight, one notable trend in marketing is the growing role of ***aftermarketing,*** that is, those marketing activities that occur *after* customer purchase. Innovative design, thorough testing, quality production, and effective communication—through mass customization or any other means—are without question the most important considerations in enhancing product consumption experiences that build brand equity.

In many cases, however, they may only be necessary and not sufficient conditions for brand success, and marketers may need to use other means to enhance consumption experiences. Here we consider the role of user manuals, customer service programs, and loyalty programs.

User Manuals.   Instruction or user manuals for many products are too often an afterthought, put together by engineers who use overly technical terms and convoluted language. Online help forums put the consumer at the mercy of other equally ignorant users or so-called experts who may not understand or appreciate the obstacles the average consumer faces.

As a result, consumers' initial product experiences may be frustrating or, even worse, unsuccessful. Even if consumers are able to figure out how to make the product perform its basic functions, they may not learn to appreciate some of its more advanced features, which are usually highly desirable and possibly unique to the brand.

To enhance consumers' consumption experiences, marketers must develop user manuals or help features that clearly and comprehensively describe both what the product or service can do for consumers and how they can realize these benefits. With increasing globalization, writing easy-to-use instructions has become even more important because they often require translation into multiple languages.[28] Manufacturers are spending more time designing and testing instructions to make them as user friendly as possible.

User manuals increasingly may need to appear in online and multimedia formats to most effectively demonstrate product functions and benefits. Intuit, makers of the Quicken personal finance management software package, routinely sends researchers home with first-time buyers to check that its software is easy to install and to identify any sources of problems that might arise. Corel software adopts a similar "Follow Me Home" strategy and also has "pizza parties" at the company where marketing, engineering, and quality assurance teams analyze the market research together, so that marketing does not just hand down conclusions to other departments.[29]

Customer Service Programs.   Aftermarketing, however, is more than the design and communication of product instructions. As one expert in the area notes, "The term 'aftermarketing' describes a necessary new mind-set that reminds businesses of the importance of building a lasting relationship with customers, to extend their lifetimes. It also points to the crucial need to better balance the allocation of marketing funds between conquest activities (like advertising) and retention activities (like customer communication programs)."[30]

Creating stronger ties with consumers can be as simple as creating a well-designed customer service department. Research by Accenture in 2010 found that two in three customers switched companies in the past year due to poor customer service.[31] In the auto industry, aftersales service from the dealer is a critical determinant of loyalty and repeat buying of a brand. Routine maintenance and unplanned repairs are an opportunity for dealers to strengthen their ties with customers.[32]

Aftermarketing can include the sale of complementary products that help make up a system or in any other way enhance the value of the core product. Printer manufacturers such as Hewlett-Packard derive much of their revenue from high-margin postpurchase items such as inkjet cartridges, laser toner cartridges, and paper specially designed for PC printers. The average owner of a home PC printer spends much more on consumables over the lifetime of the machine than on the machine itself.[33]

Aftermarketing can be an important determinant of profitability. For example, roughly three-quarters of revenue for aerospace and defense providers comes from aftermarket support and related sales. Aftermarket sales are strongest when customers are locked in to buying from the company that sold them the primary product due to service contracts, proprietary technology or patents, or unique service expertise.[34]

HP makes much more money selling printer cartridges than from selling the printer itself.
Source: Brown Adrian/SIPA/ Newscom

Loyalty Programs. *Loyalty* or *frequency programs* have become one popular means by which marketers can create stronger ties to customers.[35] Their purpose is "identifying, maintaining, and increasing the yield from a firm's 'best' customers through long-term, interactive, value-added relationships."[36] Firms in all kinds of industries—most notably the airlines—have established loyalty programs through different mixtures of specialized services, newsletters, premiums, and incentives. Often they include extensive co-branding arrangements or brand alliances.

AMERICAN AIRLINES

In 1981, American Airlines founded the first airline loyalty program, called AAdvantage. This frequent-flier program rewarded the airline's top customers with free trips and upgrades based on mileage flown. By recognizing customers for their patronage and giving them incentives to bring their business to American Airlines, the airline hoped to increase loyalty among its passengers. The program was an instant success, and other airlines quickly followed suit. These days, members can earn miles at more than 1,000 participating companies, which include over 35 hotel chains representing more than 75 brands, more than 20 airlines, eight car rental companies, and approximately 25 major retail/financial companies. In addition, members can earn miles when making purchases with one of more than 60 affinity card products in 30 countries. Today, scores of frequent-traveler programs exist, but American Airlines is still one of the largest, with membership of over 67 million in 2011.[37]

Many businesses besides airlines introduced loyalty programs in the intervening years because they often yield results.[38] As one marketing executive said, "Loyalty programs reduce defection rates and increase retention. You can win more of a customer's purchasing share." The value created by the loyalty program creates switching costs for consumers, reducing price competition among brands.

To get discounts, however, consumers must typically hand over personal data, raising privacy concerns. When the loyalty program is tied into a credit card, as is sometimes the case, privacy concerns are even more acute. Nevertheless, the lure of special deals can be compelling to consumers, and in 2011, there were more than 2 billion memberships in loyalty programs, with an average value of $622 points issues per household. A third of these rewards, however, remain unredeemed.[39]

The appeal to marketers is clear too. Fifteen percent of a retailer's most loyal customers can account for as much as half its sales, and it can take between 12 and 20 new customers to replace a lost loyal customer.[40] Some tips for building effective loyalty programs follow:[41]

- *Know your audience:* Most loyalty marketers employ sophisticated databases and software to determine which customer segment to target with a given program. Target customers whose purchasing behavior can be changed by the program.
- *Change is good:* Marketers must constantly update the program to attract new customers and prevent other companies in their category from developing "me-too" programs. "Any loyalty program that stays static will die," said one executive.

- *Listen to your best customers:* Suggestions and complaints from top customers deserve careful consideration, because they can lead to improvements in the program. Because they typically represent a large percentage of business, top customers must also receive better service and more attention.
- *Engage people:* Make customers want to join the program. Make the program easy to use and offer immediate rewards when customers sign up. Once they become members, make customers "feel special," for example, by sending them birthday greetings, special offers, or invitations to special events.

Summary

The product is at the heart of brand equity. Marketers must design, manufacture, market, sell, deliver, and service products in a way that creates a positive brand image with strong, favorable, and unique brand associations; elicits favorable judgments and feelings about the brand; and fosters greater degrees of brand resonance.

Product strategy entails choosing both tangible and intangible benefits the product will embody and marketing activities that consumers desire and the marketing program can deliver. A range of possible associations can become linked to the brand—some functional and performance-related, and some abstract and imagery-related. Perceived quality and perceived value are particularly important brand associations that often drive consumer decisions.

Because of the importance of loyal customers, relationship marketing has become a branding priority. Consequently, consumers' actual product experiences and aftermarketing activities have taken on increased importance in building customer-based brand equity. Those marketers who will be most successful at building CBBE will take the necessary steps to make sure they fully understand their customers and how they can deliver superior value before, during, and after purchase. A company doing just that is CVS.

CVS

Drugstore chain leader CVS has taken a number of steps to ensure customer loyalty. Data from its ExtraCare loyalty program is used to tailor offerings to its 67 million plus members. Interactive ExtraCare Coupon Centers in the stores let shoppers scan their loyalty cards to receive targeted offers before checking out, based on past purchases. Coupon Centers can also check product prices and dispense ExtraBucks rewards. In addition to coupons, the program offers customers 2 percent cash back on every dollar spent. The company notes that the average purchase by ExtraCare customers is higher (averaging 4.5 items for $15) than by non-ExtraCare customers (averaging 3.6 items for $12). CVS's rewards program set it apart from rival Walgreens, which did not originally have a loyalty card. Within five years, the ExtraCare card became associated with 60 percent of front-store transactions.[42]

CVS has found that its ExtraCare loyalty program creates more profitable customers.
Source: CVS

PRICING STRATEGY

Price is the one revenue-generating element of the traditional marketing mix, and price premiums are among the most important benefits of building a strong brand. This section considers the different kinds of price perceptions that consumers might form, and different pricing strategies that the firm might adopt to build brand equity.

Consumer Price Perceptions

The pricing strategy can dictate how consumers categorize the price of the brand (as low, medium, or high), and how firm or how flexible they think the price is, based on how deeply or how frequently it is discounted.

Consumers often rank brands according to price tiers in a category.[43] For example, Figure 5-3 shows the price tiers that resulted from a study of the ice cream market.[44] In that market, as the figure shows, there is also a relationship between price and quality. Within any price tier, there is a range of acceptable prices, called **price bands**, that indicate the flexibility and breadth marketers can adopt in pricing their brands within a tier. Some companies sell multiple brands to better compete in multiple categories. Figure 5-4 displays clothing offerings from Phillips Van Huesen that at one time covered a wide range of prices and corresponding retail outlets.[45]

Besides these descriptive "mean and variance" price perceptions, consumers may have price perceptions that have more inherent product meaning. In particular, in many categories, they may infer the quality of a product on the basis of its price and use perceived quality and price to arrive at an assessment of perceived value. Costs here are not restricted to the actual monetary price but may reflect opportunity costs of time, energy, and any psychological involvement in the decision that consumers might have.[46]

Consumer associations of perceived value are often an important factor in purchase decisions. Thus many marketers have adopted **value-based pricing strategies**—attempting to sell the right product at the right price—to better meet consumer wishes, as described in the next section.

In short, price has complex meaning and can play multiple roles to consumers. The Science of Branding 5-2 provides insight into how consumers perceive and process prices as part of their shopping behavior. Marketers need to understand all price perceptions that consumers have for a brand, to uncover quality and value inferences, and to discover any price premiums that exist.

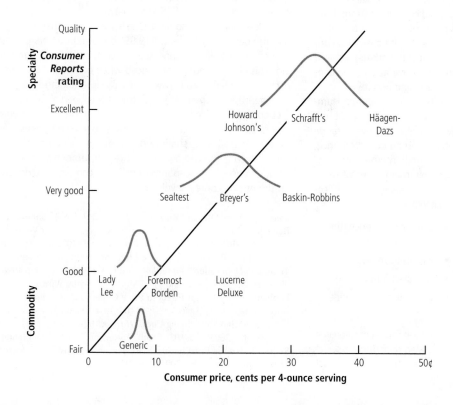

FIGURE 5-3

Price Tiers in the Ice Cream Market

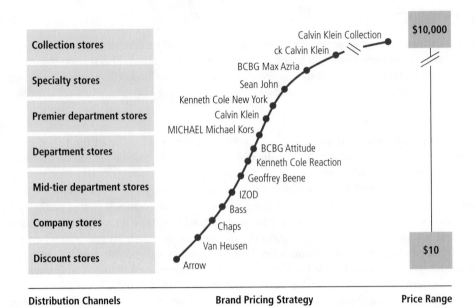

FIGURE 5-4

Phillips Van-Heusen
Brand Price Tiers

| Distribution Channels | Brand Pricing Strategy | Price Range |

THE SCIENCE OF BRANDING 5-2

Understanding Consumer Price Perceptions

Economists traditionally assumed that consumers were "price takers" who accepted prices as given. However, as Ofir and Winer note, consumers and customers often actively process price information, interpreting prices in terms of their knowledge from prior purchasing experience, formal communications such as advertising, informal communications from friends or family members, and point-of-purchase or online information. Consumer purchase decisions are based on consumers' perceived prices, however, not the marketer's stated value. Understanding how consumers arrive at their perceptions of prices is thus an important marketing priority.

Much research has shown that surprisingly few consumers can recall specific prices of products accurately, although they may have fairly good knowledge of the relevant range of prices. When examining or considering an observed price, however, consumers often compare it with internal frames of reference (prices they remember) or external frames of reference (a posted "regular retail price"). Internal reference prices occur in many forms, such as the following:

- "Fair price" (what product should cost)
- Typical price
- Last price paid
- Upper-bound price (the most consumer would pay)
- Lower-bound price (the least consumer would pay)
- Competitive prices
- Expected future price
- Usual discounted price

When consumers evoke one or more of these frames of reference, their perceived price can vary from the stated price. Most research on reference prices has found that "unpleasant surprises," such as a stated price higher than the perceived price, have a greater impact on purchase likelihood than pleasant surprises.

Consumer perceptions of prices are also affected by alternative pricing strategies. For example, research has shown that a relatively expensive item can seem less expensive if the price is broken down into smaller units (a $500 annual membership seems pricier than "less than $50 a month"). One reason prices often end with the number nine (as in, say, $49.99) is that consumers process prices in a left-to-right manner rather than holistically or by rounding. This effect is more pronounced when competing products' prices are numerically and psychologically closer together.

Even the competitive environment has been shown to affect consumer price judgments: deep discounts (like everyday low pricing or EDLP) can lead to lower perceived prices over time than frequent, shallow discounts (high-low pricing or HILO), even if the average prices are the same in both cases. Clearly, consumer perceptions of price are complex and depend on the pricing context involved.

Sources: Chezy Ofir and Russell S. Winer, "Pricing: Economic and Behavioral Models," in *Handbook of Marketing*, eds. Bart Weitz and Robin Wensley (New York: Sage Publications, 2002): 5–86; John T. Gourville, "Pennies-a-Day: The Effect of Temporal Reframing on Transaction Evaluation," *Journal of Consumer Research* (March 1998): 395–408; Manoj Thomas and Vicki Morwitz, "Penny Wise and Pound Foolish: The Left-Digit Effect in Price Cognition," *Journal of Consumer Research* 26 (June 2005): 54–64; Eric Anderson and Duncan Simester, "Mind Your Pricing Cues," *Harvard Business Review* 81, no. 9 (September 2003): 96–103; Tridib Mazumdar, S. P. Raj, and Indrajit Sinha, "Reference Price Research: Review and Propositions," *Journal of Marketing* 69 (October 2005): 84–102.

Setting Prices to Build Brand Equity

Choosing a pricing strategy to build brand equity means determining the following:

- A method for setting current prices
- A policy for choosing the depth and duration of promotions and discounts

There are many different approaches to setting prices, and the choice depends on a number of considerations. This section highlights a few of the most important issues as they relate to brand equity.[47]

Factors related to the costs of making and selling products and the relative prices of competitive products are important determinants in pricing strategy. Increasingly, however, firms are placing greater importance on consumer perceptions and preferences. Many firms now are employing a value-pricing approach to setting prices and an everyday-low-pricing (EDLP) approach to determining their discount pricing policy over time. Let's look at both.

Value Pricing.   The objective of ***value pricing*** is to uncover the right blend of product quality, product costs, and product prices that fully satisfies the needs and wants of consumers and the profit targets of the firm. Marketers have employed value pricing in various ways for years, sometimes learning the hard way that consumers will not pay price premiums that exceed their perceptions of the value of a brand. Perhaps the most vivid illustration was the legendary price cut for Philip Morris's leading cigarette brand, Marlboro, described in Branding Brief 5-1.[48]

BRANDING BRIEF 5-1

Marlboro's Price Drop

On April 2, 1993, or "Marlboro Friday," Philip Morris dropped a bombshell in the form of a three-page announcement: "Philip Morris USA . . . announced a major shift in business strategy designed to increase market share and grow long-term profitability in a highly price sensitive market environment." Quoting tobacco unit president and CEO William I. Campbell, the statement continued, "We have determined that in the current market environment caused by prolonged economic softness and depressed consumer confidence, we should take those steps necessary to grow our market share rather than pursue rapid income growth rates that might erode our leading marketplace position."

Philip Morris announced four major steps, the fourth of which caught the eye of marketers and Wall Street alike: a major promotional cut in the price of Marlboro (roughly 40 to 50 cents a pack), which was expected to decrease earnings in Philip Morris's most profitable unit by 40 percent. The action was justified by the results of a month-long test in Portland, Oregon, the previous December in which a 40-cent decrease in pack price had increased market share by 4 points.

The stock market reaction to the announcement was swift. By day's end, Philip Morris's stock price had declined from $64.12 to $49.37, a 23 percent drop that represented a one-day loss of $13 billion in shareholder equity! There was a ripple effect in the stock market, with significant stock price declines for other consumer goods companies with major brands like Sara Lee, Kellogg's, General Mills, and Procter & Gamble. A company that took one of the biggest hits was Coca-Cola, whose shareholders lost $5 billion in paper earnings in the days following "Black Friday."

A number of factors probably led Marlboro to cut prices so dramatically. The economy certainly was still sluggish, coming out of a recession. Private-label or store-brand cigarettes had been increasing in quality and were receiving more attention from customers and retailers. A prime consideration suggested by many was related to Philip Morris's hefty price increases. These had often occurred two to three times a year, so that the retail price of a pack of Marlboros more than tripled between 1980 and 1992. The 80 cents to $1 difference between premium brands and discount brands that prevailed at that time was thought to have resulted in steady sales increases for the discount brands at the expense of Marlboro's market share, which had dropped to 22 percent and was projected to decline further to 18 percent if Philip Morris made no changes.

Although much of the popular press attempted to exploit Marlboro's actions to proclaim that "brands were dead," nothing could have been further from the truth. In fact, a more accurate interpretation of the whole episode is that it showed that new brands were entering the scene, as evidenced by the ability of discount brands to create their own brand equity on the basis of strong consumer associations to "value."

At the same time, existing brands, if properly managed, can command loyalty, enjoy price premiums, and still be extremely profitable. By cutting the difference between discount cigarettes and Marlboro to roughly 40 cents, Philip Morris was able to woo back many customers. Within nine months after the price drop, its market share increased to almost 27 percent. Years later, Marlboro currently owns 42 percent of the market. Priced at $5.70 a pack, the brand commands a significant premium over the average $4.21 price for the cheapest brands on the market.

Sources: Laura Zinn, "The Smoke Clears at Marlboro," *BusinessWeek*, 31 January 1994, 76–77; Al Silk and Bruce Isaacson, "Philip Morris: Marlboro Friday (A)," Harvard Business School Case 9–596–001; Michael Felberbaum, "Altria 1Q Net Rises, but Marlboro Loses Ground," *Bloomberg BusinessWeek*, 20 April 2011.

Walmart's "Save Money. Live Better" slogan succinctly summarizes its strong value positioning.

Source: Beth Hall/ Bloomberg via Getty Images

Two important and enduring branding lessons emerged from the Marlboro episode. First, strong brands can command price premiums. Once Marlboro's price entered a more acceptable range, consumers were willing to pay the still-higher price, and sales of the brand started to increase. Second, strong brands cannot command an excessive price premium. The clear signal sent to marketers everywhere is that price hikes without corresponding investments in the value of the brand may increase the vulnerability of the brand to lower-priced competition. In these cases, consumers may be willing to "trade down" because they no longer can justify to themselves that the higher-priced brand is worth it. Although the Marlboro price discounts led to short-term profitability declines, they also led to regained market share that put the brand on a stronger footing over the longer haul.

In today's challenging new climate, several firms have been successful by adopting a value-pricing strategy. For example, Walmart's slogan, "Save Money. Live Better," describes the pricing strategy that has allowed it to become the world's largest retailer. Southwest Airlines combined low fares with no-frills—but friendly—service to become a powerful force in the airline industry. The success of these and other firms has dramatized the potential benefits of implementing a value-pricing strategy.

As you might expect, there are a number of opinions regarding the keys for success in adopting a value-based pricing approach. In general, however, an effective value-pricing strategy should strike the proper balance among three key components:

- Product design and delivery
- Product costs
- Product prices

In other words, as we've seen before, the right kind of product has to be made the right way and sold at the right price. We look at each of these three elements below. Meanwhile, a brand that has experienced much success in recent years balancing this formula is Hyundai.

HYUNDAI

Taking a page from the Samsung playbook, Korean upstart automaker Hyundai is trying to do to Toyota and Honda what Samsung successfully did to Sony—provide an affordable alternative to a popular market leader. Like Samsung, Hyundai has adopted a well-executed value pricing strategy that combines advanced technology, reliable performance, and attractive design with lower prices. As the head of U.S. design noted in discussing the 2011 Sonata sedan and revamped Tucson crossover, "The basic idea is a car that looks like a premium car, but not at a premium price. We're looking to pull people out of Camrys and Accords and give them something different." Hyundai's 10-year or 100,000 mile power train warranty programs brand positive reviews from car analysts such as J. D. Power provided additional reassurance to potential buyers of the quality of the products and the company's stability. To maintain momentum during the recession, Hyundai's "Assurance" program, featuring a highly publicized Super Bowl TV spot, allowed new buyers to return their Hyundai vehicles if they lost their job. All these efforts were met with greater customer acceptance: the number of potential U.S. buyers who say they would "definitely" consider a Hyundai tripled from 2000 to 2009. Hyundai's current Assurance program is centered on a new Trade-in Value Guarantee that preserves the market value of a new Hyundai by guaranteeing to customers at the time of purchase exactly how much it would be worth, two, three, or four years from now.[49]

Hyundai has a strong value proposition, anchored by its 10-year or 100,000-mile warranty.

Source: Hyundai Motor America

Product Design and Delivery. The first key is the proper design and delivery of the product. Product value can be enhanced through many types of well-conceived and well-executed marketing programs, such as those covered in this and other chapters of the book. Proponents of value pricing point out that the concept does not mean selling stripped-down versions of products at lower prices. Consumers are willing to pay premiums when they perceive added value in products and services.

Some companies actually have been able to *increase* prices by skillfully introducing new or improved "value-added" products. Some marketers have coupled well-marketed product innovations and improvements with higher prices to strike an acceptable balance to at least some market segments. Here are two examples of Procter & Gamble brands that used that formula to find marketplace success in the midst of the deep recession of 2008–2010.

- P&G introduced its most expensive Gillette razor ever, the Fusion ProGlide, by combining an innovative product with strong marketing support. Its "Turning Shaving into Gliding and Skeptics into Believers" campaign for Fusion ProGlide gave sample razors to bloggers and ran ads online and on TV showing men outside their homes given impromptu shaves with the new razor.[50]
- P&G's Pepto-Bismol stomach remedy liquid was able to command a 60 percent price premium over private labels through a blend of product innovation (new cherry flavors) and an engaging advertising campaign that broke copy-testing research records for the brand ("Coverage" featuring a headset-wearing, pink-vested "Pepto Guy" fielding calls and offering humorous advice to gastrointestinally challenged callers).[51]

With the advent of the Internet, many critics predicted that customers' ability to perform extensive, assisted online searches would result in only low-cost providers surviving. In reality, the advantages of creating strong brand differentiation have led to price premiums when brands are sold online just as much as when sold offline. For example, although undersold by numerous book and music sellers online, Amazon.com was able to maintain market leadership, eventually forcing low-priced competitors such as Books.com and others out of business.[52]

Product Costs. The second key to a successful value-pricing strategy is to lower costs as much as possible. Meeting cost targets invariably requires finding additional cost savings through productivity gains, outsourcing, material substitution (less expensive or less wasteful materials),

Famous athletes and celebrities—such as NBA player Tony Parker, WWE wrestler John Cena, and TV sportscaster Erin Andrews—have promoted Gillette's latest Fusion ProGlide razor and its innovative performance features.

Source: mZUMA Press/Newscom

product reformulations, and process changes like automation or other factory improvements.[53] As one marketing executive once put it:

> The customer is only going to pay you for what he perceives as real value-added. When you look at your overhead, you've got to ask yourself if the customer is really willing to pay for that. If the answer is no, you've got to figure out how to get rid of it or you're not going to make money.[54]

To reduce its costs to achieve value pricing, Procter & Gamble cut overhead according to four simple guidelines: change the work, do more with less, eliminate work, and reduce costs that cannot be passed on to consumers. P&G simplified the distribution chain to make restocking more efficient through continuous product replenishment. The company also scaled back its product portfolio by eliminating 25 percent of its stock-keeping units.

Firms have to be able to develop business models and cost structures to support their pricing plans. Taco Bell reduced operating costs enough to lower prices for many items on the menu to under $1, sparking an industry-wide trend in fast foods. Unfortunately, many other fast food chains found it difficult to lower their overhead costs enough or found that their value menu cannibalized more profitable items.[55]

Cost reductions certainly cannot sacrifice quality, effectiveness, or efficiency. Toyota and Johnson & Johnson's Tylenol both experienced brand crises due to product problems, which analysts and even some of the management of the two firms attributed to overly zealous cost reductions. When H&R Block cut costs as it moved into new areas outside tax preparation, customer service suffered and customers began to complain about long wait times and rudeness.[56]

Product Prices.   The final key to a successful value-pricing strategy is to understand exactly how much value consumers perceive in the brand and thus to what extent they will pay a premium over product costs.[57] A number of techniques are available to estimate these consumer value perceptions. Perhaps the most straightforward approach is to directly ask consumers their perceptions of price and value in different ways.

The price suggested by estimating perceived value can often be a starting point for marketers in determining actual marketplace prices, adjusting by cost and competitive considerations as necessary. For example, to halt a precipitous slide in market share for its flagship 9-Lives brand, the pet products division of H. J. Heinz took a new tack in its pricing strategy. The company found from research that consumers wanted to be able to buy cat food at the price of "four cans for a dollar," despite the fact that its cat food cost between 29 and 35 cents per can. As a result, Heinz reshaped its product packaging and redesigned its manufacturing processes to be able to hit the necessary cost, price, and margin targets. Despite lower prices, profits for the brand doubled.

Communicating Value.   Combining these three components in the right way to create value is crucial. Just delivering good value, however, is necessary but not sufficient for achieving pricing success—consumers have to actually understand and appreciate the value of the brand. In many cases, that value may be obvious—the product or service benefits are clear and comparisons with competitors are easy. In other cases, however, value may not be obvious, and consumers may too easily default to purchasing lower-priced competitors. Then marketers may need to engage in marketing communications to help consumers better recognize the value. In some cases, the solution may simply require straightforward communications that expand on the value equation for the brand, such as stressing quality for price. In other cases, it may involve "framing" and convincing consumers to think about their brand and product decisions differently.

For example, take a premium-priced brand such as Procter & Gamble's Pantene. It faces pressure from many competing brands, but especially private-label and store and discount brands that may cost much less. In tough times, even small cost savings may matter to penny-pinching consumers. Assume a bottle of Pantene cost a $1 more than its main competitors but could be used for up to 100 shampoos. In that case, the price difference is really only one cent *per shampoo*. By framing the purchase decision in terms of cost per shampoo, P&G could then advertise, "Isn't it worth a penny more to get a better-looking head of hair?"

Price Segmentation.   At the same time, different consumers may have different value perceptions and therefore could—and most likely should—receive different prices. Price segmentation sets and adjusts prices for appropriate market segments. Apple has a three-tier pricing scheme for iTunes downloads—a base price of 99 cents, but $1.29 for popular hits and 69 cents for oldies-but-not-so-goodies.[58] Starbucks similarly has raised the prices of some of its specialty beverages while charging less for some basic drinks.[59]

In part because of wide adoption of the Internet, firms are increasingly employing ***yield management principles*** or ***dynamic pricing***, such as those adopted by airlines to vary their prices for different market segments according to their different demand and value perceptions. Here are several examples:

- Allstate Insurance embarked on a yield management pricing program, looking at drivers' credit history, demographic profile, and other factors to better match automobile policy premiums to customer risk profiles.[60]
- To better compete with scalpers and online ticket brokers such as StubHub, concert giant Ticketmaster has begun to implement more efficient variable pricing schemes based on demand that charge higher prices for the most sought-after tickets and lower prices for less-desirable seats for sporting events and concerts.[61]
- The San Francisco Giants now uses a software system that allows the team to look at different variables such as current ticket sales, weather forecasts, and pitching matchups to determine whether it should adjust prices—right up until game day. The software allows the team to take the price-tier strategy baseball has traditionally used and make it more dynamic.[62]
- New start-up Village Vines offers a demand-management solution to restaurants that allows them to effectively price discriminate by offering deal-prone customers the option of making reservations for 30 percent off the entire bill on select (less desirable) days and times.[63]

Everyday Low Pricing.   ***Everyday low pricing (EDLP)*** has received increased attention as a means of determining price discounts and promotions over time. EDLP avoids the sawtooth, whiplash pattern of alternating price increases and decreases or discounts in favor of a more consistent set of "everyday" base prices on products. In many cases, these EDLP prices are based on the value-pricing considerations we've noted above.

The P&G Experience.   In the early 1990s, Procter & Gamble made a well-publicized conversion to EDLP.[64] By reducing list prices on half its brands and eliminating many temporary discounts, P&G reported that it saved $175 million in 1991, or 10 percent of its previous year's profits. Advocates of EDLP argue that maintaining consistently low prices on major items every day helps build brand loyalty, fend off private-label inroads, and reduce manufacturing and inventory costs.[65]

The San Francisco Giants have used yield pricing at their AT&T Park home, basing prices for any seat at any game on a number of different factors.

Source: Aurora Photos/ Alamy

Even strict adherents of EDLP, however, see the need for some types of price discounts over time. When P&G encountered some difficulties in the late 1990s, it altered its value-pricing strategy in some segments and reinstated selected price promotions. More recently, P&G has adopted a more fluid pricing strategy in reaction to market conditions.[66] Although P&G lowered prices in 2010 to try to gain market share in the depths of a severe recession, the company actually raised some prices to offset rising commodity costs in 2011. Management felt confident about the strength of some of the firm's popular premium-priced brands—such as Fusion ProGlide, Crest 3-D products, and Old Spice body wash—where demand had actually even exceeded supply.

As Chapter 6 will discuss, well-conceived, timely sales promotions can provide important financial incentives to consumers and induce sales. As part of revenue-management systems or yield-management systems, many firms have been using sophisticated models and software to determine the optimal schedule for markdowns and discounts.[67]

Reasons for Price Stability.   Why then do firms seek greater price stability? Manufacturers can be hurt by an overreliance on trade and consumer promotions and the resulting fluctuations in prices for several reasons.

For example, although trade promotions are supposed to result in discounts on products only for a certain length of time and in a certain geographic region, that is not always the case. With *forward buying,* retailers order more product than they plan to sell during the promotional period so that they can later obtain a bigger margin by selling the remaining goods at the regular price after the promotional period has expired. With *diverting*, retailers pass along or sell the discounted products to retailers outside the designated selling area.

From the manufacturer's perspective, these retailer practices created production complications: factories had to run overtime because of excess demand during the promotion period but had slack capacity when the promotion period ended, costing manufacturers millions. On the demand side, many marketers felt that the seesaw of high and low prices on products actually trained consumers to wait until the brand was discounted or on special to buy it, thus eroding its perceived value. Creating a brand association to "discount" or "don't pay full price" diminished brand equity.

Summary

To build brand equity, marketers must determine strategies for setting prices and adjusting them, if at all, over the short and long run. Increasingly, these decisions will reflect consumer perceptions of value. Value pricing strikes a balance among product design, product costs, and product prices. From a brand equity perspective, consumers must find the price of the brand appropriate and fair given the benefits they feel they receive by the product and its relative advantages with respect to competitive offerings, among other factors. Everyday low pricing is a complementary pricing approach to determine the nature of price discounts and promotions over time that maintains consistently low, value-based prices on major items on a day-to-day basis.

There is always tension between lowering prices on the one hand and increasing consumer perceptions of product quality on the other. Academic researchers Lehmann and Winer believe that although marketers commonly use price reductions to improve perceived value, in reality discounts are often a more expensive way to add value than brand-building marketing activities.[68] Their argument is that the lost revenue from a lower margin on each item sold is often much greater than the additional cost of value-added activities, primarily because many of these costs are fixed and spread over *all* the units sold, as opposed to the per unit reductions that result from lower prices.

CHANNEL STRATEGY

The manner by which a product is sold or distributed can have a profound impact on the equity and ultimate sales success of a brand. *Marketing channels* are defined as "sets of interdependent organizations involved in the process of making a product or service available for use or consumption."[69] Channel strategy includes the design and management of intermediaries such as wholesalers, distributors, brokers, and retailers. Let's look at how channel strategy can contribute to brand equity.[70]

Channel Design

A number of possible channel types and arrangements exist, broadly classified into direct and indirect channels. *Direct channels* mean selling through personal contacts from the company to prospective customers by mail, phone, electronic means, in-person visits, and so forth. *Indirect channels* sell through third-party intermediaries such as agents or broker representatives, wholesalers or distributors, and retailers or dealers.

Increasingly, winning channel strategies will be those that can develop "integrated shopping experiences" that combine physical stores, Internet, phone, and catalogs. For example, consider the wide variety of direct and indirect channels by which Nike sells its shoes, apparel, and equipment products:[71]

- *Branded Niketown stores:* Over 500 Niketown stores, located in prime shopping avenues in metropolitan centers around the globe, offer a complete range of Nike products and serve as showcases for the latest styles. Each store consists of a number of individual shops or pavilions that feature shoes, clothes, and equipment for a different sport (tennis, jogging, biking, or water sports) or different lines within a sport (there might be three basketball shops and two tennis shops). Each shop develops its own concepts with lights, music, temperature, and multimedia displays. Nike is also experimenting with newer, smaller stores that target specific customers and sports (a running-only store in Palo Alto, CA; a soccer-only store in Manchester, England).
- *NikeStore.com:* Nike's e-commerce site allows consumers to place Internet orders for a range of products or to custom-design some products through NIKEiD, which surpassed $100 million in sales in 2010.
- *Outlet stores:* Nike's outlet stores feature discounted Nike merchandise.
- *Retail:* Nike products are sold in retail locations such as shoe stores, sporting goods stores, department stores, and clothing stores.

Nike uses a variety of different channels for different purposes. Its Niketown stores have been very useful as a brand-building tool.

Source: AP Photo/Marcio Jose Sanchez

- *Catalog retailers:* Nike's products appear in numerous shoe, sporting goods, and clothing catalogs.
- *Specialty stores:* Nike equipment from product lines such as Nike Golf is often sold through specialty stores such as golf pro shops.

Much research has considered the pros and cons of selling through various channels. Although the decision ultimately depends on the relative profitability of the different options, some more specific guidelines have been proposed. For example, one study for industrial products suggests that direct channels may be preferable when product information needs are high, product customization is high, product quality assurance is important, purchase lot size is important, and logistics are important. On the other hand, this study also suggests that indirect channels may be preferable when a broad assortment is essential, availability is critical, and after-sales service is important. Exceptions to these generalities exist, especially depending on the market segments.[72]

From the viewpoint of consumer shopping and purchase behaviors, we can see channels as blending three key factors: information, entertainment, and experiences.

- Consumers may learn about a brand and what it does and why it is different or special.
- Consumers may also be entertained by the means by which the channel permits shopping and purchases.
- Consumers may be able to participate in and experience channel activities.

It is rare that a manufacturer will use only a single type of channel. More likely, the firm will choose a hybrid channel design with multiple channel types.[73] Marketers must manage these channels carefully, as Tupperware found out.

TUPPERWARE

In the 1950s, Tupperware pioneered the plastic food-storage container business and the means by which the containers were sold. With many mothers staying at home and growth in the suburbs exploding, Tupperware parties with a local neighborhood host became a successful avenue for selling. Unfortunately, with more women entering the workforce and heightened competition from brands such as Rubbermaid, Tupperware sales closed out the twentieth century with a 15-year decline. Sales turned around only with some new approaches to selling, including booths at shopping malls and a move to the Internet. The decision to place products in all 1,148 Target stores, however, was a complete disaster. In-store selling was difficult given the very different retail environment. Moreover, because the product was made more widely available, interest in traditional in-home parties plummeted. Frustrated, many salespeople dropped out and fewer new ones were recruited. Although the products were yanked from the stores, the damage was done and profit plunged almost 50 percent. As one key distributor commented, "We just bit off more than we could chew."[74]

Tupperware made a serious mistake revising its channel strategy to sell through Target.
Source: Justin Sullivan/Getty Images

The risk in designing a hybrid channel system is having too many channels (leading to conflict among channel members or a lack of support), or too few channels (resulting in market opportunities being overlooked). The goal is to maximize channel coverage and effectiveness while minimizing channel cost and conflict.

Because marketers use both direct and indirect channels, let's consider the brand equity implications of the two major channel design types.

Indirect Channels

Indirect channels can consist of a number of different types of intermediaries, but we will concentrate on retailers. Retailers tend to have the most visible and direct contact with customers and therefore have the greatest opportunity to affect brand equity. As we will outline in greater detail in Chapter 7, consumers may have associations to any one retailer on the basis of product assortment, pricing and credit policy, and quality of service, among other factors. Through the products and brands they stock and the means by which they sell, retailers strive to create their own brand equity by establishing awareness and strong, favorable, and unique associations.

At the same time, retailers can have a profound influence on the equity of the brands they sell, especially in terms of the brand-related services they can support or help create. Moreover, the interplay between a store's image and the brand images of the products it sells is an important one. Consumers make assumptions such as "this store only sells good-quality, high-value merchandise, so this particular product must also be good quality and high value."

Push and Pull Strategies.   Besides the indirect avenue of image transfer, retailers can directly affect the equity of the brands they sell. Their methods of stocking, displaying, and selling products can enhance or detract from brand equity, suggesting that manufacturers must take an active role in helping retailers add value to their brands. A topic of great interest in recent years in that regard is shopper marketing.

Though defined differently by different people, at its core ***shopper marketing*** emphasizes collaboration between manufacturers and retailers on in-store marketing like brand-building displays, sampling promotions, and other in-store activities designed to capitalize on a retailer's capabilities and its customers. Vlasic is a brand that has ramped up its shopper marketing program.

VLASIC

Although many homes keep a jar of pickles in their refrigerator, too often it ends up in the back of a shelf, where it is forgotten. When summer barbecue season rolls along, pickle consumption increases, although still not as much as market leader Vlasic would like. Company research revealed that about 80 percent of pickles consumed in U.S. homes accompany a hamburger or other sandwich, but only 3 percent of all sandwiches consumed are served with pickles. Compounding the consumption problem is a shopping obstacle. Pickles typically are stocked in the center aisles of stores, where only about 20 percent of shoppers turn on any given trip, compared with the produce or deli aisles on the perimeter of the store, where about 60 percent shop. Vlasic did have one advantage with which to work. Through the years, its iconic brand character—a stork with a Groucho Marx look and personality—had become widely recognizable from all its advertising appearances. For the 2011 summer selling season, Vlasic decided to pull all those factors together to try something different in its marketing. In-store ad cutouts with the stork began to appear in sections of the supermarket away from where pickles were stocked. In the meat section, for example, an ad was placed that included a speech balloon near the stork's beak proclaiming: "Pro tip: Serve your burgers with a Vlasic pickle. Amateur tip: Don't." Similar type ads appeared near the hamburger buns in the bread aisle and all through the cheese aisles. The ads also appeared on shopping carts and on vinyl ads on the supermarket floor. To provide further marketing support outside the store, print ads for the brand stating "Bring On the Bite" appeared in magazines and on Web sites.[75]

Vlasic's concerted shopper marketing program paid off nicely in the marketplace.
Source: Pinnacle Foods Group LLC

Such collaborative efforts can spur greater sales of a brand. Yet, at the same time, much conflict has also emerged in recent years between manufacturers and the retailers making up their channels of distribution. Because of greater competition for shelf space among what many retailers feel are increasingly undifferentiated brands, retailers have gained power and are now in a better position to set the terms of trade with manufacturers. Increased power means that retailers can command more frequent and lucrative trade promotions.

One way for manufacturers to regain some of their lost leverage is to create strong brands through some of the brand-building tactics described in this book, for example, by selling innovative and unique products—properly priced and advertised—that consumers demand. In this way, consumers may ask or even pressure retailers to stock and promote manufacturers' products.

By devoting marketing efforts to the end consumer, a manufacturer is said to employ a ***pull strategy***, since consumers use their buying power and influence on retailers to "pull" the product through the channel. Alternatively, marketers can devote their selling efforts to the channel members themselves, providing direct incentives for them to stock and sell products to the end consumer. This approach is called a ***push strategy***, because the manufacturer is attempting to reach the consumer by "pushing" the product through each step of the distribution chain.

Although certain brands seem to emphasize one strategy more than another (push strategies are usually associated with more selective distribution, and pull strategies with broader, more intensive distribution), the most successful marketers—brands like Apple, Coca-Cola, and Nike—skillfully blend push *and* pull strategies.

Marketing research	Gathering information necessary for planning and facilitating interactions with customers
Communications	Developing and executing communications about the product and service
Contact	Seeking out and interacting with prospective customers
Matching	Shaping and fitting the product/service to the customer's requirements
Negotiations	Reaching final agreement on price and other terms of trade
Physical distribution	Transporting and storing goods (inventory)
Financing	Providing credit or funds to facilitate the transaction
Risk-taking	Assuming risks associated with getting the product or service from firm to customer
Service	Developing and executing ongoing relationships with customers, including maintenance and repair

FIGURE 5-5

Services Provided by Channel Members

Source: Reprinted from Donald Lehmann and Russell Winer, *Product Management,* 2nd ed (Burr Ridge, IL: Irwin, 1997), Figure 13-8 on p. 379. © The McGraw-Hill Companies.

Channel Support.   A number of different services provided by channel members can enhance the value to consumers of purchasing and consuming a brand name product (see Figure 5-5). Although firms are increasingly providing some of the services themselves through toll-free numbers and Web sites, establishing a "marketing partnership" with retailers may nevertheless be critical to ensuring proper channel support and the execution of these various services.

Manufacturers can take a number of steps to keep retail partners happy and prevent breaks in the supply chain. Resellers often sink significant amounts of money into maintaining their facilities and paying sales staffs. To compensate them, manufacturers can offer dealers exclusive access to new products, or branded variants, as described below. Experts also advise that manufacturers stick to fixed prices when they offer products directly to consumers. If they do offer big discounts, they should offer them at outlet malls, where they won't confuse customers.

Manufacturers also can back up their distributors by educating them about their products so the retail partners can shape an effective sales force. When makeup giant Mary Kay began selling its cosmetics online in 1997, it also helped the members of its direct sales force set up their own online stores. Sharing product information and also doing good advertising contributes to distributors' success. John Deere effectively partnered with its channel members on customer service.

JOHN DEERE

John Deere was founded in 1837 by a blacksmith who devised a new type of cast-steel plow that revolutionized Midwest farming. The firm is now best known, however, for its tractors and residential and commercial-use products, such as mowers, ATVs, and saws. Over the decades, Deere dealers sprouted throughout the country, growing to more than 10,000 in the 1920s. Consolidation led to a contraction of the dealer network, a trend that Deere has actively encouraged in recent years as it tries to ensure that dealers have the necessary technological and business expertise to deal with increasingly large and sophisticated farm conglomerates. In 2003, John Deere expanded beyond its mainly rural network of more than 2,500 dealers to gain access to an additional 100,000 customers by selling its products through Home Depot. In doing so, Deere avoided conflict by assigning dealers to handle the service for purchases made from the mass channel, ensuring that they gained immediate revenue and an opportunity for future sales.[76]

Ultimately, companies have to share the power to make decisions with their distributors and recognize that dealers' success benefits them too. In many markets, dealers have captured more of the retail sales, so manufacturers must keep them happy and profitable if they want the benefits of a smooth supply chain. Two important components of partnership strategies are retail segmentation activities and cooperative advertising programs.

Retail Segmentation.   Retailers are "customers" too. Because of their different marketing capabilities and needs, retailers may need to be divided into segments or even treated individually so they will provide the necessary brand support.[77] Consider how the following packaged goods companies have customized their marketing efforts to particular retailers:[78]

- Frito-Lay developed a tailored supply-chain system for its corn chip and potato chip markets, making fast and broad distribution possible, reducing stock-outs, and creating better-turning store displays for its various retail customers.
- SC Johnson has leveraged customized market research insights to develop unique category management solutions to its strategic retail customers.
- Scotts Miracle-Gro customizes its product lines, marketing events, and supply chain for "big box," club, and hardware co-op channels.

Different retailers may need different product mixes, special delivery systems, customized promotions, or even their own branded version of the products.

Branded variants have been defined as branded items in a diverse set of durable and semi-durable goods categories that are not directly comparable to other items carrying the same brand name.[79] Manufacturers create branded variants in many ways, including making changes in color, design, flavor, options, style, stain, motif, features, and layout. For example, portable stereo "boom boxes" from brands like Sony, Panasonic, and Toshiba come in a broad assortment of variants, varying in speaker size, total weight, number of audio controls, recording features, and SKU number.

Branded variants are a means to reduce retail price competition because they make direct price comparisons by consumers difficult. Thus, different retailers may be given different items or models of the same brand to sell. Shugan and his colleagues show that as the manufacturer of a product offers more branded variants, a greater number of retail stores carry the product, and these stores offer higher levels of retail service for these products.[80]

Cooperative Advertising.   One relatively neglected means of increasing channel support is well-designed cooperative advertising programs. Traditionally, with co-op advertising, a manufacturer pays for a portion of the advertising that a retailer runs to promote the manufacturer's product and its availability in the retailer's place of business. To be eligible to receive co-op funds, the retailer usually must follow the manufacturer's stipulations as to the nature of brand exposure in the ad. Manufacturers generally share the cost of the advertising on a percentage basis up to a certain limit but usually 50–50. The total amount of cooperative advertising funds the manufacturer provides to the retailer is usually based on a percentage of dollar purchases made by the retailer from the manufacturer.[81]

The rationale behind cooperative advertising for manufacturers is that it concentrates some of the communication efforts at a local level where they may have more relevance and selling impact with consumers. Unfortunately, the brand image communicated through co-op ads is not as tightly controlled as when the manufacturer runs its own ads, and there is a danger that the emphasis in a co-op ad may be on the store or on a particular sale it is running rather than on the brand. Perhaps even worse, there is also a danger that a co-op ad may communicate a message about the brand that runs counter to its desired image.

An ideal situation is to achieve synergy between the manufacturer's own ad campaigns for a brand and its corresponding co-op ad campaigns with retailers. The challenge in designing effective co-op ads will continue to be striking a balance between pushing the brand and the store at the same time. In that sense, cooperative advertising will have to live up to its name, and manufacturers will have to get involved in the design and execution of retailers' campaigns rather than just handing over money or supplying generic, uninspired ads.

Summary.   In eliciting channel support, manufacturers must be creative in the way they develop marketing and merchandising programs aimed at the trade or any other channel members.

They should consider how channel activity can encourage trial purchase and communicate or demonstrate product information, to build brand awareness and image and to elicit positive brand responses.

Direct Channels

For some of the reasons we've already noted, manufacturers may choose to sell directly to consumers. Let's examine some of the brand equity issues of selling through direct channels.

Company-Owned Stores. To gain control over the selling process and build stronger relationships with customers, some manufacturers are introducing their own retail outlets, as well as selling their product directly to customers through various means. These channels can take many forms, the most complex of which, from a manufacturer's perspective, is company-owned stores. Hallmark, Goodyear, and others have sold their own products in their own stores for years. They have eventually been joined by a number of other firms—including some of the biggest marketers around.

For example, in December 1994, after the Federal Trade Commission amended a 16-year ban on the jeans maker selling its own wares, Levi Strauss began to open up Levi's Stores in the United States and abroad, located mostly in downtown areas and upscale suburban malls.[82] Only launched in 2001, Apple now derives 20 percent of its revenue from its physical stores, generating revenue at a rate of about $4,000 per square foot a year. Apple's own-store success is attributed to strong customer service, a clear link between the retail space and the product's user-friendly design, and the "community center" environment that add up to create a distinctively Apple retail experience.[83]

A number of other brands of all kinds have created their own stores, such as Bang & Olufsen audio equipment, OshKosh B'Gosh children's wear, Dr. Martens boots and shoes, and Warner Bros. entertainment. But not all company stores are big structures with extensive inventory. One recent trend is the launching of pop-up stores—temporary stores that blend retail and event marketing.[84]

POP-UP STORES

As a means to complement their existing channels and even own brick-and-mortar stores, some companies are introducing temporary store locations, especially during the holiday season. One popular location is New York City, which at times can have many appealing vacant spaces to choose from. During the 2010 holiday season, Procter & Gamble's 4,000-square-foot pop-up location on Fifty-Seventh Street in Manhattan drew 14,000 visitors in the first 10 days it was open. P&G's store, with tinted windows and neon lights, was designed as a flashy means to distribute samples of its products and experiences—from a full CoverGirl makeover or Head & Shoulders wash-and-blow-dry to free Febreze scented candles. Levi Strauss's 10,000-square-foot "workshop" in a former art gallery in Manhattan's SoHo district was designed to reinforce craftsmanship and collaboration themes in its "Go Forth" ad campaign. Target's Liberty of London pop-up shop closed a day early when it sold out of all its merchandise. For all these companies, pop-up stores are a way to create buzz, try out some new products and merchandising, and connect with some consumers in a unique way.

Temporary pop-up stores have given marketers a creative way to generate consumer interest and involvement.

Source: Andrew H. Walker/Getty Images for Target

Company stores provide many benefits.[85] Primarily, they are a means to showcase the brand and all its different product varieties in a manner not easily achieved through normal retail channels. For example, Nike might find its products spread all through department stores and athletic specialty stores. These products may not be displayed in a logical, coordinated fashion, and certain product lines may not even be stocked. By opening its own stores, Nike was able to effectively put its best foot forward by showing the depth, breadth, and variety of its branded products. Company stores can provide the added benefit of functioning as a test market to gauge consumer response to alternative product designs, presentations, and prices, allowing firms to keep their fingers on the pulse of consumers' shopping habits.

A disadvantage of company stores is that some companies lack the skills, resources, or contacts to operate effectively as a retailer. For example, The Disney Store, started in 1987, sells exclusive Disney-branded merchandise, ranging from toys and videos to collectibles and clothing, priced from $3 to $3,000. Disney views the stores as an extension of the "Disney experience," referring to customers as "guests" and employees as "cast members," just as it did in its theme parks. The company has struggled, however, to find the right retail formula through the years, even selling the chain of stores in Japan and North America to a set of other companies before eventually buying them back.[86]

Another issue with company stores, of course, is potential conflict with existing retail channels and distributors. In many cases, however, company stores can be a means of bolstering brand image and building brand equity rather than as direct sales devices. For example, Nike views its stores as essentially advertisements and tourist attractions. The company reports that research studies have confirmed that Niketown stores enhanced the Nike brand image by presenting the full scope of its sports and fitness lines to customers and "educating them" on the value, quality, and benefits of Nike products. The research also revealed that although only about 25 percent of visitors actually made a purchase at a Niketown store, 40 percent of those who did not buy during their visit eventually purchased Nike products from some other retailer.

These manufacturer-owned stores can also be seen as a means of hedging bets with retailers who continue to push their own labels. With one of its main distributors, JCPenney, pushing its own Arizona brand of jeans, Levi's can protect its brand franchise to some extent by

BRANDING BRIEF 5-2

Goodyear's Partnering Lessons

Goodyear is a good example of some of the challenges in managing channel conflict, having had to work hard to recover from missteps it took with the middlemen it uses to distribute its tires. A well-respected brand that once managed the top tire reseller network in the United States, Goodyear earned dealer loyalty in the 1970s and 1980s through competitive pricing, on-time deliveries, and very visible marketing in the form of the Goodyear blimp.

Subsequent years produced a number of problems. Goodyear managed to damage its own reputation through its apparent indifference to the distributors who sold its products. The company's prices varied from month to month, and when distributors ordered tires, often only 50 percent of their order would be filled. Distributors nationwide said it was just getting hard to do business with Goodyear and many began hawking other brands instead.

Goodyear announced a distribution deal with Sears, even though the company had previously promised dealers that it would not sell tires through discount retailers, and then made similar deals with Walmart and Sam's Club. To increase sales, the company began to offer the big retailers bulk discounts. As a result, smaller individually owned dealers had to pay as much for their tires as customers could pay at other retailers.

Shortly after Firestone was forced to recall 6.5 million tires in 2000, Goodyear management annoyed many of its distributors instead of taking advantage of its competitor's legal and image problems. Goodyear dealership owners complained of pressure to buy more tires than they needed, uneven pricing, and poor quality. At that time, Goodyear had 5,300 authorized dealers, about the same number it had had since 1994. While overall U.S. tire sales grew during that time, Goodyear's replacement tire sales slumped 14 percent, representing a loss of about $550 million in sales.

Goodyear has taken a number of steps in trying to win back its dealers since that time, including originally selling its popular Assurance tires exclusively through authorized dealers. Recent Goodyear price hikes, however, have forced dealers to take lower profits in selling its tires.

Sources: Kevin Kelleher, "Giving Dealers a Raw Deal," *Business 2.0*, December 2004; Nirmalya Kumar, "Living with Channel Conflict," *CMO Magazine*, October 2004; Louis Uchitelle, "Oil Prices Raise Cost of Making a Range of Goods," *New York Times*, 8 June 2008.

establishing its own distribution channel. Nevertheless, many retailers and manufacturers are dancing around the turf issue, avoiding head-on clashes in establishing competitive distribution channels. Manufacturers in particular have been careful to stress that their stores are not a competitive threat to their retailers but rather a "showcase" that can help sell merchandise for any retailer carrying their brand. Branding Brief 5-2 describes some of Goodyear's channel conflict experiences.

Store-Within-a-Store.   Besides creating their own stores, some marketers—such as Nike, Polo, and Levi Strauss (with Dockers)—are attempting to create their own shops within major department stores. More common in other parts of the world such as Asia, these approaches can offer the dual benefits of appeasing retailers—and perhaps even allowing them to benefit from the retailer's brand image—while at the same time allowing the firm to retain control over the design and implementation of the product presentation at the point of purchase.[87]

The store-within-a-store concept can take hold through actual leasing arrangements or less formal arrangements where branded mini-stores are used. For retailers, these arrangements help drive foot traffic and acquire new capabilities quickly. For smaller brands, like Murray's Cheese Shop, which has an arrangement with Kroger, they allow for quick distribution growth.

Retailers are also combining with other retailers to seek similar benefits.[88] Sears has partnered with much trendier retailer Forever 21 to upgrade its image as well as established in-store leases with Edwin Watts Golf Shops, uniform apparel seller Work N' Gear, and Whole Foods organic foods grocer. Macy's has partnered with Sunglass Hut, maternity apparel brand Destination Modernity, and UK toiletries brand Lush.

The goal in all these situations is to find "win–win" solutions that benefit channel partners and consumers alike. In explaining the rationale of hosting beauty-products retailer Sephora in its stores, one JCPenny's executive noted, "Longtime Sephora fanatics come in and wind up becoming loyal JCPenney shoppers, and vice versa."[89]

Other Means.   Finally, another channel option is to sell directly to consumers via phone, mail, or electronic means. Retailers have sold their goods through catalogs for years. Many mass marketers, especially those that also sell through their own retail stores, are increasingly using direct selling, a long-successful strategy for brands such as Mary Kay and Avon. These vehicles not only help sell products but also contribute to brand equity by increasing consumer awareness of the range of products associated with a brand and increasing consumer understanding of the key benefits of those products. Marketers can execute direct marketing efforts in many ways, such as catalogs, videos, or physical sites, all of which are opportunities to engage in a dialogue and establish a relationship with consumers.

Beauty-products retailer Sephora has found success with its "store-within-a-store" retail strategy with JCPenney.

Source: J. C. Penney Company Inc.

Online Strategies

The advantages of having both a physical "brick and mortar" channel and a virtual, online retail channel are becoming clearer to many firms. Integrated channels allow consumers to shop when and how they want. Many consumers value the convenience of ordering from companies online or over the phone and picking up the physical product at their local store rather than having it shipped. They also want to be able to return merchandise at a store even if they originally bought it and had it shipped outside the store.[90]

Many consumers also like the convenience of being able to access their online account inside the store and use Internet kiosks to research purchase decisions in the store itself.[91] The influence of the Internet extends outside the store too. In a Forrester research report, it was estimated that 16 percent of all store sales were influenced by consumers initially searching on the Web outside the store.[92]

Integrating channels does not benefit only consumers. Figure 5-6 shows an analysis of JCPenney's channel mix, which reveals that its most profitable customers were those who shopped multiple channels. Similarly, a Deloitte study revealed that multichannel shoppers spent 82 percent more in each transaction than those who shopped in only one store.[93]

The Boston Consulting Group concluded that multichannel retailers were able to acquire customers at half the cost of Internet-only retailers, citing a number of advantages for the multichannel retailers:[94]

- They have market clout with suppliers.
- They have established distribution and fulfillment systems (L.L. Bean and Land's End).
- They can cross-sell between Web sites and stores (The Gap and Barnes & Noble).

Many of these same advantages are realized by multichannel product manufacturers. Recognizing the power of integrated channels, many Internet-based companies are also engaging in "physical world" activities to boost their brand. For example, Yahoo! opened a promotional store in New York's Rockefeller Center, and eTrade.com opened a flagship own-brand financial center on New York's Madison Avenue as well as mini-centers and kiosks in Target stores.

Summary

Channels are the means by which firms distribute their products to consumers. Channel strategy to build brand equity includes designing and managing direct and indirect channels to build brand awareness and improve the brand image. Direct channels can enhance brand equity by allowing consumers to better understand the depth, breadth, and variety of the products associated with the brand as well as any distinguishing characteristics. Indirect channels can influence brand equity through the actions and support of intermediaries such as retailers, and the transfer of any associations that these intermediaries might have to the brand.

FIGURE 5-6

JCPenney Customer Channel Value Analysis

Source: Customer Values Analysis, Doublecheck (2004). Courtesy of Abacus Direct, LLC.

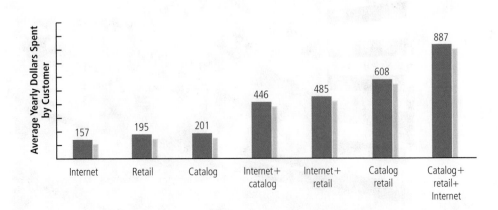

Direct and indirect channels offer varying advantages and disadvantages that marketers must thoughtfully combine, both to sell products in the short run, and maintain and enhance brand equity in the long run. As is often the case with branding, the key is to mix and match channel options so that they collectively realize these goals. Thus, it is important to assess each possible channel option in terms of its direct effect on product sales and brand equity, as well as its indirect effect through interactions with other channel options.

REVIEW

Marketing activities and programs are the primary means that firms build brand equity. Brand-building product, pricing, channel, and communication strategies must be put into place. In terms of product strategies, both tangible and intangible aspects of the brand will matter. Successful brands often create strong, favorable, and unique brand associations to both functional and symbolic benefits. Although perceived quality is often at the heart of brand equity, there is a wide range of associations that consumers may make to the brand.

Marketers are personalizing their consumer interactions through experiential and relationship marketing. Experiential marketing promotes a product by not only communicating a product's features and benefits but also connecting it with unique and interesting consumer experiences. Relationship marketing includes marketing activities that deepen and broaden the way consumers think and act toward the brand. Mass customization, one-to-one, and permission marketing are all means of getting consumers more actively engaged with the product or service. Aftermarketing and loyalty programs are also ways to help create holistic, personalized buying experiences.

In terms of pricing strategies, marketers should fully understand consumer perceptions of value. Increasingly, firms are adopting value-based pricing strategies to set prices and everyday-low-pricing strategies to guide their discount pricing policy over time. Value-based pricing strategies attempt to properly balance product design and delivery, product costs, and product prices. Everyday-low-pricing strategies establish a stable set of "everyday" prices and introduce price discounts very selectively.

In terms of channel strategies, marketers need to appropriately match brand and store images to maximize the leverage of secondary associations, integrate push strategies and shopper marketing activities for retailers with pull strategies for consumers, and consider a range of direct and indirect distribution options.

In the next chapter, we consider how to develop integrated marketing communication programs to build brand equity.

DISCUSSION QUESTIONS

1. Have you had any experience with a brand that has done a great job with relationship marketing, permission marketing, experiential marketing, or one-to-one marketing? What did the brand do? Why was it effective? Could others learn from that?

2. Think about the products you own. Assess their product design. Critique their aftermarketing efforts. Are you aware of all of the products' capabilities? Identify a product whose benefits you feel you are not fully capitalizing on. How might you suggest improvements?

3. Choose a product category. Profile all the brands in the category in terms of pricing strategies and perceived value. If possible, review the brands' pricing histories. Have these brands set and adjusted prices properly? What would you do differently?

4. Visit a department store and evaluate the in-store marketing effort. Which categories or brands seem to be receiving the biggest in-store push? What unique in-store merchandising efforts do you see?

5. Take a trip to a supermarket and observe the extent of private-label brands. In which categories do you think private labels might be successful? Why?

BRAND FOCUS 5.0

Private-Label Strategies and Responses

This appendix considers the issue of private labels or store brands. After portraying private-label branding strategies, it describes how major manufacturers' brands have responded to their threat.

Private Labels

Although different terms and definitions are possible, **private labels** can be defined as products marketed by retailers and other members of the distribution chain. Private labels can be called **store brands** when they actually adopt the name of the store itself in some way (such as Safeway Select). Private labels should not be confused with **generics**, whose simple black-and-white packaging typically provides no information about who made the product.

Private-label brands typically cost less to make and sell than the national or manufacturer brands with which they compete. Thus, the appeal to consumers of buying private labels and store brands often is the cost savings involved; the appeal to retailers of selling private labels and store brands is that their gross margin is often 25 percent to 30 percent—nearly twice that of national brands.

The history of private labels is one of many ups and downs. The first private-label grocery products in the United States were sold by the Great Atlantic and Pacific Tea Company (later known as A&P), which was founded in 1863. During the first half of the twentieth century, a number of store brands were successfully introduced. Under competitive pressure from the sophisticated mass-marketing practices adopted by large packaged-goods companies in the 1950s, private labels fell out of favor with consumers.

Because the appeal of private labels to consumers has traditionally been their lower cost, the sales of private labels generally have been highly correlated with personal disposable income. The recession of the 1970s saw the successful introduction of low-cost, basic-quality, and minimally packaged generic products that appealed to bargain-seeking consumers. During the subsequent economic upswing, though, the lack of perceived quality eventually hampered sales of generics, and many consumers returned to national or manufacturers' brands.

To better compete in today's marketplace, private-label makers have begun improving quality and expanding the variety of their private-label offerings to include premium products. In recognition of the power of bold graphics, supermarket retailers have been careful to design attractive, upscale packages for their own premium branded products. Because of these and other actions, private-label sales have recently made some major inroads in new markets. Retailers value private labels for their profit margins and their means of differentiation to drive customer loyalty. Retailer Target has introduced a steady stream of exclusives through the years, such as its stylish Mossimo apparel and Michael Graves houseware brands.[95]

Private-Label Status

The major recession that began in 2008 heightened interest once again in private labels. Given retailers' success in improving private-label quality and developing cohesive branding and marketing programs, many critics wondered whether this time things would be different and sales would not drop after the end of the recession.[96]

In the United States, private-label goods have accounted for roughly 16–17 percent of total supermarket dollar volume. In other countries, these percentages are often quite higher, on average twice as much. For example, Western Europe dominates the market for private labels in the supermarket, with the biggest being Switzerland at 45 percent, Germany at 30 percent, Spain at 26 percent, and Belgium at 25 percent.[97]

Private labels in the United Kingdom make up over a third of sales at grocery stores, in part because the grocery industry is more concentrated. Two of the largest UK grocery chains are Tesco and Sainsbury.[98]

- Tesco, with the brand slogan "Every Little Helps," has a number of its own private-label brands, ranging from Value to Finest, and has its own lifestyle brands, such as Organic, Free Form, and Healthy Living, positioned as "Making Life Taste Better."

- Sainsbury's originally used its name to introduce a wide variety of fruit, vegetables, grocery, and household products, later expanding to clothing, housewares, and other non-supermarket products. Sainsbury's own brand products are categorized into one of three quality tiers; for example, the lasagna range is comprised of the Basics sub-brand for "good," the core, Sainsbury's label line for "better," and the premium "Taste the Difference" line for "best." Sainsbury's began a major overhaul of these various brand lines in 2010.

Private-label appeal is widespread. In supermarkets, private-label sales have always been strong in product categories such as dairy goods, vegetables, and beverages. More recently, private labels have been successful in previously "untouchable" categories such as cigarettes, disposable diapers, and cold remedies. *Consumer Reports* conducted a study on private labels published in September 2010. Key findings included the facts that 84 percent of U.S. consumers have purchased a store brand and 93 percent of store-brand shoppers indicated that they would continue to purchase private labels even as the economy recovered.[99]

Nevertheless, some categories have not seen a strong private-label presence. Many shoppers, for example, still seem unwilling to trust their hair, complexion, or dental care to store brands. Private labels also have been relatively unsuccessful in categories such as candy, cereal, pet foods, baby food, and beer.

One implication that can be drawn from this pattern of product purchases is that consumers are being more selective in what they buy, no longer choosing to buy only national brands. For less important products in particular, consumers seem to feel "that the very best is unnecessary and good is good enough." Categories that are particularly vulnerable to private-label advances are those in which there is little perceived quality differences among brands in the eyes of a sizable group of consumers, for example, over-the-counter pain relievers, bottled water, plastic bags, paper towels, and dairy products.

Private-Label Branding Strategy

Although the growth of private labels has been interpreted by some as a sign of the decline of brands, the opposite conclusion may in fact be more valid: private-label growth could be seen in some ways as a consequence of cleverly designed branding strategies. In terms of building brand equity, the key point-of-difference for private labels in consumers' eyes has always been "good value," a desirable and transferable association across many product categories. As a result, private labels can be extremely broad, and their name can be applied across many diverse products.

As with national brands, implementing a value-pricing strategy for private labels requires determining the right price and product offering. For example, one reported rule of thumb is that the typical "no-name" product has to sell for at least 15 percent less than a national brand, on average, to be successful. The challenge for private labels has been to determine the appropriate product offering.

Specifically, to achieve the necessary points-of-parity, or even to create their own points-of-difference, private labels have been improving quality, and as a result are now aggressively positioning against even national brands. In its September 2010 study, *Consumer Reports* conducted taste tests in 21 categories comparing the two and found that national brands won seven times, private labels won three times, with the rest resulting in a tie. *Consumer Reports* concluded that consumers could cut their costs by as much as half by switching to a store brand.[100]

Many supermarket chains have introduced their own premium store brands, such as Safeway Select, Von's Royal Request, and Ralph's Private Selection. For example, A&P positioned its premium Master Choice brand to fill the void between the mass-market national brands and the upscale specialty brands it sells. It has used the brand across a wide range of products, such as teas, pastas, sauces, and salad dressings. Trader Joe's offers 2,000 private-label products—only 10 percent of what would be found in a typical supermarket—but creates a fun, roomy atmosphere for bargain seekers wanting the best in gourmet-style foods, health food supplements, and wines.[101]

Sellers of private labels are also adopting more extensive marketing communication programs to spread the word about their brands. For example, Walgreens launched its first national advertising campaign for Walgreens-branded health and wellness products in February 2011. The campaign emphasized the durability and quality of the Walgreens-brand products, using the store's 26,000 pharmacists as endorsers.[102] Loblaws has been a pioneer in marketing its private-label brands.

LOBLAWS

Loblaws is Canada's largest food distributor. In 1978, Loblaws was the first store in Canada to introduce generics, reflecting a carefully crafted strategy to build an image of quality and high value in six areas. By 1983, Loblaws carried over 500 generic products that accounted for 10 percent of store sales. This success was due to innovative marketing, low costs, and a large network of suppliers. In 1984, Loblaws chose to introduce a private-label brand, President's Choice, which was designed to offer unique value through exceptional quality and moderate prices. These categories ranged from basic supermarket categories such as chocolate chip cookies, colas, and cereals to more exotic categories such as Devonshire custard from England and gourmet Russian mustard. These products also used distinctive and attractive packaging with modern lettering and colorful labels and names ("decadent" cookies, "ultimate" frozen pizza, "and "too good to be true" peanut butter). In terms of marketing communications, Loblaws put into place a strong promotional program with much in-store merchandising. Loblaws also introduced its *Insider's Report,* a quarterly publication featuring its own store brands and offering consumers shopping tips.[103]

Major Brand Response to Private Labels

Procter & Gamble's value-pricing program was one strategy to combat competitive inroads from private labels and other brands. To compete with private labels, a number of different other tactics also have been adopted by marketers of major national or manufacturer brands (see Figure 5-7).

First, marketers of major brands have attempted to decrease costs and reduce price to negate the primary point-of-difference of private labels and achieve a critical point-of-parity. In many categories, prices of major brands had crept up to a point at which price premiums over private labels were 30–50 percent, or even 100 percent. In those categories in which consumers make frequent purchases, the cost savings of "trading down" to a private label brand were therefore quite substantial.

In instances in which major brands and private labels are on a more equal footing with regard to price, major brands often compete well because of other favorable brand perceptions that consumers might have. Procter & Gamble, Colgate, and Unilever cut prices on a number of old standbys during the recent recession to help fend off private-label competition.

One problem faced by marketers of major brands is that it can be difficult to actually lower prices even if they so desire. Supermarkets may not pass along the wholesale price cuts they are given. Moreover, marketers of major brands may not want to alienate retailers by attacking their store brands too forcefully, especially in zero-sum categories in which their brands could be easily replaced.

Decrease costs.

Cut prices.

Increase R&D expenditures to improve products and identify new product innovations.

Increase advertising and promotion budgets.

Eliminate stagnant brands and extensions and concentrate efforts on smaller number of brands.

Introduce discount "fighter" brands.

Supply private label makers.

Track store brands' growth and compete market-by-market.

FIGURE 5-7

Major Brand Response to Private Labels

Besides these various pricing moves to achieve points-of-parity, marketers of major brands have used other tactics to achieve additional points-of-difference to combat the threat of private labels. They have increased R&D expenditures to improve products and identify new product innovations, as was the case with Kimberly-Clark and its Kleenex brand.[104]

KLEENEX

Kleenex has dominated the facial tissue category for years, currently holding 46 percent market share. In recent years, with the economic downturn, more consumers are switching to less-expensive store brands as private labels in the category have increased quality to provide a more viable alternative. Kimberly-Clark—maker of Kleenex—chose to respond through product innovation. The average home purchases facial tissues about eight times a year and contains four boxes at any point in time. Increasingly, those boxes are not placed inside a decorative cover. Much of that is due to Kimberly-Clark's innovative efforts to improve the design aesthetics of the Kleenex box. Oval-shaped packages and embossed wallpaper-like patterns have been introduced as well as seasonal offerings. An oval package with a pattern of Christmas lights was introduced that actually flickered when a tissue was taken out. To boost summer sales—when revenue typically drops by as much as 60 percent from the winter months—new packages were launched that resembled wedges of fruit such as watermelon, orange, and lime. Through all these packaging innovations, Kimberly-Clark hopes to keep Kleenex differentiated as the market leader.

By emphasizing packaging innovation and design, Kimberly-Clark has been able to fend off private label competition for its Kleenex brand.

Source: David Paul Morris/Bloomberg via Getty Images

Marketers of major brands have also increased advertising and promotion budgets. They have also tracked store-brand growth more closely than in the past and are competing on a market-by-market basis. Marketers of major brands have also adjusted their brand portfolios. They have eliminated stagnant brands and extensions and concentrated their efforts on smaller numbers of brands. They have introduced discount "fighter" brands that are specially designed and promoted to compete with private labels.

Marketers of major brands have also been more aggressive about legally protecting their brands. For example, Unilever filed suit against global supermarket giant Ahold alleging trademark and trade dress (the design and visual appearance of the product and package) infringement across four of its European margarine brands. Unilever also filed suit against Lipton iced tea and Bertolli olive oil, maintaining that their packaging looked too similar to its own brands.[105]

One controversial move by some marketers of major brands is to actually supply private-label makers. For example, Sara Lee, Del Monte, and Birds Eye have all supplied products—sometimes lower in quality—to be used for private labels in the past. Other marketers, however, criticize this "if you can't beat 'em, join 'em" strategy, maintaining that these actions, if revealed, may create confusion or even reinforce a perception by consumers that all brands in a category are essentially the same.

Future Developments

Many marketers feel that the brands most endangered by the rise of private labels are second-tier brands that have not been as successful at establishing a clear identity as market leaders have. For example, in the laundry detergent category, the success of a private-label brand such as Walmart's Ultra Clean is more likely to come at the expense of brands such as Oxydol, All, or Fab rather than market leader Tide.

In Britain, one study showed that the average share of 52 leading brands measured fell only from 34.2 percent to 32.6 percent between 1975 and 1999—the "losers" were the smaller "trade dependent" brands that invest less in marketing and attempt to compete on price with private labels.[106] Thus, highly priced, poorly differentiated and undersupported brands are especially vulnerable to private-label competition.

At the same time, if nothing else, retailers will need the quality and image that go along with well-researched, efficiently manufactured, and professionally marketed major brands, because of consumer demand. When A&P let store brands soar to 35 percent of its dry grocery sales mix in the 1960s, many shoppers defected, and the store was forced to drop the percentage to under 20 as a result. Similarly, Federated Department Stores, owner of private-label wizard Macy's, has vowed to keep its percentage of revenue from private labels at under 20 percent.

Notes

1. Philip Kotler and Kevin Lane Keller, *Marketing Management*, 14th ed. (Upper Saddle River, NJ: Prentice Hall, 2012).
2. Ibid.
3. For an interesting examination of some of the different low-level effects to brand exposure, see S. Adam Brasal and James Gips, "Red Bull Gives You 'Wings' for Better or for Worse: A Double-Edged Impact of Brand Exposure on Consumer Performance," *Journal of Consumer Psychology* 21 (2011): 57–64.
4. Don E. Schultz, Stanley I. Tannenbaum, and Robert F. Lauterborn, *Integrated Marketing Communications* (Lincolnwood, IL: NTC Business Books, 1993).

5. For a description of their methodology to help identify and prioritize brand contact points, see Amitava Chattopadhyay and Jean-Louis Laborie, "Managing Brand Experience: The Market Contact Audit," *Journal of Advertising Research* (March 2005): 9–16.

6. David Goetzel, "Moosejaw Touts 'Humanization' e-Marketing," *MediaPost*, 4 May 2011; Bruce Britt, "For Crying Out Loud," *Deliver* (February 2011): 29–32; Richard H. Levey, "Crying Tomatoes, Laughing Customers," *Chief Marketer*, 1 June 2010; Brian Quinton, "Young But Not Stupid," *Promo*, 1 February 2008; "The Moose is Loose," *Chain Store Age*, 30 July 2007.

7. Peter Post, "Beyond Brand—The Power of Experience Branding," *ANA/The Advertiser*, October/November 2000.

8. B. Joseph Pine and James H. Gilmore, *The Experience Economy: Work Is Theatre and Every Business a Stage* (Cambridge, MA: Harvard University Press, 1999).

9. Bernd H. Schmitt and David L. Rogers, *Handbook on Brand and Experience Management* (Northampton, MA: Edward Elgar Publishing, 2008); Bernd H. Schmitt, *Customer Experience Management: A Revolutionary Approach to Connecting with Your Customers* (Hoboken, NJ: John Wiley & Sons, 2003); Bernd H. Schmitt, *Experiential Marketing: How to Get Customers to Sense, Feel, Think, Act, and Relate to Your Company and Brands* (New York: Free Press, 1999);

10. Liz Zarantonello and Bernd H. Schmitt, "Using the Brand Experience Scale to Profile Consumers and Predict Consumer Behaviour," *Journal of Brand Management* 17 (June 2010): 532–540.

11. Christopher Meyer and Andre Schwager, "Understanding Customer Experience," *Harvard Business Review*, February 2007.

12. Jennifer Aaker, Susan Fournier, and S. Adam Brasel, "When Good Brands Do Bad," *Journal of Consumer Research* 31 (June 2004): 1–16; Pankaj Aggarwal, "The Effects of Brand Relationship Norms on Consumer Attitudes and Behavior," *Journal of Consumer Research* 31 (June 2004): 87–101; Pankaj Aggarwal and Sharmistha Law, "Role of Relationship Norms in Processing Brand Information," *Journal of Consumer Research* 32 (December 2005): 453–464.

13. Frederick F. Reichheld, *The Loyalty Effect* (Boston: Harvard Business School Press, 1996); Robert W. Palmatier, Rajiv P. Dant, Dhruv Grewal, and Kenneth R Evans, "Factors Influencing the Effectiveness of Relationship Marketing: A Meta-Analysis," *Journal of Marketing* 70 (October 2006): 136–153.

14. Dave Sloan, "5 Signs That Customer Co-creation Is a Trend to Watch," www.venturebeat.com, 19 July 2010.

15. Roland T. Rust, Christine Moorman, and Peter R. Dickson, "Getting Returns from Service Quality: Revenue Expansion, Cost Reduction, or Both?," *Journal of Marketing* 66 (October 2002): 7–24.

16. Chris Woodyard, "Mass Production Gives Way to Mass Customization," *USA Today*, 16 February 1998, 3B.

17. Sloan, "5 Signs That Customer Co-creation Is a Trend to Watch."

18. Don Peppers and Martha Rogers, *The One to One Future: Building Relationships One Customer at a Time* (New York: Doubleday, 1997); Don Peppers and Martha Rogers, *Enterprise One to One: Tools for Competing in the Interactive Age* (New York: Doubleday, 1999); Don Peppers and Martha Rogers, *The One to One Fieldbook: The Complete Toolkit for Implementing a 1 to 1 Marketing Program* (New York: Doubleday, 1999). For some more recent discussion from these authors, see Don Peppers and Martha Rogers, *Return on Customer: Creating Maximum Value from Your Scarcest Resource* (Currency, 2005). See also Sunil Gupta and Donald R. Lehmann, *Managing Customers as Investments: The Strategic Value of Customers in the Long Run* (Cambridge, MA: Harvard Business School Press, 2005).

19. Don Peppers and Martha Rogers, "Welcome to the 1:1 Future," *Marketing Tools*, 1 April 1994.

20. Sallie Burnett, "Tesco Revamps Loyalty Program," www.customerinsightgroup.com, 20 September 2010; Mary-Louise Clews, "Tesco Unveils Plan for Next Generation of Loyalty Card," *MarketingWeek*, 22 April 2009; Zoe Wood and Teena Lyons, "Clubcard Couple Head for Checkout at Tesco," *The Guardian*, 29 October 2010.

21. Seth Godin, *Permission Marketing: Turning Strangers into Friends, and Friends into Customers* (New York: Simon & Schuster, 1999).

22. Susan Fournier, Susan Dobscha, and David Mick, "Preventing the Premature Death of Relationship Marketing," *Harvard Business Review* (January–February 1998): 42–51. See also Erwin Danneels, "Tight-Loose Coupling with Customers: The Enactment of Customer Orientation," *Strategic Management Journal* 24 (2003): 559–576.

23. Mark Dolliver, "Permission-Based Email Affects Purchase Decisions," *Advertising Age*, 24 February 2009.

24. "Click to Download," *Economist*, 19 August 2006, 57–58; Robert D. Hof, "Jeff Bezos' Risky Bet," *BusinessWeek*, 13 November 2006; Erick Schonfield, "The Great Giveaway," *Business 2.0*, April 2005, 80–86; Elizabeth West, "Who's Next?," *Potentials*, February 2004, 7–8; Robert D. Hof, "The Wizard of Web Retailing," *BusinessWeek*, 20 December 2004, p. 18; Chris Taylor, "Smart Library," *Time*, 17 November 2003, 68; Deborah Solomon, "Questions for Jeffrey P. Bezos," *The New York Times*, 2 December 2009; Patrick Seitz, "Amazon.com Whiz Jeff Bezos Keeps Kindling Hot Concepts," *Investors' Daily Business*, 31 December 2009; *Amazon.com*. Amazon.com, 2009 Annual Report.

25. Neeli Bendapudi and Robert P. Leone, "Psychological Implications of Customer Participation in Co-Production," *Journal of Marketing* 67 (January 2003): 14–28.

26. Stratford Sherman, "How to Prosper in the Value Decade," *Fortune*, 30 November 1992, 91.

27. David Garvin, "Product Quality: An Important Strategic Weapon," *Business Horizons* 27 (May–June 1985): 40–43; Philip Kotler, *Marketing Management*, 10th ed. (Upper Saddle River, NJ: Prentice Hall, 2000).

28. Jessica Mintz, "Using Hand, Grab Hair. Pull," *Wall Street Journal*, 23 December 2004, B1, B5.

29. Jacqueline Martense, "Get Close to Your Customers," *Fast Company*, August 2005, 37.

30. Terry Vavra, *Aftermarketing: How to Keep Customers for Life Through Relationship Marketing* (Chicago: Irwin Professional Publishers, 1995).

31. Accenture 2010 Global Consumer Research executive summary, white paper, www.accenture.com, 2011.

32. Lori Flees and Todd Senturia, "After-Sales Service Key to Retaining Car Buyers," *Bloomberg Business-Week*, 23 September 2008.

33. Clif Edwards, "HP Gets Tough on Ink Counterfeiters," *Bloomberg BusinessWeek*, 28 May 2009; Tom Spring, "Why Do Ink Cartridges Cost So Much?," *PCWorld*, 28 August 2003.

34. Michael Bean, "Developing an Aftermarket Strategy," *Forio's Forum*, 29 June 2003.

35. "Loyal, My Brand, to Thee," *Promo*, 1 October 1997; Arthur Middleton Hughes, "How Safeway Built Loyalty—Especially Among Second-Tier Customers," *Target Marketing*, 1 March 1999; Laura Bly, "Frequent Fliers Fuel a Global Currency," *USA Today*, 27 April 2001.

36. www.frequencymarketing.com, accessed December 10, 2011.

37. "After 30 Years, the AAdvantage Program Still Offers Members the Best Travel Awards During 'Deal 30' Promotion," www.aa.com, 18 April 2011.

38. James L. Heskett, W. Earl Sasser Jr., and Leonard A. Schlesinger, *The Service Profit Chain* (New York: Simon & Schuster, 1997); Michael Lewis, "The Influence of Loyalty Programs and Short-Term Promotions on Customer Retention," *Journal of Marketing Research* 41 (August 2004), 281–292; Yuping Liu, "The Long-Term Impact of Loyalty Programs on Consumer Purchase Behavior and Loyalty," *Journal of Marketing* 71 (October 2007): 19–35.

39. Dennis Armbruster, "Understanding What's in Consumers' Wallets, and on the Table," *Colloquy*, 21 April 2011.

40. Elizabeth Holmes, "Why Pay Full Price?," *Wall Street Journal*, 5 May 2011.

41. Grahame R. Dowling and Mark Uncles, "Do Customer Loyalty Programs Really Work?" *Sloan Management Review* (Summer 1997): 71–82. See also Steven M. Shugan, "Brand Loyalty Programs: Are They Shams?" *Marketing Science* 24 (Spring 2005): 185–193.

42. Elizabeth Holmes, "Why Pay Full Price?," *Wall Street Journal*, 5 May 2011; Carol Angrisani, "CVS Moves to Personalization," *Supermarket News*, 24 March 2008; "ExtraCare Bolsters Bonds with Customers," *Chain Drug Review*, 28 April 2008.

43. Robert C. Blattberg and Kenneth Wisniewski, "Price-Induced Patterns of Competition," *Marketing Science* 8 (Fall 1989): 291–309.

44. Elliot B. Ross, "Making Money with Proactive Pricing," *Harvard Business Review* (November–December 1984): 145–155.

45. www.pvh.com/annual_pdfs/pdf_2004/corp_strategy. pdf. All brands in the figure are registered trademarks of Phillips-Van Heusen or its licensors.

46. Kotler and Keller, *Marketing Management.*

47. For a more detailed and comprehensive treatment of pricing strategy, see Thomas T. Nagle and Reed K. Holden, *The Strategy and Tactics of Pricing: A Guide to Profitable Decision-Making*, 5th ed. (Upper Saddle River, NJ: Prentice Hall, 2011); Kent B. Monroe, *Pricing: Making Profitable Decisions*, 3rd ed. (New York: McGraw-Hill/Irwin, 2002); and Robert J. Dolan and Hermann Simon, *Power Pricing* (New York: Free Press, 1997).

48. Ira Teinowitz, "Marlboro Friday: Still Smoking," *Advertising Age*, 28 March 1994, 24.

49. Alan Ohnsman and Seonjin Cha, "Restyling Hyundai for the Luxury Market," *Bloomberg BusinessWeek*, 28 December 2009; Hannah Elliott, "Best New-Car Incentives," *Forbes*, 3 February 2010; Alex Taylor III, "Hyundai Smokes the Competition," *Fortune*, 18 January 2010, 62–71; Moon Ihlwan and David Kiley, "Hyundai Gains With Marketing Blitz, *BusinessWeek*, 17 September 2009; Moon Ihlwan and David Kiley," Hyundai Floors it in the U.S., *BusinessWeek*, 27 February 2009, 30–31.

50. Jack Neff, "Gillette Fusion ProGlide," *Advertising Age*, 15 November 2010; Claudia H. Deutsch, "Gillette Is Betting That Men Want an Even Closer Shave," *New York Times*, 15 September 2005.

51. Jack Neff, "Pepto Beats Private-Label Despite 60% Price Premium," *Advertising Age*, 21 September 2009.

52. Peter Coy, "The Power of Smart Pricing," *BusinessWeek*, 10 April 2000, 600–164.

53. Allan J. Magrath, "Eight Timeless Truths About Pricing," *Sales & Marketing Management* (October 1989): 78–84.

54. Thomas J. Malott, CEO of Siemens, which makes heavy electrical equipment and motors, quoted in Stratford Sherman, "How to Prosper in the Value Decade," *Fortune*, 30 November 1992, 90–103.

55. Emily Bryson York, "Burger King Franchisee in New York Shutters Stores, Blames Dollar Offerings," *Advertising Age*, 31 March 2008.

56. Rose Gordon, "H&R Block Bets on Customer Service For Turnaround," *Direct Marketing News*, 30 June 2010.

57. For a discussion of the pros and cons of customer value mapping (CVM) and economic value mapping (EVM), see Gerald E. Smith and Thomas T. Nagle, "Pricing the Differential," *Marketing Management*, May/June 2005, 28–32.

58. Brad Stone, "Making Sense of New Prices on Apple's iTunes," *New York Times*, 7 April 2009.

59. Claire Cain Miller, "Will the Hard-Core Starbucks Customer Pay More? The Chain Plans to Find Out," *New York Times*, 21 August 2009.

60. Adrienne Carter, "Telling the Risky from the Reliable," *BusinessWeek*, 1 August 2005, 57–58.

61. Ben Sisario, "Ticketmaster Plans to Use a Variable Pricing Policy," *New York Times*, 18 April 2011.

62. Ken Belson, "Baseball Tickets Too Much? Check Back Tomorrow," *New York Times*, 18 May 2009.

63. Howard Greenstein, "Demand Management Provides a Business Model," *Inc.*, 17 September 2010.

64. Alecia Swasy, "In a Fast-Paced World, Procter & Gamble Sets Its Store in Old Values," *Wall Street Journal*, 21 September 1989, A1; Zachary Schiller, "The Marketing Revolution at Procter & Gamble," *BusinessWeek*, 25 July 1988, 72; Bill Saporito, "Behind the Tumult at

P&G," *Fortune*, 7 March 1994, 74–82; Zachary Schiller, "Procter & Gamble Hits Back," *BusinessWeek*, 19 July 1993, 20–22; Zachary Schiller, "Ed Artzt's Elbow Grease Has P&G Shining," *BusinessWeek*, 10 October 1994, 84–86; Zachary Schiller, "Make It Simple," *BusinessWeek*, 9 September 1996, 96–104; "Executive Update: Value Pricing Plan Helps Push Products," *Investor's Business Daily*, 30 August 1995. For an interesting analysis, see Kusum L. Ailawadi, Donald R. Lehmann, and Scott A. Neslin, "Market Response to a Major Policy Change in the Marketing Mix: Learning from P&G's Value Pricing Strategy," *Journal of Marketing* 65, no. 1 (2001): 71–89.

65. Richard Gibson, "Broad Grocery Price Cuts May Not Pay," *Wall Street Journal*, 7 May 1993, B1.

66. Ellen Byron, "P&G Puts Up Its Dukes Over Pricing," *Wall Street Journal*, 30 April 2010; Jack Neff and E. J. Schultz, "P&G, Colgate, Clorox to Raise Prices, Marketing Spending," *Advertising Age*, 25 February 2011.

67. Amy Merrick, "Retailers Try to Get Leg Up on Markdowns with New Software," *Wall Street Journal*, 7 August 2001, A1, A6; Kinshuk Jerath, Serguei Netessine, and Senthil Kumar Veeraraghavan, "Revenue Management with Strategic Customers: Last-Minute Selling and Opaque Selling," *Management Science* 56 (March 2010): 430–448; Eyal Biyalogorsky and Eitan Gerstner, "Contingent Pricing to Reduce Price Risks," *Marketing Science* 23 (Winter 2004): 146–155; Ramarao Desiraju and Steven M. Shugan, "Strategic Service Pricing and Yield Management," *Journal of Marketing* 63 (January 1999): 44–56.

68. Donald R. Lehmann and Russell S. Winer, *Product Management*, 4th ed. (New York: McGraw-Hill, 2007).

69. Kotler and Keller, *Marketing Management*.

70. For a more detailed and comprehensive treatment of channel strategy, see Anne T. Coughlan, Erin Anderson, Louis W. Stern, and Adel I. El-Ansary, *Marketing Channels*, 7th ed. (Upper Saddle River, NJ: Prentice Hall, 2006).

71. Erik Siemers, "Nike Veers from Large Niketown Format," *Portland Business Journal*, 16 May 2010; Mark Brohan, "Nike's Web Sales Flourish in Fiscal 2010," www.internetretailer.com, 30 June 2010.

72. V. Kasturi Rangan, Melvyn A. J. Menezes, and E. P. Maier, "Channel Selection for New Industrial Products: A Framework, Method, and Applications," *Journal of Marketing* 56 (July 1992): 69–82.

73. Rowland T. Moriarty and Ursula Moran, "Managing Hybrid Marketing Systems," *Harvard Business Review* 68 (1990): 146–155.

74. Rick Brooks, "A Deal with Target Put Lid on Revival at Tupperware," *Wall Street Journal*, 18 February 2004, A1, A9; Diane Brady, "In France, Vive la Tupperware," *Bloomberg BusinessWeek*, 15 May 2011, 21–23.

75. Andrew Adam Newman, "Taking Pickles Out of the Afterthought Aisle," *New York Times*, 25 April 2011; Dale Buss, "Vlasic Enhances Brand Awareness with Clever Signage Strategy," www.cpgmatters.com, June 2011; Sarah Gilbert, "Picklemakers Finding Their Way Out of a Pickle," www.walletpop.com, 29 April 2011.

76. Mya Frazier, "John Deere Cultivates Its Image," *Advertising Age*, 25 July 2005, 6; Ilan Brat and Timothy Aeppel, "Why Deere Is Weeding Out Dealers Even as Farms Boom," *Wall Street Journal*, 14 August 2007.

77. For a discussion of CRM issues with multichannel retailers, see Jacquelyn S. Thomas and Ursula Y. Sullivan, "Managing Marketing Communications," *Journal of Marketing* 69 (October 2005): 239–251.

78. Matthew Egol, Karla Martin, and Leslie Moeller, "One Size Fits All," *Point*, September 2005, 21–24; Matthew Egol, Paul Leinwand, Leslie Moeller, "Beyond the Brand: Fighting the Retail Wars with Smart Customization," Booz Allen Hamilton white paper, www.booz.com, 2005.

79. Steven M. Shugan, "Branded Variants," *Research in Marketing,* AMA Educators' Proceedings, Series no. 55 (Chicago: American Marketing Association, 1989), 33–38. Shugan cites alarm clocks, answering machines, appliances, baby items, binoculars, dishwashers, luggage, mattresses, microwaves, sports equipment, stereos, televisions, tools, and watches as examples.

80. Mark Bergen, Shantanu Dutta, and Steven M. Shugan, "Branded Variants: A Retail Perspective," *Journal of Marketing Research* (February 1995): 9; Yuxin Chen and Tony Haitao Cui, "The Benefit of Uniform Price for Branded Variants," working paper, Kellogg School of Management, Northwestern University, 2011.

81. George E. Belch and Michael A. Belch, *Introduction to Advertising and Promotion* (Chicago: Irwin, 1995).

82. Bill Richards, "Levi-Strauss Plans to Open 200 Stores in 5 Years, with Ending of FTC Ban," *Wall Street Journal*, 22 December 1994, A2.

83. Katie Hafner, "Inside Apple Stores, a Certain Aura Enchants the Faithful," *New York Times*, 27 December 2007.

84. Matt Townsend, "The Staying Power of Pop-Up Stores," *Bloomberg BusinessWeek*, 11 November 2010; Keith Mulvihill, "Pop-Up Stores Become Popular for New York Landlords," *New York Times*, 22 June 2010.

85. Mary Kuntz, "These Ads Have Windows and Walls," *BusinessWeek*, 27 February 1995, 74.

86. "Disney Takes Back Disney Stores from Children's Place," *Associated Press*, 1 May 2008; Brooks Barnes, "Disney's Retail Plan Is a Theme Park in Its Stores," *New York Times*, 12 October 2009.

87. Kinshuk Jerath and Z. John Zhang, "Store Within a Store," *Journal of Marketing Research*, 42 (August 2010): 748–763.

88. Kit R. Roane, "Stores Within a Store, www.cnnmoney.com, 24 January 2011.

89. David Kaplan, "Stores That Dwell in Stores," *Houston Chronicle*, 10 January 2001.

90. "Clicks, Bricks, and Bargains," *The Economist*, 3 December 2005, 57–58.

91. "Catering to Multichannel Consumers," www.emarketer.com, 8 September 2008.

92. Tamara Mendelsohn, "The Web's Impact on In-Store Sales: US Cross-Channel Sales Forecast, 2006 To 2012," *Forrester Research*, May 2007.

93. Chloe Rigby, "Multichannel Shoppers Spend 82% More," *InternetRetailing*, 14 December 2010.

94. "The Real Internet Revolution," *The Economist,* 21 August 1999, 53–54; Scott A. Neslin and Venkatesh Shankar, "Key Issues in Multichannel Customer Management: Current Knowledge and Future Directions," *Journal of Interactive Marketing* 23 (February 2009), 70–81; Jie Zhang, Paul Farris, Tarun Kushwaha, John Irvin, Thomas J. Steenburgh, and Barton Weitz, "Crafting Integrated Multichannel Retailing Strategies," *Journal of Interactive Marketing*, 24 (May 2010): 168–180; Jill Avery, Thomas J. Steenburgh, John Deighton, and Mary Caravella, "Adding Bricks to Clicks: Predicting the Patterns of Cross-Channel Elasticities over Time," *Journal of Marketing*, forthcoming.

95. Lorrie Grant, "Retailers Private Label Brands See Sales Growth Boom," *USA Today*, 15 April 2004.

96. Noreen O'Leary, "New & Improved Private Label Brands," *Adweek*, 22 October 2007.

97. George Anderson, "Private Labels: The Global View," www.retailwire.com, October 2010.

98. "Tesco and Sainsbury's Expand Private Label Beverages," www.storebrandsdecisions.com, 3 August 2010; "Sainsbury's Revamps Entire Private Label Line," www.storebrandsdecisions.com, 17 May 2011.

99. "Consumer Reports Latest Taste Tests Find Some Store Brands at Least as Good as National Brands," *PR Newswire*, 7 September 2010.

100. Ibid.

101. Irwin Speizer, "The Grocery Store That Shouldn't Be," *Fast Company*, February 2004, 31; Beth Kowitt, "Inside the Secret World of Trader Joe's," *Fortune*, 23 August 2010.

102. Tanzina Vega, "Walgreens Launches Campaign to Push Store-Brand Products," *New York Times*, 10 February 2011.

103. Mary L. Shelman and Ray A. Goldberg, "Loblaw Companies Limited," Case 9–588–039 (Boston: Harvard Business School, 1994); Gordon H. G. McDougall and Douglas Snetsinger, "Loblaws," in *Marketing Challenges*, 3rd ed., eds. Christopher H. Lovelock and Charles B. Weinberg (New York: McGraw-Hill, 1993), 169–185; "Loblaw Launches a New Line of Discount Store Brands," www.storebrandsdecisions.com, 16 February 2010; Marina Strauss, "Loblaws Takes Aim at Rivals, *The Globe and Mail*, 10 February 2010; www.loblaws.ca.

104. Andrew Adam Newman, "A Sharp Focus on Design When the Package Is Part of the Product," *New York Times*, 8 July 2010.

105. Jack Neff, "Marketers Put Down Foot on Private-Label Issue," *Advertising Age*, 4 April 2005, 14.

106. Chris Hoyt, "Kraft's Private Label Lesson," *Reveries*, February 2004.

Integrating Marketing Communications to Build Brand Equity

6

Learning Objectives

After reading this chapter, you should be able to

1. Describe some of the changes in the new media environment.
2. Outline the major marketing communication options.
3. Describe some of the key tactical issues in evaluating different communication options.
4. Identify the choice criteria in developing an integrated marketing communication program.
5. Explain the rationale for mixing and matching communication options.

Ford launched its new Fiesta model in the United States with a combination of events, traditional media, and a heavy dose of social media.

Source: Ford Motor Company

Preview

The preceding chapter described how various marketing activities and product, price, and distribution strategies can contribute to brand equity. This chapter considers the final and perhaps most flexible element of marketing programs. *Marketing communications* are the means by which firms attempt to inform, persuade, and remind consumers—directly or indirectly—about the brands they sell. In a sense, marketing communications represent the voice of the brand and are a means by which the brand can establish a dialogue and build relationships with consumers. Although advertising is often a central element of a marketing communications program, it is usually not the only element—or even the most important one—for building brand equity. Figure 6-1 displays some of the common marketing communication options for the consumer market.

Designing marketing communication programs is a complex task. We begin by describing the rapidly changing media landscape and the new realities in marketing communications. To provide necessary background, we next evaluate how the major communication options contribute to brand equity and some of their main costs and benefits. We conclude by considering how to mix and match communication options—that is, how to employ a range of communication options in a coordinated or integrated fashion—to build brand equity. We consider some of what we have learned about advertising in Brand Focus 6.0. For the sake of brevity, we will not consider specific marketing communication issues such as media scheduling, budget estimation techniques, and research approaches or the topic of personal selling.[1]

Media advertising
TV
Radio
Newspaper
Magazines

Direct response advertising
Mail
Telephone
Broadcast media
Print media
Computer-related
Media-related

Place advertising
Billboards and posters
Movies, airlines, and lounges
Product placement
Point of purchase

Point-of-purchase advertising
Shelf talkers
Aisle markers
Shopping cart ads
In-store radio or TV

Trade promotions
Trade deals and buying allowances
Point-of-purchase display allowances
Push money
Contests and dealer incentives
Training programs
Trade shows
Cooperative advertising

Consumer promotions
Samples
Coupons
Premiums
Refunds and rebates
Contests and sweepstakes
Bonus packs
Price-offs

Interactive
Web sites
E-mails
Banner ads
Rich media ads
Search
Videos
Message boards and forums
Chat rooms
Blogs
Facebook
Twitter
YouTube

Event marketing and sponsorship
Sports
Arts
Entertainment
Fairs and festivals
Cause-related

Mobile
SMS & MMS messages
Ads
Location-based services

Publicity and public relations
Word-of-mouth
Personal selling

FIGURE 6-1
Marketing
Communications
Options

THE NEW MEDIA ENVIRONMENT

Although advertising and other communication options can play different roles in the marketing program, one important purpose they all serve is to contribute to brand equity. According to the customer-based brand equity model, marketing communications can contribute to brand equity in a number of different ways: by creating awareness of the brand; linking points-of-parity and points-of-difference associations to the brand in consumers' memory; eliciting positive brand judgments or feelings; and facilitating a stronger consumer–brand connection and brand resonance. In addition to forming the desired brand knowledge structures, marketing communication programs can provide incentives eliciting the differential response that makes up customer-based brand equity.

The flexibility of marketing communications comes in part from the number of different ways they can contribute to brand equity. At the same time, brand equity helps marketers determine how to design and implement different marketing communication options. In this chapter, we consider how to develop marketing communication programs to build brand equity. We will assume the other elements of the marketing program have been properly put into place. Thus, the optimal brand positioning has been defined—especially in terms of the desired target market—and product, pricing, distribution, and other marketing program decisions have largely been made.

Complicating the picture for marketing communications programs, however, is that fact that the media environment has changed dramatically in recent years. Traditional advertising media such as TV, radio, magazines, and newspapers seem to be losing their grip on consumers due to increased competition for consumer attention. The digital revolution offers a host of new ways for consumers to learn and talk about brands with companies or with each other.

This changing media landscape has forced marketers to reevaluate how they should best communicate with consumers.[2] Consider how Ford defied convention in launching a new vehicle.

FIESTA

The Ford Fiesta was a vital new product introduction for the company, given the tough economic times and financial challenges faced by the auto industry. Its success was due, in part, to a comprehensive, carefully integrated marketing communications program. Before the U.S. launch took place in April 2010, 150 Fiestas toured the country for test drives, and 100 were given to bloggers for six months to allow them to share their experiences. People were chosen based on their online experience with blogging and social-media friends and a video they submitted testifying to their desire for adventure. After six months, the campaign had 4.3 million YouTube views, over 500,000 Flickr views, over 3 million Twitter impressions, and 50,000 interested potential customers, 97 percent of whom didn't already own a Ford. After launch, more traditional advertising and other forms of promotion kicked in, but a second phase of the social media campaign was also introduced. Twenty pairs of agents selected from 1,000 applicants were assigned to a major market where they tweeted messages and promoted the Fiesta virally via a series of online and local challenges.[3]

Challenges in Designing Brand-Building Communications

The new media environment has further complicated marketers' perennial challenge to build effective and efficient marketing communication programs. The Fiesta example illustrates the creativity and scope of what will characterize successful twenty-first century marketing communication programs. Skillfully designed and implemented marketing communications programs require careful planning and a creative knack. Let's first consider a few useful tools to provide some perspective.

Perhaps the simplest—but most useful—way to judge any communication option is by its ability to contribute to brand equity. For example, how well does a proposed ad campaign contribute to brand awareness or to creating, maintaining, or strengthening certain brand associations? Does a sponsorship cause consumers to have more favorable brand judgments and feelings? To what extent does an online promotion encourage consumers to buy more of a product? At what price premium? Figure 6-2 displays a simple three-step model for judging the effectiveness of advertising or any communication option to build brand equity.

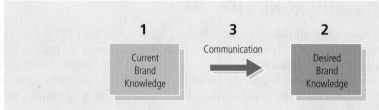

FIGURE 6-2

Simple Test for
Marketing
Communication
Effectiveness

1. What is your current brand knowledge? Have you created a detailed
    mental map?

2. What is your desired brand knowledge? Have you defined optimal points-
    of-parity and points-of-difference and a brand mantra?

3. How does the communication option help the brand get from current to
    desired knowledge with consumers? Have you clarified the specific effects
    on knowledge engendered by communications?

Information Processing Model of Communications.   To provide some perspective, let's
consider in more depth the process by which marketing communications might affect consumers. A number of different models have been put forth over the years to explain communications
and the steps in the persuasion process—recall the discussion on the hierarchy of effects model
from Brand Focus 2.0. For example, for a person to be persuaded by any form of communication
(a TV advertisement, newspaper editorial, or blog posting), the following six steps must occur:[4]

1. *Exposure:* A person must see or hear the communication.
2. *Attention:* A person must notice the communication.
3. *Comprehension:* A person must understand the intended message or arguments of the
    communication.
4. *Yielding:* A person must respond favorably to the intended message or arguments of the
    communication.
5. *Intentions:* A person must plan to act in the desired manner of the communication.
6. *Behavior:* A person must actually act in the desired manner of the communication.

You can appreciate the challenge of creating a successful marketing communication program when you realize that each of the six steps must occur for a consumer to be persuaded. If
there is a breakdown or failure in any step along the way, then successful communication will
not result. For example, consider the potential pitfalls in launching a new advertising campaign:

1. A consumer may not be exposed to an ad because the media plan missed the mark.
2. A consumer may not notice an ad because of a boring and uninspired creative strategy.
3. A consumer may not understand an ad because of a lack of product category knowledge or
    technical sophistication, or because of a lack of awareness and familiarity about the brand
    itself.
4. A consumer may fail to respond favorably and form a positive attitude because of irrelevant
    or unconvincing product claims.
5. A consumer may fail to form a purchase intention because of a lack of an immediate per-
    ceived need.
6. A consumer may fail to actually buy the product because he or she doesn't remember any-
    thing from the ad when confronted with the available brands in the store.

To show how fragile the whole communication process is, assume that the probability of
each of the six steps being successfully accomplished is 50 percent—most likely an extremely
generous assumption. The laws of probability suggest that the likelihood of all six steps successfully occurring, assuming they are independent events, is $0.5 \times 0.5 \times 0.5 \times 0.5 \times 0.5 \times 0.5$, which
equals 1.5625 percent. If the probability of each step's occurring, on average, were a more pessi-
mistic 10 percent, then the joint probability of all six events occurring is .000001. In other words,
only 1 in 1,000,000! No wonder advertisers sometimes lament the limited power of advertising.

One implication of the information processing model is that to increase the odds for a successful marketing communications campaign, marketers must attempt to increase the likelihood that *each* step occurs. For example, from an advertising standpoint, the ideal ad campaign would ensure that:

1. The right consumer is exposed to the right message at the right place and at the right time.
2. The creative strategy for the advertising causes the consumer to notice and attend to the ad but does not distract from the intended message.
3. The ad properly reflects the consumer's level of understanding about the product and the brand.
4. The ad correctly positions the brand in terms of desirable and deliverable points-of-difference and points-of-parity.
5. The ad motivates consumers to consider purchase of the brand.
6. The ad creates strong brand associations to all these stored communication effects so that they can have an effect when consumers are considering making a purchase.

Clearly, marketers need to design and execute marketing communication programs carefully if they are to have the desired effects on consumers.

Role of Multiple Communications

How much and what kinds of marketing communications are necessary? Economic theory suggests placing dollars into a marketing communication budget and across communication options according to marginal revenue and cost. For example, the communication mix would be optimally distributed when the last dollar spent on each communication option generated the same return.

Because such information may be difficult to obtain, however, other models of budget allocation emphasize more observable factors such as stage of brand life cycle, objectives and budget of the firm, product characteristics, size of budget, and media strategy of competitors. These factors are typically contrasted with the different characteristics of the media.

For example, marketing communication budgets tend to be higher when there is low channel support, much change in the marketing program over time, many hard-to-reach customers, more complex customer decision making, differentiated products and nonhomogeneous customer needs, and frequent product purchases in small quantities.[5]

Besides these efficiency considerations, different communication options also may target different market segments. For example, advertising may attempt to bring new customers into the market or attract competitors' customers to the brand, whereas promotions might attempt to reward loyal users of the brand.

Invariably, marketers will employ multiple communications to achieve their goals. In doing so, they must understand how each communication option works and how to assemble and integrate the best set of choices. The following section presents an overview and critique of four major marketing communication options from a brand-building perspective.

FOUR MAJOR MARKETING COMMUNICATION OPTIONS

Our contention is that in the future there will be four vital ingredients to the best brand-building communication programs: (1) advertising and promotion, (2) interactive marketing, (3) events and experiences, and (4) mobile marketing. We consider each in turn.

Advertising

Advertising is any paid form of nonpersonal presentation and promotion of ideas, goods, or services by an identified sponsor. Although it is a powerful means of creating strong, favorable, and unique brand associations and eliciting positive judgments and feelings, advertising is controversial because its specific effects are often difficult to quantify and predict. Nevertheless, a number of studies using very different approaches have shown the potential power of advertising on brand sales. As Chapter 1 noted, the latest recession provided numerous examples of brands benefiting from increased advertising expenditures. A number of prior research studies are consistent with that view.[6]

Given the complexity of designing advertising—the number of strategic roles it might play, the sheer number of specific decisions to make, and its complicated effect on consumers—it is difficult to provide a comprehensive set of detailed managerial guidelines. Different advertising media clearly have different strengths, however, and therefore are best suited to play certain roles in a communication program. Brand Focus 6.0 provides some empirical generalizations about advertising. Now we'll highlight some key issues about each type of advertising medium in turn.

Television.   Television is a powerful advertising medium because it allows for sight, sound, and motion and reaches a broad spectrum of consumers. Virtually all U.S. households have televisions, and the average hours viewed per person per week in the United States in 2010 was 34 hours, an all-time high.[7] The wide reach of TV advertising translates to low cost per exposure.

Pros & Cons.   From a brand equity perspective, TV advertising has two particularly important strengths. First, it can be an effective means of vividly demonstrating product attributes and persuasively explaining their corresponding consumer benefits. Second, TV advertising can be a compelling means for dramatically portraying user and usage imagery, brand personality, emotions, and other brand intangibles.

On the other hand, television advertising has its drawbacks. Because of the fleeting nature of the message and the potentially distracting creative elements often found in a TV ad, consumers can overlook product-related messages and the brand itself. Moreover, the large number of ads and nonprogramming material on television creates clutter that makes it easy for consumers to ignore or forget ads. The large number of channels creates fragmentation, and the widespread existence of digital video recorders gives viewers the means to skip commercials.

Another important disadvantage of TV ads is the high cost of production and placement. In 2010, for example, a 30-second spot to air during the popular *American Idol* on FOX ran between $360,000 and $490,000. A 30-second spot on even a new network show typically costs over $100,000.[8] Although the price of TV advertising has skyrocketed, the share of the prime time audience for the major networks has steadily declined. By any number of measures, the effectiveness of any one ad, on average, has diminished.

Nevertheless, properly designed and executed TV ads can affect sales and profits. For example, over the years, one of the most consistently successful TV advertisers has been Apple. The "1984" ad for the introduction of its Macintosh personal computer—portraying a stark Orwellian future with a feature film look—ran only once on TV, but is one of the best-known ads ever. In the years that followed, Apple advertising successfully created awareness and image for a series of products, more recently with the acclaimed "Get a Mac" global ad campaign.[9]

APPLE

Apple Computer's highly successful "Get a Mac" ad campaign—also known as "Mac vs. PC"—featured two actors bantering about the merits of their respective brands: one is hip looking (Apple), the other nerdy looking (PC). The campaign quickly went global. Apple, recognizing its potential, dubbed the ads for Spain, France, Germany, and Italy; however, it chose to reshoot and rescript for the United Kingdom and Japan—two important markets with unique advertising and comedy cultures. The UK ads followed a similar formula but used two well-known actors in character and tweaked the jokes to reflect British humor. The Japanese ads avoided direct comparisons and were more subtle in tone. Played by comedians from a local troupe called the Rahmens, the two characters were more similar in nature but represented work (PC) versus home (Mac). Creative but effective in any language, the ads helped provide a stark contrast between the two brands, making the Apple brand more relevant and appealing to a whole new group of consumers.

Guidelines.   In designing and evaluating an ad campaign, marketers should distinguish the *message strategy* or positioning of an ad (what the ad attempts to convey about the brand) from its *creative strategy* (the way the ad expresses the brand claims). Designing effective advertising campaigns is both an art and a science: The artistic aspects relate to the creative strategy of the ad and its execution; the scientific aspects relate to the message strategy and the brand claim information the ad contains. Thus, as Figure 6-3 describes, the two main concerns in devising an advertising strategy are as follows:

- Defining the proper positioning to maximize brand equity
- Identifying the best creative strategy to communicate or convey the desired positioning

DEFINE POSITIONING TO ESTABLISH BRAND EQUITY

Competitive frame of reference

Nature of competition

Target market

Point-of-parity attributes or benefits

Category

Competitive

Correlational

Point-of-difference attributes or benefits

Desirable

Deliverable

Differentiating

IDENTIFY CREATIVE STRATEGY TO COMMUNICATE POSITIONING CONCEPT

Informational (benefit elaboration)

Problem–solution

Demonstration

Product comparison

Testimonial (celebrity or unknown consumer)

Transformational (imagery portrayal)

Typical or aspirational usage situation

Typical or aspirational user of product

Brand personality and values

Motivational ("borrowed interest" techniques)

Humor

Warmth

Sex appeal

Music

Fear

Special effects

FIGURE 6-3

Factors in Designing Effective Advertising Campaigns

Source: Based in part on an insightful framework put forth in John R. Rossiter and Larry Percy, *Advertising and Promotion Management*, 2nd ed. (New York: McGraw-Hill, 1997).

Chapter 3 described a number of issues with respect to positioning strategies to maximize brand equity. Creative strategies tend to be either largely *informational*, elaborating on a specific product-related attribute or benefit, or largely *transformational*, portraying a specific non-product-related benefit or image.[10] These two general categories each encompass several different specific creative approaches.

Regardless of which general creative approach marketers take, however, certain motivational or "borrowed interest" devices can attract consumers' attention and raise their involvement with an ad. These devices include cute babies, frisky puppies, popular music, well-liked celebrities, amusing situations, provocative sex appeals, and fear-inducing threats. Many believe such techniques are necessary in the tough new media environment characterized by low-involvement consumer processing and much competing ad and programming clutter.

Unfortunately, these attention-getting tactics are often *too* effective and distract from the brand or its product claims. Thus, the challenge in arriving at the best creative strategy is figuring out how to break through the clutter to attract the attention of consumers but still deliver the intended message. Consider how the SNICKERS® candy bar achieved that.

SNICKERS® BRAND

Facing slumping sales, SNICKERS® needed to build on its key point-of-difference as a deliciously filling hunger-satisfier to extend its reach beyond its core audience of young males. With a campaign theme of "You're Not You When You're Hungry®," humorous ads were created that showed everyday people acting like—and literally becoming—different people in different situations because of their hunger. Only when they eat a SNICKERS® bar do they snap back to reality and become themselves again. In the high-profile 2010 Super Bowl launch ad for the U.S. market, a guy in a playground football game is snidely told he is playing like famed comedienne Betty White—who actually is shown playing—until he gets his bite of SNICKERS®. In a follow-up spot, one of four guys on a road trip is told he is acting like a diva in the form of legendary soul singer Aretha Franklin until he is given a SNICKERS® bar. Strong PR, complementary print, and extensive digital activation and Facebook, YouTube, and Twitter presence all further reinforced the message. The well-conceived and executed campaign received an EFFIE award from the American Marketing Association in recognition of its marketplace sales success.[11]

Humorous ads for **SNICKERS®** have reinforced its value as a hunger satisfier.

Source: SNICKERS® is a registered trademark of Mars, Incorporated and its affiliates. This trademark is used with permission. Mars, Incorporated is not associated with Pearson Education, Inc. The SNICKERS® advertisement is printed with permission of Mars, Incorporated.

What makes an effective TV ad?[12] Fundamentally, a TV ad should contribute to brand equity in some demonstrable way, for example, by enhancing awareness, strengthening a key association or adding a new association, or eliciting a positive consumer response. Earlier, we identified six broad information-processing factors as affecting the success of advertising: consumer targeting, the ad creative, consumer understanding, brand positioning, consumer motivation, and ad memorability.

Although managerial judgment using criteria such as these can and should be employed in evaluating advertising, research also can play a productive role. Advertising strategy research is often invaluable in clarifying communication objectives, target markets, and positioning alternatives. To evaluate the effectiveness of message and creative strategies, *copy testing* is often conducted, in which a sample of consumers is exposed to candidate ads and their reactions are gauged in some manner.

Unfortunately, copy-testing results vary considerably depending on exactly how tests are conducted. Consequently, the results must be interpreted as only one possible data point that should be combined with managerial judgment and other information in evaluating the merits of an ad. Copy testing is perhaps most useful when managerial judgment reveals some fairly clear positive and negative aspects to an ad and is therefore somewhat inconclusive. In this case, copy-testing research may shed some light on how these various conflicting aspects "net out" and collectively affect consumer processing.

Regardless, copy-testing results should not be seen as a means of making a "go" or "no go" decision; ideally, they should play a diagnostic role in helping to understand *how* an ad works. As an example of the potential fallibility of pretesting, consider NBC's experiences with the popular TV series *Seinfeld.*

SEINFELD

In October 1989, *The Seinfeld Chronicles,* as it was called then, was shown to several groups of viewers in order to gauge the show's potential, like most television pilot projects awaiting final network approval. The show tested badly—very badly. The summary research report noted that "no segment of the audience was eager to watch the show again." The reaction to Seinfeld himself was "lukewarm" because his character was seen as "powerless, dense, and naïve." The test report also concluded that "none of the supports were particularly liked and viewers felt that Jerry needed a better back-up ensemble." Despite the weak reaction, NBC decided to go ahead with what became one of the most successful television shows of the 1990s. Although NBC also changed its testing methods, this experience reinforces the limitations of testing and the dangers of relying on single numbers.[13]

Future Prospects.   In the new Internet era, the future of television and traditional mass marketing advertising is uncertain as top marketers weigh their new communication options. Some "New Year's Resolutions" drafted for 2010 reveal their changing mind-set:[14]

- Richard Gerstein, senior VP of marketing at Sears: "Stay focused on creating personalized digital relationships with our customers by meeting their individual needs in an integrated way through our stores, Web sites, call center, and innovative mobile shopping sites."
- Keith Levy, VP of marketing at Anheuser-Busch: "To find the next Facebook or Twitter phenomenon . . . making sure we're in the places our consumers are increasingly headed and being there in an authentic way."

Although digital has captured the imagination of marketers everywhere, at least for some, the power of TV ads remains. In a series of interviews in 2011, many CMOs also continued to show their support for TV advertising. Procter & Gamble CMO Marc Pritchard put it directly when he said, "TV will continue to be an essential part of our marketing mix to reach people with our brands."[15] TV spending is forecast to continue to make up almost 40 percent of all U.S. ad spending through 2015.

Radio.   Radio is a pervasive medium: 93 percent of all U.S. consumers 12 years and older listen to the radio daily and, on average, for over 15 hours a week, although often only in the background.[16] Perhaps the main advantage to radio is flexibility—stations are highly targeted, ads are relatively inexpensive to produce and place, and short closings allow for quick responses.

Radio is a particularly effective medium in the morning and can effectively complement or reinforce TV ads. Radio also enables companies to achieve a balance between broad and localized market coverage. Obvious disadvantages of radio, however, are the lack of visual image and the relatively passive nature of consumer processing that results. Several brands, however, have effectively built brand equity with radio ads.

MOTEL 6

One notable radio ad campaign is for Motel 6, the nation's largest budget motel chain, which was founded in 1962 when the "6" stood for $6 a night. After finding its business fortunes hitting bottom in 1986 with an occupancy rate of only 66.7 percent, Motel 6 made a number of marketing changes, including the launch of a radio campaign of humorous 60-second ads featuring folksy contractor-turned-writer Tom Bodett. Containing the clever tag line "We'll Leave the Light on for You," the campaign is credited with a rise in occupancy and a revitalization of the brand that continues to this day.[17]

Using the clever slogan, "We'll Leave the Light on for You,"
radio—complemented by magazine ads like this—has been
a highly effective brand-building medium for Motel 6.
Source: Accor North America

What makes an effective radio ad?[18] Radio has been less studied than other media. Because of its low-involvement nature and limited sensory options, advertising on radio often must be fairly focused. For example, the advertising pioneer David Ogilvy believed four factors were critical:[19]

1. Identify your brand early in the commercial.
2. Identify it often.
3. Promise the listener a benefit early in the commercial.
4. Repeat it often.

Nevertheless, radio ads can be extremely creative. Some see the lack of visual images as a plus because they feel the clever use of music, sounds, humor, and other creative devices can tap into the listener's imagination in a way that creates powerfully relevant and liked images.

Print.   Print media has taken a huge hit in recent years as more and more consumers choose to collect information and seek entertainment online. In response, publishers are doing their own digital innovation in the form of iPad apps and a stronger Web presence.

Print media does offer a stark contrast to broadcast media. Most importantly, because they are self-paced, magazines and newspapers can provide detailed product information. At the same time, the static nature of the visual images in print media makes it difficult to provide dynamic presentations or demonstrations. Another disadvantage of print advertising is that it can be a fairly passive medium.

Pros & Cons.   The two main print media—magazines and newspapers—have many of the same advantages and disadvantages. Magazines are particularly effective at building user and usage imagery. They can also be highly engaging: one study showed that consumers are more likely to view magazine ads as less intrusive, more truthful, and more relevant than ads in other media and are less likely to multitask while reading.[20]

Newspapers, however, are more timely and pervasive. Daily newspapers are read by 30 percent of the population—although that number has been declining for years as more consumers go online to get their news—and tend to be used for local (especially retailer) advertising.[21] On the other hand, although advertisers have some flexibility in designing and placing newspaper ads, poor reproduction quality and short shelf life can diminish some of the possible impact of newspaper advertising. These are disadvantages that magazine advertising usually doesn't share.

Although print advertising is particularly well suited to communicate product information, it can also effectively communicate user and usage imagery. Fashion brands such as Calvin Klein, Ralph Lauren, and Guess have also created strong nonproduct associations through print advertising. Some brands attempt to communicate both product benefits and user or usage imagery in their print advertising, for example, car makers such as Ford, Volkswagen, and Volvo or cosmetics makers such as Maybelline and Revlon.

One of the longest-running and perhaps most successful print ad campaigns ever is for Absolut vodka.[22]

ABSOLUT

In 1980, Absolut was a tiny brand, selling 100,000, nine-liter cases a year. Research pointed out a number of liabilities for the brand: the name was seen as too gimmicky; the bottle shape was ugly, and bartenders found it hard to pour; shelf prominence was limited; and there was no credibility for a vodka brand made in Sweden. Michel Roux, president of Carillon (Absolut's importer), and TBWA (Absolut's New York ad agency) decided to use the oddities of the brand—its quirky name and bottle shape—to create brand personality and communicate quality and style in a series of creative print ads. Each ad in the campaign visually depicted the product in an unusual fashion and verbally reinforced the image with a simple, two-word headline using the brand name and some other word in a clever play on words. For example, the first ad showed the bottle prominently displayed, crowned by an angel's halo, with the headline "Absolut Perfection" appearing at the bottom of the page. Follow-up ads explored various themes (seasonal, geographic, celebrity artists) but always attempted to put forth a fashionable, sophisticated, and contemporary image. By 2001, Absolut had become the leading imported vodka in the United States, and by 2006, it was the third-largest premium spirits brand in the world, with sales of 9.8 million nine-liter cases. Facing slowing sales in 2007, however, the firm launched its first new campaign in 25 years, "In an Absolut World." The goal of the campaign was to focus on the uniqueness of the brand by showing a fantasy world where lying leaders are exposed by their Pinocchio noses, protesters and the police wage street fights with feather pillows, nice Manhattan apartments cost $300 a month, and it takes only one lap in a pool to turn fat into muscle. Later ads expanded the meaning of an "Absolut World" to include special, offbeat, or unusual events, people, and things by including celebrities such as Kate Beckinsale and Zooey Deschanel. In 2011, a new multimedia campaign, ABSOLUT BLANK, was launched with the tag line, "It All Starts with an Absolute Blank." Twenty artists—from drawing, painting, and sculpting to film making and digital art—used the iconic Absolut bottle as a blank canvas and creatively filled it with their artistic expression.

Absolut's new print ad campaign has returned to a creative strategy that emphasizes the product's packaging and appearance. This ad featured artist Dave Kinsey.

Source: © The Absolut Company AB. Used under permission from The Absolut Company AB.

Guidelines. What makes an effective print ad? The evaluation criteria we noted earlier for television advertising apply, but print advertising has some special requirements and rules. For example, research on print ads in magazines reveals that it is not uncommon for two-thirds of a magazine audience to not even notice any one particular print ad, or for only 10 percent or so of the audience to read much of the copy of any one ad. Many readers only glance at the most visible elements of a print ad, making it critical that an ad communicate clearly, directly, and consistently in the ad illustration and headline. Finally, many consumers can easily overlook the brand name if it is not readily apparent. We can sum the creative guidelines for print ads in three simple criteria: clarity, consistency, and branding.

Direct Response. In contrast to advertising in traditional broadcast and print media, which typically communicates to consumers in a nonspecific and nondirective manner, *direct response* uses mail, telephone, Internet, and other contact tools to communicate with or solicit a response from specific customers and prospects. Direct response can take many forms and is not restricted to solicitations by mail, telephone, or even within traditional broadcast and print media.

Direct mail still remains popular, with U.S. businesses generating $571 billion in sales from direct mail in 2010.[23] Marketers are exploring other options, though. One increasingly popular means of direct marketing is infomercials, formally known as direct response TV marketing.[24] In a marketing sense, infomercials attempt to combine the sell of commercials with the draw of educational information and entertainment. We can therefore think of them as a cross between a sales call and a television ad. According to Infomercial DRTV, a trade Web site, infomercials are typically 28 minutes and 30 seconds long with an average cost in the $150,000–250,000 range (although production can cost as little as $75,000 and as much as $500,000).[25]

Starting with infomercials, although now moving online and also employing social media, Guthy-Renker enjoys about $800 million in revenue from its Proactiv acne treatment, endorsed by celebrities Justin Bieber, Jennifer Love-Hewitt, Katy Perry, Avril Lavigne, and Jenna Fischer. Many infomercial products are now showing up in stores carrying little "As Seen on TV" signs. Telebrands has sold 35 million of the PedEgg used to smooth rough feet and generates 90 percent of sales of all its products from major retailers such as CVS and Target. By 2014, direct-response TV marketing is expected to drive sales of $174 billion—a 30% increase from 2010 levels.[26]

Guidelines. The steady growth of direct marketing in recent years is a function of technological advances like the ease of setting up toll-free numbers and Web sites; changes in consumer behavior, such as the increased demand for convenience; and the needs of marketers, who want to avoid wasteful communications to nontarget customers or customer groups. The advantage of direct response is that it makes it easier for marketers to establish relationships with consumers.

Direct communications through electronic or physical newsletters, catalogs, and so forth allow marketers to explain new developments with their brands to consumers on an ongoing basis as well as allow consumers to provide feedback to marketers about their likes and dislikes and specific needs and wants. By learning more about customers, marketers can fine-tune marketing programs to offer the right products to the right customers at the right time. In fact, direct marketing is often seen as a key component of relationship marketing—an important marketing trend we reviewed in Chapter 5. Some direct marketers employ what they call *precision marketing*—combining data analytics with strategic messages and compelling colors and designs in their communications.[27]

As the name suggests, the goal of direct response is to elicit some type of behavior from consumers; given that, it is easy to measure the effects of direct marketing efforts—people either respond or they do not. The disadvantages to direct response, however, are intrusiveness and clutter. To implement an effective direct marketing program, marketers need the three critical ingredients of (1) developing an up-to-date and informative list of current and potential future customers, (2) putting forth the right offer in the right manner, and (3) tracking the effectiveness of the marketing program. To improve the effectiveness of direct marketing programs, many marketers are embracing database marketing, as highlighted by The Science of Branding 6-1.

Place. The last category of advertising is also often called "nontraditional," "alternative," or "support" advertising, because it has arisen in recent years as a means to complement more traditional advertising media. *Place advertising*, also called *out-of-home advertising*, is a

THE SCIENCE OF BRANDING 6-1

The Importance of Database Marketing

Formally, **database marketing** has been defined as "managing a computerized relational database, in real time, of comprehensive, up-to-date, relevant data on customers, inquiries, prospects and suspects, to identify our most responsive customers for the purpose of developing a high quality, long-standing relationship of repeat business by developing predictive models which enable us to send desired messages at the right time in the right form to the right people—all with the result of pleasing our customers, increasing our response rate per marketing dollar, lowering our cost per order, building our business, and increasing our profits."

Regardless of the particular means of direct marketing, database marketing can help create targeted communication and marketing programs tailored to the needs and wants of specific consumers. When customers place orders, send in a coupon, fill out a warranty card, or enter a sweepstakes, database marketers collect their names and information about their attitudes and behavior, which they compile in a comprehensive database.

Database marketing is generally more effective at helping firms retain existing customers than in attracting new ones. Many marketers believe it makes more sense the higher the price of the product and the more often consumers buy it. Database marketing is often at the heart of a successful loyalty rewards program. Best Western uses both online and mail outlets to contact its program participants and relies on database information to improve the relevance and timeliness of its messages.

Database marketing pioneers include a number of financial services firms and airlines. Even packaged-goods companies, however, are exploring the possible benefits of database marketing. For example, Procter & Gamble created a database to market Pampers disposable diapers, allowing it to send out individualized birthday cards for babies and reminder letters to parents to move their child up to the next size. Combining this effort with a well-developed help line and Web site and in-store couponing, P&G is creating interactive, individualized, value-added contacts.

Database management tools will become a priority to marketers as they attempt to track the lifetime value (LTV) of customers. Some database marketing activities that can occur through the application of LTV analysis include predictive modeling, multiple campaign management, targeted promotions, up-selling, cross-selling, segmentation, churn management, multichannel management, product personalization, and acquisition and retention management.

Sources: Robert C. Blattberg, Byung-Do Kim, and Scott A. Neslin, *Database Marketing: Analyzing and Managing Customers* (New York: Springer Science + Business, 2008); James Tenser, "'Behavior-Activated Research' Benefits P&G's Pampers Brand," www.cpgmatters.com; Thomas Haire, "Best Western Melds Old and New," *Response*, March 2009.

broadly defined category that captures advertising outside traditional media. Increasingly, ads and commercials are showing up in unusual spots, sometimes as parts of experiential marketing programs.

The rationale is that because traditional advertising media—especially television advertising—are becoming less effective, marketers are better off reaching people in other environments, such as where they work, play, and, of course, shop. Out-of-home advertising picked up as the economy started to pick up in 2010, when it was estimated that $6.1 billion was spent.[28] Some of the options include billboards and posters; movies, airlines, lounges, and other places; product placement; and point-of-purchase advertising.

Billboards and Posters.   Billboards have a long history but have been transformed over the years and now employ colorful, digitally produced graphics, backlighting, sounds, movement, and unusual—even three-dimensional—images to attract attention. The medium has improved in terms of effectiveness (and measurability), technology (some billboards are now digitized), and provide a good opportunity for companies to sync their billboard strategies with mobile advertising.

Billboard-type poster ads are now showing up everywhere in the United States each year to increase brand exposure and goodwill. Transit ads on buses, subways, and commuter trains—around for years—have now become a valuable means to reach working women. Street furniture (bus shelters, kiosks, and public areas) has also become a fast-growing area. In Japan, cameras and sensors are being added to signs and electronic public displays so that—combined with cell-phone technology—they can become more interactive and personalized.[29]

Billboards do not even necessarily have to stay in one place. Marketers can buy ad space on billboard-laden trucks that are driven around all day in marketer-selected areas. Oscar Mayer sends seven "Wienermobiles" traveling across the country each year. New York City became the

Oscar Meyer's Weinermobile, with its two Hotdoggers drivers, tour the country and make appearances at various events.

Source: ZUMA Press/ Newscom

first major city to allow its taxi cabs to advertise via onboard television screens. Between 2009 and 2010, the number of taxi advertisers doubled, and included brands such as AOL, Citibank, and Sprint. Research has shown that passengers keep the TVs on 85 percent of the time.[30]

Advertisers can now buy space in stadiums and arenas and on garbage cans, bicycle racks, parking meters, airport luggage carousels, elevators, gasoline pumps, the bottom of golf cups, airline snacks, and supermarket produce in the form of tiny labels on apples and bananas. Leaving no stone unturned, advertisers can even buy space in toilet stalls and above urinals, which, according to research studies, office workers visit an average of three to four times a day for roughly four minutes per visit. At Chicago O'Hare airport, digital commercials are now being shown in 150 bathroom mirrors above lavatory sinks.[31] Figure 6-4 displays some of the most successful outdoor advertisers.

Movies, Airlines, Lounges, and Other Places. Increasingly, advertisers are placing traditional TV and print ads in unconventional places. Companies such as Whittle Communication and Turner Broadcasting have tried placing TV and commercial programming in classrooms, airport lounges, and other public places. Airlines now offer media-sponsored audio and video programming that accepts advertising (*USA Today Sky Radio* and *National Geographic Explorer*) and include catalogs in seat pockets for leading mail-order companies (*SkyMall* magazine). Movie theater chains such as Loews Cineplex now run 30-, 60-, or 90-second ads on 2,000-plus screens. Although the same ads that appear on TV or in magazines often appear in these unconventional places, many advertisers believe it is important to create specially designed ads for these out-of-home exposures to better meet consumer expectations.

FIGURE 6-4

Obie Hall of Fame Winners (as selected by the Outdoor Advertising Association of America)

Chick-fil-A (2006)

Walt Disney Company (2007)

Altoids (2008)

Absolut (2009)

MINI Cooper (2010)

Cracker Barrel Old Country Store (2011)

Product Placement.   Many major marketers pay fees of $50,000–100,000 and even higher so their products can make cameo appearances in movies and on television, with the exact fee depending on the amount and nature of the brand exposure. This practice got a boost in 1982 when—after Mars declined an offer for use of its M&M's brand—sales of Reese's Pieces increased 65 percent after the candy appeared prominently in the blockbuster movie *E.T.: The Extraterrestrial*.[32]

More recently, many brands such as Chase, Hilton, AT Cross, and Heineken have paid to be featured in the popular TV series *Mad Men*.[33] Marketers combine product placements with special promotions to publicize a brand's entertainment tie-ins and create "branded entertainment." For example, BMW complemented product placement in the James Bond film *Goldeneye* with an extensive direct mail and advertising campaign to help launch its Z3 roadster.

Some firms benefit from product placement at no cost by either supplying their product to the movie company in return for exposure or simply because of the creative demands of the storyline. *Mad Men* has also prominently featured such iconic brands as Cadillac, Kodak, and Utz potato chips for free because of plot necessities. To test the effects of product placement, marketing research companies such as CinemaScore conduct viewer exit surveys to determine which brands were actually noticed during movie showings.

Point of Purchase.   Myriad possibilities have emerged in recent years as ways to communicate with consumers at the point of purchase. In-store advertising includes ads on shopping carts, cart straps, aisles, or shelves as well as promotion options such as in-store demonstrations, live sampling, and instant coupon machines. Point-of-purchase radio provides FM-style programming and commercial messages to thousands of food stores drugstores nationwide. Programming includes a store-selected music format, consumer tips, and commercials. The Walmart Smart Network is beamed to over 2,700 of the retail giant's stores and is a mixture of information content and advertising.[34]

The appeal of point-of-purchase advertising lies in the fact that, as numerous studies have shown, consumers in many product categories make the bulk of their final brand decisions in the store. In-store media are designed to increase the number and nature of spontaneous and planned buying decisions. One company placing ads on the entryway security panels of major retail chains reported that the advertised brands experienced an average increase in sales of 20 percent over the four-week period in which their ads appeared.[35]

Guidelines.   Nontraditional or place media present some interesting options for marketers to reach consumers in new ways. Ads now can appear virtually any place where consumers have a

Mad Men has been popular not just with viewers—a number of marketers have paid for product placement for their brands.

Source: Pictorial Press Ltd / Alamy

few spare minutes or even seconds and thus enough time to notice them. The main advantage of nontraditional media is that they can reach a very precise and captive audience in a cost-effective and increasingly engaging manner.

Because the audience must process out-of-home ads quickly, however, the message must be simple and direct. In fact, outdoor advertising is often called the "15-second sell." In noting how out-of-home aligns with twenty-first century consumers, one commentator observed that with people on-the-go and wanting content in short bursts, "Billboards are the original tweets—you get a quick image or piece of knowledge than move on."[36] In that regard, strategically, out-of-home advertising is often more effective at enhancing awareness or reinforcing existing brand associations than at creating new ones.

The challenge with nontraditional media is demonstrating their reach and effectiveness through credible, independent research. Another danger of nontraditional media is consumer backlash against overcommercialization. Perhaps because of the sheer pervasiveness of advertising, however, consumers seem to be less bothered by nontraditional media now than in the past.

Consumers must be favorably affected in some way to justify the marketing expenditures for nontraditional media, and some firms offering ad placement in supermarket checkout lines, fast-food restaurants, physicians' waiting rooms, health clubs, and truck stops have suspended business at least in part because of lack of consumer interest. The bottom line, however, is that there will always be room for creative means of placing the brand in front of consumers—the possibilities are endless.

Promotion

Although they do very different things, advertising and promotion often go hand-in-hand. *Sales promotions* are short-term incentives to encourage trial or usage of a product or service.[37] Marketers can target sales promotions to either the trade or end consumers. Like advertising, sales promotions come in all forms. Whereas advertising typically provides consumers a *reason* to buy, sales promotions offer consumers an *incentive* to buy. Thus, sales promotions are designed to do the following:

- Change the behavior of the trade so that they carry the brand and actively support it
- Change the behavior of consumers so that they buy a brand for the first time, buy more of the brand, or buy the brand earlier or more often

Analysts maintain that the use of sales promotions grew in the 1980s and 1990s for a number of reasons. Brand management systems with quarterly evaluations were thought to encourage short-term solutions, and an increased need for accountability seemed to favor communication tools like promotions, whose behavioral effects are more quickly and easily observed than the often "softer" perceptual effects of advertising. Economic forces worked against advertising effectiveness as ad rates rose steadily despite what marketers saw as an increasingly cluttered media environment and fragmented audience. Consumers were thought to be making more in-store decisions, and to be less brand loyal and more immune to advertising than in the past. Many mature brands were less easily differentiated. On top of it all, retailers became more powerful.

For all these reasons, some marketers began to see consumer and trade promotions as a more effective means than advertising to influence the sales of a brand. There clearly are advantages to sales promotions. Consumer sales promotions permit manufacturers to price discriminate by effectively charging different prices to groups of consumers who vary in their price sensitivity. Besides conveying a sense of urgency to consumers, carefully designed promotions can build brand equity through information or actual product experience that helps to create strong, favorable, and unique associations. Sales promotions can encourage the trade to maintain full stocks and actively support the manufacturer's merchandising efforts.

On the other hand, from a consumer behavior perspective, there are a number of disadvantages of sales promotions, such as decreased brand loyalty and increased brand switching, decreased quality perceptions, and increased price sensitivity. Besides inhibiting the use of franchise-building advertising or other communications, diverting marketing funds into coupons or other sales promotion sometimes has led to reductions in research and development budgets and staff. Perhaps most importantly, the widespread discounting arising from trade promotions may have led to the increased importance of price as a factor in consumer decisions, breaking down traditional brand loyalty patterns.

Another disadvantage of sales promotions is that in some cases they may merely subsidize buyers who would have bought the brand anyway. Interestingly, the more affluent, educated, suburban, and ethnically Caucasian a household is, the more likely it is to use coupons, mainly because

Some consumers have created Web sites to share their expertise in using coupons and promotions with others.
Source: Gina Lincicum/Moneywise Moms

its members are more likely to read newspapers where the vast majority of coupons appear. Sales promotions also may just subsidize "coupon enthusiasts" who use coupons frequently and broadly (on as many 188 items a year and up). Eighty-one percent of the products purchased using manufacturer coupons in the first half of 2009 came from just 19 percent of U.S. households. One "extreme" couponer prides herself on the fact that she saves 40–60 percent off her weekly grocery trips and even hosts a blog (www.MoneyWiseMoms.com) to share her couponing tips.[38]

Another drawback to sales promotions is that new consumers attracted to the brand may attribute their purchase to the promotion and not to the merits of the brand per se and, as a result, may not repeat their purchase when the promotional offer is withdrawn. Finally, retailers have come to expect and now demand trade discounts. The trade may not actually provide the agreed-upon merchandising and take advantage of promotions by engaging in nonproductive activities such as forward buying (stocking up for when the promotion ends) and diversion (shipping products to areas where the promotion was not intended to go).[39]

Promotions have a number of possible objectives.[40] With consumers, objectives may target new category users, existing category users, and/or existing brand users. With the trade, objectives may center on distribution, support, inventories, or goodwill. Next, we consider some specific issues related to consumer and trade promotions.

Consumer Promotions. Consumer promotions are designed to change the choices, quantity, or timing of consumers' product purchases. Although they come in all forms, we distinguish between customer franchise building promotions like samples, demonstrations, and educational material, and noncustomer franchise building promotions such as price-off packs, premiums, sweepstakes, and refund offers.[41] Customer franchise building promotions can enhance the attitudes and loyalty of consumers toward a brand—in other words, affect brand equity.

For example, sampling is a means of creating strong, relevant brand associations while also perhaps kick-starting word-of-mouth among consumers. Marketers are increasingly using sampling at the point of use, growing more precise about where and how they deliver samples to maximize brand equity. For a $10 monthly subscription, one new firm, Birchbox, sends consumers a box of deluxe-size samples from such notable beauty brands as Benefit, Kiehl's, and Marc Jacobs. Members can go to the Web site to collect more information, provide feedback, and earn points for full-sized products. The beauty brands like the selectivity and customer involvement of the promotion.[42]

Thus, marketers increasingly judge sales promotions by their ability to contribute to brand equity as well as generate sales. Creativity is as critical to promotions as it is to advertising or any other form of marketing communications. The Promotion Marketing Association (PMA) bestows Reggie awards to recognize "superior promotional thinking, creativity, and execution across the full spectrum of promotional marketing." In 2011, Walgreens won the Super Reggie award for its highly integrated promotional program.

WALGREENS

The main objective of Walgreens's "Arm Yourself for the Ones You Love" campaign was to convince 5 million people to get their flu shots at Walgreens in the winter of 2010. Research uncovered a subset of untapped consumers most receptive to getting a flu shot at Walgreens: "Well-Intender Moms" were 15–18 percent of the female population who had every intention of getting a flu shot the previous year but did not follow through. Busy doing things for others (including making sure their family got flu shots), they gave less priority to getting a shot for themselves. The campaign aimed to show these moms that getting their shot was a real priority and just as important to the health and well-being of their families. Walgreens's ad agency employed a holistic communication approach, using a range of communication options from broadcast media seen at home to the Web, circulars, outdoor ads, and in-store displays. The centerpiece was an "I got my flu shot for _____" bandage/sticker so people could proudly display that they had gotten their flu shots to protect themselves and a loved one. Here are some notable activation tactics:

- Thousands of photos of employees "showing their hearts" were used to kick off the campaign in Times Square.
- Walgreens pharmacists appeared on national TV (MSNBC, CNN, etc.) and popular shows like *The Dr. Oz Show*, administering flu shots to anchors and discussing the benefits.
- Zoned in-store messaging let shoppers know how and where they could "arm themselves."
- Regional print ads showcased local heroes "arming themselves."
- Digital and social media allowed people to show their love with their network of family and friends.
- Street-level outdoor media ads were placed where people were most likely to be thinking about getting exposed to the flu (bus stops, airports, and hospitals).
- "Arm Yourself" commercials brought the message to TV.

The "Arm Yourself for the Ones You Love" campaign far exceeded its goal, inspiring 5.4 million people to get their flu shot in just five weeks.[43]

Walgreen's award-winning "Arm Yourself for the Ones You Love" campaign used a variety of different communication options.
Source: Walgreens

Promotion strategy must reflect the attitudes and behavior of consumers. The percentage of coupons consumers redeem dropped steadily for years—in part due to the clutter of coupons that were increasingly being distributed—before experiencing an uptick more recently: redemption rates peaked in 1992 but fell for the next 15 years until experiencing an increase in the tough economic climate of late 2008. Almost 90 percent of all coupons appear in free-standing inserts (FSIs) in Sunday newspapers.

One area of promotional growth is in-store coupons, which marketers have increasingly turned to given that their redemption rates far exceed those of traditional out-of-store coupons. Another growing area is digital coupons, whose redemption rate (6 percent) is the highest of all types of coupons and 10 times higher than for newspaper coupons. Groupon created a clever promotional scheme that has met with some apparent success; the firm also turned down a $6 billion purchase offer from Google in 2010.[44]

GROUPON

Groupon launched in 2008 as a company offering a new marketing vehicle to businesses. By leveraging the Internet and e-mail, the company helps businesses use promotions as a form of advertisement. Specifically, Groupon maintains a large base of subscribers who receive a humorously worded daily deal—a specific percentage or dollar amount off the regular price—for a specific branded product or service. Through these e-mail discounts, Groupon offers three benefits to businesses: increased consumer exposure to the brand, the ability to price discriminate, and the creation of a "buzz factor." For these benefits, Groupon takes a 40–50 percent cut in the process. Many promotions are offered on behalf of local retailers such as spas, fitness centers, and restaurants, but Groupon also manages deals on behalf of national brands such as Gap, Southwest Airlines, and FTD. In 2010, Groupon expanded from 1 to 35 countries, grew its subscriber base from 2 million to over 50 million, partnered with 58,000 local businesses to promote over 100,000 deals, and saved consumers over $1.5 billion. Although some businesses complain that Groupon just attracts deal-seekers and is not as effective in converting regular customers, its 2011 revenue was reported to be between $3 billion and $4 billion. Groupon now faces several competitors in the market it helped create, including LivingSocial, Bloomspot, and Buywithme. Partly in response, Groupon Now was launched. Leveraging its massive sales force to sell Groupon Now, Groupon enlists local businesses to offer time and location-specific deals that customers can obtain via the Web or their smartphone. The iPhone app for the new service has two buttons, "I'm Bored" and "I'm Hungry" to trigger possible deals in real time. For businesses, the service is a way to boost traffic at otherwise slow times. Even a popular restaurant might still consider some midday and midweek discounts knowing the place is rarely full then.

Groupon devised a completely new way to send timely promotions to consumers by digital means.

Source: Groupon Inc.

Trade Promotions.   Trade promotions are often financial incentives or discounts given to retailers, distributors, and other channel members to stock, display, and in other ways facilitate the sale of a product through slotting allowances, point-of-purchase displays, contests and dealer incentives, training programs, trade shows, and cooperative advertising. Trade promotions are typically designed either to secure shelf space and distribution for a new brand, or to achieve more prominence on the shelf and in the store. Shelf and aisle positions in the store are important because they affect the ability of the brand to catch the eye of the consumer—placing a brand on a shelf at eye level may double sales over placing it on the bottom shelf.[45]

Because of the large amount of money spent on trade promotions, there is increasing pressure to make trade promotion programs more effective. Many firms are failing to see the brand-building value in trade promotions and are seeking to reduce and eliminate as much of their expenditures as possible.

Online Marketing Communications

The first decade of the twenty-first century has seen a headlong rush by companies into the world of interactive, online marketing communications. With the pervasive incorporation of the Internet into everyday personal and professional lives, marketers are scrambling to find the right places to be in cyberspace. The main advantages to marketing on the Web are the low cost and the level of detail and degree of customization it offers. Online marketing communications can accomplish almost any marketing communication objective and are especially valuable in terms of solid relationship building.

Leading trade publication *Advertising Age*'s 2010 Media Vanguard Awards for innovative uses of technology in media planning showed the wide range of online applications that exist. Among the winners were Martha Stewart for her "multimedia vision," *Financial Times* for successfully managing its free Web site alongside its paid online product, Kmart for showcasing a series of online videos to promote merchandising in its stores, and Allstate's relaunch of its Teen Driver Web site to better "speak" in teen language and use interactive games and features to engage them.

Reviewing all the guidelines for online marketing communications is beyond the scope of this text.[46] Here, we'll concentrate on three particularly crucial online brand-building tools: (1) Web sites, (2) online ads and videos, and (3) social media.

Web Sites.   One of the earliest and best-established forms of online marketing communications for brands is company-created Web sites. By capitalizing on the Web's interactive nature, marketers can construct Web sites that allow any type of consumer to choose the brand information relevant to his or her needs or desires. Even though different market segments may have different levels of knowledge and interest about a brand, a well-designed Web site can effectively communicate to consumers regardless of their personal brand or communications history.

Because consumers often go online to seek information rather than be entertained, some of the more successful Web sites are those that can convey expertise in a consumer-relevant area. For example, Web sites such as P&G's www.pampers.com and General Mills's www.cheerios.com offer baby care and parenting advice. Web sites can store company and product information, press releases, and advertising and promotional information as well as links to partners and key vendors. Web marketers can collect names and addresses for a database and conduct e-mail surveys and online focus groups.

Brand-building is increasingly a collaborative effort between consumers and brand marketers. As part of this process, there will be many consumer-generated Web sites and pages that may include ratings, reviews, and feedback on brands. Many consumers also post opinions and reviews or seek advice and feedback from others at commercial sites such as Yelp, TripAdvisor, and Epinions. As will be discussed in greater detail below, marketers must carefully monitor these different forums and participate where appropriate.

In creating online information sources for consumers at company Web sites, marketers must provide timely and reliable information. Web sites must be updated frequently and offer as much customized information as possible, especially for existing customers. Designing Web sites requires creating eye-catching pages that can sustain browsers' interest, employing the latest technology and effectively communicating the brand message. Web site design is crucial, because if consumers do not have a positive experience, it may be very difficult to entice them back in the highly competitive and cluttered online world.

Online Ads and Videos.   Internet advertising comes in a variety of forms—banner ads, rich-media ads, and other types of ads. Advertising on the Internet has grown rapidly—in 2010 it totaled $26 billion in the United States, surpassing newspaper advertising ($22.8 billion) to rank second behind TV advertising ($28.6 billion).[47]

A number of potential advantages exist for Internet advertising: It is accountable, because software can track which ads went to which sales; it is nondisruptive, so it doesn't interrupt consumers; and it can target consumers so that only the most promising prospects are contacted, who can then seek as much or as little information as they desire. Online ads and videos also can extend the creative or legal restrictions of traditional print and broadcast media to persuasively communicate brand positioning and elicit positive judgments and feelings.

Unfortunately, there are also many disadvantages. Many consumers find it easy to ignore banner ads and screen them out with pop-up filters. The average click-through rate for a standard banner ad in the United States was 0.08 percent in 2010, although that number increased to 0.14 percent for an expandable rich media banner. Similar percentages could be found in European and Latin American countries. Even in ad categories drawing exceptional interest from consumers, the percentages barely increased (to 1.02 percent for auto in Italy, 1.9 percent for health and beauty in Poland, and the biggest percentage, almost 8 percent for restaurants in Belgium).[48]

Increasingly, Web messages like streaming ads are drawing closer to traditional forms of television advertising. Videos take that one step further by virtually becoming short films. BMW, one of the pioneers, created a series of highly successful made-for-the-Web movies using well-known directors such as Guy Ritchie and actors such as Madonna. The advantage of videos is the enormous potential pass-along that exists if an imaginative video strikes a chord with consumers, as was the case for Coke.[49]

COKE'S "HAPPINESS MACHINE"

Coca-Cola's "Open Happiness" global brand slogan and platform lends itself to many different creative ideas and executions. Besides its usual iconic ads, the company decided it also wanted to activate the idea digitally in an equally inspired way. To do so, Coca-Cola rigged up a special vending machine at St. John's University in Queens, New York, dubbed the "Happiness Machine." The back of the machine was connected to a storeroom filled with all the people and props necessary to execute the stunt. When unsuspecting students started to use the machine, they first just received Cokes, but after that, all kinds of goodies began to appear—a bouquet of sunflowers, balloon animals, six-foot subs, and even a hot pepperoni pizza. Their astonished and gleeful reactions were caught by hidden cameras and fed into YouTube videos that received millions of hits and even became the basis of a 30-second TV spot shown all over the world.

Coca-Cola's "Happiness Machine" was a clever
brand-building stunt that was seen virally all over the world.
Source: Photographed by Lauren Nicole Maddox

As suggested by the Coke example, the Google-owned YouTube video-sharing Web site has become an especially important vehicle for distributing videos and initiating dialogue and cultivating a community around a brand.

With Internet-connected HDTV sales climbing, video opportunities for brand building can only continue to grow.[50] Any size brand can benefit. Tipp-Ex's "A Hunter Shoots a Bear" campaign became a viral YouTube sensation with millions and millions of views. In the video, a hunter finds a bear approaching his tent but decides not to shoot it. Using Tipp-Ex, he whites out the verb "shoot" and invites viewers to add their own verbs. For each inserted verb, a stored video response is played to humorously depict the action.[51]

As a manifestation of permission marketing, e-mail ads in general—often including advanced features such as personalized audio messages, color photos, and streaming video—have increased in popularity. E-mail ads often receive response rates of 20–30 percent at a cost less than that of banner ads. Tracking these response rates, marketers can fine-tune their messages. The key, as with direct marketing, is to create a good customer list.

Another alternative to banner ads that a great many marketers employ is search advertising, in which users are presented with sponsored links relevant to their search words alongside unsponsored search results. Since these links are tied to specific keywords, marketers can target them more effectively than banner ads and thus generate higher response rates. Almost half of all Internet advertising in 2010 (over $12 billion) was devoted to search.[52]

Google pioneered search advertising and helped make it a cost-effective option for online advertisers by offering "cost-per-click" pricing, wherein advertisers were charged based on the number of times a sponsored link was actually clicked. Companies have developed extensive search advertising strategies, based, for example, on how much to bid for keywords.

Social Media.   Social media is playing an increasingly important brand communication role due its massive growth. Social media allows consumers to share text, images, audio, and video online with each other and—if they choose—with representatives from companies. Social media comes in many forms, but six key options are: (1) message boards and forums, (2) chat rooms, (3) blogs, (4) Facebook, (5) Twitter, and (6) YouTube.

The numbers associated with social media are truly staggering. In November 2010, nearly one in four page views in the United States took place on Facebook. One forecast projected that by 2014, roughly two-thirds of U.S. Internet users will be regular visitors to social media networks.[53]

Social media offers many benefits to marketers. It allows brands to establish a public voice and presence on the Web. It complements and reinforces other communication activities. It helps promote innovation and relevance for the brand. By permitting personal, independent expression, message boards, chat rooms, and blogs can create a sense of community and foster active engagement.

Some social networks, such as Sugar and Gawker, provide an easy means for consumers to learn from and express attitudes and opinions to others. They also permit feedback that can improve all aspects of a brand's marketing program. Dr. Pepper has an enormous 8.5 million fan base on Facebook. Careful tracking and testing with Facebook users who state that they the "like" the brand has allowed the brand to fine-tune its marketing messages. With consumers increasingly avoiding surveys, many marketing researchers are excited about the potential of social networks to yield market insights.[54]

Social media clearly offers enormous opportunities for marketers to connect with consumers in ways that were not possible before. Although some marketers were uncertain as to whether they should engage in social media, many have come to realize that online conversations will occur whether they want them to or not, so the best strategy seems to be to determine how to best participate and be involved. Accordingly, many companies now have official Twitter handles and Facebook pages for their brands.

Different social media can accomplish different objectives. Landor's Allen Adamson views the chief role of Twitter—with its 140 character text-based limit for posting—as an "early warning system" so marketers know exactly what is happening in the marketplace and how to respond at any one point in time. For example, when a customer tweeted about a bad customer experience with Zappos, because the company was monitoring social media, it was able to immediately send an explanation, apology, and coupon.[55]

Facebook, on the other hand, is more about long-term relationship building and can be used to engage consumers and delve more deeply into their interests and passions. As popular as

Facebook is, it is not the only game in town. Special-interest community sites such as GoFISHn, with over 150,000 loyal anglers, and Dogster, with over 600,000 dog lovers, present even more focused targets.[56]

Some brands have fully embraced social media. Lego has always involved lead users and fans in its brand marketing activities, so it is no surprise it has thousands of YouTube videos and Flickr photos. Even top executives of some brands, such as Virgin's Richard Branson and Zappos's Tony Hsieh, weigh in with their comments. When companies choose to engage in social media, speed of response and the proper tone is critical.

There is no question that some consumers are choosing to become engaged with a brand at a deeper and broader level, and marketers must do everything they can to encourage them to do so. P&G invested heavily in 2010 to expand its Facebook presence with its brands. Fifteen of its brands quickly gained over 100,000 followers, and Pringles and Old Spice gained 9 million and 1.3 million, respectively. Its "Mean Girls Stink" antibullying Facebook app for Secret deodorant was downloaded more than 250,000 times.[57]

As exciting as these kinds of prospects are, marketers must also bear in mind that not everyone actively participates in social media. Only *some of the consumers* want to get involved with only *some of the brands* and, even then, only *some of the time*. Understanding how to best market a brand given such diversity in consumer backgrounds and interests is crucially important and will separate digital marketing winners and losers in the years to come.

Putting It All Together.   Interactive marketing communications work well together. Attention-getting online ads and videos can drive consumers to a brand's Web sites, where they can learn and experience more about the brand. Company-managed bulletin boards and blogs may then help create more engagement. Interactive marketing communications reinforces other forms of marketing communications as well.

Many experts maintain that a successful digitally based campaign for a brand often skillfully blends three different forms of media: paid, owned, and earned media. *Paid media* is all the various forms of more traditional advertising media described above, including TV and print. *Owned media* are those media channels the brand controls to some extent—Web sites, e-mails, social media, etc. *Earned media* are when consumers themselves communicate about the brand via social media, word-of-mouth, etc. It should be recognized that the lines sometimes blur, and communications can perform more than one function. For example, YouTube costs marketers to maintain, is under their control, but is also importantly social.

The interplay between the three forms of media is crucial. As one critic noted, "Paid media jump starts owned; owned sustains earned; and earned drives costs down and effectiveness up."[58] Procter & Gamble's highly successful "The Man Your Man Could Smell Like" starring ex-football player Isaiah Mustafa started with humorous tongue-in-cheek ads (paid media) that migrated online to YouTube, Facebook, and a brand microsite (owned media) before gaining heightened public attention via word-of-mouth, media reports, and social network interactions (earned media).

It is important to track all form of social media formally and informally. A number of firms have popped up to assist firms in this pursuit. For its Gatorade brand, PepsiCo actually created its own "Mission Control" where four full-time employees monitor social-media posts 24 hours a day. Any mention of Gatorade on Twitter, Facebook, or elsewhere is flagged, allowing the company to join conversations when needed and appropriate, such as when a Facebook poster incorrectly noted that Gatorade contains high-fructose corn syrup.[59]

Marketers have become more thoughtful about how to measure social media and classify interactive marketing success. The fact is, no matter how many they are, Facebook fans and Twitter followers will not matter if they are not engaged with the brand. Popular viral videos—like Burger King's "Subservient Chicken"—will mean little if they don't help to drive sales in some way.[60]

Events and Experiences

As important as online marketing is to brand management, events and experiences play an equally important role. Brand building in the virtual world must be complemented with brand building in the real or physical world. Events and experiences range from an extravagant multimillion dollar sponsorship of a major international event to a simple local in-store product demonstration or sampling program. What all these different kinds of events and experiences share is that, one way or another, the brand engages the consumers' senses and imagination, changing brand knowledge in the process.

Experiences can take all forms and are limited only by the marketers' imagination. To create awareness of its Lumix ZX1 camera, with its optical zoom lens capable of rendering anything eight times its normal size, Panasonic placed gigantic attention-getting sculptures—an over-sized pigeon, traffic cone, coffee cup, and so on—around London, Edinburgh, and four other UK cities. The campaign was reinforced digitally by a Facebook contest in which camera users could shoot their own images distorting everyday objects with the camera's zoom lens.[61]

Formally, *event marketing* can be defined as public sponsorship of events or activities related to sports, art, entertainment, or social causes. According to the International Events Group, event sponsorship has grown rapidly in recent years, to total $46.3 billion globally in 2010. The vast majority of event expenditures—68 percent—occur in the world of sports. Other categories are entertainment tours and attractions (10 percent), causes (9 percent), arts (5 percent); festivals, fairs and annual events (5 percent), and associations and membership organizations (3 percent).

Once employed mostly by cigarette, beer, and auto companies, sports marketing is now being embraced by virtually every type of company. Moreover, seemingly every sport—from dogsled racing to fishing tournaments and from tractor pulls to professional beach volleyball—now receives corporate backing of some kind. Chapter 7 examines the issues of event marketing and sponsorship in terms of the secondary associations that they bring to the brand.

Rationale. Event sponsorship provides a different kind of communication option for marketers. By becoming part of a special and personally relevant moment in consumers' lives, sponsors can broaden and deepen their relationship with their target market. Marketers report a number of reasons why they sponsor events:[62]

- *To identify with a particular target market or lifestyle:* Marketers can link their brands to events popular with either a select or broad group of consumers. They can target customers geographically, demographically, psychographically, or behaviorally, according to the sponsored events. In particular, marketers can choose events based on attendees' attitudes and usage of certain products or brands. No athletic event in the United States attracts more "pentamillionaires"—those with a net worth of more than $5 million—than the U.S. Open tennis tournament. Perhaps it is no surprise that its sponsors include luxury brands such as Lexus, Tiffany, American Express, and Heineken, which largely target affluent customers.[63]

- *To increase awareness of the company or product name:* Sponsorship often offers sustained exposure to a brand, a necessary condition to building brand recognition. By skillfully choosing sponsorship events or activities, marketers can enhance identification with a product and thus also brand recall. Waterford Crystal is well known for providing the crystal ball that drops down at midnight in New Year's Eve in Times Square.

- *To create or reinforce consumer perceptions of key brand image associations:* Events themselves have their own associations that help to create or reinforce brand associations. Seiko has been the official timer of the Olympics and other major sporting events for years. Subaru believes there is a match in interests between skiing events and potential buyers of its all-wheel-drive vehicles.

- *To enhance corporate image dimensions:* Sponsorship is a soft sell and a means to improve perceptions that the company is likable, prestigious, and so forth. Marketers hope consumers will credit the company for its sponsorship and favor it in later product choices. Mountain Dew created the multicity Dew Tour, in which athletes compete in different skateboarding, BMX, and freestyle motocross events to reach and make a favorable impression with the coveted but fickle 12- to 24-year-old target market.

- *To create experiences and evoke feelings:* Events can be part of an experiential marketing program. The feelings engendered by an exciting or rewarding event may indirectly link to the brand. Marketers can also use the Web to provide further event support and additional experiences. At the "LG Experience" at the NCAA Final Four Bracket Town Fan Experience in March 2011, LG showcased its new line of 3-D televisions, mobile phones, and home appliances. The goal was to tap into the passion of spectators and transfer that passion to its brands and products. A bar-coded, scannable Fan Pass allowed LG to track attendees and what they saw and for how long.[64]

- *To express commitment to the community or on social issues:* Often called cause-related marketing, sponsorships dedicated to the community or to promoting social issues create corporate tie-ins with nonprofit organizations and charities (see Chapter 11). For over 20 years, Colgate-Palmolive has sponsored the Starlight Children's Foundation, which grants wishes to young people who are critically ill.
- *To entertain key clients or reward key employees:* Many events have lavish hospitality tents and other special services or activities that are available only for sponsors and their guests. Bank of Boston's sponsorship of musical performances and Bank of America's golf tournament sponsorship include special events for clients. Involving clients with the event in these and other ways can engender goodwill and establish valuable business contacts. From an employee perspective, events can build participation and morale or create an incentive.
- *To permit merchandising or promotional opportunities:* Many marketers tie in contests or sweepstakes, in-store merchandising, and direct response or other marketing activities with their event. Warner-Lambert sponsors the "Taste of Chicago" promotion in part so it can gain shelf space in stores and participate in retailer co-op advertising.

Despite these potential advantages, there are a number of potential disadvantages to sponsorship. The success of an event can be unpredictable and out of the sponsor's control. There can be much clutter in sponsorship. Finally, although many consumers will credit sponsors for providing necessary financial assistance to make an event possible, some consumers may still resent the commercialization of events through sponsorship.

Guidelines.   Developing successful event sponsorship means choosing the appropriate events, designing the optimal sponsorship program, and measuring the effects of sponsorship on brand equity.

Choosing Sponsorship Opportunities.
Because of the huge amount of money involved and the number of event opportunities, many marketers are thinking more strategically about the events with which they will get involved and the manner by which they will do so.

There are a number of potential guidelines for choosing events. First, the event must meet the marketing objectives and communication strategy defined for the brand. That is, the audience delivered by the event must match the target market of the brand. Moreover, the event must have sufficient awareness, possess the desired image, and be capable of creating the desired effects with that target market. Of particular concern is whether consumers make favorable attributions to the sponsor for its participation.

An "ideal event" might be one whose audience closely matches the ideal target market, that generates much favorable attention, that is unique but not encumbered with many sponsors, that lends itself to ancillary marketing activities, and that reflects or even enhances the brand or corporate image of the sponsor.

Of course, rather than linking themselves to an event, some sponsors create their own. Branding Brief 6-1 describes how cable sports network ESPN created the X Games to appeal to a market segment not easily attracted by traditional sports.

More and more firms are also using their names to sponsor the arenas, stadiums, and other venues that actually hold the events. Staples paid $100 million over 20 years to name the downtown Los Angeles arena where the NBA Lakers and Clippers and the NHL Kings play, and where concerts and other events are also held. Although stadium naming rights can command high fees, its direct contribution to building brand equity is primarily in creating brand recognition—not brand recall—and marketers can expect it to do little for brand image except perhaps to convey a certain level of scope and size.

Designing Sponsorship Programs.
Many marketers believe that the marketing program accompanying a sponsorship is what ultimately determines its success. A sponsor can strategically identify itself at an event in a number of ways, including banners, signs, and programs. For more significant and broader impact, however, sponsors typically supplement such activities with samples, prizes, advertising, retail promotions, publicity, and so forth. Marketers often note that the budget for related marketing activities should be at least two to three times the amount of the sponsorship expenditure.

BRANDING BRIEF 6-1

Brand Building via the X Games

Although the action sports industry contains a variety of high-energy and sometimes potentially high-risk sports, it is largely defined by various forms of skateboarding, snowboarding, surfing, and BMX biking. Action sports continue on a growth trajectory in terms of legitimacy, participation, public interest, and sponsor/business investment. They have become increasingly profitable, with skate, snow and surf gear, apparel, and accessories jumping from a $5 billion to an $11 billion market in the last eight years. Analysts predict that kind of exponential growth—although hard to track—reflects the future of action sports, as more youth and adults in the United States and globally become involved and retailers continue to evolve their brands.

ESPN's X Games, begun as a biannual event in 1995, remain at the forefront of the industry. They are ESPN's largest owned and operated property and are regarded as the gold standard in the action sports world. While the public initially saw the X Games as "the circus coming to town" or as a showcase for death-defying stunts and tricks, people have begun to realize that the riders are legitimate athletes in a sustainable business. Viewers 18 and younger, especially, have grown up with the X Games and consider it their own Olympics.[65]

X Games quickly grew into a franchise that has staged more than 65 events attended by more than 2.5 million fans. It has successfully launched a variety of brand extensions in consumer products and home entertainment and touches all seven continents. ESPN believes the evolution and growth of all elements of the X Games have positioned it well for continued successes—in brand perception and relevance, live event attendance, record-setting broadcast viewership and ratings, increased sponsor investment, and overall popularity and incorporation into the mainstream. As one top X Games executive, Rick Alessandri, noted, X "represents the best in action sports, innovation, creativity, and progression. It's constantly moving forward . . . we're right on track. We're going on the fifteenth year . . . sports get added and removed, new athletes come along . . . we're continually evolving."

The four-day and final attendance for X Games 17 in the summer of 2011 was 141,500 and included the following events:

- **BMX:** Big Air, Freestyle Vert, Park, Street
- **Moto X:** Best Trick, Best Whip, Enduro X (Men's and Women's), Freestyle, Racing (Women's), Speed & Style, Step Up
- **Skateboard:** Big Air, Game of SK8, Park, Real Street, Street (Men's & Women's), Vert
- **Rally:** Rally Car Racing, RallyCross

Partners for X Games 17 in the summer of 2011 were chosen based on their ability to meet the various needs of the sponsors, the X Games franchise, and ESPN as a whole. Sponsors were eventually matched because:

- ESPN sales teams and agencies pitched the X Games property to sponsors based on perceived fit and common objectives.

The X Games, with top action-sports athletes like Shaun White, have been an excellent vehicle for advertisers to reach and engage a young adult segment.
Source: ZUMA Press/Newscom

- Advertisers specifically requested X Games.
- Advertisers wanted to target a certain demographic (males 18–34) and asked the ESPN sales team for recommendations.
- Advertisers wanted to conduct a promotion/push a certain product or air commercials within a particular time, and X Games event timing matched.
- Advertisers had a certain budget/amount of money to spend, and the ESPN sales team offered the X Games property based on that budget and the perceived fit.

The final sponsor roster included partners that were culturally aligned with ESPN, the X Games franchise, and the parent Walt Disney Company, and that satisfied minimum investment criteria established by ESPN and X Games. Sponsors with adult-oriented products such as alcoholic beverages, for example, have traditionally not been included. Figure 6-5 provides some detail on the official and event sponsors.

Official Sponsors

BFGoodrich—BFGoodrich's national marketing efforts included television spots, print collateral, digital advertising, on-site activations, and competition course signage.

Ford—Ford's national marketing efforts included television spots, print collateral, digital advertising, on-site activations, and competition course signage.

America's Navy—Navy's national marketing efforts included television spots, print collateral, digital advertising, radio campaigns, on-site activations, and competition course signage

Red Bull—Red Bull's national marketing efforts included television spots, print collateral, digital ad space, on-site activations, and unique competition course signage.

Event Sponsors

Casio G'zOne Commando—Casio's national marketing efforts included television spots, online advertising, on-site activations, and competition course signage.

Shark Week—Discovery's national marketing efforts included television spots, print collateral, online advertising, on-site activations, and competition course signage.

Mobil 1—Mobil 1's national marketing efforts included television spots, online advertising, radio campaigns, and competition course signage.

Sony—Sony's national marketing efforts included television spots, online advertising, on-site TV displays, and competition course signage.

FIGURE 6-5

X Games 17 Sponsorship Information.

Source: Fay Wells, 'ESPN X Games: Launching a New Category,"in *Best Practice Cases in Branding*, 4th ed. Kevin Lane Keller and Lowey Sichol (Upper Saddle River, NJ: Pearson, 2013).

Measuring Sponsorship Activities.   There are two basic approaches to measuring the effects of sponsorship activities: the ***supply-side method*** focuses on potential exposure to the brand by assessing the extent of media coverage, and the ***demand-side method*** focuses on reported exposure from consumers.

Supply-side methods attempt to approximate the amount of time or space devoted to the brand in media coverage of an event. For example, we can estimate the number of seconds the brand is clearly visible on a television screen, or the column inches of press clippings covering an event that mention the brand. Then we can translate this measure of potential impressions delivered by an event sponsorship into an equivalent value in advertising dollars, according to the fees associated with actually advertising in the particular media vehicle.

Although supply-side exposure methods provide quantifiable measures, equating media coverage with advertising exposure ignores the content of the respective communications that consumers receive. The advertiser uses media space and time to communicate a strategically designed message. Media coverage and telecasts only expose the brand, and don't necessarily embellish its meaning in any direct way. Some public relations professionals maintain that positive editorial coverage can be worth 5–10 times the advertising equivalency value, but it is rare that sponsorship affords the brand such favorable treatment. As one group of critics noted:

Equating incidental visual and audio exposures with paid advertising time is, we feel, questionable at best. A commercial is a carefully crafted persuasive declaration of a product's virtues. It doesn't compete for attention with the actual on-camera action of a game or race. A 30-second exposure of a billboard in the background can't match the value of 30 seconds in which the product is the only star.[66]

An alternative measurement approach is the demand-side method, which attempts to identify the effects that sponsorship has on consumers' brand knowledge structures. Thus, tracking or custom surveys can explore the ability of the event sponsorship to affect awareness, attitudes, or even sales. We can identify and survey event spectators after the event to measure recall of the event's sponsor, as well as attitudes and intentions toward the sponsor as a result of the event. We can also conduct internal tracking to see how different aspects of the sales process are impacted.

NATIONWIDE

Nationwide Insurance has a highly successful partnership with NASCAR racing. It sponsors the NASCAR Nationwide Series of stock car races and is also the official auto, home, and life insurance partner of NASCAR. After the third year of a seven-year deal, Nationwide research showed that the insurance company was up 183 percent on lead generation, had raised brand awareness among NASCAR fans by 50 percent, and had increased buying rates for three consecutive years. Nationwide had anticipated NASCAR fans' legendary loyalty, but its executives were still surprised by the quality and profitability of the relationships they built. As one executive noted: "They're a higher-value consumer. They tend to buy more than one product and be more responsible, resulting in fewer claims." Nationwide has also developed business-to-business relationships with other sponsors, racing teams, and tracks. As a result of all these developments, the sponsorship broke even early in the third year of the sponsorship, sooner than expected.[67]

Nationwide has been surprised and pleased at the marketing value it has gained from its NASCAR sponsorship and partnership.

Source: Chris Graythen/Getty Images

Mobile Marketing

A fourth broad communication option has emerged in recent years and will undoubtedly play a greater role in brand building in the future. As smartphones are playing an increasingly significant role in consumers' lives, more marketers are taking notice, and mobile ad spending passed $1 billion in 2011.[68]

Because consumers already use smartphones for information and entertainment as well as communication—and are beginning to use them as shopping devices and payment methods—investment in mobile marketing from a whole range of different sectors looking to tap into a new revenue stream is expected to grow rapidly. Handset makers are racing to produce ever better smartphones, with bigger and higher definition screens, faster processors, and easier access to social networks. These new technologies are creating more targeted, interactive, and useful mobile ads than ever before.[69]

One of the fastest-growing areas in mobile ad spending is Apple's new iAd mobile network, which allows marketers to place interactive banner ads in iPhone, iPod Touch, and iPad software applications, or apps. Unilever successfully used iAd to promote its Dove soap. When touched, Unilever's banner ad opened into a library of videos and other content promoting Dove. More than 20 percent of people who opened the ad returned to it a second time.[70] Many ads are also being developed for Google's Android operating system.

Smartphones present a unique opportunity for marketers because they can be in consumers' hands at the point of sale or consumption.[71] IHOP restaurants experienced a 10 percent mobile coupon redemption rate with one of its campaigns. The goal of Domino's mobile campaign was to increase awareness about the new Legends Pizza, drive foot traffic to store locations, and increase sales. A marketer can put different short-code key words into calls for consumers to text the various print and electronic media and then determine which ad medium is most effective in driving consumer awareness and interaction.

Geotargeting occurs when marketers take advantage of digital technology to send messages to consumers based on their location and the activities they are engaging in.[72] A simple application uses Web IP addresses to display ads letting browsers know of opportunities in their area. Some of the more exciting recent developments include using mobile phones in this way as marketers strive to find when and how to reach consumers as they travel through their days.

Enormous privacy and regulatory concerns surround mobile advertising. *Opt-in* advertising will be key, whereby users agree to allow advertisers to use specific, individual information about time, location, and shopping preferences in order to send them targeted ads and promotions.[73] Increasingly, consumers are choosing to opt in to different services and share their locations in return for coupons, discounts, and more relevant promotional material and messages. One popular example is Foursquare.[74]

FOURSQUARE

Created in 2009 by Dennis Crowley and Naveen Selvadurai, Foursquare is a Web and mobile application that allows registered users to connect with friends and update their location. When they arrive at a restaurant, bar, or other site, users can "check in" and announce their location to others on social networking sites such as Facebook and Twitter. Points awarded for checking in at venues can be used for discounts and prizes. The title of "Mayor" is bestowed to users who check in the most times at a certain location over a 60-day period. Foursquare is experiencing rapid growth, as companies such as Starbucks, Bergdorf Goodman, and Crunch gyms have experimented with ways to leverage its location-based knowledge to offer customer promotions.

With the phenomenal adoption of smartphones by consumers, location-based social networking services like Foursquare are poised for growth.

Source: Foursquare Labs, Inc.

Unlike the Foursquare app, the Shopkick app lets marketers know when users are actually inside a store, not just nearby. Users can scan bar codes at participating stores—Macy's, Best Buy, Target—to earn "kickbucks," reward points toward gift certificates. Retailers pay Shopkick to be included in the app and featured in special promotions. Costing less than $1 per user store visit, "It definitely drove traffic into the stores," as one participating CMO noted. Different shopping behaviors—trying on clothes, inspecting a product, and so on—earn different points. Ten percent of users reportedly use the app every single day.[75]

Online retailers are also recognizing the power of m-commerce—selling through mobile devices—by launching mobile apps and revamping online stores to handle mobile traffic more easily. In 2010, eBay estimated it had sold $1.5 billion worth of goods over mobile devices. At Gilt, as much as 20 percent of revenue comes from mobile devices on nights and weekends.[76]

Several years ago, the idea of mobile marketing was met with fear that marketers would alienate customers with annoying product pitches. But creative messages that pull willing consumers into dialogue with the brand have evolved into an appealing way to increase brand awareness, especially when it is part of a larger campaign in other media.

BRAND AMPLIFIERS

Complementing these four broad sets of marketing communication activities are efforts to engage consumers and the public via word-of-mouth and public relations and publicity. Although they can perform many different functions, they are especially well-suited at amplifying the effects created by other marketing activities.[77]

Public Relations and Publicity

Public relations and publicity relate to a variety of programs and are designed to promote or protect a company's image or its individual products. *Publicity* is nonpersonal communications such as press releases, media interviews, press conferences, feature articles, newsletters, photographs, films, and tapes. *Public relations* may also include annual reports, fund-raising and membership drives, lobbying, special event management, and public affairs.

The marketing value of public relations got a big boost in 1983 when public relations firm Burson-Marsteller's skillful handling of Johnson & Johnson's Tylenol product tampering incident was credited with helping to save the brand. Brand Focus 11.0 provides a comprehensive account of that landmark campaign. Around that time, politicians also discovered the power of campaign sound bites that were picked up by the press as a means of broad, cost-efficient candidate exposure.

Marketers now recognize that although public relations are invaluable during a marketing crisis, it also needs to be a routine part of any marketing communications program. Even companies that primarily use advertising and promotions can benefit from well-conceived and well-executed publicity. Winner of *PR Week*'s Campaign of the Year for 2011, Mattel's PR campaign for the Barbie "I Can Be . . ." career doll line let young girls vote for the first time on the 50-year old doll's next career move. Over 1 million online votes were cast, and after 125 different careers—including astronaut, veterinarian, and even U.S. president—the winning job was computer engineer. The buzz behind the campaign increased sales and expanded the brand outside its core territory.[78]

Word-of-Mouth

Publicity and PR often serve another important role—they get people talking. Word-of-mouth is a critical aspect of brand building as consumers share their likes, dislikes, and experiences with brands with each other.[79] The power of word-of-mouth is the credibility and relevance it often brings. Study after study has shown that the most trusted source of product information is friends and families.

If marketers do their job right and create marketing programs that offer consumers superior delivery of desired benefits, people will write and talk about the brand, amplifying any marketing effects. In effect, a buzz has been created among consumers. Companies are attempting to create this consumer word-of-mouth through various techniques often called *buzz marketing*.[80]

Established companies do not have the luxury of time, so they often attempt to catalyze the buzz marketing effect for new product introductions. One popular method is to allow consumers who are likely to influence other consumers to "discover" the product in the hopes that they will pass a positive endorsement on to their peers. Procter & Gamble has created a program specifically designed to enhance buzz.

TREMOR

Procter & Gamble's proprietary word-of-mouth technology, Tremor, consists of 500,000 women who are part of their Vocalpoint panel and qualify as "connectors." According to P&G, a connector is a person with a social network five to six times larger than the average person's, and with a deep propensity to talk about ideas with that network. To identify a connector, a questionnaire weeds out 90 percent of potential respondents. Connectors, who are not paid, are attracted to the idea of hearing things first and being able to communicate directly back to the company. P&G has used Tremor for its own products, such as Noxzema and Pringles, and leased it to other companies, including WD-40, Kashi, and Kellogg. For its own Secret deodorant, it created a disruptive message, "The More You Move, the Better You Smell," to counteract the perception that activity equates with sweat and a worse smell. The message was a well-designed complement to the advertising message, "Live Life. Don't Sweat It," and 51,000 posts were made to its Web site as a result. Steve Knox, former CEO of the P&G unit, claims the real key to success is creating messaging that creates word-of-mouth. "The way we phrase this to people is there's a message that the consumer wants to hear and then there's a message they want to share with their friends and those are two different messages." He claims the biggest mistake made with word-of-mouth is to say, "Here's my marketing message. Make them talk about this." Based in part on the success of Tremor, General Mills and Kraft launched their own word-of-mouth marketing programs in 2008.[81]

Buzz marketing works well when the marketing message appears to originate with an independent source and not with the brand. Because consumers are becoming increasingly skeptical and wary of traditional advertising, buzz marketers seek to expose consumers to their brands in a unique and innocuous fashion.[82] One approach is to enlist genuine consumers able to give authentic-seeming endorsements of the brand. An ad executive with Bates USA explained the goal of this strategy: "Ultimately, the brand benefits because an accepted member of the social circle will always be more credible than any communication that could ever come directly from the brand."[83]

Some criticize buzz marketing as "a form of cultural corruption" in which marketers are actually creating the culture at a fundamental level. Critics claim that buzz marketing's interference in consumers' lives is insidious because participants cannot always detect the pitch. Another potential problem with buzz marketing is that it requires a buzz-worthy product. As one marketing expert said, "The bad news is that [buzz marketing] only works in high-interest product categories."

DEVELOPING INTEGRATED MARKETING COMMUNICATION PROGRAMS

We've examined in depth the various communication options available to marketers. Now we consider how to develop an integrated marketing communication (IMC) program by choosing the best set options and managing the relationships between them.[84] Our main theme is that marketers should "mix and match" communication options to build brand equity—that is,

Kellogg's "Share Your Breakfast" campaign—shown here at a press event with actress Melissa Joan Hart at New York's Grand Central Terminal—was backed by a fully integrated marketing communications program.

Source: Otero Andres/SIPA/Newscom

choose a variety of different communication options that share common meaning and content but also offer different, complementary advantages so that the whole is greater than the sum of the parts.[85]

Numerous firms are embracing this broad-based approach to developing their communications program. Kellogg launched its largest integrated marketing campaign ever in Q1 2011.[86] The campaign, called "Share Your Breakfast," included a Web site where consumers could upload pictures of their breakfast and for which Kellogg, in turn, would donate a meal through a partnership with the nonprofit, Action for Healthy Kids. In addition to the Web site, the campaign included broadcast, digital, social, and print media. Kellogg worked with several different agencies across different media. The campaign extended to specific retailer promotions and applied across many of the company's brands.

Criteria for IMC Programs

In assessing the collective impact of an IMC program, the marketer's overriding goal is to create the most effective and efficient communication program possible. Here are six relevant criteria, known as "the 6 Cs" for short:[87]

1. Coverage
2. Contribution
3. Commonality
4. Complementarity
5. Conformability
6. Cost

After considering the concept of coverage and how it relates to the other five criteria, let's look quickly at each in turn.

Coverage.   Coverage is the proportion of the audience reached by each communication option, as well as how much overlap exists among communication options. In other words, to what extent do different communication options reach the designated target market, and the same or different consumers making up that market? As Figure 6-6 shows, the unique aspects of coverage relate to the direct main effects of any communication; the common aspects relate to the interaction or multiplicative effects of two communication options working together.

The unique aspect of coverage is the inherent communication ability of a marketing communication option, as suggested by the second criterion, contribution. If there is some overlap in communication options, however, marketers must decide how to design their communication program to reflect the fact that consumers may already have some communication effects in memory prior to exposure to any particular communication option.

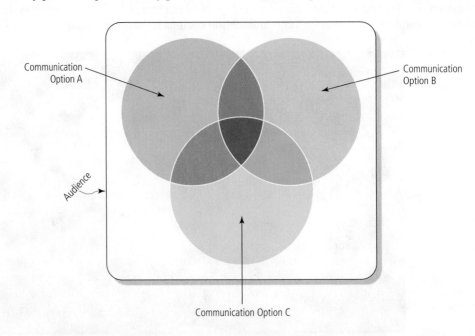

FIGURE 6-6

IMC Audience
Communication
Option Overlap

A communication option can either reinforce associations and strengthen linkages that are also the focus of other communication options, or it can address other associations and linkages, as suggested by the third and fourth criteria, commonality and complementarity. Moreover, if less than perfect overlap exists—which is almost always the case—marketers can design a communication option to reflect the fact that consumers may or may not have seen other communication options, as suggested by the fifth criterion, conformability. Finally, all of these considerations must be offset by their cost, as suggested by the sixth criterion.

Contribution.   Contribution is the inherent ability of a marketing communication to create the desired response and communication effects from consumers *in the absence of exposure to any other communication option.* In other words, contribution describes the main effects of a marketing communication option in terms of how it affects consumers' processing of a communication and the resulting outcomes. As we noted earlier, marketing communications can play many different roles, like building awareness, enhancing image, eliciting responses, and inducing sales, and the contribution of any marketing communication option will depend on how well it plays that role. Also as we noted earlier, much prior research has considered this aspect of communications, generating conceptual guidelines and evaluation criteria in the process. Given that overlap with communication options exists, however, marketers must consider other factors, as follows.

Commonality.   Regardless of which communication options marketers choose, they should coordinate the entire marketing communication program to create a consistent and cohesive brand image in which brand associations share content and meaning. The consistency and cohesiveness of the brand image is important because the image determines how easily consumers can recall existing associations and responses and how easily they can link additional associations and responses to the brand in memory.

Commonality is the extent to which *common* information conveyed by different communication options shares meaning across communication options. Most definitions of IMC emphasize only this criterion. For example, Burnett and Moriarty define integrated marketing communications as the "practice of unifying all marketing communication tools—from advertising to packaging—to send target audiences a consistent, persuasive message that promotes company goals."[88]

In general, we learn and recall information that is consistent in meaning more easily than unrelated information—though the unexpectedness of inconsistent information sometimes can lead to more elaborate processing and stronger associations than consistent information.[89] Nevertheless, with inconsistent associations and a diffuse brand image, consumers may overlook some associations or, because they are confused about the meaning of the brand, form less strong and less favorable new associations.

Therefore, in the long run, marketers should design different communication elements and combine them so that they work effectively together to create a consistent and cohesive brand image. The more abstract the association to be created or reinforced by marketing communications, the more likely it would seem that we could effectively reinforce it in different ways across heterogeneous communication options.[90]

For example, if the association we desire is "contemporary," then there may be a number of different ways we can make a brand seem modern and relevant. On the other hand, if our desired association is a concrete attribute, say, "rich chocolate taste," then it may be difficult to convey it in communication options that do not permit explicit product statements, such as sponsorship.

Take Heineken. The brand seeks to achieve a strong premium image and positioning in it communications. Heineken's "Walk-In Fridge" campaign started as a video and then a TV ad that first showed a group of girlfriends jumping up and down and shrieking with joy when one of them gets a walk-in wardrobe closet, followed by a group of guys equally ecstatic over a walk-in refrigerator lined with Heineken. Heineken next placed gigantic cardboard boxes labeled "Walk-In Fridge" all over Amsterdam as if put out in the trash. Finally, Heineken placed real walk-in fridges at various beer festivals, allowing groups of friends to mimic the ad and video and upload their own video to YouTube.[91]

Finally, another commonality issue is the extent of executional consistency across communication options—that is, the extent to which we convey non-product-related information in different communication options. The more coordinated executional information is, the more likely it is that this information can serve as a retrieval cue to other communication effects.[92] In other words, if a symbol is established in one communication option, like a feather in a TV ad for a deodorant to convey mildness and softness, then marketers can use it in other communications to help trigger the knowledge, thoughts, feelings, and images stored in memory from exposure to a previous communication.

Complementarity. Communication options are often more effective when used in tandem. *Complementarity* describes the extent to which *different* associations and linkages are emphasized across communication options. The ideal marketing communication program would ensure that the communication options chosen are mutually compensatory and reinforcing to create desired consumer knowledge structures.

Marketers might most effectively establish different brand associations by capitalizing on those marketing communication options best suited to eliciting a particular consumer response or establishing a particular type of brand association. For example, some media, like sampling and other forms of sales promotion, are demonstrably better at generating trial than engendering long-term loyalty. Research with some industrial distributors has shown that follow-up sales efforts generate higher sales productivity when firms have already exposed customers to its products at a trade show.[93]

The Science of Branding 6-2 describes how communication options may need to be explicitly tied together to capitalize on complementarity to build brand equity.

Conformability. Conformability refers to the extent that a marketing communication option is robust and effective for different groups of consumers. There are two types of conformability: communication and consumer. The reality of any IMC program is that when consumers are exposed to a particular marketing communication, some consumers will have already been exposed to other marketing communications for the brand, and others will not. The ability of a marketing communication to work at two levels—effectively communicating to both groups—is critically important. We consider a marketing communication option conformable when it achieves its desired effect *regardless* of consumers' past communication history.

Besides this communication conformability, we can also judge a communication option in terms of broader consumer conformability, that is, how well does it inform or persuade consumers who vary on dimensions other than communication history? Communications directed at primarily creating brand awareness, like sponsorship, may be more conformable by virtue of their simplicity.

There seem to be two possible means of achieving this dual communication ability:

1. *Multiple information provision strategy:* Provide different information within a communication option to appeal to the different types of consumers. An important issue here is how information designed to appeal to one target market of consumers will be processed by other consumers and target markets. Issues of information overload, confusion, and annoyance may come into play if communications become burdened with a great deal of detail.
2. *Broad information provision strategy:* Provide information that is rich or ambiguous enough to work regardless of prior consumer knowledge. The important issue here is how potent or successful marketers can make that information. If they attempt to appeal to the lowest common denominator, the information may lack precision and sufficient detail to have any meaningful impact on consumers. Consumers with disparate backgrounds will have to find information in the communication sufficiently relevant to satisfy their goals, given their product or brand knowledge or communications history.

Cost. Finally, evaluations of marketing communications on all of the preceding criteria must be weighed against their cost to arrive at the most effective *and* efficient communication program.

Using IMC Choice Criteria

The IMC choice criteria can provide some guidance for designing integrated marketing communication programs. Two key steps are evaluating communication options and establishing priorities and trade-offs.

THE SCIENCE OF BRANDING 6-2

Coordinating Media to Build Brand Equity

For brand equity to be built, it is critical that communication effects created by advertising be linked to the brand. Often, such links are difficult to create. TV ads in particular do not "brand" well. There are a number of reasons why:

- Competing ads in the product category can create interference and consumer confusion as to which ad goes with which brand.

- "Borrowed interest" creative strategies and techniques—humor, music, special effects, sex appeals, fear appeals, etc—may grab consumers' attention, but result in the brand being overlooked in the process.

- Delaying brand identification or providing few brand mentions may raise processing intensity but direct attention away from the brand.

- Limited brand exposure time in the ad may allow little opportunity for elaboration of existing brand knowledge.

- Consumers may not have any inherent interest in the product or service category or may lack knowledge of the specific brand.

- A change in advertising strategy may make it difficult for consumers to easily relate new information to existing brand knowledge.

Strategies to Strengthen Communication Effects

For a variety of reasons, advertising may "succeed" in the sense that communication effects are stored in memory, yet "fail" at the same time in that these communication effects are not accessible when critical brand-related decisions were made.

To address this problem, one common tactic marketers employ is to make the brand name and package information prominent in the ad. Unfortunately, this increase in brand emphasis means that communication effects and brand associations are less likely to be able to be created by the ad and stored in consumer memory. In other words, although consumers are better able to recall the advertised brand, there is *less* other information about the brand to actually recall. Three potentially more effective strategies are brand signatures, ad retrieval cues, and media interactions.

Brand Signatures

Perhaps the easiest way to increase the strength of brand links to communication effects is to create a more powerful and compelling brand signature. The *brand signature* is the manner by which the brand is identified in a TV or radio ad or displayed within a print ad. The brand signature must creatively engage the consumer and cause him or her to pay more attention to the brand itself and, as a consequence, increase the strength of brand associations created by the ad.

An effective brand signature often dynamically and stylistically provides a seamless connection to the ad as a whole. For example, the famous "Got Milk?" campaign always displayed that tag line or slogan in a manner fitting the ad (in flames for the "yuppie in hell" ad or in primary-school print for the "school lunchroom

bully" ad). As another example, the introductory Intel Inside ad campaign always ended with a swirling image from which the Intel Inside logo dramatically appeared, in effect stamping the end of the ad with Intel Inside in an "in your face" manner.

Ad Retrieval Cues

Another effective tactic to use *advertising retrieval cues*—visual or verbal information uniquely identified with an ad that is evident when consumers are making a product or service decision. The purpose is to maximize the probability that consumers who have seen or heard the cued ad will retrieve the communication effects stored in long-term memory. Ad retrieval cues may consist of a key visual, a catchy slogan, or any unique advertising element that serves as an effective reminder to consumers. For example, in an attempt to remedy a problem of mistaken attributions, Quaker Oats placed a photograph of the "Mikey" character from the popular Life cereal ad on the front of the package. More recently, Eveready featured a picture of its pink bunny character on packages of Energizer batteries to reduce consumer confusion with Duracell.

Media Interactions

Finally, print and radio reinforcement of TV ads (in which the video and audio components of a TV ad serve as the basis for the respective type of ads) can be an effective means to leverage existing communication effects from TV ad exposure and more strongly link them to the brand. Cueing a TV ad with an explicitly linked radio or print ad can create similar or even enhanced processing outcomes that can substitute for additional TV ad exposures. Moreover, a potentially useful, although rarely employed, media strategy is to run explicitly linked print or radio ads *prior* to the accompanying TV ad. The print and radio ads in this case function as teasers and increase consumer motivation to process the more complete TV ad consisting of both audio and video components.

Sources: Raymond R. Burke and Thomas K. Srull, "Competitive Interference and Consumer Memory for Advertising," *Journal of Consumer Research* 15 (June 1988): 55–68; Kevin Lane Keller, "Memory Factors in Advertising: The Effect of Advertising Retrieval Cues on Brand Evaluations," *Journal of Consumer Research* 14 (December 1987): 316–333; Robert J. Kent and Chris T. Allen, "Competitive Interference Effects in Consumer Memory for Advertising: The Role of Brand Familiarity," *Journal of Marketing* 58 (July 1994): 97–105; Kevin Lane Keller, Susan Heckler, and Michael J. Houston, "The Effects of Brand Name Suggestiveness on Advertising Recall," *Journal of Marketing* 62 (January 1998): 48–57; William E. Baker, Heather Honea, and Cristel Antonia Russell, "Do Not Wait to Reveal the Brand Name: The Effect of Brand-Name Placement on Television Advertising Effectiveness," *Journal of Advertising* 33 (Fall 2004): 77–85; Micael Dahlén and Sara Rosengren, "Brands Affect Slogans Affect Brands? Competitive Interference, Brand Equity and the Brand-Slogan Link," *Journal of Brand Management* 12 (February 2005): 151–164; Peter J. Danaher, André Bonfrer, and Sanjay Dhar, "The Effect of Competitive Advertising Interference on Sales for Packaged Goods," *Journal of Marketing Research* 45 (April 2008): 211–225.

Evaluating Communication Options.   We can judge marketing communication options or communication types according to the response and communication effects they can create, as well as how they rate on the IMC choice criteria. Different communication types and options have different strengths and weaknesses and raise different issues.

Several points about the IMC choice criteria are worth noting. First, there are not necessarily any inherent differences across communication types for contribution and complementarity, because each communication type, if properly designed, can play a critical and unique role in achieving those communication objectives. Similarly, all marketing communications appear expensive, although some differences in cost per thousands can prevail. Communication types vary, however, in their breadth and depth of audience coverage, and in terms of commonality and conformability according to the number of modalities they employ: The more modalities available with a communication type, the greater its potential commonality and conformability.

Arriving at a final mix requires making decisions on priorities and tradeoffs among the IMC choice criteria, discussed next.

Establishing Priorities and Trade-Offs.   The IMC program a marketer adopts, after profiling the various options, will depend in part on how he or she ranks the choice criteria. Because the IMC choice criteria themselves are related, the marketer must also make tradeoffs. The objectives of the marketing communication program, and whether they are short run or long run, will set priorities along with a host of factors beyond the scope of this chapter. We identify three possible tradeoffs with the IMC choice criteria that result from overlaps in coverage.

- *Commonality and complementarity will often be inversely related.* The more various marketing communication options emphasize the same brand attribute or benefit, all else being equal, the less they can effectively emphasize other attributes and benefits.
- *Conformability and complementarity will also often be inversely related.* The more a communication program accounts for differences in consumers across communication options, the less necessary it is that any one communication be designed to appeal to many different groups.
- *Commonality and conformability do not share an obvious relationship.* It may be possible, for example, to develop a sufficiently abstract message, like "Brand X is contemporary," to effectively reinforce the brand across multiple communication types including advertising, interactive, sponsorship, and promotions.

REVIEW

This chapter provided conceptual frameworks and managerial guidelines for how marketing communications can be integrated to enhance brand equity. The chapter addressed this issue from the perspective of customer-based brand equity, which maintains that brand equity is fundamentally determined by the brand knowledge created in consumers' minds by the supporting marketing program. Four main types of communications were identified as being critical: (1) advertising and promotion, (2) interactive marketing, (3) events and experiences, and (4) mobile marketing

A number of specific communication options—broadcast, print, direct response, and place advertising media; consumer and trade promotions; Web sites, online ads and videos, and social media online marketing; and events and experiences—were reviewed in terms of basic characteristics as well as success factors for effectiveness. Brand amplifiers that enhance these effects in the form of publicity and public relations, word-of-mouth, and buzz marketing were also discussed. The chapter also provided criteria as to how different communication options should be combined to maximally build brand equity.

Two key implications emerge from this discussion. First, from the perspective of customer-based brand equity, all possible communication options should be evaluated in terms of their ability to affect brand equity. In particular, the CBBE concept provides a common denominator by which the effects of different communication options can be evaluated: Each

1. *Be analytical:* Use frameworks of consumer behavior and managerial decision making to develop well-reasoned communication programs.

2. *Be curious:* Better understand customers by using all forms of research, and always be thinking of how you can create added value for consumers.

3. *Be single-minded:* Focus your message on well-defined target markets (less can be more).

4. *Be integrative:* Reinforce your message through consistency and cuing across all communication options and media.

5. *Be creative:* State your message in a unique fashion; use alternative promotions and media to create favorable, strong, and unique brand associations.

6. *Be observant:* Keep track of competition, customers, channel members, and employees through monitoring and tracking studies.

7. *Be patient:* Take a long-term view of communication effectiveness to build and manage brand equity.

8. *Be realistic:* Understand the complexities involved in marketing communications.

FIGURE 6-7

General Marketing Communication Guidelines: The "Keller Bs"

communication option can be judged in terms of the effectiveness and efficiency by which it affects brand awareness and by which it creates, maintains, or strengthens favorable and unique brand associations. Different communication options have different strengths and can accomplish different objectives. Thus, it is important to employ a mix of different communication options, each playing a specific role in building or maintaining brand equity.

The second important insight that emerges from the conceptual framework is that the marketing communication program should be put together in a way such that the whole is greater than the sum of the parts. In other words, as much as possible, there should be a match among certain communication options so that the effects of any one communication option are enhanced by the presence of another option.

In closing, the basic message of this chapter is simple: marketers need to evaluate marketing communication options strategically to determine how they can contribute to brand equity. To do so, marketers need some theoretical and managerial guidelines by which they can determine the effectiveness and efficiency of various communication options both singularly and in combination with other communication options. Figure 6-7 provides the author's philosophy concerning the design, implementation, and interpretation of marketing communication strategies.

DISCUSSION QUESTIONS

1. Pick a brand and gather all its marketing communication materials. How effectively has the brand mixed and matched marketing communications? Has it capitalized on the strengths of different media and compensated for their weaknesses at the same time? How explicitly has it integrated its communication program?

2. What do you see as the role of the Internet in building brands? How would you evaluate the Web site for a major brand—for example, Nike, Disney, or Levi's? How about one of your favorite brands?

3. Pick up a current issue of a popular magazine. Which print ad do you feel is the best, and which ad do you feel is the worst based on the criteria described in this chapter?

4. Look at the coupon supplements in a Sunday newspaper. How are they building brand equity, if at all? Try to find a good example and a poor example of brand-building promotions.

5. Choose a popular event. Who sponsors it? How are they building brand equity with their sponsorship? Are they integrating the sponsorship with other marketing communications?

BRAND FOCUS 6.0

Empirical Generalizations in Advertising

In a comprehensive academic endeavor, a number of researchers have worked together to accumulate what they call "empirical generalizations" (EG) of advertising. In putting this research into context, the lead authors Jerry Wind and Byron Sharp note: "Even advertising has scientific laws, empirical patterns that generalize across a wide range of known conditions. These empirical generalizations provide us with benchmarks, predictions, and valuable insights into how the digital revolution may affect advertising."

Empirical generalizations emerge from careful, thoughtful research. The authors are quick to add several caveats. Empirical generalizations are not formal laws themselves and there may be important exceptions and boundary conditions as to when they operate. Nevertheless, they suggest three possible benefits to having some empirical generalizations: (1) as a starting point in the development of an advertising strategy; (2) as an initial set of tentative rules that management can follow; and (3) as a benchmark, giving management some sense of how much change to expect when advertising is launched or something changes in the advertising environment.

The empirical generalizations they identified can be grouped into four broad topics: ROI, 360-degree media planning, value of TV, and creative quality.

ROI

- Advertising typically has a half-life of three to four weeks. If advertising is to be sales-effective in the long term, it must show immediate sales effects in single-source data.

- Based on the established EG that advertising elasticity is approximately 0.1, net profit is optimized by setting the advertising budget to be 10 percent of gross profit. If the elasticity is 0.15, then the advertising budget should be 15 percent of gross profit, and so on.

- Brand advertising often has a pronounced short-term sales impact (as shown in single-source data). This impact decays over time. The most dramatic influence on short-term effect is creative copy.

- Even with no clicks or minimal clicks, online display advertisements generate lift in site visitation, trademark search queries, and lift in both online and offline sales.

- In-store digital signage featuring "newsworthy" information (e.g., new items, seasonal offers, promotions) has a markedly favorable impact on sales. This effect is stronger for hedonic (food and entertainment) products.

- TV advertising for consumer services follow a 70:30 rule (70 percent of the efforts create interest, 30 percent create action). And 90 percent of TV advertising for consumer services dissipates within three months (versus four months for consumer goods).

- If advertising changes by 1 percent, sales or market share will change by about 0.1 percent. (That is, advertising elasticity is 0.1.) The advertising elasticity is higher in Europe relative to the United States, for durables relative to nondurables, in

early relative to late stages of the product life cycle, and in print over TV.

- There is a greater than 50 percent chance that the typical TV advertising campaign will lose money both short term and long term. The risk of losing money fluctuates over the years, but has been over 50 percent. The average elasticity of TV advertising has fluctuated between 0.043 and 0.163 over the past 25 years.

- The advertising response curve is "convex"—the greatest marginal response is from the first exposures. As the number of cumulative exposures in a period increases, the marginal effect of the advertising drops.

360-Degree Media Planning

- A retail store layout that makes shopping quicker results in increased shopper spending.

- Approximately 20 percent of word-of-mouth (WOM) about brands refers to paid advertising in media. The level and effectiveness of WOM are substantially increased when stimulated, encouraged, and/or supported by advertising, increasing the probability by about 20 percent that a consumer will make a strong recommendation to buy or try a product.

- If the advertisements recently recalled were on traditional media, they were more likely to have left a positive impression than if they were on digital media. If the consumers had a previous positive impression of the brand or product advertised for advertisements recently recalled, the advertisements were more likely to have left a positive impression, regardless of the media.

- Doubling the clutter does not halve the number of advertisements recalled. Advertisements recalled in high clutter are more likable on average.

- Repeat viewing is 38 percent, and this does not alter when a program changes time. Repeat viewing is lower for comedies than police dramas and for low rating shows, but within these program types or ratings levels repeat viewing remains at a consistent low or high value across time changes.

- Where TV, radio, and magazines (and even special interest ones) claim to attract a specific audience, the target group is typically less than half of the media's total audience, and rival outlets often outperform them in reaching this subsegment.

- Spaced multiple exposures (distributed) produce greater learning than repeated exposures with short intervals (massed). Longer intervals between exposures result in better learning than shorter intervals.

Value of TV

- Over the past 15 years, TV has not declined in its effectiveness at generating sales lift, and appears to be more effective than either online or print at generating brand awareness and recognition.

- Households with DVRs are similar to non-DVR households in the basic measures of advertising effectiveness (recall and recognition).

- TV still has very high reach. Declining ratings are due to fragmentation (more channels), not to reduced TV viewing levels that are remarkably resilient to social and technological changes and to the emergence of "new media." Average ratings halve if the number of channels doubles. In addition, the double jeopardy law applies to TV channels. Bigger channels have more viewers, and these viewers watch the channel for more hours.

- Despite increase in TV channels and fragmentation of audience, TV appears to retain its perceived clout among target audiences in Asia, Europe, and North America and holds across recent years. While the influence of digital media has grown, it has not caused a corresponding decrease in TV perceived clout.

Creative Quality

- Advertising that communicates a unique selling proposition (USP) outperforms advertising, which does not. Ideally, the USP should be based on an important benefit; alternatively and riskier, it could be based on a feature that

clearly implies a benefit. It is effective if it is unique in the minds of consumers even though other brands could make the same claim. However, it is especially effective if it cannot be easily matched by competitors.

- The number of times a brand visually appears in a TV commercial increases the degree of correct brand association with that commercial.

- Emotional response to a TV advertisement influences both branded engagement (directly) and persuasion (indirectly), and therefore the likelihood of short-term sales. This pattern holds for TV advertisements across Argentina, Brazil, and Mexico, but the magnitude of effect is different.

Sources: Yoram Wind and Byron Sharp, "Advertising Empirical Generalizations: Implications for Research and Action," *Journal of Advertising Research* 49 (June 2009): 246–252. See also Scott Koslow and Gerard J. Tellis, "What Scanner Panel Data Tell Us About Advertising: A Detective Story with a Dark Twist," *Journal of Advertising Research* 51 (March 2011): 87–100; Raj Sethuraman, Gerard J. Tellis, and Richard A. Briesch, "How Well Does Advertising Work? Generalizations from Meta-Analysis of Brand Advertising Elasticities," *Journal of Marketing Research* 48 (June 2011): 457–471.

Notes

1. To obtain a broader perspective, it is necessary to consult good advertising texts, such as George E. Belch and Michael A. Belch, *Advertising and Promotion: An Integrated Marketing Communications Perspective*, 9th ed. (Homewood, IL: McGraw-Hill, 2012); Thomas C. O'Guinn, Richard J. Seminik, and Chris T. Allen, *Advertising and Integrated Brand Promotion*, 6th ed. (Cincinnati, OH: South-Western, 2012); or John R. Rossiter and Larry Percy, *Advertising and Promotion Management*, 2nd ed. (New York: McGraw-Hill/Irwin, 1997).

2. For a provocative but also practical treatment of the new rules in brand building, see Christopher Grams, *The Ad-Free Brand: Secrets to Building Successful Brands in a Digital World* (Indianapolis, IN: Que Publishing, 2012). See also Allen P. Adamson, *Brand Digital: Simple Ways Top Brands Succeed in a Digital World* (New York: Palgrave Macmillan, 2008).

3. Elaine Wong, "Ford 'Agents' Hit the Road," *Adweek*, 1 March 2010; Keith Barry, "Fiesta Stars in Night of the Living Social Media Campaign," *Wired*, 21 May 2010; Matthew Dolan, "Ford Takes Online Gamble with New Fiesta," *Wall Street Journal*, 8 April 2009; John Frank, "Beep! Beep! Coming Through," *Marketing News*, 30 September, 2009, 12–14; David Kiley, "Ford's Savior?" *BusinessWeek*, March 16, 2009, 31–34; Alex Taylor III, "Fixing Up Ford," *Fortune*, 25 May, 2009, 45–50; David Kiley, "One Ford for the Whole Wide World," *BusinessWeek*, 15 June, 2009, 58–59.

4. William J. McGuire, "The Nature of Attitudes and Attitude Change," in *The Handbook of Social Psychology*, Vol. 3, 2nd ed., eds. G. Lindzey and E. Aronson (Reading, MA: Addison-Wesley, 1969):136–314; Robert J. Lavidge and Gary A. Steiner, "A Model for Predictive Measurements of Advertising Effectiveness," *Journal of Marketing* 25 (October): 59–62; Thomas E. Barry and Daniel J. Howard, "A Review and Critique of the Hierarchy of Effects in Advertising," *International Journal of Advertising* 9, no. 2 (1990): 121–135.

5. Thomas C. Kinnear, Kenneth L. Bernhardt, and Kathleen A. Krentler, *Principles of Marketing*, 4th ed. (New York: HarperCollins, 1995).

6. Alexander L. Biel, "Converting Image into Equity," in *Brand Equity and Advertising*, eds. David A. Aaker and Alexander L. Biel (Hillsdale, NJ: Lawrence Erlbaum Associates, 1993), 67–82.

7. "TV Viewing at All-Time High," *Adweek Media*, 13 December 2010.

8. Brian Sternberg, "'Sunday Night Football' Remains Costliest Show," *Advertising Age*, 26 October, 2009.

9. Geoffrey Fowler, Brian Steinberg, and Aaron O. Patrick, "Globalizing Apple's Ads," *Wall Street Journal*, 1 March 2007; Joan Voight, "Best Campaign of the Year: Apple "Mac vs. PC," *Adweek*, 17 July 2007.

10. Rossiter and Percy, *Advertising and Promotion Management*.

11. "A Spot Sure to Satisfy: SNICKERS® Will Unveil Newest 'You're Not You When You're Hungry' Spot During Super Bowl XLV," *PR Newswire* 27 January 2011; http://www.effie.org/winners/showcase/2011/5176; www.snickers.com.

12. The American Marketing Association gives EFFIE awards for advertising campaigns that can demonstrate an impact on sales and profits. They are awarded based on the following subjective criteria: background/strategy (marketing challenge, target

insight, campaign objective), creative (idea, link to strategy, and quality of execution), and media (link to market strategy, link to creative strategy), which together account for 70 percent of an ad campaign's score. Proof of results accounts for 30 percent. See www.effie.org.

13. Max Robins, "Seinfeld Aces Ultimate Test," *TV Guide*, 81; Mike Duffy, "Give Thanks for the 'Seinfeld Story,'" *Knight Ridder Newspapers*, 24 November 2004.

14. "Marketing World's New Year Resolution: to Further Evolution," *Advertising Age*, 11 January 2010.

15. "For Top CMOs, TV Remains Surest Bet for Advertising," *Advertising Age*, 17 April 2011.

16. "Radio Today: How Americans Listen to Radio," 2009 edition, www.arbitron.com.

17. Steve Krajewski, "Motel 6 Keeps Light On," *Adweek*, 4 May 1998; "Motel 6 Earns Grand Prize at Radio Mercury Awards," www.motel6.com, 1 July 2009; "Mercurys Give the Richards Group Top Honors for Motel 6 Spot," www.rbr.com, 18 June 2009.

18. For a comprehensive overview, see Bob Schulberg, *Radio Advertising: The Authoritative Handbook* (Lincolnwood, IL: NTC Business Books, 1990).

19. David Ogilvy, *Ogilvy on Advertising* (New York: Vintage Books, 1983).

20. Magazine Publishers of America, "How Do You Measure a Smile?" *Advertising Age*, 26 September 2005, M6.

21. "Internet Gains on Television as Public's Main News Source," Pew Research Center for the People & Press, 4 January 2011.

22. Stuart Elliott, "In an 'Absolut World,' a Vodka Could Use the Same Ads for More Than 25 Years," *New York Times*, 27 April 2007; Stuart Elliott, "Loved the Ads? Now Pour the Drinks," *New York Times*, 27 August 2008; Media Decoder, "Absolut Adds Star Power," *New York Times*, 1 December 2009; "Absolut Inspires a New Movement of Creativity with an Absolut Blank," www.absolutcompany.com, 12 July 2011. Absolut ® Vodka. Absolut country of Sweden vodka and logo, Absolut bottle design and Absolut calligraphy are trademarks owned by the Absolut Company AB.

23. "By the Numbers," *Deliver*, 5 April 2011.

24. Matt Robinson, "As Seen on TV—and Sold at Your Local Store," *BusinessWeek*, 1 August 2010, 21–22; Lacey Rose, "Shill Shocked," *Forbes*, 22 November 2010, 146–148.

25. Peter Koeppel, "What You Should Know About Infomercial Production," www.infomercialdrtv.com.

26. Matt Robinson, "The Infomercial Business Goes Mainstream," *BusinessWeek*, 22 July 2010; Jim Edwards, "The Art of the Infomercial," *Brandweek*, 3 September 2001, 14–19.

27. Bruce Britt, "The Medium Gets Larger," *Deliver*, April 2011, 15–17; Jeff Zabin and Gresh Brebach, *Precision Marketing: The New Rules for Attracting, Retaining and Leveraging Profitable Customers* (Hoboken, NJ: John Wiley & Sons, Inc., 2004).

28. "Out of Home Advertising Revenue up 4.1% in 2010," Outdoor Advertising Association of America, 24 February 2011.

29. Daisuke Wakabayashi, "Billboards That Can See You," *Wall Street Journal*, 2 September 2010; Emily Steel, "The Billboard That Knows," *Wall Street Journal*, 28 February 2011.

30. Michael N. Grynbaum, "Taxi TV Screens Gain Ad Business in New York," *New York Times*, 12 December 2010.

31. Jeff Pelline, "New Commercial Twist in Corporate Restrooms," *San Francisco Chronicle*, 6 October 1986; Ben Mutzabaugh, "Wash Your Hands, Watch a Commercial," *USA Today*, 12 March 2011.

32. David T. Friendly, "Selling It at the Movies," *Newsweek*, 4 July 1983, 46.

33. "Mad Men Is Back and So Is Product Placement," www.money.cnn.com, 10 July 2010.

34. "Walmart Updates In-Store TV Network," *Promo*, 8 September 2008.

35. "Michael Applebaum, "Run from Interactive Digital Displays to Traditional Billboards, Out-of-Home is on an Upswing," *Adweek*, 15 April 2011.

36. "Michael Applebaum, "Run from Interactive Digital Displays to Traditional Billboards, Out-of-Home is on an Upswing," *Adweek*, 15 April 2011.

37. For a classic summary of issues related to the type, scope, and tactics of sales promotions design, see John A. Quelch, "Note on Sales Promotion Design," Teaching Note N-589-021 (Boston: Harvard Business School, 1988).

38. Jack Neff, "Coupons Are Hot, But Are They a Bargain for Brands?," *Advertising Age*, 11 July 2011, 10; Kunar Patel, "Marketers: Beware the Coupon Mom, *Advertising Age*, 11 July 2011, 1, 11–12; Kenneth Hein, "Coupon Enthusiasts Drive Up Redemption Rates," *Adweek*, 8 September 2009; Teddy Wayne, "Coupons Are Making a Comeback," *New York Times*, 8 September 2009.

39. Andrew Ehrenberg and Kathy Hammond, "The Case Against Price-Related Promotions," *Admap*, June 2001.

40. Quelch, "Note on Sales Promotion Design."

41. Michael L. Ray, *Advertising and Communication Management* (Upper Saddle River, NJ: Prentice Hall, 1982).

42. Suzy Evans, "Random Samples No More," *Fast Company*, February 2011, 35.

43. "Walgreens 'Arm Yourself for the Ones You Love' Campaign Takes Home the Super REGGIE Award," www.donnaspromotalk.com, 10 April 2011; www.pmalink.org; "Walgreens Kicks Off Flu Season Public Awareness Campaign," www.chaindrugreview.com, 8 September 2009.

44. Cassie Lancellotti-Young, "Groupon Case," Glassmeyer/McNamee Center for Digital Strategies, Dartmouth College, 2011; Brad Stone and Douglas MacMillan, "Are These Four Words Worth $25 Billion," *Bloomberg BusinessWeek*, 27 March 2011; Brad Stone, "Coupon Deathmatch, Party of Two?," *Bloomberg BusinessWeek*, 10 October 2010.

45. Rossiter and Percy, *Advertising and Promotion Management*.

46. See Jakki J. Mohr, Sanjit Sengupta, and Stanley J. Slater, *Marketing of High-Technology Products and Innovations*, 3rd ed. (Upper Saddle River, NJ: Prentice Hall, 2010) and Eloise Coupey, *Digital Business: Concepts & Strategies*, 2nd ed. (Upper Saddle River, NJ: Prentice Hall, 2005).

47. Erick Schonfeld, "IAB: Internet Advertising Reached $26 Billion in 2010, Display Grew Twice as Fast as Search," www.techcrunch.com, 13 April 2011.

48. Mike Chapman, "What Clicks Worldwide," *Adweek*, 30 May 2011, 12–13.

49. "Coke's Happiness Machine," *Adweek*, 1 November 2010; "Machine Dispenses Happiness for Unsuspecting College Students in Viral Video Hit," *PR Newswire*, 15 January 2010; "How Coca-Cola Created Its 'Happiness Machine,'" www.mashable.com, 21 July 2010.

50. Mark Borden, "Repeat Offenders," *Fast Company*, May 2010, 96–99.

51. "Helping Marketers Harness Consumers," *Adweek*, 21 January 2011.

52. Tanzina Vega, "Online Ad Revenue Continues to Rise," *New York Times*, 13 April 2011.

53. "Social Net Growth: No End in Sight," *Adweek*, 11 August 2010.

54. Geoffrey Fowler, "Are You Talking to Me?," *Wall Street Journal*, 25 April 2011; Jack Neff, "Why Social Networks Are Cool on Sharing," *Advertising Age*, 2 May 2011.

55. Allen Adamson, "No Contest: Twitter and Facebook Can Both Play a Role in Branding," *Forbes*, 6 May 2009.

56. Douglas MacMillan, "With Friends Like This, Who Needs Facebook," *Bloomberg BusinessWeek*, 10 September 2010.

57. Jack Neff, "Digital A-List: P&G," *Advertising Age*, 28 February 2011, 34–35.

58. Kirk Cheyfitz, "Advertising's Future Is 3 Simple Words: Paid. Owned. Earned.," *Huffington Post*, 27 October 2010.

59. Valerie Bauerlein, "Gatorade's 'Mission'," *Wall Street Journal*, 13 September 2010.

60. Dan Ouellette, "The Value of Social Media," *Adweek*, 21 January 2011; Simon Dumenco, "Metrics Mess: Five Sad Truths About Measurement Right Now," *Advertising Age*, 28 February 2011; Rance Crain, "Just How Influential Is Your Social-Media Program If It Isn't Helping to Sell Product?," *Advertising Age*, 17 January 2011, 14.

61. David Kiley and Robert Klara, "Panasonic '8x Life'," *Adweek Media*, 1 November 2010, 14.

62. See also "IEG's Guide to Why Companies Sponsor," www.sponsorship.com.

63. Tom Van Riper, "Open Sponsors, Open Wallets," *Forbes*, 6 September 2007.

64. "LG Experience at NCAA Final Four Nets Big Results," *Event Marketer*, 7 June 2011.

65. Interview with Rick Alessandri, senior vice president and managing director of ESPN X Game's franchise, November 2008.

66. William L. Shankin and John Kuzma, "Buying That Sporting Image," *Marketing Management* (Spring 1992): 65.

67. Noreen O'Leary, "Nationwide CMO Talks Sports Sponsorship and ROI, *Adweek*, 19 October 2010; Nate Ryan, "NASCAR Sponsorship Proves a Boon for Nationwide Insurance," *USA TODAY*, 27 August 2010.

68. "U.S. Mobile Ad Spending to Top $1 Billion for First Time This Year," www.iab.net, 4 October 2011.

69. Tom Farrell, "Selling Smart with Smartphones," *Adweek*, 23 May 2011.

70. Olga Kharif, "Apple Takes Share from Google in Mobile Ads," *Bloomberg BusinessWeek*, 10 October 2010, 40; Yukari Iwatani, "Apple's Ad Service Off to a Bumpy Start," *Wall Street Journal*, 16 August 2010.

71. Dan Butcher, "Macy's, Domino's and Unilever's Dove Case Studies Shared at Mobile Marketing Day," *Mobile Commerce Daily*, 5 March 2010.

72. Bette Marston, "Where in the World?," *Marketing News*, 30 September 2010, 6.

73. Ruth Bender, "Mobile-Ad Market Still Faces Hurdles," *Wall Street Journal*, 18 February 2011.

74. Spencer E. Ante, "Foursquare Locates New Funds to Expand," *Wall Street Journal*, 28 June 2010; Geoffrey Fowler, "Mobile Apps Drawing in Shoppers, Marketers," *Wall Street Journal*, 31 January 2011.

75. Ozier Muhammad, "Aisle by Aisle, an App That Pushes Bargains, *New York Times*, 16 August 2010; Sarah Lacy, "The Power of Velveeta: Shopkick Announces 3 Million Product Scans," *Wall Street Journal*, 8 February 2011; Jennifer Valentino-DeVries, "Paying People to 'Check In' and Promote Products," *Wall Street Journal*, 18 June 2010.

76. Cate R. Corcoran and Jean E. Palmieri, "M-Commerce Gets Ready for Takeoff as Men Go Mobile," *Menswear*, February 2011, 36–37.

77. John E. Hogan, Katherine N. Lemon, and Barak Libai, "Quantifying the Ripple: Word-of-Mouth and Advertising Effectiveness," *Journal of Advertising Research* (September 2004): 271–280.

78. "Ketchum and Mattel Capture *PRWeek*'s 2011 Campaign of the Year Award, Marking an Unprecedented Third Time an Agency Takes the Honor," *PR Newswire*, 11 March 2011.

79. Jonah Berger and Eric Schwartz, "What Drives Immediate and Ongoing Word-of-Mouth?," *Journal of Marketing Research* 48 (October 2011): 869–880.

80. Gerry Khermouch, "Buzz Marketing," *BusinessWeek*, 30 July 2001; Mark Hughes, *Buzzmarketing: Get People to Talk About Your Stuff* (New York: Penguin Books, 2005); "What's the Buzz About Buzz Marketing?," *Knowledge@Wharton*, 12 January 2005.

81. Steve Knox, "Why Effective Word-of-Mouth Disrupts Schemas," *Advertising Age*, 25 January 2010; Elaine Wong, "General Mills, Kraft Launch Word of Mouth Networks," *Adweek*, 5 October 2008; Todd Wasserman, "P&G Buzz Program Tremor Moving on to Mothers," *Brandweek*, 26 September 2006, 15; Robert Berner, "I Sold It Through the Grapevine," *BusinessWeek*, 29 May 2006; www.tremor.com.

82. Mark Hughes, *Buzzmarketing* (New York: Penguin/Portfolio, 2005).

83. Gerry Khermouch, "Buzz Marketing: Suddenly This Stealth Strategy Is Hot," *BusinessWeek*, 30 July 2001, 50.

84. For a review of some academic and practitioner issues with IMC, see Prasad A. Naik, "Integrated Marketing Communications: Provenance, Practice and Principles," in *Handbook of Advertising*, eds. Gerard J. Tellis and Tim Ambler (Thousands Oaks, CA: Sage Publications, 2007); and Tom Duncan and Frank Mulhern, eds., "A White Paper on the Status, Scope, and Future of IMC," March 2004, Daniels College of Business at the University of Denver.

85. Prasad A. Naik, Kalyan Raman, and Russ Winer, "Planning Marketing-Mix Strategies in the

Presence of Interactions," *Marketing Science* 24, no. 10 (2005): 25–34.

86. Tanzina Vega, "Taking Photos of Breakfast and Giving Meals to Children," *New York Times*, 7 March 2011.

87. This discussion assumes that the marketer has already thoroughly researched the target market and fully understands who they are—their perceptions, attitudes, and behaviors—and therefore knows exactly what needs to be done with them in terms of communication objectives.

88. Sandra Moriarty, Nancy D. Mitchell, and William D. Wells, *Advertising & IMC: Principles & Practice*, 9th ed. (Upper Saddle River, NJ: Prentice Hall, 2012).

89. Susan E. Heckler and Terry L. Childers, "The Role of Expectancy and Relevancy in Memory for Verbal and Visual Information: What Is Incongruency?" *Journal of Consumer Research* 18 (March 1992): 475–492; Michael J. Houston, Terry L. Childers, and Susan E. Heckler, "Picture-Word Consistency and the Elaborative Processing of Advertisements," *Journal of*

Marketing Research 24 (November 1987): 359–369; Thomas K. Srull and Robert S. Wyer, "Person Memory and Judgment," *Psychological Review* 96, no. 1 (1989): 58–83.

90. Michael D. Johnson, "Consumer Choice Strategies for Comparing Noncomparable Alternatives," *Journal of Consumer Research* 11 (December 1984): 741–753.

91. David Kiley and Robert Klara, "Heineken's 'Walk-In Fridge'," *Adweek Media*, 1 November 2010, 15.

92. Julie A. Edell and Kevin Lane Keller, "The Information Processing of Coordinated Media Campaigns," *Journal of Marketing Research* 26 (May 1989): 149–163; Julie Edell and Kevin Lane Keller, "Analyzing Media Interactions: The Effects of Coordinated Print-TV Advertising Campaigns," *Marketing Science Institute Report*, no. 99–120.

93. Timothy M. Smith, Srinath Gopalakrishna, and Paul M. Smith, "The Complementary Effect of Trade Shows on Personal Selling," *International Journal of Research in Marketing* 21, no. 1 (2004): 61–76.

Leveraging Secondary Brand Associations to Build Brand Equity

7

Learning Objectives

After reading this chapter, you should be able to

1. Outline the eight main ways to leverage secondary associations.

2. Explain the process by which a brand can leverage secondary associations.

3. Describe some of the key tactical issues in leveraging secondary associations from different entities.

If Salomon decided to extend from skis to tennis racquets, there are a number of different ways it could leverage secondary brand associations.

Source: Karl Mathis/EPA/Newscom

Preview

The preceding chapters described how we can build brand equity through the choice of brand elements (Chapter 4) or through marketing program activities and product, price, distribution, and marketing communication strategies (Chapters 5 and 6). This chapter considers the third means of building brand equity—namely, through the leverage of related or secondary brand associations.

Brands themselves may be linked to other entities that have their own knowledge structures in the minds of consumers. Because of these linkages, consumers may assume or infer that some of the associations or responses that characterize the other entities may also be true for the brand. In effect, the brand "borrows" some brand knowledge and, depending on the nature of those associations and responses, perhaps some brand equity from other entities.

This indirect approach to building brand equity is *leveraging secondary brand associations* for the brand. Secondary brand associations may be quite important to creating strong, favorable, and unique associations or positive responses if existing brand associations or responses are deficient in some way. It can also be an effective way to reinforce existing associations and responses in a fresh and different way.

This chapter considers the different means by which we can leverage secondary brand associations by linking the brand to the following (see Figure 7-1 for a fuller depiction):

1. Companies (through branding strategies)
2. Countries or other geographic areas (through identification of product origin)
3. Channels of distribution (through channel strategy)
4. Other brands (through co-branding)
5. Characters (through licensing)
6. Spokespersons (through endorsements)
7. Events (through sponsorship)
8. Other third-party sources (through awards or reviews)

The first three entities reflect source factors: who makes the product, where the product is made, and where it is purchased. The remaining entities deal with related people, places, or things.

As an example, suppose that Salomon—makers of alpine and cross-country ski bindings, ski boots, and skis—decided to introduce a new tennis racquet called "the Avenger." Although Salomon has been selling safety bindings for skis since 1947, much of its growth was fueled by its diversification into ski boots and the introduction of a revolutionary new type of ski called the Monocoque in 1990. Salomon's innovative, stylish, and top-quality products have led to strong leadership positions.

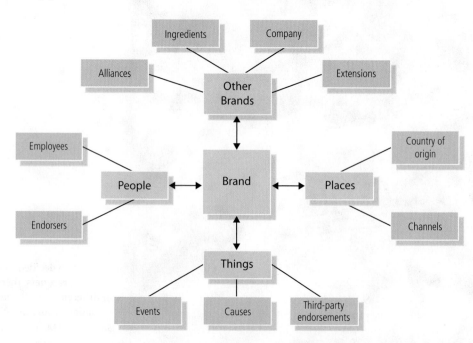

FIGURE 7-1

Secondary Sources of
Brand Knowledge

In creating the marketing program to support the new Avenger tennis racquet, Salomon could attempt to leverage secondary brand associations in a number of different ways.

- Salomon could leverage associations to the corporate brand by sub-branding the product—for example, by calling it "Avenger by Salomon." Consumers' evaluations of the new product extension would be influenced by the extent to which they held favorable associations about Salomon as a company or brand because of its skiing products, and how strongly they felt that such knowledge could predict the quality of a Salomon tennis racquet.
- Salomon could try to rely on its European origins (it is headquartered near Lake Annecy at the foot of the Alps), although such a location would not seem to have much relevance to tennis.
- Salomon could also try to sell through upscale, professional tennis shops and clubs in hopes that these retailers' credibility would rub off on the Avenger brand.
- Salomon could attempt to co-brand by identifying a strong ingredient brand for its grip, frame, or strings (as Wilson did by incorporating Goodyear tire rubber on the soles of its ProStaff Classic tennis shoes).
- Although it is doubtful that a licensed character could be effectively leveraged, Salomon obviously could attempt to find one or more top professional players to endorse the racquet or could choose to become a sponsor of tennis tournaments, or even the entire professional ATP men's or WTA women's tennis tour.
- Salomon could attempt to secure and publicize favorable ratings from third parties like *Tennis* magazine.

Thus, independent of the associations created by the racquet itself, its brand name, or any other aspects of the marketing program, Salomon may be able to build equity by linking the brand to other entities in various ways.

This chapter first considers the nature of brand knowledge that marketers can leverage or transfer from other entities, and the process for doing it. We then consider in detail each of the eight different means of leveraging secondary brand associations. The chapter concludes by considering the special topic of Olympic sponsorship in Brand Focus 7.0.

CONCEPTUALIZING THE LEVERAGING PROCESS

Linking the brand to some other entity—some source factor or related person, place, or thing—may create a new set of associations from the brand to the entity, as well as affecting existing brand associations. Let's look at both these outcomes.[1]

Creation of New Brand Associations

By making a connection between the brand and another entity, consumers may form a mental association from the brand to this other entity and, consequently, to any or all associations, judgments, feelings, and the like linked to that entity. In general, these secondary brand associations are most likely to affect evaluations of a new product when consumers lack either the motivation or the ability to judge product-related concerns. In other words, when consumers either don't care much about or don't feel that they possess the knowledge to choose the appropriate brand, they may be more likely to make brand decisions on the basis of secondary considerations such as what they think, feel, or know about the country from which the product came, the store in which it is sold, or some other characteristic.

Effects on Existing Brand Knowledge

Linking the brand to some other entity may not only create new brand associations to the entity but also affect existing brand associations. The basic mechanism is this. Consumers have some knowledge of an entity. When a brand is identified as linked to that entity, consumers may infer that some of the particular associations, judgments, or feelings that characterize the entity may also characterize the brand. A number of different theoretical mechanisms from psychology predict this type of inference. One is "cognitive consistency"—in other words, in the minds of consumers, what is true for the entity, must be true for the brand.[2]

To describe the process more formally, here are three important factors in predicting the extent of leverage from linking the brand to another entity:

1. *Awareness and knowledge of the entity:* If consumers have no awareness or knowledge of the secondary entity, then obviously there is nothing they can transfer from it. Ideally, consumers would be aware of the entity; hold some strong, favorable, and perhaps even unique associations about it; and have positive judgments and feelings about it.
2. *Meaningfulness of the knowledge of the entity:* Given that the entity evokes some positive associations, judgments, or feelings, is this knowledge relevant and meaningful for the brand? The meaningfulness may vary depending on the brand and product context. Some associations, judgments, or feelings may seem relevant to and valuable for the brand, whereas others may seem to consumers to have little connection.
3. *Transferability of the knowledge of the entity:* Assuming that some potentially useful and meaningful associations, judgments, or feelings exist regarding the entity and could possibly transfer to the brand, how strongly will this knowledge actually become linked to the brand?

In other words, the basic questions we want to answer about transferring secondary knowledge from another entity are: What do consumers know about the other entity? and, Does any of this knowledge affect what they think about the brand when it becomes linked or associated in some fashion with this other entity?

Theoretically, consumers can infer any aspect of knowledge from other entities to the brand (see Figure 7-2), although some types of entities are more likely to inherently create or affect certain kinds of brand knowledge than others. For example, events may be especially conducive to the creation of experiences; people may be especially effective for the elicitation of feelings; other brands may be especially well suited for establishing particular attributes and benefits; and so on. At the same time, any one entity may be associated with multiple dimensions of knowledge, each of which may affect brand knowledge directly or indirectly.

For example, consider the effects on knowledge of linking the brand to a cause, like Avon's Breast Cancer Crusade. A cause marketing program could build brand awareness via recall and recognition; enhance brand image in terms of attributes such as brand personality or user imagery like kind and generous; evoke brand feelings like social approval and self-respect; establish brand attitudes such as trustworthy and likable; and create experiences through a sense of community and participation in cause-related activities.

Judgments or feelings may transfer more readily than more specific associations, which are likely to seem irrelevant or be too strongly linked to the original entity to transfer. As we'll see in Chapter 12, the inferencing process depends largely on the strength of the linkage or connection in consumers' minds between the brand and the other entity. The more consumers see similarity between the entity and the brand, the more likely they will infer similar knowledge about the brand.

Guidelines

Leveraging secondary brand associations may allow marketers to create or reinforce an important point-of-difference or a necessary or competitive point-of-parity versus competitors. When choosing to emphasize source factors or a particular person, place, or thing, marketers

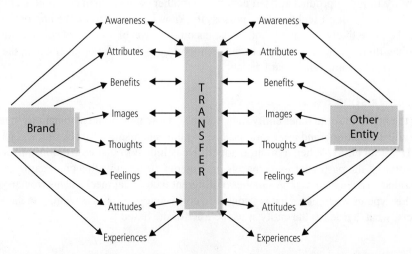

FIGURE 7-2

Understanding Transfer of Brand Knowledge

should take into account consumers' awareness of that entity, as well as how the associations, judgments, or feelings for it might become linked to the brand or affect existing brand associations.

Marketers can choose entities for which consumers have some or even a great deal of similar associations. A *commonality* leveraging strategy makes sense when consumers have associations to another entity that are congruent with desired brand associations. For example, consider a country such as New Zealand, which is known for having more sheep than people. A New Zealand sweater manufacturer that positioned its product on the basis of its "New Zealand wool" presumably could more easily establish strong and favorable brand associations because New Zealand may already mean "wool" to many people.

On the other hand, there may be times when entities are chosen that represent a departure for the brand because there are few if any common or similar associations. Such *complementarity* branding strategies can be strategically critical in terms of delivering the desired position. The marketer's challenge here is to ensure that the less congruent knowledge for the entity has either a direct or an indirect effect on existing brand knowledge. This may require skillfully designed marketing programs that overcome initial consumer confusion or skepticism. For example, when Buick signed Tiger Woods as an endorser, many questioned whether consumers would find a fit or consistency between the golfer and the car maker, and, if not, how much value the endorsement would add to the Buick brand.

Even if consumers buy into the association one way or another, leveraging secondary brand associations may be risky because the marketer gives up some control of the brand image. The source factors or related person, place, or thing will undoubtedly have a host of other associations, of which only some smaller set will be of interest to the marketer. Managing the transfer process so that only the relevant secondary knowledge becomes linked to the brand may be difficult. Moreover, this knowledge may change over time as consumers learn more about the entity, and these new associations, judgments, or feelings may or may not be advantageous for the brand.

The following sections consider some of the main ways by which we can link secondary brand associations to the brand.

COMPANY

Branding strategies are an important determinant of the strength of association from the brand to the company and any other existing brands. Three main branding options exist for a new product:

1. Create a new brand.
2. Adopt or modify an existing brand.
3. Combine an existing and a new brand.

Existing brands may be related to the corporate brand, say Samsung, or a specific product brand like Samsung Galaxy S 4G mobile phone. If the brand is linked to an existing brand, as with options 2 and 3, then knowledge about the existing brand may also become linked to the brand.

In particular, a corporate or family brand can be a source of much brand equity. For example, a corporate brand may evoke associations of common product attributes, benefits, or attitudes; people and relationships; programs and values; and corporate credibility. Branding Brief 7-1 describes the corporate image campaign for IBM.

Leveraging a corporate brand may not always be useful, however. In fact, in some cases, large companies have deliberately introduced new brands or bought successful niche brands in an attempt to convey a "smaller" image. Examples of the latter strategy—that might even surprise their existing customers!—include Ben and Jerry's (Unilever), Kashi (Kellogg's), Odwalla (Coca-Cola), and Tom's of Maine (Colgate-Palmolive). Clorox paid almost $1 billion for Burt's Bees—famous for beeswax lip balm, lotions, soaps and shampoos—in part because of the market opportunity, but also to better learn about best practices for environmental sustainability, an emerging corporate priority.[3] Anheuser-Busch acquired the successful Midwest craft beer Goose Island in part to better compete with rival MillerCoors's highly successful Blue Moon brand.[4]

BRANDING BRIEF 7-1

IBM Promotes a Smarter Planet

IBM's long tradition as "Big Blue" helped it become one of the world's most successful companies of the twentieth century. Unfortunately, many of the product areas on which this success was built became highly competitive and increasingly commoditized in the new millenium. As a result, IBM decided it needed to radically transform itself from a product-focused company to a value-added, services-oriented company.

IBM Chairman and CEO Sam Palmisano spun off the company's famous PC division and began to invest heavily in software and business consulting. Another critical aspect of the transformation was aligning the public perception of IBM with this new vision. The vision itself—and thus the corresponding marketing communication program—was rooted in a basic belief that the world was changing in three significant ways that provided clear direction to IBM's new mission. In other words, the world was becoming:

- Instrumented ("Instrument the world's systems")
- Interconnected ("Interconnect them")
- Intelligent ("Make them intelligent")

IBM wanted to be the leader in each of these three areas. The original name chosen to reflect this new positioning was the very literal "Integrated Intelligent Infrastructure," but further work led to the snappier, more inspiring "Smarter Planet" phrase that also became the slogan for the corporate campaign. The basic premise of the campaign was that every business would become a technology company and be forced to face new and challenging policy changes, especially with respect to sustainability, security, and privacy. IBM was positioned to be the ideal partner to assist in these efforts. Given the ambitious scope of the positioning, government officials became the target as much as business leaders.

The "Smarter Planet" positioning had its roots in some of IBM's recent accomplishments. For example, in Stockholm, Sweden, IBM smart traffic systems cut gridlock by 20 percent, reduced emissions by 12 percent, and resulted in a dramatic increase in the use of public transportation. Smart grid projects in various locales had already helped consumers save 10 percent on their bills and reduced peak demand by 15 percent.

With these accomplishments in mind, the initial goal of the "Smarter Planet" campaign was to position IBM as a leader in solving the world's most pressing problems. Specifically, the marketing objectives were to:

- Be established in 50+ countries.
- Create 300 new client references and business opportunities.
- Change perceptions of and likelihood of doing business with IBM.

Launched in November 2008, one of the first campaign activities was an op-ad series, "Building a Smarter Planet," targeting forward-thinking leaders. The full-page ads appeared in major newspapers such as the *Wall Street Journal*, *New York Times* and *Financial Times*. They were unusual in the lengthy text that they included. Figure 7-3 has an excerpt from the first ad that describes the rationale behind the campaign.

IBM's "Smarter Planet" positioning has strengthened the corporate brand, benefiting all the company's associated product and services.

Source: Courtesy of International Business Machines Corporation, © International Business Machines Corporation.

The campaign also included TV ads and targeted ads to three groups: business and government leaders in large organizations, IT professionals, and the mid-market. It included a strong digital component, with an expanded IBM Web site and a Smarter Planet blog. Videos were created and distributed across eight of the largest video-sharing sites. IBM also launched a "Smarter Cities" global tour to bring key policy and decision makers together to discuss the topical issues they faced, such as transportation, energy, health care, education, and public safety.

IBM analysts estimated that the Smarter Planet strategy expanded its market potential by as much as 40 percent globally, or by an additional $2.3 billion in revenue. IBM's brand tracking revealed increases across the board on a variety of image measures (such as "making the world a better place" and "an expert in how the world works") and overall judgments related to consideration, preference, and likelihood of doing business. IBM's stock price during the campaign increased by 64 percent, while the Dow index grew only 14 percent over the same time.

Just over a year ago, we began a global conversation about how the planet is becoming smarter. By smarter, we mean that intelligence is being infused into the systems and processes that make the world work—into things no one would recognize as computers: cars, appliances, roadways, power grids, clothes, even natural systems such as agriculture and waterways.

Trillions of digital devices, connected through the Internet, are producing a vast ocean of data. And all this information—from the flow of markets to the pulse of societies—can be turned into knowledge because we now have the computational power and advanced analytics to make sense of it. With this knowledge we can reduce costs, cut waste, and improve the efficiency, productivity and quality of everything from companies to cities.

A year into this new era, the signs of a smarter planet are all around us. Smarter systems are being implemented and are creating value in every major industry, across every region in both the developed and developing worlds. This idea isn't a metaphor, or a vision, or a proposal—it's a rapidly emerging reality.

FIGURE 7-3
Excerpt from IBM's "Building a Smarter Planet" First Op-Ad Piece

Source: www.ibm.com/ smarterplanet; www.ibm. com. Used with permission of IBM.

Sources: Talk given by Jon Iwata, SVP, Marketing & Communications, IBM, at the Tuck School of Business at Dartmouth College, 10 February 2010; "Let's Build a Smarter Planet," 2010 Gold Effie Winner, www.effie.org/ winners/showcase/2010/4625; www.ibm.com/smarterplanet; www.ibm.com.

BLUE MOON

Although the U.S. beer market has been in a slowdown in recent years, a bright spot is craft beers, which have been able to combine quality, heritage, and some unique characteristics to command a premium price. Blue Moon was named for the second full moon in a calendar month. Launched in 1995 by Coors in Denver, Colorado, it was positioned as a uniquely flavored, highly drinkable, handcrafted Belgian-style wheat beer. Brewed with oats for creaminess and spiced with orange peel and coriander, Blue Moon Belgian White is often served with a slice of orange. Coors downplays its connection, and the beer is branded as brewed by the "Blue Moon Brewing Company." Deemed the leading craft beer by many, the beer has received extensive marketing support. Its brand slogan—"Artfully Crafted," describing how the beer is made—has also served as the basis for a multimedia communication program. TV and print ads have featured hand-painted images of Blue Moon beer bottles and glasses. Taking the campaign online, a contest gave Blue Moon fans the chance to upload their own "Artfully Crafted" photos to the Photo Crafter tab on the brand's Facebook page. An application there transformed the photo into artfully crafted Blue Moon paintings and entered fans into the contest to win prizes.[5]

Sometimes companies want to downplay their corporate associations, as when Coors launched the craft-beer-like Blue Moon.

Source: Francis Vachon/Alamy

Finally, brands and companies are often unavoidably linked to the category and industry in which they compete, sometimes with adverse consequences. Some industries are characterized by fairly divided opinions, but consider the challenges faced by brands in the oil and gas or financial services industry which consumers have generally viewed in a negative light.[6] By virtue of membership in the category in which it competes, an oil company may expect to face a potentially suspicious or skeptical public *regardless* of what it does.

Chapters 11 and 12 describe in detail how marketers can leverage the equity of existing brands to launch their new products.

COUNTRY OF ORIGIN AND OTHER GEOGRAPHIC AREAS

Besides the company that makes the product, the country or geographic location from which it originates may also become linked to the brand and generate secondary associations.[7] Many countries have become known for expertise in certain product categories or for conveying a particular type of image.

The world is becoming a "cultural bazaar" where consumers can pick and choose brands originating in different countries, based on their beliefs about the quality of certain types of products from certain countries or the image that these brands or products communicate.[8] Thus, a consumer from anywhere in the world may choose to wear Italian suits, exercise in U.S. athletic shoes, listen to a Japanese or Korean MP3 player, drive a German car, or drink English ale.

Choosing brands with strong national ties may reflect a deliberate decision to maximize product utility and communicate self-image, based on what consumers believe about products from those countries. A number of brands are able to create a strong point-of-difference, in part because of consumers' identification of and beliefs about the country of origin. For example, consider the following strongly linked brands and countries:

Levi's jeans—United States	Dewar's whiskey—Scotland
Chanel perfume—France	Kikkoman soy sauce—Japan
Foster's beer—Australia	Cadbury—England
Barilla pasta—Italy	Gucci shoes and purses—Italy
BMW—Germany	Mont Blanc pens—Switzerland

Puerto Rico rum makers have leveraged their geographical roots to establish a dominant market position.

Source: Donald Bowers/ Getty Images

Other geographic associations besides country of origin are possible, such as states, regions, and cities. Three classic U.S. tourism slogans, "I Love New York," "Virginia Is for Lovers," and Las Vegas's "What Happens Here, Stays Here," are for these more specific types of locales.

Marketers can establish a geographic or country-of-origin association in different ways. They can embed the location in the brand name, such as Idaho potatoes, Irish Spring soap, or South African Airways, or combine it with a brand name in some way as in Bailey's Irish Cream. Or they can make the location the dominant theme in brand advertising, as has been the case for Coors with Foster's beer.

Some countries have even created advertising campaigns to promote their products. For example, "Rums of Puerto Rico" advertise that they are the finest-quality rums, leading to a 70 percent share of U.S. brand sales.[9] Other countries have developed and advertised labels or seals for their products.[10] Branding Brief 7-2 describes how New Zealand's launch of its "The New Zealand Way" brand has led to much marketing success for the country.

Because it's typically a legal necessity for the country of origin to appear somewhere on the product or package, associations to the country of origin almost always have the potential to be created at the point of purchase and to affect brand decisions there. The question really is one of relative emphasis, and the role of country of origin or other geographic regions throughout the marketing program. Becoming strongly linked to a country of origin or specific geographic region is not without potential disadvantages. Events or actions associated with the country may color people's perceptions.[11]

BRAND AMERICA

The turn of the century and George W. Bush's presidency coincided with sharp drop in the image of the United States in the eyes of the world's citizens. A comprehensive analysis by Pew Research Center in 2008 concluded:[12]

> The U.S. image abroad is suffering almost everywhere. Particularly in the most economically developed countries, people blame America for the financial crisis. Opposition to key elements of American foreign policy is widespread in Western Europe, and positive views of the U.S. have declined steeply among many of America's longtime European allies. In Muslim nations, the wars in Afghanistan and particularly Iraq have driven negative ratings nearly off the charts. The United States earns positive ratings in several Asian and Latin American nations, but usually by declining margins.

One BBC-commissioned poll of 26,000 respondents in the 25 largest countries in 2007 found that roughly half thought the United States had a "mostly negative" influence on the world. A global economic recession, unpopular wars, and disagreements on various social and environmental policies took their toll. Although few global U.S. companies experienced the same erosion in reputation—many people seemed willing to compartmentalize politics and commerce—restoring U.S. image became a popular theme with the election of Barack Obama in 2008. Recognizing the importance of tourism to the U.S. economy—one in nine U.S. jobs is in a travel or tourism-related sector—the U.S. Travel Association has been aggressively marketing visits to the United States to the international travel industry.[13]

Finally, consider the favorability of a country-of-origin association from both a domestic and a foreign perspective. In the domestic market, country-of-origin perceptions may stir consumers' patriotic notions or remind them of their past. As international trade grows, consumers may view certain brands as symbolically important of their own cultural heritage and identity. Some research found that domestic brands were more strongly favored in collectivistic countries such as Japan and other Asian countries that have strong group norms and ties to family and country. In individualistic societies such as the United States and other Western countries that are more guided by self-interest and personal goals, consumers demand stronger evidence of product superiority.[14]

Patriotic appeals have been the basis of marketing strategies all over the world. However, they can lack uniqueness and even be overused. For example, during the Reagan administration in the 1980s, a number of different U.S. brands in a diverse range of product categories including cars, beer, and clothing used pro-U.S. themes in their advertising, perhaps diluting the efforts of all as a result. In recent years, the debate over outsourcing and offshoring and, tragically, the events of September 11, 2001, raised the visibility of patriotic appeals once again.

BRANDING BRIEF 7-2

Selling Brands the New Zealand Way

In November 2010, New Zealand was ranked as the third-strongest country brand in the world—ahead of the United States—by brand consultancy FutureBrand's Country Brand Index. The ranking was a credit to the country's remarkable qualities, but also to its concerted marketing program through the years.

Back in 1991, New Zealand began a branding initiative called "The New Zealand Way." The key objectives of the New Zealand Way brand campaign were to reposition New Zealand to reflect its contemporary positioning and undertake a sustained campaign that could be a powerful force to benefit trade and tourism in the global marketplace. The innovative programme was owned and funded by the New Zealand Tourism Board, and New Zealand Trade & Enterprise (NZTE, the government's official economicDevelopment Agency), working with the best businesses across tourism and trade, known as "Brand Partners."

New Zealand has benefited from popular films and a concerted marketing effort to build the country brand.

Source: © Tourism New Zealand www.tourismnewzealand.com +64 4 462 8000

The New Zealand Way brand campaign promoted the country, its tourism and trade products and services, and its famous people, known as "Brand Ambassadors."

From this research and focus groups, a fern logo was developed and intellectually protected as a new icon for New Zealand. It represented New Zealand's green provenance and leveraged the well-known existing silver fern used by many sports teams (such as the rugby team the All Blacks) and some industries (such as Anchor butter). From research, a set of brand values were also agreed on by New Zealanders to inform the repositioning.

In 1999, a decision was made to develop a more focused campaign for tourism and Tourism New Zealand sharpened its destination global marketing with its campaign: "100% Pure New Zealand." For the next decade the campaign combined a number of different activities but concentrating on the Internet, international media partnerships, events and close engagement and training with tourism operators. The campaign focused on building awareness of New Zealand as a unique holiday destination due its spectacular natural landscapes and fascinating culture and people. Purity was defined in a natural, wholesome way, but also in the genuineness and down-to-earth nature of the people.

Buoyed also by publicity from the highly popular *Lord of the Rings* film trilogy, which was filmed there, plus the profile from the America's Cup which Tourism New Zealand cleverly used for promotion, the number of visitors to the country increased by 50% during this time. NZTE chose to focus its branding efforts on international business development reflecting emerging and relevant values for enterprise such as innovation, creativity, and integrity. This complemented the ongoing successes of the primary sector and New Zealand's clean and green environment.

In 2011, the tag line for the tourism campaign was changed to "100% Pure You" with the subline, "It's About Time." The intent was to build on the prior campaign to target people who were actively considering New Zealand for a holiday vacation and to encourage them to travel soon. The focus was online, incorporating SEM, standard and rich media online ads, social media, and integrated partnership with the trade. The campaign was localized for each key market, for example, "It's About Time" for the U.K., "Discover" for Germany, and "Revive" for Asia.

So that the right message is sent, the country home page (www.newzealand.com) directs visitors to either the tourism or business Web sites, depending on expressed preference.

Sources: www.newzealand.com; Valarie Tjolle, "Tourism New Zealand Unveils New Digital Marketing Campaign," www.travelmole.com, 21 February 2011; Grant McPherson, "Branding Debate Goes Beyond Logos," www.nzte.govt.nz, 23 August 2011; Magdalena Florek and Andrea Insch, "The Trademark Protection of Country Brands: Insights From New Zealand," *Journal of Place Management and Development* 1, no. 3 (2008): 292–305.

Another challenge with country-of-origin is how consumers actually define it and under what circumstances they care. Many U.S. companies are moving their manufacturing offshore. Although they may still base their headquarters on U.S. soil, some very iconic brands—including Converse, Levi's, Mattel, and Rawlings baseballs—are no longer manufactured in the United States. Some other famous U.S. brands, such as Ben & Jerry's, Budweiser, and Gerber, are actually owned by foreign corporations.

In an increasingly globally connected world, the concept of country-of-origin is likely to become very confusing at times. Governments in some countries have even taken steps to protect their popular industries. Swiss lawmakers have stipulated that local watchmakers can label their products Swiss-made only if non-Swiss parts equal less than 50 percent of the value of the watch's movement, or motor.[15]

CHANNELS OF DISTRIBUTION

Chapter 5 described how members of the channels of distribution can directly affect the equity of the brands they sell. Let's next consider how retail stores can indirectly affect brand equity through an "image transfer" process because of consumers' associations linked to the retail stores.

Because of associations to product assortment, pricing and credit policy, quality of service, and so on, retailers have their own brand images in consumers' minds. The Science of Branding 7-1 summarizes academic research into the dimensions of retailer images. Retailers create these associations through the products and brands they stock and the means by which they sell them. To more directly shape their images, many retailers aggressively advertise and promote directly to customers.

A consumer may infer certain characteristics about a brand on the basis of where it is sold. "If it's sold by Nordstrom, it must be good quality." Consumers may perceive the same brand differently depending on whether it is sold in a store seen as prestigious and exclusive, or in a store designed for bargain shoppers and having more mass appeal.

The transfer of store image associations can be either positive or negative for a brand. For many high-end brands, a natural growth strategy is to expand the customer base by tapping new channels of distribution. Such strategies can be dangerous, however, depending on how existing customers and retailers react. When Vera Wang decided to also distribute her wares through Kohl's, Macy's decided to drop her popular lingerie line. The retailer also cut ties with Liz Claiborne when the fashion brand decided to offer a line called Liz & Co. to JCPenney.[16]

CO-BRANDING

We've noted that through a brand extension strategy, a new product can become linked to an existing corporate or family brand that has its own set of associations. An existing brand can also leverage associations by linking itself to other brands from the same or different company. *Co-branding*—also called brand bundling or brand alliances—occurs when two or more existing brands are combined into a joint product or are marketed together in some fashion.[17] A special case of this strategy is ingredient branding, which we'll discuss in the next section.[18]

Co-branding has been around for years; for example, Betty Crocker paired with Sunkist Growers in 1961 to successfully market a lemon chiffon cake mix.[19] Interest in co-branding as a means of building brand equity has increased in recent years. For example, Hershey's Heath toffee candy bar has not only been extended into several new products—Heath Sensations (bite-sized candies) and Heath Bits and Bits of Brickle (chocolate-covered and plain toffee baking products)—but also has been licensed to a variety of vendors, such as Dairy Queen (with its Blizzard drink), Ben & Jerry's, and Blue Bunny (with its ice cream bar).

Some other notable supermarket examples of co-branding are Yoplait Trix yogurt, Betty Crocker's brownie mix with Hershey's chocolate syrup, and Kellogg's Cinnabon cereal. In the credit card market, co-branding often links three brands, as in the Shell Gold MasterCard from Citi Cards. With airlines, brand alliances can unite a host of brands, such as Star Alliance, which includes 16 different airlines such as United Airlines, Lufthansa, and Singapore Airlines.

THE SCIENCE OF BRANDING 7-1

Understanding Retailers' Brand Images

Like the brands they sell, retailers have brand images that influence consumers and must be carefully constructed and maintained. Academics have identified the following five dimensions of a retailer's brand image:

Access

The location of a store and the distance that consumers must travel to shop are basic criteria in their store choice decisions. Access is a key component in consumers' assessment of total shopping costs, and is especially important for retailers who wish to get a substantial share of wallet from fill-in trips and small-basket shoppers.

Store Atmosphere

Different elements of a retailer's in-store environment, like color, music, and crowding, can influence consumers' perceptions of its atmosphere, whether or not they visit a store, how much time they spend in it, and how much money they spend there. A pleasing in-store atmosphere provides substantial hedonic utility to consumers and encourages them to visit more often, stay longer, and buy more. Although it improves consumers' perceptions of the quality of merchandise in the store, consumers also tend to associate it with higher prices. An appealing in-store atmosphere also offers much potential in terms of crafting a unique store image and establishing differentiation. Even if the products and brands stocked by a retailer are similar to those sold by others, the ability to create a strong in-store personality and rich experiences can play a crucial role in building retailer brand equity.

Price and Promotion

A retailer's price image is influenced by attributes like average level of prices, how much variation there is in prices over time, the frequency and depth of promotions, and whether the retailer positions itself on a continuum between EDLP (everyday low price) and HILO (high-low promotional) pricing. Consumers are more likely to develop a favorable price image when retailers offer frequent discounts on a large number of products than when they offer less frequent, but steeper discounts. Further, products that have high unit price and are purchased more frequently are more salient in determining the retailer's price image. One pricing format does not dominate another,

but research has shown that large-basket shoppers prefer EDLP stores while small-basket shoppers prefer HILO, and it is optimal for HILO stores to charge an average price that is higher than the EDLP. Finally, price promotions are associated with store switching, but the effect is indirect, altering consumers' category purchase decisions while they are in the store rather than their choice of which store to visit.

Cross-Category Assortment

Consumers' perception of the breadth of different products and services offered by a retailer under one roof significantly influences store image. A broad assortment can create customer value by offering convenience and ease of shopping. It is risky to extend too far too soon, but staying too tightly coupled to the current assortment and image may unnecessarily limit the retailer's range of experimentation. The logic and sequencing of a retailer's assortment policy are critical to its ability to successfully expand its meaning and appeal to consumers over time.

Within-Category Assortment

Consumers' perceptions of the depth of a retailer's assortment within a product category are an important dimension of store image and a key driver of store choice. As the perceived assortment of brands, flavors, and sizes increases, variety-seeking consumers will perceive greater utility, consumers with uncertain future preferences will believe they have more flexibility in their choices, and, in general, consumers are more likely to find the item they desire. A greater number of SKUs need not directly translate to better perceptions. Retailers often can reduce the number of SKUs substantially without adversely affecting consumer perceptions, as long as they pay attention to the most preferred brands, the organization of the assortment, and the availability of diverse product attributes.

Sources: Kusum L. Ailawadi and Kevin Lane Keller, "Understanding Retail Branding: Conceptual Insights and Research Priorities," *Journal of Retailing* 80 (2004): 331–342; Dennis B. Arnett, Debra A. Laverie, and Amanda Meiers, "Developing Parsimonious Retailer Equity Indexes Using Partial Least Squares Analysis: A Method and Applications," *Journal of Retailing* 79 (2003): 161–170; Dhruv Grewal and Michael Levy, "Emerging Issues in Retailing Research," *Journal of Retailing* 85 (December 2009): 522–526.

Figure 7-4 summarizes the advantages and disadvantages of co-branding and licensing. The main advantage of co-branding is that a product may be uniquely and convincingly positioned by virtue of the multiple brands in the campaign. Co-branding can create more compelling points-of-difference or points-of-parity for the brand—or both—than otherwise might have been feasible. As a result, it can generate greater sales from the existing target market as well as open additional opportunities with new consumers and channels. When Kraft adds Dole fruit to its popular Lunchables lunch combinations line for kids, it was partly to help address health concerns and criticism from nutrition critics.[20]

Advantages

Borrow needed expertise
Leverage equity you don't have
Reduce cost of product introduction
Expand brand meaning into related categories
    Broaden meaning
    Increase access points
Source of additional revenue

Disadvantages

Loss of control
Risk of brand equity dilution
Negative feedback effects
Lack of brand focus and clarity
Organizational distraction

FIGURE 7-4

Advantages and Disadvantages of Co-Branding and Licensing

Co-branding can reduce the cost of product introduction because it combines two well-known images, accelerating potential adoption. Co-branding also may be a valuable means to learn about consumers and how other companies approach them. In poorly differentiated categories especially, co-branding may be an important means of creating a distinctive product.[21]

The potential disadvantages of co-branding are the risks and lack of control that arise from becoming aligned with another brand in the minds of consumers. Consumer expectations about the level of involvement and commitment with co-brands are likely to be high. Unsatisfactory performance thus could have negative repercussions for both (or all) brands.[22] If the brands are very distinct, consumers may be less sure about what each brands represents.[23] If the other brand has entered into a number of co-branding arrangements, there also may be a risk of overexposure that would dilute the transfer of any association. It may also result in distraction and a lack of focus on existing brands.

Guidelines

The Science of Branding 7-2 provides some academic insight about how consumers evaluate co-branded products. To create a strong co-brand, both brands should have adequate brand awareness; sufficiently strong, favorable, and unique associations; and positive consumer judgments and feelings. Thus, a necessary but not sufficient condition for co-branding success is that the two brands *separately* have some potential brand equity. The most important requirement is a logical fit between the two brands, so that the combined brand or marketing activity maximizes the advantages of the individual brands while minimizing the disadvantages.[24]

SMART CAR

Some eyebrows were raised when DaimlerChrysler AG's Mercedes Benz unit agreed to manufacture a "Swatchmobile," named after SMH's colorful and fashionable lines of Swatch watches. Personally championed by SMH's charismatic chairman, Nicolas Hayek, the Smart Car, as it came to be known, was designed to be small (less than 10 feet long) and low cost (under $10,000). The car combined the three most important features of Swatch watches—affordability, durability, and stylishness—with important features of a Mercedes Benz automobile—safety and security in a crash. A number of critics believed the Mercedes-Benz image could suffer if the car was unsuccessful, which was a possible outcome given the fact that many products bearing the Swatch name (like clothes, bags, telephones, pagers, and sunglasses) had disappointing sales or were dropped altogether. However, those concerns were quickly proven to be incorrect, with their successful launch in Europe. Since then Smart has been a worldwide hit with the Smart Fortwo being sold in over 35 countries worldwide.[25]

The Smart car has built its equity on its own novel features and not on any corporate brand associations.

Source: Courtesy of Daimler AG

Besides these strategic considerations, marketers must enter into and execute co-branding ventures carefully. They must ensure the right kind of fit in values, capabilities, and goals in addition to an appropriate balance of brand equity. When it comes to execution, marketers need detailed plans to legalize contracts, make financial arrangements, and coordinate marketing programs. As one executive at Nabisco put it, "Giving away your brand is a lot like giving away your child—you want to make sure everything is perfect." The financial arrangement between brands may vary, although typically the firm using the other brand will pay some type of licensing fee and/or royalty from sales. The aim is for the licensor and the licensee to benefit from these agreements as a result of the shared equity, increased awareness for the licensor, and greater sales for the licensee.

More generally, brand alliances, such as co-branding, require marketers to ask themselves a number of questions, such as:

- What capabilities do we *not* have?
- What resource constraints do we face (people, time, money)?
- What growth goals or revenue needs do we have?

In assessing a joint branding opportunity, marketers will ask themselves:

- Is it a profitable business venture?
- How does it help to maintain or strengthen brand equity?
- Is there any possible risk of dilution of brand equity?
- Does it offer any extrinsic advantages such as learning opportunities?

One of the highest-profile brand alliances was that of Disney and McDonald's, which had the exclusive global rights from 1996 to 2006 in the fast-food industry to promote everything from Disney movies and videos to TV shows and theme parks. McDonald's has partnerships with a number of different brands, including leading toy and entertainment companies for its Happy Meals, and Kraft's Oreo, Hershey's M&M's, and Rolo brands for its McFlurry dessert.

Ingredient Branding

A special case of co-branding is ***ingredient branding***, which creates brand equity for materials, components, or parts that are necessarily contained within other branded products.[27] Some successful ingredient brands over the years include Dolby noise reduction, Gore-Tex water-resistant fibers, Teflon nonstick coatings, Stainmaster stain-resistant fibers, and Scotchgard fabrics. Ingredient brands attempt to create enough awareness and preference for their product that consumers will not buy a host product that does not contain the ingredient.

THE SCIENCE OF BRANDING 7-2

Understanding Brand Alliances

Brand alliances, which combine two brands in some way, come in all forms.[26] Academic research has explored the effects of co-branding and ingredient branding strategies.

Co-Branding

Park, Jun, and Shocker compare co-brands to the notion of "conceptual combinations" in psychology. A conceptual combination ("apartment dog") consists of a modifying concept, or "modifier" (*apartment*) and a modified concept, or "header" (*dog*). Experimentally, Park and his colleagues explored the different ways that Godiva (associated with expensive, high-calorie boxed chocolates) and Slim-Fast (associated with inexpensive, low-calorie diet food) could hypothetically introduce a chocolate cake mix separately or together through a co-brand.

They found that the co-branded version of the product was better accepted than if either brand attempted to extend individually into the cake mix category. They also found that consumers' impressions of the co-branded concept were driven by the header brand—Slim-Fast chocolate cake mix by Godiva was seen as lower calorie than if the product was called Godiva chocolate cake mix by Slim-Fast; the reverse was true for associations of richness and luxury. Similarly, consumers' impressions of Slim-Fast after exposure to the co-branded concept were more likely to change when it was the header brand than when it was the modifier brand. The findings show how carefully selected brands can be combined to overcome the potential problems of negatively correlated attributes (here, rich taste and low calories).

Simonin and Ruth found that consumers' attitudes toward a brand alliance could influence subsequent impressions of each partner's brands (spillover effects existed), but that these effects also depended on other factors such as product fit or compatibility and brand fit or image congruity. Brands less familiar than their partners contributed less to an alliance but experienced stronger spillover effects than their more familiar partners. Voss and Tansuhaj found that consumer evaluations of an unknown brand from another country were more positive when it was allied with a well-known domestic brand.

Levin and Levin explored the effects of dual branding, which they defined as a marketing strategy in which two brands, usually restaurants, share the same facilities while providing consumers with the opportunity to use either one or both brands. Kumar found that introducing a co-branded extension into a new product category made it less likely that a brand from the new category could turn around and introduce a counterextension into the original product category. LeBar and colleagues found that joint branding helped to increase a brand's perceived differentiation, but also sometimes decreased consumers' perceived esteem for the brand and knowledge about the brand.

Ingredient Branding

Desai and Keller conducted a laboratory experiment to consider how ingredient branding affected consumer acceptance of an initial line extension, as well as the ability of the brand to introduce future category extensions. They studied two particular types of line extensions, defined as brand expansions: (1) *slot filler expansions*, in which the level of one existing product attribute changed (a new type of scent in Tide detergent), and (2) *new attribute expansions*, in which an entirely new attribute or characteristic was added to the product (cough relief liquid added to LifeSavers candy). They examined two types of ingredient branding strategies by branding the target attribute ingredient for the brand expansion with either a new name as a *self-branded ingredient* (Tide with its own EverFresh scented bath soap) or an established, well-respected name as a *co-branded ingredient* (Tide with Irish Spring scented bath soap).

The results indicated that with slot filler expansions, although a co-branded ingredient eased initial acceptance of the expansion, a self-branded ingredient led to more favorable later extension evaluations. With more dissimilar new attribute expansions, however, a co-branded ingredient led to more favorable evaluations of both the initial expansion and the subsequent extension.

Venkatesh and Mahajan derived an analytical model based on bundling and reservation price notions to help formulate optimal pricing and partner selection decisions for branded components. In an experimental application in the context of a university computer store selling 486-class laptop computers, they showed that at the bundle level, an all-brand Compaq PC with Intel 486 commanded a clear price premium over other alternatives. The relative brand strength of the Intel brand, however, was shown to be stronger in some senses than that of the Compaq brand.

Sources: C. Whan Park, Sung Youl Jun, and Allan D. Shocker, "Composite Branding Alliances: An Investigation of Extension and Feedback Effects," *Journal of Marketing Research* (November 1996): 453–467; Bernard L. Simonin and Julie A. Ruth, "Is a Company Known by the Company It Keeps? Assessing the Spillover Effects of Brand Alliances on Consumer Brand Attitudes," *Journal of Marketing Research* 35, no. 2 (1998): 30–42; Piyush Kumar, "The Impact of Cobranding on Customer Evaluation of Brand Counterextensions," *Journal of Marketing* 69 (July 2005): 1–18; Kalpesh Desai and Kevin Lane Keller, "The Effects of Brand Expansions and Ingredient Branding Strategies on Host Brand Extendibility," *Journal of Marketing* 66 (January 2002): 73–93; Mrinal Ghosh and George John, "When Should Original Equipment Manufacturers Use Branded Component Contracts with Suppliers?," *Journal of Marketing Research* 46 (October 2009): 597–611; Alokparna Basu Monga and Loraine Lau-Gesk, "Blending Cobrand Personalities: An Examination of the Complex Self," *Journal of Marketing Research* 44 (August 2007): 389–400.

From a consumer behavior perspective, branded ingredients are often a signal of quality. In a provocative academic research study, Carpenter, Glazer, and Nakamoto found that the inclusion of a branded attribute ("Alpine Class" fill for a down jacket) significantly affected consumer choices even when consumers were explicitly told that the attribute was not relevant to their decision.[28] Clearly, consumers inferred certain quality characteristics as a result of the branded ingredient.

The uniformity and predictability of ingredient brands can reduce risk and reassure consumers. As a result, ingredient brands can become industry standards and consumers will not want to buy a product that does not contain the ingredient. In other words, ingredient brands can become, in effect, a category point-of-parity. Consumers do not necessarily have to know exactly how the ingredient works—just that it adds value.

Ingredient branding has become more prevalent as mature brands seek cost-effective means to differentiate themselves on the one hand, and potential ingredient products seek means to expand their sales opportunities on the other hand. Some companies create their own ingredient brands, such as Chevron with its Techron gasoline additive, Westin with its Heavenly Bed, and Best Buy with its Geek Squad technical support team.[29] To illustrate the range of alternatives in ingredient branding, consider how Singapore Airlines uses both co-branded and self-branded ingredients in their service delivery.

SINGAPORE AIRLINES

In its Suites class of service, Singapore Airlines offers bedding and tableware from Givenchy as well as new chairs hand stitched by "master Italian craftsman" Poltrona Frau. The First Class SkySuites feature leather seats trimmed with Burrwood. The airline offers the Krisworld entertainment system and Givenchy fleece blankets. In the more expensive Suites, first, and business classes, customers can enjoy Bose QuietComfort 2 acoustic noise-canceling headphones (economy flyers get Dolby). For its cuisine, Singapore Airlines's meals are prepared by its International Culinary Panel and premium classes enjoy ethnically branded meals such as Shahi Thali (Suites and first class) and Hanakoireki (business class). All passengers can join the KrisFlyer frequent flyer program.[30]

Singapore Airlines uses a combination of co-branded and self-branded ingredients in branding its services.
Source: Eric Piermont/AFP/Getty Images

Thus, as in this example, one product may contain a number of different branded ingredients. Ingredient brands are not restricted to products and services. For example, through the years, electronics specialty retailer RadioShack has established strategic alliances with Hewlett Packard, Microsoft, RCA, Sprint, Verizon Wireless, and others that let the manufacturers set up kiosks within many of RadioShack's 7,000 U.S. stores. RadioShack itself has set up mobile phone kiosks in almost 1,500 Target stores in the United States, served by Radio Shack's own black-shirted employees and using its own point-of-sale systems.[31]

Advantages and Disadvantages. The pros and cons of ingredient branding are similar to those of co-branding.[32] From the perspective of the firm making and supplying the ingredient, the benefit of branding its products as ingredients is that by creating consumer pull, the firm can generate greater sales at a higher margin. There may also be more stable and broader customer demand and better long-term supplier–buyer relationships. Enhanced revenues may accrue from having two revenue streams—the direct revenue from the cost of the supplied ingredients, as well as possible extra revenue from the royalty rights paid to display the ingredient brand.

From the standpoint of the manufacturer of the host product, the benefit is in leveraging the equity from the ingredient brand to enhance its own brand equity. On the demand side, the host product brands may achieve access to new product categories, different market segments, and more distribution channels than they otherwise could have expected. On the supply side, the host product brands may be able to share some production and development costs with the ingredient supplier.

Ingredient branding is not without its risks and costs. The costs of a supporting marketing communication program can be high—advertising to sales ratios for consumer products often surpass 5 percent—and many suppliers are relatively inexperienced at designing mass media communications that may have to contend with inattentive consumers and noncooperative middlemen. As with co-branding, there is a loss of control, because marketing programs for the supplier and manufacturer may have different objectives and thus may send different signals to consumers.

Some manufacturers may be reluctant to become supplier dependent or may not believe that the branded ingredient adds value, resulting in a loss of possible accounts. Manufacturers may resent any consumer confusion about what is the "real brand" if the branded ingredient gains too much equity. Finally, the sustainability of the competitive advantage may be somewhat uncertain, because brands that follow may benefit from consumers' increased understanding of the role of the ingredient. As a result, follower brands may have to communicate not so much the importance of the ingredient as why their particular ingredient brand is better than the pioneer or other brands.

Guidelines. Ingredient branding programs build brand equity in many of the same ways that conventional branding programs do. Branding Brief 7-3 describes ingredient branding efforts at DuPont, which has successfully introduced a number of such brands.

Turning to the other side of the equation, what are some specific requirements for successful ingredient branding? In general, ingredient branding must accomplish four tasks:

1. Consumers must first perceive that the ingredient matters to the performance and success of the end product. Ideally, this intrinsic value is visible or easily experienced.
2. Consumers must then be convinced that not all ingredient brands are the same and that the ingredient is superior. Ideally, the ingredient would have an innovation or some other substantial advantage over existing alternatives.
3. A distinctive symbol or logo must be designed to clearly signal to consumers that the host product contains the ingredient. Ideally, the symbol or logo would function essentially as a "seal" and would be simple and versatile—it could appear virtually anywhere—and credibly communicate quality and confidence to consumers.
4. Finally, a coordinated push and pull program must be put into place such that consumers understand the importance and advantages of the branded ingredient. Often this will include consumer advertising and promotions and, sometimes in collaboration with manufacturers, retail merchandising and promotion programs. As part of the push strategy, some communication efforts may also need to be devoted to gaining the cooperation and support of manufacturers or other channel members.

LICENSING

Licensing creates contractual arrangements whereby firms can use the names, logos, characters, and so forth of other brands to market their own brands for some fixed fee. Essentially, a firm is "renting" another brand to contribute to the brand equity of its own product. Because it can be a shortcut means of building brand equity, licensing has gained in popularity in recent years. The top 125 global licensors drove more than $184 billion in sales of licensed products in 2010. Perhaps the champion of licensing is Walt Disney.[33]

BRANDING BRIEF 7-3

Ingredient Branding the DuPont Way

Perhaps one of the most successful ingredient brand marketers of all times is DuPont, which was founded in Delaware as a black-powder manufacturer in 1802 by Frenchman E. I. duPont de Nemours. Over the years, the company introduced a number of innovative products for use in markets ranging from apparel to aerospace. Many of the company's innovations, such as Lycra and Stainmaster fabrics, Teflon coating, and Kevlar fiber, became household names as ingredient brands in consumer products manufactured by many other companies. Although some have been spun off, the company still maintains a healthy roster of consumer products.

Early on, DuPont learned an important branding lesson the hard way. Because the company did not protect the name of its first organic chemical fiber, nylon, it was not trademarkable and became generic. The brands created by DuPont through the years have been components in a wide variety of products that are marketed to make everyday life better, safer, and healthier.

In 2010, DuPont recorded more than $9.5 billion in revenue from new products and applications launched between 2007 and 2010, representing 31 percent of total revenue. These innovations have been the result of the company's massive R&D program ($1.7 billion spent in 2010). DuPont has over 75 R&D facilities globally, including 35 outside the United States. The highest proportion of the R&D budget—approximately 50 percent—is dedicated to agriculture and nutrition, which is currently its fastest-growing business segment.

A key question that DuPont constantly confronts is whether to brand a product as an ingredient brand. To address this question, the firm has traditionally applied several criteria, both quantitative and qualitative.

- On the *quantitative* side, DuPont has a model that estimates the return on investment of promoting a product as an ingredient brand. Inputs to the model include brand resource allocations such as advertising and trade support; outputs relate to favorability ratings and potential sales. The goal of the model is to determine whether branding an ingredient can be financially justified, especially in industrial markets.

- On the *qualitative* side, DuPont assesses how an ingredient brand can help a product's positioning. If competitive

As one of the most successful ingredient brand marketers, DuPont knows the importance of having a strong corporate brand, as reflected in its long-time sponsorship of NASCAR driver Jeff Gordon.
Source: ZUMA Press/Newscom

and consumer analyses reveal that conveying certain associations would boost sales, DuPont is more likely to brand the ingredient. For example, one reason that DuPont launched its stain-resistant carpet fiber under the ingredient brand Stainmaster was that the company felt a "tough" association would be highly valued in the market.

DuPont maintains that an appropriate, effective ingredient branding strategy leads to a number of competitive advantages, such as higher price premiums (often as much as 20 percent), enhanced brand loyalty, and increased bargaining power with other members of the value chain. DuPont employs both push and pull strategies to create its ingredient brands. Consumer advertising creates consumer pull by generating interest in the brand and a willingness to specifically request it. Extensive trade support in the form of co-op advertising, training, and trade promotions creates push by fostering a strong sense of loyalty to DuPont from other members of the value chain. This loyalty helps DuPont negotiate favorable terms from distributors and leads to increased cooperation when new products are introduced.

Sources: Nigel Davis, "DuPont Innovating a Way Out of a Crisis," www.icis.com, 23 June 2009; Kevin Lane Keller, "DuPont: Managing a Corporate Brand," *Best Practice Cases in Branding*, 3rd ed. (Upper Saddle River, NJ: Pearson Prentice Hall, 2008); "2010 DuPont Annual Review," www.dupont.com.

DISNEY CONSUMER PRODUCTS

The Walt Disney Company is recognized as having one of the strongest brands in the world. Much of its success lies in its flourishing television, movie, theme park, and other entertainment ventures. These different vehicles have created a host of well-loved characters and a reputation for quality entertainment. Disney Consumer Products (DCP) is designed to keep the Disney name and characters fresh in the consumer's mind through various lines of business: Disney Toys, Disney Fashion & Home, Disney Food, Health & Beauty, and Disney Stationery.

DCP has a long history, which can be traced back to 1929 when Walt Disney licensed the image of Mickey Mouse for use on a children's writing tablet. Disney started licensing its characters for toys made by Mattel in the 1950s. Disney Consumer Products (DCP) ranked as the number-one global licensor in 2010, reporting $28.6 billion in retail sales of licensed merchandise worldwide. DCP's *Toy Story* franchise, driven by box office success and merchandise demand for *Toy Story 3*, was the most dominant property of the year at retail, generating $2.4 billion in retail sales. The timeless Mickey Mouse and Winnie the Pooh franchises combine to make up roughly a third of the division's total revenue. Much newer franchises—Disney Princesses and Disney Fairies launched in 2000 and 2002 respectively—already combine to make almost a quarter of DCP's total revenue. Artists in Disney Licensing's Creative Resources department work closely with manufacturers on all aspects of product marketing, including design, prototyping, manufacturing, packaging, and advertising. Disney's acquisition of Marvel Entertainment in August 2009 for $4 billion, a wholly owned subsidiary, opened a new world of comic book characters and popular film adaptations such as *Thor* and *Captain America* in 2011 and *The Avengers* and *The Amazing Spider-Man* in 2012. Marvel produced worldwide retail sales of licensed merchandise for 2010 of $5.6 billion.

Popular films such as *Toy Story* have helped to create a multibillion-dollar licensing business for Disney Consumer Products.

Source: ZUMA Press/Newscom

Entertainment licensing has certainly become big business in recent years. Successful licensors include movie titles and logos like *Harry Potter, Transformers,* and *Spider-Man*; comic strip characters such as *Garfield* and *Peanuts* characters; and television and cartoon characters from *Sesame Street, The Simpsons, SpongeBob SquarePants,* and others. Every summer, marketers spend millions of dollars in movie tie-ins as marketers look for the next blockbuster franchise.

Licensing can be quite lucrative for the licensor. It has long been an important business strategy for designer apparel and accessories, for example. Designers such as Donna Karan, Calvin Klein, Pierre Cardin, and others command large royalties for the right to use their name on a variety of merchandise such as clothing, belts, ties, and luggage. Over the course of three decades, Ralph Lauren became the world's most successful designer, creating a $5-billion-dollar business licensing his Ralph Lauren, Double RL, and Polo brands to many different kinds of products. Everyone seems to get into the act with licensing. Sports licensing of clothing apparel and other products has grown considerably to become a multibillion-dollar business.

Licensing can also provide legal protection for trademarks. Licensing the brand for use in certain product categories prevents other firms or potential competitors from legally using the brand name to enter those categories. For example, Coca-Cola entered licensing agreements in a number of product areas, including radios, glassware, toy trucks, and clothes, in part as legal protection. As it turns out, its licensing program has been so successful the company now sells a variety of products bearing the Coca-Cola name directly to consumers.

Licensing certainly carries risks, too. A trademark can become overexposed if marketers adopt a saturation policy. Consumers do not necessarily know the motivation or marketing arrangements behind a product and can become confused or even angry if the brand is licensed to a product that seemingly bears no relation. Moreover, if the product fails to live up to consumer expectations, the brand name could become tarnished.

Guidelines

One danger in licensing is that manufacturers can get caught up in licensing a brand that might be popular at the moment but is only a fad and produces short-lived sales. Because of multiple licensing arrangements, licensed entities can also easily become overexposed and wear out quickly as a result. Sales of Izod Lacoste, with its familiar alligator crest, peaked at $450 million in 1982 but dwindled to an estimated $150 million in shirt sales in 1990 after the brand became overexposed and discount priced.[34] Subsequently purchased by Phillips-Van Heusen, the brand has been making a comeback as the result of more careful marketing.

Firms are taking a number of steps to protect themselves in their licensing agreements, especially those firms that have little brand equity of their own and rely on the image of their licensor.[35] For example, firms are obtaining licensing rights to a broad range of licensed entities—some of which are more durable—to diversify their risk. Licensees are developing unique new products and sales and marketing approaches so that their sales are not merely a function of the popularity of other brands. Some firms conduct marketing research to ensure the proper match of product and licensed entity or to provide more precise sales forecasts for effective inventory management.

Corporate trademark licensing is the licensing of company names, logos, or brands for use on various, often unrelated products. For example, in the depths of a financial crisis a number of years ago, Harley-Davidson chose to license its name—synonymous with motorcycles and a certain lifestyle—to a polo shirt, a gold ring, and even a wine cooler. Once it regained firmer financial footing, the company developed a much more concerted strategy, meeting with much success as described in its 10K report in 2011.

> The Company creates an awareness of the Harley-Davidson brand among its customers and the non-riding public through a wide range of products for enthusiasts by licensing the name "Harley-Davidson" and other trademarks owned by the Company. The Company's licensed products include t-shirts, vehicles and vehicle accessories, jewelry, small leather goods, toys and numerous other products. Although the majority of licensing activity occurs in the U.S., the Company continues to expand these activities in international markets. Royalty revenues from licensing, included in Motorcycles segment net revenue, were $39.8 million, $38.3 million and $45.4 million in 2010, 2009 and 2008, respectively.

Other seemingly narrowly focused brands such as Jeep, Caterpillar, Deere, and Jack Daniels have also entered a broad portfolio of licensing arrangements.

In licensing their corporate trademarks, firms may have different motivations, including generating extra revenues and profits, protecting their trademarks, increasing their brand exposure, or enhancing their brand image. The profit appeal can be enticing because there are no inventory expenses, accounts receivables, or manufacturing expenses. In an average deal, a licensee pays a corporation a royalty of about 5 percent of the wholesale price of each product, although the actual percentage can vary from 2 percent to 10 percent. As noted in Chapter 5, some firms now sell licensed merchandise through their own catalogs.

As in any co-branded arrangement, however, the risk is that the product will not live up to the reputation established by the brand. Inappropriate licensing can dilute brand meaning with consumers and marketing focus within the organization. Consumers don't care about the financial arrangements behind a particular product or service; if the brand is used, the brand promise must be upheld.

CELEBRITY ENDORSEMENT

Using well-known and admired people to promote products is a widespread phenomenon with a long marketing history. Even the late U.S. president Ronald Reagan was a celebrity endorser, pitching several different products, including cigarettes, during his acting days. Some U.S. actors or actresses who refuse to endorse products in the United States are willing to do so in overseas markets. For example, rugged American actors Arnold Schwarzenegger (Bwain drink), Brad Pitt (Softbank), and Harrison Ford (Kirin beer) have all done ads for brands in Japan. Although Millward Brown estimates that celebrities show up in 15 percent of U.S. ads, that number jumps to 24 percent for India and 45 percent for Taiwan.[36]

The rationale behind these strategies is that a famous person can draw attention to a brand and shape the perceptions of the brand, by virtue of the inferences that consumers make based on the knowledge they have about the famous person. The hope is that the celebrities' fans will also become fans of their products or services. The celebrity must be well enough known to improve awareness, image, and responses for the brand.

In particular, a celebrity endorser should have a high level of visibility and a rich set of potentially useful associations, judgments, and feelings.[37] Ideally, he or she would be credible in terms of expertise, trustworthiness, and likability or attractiveness, as well as having specific associations that carry potential product relevance. One person who has done a remarkable job building and leveraging a highly credible brand is Oprah Winfrey.

OPRAH WINFREY

One of the most successful and valuable person brands in the world is Oprah Winfrey—*Forbes* magazine estimates her net worth at a staggering $2.7 billion. Overcoming a childhood of poverty and other personal challenges and driven by her own motto, "Live Your Best Life," she has parlayed her relentless optimism and drive for self-improvement into an entertainment franchise covering all media markets and corners of the globe. Her empathetic connection with her audience has created a marketing gold mine in the process. At its peak, her television talk show was seen by 12 million viewers daily in the United States alone, while also airing in 144 countries around the world. Her Harpo production company, shrewdly formed early in her show's syndication life, has also launched hit spin-off shows for some of her most of popular guests such as Dr. Phil, Dr. Oz, Rachel Ray, and design expert Nate Berkus. Her magazine, *O, the Oprah Magazine*, published by Hearst, has a circulation of roughly 2.5 million. Winfrey has produced Broadway shows, feature films, and television movies and has her own satellite radio station. After ending the 25-year run of her broadcast television show on May 25, 2011, she turned her energy to her new cable channel, OWN. Her sincere nature and credibility with her audience has made any product or brand endorsements instant hits. "Oprah's Book Club" launched many best-sellers and is credited by some with saving the publishing industry. Her annual infomercial-like "Favorite Things" show transformed sometimes low-profile brands into overnight successes. When Greenburg Smoked Turkey from Tyler, TX got a 42-second mention on one such show, it received $1 million in orders for the upcoming holiday season.[38]

One of the most valuable person brands in the world is Oprah Winfrey, shown here at a promotional filming of her show at the Sydney Opera House in Australia.
Source: George Burns//AFP/Getty Images/Newscom

Potential Problems

Despite the potential upside of linking a celebrity endorser to a brand, there are a number of potential problems. First, celebrity endorsers can endorse so many products that they lack any specific product meaning or are seen as opportunistic or insincere. Although

NFL star quarterback Peyton Manning has parlayed success on the football field and his "Aw shucks" personality into endorsement contracts for a number of different brands—DirectTV, Gatorade, MasterCard, Oreo, Reebok, and Sprint, among others—he runs the risk of overexposure, especially given that so many of his ads run concurrently with the football season.[39]

Second, there must be a reasonable match between the celebrity and the product.[40] Many endorsements would seem to fail this test. Despite being featured in their ads, NBA star Kobe Bryant and race car driver Danica Patrick would seem to have no logical connection to Turkish Airlines and Go Daddy Internet domain registrar and Web hosting company, respectively. Some better matches in recent years include comedian Bill Cosby's playful tone for Jell-O and champion cyclist and cancer-survivor Lance Armstrong for Bristol-Myers Squibb's cancer medicines.

Third, celebrity endorsers can get in trouble or lose popularity, diminishing their marketing value to the brand, or just fail to live up to expectations. Most companies conduct background checks before signing celebs, but that doesn't guard against bad behavior in the future. A number of spokespeople over the years have run into legal difficulties, personal problems, or controversies of some form that diminished their marketing value, such as O.J. Simpson, Martha Stewart, and Michael Jackson.[41] Figure 7-5 is a rogue's gallery of high-profile celebrity endorsement mishaps. To broaden the appeal and reduce the risks of linking to one celebrity, some marketers have begun to employ several different celebrities or even celebrities who are deceased and therefore a known commodity—dead celebrities were estimated to generate $2.25 billion in revenue in North America in 2009.[42]

Celebrity & Brand	Mishap
James Garner and Cybil Shepherd for Beef	Both actors were dropped as spokespersons after Garner had heart trouble and Shepherd reported in a magazine interview that she did not eat red meat.
Martina Hingis for Sergio Tacchini	In the midst of a 5-year contract, the one-time women's tennis champ sued the Italian maker of her tennis shoes for $35 million after she claimed they gave her a chronic foot injury.
Michael Vick for Nike, Reebok, Upper Deck, and others	When a dog-fighting conviction led to a prison sentence, pro football star Vick reportedly lost over $50 million in endorsement contracts after being dropped by companies.
Whoopi Goldberg for SlimFast	The comic actress was dropped as an endorser after she made critical comments about then-President George W. Bush during a Democratic fundraiser.
Kobe Bryant for McDonald's, Sprite, and Nutella	The basketball star lost millions in endorsements after being charged with sexual assault.
Kate Moss for H&M, Pepsi, Burberry, and Chanel	The model was dropped as spokesperson by a number of companies after tabloid newspapers showed her using cocaine.
Michael Phelps for Kellogg	The Olympic champion swimmer was dropped after being photographed smoking marijuana.
Tiger Woods for Accenture, Gillette, Gatorade, and AT&T	The golf champion lost numerous endorsements as reports of his serial infidelity emerged.

FIGURE 7-5 Celebrity Endorsement Mishaps

Sources: Based on Jack Trout, "Celebs Who Un-Sell Products," *Forbes*, 13 September 2007; Mike Chapman, "Celebrities Moving Products? Not So Much," *Adweek*, 8 June 2011; Steve McKee, "The Trouble With Celebrity Endorsements," *Bloomberg BusinessWeek*, 14 November 2008.

Fourth, many consumers feel celebrities are doing the endorsement only for the money and do not necessarily believe in or even use the brand. Even worse, some feel the fees celebrities earn to appear in commercials add a significant and unnecessary cost to the brand. In reality, celebrities often do not come cheap and can demand literally millions of dollars for endorsements.

Celebrities also can be difficult to work with and may not willingly follow the marketing direction of the brand. Tennis player Andre Agassi tried Nike's patience when—at the same time he was advertising for Nike—he appeared in commercials for the Canon Rebel camera. In these ads, he looked into the camera and proclaimed "Image Is Everything"—the antithesis of the "authentic athletic performance" positioning that has been the foundation of Nike's brand equity. Winning the French Open, however, put Agassi back in Nike's good graces.

Finally, as noted in Chapter 6, celebrities may distract attention from the brand in ads so that consumers notice the stars but have trouble remembering the advertised brand. PepsiCo decided to drop singers Beyoncé Knowles and Britney Spears from high-profile ad campaigns when they felt the Pepsi brand did not get the same promotion boost from the campaign that the stars were getting. The firm decided to put the spotlight back on the product with its endorsement-free follow-up, "Pepsi. It's the Cola." After signing Celine Dion for a three-year, $14 million deal, Chrysler dumped her in the first year when commercials featuring Dion driving a Pacifica produced great sales for the singer, but not for the car!

Brands can become overreliant on a celebrity. Founder and chairman Dave Thomas was an effective pitchman for his Wendy's restaurant chain because of his down-home, unpretentious, folksy style and strong product focus. Recognized by over 90 percent of adult consumers, he appeared in hundreds of commercials over a 12-year period until his death in early 2002.[43] The brand struggled for years afterward, however, trying to find the right advertising approach to replace him.

Guidelines

To overcome these problems, marketers should strategically evaluate, select, and use celebrity spokespeople. First, choose a well-known and well-defined celebrity whose associations are relevant to the brand and likely to be transferable. For example, despite false starts for his retirement, Brett Favre's rugged, down-to-earth persona fits well for the backyard football games in the "Real. Comfortable. Jeans." Wrangler ads.

Then, there must be a logical fit between the brand and the person.[44] To reduce confusion or dilution, the celebrity ideally will not be linked to a number of other brands or be overexposed. Popular Hong Kong actor Jackie Chan has been criticized for endorsing too many

Although Jackie Chan has endorsed a wide range of products, his track record has been mixed.

Source: Toshifumi Kitamura/AFP/Getty Images/Newscom

products—from electric bikes to antivirus software to frozen dumplings and more. Unfortunately, many of the products he has endorsed have run into problems—a shampoo was alleged to contain carcinogens, an auto repair school was hit by a diploma scandal, and makers of both video compact discs and an educational computer went out of business. As one Chinese editorial commented: "He has become the coolest spokesperson in history—a man who can destroy anything!"[45]

Third, the advertising and communication program should use the celebrity in a creative fashion that highlights the relevant associations and encourages their transfer. Dennis Haysbert has played the president of the United States in the TV series *24* and adopts a similarly stately, reassuring tone for his spokesperson role in the "You're in Good Hands" ads for Allstate insurance. William Shatner's humorous Priceline ads take a completely different tack and take advantage of the actor's self-deprecating, campy wit to draw attention to its discount message.

Finally, marketing research must help identify potential endorser candidates and facilitate the development of the proper marketing program, as well as track its effectiveness.

Q SCORES

Marketing Evaluations conducts surveys to determine "Q Scores" for a broad range of entertainers and other public figures like TV performers, news and sports anchors, and reporters, athletes, and models. Each performer is rated on the following scale: "One of My Favorites," "Very Good," "Good," "Fair," "Poor," and "Never Seen or Heard of Before." The sum of the "Favorite" through "Poor" ratings is "Total Familiar." Because some performers are not very well known, a positive Q Score is a ratio of the "One of My Favorites" rating to the "Total Familiar" rating and a negative Q Score is a ratio of the sum of "Poor" and "Fair" ratings to the "Total Familiar" rating. Q Scores thus capture how appealing or unappealing a public figure is among those who do know him or her. Q Scores will move around, depending on the fame and fortune of the subject. In January 2010, in a poll of the general population, 24 percent of people viewed NBA star Lebron James in a positive light, compared to 22 percent who had a negative opinion. These were the highest scores ever seen by Marketing Evaluations for an athlete—the average sports personality has a 15 percent positive score and 24 percent negative score. After James's "decision" and his messy departure from Cleveland to play for the Miami Heat, a September 2010 poll revealed that only 14 percent of the population saw him in a positive light, while 39 percent had a negative opinion, the steepest decline for a sports personality in the 45-year history of Q Scores. By February 2011, the positive and negative scores had improved to 17 percent and 33 percent—progress, but still a far cry from his peak. James's tarnished image certainly did not immediately affect his endorsement portfolio, however, which was estimated to total over $48 million in 2011, landing him in the Top 10 of *Forbes* magazine's Celebrity 100 ranking of power.[46]

Celebrities themselves must manage their own "brands" to ensure that they provide value. By the same token, anyone with a public profile, even if just within the company in which he or she works, should consider how to best manage his or her brand image.[47] Branding Brief 7-4 offers some thoughts about how personal branding works in general and how it differs from more traditional branding for products and services.

SPORTING, CULTURAL, OR OTHER EVENTS

As Chapter 6 described, events have their own set of associations that may become linked to a sponsoring brand under certain conditions. Sponsored events can contribute to brand equity by becoming associated to the brand and improving brand awareness, adding new associations, or improving the strength, favorability, and uniqueness of existing associations.[48]

The main means by which an event can transfer associations is credibility. A brand may seem more likable or perhaps even trustworthy or expert by virtue of becoming linked to an event. The extent to which this transfer takes place will depend on which events are selected and how the sponsorship program is designed and integrated into the entire marketing program to build brand equity. Brand Focus 7.0 discusses sponsorship strategies for the Olympic Games. Pepsico is one of the leading companies making major investments in sports marketing.

BRANDING BRIEF 7-4

Managing a Person Brand

Although many branding principles apply, there are some important differences between a person brand and a product or service brand. Here are some of the main differences to consider:

1. Person brands are more abstract and intangible but have very rich imagery.

2. Person brands are more difficult to compare because competition is very broad and often not easily relatable.

3. Person brands can be difficult to control and keep consistent. A person brand can have many facets, and many interactions and experiences with many different people over time, all adding to the complexity of brand management.

4. People may adopt different personas for different situations (such as work vs. play) that will affect the dimensionality of their brand.

5. Repositioning a person brand can be tricky because people like to categorize other people, but it is not impossible. Actors/entertainers such as Mark Wahlberg and Madonna have changed their images, whereas others such as Sylvester Stallone and Jim Carrey have found it more difficult.

As guidelines for managing a person brand, consider the following recommendations:

1. A person brand must manage brand elements. Names can be shortened and nicknames adopted. Even though a person does not necessarily have a logo or symbol, appearance in terms of dress and look can still help to create a brand identity.

2. A person brand is built by the words and actions of that person. Given the intangible nature of a person brand, however, it is hard to form judgments at one point in time—repeated exposures are usually necessary.

3. A person brand can borrow brand equity through secondary associations such as geographical regions, schools and universities, and the like. A person brand can employ strategic partnerships with other people to enhance brand equity.

4. Credibility is key for a person brand. Trustworthiness is important, but so is likability and appeal in terms of eliciting more emotional responses.

5. Person brands can use multiple media channels—online is especially useful in terms of social networking and community building.

6. A person brand must stay fresh and relevant and properly innovate and invest in key person traits.

7. A person brand should consider optimal positioning in terms of brand potential and associated points-of-parity and points-of-difference. A clear and compelling point-of-difference is especially important in terms of carving out a unique identity in the workplace or market.

8. Brand architecture is simpler for a person brand—sub-branding is less relevant—but brand extensions can occur, for instance when a person adds to his or her perceived capabilities.

9. A person brand must live up to the brand promise at all times. Reputations and brands are built over years but can be harmed or even destroyed in days. One slip can be devastating and difficult to recover from.

10. A person brand must be a self-advocate and help to shape impressions.

PEPSICO

Pepsico has been a major sponsor of sports all over the world for a number of years. In the United States, it has official alliances with the National Football League, Major League Baseball, National Hockey League and Major League Soccer; it is title sponsor of the AST (Mountain) Dew Action Sports Tour; and it has naming rights at the Pepsi Center in Denver (an indoor sports facility that is home to the NHL's Avalanche and NBA's Nuggets, among others). With NASCAR auto racing, Pepsi is the title sponsor of the Pepsi Max 400 and has numerous pouring rights at various tracks. Pepsi also has endorsement deals with many athletes in these sports and has spent over $100 million in the course of a given year running ads—often featuring these athletes—in network sports programming. Overseas, other sports take center stage, such as cricket in India, Pakistan, and other Commonwealth countries. Pepsi takes a strategic approach to its sports marketing. Sports marketing played a prominent role in the Pepsi Refresh Project, a cause-based program offering Pepsi grants for worthy ideas to benefit communities throughout the United States. Pepsi also elevated the importance of Pepsi Max in its sport sponsorships in 2010 to help boost the struggling brand. Pepsi Max became the new face of the brand's NFL sponsorship, and the Pepsi 400 NASCAR race was renamed as Pepsi Max 400.[49]

Pepsi Max has become an NFL sponsor as means to boost its appeal.
Source: Warren Little/Getty Images

THIRD-PARTY SOURCES

Finally, marketers can create secondary associations in a number of different ways by linking the brand to various third-party sources. For example, the *Good Housekeeping* seal has been seen as a mark of quality for decades, offering product replacement or refunds for defective products for up to two years from purchase. Endorsements from leading magazines like *PC* magazine, organizations like the American Dental Association, acknowledged experts such as film critic Roger Ebert, or carefully selected Elite critics of the online Yelp consumer review site can obviously improve perceptions of and attitudes toward brands.

Third-party sources can be especially credible sources. As a result, marketers often feature them in advertising campaigns and selling efforts. J.D. Power and Associates' well-publicized Customer Satisfaction Index helped to cultivate an image of quality for Japanese automakers in the 1980s, with a corresponding adverse impact on the quality image of their U.S. rivals. In the 1990s, they began to rank quality in other industries, such as airlines, credit cards, rental cars, and phone service, and top-rated brands in these categories began to feature their awards in ad campaigns. Grey Goose vodka cleverly employed a third-party endorsement to drive sales.

GREY GOOSE

Sidney Frank first found success in the liquor industry with a little-known German liqueur, Jagermeister, which he began to market in the United States in the mid-1980s and drove to 700,000 annual cases in sales and market leadership by 2001. Turning his sights to the high-margin super-premium market, Frank decided to create a French vodka that would use water from the Cognac region and be distilled by the makers of Cardin brandy. Branded as "Grey Goose," the product had distinctive packaging— a must in the category—with a bottle taller than competitors that combined clear and frosted glass with a cutaway of geese in flight and the French flag. But perhaps the most important factor in the brand's eventual success was a taste-test result from the Beverage Testing Institute that ranked Grey Goose as the number-one imported vodka. Fueled by exhaustive advertising that trumpeted its big win as "the World's Best-Tasting Vodka," Grey Goose became a top seller. Frank eventually sold Grey Goose Vodka brand to Bacardi in 2004 for a stunning $2.2 billion. Its success continues to this day. Despite the fact that vodka has been characterized as essentially odorless and tasteless, it is consistently ranked as the top brand of vodka brand in consumer loyalty polls on the basis of image, versatility, and smoothness.[50]

Distinctive packaging and taste-test awards have propelled Grey Goose to a leadership position in the vodka category.

Source: AP Photo/PRNewsFoto/GREY GOOSE(R) Vodka

With the growth of social networks and blogs, a whole range of new online opinion leaders are emerging that can influence the fate of brands. Some come with credentials from traditional businesses or organizations. For example, *Wall Street Journal* technology columnist Walter Mossberg and colleague Kara Swisher have created their own successful technology-focused Web site, www.allthingsd.com. The pair also run an influential annual technology conference, "D: All Things Digital," where top technology leaders such as Bill Gates and Steve Jobs have appeared in unscripted interviews.

Other opinion leaders gain influence in different ways through a sequence of events. Justine Ezarik (aka iJustine) had begun "lifecasting" her activities on the Internet, but she really gained fame in August 2007 after posting a viral video of the 300-page AT&T bill she received for her first-generation iPhone. The attention she received for her role in persuading AT&T to change its billing policy—it began to provide usage summaries instead—was the first step in developing a significant YouTube presence. Her videos have since been seen hundreds of millions of times, and she has developed partnerships with companies such as GE, Intel, and Mattel, which value her credibility.[51]

REVIEW

This chapter considered the process by which other entities can be leveraged to create secondary associations. These other entities include source factors such as the company that makes a product, where the product is made, and where it is purchased, as well as related people, places, or things. When they link the brand to other entities with their own set of associations, consumers may expect that some of these same associations also characterize the brand.

Thus, independent of how a product is branded, the nature of the product itself, and its supporting marketing program, marketers can create brand equity by "borrowing" it from other sources. Creating secondary associations in this fashion may be quite important if the corresponding brand associations are deficient in some way. Secondary associations may be especially valuable as a means to link favorable brand associations that can serve as points-of-parity or to create unique brand associations that can serve as points-of-difference in positioning a brand.

Eight different ways to leverage secondary associations to build brand equity are linking the brand to (1) the company making the product; (2) the country or some other geographic location in which the product originates; (3) retailers or other channel members that sell the product; (4) other brands, including ingredient brands; (5) licensed characters; (6) famous spokespeople or endorsers; (7) events; and (8) third-party sources.

In general, the extent to which any of these entities can be leveraged as a source of equity depends on consumer knowledge of the entity and how easily the appropriate associations or responses to the entity transfer to the brand. Overall credibility or attitudinal dimensions may be more likely to transfer than specific attribute and benefit associations, although the latter can be transferred, too. Linking the brand to other entities, however, is not without risk. Marketers give up some control, and managing the transfer process so that only the relevant secondary associations become linked to the brand may be a challenge.

DISCUSSION QUESTIONS

1. The Boeing Company makes a number of different types of aircraft for the commercial airline industry, for example, the 727, 747, 757, 767, 777, and now the 787 jet models. Is there any way for Boeing to adopt an ingredient branding strategy with its jets? How? What would be the pros and cons?
2. After winning major championships, star players often complain about their lack of endorsement offers. Similarly, after every Olympics, a number of medal-winning athletes lament their lack of commercial recognition. From a branding perspective, how would you respond to the complaints of these athletes?
3. Think of the country in which you live. What image might it have with consumers in other countries? Are there certain brands or products that are highly effective in leveraging that image in global markets?
4. Which retailers have the strongest image and equity in your mind? Think about the brands they sell. Do they contribute to the equity of the retailer? Conversely, how does that retailer's image help the image of the brands it sells?
5. Pick a brand. Evaluate how it leverages secondary associations. Can you think of any ways that the brand could more effectively leverage secondary brand associations?

BRAND FOCUS 7.0

Going for Corporate Gold at the Olympics

Competition at the Olympics is not restricted to just the athletes. A number of corporate sponsors also vie to maximize the return on their sponsorship dollars. Corporate sponsorship is a significant part of the business side of the Olympics and contributes almost one-third of the revenue of the International Olympic Committee (IOC). Countries themselves vie for the rights to host the Games. Rio de Janeiro, Brazil, won the rights to host the 2016 Games over Chicago, Madrid, and Tokyo.

Corporate Sponsorship

Corporate sponsorship of the Olympics exploded with the commercial success of the 1984 Summer Games in Los Angeles. At that time, many international sponsors, like Fuji, achieved positive image building and increased market share.

Eleven companies have paid for the highest level of Olympic sponsorship (TOP)—estimated to cost in the neighborhood of $80 million—for exclusive worldwide marketing rights to the Summer, Winter, and Youth Olympic Games: Acer, Atos Origin, Coca-Cola, Dow, GE, McDonald's, Omega, Panasonic, Procter & Gamble, Samsung, and Visa.[52] In addition to exclusive worldwide marketing opportunities, partners receive:

- Use of all Olympic imagery, as well as appropriate Olympic designations on products
- Hospitality opportunities at the Olympic Games
- Direct advertising and promotional opportunities, including preferential access to Olympic broadcast advertising
- On-site concessions/franchise and product sale/showcase opportunities
- Ambush marketing protection (see below)
- Acknowledgement of their support though a broad Olympic sponsorship recognition program

Other tiers at lower levels of sponsorship also exist. For example, London 2012 Official Partners included Adidas, BP, British Airways, BT, EDF Energy, Lloyds TSB, and Nortel.

Besides direct expenditures, firms spent hundreds of millions more on related marketing efforts. A long-time Olympics supporter since the 1976 Summer Games in Montreal, McDonald's always runs a number of promotional campaigns to tie in with its sponsorship. Building on prior McDonald's kids' programs at the Olympic Games in Beijing and Vancouver, McDonald's "Champions of Play for the Olympic Games" brought up to 200 children from around the world to London (each with a guardian) as part of a new global program to encourage a balanced approach to nutrition and activity for children.[53]

Participating McDonald's countries initiated grassroots activities for children ages 6–10.

"For the first time ever, McDonald's Champions of Play for the Olympic Games will tour and play with athletes at the actual Olympic venues," said Kevin Newell, McDonald's global chief brand officer. "This will be an unforgettable, inspiring moment for our champions, along with attending the Games, seeing McDonald's Chef demonstrations, taking an exclusive tour of the Olympic Village dining area, visiting London's cultural sites, and making new friends."

McDonald's Olympic Games program also targeted families across the globe through:

- A Web site offering balanced eating and fun play facts, and challenges.

- Digital engagement—allowing kids everywhere to track their physical activities online.

- Special Happy Meal packaging featuring information and tips on balanced eating and fun play.

McDonald's also selected 2,000 of its top-performing restaurant staff from the UK and around the world—the largest Olympic team ever assembled—to serve the world's top athletes, coaches, spectators, media, and officials at the Games. In 2012, these brand ambassadors had the opportunity to meet Olympic athletes, attend competitions, participate in their own sports and activities in the Royal Parks, visit cultural sites in London, and socialize with their international peers.

A relative newcomer beginning its sponsorship with the Vancouver Olympics in 2010, Procter & Gamble launched its "Proud Sponsor of Mums (or Moms)" campaign that it extended throughout P&G's sponsorship of the London 2012 Olympic Games. P&G's Olympic Games partnership is the first to cover multiple brands under one sponsor and will span the next 10 years, more than 30 product categories, and 205 National Olympic Committees to raise awareness of and reward mothers' contributions globally.[54]

GE, Coca-Cola, Dow, Omega, and Visa have also extended their sponsorship through 2020. In announcing GE's sponsorship, Jeff Immelt, chairman and CEO, stated, "The Olympic Games provide a unique opportunity to showcase our innovative technologies and services. Hosting a successful Olympic Games is a transformational opportunity for every host city. We are committed to working with the IOC and the local organizing committees to deliver world-class infrastructure solutions and a sustainable legacy to future generations."

GE works closely with host countries, cities, and organizing committees to provide infrastructure solutions for Olympic Games venues including power, water treatment, transportation and security, and to supply hospitals with ultrasound and MRI equipment to help doctors treat athletes.[55]

Sponsorship ROI

Although several firms have long-term relationships and commitments with the Olympics, in recent years other long-time sponsors have cut their ties. Kodak ended over a century of sponsorship after the Beijing Olympic Games, and General Motors ended its decades-long support at that time too. Other TOP partners that chose not to renew after the 2008 Games included Johnson & Johnson, Lenovo, and Manulife.

Although many factors affect the decision to engage in or renew an Olympic sponsorship, its marketing impact is certainly widely debated. For example, one survey of 1,500 Chinese city residents just prior to the 2008 Beijing Games revealed that only 15 percent could name two of the 12 global sponsors, and just 40 percent could name one: Coca-Cola. After virtually every Olympic Games, surveys show that many spectators at the Games and even avid viewers of the broadcasts mistakenly indentify a nonsponsoring company as an official sponsor.[56]

Ambush Marketing

In some cases, sponsorship confusion may be due to ***ambush marketing***, in which advertisers attempt to give consumers the false impression they are Olympic sponsors without paying for the right to do so. Nonsponsoring companies attempt to attach themselves to the Games by, for instance, running Olympic-themed ads that publicize other forms of sponsorship like sponsoring a national team, by identifying the brand as an official supplier, or by using current or former Olympians as endorsers.[57]

For the Beijing Games, not only did popular former Chinese gymnastics champion Li Ning light the Olympic cauldron in the opening ceremony, he did so wearing shoes from the sportswear company he had founded. His actions drew tremendous attention to the Li Ning line while the official athletic sponsor, Adidas, which had spent millions for its rights, could only sit and watch. To improve the marketing effectiveness of sponsorship, the Olympic Committee has declared that it will vigorously fight ambush marketing. It has reduced the number of sponsors to avoid clutter.[58]

Containing ambush marketing requires much diligence. In the 2010 Winter Olympics in Vancouver, Canada, free Ocean Spray Cranberry Cocktail drinks were handed out to commuters at the Games as a promotion despite Coca-Cola's being the official beverage sponsor. Bank of Nova Scotia launched a navigational mobile application to help people get around the Games while Royal Bank of Canada was the official banking sponsor, and Subway ran an advertising campaign featuring U.S. Olympic swim champion Michael Phelps although McDonald's was the official restaurant of the Olympics. In each case, the IOC warned the offending company of employing ambush marketing tactics.[59]

Beijing 2008 Summer Games

Every Olympic Games presents special opportunities for host countries and sponsoring companies. The 2008 Summer Games in Beijing held special appeal for some advertisers because the Games represented a connection to the burgeoning Chinese market. General Electric began its first global campaign revolving around the Beijing Games in 2005. GE chose the Olympics to position the company as global and innovative to Chinese consumers.

UPS also chose the Beijing games to strengthen its brand presence in China. UPS was a global Olympic sponsor in 1996, 1998, and 2000 but then dropped out of the Games after 2000, saying its brand awareness goals had been achieved. But in 2005, UPS announced it would rejoin the Olympics for 2008, this time in a limited deal that allowed the company to use the Olympic logo for marketing in China only—not in the United States. International and local sponsors were estimated to have spent a total of $1 billion on the Beijing Olympics, aided partly by the nationalist spirit that drove some Chinese companies to sponsor the Games.

London 2012 Summer Games

Every Olympic Games also presents the opportunity to learn from past successes and mistakes and to run an event that will benefit athletes, spectators, viewers, and sponsors alike. Recognizing the important financial contribution of sponsorship, the London Games were supported by the British government's introduction of extensive antiambush legislation. Banned were activities such as sky-writing, flyers, posters, billboards, and projected advertising within 200 meters of any Olympic venue. The government also passed legislation to forbid a variety of words such as "Games," "2012," "Two Thousand and Twelve," and "Twenty Twelve" to be used in combination with words such as, "Gold," "Silver," "Bronze," "London," "Medals," "Sponsor," or "Summer" in an unauthorized manner such that general public would think there was an association with the London Olympics.[60]

Ticket revenue is also critical to the success of the Olympics, so organizers of the London Games also embarked on a multimillion-dollar advertising campaign, "The Greatest Tickets on Earth," in hope of raising £500 million from ticket sales. Twelve ads showcased likely Olympic stars, including local favorites gymnast Beth Twiddle and diver Tom Daley. Over half of all tickets to the most popular events, however, were earmarked for corporate sponsors and their employees or guests.[61]

Outside the country, the government also embarked on a "Visit Britain" and "Visit London" promotional campaign to attract tourists. The campaigns set out strategically to emphasize the "timeless," "dynamic," and "genuine" qualities—based on the people, places, and culture—that define the British brand.[62]

City and Country Effects

Another hotly debated Olympics topic is the value of the payback to the host city, region, and country. Bringing an aggressive new sponsorship approach to the Los Angeles Olympics resulted in those Games being a financial success, but other Games since then have been a mixed bag. However, a number of benefits may be evident for a host country that can be hard to quantify.[63]

One important psychological benefit is civic pride and patriotism for serving as host to such an iconic global sporting event. With a worldwide television audience for two weeks and more, the Games also serve as a huge advertising and public relations opportunity to aid tourism, real estate, and commercial business. Both the 1992 Barcelona and 2000 Sydney Games enjoyed these broad sets of benefits.

Another often-overlooked benefit is the investment in improving infrastructure that often leads up to hosting the Games. Beijing added new subway lines, highways, an airport to ease transportation, and new parks alongside to add to the scenery, providing some badly needed improvements in transportation and quality of life for residents of the city.

Nevertheless, the financial stakes are high, and only careful planning and execution and the right circumstances can result in success for the Olympics host city, region, and country. The 1976 Montreal and 2004 Athens Games, for example, had a much less positive effect on the host countries. It took Montreal almost 30 years to pay back the $2.7 billion in debt it incurred in hosting the Games.

Summary

Olympic sponsorship remains highly controversial. Many corporate sponsors continue to believe that their Olympic sponsorship yields many significant benefits, creating an image of goodwill for their brand, serving as a platform to enhance awareness and communicate messages, and affording numerous opportunities to reward employees and entertain clients. Others view the Games as overly commercialized, despite the measures undertaken by the IOC and USOC to portray the Olympics as wholesome. In any case, the success of Olympic sponsorship—like that of any sports sponsorship—depends in large part on how well it is executed and incorporated into the entire marketing plan.

Notes

1. Kevin Lane Keller, "Brand Synthesis: The Multi-Dimensionality of Brand Knowledge," *Journal of Consumer Research* 29, no. 4 (2003): 595–600.

2. For an examination of lower-level transfer effects, see Claudiu V. Dimofte and Richard F. Yalch, "The Mere Association Effect and Brand Evaluations," *Journal of Consumer Psychology* 21 (2011): 24–37.

3. Louise Story, "Can Burt's Bees Turn Clorox Green?," *New York Times*, 6 January 2008.

4. Heather Landi, "A-B Gets the Golden Egg," *Beverage World*, April 2011.

5. www.sabmiller.com; "Blue Moon to Raise Awareness Through 'Artfully Crafted' Campaign," *The Drum*, 23 June 2011; Brady Walen, "Blue Moon Artfully Crafted Facebook Photo Contest," www.craftedsocialmedia. com, 29 June 2011; Joseph T. Hallinan, "Craft Beers Have Big Breweries Thinking Small," *Wall Street Journal*, 20 November 2006.

6. Jeff Smith, "Reputation Winners and Losers: Highlights from Prophet's 2010–2011 U.S. Reputation Study," white paper, 1 March 2011, www.prophet.com.

7. Wai-Kwan Li and Robert S. Wyer Jr., "The Role of Country of Origin in Product Evaluations: Informational and Standard-of-Comparison Effects," *Journal of Consumer Psychology* 3, no. 2 (1994): 187–212.

8. Tülin Erdem, Joffre Swait, and Ana Valenzuela, "Brands as Signals: A Cross-Country Validation Study," *Journal of Marketing* 70 (January 2006): 34–49; Yuliya Strizhakova, Robin Coulter, and Linda Price. Branding in a Global Marketplace: The Mediating Effects of Quality and Self-Identity Brand Signals," *International Journal of Research in Marketing* 28 (December 2011): 342–351.

9. "Rums of Puerto Rico Uncorks New Ad Campaign," *Caribbean Business*, 17 August 2011; "Rums of Puerto Rico Encourages Consumers to 'Just Think, Puerto Rican Rum,'" *PR Newswire*, 23 February 2011.

10. For a broader discussion of "nation branding," see Philip Kotler, Somkid Jatusriptak, and Suvit Maesincee, *The Marketing of Nations: A Strategic Approach to Building National Wealth* (New York: Free Press, 1997); Wally Olins, "Branding the Nation—The Historical Context," *Journal of Brand Management* 9 (April 2002): 241–248; and for an interesting analysis in the context of Iceland, see Hlynur Gudjonsson, "Nation Branding," *Place Branding* 1, no. 3 (2005): 283–298.

11. For stimulating and enlightening discussion, see www. strengtheningbrandamerica.com.

12. "Global Public Opinion in the Bush Years (2001–2008)," Pew Research Center, 18 December 2008.

13. John A. Quelch and Katherine E. Jocz, "Can Brand Obama Rescue Brand America?," *The Brown Journal of World Affairs*, Fall 2009; "View of U.S. Global Role 'Worse,'" *BBC News*, 23 January 2007; Alex Y. Vergara, "'Brand America'—How U.S. Tourism Plans to Recover Lost Ground," *Philippine Daily Inquirer*, 19 June 2011; Bill Marriott Jr., "America Needs More Tourists," *Fortune*, 1 June 2011.

14. Zeynep Gurhan-Canli and Durairaj Maheswaran, "Cultural Variations in Country of Origin Effects," *Journal of Marketing Research* 37 (August 2000): 309–317.

15. Thomas Mulier, "Clash of the Angry Swiss Watchmakers," *Bloomberg BusinessWeek*, 8 May 2011.

16. Eric Wilson and Michael Barbaro, "Big Names in Retail Fashion Are Trading Teams," *New York Times*, 8 March 2008; Stephanie Rosenbloom, "Liz Claiborne to Be Sold Only at J.C. Penney Stores, *New York Times*, 9 October 2009.

17. Akshay R. Rao and Robert W. Ruekert, "Brand Alliances as Signals of Product Quality," *Sloan Management Review* (Fall 1994): 87–97; Akshay R. Rao, Lu Qu, and Robert W. Ruekert, "Signalling Unobservable Product Quality through Brand Ally," *Journal of Marketing Research* 36, no. 2 (May 1999): 258–268; Mark B. Houston, "Alliance Partner Reputation as a Signal to the Market: Evidence from Bank Loan Alliances," *Corporate Reputation Review* 5 (Winter 2003): 330–342; Henrik Uggla, "The Brand Association Base: A Conceptual Model for Strategically Leveraging Partner Brand Equity," *Journal of Brand Management* 12 (November 2004):105–123.

18. Robin L. Danziger, "Cross Branding with Branded Ingredients: The New Frontier," paper presented at the ARF Fourth Annual Advertising and Promotion Workshop, February 1992.

19. Kim Cleland, "Multimarketer Melange an Increasingly Tasty Option on the Store Shelf," *Advertising Age*, 2 May 1994, S-10.

20. E. J. Schultz, "How Kraft's Lunchable Is Evolving in the Anti-Obesity Era," *Advertising Age*, 19 April 2011.

21. Ed Lebar, Phil Buehler, Kevin Lane Keller, Monika Sawicka, et al., "Brand Equity Implications of Joint Branding Programs," *Journal of Advertising Research* 45, no. 4 (2005).

22. Nicole L. Votolato and H. Rao Unnava, "Spillover of Negative Information on Brand Alliances," *Journal of Consumer Psychology* 16, no. 2 (2006): 196–202.

23. Ed Lebar, Phil Buehler, Kevin Lane Keller, Monika Sawicka, Zeynep Aksehirli, and Keith Richey, "Brand Equity Implications of Joint Branding Programs," *Journal of Advertising Research* 45, no. 4 (2005): 413–425; Tansev Geylani, J. Jeffrey Inman, and Frenkel Ter Hofstede, "Image Reinforcement or Impairment: The Effects of Co-Branding on Attribute Uncertainty," *Marketing Science*, 27 (July–August 2008): 730–744.

24. For general background, see Akshay R. Rao, "Strategic Brand Alliances," *Journal of Brand Management* 5, no. 2 (1997): 111–119; Akshay R. Rao, L. Qu, and Robert W. Ruekert, "Signaling Unobservable Product Quality through a Brand Ally," *Journal of Marketing Research* (May 1999): 258–268; Allen D. Shocker, Raj K. Srivastava, and Robert W. Ruekert, "Challenges and Opportunities Facing Brand Management: An Introduction to the Special Issue," *Journal of Marketing Research* 31 (May 1994): 149–158; Tom Blackett and Bob Boad, *Co-Branding—The Science of Alliance* (London: Palgrave MacMillan, 1999).

25. Kevin Helliker, "Can Wristwatch Whiz Switch Swatch Cachet to an Automobile?" *Wall Street Journal*, 4 March 1994, A1; Beth Demain Reigber, "DaimlerChrysler Smarts as BMW Mini Looms," *Dow Jones Newswire*, 20 June 2001; Chris Reiter, "U.S. Sales of Daimler's Smart Brand Minicar Plummet," *Washington Post*, 11 January 2010; "2012 Smart Fortwo Electric Drive Hits 75 mph, Whizzes to 60 in 13 Seconds," www.autoblog.com, 16 August 2011.

26. For a sports marketing application, see Yupin Yang, Mengze Shi, and Avi Goldfarb, "Estimating the Value of Brand Alliances in Professional Team Sports," *Marketing Science* 28 (November–December 2009): 1095–1111.

27. Philip Kotler and Waldemar Pfoertsch, *Ingredient Branding: Making the Invisible Visible* (New York: Springer, 2010); John Quelch, "How to Brand an Ingredient," www.blogs.hbr.org, 8 October 2007.

28. Gregory S. Carpenter, Rashi Glazer, and Kent Nakamoto, "Meaningful Brands from Meaningless Differentiation: The Dependence on Irrelevant Attributes," *Journal of Marketing Research* (August 1994): 339–350. See also Christina Brown and Gregory Carpenter, "Why Is the Trivial Important? A Reasons-Based Account for the Effects of Trivial Attributes on Choice," *Journal of Consumer Research*, 26 (March 2000): 372–385; Susan M. Broniarczyk and Andrew D. Gershoff, "The Reciprocal Effects of Brand Equity and Trivial Attributes," *Journal of Marketing Research* 41 (2003): 161–175.

29. Martin Bishop, "Ingredient Branding, Or, Finding Your Nemo," www.landor.com, July 2010.

30. www.singaporeair.com; Bettina Wassener, "Airlines in Asia Resist the No-Frills Trend," *New York Times*, 24 December 2009.

31. Kit R. Roane, "Stores Within Stores: Retail's Savior?," www.money.cnn.com, 24 January 2011. See also, Kinshuk Jerath and Z. John Zhang, "Store Within a Store," *Journal of Marketing Research* 47 (August 2010), 748–763.

32. Philip Kotler and Waldemar Pfoertsch, *Ingredient Branding: Making the Invisible Visible* (New York: Springer, 2010); Donald G. Norris, "Ingredient Branding: A Strategy Option with Multiple Beneficiaries," *Journal of Consumer Marketing* 9, no. 3 (1992): 19–31.

33. "Top 125 Global Licensors," *License*, May 2011; "Disney's 2011 Investor Conference: Disney Consumer Products," www.disney.com/investors, 17 February 2011; Bruce Orwall, "Disney's Magic Transformation?" *Wall Street Journal*, 4 October 2000.

34. Teri Agins, "Izod Lacoste Gets Restyled and Repriced," *Wall Street Journal*, 22 July 1991, B1.

35. Udayan Gupta, "Licensees Learn What's in a Pop-Culture Name: Risk," *Wall Street Journal*, 8 August 1991, B2.

36. Cate Doty, "For Celebrities, Ads Made Abroad Shed Some Stigma," *New York Times*, 4 February 2008; Dean Crutchfield, "Celebrity Endorsements Still Push Product," *Advertising Age*, 22 September 2010.

37. Grant McCracken, "Who Is the Celebrity Endorsor? Cultural Foundations of the Endorsement Process," *Journal of Consumer Research* 16 (December 1989): 310–321.

38. Susan Berfield, "Marketing Lessons from Brand Oprah," *Bloomberg BusinessWeek*, 29 May 2011; Patricia Sellers, "Oprah's Next Act: Full Version, *Fortune*, 30 September 2010; Dorothy Pomerantz, "Lady Gaga Tops Celebrity 100 List," *Forbes*, 18 May 2011.

39. "Manning's Roster of Endorsements," *USA Today*, 16 November 2006; Curtis Eichelberger, "Colts Victory May Bring Manning $3 Million More in Endorsements," www.bloomberg.com, 5 February 2010.

40. Shekhar Misra and Sharon E. Beatty, "Celebrity Spokesperson and Brand Congruence," *Journal of Business Research* 21 (1990): 159–173.

41. Eugenia Levenson, "Risky Business," *Fortune*, 17 October 2005; Steve McKee, "The Trouble with Celebrity Endorsements," *Bloomberg BusinessWeek*, 14 November 2008.

42. Jonathan Keehner and Lauren Coleman-Lochner, "In Death, Endorsements Are a Girl's Best Friend," *Bloomberg BusinessWeek*, 23 January 2011; "I See Dead People," *Adweek Media*, 14 March 2011.

43. John Grossman, "Dave Thomas' Recipe for Success," *Sky*, November 2000, 103–107; Bruce Horvitz, "Wendy's Icon Back at Work," *USA Today*, 31 March 1997, B1–B2.

44. Misra and Beatty, "Celebrity Spokesperson and Brand Congruence."

45. David Pierson, "If Jackie Chan Says It's Good—Well, Get a Second Opinion, *Los Angeles Times*, 23 August 2010; for a more charitable view of Jackie Chan, see Ron Gluckman, "Kicking It Up for Kids," *Forbes*, 18 July 2011.

46. Darren Rovell, "LeBron's Q Score Takes Huge Hit," www.cnbc.com, 14 September 2010; Darren Rovell, "New Q Scores Show Vick, LeBron Image Recovery, No Change on Tiger," www.cnbc.com, 21 March 2011; Kurt Badenhausen, "LeBron Looks to Conquer the World," *Forbes*, 18 May 2011.

47. Tom Peters, "A Brand Called You," *Fast Company*, 31 August 1997; Dorie Clark, "Reinventing Your Personal Brand," *Harvard Business Review*, March 2011, 78–81.

48. For general background and in-depth research on a number of sponsorship issues, consult the *Journal of Sponsorship*, a Henry Stewart publication.

49. Barry Janoff with Ralph Santana, "Pepsi Makes Heavy Play in Sports Marketing Field," *Brandweek*, 3 March 2008; Terry Lefton, Pepsi's Sport Sponsorship Muscle Behind Max, *Street & Smith's SportsBusiness Journal*, 27 September 2010; Barry Janoff, "Cause and Effect: Pepsi Is Using Sports to Drive Refresh Project, but Is It Scoring with Consumers?" www.nysportsjournalism.com, 17 June 2010.

50. David Kiley, "World's Best Vodka? It's Anybody's Guess," *Bloomberg BusinessWeek*, 23 May 2008; "Vodka" *Adweek*, 1 July 2010; "Grey Goose Vodka Continues to Soar in the U.S. Despite the Economy," Reuters, 6 April 2009.

51. Mark Borden, "The *New* Influentials," *Fast Company*, November 2010, 125–131.

52. "Olympic Marketing Fact File," 2011 edition, www.olympic.org.

53. www.aboutmcdonalds.com; "McDonald's, Shawn Johnson Offer Invitations to Olympics," *QSR*, 30 September 2009.

54. www.pg.com; Michelle Warren, "P&G to Give Moms an Olympic Salute," *Marketing*, 5 August 2011.

55. "GE Extends Olympic Sponsorship Through 2020," *BusinessWire*, 29 June 2011.

56. Frederik Balfour and Reena Jana, "Are Olympic Sponsorships Worth It?," *Bloomberg BusinessWeek*, 31 July 2008; "Kodak to End 100-Year Olympic Sponsorship Tie," *Marketing*, 17 October 2007.

57. "Ambush Marketing: Dirty Play at the Olympics?," www.brandstoke.com, 17 February 2010; David Wolf, "Let the Ambush Games Begin," *Advertising Age*, 11 August 2008.

58. John Grady, Steve McKelvey, and Matthew J. Bernthal, "From Beijing 2008 to London 2012: Examining Event-Specific Olympic Legislation Vis-à-Vis the Rights and Interests of Stakeholders," *Journal of Sponsorship* 3 (February 2010): 144–156; Nicholas Burton and Simon Chadwick, "Ambush Marketing in Sport: An Analysis of Sponsorship Protection Means and Counter-Ambush Measures," *Journal of Sponsorship* 2 (September 2009): 303–315.

59. Marina Palomba, "Ambush Marketing and the Olympics 2012," *Journal of Sponsorship* 4 (June 2011): 245–252; Dana Ellis, Marie-Eve Gauthier, and Benoit Séguin, "Ambush Marketing, the Olympic and Paralympic Marks Act and Canadian Sports Organisations: Awareness, Perceptions and Impacts," *Journal of Sponsorship* 4 (June 2011): 253–271.

60. Kirsten Toft, "United Kingdom: Ambush Marketing and the London Olympics 2012," *Newswire*, 28 August 2009; Jacquelin Magnay, "London 2012 Olympics: Government Unveils Plans to Ban Ambush Marketing and Bolster Games Security," *Telegraph*, 7 March 2011; "Ambush Marketing & the London Olympics," www.slingshotsponsorship.com, 14 February 2011.

61. "Olympic Advertising Aims to Sell £500m in Tickets," *Marketing News*, 21 March 2011; Sam Greenhill, "The Freebie Olympics: Corporate Fat Cats Get More Than Half of Top Games Tickets," *Daily Mail*, 3 June 2011; www.visitbritain.org.

62. www.visitbritain.org.

63. "Do Olympic Host Cities Ever Win?," *New York Times*, 2 October 2009; "The Economic Impact of the Olympic Games," *PricewaterhouseCoopers European Economic Outlook*, June 2004.

Developing a Brand Equity Measurement and Management System

8

Learning Objectives

After reading this chapter, you should be able to

1. Describe the new accountability in terms of ROMI.

2. Outline the two steps in conducting a brand audit.

3. Describe how to design, conduct, and interpret a tracking study.

4. Identify the steps in implementing a brand equity management system.

Marketers must adopt research methods and procedures so they understand when, where, how, and why consumers buy.

Source: David Noton Photography/Alamy

Preview

The previous six chapters, which made up Parts II and III of the text, described various strategies and approaches to building brand equity. In the next three chapters, which make up Part IV, we take a detailed look at what consumers know and feel about and act toward brands and how marketers can develop measurement procedures to assess how well their brands are doing.

The customer-based brand equity (CBBE) concept provides guidance about how we can measure brand equity. Given that customer-based brand equity is the differential effect that knowledge about the brand has on customer response to the marketing of that brand, two basic approaches to measuring brand equity present themselves. An *indirect approach* can assess potential sources of customer-based brand equity by identifying and tracking consumers' brand knowledge—all the thoughts, feelings, images, perceptions, and beliefs linked to the brand. A *direct approach*, on the other hand, can assess the actual impact of brand knowledge on consumer response to different aspects of the marketing program.

The two approaches are complementary, and marketers can and should use both. In other words, for brand equity to provide a useful strategic function and guide marketing decisions, marketers must fully understand the sources of brand equity, how they affect outcomes of interest such as sales, and how these sources and outcomes change, if at all, over time. Chapter 3 provided a framework for conceptualizing consumers' brand knowledge structures. Chapter 9 uses this information and reviews research methods to measure sources of brand equity and the customer mind-set. Chapter 10 reviews research methods to measure outcomes, that is, the various benefits that may result from creating these sources of brand equity.

Before we get into specifics of measurement, this chapter offers some big-picture perspectives of how to think about brand equity measurement and management. Specifically, we'll consider how to develop and implement a brand equity measurement system. A *brand equity measurement system* is a set of research procedures designed to provide marketers with timely, accurate, and actionable information about brands so they can make the best possible tactical decisions in the short run and strategic decisions in the long run. The goal is to achieve a full understanding of the sources and outcomes of brand equity and to be able to relate the two as much as possible.

The ideal brand equity measurement system would provide complete, up-to-date, and relevant information about the brand and its competitors to the right decision makers at the right time within the organization. After providing some context about the heightened need for marketing accountability, we'll look in detail at three steps toward achieving that ideal—conducting brand audits, designing brand tracking studies, and establishing a brand equity management system.

THE NEW ACCOUNTABILITY

Although senior managers at many firms have embraced the marketing concept and the importance of brands, they often struggle with questions such as: How strong is our brand? How can we ensure that our marketing activities create value? How do we measure that value?

Virtually every marketing dollar spent today must be justified as both effective and efficient in terms of *return of marketing investment* (ROMI).[1] This increased accountability has forced marketers to address tough challenges and develop new measurement approaches.

Complicating matters is that, depending on the particular industry or category, some observers believe up to 70 percent (or even more) of marketing expenditures may be devoted to programs and activities that improve brand equity but cannot be linked to short-term incremental profits.[2] Measuring the long-term value of marketing in terms of both its full short-term and long-term impact on consumers is thus crucial for accurately assessing return on investment.

Clearly marketers need new tools and procedures that clarify and justify the value of their expenditures, beyond ROMI measures tied to short-term changes in sales. In Chapter 3, we introduced the brand resonance model and brand value chain, structured means to understand how consumers build strong bonds with brands and how marketers can assess the success of their branding efforts. In the remainder of this chapter, we offer several additional concepts and perspectives to help in that pursuit.

CONDUCTING BRAND AUDITS

To learn how consumers think, feel, and act toward brands and products so the company can make informed strategic positioning decisions, marketers should first conduct a brand audit. A *brand audit* is a comprehensive examination of a brand to discover its sources of brand equity. In accounting, an audit is a systematic inspection by an outside firm of accounting records including analyses, tests, and confirmations.[3] The outcome is an assessment of the firm's financial health in the form of a report.

A similar concept has been suggested for marketing. A *marketing audit* is a "comprehensive, systematic, independent, and periodic examination of a company's—or business unit's—marketing environment, objectives, strategies, and activities with a view of determining problem areas and opportunities and recommending a plan of action to improve the company's marketing performance."[4] The process is a three-step procedure in which the first step is agreement on objectives, scope, and approach; the second is data collection; and the third and final step is report preparation and presentation. This is an internally, company-focused exercise to make sure marketing operations are efficient and effective.

A brand audit, on the other hand, is a more externally, consumer-focused exercise to assess the health of the brand, uncover its sources of brand equity, and suggest ways to improve and leverage its equity. A brand audit requires understanding the sources of brand equity from the perspective of both the firm and the consumer. From the perspective of the firm, what products and services are currently being offered to consumers, and how they are being marketed and branded? From the perspective of the consumer, what deeply held perceptions and beliefs create the true meaning of brands and products?

The brand audit can set strategic direction for the brand, and management should conduct one whenever important shifts in strategic direction are likely.[5] Are the current sources of brand equity satisfactory? Do certain brand associations need to be added, subtracted, or just strengthened? What brand opportunities exist and what potential challenges exist for brand equity? With answers to these questions, management can put a marketing program into place to maximize sales and long-term brand equity.

Conducting brand audits on a regular basis, such as during the annual planning cycle, allows marketers to keep their fingers on the pulse of their brands. Brand audits are thus particularly useful background for managers as they set up their marketing plans and can have profound implications on brands' strategic direction and resulting performance.

DOMINO'S PIZZA

In late 2009, Domino's was a struggling business in a declining market. Pizza sales were slumping as consumers defected to healthier and fresher dining options at one end or to less expensive burger or sandwich options at the other end. Caught in the middle, Domino's also found its heritage in "speed" and "best in delivery" becoming less important; even worse, it was undermining consumer's perceptions of the brand's taste, the number-one driver of choice in the pizza category. To address the problem, Domino's decided to conduct a detailed brand audit with extensive qualitative and quantitative research. Surveys, focus groups, intercept interviews, social media conversations, and ethnographic research generated a number of key insights. The taste problem was severe—some consumers bluntly said that Domino's tasted more like the box than the pizza. Research also revealed that consumers felt betrayed by a company they felt they no longer knew. A focus on impersonal, efficient service meant that in consumers' minds, there was no Domino's kitchens, no chefs, not even ingredients. Consumers were skeptical of "new and improved" claims and felt companies never admitted they were wrong. Based on these and other insights, Domino's began its brand comeback. Step one—new recipes for crust, sauce, and cheese that resulted in substantially better taste-test scores. Next, Domino's decided not to run from criticism and launched the "Oh Yes We Did" campaign. Using traditional TV and print media and extensive online components, the company made clear that it had listened and responded by creating a better pizza. Documentary-type filming showed Domino's CEO and other executives observing the original consumer research and describing how they took it to heart. Surprise visits were made to harsh critics from the focus groups, who tried the new pizza on camera and enthusiastically praised it. Domino's authentic, genuine approach paid off. Consumer perceptions dramatically improved and growth in sales in 2010 far exceeded the competitors'.[6]

A thorough, insightful brand audit helped to convince Domino's they needed to confront their perceived flaws head on.

Source: Domino's Pizza LLC

The brand audit consists of two steps: the brand inventory and the brand exploratory. We'll discuss each in turn. Brand Focus 8.0 illustrates a sample brand audit using the Rolex brand as an example.

Brand Inventory

The purpose of the *brand inventory* is to provide a current, comprehensive profile of how all the products and services sold by a company are marketed and branded. Profiling each product or service requires marketers to catalogue the following in both visual and written form for each product or service sold: the names, logos, symbols, characters, packaging, slogans, or other trademarks used; the inherent product attributes or characteristics of the brand; the pricing, communications, and distribution policies; and any other relevant marketing activity related to the brand.

Often firms set up a "war room" where all the various marketing activities and programs can be displayed or accessed. Visual and verbal information help to provide a clearer picture. Figure 8-1 shows a wall that software pioneer Red Hat created of all its various ads, brochures, and other marketing materials. Managers were pleasantly surprised when they saw

FIGURE 8-1

Red Hat Brand Wall

Source: Photo courtesy of Red Hat, Inc.

how consistent all the various items were in form, look, and content, although they were left scratching their heads as to why the Red Hat office in Australia had created branded underwear as a promotional gift. Needless to say, the "tighty whities" were dropped after being deemed off-brand.[7]

The outcome of the brand inventory should be an accurate, comprehensive, and up-to-date profile of how all the products and services are branded in terms of which brand elements are employed and how, and the nature of the supporting marketing program. Marketers should also profile competitive brands in as much detail as possible to determine points-of-parity and points-of-difference.

Rationale. The brand inventory is a valuable first step for several reasons. First, it helps to suggest what consumers' current perceptions may be based on. Consumer associations are typically rooted in the *intended* meaning of the brand elements attached to them—but not always. The brand inventory therefore provides useful information for interpreting follow-up research such as the brand exploratory we discuss next.

Although the brand inventory is primarily a descriptive exercise, it can supply some useful analysis too, and initial insights into how brand equity may be better managed. For example, marketers can assess the consistency of all the different products or services sharing a brand name. Are the different brand elements used on a consistent basis, or are there many different versions of the brand name, logo, and so forth for the same product—perhaps for no obvious reason—depending on which geographic market it is being sold in, which market segment it is being targeted to, and so forth? Similarly, are the supporting marketing programs logical and consistent across related brands?

As firms expand their products geographically and extend them into other categories, deviations—sometimes significant in nature—commonly emerge in brand appearance and marketing. A thorough brand inventory should be able to reveal the extent of brand consistency. At the same time, a brand inventory can reveal a lack of perceived differences among different products sharing the brand name—for example, as a result of line extensions—that are designed to differ on one or more key dimensions. Creating sub-brands with distinct positions is often a marketing priority, and a brand inventory may help to uncover undesirable redundancy and overlap that could lead to consumer confusion or retailer resistance.

Brand Exploratory

Although the supply-side view revealed by the brand inventory is useful, actual consumer perceptions, of course, may not necessarily reflect those the marketer intended. Thus, the second step of the brand audit is to provide detailed information about what consumers actually think of the brand by means of the **brand exploratory**. The brand exploratory is research directed to understanding what consumers think and feel about the brand and act toward it in order to better understand sources of brand equity as well as any possible barriers.

Preliminary Activities. Several preliminary activities are useful for the brand exploratory. First, in many cases, a number of prior research studies may exist and be relevant. It is important to dig through company archives to uncover reports that may have been buried, and perhaps even long forgotten, but that contain insights and answers to a number of important questions or suggest new questions that may still need to be posed.

Second, it is also useful to interview internal personnel to gain an understanding of their beliefs about consumer perceptions for the brand and competitive brands. Past and current marketing managers may be able to share some wisdom not necessarily captured in prior research reports. The diversity of opinion that typically emerges from these internal interviews serves several functions, increasing the likelihood that useful insights or ideas will be generated, as well as pointing out any inconsistencies or misconceptions that may exist internally for the brand.

Although these preliminary activities are useful, additional research is often required to better understand how customers shop for and use different brands and what they think and feel about them. To allow marketers to cover a broad range of issues and to pursue some in greater depth, the brand exploratory often employs qualitative research techniques as a first step, as summarized in Figure 8-2, followed by more focused and definitive survey-based quantitative research.

Free association	Day/Behavior reconstruction
Adjective ratings and checklists	Photo/Written journal
Confessional interviews	Participatory design
Projective techniques	Consumer-led problem solving
Photo sorts	Real-life experimenting
Archetypal research	Collaging and drawing
Bubble drawings	Consumer shadowing
Store telling	Consumer–product interaction
Personification exercises	Video observation
Role playing	
Metaphor elicitation*	

*ZMET trademark

FIGURE 8-2

Summary of Qualitative Techniques

Interpreting Qualitative Research.   There are a wide variety of qualitative research techniques. Marketers must carefully consider which ones to employ.

Criteria.   Levy identifies three criteria by which we can classify and judge any qualitative research technique: direction, depth, and diversity.[8] For example, any projective research technique varies in terms of the nature of the stimulus information (is it related to the person or the brand?), the extent to which responses are superficial and concrete as opposed to deeper and more abstract (and thus requiring more interpretation), and the way the information relates to information gathered by other projective techniques.

In Figure 8-2, the tasks at the top of the left-hand list ask very specific questions whose answers may be easier to interpret. The tasks on the bottom of the list ask questions that are much richer but also harder to interpret. Tasks on the top of the right-hand list are elaborate exercises that consumers undertake themselves and that may be either specific or broadly directed. Tasks at the bottom of the right-hand list consist of direct observation of consumers as they engage in various behaviors.

According to Levy, the more specific the question, the narrower the range of information given by the respondent. When the stimulus information in the question is open-ended and responses are freer or less constrained, the respondent tends to give more information. The more abstract and symbolic the research technique, however, the more important it is to follow up with probes and other questions that explicitly reveal the motivation and reasons behind consumers' responses.

Ideally, qualitative research conducted as part of the brand exploratory should vary in direction and depth as well as in technique. The challenge is to provide accurate interpretation—going beyond what consumers explicitly state to determine what they implicitly mean. Chapter 9 reviews how to best conduct qualitative research.

Mental Maps and Core Brand Associations.   One useful outcome of qualitative research is a mental map. A *mental map* accurately portrays in detail all salient brand associations and responses for a particular target market. One of the simplest means to get consumers to create a mental map is to ask them for their top-of-mind brand associations ("When you think of this brand, what comes to mind?"). The brand resonance pyramid from Chapter 3 helps to highlight some of the types of associations and responses that may emerge from the creation of a mental map.

It is sometimes useful to group brand associations into related categories with descriptive labels. *Core brand associations* are those abstract associations (attributes and benefits) that characterize the 5–10 most important aspects or dimensions of a brand. They can serve as the basis of brand positioning in terms of how they create points-of-parity and points-of-difference. For example, in response to a Nike brand probe, consumers may list LeBron James, Tiger Woods, Roger Federer, or Lance Armstrong, whom we could call "top athletes." The challenge is to include all relevant associations while making sure each is as distinct as possible. Figure 8-3 displays a hypothetical mental map and some core brand associations for MTV.

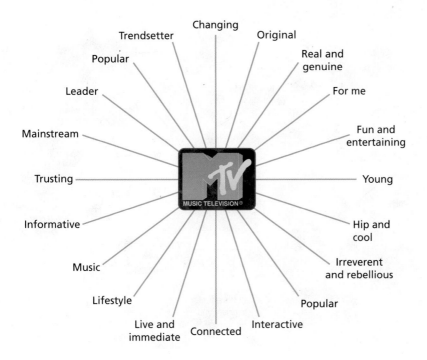

FIGURE 8-3a

Classic MTV Mental Map

Source: MTV logo, MCT/Newscom

Music
What's hot and what's new

Credibility
Expert, trusting, reality

Personality
Irreverent, hip, cool

Accessibility
Relevant, for everyone

Interactivity
Connected and participatory

Community
Shared experience (literally and talk value)

Modern
Hip, cool

Spontaneity
Up-to the-minute, immediate

Originality
Genuine, creative

Fluidity
Always changing and evolving

FIGURE 8-3b

Possible MTV Core Brand Associations

A related methodology, brand concept maps (BCM), elicits brand association networks (brand maps) from consumers and aggregates individual maps into a consensus map.[9] This approach structures the brand elicitation stage of identifying brand associations by providing survey respondents with a set of brand associations used in the mapping stage. The mapping stage is also structured and has respondents use the provided set of brand associations to build an individual brand map that shows how brand associations are linked to each other and to the brand, as well as how strong these linkages are. Finally, the aggregation stage is also structured and analyzes individual brand maps step by step, uncovering the common thinking involved. Figure 8-4 displays a brand concept map for the Mayo Clinic (the subject of Branding Brief 8-2) provided by a sample of patients.

One goal from qualitative, as well as quantitative, research in the brand exploratory is a clear, comprehensive profile of the target market. As part of that process, many firms are literally creating personas to capture their views as to the target market, as summarized in The Science of Branding 8-1.

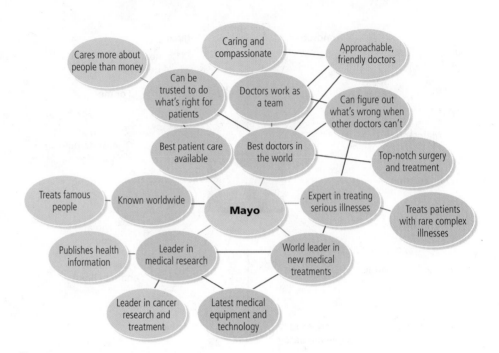

FIGURE 8-4

Sample Mayo Clinic
Brand Concept Map

Conducting Quantitative Research.   Qualitative research is suggestive, but a more definitive assessment of the depth and breadth of brand awareness and the strength, favorability, and uniqueness of brand associations often requires a quantitative phase of research.

The guidelines for the quantitative phase of the exploratory are relatively straightforward. Marketers should assess all potentially salient associations identified by the qualitative research phase according to their strength, favorability, and uniqueness. They should examine both specific brand beliefs and overall attitudes and behaviors to reveal potential sources and outcomes of brand equity. And they should assess the depth and breadth of brand awareness by employing various cues. Typically, marketers will also need to conduct similar types of research for competitors to better understand their sources of brand equity and how they compare with the target brand.

Much of the above discussion of qualitative and quantitative measures has concentrated on associations to the brand name—for example, what do consumers think about the brand when given its name as a probe? Marketers should study other brand elements in the brand exploratory as well, because they may trigger other meanings and facets of the brand.

For instance, we can ask consumers what inferences they make about the brand on the basis of the product packaging, logo, or other attribute alone, such as, "What would you think about the brand just on the basis of its packaging?" We can explore specific aspects of the brand elements—for example, the label on the package or the shape of the package itself—to uncover their role in creating brand associations and thus sources of brand equity. We should also determine which of these elements most effectively represents and symbolizes the brand as a whole.

Brand Positioning and the Supporting Marketing Program

The brand exploratory should uncover the current knowledge structures for the core brand and its competitors, as well as determining the desired brand awareness and brand image and points-of-parity and points-of-difference. Moving from the current brand image to the desired brand image typically means adding new associations, strengthening existing ones, or weakening or eliminating undesirable ones in the minds of consumers according to the guidelines outlined in Chapter 2.

John Roberts, one of Australia's top marketing academics, sees the challenge in achieving the ideal positioning for a brand as being able to achieve congruence among four key considerations: (1) what customers currently believe about the brand (and thus find credible), (2) what customers will value in the brand, (3) what the firm is currently saying about the brand, and (4) where the firm would like to take the brand (see Figure 8-5).[10] Because each of the four considerations may suggest or reflect different approaches to positioning, finding a positioning that balances the four considerations as much as possible is key.

A number of different internal management personnel can be part of the planning and positioning process, including brand, marketing research, and production managers, as can relevant outside

THE SCIENCE OF BRANDING 8-1

The Role of Brand Personas

To crystalize all the information and insights they have gained about their target market(s), researchers can employ personas. **Personas** are detailed profiles of one, or perhaps a few, target market consumers. They are often defined in terms of demographic, psychographic, geographic, or other descriptive attitudinal or behavioral information. Researchers may use photos, images, names, or short bios to help convey the particulars of the persona.

The rationale behind personas is to provide exemplars or archetypes of how the target customer looks, acts, and feels that are as true-to-life as possible, to ensure marketers within the organization fully understand and appreciate their target market and therefore incorporate a nuanced target customer point of view in all their marketing decision-making. Personas are fundamentally designed to bring the target consumer to life.

A good brand persona can guide all marketing activities. Burger King's brand persona is a cool, youngish uncle, who—although somewhat older than the chain's early-teens male target—is younger than their parents. The corresponding brand voice appears online, in ads and promotions, and wherever the brand expresses itself.

Although personas can provide a very detailed and accessible perspective on the target market, it can come at a cost. Overly focusing on a narrow slice of the target market can lead to oversimplification and erroneous assumptions about how the target market as a whole thinks, feels, or acts. The more heterogeneity in the target market, the more problematic the use of personas can be.

To overcome the potential problem of overgeneralization, some firms are creating multiple personas to provide a richer tapestry of the target market. There can also be varying levels of personas, such as primary (target consumer), secondary (target consumer with differing needs, targets, goals), and negative (false stereotypes of users).

Burger King adopted a persona as the "cool youngish uncle" to help guide the irreverent tone and personality of its marketing communications.

Source: Charles Harris/AdMedia/Newscom

Sources: Allen P. Adamson, *Brand Digital: Simple Ways Top Brands Succeed in the Digital Age* (New York: Palgrave-MacMillan, 2008); Lisa Sanders, "Major Marketers Get Wise to the Power of Assigning Personas," *Advertising Age*, 9 April 2007, 36; Stephen Herskovitz and Malcolm Crystal, "The Essential Brand Persona: Storytelling and Branding," *Journal of Business Strategy* 31, no. 3 (2010): 21. For additional information on storytelling, see Edward Wachtman and Sheree Johnson, "Discover Your Persuasive Story," *Marketing Management* (March/April 2009): 22–27.

marketing partners like the marketing research suppliers and ad agency team. Once marketers have a good understanding from the brand audit of current brand knowledge structures for their target consumers and have decided on the desired brand knowledge structures for optimal positioning, they may still want to do additional research testing alternative tactical programs to achieve that positioning.

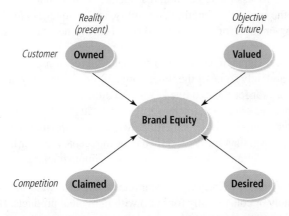

FIGURE 8-5

John Roberts's Brand Positioning Considerations

Source: Used with permission of John Roberts, ANU College of Business and Economics, The Australian National University.

DESIGNING BRAND TRACKING STUDIES

Brand audits are a means to provide in-depth information and insights essential for setting long-term strategic direction for the brand. But to gather information for short-term tactical decisions, marketers will typically collect less detailed brand-related information through on-going tracking studies.

Brand tracking studies collect information from consumers on a routine basis over time, usually through quantitative measures of brand performance on a number of key dimensions that marketers can identify in the brand audit or other means. They apply components from the brand value chain to better understand where, how much, and in what ways brand value is being created, offering invaluable information about how well the brand has achieved its positioning.

As more marketing activity surrounds the brand—as the firm introduces brand extensions or incorporates an increasing variety of communication options in support of the brand—it becomes difficult and expensive to research each one. Regardless of how few or how many changes are made in the marketing program over time, however, marketers need to monitor the health of the brand and its equity so they can make adjustments if necessary.

Tracking studies thus play an important role by providing consistent baseline information to facilitate day-to-day decision making. A good tracking system can help marketers better understand a host of important considerations such as category dynamics, consumer behavior, competitive vulnerabilities and opportunities, and marketing effectiveness and efficiency.

What to Track

Chapter 3 provided a detailed list of potential measures that correspond to the brand resonance model, all of which are candidates for tracking. It is usually necessary to customize tracking surveys, however, to address the specific issues faced by the brand or brands in question. Each brand faces a unique situation that the different types of questions in its tracking survey should reflect.

Product–Brand Tracking.   Tracking an individual branded product requires measuring brand awareness and image, using both recall and recognition measures and moving from more general to more specific questions. Thus, it may make sense to first ask consumers what brands come to mind in certain situations, to next ask for recall of brands on the basis of various product category cues, and to then finish with tests of brand recognition (if necessary).

Moving from general to more specific measures is also a good idea in brand tracking surveys to measure brand image, especially specific perceptions like what consumers think characterizes the brand, and evaluations such as what the brand means to consumers. A number of specific brand associations typically exist for the brand, depending on the richness of consumer knowledge structures, which marketers can track over time.

Given that brands often compete at the augmented product level (see Chapter 1), it is important to measure all associations that may distinguish competing brands. Thus, measures of specific, "lower-level" brand associations should include all potential sources of brand equity such as performance and imagery attributes and functional and emotional benefits. Benefit associations often represent key points-of-parity or points-of-difference, so it is particularly important to track them as well. To better understand any changes in benefit beliefs for a brand, however, marketers may also want to measure the attribute beliefs that underlie those benefit beliefs. In other words, changes in descriptive attribute beliefs may help to explain changes in more evaluative benefit beliefs for a brand.

Marketers should assess those key brand associations that make up the potential sources of brand equity on the basis of strength, favorability, and uniqueness *in that order.* Unless associations are strong enough for consumers to recall them, their favorability does not matter, and unless they are favorable enough to influence consumers' decisions, their uniqueness does not matter. Ideally, marketers will collect measures of all three dimensions, but perhaps for only certain associations and only some of the time; for example, favorability and uniqueness may be measured only once a year for three to five key associations.

At the same time, marketers will track more general, "higher-level" judgments, feelings, and other outcome-related measures. After soliciting their overall opinions, consumers can be asked whether they have changed their attitudes or behavior in recent weeks or months and, if so, why. Branding Brief 8-1 provides an illustrative example of a simple tracking survey for McDonald's.

Corporate or Family Brand Tracking.   Marketers may also want to track the corporate or family brand separately or concurrently (or both) with individual products. Besides the measures

BRANDING BRIEF 8-1

Sample Brand Tracking Survey

Assume McDonald's is interested in designing a short online tracking survey. How might you set it up? Although there are a number of different types of questions, your tracking survey might take the following form.

Introduction: We're conducting a short online survey to gather consumer opinions about quick-service or "fast-food" restaurant chains.

Brand Awareness and Usage

a. What brands of quick-service restaurant chains are you aware of?

b. At which brands of quick-service restaurant chains would you consider eating?

c. Have you eaten in a quick-service restaurant chain in the last week? Which ones?

d. If you were to eat in a quick-service restaurant tomorrow for lunch, which one would you go to?

e. What if you were eating dinner? Where would you go?

f. Finally, what if you were eating breakfast? Where would you go?

g. What are your favorite quick-service restaurant chains?

We want to ask you some general questions about a particular quick-service restaurant chain, McDonald's.

Have you heard of this restaurant? [Establish familiarity.]

Have you eaten at this restaurant? [Establish trial.]

When I say McDonald's, what are the first associations that come to your mind? Anything else? [List all.]

Brand Judgments

We're interested in your overall opinion of McDonald's.

a. How favorable is your attitude toward McDonald's?

b. How well does McDonald's satisfy your needs?

c. How likely would you be to recommend McDonald's to others?

d. How good a value is McDonald's?

e. Is McDonald's worth a premium price?

f. What do you like best about McDonald's? Least?

g. What is most unique about McDonald's?

h. To what extent does McDonald's offer advantages that other similar types of quick-service restaurants cannot?

i. To what extent is McDonald's superior to other brands in the quick-service restaurant category?

j. Compared to other brands in the quick-service restaurant category, how well does McDonald's satisfy your basic needs?

A whole range of questions can be used to understand McDonald's sources and outcomes of brand equity in a tracking survey.
Source: Kim Karpeles/Alamy

We now want to ask you some questions about McDonald's as a company. Please indicate your agreement with the following statements.

McDonald's is . . .

a. Innovative

b. Knowledgeable

c. Trustworthy

d. Likable

e. Concerned about their customers

f. Concerned about society as a whole

g. Likable

h. Admirable

Brand Performance

We now would like to ask some specific questions about McDonald's. Please indicate your agreement with the following statements.

McDonald's . . .

a. Is convenient to eat at

b. Provides quick, efficient service

c. Has clean facilities

d. Is ideal for the whole family

e. Has delicious food

f. Has healthy food

g. Has a varied menu

h. Has friendly, courteous staff

i. Offers fun promotions

j. Has a stylish and attractive look and design

k. Has high-quality food

Brand Imagery

a. To what extent do people you admire and respect eat at McDonald's?

b. How much do you like people who eat at McDonald's?

c. How well do each of the following words describe McDonald's?

   Down-to-earth, honest, daring, up-to-date, reliable, successful, upper class, charming, outdoorsy

d. Is McDonald's a restaurant that you can use in a lot of different meal situations?

e. To what extent does thinking of McDonald's bring back pleasant memories?

f. To what extent do you feel that you grew up with McDonald's?

Brand Feelings

Does McDonald's give you a feeling of . . .

a. Warmth?

b. Fun?

c. Excitement?

d. Sense of security or confidence?

e. Social approval?

f. Self-respect?

Brand Resonance

a. I consider myself loyal to McDonald's.

b. I buy McDonald's whenever I can.

c. I would go out of my way to eat at McDonald's.

d. I really love McDonald's.

e. I would really miss McDonald's if it went away.

f. McDonald's is special to me.

g. McDonald's is more than a product to me.

h. I really identify with people who eat at McDonald's.

i. I feel a deep connection with others who eat at McDonald's.

j. I really like to talk about McDonald's to others.

k. I am always interested in learning more about McDonald's.

l. I would be interested in merchandise with the McDonald's name on it.

m. I am proud to have others know I eat at McDonald's.

n. I like to visit the McDonald's Web site.

o. Compared to other people, I follow news about McDonald's closely.

of corporate credibility we identified in Chapter 2, you can consider other measures of corporate brand associations including the following (illustrated with the GE corporate brand):

- How well managed is GE?
- How easy is it to do business with GE?
- How concerned is GE with its customers?
- How approachable is GE?
- How accessible is GE?
- How much do you like doing business with GE?
- How likely are you to invest in GE stock?
- How would you feel if a good friend accepted employment with GE?

The actual questions should reflect the level and nature of experience your respondents are likely to have had with the company.

When a brand is identified with multiple products, as in a corporate or family branding strategy, one important issue is which particular products the brand reminds consumers of. At the same time, marketers also want to know which particular products are most influential in affecting consumer perceptions about the brand.

To identify these more influential products, ask consumers which products they associate with the brand on an unaided basis ("What products come to mind when you think of the Nike brand?") or an aided basis by listing sub-brand names ("Are you aware of Nike Air Force basketball shoes? Nike Sphere React tennis apparel? Nike Air Max running shoes?"). To better understand the dynamics between the brand and its corresponding products, also ask consumers about their relationship between them ("There are many different products associated with Nike. Which ones are most important to you in formulating your opinion about the brand?").

Global Tracking. If your tracking covers diverse geographic markets—especially in both developing and developed countries—then you may need a broader set of background measures to

We power.
We are making
energy independence a reality.
From cutting-edge, thin-film solar panels
to advanced gas turbines,
we create the high-tech machines that
create over a quarter of the world's energy.
Cleaner energy, renewable energy, more energy.
This is not talking, this is doing.

GE works.
Powering the world.

GE.com/stories   *GE* imagination at work

It is perhaps no coincidence that one of the strongest B-to-B brands—GE—is also one of the best-managed.
Source: Courtesy of GE

put the brand development in those markets in the right perspective. You would not need to collect them frequently, but they could provide useful explanatory information (see Figure 8-6 for some representative measures).

How to Conduct Tracking Studies

Which elements of the brand should you use in tracking studies? In general, marketers use the brand name, but it may also make sense to use a logo or symbol in probing brand structures, especially if these elements can play a visible and important role in the decision process.

You also need to decide whom to track, as well as when and where to track.

Whom to Track.   Tracking often concentrates on current customers, but it can also be rewarding to monitor nonusers of the brand or even of the product category as a whole, for example, to suggest potential segmentation strategies. Marketers can track those customers loyal to the brand against those loyal to other brands, or against those who switch brands. Among current customers, marketers can distinguish between heavy and light users of the brand. Dividing up the market typically requires different questionnaires (or at least sections of a basic questionnaire) to better capture the specific issues of each segment.

It's often useful to closely track other types of customers, too, such as channel members and other intermediaries, to understand their perceptions and actions toward the brand. Of particular interest is their image of the brand and how they feel they can help or hurt its equity. Retailers can answer direct questions such as, "Do you feel that products in your store sell faster if they have [the brand name] on them? Why or why not?" Marketers might also want to track employees such as salespeople, to better understand their beliefs about the brand and how they feel they're contributing to its equity now or could do so in the future. Such tracking may be especially important with service organizations, where employees play profound roles in affecting brand equity.

When and Where to Track.   How often should you collect tracking information? One useful approach for monitoring brand associations is continuous tracking studies, which collect information from consumers continually over time. The advantage of continuous tracking is that it smoothes out aberrations or unusual marketing activities or events like a high profile new digital campaign or an unlikely occurrence in the marketing environment to provide a more representative set of baseline measures.

The frequency of such tracking studies, in general, depends on the frequency of product purchase (marketers typically track durable goods less frequently because they are purchased less

Economic Indicators
Gross domestic product
Interest rates
Unemployment
Average wage
Disposable income
Home ownership and
    housing debt
Exchange rates, share markets,
    and balance of payments

Retail
Total spent in supermarkets
Change year to year
Growth in house brand

Technology
Computer at home
DVR
Access to and use of Internet
Phones
PDA
Microwaves
Television

Personal Attitudes and Values
Confidence
Security
Family
Environment
Traditional values
Foreigners vs. sovereignty

Media Indicators
Media consumption: total time
    spent watching TV, consuming
    other media
Advertising expenditure: total, by
    media and by product category

Demographic Profile
Population profile: age, sex, income,
    household size
Geographic distribution
Ethnic and cultural profile

Other Products and Services
Transport: own car—how many
Best description of car
Motorbike
Home ownership or renting
Domestic trips overnight in last year
International trips in last two years

Attitude to Brands and Shopping
Buy on price
Like to buy new things
Country of origin or manufacture
Prefer to buy things that have been
    advertised
Importance of familiar brands

FIGURE 8-6
Brand Context Measures

often), and on the consumer behavior and marketing activity in the product category. Many companies conduct a certain number of interviews of different consumers every week—or even every day—and assemble the results on a rolling or moving average basis for monthly or quarterly reports.

MILLWARD BROWN

Millward Brown has led the innovation and implementation of tracking studies for the last 30 years. In general, the firm interviews 50–100 people a week and looks at the data with moving averages trended over time. Then it relates specific marketing activity and events to the trend data to understand their impact. Client brands are typically compared to a competitive set to determine relative performance within the product category. Millward Brown collects data on a variety of topics as dictated by the client needs. Modules include brand equity (current and future potential), brand positioning, value perceptions, awareness and response to marketing communications and in-store promotions, consumer profiles, and so on. The survey data is analyzed in conjunction with a variety of other data sources (traditional and social media, search data, sales data, etc.) to provide guidance on improving marketing ROI. Interviews on average run from 15 to 20 minutes in length (on the Web, the phone—both landline and mobile—and in-person in emerging markets). A 20-minute weekly interview with 50 nationally representative consumers can cost roughly $300,000 annually for a typical consumer product, depending on modality.[11]

When the brand has more stable and enduring associations, tracking on a less frequent basis can be enough. Nevertheless, even if the marketing of a brand does not appreciably change over time, competitive entries can change consumer perceptions of the dynamics within the market, making tracking critical. Finally, the stage of the product or brand life cycle will affect your decision about the frequency of tracking: Opinions of consumers in mature markets may not change much, whereas emerging markets may shift quickly and perhaps unpredictably.

How to Interpret Tracking Studies

To yield actionable insights and recommendations, tracking measures must be as reliable and sensitive as possible. One problem with many traditional measures of marketing phenomena is that they don't change much over time. Although this stability may mean the data haven't changed much, it may also be that one or more brand dimensions have changed to some extent but the measures themselves are not sensitive enough to detect subtle shifts. To develop sensitive tracking measures, marketers might need to phrase questions in a comparative way—"compared to other brands, how much . . ." or in terms of time periods—"compared to one month or one year ago, how much . . ."

Another challenge in interpreting tracking studies is deciding on appropriate benchmarks. For example, what is a sufficiently high level of brand awareness? When are brand associations sufficiently strong, favorable, and unique? How positive should brand judgments and feelings be? What are reasonable expectations for the amount of brand resonance? The cutoffs must not be unreasonable and must properly reflect the interests of the intended internal management audience. Appropriately defined and tested targets can help management benchmark against competitors and assess the productivity of brand marketing teams.

Marketers may also have to design these targets with allowance for competitive considerations and the nature of the category. In some low-involvement categories like, say, lightbulbs, it may be difficult to carve out a distinct image, unlike the case for higher-involvement products like cars or computers. Marketers must allow for and monitor the number of respondents who indicate they "don't know" or have "no response" to the brand tracking measures: the more of these types of answers collected, the less consumers would seem to care.

One of the most important tasks in conducting brand tracking studies is to identify the determinants of brand equity.[12] Which brand associations actually influence consumer attitudes and behavior and create value for the brand? Marketers must identify the real value drivers for a brand—that is, those tangible and intangible points-of-difference that influence and determine consumers' product and brand choices. Similarly, marketers must identify the marketing activities that have the most effective impact on brand knowledge, especially consumer exposure to advertising and other communication mix elements.

Carefully monitoring and relating key sources and outcome measures of brand equity should help to address these issues. The brand resonance and brand value chain models suggest many possible links and paths to explore for their impact on brand equity. (Chapters 9 and 10 discuss several measures in more detail.)

ESTABLISHING A BRAND EQUITY MANAGEMENT SYSTEM

Brand tracking studies, as well as brand audits, can provide a huge reservoir of information about how best to build and measure brand equity. To get the most value from these research efforts, firms need proper internal structures and procedures to capitalize on the usefulness of the brand equity concept and the information they collect about it. Although a brand equity measurement system does not ensure that managers will always make "good" decisions about the brand, it should increase the likelihood they do and, if nothing else, decrease the likelihood of "bad" decisions.

Embracing the concept of branding and brand equity, many firms constantly review how they can best factor it into the organization. Interestingly, perhaps one of the biggest threats to brand equity comes from *within* the organization, and the fact that too many marketing managers remain on the job for only a limited period of time. As a result of these short-term assignments, marketing managers may adopt a short-term perspective, leading to an overreliance on quick-fix sales-generating tactics such as line and category extensions, sales promotions, and so forth. Because these managers lack an understanding and appreciation of the brand equity concept, some critics maintain, they are essentially running the brand "without a license."

To counteract these and other potential forces within an organization that may lead to ineffective long-term management of brands, many firms have made internal branding a top priority, as we noted in Chapter 2. As part of these efforts, they must put a brand equity management system into place. A *brand equity management system* is a set of organizational processes designed to improve the understanding and use of the brand equity concept within a firm. Three major steps help to implement a brand equity management system: creating brand charters, assembling brand equity reports, and defining brand equity responsibilities. The following subsections discuss each of these in turn. Branding Brief 8-2 describes how the Mayo Clinic has developed a brand equity measurement and management system.

BRANDING BRIEF 8-2

Understanding and Managing the Mayo Clinic Brand

Mayo Clinic was founded in the late 1800s by Dr. William Worral Mayo and his two sons, who later pioneered the "group practice of medicine" by inviting other physicians to work with them in Rochester, Minnesota. The Mayos believed that "two heads are better than one, and three are even better." From this beginning on the frontier, Mayo Clinic grew to be a worldwide leader in patient care, research, and education and became renowned for its world-class specialty care and medical research. In addition to the original facilities in Rochester, Mayo later built clinics in Jacksonville, Florida, and Scottsdale, Arizona, during the 1980s. More than 500,000 patients are cared for in Mayo's inpatient and outpatient practice annually.

In 1996, Mayo undertook its first brand equity study and since then has conducted regular, national qualitative and quantitative studies. Mayo's research identifies seven key brand attributes or values, including (1) integration, (2) integrity, (3) longevity, (4) exclusivity, (5) leadership, (6) wisdom, and (7) dedication. Although some of these values also characterize other high-quality medical centers, integration and integrity are more nearly unique to Mayo.

In terms of integration, respondents described Mayo as bringing together a wealth of resources to provide the best possible care. They perceived Mayo to be efficient, organized, harmonious, and creating a sense of participation and partnership. For example, one person described Mayo as "A well conducted symphony . . . works harmoniously . . . One person can't do it alone . . . Teamwork, cooperation, compatibility."

For integrity, respondents placed great value on the fact that Mayo is noncommercial and committed to health and healing over profit. One participant said, "The business element is taken out of Mayo. . . . Their ethics are higher . . . which gives me greater faith in their diagnosis."

Although none of Mayo Clinic's brand attributes are solely negative, perceptions of exclusivity pose some specific challenges. This attribute was sometimes described positively, in perceptions that Mayo offers the highest quality care and elite doctors, but inaccurate beliefs that it serves only the rich and famous and the sickest of the sick were emotionally distancing and made Mayo seem inaccessible.

In a more recent quantitative study, overall awareness of Mayo Clinic in the United States was 90.2 percent, and a remarkable one-third knew at least one Mayo patient. One of the key questions in the survey asked, "Suppose your health plan or personal finances permitted you to go anywhere in the U.S. for a serious medical condition which required highly specialized care, to which one institution would you prefer to go?" Mayo Clinic was the most popular choice, earning 18.6 percent of the responses, compared with 5.0 percent for the next most frequently mentioned medical center. Word-of-mouth has the most influence on these preferences for highly specialized medical care.

From its research, Mayo Clinic understands that its brand "is precious and powerful." Mayo realized that while it had an overwhelmingly positive image, it was vital to develop guidelines to protect the brand. In 1999, the clinic created a brand

The Mayo Clinic knows the importance and value of its brand and carefully monitors and manages its image and equity.
Source: Courtesy Mayo Clinic

management infrastructure to be the "institutional clearinghouse for ongoing knowledge about external perceptions of Mayo Clinic and its related activities." Mayo Clinic also established guidelines for applying the brand to products and services. Its brand management measures work to ensure that the clinic preserves its brand equity, as well as allowing Mayo to continue to accomplish its mission:

> To inspire hope and contribute to health and well-being by providing the best care to every patient through integrated clinical practice, education and research.

Sources: Thanks to Mayo Clinic's John La Forgia, Kent Seltman, Scott Swanson, and Amy Davis for assistance and cooperation, including interviews in October 2011; www.mayoclinic.org; "Mayo Clinic Brand Management," internal document, 1999; Leonard L. Berry and Neeli Bendapudi, "Clueing in Customers," *Harvard Business Review* (February 2003): 100–106; Paul Roberts, "The Agenda—Total Teamwork," *Fast Company*, April 1999, 148; Leonard L. Berry and Kent D. Seltman, *Management Lessons from Mayo Clinic: Inside One of the World's Most Admired Service Organizations* (New York: McGraw Hill, 2008).

Brand Charter

The first step in establishing a brand equity management system is to formalize the company view of brand equity into a document, the ***brand charter***, or brand bible as it is sometimes called, that provides relevant guidelines to marketing managers within the company as well as to key marketing partners outside the company such as marketing research suppliers or ad agency staff. This document should crisply and concisely do the following:

- Define the firm's view of branding and brand equity and explain why it is important.
- Describe the scope of key brands in terms of associated products and the manner by which they have been branded and marketed (as revealed by historical company records as well as the most recent brand audit).
- Specify what the actual and desired equity is for brands at all relevant levels of the brand hierarchy, for example, at both the corporate and the individual product level (as outlined in Chapter 11). The charter should define and clarify points-of-parity, points-of-difference, and the brand mantra.
- Explain how brand equity is measured in terms of the tracking study and the resulting brand equity report (described shortly).
- Suggest how marketers should manage brands with some general strategic guidelines, stressing clarity, consistency, and innovation in marketing thinking over time.
- Outline how to devise marketing programs along specific tactical guidelines, satisfying differentiation, relevance, integration, value, and excellence criteria. Guidelines for specific brand management tasks such as ad campaign evaluation and brand name selection may also be offered.
- Specify the proper treatment of the brand in terms of trademark usage, design considerations, packaging, and communications. As these types of instructions can be long and detailed, it is often better to create a separate *Brand or Corporate Identity Style Manual* or guide to address these more mechanical considerations.

Although parts of the brand charter may not change from year to year, the firm should nevertheless update it on an annual basis to provide decision makers with a current brand profile and to identify new opportunities and potential risks for the brand. As marketers introduce new products, change brand programs, and conduct other marketing initiatives, they should reflect these adequately in the brand charter. Many of the in-depth insights that emerge from brand audits also belong in the charter.

Skype's brand bible, for example, outlines the branding and image of its products and services.[13] The document clearly states how Skype wants to be seen by consumers, how the firm uses its branding to achieve that, and why this is important. It also explains how Skype's logo of clouds and the vivid blue color are designed to make clean lines and foster a creative and simple look. The brand bible explains the "do's and don'ts" of marketing Skype's products and services and the dangers for the company image of working outside the brand guidelines.

Skype's brand bible provides important guidelines about how the brand should look and behave.

Source: Skype

Brand Equity Report

The second step in establishing a successful brand equity management system is to assemble the results of the tracking survey and other relevant performance measures for the brand into a brand equity report or scorecard to be distributed to management on a regular basis (weekly, monthly, quarterly, or annually). Much of the information relevant to the report may already exist within the organization. Yet it may have been presented to management in disjointed chunks so that no one has a holistic understanding of it. The brand equity report attempts to effectively integrate all these different measures.[14]

Contents.   The brand equity report should describe *what* is happening with the brand as well as *why* it is happening. It should include all relevant internal measures of operational efficiency and effectiveness and external measures of brand performance and sources and outcomes of brand equity.[15]

In particular, one section of the report should summarize consumers' perceptions of key attribute or benefit associations, preferences, and reported behavior as revealed by the tracking study. Another section of the report should include more descriptive market-level information such as the following:

- Product shipments and movement through channels of distribution
- Retail category trends
- Relevant cost breakdowns
- Price and discount schedules where appropriate
- Sales and market share information broken down by relevant factors (such as geographic region, type of retail account, or customer)
- Profit assessments

These measures can provide insight into the market performance component of the brand value chain. Management can compare them to various frames of reference—performance last month/quarter/year—and color code them green, yellow, or red, depending on whether the trends are positive, neutral, or negative, respectively. Internal measures might focus on how much time, money, and labor was being spent on various marketing activities.[16]

Dashboards.   As important as the information making up the brand equity report is the *way* the information is presented. Thus firms are now also exploring how best to display the right data to influence marketing decision makers. Top digital agency R/GA, for example, has created a data-visualization department to reflect the growing importance of presenting information to its clients.[17]

A number of firms have implemented **marketing dashboards** to provide comprehensive but actionable summaries of brand-related information. A marketing dashboard functions just like the dashboard of a car. Although they can be valuable tools for companies, if not designed and implemented properly dashboards also can be a big waste of time and money. An early leader on the subject, Pat LaPointe has identified four success factors in developing a successful dashboard:[18]

1. Senior-level executives must devote the necessary resources to its development and stay actively involved—delegating the task to lower levels of the organization rarely pays off.
2. The investment in resources doesn't stop with launch. Additional resources are required to gather, align, and properly interpret the right information.
3. Graphics and analytics matter. Excel may be cheap and easy to use, but it can also constrain thinking.
4. Executives should focus on what can be measured today but also learn more about how to improve the dashboard in the future.

IT company Unisys successfully developed a dashboard that covered all its geographical areas and applied to all its divisions and business units. Data was collected from a variety of sources—brand tracking, CRM programs, tradeshows, media reports, satisfaction studies, and Web logs—offering views for all levels right up to the CMO.[19]

To provide feedback on marketing performance to boards of directors, former Harvard Business School faculty Gail McGovern and John Quelch advocate quarterly tracking reports of the three or four marketing or customer-related metrics that truly drive and predict the company's

Harrah's has an
extensive customer
information system that
helps the company track
key metrics.
Source: Craig Moran/
Rapport Press/Newscom

business performance—the behavioral measures specific to a company's business model.[20] As an example, they note how the board of casino operator Harrah's focuses on three metrics: share of its customer's gaming dollars (share of wallet), loyalty program updates (an indicator of increased concentration of a customer's gaming at Harrah's), and percent of revenue from customers visiting more than one of Harrah's 30 casinos (an indicator of cross-selling). To support its tracking, Harrah's has spent $50 million annually on a customer information system.

Similarly, Ambler and Clark offer three recommendations.[21] First, marketers must work with their CFO to develop marketing dashboards and to shift metrics and forecasting responsibilities to the finance department. Second, marketers should develop with each agency a detailed brief with measurable objectives and a results-driven compensation component (for agencies). Third, marketers need to dedicate extra time to securing buy-in from colleagues on their business model, strategy, and metrics.

In terms of choosing specific metrics for a brand equity report or dashboard, Ambler and Clark offer three additional guidelines.[22] First, marketers must select metrics that suit their business model and strategy. Two, they need to balance their metrics portfolio across audiences, comprehensiveness, efficiency, and other considerations. Three, marketers should review and modify their metrics portfolio as their needs change.

With advances in computer technology, it will be increasingly easy for firms to place the information that makes up the brand equity report online, so managers can access it through the firm's intranet or some other means. For example, early research pioneer NFO MarketMind developed a brand management database system that integrated continuous consumer tracking survey data, media weight (or cost) data, warehouse sales and retail scan data, and PR and editorial content.

Brand Equity Responsibilities

To develop a brand equity management system that will maximize long-term brand equity, managers must clearly define organizational responsibilities and processes with respect to the brand. Brands need constant, consistent nurturing to grow. Weak brands often suffer from a lack of discipline, commitment, and investment in brand building. In this section, we consider internal issues of assigning responsibilities and duties for properly managing brand equity, as well as external issues related to the proper roles of marketing partners. The Science of Branding 8-2 describes some important principles in building a brand-driven organization.

THE SCIENCE OF BRANDING 8-2

Maximizing Internal Branding

Internal branding doesn't always receive as much time, money, or effort as external branding programs receive. But although it may require significant resources, it generates a number of benefits. Internal branding creates a positive and more productive work environment. It can also be a platform for change and help foster an organization's identity. For example, after employee turnover became too high, Yahoo! created the "What Sucks" program in which employees could send their concerns straight to the CEO.

Branding expert Scott Davis offers a number of insights into what it takes to make a brand-driven organization. According to Davis, for employees to become passionate brand advocates, they must understand what a brand is, how it is built, what their organization's brand stands for, and what their role is in delivering on the brand promise. Formally, he sees the process of helping an organization's employees assimilate the brand as three stages:

1. *Hear It:* How do we best get it into their hands?

2. *Believe It:* How do we best get it into their heads?

3. *Live It:* How do we best get it into their hearts?

Davis also argues that six key principles should guide the brand assimilation process within an organization, offering the following examples.

1. *Make the brand relevant.* Each employee must understand and embrace the brand meaning. Nordstrom, whose brand relies on top-notch customer service, empowers sales associates to approve exchanges without manager approval.

2. *Make the brand accessible.* Employees must know where they can get brand knowledge and answers to their brand-related questions. Ernst & Young launched "The Branding Zone" on its intranet to provide employees easy access to information about its branding, marketing, and advertising programs.

3. *Reinforce the brand continuously.* Management must reinforce the brand meaning with employees beyond the initial rollout of an internal branding program. Southwest Airlines continually reinforces its brand promise of "a symbol of freedom" through ongoing programs and activities with a freedom theme.

4. *Make brand education an ongoing program.* Provide new employees with inspiring and informative training. Ritz-Carlton ensures that each employee participates in an

Part of the success of Nordstrom's legendary customer service is that it empowers employees to take brand-consistent actions.
Source: REUTERS/Rick Wilking

intensive orientation called "The Gold Standard" that includes principles to improve service delivery and maximize guest satisfaction.

5. *Reward on-brand behaviors.* An incentive system to reward employees for exceptional support of the brand strategy should coincide with the roll-out of an internal branding program. Prior to its merger with United, Continental Airlines rewarded employees with cash bonuses each month that the airline ranked in the top five of on-time airlines.

6. *Align hiring practices.* HR and marketing must work together to develop criteria and screening procedures to ensure that new hires are good fits for the company's brand culture. Pret A Manger sandwich shops has such a carefully honed screener that only 20 percent of applicants end up being hired.

Davis also emphasizes the role of senior management in driving internal branding, noting that the CEO ultimately sets the tone and compliance with a brand-based culture and determines whether proper resources and procedures are put into place.

Sources: Scott M. Davis, *Building the Brand-Driven Business: Operationalize Your Brand to Drive Profitable Growth* (San Francisco, CA: Jossey-Bass, 2002); Scott M. Davis, "Building a Brand-Driven Organization," in *Kellogg on Branding*, eds. Alice M. Tybout and Tim Calkins (Hoboken, NJ: John Wiley & Sons, 2005); Scott M. Davis, *The Shift: The Transformation of Today's Marketers into Tomorrow's Growth Leaders* (San Francisco, CA: Jossey-Bass, 2009).

Overseeing Brand Equity.   To provide central coordination, the firm should establish a position responsible for overseeing the implementation of the brand charter and brand equity reports, to ensure that product and marketing actions across divisions and geographic boundaries reflect their spirit as closely as possible and maximize the long-term equity of the brand. A natural place to house such oversight duties and responsibilities is in a corporate marketing group that has a senior management reporting relationship.

Scott Bedbury, who helped direct the Nike and Starbucks brands during some of their most successful years, is emphatic about the need for "top-down brand leadership."[23] He advocates the addition of a chief brand officer (CBO) who reports directly to the CEO of the company and who:

- ***Is an omnipresent conscience whose job is to champion and protect the brand—the way it looks and feels—both inside and outside the company.*** The CBO recognizes that the brand is the sum total of everything a company does and strives to ensure that all employees understand the brand and its values, creating "brand disciples" in the process.
- ***Is an architect and not only helps build the brand but also plans, anticipates, researches, probes, listens, and informs.*** Working with senior leadership, the CBO helps envision not just what works best for the brand today but also what can help drive it forward in the future.
- ***Determines and protects the voice of the brand over time by taking a long-term (two to three years) perspective.*** The CBO can be accountable for brand-critical and corporate-wide activities such as advertising, positioning, corporate design, corporate communications, and consumer or market insights.

Bedbury also advocates periodic brand development reviews (full-day meetings quarterly, or even half-day meetings monthly) for brands in difficult circumstances. As part of a brand development review, he suggests the following topics and activities:[24]

- *Review brand-sensitive material:* For example, review brand strength monitors or tracking studies, brand audits, and focus groups, as well as less formal personal observations or "gut feelings."
- *Review the status of key brand initiatives:* Because brand initiatives include strategic thrusts to either strengthen a weakness in the brand or exploit an opportunity to grow the brand in a new direction, customer perceptions may change and marketers therefore need to assess them.
- *Review brand-sensitive projects:* For example, evaluate advertising campaigns, corporate communications, sales meeting agendas, and important human resources programs (recruitment, training, and retention that profoundly affect the organization's ability to embrace and project brand values).
- *Review new product and distribution strategies with respect to core brand values:* For example, evaluate licensing the brand to penetrate new markets, forming joint ventures to develop new products or brands, and expanding distribution to nontraditional platforms such as large-scale discount retailers.
- *Resolve brand positioning conflicts:* Identify and resolve any inconsistencies in positioning across channels, business units, or markets.

Even strong brands need careful watching to prevent managers from assuming it's acceptable to "make one little mistake" with brand equity or to "let it slide." A number of top companies like Colgate-Palmolive, Canada Dry, Quaker Oats, Pillsbury, Coca-Cola, and Nestlé Foods have created brand equity gatekeepers for some or all their brands at one time.[25] Branding Brief 8-3 contains a checklist by which firms can assess their marketing skills and performance.

One of senior management's important roles is to determine marketing budgets and decide where and how to allocate company resources within the organization. The brand equity management system must be able to inform and provide input to decision makers so that they can recognize the short-term and long-term ramifications of their decisions for brand equity. Decisions about which brands to invest in, and whether to implement brand-building marketing programs or leverage brand equity through brand extensions instead, should reflect the current and desired state of the brand as revealed through brand tracking and other measures.

Organizational Design and Structures.   The firm should organize its marketing function to optimize brand equity. Several trends have emerged in organizational design and structure

BRANDING BRIEF 8-3

How Good Is Your Marketing? Rating a Firm's Marketing Assessment System

Famed former London Business School professor Tim Ambler has a wealth of experience in working with companies. He notes that in his interactions, "most companies do not have a clear picture of their own marketing performance which may be why they cannot assess it." To help companies evaluate if their marketing assessment system is good enough, he suggests that they ask the following 10 questions—the higher the score, the better the assessment system.

1. Does the senior executive team regularly and formally assess marketing performance?

   a. Yearly—10

   b. Six-monthly—10

   c. Quarterly—5

   d. More often—0

   e. Rarely—0

   f. Never—0

2. What does the senior executive team understand by "customer value"?

   a. Don't know. We are not clear about this—0

   b. Value of the customer to the business (as in "customer lifetime value")—5

   c. Value of what the company provides from the customers' point of view—10

   d. Sometimes one, sometimes the other—10

3. How much time does the senior executive team give to marketing issues?

   a. >30%—10

   b. 20–30%—6

   c. 10–20%—4;

   d. <10%—0

4. Does the business/marketing plan show the non-financial corporate goals and link them to market goals?

   a. No/no plan—0

   b. Corporate no, market yes—5

   c. Yes to both—10

5. Does the plan show the comparison of your marketing performance with competitors or the market as a whole?

   a. No/no plan—0

   b. Yes, clearly—10

   c. In between—5

6. What is your main marketing asset called?

   a. Brand equity—10

   b. Reputation—10

   c. Other term—5

   d. We have no term—0

7. Does the senior executive team's performance review involve a quantified view of the main marketing asset and how it has changed?

   a. Yes to both—10

   b. Yes but only financially (brand valuation)—5

   c. Not really—0

8. Has the senior executive team quantified what "success" would look like 5 or 10 years from now?

   a. No—0

   b. Yes—10

   c. Don't know—0

9. Does your strategy have quantified milestones to indicate progress toward that success?

   a. No—0

   b. Yes—10

   c. What strategy?—0

10. Are the marketing performance indicators seen by the senior executive team aligned with these milestones?

    a. No—0

    b. Yes, external (customers and competitors)—7

    c. Yes, internal (employees and innovativeness)—5

    d. Yes, both—10

Sources: Adapted from Tim Ambler, "10 Ways to Rate Your Firm's Marketing Assessment System," www.zibs.com, September 2005; Tim Ambler, *Marketing and the Bottom Line*, 2nd ed. (London: FT Prentice Hall, 2004).

Many leading manufacturers such as Procter & Gamble are assuming the role of category captain to help retailers manage sections of their stores.
Source: HolgerBurmeister/ Alamy

that reflect the growing recognition of the importance of the brand and the challenges of managing brand equity carefully. For example, an increasing number of firms are embracing brand management. Firms from more and more industries—such as the automobile, health care, pharmaceutical, and computer software and hardware industries—are introducing brand managers into their organizations. Often, they have hired managers from top packaged-goods companies, adopting some of the same brand marketing practices as a result.

Interestingly, packaged-goods companies, such as Procter & Gamble, continue to evolve the brand management system. With category management, manufacturers offer retailers advice about how to best stock their shelves. An increasing number of retailers are also adopting category management principles. Although manufacturers functioning as category captains can improve sales, experts caution retailers to exercise their own insights and values to retain their distinctiveness in the marketplace.

Many firms are thus attempting to redesign their marketing organizations to better reflect the challenges faced by their brands. At the same time, because of changing job requirements and duties, the traditional marketing department is disappearing from a number of companies that are exploring other ways to conduct their marketing functions through business groups, multidisciplinary teams, and so on.[26]

The goal in these new organizational schemes is to improve internal coordination and efficiencies as well as external focus on retailers and consumers. Although these are laudable goals, clearly one of the challenges with these new designs is to ensure that brand equity is preserved and nurtured, and not neglected due to a lack of oversight.

With a multiple-product, multiple-market organization, the difficulty often lies in making sure that both product and place are in balance. As in many marketing and branding activities, achieving the proper balance is the goal, in order to maximize the advantages and minimize the disadvantages of both approaches.

Managing Marketing Partners. Because the performance of a brand also depends on the actions taken by outside suppliers and marketing partners, firms must manage these relationships carefully. Increasingly, firms have been consolidating their marketing partnerships and reducing the number of their outside suppliers.

This trend has been especially apparent with global advertising accounts, where a number of firms have placed most, if not all, their business with one agency. For example, Colgate-Palmolive has worked largely with just Young & Rubicam, and American Express and IBM with Ogilvy & Mather.

Factors like cost efficiencies, organizational leverage, and creative diversification affect the number of outside suppliers the firm will hire in any one area. From a branding perspective, one advantage of dealing with a single major supplier such as an ad agency is the greater consistency in understanding and treatment of a brand that can result.

Other marketing partners can also play an important role. For example, Chapter 5 described the importance of channel members and retailers in enhancing brand equity and the need for cleverly designed push programs. One important function of having a brand charter or bible is to inform and educate marketing partners so that they can provide more brand-consistent support.

REVIEW

A brand equity measurement system is defined as a set of research procedures designed to provide timely, accurate, and actionable information for marketers regarding brands so that they can make the best possible tactical decisions in the short run as well as strategic decisions in the long run. Implementing a brand equity measurement system involves two steps: conducting brand audits, designing brand tracking studies, and establishing a brand equity management system.

A brand audit is a consumer-focused exercise to assess the health of the brand, uncover its sources of brand equity, and suggest ways to improve and leverage its equity. It requires understanding brand equity from the perspective of both the firm and the consumer. The brand audit consists of two steps: the brand inventory and the brand exploratory.

The purpose of the brand inventory is to provide a complete, up-to-date profile of how all the products and services sold by a company are marketed and branded. Profiling each product or service requires us to identify the associated brand elements as well as the supporting marketing program. The brand exploratory is research activity directed to understanding what consumers think and feel about the brand to identify sources of brand equity.

Brand audits can be used to set the strategic direction for the brand. As a result of this strategic analysis, a marketing program can be put into place to maximize long-term brand equity. Tracking studies employing quantitative measures can then be conducted to provide marketers with current information as to how their brands are performing on the basis of a number of key dimensions identified by the brand audit.

Tracking studies involve information collected from consumers on a routine basis over time and provide valuable tactical insights into the short-term effectiveness of marketing programs and activities. Whereas brand audits measure "where the brand has been," tracking studies measure "where the brand is now" and whether marketing programs are having their intended effects.

Three major steps must occur as part of a brand equity management system. First, the company view of brand equity should be formalized into a document, the brand charter. This document serves a number of purposes: It chronicles the company's general philosophy with respect to brand equity; summarizes the activity and outcomes related to brand audits, brand tracking, and so forth; outlines guidelines for brand strategies and tactics; and documents proper treatment of the brand. The charter should be updated annually to identify new opportunities and risks and to fully reflect information gathered by the brand inventory and brand exploratory as part of any brand audits.

Second, the results of the tracking surveys and other relevant outcome measures should be assembled into a brand equity report that is distributed to management on a regular basis (monthly, quarterly, or annually). The brand equity report should provide descriptive information as to *what* is happening to a brand as well as diagnostic information as to *why* it is happening. These reports are often being displayed in marketing dashboards for ease of review.

Finally, senior management must be assigned to oversee how brand equity is treated within the organization. The people in that position would be responsible for overseeing the implementation of the brand charter and brand equity reports to make sure that, as much as possible, product and marketing actions across divisions and geographic boundaries are performed in a way that reflects the spirit of the charter and the substance of the report so as to maximize the long-term equity of the brand.

DISCUSSION QUESTIONS

1. What do you see as the biggest challenges in conducting a brand audit? What steps would you take to overcome them?
2. Pick a brand. See if you can assemble a brand inventory for it.
3. Consider the McDonald's tracking survey presented in Branding Brief 8-1. What might you do differently? What questions would you change or drop? What questions might you add? How might this tracking survey differ from those used for other products?
4. Can you develop a tracking survey for the Mayo Clinic? How might it differ from the McDonald's tracking survey?
5. Critique the Rolex brand audit in Brand Focus 8.0. How do you think it could be improved?

BRAND FOCUS 8.0

Rolex Brand Audit

For over a century, Rolex has remained one of the most recognized and sought-after luxury brands in the world. In 2009, *Businessweek*/Interbrand ranked Rolex as the 71st most valuable global brand, with an estimated brand value of $5 billion.[27] A thorough audit can help pinpoint opportunities and challenges for Rolex, whose brand equity has been historically strong, as much is at stake.

> *"The name of Rolex is synonymous with quality. Rolex—with its rigorous series of tests that intervene at every stage—has redefined the meaning of quality."*

—**www.rolex.com**

BACKGROUND

History

Rolex was founded in 1905 by a German named Hans Wilsdorf and his brother-in-law, William Davis, as a watch-making company, Wilsdorf & Davis, with headquarters in London, England. Wilsdorf, a self-proclaimed perfectionist, set out to improve the mainstream pocket watch right from the start. By 1908, he had created a timepiece that kept accurate time but was small enough to be worn on the wrist. That same year, Wilsdorf trademarked the name "Rolex" because he thought it sounded like the noise a watch made when it was wound. Rolex was also easy to pronounce in many different languages.

In 1912, Rolex moved its headquarters to Geneva, Switzerland, and started working on improving the reliability of its watches. Back then, dust and moisture could enter the watch case and cause damage to the movement or internal mechanism of the watch. As a result, Wilsdorf invented a screw crown and waterproof casebook mechanism that revolutionized the watch industry. In 1914, the Rolex wristwatch obtained the first Kew "A" certificate after passing the world's toughest timing test, which included testing the watch at extreme temperature levels.

Twelve years later, Wilsdorf developed and patented the now famous Oyster waterproof case and screw crown. This mechanism became the first true protection against water, dust, and dirt. To generate publicity for the watch, jewelry stores displayed fish tanks in their windows with the Oyster watch completely submerged in it. The Oyster was put to the test on October 7, 1927, when Mercedes Gleitze swam the English Channel wearing one. She emerged 15 hours later with the watch functioning perfectly, much to the amazement of the media and public. Gleitze became the first of a long list of "ambassadors" that Rolex has used to promote its wristwatches.

Over the years, Rolex has pushed innovation in watches to new levels. In 1931, the firm introduced the Perpetual self-winding rotor mechanism, eliminating the need to wind a watch. In 1945, the company invented the first watch to display a number date at the 3 o'clock position and named it the Datejust. In 1953, Rolex launched the Submariner—the first diving watch that was water-resistant and pressure-resistant to 100 meters. The sporty watch appeared in various James Bond movies in the 1950s and became an instant symbol of prestige and durability.

For decades, Swiss-made watches owned the middle and high-end markets, remaining virtually unrivaled until the invention of the quartz watch in 1969. Quartz watches kept more accurate time, were less expensive to make, and quickly dominated the middle market. Within 10 years, quartz watches made up approximately half of all watch sales worldwide.[28] Joe Thompson, editor of *Modern Jeweler*, a U.S. trade publication, explained, "By 1980, people thought the mechanical watch was dead."[29]

Rolex proved the experts wrong. The company would not give in to the quartz watch rage. In order to survive, however, Rolex was forced to move into the high-end market exclusively—leaving the middle to the quartz people—and create a strategy to defend and build its position there.

Private Ownership

Rolex is a privately owned company and has been controlled by only three people in its 100-year history. Before Wilsdorf died, he set up the Hans Wilsdorf Foundation, ensuring that some of the company's income would go to charity and that control of the company lay with the foundation.[30] This move was a critical step toward the long-term success of Rolex as a high-end brand. Over the years, many luxury brands have been forced to

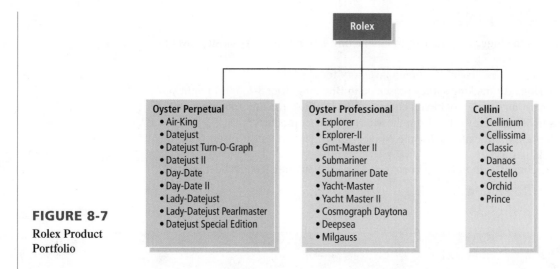

FIGURE 8-7
Rolex Product
Portfolio

affiliate with conglomerates in order to compete, but by staying an independent entity, Rolex has remained focused on its core business. André Heiniger, managing chairman of Rolex through the 1980s, explained, "Rolex's strategy is oriented to marketing, maintaining quality, and staying out of fields where we are not prepared to compete effectively."

Brand Portfolio

Rolex includes three family brands of wristwatches, called "collections"; each has a subset of brands (see Figure 8-7).

- The *Oyster Perpetual Collection* includes the "traditional" Rolex wristwatch, and has eight sub-brands that are differentiated by features and design. The Perpetual Collection targets affluent men and women.

- The *Professional Collection* targets specific athletic and adventurer user groups through its features and imagery. The Oyster Professional Collection includes seven sub-brands.

- The *Cellini Collection* focuses on formal occasions through its elegant designs, and encompasses seven sub-brands. These watches incorporate fashion and style features like colored leather bands and an extensive use of diamonds.

In addition to the three collections, Rolex owns a separate "fighter" brand called Tudor, developed in 1946 to stave off competition from mid-range watches such as Tag Heuer, Citizen, and Rado. Tudor has its own range of family brands, or collections, namely Prince, Princess, Monarch, and Sport, each of which encompasses a number of sub-brands. Tudor watches are sold at own-brand specialty stores and through the network of exclusive Rolex dealers. Although they are no longer for sale in the United States, there are many outlets in Europe and Asia. Tudor targets younger consumers and offers watches at a lower price range. The brand is distinctly separate, and the Rolex name does not appear on Tudor watches.

BRAND INVENTORY

Rolex's success as the largest single luxury watch brand can be credited to several factors. The company not only produces extremely high-quality timepieces, but also tightly controls how its watches are sold, ensuring high demand and premium prices. In addition, Rolex's sophisticated marketing strategy has created an

exclusive and premium brand that many aspire to own. The brand inventory will describe each of these factors in more depth.

Brand Elements

Rolex's most distinguishable brand element is its Crown logo. Trademarked in 1925, the Crown made its appearance on the watches in 1939. The logo has undergone few revisions, keeping its signature five-point crown intact over the years. Rolex watches feature the name "Rolex" on the dial, a tradition dating to 1926. This development initially helped increase brand recognition. Many Rolex watches also have a distinct look, including a big round face and wide wrist band.

Rolex watches have a classic design and look.
Source: Lee Hacker/Alamy

Product

Throughout the years, Rolex timepieces have maintained the high quality, durability, and prestige on which the company built its name. In particular, the firm has maintained a keen focus on delivering a highly accurate watch of superior craftsmanship, using only the finest premium materials such as gold, platinum, and jewels. It continually works on improving the functionality of its watches with better movements and new, sophisticated features. As a result, Rolex watches are complex mechanisms compared to most mass-produced watches. A quartz watch, for example, has between 50 and 100 parts; a Rolex Oyster chronometer has 220.[31]

Each Rolex watch consists of 10 unique features identified as the company's "10 Golden Rules:"

1. A waterproof case
2. The Perpetual rotor
3. The case back
4. The Oyster case
5. The winding crown
6. The finest and purest materials
7. Quality control
8. Rolex self-winding movement
9. Testing from the independent Controle Official Suisse des Chronometres
10. Rolex testing

The company does not license its brand or produce any other product besides watches. Its product portfolio is clear, concise, and focused.

Rolex spends more time and money than any other watch company fighting counterfeiters. Today, it is often hard to spot the differences between a $25 counterfeit and a $10,000 authentic Rolex watch. Counterfeiting Rolex watches has become a sophisticated industry, with sales exceeding $1.8 billion per year.

Pricing

By limiting production to approximately 2,000 watches a day, Rolex keeps consumer demand high and prices at a premium.

Prices start around $2,500 for the basic Oyster Perpetual and can reach $200,000, depending on the specific materials used such as steel, yellow gold, or platinum. Scarcity also helps positively influence the resale value of Rolex watches. One report indicated that "almost all older Rolex models are valued above their initial selling price."[32]

Distribution

Rolex carefully monitors how its timepieces are sold, distributing them only through its approximately 60,000 "Official Rolex Dealers" worldwide. Official dealers must meet several criteria, including a high-end image, adequate space, attractive location, and outstanding service. In addition, a large secondary market exists for Rolex, both through online auction sites such as eBay and at live auctions run by Christies and Sotheby's.

Communications

Rolex's marketing and communications strategy strives to create a high-quality, exclusive brand image. The company associates itself with "ambassadors"—established artists, top athletes, rugged adventurers, and daring explorers—to help create this imagery. Rolex also sponsors various sports and cultural events as well as philanthropy programs to help align with targeted demographics as well as create positive associations in consumers' minds.

Advertising.   Rolex is the number-one watch advertiser in the world. In 2008, the firm spent over $49 million on advertising, $20 million more than the number-two contender, Breitling.[33] One of the company's largest expenditures is for magazine advertising. Rolex's print ads are often simple and austere, usually featuring one of its many brand ambassadors or a close-up photo of one of its watches with the tagline "Rolex. A Crown for Every Achievement." Rolex does not advertise extensively on television, but does sponsor some events that are televised.

Ambassadors.   Rolex's celebrity endorsers are continuously added and dropped depending on their performance. These ambassadors fall into four categories: athletes, artists, explorers,

Rolex sponsors a number of different sporting events, including sailing races.
Source: AP Photo/J Pat Carter

Artists	Explorers	Golfers	Racing
Cecilia Bartoli	David Doubilet	Paul Casey	Sir Jackie Stewart
Michael Buble	Sylvia Earle	Luke Donald	Tom Kristensen
Placido Domingo	Alain Hubert	Ricky Fowler	Rolex 24 at Daytona
Gustavo Dudamel	Jean Troillet	Retief Goosen	Goodwood Revival
Renee Fleming	Ed Viesturs	Charles Howell	24 Hours at Le Mans
Sylvie Guillem	Chuck Yeager	Trevor Immelman	
Jonas Kaufmann	Setting Out to Conquer the World	Martin Kaymer	Tennis
Diana Krall	Deepsea Under the Pole	Matteo Manassero	Roger Federer
Yo-Yo Ma	The Deep	Phil Mickelson	Justine Henin
Anoushka Shankar	The Deepest Dive	Jack Nicklaus	Ana Ivanovic
Bryn Terfel		Lorena Ochoa	Zheng Jie
Rolando Villazon	Yachting	Arnold Palmer	Juan Martín del Potro
Yuja Wang	Robert Scheidt	Gary Player	Li Na
Royal Opera House	Paul Cayard	Adam Scott	Jo-Wilfried Tsonga
Teatro Alla Scalla	Rolex Sydney Hobart	Annika Sorenstam	Caroline Wosniacki
Wiener Philharmoniker	Maxi Yacht Rolex Cup	Camilo Villegas	Wimbledon
	Rolex Fastnet Race	Tom Watson	Australian Open
	Rolex Farr 40 World Championship	U.S. Open Championship	Monte-Carlo Rolex Masters
	Rolex Swan Cup	The Open Championship	Shanghai Rolex Masters
		The Ryder Cup	
	Equestrian	The President's Cup	Skiing
	Rodrigo Pessoa	Evian Masters	Hermann Maier
	Gonzalo Pieres, Jr.	The Solheim Cup	Lindsay Vonn
			Carlo Janka
			The Hahnenkamm Races

FIGURE 8-8 2011 Rolex Ambassadors

and yachtsmen (see Figure 8-8). Aligning with acclaimed artists symbolizes the pursuit of perfection. Association with elite sports figures is meant to signify the company's quest for excellence. Its support of sailing events, for example, highlights the company's core values: excellence, precision, and team spirit.[34] Explorers also test the excellence and innovation of Rolex's watches at extreme conditions. Rolex ambassadors have scaled Mt. Everest, broken the speed of sound, reached the depths of the ocean, and traveled in space. A print ad will usually feature one ambassador and one specific watch, with the goal of targeting a very specific demographic or consumer group.

In 2011, much to the surprise of industry experts, Rolex signed golfer Tiger Woods as a Rolex ambassador. Woods has had a long and complicated history as a celebrity endorser of watches. In 1997, just after he turned pro, Rolex's Tudor watch signed him to a partnership that lasted almost five years. Woods backed out of the contract in 2002 to sign with rival Tag Heuer, which paid him approximately $2 million annually. Woods rationalized his decision to end ties with Tudor by explaining, "My tastes have changed," and that he didn't "feel a connection with that company."[35] In 2009, the tables turned when Tag Heuer announced it had ended the relationship following Woods's involvement in a sex scandal.

Rolex's sponsorship marked the golfer's first celebrity endorsement since 2009. The company said it was "convinced that Tiger Woods still has a long career ahead of him and that he has all the qualities required to continue to mark the history of golf. The brand is committed to accompanying him in his new challenges . . . This association pays tribute to the exceptional stature of Tiger Woods and the leading role he plays in forging the sport's global appeal. It also constitutes a joint commitment to the future."[36]

Sports and Culture.   Rolex sponsors a variety of elite athletic and cultural events to reinforce the same messages, values, and associations as it does through its ambassador endorsements. These include a quest for excellence, pursuit of perfection, teamwork, and ruggedness. Rolex sponsors sporting events in golf (U.S. Open Championship, the Open Championship, and the Ryder Cup), tennis (Wimbledon and the Australian Open), skiing (the Hahnenkamm Races), racing (Rolex 24 at Daytona), and equestrian events.

Rolex also sponsors several sailing races, including the Rolex Sydney, Rolex Fastnet Race, and Maxi Yacht Rolex Cup. The company has partnered with extreme exploration expeditions, including The Deepest Dive and Deepsea Under the Pole. It is a major contributor to establishments such as the Royal Opera House in London and the Teatro alla Scala in Milan to align with a more cultural audience.

Philanthropy.   Rolex gives back through three established philanthropic programs:

1. The *Awards for Enterprise* program supports individuals whose work focuses on benefiting their communities and the world. These projects are focused on science and health, applied technology, exploration and discovery, the environment, and cultural heritage.[37]

2. The *Young Laureates Programme* is part of the Awards for Enterprise program, providing support for outstanding innovators between the ages of 18 and 30.[38]

3. The *Rolex Mentor and Protégé Arts Initiative* seeks out extraordinarily gifted young artists around the world and pairs them with established masters. Young artists have been paired with accomplished filmmakers, dancers, artists, composers, and actors.[39]

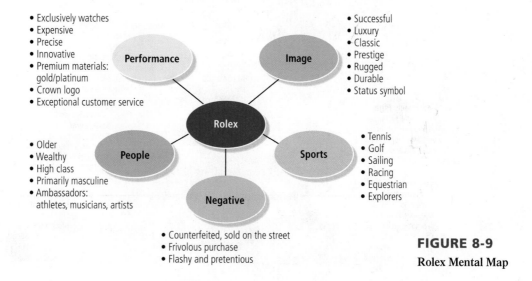

FIGURE 8-9

Rolex Mental Map

BRAND EXPLORATORY

Consumer Knowledge

Rolex has successfully leveraged its history and tradition of excellence along with innovation to become the most powerful and recognized watchmaker in the world. Some positive consumer brand associations for Rolex might be "sophisticated," "prestigious," "exclusive," "powerful," "elegant," "high quality." Some negative brand associations that some consumers may link to the brand, however, could include "flashy" or "snobby." Figure 8-9 displays a hypothetical Rolex mental map.

In one report by the Luxury Institute research group in New York, consumers had positive attitudes in terms of purchase intent toward Rolex. Wealthy people said they were more likely to buy a Rolex than any other brand for their next watch. The Rolex brand was far more recognizable (84 percent knew it) than Bulgari (39 percent) and even Cartier (63 percent), although several rivals outranked Rolex for perceived quality and exclusivity.[40]

A 2008 Mintel survey on the watch industry revealed that "women are still likely to view watches as an accessory, with many buyers choosing their watch based on looks alone. However, at the top end of the luxury market there is a growing number of women who are interested in mechanical watches. The study also found that women are increasingly choosing androgynous or unisex watches."[41]

Many older, affluent people place a high value on owning a Rolex, whether new or collectible. In 2011, a Rolex sold for $1 million for the first time. The watch—an oversized stainless-steel split-second chronograph wristwatch manufactured in 1942—was purchased at Christie's Geneva auction for $1,163,340, an all-time high price paid for any Rolex.[42]

While the brand and product line seem to resonant well with older, wealthy individuals, Rolex struggles somewhat to connect with younger consumers. In a NPD Group poll, 36 percent of people under the age of 25 didn't wear a watch.[43] Another study by Piper Jaffray revealed that 59 percent of teenagers said they never wear a watch and 82 percent said they didn't plan to buy one in the next six months.

Brand Resonance Pyramid

The Rolex brand resonance model pyramid (see Chapter 3) is equally strong on the left-hand and right-hand sides. There is great synergy between the two sides of the pyramid; the

functional and emotional benefits Rolex strives to deliver are in harmony with consumers' imagery and feelings about the brand. The pyramid is also strong from bottom to top, enjoying the highest brand awareness of any luxury brand as well as high repeat purchase rates and high customer loyalty. Rolex has successfully focused on both the superior product attributes and the imagery associated with owning and wearing a Rolex. Figure 8-10 highlights some key aspects of the Rolex brand resonance pyramid.

Competitive Analysis

Rolex has many competitors in the $26.5 billion watch industry; however, only a few brands compete in the very high-end market.[44] Through its pricing and distribution strategies, Rolex has positioned itself as a high-end luxury watch brand. On the lower end of the spectrum it competes with companies such as TAG Heuer and OMEGA, and on the high end with brands such as Patek Philippe, maker of the world's most expensive wristwatch.

TAG Heuer. A leader in the luxury watch industry, the Swiss firm TAG Heuer distinguishes itself by focusing on extreme chronograph precision in its watches, and on sports and auto-racing sponsorship in its advertising. Founded by Edouard Heuer in 1876, TAG Heuer has been a mainstay in the luxury watch business. In 1887, the firm created the first oscillating pinion, a technology that significantly improved the chronograph industry and is still used in many of its watches today. In 1895, it developed and patented the first water-resistant case for pocket watches. TAG Heuer expanded into the United States in 1910, introduced a chronograph wristwatch in 1914, and has continued to focus on chronograph innovation ever since.

TAG's image and positioning is inextricably connected to chronograph precision. Its timepieces were the official stopwatches of the Olympic Games in 1920, 1924, and 1928. The firm was a Ferrari team sponsor of Formula 1 from 1971 to 1979 and was part of the TAG-McLaren racing team from 1985 to 2002. It was also the official timekeeper of the F-1 race series for much of the 1990s and early 2000s.[45] TAG Heuer has sponsored numerous Americas Cup teams and other yacht racing teams over the years.

TAG Heuer uses officially licensed retailers to sell its watches both in stores and online. These licensed retailers range from exclusive jewelers to department stores such as Nordstrom and Macy's. The watchmaker generates brand awareness through

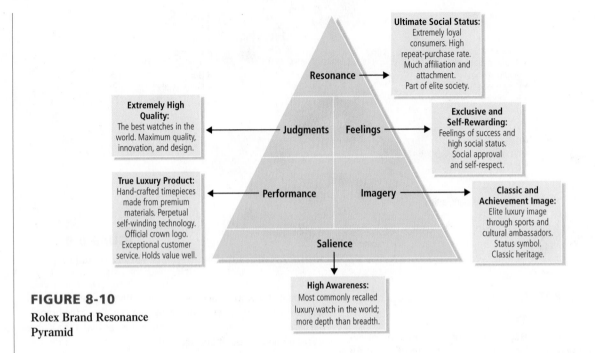

FIGURE 8-10

Rolex Brand Resonance
Pyramid

brand ambassadors and sponsoring sporting events and advertises extensively in magazines. In 1999, TAG Heuer was purchased by luxury goods conglomerate LVHM.

OMEGA. Founded in 1848 by Louis Brandt, OMEGA has long prided itself on the precision of its watches and timing devices. It built what was Amelia Earhart's watch of choice during one of her transatlantic flights and has been involved in aviation and athletic timing ever since. OMEGA was the time equipment selected for the 1936 Winter Olympics, which saw the first use of synchronized chronographs. By 1937, the company had launched its first waterproof wristwatch, and in 1967 it invented the first underwater touchpad timing equipment, which was used in Olympic swimming competitions. OMEGA watches accompanied the expedition to locate the exact position of the North Pole, and boarded the Apollo 11 mission to become the first and only watch ever to land on the moon. OMEGA is now owned by watch conglomerate, Swatch Group.

Like Rolex and TAG Heuer, OMEGA employs ambassadors to generate brand awareness, including athletes Michael Phelps, Alexander Popov, Ernie Els, and race car driver Michael Schumacher as well as Hollywood stars Nicole Kidman and Cindy Crawford. In 1995, OMEGA became the official watch of the *James Bond* film franchise.

OMEGA watches are offered in both women's and men's styles in four different collections: Constellation, Seamaster, Speedmaster, and De Ville. Prices vary greatly even within individual collections. Watches in the De Ville collection range from $1,650 to over $100,000.

Patek Philippe. In 1839, Antoine Norbert de Patek and François Czapek started a Swiss-based watch company built upon 10 values: independence, innovation, tradition, quality and workmanship, rarity, value, aesthetics, service, emotion, and heritage. After several name changes during its formative years, the company was finally named Patek Philippe. The innovator of many technologies found in today's high-end watch, it represents the absolute pinnacle of luxury timepieces.

In particular, the firm prides itself on creating many of the world's most complicated watches through innovations with split-second chronograph and perpetual date technology.

Unlike other leading luxury watchmakers, Patek Philippe does not rely on event sponsorship or brand ambassadors to generate name recognition. However, since 1851, the firm has made watches for royalty throughout Europe. Its watches are only sold through authorized retailers, of which there are 600 worldwide. In 1996, the brand started its "Generations" campaign, building on its values of heritage and tradition and featuring the tag line, "You Never Actually Own a Patek Philippe, You Merely Look After It for the Next Generation."

Patek Philippe evaluates every authorized dealer's storefront to ensure that it meets the watchmaker's quality standards. It also separates itself from other watchmakers on price, with its least expensive noncustomized watch retailing at $11,500 and its most expensive at over $600,000.

STRATEGIC RECOMMENDATIONS
Positioning

Figure 8-11 summarizes some positioning analysis and possible points-of-parity and points-of-difference, as described below.

Brand Mantra:
"Classic Designs, Timeless Status"

Points-of-Parity	Points-of-Difference
• Swiss watchmaker	• Innovative products
• Durable	• Unique appearance
• Fine materials	Big face; wide wrist band
• Quality craftsmanship	• Iconic crown logo
• Accurate	• Exclusive, prestigious imagery
• Attractive	• Rich history and heritage
	• Enduring premium value

FIGURE 8-11

Possible Rolex Brand Positioning

Points-of-Parity.   Rolex is similar to other watchmakers in the high-end luxury watch market on several levels. They all make their watches in Switzerland, which is renowned for superior craftsmanship in watch making, and they all deliver high quality. All pride themselves on their attention to detail and ongoing innovation in the watch industry.

Points-of-Difference.   Rolex separates itself from the competition in several ways. One, Rolex watches have a distinct look with their Crown logo, big face, and wide band. Two, Rolex has kept a strategically tight control on its distribution channel and production levels, creating a sense of prestige, importance, and exclusivity in the minds of consumers. Three, it has kept the brand pure, remaining focused only on watches and never licensing its name. Through careful selection of event sponsorships and brand ambassadors, Rolex has cut through the clutter, resonated with consumers around the world, and maintained an air of prestige.

Brand Mantra.   Rolex has been extremely successful in building a global name through clever marketing and communications, without compromising the integrity of the brand. It has nurtured the belief that acquiring a Rolex represents a milestone in one's life and has built a well-known brand recognized for its elegance and status throughout the entire world. A brand mantra that captures these ideas might be, "Classic Designs, Timeless Status."

TACTICAL RECOMMENDATIONS

The Rolex brand audit proved that Rolex is a very strong brand with significant brand equity. It also identified a few opportunities and challenges:

Leverage the Company's Independent, Continuous Heritage and Focus

- Rolex is the largest and most successful watch company in the world. As a result, many consumers don't realize it is privately owned and competes against major conglomerates such as TAG Heuer's parent company, LVMH, and OMEGA's parent company, Swatch Group. While being privately owned is a good thing for many reasons, it also brings up several challenges. For example, Rolex has to compete against companies that are 10 times its size. Larger companies have lower labor costs, wider distribution, and significant advertising synergies.

- Rolex may want to leverage and promote the fact that in some ways it has to work harder to succeed. It is doing what it has done for 100 years—making durable, reliable, premium watches on its own. Due to the currently popular anti-Wall Street vibe, this positioning may resonant well with consumers.

Leverage the Company's Elite Craftsmanship and Innovation

- Research from the Luxury Institute group suggested that consumers do not consider Rolex the top brand in quality and exclusivity. History has proved that Rolex watches are in fact leaders in both craftsmanship and innovation and Rolex may want to run a campaign focused more on these aspects.

Connect with the Female Consumer

- Women make up the majority of jewelry and watch purchases. However, as Mintel's 2008 study revealed, women are more and more interested in purchasing unisex mechanical watches rather than feminine-styled watches. This is a great opportunity for Rolex, whose watches are primarily masculine in design. The firm could move away from its decorative, jeweled watches and introduce more powerful, gender-neutral watches. Its 2009 Oyster Perpetual Datejust Rolesor 36 mm is one example—robust, with large utilitarian numbers, and waterproof to a depth of 100 meters.[46] However, its floral dial design and diamond-set bezel possibly give it an unnecessary feminine angle.

- Rolex may want to tweak its female ambassador list to coincide with a more unisex product line. Women who have succeeded in a male-dominated environment such as Condoleezza Rice or Katie Couric could be powerful brand endorsers.

Attack the Online Counterfeit Industry

- Counterfeits damage the company's brand equity and present a huge risk to the brand. The boom in e-commerce has taken counterfeit Rolexes from the street corner to the Internet, where fakes can reach far more consumers. Consequently, the age-old problem of counterfeiting is a bigger threat than ever before. To maintain its limited distribution, Rolex does not authorize any of its watches to be sold on the Internet. In order to combat the online sale of counterfeits, however, Rolex might consider building an exclusive online store, or an exclusive distribution site to which all official e-retailers must link. In fact, Rolex dedicates extensive resources to fight the illegal use of the brand, including sponsoring the International Anti-Counterfeiting Coalition and suing companies that allow the sale of counterfeit Rolexes.

Use Marketing to Reach Younger Consumers

- Research has shown that younger consumers do not value watches the same way older generations did. As a result, Rolex should be researching the questions: How will prestige be defined in the twenty-first century? Who or what symbolizes prestige, ruggedness, precision? Will the same formula work for the millennial generation as they age and move into the Rolex target market?

Communicate Long-Term Value

- Rolex competes for a share of the luxury buyer's wallet with a host of other types of goods, such as clothes, shoes, and handbags. Many are less durable over time than a Rolex watch and are susceptible to falling out of fashion. Rolex should leverage its superior value retention—both in its resale value and in its "heirloom" quality—in order to better compete for luxury spending with brands outside its category.

- Swiss luxury watch competitor Patek Philippe used print advertising to communicate the heirloom quality of its watches. Rolex could pursue a similar approach, perhaps using its more visible ambassadors, to communicate its own heirloom quality.

Notes

1. Frederick E. Webster, Jr., Alan J. Malter, and Shankar Ganesan, "Can Marketing Regain Its Seat at the Table?" *Marketing Science Institute Report* No. 03–113, Cambridge, MA, 2003. See also Frederick E. Webster Jr., Alan J. Malter, and Shankar Ganesan, "The Decline and Dispersion of Marketing Competence," *MIT Sloan Management Review* 46, no. 4 (Summer 2005): 35–43.

2. Patrick LaPointe, *Marketing by the Dashboard Light—How to Get More Insight, Foresight, and Accountability from Your Marketing Investment* (New York: Association of National Advertisers, 2005).

3. Clyde P. Stickney, Roman L. Weil, Katherine Schipper, and Jennifer Francis, *Financial Accounting: An Introduction to Concepts, Methods, and Uses* (Mason, OH: Southwestern Cengage Learning, 2010).

4. Phillip Kotler, William Gregor, and William Rogers, "The Marketing Audit Comes of Age," *Sloan Management Review* 18, no. 2 (Winter 1977): 25–43.

5. Laurel Wentz, "Brand Audits Reshaping Images," *Ad Age International* (September 1996): 38–41.

6. Grand Ogilvy Winner, "Pizza Turnaround: Speed Kills. Good Taste Counts," *Journal of Advertising Research* (September 2011): 463–466; Seth Stevenson, "Like Cardboard," *Slate*, 11 January 2010; Ashley M. Heher, "Domino's Comes Clean With New Pizza Ads," *Associated Press*, 11 January 2010; Bob Garfield, "Domino's Does Itself a Disservice by Coming Clean About Its Pizza," *Advertising Age*, 11 January 2010; www.pizzaturnaround.com.

7. Private correspondence with Chris Grams and John Adams from Red Hat.

8. Sidney J. Levy, "Dreams, Fairy Tales, Animals, and Cars," *Psychology and Marketing* 2 (Summer 1985): 67–81.

9. Deborah Roeddder John, Barbara Loken, Kyeongheui Kim, and Alokparna Basu Monga, "Brand Concept Maps: A Methodology for Identifying Brand Association Networks," *Journal of Marketing Research* 43 (November 2006): 549–563.

10. John Roberts, professor of marketing, Australian National University, personal correspondence, 23 June 2011.

11. Nigel Hollis, executive vice president and chief global analyst at Millward Brown, personal correspondence, 6 October 2011.

12. Na Woon Bong, Roger Marshall, and Kevin Lane Keller, "Measuring Brand Power: Validating a Model for Optimizing Brand Equity," *Journal of Product and Brand Management* 8, no. 3 (1999): 170–184.

13. http://download.skype.com/share/brand/Skype BrandBook.zip.

14. Joel Rubinson, "Brand Strength Means More Than Market Share," paper presented at the ARF Fourth Annual Advertising and Promotion Workshop, New York, 1992.

15. Tim Ambler, *Marketing and the Bottom Line*, 2nd ed. (London: FT Prentice Hall, 2004).

16. Michael Krauss, "Marketing Dashboards Drive Better Decisions," *Marketing News*, 1 October 2005.

17. Kunur Patel, "Data Moves From Research to Consumer Lure," *Advertising Age*, 6 June 2011, 4.

18. Pat LaPointe, "Dashboards—Huge Value or Big Expense," www.marketingNPV.com, 10 August 2010; see also, Koen Pauwels, Tim Ambler, Bruce Clark, Pat LaPointe, David Reibstein, Bernd Skiera, Berend Wierenga, Thorsten Wiesel, *Dashboards & Marketing: Why, What, How and What Research Is Needed?*, Report no. 08-203, Marketing Science Institute Electronic Working Paper series, 2008.

19. Amy Miller and Jennifer Cloffi, "Measuring Marketing Effectiveness and Value: The Unisys Marketing Dashboard," *Journal of Advertising Research* 44 (September 2004): 237–243; "Unisys Overcomes 6 Common Dashboard Mistakes," www.marketingnpv.com, 4 October 2004.

20. Gail McGovern and John Quelch, "Sarbox Still Putting the Squeeze on Marketing," *Advertising Age*, 19 September 2005, 28.

21. Tim Ambler and Bruce Clark, "What Will Matter Most to Marketers Three Years from Now?" paper presented at Marketing Science Institute Conference, *Does Marketing Measure Up? Performance Metrics: Practices and Impacts*, 21–22 June 2004, London, United Kingdom. See also Bruce H. Clark and Tim Ambler, "Marketing Performance Measurement: Evolution of Research and Practice," *International Journal of Business Performance Management* 3, nos. 2/3/4 (2001): 231–244; and Bruce H. Clark, Andrew Abela, and Tim Ambler, "Organizational Motivation, Opportunity and Ability to Measure Marketing Performance," *Journal of Strategic Marketing* 13 (December 2005): 241–259.

22. Bruce Clark and Tim Ambler, "Managing the Metrics Portfolio," *Marketing Management* (Fall 2011): 16–21.

23. Scott Bedbury, *A New Brand World* (New York: Viking Press, 2002).

24. Bedbury, *A New Brand World*.

25. Betsy Spethman, "Companies Post Equity Gatekeepers," *Brandweek*, 2 May 1994, 5.

26. "The Death of the Brand Manager," *The Economist*, 9 April 1994, 67–68.

27. www.businessweek.com; www.interbrand.com; "Best Global Brands 2010."

28. David Liebeskind, "What Makes Rolex Tick?" *Stern Business*, Fall/Winter 2004.

29. Peter Passell, "Watches That Time Hasn't Forgotten?" *New York Times*, 24 November 1995.

30. Gene Stone, *The Watch* (New York: ABRAMS, 2006).

31. David Liebeskind, "What Makes Rolex Tick?" *Stern Business*, Fall/ Winter 2004.

32. Ibid.

33. Joe Thomas, "Rolex Leads U.S. Watch Advertiser Pack." *Watch Time Magazine*, 12 July 2009.

34. www.rolex.com, accessed 15 November 2011.

35. Suzanne Vranica and Sam Walker, "Some Find Tiger's Move Untimely—Golfer Switches Watches to TAG

Heuer From Rolex; Brand Experts Disapprove," *Wall Street Journal*, 7 October 2002.

36. "Tiger Woods Signs Endorsement Deal with Tiger," *Watch Time Magazine*, October 2011.

37. www.rolex.com, accessed November 15, 2011.

38. Ibid.

39. Ibid.

40. Christina Binkley, "Fashion Journal: Celebrity Watch: Are You a Brad or a James?" *Wall Street Journal*, 11 January 2007.

41. Jemima Sissons, "Haute Couture Takes On Horlogerie: Fashion's Big Guns Continue to Impress in the Battle for Women's Wrists," *Wall Street Journal*, 19 March 2010.

42. "Christie's Achieves World Record Price for Any Rolex Sold at Auction," *Watch Time Magazine*, 27 May 2011.

43. Hurt Harry, "The 12-Watches-a-Year Solution," *New York Times*, 1 July 2006.

44. Women's Wear Daily, July 2005; www.fashion products.com; Federation of Swiss Watch Industry, 2010.

45. http://www.f1scarlet.com/historyoftag_f1.html.

46. Sissons, "Haute Couture Takes on Horlogerie."

9 Measuring Sources of Brand Equity: Capturing Customer Mind-Set

Learning Objectives

After reading this chapter, you should be able to

1. Describe effective qualitative research techniques for tapping into consumer brand knowledge.

2. Identify effective quantitative research techniques for measuring brand awareness, image, responses, and relationships.

3. Profile and contrast some popular brand equity models.

Marketers strive to learn everything about how consumers use the products they sell. For pillow manufacturers, that might mean knowing how many consumers fold, stack, or just hug their pillows.

Source: Jose Luis Pelaez/Stone/Getty Images

Preview

Understanding the current and desired brand knowledge structures of consumers is vital to effectively building and managing brand equity. Ideally, marketers would be able to construct detailed "mental maps" to understand exactly what exists in consumers' minds—all their thoughts, feelings, perceptions, images, beliefs, and attitudes toward different brands. These mental blueprints would then provide managers with the insights to develop a solid brand positioning with the right points-of-parity and points-of-difference and the strategic guidance to help them make good brand decisions. Unfortunately, such brand knowledge structures are not easily measured because they reside only in consumers' minds.

Nevertheless, effective brand management requires us to thoroughly understand the consumer. Often a simple insight into how consumers think of or use products and the particular brands in a category can help create a profitable change in the marketing program. That's why many large companies conduct exhaustive research studies (or brand audits, as described in Chapter 8) to learn as much as possible about consumers.

A number of detailed, sophisticated research techniques and methods now exist to help marketers better understand consumer knowledge structures. A host of primary and secondary data sources exist online. Many industry or company studies can be accessed and surveys can be efficiently distributed and collected. This chapter highlights some of the important considerations critical to the measurement of brand equity.[1] Figure 9-1 outlines general considerations in understanding consumer behavior, and Branding Brief 9-1 describes the lengths to which marketers have gone in the past to learn about consumers.

According to the brand value chain, sources of brand equity arise from the customer mind-set. In general, measuring sources of brand equity requires that the brand manager fully understand how customers shop for and use products and services and, most important, what customers know, think, and feel about and act toward various brands. In particular, measuring sources of customer-based brand equity requires us to measure various aspects of brand awareness and brand image that can lead to the differential customer response making up brand equity.

Consumers may have a holistic view of brands that is difficult to divide into component parts. But many times we can, in fact, isolate perceptions and assess them in greater detail. The remainder of this chapter describes qualitative and quantitative approaches to identifying potential sources of brand equity—that is, capturing the customer mind-set.

QUALITATIVE RESEARCH TECHNIQUES

There are many different ways to uncover the types of associations linked to the brand and their corresponding strength, favorability, and uniqueness. *Qualitative research techniques* often identify possible brand associations and sources of brand equity. These are relatively unstructured measurement approaches that permit a range of both questions and answers and so can often be a useful first step in exploring consumer brand and product perceptions.

Who buys our product or service?
Who makes the decision to buy the product?
Who influences the decision to buy the product?
How is the purchase decision made? Who assumes what role?
What does the customer buy? What needs must be satisfied?
Why do customers buy a particular brand?
Where do they go or look to buy the product or service?
When do they buy? Any seasonality factors?
What are customers' attitudes toward our product?
What social factors might influence the purchase decision?
Does the customers' lifestyle influence their decisions?
How is our product perceived by customers?
How do demographic factors influence the purchase decision?

FIGURE 9-1

Understanding
Consumer Behavior

Source: Based on a list from George Belch and Michael Belch, *Advertising and Communication Management*, 3rd ed. (Homewood, IL: Irwin, 1995).

BRANDING BRIEF 9-1

Digging Beneath the Surface to Understand Consumer Behavior

Because the consumer behavior we observe can differ from the behavior consumers report in surveys, useful marketing insights sometimes emerge from unobtrusively observing consumers rather than talking to them. For example, Hoover became suspicious when people claimed in surveys that they vacuumed their houses for an hour each week. To check, the company installed timers in certain models and exchanged them for the same models in consumers' homes. The timers showed that people actually spent only a little over *half* an hour vacuuming each week. One researcher analyzed household trash to determine the types and quantities of food people consumed, finding that people really don't have a very good idea of how much and what types of food they eat. Similarly, much research has shown that people report they eat healthier food than would appear to be case if you opened their cabinets!

DuPont commissioned marketing studies to uncover personal pillow behavior for its Dacron polyester unit, which supplies filling to pillow makers and sells its own Comforel brand (now part of INVISTA). One challenge: people don't give up their old pillows. Thirty-seven percent of one sample described their relationship with their pillow as like "an old married couple," and an additional 13 percent characterized their pillow like a "childhood friend." The researchers found that people fell into distinct groups in terms of pillow behavior: stackers (23 percent), plumpers (20 percent), rollers or folders (16 percent), cuddlers (16 percent), and smashers, who pound their pillows into a more comfy shape (10 percent). Women were more likely to plump, while men were more likely to fold. The prevalence of stackers led the com-

pany to sell more pillows packaged as pairs, as well as to market different levels of softness or firmness.

Much of this type of research has its roots in *ethnography*, the anthropological term for the study of cultures in their natural surroundings. The intent behind these in-depth, observational studies is for consumers to drop their guard and provide a more realistic portrayal of who they are rather than who they would like to be. On the basis of ethnographic research that uncovered consumers' true feelings, ad campaigns have been created for a Swiss chocolate maker with the theme "The True Confessions of a Chocoholic" (because chocolate lovers often hid stashes all though the house), for Tampax tampons with the theme "More Women Trust Their Bodies to Tampax" (because teen users wanted the freedom to wear body-conscious clothes), and for Crisco shortening with the theme "Recipe for Success" (because people often baked pies and cookies in a celebratory fashion).

Sources: Russell Belk, ed., *Handbook of Qualitative Research Method in Marketing* (Northampton, MA: Edward Elgar Publishing, 2006); Eric J. Arnould and Amber Epp, "Deep Engagement with Consumer Experience: Listening and Learning with Qualitative Data," in *The Handbook of Marketing Research: Uses, Misuses, and Future Advances*, eds. Rajiv Grover and Marco Vriens (Thousand Oaks, CA: Sage Press, 2006): 51–58; Jennifer Chang Coupland, "Invisible Brands: An Ethnography of Households and the Brands in Their Kitchen Pantries," *Journal of Consumer Research* 32 (June 2005): 106–118; John Koten, "You Aren't Paranoid If You Feel Someone Eyes You Constantly," *Wall Street Journal*, 2 March 1985; Susan Warren, "Pillow Talk: Stackers Outnumber Plumpers; Don't Mention Drool," *Wall Street Journal*, 8 January 1998, B1.

Qualitative research has a long history in marketing. Ernest Dichter, one of the early pioneers in consumer psychoanalytic research, first applied these research principles in a study for Plymouth automobiles in the 1930s.[2] His research revealed the important—but previously overlooked—role that women played in the automobile purchase decision. Based on his consumer analysis, Plymouth adopted a new print ad strategy that highlighted a young couple gazing admiringly at a Plymouth automobile under the headline "Imagine Us in a Car Like That." Dichter's subsequent work had an important impact on a number of different ad campaigns.[3]

Some of his assertions were fairly controversial. For instance, he equated convertibles with youth, freedom, and the secret wish for mistresses; argued that women used Ivory soap to wash away their sins before a date; and maintained that baking was an expression of femininity and pulling a cake or loaf out of an oven for women was "in a sense like giving birth." His suggested tagline "Putting a Tiger in the Tank" for Exxon resulting in a long-running and successful ad campaign, however.[4]

This section next reviews a number of qualitative research techniques for identifying sources of brand equity such as brand awareness, brand attitudes, and brand attachment. These techniques also can identify outcomes of brand equity such as price elasticities and brand choice and preference.

Free Association

The simplest and often the most powerful way to profile brand associations is free association tasks, in which subjects are asked what comes to mind when they think of the brand, without any more specific probe or cue than perhaps the associated product category. ("What does the Rolex name mean to you?" or "Tell me what comes to mind when you think of Rolex watches.")

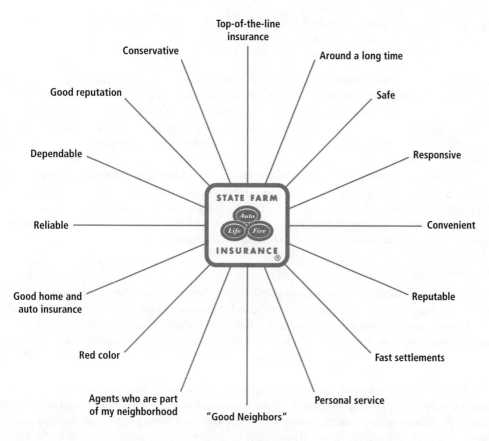

FIGURE 9-2

Sample State Farm
Mental Map

Source: Logo used with
permission of State Farm
Insurance

Marketers can use the resulting associations to form a rough mental map for the brand (see Figure 9-2 for a sample mental map for State Farm insurance).

Marketers use free association tasks mainly to identify the range of possible brand associations in consumers' minds, but free association may also provide some rough indication of the relative strength, favorability, and uniqueness of brand associations.[5] Coding free association responses in terms of the order of elicitation—whether they are early or late in the sequence—at least gives us a rough measure of their strength.[6] For example, if many consumers mention "fast and convenient" as one of their first associations when given "McDonald's restaurants" as a probe, then the association is probably a relatively strong one and likely able to affect consumer decisions. Associations later in the list may be weaker and thus more likely to be overlooked during consumer decision making. Comparing associations with those elicited for competitive brands can also tell us about their relative uniqueness. Finally, we can discern even favorability, to some extent, on the basis of how consumers phrase their associations.

Answers to free-association questions help marketers clarify the range of possible associations and assemble a brand profile.[7] To better understand the favorability of associations, we can ask consumers follow-up questions about the favorability of associations they listed or, more generally, what they like best about the brand. Similarly, we can ask them follow-up questions about the uniqueness of associations they listed or, more generally, about what they find unique about the brand. Useful questions include the following:

1. What do you like best about the brand? What are its positive aspects or advantages?
2. What do you like least about the brand? What are its negative aspects or disadvantages?
3. What do you find unique about the brand? How is it different from other brands?

These simple, direct measures can be extremely valuable for determining core aspects of a brand image. To elicit more structure and guidance, consumers can be asked further follow-up questions about what the brand means to them in terms of the classic journalism "who, what, when, where, why, and how" questions:

1. Who uses the brand? What kind of person?
2. What types of situations do they use the brand?
3. When and where do they use the brand?

4. Why do people use the brand? What do they get out of using it?

5. How do they use the brand? What do they use it for?

Guidelines.   The two main issues to consider in conducting free association tasks are what types of probes to give to subjects, and how to code and interpret the resulting data. In order not to bias results, it is best to move from general considerations to more specific considerations, as we illustrated earlier. Thus, ask consumers first what they think of the brand as a whole without reference to any particular category, followed by specific questions about particular products and aspects of the brand image.

Consumers' responses to open-ended probes can be either oral or written. The advantage of oral responses is that subjects may be less deliberate and more spontaneous in their reporting. In terms of coding the data, divide the protocols each consumer provides into phrases and aggregate them across consumers in categories. Because of their more focused nature, responses to specific probes and follow-up questions are naturally easier to code.

Projective Techniques

For marketers to succeed in uncovering the sources of brand equity, they must profile consumers' brand knowledge structures as accurately and completely as possible. Unfortunately, under certain situations, consumers may feel that it would be socially unacceptable or undesirable to express their true feelings—especially to an interviewer they don't even know! As a result, they may find it easier to fall back on stereotypical, pat answers they believe would be acceptable or perhaps even expected by the interviewer.

Consumers may be particularly unwilling or unable to reveal their true feelings when marketers ask about brands characterized by a preponderance of imagery associations. For example, it may be difficult for consumers to admit that a certain brand name product has prestige and enhances their self-image. They may instead refer to some particular product feature as the reason they like or dislike the brand. Or they may simply find it difficult to identify and express their true feelings when asked directly, *even if they attempt to do so.* For either of these reasons, it might be impossible to obtain an accurate portrayal of brand knowledge structures without some rather unconventional research methods.

Projective techniques are diagnostic tools to uncover the true opinions and feelings of consumers when they are unwilling or otherwise unable to express themselves on these matters.[8] Marketers present consumers with an incomplete stimulus and ask them to complete it, or they give consumers an ambiguous stimulus and ask them to make sense of it. The idea is that in the process consumers will reveal some of their true beliefs and feelings. Thus, projective techniques can be especially useful when deeply rooted personal motivations or personally or socially sensitive subjects are at issue.

In psychology, the most famous example of a projective technique is the *Rorschach test*, in which experimenters present ink blots to subjects and ask them what the ink blots remind them of. In responding, subjects may reveal certain facets of their own, perhaps subconscious, personality. Psychologists also use dream analysis or probe the earliest and most defining memories a person has on a topic.[9]

Projective techniques have a long history in marketing, beginning with the motivation research of the late 1940s and 1950s.[10] A classic example is an experiment exploring hidden feelings toward instant coffee conducted by Mason Haire in the late 1940s, summarized in Branding Brief 9-2.[11] Although projective techniques don't always yield results as powerful as in that example, they often provide useful insights that help to assemble us a more complete picture of consumers and their relationships with brands. Many kinds of projective techniques are possible. We'll highlight a few here.[12]

Completion and Interpretation Tasks.   Classic projective techniques use incomplete or ambiguous stimuli to elicit consumer thoughts and feelings. One approach is "bubble exercises," which depict different people buying or using certain products or services. Empty bubbles, as in cartoons, are placed in the scenes to represent the thoughts, words, or actions of one or more of the participants. Marketers then ask consumers to "fill in the bubble" by indicating what they believe is happening or being said in the scene. The stories and conversations told this way can be especially useful for assessing user and usage imagery for a brand.

BRANDING BRIEF 9-2

Once Upon a Time . . . You Were What You Cooked

One of the most famous applications of psychographic techniques was made by Mason Haire in the 1940s. The purpose of the experiment was to uncover consumers' true beliefs and feelings toward Nescafé instant coffee.

The impetus for the experiment was a survey conducted to determine why the initial sales of Nescafé instant coffee were so disappointing. The majority of the people who reported they didn't like the product stated that the reason was the flavor. On the basis of consumer taste tests, however, Nescafé's management knew consumers found the taste of instant coffee acceptable when they didn't know what type of coffee they were drinking. Suspecting that consumers were not expressing their true feelings, Haire designed a clever experiment to discover what was really going on.

Haire set up two shopping lists containing the same six items. Shopping List 1 specified Maxwell House drip ground coffee, whereas Shopping List 2 specified Nescafé instant coffee, as follows:

Shopping List 1	Shopping List 2
Pound and a half of hamburger	Pound and a half of hamburger
2 loaves Wonder bread	2 loaves Wonder bread
Bunch of carrots	Bunch of carrots
1 can Rumford's Baking Powder	1 can Rumford's Baking Powder
Maxwell House coffee (drip ground)	Nescafé instant coffee
2 cans Del Monte peaches	2 cans Del Monte peaches
5 lbs. potatoes	5 lbs. potatoes

Two groups of matched subjects were each given one of the lists and asked to "Read the shopping list. . . . Try to project yourself into the situation as far as possible until you can more or less characterize the woman who bought the groceries." Subjects then wrote a brief description of the personality and character of that person.

After coding the responses into frequently mentioned categories, Haire found that two starkly different profiles emerged:

	List 1 (Maxwell House)	List 2 (Nescafé)
Lazy	4%	48%
Fails to plan household purchases and schedules well	12%	48%
Thrifty	16%	4%
Not a good wife	0%	16%

Haire interpreted these results as indicating that instant coffee represented a departure from homemade coffee and traditions

Marketers of Nescafé instant coffee had to go to great lengths when the product was introduced to figure out what consumers really thought of it.

Source: Helen Sessions/Alamy

with respect to caring for one's family. In other words, at that time, the "labor-saving" aspect of instant coffee, rather than being an asset, was a liability in that it violated consumer traditions. Consumers were evidently reluctant to admit this fact when asked directly but were better able to express their true feelings when asked to project to another person.

The strategic implications of this new research finding were clear. Based on the original survey results, the obvious positioning for instant coffee with respect to regular coffee would have been to establish a point-of-difference on "convenience" and a point-of-parity on the basis of "taste." Based on the projective test findings, however, it was obvious that there also needed to be a point-of-parity on the basis of user imagery. As a result, a successful ad campaign was launched that promoted Nescafé coffee as a way for housewives to free up time so they could devote additional time to more important household activities.

Sources: Mason Haire, "Projective Techniques in Marketing Research," *Journal of Marketing* (April 1950): 649–652; J. Arndt, "Haire's Shopping List Revisited," *Journal of Advertising Research* 13 (1973): 57–61; G. S. Lane and G. L. Watson, "A Canadian Replication of Mason Haire's 'Shopping List' Study," *Journal of the Academy of Marketing Science* 3 (1975): 48–59; William L. Wilkie, *Consumer Behavior*, 3rd ed. (New York: John Wiley and Sons, 1994).

Comparison Tasks.   Another useful technique is comparison tasks, in which we ask consumers to convey their impressions by comparing brands to people, countries, animals, activities, fabrics, occupations, cars, magazines, vegetables, nationalities, or even other brands.[13] For example, we might ask consumers, "If Dannon yogurt were a car, which one would it be? If it were an animal, which one might it be? Looking at the people depicted in these pictures, which ones do you think would be most likely to eat Dannon yogurt?" In each case, we would ask a follow-up question about why subjects made the comparison they did. The objects people choose to represent the brand and their reasons can provide glimpses into the psyche of the consumer with respect to a brand, particularly useful in understanding imagery associations.

By examining the answers to probes, researchers may be better able to assemble a rich image for the brand, for example, identifying key brand personality associations. Branding Brief 9-3 outlines how hotel chain Joie de Vivre uses magazine imagery to clarify its brand positions.

Archetypes.   Archetype research is one technique for eliciting deeply held consumer attitudes and feelings. According to cultural anthropologist G. C. Rapaille, consumers often make purchase decisions based on factors of which they are only subconsciously aware. Conventional market research typically does not uncover these motivations, so Rapaille employs the archetype research technique to find them.[14]

Rapaille believes children experience a significant initial exposure to an element of their world called the "imprinting moment." The pattern that emerges when we generalize these imprinting moments for the entire population is the *archetype*, a fundamental psychological association, shared by the members of the culture, with a given cultural object. Different cultures have dramatically different archetypes for the same objects. In France, the archetype for cheese is "alive" because age is its most important trait. By contrast, the U.S. archetype for cheese is "dead"; it is wrapped in plastic ("a body-bag"), put in the refrigerator ("a morgue"), and pasteurized ("scientifically dead").

Rapaille uses relaxation exercises and visualization with consumers to find the imprinting moments appropriate to the product he is researching. For example, at a focus group, he will dim the lights, play soothing music, and coax the subjects into a meditative state. He will then elicit stories about the product from the subjects and analyze these stories to illuminate the archetype.

Zaltman Metaphor Elicitation Technique

One interesting approach to better understand how consumers view brands is the Zaltman Metaphor Elicitation Technique (ZMET).[15] ZMET is based on a belief that consumers often have subconscious motives for their purchasing behavior. "A lot goes on in our minds that we're not aware of," said former Harvard Business School professor Gerald Zaltman. "Most of what influences what we say and do occurs below the level of awareness. That's why we need new techniques to get at hidden knowledge—to get at what people don't know they know."

To access this hidden knowledge, he developed the Zaltman Metaphor Elicitation Technique. As described in its U.S. patent, ZMET is "a technique for eliciting interconnected constructs that influence thought and behavior." The word *construct* refers to "an abstraction created by the researcher to capture common ideas, concepts, or themes expressed by customers." For example, the construct "ease of use" might capture the statements "simple to operate," "works without hassle," and "you don't really have to do anything."

ZMET stems from knowledge and research from varied fields such as "cognitive neuroscience, neurobiology, art critique, literary criticism, visual anthropology, visual sociology, semiotics . . . art therapy, and psycholinguistics." The technique is based on the idea that "most social communication is nonverbal" and, as a result, approximately two-thirds of all stimuli received by the brain are visual. Using ZMET, Zaltman teases out consumers' hidden thoughts and feelings about a particular topic, which often can be expressed best using metaphors.

Zaltman defines a metaphor as "a definition of one thing in terms of another, [which] people can use . . . to represent thoughts that are tacit, implicit, and unspoken." ZMET focuses on surface, thematic, and deep metaphors. Some common deep metaphors include "transformation," "container," "journey," "connection," and "sacred and profane."

A ZMET study starts with a group of participants who are asked in advance to think about the research topic at hand and collect a set of images from their own sources (magazines, catalogs, and family photo albums) that represent their thoughts and feelings about the research topic. The participants bring these images with them for a personal one-on-one two-hour interview

BRANDING BRIEF 9-3

Brand Imagery at Joie de Vivre

Joie de Vivre Hospitality LLC operates a chain of boutique hotels, restaurants, and resorts in California, Arizona, and Chicago. Chip Conley founded the company in 1987 when he purchased a rundown motel in a seedy area of San Francisco and converted it into the Phoenix, a fashionable destination popular among entertainment celebrities. In establishing Joie de Vivre, Conley's goal was "to create a company with hip hotel concepts that appealed to a younger consumer base."

Since launching the Phoenix, the company has grown to a total of 34 hotels, the largest group of boutique hotels in California, and is now going national. "Each hotel is a specific world of style and service catering to the needs and wishes of like-minded travelers." Each property's unique décor, quirky amenities, and thematic style are loosely based on a popular magazine. Conley explains the design choices for the hotels and resorts as follows:

> What we've learned over time is that people choose their hotels based on the brand as a mirror. So every time we create a new hotel, spa, or resort, we imagine a magazine that defines the hotel. We choose five words that define the magazine, and by doing that, we get the psychographic fit.

For example, the Phoenix is represented by *Rolling Stone.* The five words used by Conley to describe the magazine are "adventurous, hip, irreverent, funky, and young at heart." The Hotel del Sol—a converted motel bearing a yellow exterior and surrounded by palm trees wrapped with festive lights—is described as "kind of *Martha Stewart Living* meets *Islands* magazine."

Joie de Vivre hotels strive to combine style and flavor with comfort and service. The boutique concept enables the hotels to offer personal touches for its clients, such as LCD flat-screen TVs with HD channels in rooms, billiards tables, and complimentary Wi-Fi, morning coffee, afternoon tea service, and wine hour. The Rex Hotel has a library and a literary flavor. One of the newer offerings, the Hotel Vitale, showcases yoga classes in the rooftop penthouse of its Financial District building. It is described as *Real Simple* magazine meets *Dwell* magazine; the five words that define it are "nurturing, fresh, modern, urbane, and revitalizing."

In addition to providing comfort considerations, Joie de Vivre creates loyalty among its customers with a dedication to customer service. The company condenses all pertinent service information onto a small laminated card that all employees carry with them while they work. By way of introducing the staff to the guests, the company displays "Host Profiles" at the check-in desk that give useful and interesting information about the employees. Various hotel staff contributed to a set of 20 free guides to San Francisco that guests can use to find out about the city from a local's perspective. Joie de Vivre also developed a loyalty program, called the Joy of Life Club, whereby frequent guests earn redeemable points based on what they spend during each stay at one of the company's properties.

The personal touches and unique personality offered by Joie de Vivre hotels have helped the company build a loyal customer

All Joie de Vivre's properties have a unique brand personality. Hotel Rex is sophisticated with a literary theme; Hotel del Sol is fun, colorful and casual.

Source: Joie de Vivre Hotels

base (see the accompanying photos). One repeat customer referred to the company's Hotel Rex as "a home away from home." To help first-time visitors choose the right hotel for them, the company's Web site includes a Hotel Matchmaker personality test offered by a fictional character, "Yvette," that offers recommendations based on answers to five key questions.

Sources: Neal Templin, "Boutique-Hotel Group Thrives on Quirks," *Wall Street Journal*, 18 March 1999; Clifford Carlsen, "Joie de Vivre Resorts to New Hospitality Strategy," *San Francisco Business Times*, 18 June 1999; Chip Conley, *The Rebel Rules* (New York: Fireside, 2001); "On the Record," *San Francisco Chronicle*, 7 August 2005; Tom Osborne, "What Is Your Brand Personality?," *Viget Inspire*, www.viget.com, 2 February 2009; www.jdvhospitality.com, accessed 20 December 2011.

with a study administrator, who uses advanced interview techniques to explore the images with the participant and reveal their deep ideas, archetypes, themes, and emotions through a "guided conversation."

The interview consists of a series of steps, each with a specific purpose in mind:

1. *Storytelling:* Exploring individual visual metaphors
2. *Expand the Frame:* Expanding the metaphoric meaning of images
3. *Sensory Metaphor:* Eliciting metaphors about the research topic from each sensory modality
4. *Vignette:* Using the mind's eye to create a short story about the research topic
5. *Digital Image:* Integrating the images to create a visual summary of the research topic

Once the participants' interviews have been completed, researchers identify key themes or constructs, code the data, and assemble a consensus map of the most important constructs. Quantitative analyses of the data can provide information for advertising, promotions, and other marketing decisions.

ZMET has been applied in a variety of different ways, including as a means to help understand consumers' images of brands, products, and companies. Marketers can employ ZMET for a variety of consumer-insight research topics. Zaltman lists several of these:

> ZMET is useful in understanding consumers' images of brands, products, companies, brand equity, product concepts and designs, product usage and purchase experiences, life experiences, consumption context, and attitudes toward business.

For example, DuPont enlisted Zaltman to research women's attitudes toward hosiery. Conventional research yielded the conclusion that "women mostly hated wearing pantyhose," but DuPont market researchers were not convinced that this conclusion provided a complete picture. Zaltman used ZMET with 20 subjects in order to uncover deeper answers to the question, "What are your thoughts and feelings about buying and wearing pantyhose?" He discovered that women had a "like–hate" relationship with pantyhose; they disliked the discomfort and run-proneness of pantyhose but liked the feel of elegance and sexiness they got from wearing it. This discovery prompted a number of hosiery manufacturers to include more sexy and alluring imagery in their advertising. Figure 9-3 displays a consensus map that emerged from a study of intimate apparel.

Neural Research Methods

Taking ZMET one step further to dig even deeper into the subconscious, some marketing researchers are bypassing any verbal response from consumers to literally get inside the minds of consumers through various neural research methods. *Neuromarketing* is the study of how the

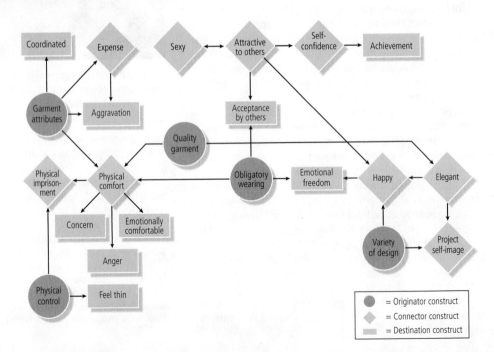

FIGURE 9-3

Application of ZMET to Intimate Apparel Market

brain responds to marketing stimuli, including brands.[16] For example, some firms are applying sophisticated techniques such as EEG (elector encephalograph) technology to monitor brain activity and better gauge consumer responses to marketing.

Neurological research has been applied many ways in marketing.[17] It has been used to measure the type of emotional response consumers exhibit when presented with marketing stimuli. Neurological research has shown that people activate different regions of the brain in assessing the personality traits of people than they do when assessing brands.

One major research finding to emerge from neurological consumer research is that many purchase decisions appear to be characterized less by the logical weighing of variables and more "as a largely unconscious habitual process, as distinct from the rational, conscious, information-processing model of economists and traditional marketing textbooks." Even basic decisions, such as the purchase of gasoline, seem to be influenced by brain activity at the subrational level.

Firms as varied as Intel, Paypal, Google, HP, Citi, and Microsoft have employed neurological marketing research studies. Frito-Lay hired neuromarketing firm NeuroFocus to study how consumers responded to their Cheetos cheese-flavored snack. Scanning the brains of a carefully chosen group of consumers revealed that their most powerful response was to the product's messy outer coating. The research study's insight led to an award-winning ad campaign.[18]

By adding neurological techniques to their research arsenal, marketers are trying to move toward a more complete picture of what goes on inside consumers' heads.[19] Although it may be able to offer different insights from conventional techniques, neurological research at this point is very costly, running as much as $100,000 or even more per project. Given the complexity of the human brain, however, many researchers caution that neurological research should not form the sole basis for marketing decisions. These research activities have not been universally accepted. The measurement devices to capture brain activity can be highly obtrusive, such as with skull caps studded with electrodes, creating artificial exposure conditions. Others question whether they offer unambiguous implications for marketing strategy. Brian Knutson, a professor of neuroscience and psychology at Stanford University, compares the use of EEG to "standing outside a baseball stadium and listening to the crowd to figure out what happened."

Brand Personality and Values

As defined in Chapter 2, brand personality is the human characteristics or traits that consumers can attribute to a brand. We can measure it in different ways. Perhaps the simplest and most direct way is to solicit open-ended responses to a probe such as the following:

> If the brand were to come alive as a person, what would it be like? What would it do? Where would it live? What would it wear? Who would it talk to if it went to a party (and what would it talk about)?

If consumers have difficulty getting started in their descriptions, an easily understood example or prompt serves as a guide. For example, if Campbell's soup were to be described as a person, one possible response might be as follows:[20]

> Mrs. Campbell is a rosy-cheeked and plump grandmother who lives in a warm, cozy house and wears an apron as she cooks wonderful things for her grandchildren.

Other means are possible to capture consumers' points of view. For example, marketers can give consumers a variety of pictures or a stack of magazines and ask them to assemble a profile of the brand. Ad agencies often conduct "picture sorting" studies to clarify who are typical users of a brand.

As Chapter 3 noted, brand personality and user imagery may not always agree. When *USA Today* was first introduced, a research study exploring consumer opinions of the newspaper indicated that the benefits readers and nonreaders perceived were highly consistent. Perceptions of the *USA Today* brand personality—as colorful, friendly, and simple—were also highly related. User imagery, however, differed dramatically: Nonreaders viewed a typical *USA Today* reader as a shallow "air head"; readers, on the other hand, saw a typical *USA Today* reader as a well-rounded person interested in a variety of issues. Based on these findings, an advertising campaign was introduced to appeal to nonreaders that showed how prominent people endorsed the newspaper.[21]

When *USA Today* launched, readers and nonreaders had very different brand imagery perceptions.

Source: Keri Miksza

The Big Five. We can assess brand personality more definitively through adjective checklists or ratings. Jennifer Aaker conducted a research project that provides an interesting glimpse into the personality of a number of well-known brands, as well as a methodology to examine the personality of any one brand. Based on an extensive data collection of ratings of 114 personality traits on 37 brands in various product categories by over 600 individuals representative of the U.S. population, she created a brand personality scale that reflected the following five factors (with underlying facets) of brand personality:[22]

1. Sincerity (down-to-earth, honest, wholesome, and cheerful)
2. Excitement (daring, spirited, imaginative, and up-to-date)
3. Competence (reliable, intelligent, and successful)
4. Sophistication (upper class and charming)
5. Ruggedness (outdoorsy and tough)

Figure 9-4 depicts the specific trait items that make up the Aaker brand personality scale. Respondents in her study rated how descriptive each personality trait was for each brand according to a seven-point scale (1 = not at all descriptive; 7 = extremely descriptive). Aaker averaged responses to provide summary measures. Some brands tend to be strong on one particular factor; some brands like Nike are high on more than one factor; some brands score poorly on all factors.

A cross-cultural study exploring the generalizability of this scale outside the United States found that three of the five factors applied in Japan and Spain, but that a "peacefulness" dimension replaced "ruggedness" both in Japan and Spain, and a "passion" dimension emerged in Spain instead of "competency."[23] Research on brand personality in Korea revealed that two culture-specific factors emerge ("passive likeableness" and "ascendancy"), reflecting the importance of Confucian values in Korea's social and economic systems.[24]

Ethnographic and Experiential Methods

More than ever, researchers are working to improve the effectiveness of their qualitative approaches, as well as to go beyond traditional qualitative techniques to research consumers in their natural environment.[25] The rationale is that no matter how clever the research design, consumers may not be able to fully express their true selves as part of a formalized research study. By tapping more directly into consumers' actual home, work, or shopping behaviors, researchers might be able to elicit more meaningful responses.[26] As markets become more competitive

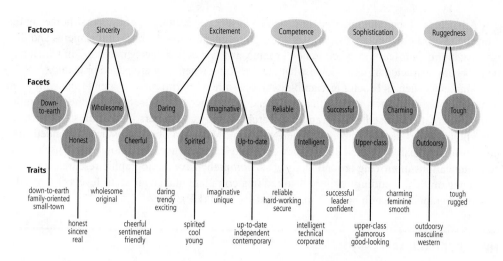

FIGURE 9-4
Brand Personality Scale Measures

and many brand differences are threatened, any insight that helps to support a stronger brand positioning or create a stronger link to consumers is valuable (see Branding Brief 9-4).

We've noted that much of this type of research has its roots in ethnographic research originally used by anthropologists. Ethnographic research uses "thick description" based on participant observation. In marketing, the goal of ethnographic research is to extract and interpret the deep cultural meaning of events and activities through various research techniques such as consumer immersion, site visits, shop-alongs, embedded research, etc.[27]

BRANDING BRIEF 9-4

Making the Most of Consumer Insights

Consumer research plays a significant role in uncovering information valuable to consumer-focused companies. David Taylor, founder of the Brand Gym consultancy, cautions that not all findings from consumer research can be considered insights. He defines an insight as "a penetrating, discerning understanding that unlocks an opportunity."

According to Taylor, an insight holds far more potential than a finding. Using Microsoft as an example, Taylor draws the contrast between the finding that "people need to process more and more information and data" and the insight that "information is the key to power and freedom." This insight might help Microsoft develop products that appeal to a larger consumer base than if the company relied solely on the finding.

Taylor developed a set of criteria to evaluate insights:

- *Fresh:* An insight might be obvious and, in fact, be overlooked or forgotten as a result. Check again.

- *Relevant:* An insight when played back to other target consumers should strike a chord.

- *Enduring:* By building on a deep understanding of consumers' beliefs and needs, a true consumer insight should have potential to remain relevant over time.

- *Inspiring:* All the team should be excited by the insight and see different but consistent applications.

Insights can come from consumer research such as focus groups, but also from using what Taylor describes

as the "core insight drills." A sample of these drills follows:

- How could the brand/category do more to help improve people's lives?

- What do people really value in the category? What would they not miss?

- What conflicting needs do people have? How can these tradeoffs be solved?

- What bigger market is the brand really competing in from a consumer viewpoint? What could the brand do more of to better meet these "higher-order" needs?

- What assumptions do people make about the market that could be challenged?

- How do people think the product works, and how does it work in reality?

- How is the product used in reality? What other products are used instead of the brand, where the brand could do a better job?

These "drills" can help companies unearth consumer insights that lead to better products and services, and ultimately to stronger brands.

Source: David Taylor, "Drilling for Nuggets: How to Use Insight to Inspire Innovation," *Brand Strategy*, March 2000. Used with permission of Brand Strategy, www.brandstrategy.co.uk.

Advocates of the ethnographic approach have sent researchers to consumers' homes in the morning to see how they approach their days, given business travelers digital cameras and diaries to capture their feelings when in hotel rooms, and conducted "beeper studies" in which participants are instructed to write down what they're doing when they are paged or texted.[28]

Marketers such as Procter & Gamble seek consumers' permission to spend time with them in their homes to see how they actually use and experience products. Some of the many other companies that have used ethnographic research to study consumers include Best Western (to learn how seniors decide when and where to shop), Moen (to observe over an extended time how customers really use their shower devices), and Intel (to understand how people use mobile communications in moving around a city).[29] A comprehensive ethnographic research study for JCPenney on their wedding registry resulted in a complete makeover at all levels.[30] Consider how ethnographic research paid off for Hewlett-Packard (HP).

HEWLETT-PACKARD (HP)

To better understand how surgeons operate, HP's medical products division sent a set of researchers into hospitals to observe. Surgeons need to carefully monitor their scalpel movements on a video monitor. During an operation, however, the researchers observed that many other staff members would cross in front of the monitor, obscuring the surgeon's line of sight. Because these staff members were going about their duties, the surgeons had failed to complain and prior research had failed to uncover the problem. Based on this research insight, HP developed a surgical helmet with goggles that cast images right in front of a surgeon's eyes, circumventing the problem.[31]

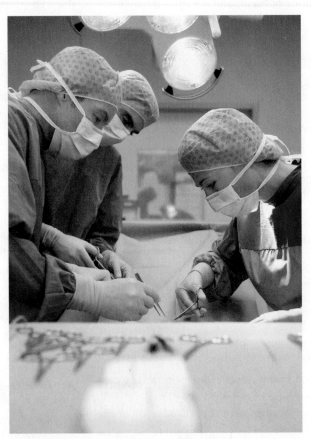

An ethnographic research study by HP led to a breakthrough new medical product.
Source: moodboard/Alamy

Business-to-business firms can also benefit from company visits that help to cement relationships and supplement research efforts. Technology firms such as Hewlett-Packard use cross-functional customer visits as a market research tool to gain a competitive advantage.

1. Send an advance letter of confirmation with an agenda so customers know what to expect and can be prepared.
2. Send small cross-functional teams.
3. Select customers according to a plan and visit at least a dozen.
4. Don't keep going back to the same small group of favorite customers.
5. Interview people at each site who represent each stage of the purchasing decision.
6. Get support from local account management.
7. Use a two- to three-page discussion guide in outline form.
8. Assign roles to team members (moderator, listener, note taker, etc.).
9. Use open-ended questions.
10. Don't ask customers to give solutions—get them to identify problems.
11. Don't talk too much and don't show off your expertise.
12. Probe deeper by using follow-up questions.
13. Debrief immediately.
14. Highlight verbatim quotes in reports.
15. A summary report should emphasize big news and be organized by major themes.
16. Archive the report online with other marketing research and intelligence.

FIGURE 9-5

Tips for Conducting
Good Customer Visits

Figure 9-5 offers advice from one expert on the subject, Ed McQuarrie, about best practices for an outbound or inbound customer visit.[32]

Service companies often employ *mystery shoppers*, paid researchers who pose as customers to learn about the service experience provided by a company. Sometimes the results can be eye-opening. When the president of Office Depot decided to pose as a mystery shopper himself, he found that employees were spending too much time keeping stores clean and well-stocked and not enough time actually building relationships with customers. As a result, the company reduced the size of stores, retrained and incentivized employees to focus more on customers, and added other products and services that customers wanted that were not currently available.[33]

Through the years, companies have changed the way they gain customer insights. Microsoft employs ethnographic research with in-depth studies of consumer online search attitudes and behavior. Observing consumers inside and outside the home in a series of research studies, the company learned of changes over time in the way consumers explore and learn about new things online.[34]

- An initial study in 2004 revealed that consumers were just trying to find out what experts say, because they felt that experts "knew it all."
- A follow-up study in 2007 showed that consumers believed all the information they needed to learn was actually available through search engines—they just needed to figure out how to use the search engines.
- By 2010, however, ethnographic research showed that people felt they actually created their own knowledge. Search engines were just enablers.

Of special research importance to many companies are lead or leading users. Many firms ask online groups of their most progressive consumers to give feedback via instant-messages or chat rooms. PepsiCo's DEWmocracy 2 program, launched in July 2009, was a 12-month, seven-stage campaign to create another consumer-generated version of its Mountain Dew soft drink, as had happened when the first DEWmocracy produced the highly successful Mountain Dew Voltage. The new campaign tapped into DEW labs, the brand's private online community of its most loyal customers, but also Facebook, Twitter, USTREAM, a 12-second TV video contest, and a dedicated YouTube channel.[35] Another company with close ties to leading-edge users is Burton Snowboards.

BURTON SNOWBOARDS

The best-known snowboard brand, Burton Snowboards, saw its market share increase from 30 percent to 40 percent by focusing on one objective—providing the best equipment to the largest number of snowboarders. To accomplish this goal, Burton engages in a number of activities. Burton puts much emphasis on its many professional riders worldwide, including a smaller percentage who are on its sponsored team. Staff members talk to the riders—on the slopes or on the phone—almost every day, and riders help to design virtually every Burton product. Company researchers immerse themselves in the riders' lives, watching where they shop, what they buy, and what they think about the sport and the equipment. To make sure it doesn't lose touch with its rank-and-file consumers, however, the company makes sure its sales representatives hit the slopes on the weekend to interact with amateur snowboarders. All employees also get a free season pass for the slopes and are allowed to use any new Burton gear for a few days to test and promote it. In 2010, the Burton Demo Tour became the largest consumer interactive product demo in the snowboard world, with over 2,000 riders testing Burton gear on slopes all over North America. Burton also has the eTeam—an online community of 25,000 kids who provide real-time feedback in exchange for free product trials. All of this information is fed into Burton's state-of-the-art innovation center, "Craig's," named after the late snowboarding pioneer Craig Kelly, where advanced prototypes are developed and tested almost daily.[36]

Burton collects information from casual and professional riders to help it design innovative snowboards and other products.
Source: Olivier Maire/EPA/Newscom

Compact video cameras make capturing participants' words and actions easier, and short films are often part of the research output that is reported to help bring the research to life.[37] Every research method, however, has its advantages and disadvantages.[38] Two of the more significant downsides to ethnographic research are that it is time-consuming and expensive. Moreover, because it is based on subjective interpretation, multiple points of view may prevail.

Summary

Qualitative research techniques are a creative means of ascertaining consumer perceptions that may otherwise be difficult to uncover. The range of possible qualitative research techniques is limited only by the creativity of the marketing researcher.

Qualitative research, however, also has its drawbacks. The in-depth insights that emerge have to be tempered by the realization that the samples are often very small and may not necessarily generalize to broader populations. Moreover, given the qualitative nature of the data, there may be questions of interpretation. Different researchers examining the same results from a qualitative research study may draw different conclusions.

QUANTITATIVE RESEARCH TECHNIQUES

Although qualitative measures are useful in identifying the range of possible associations with a brand and some initial insights into their strength, favorability, and uniqueness, marketers often want a more definitive portrait of the brand to allow them to make more confident and defensible strategic and tactical recommendations.

Some say qualitative research strives to uncover and discover, while quantitative research aims to prove or disprove. Whereas qualitative research typically elicits some type of verbal response from consumers, *quantitative research* typically employs various types of scale questions from which researchers can draw numerical representations and summaries.

Quantitative measures of brand knowledge can help to more definitively assess the depth and breadth of brand awareness; the strength, favorability, and uniqueness of brand associations; the positivity of brand judgments and feelings; and the extent and nature of brand relationships. Quantitative measures are often the primary ingredient in tracking studies that monitor brand knowledge structures of consumers over time, as we discussed in Chapter 8.

Brand Awareness

Recall that brand awareness is related to the strength of the brand in memory, as reflected by consumers' ability to identify various brand elements like the brand name, logo, symbol, character, packaging, and slogan under different conditions. Brand awareness describes the likelihood that a brand will come to mind in different situations, and the ease with which it does so given different types of cues.

Marketers use several measures of awareness of brand elements.[39] Choosing the right one is a matter of knowing the relative importance of brand awareness for consumer behavior in the category and the role it plays in the success of the marketing program, as we discussed in Chapter 2. Let's look at some of these awareness issues.

Recognition.   Brand recognition requires consumers to identify the brand under a variety of circumstances and can rest on the identification of any of the brand elements. The most basic recognition test gives consumers a set of individual items visually or orally and asks them whether they think they've previously seen or heard of these items. To provide a more sensitive test, it is often useful to include decoys or lures—items consumers could not possibly have seen. In addition to "yes" or "no" responses, consumers can also rate how confident they are in their recognition of an item.

Other, somewhat more subtle, recognition measures test "perceptually degraded" versions of the brand, which are masked or distorted in some way or shown for extremely brief duration. For example, we can test brand name recognition with missing letters. Figure 9-6 tests your ability to recognize brand names with less than full information. These more subtle measures may be particularly important for brands that have a high level of recognition, in order to provide more sensitive assessments.[40]

A brand name with a high level of awareness will be recognized under less than ideal conditions. Consider the following list of incomplete names (i.e., word fragments). Which ones do you recognize? Compare your answers to the answer key in the footnote to see how well you did.

1. D _ _ N E _
2. K O _ _ K
3. D U _ A C _ _ _
4. H Y _ T _
5. A D _ _ L
6. M _ T _ E L
7. D _ L T _
8. N _ Q U _ L
9. G _ L L _ T _ _
10. H _ _ S H _ Y
11. H _ L L _ _ R K
12. M _ C H _ _ I N
13. T _ P P _ R W _ _ E
14. L _ G _
15. N _ K _

Answers: (1) Disney; (2) Kodak; (3) Duracell; (4) Hyatt; (5) Advil; (6) Mattel; (7) Delta; (8) NyQuil; (9) Gillette; (10) Hershey; (11) Hallmark; (12) Michelin; (13) Tupperware; (14) Lego; (15) Nike.

FIGURE 9-6

Don't Tell Me, It's On the Tip of My Tongue

Brand recognition is especially important for packaging, and some marketing researchers have used creative means to assess the visibility of package design. As a starting point, they consider the benchmark or "best case" of the visibility of a package when a consumer (1) with 20–20 vision (2) is face-to-face with a package (3) at a distance of less than five feet (4) under ideal lighting conditions.

A key question then is whether the package design is robust enough to be still recognizable if one or more of these four conditions are not present. Because shopping is often not conducted under "ideal" conditions, such insights are important. For example, many consumers who wear eyeglasses do not wear them when shopping in a supermarket. Is the package still able to effectively communicate to consumers under such conditions?

Research methods using tachistoscopes (T-scopes) and eye tracking techniques exist to test the effectiveness of alternative package designs according to a number of specific criteria:

- Degree of shelf impact
- Impact and recall of specific design elements
- Perceived package size
- Copy visibility and legibility
- Distance at which the package can first be identified
- Angle at which the package can first be identified
- Speed with which the package can be identified

These additional measures can provide more sensitive measures of recognition than simple "yes" or "no" tasks. By applying these direct and indirect measures of brand recognition, marketers can determine which brand elements exist in memory and, to some extent, the strength of their association. One advantage that brand recognition measures have over recall measures is the chance to use visual recognition. It may be difficult for consumers to describe a logo or symbol in a recall task; it's much easier for them to assess the same elements visually in a recognition task.

Nevertheless, brand recognition measures provide only an approximation of *potential* recallability. To determine whether consumers will actually recall the brand elements under various circumstances, we need measures of brand recall.

Recall.   To demonstrate brand recall, consumers must retrieve the actual brand element from memory when given some related probe or cue. Thus, brand recall is a more demanding memory task than brand recognition because consumers are not just given a brand element and asked to say whether they've seen it before.

Different measures of brand recall are possible depending on the type of cues provided to consumers. *Unaided recall* on the basis of "all brands" provided as a cue is likely to identify

Before a new package ever hits the shelf, marketers often conduct research to understand its likely impact even in the store itself.

Source: Paul Burns Cultura/Newscom

only the very strongest brands. *Aided recall* uses various types of cues to help consumer recall. One possible sequence of aided recall might use progressively narrower cues—such as product class, product category, and product type labels—to provide insight into the organization of consumers' brand knowledge structures.

For example, if recall of the Porsche 911—a high-performance German sports car—in non-German markets were of interest, recall probes could begin with "all cars" and move to more and more narrowly defined categories such as "sports cars," "foreign sports cars," or even "high-performance German sports cars." Marketers could ask consumers: "When you think of foreign sports cars, which brands come to mind?"

Other types of cues can help measure brand recall. For example, marketers can ask about product attributes ("When you think of chocolate, which brands come to mind?) or usage goals ("If you were thinking of having a healthy snack, which brands come to mind?"). Often, to capture the breadth of brand recall and to assess brand salience, we might need to examine the context of the purchase decision or consumption situation, such as different times and places. The stronger the brand associations to these non-product considerations, the more likely it is that consumers will recall them when given those situational cues.

When combined, measures of recall based on product attribute or category cues and situational or usage cues give an indication of breadth and depth of recall. We can further distinguish brand recall according to the order as well as the latency or speed of recall. In many cases, people will recognize a brand when it is shown to them and will recall it if they are given a sufficient number of cues. Thus, potential recallability is high. The more important issue is the salience of the brand: Do consumers think of the brand under the right circumstances, for example, when they could be either buying or using the product? How quickly do they think of the brand? Is it automatically or easily recalled? Is it the first brand they recall?

Corrections for Guessing.

Any research measure must consider the issue of consumers making up responses or guessing. That problem may be especially evident with certain types of aided awareness or recognition measures for the brand. Spurious awareness occurs when consumers erroneously claim they recall something they really don't and that may not even exist. For example, one market research firm, Oxtoby-Smith, conducted a benchmark study of awareness of health and beauty products.[41] In the study, the firm asked consumers questions like this:

> "The following is a list of denture adhesive brand names. Please answer yes if you've heard the name before and no if you haven't. Okay? Orafix? Fasteeth? Dentu-Tight? Fixodent?"

Although 16 percent of the sample reported that they had heard of Dentu-Tight, there was one problem: it didn't exist! Similarly high levels of reported recall were reported for plausible-sounding but fictitious brands such as Four O'Clock Tea (8 percent), Leone Pasta (16 percent), and Mrs. Smith's Cake Mix (31 percent). On the basis of this study, Oxtoby-Smith found that spurious awareness was about 8 percent for new health and beauty products and even higher in some other product categories. In one case, a proposed line extension was mistakenly thought to already exist by about 50 percent of the sample (a finding that no doubt sent a message to the company that it should go ahead and introduce the product!).

From a marketing perspective, the problem with spurious awareness is that it may send misleading signals about the proper strategic direction for a brand. For example, Oxtoby-Smith reported that one of its clients was struggling with a 5 percent market share despite the fact that 50 percent of survey respondents reported they were aware of the brand. On the surface, it would seem a good idea to improve the image of the brand and attitudes toward it in some way. Upon further examination, marketers determined that spurious awareness accounted for *almost half* the survey respondents who reported brand awareness, suggesting that a more appropriate solution to the true problem would be to first build awareness to a greater degree. Marketers should be sensitive to the possibilities of misleading signals because of spurious brand awareness, especially with new brands or ones with plausible-sounding names.

Strategic Implications.

The advantage of aided recall measures is that they yield insight into how brand knowledge is organized in memory and what kind of cues or reminders may be necessary for consumers to be able to retrieve the brand from memory. Understanding recall when

For a unique sports car like Porsche, it is important for marketers to understand the breadth and depth of its brand awareness.

Source: Hand-out/PORSCHE CANADA/Newscom

we use different levels of product category specificity as cues is important, because it has implications for how consumers form consideration sets and make product decisions.

For example, again consider the Porsche 911. Assume consumer recall of this particular car model was fairly low when all cars were considered but very high when foreign sports cars were considered. In other words, consumers strongly categorized the Porsche 911 as a prototypical sports car but tended to think of it in only that way. If that were the case, for more consumers to entertain the possibility of buying a Porsche 911, we might need to broaden the meaning of Porsche so that it has a stronger association to cars in general. Of course, such a strategy risks alienating existing customers who had been initially attracted by the "purity" and strong identification of the Porsche 911 as a sports car. The choice of appropriate strategy would depend on the relative costs and benefits of targeting the two different segments.

The point is that the category structure that exists in consumers' minds—as reflected by brand recall performance—can have profound implications for consumer choice and marketing strategy, as demonstrated by The Science of Branding 9-1. The insights gleaned from measuring brand recall are also valuable for developing brand identity and integrated marketing communication programs, as we showed in Chapters 4 and 6. For example, we can examine brand recall for each brand element to explore the extent to which any one of these (name, symbol, or logo) suggests any other. Are consumers aware of all the different brand elements and how they relate?

We also need a complete understanding of brand image, as covered in the following section.

Brand Image

One vitally important aspect of the brand is its image, as reflected by the associations that consumers hold for it. It is useful for marketers to make a distinction between lower-level considerations, related to consumer perceptions of specific performance and imagery attributes and benefits, and higher-level considerations related to overall judgments, feelings, and relationships. There is an obvious connection between the two levels, because consumers' overall responses and relationship with a brand typically depend on perceptions of specific attributes and benefits of that brand. This section considers some issues in measuring lower-level brand performance and imagery associations.

Beliefs are descriptive thoughts that a person holds about something (for instance, that a particular software package has many helpful features and menus and is easy to use).[42] Brand association beliefs are those specific attributes and benefits linked to the brand and its competitors.

THE SCIENCE OF BRANDING 9-1

Understanding Categorical Brand Recall

A classic experiment by Prakash Nedungadi provides a compelling demonstration of the importance of understanding the category structure that exists in consumer memory as well as the value of strategies for increasing the recallability or accessibility of brands during choice situations. As a preliminary step in his research study, Nedungadi first examined the category structure for fast-food restaurants that existed in consumers' minds. He found that a "major subcategory" was "hamburger chains" and a "minor subcategory" was "sandwich shops." He also found, on the basis of usage and linking surveys, that within the major subcategory of national hamburger chains, a major brand was McDonald's and a minor brand was Wendy's, and within the minor subcategory of local sandwich shops, a major brand was Joe's Deli (a brand in his survey area) and a minor brand was Subway. Consistent with this reasoning, in an unaided recall and choice task, consumers were more likely to remember and select a brand from a major subcategory than from a minor subcategory and, within a subcategory, a major brand rather than a minor brand.

Nedungadi next looked at the effects of different brand "primes" on subsequent choices among the four fast-food restaurants. Brands were primed by having subjects in the experiment first answer a series of seemingly unrelated questions—including some about the brand to be primed—before making their brand selections. Two key findings emerged. First, a major brand that was primed was more likely to be selected in the later choice task even though attitudes toward the brand were no different from those of a control group. In other

words, merely making the brand more accessible in memory increased the likelihood that it would be chosen *independent of any differences in brand attitude*. Second, priming a minor brand in a minor subcategory actually benefited the *major* brand in that subcategory more. In other words, by drawing attention to the minor subcategory of sandwich shops—which could easily be overlooked—the minor brand, Subway, indirectly primed the major brand, Joe's Deli, in the subcategory. The implications of Nedungadi's research are that marketers must understand how consumers' memory is organized and, as much as possible, ensure that the proper cues and primes are evident to prompt brand recall.

In sum, brand recall provides insight into category structure and brand positioning in consumers' minds. Brands tend to be recalled in categorical clusters when consumers are given a general probe. Certain brands are grouped together in memory because they share certain associations and are thus likely to cue and remind consumers of each other if one is recalled.

Sources: Prakash Nedungadi, "Recall and Consumer Consideration Sets: Influencing Choice Without Altering Brand Evaluations," *Journal of Consumer Research* 17 (December 1990): 263–276; Joseph W. Alba and J. Wesley Hutchinson, "Dimensions of Consumer Expertise," *Journal of Consumer Research* 13 (March 1987): 411–454; Kalpesh Kaushik Desai and Wayne D. Hoyer, "Descriptive Characteristics of Memory-Based Consideration Sets: Influence of Usage Occasion Frequency and Usage Location Familiarity," *Journal of Consumer Research* 27 (2000): 309–323.

For example, consumers may have brand association beliefs for Sony PlayStation 3 entertainment system such as "fun and exciting," "cool and hip," "colorful," "great graphics," "advanced technology," "variety of game titles," and "sometimes violent." They may also have associations to the brand logo and the slogan, "It Only Does Everything." PlayStation 3 user imagery may be "used by teenagers or 20-something males who are serious about playing video games, especially sports games."

In Chapter 2, we provided a structured set of measures to tap into performance and imagery associations. The qualitative research approaches we described earlier are useful in uncovering the different types of specific brand associations making up the brand image. To better understand their potential ability to serve as basis for brand positioning and how they might contribute to brand equity, we can assess belief associations on the basis of one or more of the three key dimensions—strength, favorability, and uniqueness—making up the sources of brand equity.

As a first cut, we can use open-ended measures that tap into the strength, favorability, and uniqueness of brand associations, as follows:

1. What are the strongest associations you have to the brand? What comes to mind when you think of the brand? (Strength)
2. What is good about the brand? What do you like about the brand? What is bad about the brand? What do you dislike about the brand? (Favorability)
3. What is unique about the brand? What characteristics or features does the brand share with other brands? (Uniqueness)

1. To what extent do you feel the following product characteristics are descriptive of Lipton iced tea (where 1 = strongly disagree and 7 = strongly agree)?

   _____ convenient
   _____ refreshing and thirst quenching
   _____ real and natural
   _____ good-tasting
   _____ contemporary and relevant
   _____ used by young professionals

2. How good or bad is it for iced tea to have the following product characteristics (where 1 = very bad and 7 = very good)?

   _____ convenient
   _____ refreshing and thirst quenching
   _____ real and natural
   _____ good-tasting
   _____ contemporary and relevant
   _____ used by young professionals

3. How unique is Lipton iced tea in terms of the following product characteristics (where 1 = not at all unique and 7 = highly unique)?

   _____ convenient
   _____ refreshing and thirst quenching
   _____ real and natural
   _____ good-tasting
   _____ contemporary and relevant
   _____ used by young professionals

FIGURE 9-7

Example of Brand Association Ratings in Terms of Strength, Favorability, and Uniqueness

To gain more specific insights, we could rate these belief associations according to strength, favorability, and uniqueness, as Figure 9-7 illustrates with Lipton iced tea. Indirect tests also can assess the derived importance and favorability of these brand associations (through multivariate regression techniques).

Other Approaches.   A more complicated quantitative technique to assess overall brand uniqueness is multidimensional scaling, or perceptual maps. *Multidimensional scaling* (MDS) is a procedure for determining the perceived relative images of a set of objects, such as products or brands. MDS transforms consumer judgments of similarity or preference into distances represented in perceptual space. For example, if brands A and B are judged by respondents to be the most similar of a set of brands, the MDS algorithm will position brands A and B so that the distance between them in multidimensional space is smaller than the distance between any other two pairs of brands. Respondents may base their similarity between brands on any basis—tangible or intangible.[43]

Figure 9-8 displays a hypothetical perceptual map of restaurants in a particular market. Segment 1 is more concerned with health than taste and is well targeted by Brand B; segment 2 is more concerned with taste and is well targeted by Brand C. Brand A is trapped in the middle. It either must improve taste to provide a healthy alternative to Brand C for segment 2, or it must improve healthiness to prove a tastier alternative to Brand B for segment 1.

Brand Responses

The purpose of measuring more general, higher-level considerations is to find out how consumers combine all the more specific, lower-level considerations about the brand in their minds to form different types of brand responses and evaluations. Chapter 2 provided examples of measures of key brand judgments and feelings. Here we delve into more detail.

Purchase Intentions.   Another set of measures closely related to brand attitudes and consideration looks at purchase intentions[44] and focus on the likelihood of buying the brand or of switching to another brand. Research in psychology suggests that purchase intentions are most likely to

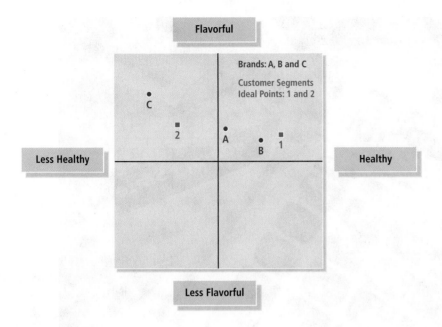

FIGURE 9-8

Hypothetical Restaurant
Perceptual Map

be predictive of actual purchase when there is correspondence between the two in the following
dimensions:[45]

- Action (buying for own use or to give as a gift)
- Target (specific type of product and brand)
- Context (in what type of store based on what prices and other conditions)
- Time (within a week, month, or year)

In other words, when asking consumers to forecast their likely purchase of a product or a brand,
we want to specify *exactly* the circumstances—the purpose of the purchase, the location of the
purchase, the time of the purchase, and so forth. For example, we could ask consumers:

> "Assume your refrigerator broke down over the next weekend and could not be inex-
> pensively repaired. If you went to your favorite appliance store and found all the dif-
> ferent brands competitively priced, how likely would you be to buy a General Electric
> refrigerator?"

Consumers could indicate their purchase intention on an 11-point probability scale that
ranges from 0 (definitely would not buy) to 10 (definitely would buy).

Likelihood to Recommend.   Bain's Frederick Reichheld suggests there is only one customer
question that really matters: "How likely is it that you would recommend this product or service to a friend or colleague?" According to Reichheld, a customer's willingness to recommend
results from all aspects of a customer's experience.[46]

Reichheld uses answers to this question to create what he calls a Net Promoter Score
(NPS). Specifically, in a survey, customers are asked to rate their likelihood to recommend on
a 0–10-point scale. Marketers then subtract *detractors* (those who gave a 0–6) from *promot-
ers* (those who gave a 9 or 10) to arrive at the NPS score. Customers who rate the brand with a
7 or 8 are deemed *passively satisfied* and are not included. A typical set of NPS scores falls in
the 10–30 percent range, but world-class companies can score over 50 percent. Some firms with
top NPS scores include USAA (89 percent), Apple (77 percent), Amazon.com (74 percent), and
Google (71 percent).

Several companies have seen benefits from adopting NetPromoter scores as a means of
tracking brand health. When the European unit of GE Healthcare overhauled its call center and
put more specialists in the field, GE Healthcare's Net Promoter scores jumped 10–15 points.
BearingPoint found clients who gave it high Net Promoter scores showed the highest revenue
growth. When Intuit applied Net Promoter to its TurboTax product, feedback revealed dissatisfaction with the software's rebate procedure. After Intuit dropped the proof-of-purchase requirement, sales jumped 6 percent.

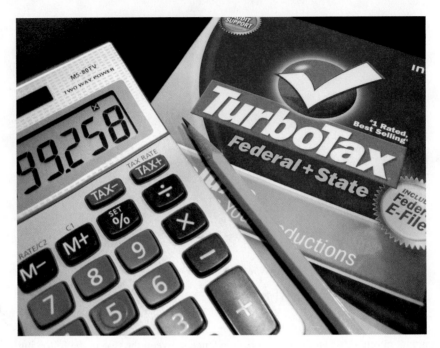

TurboTax used
NetPromoter scores
to help fine-tune its
marketing program.
Source: AP Photo/
RIGELHAUPT SAMUEL/SIPA

Brand Relationships

Chapter 2 characterized brand relationships in terms of brand resonance and offered possible measures for each of the four key dimensions: behavioral loyalty, attitudinal attachment, sense of community, and active engagement. This section considers additional considerations with respect to each of those four dimensions. Figure 9-9 displays a scale, although developed by its authors to measure overall brand engagement, could easily be adapted to measure brand resonance by replacing mentions of brands with a specific brand. For example, instead of saying, "I have a special bond with the brands I like," it could say, "I have a special bond with my Saab automobile," and so on.

Behavioral Loyalty.   To capture reported brand usage and behavioral loyalty, we could ask consumers several questions directly. Or we could ask them what percentage of their last purchases in the category went to the brand (past purchase history) and what percentage of their planned next purchases will go to the brand (intended future purchases). For example, the marketers or brand managers of Duracell batteries might ask the following questions:

- Which brand of batteries do you usually buy?
- Which brand of batteries did you buy last time?
- Do you have any batteries on hand? Which brand?
- Which brands of batteries did you consider buying?
- Which brand of batteries will you buy next time?

These types of questions can provide information about brand attitudes and usage for Duracell, including potential gaps with competitors and the names of other brands that might be in the consideration set at the time of purchase.

Marketers can make their measures open ended, force consumers to choose one of two brands, or offer multiple choice or rating scales. They can compare the answers with actual measures of consumer behavior to assess whether consumers are accurate in their predictions. For example, if 30 percent of consumers reported, on average, that they thought they would take their vitamins daily over the next two weeks, but only 15 percent of consumers reported two weeks later that they actually had done so during that period, then Centrum brand managers might need to devise strategies to better convert intentions to actual behavior.

In a business-to-business setting, Narayandas advocates analyzing sales records, talking to sales teams, and conducting surveys to assess where customers stand on a "loyalty ladder."[47]

1. I have a special bond with the brands I like.
2. I consider my favorite brands to be part of myself.
3. I often feel a personal connection between my brands and me.
4. Part of me is defined by important brands in my life.
5. I feel as if I have a close personal connection with the brands I most prefer.
6. I can identify with important brands in my life.
7. There are links between the brands that I prefer and how I view myself.
8. My favorite brands are an important indication of who I am.

FIGURE 9-9

A Brand Engagement Scale

Source: David Sprott, Sandor Czellar, and Eric Spangenberg, "The Importance of a General Measure of Brand Engagement on Market Behaviour: Development and Validation of a Scale," *Journal of Marketing Research* 46 (February 2009): 92–104.

Attitudinal Attachment.   Several different approaches have been suggested to measure the second component of brand resonance—brand attachment.[48] Some researchers like to characterize it in terms of brand love.[49] One study proposed a brand love scale that consists of 10 items: (1) This is a wonderful brand; (2) This brand makes me feel good; (3) This brand is totally awesome; (4) I have neutral feelings about this brand (reverse-coded item); (5) This brand makes me very happy; (6) I love this brand; (7) I have no particular feelings about this brand (reverse-coded item); (8) This brand is a pure delight; (9) I am passionate about this brand; and (10) I am very attached to this brand.[50]

Another study found 11 dimensions that characterized brand love:[51]

1. Passion (for the brand).
2. Duration of the relationship (the relationship with the brand exists for a long time).
3. Self-congruity (congruity between self-image and product image).
4. Dreams (the brand favors consumer dreams).
5. Memories (evoked by the brand).
6. Pleasure (that the brand provides to the consumer).
7. Attraction (feel toward the brand).
8. Uniqueness (of the brand and/or of the relationship).
9. Beauty (of the brand).
10. Trust (the brand has never disappointed).
11. Declaration of affect (feel toward the brand).

One promising approach defines brand attachment in terms of two underlying constructs—brand-self connections and brand prominence—where each of those two dimensions have two subdimensions, suggesting the following sets of measures:[52]

1. **Brand-Self Connection**
   a. *Connected*: "To what extent do you feel that you are personally connected to (Brand)?"
   b. *Part of Who You Are*: "To what extent is (Brand) part of you and who you are?"

2. **Brand Prominence**
   a. *Automatic*: "To what extent are your thoughts and feelings towards (Brand) often automatic, coming to mind seemingly on their own?"
   b. *Naturally*: "To what extent do your thoughts and feelings towards (Brand) come to you naturally and instantly?"

Sense of Community.   Although measuring behavioral loyalty and attitudinal attachment may require a fairly structured set of questions, both sense of community and active engagement could call for more varied measures because of their diverse set of issues.

One interesting concept that has been proposed with respect to community is *social currency*, developed by brand consultants Vivaldi Partners. They define social currency as "the extent to which people share the brand or information about the brand as part of their everyday social lives at work or at home." Figure 9-10 displays the different dimensions that make up the social currency concept according to Vivaldi Partners.

Dimension	Key Question	Value of Dimension
Conversation	What share of your brand users recognizes and stirs buzz?	Customers proactively talk about a brand.
Advocacy	How many act as disciples and stand up for your brand?	Customers are willing to tell others about a brand or recommend it further.
Information	How many feel they exchange fruitful information with others?	The more information customers have about a brand the more likely they are to develop preferences for the brand.
Affiliation	What share of users has a sense of community?	Value of brand is closely related to sense of community it creates among other like-minded people.
Utility	How much value do consumers derive from interacting with others?	Social exchange with others involving a brand is an integral part of people's lives.
Identity	How many of your users can identify with other users?	Customers develop strong sense of identity and ability to express themselves to others by using a brand.

FIGURE 9-10

Vivaldi Partners' Social Currency Model

Source: Used with permission from Erich Joachimsthaler at Vivaldi Partners.

Active Engagement. According to the brand resonance model, *active engagement* for a brand is defined as the extent to which consumers are willing to invest their own personal resources—time, energy, money, and so on—on the brand beyond those resources expended during purchase or consumption of the brand.

For example, in terms of engagement, in-depth measures could explore word-of-mouth behavior, online behavior, and so forth. For online behavior, measures could explore the extent of customer-initiated versus firm-initiated interactions, the extent of learning and teaching by the customer versus by the firm, the extent of customers teaching other customers, and so on.[53]

The key to such metrics is the qualitative nature of the consumer-brand interaction and how well it reflects intensity of feelings. One mistake many Internet firms made was to put too much emphasis on "eyeballs" and "stickiness"—the number and duration of page views at a Web site, respectively. The depth of the underlying brand relationships of the customers making those visits, however, and the manner in which those relationships manifest themselves in brand-beneficial actions, will typically be more important.

Accordingly, researchers are attempting to determine the brand value of different online and social media activities.[54] For example, how important is a "like" from a user on Facebook? One firm estimated that bringing a user on as a fan could be worth between 44 cents and $3.60 in equivalent media value from increased impressions generated from the Facebook newsfeed. Critics of the study, however, pointed out that not all fans are created equal.[55]

Several different specific approaches have been suggested to measure brand engagement. The Science of Branding 9-2 provides a detailed breakdown of the concept.

Fournier's Brand Relationship Research. Boston University's Susan Fournier argues that brands can and do serve as viable relationship partners, and she suggests a reconceptualization of the notion of brand personality within this framework.[56] Specifically, the everyday execution of marketing mix decisions constitutes a set of behaviors enacted on the part of the brand. These actions trigger a series of inferences regarding the implicit *contract* that appears to guide the engagement of the consumer and brand and, hence, the type of relationship formed.

Brand personality as conceptualized within this framework describes the *relationship role* enacted by the brand in its partnership capacity. For example, if the brand expresses behaviors that signal commitment to the consumer, and further if it sends gifts as symbols of affection, the consumer may infer a courtship or marriage type of engagement with the brand.

Fournier identifies a typology of 15 different relationship types characterizing consumers' engagement with brands (see Figure 9-11). Fournier argues that this relationship role view of brand personality provides more actionable guidance to managers who wish to create and manage their brand personalities in line with marketing actions than does the trait-based

THE SCIENCE OF BRANDING 9-2

Understanding Brand Engagement

There are several different ways to think of brand engagement. *Actual brand engagement* is the activities with which the consumer currently is engaged with the brand and is typically what is measured with the brand resonance model. Two other approaches provide interesting contrasts. *Ideal brand engagement* is the activities the brand consumer wishes they could do with the brand. *Market brand engagement* is the activities the consumer believes other consumers are doing with the brand.

Market brand engagement will be closely related to measures of *brand momentum*—how much progress the brand appears to be making with consumers in the marketplace. Both sets of measures deal with consumer perceptions of how other consumers are connecting to a brand.

Measures of actual brand engagement can take two forms—more general, macro measures or more specific, micro measures. Macro measures focus on the types of resources expended, for example:

Time: "It is worth spending more time on the brand (or going out of the way for it)."
Energy: "It is worth investing extra effort on the brand."
Money: "It is worth spending more money on the brand."

Micro sets of measures focus on specific categories of brand-related activities. These activities fall into three categories depending on whether they relate to: (1) collecting brand information, (2) participating in brand marketing activities, or (3) interacting with other people and having a sense of community. Here are some possible questions.

Collecting Brand Information

I like learning about this brand.
If this brand has any new products or services, I tend to notice it.
If I see a newspaper or magazine article about this brand, I tend to read it.
If I hear a TV or radio story about this brand, I tend to listen to it.
If I see a news story online about this brand, I tend to open and read it.

I like to visit this brand's Web site.
I like to read online blogs about this brand.

Participating in Brand Marketing Activities

If I notice an ad for this brand, I tend to pay attention to it.
If I notice a sales promotion from this brand, I tend to pay attention to it.
If I get something in the mail from this brand, I tend to open it.
If this brand sponsors a sports, entertainment or arts event, I tend to notice it.
If I see a billboard or any outdoor type ad for this brand, I tend to notice it.
If this brand has a display or demonstration in the store, I tend to notice it.
If this brand shows up in a movie or television show, I tend to notice it.
If I get a chance to sample one of this brand's new products, I tend to try it.
I like to buy licensed products from this brand.

Interacting with Other People

I like to talk to others about this brand.
I like to talk to people at work about this brand.
I like to talk to my friends and family about this brand.
I like to seek out others who use this brand.
I have joined or would like to join an online community with other users of this brand.
I have joined or would like to join an online community with others who like this brand.
I have joined or would like to join an online community with people from the company who makes this brand.
I am active in a loyalty program for this brand.
I tend to notice when other people are using this brand.

These are only some representative examples of the types of survey measures that could be employed to assess brand engagement. Depending on the category and circumstances, a variety of other questions could be devised and fruitfully applied.

view, which identifies general personality tendencies that might or might not be connected to marketing strategies and goals.

Fournier has conducted fascinating research that reframes the conceptualization and measurement of brand strength strictly in relationship terms. It defines a brand's strength in terms of the strength, depth, and durability of the consumer-brand relational bond using the multifaceted concept of **brand relationship quality**, or BRQ. Extensive validation work supported a multifaceted hierarchical structure for the BRQ construct that includes six main dimensions of relationship strength, many with important subfacets. The main facets are (1) interdependence, (2) self-concept connection, (3) commitment, (4) love/passion, (5) intimacy, and (6) brand partner quality.

Relationship Form	Case Examples
Arranged marriage: Nonvoluntary union imposed by preferences of third party. Intended for long-term, exclusive commitment.	Karen's husband's preferred brands (e.g., Mop'n Glo, Palmolive, Hellman's); Karen's Esteé Lauder, imposed through gift-giving; Jean's use of Murphy's Oil Soap as per manufacturer recommendation.
Casual friend/buddy: Friendship low in affect and intimacy, characterized by infrequent or sporadic engagement and few expectations of reciprocity or reward.	Karen and her household cleaning brands.
Marriage of convenience: Long-term, committed relationship precipitated by environmental influence rather than deliberate choice, and governed by satisfying rules.	Vicki's switch to regional Friend's Baked Beans brand from favored B&M brand left behind; Jean's loyalty to DeMoulas salad dressing brand left behind by client at the bar.
Committed partnership: Long-term, voluntarily imposed, socially supported union high in love, intimacy, trust, and commitment to stay together despite adverse circumstances. Adherence to exclusivity rules expected.	Jean and virtually all her cooking, cleaning, and household appliance brands; Karen and Gatorade.
Best friendship: Voluntary union based on reciprocity principle, the endurance of which is ensured through continued provision of positive rewards. Characterized by revelation of true self, honesty, and intimacy. Congruity in partner images and personal interests common.	Karen and Reebok running shoes; Vicki and Crest or Ivory.
Compartmentalized friendship: Highly specialized, situationally confined, enduring friendship characterized by lower intimacy than other friendship forms but higher socio-emotional rewards and interdependence. Easy entry and exit.	Vicki and her stable of shampoos, perfumes, and lingerie brands.
Kinship: Nonvoluntary union with lineage ties.	Vicki's preferences for Tetley tea or Karen's for Ban, Joy, and Miracle Whip, all of which were inherited through their mothers.
Rebound relationship: Union precipitated by desire to replace prior partner, as opposed to attraction to replacement partner.	Karen's use of Comet, Gateway, and Success Rice.
Childhood friendship: Infrequently engaged, affective relation reminiscent of childhood times. Yields comfort and security of past self.	Jean and Jell-O pudding.
Courtship: Interim relationship state on the road to committed partnership contract.	Vicki and her Musk scent brands.
Dependency: Obsessive, highly emotional, selfish attractions cemented by feeling that the other is irreplaceable. Separation from other yields anxiety. High tolerance of other's transgressions results.	Karen and Mary Kay; Vicki and Soft 'n Dry.
Fling: Short-term, time-bounded engagement of high emotional reward. Devoid entirely of commitment and reciprocity demands.	Vicki's trial-size shampoo brands.
Enmity: Intensely involving relationship characterized by negative affect and desire to inflict pain or revenge on the other.	Karen and her husband's brands, postdivorce; Jean and her other-recommended-but-rejected brands (e.g., ham, peanut butter, sinks).
Enslavement: Nonvoluntary relationship union governed entirely by desires of the relationship partner.	Karen and Southern Bell, Cable Vision. Vicki and Playtex, a bra for large-breasted women.
Secret affair: Highly emotive, privately held relationship considered risky if exposed to others.	Karen and the Tootsie Pops she sneaks at work.

FIGURE 9-11

A Typology of Consumer-Brand Relationships

Fournier argues that these facets and their subfacets (such as trust within the partner quality facet or consumer-to-firm and firm-to-consumer intimacy) have superior diagnostic value over competing strength measures, and she suggests they have greater managerial utility in their application. In her experience, BRQ measures have been successfully incorporated in brand tracking studies, where they provide profiles of brand strength versus competitors, useful ties to marketplace performance indicators, and specific guidance for the enhancement and dilution of brand equity through managerial actions in the marketplace. Although brand relationship quality shares some characteristics with brand resonance, it provides valuable additional perspectives and insights.

The six main facets of brand relationship quality are as follows:

- *Interdependence:* The degree to which the brand is ingrained in the consumer's daily course of living, both behaviorally (in terms of frequency, scope, and strength of interactions) and cognitively (in terms of longing for and preoccupation with anticipated brand interactions). Interdependence is often revealed through the presence of routinized behavioral rituals surrounding brand purchase and use, and through separation anxiety experienced during periods of product deprivation. At its extremes, interdependence becomes dependency and addiction.

- *Self-concept connection:* The degree to which the brand delivers on important identity concerns, tasks, or themes, thereby expressing a significant part of the self-concept, both past (including nostalgic references and brand memories) and present, and personal as well as social. Grounding of the self provides feelings of comfort, connectedness, control, and security. In its extreme form, self-connection reflects integration of concepts of brand and self.

- *Commitment:* Dedication to continued brand association and betterment of the relationship, despite circumstances foreseen and unforeseen. Commitment includes professed faithfulness and loyalty to the other, often formalized through stated pledges and publicized intentions. Commitment is not defined solely by sunk costs and irretrievable investments that pose barriers to exit.

- *Love/passion:* Affinity toward and adoration of the brand, particularly with respect to other available alternatives. The intensity of the emotional bonds joining relationship partners may range from feelings of warmth, caring, and affection to those of true passion. Love includes the belief that the brand is irreplaceable and uniquely qualified as a relationship partner.

- *Intimacy:* A sense of deep familiarity with and understanding of both the essence of the brand as a partner in the relationship and the nature of the consumer-brand relationship itself. Intimacy is revealed in the presence of a strong consumer-brand relationship culture, the sharing of little-known personal details of the self, and an elaborate brand memory containing significant experiences or associations. Intimacy is a two-dimensional concept: the consumer develops intimate knowledge of the brand, and also feels a sense of intimacy exhibited on the part of the brand toward the individual as a consumer.

- *Partner quality:* Perceived partner quality involves a summary judgment of the caliber of the role enactments performed by the brand in its partnership role. Partner quality includes three central components: (1) an empathic orientation toward the other (ability of the partner to make the other feel wanted, cared for, respected, noticed, and important; responsiveness to needs); (2) a character of reliability, dependability, and predictability in the brand; and (3) trust or faith in the belief that the brand will adhere to established relationship rules and be held accountable for its actions.

COMPREHENSIVE MODELS OF CONSUMER-BASED BRAND EQUITY

The customer-based brand equity model presented in this text provides a comprehensive, cohesive overview of brand building and brand equity. Other researchers and consultants have also put forth consumer-based brand equity models that share some of the same principles and philosophy as the CBBE model, although developed in a different way. Brand Focus 9.0 presents a detailed account of arguably the most successful and influential industry branding model, Young and Rubicam's BrandAsset Valuator. Another influential model is Millward Brown's BrandDynamics.[57]

BrandDynamics

Marketing research agency Millward Brown's BrandDynamics model offers a graphical model to represent the emotional and functional strength of relationship consumers have with

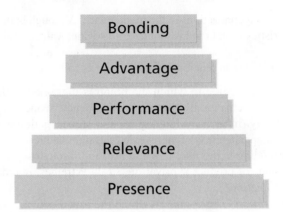

a brand. As Figure 9-12 shows, the BrandDynamics model adopts a hierarchical approach to determine the strength of relationship a consumer has with a brand. The five levels of the model, in ascending order of an increasingly intense relationship, are presence, relevance, performance, advantage, and bonding. Consumers are placed into one of the five levels depending on their brand responses. By comparing the pattern across brands, we can uncover relative strengths and weaknesses and see where brands can focus their efforts to improve their loyalty relationships.

Relationship to the CBBE Model

We can easily relate the five sequenced stages of Millward Brown's BrandDynamics model—presence, relevance, performance, advantage, and bonding—to the four ascending steps of the CBBE model (identity, meaning, responses, and relationships) and specific CBBE model concepts (such as salience, consideration, performance or quality, superiority, and resonance).

Thus, the CBBE model synthesizes the concepts and measures from a leading industry model and at the same time provides much additional substance and insight. Several particularly noteworthy aspects of the CBBE model are (1) its emphasis on brand salience and breadth and depth of brand awareness as the foundation of brand building; (2) its recognition of the dual nature of brands and the significance of both rational and emotional considerations in brand building; and (3) the importance it places on brand resonance as the culmination of brand building and a more meaningful way to view brand loyalty.

REVIEW

According to the brand value chain, sources of brand equity arise from the customer mind-set. In general, measuring sources of brand equity requires that the brand manager fully understand how customers shop for and use products and services and, most important, what customers know, think, and feel about various brands. In particular, measuring sources of customer-based brand equity requires measuring various aspects of brand awareness and brand image that lead to the customer response that creates brand equity.

This chapter described both qualitative and quantitative approaches to measure consumers' brand knowledge structures and identify potential sources of brand equity—that is, measures to capture the customer mind-set. Qualitative research techniques are a means to identify possible brand associations. Quantitative research techniques are a means to better approximate the breadth and depth of brand awareness; the strength, favorability, and uniqueness of brand associations; the favorability of brand responses; and the nature of brand relationships. Because of their unstructured nature, qualitative measures are especially well suited to provide an in-depth glimpse of what brands and products mean to consumers. To obtain more precise and generalizable information, however, marketers typically use quantitative scale measures.

Figure 9-13 summarizes some of the different types of measures that were discussed in the chapter.

I. **Qualitative Research Techniques**
    Free association
    Adjective ratings and checklists
    Projective techniques
    Photo sorts
    Bubble drawings
    Story telling
    Personification exercises
    Role playing
    Experiential methods

II. **Quantitative Research Techniques**
    A. Brand Awareness
        Direct and indirect measures of brand recognition
        Aided and unaided measures of brand recall
    B. Brand Image
        Open-ended and scale measures of specific brand attributes and benefits
            Strength
            Favorability
            Uniqueness
        Overall judgments and feelings
        Overall relationship measures
            Intensity
            Activity

FIGURE 9-13
Summary of Qualitative and Quantitative Measures

DISCUSSION QUESTIONS

1. Pick a brand. Employ projective techniques to attempt to identify sources of its brand equity. Which measures work best? Why?
2. Run an experiment to see whether you can replicate Mason Haire's instant coffee experiment (see Branding Brief 9-2). Do the same attributions still hold? If not, can you replace coffee with a brand combination from another product category that would produce pronounced differences?
3. Pick a product category. Can you profile the brand personalities of the leading brands in the category using Aaker's brand personality inventory?
4. Pick a brand. How would you best profile consumers' brand knowledge structures? How would you use quantitative measures?
5. Think of your brand relationships. Can you find examples of brands that fit into Fournier's different categories?

BRAND FOCUS 9.0

Young & Rubicam's BrandAsset Valuator

This appendix summarizes BrandAsset® Valuator (BAV), originally developed by Young & Rubicam, now overseen and expanded by BAV Consulting.[58] It is the world's largest database of consumer-derived information on brands. The BAV model is developmental in that it explains how brands grow, how they get into trouble, and how they recover.

BAV measures brands on four fundamental measures of equity value plus a broad array of perceptual dimensions. It provides comparative measures of the equity value of thousands of brands across hundreds of different categories, as well as a set of strategic brand management tools for planning: brand positioning, brand extensions, joint branding ventures, and other strategies designed to assess and direct brands and their growth. BAV is also linked to financial metrics and is used to determine a brand's contribution to a company's valuation.

Since 1993, BAV has carried out research with almost 800,000 consumers in 51 countries, enabling BAV to follow truly global brand trends. Consumers' perceptions of approximately 45,000 brands have been collected across the same set of 72 dimensions, including 48 image attributes, usage, consideration, and cultural and customer values. These elements are incorporated into a specially developed set of brand loyalty measures.

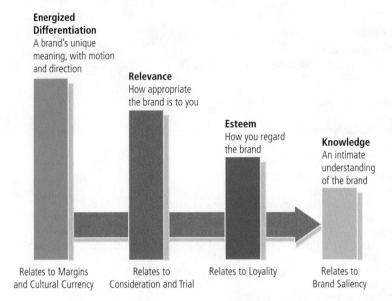

FIGURE 9-14

Four Pillars Assess
Brand Health,
Development, and
Momentum

Source: BrandAsset
Consulting. Used with
permission.

BAV represents a unique brand equity research tool. Unlike most conventional brand image surveys that adhere to a narrowly defined product category, respondents evaluate brands in a category-agnostic context. Brands are percentile ranked against *all* brands in the study for each brand metric. Thus, by comparing brands across as well as within categories, BAV is able to draw the broadest possible conclusions about how consumer-level brand equity is created and built—or lost. In the United States for the past 10 years, data has been collected quarterly from an 18,000-person panel, which enables the identification and analysis of short-term branding trends and phenomena.

Four Pillars

There are four key components of brand health in BAV (see Figure 9-14). Each pillar is derived from various measures that relate to different aspects of consumers' brand perceptions. Taken together, the four pillars trace the progression of a brand's development.

- *Energized Differentiation* measures the degree to which a brand is seen as different from others, and captures the brand's direction and momentum. This is a necessary condition for profitable brand building. It relates to pricing power and is often the key brand pillar in explaining valuation multiples like market value to sales.

- *Relevance* measures the appropriateness of the brand to consumers and the overall size of a brand's potential franchise or penetration.

- *Esteem* measures how well the brand is regarded and respected—in short, how well it's liked. Esteem is related to loyalty.

- *Knowledge* measures how intimately familiar consumers are with a brand, related to the saliency of the brand. Interestingly, high knowledge is inversely related to a brand's potential.

Relationship Among the Pillars

Examining the relationships between these four dimensions—a brand's "pillar patterns"—reveals much about a brand's current and future status (see Figure 9-15). It is not enough to look at each brand pillar in isolation; it is the relationships between the pillars that tell a story about brand health and opportunities. Here are some key relationships:

- When Energized Differentiation is greater than Relevance, the brand is standing out and receiving attention in the marketplace. It now has the potential to channel this point of difference and energy into building meaningfulness for consumers by driving Relevance.

- But if a brand is more Relevant than Differentiated, this suggests commoditization. While the brand is appropriate and meaningful within the lives of consumers, it is perceived as interchangeable with other players in the category. Therefore, consumers will not go out of their way for this brand, remain loyal to it, or pay a premium for it, since it lacks that special something we quantify as Energized Differentiation. Convenience, habit and price become drivers of brand choice in this scenario.

- Leadership brands are strong on both pillars, resulting in consumer passion as well as market penetration.

Brands often strive to build awareness, but if the brand's pillars are not in the proper alignment, then consumer knowledge of a brand becomes an obstacle that may need to be surmounted before the brand can continue to build healthy momentum.

- When a brand's Esteem is greater than its Knowledge, this tells us that consumers like what they know about the brand so far, and typically want to find out more, suggesting growth potential.

- But if brand Knowledge is greater than Esteem, then consumers feel that they know more than enough about the brand and they are not interested in getting to know it any better. In this case, Knowledge is an impediment that the brand must try to overcome if it wishes to attract more consumers.

Energized Differentiation > Relevance

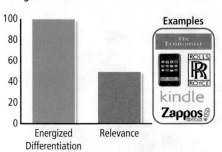

Brand has captured attention and now has potential to grow and to build Relevance: Brand has momentum

Energized Differentiation < Relevance

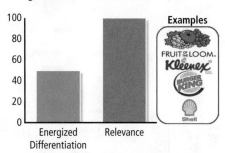

Uniqueness has faded, price or convenience has become dominant reason to buy: Brand has lost pricing power

Esteem > Knowledge

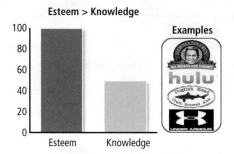

Brand is better liked than known: Desire to find out more

Esteem < Knowledge

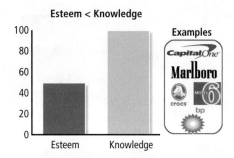

Brand is better known than liked: Too much knowledge is becoming a dangerous thing

FIGURE 9-15

Pillar Patterns Tell a Story

Source: BrandAsset Consulting. Used with permission.

The Powergrid

BrandAsset® Valuator has integrated the two macro dimensions of Brand Strength (Energized Differentiation and Relevance) and Brand Stature (Esteem and Knowledge) into a visual analytical representation known as the PowerGrid (see Figure 9-16). The PowerGrid depicts the stages in the cycle of brand development—each with its characteristic pillar patterns—in successive quadrants.

Brands generally begin their life in the lower left quadrant, where they first need to develop Relevant Differentiation and establish their reason for being. Most often, the movement from there is "up" into the top left quadrant. Increased Differentiation, followed by Relevance, initiates growth in Brand Strength. These developments occur before the brand has acquired significant Esteem or is widely known.

This quadrant represents two types of brands. For brands destined for a mass target, like Yelp and Kindle, this is the stage of emerging potential. Specialized or narrowly targeted brands, however, tend to remain in this quadrant (when viewed from the perspective of a mass audience) and can use their strength to occupy a profitable niche. This incudes brands like Method and W Hotels. From the point of view of brand leaders, new potential competitors will emerge from this quadrant.

The upper right quadrant, the Leadership Quadrant, is populated by brand leaders—those that have high levels of both Brand Strength and Brand Stature. Both older and relatively new brands can be in this quadrant, meaning that brand leadership is truly a function of the pillar measures, not of longevity. When properly managed, a brand can build and maintain a leadership position indefinitely. Examples of brands in the leadership position include Facebook, Levi's, and Nike.

Although declining brand equity is not inevitable, brands for whom strength has declined (usually driven by declining Energized Differentiation) can also be seen in this same quadrant. Brands whose Strength has started to dip below the level of their Stature display the first signs of weakness, which may well be masked by their still-buoyant sales and wide penetration. Examples include such brands as Macy's and Visa.

Brands that fail to maintain their Brand Strength—their Relevant Differentiation—begin to fade and move "down" into the bottom right quadrant. These brands become vulnerable not just to existing competitors, but also to the depredations of discount price brands, and they frequently end up being drawn into heavy and continuous price promotion in order to defend their consumer franchise and market share. American Airlines and TV Guide fall into this category.

Significant investigation has been done on relating BAV metrics to financial performance and stock price. First, the position of a brand on the PowerGrid indicates the level of intangible value (market value of brand or company-invested capital) per dollar of sale. The leadership quadrant produces brands with the largest intangible value per dollar of sale. Next, through extensive modeling, BAV has shown that a change in brand assets impacts stock price. From a macro perspective, two-thirds of the change in brand assets directly impacts stock price and the expectation for future returns. One-third of the change in brand assets impacts curent earnings. The importance of brand assets on stock price and company valuation is highly dependent on the category or economic sector.

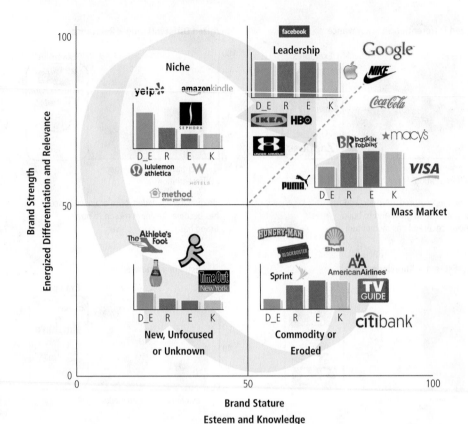

FIGURE 9-16

Brand Development
Cycle as Illustrated by
the Power Grid

Source: BrandAsset
Consulting. Used with
permission.

Applying BAV to Google

The best way to understand the BAV model is to apply it to a brand and category. Google is a dramatic example. Google achieved leadership status faster than any other brand measured in BAV. Google built each brand pillar, beginning with Energized Differentiation, both quickly and strongly. After rapidly establishing Energized Differentiation, Google built the other three pillars. It took only three years for Google's percentile-ranking on all four pillars to reach the high 90s.

At the same time, AOL began to falter, losing first Energized Differentiation, then Relevance and Esteem. For a while, AOL's Knowledge remained high, but with declining Relevance, eroding Differentiation and less Esteem, consumers began to lose interest until finally, AOL's Knowledge pillar followed the other pillars and began to decline. Figure 9-17 displays the sharp contrast in brand development between the two.

How has Google developed and maintained brand leadership? From the BAV perspective, there are three main contributing factors: (1) consistently strong brand attributes that translate into competitive advantages, (2) successful brand extensions into new categories, and (3) successful expansion into global markets and the fast establishment of brand leadership.

Competitive Advantages on Brand Attributes

Google's leadership is supported by competitive advantages on the factors that contribute to the strength of the key pillars. The BAV factors are created from the 48 brand image attributes, using data compiled from Google and its competitor brands. The individual attributes within each factor are the dimensions most correlated with each other through the eyes of consumers when

considering Google and its competitive set; thus, factors define how consumers view the category and the brands within it.

As shown in Figure 9-18, Google is stonger than the competitive average on the *Cutting Edge* (innovation) factor and the *Bold* personality factor. Both of these factors build Google's Energized Differentiation. Google's advantage on the *Dependability* (trust) factor helps keep the Relevance pillar strong, and Google's strength on the *Superiority* (best brand) factor supports both the Relevance and the Esteem pillars.

Successful Category Extensions

Google has done a masterful job of entering new categories with sub-brands. In many of these categories—such as Google Maps, Android by Google, and Gmail—the Google entrant has become the category leader. Most of the sub-brands also have very high Brand Strength, which helps replenish the Brand Strength of the Google corporate brand (see Figure 9-19). In this way, , the leadership of the sub-brands helps support the parent brand, a common theme among strong parent brands with sub-brands.

The significant strength of Google's image profile has made entrance into new categories easier. Google does not face the entrance issues that weaker brands have when their image profiles are not robust enough to create differentiation in the new category, a key condition for a successful extension.

Successful Global Expansion

BAV metrics uniquely gauge the nature of international marketing opportunities. BAV shows global brands must build consistently strong Brand Strength, Brand Stature, and power on key factors that drive brand pillars and meaning *in each market*.

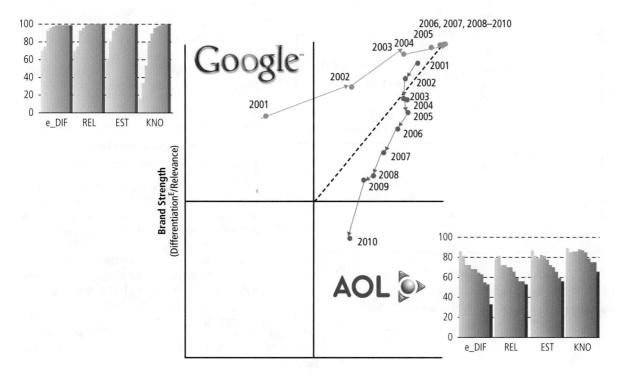

FIGURE 9-17 Google vs. AOL Brand Development

Source: BrandAsset Consulting. Used with permission.

Key Category Factors

Factor and Attribute Percentile Rank

CUTTING EDGE
(Drives DIF and ENE)

Innovative
Progressive
Visionary

BOLD
(Drives ENE)

Fun
Dynamic
Social

DEPENDABLE
(Drives REL)

Reliable
Intelligent
Trustworthy

SUPERIOR
(Drives REL and EST)

Best Brand
Leader
Worth More

	Competitor's Avg	Google
CUTTING EDGE	65.7	72.2
Innovative	92.0	99.5
Progressive	9.9	17.5
Visionary	95.2	99.5
BOLD	82.8	93.8
Fun	70.2	87.1
Dynamic	90.2	98.3
Social	88.0	96.0
DEPENDABLE	81.6	97.4
Reliable	76.1	98.3
Intelligent	93.7	99.0
Trustworthy	75.1	94.8
SUPERIOR	70.7	81.1
Best Brand	68.1	98.5
Leader	88.8	99.3
Worth More	55.9	44.6

FIGURE 9-18

Google Maintains Competitive Superiority on Key Factors Driving Brand Pillars

Source: BrandAsset Consulting. Used with permission.

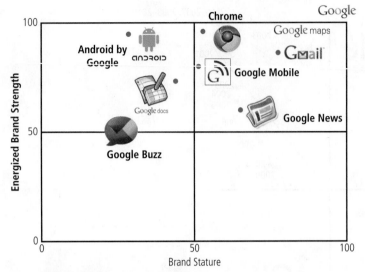

FIGURE 9-19 Google's Successful New Product Introductions

Source: BrandAsset Consulting. Used with permission.

Specifically, financial analysis of global brands has shown that brands that have consistently high Brand Strength and consistently high common meaning (attribute factor scores) will deliver better margin growth rates and are more efficient at producing higher pretax margins.

Google has achieved leadership status in global markets the same way it achieved leadership status in the USA—by quickly "maxing out" on Brand Strength and Brand Stature. In all countries recently surveyed, Google is a super-leadership brand on the PowerGrid (see Figure 9-20). Reviewing the key image factors across countries shows that Google ranks in the high 90s on each factor and each dimension, *according to consumers in each local market*. This is true consistency, which Google has built by focusing on the important factors within each local market.

Summary

There is a lot of commonality between the basic BAV model and the brand resonance model. The four factors in the BAV model can easily be related to specific components of the brand resonance model:

- BAV's Differentiation relates to brand superiority.
- BAV's Relevance relates to brand consideration.
- BAV's Esteem relates to brand credibility.
- BAV's Knowledge relates to brand resonance.

Note that brand awareness and familiarity are handled differently in the two approaches. The brand resonance framework maintains that brand salience and breadth and depth of awareness is a necessary *first* step in building brand equity. The BAV model treats familiarity in a more affective manner—almost in a warm feeling or friendship sense—and thus sees it as the *last* step in building brand equity, more akin to the resonance component itself.

The main advantage of the BAV model is that it provides rich category-agnostic descriptions and profiles across a large number of brands. It also provides focus on four key branding dimensions. It provides a brand landscape in which marketers can see where their brands stand relative to other prominent brands in many different markets.

The descriptive nature of the BAV model does mean, however, that there is potentially less insight as to exactly *how* a brand could rate highly on those factors. Because the measures underlying the four factors have to be relevant across a very disparate range of product categories, the measures (and, consequently, the factors) tend to be abstract in nature and not related directly to product attributes and benefits, or more specific marketing concerns. Nevertheless, the BAV model represents a landmark study in terms of its ability to enhance marketers' understanding of what drives top brands and where their brands fit in a vast brandscape.

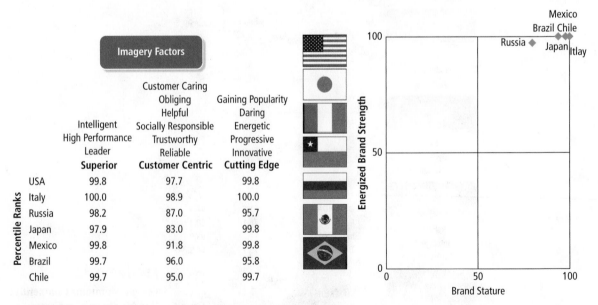

FIGURE 9-20 Google Is Consistently a Global Brand Leader

Source: BrandAsset Consulting. Used with permission.

Notes

1. Some leading textbooks in this area are J. Paul Peter and Jerry C. Olson, *Consumer Behavior and Marketing Strategy*, 8th ed. (Homewood, IL: McGraw-Hill/Irwin, 2007); Wayne D. Hoyer and Deborah J. MacInnis, *Consumer Behavior*, 5th ed. (Mason, OH: South-Western, 2010); and Michael R. Solomon, *Consumer Behavior: Buying, Having, and Being*, 9th ed. (Upper Saddle River, NJ: Prentice Hall, 2011).

2. John Motavalli, "Probing Consumer Minds," *Adweek*, 7 December 1987, 4–8.

3. Ernest Dichter, *Handbook of Consumer Motivations* (New York: McGraw-Hill, 1964).

4. "Retail Therapy: How Ernest Dichter, An Acolyte of Sigmund Freud, Revolutionized Marketing," *The Economist*, 17 December 2011.

5. H. Shanker Krishnan, "Characteristics of Memory Associations: A Consumer-Based Brand Equity Perspective," *International Journal of Research in Marketing* (October 1996): 389–405; Geraldine R. Henderson, Dawn Iacobucci, and Bobby J. Calder, "Using Network Analysis to Understand Brands," in *Advances in Consumer Research* 29, eds. Susan M. Broniarczyk and Kent Nakamoto (Valdosta, GA: Association for Consumer Research, 2002): 397–405.

6. J. Wesley Hutchinson, "Expertise and the Structure of Free Recall," in *Advances in Consumer Research* 10, eds. Richard P. Bagozzi and Alice M. Tybout (Ann Arbor, MI: Association of Consumer Research, 1983): 585–589; see also Chris Janiszewski and Stijn M. J. van Osselaer, "A Connectionist Model of Brand–Quality Associations," *Journal of Marketing Research* 37 (August 2000): 331–350.

7. Yvan Boivin, "A Free Response Approach to the Measurement of Brand Perceptions," *International Journal of Research in Marketing* 3 (1986): 11–17; Jeffrey E. Danes, Jeffrey S. Hess, John W. Story, and Keith Vorst, "On the Validity of Measuring Brand Images by Rating Concepts and Free Associations," *Journal of Brand Management*, 2012, in press.

8. Jean Bystedt, Siri Lynn, and Deborah Potts, *Moderating to the Max* (Ithaca, NY: Paramount Market Publishing, 2003).

9. For an application in marketing, see Kathryn A. Braun-LaTour, Michael S. LaTour, and George M. Zinkhan, "Using Childhood Memories to Gain Insight Into Brand Meaning," *Journal of Marketing* 71 (April 2007): 45–60.

10. Sydney J. Levy, "Dreams, Fairy Tales, Animals, and Cars," *Psychology and Marketing* 2, no. 2 (1985): 67–81.

11. Mason Haire, "Projective Techniques in Marketing Research, *Journal of Marketing* (April 1950): 649–656. Interestingly, a follow-up study conducted several decades later suggested that instant coffee users were no longer perceived as psychologically different from drip grind users. See Frederick E. Webster Jr. and Frederick Von Pechmann, "A Replication of the 'Shopping List' Study," *Journal of Marketing* 34 (April 1970): 61–63.

12. Levy, "Dreams, Fairy Tales."

13. Jeffrey Durgee and Robert Stuart, "Advertising Symbols and Brand Names That Best Represent Key Product Meanings," *Journal of Consumer Marketing* 4, no. 3 (1987): 15–24.

14. Clotaire Rapaille, *Culture Code* (New York: Broadway, 2006); Alexandra Harrington, "G. C. Rapaille: Finding the Keys in the Cultural Unconscious," *Response TV*, 1 September 2001; Jeffrey Ball, "'But How Does It Make You Feel?'" *Wall Street Journal*, 3 May 1999; Jack Hitt, "Does the Smell of Coffee Brewing Remind You of Your Mother?" *New York Times Magazine*, 7 May 2000.

15. Gerald Zaltman and Robin Higie, "Seeing the Voice of the Customer: Metaphor-Based Advertising Research," *Journal of Advertising Research* (July/August 1995): 35–51; Daniel H. Pink, "Metaphor Marketing," *Fast Company*, April 1998; Gerald Zaltman, "Metaphorically Speaking," *Marketing Research* (Summer 1996); www.olsonzaltman.com; Gerald Zaltman, "How Customers Think: Essential Insights into the Mind of the Market," *Harvard Business School Press* (2003); Wendy Melillo, "Inside the Consumer Mind: What Neuroscience Can Tell Us About Marketing," *Adweek*, 16 January 2006; Torsten Ringberg, Gaby Odekerken-Schröder, and Glenn L. Christensen, "A Cultural Models Approach to Segmenting Consumer Recovery Expectations," *Journal of Marketing* 71 (July 2007): 194–214; Gerald Zaltman and Lindsay Zaltman, *Marketing Metaphoria: What Deep Metaphors Reveal About the Minds of Consumers* (Boston: Harvard Business School Press, 2008).

16. For some provocative research, see Carolyn Yoon, Angela H. Gutchess, Fred M. Feinberg, and Thad A. Polk, "A Functional Magnetic Resonance Imaging Study of Neural Dissociations between Brand and Person Judgments," *Journal of Consumer Research* 33 (June 2006): 31–40; Samuel M. McClure, Jian Li, Damon Tomlin, Kim S. Cypert, Latané M. Montague, and P. Read Montague, "Neural Correlates of Behavioral Preference for Culturally Familiar Drinks," *Neuron* 44, no. 2 (October 2004): 379–387; Hilke Plassmann, Carolyn Yoon, Fred M. Feinberg, and Baba Shiv, "Consumer Neuroscience," in *Wiley International Encyclopedia of Marketing, Volume 3: Consumer Behavior*, eds. Richard P. Bagozzi and Ayalla Ruvio (West Sussex, UK: John Wiley, 2010). Martin Lindstrom, *Buyology: Truth and Lies About Why We Buy* (New York: Doubleday, 2008).

17. For foundational research, see Giovanna Egidi, Howard C. Nusbaum, and John T. Cacioppo, "Neuroeconomics," in *The Handbook of Consumer Psychology*, eds. Curtis Haugvedt, Paul Herr, and Frank Kardes, Vol. 57 (Mahwah, NJ: Lawrence Erlbaum Associates, 2007): 1177–1214.

18. Adam Penenberg, "They Have Hacked Your Brain," *Fast Company*, September 2011.

19. Tom Abate, "Coming to a Marketer Near You: Brain Scanning," *San Francisco Chronicle*, 19 May 2008; Brian Sternberg, "How Coach Potatoes Watch TV

Could Hold Clues for Advertisers," *Boston Globe*, 6 September 2009, G1, G3.

20. Jennifer Aaker, "Dimensions of Brand Personality," *Journal of Marketing Research* 34, no. 8 (1997): 347–356.

21. Jay Dean, "A Practitioner's Perspective on Brand Equity," in *Proceedings of the Society for Consumer Psychology*, eds. Wes Hutchinson and Kevin Lane Keller (Clemson, SC: CtC Press, 1994), 56–62.

22. Aaker, "Dimensions of Brand Personality." See also Jennifer Aaker, "The Malleable Self: The Role of Self-Expression in Persuasion," *Journal of Marketing Research* 36, no. 2 (1999): 45–57; Joseph T. Plummer, "Brand Personality: A Strategic Concept for Multinational Advertising," in *Marketing Educators' Conference* (New York: Young & Rubicam 1985): 1–31.

23. Jennifer L. Aaker, Veronica Benet-Martinez, and Jordi Garolera, "Consumption Symbols as Carriers of Culture: A Study of Japanese and Spanish Brand Personality Constructs," *Journal of Personality and Social Psychology* 81, no. 3 (2001): 492–508.

24. Yongjun Sung and Spencer F. Tinkham, "Brand Personality Structures in the United States and Korea: Common and Culture-Specific Factors," *Journal of Consumer Psychology* 15, no. 4 (2005): 334–350.

25. Gil Ereaut and Mike Imms, "'Bricolage': Qualitative Market Research Redefined," *Admap*, December 2002, 16–18.

26. Jennifer Chang Coupland, "Invisible Brands: An Ethnography of Households and the Brands in Their Kitchen Pantries," *Journal of Consumer Research* 32 (June 2005): 106–118; Mark Ritson and Richard Elliott, "The Social Uses of Advertising: An Ethnographic Study of Adolescent Advertising Audiences," *Journal of Consumer Research* 26 (December 1999): 260–277.

27. Donna Kelly and Michael Gibbons, "Ethnography: The Good, the Bad, and the Ugly," *Journal of Medical Marketing* 8, no. 4 (2008): 279–285; Special Issue on Ethnography, *International Journal of Marketing Research* 49, no. 6 (2007).

28. Melanie Wells, "New Ways to Get into Our Heads," *USA Today*, 2 March 1999, B1–B2.

29. Gerry Kermouch, "Consumers in the Mist," *Business Week*, 26 February 2001, 92–94; Alfred Hermida, "Bus Ride to the Future," www.bbc.co.uk, 3 December 2001.

30. Eric J. Arnould and Amber Epp, "Deep Engagement with Consumer Experience: Listening and Learning with Qualitative Data," in *The Handbook of Marketing Research: Uses, Misuses, and Future Advances*, eds. Rajiv Grover and Marco Vriens (Thousand Oaks, CA: Sage Press, 2006): 51–58.

31. Dev Patnik and Robert Becker, "Direct Observation: Some Practical Advice," *Marketing News*, Fall 1999; A. Parasuraman, Dhruv Grewal, and R. Krishnan, *Marketing Research*, 2nd ed. (Boston: Houghton Mifflin, 2007).

32. Edward F. McQuarrie, "Taking a Road Trip," *Marketing Management* 3 (Winter 1995): 9–21; Edward F. McQuarrie, *Customer Visits: Building a Better Market Focus*, 3rd ed. (Armonk, NY: M. E. Sharpe, 2008);

"How to Conduct Good Customer Visits: 16 Tips from Ed McQuarrie," www.managementroundtable.com.

33. Kevin Peters, "How 'Mystery Shopping' Helped Spark a Turnaround," *Harvard Business Review* (November 2011): 47–50.

34. Gord Hotchkiss, "Exploring the Shift in Search Behaviors with Microsoft's Jacquelyn Krones," www.searchengineland.com, 15 July 2011.

35. Jennifer Cirillo, "DEWmocracy 2 Continues to Buzz," *Beverage World*, 11 March 2010.

36. Rekha Balu, "Listen Up! (It Might Be Your Customer Talking)," *Fast Company*, May 2000, 304–316; Joseph Manez and Jennifer Reingold, "Burton Snowboards," *Fast Company*, September 2006, 58–59; www.burton.com; Justin Gural, "Craig's: Burton Snowboards' Future Lab," *USA Today*, 14 January 2011; Roger Brooks, "Jake Burton Charts a New Course in Snowboarding," *Success*, February 2010; Russ Edelman, "Burton Snowboards: Passion, Innovation and Profit," www.cnbc.com, 22 November 2011.

37. Russell W. Belk and Robert V. Kozinets, "Videography in Marketing and Consumer Research," *Qualitative Market Research* 8, no. 2 (2005): 128–142.

38. Louella Miles, "Market Research: Living Their Lives," www.brandrepublic.com, 11 December 2003.

39. Judith A. Howard and Daniel G. Renfrow, "Social Cognition," in *Handbook of Social Psychology*, ed. John Delamater (New York: Springer Science+Business, 2006), 259–282; Robert S. Wyer, "The Role of Information Accessibility in Cognition and Behavior: Implications for Consumer Information Processing," in *The Handbook of Consumer Psychology*, eds. Curtis Haugvedt, Paul Herr, and Frank Kardes, Vol. 57 (Mahwah, NJ: Lawrence Erlbaum Associates, 2007), 31–76; Barbara Loken, Larry Barsalou, and Christopher Joiner, "Categorization Theory and Research in Consumer Psychology: Category Representation and Category-Based Inference," in *The Handbook of Consumer Psychology*, eds. Curtis Haugvedt, Paul Herr, and Frank Kardes, Vol. 57 (Mahwah, NJ: Lawrence Erlbaum Associates, 2007), 453–485.

40. For an interesting related topic, see Henrik Hagtvedt, "The Impact of Incomplete Typeface Logos on Perceptions of the Firm," *Journal of Marketing* 75 (July 2011): 86–93.

41. Raymond Gordon, "Phantom Products," *Forbes*, 21 May 1984, 202–204.

42. Philip Kotler and Kevin Lane Keller, *Marketing Management: Analysis, Planning, Implementation, and Control*, 14th ed. (Upper Saddle River, NJ: Prentice Hall, 2012).

43. Joseph F. Hair Jr., Rolph E. Anderson, Ronald Tatham, and William C. Black, *Multivariate Data Analysis*, 4th ed. (Englewood Cliffs, NJ: Prentice Hall, 1995); James Lattin, Douglas Carrol, and Paul Green, *Analyzing Multivariate Data*, 5th ed. (Pacific Grove, CA: Duxbury Press, 2003).

44. J. Scott Armstrong, Vicki G. Morwitz, and V. Kumar, "Sales Forecasts for Existing Consumer Products and Services: Do Purchase Intentions Contribute to Accuracy?" *International Journal of Forecasting* 16 (2000): 383–397.

45. Icek Ajzen and Martin Fishbein, *Understanding Attitudes and Predicting Social Behavior* (Englewood Cliffs, NJ: Prentice Hall, 1980); Vicki G. Morwitz, Joel Steckel, and Alok Gupta, "When Do Purchase Intentions Predict Sales?," *International Journal of Forecasting* 23, no. 3, (2007): 347–364; Pierre Chandon, Vicki G. Morwitz, and Werner J. Reinartz, "Do Intentions Really Predict Behavior? Self-Generated Validity Effects in Survey Research," *Journal of Marketing* 69 (April 2005): 1–14.

46. Fred Reichheld, *Ultimate Question: For Driving Good Profits and True Growth* (Cambridge, MA: Harvard Business School Press, 2006); Jena McGregor, "Would You Recommend Us?" *BusinessWeek*, 30 January 2006, 94–95; Kathryn Kranhold, "Client-Satisfaction Tool Takes Root," *Wall Street Journal*, 10 July 2006; Timothy L. Keiningham, Bruce Cooil, Tor Wallin Andreassen, and Lerzan Aksoy, "A Longitudinal Examination of Net Promoter and Firm Revenue Growth," *Journal of Marketing* 71 (July 2007): 39–51; Neil A. Morgan and Lopo Leotte Rego, "The Value of Different Customer Satisfaction and Loyalty Metrics in Predicting Business Performance," *Marketing Science* 25 (September–October 2006): 426–439; Timothy L. Keiningham, Lerzan Aksoy, Bruce Cooil, and Tor W. Andreassen, "Linking Customer Loyalty to Growth," *MIT Sloan Management Review* (Summer 2008): 51–57.

47. Das Narayandas, "Building Loyalty in Business Markets," *Harvard Business Review* (September 2005): 131–138.

48. For more general discussion of consumer attachment, see Susan S. Kleine and Stacy M. Baker, "An Integrative Review of Material Possession Attachment," *Academy of Marketing Science Review* 8, no. 4 (2004): 1–39; Rosellina Ferraro, Jennifer Edson Escalas, and James R. Bettman, "Our Possessions, Our Selves: Domains of Self-Worth and the Possession-Self Link," *Journal of Consumer Psychology* 21, no. 2 (2011): 169–177.

49. See, for example, Lars Bergkvist and Tino Bech-Larsen, "Two Studies of Consequences and Actionable Antecedents of Brand Love," *Journal of Brand Management* 17 (June 2010): 504–518.

50. Barbara A. Carroll and Aaron C. Ahuvia, "Some Antecedents and Outcomes of Brand Love," *Marketing Letters* 17 (2006): 79–89.

51. Rajeev Batra, Aaron Ahuvia, and Richard P Bagozzi, "Brand Love," *Journal of Marketing* (2012), in press.

52. C.W. Park, Deborah J. Macinnis, Joseph Priester, Andreas B. Eisingerich, and Dawn Iacobucci, "Brand Attachment and Brand Attitude Strength: Conceptual and Empirical Differentiation of Two Critical Brand Equity Drivers," *Journal of Marketing* 74 (November 2010): 1–17.

53. Vikas Mittal and Mohanbir S. Sawhney, "Managing Customer Retention in the Attention Economy," working paper, University of Pittsburgh, 2001.

54. For a broad overview, see "Digital Marketing: Special Advertising Section," *Adweek*, 28 October 2011.

55. Jon Bruner, "What's a 'Like' Worth?," *Forbes*, 8 August 2011; Brian Morrisey, "Value of a 'Fan' on Social Media: $3.60," *Adweek*, 13 April 2010; www.vitrue.com, accessed 23 June 2011.

56. Susan M. Fournier, "Consumers and Their Brands: Developing Relationship Theory in Consumer Research," *Journal of Consumer Research* 24 (March 1998): 343–373; Susan M. Fournier, Susan Dobscha, and David G. Mick, "Preventing the Premature Death of Relationship Marketing," *Harvard Business Review* (January–February 1998): 42–51; Susan M. Fournier and Julie L. Yao, "Reviving Brand Loyalty: A Reconceptualization Within the Framework of Consumer–Brand Relationships," *International Journal of Research in Marketing* 14 (1997): 451–472; Susan Fournier, "Lessons Learned About Consumers' Relationships with Their Brands," in *Handbook of Brand Relationships*, eds. Joseph Priester, Deborah MacInnis, and C. W. Park (NY: Society for Consumer Psychology and M.E. Sharp, 2009), 5–23; Susan Fournier, Michael Breazeale, Marc Fetscherin, and T. C. Melewar, eds., *Consumer–Brand Relationships: Theory and Practice* (London: Routledge Taylor & Francis Group, 2012).

57. For a helpful review of different perspectives, see Jonathan Knowles, "In Search of a Reliable Measure of Brand Equity," *MarketingNPV* 2, no. 3 (July 2005).

58. This section greatly benefited from helpful and insightful contributions by Ed Lebar, John Gerzama, Scott Stiff, and Paul Fox.

10 Measuring Outcomes of Brand Equity: Capturing Market Performance

Learning Objectives

After reading this chapter, you should be able to

1. Recognize the multidimensionality of brand equity and the importance of multiple methods to measure it.

2. Contrast different comparative methods to assess brand equity.

3. Explain the basic logic of how conjoint analysis works.

4. Review different holistic methods for valuing brand equity.

5. Describe the relationship between branding and finance.

Intel tracks the price premiums it enjoys over competitors as a measure of its brand strength.
Source: Intel Corporation

Preview

Ideally, to measure brand equity, we would create a "brand equity index"—one easily calculated number that summarizes the health of the brand and completely captures its brand equity. But just as a thermometer measuring body temperature provides only one indication of how healthy a person is, so does any one measure of brand equity provide only one indication of the health of a brand. Brand equity is a multidimensional concept, and complex enough to require many different types of measures. Applying multiple measures increases the diagnostic power of marketing research and the likelihood that managers will better understand what is happening to their brands and, perhaps more important, why.[1]

In arguments suggesting that researchers should employ multiple measures of brand equity, writers have drawn interesting comparisons between measuring brand equity and assessing the performance of an aircraft in flight or a car on the road; for example:

> The pilot of the plane has to consider a number of indicators and gauges as the plane is flown. There is the fuel gauge, the altimeter, and a number of other important status indicators. All of these dials and meters tell the pilot different things about the health of the plane. There is no one gauge that summarizes everything about the plane. The plane needs the altimeter, compass, radar, and the fuel gauge. As the pilot looks at the instrument cluster, he has to take all of these critical indicators into account as he flies.[2]

The dashboard of a car or the gauges on the plane, which together measure its "health" while being driven or flown, are analogous to the multiple measures of brand equity necessary to assess the health of a brand.

The preceding chapter described different approaches to measuring brand knowledge structures and the customer mind-set that marketers can use to identify and quantify potential sources of brand equity. By applying these measurement techniques, we should gain a good understanding of the depth and breadth of brand awareness; the strength, favorability, and uniqueness of brand associations; the positivity of brand responses; and the nature of brand relationships for their brands. As we described in Chapters 1 and 2, a product with positive brand equity can enjoy the following six important customer-related benefits:

1. Perception of better product or service performance
2. Greater loyalty and less vulnerability to competitive marketing actions and marketing crises
3. Larger margins and more inelastic responses to price increases and elastic responses to price decreases
4. Greater trade cooperation and support
5. Increased marketing communication effectiveness
6. Opportunity for successful licensing and brand extension

The customer-based brand equity model maintains that these benefits, and thus the ultimate value of a brand, depend on the underlying components of brand knowledge and sources of brand equity. As Chapter 9 described, we can measure these individual components; however, to provide more direct estimates, we still must assess their resulting value in some way. This chapter examines measurement procedures to assess the effects of brand knowledge structures on these and other measures that capture market performance for the brand.[3]

First, we review comparative methods, which are means to better assess the effects of consumer perceptions and preferences on consumer response to the marketing program and the specific benefits of brand equity. Next, we look at holistic methods, which attempt to estimate the overall or summary value of a brand.[4] Some of the interplay between branding and financial considerations is included in Brand Focus 10.0.

COMPARATIVE METHODS

Comparative methods are research studies or experiments that examine consumer attitudes and behavior toward a brand to directly estimate specific benefits arising from having a high level of awareness and strong, favorable, and unique brand associations. There are two types of comparative methods.

- *Brand-based comparative approaches* use experiments in which one group of consumers responds to an element of the marketing program or some marketing activity when it is attributed to the target brand, and another group responds to that same element or activity when it is attributed to a competitive or fictitiously named brand.
- *Marketing-based comparative approaches* use experiments in which consumers respond to changes in elements of the marketing program or marketing activity for the target brand or competitive brands.

The brand-based approach holds the marketing program fixed and examines consumer response based on changes in brand identification, whereas the marketing-based approach holds the brand fixed and examines consumer response based on changes in the marketing program. We'll look at each of these two approaches in turn and then describe conjoint analysis as a technique that, in effect, combines the two.

Brand-Based Comparative Approaches

Competitive brands can be useful benchmarks in brand-based comparative approaches. Although consumers may interpret marketing activity for a fictitiously named or unnamed version of the product or service in terms of their general product category knowledge, they may also have a particular brand, or *exemplar*, in mind. This exemplar may be the category leader or some other brand that consumers feel is representative of the category, like their most preferred brand. Consumers may make inferences to supply any missing information based on their knowledge of this particular brand. Thus, it may be instructive to examine how consumers evaluate a proposed new ad campaign, new promotion offering, or new product when it is also attributed to one or more major competitors.

Applications.   The classic example of the brand-based comparative approach is "blind testing" research studies in which different consumers examine or use a product with or without brand identification. Invariably, differences emerge. For example, in one study, people who were asked to blind test Coca-Cola and two store brands of cola split their preferences almost evenly among the three—31 percent for Coke and 33 percent and 35 percent for the others. But when the samples were identified, 50 percent of other participants in the experiment said they preferred Coke.[5]

One natural application of the brand-based comparative approach is product purchase or consumption research for new or existing products, as long as the brand identification can be hidden in some way for the "unbranded" control group. Brand-based comparative approaches are also useful to determine brand equity benefits related to price margins and premiums.

T-MOBILE

Deutsche Telecom invested much time and money in recent years in building its T-Mobile mobile communication brand. In the United Kingdom, however, the company has leased or shared its network lines with competitor Virgin Mobile. As a result, the audio quality of the signal that a T-Mobile customer received in making a call should have been virtually identical to the audio quality of the signal for a Virgin Mobile customer. After all, the same network was being used to send the signal. Despite that fact, research showed that Virgin Mobile customers rated their signal quality significantly higher than did T-Mobile customers. The strong Virgin brand image appeared to cast a halo over its different service offerings, literally causing consumers to change their impressions of product performance.[6]

Virgin's brand is so strong that consumers may evaluate the same product or service more favorably if they think it comes from Virgin.

Source: AP Photo/Jacques Brinon

Critique.   The main advantage of a brand-based comparative approach is that because it holds all aspects of the marketing program fixed for the brand, it isolates the value of a brand in a very real sense. Understanding exactly how knowledge of the brand affects consumer responses to prices, advertising, and so forth is extremely useful in developing strategies in these different areas. At the same time, we could study an almost infinite variety of marketing activities, so what we learn is limited only by the number of different applications we examine.

Brand-based comparative methods are particularly applicable when the marketing activity under consideration represents a change from past marketing of the brand, for example, a new sales or trade promotion, ad campaign, or proposed brand extension. If the marketing activity under consideration is already strongly identified with the brand—like an ad campaign that has been running for years—it may be difficult to attribute some aspect of the marketing program to a fictitiously named or unnamed version of the product or service in a believable fashion.

Thus, a crucial consideration with the brand-based comparative approach is the realism we can achieve in the experiment. We usually have to sacrifice some realism in order to gain sufficient control to isolate the effects of brand knowledge. When it is too difficult for consumers to examine or experience some element of the marketing program without being aware of the brand, we can use detailed concept statements of that element instead. For example, we can ask consumers to judge a proposed new product when it is either introduced by the firm as a brand extension or introduced by an unnamed firm in that product market. Similarly, we can ask about acceptable price ranges and store locations for the brand name product or a hypothetical unnamed version.

One concern about brand-based comparative approaches is that the simulations and concept statements may highlight the particular product characteristics enough to make them more salient than they would otherwise be, distorting the results.

Marketing-Based Comparative Approaches

Marketing-based comparative approaches hold the brand fixed and examine consumer response based on changes in the marketing program.

Applications. There is a long academic and industry tradition of exploring price premiums using marketing-based comparative approaches. In the mid-1950s, Edgar Pessemier developed a dollar-metric measure of brand commitment that relied on a step-by-step increase of the price difference between the brand normally purchased and an alternative brand.[7] To reveal brand-switching and loyalty patterns, Pessemier plotted the percentage of consumers who switched from their regular brand as a function of the brand price increases.

A number of marketing research suppliers have adopted variations of this approach to derive similar types of demand curves, and many firms now try to assess price sensitivity and willingness-to-pay thresholds for different brands.[8] For example, Intel would routinely survey computer shoppers to find out how much of a discount they would require before switching to a personal computer that did not have an Intel microprocessor in it (say, an AMD chip) or, conversely, what premium they would be willing to pay to buy a personal computer that did have an Intel microprocessor in it.

We can apply marketing-based comparative approaches in other ways, assessing consumer response to different advertising strategies, executions, or media plans through multiple test markets. For example, SymphonyIRI's electronic test markets and similar research methodologies can permit tests of different advertising weights or repetition schedules as well as ad copy tests. By controlling for other factors, we can isolate the effects of the brand and product. Recall from Chapter 2 how Anheuser-Busch conducted an extensive series of test markets that revealed that Budweiser beer had such a strong image with consumers that advertising could be cut, at least in the short run, without hurting sales performance.

Marketers can also explore potential brand extensions by collecting consumer evaluations of a range of concept statements describing brand extension candidates. For example, Figure 10-1 displays the results of a consumer survey conducted at one time to examine reactions to hypothetical extensions of the Planters nuts brand. Contrasting those extensions provides some indication of the equity of the brand.

In this example, the survey results suggested that consumers expected any Planters brand extension to be "nut-related." Appropriate product characteristics for a possible Planters brand extension seemed to be "crunchy," "sweet," "salty," "spicy," and "buttery." In terms of where in the store consumers would have expected to find new Planters products, the snack and candy sections seemed most likely. On the other hand, consumers did not seem to expect to find new Planters products in the breakfast food aisle, bakery product section, refrigerated section, or frozen food section.

Average Scale Rating[a]	Proposed Extensions
10	Peanuts
9	Snack mixes, nuts for baking
8	—
7	Pretzels, chocolate nut candy, caramel corn
6	Snack crackers, potato chips, nutritional granola bars
5	Tortilla chips, toppings (ice cream/dessert)
4	Lunchables/lunch snack packs, dessert mixes (cookie/cake/brownie)
3	Ice cream/ice cream bars, toppings (salad/vegetable)
2	Cereal, toaster pastries, Asian entrees/sauces, stuffing mix, refrigerated dough, jams/jellies
1	Yogurt

FIGURE 10-1

Reactions to Proposed Planters Extensions

[a]Consumers rated hypothetical proposed extensions on an 11-point scale anchored by 0 (definitely would *not* expect Planter's to sell it) and 10 (definitely would expect Planter's to sell it).

A brand like Planters has many extension opportunities that it should research carefully.

Source: Jarrod Weaton/ Weaton Digital, Inc.

Consistent with these survey results, besides selling a variety of nuts (peanuts, mixed nuts, cashews, almonds, pistachios, walnuts, and so on), Planters now sells trail mix, sunflower seeds, peanut bars, and peanut butter.

Critique. The main advantage of the marketing-based comparative approach is ease of implementation. We can compare virtually any proposed set of marketing actions for the brand. At the same time, the main drawback is that it may be difficult to discern whether consumer responses to changes in the marketing stimuli are being caused by brand knowledge or by more generic product knowledge. In other words, it may be that for *any* brand in the product category, consumers would be willing to pay certain prices, accept a particular brand extension, and so forth. One way to determine whether consumer response is specific to the brand is to conduct similar tests of consumer response with competitive brands. A statistical technique well suited to do just that is described next.

Conjoint Analysis

Conjoint analysis is a survey-based multivariate technique that enables marketers to profile the consumer decision process with respect to products and brands.[9] Specifically, by asking consumers to express preferences or choose among a number of carefully designed product profiles, researchers can determine the trade-offs consumers are making between various brand attributes, and thus the importance they are attaching to them.[10]

Each profile consumers see is made up of a set of attribute levels chosen on the basis of experimental design principles to satisfy certain mathematical properties. The value consumers attach to each attribute level, as statistically derived by the conjoint formula, is called a **part worth**. We can use the part worths in various ways to estimate how consumers would value a new combination of the attribute levels. For example, one attribute is the brand name. The part worth for the "brand name" attribute reflects its value.

One classic study of conjoint analysis, reported by Green and Wind, examined consumer evaluations of a spot-remover product on five attributes: package design, brand name, price, *Good Housekeeping seal*, and money-back guarantee.[11] These same authors also applied conjoint analysis in a landmark research study to arrive at the design that became the Courtyard by Marriott hotel chain.[12]

Applications. Conjoint analysis has a number of possible applications. In the past, Ogilvy & Mather ad agency used a brand/price trade-off methodology as a means of assessing advertising effectiveness and brand value.[13] Brand/price trade-off is a simplified version of

A comprehensive conjoint analysis project helped design Courtyard by Marriott to better satisfy consumer needs and desires.

Source: AP Photo/ PRNewsFoto/Marriott International, Inc.

conjoint measurement with just two variables—brand and price. Consumers make a series of simulated purchase choices between different combinations of brands and prices. Each choice triggers an increase in the price of the selected brand, forcing the consumer to choose between buying a preferred brand and paying less. In this way, consumers reveal how much their brand loyalty is worth and, conversely, which brands they would relinquish for a lower price.

Academic researchers with an interest in brand image and equity have used other variations and applications of conjoint analysis. For example, Rangaswamy, Burke, and Oliva use conjoint analysis to explore how brand names interact with physical product features to affect the extendability of brand names to new product categories.[14] Barich and Srinivasan apply conjoint analysis to corporate image programs, to show how it can determine the company attributes relevant to customers, rank the importance of those attributes, estimate the costs of making improvements (or correcting customer perceptions), and prioritize image goals to obtain the maximum benefit, in terms of improved perceptions, for the resources spent.[15]

Critique.   The main advantage of the conjoint-based approach is that it allows us to study different brands and different aspects of the product or marketing program (product composition, price, distribution outlets, and so on) simultaneously. Thus, we can uncover information about consumers' responses to different marketing activities for both the focal and competing brands.

One of the disadvantages of conjoint analysis is that marketing profiles may violate consumers' expectations based on what they already know about brands. Thus, we must take care that consumers do not evaluate unrealistic product profiles or scenarios. It can also be difficult to specify and interpret brand attribute levels, although some useful guidelines have been put forth to more effectively apply conjoint analysis to brand positioning.[16]

HOLISTIC METHODS

We use comparative methods to approximate specific benefits of brand equity. ***Holistic methods*** place an overall value on the brand in either abstract utility terms or concrete financial terms. Thus, holistic methods attempt to "net out" various considerations to determine the unique contribution of the brand. The ***residual approach*** examines the value of the brand by subtracting consumers' preferences for the brand—based on physical product attributes alone—from their overall brand preferences. The ***valuation approach*** places a financial value on brand equity for accounting purposes, mergers and acquisitions, or other such reasons. After an example from Liz Claiborne, we'll look at each of these approaches.

LIZ CLAIBORNE

A company that found great success selling popular fashions to working women in the 1980s—generating $2 billion in annual sales by the early 1990s—Liz Claiborne found itself in serious trouble two decades later when sales started to cool. A brand transformation that eliminated some slower-selling older lines to focus on younger customers failed to turn the business around. Aging core customers deserted the brand, and department stores began to replace it with their own private labels. The company was posting annual losses by 2006, and sales dropped by half over the next five years. Management decided to retrench in 2011 and focus its resources on its faster-selling brands—Kate Spade, Lucky Brands Jeans, and Juicy Couture. The Claiborne and Monet brands were sold to JCPenney for $288 million, and as part of the sales agreement, Liz Claiborne was given one year to change its name. The firm was making another financial bet on a new brand strategy it hoped would prove more fruitful than the last one, while JCPenney was betting there was life left in the Liz Claiborne brand on which it could capitalize.[17]

Liz Claiborne decided to sell its own brand in order to concentrate on more financially promising brands like Juicy Couture.
Source: Nick Baylis/Alamy

Residual Approaches

The rationale behind residual approaches is the view that brand equity is what remains of consumer preferences and choices after we subtract physical product effects. The idea is that we can infer the relative valuation of brands by observing consumer preferences and choices *if* we take into account as many sources of measured attribute values as possible. Several researchers have defined brand equity as the incremental preference over and above what would result without brand identification. In this view, we can calculate brand equity by subtracting preferences for objective characteristics of the physical product from overall preference.[18]

Scanner Panel.   Some researchers have focused on analysis of brand value based on data sets from supermarket scanners of consumer purchases. In an early study, Kamakura and Russell proposed a measure that employs consumer purchase histories from supermarket scanner data to estimate brand equity through a residual approach.[19] Specifically, their model explains the choices observed from a panel of consumers as a function of the store environment (actual shelf prices, sales promotions, displays), the physical characteristics of available brands, and a residual term dubbed brand equity. By controlling for other aspects of the marketing mix, they estimate that aspect of brand preference that is unique to a brand and not currently duplicated by competitors.

More recently, a variation proposed by Ailawadi, Lehmann, and Neslin employs actual retail sales data to calculate a "revenue premium" as an estimate of brand equity, by calculating the difference in revenues between a brand and a generic or private label in the same category.[20] Sriram, Balachandar, and Kalwani similarly use store-level scanner data to track brand equity and key drivers of brand equity over time.[21]

Choice Experiments.   Swait, Erdem, and colleagues have proposed a related approach to measuring brand equity with choice experiments that account for brand names, product attributes, brand image, and differences in consumer sociodemographic characteristics and brand usage.[22] They define the ***equalization price*** as the price that equates the utility of a brand to the utilities that could be attributed to a brand in the category where no brand differentiation occurred. We can consider equalization price a proxy for brand equity.[23]

Multi-Attribute Attitude Models.   Srinivasan, Park, and Chang have proposed a comprehensive residual methodology to measure brand equity based on the multiattribute attitude model.[24] Their approach reveals the relative sizes of different bases of brand equity by dividing brand equity into three components: brand awareness, attribute perception biases, and nonattribute preference.

- The ***attribute-perception biased component*** of brand equity is the difference between subjectively perceived attribute values and objectively measured attribute values. Objectively measured attribute values come from independent testing services such as *Consumer Reports* or acknowledged experts in the field.
- The ***nonattribute preference component*** of brand equity is the difference between subjectively perceived attribute values and overall preference. It reflects the consumer's overall appraisal of a brand that goes beyond the utility of individual product attributes.

The researchers also incorporate the effects of enhancing brand awareness and preference on consumer "pull" and the brand's availability. They propose a survey procedure to collect information for estimating these different perception and preference measures.

Dillon and his colleagues have presented a model for decomposing attribute ratings of a brand into two components: (1) brand-specific associations, meaning features, attributes, or benefits that consumers link to a brand; and (2) general brand impressions based on a more holistic view of a brand.[25]

Critique.   Residual approaches provide a useful benchmark for interpreting brand equity, especially when we need approximations of brand equity or a financially oriented perspective on it. The disadvantage of residual approaches is that they are most appropriate for brands with a lot of product-related attribute associations, because these measures are unable to distinguish between different types of non-product-related attribute associations. Consequently, the residual approach's diagnostic value for strategic decision making in other cases is limited.

More generally, residual approaches take a fairly static view of brand equity by focusing on consumer *preferences*. This contrasts sharply with the process view advocated by the customer-based brand equity framework. The brand-based and marketing-based comparative approaches stress looking at consumer *response* to the marketing of a brand and attempting to uncover the extent to which that response is affected by brand knowledge.

This distinction is also relevant for the issue of "separability" in brand valuation that various researchers have raised. For example, Barwise and his colleagues note that marketing efforts to create an extended or augmented product, say, with extra features or service plus other means to enhance brand value, "raise serious problems of separating the value of the brand name and trademark from the many other elements of the 'augmented' product."[26] According to customer-based brand equity, those efforts could affect the favorability, strength, and uniqueness of various brand associations, which would, in turn, affect consumer response to *future* marketing activities.

For example, imagine that a brand becomes known for providing extraordinary customer service because of certain policies and favorable advertising, publicity, or word-of-mouth (like Nordstrom department stores or Singapore Airlines). These favorable perceptions of customer service and the attitudes they engender could create customer-based brand equity by affecting consumer response to a price policy (consumers would be willing to pay higher prices), a new ad campaign (consumers would accept an ad illustrating customer satisfaction), or a brand extension (customers would become interested in trying a new type of retail outlet).

Much of the company value of Prada has been attributed to the value of the brand.

Source: Pascal Sittler/REA/ Redux Pictures

Valuation Approaches

An increasingly widely held belief is that much of the corporate value of many companies is wrapped up in intangible assets, including the brand. Many studies have reinforced this point:[27]

- A survey reported by *Fortune* magazine in 2006 suggested that 72 percent of the Dow Jones market cap was made up of intangible assets.
- Accenture estimated that intangibles accounted for almost 70 percent of the value of the S&P 500 in 2007, up from 20 percent in 2007.
- Brand consultancy Brand Finance has estimated that brand value for Nike and Prada made up as much as 84 percent and 73 percent of total company value, respectively, in 2006.

Recognizing that fact, many firms are interested in exactly what that brand value is. The ability to put a specific price tag on a brand's value may be useful for a number of reasons:

- *Mergers and acquisitions:* Both to evaluate possible purchases as well as to facilitate disposal
- *Brand licensing:* Internally for tax reasons and to third parties
- *Fund raising:* As collateral on loans or for sale or leaseback arrangements
- *Brand portfolio decisions:* To allocate resources, develop brand strategy, or prepare financial reports

For example, many companies appear to be attractive acquisition candidates because of the strong competitive positions of their brands and their reputation among consumers.

Unfortunately, the value of the brand assets in many cases is largely excluded from the company's balance sheet and is therefore of little use in determining overall value. It has been argued that adjusting the balance sheet to reflect the true value of a company's brands permits us to take a more realistic view and assess the purchase premium to book value that might be earned from the brands after acquisition. Such a calculation, however, would also require estimates of capital required by brands and the expected after-acquisition return on investment (ROI) of a company.

Separating out the percentage of revenue or profits attributable to brand equity is a difficult task. In the United States, there is no conventional accounting method for doing so.[28] Some of Coca-Cola's experiences with brand valuation are instructive here.

COCA-COLA BRAND VALUATION

Despite the fact that expert analysts estimate the value of the Coca-Cola name in the billions of dollars, due to accounting convention, it appears in the company's books as only $25 *million.* Based on accounting rules, Coca-Cola's assets in 2004 had a book value of $31.3 billion, with various intangible assets assessed at $3.8 billion and a market cap of $100 billion. On June 7, 2007, Coca-Cola acquired Energy Brands, also known as glacéau, maker of enhanced water brands such as vitaminwater, fruit-water, and smartwater, for approximately $4.1 billion. Because these brands were acquired, different accounting rules apply to them. Based upon a preliminary purchase price allocation, approximately $2.8 billion was allocated to trademarks, $2.2 billion to goodwill, $200 million to customer relation-ships, and $900 million to deferred tax liabilities. At the end of 2007, Coke had trademarks on its balance sheet with a book value of $5.135 billion. Of this figure, about $2.8 billion is associated with Energy Brands.[29]

Although the Coke brand is estimated to be worth billions, for accounting purposes it is on the books for mere millions.
Source: Chen Jianli/ZUMA Press/Newscom

As the Coca-Cola experiences show, market-based estimates of value can differ dramatically from those based on U.S. accounting conventions.[30] Other countries, however, are trying to cap-ture that value. How do we calculate the financial value of a brand? This section, after providing some accounting background and historical perspective, describes several leading brand valuation approaches.[31] Brand Focus 10.0 reviews some financial considerations in the relationship of brand equity to the stock market and provides additional perspective on accounting issues in branding.

Accounting Background. The assets of a firm can be either tangible or intangible. ***Tangible assets*** include property, plant, and equipment; current assets (inventories, marketable securities, and cash); and investments in stocks and bonds. We can estimate the value of tangible assets using accounting book values and reported estimates of replacement costs.

Intangible assets, on the other hand, are any factors of production or specialized resources that permit the company to earn cash flows in excess of the return on tangible assets. In other words, intangible assets augment the earning power of a firm's physical assets. They are typi-cally lumped under the heading of ***goodwill*** and include things such as patents, trademarks, and licensing agreements, as well as "softer" considerations such as the skill of the management and customer relations.

In an acquisition, the goodwill item often includes a premium paid to gain control, which, in certain instances, may even exceed the value of tangible and intangible assets. In Britain and certain other countries, it has been common to write off the goodwill element of an acquisition against reserves; tangible assets, on the other hand, are transferred straight to the acquiring com-pany's balance sheet.

Historical Perspectives. Brand valuation's more recent past started with Rupert Murdoch's News Corporation, which included a valuation of some of its magazines on its balance sheets in 1984, as permitted by Australian accounting standards. The rationale was that the goodwill element of publishing acquisitions—the difference in value between net

By taking advantage of Australian accounting standards to put brand value on balance sheets, Rupert Murdoch was able to build a media giant with News Corporation.

Source: Jeremy Sutton-Hibbert/Alamy

assets and the price paid—was often enormous and negatively affecting the balance sheet. News Corporation used the recognition that the titles themselves contained much of the value of the acquisition to justify placing them on the balance sheet, improving the debt/equity ratio and allowing the company to get some much-needed cash to finance acquisition of some foreign media companies.

In the United Kingdom, Grand Metropolitan was one of the first British companies to place a monetary value on the brands it owned and to put that value on its balance sheet. When Grand Met acquired Heublein distributors, Pearle eye care, and Sambuca Romana liqueur in 1987, it placed the value of some of its brands—principally Smirnoff—on the balance sheet for roughly $1 billion. In doing so, Grand Met used two different methods. If a company consisted of primarily one brand, it figured that the value of the brand was 75 percent of the purchase price, whereas if the company had many brands, it used a multiple of an income figure.

British firms used brand values primarily to boost their balance sheets. By recording their brand assets, the firms maintained, they were attempting to bring their shareholder funds nearer to the market capitalization of the firm. In the United Kingdom, Rank Hovis McDougal (RHM) succeeded in putting the worth of the company's existing brands as a figure on the balance sheet to fight a hostile takeover bid in 1988. With the brand value information provided by Interbrand, the RHM board was able to go back to investors and argue that the bid was too low, and eventually to repel it.

Accounting firms in favor of valuing brands argue that it is a way to strengthen the presentation of a company's accounts, to record hidden assets so they are disclosed to company's shareholders, to enhance a company's shareholders' funds to improve its earnings ratios, to provide a realistic basis for management and investors to measure a company's performance, and to reveal detailed information on brand strengths so that management can formulate appropriate brand strategies. In practical terms, however, recording brand value as an intangible asset from the firm's perspective is a means to increase the asset value of the firm.

Actual practices have varied from country to country. Brand valuations have been accepted for inclusion in the balance sheets of companies in countries such as the United Kingdom, Australia, New Zealand, France, Sweden, Singapore, and Spain. In the United Kingdom, Martin Sorrell improved the balance sheet of WPP by attaching brand value to its primary assets, including J. Walter Thompson Company, Ogilvy & Mather, and Hill & Knowlton, stating in the annual report that:

> Intangible fixed assets comprise certain acquired separable corporate brand names. These are shown at a valuation of the incremental earnings expected to arise from the ownership of brands. The valuations have been based on the present value of notional royalty savings arising from [ownership] and on estimates of profits attributable to brand loyalty.[32]

In the United States, generally accepted accounting principles (blanket amortization principles) mean that placing a brand on the balance sheet would require amortization of that asset for up to 40 years. Such a charge would severely hamper firm profitability; as a result, firms avoid such accounting maneuvers. On the other hand, certain other countries (including Canada, Germany, and Japan) have gone beyond tax deductibility of brand equity to permit some or all of the goodwill arising from an acquisition to be deducted for tax purposes.

General Approaches.   In determining the value of a brand in an acquisition or merger, firms can choose from three main approaches: the cost, market, and income approaches.[33]

The cost approach maintains that brand equity is the amount of money that would be required to reproduce or replace the brand (including all costs for research and development, test marketing, advertising, and so on). One common criticism of approaches relying on historic or replacement cost is that they reward past performance in a way that may bear little relation to future profitability—for example, many brands with expensive introductions have been unsuccessful. On the other hand, for brands that have been around for decades (such as Heinz, Kellogg's, and Chanel), it would be virtually impossible to find out what the investment in brand development was—and largely irrelevant as well.

It is also obviously easier to estimate costs of tangible assets than intangible assets, but the latter often may lie at the heart of brand equity. Similar problems exist with a replacement cost approach; for example, the cost of replacing a brand depends a great deal on how quickly the process would take and what competitive, legal, and logistical obstacles might be encountered.

According to the second approach, the market approach, we can think of brand equity as the present value of the future economic benefits to be derived by the owner of the asset. In other words, it is the amount an active market would allow so that the asset would exchange between a willing buyer and willing seller. The main problems with this approach are the lack of open market transactions for brand name assets, and the fact that the uniqueness of brands makes extrapolating from one market transaction to another problematic.

The third approach to determining the value of a brand, the income approach, argues that brand equity is the discounted future cash flow from the future earnings stream for the brand. Three such income approaches are as follows:

1. Capitalizing royalty earnings from a brand name (when these can be defined)
2. Capitalizing the premium profits that are earned by a branded product (by comparing its performance with that of an unbranded product)
3. Capitalizing the actual profitability of a brand after allowing for the costs of maintaining it and the effects of taxation

For example, as an example of the first income approach, brand consultancy Brand Finance uses a Royalty Relief methodology for brand valuation. Their approach is based on the premise that brand value can be thought of in terms of what a company avoids in paying a license fee from actually owning the trademark. Their rationale is that such an approach has much credibility with accountants, lawyers, and tax experts because it calculates brand values on the basis of comparable third-party transactions. They use publically available information to estimate future, post-tax royalties of a brand and thus its net present value and overall brand value.[34]

The next sections and The Science of Branding 10-1 describe other income-based valuation approaches.[35]

Simon and Sullivan's Brand Equity Value.   In a seminal academic research study, Simon and Sullivan developed a technique for estimating a firm's brand equity derived from financial market estimates of brand-related profits.[37] They define brand equity as the incremental cash flows that accrue to branded products over and above the cash flows that would result from the sale of unbranded products.

To implement their approach, they begin by estimating the current market value of the firm. They assume the market value of the firm's securities to provide an unbiased estimate of the future cash flows attributable to all the firm's assets. Their methodology attempts to extract the value of a firm's brand equity from the value of the firm's other assets. The result is an estimate of brand equity based on the financial market valuation of the firm's future cash flows.

THE SCIENCE OF BRANDING 10-1

The Prophet Brand Valuation Methodology

Prophet's brand valuation methodology starts with the realization that accountants define an asset as "a resource, under the control of an enterprise, to which future economic benefits will flow." In the context of a brand, a resource is something a company owns that it uses to achieve an end or fulfill a function, namely to identify the company's product or service so that consumers can identify it and attach perceptions to it.

Fundamental to Prophet's approach is that brands generate future economic benefits, in that consumers who know of a brand and prefer it to other choices will spend money buying it now and in the future. The purpose of marketing, according to Prophet, is to find these customers in the first place and keep them over time. Prophet maintains that a credible brand valuation methodology must reflect this definition, which is why it is at the foundation of Prophet's approach.

Prophet's brand valuation methodology is also constructed on the basis of sound corporate finance principles and complies with the standards laid down by the U.S. Marketing Accountability Standards Board (MASB). Specifically, it has four steps:

1. Finance

Economic profit (EP) is the profit a company earns that exceeds its cost of capital.[36] Only firms that have developed sustainable competitive advantages over time are able to earn this class of profit. It is generally acknowledged that brands are a major cause of a company earning and sustaining economic profit. The starting point for any valuation is therefore to extract from the income statement and balance sheet the economic profit earned by the brand being valued.

2. Brand Contribution

The Prophet brand contribution is a procedure that breaks economic profit into a set of drivers and then isolates the portion that is attributable to the brand's equity or strength. The Prophet approach employs a classical qualitative/quantitative technique in the following five steps:

1. Using a modified focus group format, senior company management generates a list of probable EP drivers. These are reduced by various rating and ranking methods to between 10 and 15.

2. A panel of about 50 respondents knowledgeable about the category is assembled, and participants are briefed to participate in a two- or three-round set of quantitative questions. These require them to evaluate the driver set and allocate ratings according to relative importance. Thus the list is reduced still further to between 5 and 9.

3. The respondents are asked to evaluate the market competitiveness of each of the drivers in the set, using market-based asset as the criteria. A score out of 100 indicates each one's relative importance.

4. Finally, respondents are asked to assess each driver's dependence on, or independence from, the brand's external equity.

5. The brand equity scores are multiplied by the driver weightings. The products are summed to produce the percentage that is then applied to economic profit to identify the brand portion or contribution. In the model, this profit is called brand premium profit (BPP).

3. Category Expected Life

The profit a brand can earn is to a large extent dictated by the nature of the category in which it sells. A category might be as broad as financial services, which can be narrowed to banking and insurance, or as precise as toothpaste, which can be expanded to dental care. Within the category, supply and demand pressures will exert an influence on the price range consumers will tolerate, which in turn determines profit margins brand owners can achieve.

The Prophet model uses an evaluation of the category to measure the extent to which the category encourages or inhibits the earning of economic profit for the brands that compete within it. It does this by looking at four variables: how mature is the category; are brand shares stable or volatile; does competitive activity create high barriers to entry or not; and, how vulnerable is the category to external pressures such as government regulation, raw material supply, and changing fashions. The outcome of this evaluation is to set parameters in years of expected economic life for a strong (dominant) and weak (marginal) brand.

4. Brand Knowledge Structure (BKS)

Brand knowledge structure, or BKS, is the bundle of knowledge consumers hold in memory and use to decide what products they need and which of the available brands they will buy. The comparative strength with which this information is held by the category community of users determines the success of the competing brands. It is also a good proxy for risk: the stronger the brand, the more likely consumers are to continue to buy in the future. Brand strength ensures future cash flows. The opposite is equally true. The Prophet method uses market research–based measurements of brand strength and preference to set the number of years in the cash flow projection: the stronger the brand relative to its competitors, the more years in the model.

The Valuation

The model calculates the value of the brand by working out how many years to project the growing part of the cash flows and then the shape and duration of a theoretical decay period. It does this by merging the BKS data with the category expected life results. The value is the resulting capitalized value of the projected cash flows. The discount rate is a classical weighted average cost of capital (WACC), and risk is taken into account by specially constructed probability weightings of the near term cash flows.

Key Differences

A few characteristics distinguish the Prophet brand valuation methodology. Other models typically look at only five years of future cash flows, add a perpetuity based on a discounted sixth year, and simply divide the sixth year by the discount rate. Frequently the perpetuity represents one-quarter to one-third of the total brand value; the five-year discounted cash flow into which most of the work has been invested results in only a small amount of the valuation.

The Prophet approach models the entire expected economic life of the brand in terms of the franchise run (its rise) and decay (its decline). The nature of the brand category (category expected life) and the relative strength of the brand as measured by the BKS determine the total number of years for the present-value calculation. The proportions are reversed compared to many other models, with the major portion of the Prophet valuation located in the early franchise run, which includes the five-year discounted part of the cash flow projection. This makes the valuation sensitive to changes in the BKS and early cash flows.

Also, like most corporate finance valuations, the Prophet approach uses a classically estimated weighted average cost of capital (WACC). It takes specific risk into account in the cash flows, as opposed to the discount rate. Other methodologies use the market risk and beta components of WACC to insert their consumer-driven brand risk premiums.

Source: Based on the research and writings of Prophet's Roger Sinclair whose considerable input is gratefully acknowledged. For more information, visit www.prophet.com.

From these basic premises, Simon and Sullivan derive their methodology to extract the value of brand equity from the financial market value of the firm. The total asset value of the firm is the sum of the market value of common stock, preferred stock, long-term debt, and short-term debt. The value of intangible assets is captured in the ratio of the market value of the firm to the replacement cost of its tangible assets. There are three categories of intangible assets: brand equity, nonbrand factors that reduce the firm's costs relative to competitors like R&D and patents, and industry-wide factors that permit monopoly profits, such as regulation. By considering factors such as the age of the brand, order of entry in the category, and current and past advertising share, Simon and Sullivan then provide estimates of brand equity.

Interbrand's Brand Valuation Methodology.   Interbrand is probably the premier brand valuation firm. Figure 1-5 from Chapter 1 listed the 25 most valuable global brands according to Interbrand. In developing its brand valuation methodology, Interbrand approached the problem by assuming that the value of a brand, like the value of any other economic asset, was the present worth of the benefits of future ownership. In other words, according to Interbrand, brand valuation is based on an assessment of what the value is today of the earnings or cash flow the brand can be expected to generate in the future.[38]

Because Interbrand's approach looks at the ongoing investment and management of the brand as an economic asset, it takes into account all the different ways in which a brand benefits

According to Simon and Sullivan's analysis, in the highly competitive candy category, Tootsie Roll's brand name was a valuable financial asset.

Source: Tootsie Roll Industries, Inc.

an organization both internally and externally—from attracting and retaining talent to delivering on customer expectations. One advantage of the Interbrand valuation approach is that it is very generalizable and can be applied to virtually any type of brand or product.

Three key components contribute to the brand value assessment: (1) the financial performance of the branded products or services, (2) the role of brand in the purchase decision process, and (3) the strength of the brand.[39] Here's how Interbrand addresses each of these three components.

Brand Financial Performance. Financial performance for the brand reflects an organization's raw financial return to the investors and is analyzed as economic profit, a concept akin to economic value added (EVA). To determine economic profit, subtract taxes from net operating profit to arrive at net operating profit after tax (NOPAT). From NOPAT, subtract a capital charge to account for the capital used to generate the brand's revenues, yielding the economic profit for each year analyzed. The capital charge rate is set by the industry-weighted average cost of capital (WACC). The financial performance is analyzed for a five-year forecast and for a terminal value. The terminal value represents the brand's expected performance beyond the forecast period. The economic profit that is calculated is then multiplied by the role of brand (a percentage, as described below) to determine the branded earnings that contribute to the valuation total.

Role of Brand. Role of brand measures the portion of the customer decision to purchase that is attributable to brand—exclusive of other purchase drivers such as price or product features. Conceptually, role of brand reflects the portion of demand for a branded product or service that exceeds what the demand would be for the same product or service if it were unbranded. We can determine role of brand in different ways, including primary research, a review of historical roles of brand for companies in that industry, and expert panel assessment. We multiply the percentage for the role of brand by the economic profit of the branded products or services to determine the amount of branded earnings that contribute to the valuation total.

Brand Strength. Brand strength measures the ability of the brand to secure the delivery of expected future earnings. Brand strength is reported on a scale of 0–100 based on an evaluation across 10 dimensions of brand activation. Performance in these dimensions is generally judged relative to other brands in the industry. The brand strength inversely determines a discount rate, through a proprietary algorithm. That rate is used to discount branded earnings back to a present value, based on the likelihood that the brand will be able to withstand challenges and deliver the expected earnings.

Summary. Brand valuation and the "brands on the balance sheet" debate are controversial subjects. There is no one universally agreed-upon approach.[40] In fact, many marketing experts feel it is impossible to reduce the richness of a brand to a single, meaningful number, and that any formula that tries to do so is an abstraction and arbitrary.

The primary disadvantage of valuation approaches is that they necessarily have to make a host of potentially oversimplified assumptions to arrive at one measure of brand equity. For example, Sir Michael Perry, former chairman of Unilever, once objected for philosophical reasons:

> The seemingly miraculous conjuring up of intangible asset values, as if from nowhere, only serves to reinforce the view of the consumer skeptics, that brands are just high prices and consumer exploitation.[41]

Wharton's Peter Fader points out a number of limitations of valuation approaches: they require much judgmental data and thus contain much subjectivity; intangible assets are not always synonymous with brand equity; the methods sometimes defy common sense and lack "face validity"; the financial measures generally ignore or downplay current investments in future equity like advertising or R&D; and the strength of the brand measures may be confounded with the strength of the company.[42]

At the heart of much of the criticism is the issue of separability we identified earlier. An *Economist* editorial put it this way: "Brands can be awkward to separate as assets. With Cadbury's Dairy Milk, how much value comes from the name Cadbury? How much from Dairy Milk? How much merely from the product's (replicable) contents or design?"[43]

To draw a sports analogy, extracting brand value may be as difficult as determining the value of the coach to a team's performance. And the way a brand is managed can have a large effect, positive or negative, on its value. Branding Brief 10-1 describes several brand acquisitions that turned out unsuccessfully for firms.

As a result of these criticisms, the climate regarding brand valuation has changed. See Brand Focus 10.0 for more on how accounting standards have changed to accommodate the concept of brand value.

BRANDING BRIEF 10-1

Beauty Is in the Eye of the Beholder

Companies make acquisitions because they wish to grow and expand their business. In making acquisitions, a company has to determine what it feels the acquired brands are worth. In some instances, the hoped-for brand value has failed to materialize, serving as a reminder that the value of a brand is partly a function of what you do with it. The booming business environment of the 1990s witnessed many such failures.

A classic example is Quaker Oats's $1.7 billion acquisition of Snapple in 1994. Snapple had become a popular national brand through powerful grassroots marketing and a willingness to distribute to small outlets and convenience stores. Quaker changed Snapple's ad campaign—abandoning the rotund and immensely popular Snapple Lady—and revamped its distribution system. Quaker also changed the packaging by updating the label and putting Snapple in 64-ounce bottles, moves that did not sit well with

A brand is partly worth what you can do with it—a lesson Quaker Oats learned the hard way after it mismanaged the Snapple brand after acquiring it.
Source: Ramin Talaie/Bloomberg via Getty Images

loyal customers. The results were disastrous: Snapple began losing money and market share, allowing a host of competitors to move in. Unable to revive the foundering brand, Quaker sold the company in 1997 for $300 million to Triarc, which owned other beverages such as Royal Crown Cola and Diet Rite.

Another unsuccessful acquisition occurred when Quality Dining bought Bruegger's Bagels in 1996 with $142 million in stock. Within one year, Quality Dining agreed to sell the bagel chain back to its original owners for $50 million after taking a $203 million charge on the acquisition. Experts blamed an overly ambitious expansion strategy. Quality Dining planned to expand to 2,000 stores within four years, despite the fact that before the acquisition, Bruegger's had posted two consecutive annual losses due to its expansion to 339 stores. The new ownership also set the lofty goal of entering the top 60 domestic markets, which limited the amount of advertising and promotional support each market received. As Bruegger's fortunes turned, competitor Einstein/Noah Bagel overtook the company as the market leader in the United States. One franchisee commented, "[Quality Dining] would have had to stay up pretty late at night to screw up anything more than they did."

More recently, despite much success with its Ford brand, Ford Motor Company could never seem to find the right

formula for the overseas acquisitions that made up its Premier Automotive Group collection. The company sold the Jaguar and Land Rover brands to India's Tata Motors in March 2008 for $1.7 billion—roughly a third of the price it had paid for the two luxury brands ($2.5 billion in 1989 and $2.7 billion in 2000, respectively). After paying $6.5 billion for Volvo in 1999, Ford sold it to China's Geely for $1.5 billion in 2010. Ford's decision was motivated by a lack of success with its luxury brands and a desire to focus on its more promising Ford brand.

In all these case, despite the best of intentions, brands were sold with an implicit assumption that could be more profitably marketed by someone else.

Sources: "Cadbury Is Paying Triarc $1.45 Billion for Snapple Unit," *Baltimore Sun*, 19 September 2000; Thomas M. Burton, "The Profit Center of the Bagel Business Has Quite a Big Hole," *Wall Street Journal*, 6 October 1997; "Ford Sells Luxury Brands for $1.7 Billion," Associated Press, 26 March 2008; "Ford Sells Volvo to Chinese Carmaker Geely for $1.5 Billion," *New York Daily News*, 3 August 2010. For an interesting academic analyses, see S. Cem Bahadir, Sundar G. Bharadwaj, and Rajendra K. Srivastava, "Financial Value of Brands in Mergers and Acquisitions: Is Value in the Eye of the Beholder?," *Journal of Marketing* 72 (November 2008): 49–64; Michael A. Wiles, Neil A. Morgan, and Lopo L. Rego, "The Effect of Brand Acquisition and Disposal on Stock Returns," *Journal of Marketing*, 2012, in press.

REVIEW

This chapter considered the two main ways to measure the benefits or outcomes of brand equity: comparative methods (a means to better assess the effects of consumer perceptions and preferences on aspects of the marketing program) and holistic methods (attempts to come up with an estimate of the overall value of the brand). Figure 10-2 summarizes the different but complementary approaches. In fact, understanding the particular range of benefits for a brand on the basis of comparative methods may be useful as an input in estimating the overall value of a brand by holistic methods.

Combining these outcome measures with the measures of sources of brand equity from Chapter 9 as part of the brand value chain can provide insight into the effectiveness of marketing actions. Nevertheless, assessing the ROI of marketing activities remains a challenge.[44] Here are four general guidelines for creating and measuring ROI from brand marketing activities:

1. *Spend wisely—focus and be creative.* To be able to measure ROI, we need to be earning a return to begin with! Investing in distinctive and well-designed marketing activities increases the chance for a more positive and discernible ROI.
2. *Look for benchmarks—examine competitive spending levels and historical company norms.* It is important to get the lay of the land in a market or category in order to understand what we may expect.
3. *Be strategic—apply brand equity models.* Use models such as the brand resonance model and the brand value chain to provide discipline and a structured approach to planning, implementing, and interpreting marketing activity.
4. *Be observant—track both formally and informally.* Qualitative and quantitative insights can help us understand brand performance.

Perhaps the dominant theme of this chapter and the preceding chapter on measuring sources of brand equity is the importance of using multiple measures and research methods to capture the richness and complexity of brand equity. No matter how carefully we apply them, single measures of brand equity provide at best a one- or two-dimensional view of a brand and risk

---

Comparative methods: Use experiments that examine consumer attitudes and behavior toward a brand, to more directly assess the benefits arising from having a high level of awareness and strong, favorable, and unique brand associations.

- *Brand-based comparative approaches:* Experiments in which one group of consumers responds to an element of the marketing program when it is attributed to the brand and another group responds to that same element when it is attributed to a competitive or fictitiously named brand.

- *Marketing-based comparative approaches:* Experiments in which consumers respond to changes in elements of the marketing program for the brand or competitive brands.

- *Conjoint analysis:* A survey-based multivariate technique that enables marketers to profile the consumer buying decision process with respect to products and brands.

Holistic methods: Attempt to place an overall value on the brand in either abstract utility terms or concrete financial terms. Thus, holistic methods attempt to "net out" various considerations to determine the unique contribution of the brand.

- *Residual approach:* Examines the value of the brand by subtracting out from overall brand preferences consumers' preferences for the brand based on physical product attributes alone.

- *Valuation approach:* Places a financial value on the brand for accounting purposes, mergers and acquisitions, or other such reasons.

FIGURE 10-2

Measures of Outcomes of Brand Equity

missing important dimensions of brand equity. Recall the problems encountered by Coca-Cola from its overreliance on blind taste tests, described in Branding Brief 1-1.

No single number or measure fully captures brand equity.[45] Rather, we should think of brand equity as a multidimensional concept that depends on what knowledge structures are present in the minds of consumers, and what actions a firm takes to capitalize on the potential that these knowledge structures offer.

There are many different sources of, and outcomes from, brand equity, depending on the marketers' skill and ingenuity. Firms may be more or less able to maximize the potential value of a brand according to the type and nature of their marketing activities. As Wharton's Peter Fader says:

> The actual value of a brand depends on its fit with buyer's corporate structure and other assets. If the acquiring company has manufacturing or distribution capabilities that are synergistic with the brand, then it might be worth paying a lot of money for it. Paul Feldwick, a British executive, makes the analogy between brands and properties on the Monopoly game board. You're willing to pay a lot more for Marvin Gardens if you already own Atlantic and Ventnor Avenues![46]

The customer-based brand equity framework therefore emphasizes employing a range of research measures and methods to fully capture the multiple potential sources and outcomes of brand equity.

DISCUSSION QUESTIONS

1. Choose a product. Conduct a branded and unbranded experiment. What do you learn about the equity of the brands in that product class?
2. Can you identify any other advantages or disadvantages of the comparative methods?
3. Pick a brand and conduct an analysis similar to that done with the Planters brand. What do you learn about its extendability as a result?
4. What do you think of the Interbrand methodology? What do you see as its main advantages and disadvantages?
5. How do you think Young & Rubicam's BrandAsset Valuator relates to the Interbrand methodology (see Brand Focus 9.0)? What do you see as its main advantages and disadvantages?

BRAND FOCUS 10.0

Branding and Finance

Marketers increasingly must be able to quantify their activities directly or indirectly in financial terms. One important topic that has received increasing academic interest is the relationship between brand equity and brand strategies and stock market information and performance. Another important topic is the accounting implications of branding. We review issues around these two topics in this appendix.

Stock Market Reactions

Several researchers have studied how the stock market reacts to the brand equity and marketing activities for companies and products.

Brand Equity.   In a classic study, David Aaker and Robert Jacobson examined the association between yearly stock return and yearly brand changes (as measured by EquiTrend's perceived quality rating of brand equity) for 34 companies during the

years 1989–1992.[47] They also compared the accompanying changes in current-term return on investment (ROI).

They found that, as expected, stock market return was positively related to changes in ROI. Interestingly, they also uncovered a strong positive relationship between brand equity and stock return. Firms that experienced the largest gains in brand equity saw their stock return average 30 percent. Conversely, those firms with the largest losses in brand equity saw stock return average a negative 10 percent. The researchers concluded that investors can and do learn about changes in brand equity—not necessarily through EquiTrend studies (which may have little exposure to the financial community) but by learning about a company's plans and programs.[48]

In a follow-up study, using data for firms in the computer industry in the 1990s, Aaker and Jacobson found that changes in brand attitude were associated contemporaneously with stock return and led accounting financial performance.[49]

They also found five factors (new products, product problems, competitor actions, changes in top management, and legal actions) that were associated with significant changes in brand attitudes. Awareness that did not translate into more positive attitudes, however, did little to the stock price (Ameritrade, Juno, and Priceline). The authors conclude, "So it's not the brands customers know, but the brands customers respect, that are ultimately successful." Similarly, using *Financial World* estimates of brand equity, another comprehensive study found that brand equity was positively related to stock return and that this effect was incremental to other accounting variables such as the firm's net income.[50]

Madden, Fehle, and Fournier found that strong brands not only delivered greater returns to stockholders versus a relevant market benchmark, they did so with less risk.[51] Fornell and his colleagues find similar benefits of higher returns and lower risk for satisfied, loyal customers.[52]

Marketing Activities. Adopting an event study methodology, Lane and Jacobson were able to show that stock market participants' response to brand extension announcements, consistent with the trade-offs inherent in brand leveraging, depend interactively and nonmonotonically on brand attitude and familiarity.[53]

Specifically, the stock market responded most favorably to extensions of high-esteem, high-familiarity brands (Hershey, Coke, Norton/Symantec) and to low-esteem, low-familiarity brands (in the latter case, presumably because there was little to risk and much to gain with extensions). The stock market reaction was less favorable (and sometimes even negative!) for extensions of brands for which consumer familiarity was disproportionately high compared with consumer regard and to extensions of brands for which consumer regard was disproportionately high compared with familiarity.

In another event study of 58 firms that changed their names in the 1980s, Horsky and Swyngedouw found that for most of the firms, name changes were associated with improved performance; the greatest improvement tended to occur in firms that produced industrial goods and whose performance prior to the change was relatively poor.[54] Not all changes, however, were successful. The researchers interpreted the act of a name change as a signal that other measures to improve performance (changes in product offerings and organizational changes) will be seriously and successfully undertaken.

Rao and his colleagues analyzed financial performance of 113 firms over a five-year period and found that corporate branding strategies were associated with higher values of Tobin's Q.[55] Tobin's Q is a forward-looking measure of intangible assets and a firm's future profit potential, calculated as the ratio of the market value of the firm to the replacement cost of the firm's assets.

A mixed branding strategy (where a firm used corporate names for some products and individual names for others) was associated with lower values of Tobin's Q. The researchers also concluded that most firms would have been able to improve their Tobin's Q had they adopted a branding strategy different from the one suggested by examining their brand portfolios.

Similarly, Morgan, Rego, and colleagues showed how five brand portfolio characteristics (number of brands owned, number of segments in which they are marketed, degree to which the brands in the firm's portfolio compete with one another, and consumer perceptions of the quality and price of the brands in the firm's portfolio) affected a firm's marketing effectiveness and efficiency and financial performance.[56]

Finally, Mizik and Jacobson found that the stock market reacted favorably when a firm increased its emphasis on value appropriation (extracting profits in the marketplace) over value creation (innovating, producing, and delivering products to the market), although certain qualifying conditions prevailed.[57]

Accounting Perspectives on Brands[58]

In the period following the Second World War, investors used the physical, tangible assets owned by a company to assess its value. Records show that the market value of companies on major stock markets more or less equaled their book value. Any surplus over book value was called goodwill and was considered to be a reflection of relationships the company had built with suppliers and customers and never amounted to much.

Coinciding with the introduction to business of the mainframe computer in the 1970s and the personal computer in the 1980s, the gap started to open. At the peak of the "dot.com" boom, market value was measured at five times book value.

Traditionally, company annual financial accounts were based on "historic cost"—a record on the balance sheet of what was paid for the tangible assets a company needed to operate the business. But the cost and the value of the asset at current market prices often differed. Asset strippers could buy a company based on the historic cost of its assets and then sell off the assets at market value and make a handsome profit. Since the dot.com bust in 2000, the ratio of market to book has dropped sharply to stabilize over the last 10 years at about 2.8.[59] At the time of the 2008 financial crisis, it dropped below 2 before recovering somewhat afterward.

To provide investors with more readily useful information for making investment decisions, the major accounting bodies, the Financial Accounting Standards Board (FASB) in the United States and the International Accounting Standards Board (IASB) representing accountants in the rest of the world, took two steps:

1. They moved from historic cost to fair value, which is the price that would be received if an asset were sold in an orderly market between two market participants, that is, the current market value.

2. They began to develop accounting standards to take account of assets that have no monetary value and no physical substance—that is, intangible assets.

Over the past decade, FASB and the IASB have worked on the following four standards relevant to brands.[60]

IFRS 3 *Business Combinations*. The purpose of this standard is to guide preparers of financial statements in the treatment of companies after a merger or acquisition. A radical aspect of this standard is that it requires acquired goodwill to be allocated to cash generating units. This replaces goodwill as the arithmetic difference between net tangible value and the price paid and calls for it to be broken down into identifiable items. The standard specifies that trademarks and brands will feature among the marketing-based intangibles to be valued and included in the accounts.

IAS 38 *Intangible Assets*. This standard still has a label that indicates it has not been updated. When this happens, it will take on the IFRS appellation. In its current form, it contradicts IFRS 3 in that it states that brands developed by a company do not qualify to be described as assets. They fail to meet the recognition criteria. This is an anomaly that is known and understood by the accounting standard setters. Work had been invested in bringing IAS 38 into line but was delayed as the accounting boards dealt with the financial crisis of 2008 and other matters.[61]

IFRS 13 *Fair Value Measurement.* This standard was issued formally during the course of 2011. As its name implies, it explains in considerable detail how an asset should be measured at its fair value. While it doesn't specify brands, it makes allowance for a class of assets that can be difficult to value because they lack publicly available data. This standard provides substantial guidance on how brands should be valued.

IFRS 36 *Impairment of Assets.* Accounting principles state that an asset should not be held on the balance sheet at its original value if that value no longer applies. IFRS 36 requires assets to be tested annually, and if the value has fallen below what is called the carrying amount, the difference must be treated as a loss in the income statement. That rarely applies to brands, which tend to increase in value over time, yet there is no allowance at this stage for the opposite of impairment, which is accretion. What makes the standard useful to brand owners is the clear explanation of how the annual measurement process should be conducted.

Notes

1. C. B. Bhattacharya and Leonard M. Lodish, "Towards a System for Monitoring Brand Health," *Marketing Science Institute Working Paper Series* (00–111) (July 2000).
2. Richard F. Chay, "How Marketing Researchers Can Harness the Power of Brand Equity," *Marketing Research* 3, no. 2 (1991): 10–30.
3. For an interesting approach, see Martin R. Lautman and Koen Pauwels, "Metrics That Matter: Identifying the Importance of Consumer Needs and Wants," *Journal of Advertising Research* (September 2009): 339–359.
4. Peter Farquhar and Yuji Ijiri have made several other distinctions in classifying brand equity measurement procedures. Peter H. Farquhar, Julia W. Han, and Yuji Ijiri, "Recognizing and Measuring Brand Assets," *Marketing Science Institute Report* (1991): 91–119. They describe two broad classes of measurement approaches to brand equity: separation approaches and integration approaches. Separation approaches view brand equity as the value added to a product. Farquhar and Ijiri categorize separation approaches into residual methods and comparative methods. Residual methods determine brand equity by what remains after subtracting physical product effects. Comparative methods determine brand equity by comparing the branded product with an unbranded product or an equivalent benchmark.

   Integration approaches, on the other hand, typically define brand equity as a composition of basic elements. Farquhar and Ijiri categorize integration approaches into association and valuation methods. Valuation methods measure brand equity by its cost or value as an intangible asset for a particular owner and intended use. Association methods measure brand equity in terms of the favorableness of brand evaluations, the accessibility of brand attitudes, and the consistency of brand image with consumers.

   The previous chapter described techniques that could be considered association methods. This chapter considers techniques related to the other three categories of methods.
5. Jennifer E. Breneiser and Sarah N. Allen, "Taste Preference for Brand Name versus Store Brand Sodas," *North American Journal of Psychology* 13, no. 2 (2011): 281–290.
6. Julian Clover, "Virgin Connects Mobile Network with Orange," *Broadband TV News*, 10 October 2011; Chris Martin, "Virgin Media Mobile Customers Will Get Orange Network Coverage," *The Inquirer*, 7 October 2011; www.virginmobile.com.
7. Edgar Pessemier, "A New Way to Determine Buying Decisions," *Journal of Marketing* 24 (1959): 41–46.
8. Björn Höfer and Volker Bosch, "Brand Equity Measurement with GfK Price Challenger, *Yearbook of Marketing and Consumer Research*, Vol. 5 (2007): 21–39.
9. Paul E. Green and V. Srinivasan, "Conjoint Analysis in Consumer Research: Issues and outlook," *Journal of Consumer Research* 5 (1978): 103–123; Paul E. Green and V. Srinivasan, "Conjoint Analysis in Marketing: New Developments with Implications for Research and Practice," *Journal of Marketing* 54 (1990): 3–19; David Bakken and Curtis Frazier, "Conjoint Analysis: Understanding Consumer Decision Making," Chapter 15 in *Handbook of Marketing Research: Uses, Misuses, and Future Advances*, eds. Rajiv Grover and Marco Vriens (Thousand Oaks, CA: Sage Publications, 2006): 288–311.
10. For more details, see Betsy Sharkey, "The People's Choice," *Adweek*, 27 November 1989, MRC 8.
11. Paul E. Green and Yoram Wind, "New Ways to Measure Consumers' Judgments," *Harvard Business Review* 53 (July–August 1975): 107–111.
12. Jerry Wind, Paul E. Green, Douglas Shifflet, and Marsha Scarbrough, "Courtyard by Marriott: Designing a Hotel Facility with Consumer-Based Marketing Models," *Interfaces* 19 (January–February 1989): 25–47.
13. Max Blackstone, "Price Trade-Offs as a Measure of Brand Value," *Journal of Advertising Research* (August/September 1990): RC3–RC6.
14. Arvind Rangaswamy, Raymond R. Burke, and Terence A. Oliva, "Brand Equity and the Extendibility of Brand Names," *International Journal of Research in Marketing* 10 (March 1993): 61–75. See also Moonkyu Lee, Jonathan Lee, and Wagner A. Kamakura, "Consumer Evaluations of Line Extensions: A Conjoint Approach," in *Advances in Consumer Research*, Vol. 23

(Ann Arbor, MI: Association of Consumer Research, 1996), 289–295.

15. Howard Barich and V. Srinivasan, "Prioritizing Marketing Image Goals under Resource Constraints," *Sloan Management Review* (Summer 1993): 69–76.

16. Marco Vriens and Curtis Frazier, "The Hard Impact of the Soft Touch: How to Use Brand Positioning Attributes in Conjoint," *Marketing Research* (Summer 2003): 23–27.

17. Nicholas Rubino, "McComb Played a Bad Hand Well," *Wall Street Journal*," 20 October 2011; Dana Mattiolo, "Liz Claiborne Must Say Adieu to Liz," *Wall Street Journal*, 13 October 2011; Associated Press, "Liz Claiborne to Sell Several Brands, Change Name, *USA Today*, 12 October 2011.

18. V. Srinivasan, "Network Models for Estimating Brand-Specific Effects in Multi-Attribute Marketing Models," *Management Science* 25 (January 1979): 11–21; V. Srinivasan, Chan Su Park, and Dae Ryun Chang, "An Approach to the Measurement, Analysis, and Prediction of Brand Equity and Its Sources," *Management Science* 51, no. 9 (September 2005): 1433–1448.

19. Wagner A. Kamakura and Gary J. Russell, "Measuring Brand Value with Scanner Data," *International Journal of Research in Marketing* 10 (1993): 9–22.

20. Kusum Ailawadi, Donald R. Lehmann, and Scott A. Neslin, "Revenue Premium as an Outcome Measure of Brand Equity," *Journal of Marketing* 67 (October 2003): 1–17. See also Avi Goldfarb, Qiang Lu, and Sridhar Moorthy, "Measuring Brand Value in an Equilibrium Framework," *Marketing Science* 28 (January–February 2009): 69–86; C. Whan Park, Deborah J. MacInnis, Xavier Dreze, and Jonathan Lee, "Measuring Brand Equity: The Marketing Surplus & Efficiency (MARKSURE)–Based Brand Equity Measure," in *Brands and Brand Management: Contemporary Research Perspectives*, eds. Barbara Loken, Rohini Ahluwalia, and Michael J. Houston (London: Taylor and Francis Group Publishing, 2010), 159–188.

21. S. Sriram, Subramanian Balachander, and Manohar U. Kalwani, "Monitoring the Dynamics of Brand Equity Using Store-level Data," *Journal of Marketing* 71 (April 2007): 61–78.

22. Joffre Swait, Tülin Erdem, Jordan Louviere, and Chris Dubelar, "The Equalization Price: A Measure of Consumer-Perceived Brand Equity," *International Journal of Research in Marketing* 10 (1993): 23–45; Tülin Erdem and Joffre Swait, "Brand Equity as a Signaling Phenomenon," *Journal of Consumer Psychology* 7, no. 2 (1998): 131–157; Tülin Erdem, Joffre Swait, and Ana Valenzuela, "Brands as Signals: A Cross-Country Validation Study," *Journal of Marketing* 70 (January 2006): 34–49; Joffre Swait and Tülin Erdem, "Characterizing Brand Effects on Choice Set Formation and Preference Discrimination Under Uncertainty," *Marketing Science* 26 (September–October 2007): 679–697.

23. See also Eric L. Almquist, Ian H. Turvill, and Kenneth J. Roberts, "Combining Economic Analysis for Breakthrough Brand Management," *Journal of Brand Management* 5, no. 4 (1998): 272–282.

24. V. Srinivasan, Chan Su Park, and Dae Ryun Chang, "An Approach to the Measurement, Analysis, and Prediction of Brand Equity and Its Sources," *Management Science* 51 (September 2005): 1433–1448. See also Chan Su Park and V. Srinivasan, "A Survey-Based Method for Measuring and Understanding Brand Equity and Its Extendability," *Journal of Marketing Research* 31 (May 1994): 271–288. See also Na Woon Bong, Roger Marshall, and Kevin Lane Keller, "Measuring Brand Power: Validating a Model for Optimizing Brand Equity," *Journal of Product and Brand Management* 8, no. 3 (1999): 170–184; Randle Raggio and Robert P. Leone, "Producing a Measure of Brand Equity by Decomposing Brand Beliefs into Brand and Attribute Sources," ICFAI Press, 2007.

25. William R. Dillon, Thomas J. Madden, Amna Kirmani, and Soumen Mukherjee, "Understanding What's in a Brand Rating: A Model for Assessing Brand and Attribute Effects and Their Relationship to Brand Equity," *Journal of Marketing Research* 38 (November 2001): 415–429.

26. Patrick Barwise (with Christopher Higson, Andrew Likierman, and Paul Marsh), "Brands as 'Separable Assets,'" *Business Strategy Review* (Summer 1990): 49.

27. "The Battle for the Best," *The Economist*, 16 November 2006; John Gerzema and Edward Lebar, "The Danger of a Brand Bubble," *Market Leader* (Quarter 4, 2009): 30–34; John Gerzema and Edward Lebar, *The Brand Bubble: The Looming Crisis in Brand Value and How to Avoid It* (San Francisco: Jossey-Bass, 2008); www.brandfinance.com.

28. For some accounting perspectives on intangible assets, see Baruch Lev, *Intangibles: Management, Measurement, and Reporting* (Washington, D.C.: Brookings Institution Press, 2001); Leslie A. Robinson and Richard Sansing, "The Effect of 'Invisible' Tax Preferences on Investment and Tax Preference Measures," *Journal of Accounting and Economics* 46 (2008). The helpful input of Richard Sansing on this topic is gratefully acknowledged.

29. Andrew Ross Sorkin and Andrew Martin, "Coca-Cola Agrees to Buy Vitaminwater," *New York Times*, 26 May 2007; "Coca-Cola 2007 Annual Report," www.thecoca-colacompany.com.

30. Bernard Condon, "Gaps in GAAP," *Forbes*, 25 January 1999, 76–80.

31. For a comprehensive and insightful summary of key issues, see Gabriela Salinas, *The International Brand Valuation Manual* (West Sussex, United Kingdom: John Wiley & Sons, 2009), as well as Gabriela Salinas and Tim Ambler, "A Taxonomy of Brand Valuation Practice: Methodologies and Purposes," *Journal of Brand Management* 17 (September 2009): 39–61. Another helpful guide is Jan Lindemann, *The Economy of Brands* (London: Palgrave Macmillan, 2010).

32. Quoted in "What's a Brand Worth? [editorial]," *Advertising Age*, 18 July 1994.

33. Lew Winters, "Brand Equity Measures: Some Recent Advances," *Marketing Research* (December 1991): 70–73; Gordon V. Smith, *Corporate Valuation: A Business and Professional Guide* (New York: John Wiley & Sons, 1988).

34. www.brandfinance.com.

35. The Science of Branding 10-1 is based on the research and writings of Prophet's Roger Sinclair, whose

considerable input is gratefully acknowledged. For more information, visit www.prophet.com.

36. Investors put capital into a company to ensure it can operate on a day-to-day basis. This money does not come free, as investors expect a return on their investment. While accountants are happy to accept the difference between revenue and expenses as the company's profit, economists believe that true profit is accounting profit less the expected return on the company's capital employed: the investors' funds.

37. Carol J. Simon and Mary W. Sullivan, "Measurement and Determinants of Brand Equity: A Financial Approach," *Marketing Science* 12, no. 1 (Winter 1993): 28–52.

38. Michael Birkin, "Assessing Brand Value," in *Brand Power*, ed. Paul Stobart (Washington Square, NY: New York University Press, 1994).

39. http://www.interbrand.com/en/best-global-brands/best-global-brands-methodology/Overview.aspx; Jan Lindemann, *The Economy of Brands* (London: Palgrave Macmillan, 2010).

40. For example, brand characteristics have been show to improve brand valuation accuracy. See Natalie Mizik and Robert Jacobson, "Valuing Branded Businesses," *Journal of Marketing* 73 (November 2009): 137–153.

41. Diane Summers, "IBM Plunges in Year to Foot of Brand Name Value League," *Financial Times*, 11 July 1994.

42. Peter Fader, course notes, Wharton Business School, University of Pennsylvania, 1998.

43. "On the Brandwagon," *The Economist*, 20 January 1990.

44. Koen Pauwels and Martin Lautman, "What Is Important? Identifying Metrics That Matter," *Journal of Advertising Research* 49 (September 2009), 339–359.

45. For an interesting empirical application, see Manoj K. Agarwal and Vithala Rao, "An Empirical Comparison of Consumer-Based Measures of Brand Equity," *Marketing Letters* 7, no. 3 (1996): 237–247.

46. Fader, course notes.

47. David A. Aaker and Robert Jacobson, "The Financial Information Content of Perceived Quality," *Journal of Marketing Research* 31 (May 1994): 191–201.

48. For a more recent illustration, see Robert A. Peterson and Jaeseok Jeong, "Exploring the Impact of Advertising and R&D Expenditures on Corporate Brand Value and Firm-Level Financial Performance," *Journal of the Academy of Marketing Science* 38, no. 6 (2010): 677–690.

49. David A. Aaker and Robert Jacobson, "The Value Relevance of Brand Attitude in High-Technology Markets," *Journal of Marketing Research* 38 (November 2001): 485–493.

50. M. E. Barth, M. Clement, G. Foster, and R. Kasznik, "Brand Values and Capital Market Valuation," *Review of Accounting Studies* 3 (1998): 41–68.

51. Thomas J. Madden, Frank Fehle, and Susan M. Fournier, "Brands Matter: An Empirical Demonstration of the Creation of Shareholder Value through Brands," *Journal of the Academy of Marketing Science* 34, no. 2 (2006): 224–235; Frank Fehle, Susan M. Fournier, Thomas J. Madden, and David G. Shrider, "Brand Value and Asset Pricing," *Quarterly Journal of Finance & Accounting* 47, no. 1 (2008): 59–82. See also, Lopo L. Rego, Matthew T. Billet, and Neil A. Morgan, "Consumer-Based Brand Equity and Firm Risk," *Journal of Marketing* 73 (November 2009): 47–60.

52. Clas Fornell, Sunil Mithas, Forrest V. Morgeson III, and M. S. Krishnan, "Customer Satisfaction and Stock Prices: High Returns, Low Risk," *Journal of Marketing* 70 (January 2006): 3–14.

53. Vicki Lane and Robert Jacobson, "Stock Market Reactions to Brand Extension Announcements: The Effects of Brand Attitude and Familiarity," *Journal of Marketing* 59 (January 1995): 63–77.

54. Dan Horsky and Patrick Swyngedouw, "Does It Pay to Change Your Company's Name? A Stock Market Perspective," *Marketing Science* (Fall 1987): 320–335.

55. Vithala R. Rao, Manoj K. Agrawal, and Denise Dahlhoff. "How Is Manifested Branding Strategy Related to the Intangible Value of a Corporation?" *Journal of Marketing* 68 (October 2004): 126–141; see also Liwu Hsu, Susan Fournier, and Shuba Srinivasan, "How Brand Portfolio Strategy Affects Firm Value," working paper, 2011, Boston University.

56. Neil A. Morgan and Lopo L. Rego, "Brand Portfolio Strategy and Firm Performance," *Journal of Marketing* 73 (January 2009): 59–74.

57. Natalie Mizik and Robert Jacobson, "Trading Off between Value Creation and Value Appropriation: The Financial Implications of Shifts in Strategic Emphasis," *Journal of Marketing* 67 (January 2003): 63–76; see also V. Kumar and Denish Shah, "Can Marketing Lift Stock Prices?," *MIT Sloan Management Review* (Summer 2011): 24–26.

58. This section based in part on a white paper by Roger Sinclair (www.prophet.com), "The Final Barrier: Marketing and Accounting Converge at the Corporate Finance Interface," as well as his other writings and personal correspondence.

59. http://www.vectorgrader.com/indicators/price-book.html.

60. In February 2006, FASB and IASB signed a memorandum of understanding setting out the relationship priorities that would bring about a harmonization of their respective standards. We refer to the ISAB in this appendix given that the standards involved are largely harmonized.

61. In June 2011, the IASB invited comments on topics that should be included in its three-year research agenda for the period 2012 to 2015. Among others, the Marketing Accountability Standards Board (MASB) submitted a letter arguing that IAS 38 should be on the agenda in order to iron out the variability between the two standards (IFRS 3 and IAS 38). IASB stated that it would reach and announce its decision between March and May 2012. If IAS 38 were to be added to the agenda, experts believe that in all likelihood, brands would be balance sheet items within two to three years regardless of whether they are internally generated or acquired.

Designing and Implementing Brand Architecture Strategies

11

Learning Objectives

After reading this chapter, you should be able to

1. Define the key components of brand architecture.
2. Outline the guidelines for developing a good brand portfolio.
3. Assemble a basic brand hierarchy for a brand.
4. Describe how a corporate brand is different from a product brand.
5. Explain the rationale behind cause marketing and green marketing.

Honda adopted an alphanumeric-based brand architecture for its Acura brand—including the Acura TL shown here—to better compete in the luxury automobile market.

Source: American Honda Motor Co., Inc.

Preview

Parts II, III, and IV of this book examined strategies for building and measuring brand equity. Part V takes a broader perspective and considers how to sustain, nurture, and grow brand equity under various situations and circumstances.

The successful launch of new products and services is of paramount importance to firms' long-term financial prosperity. Firms must maximize brand equity across all the different brands and products and services they offer. Their brand architecture strategy determines which brand elements they apply across all their new and existing products and services and is the means by which they help consumers understand those products and services and organize them in their minds.

Many firms employ complex brand architecture strategies. For example, brand names may consist of multiple brand-name elements (Toyota Camry XLE) and may be applied across a range of products (Toyota cars and trucks). What is the best way to characterize a firm's brand architecture strategy? What guidelines exist for choosing the right combinations of brand names and other brand elements to best manage brand equity across the entire range of a firm's products?

We begin by outlining a three-step process to develop an effective brand architecture strategy. We next describe two important strategic tools—brand portfolios and brand hierarchies—which, by defining various relationships among brands and products, help characterize and formulate brand architecture strategies. We then consider corporate branding strategies. After outlining corporate image dimensions, we examine three specific issues in managing a corporate brand: corporate social responsibility, corporate image campaigns, and corporate name changes. Brand Focus 11.0 devotes special attention to the topics of cause marketing and green marketing.

DEVELOPING A BRAND ARCHITECTURE STRATEGY

The firm's **brand architecture strategy** helps marketers determine which products and services to introduce, and which brand names, logos, symbols, and so forth to apply to new and existing products. As we describe below, it defines both the brand's breadth or boundaries and its depth or complexity. Which different products or services should share the same brand name? How many variations of that brand name should we employ? The role of brand architecture is twofold:

- *To clarify brand awareness:* Improve consumer understanding and communicate similarity and differences between individual products and services.
- *To improve brand image:* Maximize transfer of equity between the brand and individual products and services to improve trial and repeat purchase.

Developing a brand architecture strategy requires three key steps: (1) defining the potential of a brand in terms of its "market footprint," (2) identifying the product and service extensions that will allow the brand to achieve that potential, and (3) specifying the brand elements and positioning associated with the specific products and services for the brand. Although we introduce all three topics here, this chapter concentrates on insights and guidelines into the first and third. Chapter 12 exclusively focuses on the second topic and how to launch successful brand extensions. The Science of Branding 11-1 describes a useful tool to help depict brand architecture strategies for a firm.

Step 1: Defining Brand Potential

The first step in developing an architecture strategy is to define the brand potential by considering three important characteristics: (1) the brand vision, (2) the brand boundaries, and (3) the brand positioning.

Articulating the Brand Vision.   *Brand vision* is management's view of the brand's long-term potential. It is influenced by how well the firm is able to recognize the current and possible future brand equity. Many brands have latent brand equity that is never realized because the firm is unable or unwilling to consider all that the brand could and should become.

THE SCIENCE OF BRANDING 11-1

The Brand–Product Matrix

To characterize the brand architecture strategy of a firm, one useful tool is the **brand–product matrix**, a graphical representation of all the brands and products sold by the firm. The matrix (or grid) has the firm's brands as rows and the corresponding products as columns (see Figure 11-1).

- The rows of the matrix represent **brand–product relationships**. They capture the firm's brand-extension strategy in terms of the number and nature of products sold under its different brands. A **brand line** consists of all products—original as well as line and category extensions—sold under a particular brand. Thus, a brand line is one row of the matrix. We want to judge a potential new product extension for a brand on how effectively it leverages existing brand equity from the parent brand to the new product, as well as how effectively the extension, in turn, contributes to the equity of the parent brand.

- The columns of the matrix represent **product–brand relationships**. They capture the brand portfolio strategy in terms of the number and nature of brands to be marketed in each category. The **brand portfolio** is the set of all brands and brand lines that a particular firm offers for sale to buyers in a particular category. Thus, a brand portfolio is one column of the matrix. Marketers design and market different brands to appeal to different market segments.

We can characterize a firm's brand architecture strategy according to its *breadth* (in terms of brand–product relationships and brand extension strategy) and its *depth* (in terms of product–brand relationships and the brand portfolio or mix). For example, a brand architecture strategy is both deep and broad if the firm has a large number of brands, many of which have been extended into various product categories.

Several other terms are useful to understanding how to characterize the brand architecture strategies of a firm.

- A **product line** is a group of products within a product category that are closely related because they function in a similar manner, are sold to the same customer groups, are marketed through the same type of outlets, or fall within given price ranges. A product line may include different brands, or a single family brand or individual brand that has been line extended. Campbell's makes a variety of different soup products, varying in flavor, type, sizes, etc.

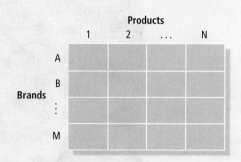

FIGURE 11-1 Brand–Product Matrix

- A **product mix** (or product assortment) is the set of all product lines and items that a particular seller makes available to buyers. Thus, product lines represent different sets of columns in the brand–product matrix that, in total, make up the product mix. In addition to soup, Campbell's sells tomato sauces, salsa, vegetable juices, and cookies and crackers.

- A **brand mix** (or brand assortment) is the set of all brand lines that a particular seller makes available to buyers. Campbell's brand lines include Prego, Pace, V8, and Pepperidge Farm.

A firm like Campbell's has to make strategic decisions about how many different product lines it should carry (the breadth of the product mix), as well as how many variants to offer in each product line (the depth of the product mix).

As another example, consider Nestlé—the biggest producer of food in the world, with over $100 billion in revenue. Understanding the brand–product matrix and developing the right brand architecture strategy for them is key. Over 1.2 billion people buy Nestlé's products daily, and 28 of its different brands are approaching or exceed $1 billion in sales. Its global approach of blending local and global brands and diversifying products paid off in the recent recession when it actually gained market share against its competitors.

Sources: Phillip Kotler and Kevin Lane Keller, *Marketing Management*, 14th ed. (Upper Saddle River, NJ: Prentice Hall, 2012); Beth Kowitt, "Nestlé," *Fortune*, 5 July 2010.

On the other hand, many brands have transcended their initial market boundaries to become much more. Waste Management is in the process of transforming itself from a "trash company" to a "one-stop, green, environmental services shop" that does a lot more than just collect and dispose of garbage. Its new tag line, "Think Green," signals the direction it is taking to find ways to extract value from the waste stream through materials-recovery facilities (MRFs) that enable "single-stream recycling."[1] Google is clearly in the process of being much more than a search engine as it offers more and more services. Another brand that has already transcended its traditional boundaries is Crayola.

Waste Management is transforming itself from a "trash company" to a "one-stop, green, environmental services shop."

Source: Waste Management

CRAYOLA

Crayola, known for its crayons, first sought to expand its brand meaning by making some fairly direct brand extensions into other drawing and coloring implements, such as markers, pencils, paints, pens, brushes, and chalk. The company further expanded beyond coloring and drawing into arts and crafts, with extensions such as Crayola Chalk, Crayola Clay, Crayola Dough, Crayola Glitter Glue, and Crayola Scissors. These extensions established a new brand meaning for Crayola as "colorful arts and crafts for kids." Crayola says its brand essence is to find the "what if" in each child:

> "We believe in unleashing, nurturing and celebrating the colorful originality in every child. We give kids an invitation that ignites, colors that inspire, and tools that transform original thoughts into visible form. We give colorful wings to the invisible things that grow in the hearts of children. Because we believe that creatively alive kids grow into inspired adults."

Subsequent category extensions allowed kids to use their imagination to create colorful jewelry, glow-in-the-dark animation, and comic books.[2]

Without a clear understanding of its current equity, however, it is difficult to understand what the brand could be built on. A good brand vision has a foot in both the present and the future. Brand vision obviously needs to be aspirational, so the brand has room to grow and improve in the future, yet it cannot be unobtainable. The trick is to strike the right balance between what the brand is and what it could become, and to identify the right steps to get it there.

Fundamentally, brand vision relates to the "higher-order purpose" of the brand, based on keen understanding of consumer aspirations and brand truths. It transcends the brand's physical product category descriptions and boundaries. P&G's legendary former CMO Jim Stengel maintains that successful brands have clear "ideals"—such as "eliciting joy, enabling connection, inspiring exploration, evoking pride or impacting society"—and a strong purpose of building customer loyalty and driving revenue growth.[3] The Science of Branding 11-2 describes one perspective on how firms can maximize a brand's long-term value according to their vision of its potential.

Defining the Brand Boundaries. Some of the world's strongest brands, such as GE, Virgin, and Apple, have been stretched across multiple categories. Defining brand boundaries thus means—based on the brand vision and positioning—identifying the products or services the brand should offer, the benefits it should supply, and the needs it should satisfy.

Although many product categories may seem to be good candidates for a brand extension, as we will develop in greater detail in Chapter 12, marketers would be wise to heed the "Spandex Rule" espoused by Scott Bedbury, former VP-Advertising for Nike and VP-Marketing for Starbucks: "Just because you can . . . doesn't mean you should!" Marketers must evaluate extending their brand carefully and launch new products selectively.

A "broad" brand is one with an abstract positioning that is able to support a higher-order promise relevant in multiple product settings. It often has a transferable point-of-difference, thanks to a widely relevant benefit supported by multiple reasons-to-believe or supporting attributes. For example, Delta Faucet Company has taken its core brand associations of "stylish" and "innovative" and successfully expanded the brand from faucets to a variety of kitchen and bathroom products and accessories.

Nevertheless, all brands have boundaries. It would be very difficult for Delta to introduce a car, tennis racquet, or lawnmower. Japanese carmakers Honda, Nissan, and Toyota chose to introduce their luxury brands in North America under new brand names, Acura, Infiniti, and Lexus, respectively. Even considering its own growth, Nike chose to purchase Cole Haan to sell into the dressier, more formal shoe market. Some brands have struggled to stretch into new markets, as did VW Phaeton.

VW PHAETON

Auto industry insiders were surprised when VW chose to introduce the $85,000 VW Phaeton luxury sedan in 2002. Named after the son of the Greek god Helios, the vehicle racked up more than $1.3 billion in development costs. Although VW also owned Audi, management wanted to make the VW brand more upscale to better compete with BMW and Mercedes. But after Phaeton failed to meet sales goals in the United States—selling only 2,253 cars from 2004 to 2006—the brand was pulled from the market in 2006. After continuing to experience annual losses in the highly competitive U.S. market, VW announced in 2011 that it would relaunch a newly redesigned Phaeton at a later date, with a higher-quality interior, renewed front and rear exterior, and new engine choices. VW sees a strong presence in the U.S. luxury car segment as vital to its goals of tripling its share in the United States and surpassing Toyota worldwide in sales and profitability.[4]

VW has struggled to successfully extend its brand upward in the U.S. luxury car market with its Phaeton sub-brand.

Source: Laurent Gillieron/EPA/Newscom

To improve market coverage, companies target different segments with multiple brands in a portfolio. They have to be careful to not over-brand, however, or attempt to support too many brands. The trend among many top marketing companies in recent years has been to focus on fewer, stronger brands. Each should be clearly differentiated and appeal to a sizable enough market segment to justify its marketing and production costs.

THE SCIENCE OF BRANDING 11-2

Capitalizing on Brand Potential

All you can ask of a brand is that it reaches its potential. The brand's long-term brand value depends on how well a firm understands and recognizes its potential and capitalizes on it in the marketplace. Let's consider all the different aspects of how long-term brand value gets created. See Figure 11-2 for a schematic summary.

Processes Affecting Long-Term Brand Value
Long-term brand value depends on two basic processes: brand vision (the ability to see the brand's inherent potential) and brand actualization (the ability to actually capitalize on the brand's potential to derive maximum revenue).

Brand Vision.   Brand vision requires defining the potential of a brand. **Inherent brand potential** is the value we could extract from a brand via optimally designed marketing strategies, programs, and activities. In other words, it reflects what brand value *could* become if, for example, we introduce different products, enter new markets, and appeal to different customers in the future. There are many different ways to expand a brand across products and markets.

Brand potential is in effect the "option value" of a brand if we recognize and capitalize on its assets. For publicly traded companies, it manifests itself in the premium a stock commands over the value explainable from cash flows in its current businesses. Viewed this way, acquiring a brand makes sense and will bring a positive return only if the acquiring firm has a better vision or ability to execute than the prior owners.

Brand Actualization.   While brand vision means understanding the brand's inherent potential, **brand actualization** means achieving that potential. Not surprisingly, due to differences in firm resources and management skill, firms vary in their ability to formulate a vision of what brand potential is and then capitalize on it to activate the brand's inherent brand potential.

Components of Long-Term Brand Value
Brand actualization (or potential actualization) depends on how successfully a firm can translate brand potential into the two key components of long-term brand value: brand persistence and brand growth.

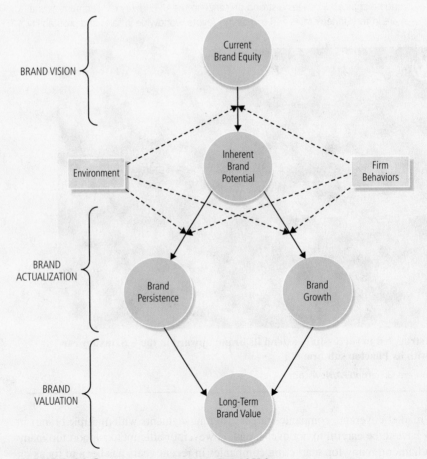

FIGURE 11-2 Achieving Long-Term Brand Value

Brand Persistence. *Brand persistence* reflects the extent to which the current customer franchise and their spending levels can be sustained over time. Without continued investments, brands can decline in value for myriad reasons. Even traditionally well-funded, high-equity brands such as Kodak, Levi-Strauss, and Borders can be vulnerable to a change in fortunes or even bankruptcy.

The endurance of a brand's position and equity depends primarily on three factors:

1. The strength, favorableness, and uniqueness of key brand associations;

2. The likelihood these characteristics will continue into the future; and

3. The firm's skill in developing and implementing marketing programs and activities that help preserve them over time.

Some brand associations are more enduring than others. For example, quality can be a relatively timeless attribute, while many imagery associations like trendiness and youthfulness often fade badly over time. Perhaps the biggest challenge to brand persistence, however, is the ability of the brand to sustain differentiation. Competitive responses, marketplace changes, and other external factors all conspire to make it difficult for a brand to be as unique as it once was.

Brand Growth. The requirements to grow thus implicitly include the ability of a brand's sales to persist and resist decay. *Brand growth* reflects the extent to which current customers actually increase their spending and new customers are attracted to the brand, with either existing or new products. Chapters 12 and 14 discuss these issues in detail.

Factors Influencing Brand Persistence and Growth

Finally, brand persistence and growth—and thus long-term brand value—depend on the risks evident in the marketing environment, the brand's vulnerability to those risks, and what the firm does to handle them.

Risks in the Marketing Environment. A number of factors in the environment work for or against the creation and realization of inherent brand potential. Broadly, the marketing environment consists of seven components: competitive, demographic, economic, physical, technological, political-legal, and social-cultural. Changes or shifts in the nature of competition; age or cultural make-up of a market; the income and tax base; the supply of natural resources; government policies and regulations; and social trends, to name just a few, can all profoundly change the fortunes of a brand and test the skills of marketers.

Long-term brand value is more predictable. It rises when firms are less vulnerable to competition and other environmental changes and are therefore better able to capitalize on their inherent brand potential. Greater consumer loyalty and high switching costs improve the odds of retention in the face of difficulties or challenges for a brand. Barriers to entry can also provide insurance against competitive actions.

Brand persistence and growth also depend on how effectively competitors operate. A key question is how equipped a company is to anticipate, withstand, and capitalize on changes and shifts that occur in the marketplace. Firms such as IBM, Microsoft, and Corning have evolved considerably through the years, building on the brand value they have accumulated, although not always smoothly or easily.

Firm Behaviors. Brand visioning and potential actualization will depend on the motivation, ability, and opportunity of a firm to recognize and maximize brand potential in the face of possible environmental changes. First, the firm must be motivated and committed to take advantage of the brand and its potential. Many brands, even after acquisition, can become neglected or forgotten, especially if the firm has an expansive set of brands.

The ability to maximize brand potential will depend in large part on the skills of the firm to recognize and define the brand's potential to begin with. If that assessment is done properly, then the question is whether the firm has—or has access to—the resources, skills, and other assets needed to cash in on the identified potential.

Finally, a firm must have the opportunity to formulate and activate the brand potential. Diverting resources, skills, and other assets to other areas makes it difficult or even impossible to achieve a brand's potential. Many best-laid plans are abandoned given the twists and turns in marketplace performance and corporate decision-making, and resulting changes in budget allocation.

A Key Implication

We've seen that achieving the brand's long-term value is a function of recognizing and realizing its potential through brand vision and brand actualization activities. One important implication is that a brand has different growth prospects depending on which firm owns it. Given the difficulty of cutting costs, the only real justification for M&A activity is a bet that the acquiring company is smarter, more knowledgeable, more creative—or has access to resources at a lower cost—than the current brand owners. Given that current owners of a brand are generally more likely to be knowledgeable about the brand than those who intend to acquire it, however, many acquirers may overestimate growth potential and overpay for the brand.

Sources: Kevin Lane Keller and Don Lehmann, "Assessing Brand Potential," in special issue, "Brand Value and Valuation," of *Journal of Brand Management* 17, eds. Randall Raggio and Robert P. Leone (September 2009): 6–17; Kevin Lane Keller and David A. Aaker, "The Effects of Sequential Introduction of Brand Extensions," *Journal of Marketing Research* 29 (February 1992): 35–50; Randle Raggio and Robert P. Leone, "The Theoretical Separation of Brand Equity and Brand Value: Managerial Implications for Strategic Planning," *Journal of Brand Management* 14 (May 2007): 380–395; S. Cem Bahadir, Sundar G. Bharadwaj, and Rajendra K. Srivastava, "Financial Value of Brands in Mergers and Acquisitions: Is Value in the Eye of the Beholder?," *Journal of Marketing* 72 (November 2008): 49–64; Yana Damoiseau, William C. Black, and Randle D. Raggio, "Brand Creation vs. Acquisition in Portfolio Expansion Strategy," *Journal of Product & Brand Management* 20, no. 4 (2011): 268–281.

Crafting the Brand Positioning.   Brand positioning puts some specificity into a brand vision. Chapter 2 reviewed brand positioning considerations in detail; the four key ingredients are: (1) competitive frame of reference, (2) points-of-difference, (3) points-of-parity, and (4) brand mantra. The brand mantra in particular can be very useful in establishing product boundaries or brand "guardrails." It should offer rational and emotional benefits and be sufficiently robust to permit growth, relevant enough to drive consumer and retailer interest, and differentiated enough to sustain longevity.

Step 2: Identifying Brand Extension Opportunities

Determining the brand vision, boundaries, and positioning in Step 1 helps define the brand potential and provides a clear sense of direction for the brand. Step 2 is to identify new products and services to achieve that potential through a well-designed and implemented brand extension strategy.

A brand extension is a new product introduced under an existing brand name. We differentiate between *line extensions*, new product introductions within existing categories (Tide Total Care laundry detergent), and *category extensions*, new product introductions outside existing categories (Tide Dry Cleaners retail outlets).

It is important to carefully plan the optimal sequence of brand extensions to achieve brand potential. The key is to understand equity implications of each extension in terms of points-of-parity and points-of-difference. By adhering to the brand promise and growing the brand carefully through "little steps," marketers can ensure that brands cover a lot of ground.

For example, through a well-planned and well-executed series of new product introductions in the form of category extensions over a 25-year period, Nike evolved from a company selling running, tennis, and basketball shoes to mostly males between the ages of 12 and 29 in North America in the mid-1980s, to a company now selling athletic shoes, clothing, and equipment across a range of sports to men and women of all ages in virtually all countries.

Launching a brand extension is harder than it might seem. Given that the vast majority of new products are extensions and the vast majority of new products fail, the clear implication is that too many brand extensions fail. An increasingly competitive marketplace will be even more unforgiving to poorly positioned and marketed extensions in the years to come. To increase the likelihood of success, marketers must be rigorous and disciplined in their analysis and development of brand extensions. Chapter 12 provides detailed guidelines for successful brand extension strategies.

Step 3: Branding New Products and Services

The final step in developing the brand architecture is to decide on the specific brand elements to use for any particular new product or service associated with the brand. New products and services must be branded in a way to maximize the brand's overall clarity and understanding to consumers and customers. What names, looks, and other branding elements are to be applied to the new and existing products for any one brand?

One way we can distinguish brand architecture strategies is by looking at whether a firm is employing an umbrella corporate or family brand for all its products, known as a "branded house," or a collection of individual brands all with different names, known as a "house of brands."

- Firms largely employing a branded house strategy include many business-to-business industrial firms, such as Siemens, Oracle, and Goldman Sachs.
- Firms largely employing a house of brands strategy include consumer product companies, such as Procter & Gamble, Unilever, and ConAgra.

The reality is that most firms adopt a strategy somewhere between these two end points, often employing various types of sub-brands. *Sub-brands* are an extremely popular form of brand extension in which the new product carries both the parent brand name and a new name (Apple iPad, Ford Fusion, and American Express Blue card).

A good sub-branding strategy can tap associations and attitudes about the company or family brand as a whole, while also allowing for the creation of new brand beliefs to position the extension in the new category. For example, Hershey's Kisses taps into the quality, heritage, and familiarity of the Hershey's brand but at the same time has a much more playful and fun

An ideal sub-brand, Hershey's Kisses adds a fun, playful dimension to Hershey's well-regarded brand image.

Source: ©The Hershey Company

brand image. An iconic brand, Hershey's Kisses ranked number one in the Harris Interactive EquiTrend brand equity study for 2010.[5]

Sub-brands play an important brand architecture role by signaling to consumers to expect similarities *and* differences in the new product. To realize these benefits, however, sub-branding typically requires significant investments and disciplined and consistent marketing to establish the proper brand meanings with consumers. In the absence of such financial commitments, marketers may be well advised to adopt the simplest brand hierarchy possible, such as using a branded house–type approach with the company or a family brand name with product descriptors. Marketers should employ sub-branding only when there is a distinctive, complementary benefit; otherwise, they should just use a product descriptor to designate the new product or service.

Summary

The three steps we outlined provide a careful and well-grounded approach to developing a brand architecture strategy. To successfully execute this process, marketers should use brand portfolio analysis for Step 1 and determining brand potential, and brand hierarchy analysis for Steps 2 and 3 and branding particular products and services. We describe both tools next.

BRAND PORTFOLIOS

A *brand portfolio* includes all brands sold by a company in a product category. We judge a brand portfolio by its ability to maximize brand equity: Any one brand in the portfolio should not harm or decrease the equity of the others. Ideally, each brand maximizes equity in combination with all other brands in the portfolio.

Why might a firm have multiple brands in the same product category? The primary reason is market coverage. Although multiple branding was originally pioneered by General Motors, Procter & Gamble is widely recognized as popularizing the practice. P&G became a proponent of multiple brands after introducing its Cheer detergent brand as an alternative to its already successful Tide detergent, resulting in higher combined product category sales.

Firms introduce multiple brands because no one brand is viewed equally favorably by all the different distinct market segments the firm would like to target. Multiple brands allow a firm to pursue different price segments, different channels of distribution, different geographic boundaries, and so forth.[6]

In designing the optimal brand portfolio, marketers must first define the relevant customer segments. How much overlap exists across segments, and how well can products be cross-sold?[7] Branding Brief 11-1 describes how Marriott has introduced different brands and sub-brands to attack different markets.

Other reasons for introducing multiple brands in a category include the following:[8]

- To increase shelf presence and retailer dependence in the store
- To attract consumers seeking variety who may otherwise switch to another brand
- To increase internal competition within the firm
- To yield economies of scale in advertising, sales, merchandising, and physical distribution

Marketers generally need to trade off market coverage and these other considerations with costs and profitability. A portfolio is too big if profits can be increased by dropping brands; it is not big enough if profits can be increased by adding brands. Brand lines with poorly differentiated brands are likely to be characterized by much cannibalization and require appropriate pruning.[9]

The basic principle in designing a brand portfolio is to *maximize market coverage* so that no potential customers are being ignored, but *minimize brand overlap* so that brands aren't competing among themselves to gain the same customer's approval. Each brand should have a distinct target market and positioning.[10]

For example, over the last 10 years or so, Procter & Gamble has sought to maximize market coverage and minimize brand overlap by pursuing organic growth from existing core brands rather than introducing a lot of new brands. The company has focused its innovation efforts on its core "billion dollar" brands—those with more than $1 billion in revenue. Numerous successful market-leading brand extensions followed, such as Crest whitening products, Pampers' training diapers, and Mr. Clean Magic Eraser products.[11]

Besides these considerations, brands can play a number of specific roles as part of a brand portfolio. Figure 11-3 summarizes some of them, which we review next.

Flankers. Certain brands act as protective flanker or "fighter" brands.[12] The purpose of flanker brands typically is to create stronger points-of-parity with competitors' brands so that more important (and more profitable) flagship brands can retain their desired positioning. In particular, as we noted in Chapter 5, many firms are introducing discount brands as flankers, to better compete with store brands and private labels and to protect their higher-priced brand companions. In Australia, Qantas launched Jetstar airlines as a discount fighter brand to compete with the recently introduced low-priced Virgin Blue airlines—which was meeting with much success—and to protect its flagship premium Qantas brand.[13]

---

1. To attract a particular market segment not currently being covered by other brands of the firm
2. To serve as a flanker and protect flagship brands
3. To serve as a cash cow and be milked for profits
4. To serve as a low-end entry-level product to attract new customers to the brand franchise
5. To serve as a high-end prestige product to add prestige and credibility to the entire brand portfolio
6. To increase shelf presence and retailer dependence in the store
7. To attract consumers seeking variety who may otherwise have switched to another brand
8. To increase internal competition within the firm
9. To yield economies of scale in advertising, sales, merchandising, and physical distribution

FIGURE 11-3

Possible Special Roles of Brands in the Brand Portfolio

In other cases, firms have repositioned existing brands in their portfolio to play that role. The one-time "champagne of bottled beer," Miller High Life, was relegated to a discount brand in the 1990s to protect premium-priced Miller Genuine Draft and Miller Lite. Similarly, P&G repositioned its one-time top-tier Luvs diaper brand to serve as a price fighter against private labels and store brands to protect the premium Pampers brand.

In designing fighter brands, marketers walk a fine line. Fighters must not be so attractive that they take sales away from their higher-priced comparison brands or referents. At the same time, if they are connected to other brands in the portfolio in any way (say, through a common branding strategy), they must not be designed so cheaply that they reflect poorly on these other brands.

Cash Cows.   Some brands may be kept around despite dwindling sales because they still manage to hold on to a sufficient number of customers and maintain their profitability with virtually no marketing support. Marketers can effectively milk these "cash cows" by capitalizing on their reservoir of existing brand equity. For example, while technological advances have moved much of the market to its newer Fusion brand of razors, Gillette still sells its older Trac II, Atra, Sensor, and Mach3 brands. Because withdrawing these may not necessarily switch customers to another Gillette brand, the company may profit more by keeping than discarding them.

Low-End, Entry-Level or High-End, Prestige Brands.   Many brands introduce line extensions or brand variants in a certain product category that vary in price and quality. These subbrands leverage associations from other brands while distinguishing themselves on price and quality. In this case, the end points of the brand line often play a specialized role.

The role of a relatively low-priced brand in the brand portfolio often may be to attract customers to the brand franchise. Retailers like to feature these traffic builders because they often are able to "trade up" customers to a higher-priced brand. For example, Verizon wireless plans allow customers to upgrade their old, sometimes cheaper cell phones to newer versions that are more expensive but still cheaper than retail.

Many of Gillette's older brands like Trac II, Atra, Sensor, and Mach III are cash cows in that they continue to sell reasonably well without any significant marketing support.

Source: Keri Miksza

BRANDING BRIEF 11-1

Expanding the Marriott Brand

Marriott International grew to an international hospitality giant from humble roots as a single root beer stand started by John and Alice Marriott in Washington, D.C., during the 1920s. The Marriotts added hot food to their root beer stand and renamed their business the Hot Shoppe, which they incorporated in 1929 when they began building a regional chain of restaurants. As the number of Hot Shoppes in the Southeast grew, Marriott expanded into in-flight catering by serving food on Eastern, American, and Capital Airlines, beginning in 1937. In 1939, Hot Shoppes began its food service management business when it opened a cafeteria in the U.S. Treasury building. The company expanded into another hospitality sector in 1957, when Hot Shoppes opened its first hotel in Arlington, Virginia. Hot Shoppes, which was renamed Marriott Corporation in 1967, grew nationally and internationally by making strategic acquisitions and entering new service categories; by 1977, sales topped $1 billion.

In pursuit of more growth, Marriott continued to diversify its business. Its 1982 acquisition of Host International made it the top U.S. operator of airport food and beverage facilities. Over the following three years, Marriott added 1,000 food service accounts by purchasing three food service companies: Gladieux, Service Systems, and Saga Corporation. Determining that its high penetration in the traditional hotel market did not offer many opportunities for growth, the company initiated a segmented marketing strategy for its hotels by introducing the moderately priced Courtyard by Marriott brand in 1983. Moderately priced hotels constituted the largest segment of the U.S. lodging industry, filled with established competitors such as Holiday Inn, Ramada, and Quality Inn. Marriott's research registered the greatest consumer dissatisfaction in this segment, so Courtyard hotels were designed to offer travelers greater convenience and amenities, such as balconies and patios, large desks and sofas, and pools and spas.

Early success with Courtyard prompted Marriott to expand further. In 1984, the company entered the vacation timesharing business by acquiring American Resorts Group. The following year, it purchased Howard Johnson Company, selling the hotels and retaining the restaurants and rest stops. The first JW Marriott luxury hotel was opened on Pennsylvania Avenue in Washington, D.C. as a tribute to the founder.

In 1987, Marriott added three new market segments: Marriott Suites, full-service suite accommodations; Residence Inn, extended-stay rooms for business travelers; and Fairfield Inn, an economy hotel brand. A company spokesman explained this rapid expansion: "There is a lot of segmentation that's going on in the hotel business. Travelers are sophisticated and have many wants and needs. In addition to that, we saw there would be a finite … ability to grow the traditional business."

In 1993, Marriott Corporation split in two, forming Host Marriott to own the hotel properties, and Marriott Interna-

Brand Category	Brands
Iconic Luxury	Bvlgari The Ritz-Carlton The Ritz-Carlton Destination Club
Luxury	JW Marriott
Lifestyle | Collections	Edition Autograph Collection Renaissance Hotels AC Hotels
Signature	Marriott Hotels and Resorts
Modern Essentials	Courtyard SpringHill Suites Fairfield Inn and Suites
Extended Stay	Residence Inn TownePlace Suites ExecuStay Marriott Executive Apartments
Vacation Clubs	Marriott Vacation Club Grand Residences

FIGURE 11-4 Marriott International Portfolio Architecture

Source: Marriott International, Inc. Used with permission.

tional to manage them and franchise its brands. Marriott International bought a minority stake in the Ritz-Carlton luxury hotel group in 1995 and purchased the remaining share in 1998. It expanded again in 1997 by acquiring the Renaissance Hotel Group and introducing TownePlace Suites, Fairfield Suites, and Marriott Executive Residences. Marriott added a new hotel brand in 1998 with the introduction of SpringHill Suites, which provide moderately priced suites that are 25 percent larger than standard hotel rooms. The following year, the company acquired corporate housing specialist ExecuStay Corporation and formed ExecuStay by Marriott, now a franchise business.

A new century saw new growth. The launch in 2007 of stylish EDITION hotels put Marriott in the luxury boutique market. Each property was distinctive and designed by famed hotel developer Ian Schrager. The Autograph Collection was also introduced in 2011, a diverse collection of high-personality, upper-upscale independent hotels. AC Hotels by Marriott was another lifestyle hotel entry in 2011, an upper-moderate tier brand targeting design-conscious younger travelers in Europe with stylish, urban properties.

The last Hot Shoppe restaurant, located in a shopping mall in Washington, D.C., closed on December 2, 1999. This closing was fitting, since the tiny restaurant in no way resembled the multinational hospitality leader it had

Like many major hotel companies, Marriott carefully manages its brand portfolio, including its Courtyard by Marriott, Marriott, and Ritz-Carlton brands.

Source: Andre Jenny Stock Connection Worldwide/Newscom; Andre Jenny Stock Connection Worldwide/Newscom; Lana Sundman/Alamy

spawned. Today, Marriott International is one of the leading hospitality companies in the world, with 3,700 properties in 72 countries and territories worldwide that brought in almost $12 billion in global revenues in 2010. In 2012, after extensive consumer research, Marriott International developed a formal brand architecture that it shared with prospective guests on its Web sites to aid them in their lodging decisions (see Figure 11-4).

Sources: www.marriott.com; Kim Clark, "Lawyers Clash on Timing of Marriott's Plan to Split," *Baltimore Sun*, 27 September 1994; Neil Henderson, "Marriott Gambles on Low-Cost, Classy Suburban Motels," *Washington Post*, 18 June 1994; Neil Henderson, "Marriott Bares Courtyard Plans," *Washington Post*, 12 June 1984; Elizabeth Tucker, "Marriott's Recipe for Corporate Growth," *Washington Post*, 1 June 1987; Paul Farhi, "Marriott to Sell 800 Restaurants," *Washington Post*, 19 December 1989; Stephane Fitch, "Soft Pillows and Sharp Elbows," *Forbes*, 10 May 2004, 66.

BMW introduced certain models into its 3-series automobiles in part as a means of bringing new customers into its brand franchise, with the hope of moving them up to higher-priced models when they traded their cars in. As the 3-series gradually moved up-market, BMW introduced the 1-series in 2004, which was built on the same production line as the 3-series and priced between the 3-series and the MINI.

On the other hand, the role of a relatively high-priced brand in the brand family is often to add prestige and credibility to the entire portfolio. For example, one analyst argued that the real value to Chevrolet of its Corvette high-performance sports car was "its ability to lure curious customers into showrooms and at the same time help improve the image of other Chevrolet cars. It does not mean a hell of a lot for GM profitability, but there is no question that it is a traffic builder."[14] Corvette's technological image and prestige cast a halo over the entire Chevrolet line.

Summary. Multiple brands can expand coverage, provide protection, extend an image, or fulfill a variety of other roles for the firm. In all brand portfolio decisions, the basic criteria are simple, even though their application can be quite complicated: to minimize overlap and get the most from the portfolio, each brand-name product must have (1) a well-defined role to fulfill for the firm and, thus, (2) a well-defined positioning indicating the benefits or promises it offers consumers. As Chapter 12 reveals, many firms find that due to product proliferation through the years, they now can cut the number of brands and product variants they offer and still profitably satisfy consumers.

BRAND HIERARCHIES

A *brand hierarchy* is a useful means of graphically portraying a firm's branding strategy by displaying the number and nature of common and distinctive brand elements across the firm's products, revealing their explicit ordering. It's based on the realization that we can brand a product in different ways depending on how many new and existing brand elements we use and how we combine them for any one product.

For example, a Dell Inspiron 17R notebook computer consists of three different brand name elements, "Dell," "Inspiron," and "17R." Some of these may be shared by many different products; others are limited. Dell uses its corporate name to brand many of its products, but Inspiron designates a certain type of computer (portable), and 17R identifies a particular model of Inspiron (designed to maximize gaming performance and entertainment and including a 17-inch screen).

We can construct a hierarchy to represent how (if at all) products are nested with other products because of their common brand elements. Figure 11-5 displays a simple characterization of ESPN's brand hierarchy. Note that ESPN is owned by Walt Disney Company and functions as a distinct family brand in that company's brand portfolio. As the figure shows, a brand hierarchy can include multiple levels.

There are different ways to define brand elements and levels of the hierarchy. Perhaps the simplest representation from top to bottom might be:

1. Corporate or company brand (General Motors)
2. Family brand (Buick)
3. Individual brand (Regal)
4. Modifier (designating item or model) (GS)
5. Product description (midsize luxury sport sedan automobile)

Levels of a Brand Hierarchy

Different levels of the hierarchy have different issues, as we review in turn.

Corporate or Company Brand Level. The highest level of the hierarchy technically always consists of one brand—the *corporate or company brand*. For simplicity, we refer to corporate and company brands interchangeably, recognizing that consumers may not necessarily draw a distinction between the two or know that corporations may subsume multiple companies.

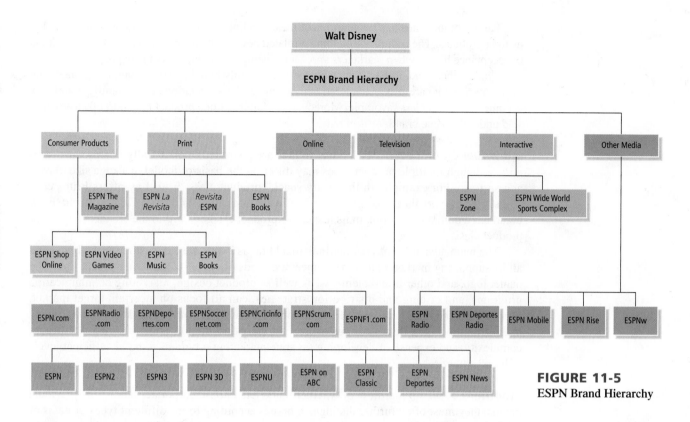

FIGURE 11-5
ESPN Brand Hierarchy

For legal reasons, the company or corporate brand is almost always present somewhere on the product or package, although the name of a company subsidiary may appear instead of the corporate name. For example, Fortune Brands owns many different companies, such as Jim Beam whiskey, Courvoisier cognac, Master Lock locks, and Moen faucets, but it does not use its corporate name on any of its lines of business.

For some firms like General Electric and Hewlett-Packard, the corporate brand is virtually the only brand. Conglomerate Siemens's varied electrical engineering and electronics business units are branded with descriptive modifiers, such as Siemens Transportation Systems. In other cases, the company name is virtually invisible and, although technically part of the hierarchy, receives virtually no attention in the marketing program. Black & Decker does not use its name on its high-end DeWalt professional power tools.

As we detail below, we can think of a ***corporate image*** as the consumer associations to the company or corporation making the product or providing the service. Corporate image is particularly relevant when the corporate or company brand plays a prominent role in the branding strategy.

Family Brand Level.   At the next-lower level, a ***family brand***, also called a ***range brand*** or ***umbrella brand***, is used in more than one product category but is not necessarily the name of the company or corporation. For example, ConAgra's Healthy Choice family brand appears on a wide spectrum of food products, including packaged meats, soups, pasta sauces, breads, popcorn, and ice cream. Some other notable family brands for companies that generate more than $1 billion in sales include Purina and Kit Kat (Nestlé); Mountain Dew, Doritos, and Quaker Foods (PepsiCo); and Oreo, Cadbury, and Maxwell House (Kraft).

Because a family brand may be distinct from the corporate or company brand, company-level associations may be less salient. Most firms typically support only a handful of family brands. If the corporate brand is applied to a range of products, then it functions as a family brand too, and the two levels collapse to one for those products.

Marketers may apply family brands instead of corporate brands for several reasons. As products become more dissimilar, it may be harder for the corporate brand to retain any product meaning or to effectively link the disparate products. Distinct family brands, on the other hand, can evoke a specific set of associations across a group of related products.[15]

Family brands thus can be an efficient means to link common associations to multiple but distinct products. The cost of introducing a related new product can be lower and the likelihood of acceptance higher when marketers apply an existing family brand to a new product.

On the other hand, if the products linked to the family brand and their supporting marketing programs are not carefully considered and designed, the associations to the family brand may become weaker and less favorable. Moreover, the failure of one product may hurt other products sold under the same brand.

Individual Brand Level.   Individual brands are restricted to essentially one product category, although multiple product types may differ on the basis of model, package size, flavor, and so forth. For example, in the "salty snack" product class, Frito-Lay offers Fritos corn chips, Doritos tortilla chips, Lays and Ruffles potato chips, and Rold Gold pretzels. Each brand has a dominant position in its respective product category within the broader salty snack product class.

The main advantage of creating individual brands is that we can customize the brand and all its supporting marketing activity to meet the needs of a specific customer group. Thus, the name, logo, and other brand elements, as well as product design, marketing communication programs, and pricing and distribution strategies, can all focus on a certain target market. Moreover, if the brand runs into difficulty or fails, the risk to other brands and the company itself is minimal. The disadvantages of creating individual brands, however, are the difficulty, complexity, and expense of developing separate marketing programs to build sufficient levels of brand equity.

Modifier Level.   Regardless of whether marketers choose corporate, family, or individual brands, they must often further distinguish brands according to the different types of items or models. A *modifier* is a means to designate a specific item or model type or a particular version or configuration of the product. Land O'Lakes offers "whipped," "unsalted," and "regular" versions of its butter. Yoplait yogurt comes as "light," "custard style," and "original" flavors.

Adding a modifier often can signal refinements or differences between brands related to factors such as quality levels (Johnnie Walker Red Label, Black Label, and Gold Label Scotch whiskey), attributes (Wrigley's Spearmint, Doublemint, Juicy Fruit, and Winterfresh flavors of chewing gum), function (Dockers Relaxed Fit, Classic Fit, Straight Fit, Slim Fit, and Extra Slim Fit pants), and so forth.[16] Thus, one function of modifiers is to show how one brand variation relates to others in the same brand family.

Modifiers help make products more understandable and relevant to consumers or even to the trade. They can even become strong trademarks if they are able to develop a unique association with the parent brand—only Uncle Ben has "Converted Rice," and only Orville Redenbacher sells "Gourmet Popping Corn."[17]

Product Descriptor.   Although not considered a brand element per se, the product descriptor for the branded product may be an important ingredient of branding strategy. The product descriptor helps consumers understand what the product is and does and also helps define the relevant competition in consumers' minds.

In some cases, it may be hard to describe succinctly what the product is, a new product with unusual functions or even an existing product that has dramatically changed. Public libraries are no longer about checking out books or taking a preschooler to story time. A full-service modern public library serves as an educational, cultural, social, and recreational community center.

In the case of a truly new product, introducing it with a familiar product name may facilitate basic familiarity and comprehension, but perhaps at the expense of a richer understanding of how the new product is different from closely related products that already exist.

Designing a Brand Hierarchy

Given the different possible levels of a brand hierarchy, a firm has a number of branding options available, depending on whether and how it employs each level. Designing the right brand hierarchy is crucial. Branding Brief 11-2 describes the firestorm Netflix encountered when it attempted to make a significant change to its brand hierarchy.

BRANDING BRIEF 11-2

Netflix Branding Stumbles

A media darling for much of his company's meteoric rise, Reed Hastings, founder and CEO of Netflix, seemingly could do no wrong. Founded in 1997, Netflix pioneered the DVD-by-mail category, successfully challenging traditional video stores and driving industry leader Blockbuster into bankruptcy in the process. Netflix's bold formula for success included flawless service delivery combined with a state-of-the-art movie recommendation engine for users. The company even famously sponsored a contest with a $1 million prize to anyone who could make its recommendation algorithm work better.

Netflix's business philosophy was captured by two credos found on its corporate Web site: "Avoid 'barnacles' that can slow down a fast-growing business" and "Make tough decisions without agonizing and focus on great results rather than process." Hard-charging and constantly seeking to innovate, Netflix dove in head-first as streaming technology evolved online and quickly found a receptive audience ready to instantaneously download and view video. That's also where the trouble began.

The difference in gross profit margins between mail order (37 percent) and streaming rentals (65 percent) was significant. In part to better account for these revenue differences, management decided in April 2011 to split the company into two brands and businesses. As the first step, customers were told on July 12, 2011, that they would begin to be charged $7.99 for each form of rental instead of $9.99 for both forms, in effect a 60 percent price increase for the 24 million subscribers who wanted to use both physical discs and streaming. In an unfortunate coincidence, at roughly the same time, cable channel Starz very publicly ended negotiations with Netflix to renew a key online deal to supply movies and TV shows.

Perceiving that they would be paying more for less, customers were decidedly unhappy. Over 600,000 terminated their accounts in the following months, catching Netflix off guard. Although the company normally conducted exhaustive consumer research on everything from the red color of its envelopes to the quality of its video streams, in this case it had decided to forgo consumer research based on its understanding that the vast majority of new customers seemed to prefer streaming. Many existing customers, however, accustomed to years of the three-at-a-time DVD rental service, viewed the online service as a free add-on to their DVD rentals, not the other way around.

The company compounded its problems with a blog post by Hastings on September 18, 2011, that many saw as only a half-hearted apology. Hastings announced that the company's movies-by-mail service would be rebranded Qwikster and would add video games to its catalog, while the Netflix brand would be devoted to streaming video only. Once again, consumer response was emphatically negative—to the strategy and even to the new name. As one critic said:

"It is as though Hastings and the Netflix crew sat in a room and brainstormed the dumbest possible names they could think of and knew they were really onto something truly stupid when they came up with Qwikster … My first

Founder Reed Hastings ran into a public relations firestorm when he attempted to split up the Netflix business to create a new brand architecture.
Source: Dan Krauss/The New York Times/Redux Pictures

reaction, when I heard the news, was, "Hey Qwikster, 1991 called, it wants its radical new company name back."

On October 10, 2011, after several weeks of negative criticism and publicity, another Hastings post announced that the company would no longer split its services in two: "It is clear that for many of our members two websites would make things more difficult, so we are going to keep Netflix as one place to go for streaming and DVDs. This means no change: one website, one account, one password … in other words, no Qwikster."

Netflix's brand architecture problems clearly slowed down the momentum the company had achieved in the marketplace and left many consumers unhappy or confused. As one disgruntled blogger noted, "Netflix does more flip-flopping than a fish on a hot deck." As the year ended, however, some signs of stability and growth emerged, and analysts were cautiously optimistic that Netflix would be able to put its problems behind it.

Sources: Michael V. Copeland, "Reed Hastings: Leader of the Pack," *Fortune* (6 December 2010): 121–130; Ronald Grover and Cliff Edwards, "Can Netflix Find Its Future by Abandoning the Past?," *Bloomberg BusinessWeek*, 22 September 2011; Cliff Edwards, "Can Netflix Regain Lost Ground?," *Bloomberg BusinessWeek*, 23 October 2011; John D. Sutter, "Netflix Whiplash Stirs Angry Mobs—Again," www.cnn.com, 10 October 2011; Doug Gross, "Customers Fume Over Netflix Changes," www.cnn.com, 20 September 2011; Logan Burruss and David Goldman, "Netflix Abandons Plan for Qwikster DVD Service," www.cnnmoney.com, 10 October 2011; Stu Woo and Ian Sherr, "Netflix Recovers Subscribers," *Wall Street Journal*, 26 January 2012.

1. Decide on which products are to be introduced.
   - *Principle of growth:* Invest in market penetration or expansion vs. product development according to ROI opportunities.
   - *Principle of survival:* Brand extensions must achieve brand equity in their categories.
   - *Principle of synergy:* Brand extensions should enhance the equity of the parent brand.
2. Decide on the number of levels.
   - *Principle of simplicity:* Employ as few levels as possible.
   - *Principle of clarity:* Logic and relationship of all brand elements employed must be obvious and transparent.
3. Decide on the levels of awareness and types of associations to be created at each level.
   - *Principle of relevance:* Create abstract associations that are relevant across as many individual items as possible.
   - *Principle of differentiation:* Differentiate individual items and brands.
4. Decide on how to link brands from different levels for a product.
   - *Principle of prominence:* The relative prominence of brand elements affects perceptions of product distance and the type of image created for new products.
5. Decide on how to link a brand across products.
   - *Principle of commonality:* The more common elements products share, the stronger the linkages.

FIGURE 11-6

Guidelines for Brand Hierarchy Decisions

Brand elements at each level of the hierarchy may contribute to brand equity through their ability to create awareness as well as foster strong, favorable, and unique brand associations and positive responses. The challenge in setting up a brand hierarchy is to decide:

1. The specific products to be introduced for any one brand.
2. The number of levels of the hierarchy to use.
3. The desired brand awareness and image at each level.
4. The combinations of brand elements from different levels of the hierarchy, if any, to use for any one particular product.
5. The best way to link any one brand element, if at all, to multiple products.

The following discussion reviews these five decisions. Figure 11-6 summarizes guidelines in each of these areas to assist in the design of brand hierarchies.

Specific Products to Introduce.   Consistent with discussions in other chapters about what products a firm should introduce for any one brand, we can note three principles here.

The ***principle of growth*** maintains that investments in market penetration or expansion versus product development for a brand should be made according to ROI opportunities. In other words, firms must make cost–benefit calcuations for investing resources in selling more of a brand's existing products to new customers versus launching new products for the brand.

In seeing its traditional networking business slow down, Cisco decided to bet big on new Internet video products. Although video has become more pervasive in almost all media (cell phones, Internet, etc.), the bulky size of files creates transmission challenges. Cisco launched Telepresence technology to permit high-definition videoconferencing for its corporate customers and is infusing its entire product line with greater video capabilities through its medianet architecture.[18]

The other two principles address the dynamics of brand extension success, as developed in great detail in Chapter 12. The ***principle of survival*** states that brand extensions must achieve brand equity in their categories. In other words, "me too" extensions must be avoided. The ***principle of synergy*** states that brand extensions should also enhance the equity of the parent brand.

Number of Levels of the Brand Hierarchy.   Given product boundaries and an extension strategy in place for a brand, the first decision to make in defining a branding strategy is, broadly, which level or levels of the branding hierarchy to use. Most firms choose to use more than one level, for two main reasons. Each successive branding level allows the firm to communicate additional, specific information about its products. Thus, developing brands at lower levels of the hierarchy allows the firm flexibility in communicating the uniqueness of its products. At the same time, developing brands at higher levels of the hierarchy is obviously an economical means of communicating common or shared information and providing synergy across the company's operations, both internally and externally.

As we noted above, the practice of combining an existing brand with a new brand is called sub-branding, because the subordinate brand is a means of modifying the superordinate brand. A sub-brand, or hybrid branding, strategy can also allow for the creation of specific brand beliefs. Pepsi is working hard to create a number of sub-brands for its Gatorade brand.

GATORADE

First created by researchers at the University of Florida in the mid-1960s—whose nickname for its sports teams the "Gators" gave the product its name—Gatorade was a carbohydrate-electrolyte beverage designed to replace what the school's athletes would lose from sweating in the intense Gainsville heat. Pioneering the sports drink market, Gatorade became an on-court and off-court staple for athletes everywhere. PepsiCo bought Quaker Oats and the brand in 2000, but after a decade of ownership, sales began to slump. A slew of new water and energy drink competitors helped erode Gatorade's sales. The "What is G?" ad campaign failed to reignite sales in 2009. That year, Pepsi marketers decided to launch the innovative new "G series" to reconnect with competitive athletes and to ensure that Gatorade was not seen as "the sports drink of my father." The G series was designed to "fuel the body before, during, and after practice, training and competition." It consisted of three product groupings:

- *Prime 01*, pregame fuel in the form of four-ounce beverage pouches packed with carbohydrates, sodium, and potassium to be consumed before athletic activity.
- *Perform 02*, the traditional Thirst Quencher and G2 beverage lines used to hydrate and refresh during periods of heavy exertion, exercise, or competition.
- *Recover 03*, a protein-packed beverage to aid hydration and muscle recovery after exercise.

Other versions of G Series were also launched. G Series Pro was initially available only for professional athletes but was later broadened to target the more serious amateur; G Series Natural contained natural ingredients like sea salt, fruit flavors, and natural sweetners. G Series Fit was a healthier and low-calorie version of the product line to be used before, during, and after personal workouts.[19]

Gatorades's dramatic repositioning included a completely new G Series brand architecture.

Source: Jarrod Weaton/Weaton Digital, Inc.

Sub-branding thus creates a stronger connection to the company or family brand and all the associations that come along with that. At the same time, developing sub-brands also allows for the creation of brand-specific beliefs. This more detailed information can help customers better understand how products vary and which particular product may be the right one for them.

Sub-brands also help organize selling efforts so that salespeople and retailers have a clear picture of how the product line is organized and how best to sell it. For example, one of the main advantages to Nike of continually creating sub-brands in its basketball line with Air Max Lebron, Air Zoom Hyperdunk, and Hyperfuse, as well as the very popular Jordan line, is to generate retail interest and enthusiasm. Ninety-two of the top-100-selling basketball shoes in 2010 were sold by Nike.[20]

Marketers can employ a host of brand elements as part of a sub-brand, including name, product form, shape, graphics, color, and version. By skillfully combining new and existing brand elements, they can effectively signal the intended similarity or fit of a new extension with its parent brand.

The *principle of simplicity* is based on the need to provide the right amount of branding information to consumers—no more and no less. The desired number of levels of the brand hierarchy depends on the complexity of the product line or product mix, and thus on the combination of shared and separate brand associations the company would like to link to any one product.

With relatively simple low-involvement products—such as light bulbs, batteries, and chewing gum—the branding strategy often consists of an individual or perhaps a family brand combined with modifiers that describe differences in product features. For example, GE has three main brands of general-purpose light bulbs (Edison, Reveal, and Energy Smart) combined with designations for basic functionality (Standard, Reader, and three-way), aesthetics (soft white and daylight), and performance (40, 60, and 100 watts).

A complex set of products—such as cars, computers, or other durable goods—requires more levels of the hierarchy. Thus, Sony has family brand names such as Cyber-Shot for its cameras, Bravia for TVs, and Handycams for its camcorders.[21] A company with a strong corporate brand selling a relatively narrow set of products, such as luxury automobiles, can more easily use nondescriptive alphanumeric product names because consumers strongly identify with the parent brand, as Acura found out.

ACURA

Honda grew from humble origins as a motorcycle manufacturer to become a top automobile import competitor in the United States. Recognizing that future sales growth would come from more upscale customers, it set out in the early 1980s to compete with European luxury cars. Since Honda's image of dependable, functional, and economical cars did not have the cachet to appeal to this segment, the company created the new Acura division. After meeting initial success, however sales began to drop. Research revealed part of the problem: Acura's Legend, Integra, and Vigor sub-brand names did not communicate luxury and order in the product line as well as the alphanumeric branding scheme of competitors BMW, Mercedes, Lexus, and Infiniti. Honda decided that the strength of the brand should lie in the Acura name. Thus, despite the fact that it had spent nearly $600 million on advertising Acura sub-brands over the previous eight years to build their equity, the firm announced a new alphanumeric branding scheme in the winter of 1995: the 2.5 TL and 3.2 TL (for Touring Luxury) sedan series, the 3.5 RL, the 2.2 CL, and 3.0 CL, and the RSX series. Acura spokesperson Mike Spencer said, "It used to be that people said they owned or drove a Legend.... Now they say they drive an Acura, and that's what we wanted." Introducing new models with new names paid off and sales subsequently rose. Although Acura solved its branding problems, a perceived lack of styling has plagued the brand, and in recent years the company has struggled to keep up with its luxury compatriots.[22]

It's difficult to brand a product with more than three levels of brand names without overwhelming or confusing consumers. A better approach might be to introduce multiple brands at the same level (multiple family brands) and expand the depth of the branding strategy.

Desired Awareness and Image at Each Hierarchy Level.   How much awareness and what types of associations should marketers create for brand elements at each level? Achieving the desired level of awareness and strength, favorability, and uniqueness of brand associations may take some time and call for a considerable change in consumer perceptions. Assuming marketers use some type of sub-branding strategy for two or more brand levels, two general principles—relevance and differentiation—should guide them at each level of the brand knowledge creation process.

The *principle of relevance* is based on the advantages of efficiency and economy. Marketers should create associations that are relevant to as many brands nested at the level below as possible, especially at the corporate or family brand level. The greater the value of an association in the firm's marketing, the more efficient and economical it is to consolidate this meaning into one brand linked to all these products.[23] For example, Nike's slogan ("Just Do It") reinforces a key point-of-difference for the brand—performance—that is relevant to virtually every product it sells.

The more abstract the association, the more likely it is to be relevant in different product settings. Thus, benefit associations are likely to be extremely advantageous because they can cut across many product categories. For brands with strong product category and attribute associations, however, it can be difficult to create a brand image robust enough to extend into new categories.

For example, Blockbuster struggled to expand its meaning from "a place to rent videos" to "your neighborhood entertainment center" in hopes of creating a broader brand umbrella with greater relevance to more products. It eventually declared bankruptcy before being acquired via auction by satellite television provider Dish Network in April 2011.[24]

The *principle of differentiation* is based on the disadvantages of redundancy. Marketers should distinguish brands at the same level as much as possible. If they cannot easily distinguish two brands, it may be difficult for retailers or other channel members to justify supporting both, and for consumers to choose between them.

Although new products and brand extensions are critical to keeping a brand innovative and relevant, marketers must introduce them thoughtfully and selectively. Without restraint, brand variations can easily get out of control.[25]

A grocery store can stock as many as 40,000 items, which raises the question: Do consumers really need nine kinds of Kleenex tissues, Eggo waffles in 16 flavors, and 72 varieties of Pantene shampoo, all of which have been available at one point in time? To better control its inventory and avoid brand proliferation, Colgate-Palmolive began to discontinue one item for each product it introduces.

Although the principle of differentiation is especially important at the individual brand or modifier levels, it's also valid at the family brand level. For example, one of the criticisms of marketing at General Motors was that the company had failed to adequately distinguish its family brands of automobiles, perhaps ultimately leading to the demise of the Oldsmobile, Pontiac, and Saturn brands.

The principle of differentiation also implies that not all products should receive the same emphasis at any level of the hierarchy. A key issue in designing a brand hierarchy is thus choosing the relative emphasis to place on the different products in it. If a corporate or family brand is associated with multiple products, which product should be the core or flagship product? What product should represent "the brand" to consumers?

A *flagship product* is one that best represents or embodies the brand to consumers. It is often the first product by which the brand gained fame, a widely accepted best seller, or a highly admired or award-winning product. For example, although other products are associated with their brands, flagship products might be soap for Ivory, credit cards for American Express, and cake mix for Betty Crocker.[26]

Flagship products play a key role in the brand portfolio in that marketing them can have short-term benefits (increased sales), as well as long-term benefits (improved brand equity). Chrysler put a lot of marketing effort behind its 300 models when they were hot sellers even though they made up only 22 percent of the brand's total sales, because the 300 also appeared to provide a halo over the rest of the Chrysler line. At a time when General Motors sales were declining by 4 percent, Chrysler's sales shot up 10 percent.[27]

Combining Brand Elements from Different Levels.   If we combine multiple brand elements from different levels of the brand hierarchy, we must decide how much emphasis to give each. For example, if we adopt a sub-brand strategy, how much prominence should we give individual brands at the expense of the corporate or family brand?

Principle of Prominence. The *prominence* of a brand element is its relative visibility compared with other brand elements. Prominence depends on several factors, such as order, size, and appearance, as well as semantic associations. A name is generally more prominent when it appears first, is larger, and looks more distinctive. Assume PepsiCo has adopted a sub-branding strategy to introduce a new vitamin-fortified cola, combining its corporate family brand name with a new individual brand name, say, "Vitacola." We could make the Pepsi name more prominent by placing it first and making it bigger: PEPSI *Vitacola*. Or we could make the individual brand more prominent by placing it first and making it bigger: Vitacola BY PEPSI.

The ***principle of prominence*** states that the relative prominence of the brand elements determines which become the primary one(s) and which the secondary one(s). Primary brand elements should convey the main product positioning and points-of-difference. Secondary brand elements convey a more restricted set of supporting associations such as points-of-parity or perhaps an additional point-of-difference. A secondary brand element may also facilitate awareness.

For example, with the Droid by Motorola series of smartphones, the primary brand element is the Droid name, which connotes its use of Google's Android operating system. The Motorola name, on the other hand, is a secondary brand element that ideally conveys credibility, quality, and professionalism. According to the principle of prominence, the more prominent a brand element, the more emphasis consumers will give it in forming their brand opinions. The relative prominence of the individual and the corporate brands will therefore affect perceptions of product distance and the type of image created for a new product.

Consumers are very literal. If the corporate or family brand is made more prominent, then its associations are more likely to dominate. If the individual brand is made more prominent, on the other hand, then it should be easier to create a more distinctive brand image. "Marriott's Courtyard" would be seen as much more of a Marriott hotel than "Courtyard by Marriott" by virtue of having the corporate name first. In "Courtyard by Marriott," the position of the corporate or family brand is signaling to consumers that the new product is not as closely related to its other products that share that name. As a result, consumers should be less likely to transfer corporate or family brand associations. At the same time, because of the greater perceived distance, the success or failure of the new product should be less likely to affect the image of the corporate

Branding for the Droid by Motorola emphasizes Google's Android operating system more than it does the Motorola corporate name.

Source: AP Photo/David Duprey

or family brand. With a more prominent corporate or family brand, however, feedback effects are probably more likely to be evident.

In some cases, the brand elements may not be explicitly linked at all. In a ***brand endorsement strategy***, a brand element—often the corporate brand name or logo—appears on the package, signage, or product appearance in some way but is not directly included as part of the brand name. The brand endorsement strategy presumably establishes the maximum distance between the corporate or family brand and the individual brands, suggesting that it would yield the smallest transfer of brand associations to the new product but, at the same time, minimize the likelihood of any negative feedback effects.

For example, General Mills places its "Big G" logo on its cereal packages but retains distinct brand names such as Cheerios, Wheaties, and Lucky Charms. Kellogg, on the other hand, adopts a sub-brand strategy that combines the corporate name with individual cereal brands, for instance Kellogg's Corn Flakes and Kellogg's Special K. Through its sub-branding strategy and marketing activities, Kellogg should be more effective than General Mills in connecting its corporate name to its products and, as a result, in creating favorable associations to its corporate name.

Branding Strategy Screen. Marketers can use the branding strategy screen displayed in Figure 11-7 to "dial up" or "dial down" different brand elements. If a potential new product or service is strongly related to the parent brand such that there is a high likelihood of parent brand equity carryover, and if there is little equity risk, a product descriptor or parent-brand-first sub-brand may make sense.[28]

On the other hand, if a potential new product or service is more removed from the parent brand such that there is a lower likelihood of parent brand equity carryover or if there is higher equity risk, then a parent-brand-second sub-brand or even a new brand may be more appropriate. In these latter cases, the parent brand may just be used as an endorser.

These pros and cons help determine whether a "branded house" or "house of brands" is the more appropriate strategy. What consumers know about and want from the brand, and how they will actually use it, is also important. Although offering multiple sub-brands as part of a detailed brand family may seem to provide more descriptive details, it can easily backfire if taken too far.

For example, when one-time technology hotshot Silicon Graphics named its new 3-D work station "Indigo^2 Solid Impact," customers chose to simplify the name by calling it simply "Solid." Creating equity for a low-level brand modifier (Solid) would certainly not be called good branding practice. Brand equity ideally resides at the highest level of the branding hierarchy possible, where it can benefit more products and services.

Linking Brand Elements to Multiple Products. So far, we've highlighted how to apply different brand elements to a particular product—the "vertical" aspects of the brand hierarchy. Next, we consider how to link any one brand element to multiple products—the "horizontal" aspects. The ***principle of commonality*** states that the more common brand elements products share, the stronger the linkages between them.

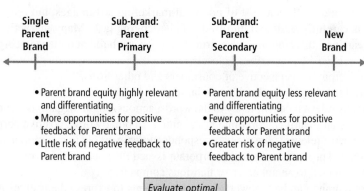

FIGURE 11-7

Branding Strategy
Screen

The simplest way to link products is to use the brand element "as is" across them. Adapting the brand, or some part of it, offers additional possibilities for making the connection.

- Hewlett-Packard capitalized on its highly successful LaserJet computer printers to introduce a number of new products using the "Jet" suffix, for example, the DeskJet, PaintJet, ThinkJet, and OfficeJet printers.
- McDonald's has used its "Mc" prefix to introduce a number of products, such as Chicken McNuggets, Egg McMuffin, and the McRib sandwich.
- Donna Karan's DKNY brand, Calvin Klein's CK brand, and Ralph Lauren's Double RL brand rely on initials.

We can also create a relationship between a brand and multiple products with common symbols. For example, corporate brands like Nabisco often place their corporate logo more prominently on their products than their name, creating a strong brand endorsement strategy.

Finally, it's often a good idea to logically order brands in a product line, to communicate how they are related and to simplify consumer decision making. We can communicate the order though colors (American Express offers Red, Blue, Green, Gold, Platinum, and "Black" or Centurion cards), numbers (BMW offers its 3-, 5-, and 7-series cars), or other means. This strategy is especially important in developing brand migration pathways for customers to switch among the brands offered by the company. The relative position of a brand within a brand line may also affect consumer perceptions and preferences.[29]

CORPORATE BRANDING

Given its fundamental importance in brand architecture, we will go into greater detail on corporate branding. A corporate brand is distinct from a product brand in that it can encompass a much wider range of associations. As detailed below, a corporate brand name may be more likely to evoke associations of common products and their shared attributes or benefits, people and relationships, programs and values, and corporate credibility.

These associations can have an important effect on the brand equity and market performance of individual products. For example, one research study revealed that consumers with a more favorable corporate image of DuPont were more likely to respond favorably to the claims made in an ad for Stainmaster carpet and therefore actually buy the product.[30]

Building and managing a strong corporate brand, however, can necessitate that the firm keep a high public profile, especially to influence and shape some of the more abstract types of associations. The CEO or managing director, if associated with a corporate brand, must also be willing to maintain a more public profile to help communicate news and information, as well as perhaps provide a symbol of current marketing activities. At the same time, a firm must also be willing to subject itself to more scrutiny and be extremely transparent in its values, activities, and programs. Corporate brands thus have to be comfortable with a high level of openness.

A corporate brand offers a host of potential marketing advantages, but only if corporate brand equity is carefully built and nurtured—a challenging task. Many marketing winners in the coming years will therefore be those firms that properly build and manage corporate brand equity. Branding Brief 11-3 describes a closely related concept—corporate reputation—and how we can look at it from the perspective of consumers and other firms.[31]

Corporate brand equity is the differential response by consumers, customers, employees, other firms, or any relevant constituency to the words, actions, communications, products, or services provided by an identified corporate brand entity. In other words, positive corporate brand equity occurs when a relevant constituency responds more favorably to a corporate ad campaign, a corporate-branded product or service, a corporate-issued PR release, and so on than if the same offering were attributed to an unknown or fictitious company.

A corporate brand can be a powerful means for firms to express themselves in a way that isn't tied to their specific products or services. The Science of Branding 11-3 describes one approach to defining corporate brand personality.

THE SCIENCE OF BRANDING 11-3

Corporate Brand Personality

The success of a twenty-first-century company will be a function of many different characteristics—its mission, structure, processes, culture, and so on. One important characteristic is its corporate brand personality.

Formally, we can define **corporate brand personality** as "a form of brand personality specific to a corporate brand" and "the human characteristics or traits that can be attributed to a corporate brand." Despite the fact that the concept of brand personality applies to both product brands and corporate brands, because corporate brands are designed to encompass a wider range of associations than the product brands that might fall under them, the dimensions are not necessarily the same.

One approach maintains that a successful twenty-first-century corporation's brand personality must reflect three core dimensions: the "heart," the "mind," and the "body" (see Figure 11-8).

- The "heart" of a company reflects two traits: it is *passionate* and *compassionate*. Employees should be passionate about their jobs, their business and industry, their firm's products and services, and what they can do for their customers. The company must also have compassion and care deeply about its customers, employees, stakeholders, the communities in which it operates, and the environment as a whole.

- The "mind" of a company is *creative* and *disciplined*. A successful twenty-first-century company must be creative in its approach to serving its customers, transcending the current status quo, finding new solutions to old problems, and overcoming the trade-offs faced by all businesses. Yet it must also be disciplined and stay focused, avoiding the "grass is greener" syndrome and the latest management fads, finding truly promising growth opportunities, and ensuring that it takes appropriate and consistent actions.

- The "body" of a company is *agile* and *collaborative*. It must anticipate changes that will be necessary in the future, move forward quickly, and nimbly react to changes in the market. A successful twenty-first-century company must also be collaborative, fostering an internal culture of interdepartmental teamwork and establishing an external network of partners that share common corporate values and beliefs and offer complementary and synergistic assets and competencies.

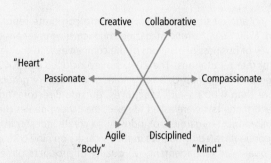

FIGURE 11-8 Corporate Personality Traits

These three core dimensions of corporate personality have a multiplicative, not merely an additive, effect. For example, passion can drive creativity in an organization. In turn, creativity spurs agility, as more creative firms are able to rapidly find solutions to problems or recognize new opportunities. Discipline engenders better collaborative efforts, as employees more readily establish and follow guidelines and partnership principles.

These dimensions of corporate personality traits are important to build in a brand, because the corporation competing in the twenty-first century will be defined "as much by *who* it is as *what* it does." This contrasts with the historical case for corporations, in which a company drew its identity primarily from products and services it sold and its actions in the market.

A company's employees are, in many cases, the outward face of the company that consumers see, and they define "who" a corporation is. They embody the personality traits the company has established. If all employees act with a "heart," "mind," and "body," then the company will be better positioned to achieve success in the twenty-first-century business environment.

Sources: Kevin Lane Keller and Keith Richey, "The Importance of Corporate Brand Personality Traits to a Successful 21st Century Business, *Journal of Brand Management* 14 (September–November 2006): 74–81; Thomas J. Brown, "Corporate Associations in Marketing: Antecedents and Consequences," *Corporate Reputation Review* 1 (Autumn 1998): 215–233; Majken Schultz, Yun Mi Antorini, and Fabian F. Csaba, eds., *Corporate Branding: Purpose, People, and Processes* (Herndon, VA: Copenhagen Business School Press, 2005); Lynn B. Upshaw and Earl L. Taylor, *The Masterbrand Mandate* (New York: John Wiley & Sons, 2000).

Corporate Image Dimensions

A corporate image will depend on a number of factors, such as the products a company makes, the actions it takes, and the manner in which it communicates to consumers. This section highlights some of the different types of associations that are likely to be linked to a corporate brand and that can affect brand equity (see Figure 11-9).[32]

Common Product Attributes, Benefits, or Attitudes. Like individual brands, a corporate or company brand may evoke in consumers a strong association to a product attribute (Hershey with "chocolate"), type of user (BMW with "yuppies"), usage situation (Club Med with "fun times"), or overall judgment (Sony with "quality").

BRANDING BRIEF 11-3

Corporate Reputations: The Most Admired U.S. Companies

Two annual surveys offer insights into corporate reputation. Every year, *Fortune* magazine conducts a comprehensive survey of business perceptions of the companies with the best corporate reputations. The 2010 survey included the 1,400 largest U.S. and non-U.S. companies in 64 industry groups. More than 4,000 senior executives, outside directors, and financial analysts were asked to select the 10 companies they admired most, regardless of industry. To create industry lists, respondents rated companies in their industry on nine criteria: (1) quality of management; (2) quality of products or services; (3) innovativeness; (4) long-term investment value; (5) financial soundness; (6) ability to attract, develop, and keep talented people; (7) responsibility to the community and the environment; (8) wise use of corporate assets; and (9) global competitiveness.

Many of the same companies make the list year after year; for example, Apple was number one from 2007 to 2010, and Procter & Gamble was in the top ten from 2005 to 2010. *Fortune*'s top ten most admired companies from 2010 and their rankings are as follows:

Rank	Company	Rank	Company
1	Apple	6	Coca-Cola
2	Google	7	Amazon.com
3	Berkshire Hathaway	8	FedEx
4	Southwest Airlines	9	Microsoft
5	Procter & Gamble	10	McDonald's

Another informative survey, the RQ 2010 study of corporate reputations, conducted each year since 1999 by Harris Interactive and the Reputation Institute, demonstrated both the enduring character of corporate reputations but their ability to change quickly at the same time. Researchers determine which companies should be rated on the basis of a preliminary sampling of over 30,000 members of the U.S. general public, utilizing the proprietary Harris Poll online panel. Respondents are asked first to identify the 60 most visible companies and then to rate them on 20 different attributes that make up the Reputation Quotient (RQ) instrument. The attributes are then grouped into six different reputation dimensions: Emotional Appeal, Products & Services, Social Responsibility, Vision & Leadership, Workplace Environment, and Financial Performance. The study also includes a number of questions that help provide a comprehensive understanding of how the public perceived firms' reputations. The 2010 rankings are as follows:

Rank	Company	Rank	Company
1	Google	6	Intel
2	Johnson & Johnson	7	Kraft Foods
3	3M	8	Amazon.com
4	Berkshire Hathaway	9	General Mills
5	Apple	10	Walt Disney Co.

Sources: "World's Most Admired Companies," *Fortune*, 22 March 2011; "Google Ranks Highest on Corporate Reputation in 12th Annual Harris Interactive U.S. Reputation Quotient® (RQ®) Survey," press release, Harris Interactive, 2 May 2011.

Common Product Attributes, Benefits, or Attitudes
Quality
Innovativeness

People and Relationships
Customer orientation

Values and Programs
Concern with environment
Social responsibility

Corporate Credibility
Expertise
Trustworthiness
Likability

FIGURE 11-9

Some Important
Corporate Image
Associations

If a corporate brand is linked to products across diverse categories, then some of its strongest associations are likely to be those intangible attributes, abstract benefits, or attitudes that span each of the different product categories. For example, companies may be associated with products or services that solve particular problems (Black & Decker), bring excitement and fun to certain activities (Nintendo), are built with the highest quality standards (Motorola), contain advanced or innovative features (Rubbermaid), or represent market leadership (Hertz).

Two specific product-related corporate image associations—high quality and innovation—deserve special attention.

A *high-quality corporate image association* creates consumer perceptions that a company makes products of the highest quality. A number of different organizations like J.D. Power, *Consumer Reports*, and various trade publications for automobiles rate products. The Malcolm Baldrige award is one of many that distinguishes companies on the basis of quality. Quality is one of the most important, if not *the* most important, decision factors for consumers.

An *innovative corporate image association* creates consumer perceptions of a company as developing new and unique marketing programs, especially with respect to product introductions or improvements. Keller and Aaker experimentally showed how different corporate image strategies—being innovative, environmentally concerned, or involved in the community—could affect corporate credibility and strategically benefit the firm by increasing the acceptance of brand extensions.[33] Interestingly, consumers saw a company with an innovative corporate image as not only expert but also trustworthy and likable. Being innovative is seen in part as being modern and up-to-date, investing in research and development, employing the most advanced manufacturing capabilities, and introducing the newest product features.

An image priority for many Japanese companies—from consumer product companies such as Kao to more technically oriented companies such as Canon—is to be perceived as innovative.[34] Perceived innovativeness is also a key competitive weapon and priority for firms in other countries. Michelin ("A Better Way Forward") describes how its commitment to the environment, security, value, and driving pleasure has been spurring innovation. Branding Brief 11-4 describes how 3M has developed an innovative culture and image.

People and Relationships.   Corporate image associations may reflect characteristics of the employees of the company. Although focusing on employees is a natural positioning strategy for service firms like Southwest Airlines, Avis car rental, and Ritz-Carlton hotels as well as retailers like Walmart, manufacturing firms like DuPont and others have also used it in the past. Their rationale is that the traits that employees exhibit will directly or indirectly influence consumers about the products the firm makes or the services it provides.

Consumers may themselves form more abstract impressions of a firm's employees, especially in a services setting. One major public utility company was described by customers as "male, 35–40 years old, middle class, married with children, wearing a flannel shirt and khaki pants, who would be reliable, competent, professional, intelligent, honest, ethical, and business-oriented." On the downside, these same customers also described the utility as "distant, impersonal, and self-focused," suggesting an important area for improvement in its corporate brand image.

Retail stores also derive brand equity from their employees. For example, from its origins as a small shoe store, Seattle-based Nordstrom has become one of the nation's leading fashion specialty retailers through a commitment to quality, value, selection, and, especially, service. Legendary for its "personalized touch" and willingness to go to extraordinary lengths to satisfy its customers, Nordstrom creates brand equity largely through the efforts of its salespeople and the relationships they develop with customers.

Thus, a *customer-focused corporate image association* creates consumer perceptions of a company as responsive to and caring about its customers. Consumers believe their voice will be

BRANDING BRIEF 11-4

Corporate Innovation at 3M

3M has fostered a culture of innovation and improvisation from its very beginnings. In 1904, the company's directors were faced with a failed mining operation, but they turned the left-over grit and waste into a revolutionary new product: sandpaper. Today, 3M makes more than 50,000 products, including adhesives, contact lenses, and optical films. Over the last century, some of its noteworthy product launches include Scotch masking and transparent tape, Scotchgard fabric protector, and Post-it Notes.

Each year, 3M launches scores of new products, and the company generates significant revenues from those introduced within the past five years. It regularly ranks among the top 10 U.S. companies each year in patents received. 3M budgets roughly 5–6 percent of sales to R&D, totaling $1–$1.5 billion annually. The firm is able to consistently produce innovations in part because it promotes a corporate environment that facilitates new discoveries:

- 3M encourages everyone, not just engineers, to become "product champions." The company's "15 percent time" lets all employees spend up to 15 percent of their time working on projects of personal interest. A culture of healthy competition among highly motivated peers helps 3M innovate and create.

- Each promising new idea is assigned to a multidisciplinary venture team headed by an "executive champion." 3M hands Golden Step awards each year to the venture teams whose new products earned more than $2 million in U.S. sales or $4 million in worldwide sales within three years of commercial introduction.

- 3M expects some failures and uses them as opportunities to learn how to make products that work. It is also very selective about acquisitions, seeing them as only supplementary to organic growth and internal innovations and developments.

- Starting in 2010, 3M has introduced social networks into its innovation process, inviting 75,000 global employees and over 1,200 other people to participate in its annual Markets of the Future brainstorming session. Over 700 new ideas have been generated, leading to nine new markets for the company to explore.

Some of the innovations that emerged from 3M in 2010 include Cubitron II industrial abrasives, which are revolutionizing how grinding and abrading are done; new low-cost,

3M's strong emphasis on R&D and innovation results in many breakthrough products, like its Cubitron industrial.
Source: 3M

maintenance-free respirators' and a new line of microprojectors for cars, classrooms, and recreational use.

Sources: www.3m.com; 3M 2010 annual report; Chuck Salter, "The Nine Passions of 3M's Mauro Porcini," *Fast Company*, October 2011; Kaomi Goetz, "How 3M Gave Everyone Days Off and Created an Innovation Dynamo," *Fast Company Design*, February 2011; Rick Swanborg, "Social Networks in the Enterprise: 3M's Innovation Process," *CIO*, 29 April 2010.

heard and that the company has their best interests in mind. Often this philosophy is reflected throughout the marketing program and communicated through advertising.

Values and Programs. Corporate image associations may reflect company values and programs that do not always directly relate to the products. Firms can run corporate-image ad campaigns to describe to consumers, employees, and others their philosophy and actions with respect to organizational, social, political, or economic issues.

For example, many recent corporate advertising campaigns have focused on environmental issues and social responsibility. A *socially responsible corporate image association* portrays the company as contributing to community programs, supporting artistic and social activities, and generally attempting to improve the welfare of society as a whole. An *environmentally concerned corporate image association* projects a company whose products protect or improve the environment and make more effective use of scarce natural resources. We consider corporate responsibility in more detail below, and Brand Focus 11.0 looks at the broader issue of cause marketing, in which British Airways has been a pioneer.

BRITISH AIRWAYS

An innovative cause marketer, British Airways has successfully introduced several noteworthy cause programs. It first partnered with UNICEF in 1994 for the cleverly titled Change for Good campaign, based on a very simple idea: foreign coins are particularly difficult to exchange at banks and currency exchanges. So passengers were asked to place any surplus coins—or bills, for that matter—in envelopes provided by British Airways, which donated them directly to UNICEF. British Airways advertised the program on the backs of seat cards, during an in-flight video, and with in-flight announcements with such success that fellow international carriers in the Oneworld Alliance began to participate. In June 2010, the program was replaced with the Flying Start program. This new program was a partnership with Comic Relief UK, a successful charity started by comedians whose aim is to "bring about positive and lasting change in the lives of poor and disadvantaged people." To publicize the new program, the airlines teamed up with Guinness World Records for the "Highest Stand-Up Comedy Gig in the World." Three comedians entertained 75 lucky passengers for a two-and-a-half-hour champagne flight. Flying Start was structured like Change for Good—donations were collected in-flight as well as online and at Travelex currency exchange locations in UK airports—but had a stronger local angle. The program raised almost $3 million in its first year, with a goal of raising $20 million by 2013 to "improve the lives of hundreds of thousands of children living in the UK and in some of the poorest countries across the world."[35]

Corporate Credibility. A particularly important set of abstract brand associations is corporate credibility. As defined in Chapter 2, corporate credibility measures the extent to which consumers believe a firm can design and deliver products and services that satisfy their needs and wants. It is the reputation the firm has achieved in the marketplace. Corporate credibility—as well as success and leadership—depend on three factors:

1. *Corporate expertise:* The extent to which consumers see the company as able to competently make and sell its products or conduct its services
2. *Corporate trustworthiness:* The extent to which consumers believe the company is motivated to be honest, dependable, and sensitive to customer needs
3. *Corporate likability:* The extent to which consumers see the company as likable, attractive, prestigious, dynamic, and so forth

While consumers who perceive the brand as credible are more likely to consider and choose it, a strong and credible reputation can offer additional benefits.[36] L.L. Bean is a company with much corporate credibility.

L.L. BEAN

A brand seen as highly credible, outdoors-product retailer L.L. Bean attempts to earn its customers' trust every step of the way—by providing prepurchase advice, secure transactions, best-in-class delivery, and easy returns and exchanges. Founded in 1912, L.L. Bean backs its efforts with a 100-percent satisfaction guarantee as well as its Golden Rule: "Sell good merchandise at a reasonable profit, treat your customers like human beings and they will always come back for more." Now a billion-dollar brand celebrating its 100th anniversary in 2012, the company retains its original image of being passionate about the outdoors and believing profoundly in honesty, product quality, and customer service.[37]

L.L. Bean's popular roving Bootmobile was a clever way to create awareness and engagement around its 100th anniversary.

Source: AP Photo/L.L. Bean, Lincoln Benedict

A highly credible company may be treated more favorably by other external constituencies, such as government or legal officials. It also may be able to attract better-qualified employees and motivate existing employees to be more productive and loyal. As one Shell Oil employee remarked as part of some internal corporate identity research, "If you're really proud of where you work, I think you put a little more thought into what you did to help get them there."

A strong corporate reputation can help a firm survive a brand crisis and avert public outrage that could otherwise depress sales or block expansion plans. As Harvard's Stephen Greyser notes, "Corporate reputation . . . can serve as a capital account of favorable attitudes to help buffer corporate trouble."

Summary.   Many intangible brand associations can transcend the physical characteristics of products, providing valuable sources of brand equity and serving as critical points-of-parity or points-of-difference.[38] Companies have a number of means—indirect or direct—of creating these associations. But they must "talk the talk" and "walk the walk" by communicating to consumers and backing up claims with concrete programs consumers can easily understand or even experience.

Managing the Corporate Brand

A number of specific issues arise in managing a corporate brand. Here we consider three: corporate social responsibility, corporate image campaigns, and corporate name changes.

Corporate Social Responsibility.   Some marketing experts believe consumers are increasingly using their perceptions of a firm's role in society in their purchase decisions. For example, consumers want to know how a firm treats its employees, shareholders, local neighbors, and other stakeholder or constituents.[39] As the head of a large ad agency put it: "The only sustainable competitive advantage any business has is its reputation."[40]

Consistent with this reasoning, 91 percent of respondents in a large global survey of financial analysts and others in the investment community agreed that a company that fails to look after its reputation will endure financial difficulties. Moreover, 96 percent said the CEO's reputation was fairly, very, or extremely important in influencing their ratings.[41]

The realization that consumers and others may be interested in issues beyond product characteristics and associations has prompted much marketing activity to establish the proper corporate image.[42] Some firms are putting corporate social responsibility at the very core of their existence.[43] Ben & Jerry's has created a strong association as a "do-gooder" by using Fair Trade ingredients and donating 7.5 percent of its pretax profits to various causes. Its annual Social and Environmental Assessment Report details the company's main social mission goals and spells out how it is attempting to achieve them.

TOMS Shoes used cause marketing to launch its brand.

TOMS SHOES

When entrepreneur and former reality-show contestant Blake Mycoskie visited Argentina in 2006, he saw masses of children who suffered health risks and interrupted schooling due to a simple lack of shoes. Once home, Mycoskie started TOMS Shoes, whose name conveys "Shoes for a Better Tomorrow" and whose One for One program delivers a free pair of shoes to a needy child for each pair sold. The shoes themselves are based on the classic *alpargata* style found in Argentina. They're sold online and through top retailers such as Whole Foods, Nordstrom, and Neiman Marcus. TOMS's donated shoes—black, uni-sex canvas slip-ons with a sturdy sole—can now be found on the feet of more than 2 million kids in developing countries such as Argentina and Ethiopia. TOMS has a strong social media presence with almost a million Facebook friends. In 2011, Mycoskie launched TOMS Eyewear, using a similar One for One model in which for every pair of glasses sold, a child in need will receive either medical care, prescription glasses, or sight-saving surgery.[44]

Founder Blake Mycoskie put social responsibility at the heart of his TOMS Shoes business.

Source: AP Images/PRNewsFoto/TOMS Shoes

Brand Focus 11.0 outlines the advantages of cause marketing, the obstacles they face, and how to successfully design a successful campaign, with particular emphasis on green marketing.

Corporate Image Campaigns. *Corporate image campaigns* are designed to create associations to the corporate brand as a whole; consequently, they tend to ignore or downplay individual products or sub-brands.[45] As we would expect, some of the biggest spenders on these kinds of campaigns are well-known firms that use their company or corporate name prominently in their branding strategies, such as GE, Toyota, British Telecom, IBM, Novartis, and Deutsche Bank.

Corporate image campaigns have been criticized as an ego-stroking waste of time, and they can be easy for consumers to ignore. However, a strong campaign can provide invaluable marketing and financial benefits by allowing the firm to express itself and embellish the meaning of its corporate brand and associations for its individual products, as Philips did.

PHILIPS

To reposition itself as a more consumer-friendly brand, Philips Consumer Electronics launched a global corporate advertising campaign in 2004 that ran for a number of years. Centered on the company's new tagline, "Sense and Simplicity," which replaced the nine-year-old "Let's Make Things Better," the ads showcased innovative Philips products like the Flat TV with Ambilight, the HDRW720 DVD recorder with built-in hard disk, and the Sonicare Elite toothbrush fitting in effortlessly with users' sophisticated lifestyles. Philips president and CEO Gerard Kleisterlee described the repositioning campaign by saying, "Our route to innovation isn't about complexity—it's about simplicity, which we believe will be the new cool."[46]

To maximize the probability of success, however, marketers must clearly define the objectives of a corporate image campaign *and* carefully measure results against them.[47] A number of different objectives are possible in a corporate brand campaign:[48]

- Build awareness of the company and the nature of its business.
- Create favorable attitudes and perceptions of company credibility.
- Link beliefs that can be leveraged by product-specific marketing.
- Make a favorable impression on the financial community.
- Motivate present employees and attract better recruits.
- Influence public opinion on issues.

In terms of building customer-based brand equity, the first three objectives are particularly critical. A corporate image campaign can enhance awareness and create a more positive image of the corporate brand that will influence consumer evaluations and increase the equity associated with individual products and any related sub-brands. In certain cases, however, the latter three objectives can take on greater importance.[49]

A corporate image campaign may be useful when mergers or acquisitions transform the company. Consolidation in the financial services industry has caused firms like Zurich and UBS to develop and implement strong corporate branding strategies.

UBS

UBS was formed in 1998 when Union Bank of Switzerland and Swiss Bank Corporation merged. The bank struggled for recognition outside Switzerland, especially in the United States. After a period of acquiring better-known companies such as SG Warburg and PaineWebber, UBS engaged in a comprehensive review of its branding strategy. The results showed product overlap among UBS businesses, a weak branding culture, and a focus on individual employees rather than the brand. The company decided to adopt the UBS brand for all its businesses, and, in order to build brand equity, it launched a global brand-building effort emphasizing the bank's scope and resources, while also playing up its one-on-one client relationships. The "You and Us" campaign debuted in 2004, with global campaign expenditures above $100 million. The goal was to assure customers that they could rely on the breadth and depth of the bank's offerings, whatever their financial needs. By 2010, the brand had become a perennial entry in Interbrand's Top 100 global brands.[50]

Like product advertising, corporate image campaigns are becoming more creative and often include digital strategies as an integral component. For its new "Solutionism. The New Optimism." campaign, Dow Chemical put up a giant 46-foot chalkboard in Soho, Manhattan. Over a series of days, an elaborate set of equations described as a mathematical poem emerged, with numbers representing significant human achievements through history, such as "the year the Great Pyramid of Giza was completed," "Golden Gate Bridge length in feet," and "GIANT leaps for mankind." The public was invited to participate and guess the meanings of different elements of the poem through Twitter (@giantchalkboard) and a giantchalkboard.com Web site. When the full equation appeared on the fifth day, its solution totaled 7 billion, the total world population.[51]

Unlike a corporate image campaign that presents the brand in abstract terms with few, if any, references to specific products, **brand line campaigns** promote a range of products associated with a brand line. By showing consumers the different uses or benefits of the multiple products offered by a brand, brand line ads or promotions can be particularly useful in building brand awareness, clarifying brand meaning, and suggesting additional usage applications. Sometimes a brand line campaign will emphasize a common thread running through all the products for a brand, as was the case with General Mills.

As part of its "Solutionism. The New Optimism" corporate image campaign, Dow Chemical put a gigantic attention-getting chalkboard up in Manhattan.

Source: The Dow Chemical Company

GENERAL MILLS

In 2004, General Mills elected to make all its cereals with 100 percent whole grains so that each provided at least half a serving (8 grams) in every bowl. Despite the many benefits of whole grains, including lowered risks of chronic diseases such as heart disease, certain cancers, and diabetes, only 5 percent of U.S. consumers at that time got the minimum three daily servings recommended by the U.S. Dietary Guidelines for Americans. Much consumer confusion existed about what whole grains were and why it mattered. Based on research showing that consumers read their cereal boxes an average of 2.7 times, General Mills decided to promote the health benefits of 100 percent whole-grain cereal on all its product packaging, using the U.S. Department of Agriculture food guide pyramid. An advertising campaign also touted the switch to whole grains. The program met with much success, essentially adding 1.5 billion servings of whole grains to the U.S. diet each year. In 2011, General Mills partnered with Dr. Travis Stork, host of a popular daytime talk show, to donate 1 million servings of whole grain to families in need.[52]

General Mills promotes the fact that its entire line of cereals is 100 percent whole grain.

Source: Keri Miksza

Corporate Name Changes.   Corporate names may have to change for many reasons, but they should be the right reasons pursued in the right way.

Rationale.   A merger or acquisition is often the impetus to reevaluate naming strategies and weigh the existing and potential equity of each brand in its new context.[53]

- A new corporate name arising from a merger or acquisition may be based on some combination of two existing names, if they are strong. For example, when Glaxo Wellcome merged with SmithKline Beecham, the new company became GlaxoSmithKline. J.P. Morgan & Co. and Chase Manhattan Corporation became JP Morgan Chase after their merger. United's name was combined with Continental's globe logo when those two air carriers merged.
- If there is an imbalance in brand equity, the firm typically chooses the name with more inherent brand equity and relegates the other to a sub-brand role or eliminates it altogether. When Citicorp merged with Travelers, the latter's name was dropped, although its familiar red umbrella symbol was retained as part of the new Citigroup brand look.
- Finally, if neither name has the desired brand equity, a completely new name can signal new capabilities. When Bell Atlantic purchased GTE in 2000, the newly merged company adopted the Verizon brand name, which combined *veritas*, the Latin word for reliability, and *horizon*, which was intended to signify a forward-looking attitude.

Corporate names also change because of divestitures, leveraged buyouts, or the sale of assets. When Andersen Consulting was allowed to separate from Arthur Andersen following an arbitrator's ruling in 2000, it was required to stop using its old name by the end of the year. After an extensive naming search and rebranding project, the firm was renamed "Accenture"—an employee suggestion meant to connote an "accent on the future." Having a new name proved especially fortuitous when Arthur Andersen was convicted of obstruction of justice in 2002 in the wake of the Enron scandal and ceased to operate as a business. Some residual negative perceptions from Arthur Andersen would likely have transferred to the Andersen Consulting brand.

Corporate names can also change to correct public misperceptions about the nature of the company's business.[54] For example, Europe's third-largest food company, BSN, renamed itself for its Danone brand—a hugely successful fresh dairy products subsidiary, second only to Coca-Cola in terms of branded sales in Europe—because many consumers didn't know what the old name stood for. Moreover, BSN was already used by other companies in other countries, including a bank in Spain, a textile firm in the United States, and a television station in Japan.[55]

Significant shifts in corporate strategy may necessitate name changes. US Steel changed its name to USX to downplay the importance of steel and metal in its product mix. Allegheny Airlines changed its name to USAir when it moved from being a regional to a national carrier, and then later to USAirways when it wanted to be seen as an international carrier. Its later acquisition of America West did not require a change in strategy or implementation but brought significant logistical hurdles.

Sometimes a name change just reflects the fact that the original name wasn't all that good and probably shouldn't have been chosen to begin with.

BOLOCO

A small New England restaurant chain selling burritos, bowls, and smoothies was called The Wrap, derived from its original name, Under Wraps. In 2005, the founders felt a name change was in order because the word "wrap" had come to mean something that was typically cold, full of lettuce, and wrapped in pita bread and then cellophane, with a packet of mayonnaise and mustard on the side. The Wrap, on the other hand, had always been about hot, grilled, fresh ingredients wrapped in steamed tortillas, more like a burrito than a wrap. The new name, Boloco, and the tag line "Inspired Burritos" were much more evocative of what the chain sold. As cofounder and CEO John S. Pepper explained, "The name has a bit of a Latin flair with 'loco,' reflecting what our menu focuses on—inspired burritos. Furthermore, Boloco—Boston Local Company—is a tribute to the city of Boston and our customers who gave us a chance to be successful."

Another reason for the name change was that The Wrap was too generic to be protected legally. Boloco was not a name shared by any other entity at the time.[56]

Boloco changed its name from The Wrap to better reflect what the small New England restaurant chain actually sold.

Source: © Boloco. Used with kind permission.

Finally, the desire to create distance from scandal can also motivate a name change. A new name cannot repair a company's damaged reputation, though, and experts advise against making a switch in the midst of bad publicity; otherwise the stigma and suspicion will follow the new name. Philip Morris Co. decided to change its name to get away from its association with tobacco and emphasize its range of companies, including Kraft Foods, so in 2003, it adopted the new name Altria Group Inc. After its name was tarnished by human rights violations, military support firm Blackwater changed its name to Xe in 2007 and then again to Academi in 2011.[57]

Guidelines. Although renaming can yield growth opportunities, experts recommend a cautious approach. Name changes are typically complicated, time-consuming, and expensive and firms should undertake them only when compelling marketing or financial considerations prevail and a proper supporting marketing program can be put into place. A new corporate name cannot hide product or other deficiencies, and it requires extensive legal and URL vetting to make sure it is available and appropriate. Rebranding campaigns also usually forfeit the brand recognition and loyalty attached to the old name.

Many of the branding issues we discussed in Chapter 4 are relevant in choosing or changing a corporate name. Given the corporate branding strategy and marketing objectives, firms should evaluate candidate names in terms of memorability, meaningfulness, likability, protectability, adaptability, and transferability. If the consumer market is the primary objective, the name may reflect or be suggestive of certain product characteristics, benefits, or values. Consolidated Foods Corporation switched to Sara Lee Corporation, Castle & Cooke, Inc. to Dole Food Company, and United Brands Company to Chiquita Brands International.

Once the firm has chosen the new name, the substantial task of introducing it to employees, customers, suppliers, investors, and the public begins—often with the launch of a new marketing campaign and the opportunity to work with a blank canvas. Corporate rebranding is a time- and resource-intensive process that demands a company's total commitment to succeed. A company with little consumer exposure may spend as much as $5 million on research, advertising, and other marketing costs (new signs, stationery, business cards, Web site, and so on) to change its identity, but a company with a high public profile may have to spend up to $100 million or more.[58]

Macy's moved too quickly in rebranding beloved Chicago department store Marshall Fields after its acquisition, raising the ire of many of its former customers.

Source: Tim Boyle/Getty Images

It is important not to move too fast in rebranding. In updating brand architecture in any way, the goal is to at least preserve if not actually enhance brand equity as much as possible. Here are two companies that got ahead of themselves in their brand makeovers.

- As part of its strategy to become more of a national retailer, Macy's acquired May Department Stores and Chicago retailing icon Marshall Field's in August 2005. The Marshall Field's flagship building on State Street, built in 1892 and covering a full city block, was designated a National Historic Landmark in 1978. The department store occupied 8 of its 12 floors, and generations of Chicagoans had shopped there. When Macy's almost immediately rebranded the store as Macy's, replacing Marshall Field's famous awnings, signage, and green shopping bags, a consumer uproar ensued. It took years for protests to die down.[59]

- When online retailer Overstock.com rebranded itself as O.co in June 2011, the company revamped its Web site and changed its advertising and sponsorship to reflect the new name. Unfortunately, many consumers began mistakenly going to the O.com Web site, which was *not* owned by the company. After six months, the company decided to return to Overstock.com on its Web site, in online ads, and in new TV ads "for now," though not abandoning O.co outright. The O.co name was to still be used internationally, on mobile efforts, and on the Oakland NFL stadium sign. "We were going too fast, and people were confused, which told us we didn't do a good job," President Jonathan Johnson admitted.[60]

Initial reaction to rebranding is almost always negative, simply because people resist change. Sometimes, however, an especially harsh reception will cause a firm to abandon a new name. As Royal Mail began to distance itself a bit from the UK government, which owned a majority share, it tried to adopt a new name, Consignia. A public outcry ensued, and within a matter of months, the name was changed back to the original.[61] PriceWaterhouseCoopers tried to spin off its consulting unit to a new firm called Monday. The name was widely mocked, and within nine months the group was sold off and absorbed into IBM. The name change and branding were largely blamed for Monday's lack of success.[62]

When UAL, the parent company of United Airlines, decided a new name was necessary to reflect the one-stop travel options that resulted from its acquisitions of Hertz car rental and Westin and Hilton International hotels, it chose the name "Allegis," a compound of "allegiance" and "aegis." Public reaction was decidedly negative. Critics maintained that the name was difficult to pronounce, sounded pretentious, and had little connection with travel services. Donald Trump, formerly a major UAL shareholder, said the new name was "better suited to the next world-class disease." After six weeks and $7 million in research and promotion expenditures, the company decided to shed its car rental and hotel businesses and rename the surviving company United Airlines, Inc.[63]

Over time, though, if properly chosen and handled, new names gain familiarity and acceptance. Guidelines that encourage uniformity and consistency in the brand's appearance and usage help make the implementation effective; these rules should be part of a revised brand charter (see Chapter 8).

BRAND ARCHITECTURE GUIDELINES

Brand architecture is a classic example of the "art and science" nature of marketing. It is important to establish rules and conventions and be disciplined and consistent. Yet at the same time, it is also important to be flexible and creative. There rarely are pure solutions to a brand architecture challenge, and no uniform agreement exists on the one type of branding strategy that all firms should adopt for all products. Even within a firm hybrid strategies often prevail, and marketers may adopt different branding strategies for different products.

For example, although Miller has long used its name across its different types of beer, with various sub-brands like Miller High Life, Miller Lite, and Miller Genuine Draft, it carefully branded its no-alcohol beer substitute as Sharp's, its ice beer as Icehouse, and its low-priced beer as Milwaukee's Best, with no overt Miller identification. The assumption was that the corporate family brand name would not be relevant to or valued by the target market in question.

The brand hierarchy may not be symmetric. Corporate objectives, consumer behavior, or competitive activity may sometimes dictate significant deviations in branding strategy and the way the brand hierarchy is organized for different products or for different markets.

Brand elements may receive more or less emphasis, or not be present at all, depending on the particular products and markets. For example, in an organizational market segment where the DuPont brand name may be more valuable, that element might receive more emphasis than associated sub-brands. In appealing to a consumer market segment, a sub-brand such as Teflon may be more meaningful; thus it received relatively more emphasis when DuPont is targeting that market. (See Figure 11-10.)

In evaluating a brand architecture strategy, we should ask a number of questions, such as:

- For the brand portfolio, do all brands have defined roles? Do brands collectively maximize coverage and minimize overlap?
- For the brand hierarchy, does the brand have extension potential? Within the category? Outside the category? Is the brand overextended?
- What positive and negative brand equity implications will transfer from the parent brand to individual products? What feedback exists from the individual products to the parent brands in turn?
- What profit streams result from different branding arrangements? How much revenue does each brand generate? At what cost? What other cross-selling opportunities exist between brands?

In answering these questions and in devising and implementing the optimal brand architecture strategy, marketers should keep the following five guidelines in mind.

1. *Adopt a strong customer focus*. Recognize what customers know and want, and how they will behave.
2. *Create broad, robust brand platforms*. Strong umbrella brands are highly desirable. Maximize synergies and flow.
3. *Avoid overbranding and having too many brands*. High-tech products, for example, are often criticized for branding every ingredient so the overall effect is like a NASCAR race car with logos and decals everywhere.

DuPont Leveraged Equity

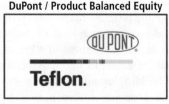

DuPont / Product Balanced Equity

Endorsement Brand

FIGURE 11-10
DuPont "Product-Endorsed" Business Strategy

Source: Courtesy of DuPont

4. *Selectively employ sub-brands*. Sub-brands can communicate relatedness *and* distinctiveness and are a means of complementing and strengthening brands.

5. *Selectively extend brands*. As Chapter 12 explains, brand extensions should establish new brand equity and enhance existing brand equity.

REVIEW

A key aspect of managing brand equity is adopting the proper branding strategy. Brand names of products typically consist of a combination of different names and other brand elements. A brand architecture strategy for a firm identifies which brand elements a firm chooses to apply across the various products or services it sells. Several tools aid in developing a brand architecture strategy. Combining the brand–product matrix, the brand portfolio, and the brand hierarchy with customer, company, and competitive considerations can help a marketing manager formulate the optimal brand architecture strategy.

The brand–product matrix is a graphical representation of all the firm's brands and products, with brands as rows and the corresponding products as columns. The rows represent brand–product relationships and capture the firm's brand extension strategy. Marketers should judge potential extensions by how effectively they leverage existing brand equity to a new product, as well as how effectively the extension, in turn, contributes to the equity of the existing parent brand. The columns of the matrix represent product–brand relationships and capture the brand portfolio strategy in terms of the number and nature of brands to be marketed in each category.

We characterize a brand architecture strategy according to its breadth in terms of brand–product relationships and brand extension strategy, and its depth in terms of product–brand relationships and the brand portfolio or mix. Breadth describes the product mix and which products the firm should manufacture or sell. Depth deals with the brand portfolio and the set of all brands and brand lines that a particular seller offers.

A firm may offer multiple brands in a category to attract different—and potentially mutually exclusive—market segments. Brands also can take on very specialized roles in the portfolio: as flanker brands to protect more valuable brands, as low-end entry-level brands to expand the customer franchise, as high-end prestige brands to enhance the worth of the entire brand line, or as cash cows to milk all potentially realizable profits. Companies must be careful to understand exactly what each brand should do for the firm and, more important, what they want it to do for the customer.

A brand hierarchy reveals an explicit ordering of all brand names by displaying the number and nature of common and distinctive brand name elements across the firm's products. By capturing the potential branding relationships among the different products sold by the firm, a brand hierarchy graphically portrays a firm's branding strategy. One simple representation of possible brand elements and thus of potential levels of a brand hierarchy is (from top to bottom): corporate (or company) brand, family brand, individual brand, and modifier.

In designing a brand hierarchy, marketers should define the number of different levels of brands (generally two or three) and the relative emphasis that brands at different levels will receive when combined to brand any one product. One common strategy to brand a new product is to create a sub-brand, combining an existing company or family brand with a new individual brand. When marketers use multiple brand names, as with a sub-brand, the relative visibility of each brand element determines its prominence. Brand visibility and prominence will depend on factors such as the order, size, color, and other aspects of the brand's physical appearance. To provide structure and content to the brand hierarchy, marketers must make clear to consumers the specific means by which a brand applies across different products and, if different brands are used for different products, the relationships among them.

In designing the supporting marketing program in the context of a brand hierarchy, marketers must define the desired awareness and image at each level of the brand hierarchy for each product. In a sub-branding situation, the desired awareness of a brand at any level will dictate the relative prominence of the brand and the extent to which associations linked to the brand will transfer to the product. In terms of building brand equity, we should link associations at any one level based on principles of relevance and differentiation. In general, we want to create associations relevant to as many brands nested at the level below as possible and to distinguish any brands at the same level.

Corporate or family brands can establish a number of valuable associations to differentiate the brand, such as common product attributes, benefits, or attitudes; people and relationships; programs and values; and corporate credibility. A corporate image will depend on a number of factors, such as the products a company makes, the actions it takes, and the manner in which it communicates to consumers. Communications may focus on the corporate brand in the abstract or on the different products making up the brand line. Any corporate name changes and rebranding efforts need to be done carefully.

An area of increasing importance for many brands is corporate social responsibility. Firms are becoming more aware of the environmental, economic, and social impact of their words and actions. Many now employ cause-marketing programs designed to align their brands with a cause of importance to their customers. Many consumers are also becoming much more aware of the environmental aspect of the products and services of a firm and how they are produced and disposed.

DISCUSSION QUESTIONS

1. Pick a company. As completely as possible, characterize its brand portfolio and brand hierarchy. How would you improve the company's branding strategies?
2. Do you think the Dow Chemical corporate image campaign described in this chapter will be successful? Why or why not? What do you see as key success factors for a corporate image campaign?
3. Contrast the branding strategies and brand portfolios of market leaders in two different industries. For example, contrast the approach by Anheuser-Busch and its Budweiser brand with that of Kellogg in the ready-to-eat cereal category.
4. What are some of the product strategies and communication strategies that General Motors could use to further enhance the level of perceived differentiation between its divisions?
5. Consider the companies listed in Branding Brief 11-3 as having strong corporate reputations. By examining their Web sites, can you determine why they have such strong corporate reputations?

BRAND FOCUS 11.0

Cause Marketing

The 1980s saw the advent of cause marketing. Formally, cause-related (or cause) marketing has been defined as "the process of formulating and implementing marketing activities that are characterized by an offer from the firm to contribute a specified amount to a designated cause when customers engage in revenue-providing exchanges that satisfy organizational and individual objectives."[64] As Varadarajan and Menon note, the distinctive feature of cause marketing is the link between the firm's contribution to a designated cause and customers' engaging in revenue-producing transactions with the firm.

Advantages of Cause Marketing

One reason for the rise in cause marketing is the positive response it elicits from consumers.[65] Cone Communications, one of the leading firms advising companies on cause-related marketing, found convincing evidence in its 2011 Cone/Echo Global CR Opportunity Study:[66]

- 81 percent of consumers say companies have a responsibility to address key social and environmental issues beyond their local communities.

- 93 percent of consumers say companies must go beyond legal compliance to operate responsibly.

- 94 percent of consumers say companies must analyze and evolve their business practices to make their impact as positive as possible.

- 94 percent would buy a product that has an environmental benefit; 76 percent have already purchased an environmental product in the past 12 months.

- 93 percent would buy a product associated with a cause; 65 percent have already purchased a cause-related product in the past 12 months.

Cause or corporate societal marketing (CSM) programs offer many potential benefits to a firm:[67]

- *Building brand awareness:* Because of the nature of the brand exposure, CSM programs can be a means of improving recognition for a brand, although not necessarily recall. Like sponsorship and other indirect forms of brand-building communications, most CSM programs may be better suited to increasing exposure to the brand rather than to tying the brand to specific consumption or usage situations, because it can be difficult or inappropriate to include product-related information. At the same time, repeated or prominent exposure to the brand as a result of the CSM program can facilitate brand recognition.

- *Enhancing brand image:* Because most CSM programs do not include much product-related information, we would not expect them to have much impact on more functional, performance-related considerations. On the other hand, we can link two types of abstract or imagery-related associations to a brand via CSM: user profiles—CSM may allow consumers to develop a positive image of brand users to which they also may aspire in terms of being kind, generous, and doing good things; and personality and values—CSM could clearly bolster the sincerity dimension of a brand's personality such that consumers would think of the people behind the brand as caring and genuine.

- *Establishing brand credibility:* CSM could affect all three dimensions of credibility, because consumers may think of a firm willing to invest in CSM as caring more about customers and being more dependable than other firms, at least in a broad sense, as well as being likable for "doing the right things."[68] Whirlpool generated much goodwill with its "More Than Houses" cause program with Habitat for Humanity, in which it donated a range and refrigerator for each new home built.

- *Evoking brand feelings:* Two categories of brand feelings that seem particularly applicable to CSM are social approval and self-respect. In other words, CSM may help consumers justify their self-worth to others or to themselves. CSM programs may need to provide consumers with external symbols to explicitly advertise or signal their affiliation to others—for example, bumper stickers, ribbons, buttons, and T-shirts. They can also give people the notion that they are doing the right thing and should feel good about themselves for having done so. External symbols in this case may not be as important as the creation of "moments of internal reflection" during which consumers are able to experience these feelings. Communications that reinforce the positive outcomes associated with the cause program—and how consumer involvement contributed to that success—could help trigger these types of experiences. To highlight the consumer contribution, it may be necessary to recommend certain actions or outcomes such as having consumers donate a certain percentage of income or a designated amount.

- *Creating a sense of brand community:* CSM and a well-chosen cause can serve as a rallying point for brand users and a means for them to connect to or share experiences with other consumers or employees of the company itself.[69] One place where communities of like-minded users exist is online. Marketers may be able to tap into the many close-knit online groups that have sprung up around cause-related issues (for instance, medical concerns such as Alzheimer's disease, cancer, and autism). The brand might even serve as the focal point or ally for these online efforts to be seen in a more positive light.

- *Eliciting brand engagement:* Participating in a cause-related activity as part of a CSM program for a brand is certainly one means of eliciting active engagement. As part of any of these activities, customers themselves may become brand evangelists and ambassadors and help communicate about the brand and strengthen the brand ties of others. A CSM program of "strategic volunteerism," whereby corporate personnel volunteer their time to help administer the non-profit program, could actively engage consumers with both the cause and the brand.

Perhaps the most important benefit of cause-related marketing is that by humanizing the firm, it may help consumers develop a strong, unique bond with the firm that transcends normal marketplace transactions. A striking success story is McDonald's, whose franchises have long been required to stay close to their local communities. Ronald McDonald House Charities provides comfort and care to sick children and their families by supporting over 300 Ronald McDonald Houses and 45 Ronald McDonald Care Mobiles in communities around the world and by making grants to other not-for-profit organizations whose programs help children in need. Ronald McDonald Houses effectively leverage the company's Ronald McDonald character and its identification with children to concretely symbolize the firm's "do-good" efforts. This well-branded cause program enhances McDonald's reputation as caring and concerned for customers.[70]

Designing Cause-Marketing Programs

Cause marketing comes in many forms related to education, health, the environment, the arts, and so on. Some firms have used cause marketing very strategically to gain a marketing advantage.[71] Toyota has run corporate advertising for years—most recently its "Moving Forward" campaign—showing it has roots in local U.S. communities. For Toyota, this campaign may go beyond cause marketing to become a means to help create a vital point-of-parity with respect to domestic car companies on "country of origin."

A danger is that the promotional efforts behind a cause-marketing program could backfire if cynical consumers question the link between the product and the cause and see the firm as self-serving and exploitive as a result. To realize brand equity benefits, firms must brand their cause-marketing efforts in the right manner. In particular, consumers must be able to make some kind of connection from the cause to the brand.[72]

The hope is that cause marketing strikes a chord with consumers and employees, improving the image of the company and energizing these constituents to act. With near-parity products, some marketers feel that a strongly held point-of-difference on the basis of community involvement and concern may in some cases be the best way—and perhaps the only way—to uniquely position a product. Two highly successful cause programs are associated with breast cancer:

- *The Avon Breast Cancer Crusade:* Founded in 1993, the Avon Breast Cancer Crusade is a U.S. initiative of Avon Products, Inc. Its mission has been to provide women, particularly those who are medically underserved, with direct access to breast cancer education and early-detection screening services such as mammograms and clinical breast exams. In the United States, Avon is the largest corporate supporter of the breast cancer cause, generating some $740 million in the first 19 years of its existence and donating it around the world. The Crusade raises funds to accomplish this mission in two ways: through the sale of special fund-raising (pink ribbon) products by Avon's nearly 6.5 million independent sales representatives worldwide, and through fund-raising walks. In the United States, the Avon Walk for Breast Cancer 2-Days, a series of two-day, 30-mile fund-raising walks in major cities nationwide, attracts thousands of participants. The Crusade has linked more than 15 million women to early-detection programs and provided $25 million for 41 research projects.[73]

- *Yoplait Save Lids to Save Lives:* Yoplait yogurt is the biggest-selling yogurt in the United States and accounted for $1.1 billion of parent company General Mills's $11.2 billion in

General Mills' "Save Lids to Save Lives" cause campaign has been a win-win success for raising funds for breast cancer research and for building the Yoplait brand.

Source: ©2012 YOPLAIT USA, INC. Yoplait and Save Lids to Save Lives are registered trademarks of YOPLAIT Marques Internationales SAS (France) used under license. ©2012 Susan G. Komen for the Cure®. Used with kind permission.

sales in 2010. General Mills started the the highly successful Save Lids to Save Lives cause-marketing program for Yoplait in 1998. For each pink lid customers redeem online or through the mail from September through December each year, Yoplait donates 10 cents to Susan G. Komen for the Cure, up to $2 million. Yoplait is also the National Series Presenting Sponsor of the Susan G. Komen Race for the Cure. The program's Web site allows participants to share stories, make dedications, and learn more about breast cancer. The program raised over $30 million in its first 13 years, boosting Yoplait sales in the process.[74]

Green Marketing

A special case of cause marketing is ***green marketing***. Although environmental issues have long affected marketing practices, especially in Europe, companies are increasingly recognizing that the environment is an important issue to their customers and shareholders and, therefore, to their bottom lines. Research shows the environment is one of the top five issues that youth care most about.

One survey revealed that two-thirds of leaders of major brands believe sustainability initiatives were critical to stay competitive. Firms like Kimberly-Clark, HP, and GE stated that it was a key priority. "For us now, it's about looking at the full spectrum of sustainability," said one senior executive at Kimberly-Clark, who noted the firm is seeking to generate 25 percent of 2015 net sales from sustainable products in its fast-moving consumer goods (FMCG) group.[75] Here is what GE is doing.

GE

Despite its industrial past, GE views eco-friendly products as a high-growth business. Spurred by environmental concerns voiced by its customers, GE and CEO Jeffrey Immelt launched Ecomagination in 2005, the name of which is a play on its ongoing corporate campaign "Imagination at Work." The initiative focused on how to effectively and efficiently "create, connect to, and use power and water" and committed $1.5 billion in annual investment to research and technology into cleaner technologies. Some of its goals were to double GE revenue from sales of products and services that provide environmental advantages, and to reduce greenhouse gas emissions and improve the energy efficiency of operations. GE built an Ecomagination advertising campaign

that targeted business-to-business customers, investors, employees, and consumers. In a 2011 letter to investors, customers, and other stakeholders to mark its progress, the company was able to note these achievements in the first five years of the program:

- **$5 billion** of clean-tech research and development
- **$85 billion** in revenue from Ecomagination products and solutions
- **22 percent** reduction in greenhouse gas emissions
- **30 percent** reduction in water use
- **$130 million** in energy efficiency savings

GE also launched a Smart Grid initiative—"a vision for a smarter, more efficient, and sustainable electrical energy grid that GE technology is helping to bring to life."[76]

On the corporate side, a host of marketing initiatives have been undertaken by a wide variety of firms with environmental overtones. The auto industry is responding to the dual motivators of concerned consumers and rising oil prices by introducing gas-saving and emission-reducing hybrid models. McDonald's has introduced a number of well-publicized environmental initiatives through the years, such as moving to unbleached paper carry-out bags and replacing polystyrene foam sandwich clamshells with paper wraps and lightweight recyclable boxes.

From a branding perspective, however, green marketing programs have not always been entirely successful.[77] What obstacles have they encountered?

Overexposure and Lack of Credibility. So many companies have made environmental claims that the public has sometimes become skeptical of their validity. What does it mean when a product claims it is "organic," "fair trade," or "eco-friendly?" Government investigations into some "green" claims, like the degradability of trash bags, and media reports of the spotty environmental track records behind others have only increased consumers' doubts. This backlash has led many consumers to consider environmental claims to be marketing gimmicks.

Efforts to provide consumers with more information have sometimes only complicated the situation. Hundreds of different product labels have been introduced, for instance. Seeking to serve as an environmental leader, Walmart announced a Sustainability Index in 2009 to grade suppliers and products on a range of environmental and sustainable factors. The company found it hard to actually implement such a formal rating, however, and later announced it was committed only to providing more product information to consumers.[78]

The challenge is that producing and consuming products always requires trade-offs—all products, regardless of how "green" they appear or claim to be, affect the environment in some way. To understand the full environmental impact of any one product, we need to understand the entire production and consumption process, from raw material inputs to ultimate disposal.

And the results of "green" actions are not always obvious. Gary Hirshberg, founder and CEO of Stonyfield Farm, notes that although many see the use of recyclable packaging as environmentally friendly, Stonyfield further reduced its carbon footprint by switching to yogurt cups that were *not* recyclable, and meant to be thrown away. These cups, made from plants that are disposed into landfills, generate far fewer greenhouse gas emissions than recycled plastic containers.

Similarly, when Patagonia examined the environmental impact of the fibers in its outdoor apparel lines, it found the most harmful one was cotton—not petroleum-based synthetics—because growing cotton requires the use of pesticides. The company switched to organic cotton, but that has its own drawbacks because it uses so much water. Manufacturing a single pair of jeans can require 1,200 gallons of water![79]

Deciphering environmental claims is thus very tricky. To help provide some clarity, the U.S. government has stepped in and demanded that companies be more specific and substantiate environmental claims. A "recycled" claim must specify how much of the product or package is recycled and whether it is "postconsumer" (previously used goods) or "preconsumer" (manufacturing waste). The Federal Trade Commission (FTC) is leading the charge, cracking down on vague, unsubstantiated claims by requiring independent product testing. For example, firms cannot use the government's Energy Star logo on their products unless third-party testing proves they are more efficient than comparable regular products.[80]

Consumer Behavior.   Like many well-publicized social trends, corporate environmental awareness is often fairly complex in reality and does not always fully match public perceptions. Several studies help put consumer attitudes toward the environment in perspective.

Although consumers often assert that they would like to support environmentally friendly products, their behavior doesn't always match their intentions.[81] In most segments, they appear unwilling to give up the benefits of other options to choose green products. For example, some consumers dislike the performance, appearance, or texture of recycled paper and household products. Others are unwilling to give up the convenience of disposable products like diapers.

Poor Implementation.   In jumping on the green marketing bandwagon, many firms initially did a poor job. Products were poorly designed, overpriced, and inappropriately promoted. Once product quality improved, advertising sometimes still missed the mark, being overly aggressive or not compelling. One research study found that assertive environmental messages were most effective for important environmental causes; otherwise, a softer touch was more beneficial.[82]

Possible Solutions.   The environmental movement in Europe and Japan has a longer history and firmer footing than in the United States. In Europe, many of Procter & Gamble's basic household items, including cleaners and detergents, are available in refills that come in throw-away pouches. P&G says U.S. customers probably would not take to the pouches. In the United States, firms continue to strive to meet the wishes of consumers concerning the environmental benefits of their products, while maintaining necessary profitability.

Notes

1. Marc Gunther, "Waste Management's New Direction," *Fortune*, 6 December 2010.
2. www.crayola.com, accessed December 30, 2011.
3. Jim Stengel, *Grow: How Ideals Power Growth and Profitability at the World's Greatest Companies* (New York: Crown Business, 2011); "Ideals Key for Top Brands," *WARC*, 4 January 2012; Jack Neff, "Just How Well-Defined Is Your Brand's Ideal?," *Advertising Age*, 16 January 2012.
4. "VW to Bring Back Phaeton to U.S. After Flop," *Automotive News Europe*, 19 August 2010; Zack Newmark, "2011 Volkswagen Phaeton Facelift In Depth," www.worldcarfans.com, 7 June 2010; Zack Newmark, "VW Phaeton to Return to U.S. Market," www.worldcarfans.com, 20 August 2010.
5. "Harris Poll Finds That Consumers Love Kisses: Hershey's Ranks Highest Overall in Brand Equity," www.harrisinteractive.com, 24 February 2010; "One of a Kind Hershey's Kisses," www.thearf.org/ogilvy-10-winners.php, accessed January 14, 2012.
6. Neil A. Morgan and Lopo Leotte do Rego, "Brand Portfolio Strategy and Firm Performance," *Journal of Marketing* 73 (January 2009): 59–74.
7. Bharat N. Anand and Ron Shachar, "Brands as Beacons: A New Source of Loyalty to Multiproduct Firms," *Journal of Marketing Research* 41 (May 2004): 135–150.
8. Kotler and Keller, *Marketing Management*; Patrick Barwise and Thomas Robertson, "Brand Portfolios," *European Management Journal* 10, no. 3 (September 1992): 277–285.
9. For a methodological approach for assessing the extent and nature of cannibalization, see Charlotte H. Mason and George R. Milne, "An Approach for Identifying Cannibalization within Product Line Extensions and Multi-brand Strategies," *Journal of Business Research* 31 (1994): 163–170. For an analytical exposition, see Preyas S. Desai, "Quality Segmentation in Spatial Markets: When Does Cannibalization Affect Product Line Design," *Marketing Science* 20 (Summer 2001): 265–283.

10. Jack Trout, *Differentiate or Die: Survival in Our Era of Killer Competition* (New York: Wiley, 2000).

11. Patricia Sellers, "P&G: Teaching an Old Dog New Tricks," *Fortune*, 31 May 2004, 166–172; Jennifer Reingold, "CEO Swap: The $79 Billion Plan," *Fortune*, 20 November 2009.

12. Mark Ritson, "Should You Launch a Fighter Brand?," *Harvard Business Review* 87 (October 2009): 65–81.

13. Mark Ritson, "Is Your Fighter Brand Strong Enough to Win the Battle?," *Advertising Age*, 13 October 2009; Mark Ritson, "Should You Launch a Fighter Brand?," *Harvard Business Review* 87 (October 2009): 65–81.

14. Paul W. Farris, "The Chevrolet Corvette," Case UVA-M-320 (Charlottesville, VA: Darden Graduate Business School Foundation, University of Virginia, 1995).

15. Zeynep Gurhan-Canli, "The Effect of Expected Variability of Product Quality and Attribute Uniqueness on Family Brand Evaluations," *Journal of Consumer Research* 30 (June 2003): 105–114.

16. Much of this section—including examples—is based on an excellent article by Peter H. Farquhar, Julia Y. Han, Paul M. Herr, and Yuji Ijiri, "Strategies for Leveraging Master Brands," *Marketing Research* (September 1992): 32–43.

17. Farquhar, Han, Herr, and Ijiri, "Strategies for Leveraging Master Brands."

18. Jon Fortt, "Cisco's Online Video Gamble," *Fortune*, 1 November 2010.

19. Natalie Zmuda, "Another Gatorade Product Line, Another Dedicated Ad Blitz," *Advertising Age*, 2 May 2011; Natalie Zmuda, "Gatorade Planning Another Facelift, New Products in 2010," *Advertising Age*, 14 December 2009; "Sports Drink Sales Get Into Shape," *Beverage Industry*, 12 July 2011.

20. "Top 100 Best Selling Basketball Shoes (November 2010)," www.counterkicks.com, accessed January 1, 2012.

21. Beth Snyder Bulik, "Tech Sector Ponders: What's in a Name?" *Advertising Age*, 9 May 2005, 24.

22. David Kiley, "I'd Like to Buy a Vowel, Drivers Say," *USA Today*, 9 August 2000; Fara Werner, "Remaking of a Legend," *Brandweek*, 25 April 1994, 23–28; Neal Templin, "Japanese Luxury-Car Makers Unveiling Cheaper Models in Bid to Attract Buyers," *Wall Street Journal*, 9 February 1995; T. L. Stanley and Kathy Tryer, "Acura Plays Numbers Game to Fortify Future," *Brandweek*, 20 February 1995, 3; Michelle Krebs, "Acura: Can Style Save Honda's Luxury Brand," *Edmunds Auto Observer*, 20 March 2008; Alan Ohnsman, "Honda Hopes New Acura ILX Helps Keep Gen-Y Out of Lexus, BMW," *Bloomberg News*, 12 December 2011; Richard Bremner, "BMW Mulls New Naming Strategies for Car Brands," www.insideline.com, 28 July 2011; Stefan Constantinescu, "Nokia to Change How They Name Devices Yet Again, Switching to BMW-like 500/600/700 Series Model Numbers," www.intomobile.com, 28 June 2011.

23. Tulin Erdem and Baohung Sun, "An Empirical Investigation of the Spillover Effects of Advertising and Sales Promotions in Umbrella Branding," *Journal of Marketing Research* 39 (November 2002): 408–420.

24. Ben Fritz, "Dish Network Wins Bidding for Assets of Bankrupt Blockbuster," *Los Angeles Times*, 7 April 2011.

25. Emily Nelson, "Too Many Choices," *Wall Street Journal*, 20 April 2001, B1, B4.

26. Deborah Roedder John, Barbara Loken, and Christopher Joiner, "The Negative Impact of Extensions: Can Flagship Products Be Diluted?," *Journal of Marketing* 62 (January 1998): 19–32.

27. Derrick Daye and Brad VanAuken, "Creating the Brand Halo Effect," www.brandingstrategyinsider.com, 21 September 2009.

28. Guido Berens, Cees B.M. van Riel, and Gerrit H. van Bruggen, "Corporate Associations and Consumer Product Responses: The Moderating Role of Corporate Brand Dominance," *Journal of Marketing* 69 (July 2005): 35–48.

29. France Leclerc, Christopher K. Hsee, and Joseph C. Nunes, "Narrow Focusing: Why the Relative Position of a Good Within a Category Matters More Than It Should," *Marketing Science* 24 (Spring 2005): 194–206.

30. "DuPont: Corporate Advertising," Case 9-593-023 (Boston: Harvard Business School, 1992); John B. Frey, "Measuring Corporate Reputation and Its Value," presentation given at Marketing Science Conference, Duke University, 17 March 1989.

31. Charles J. Fombrun, *Reputation* (Boston: Harvard Business School Press, 1996).

32. Several thoughtful reviews of corporate images are available. See, for example, James R. Gregory, *Marketing Corporate Image: the Company as Your Number One Product* (Lincolnwood, IL: NTC Business Books, 1999); Grahame R. Dowling, *Creating Corporate Reputations: Identity, Image and Performance* (Oxford, UK: Oxford University Press, 2001).

33. Kevin Lane Keller and David A. Aaker, "The Effects of Sequential Introduction of Brand Extensions," *Journal of Marketing Research* 29 (February 1992): 35–50. See also Thomas J. Brown and Peter Dacin, "The Company and the Product: Corporate Associations and Consumer Product Responses," *Journal of Marketing* 61 (January 1997): 68–84.

34. Masashi Kuga, "Kao's Strategy and Marketing Intelligence System," *Journal of Advertising Research* 30 (April/May 1990): 20–25.

35. John Williams, "British Airways Launch Flying Start in Partnership with Comic Relief," UK Business News, 16 February 2011; "BA and Comic Relief Launch Global Children's Charity," *Travel Weekly*, 30 June 2010; www.ba.com; www.comicrelief.com.

36. Tulun Erdem and Joffre Swait, "Brand Credibility, Brand Consideration and Choice," *Journal of Consumer Research* 31 (June 2004): 191–198; Marvin E. Goldberg and Jon Hartwick, "The Effects of Advertiser Reputation and Extremity of Advertising Claim on Advertising Effectiveness," *Journal of Consumer Research* 17 (September 1990): 172–179.

37. David Sharp, "L.L. Bean Hits Century Mark," *Associated Press*, 17 January 2012; www.llbean.com. Dale Northrup, "Good Ol' Bean," *Northern New England Journey*, January/February 2012; "Satisfaction Guaranteed: An Interview with Steve Fuller," *Reveries*, April 2001.

38. Majken Schultz, Mary Jo Hatch, and Mogens Holten Larsen, eds., *The Expressive Organization: Linking Identity, Reputation, and the Corporate Brand* (New York: Oxford University Press, 2000); Mary Jo Hatch and Majken Schultz, "Are the Strategic Stars Aligned for Your Corporate Brand?" *Harvard Business Review* (February 2001): 129–134; Mary Jo Hatch and Majken Schultz, *Taking Brand Initiative: How Companies Can Align Strategy, Culture, and Identity Through Corporate Branding* (San Francisco, CA: Jossey-Bass, 2008). See also James Gregory, *Leveraging the Corporate Brand* (Chicago: NTC Press, 1997); Lynn B. Upshaw and Earl L. Taylor, *The Masterbrand Mandate* (New York: John Wiley & Sons, 2000).

39. For some broad discussion, see the Special Issue on Stakeholder Marketing, *Journal of Public Policy and Marketing* 29 (May 2010).

40. Laurel Cutler, vice-chairman of FCB/Leber Katz Partners, a New York City advertising agency, quoted in Susan Caminit, "The Payoff from a Good Reputation," *Fortune*, 6 March 1995, 74. See also Michael E. Porter and Mark R. Kramer, "The Competitive Advantage of Corporate Philanthropy," *Harvard Business Review* 80 (December 2002): 56–69; Steve Hoeffler, Paul Bloom, and Kevin Lane Keller, "Understanding Stakeholder Responses to Corporate Citizenship Initiatives: Managerial Guidelines and Research Directions," *Journal of Public Policy & Management* 29 (Spring 2010): 78–88; Frank Huber, Frederik Meyer, Johannes Vogel, and Stefan Vollman, "Corporate Social Performance as Antecedent of Consumer's Brand Perception," *Journal of Brand Management* 19 (December 2011): 228–240.

41. Hill & Knowlton, Return on Reputation Study, March 2006.

42. Tillmann Wagner, Richard J. Lutz, and Barton A. Weitz, "Corporate Hypocrisy: Overcoming the Treat of Inconsistent Corporate Social Responsibility Perceptions," *Journal of Marketing* 73 (November 2009): 77–91.

43. Raj Sisodia, David B. Wolfe, and Jag Sheth, *Firms of Endearment: How World-Class Companies Profit from Passion and Purpose* (Upper Saddle River, NJ: Wharton School Publishing, 2007); John A. Quelch and Katherine E. Jocz, *Greater Good: How Good Marketing Makes for Better Democracy* (Boston, MA: Harvard Business School Press, 2007).

44. "How I Got Started … Blake Mycoskie, Founder of TOMS Shoes," *Fortune*, 22 March 2010, 72; Dan Heath and Chip Heath, "An Arms Race of Goodness," *Fast Company*, October 2009, 82–83; www.toms.com/movement-one-for-one.

45. For a review of current and past practices, see David W. Schumann, Jan M. Hathcote, and Susan West, "Corporate Advertising in America: A Review of Published Studies on Use, Measurement, and Effectiveness," *Journal of Advertising* 20 (September 1991): 35–56. See also Zeynep Gürhan-Canli and Rajeev Batra, "When Corporate Image Affects Product Evaluations: The Moderating Role of Perceived Risk," *Journal of Marketing Research* 41 (May 2004): 197–205.

46. "Sense and Simplicity: Philips Is Spending 80 Million [Euro] on a Rebranding Strategy That Will Emphasize Simplicity and Give Consumers What They Want," *ERT Weekly*, 23 September 2004; John Zerio, "Philips: Sense and Simplicity," Thunderbird Case # A12-07-013; www.philips.com, accessed February 27, 2012.

47. David M. Bender, Peter Farquhar, and Sanford C. Schulert, "Growing from the Top: Corporate Advertising Nourishes the Brand Equity from Which Profits Sprout," *Marketing Management* 4, no. 4 (1996): 10–19; Nicholas Ind, "An Integrated Approach to Corporate Branding," *Journal of Brand Management* 5, no. 5 (1998): 323–329; Cees B. M. Van Riel, Natasha E. Stroker, and Onno J. M. Maathuis, "Measuring Corporate Images," *Corporate Reputation Review* 1, no. 4 (1998): 313–326.

48. Gabriel J. Biehal and Daniel A. Shenin, "Managing the Brand in a Corporate Advertising Environment," *Journal of Advertising* 28, no. 2 (1998): 99–110.

49. Mary C. Gilly and Mary Wolfinbarger, "Advertising's Internal Audience," *Journal of Marketing* 62 (January 1998): 69–88.

50. Jestyn Thirkell-White, "UBS: Brand Building in a Global Market," *Admap*, July/August 2004; Haig Simoniam, "Three Letters Gain a Personality," *Financial Times*, 18 April 2005; "Best Global Brands 2011," www.interbrand.com, accessed December 29, 2011.

51. "Dow Chemical Company: Giant Chalkboard," www.adsoftheworld.com, September 2011; Charles Muir, "'Solutionism': Brain Busting Brand Positioning," www.corebrand.com/views, 23 September 2011.

52. Bruce Horovitz, "General Mills Cereals Go Totally Whole Grain," *USA Today*, 30 September 2004; Loraine Heller, "General Mill's Whole Grain Cereal Conversion in Retrospect,' www.foodnavigator-usa.com, 19 September 2006; "General Mills Chief Marketing Officer Mark Addicks on How Marketing Can Make a Better World," www.minnesota.publicradio.org, 25 January 2011; "General Mills Donates 1 Million Servings of Whole Grain," www.generalmills.com, 10 February 2011.

53. Richard Ettenson and Jonathan Knowles, "Merging the Brand and Branding the Merger," *MIT Sloan Management Review* (Summer 2006): 39–49.

54. Mark P. DeFanti and Paul S. Busch, "Image-Related Corporate Name Changes: Their Effect Upon Firm's Stock Prices," *Journal of Brand Management* 19, no. 3 (2011): 241–253.

55. "BSWho?" *The Economist*, 14 May 1994, 70.

56. Carolyn Sheehan, "The Name Game: The Wrap Goes Boloco," *Harvard Crimson*, 17 November 2005; Naomi R. Kooker, "The Wrap Becomes Boloco as Owner Goes National," *Boston Business Journal*, 2 January 2006; "The First Boloco Is Moving," *Fenway News*, 16 January 2010; www.boloco.com/story/our-story. Since 1997, Boloco, the Boston-based family of 18 restaurants & 300 team members, serves globally inspired burritos, bowls, smoothies & shakes in locations throughout New England. Boloco's mission is to positively impact the lives and futures of its people through bold and inspired food and practices.

57. Nathan Hodge, "Company Once Known as Blackwater Ditches Xe for Yet Another New Name," *Wall Street Journal*, 12 December 2011.

58. Dottie Enrico, "Companies Play Name-Change Game," *USA Today*, 28 December 1994, 4B.

59. Associated Press, "Protesters Gather as Chicago's Landmark Marshall Fields Store Is Replaced By Macy's," 9 September 2006; Sandra M. Jones, "A Year Later, Field's Followers Still Protesting, *Chicago Tribune*, 8 September 2007. For some discussion of the broader success of Macy's strategy, see Cotton Timberlake, "With Stores Nationwide, Macy's Goes Local," *Bloomberg BusinessWeek*, 4 October 2011.

60. Beth Snyder Bulik, "O, No! Overstock Backs Off O.co Name Change," *Advertising Age*, 14 November 2011; Matt Brownell, "Why 'O.co' Didn't Work for Overstock.com," www.mainstreet.com, 16 November 2011; George Anderson, "O.co Is out in Overstock Name Change Part Two," www.retailwire.com, 16 November 2011.

61. Mike Verdin, "Consignia: Nine Letters That Spelled Fiasco," *BBC News*, 31 May 2002.

62. Tania Mason, "PWC Defends Monday as IBM Removes Name," *Marketing*, 8 August 2002.

63. "Allegis: A $7 Million Name Is Grounded," *San Francisco Examiner*, 16 June 1987, C9.

64. P. Rajan Varadarajan and Anil Menon, "Cause-Related Marketing: A Coalignment of Marketing Strategy and Corporate Philanthropy," *Journal of Marketing* 52 (July 1988): 58–74.

65. Sankar Sen and C. B. Bhattacharya, "Does Doing Good Always Lead to Doing Better? Consumer Reactions to Corporate Social Responsibility," *Journal of Marketing Research* 38 (May 2001): 225–243; Xueming Luo and C. B. Bhattacharya, "The Debate over Doing Good: Corporate Social Performance, Strategic Marketing Levers, and Firm-Idiosyncratic Risk," *Journal of Marketing* 73 (November 2009): 198–213.

66. "Global Consumers Voice Demand for Greater Corporate Responsibility," www.coneinc.com, 4 October 2011; Paul N. Bloom, Steve Hoeffler, Kevin Lane Keller, and Carlos E. Basurto Meza, "How Social-Cause Marketing Affects Consumer Perceptions," *MIT Sloan Management Review* 47, no. 2 (2006): 49–55.

67. Paul N. Bloom, Steve Hoeffler, Kevin Lane Keller, and Carlos E. Basurto, "How Social-Cause Marketing Affects Consumer Perceptions," *MIT Sloan Management Review* (Winter 2006): 49–55; Carolyn J. Simmons and Karen L. Becker-Olsen, "Achieving Marketing Objectives through Social Sponsorships," *Journal of Marketing* 70 (October 2006): 154–169; Guido Berens, Cees B. M. van Riel, and Gerrit H. van Bruggen, "Corporate Associations and Consumer Product Responses: The Moderating Role of Corporate Brand Dominance," *Journal of Marketing* 69 (July 2005): 35–48; Donald R. Lichtenstein, Minette E. Drumwright, and Bridgette M. Braig, "The Effect of Social Responsibility on Customer Donations to Corporate-Supported Nonprofits," *Journal of Marketing* 68 (October 2004): 16–32; Stephen Hoeffler and Kevin Lane Keller, "Building Brand Equity through Corporate Societal Marketing," *Journal of Public Policy and Marketing* 21, no. 1 (Spring 2002): 78–89.

68. Note that enhanced credibility may depend on the type of brand involved; some proactive research shows how luxury brands can actually be hurt by CSR programs. See Carlos J. Torelli, Alokparna Basu Monga, and Andrew M. Kaikati, "Doing Poorly by Doing Good: Corporate Social Responsibility," *Journal of Consumer Research* (February 2012): 948–963.

69. Sankar Sen, Shuili Du, and C. B. Bhattacharya, "Building Relationships through Corporate Social Responsibility," in *Handbook of Brand Relationships*, eds. Joseph Priester, Deborah MacInnis, and C.W. Park (New York: M. E. Sharp, 2009): 195–211.

70. www.rhmc.org, accessed January 22, 2012.

71. C.B. Bhattacharya, Sankar Sen, and Daniel Korschun, "Using Corporate Social Responsibility to Win the War for Talent," *MIT Sloan Management Review* 49 (January 2008): 37–44; Xueming Luo and C. B. Bhattacharya, "Corporate Social Responsibility, Customer Satisfaction, and Market Value," *Journal of Marketing* 70 (October 2006): 1–18; Pat Auger, Paul Burke, Timothy Devinney, and Jordan J. Louviere, "What Will Consumers Pay for Social Product Features?" *Journal of Business Ethics* 42 (February 2003): 281–304; Dennis B. Arnett, Steve D. German, and Shelby D. Hunt, "The Identity Salience Model of Relationship Marketing Success: The Case of Nonprofit Marketing," *Journal of Marketing* 67 (April 2003): 89–105; C. B. Bhattacharya and Sankar Sen, "Consumer-Company Identification: A Framework for Understanding Consumers' Relationships with Companies," *Journal of Marketing* 67 (April 2003): 76–88; Sankar Sen and C. B. Bhattacharya, "Does Doing Good Always Lead to Doing Better? Consumer Reactions to Corporate Social Responsibility," *Journal of Marketing Research* 38 (May 2001): 225–244.

72. Xiaoli Nan and Kwangjun Heo, "Consumer Responses to Corporate Social Responsibility (CSR) Initiatives: Examining the Role of Brand-Cause Fit in Cause-Related Marketing," *Journal of Advertising* 36 (Summer 2007): 63–74.

73. Hamish Pringle and Marjorie Thompson, *Brand Spirit: How Cause Related Marketing Builds Brands* (Chichester, NY: Wiley, 1999); www.avonfoundation.org/breast-cancer-crusade, accessed February 27, 2012; David Hessekiel, "The Most Influential Cause-Marketing Programs of All Time," www.bestcm.posterous.com, accessed February 27, 2012.

74. David Hessekiel, "The Most Influential Cause-Marketing Programs of All Time," www.bestcm.posterous.com; www.yoplait.com; For a provocative discussion of some of the broader issues about cause marketing for breast cancer, see Gayle A. Sulik, *Pink Ribbon Blues: How Breast Cancer Culture Undermines Women's Health* (New York: Oxford University Press, 2011).

75. David Kiron, Nina Kruschwitz, Knut Haanaes, Martin Reeves, and Ingrid von Streng Velken, "Sustainability Nears a Tipping Point," *MIT Sloan Management Review* (Winter 2012): 69–74.

76. Geoff Colvin, "Grading Jeff Immelt," *Fortune*, 28 February 2011, 75–80. Beth Comstock, Ranjay Gulati, and Stephen Liguori, "Unleashing the Power of Marketing," *Harvard Business Review* (October 2010): 90–98; Bob Sechler, "GE's 'Green' Effort Fails to Strike Investors' Imagination," *Chicago Tribune*, 6 July 2008, 8; Anne Fisher, "America's Most Admired Companies," *Fortune*, 19 March 2007, 88–94; Daniel Fisher, "GE Turns Green," *Forbes*, 15 August 2005, 80–85; www.ecomagination.com/ progress/overview/letter.

77. Joanne Lipman, "Environmental Theme Hits Sour Notes," *Wall Street Journal*, 3 May 1990, B6.

78. Stephanie Rosenbloom, "Wal-Mart Unveils Plan to Make Supply Chain Greener," *New York Times*, 26 February 2010.

79. Paul Keegan, "The Trouble with Green Product Ratings, *Fortune*, 25 July 2011; Karen Weise, "Who's the Greenest of Them All?," *Bloomberg Businessweek*, 28 November 2011.

80. Wendy Koch, "Green, Green, It's Green They Say," *USA Today*, 21 April 2011.

81. Katherine White, Rhiannon MacDonnell, and John H. Ellard, "Belief in a Just World: Consumer Intentions and Behaviors Toward Ethical Products," *Journal of Marketing* 76 (January 2012): 103–118; Remi Trudel and June Cotte, "Does It Pay to Be Good?," *Sloan Management Review* 50 (Winter 2009): 61–68; Michael G. Luchs, Rebecca Walker Naylor, Julie R. Irwin, and Rajagopal Raghunathan, "The Sustainability Liability: Potential Negative Effects of Ethicality on Product Preference, *Journal of Marketing* 74 (September 2010): 18–31.

82. Ann Krorod, Amir Grinstein, and Luc Wathieu, "Go Green! Should Environmental Messages Be So Assertive?," *Journal of Marketing* 76 (January 2012): 95–102.

Introducing and Naming New Products and Brand Extensions

12

Learning Objectives

After reading this chapter, you should be able to

1. Define the different types of brand extensions.

2. List the main advantages and disadvantages of brand extensions.

3. Summarize how consumers evaluate extensions and how extensions contribute to parent brand equity.

4. Outline the key assumptions and success criteria for brand extensions.

After too many extensions began to harm its image, Gucci retrenched and adopted a more careful approach to stretching its brand that met with greater success.

Source: Lou Linwei/Alamy

403

Preview

Chapter 11 introduced the concept of brand architecture and described a process by which marketers can develop it. An important part of the process is the introduction of new products to help a brand grow and achieve its potential. Thus, this chapter considers in more detail the role of product strategy in creating, maintaining, and enhancing brand equity. Specifically, we'll develop guidelines to improve the introduction and naming of new products and brand extensions.

Let's start with a little historical perspective. For years firms tended to follow the lead of Procter & Gamble, Coca-Cola, and other major consumer goods marketers that essentially avoided introducing any new products using an existing brand name. Over time, tight economic conditions, a need for growth, and competitive realities forced firms to rethink their "one brand–one product" policies. Recognizing that brands are among their most valuable assets, many firms have since decided to leverage that value by introducing a host of new products under some of their strongest brand names.

Many seek to build "power" or "mega" brands that establish a broad market footprint, appealing to multiple customer segments with multiple products all underneath one brand umbrella. Unilever's Dove brand has made successful forays from its roots in soap into a range of skin care and body care products, backed by its "Campaign for Real Beauty" media campaign. At the same time, marketers are also realizing that too many product variations can be counterproductive, and ill-advised brand proliferation may actually repel consumers.

We've learned much about the best-practice management of brand extensions. This chapter begins by describing brand extensions and outlining their advantages and disadvantages. Then we present a simple model of how consumers evaluate brand extensions and offer managerial guidelines for introducing and naming new products and brand extensions. We conclude with a comprehensive summary of some of the key academic research findings on brand extensions. Brand Focus 12.0 provides a detailed checklist to help marketers evaluate the viability of a brand extension.

NEW PRODUCTS AND BRAND EXTENSIONS

As background, first consider the sources of growth for a firm. One useful perspective is Ansoff's product/market expansion grid, also known as the growth matrix. As in Figure 12-1, we can categorize growth strategies according to whether they rely on existing or new products, and whether they target existing or new customers or markets. Branding Brief 12-1 describes McDonald's growth strategies along these lines.

Although existing products can further penetrate existing customer markets or push into additional ones (the focus of Chapter 13), new-product introductions are often vital to the long-run success of a firm. A discussion of all the issues in effectively managing the development and introduction of new products is beyond the scope of this chapter. Here we'll simply address some brand equity implications of new products.[1]

First we'll establish some terminology. When a firm introduces a new product, it has three choices for branding it:

1. It can develop a new brand, individually chosen for the new product.
2. It can apply one of its existing brands.
3. It can use a combination of a new brand and an existing brand.

	Current Products	**New Products**
Current Markets	Market Penetration Strategy	Product Development Strategy
New Markets	Market Development Strategy	Diversification Strategy

FIGURE 12-1
Ansoff's Growth Matrix

A *brand extension* occurs when a firm uses an established brand name to introduce a new product (approach 2 or 3). As we noted in Chapter 11, when a new brand is combined with an existing brand (approach 3), the brand extension can also be a *sub-brand*. An existing brand that gives birth to a brand extension is the *parent brand*. If the parent brand is already associated with multiple products through brand extensions, then it may also be called a *family brand*.

Brand extensions fall into two general categories:[2]

- *Line extension:* Marketers apply the parent brand to a new product that targets a new market segment within a product category the parent brand currently serves. A line extension often adds a different flavor or ingredient variety, a different form or size, or a different application for the brand (like Head & Shoulders Dry Scalp shampoo).
- *Category extension:* Marketers apply the parent brand to enter a different product category from the one it currently serves (like Swiss Army watches).

The vast majority of new products in any one year are brand extensions. In 2009, 93 percent of the new food or beverage products with first-year sales that exceeded $7.5 million were brand extensions. Some notable food or beverage launches that year were Campbell's Select Harvest soups, Bud Light Lime beer, Arnold Select Sandwich Thins rolls, and Kellogg's FiberPlus snack bars.[3] Some successful nonfood or beverage launches were Tide Total Care liquid laundry detergent, Quilted Northern Ultra Plush toilet paper, Gillette Venus Embrace razor, and Bounty ExtraSoft paper towels. All these new products were launched as extensions.[4]

Nevertheless, many new products are still introduced each year as new brands. A slew of new technology brands have recently begun to make their mark, such as SurveyMonkey online survey tool, Spotify music Web site, Lookout mobile security software, and Twilio voice and text messaging application facilitator. Dropbox makes downloadable software that lets users digitally store and share documents for a fee. New brands are not restricted to technology, however—consider the Chobani story.

CHOBANI

In just a few short years, Chobani yogurt has challenged long-time market leaders Yoplait and Dannon and has become the number-one brand in the exploding Greek-style yogurt category. It even topped a January 2012 IRI InfoScan review of retail yogurt sales. Called "strained" yogurt in other parts of the world because it is typically strained in a cloth or paper bag or filter to remove the whey, Greek-style yogurt has a consistency between that of yogurt and cheese, but with yogurt's distinctive sour taste. Greek-style yogurt now makes up 25 percent of all U.S. yogurt sales, with Chobani enjoying 60 percent of those sales. The brand was started by a Turkish immigrant, Hamdi Ulukaya, who came to the United States to go to college in 1994. Intrigued when an old Kraft yogurt factory in upstate New York came up for sale, he and his initial team spent a year and a half tinkering with the product. The first Chobani yogurt was introduced in 2007. Sales exploded, especially after the brand was picked up BJ's Wholesale Club and Costco in 2009, and in less than five years, it had become a rapidly growing $700 million business. In 2011, the company made its first acquisition, an Australian dairy firm called Bead Foods, as a first step toward international distribution.[5]

The marketplace will always reward an innovative, well-marketed new product as happened with Chobani Greek yogurt.

Source: Chobani

Growing the McDonald's Brand

Over the last decade, McDonald's has faced a challenging environment. Market saturation, global health concerns, and a slumping economy have presented significant obstacles to its growth. To overcome these, the company has employed a number of different growth strategies that we can classify using the Ansoff growth share matrix. As a result of these strategies, the company's financial fortunes have rebounded, and McDonald's has outperformed many of its peers in revenue growth. The brand has even been credited with producing a "halo effect" that is "driving growth for the entire quick-service restaurant category."

Market Penetration

For a long time, McDonald's increased its market penetration just by introducing hundreds of new outlets each year. But by 2002, markets had become saturated and sales had slumped. On becoming CEO in 2004, James Skinner adopted a new corporate motto, "Better, not bigger." Rather than trying to grow by adding new restaurants, McDonald's would grow by generating greater returns from the ones it had.

Thus, instead of investing in new real estate, the firm made huge investments in upgrading the facilities and operations of existing stores. One important way McDonald's made it easier for its customers to spend more money was by expanding to 24-hour service at many stores. To better accommodate these longer hours, the menu has been constantly fine-tuned so there are offerings to suit any meal or snack opportunity.

Breakfast has become an essential part of the McDonald's revenue equation. A quarter of its domestic revenue—over $6 billion—and half its profits come from breakfast, which includes the highly successful McMuffin and McGriddle breakfast sandwiches. Snack Wraps and smoothies entice customers between meals. Snack Wraps are ideal for drive-thru customers who need to have one hand on the steering wheel; 60 percent of sales are drive-thru generated.

McDonald's decade-long "I'm Lovin' It" global advertising campaign has served as the perfect vehicle to support new product launches and enhance loyalty. Translated into a number of languages worldwide, it replaced some

One way McDonald's grows its brand is through market development and expanding in overseas markets such as Japan.
Source: Iain Masterton / Alamy

20 different ad platforms that had been running in different regions.

Market Development

McDonald's has made concerted efforts to expand globally through the years, and its progress has been astounding. There are over 33,000 restaurants worldwide in 119 different countries today, and 1.7 million employees serve 64 million customers

Even in a product category as simple and established as hamburgers—U.S. consumers eat 13 billion burgers a year, 4.3 for every man, woman, and child—new brands can appear. *Forbes* magazine dubbed Denver-based Smashburger as one of the most promising U.S. companies on the basis of its "thoughtful product design and deft execution," and the fact that it offered "more interesting fare and a (small) dash of ambience at a reasonable price premium." And Shake Shack's updated "roadside burger stand" now brings in almost a third of the profits of Union Square Hospitality Group, which owns three of the *Zagat Guide*'s top five dining establishments in Manhattan![6]

daily in the United States, Europe, the Middle East, the Asia-Pacific region, Africa, Canada, and Latin America.

One key to its global success has been McDonald's willingness to adapt its menu to different cultural preferences and regional tastes. The chain offers specialized menu items, such as the Teriyaki Burger in Japan and Vegetable McNuggets in England. In India—where beef is not consumed because cows are sacred—it introduced the Maharaja Mac, made from mutton. The company also developed spicy sauces, such as McMasala and McImli.

McDonald's targets different demographic and psychographic market segments as well. The product offerings in Happy Meals have been tweaked through the years to appeal to both children and their parents. More recently, McDonald's sought to develop a new U.S. market by attracting twenty- and thirty-something females with premium salads served with Newman's Own dressing, and other lighter menu options. McDonald's rapidly became the number-one salad brand in the United States.

Product Development

McDonald's found its popularity in its core markets under threat as international concern grew about the role of fast food in poor health and obesity, highlighted by the 2001 book *Fast Food Nation* and the 2004 movie *Super Size Me*, among other critiques. The company posted its first quarterly loss in 2002, and as a consequence, it "needed to look at why its customers weren't buying and recognize that they wanted better choices and healthier options."

McDonald's responded by overhauling its menu, removing "Super Size" options and adding healthier options such as a number of fresh salads, healthier versions of kids' Happy Meals, and adult versions that included salad, bottled water, and a pedometer to encourage exercise. Other health initiatives the firm undertook included its Balanced Lifestyles platform for children, which promoted healthy food choices, education, and physical activity; and its Go Active! campaign to promote active lifestyles. Both were endorsed by Bob Greene, Oprah Winfrey's personal trainer.

The shift in focus toward healthy eating and physical activity was emphasized by McDonald's recasting of Ronald McDonald as its "Chief Happiness Officer," a sports enthusiast who donned a more athletic version of his traditional yellow-and-red clown suit and snowboarded, skateboarded, and juggled fruit in a new TV spot.

The company also tapped into the growing premium-coffee trend in the United States by launching McDonald's Premium Roast coffee, which retails for about 35 percent less than a cup of Starbucks coffee. McDonald's also introduced a new line of premium hamburgers—one-third-of-a-pound Angus Burgers. The 20-piece Chicken McNuggets allowed the company to enter the shared-meals segment dominated by KFC.

Diversification

Although McDonald's has largely focused on expansion through market penetration, market development, and product development, it has done some diversification to target new customers with new service offerings. It extended its brand in 2001 with the opening of its first domestic McCafé, a gourmet coffee shop inspired by the success of Starbucks that had debuted in Portugal and Austria. Another extension is McTreat, an ice cream and dessert shop.

While several Golden Arch Hotels in Switzerland failed to make it and were sold off, experimentation continues. In Hong Kong, three McDonald's locations offer wedding packages for loyal couples. The basic Warm and Sweet Wedding Package for 50 guests goes for under $1,300. An additional $165 covers a rented "gown" of pearly white balloons.

Sources: Joanna Doonar, "Life in the Fast Lane," *Brand Strategy*, 6 October 2004, 20; Gina Piccolo, "Fries with That Fruit?" *Los Angeles Times*, 18 July 2005, F1; Pallavi Gogoi and Michael Arndt, "Hamburger Hell," *BusinessWeek*, 3 March 2003, 104; Kate MacArthur, "Big Mac's Back," *Advertising Age*, 13 December 2004, S1; Michael Arndt, McDonald's 24/7," *Bloomberg BusinessWeek*, 5 February 2007; "McDonald's to Diversify into 'Shared Meals' Segment," www.room54.co, 13 February 2011; Dan Malovany and Maria Pilar Clark, "McSmart and McSnackable: McDonald's New Product Strategy Boosts Bottom Line," *Stagnito's New Products Magazine*, June 2007; Stefan Michel, "McDonald's Failed Venture in Hotels," www.knowledgenetwork.thunderbird.edu, 11 July 2008; Hillary Brehnhouse, "Want Fries With That Ring? McDonald's Offers Weddings," *Time*, 7 March 2001.

Despite such success stories, most new products are branded and launched as extensions. To understand why, we'll next outline some of the main advantages and disadvantages of brand extensions.

ADVANTAGES OF EXTENSIONS

For most firms, the question is not *whether* to extend the brand, but when, where, and how to extend it. Well-planned and well-implemented extensions offer a number of advantages that we can broadly categorize as those that facilitate new-product acceptance and those that provide feedback benefits to the parent brand or company as whole (see Figure 12-2).

Facilitate New Product Acceptance

Improve brand image
Reduce risk perceived by customers
Increase the probability of gaining distribution and trial
Increase efficiency of promotional expenditures
Reduce costs of introductory and follow-up marketing programs
Avoid cost of developing a new brand
Allow for packaging and labeling efficiencies
Permit consumer variety-seeking

Provide Feedback Benefits to the Parent Brand and Company

Clarify brand meaning
Enhance the parent brand image
Bring new customers into brand franchise and increase market coverage
Revitalize the brand
Permit subsequent extensions

FIGURE 12-2

Advantages of Brand
Extension

Facilitate New-Product Acceptance

The high failure rate of new products has been well documented. Marketing analysts estimate that only 2 of 10 new products will be successful, or maybe even as few as 1 of 10. Brand extensions can certainly suffer some of the same shortcomings as any new product. Nevertheless, a new product introduced as a brand extension may be more likely to succeed, at least to some degree, because the advantages we describe below work to increase acceptance.

Improve Brand Image.   As we saw in Chapter 2, one of the advantages of a well-known and well-liked brand is that consumers form expectations of its performance over time. They can form similar inferences and expectations about the likely composition and performance of a brand extension, based on what they already know about the brand itself and the extent to which they feel this information is relevant to the new product.[7]

These inferences may improve the strength, favorability, and uniqueness of the extension's brand associations. For example, when Sony first introduced its laptop and personal computer tailored for multimedia applications, Vaio, consumers may have been more likely to feel comfortable with its anticipated performance because of their experience with and knowledge of other Sony products than if Sony had branded it as something completely new.

Reduce Risk Perceived by Customers.   One research study found that the most important factor for predicting initial trial of a new product was the extent to which it connected to a known family brand.[8] Extensions from well-known corporate brands such as General Electric, Hewlett-Packard, Motorola, or others may communicate longevity and sustainability. Although corporate brands can lack specific product associations because of the breadth of products attached to their name, their established reputation for introducing high-quality products and standing behind them may be an important risk-reducer for consumers.[9]

Perceptions of corporate credibility—in terms of the firm's expertise and trustworthiness—can be valuable associations in introducing brand extensions.[10] Similarly, although widely extended supermarket family brands such as Betty Crocker, Green Giant, Del Monte, and Pepperidge Farm may lack specific product meaning, they may still stand for product quality in the minds of consumers and, by reducing perceived risk, facilitate the adoption of brand extensions.

Increase the Probability of Gaining Distribution and Trial.   The potential for increased consumer demand for a new product introduced as an extension may convince retailers to stock and promote it. One study indicated that brand reputation was a key screening criteria of gatekeepers making new-product decisions at supermarkets.[11]

Increase Efficiency of Promotional Expenditures.   From a marketing communications perspective, one obvious advantage of introducing a new product as a brand extension is that the introductory campaign does not have to create awareness of both the brand and the new product but instead can concentrate on only the new product itself.[12]

Several research studies document this benefit. One study of 98 consumer brands in 11 markets found that successful brand extensions spent less on advertising than comparable new-name entries spent.[13] Another comprehensive study found similar results, indicating that the average advertising-to-sales ratio for brand extensions was 10 percent, compared with 19 percent for new brands.[14]

Reduce Costs of Introductory and Follow-Up Marketing Programs.   Because of these push and pull considerations in distribution and promotion, it has been estimated that a firm can save 40–80 percent on the estimated \$30–\$50 million it can cost to launch a new supermarket product nationally in the United States. Other efficiencies can result after the launch. For example, when a brand becomes associated with multiple products, advertising can be more cost-effective for the family brand as a whole.

Avoid Cost of Developing a New Brand.   Developing new brand elements is an art and a science. To conduct the necessary consumer research and employ skilled personnel to design high-quality brand names, logos, symbols, packages, characters, and slogans can be quite expensive, and there is no assurance of success. As the number of available—and appealing—brand names keeps shrinking, legal conflicts grow more likely. To avoid these, a global trademark search is a must for any major new brand launch or rebranding, and it can cost millions of dollars.

Allow for Packaging and Labeling Efficiencies.   Similar or identical packages and labels for extensions can result in lower production costs and, if coordinated properly, more prominence in the retail store where they can create a "billboard" effect. For example, Stouffer's offers a variety of frozen entrees with identical orange packaging that increases their visibility when they are stocked together in the freezer. Coca-Cola soft drinks and Pepperidge Farm cookies achieve a similar effect.

Permit Consumer Variety-Seeking.   If marketers offer a portfolio of brand variants within a product category, consumers who need a change—because of boredom or satiation—can switch without having to leave the brand family. A complement of line extensions can also encourage customers to use the brand to a greater extent or in different ways. Even to compete effectively in some categories, marketers may need to have multiple items that together form a cohesive product line. A company that seems to offer something for everyone is L'Oréal.

L'ORÉAL

Concentrating solely on beauty and personal care since its founding in 1907, L'Oréal has become a global powerhouse through its extensive brand portfolio. The firm has products for virtually every channel, price point, and market. Garnier is its fast-growing mass brand. L'Oréal Paris is at the higher end of the mass range, combining sophisticated cosmetics at accessible price points. Lancôme is the premium luxury brand. L'Oréal adheres to a strict channel exclusivity strategy. Professional products (Matrix and Redken) are sold at hair salons, consumer product brands (Maybelline and Garnier) at retail stores, including drug stores and food stores, luxury products (Biotherm and Lancôme) at specialty stores or department stores, and active cosmetic brands (La Roche-Posay) at dispensing dermatologists and pharmacies. L'Oréal also owns two retail chain brands—Kiehl's and the Body Shop. Geographically, the company casts a wide net. Many of its brands are sold in as many as 130 countries; Lancôme is sold in 160. Recently, L'Oréal has placed much importance on emerging markets, China and India in particular, and it aims to double its existing customer base of 1 billion customers worldwide by 2021. The firm invests heavily in research and development (earmarking approximately 3 percent of net sales) in the belief that science and technology and the quality of its products are the keys to success. Roughly 15–20 percent of the product lines turn over in any given year, due to product improvements or the launch of new products. The company's first CMO, Marc Speichert, was hired from Colgate in part to orchestrate marketing across the wide variety of brands. He is also putting more emphasis on digital and mobile strategies to engage customers but without abandoning the traditional magazine print ads that have served beauty brands well through the years.[15]

Lancôme is one of L'Oréal's most successful global brands.
Source: Jeffrey Ufberg/Getty Images for Lancôme

Provide Feedback Benefits to the Parent Brand

Besides facilitating acceptance of new products, brand extensions can also provide positive feedback to the parent brand in a number of ways.

Clarify Brand Meaning.   Extensions can help clarify the meaning of a brand to consumers and define the kinds of markets in which it competes, an important first step in the brand architecture process. Thus, through brand extensions, Hunt's means "tomato," Clairol means "hair coloring," Gerber means "baby care," and Nabisco means "baked cookies and crackers." Figure 12-3 shows how other brands that have introduced multiple brand extensions have broadened their meaning to consumers.

As Chapter 11 noted, broader brand meaning often is necessary so that firms avoid "marketing myopia" and do not mistakenly draw narrow boundaries around their brand, either missing market opportunities or becoming vulnerable to well-planned competitive strategies. Thus, as Harvard's Ted Levitt pointed out in a pioneering article, railroads are not just in the "railroad" business but are also in the "transportation" business.[16]

Thinking more broadly about product meaning can easily inspire different marketing programs and new-product opportunities. For example, when Steelcase introduced the slogan, "A Smarter Way to Work," it reflected the fact that the company had defined its business not as manufacturing desks, chairs, file cabinets, and credenzas but as "helping to enhance office productivity." For some brands, creating broader meaning is critical and may be the only way to expand sales.

FIGURE 12-3
Expanding Brand Meaning through Extensions

Brand	Original Product	Extension Products	New Brand Meaning
Weight Watchers	Fitness centers	Low-calorie foods	Weight loss and maintenance
Sunkist	Oranges	Vitamins, juices	Good health
Kellogg's	Cereal	Nutri-Grain bars, Special K bars	Healthy snacking
Aunt Jemima	Pancake mixes	Syrups, frozen waffles	Breakfast foods

In some cases, it is advantageous to establish a portfolio of related products that completely satisfy consumer needs in a certain area. For example, many specific-purpose cleaning products have broadened their meaning to be seen as multipurpose, including Lysol, Comet, and Mr. Clean. Similarly, the $245 billion enterprise software market is characterized by a few megabrands like Oracle and SAP that compete in multiple segments with multiple product offerings. Although at one time these different brands were limited to a few specific products, they have broadened their meaning through brand extensions and acquisitions to represent "complete business software solutions."[17]

Enhance the Parent Brand Image.   According to the customer-based brand equity model, one desirable outcome of a successful brand extension is that it may enhance the parent brand image by strengthening an existing brand association, improving the favorability of an existing brand association, adding a new brand association, or a combination of these.

One common way a brand extension affects the parent brand image is by helping clarify its core brand values and associations. Core brand associations, as we defined them in Chapter 3, are those attributes and benefits that come to characterize all the products in the brand line and, as a result, are those with which consumers often have the strongest associations. For example, Nike has expanded from running shoes to other athletic shoes, athletic clothing, and athletic equipment, strengthening its associations to "peak performance" and "sports" in the process.

Another type of association that successful brand extensions may improve is consumer perceptions of the company's credibility. For example, one research study showed that a successful corporate brand extension led to improved perceptions of the expertise, trustworthiness, and likability of the company.[18]

Choosing to launch a new product or service with a completely new brand name means forgoing these feedback benefits. In the late 1990s, with the advent of the Internet, several firms introduced online versions of their services under a separate brand name. For example, Bank One, a leading brand at the time, opened its online bank services under the Wingspan brand name. Besides increasing the difficulty and expense of launching a new brand, these companies also lost the opportunity to modernize the parent brand image and improve its technological credentials. In many cases, the new ventures failed and their capabilities were folded back into the parent organization.

Bring New Customers into the Brand Franchise and Increase Market Coverage.   Line extensions can benefit the parent brand by expanding market coverage, such as by offering a product benefit whose absence may have prevented consumers from trying the brand. For example, when Tylenol introduced a capsule form of its acetaminophen pain reliever, it was able to attract consumers who had difficulty swallowing tablets and might have otherwise avoided the brand.

Creating "news" and bringing attention to the parent brand may benefit the family brand as a whole. Through the skillful introduction of extensions, Tide as a family brand has managed to maintain its market leadership and actual market share—roughly 40 percent in the United States—from the 1950s to the present. Ocean Spray has successfully introduced a wide range of extensions to offer consumers more ways to enjoy cranberries.

OCEAN SPRAY

The growers' cooperative Ocean Spray Cranberries, Inc., found itself in a difficult position around 2004. With growth in carbonated beverages slowing, Coca-Cola and PepsiCo began to move aggressively into noncarbonated drinks, including juices. Ocean Spray contemplated selling the brand to PepsiCo, but ultimately the coop voted to remain independent. To remain competitive with these larger players, however, Ocean Spray has continued to introduce a number of brand extensions, supported by well-integrated marketing campaigns. Its expanded product mix now includes regular, diet, and light versions of many of its popular cocktail, juice drink, and blends beverages; Craisins dried cranberries and trail mix; cranberry sauce; fresh fruit; and fruit-flavored snacks. The coop has introduced new flavor varieties based on blueberry and cherry and a line of energy juice drinks and sparkling beverages.

Its "Straight from the Bog" ad campaign showed two folksy farmers waist-deep in a cranberry bog humorously extolling the virtues of various Ocean Spray products. The campaign was reinforced by a host of events, promotions, and other PR activities.[19]

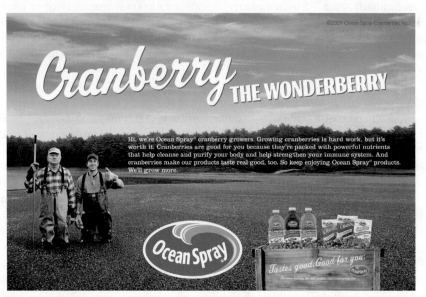

Ocean Spray has expanded its brand into a number of different markets via some creative marketing.

Source: Courtesy of Ocean Spray Cranberries, Inc.

Revitalize the Brand. Sometimes brand extensions can be a means to renew interest in and liking for the brand. A classic example is with the General Motors luxury brand name-plate Cadillac, whose sales were fading fast by the end of the 1990s. At that time, many marketing experts put the brand on life support and predicted its demise. The introduction of the sleek CTS sedan in 1999—backed by a powerful Led Zeppelin soundtrack in the launch ads—signaled that things were changing for the brand. The follow-up introduction of the flashy, muscular Escalade SUV, however, completely transformed the brand's image. Seen as urban and edgy, the Escalade further modernized the aging brand, making it more contemporary and relevant.[20]

Permit Subsequent Extensions. One benefit of a successful extension—especially a category extension—is that it may serve as the basis for subsequent extensions. Consider how Billabong transcended its surfer origins to introduce products that tapped into related lifestyle activities.

BILLABONG

The Billabong brand was established in 1973 by Gordon Merchant, who wanted to create a brand that had "functional products for surfers to help us better enjoy our sport." During the 1970s and 1980s, Billabong established its brand credibility with the young surfing community as a designer and producer of quality surf apparel. In the early 1980s, it began to sell its products in Japan, Europe, and the United States through licensees. In the late 1980s and early 1990s, the brand extended into other youth-oriented areas, such as snowboarding and skateboarding, but sticking to its core brand proposition: contemporary, relevant, innovative products of consistent high quality. In 2004, the company launched an entirely new brand called Honolua Surf Co., inspired by Hawaiian surf styles. Later years saw various brand acquisitions too: Nixon Inc., a premium watch and accessories maker in the surf, skate, and snowboard markets; Von Zipper edgy eyewear and goggles, Element shoes, Kustom footwear, and Mrs. Palmers surf wax and accessories. As a result of its consistent growth, Billabong was ranked the eighth most valuable brand in Australia, with an estimated value of $1.1 billion.[21]

Billabong's strong lifestyle appeal has allowed the brand to enter several new categories beyond surfing such as snowboarding and skateboarding.

Source: Martin Berry/Alamy

DISADVANTAGES OF BRAND EXTENSIONS

Despite their potential advantages, brand extensions have a number of disadvantages (see Figure 12-4).

Can Confuse or Frustrate Consumers

Different varieties of line extensions may confuse and perhaps even frustrate consumers about which version of the product is the "right one" for them. With 16 varieties of Coke and 35 versions of Crest toothpaste, consumers can easily feel overwhelmed.[22] For example, one study found that consumers were more likely to make a purchase after sampling a product (and being given a coupon) when there were six product flavors to sample than when there were 24.[23]

So, in some situations, greater product variety may induce shoppers to buy less. Consumers may reject new extensions for tried and true favorites or all-purpose versions that claim to supersede more specialized product versions. The global success of Colgate Total is certainly due in part to its positioning—reflected in its name—as an inclusive product that contains all the necessary or desirable toothpaste benefits.

Many retailers do not have enough shelf or display space to stock the large number of new products and brands continually being introduced even if they wanted to. So some consumers may be disappointed when they're unable to find an advertised brand extension because a retailer is unable or unwilling to stock it. If a firm launches extensions that consumers deem inappropriate, they may question the integrity and competence of the brand.

Can confuse or frustrate consumers
Can encounter retailer resistance
Can fail and hurt parent brand image
Can succeed but cannibalize sales of parent brand
Can succeed but diminish identification with any one category
Can succeed but hurt the image of parent brand
Can dilute brand meaning
Can cause the company to forgo the chance to develop a new brand

FIGURE 12-4

Disadvantages of
Brand Extension

Can Encounter Retailer Resistance

The number of consumer packaged-goods stock-keeping units (SKUs) outpaces the growth of retail space in year-on-year percentage growth. Own-brand or private-label goods also continue to grow as a percentage of total grocery sales. Many brands now come in a multitude of different forms. For example, Campbell's has introduced a number of different lines of soup—including Condensed, Home Cookin', Chunky, Healthy Request, Select, Simply Home, Ready-to-Serve Classic, and portable Soup at Hand—and offers more than 100 flavors in all.

As a result, it has become virtually impossible for a grocery store or supermarket to offer all the different varieties available across all the different brands in any one product category. Moreover, retailers often feel that many line extensions are merely "me-too" products that duplicate existing brands in a product category and should not be stocked even if there is space. Walmart, the biggest retailer in the United States, attempts to stock the items that sell best, dropping as many as 20 percent of slow-moving items from its shelves annually.[24]

Attacking brand proliferation, an influential Food Marketing Institute (FMI) study examined the effects of stock-keeping unit (SKU) reduction in six test categories (cereal, toothpaste, salad dressing, toilet tissue, spaghetti sauce, and pet food). The study showed that retailers could reduce their SKUs by 5–25 percent without hurting sales or consumer perceptions of the variety offered by their stores. The FMI "product variety" study recommended that retailers systematically identify duplicated and slow-moving items and eliminate them to maximize profitability.[25]

Many large packaged food brands took this advice to heart and began trimming their product lines in order to focus on their top-selling brands. Heinz culled 40 percent of its items over a two-year period, a move that yielded an operating income increase of 18 percent. General Mills reduced the number of products it sells by 20 percent, while Hershey Foods made similar cuts.[26] Additional academic research has shed light on how to reduce brand proliferation, as summarized in The Science of Branding 12-1.

Can Fail and Hurt Parent Brand Image

The worst possible scenario for an extension is not only to fail, but to harm the parent brand image in the process. Unfortunately, these negative feedback effects can sometimes happen.

Consider General Motors' experience with the Cadillac Cimarron. This model, introduced in the early 1980s, was a "relative" of models in other GM lines, such as the Pontiac 2000 and Chevrolet Cavalier. The target market was less-affluent buyers who were seeking a small luxury car but could not really afford a full-size Cadillac. Not only was the Cadillac Cimarron unsuccessful at generating new sales with this market segment, but existing Cadillac owners hated it. They felt it was inconsistent with the large size and prestige image they expected from Cadillac. As a result, Cadillac sales dropped significantly in the mid-1980s. Looking back, one GM executive offered the following insights:[27]

> The decision was made purely on the basis of short-sighted profit and financial analysis, with no accounting for its effect on long-run customer loyalty or, if you will, equity. A typical financial analysis would argue that the Cimarron will rarely steal sales from Cadillac's larger cars, so any sale would be one that we wouldn't have gotten otherwise. The people who were most concerned with such long-range issues raised serious objections but the bean counters said, "Oh no, we'll get this many dollars for every model sold." There was no thinking about brand equity. We paid for the Cimarron down the road. Everyone now realizes that using the model to extend the name was a horrible mistake.

Even if an extension initially succeeds, by linking the brand to multiple products, the firm increases the risk that an unexpected problem or even a tragedy with one product in the brand family can tarnish the image of some or all the remaining products. The Audi is a classic example.

THE SCIENCE OF BRANDING 12-1

When Is Variety a Bad Thing?

Today, consumers face an unprecedented number of choices. Supermarkets can contain more than 40,000 products, up from only 7,000 in the 1960s, and product features continue to multiply. Take toothpaste. A supermarket can stock over 100 varieties depending on brand name (Colgate, Crest, Tom's, Mentadent), benefits (tartar control, whitening, breath freshening, sensitive gums), flavors (regular, mint, cinnamon, citrus), and forms (gel, paste). Online shopping makes it easier to offer even more choice in many categories.

Consumers may like the idea of having more choice—the flexibility and sense of freedom it gives, the greater likelihood of finding just the right alternative—but negative consequences often arise too. Actually finding the optimal choice can require much effort and result in inner conflict and regret. The difficulty of making a decision can be overwhelming or demotivating, and some consumers may just choose to walk away.

Product assortment has been defined as the number of SKUs offered within a single product category. Consumer perception of assortment is one of the top three criteria, along with location and price, that affect their retail loyalty. Manufacturers and retailers are thus keenly interested in factors affecting the optimal product assortment size for a brand.

Consistent with the Food Marketing Institute study, much additional research has supported the conclusion that reducing the number of different items stocked does not necessarily adversely affect category volume, especially if the category already has a lot of SKUs or a few SKUs that are big sellers. Research has also found that consumer perceptions of variety assortment depend on factors such as the similarity of items for the brand, the amount of allocated shelf space, and the presence of the consumer's favorite item.

Marketers and retailers can improve perceptions of product variety in a category or for a brand. For example, organized displays have been found to be better for large brand assortments, whereas unorganized displays are better for small brand assortments. Asymmetrical assortments—in which some items for a brand appear more frequently than others—have also been found to lead to perceptions of greater assortment.

Sources: Steven M. Cristol and Peter Sealey, *Simplicity Marketing* (New York: Free Press, 2000); Sheena S. Iyengar and Mark Lepper, "When Choice Is Demotivating: Can One Desire Too Much of a Good Thing?," *Journal of Personality and Social Psychology* 79 (December 2000): 995–1006; Peter Boatwright and Joseph C. Nunes, "Reducing Assortment: An Attribute-Based Approach," *Journal of Marketing* 65 (July 2001): 50–63; Sheena S. Iyengar and Barry Schwartz, "Doing Better but Feeling Worse: Looking for the 'Best' Job Undermines Satisfaction," *Psychological Science* 17, no. 2 (2006): 143–150; Roland T. Rust, Debora Viana Thompson, and Rebecca W. Hamilton, "Defeating Feature Fatigue," *Harvard Business Review*, February 2006, 98–107; Laurens M. Sloot, Dennis Fok, and Peter C. Verhoef, "The Short- and Long-Term Impact of an Assortment Reduction on Category Sales," *Journal of Marketing Research* 43 (November 2006): 536–548; Jie Zhang and Aradhna Krishna, "Brand Level Effects of Stockkeeping Unit Reductions," *Journal of Marketing Research* 44 (November 2007): 545–559; Susan M. Broniarczyk, Wayne D. Hoyer, and Leigh McAlister, "Consumers' Perceptions of the Assortment Offered in a Grocery Category: The Impact of Item Reduction," *Journal of Marketing Research* 35 (May 1998): 166–176; Susan M. Broniarczyk, "Product Assortment," in *Handbook of Consumer Psychology*, Chapter 30, eds. Curt P. Haugtvedt, Paul M. Herr, and Frank R. Kardes (Mahwah, NJ: Lawrence Erlbaum Associates, 2008), 755–779; Susan M. Broniarczyk and Wayne D. Hoyer, "Retail Assortment: More ≠ Better," in *Retailing in the 21st Century*, eds. Manfred Krafft and Murali K. Mantrala (New York: Springer Publishing, 2005), 225–238.

The 1980s' launch of Cadillac Cimarron was a disaster for General Motors because it alienated existing customers and at the same time failed to attract new ones.

Source: Newscast/Alamy

AUDI

Starting in 1986, the Audi 5000 car suffered a tidal wave of negative publicity and word-of-mouth because it was alleged to have a "sudden acceleration" problem that resulted in an alarming number of sometimes fatal accidents. Even though there was little concrete evidence to support the claims, Audi, in a public relations disaster, attributed the problem to the clumsy way U.S. drivers operated the car, and U.S. sales declined from 74,000 in 1985 to 21,000 in 1989. As might be expected, the damage was most severe for the Audi 5000, but the adverse publicity also spilled over to the 4000 model. The Quattro was affected to a lesser extent, perhaps because it was distanced by its distinct branding and advertising strategy.[28]

Understanding when unsuccessful brand extensions may damage the parent brand is important, and later in the chapter we'll develop a conceptual model to address the topic and describe some important findings. On a more positive note, however, one reason an unsuccessful brand extension may not necessarily damage the parent brand is the very reason the extension may have been unsuccessful in the first place—hardly anyone may even have heard of it! Thus, the silver lining when a brand extension fails to achieve sufficient brand awareness or distribution is that the parent brand is more likely to survive unscathed. But as we'll argue below, product failures in which the extension is found to be inadequate on the basis of performance are more likely to hurt perceptions of the parent brand than these "market" failures.

Can Succeed but Cannibalize Sales of Parent Brand

Even if sales of a brand extension are high and meet targets, success may result merely from consumers switching from existing offerings of the parent brand—in effect cannibalizing it. Line extensions designed to establish points-of-parity with current offerings in the parent brand category particularly may result in cannibalization. Sometimes, however, such intrabrand shifts in sales are not undesirable; we can think of them as a form of "preemptive cannibalization." In other words, without the introduction of the line extension, consumers might have switched to a competing brand instead.

For example, Diet Coke's point-of-parity of "good taste" and point-of-difference of "low calories" undoubtedly took some sales from regular Coke drinkers. In fact, although U.S. sales of Coca-Cola's cola products have held steady since 1980, sales in 1980 came from Coke alone, whereas sales today include significant contributions from Diet Coke, Coke Zero, Cherry Coke, and uncaffeinated and flavored forms of Coke. Without the introduction of those extensions, however, some of Coke's sales might have gone to competing Pepsi products or other soft drinks or beverages instead.

Can Succeed but Diminish Identification with Any One Category

One risk of linking multiple products to a single brand is that the brand may not be strongly identified with any one product. Thus, brand extensions may obscure the brand's identification with its original categories, reducing brand awareness.[29] For example, when Cadbury became linked in the United Kingdom to mainstream food products such as Smash instant potatoes, its marketers may have run the risk of weakening its association to fine chocolates. Pepperidge Farm is another brand that has been accused of extending so much (into pastries, bread, and snacks) that it has lost its original meaning of "delicious, high-quality cookies."

Some notable—and fascinating—counterexamples to these dilution effects exist, however, in firms that have branded a heterogeneous set of products and still achieved a reasonable level of perceived quality for each. As we saw in Chapter 11, many Japanese firms have adopted a corporate branding strategy with a very broad product portfolio. For example, Yamaha developed a strong reputation selling an extremely diverse brand line that includes motorcycles, guitars, and pianos. Mitsubishi uses its name to brand a bank, cars, and aircraft. Canon has successfully marketed cameras, photocopiers, and office equipment.

In a similar vein, the founder of Virgin Records, Richard Branson, has conducted an ambitious, and perhaps risky, brand extension program (see Branding Brief 12-2). In all these cases, it seems the brand has been able to secure a dominant association to quality in the minds of consumers without strong product identification that might otherwise limit it.

BRANDING BRIEF 12-2

Are There Any Boundaries to the Virgin Brand Name?

Perhaps the most extensive brand extension program in recent years has been undertaken by Richard Branson with his Virgin brand. Virgin's brand strategy is to go into categories where consumer needs are not well met and do different things—and do them differently—to better satisfy consumers.

Branson founded the Virgin record label at the age of 21, and in 1984 he launched Virgin Atlantic Airways. Later, he made millions on the sale of his record label, his Virgin record retail chain, and his Virgin computer games business. After licensing the use of the Virgin name to European startup airlines that were flying the London–Athens and London–Dublin routes, Branson decided to expand the range of products carrying the Virgin brand.

Branson has since licensed the Virgin name for use on personal computers and set up joint ventures in 1994 to market Virgin Vodka and Virgin Cola. In 1997, he took over six of the United Kingdom's government rail lines and established Virgin Rail. In 1999, he launched Virgin Mobile, a wireless company that provides cellular service through a partnership with Deutsche Telecom. He branched into e-commerce that same year with the debut of Virgin.com, a portal where consumers can purchase every product or service offered by the Virgin brand.

Today, the Virgin Group employs over 50,000 people, spans 30 countries, and contains more than 300 branded companies marketing such diverse product areas as travel, lifestyle, media and mobile, money, people and planet, music, health care, and alcohol (see below). Virgin had 2011 revenues of an estimated $21 billion, and Branson's personal fortune was estimated at $4.2 billion in 2011.

Travel: Virgin Australia, V Australia, Virgin Atlantic Airways, Virgin America, Virgin Holidays, Virgin Holidays + Hip Hotels, Virgin Holidays Cruises, Virgin Limited Edition, Virgin Vacations, Blue Holidays, Virgin Galactic, Virgin Books, Virgin Limobike, Virgin Trains

Lifestyle: Virgin Active UK, Virgin Active Australia, Virgin Active Italia, Virgin Active Portugal, Virgin Active South Africa, Virgin Active Spain, Virgin Experience Days, Virgin Racing, Virgin Balloon Flights, The Virgin Voucher

Money: Virgin Money UK, Virgin Money Australia, Virgin Money South Africa, Virgin Money Giving

People and Planet: Virgin Earth Challenge, Virgin Green Fund, Virgin Unite

Music: Virgin Megastore, Virgin Radio International, Virgin Festivals

Sir Richard Branson has introduced Virgin products and services customers in all corners of the world.
Source: H. Lorren Au Jr./MCT/Newscom

Health Care: Virgin Health Bank, Virgin Health Miles, Virgin Life Care, Assura Medical

Alcohol: Virgin Wines Australia, Virgin Wines UK, Virgin Wines US

Virgin's growth and expansion has sparked debate about Branson's seemingly undisciplined extension of the brand. One branding expert criticized Virgin's rapid expansion: "Virgin makes no sense; it's completely unfocused." When Virgin ventures are poorly received, as Virgin Cola, Virgin Vodka, Virgin PCs, Virgin Jeans, Virgin Brides, and Virgin Clothing were in recent years, experts worry about the cumulative negative effect of these unsuccessful brands on the company's overall equity. One marketing executive illustrated the risk of launching an unsuccessful brand by saying, "When I'm delayed on a Virgin train, I start wondering about Virgin Atlantic. Every experience of a brand counts, and negative experiences count even more."

Some critics believe Virgin consumer products will do little more than generate publicity for Virgin airlines. They also warn of overexposure, even with the young, hip audience the Virgin brand has attracted. For example, one advertising agency executive remarked, "I would imagine the risk is that the Virgin brand name can come to mean everything to everybody, which in turn means it becomes nothing to nobody." In Branson's view, as long as a new brand adds value for the consumer, then it strengthens the Virgin image: "If the consumer benefits, I see no reason why we should be frightened about launching new products."

Among the new products Branson is launching are Virgin Oceanic for oceanic exploration and Virgin Galactic for space tourism on rocket ships. Yet Virgin has become more disciplined about its expansion in recent years: The company pursues new businesses only if they are expected to generate more than $150 million in sales within three years. Virgin is also placing great emphasis on sustainability and the environment. Its Web site describes its mission as "to contribute to creating happy and fulfilling lives which are also sustainable."

Sources: Andy Pasztor, "Virgin Galactic's Flights Seen Delayed Yet Again," *Wall Street Journal*, 26 October 2011; Jenny Wilson, "Virgin Oceanic: Just the Latest in Richard Branson's Massive Ventures," *Time*, 6 April 2011; Alan Deutscham, "The Gonzo Way of Branding," *Fast Company*, October 2004, 91; Melanie Wells, "Red Baron," *Forbes*, 3 July 2000; Quentin Sommerville, "High-Flying Brand Isn't All It Appears," *Scotland on Sunday*, 24 December 2000; Roger Crowe, "Global—A Brand Too Far?" *GlobalVue*, 28 October 1998; www.virgin.com/people-and-planet/our-vision.

Can Succeed but Hurt the Image of the Parent Brand

If customers see the brand extension's attribute or benefit associations as inconsistent or even conflicting with the corresponding associations for the parent brand, they may change their perceptions of the parent brand as a result.

In a classic example, Miller Brewing has had much difficulty creating a "hearty" association to its flagship Miller High Life beer brand, in part because of its clear bottle and its advertising heritage as the "champagne of bottled beer." It has often been argued that Miller Lite's early success—its extension-market share soared from 9.5 percent in 1978 to 19 percent in 1986—only exacerbated customers' tendency to think of Miller High Life as "watery" and not a full-bodied beer. These unfavorable perceptions may have contributed to the decline of Miller High Life, whose market share slid from 21 percent to 12 percent during that same eight-year period.

Can Dilute Brand Meaning

The potential drawbacks of a brand extension's lack of identification with any one category and a weakened image may be especially evident with high-quality or prestige brands. Consider how Gucci ran into the hazards of overexpansion.

GUCCI

In its prime, the Gucci brand symbolized luxury, status, elegance, and quality. By the 1980s, however, the label had become tarnished by sloppy manufacturing, countless knock-offs, and even a family feud among the managing Gucci brothers. The product line consisted of 22,000 items, distributed extensively across all types of department stores. Not only were there too many items, but some did not even fit the Gucci image—for example, a cheap canvas pocketbook with the double-G logo that was easily counterfeited and sold on the street for $35. Sales recovered only when Gucci refocused the brand, paring the product line to 7,000 high-end items and selling them through its own company-owned outlets. The strategy helped propel Gucci to the height of the fashion business. With sales of $21 billion in 2010, Gucci is consistently ranked in the world's top 50 brands in value by Interbrand.[30]

To protect their brands from dilution, many up-and-coming fashion companies and designers seeking to establish their brand through a family of brand extensions are now forging exclusive licensing partnerships with a single retailer. Target started with exclusive deals with architect and designer Michael Graves and continued with later deals with Todd Oldham, Mossimo, Isaac Mizrahi, and as of the 2011 holiday season, singer Gwen Stefani.[31] These exclusive licenses enable the licensor to better control the inventory, avoid discounts, and, most importantly, protect the brand.

Can Cause the Company to Forgo the Chance to Develop a New Brand

One easily overlooked disadvantage of brand extensions is that by introducing a new product as a brand extension, the company forgoes the chance to create a *new* brand, with its own unique image and equity. For example, consider the benefits Disney enjoyed from introducing Touchstone Pictures films, which attracted an audience interested in more adult themes and situations than its traditional family-oriented releases, or the boost Levi's earned from Dockers pants, which attracted a segment looking for casual pants. Amazon's runaway success with Kindle suggests another example.

KINDLE

Amazon revolutionized book retailing with the launch of its online book-selling service, "Earth's Largest Bookstore." The company has transcended its bookseller roots and now sells millions of goods and services of all kinds, from simple toys to high-definition televisions, as it continues to fine-tune its appealing combination of wide selection, helpful service, and low prices. Years of product development led to the launch of the revolutionary Kindle e-reader, with which customers could also shop for and purchase e-books and other digital media via wireless networking. Consistent with Amazon's business strategy, Kindle was priced increasingly lower with each successive generation. Subsequent models were also thinner and lighter than previous versions, with faster page turns, sharper resolution, and improved readability. When Apple launched its iPad in April 2010 and many forecast the demise of the Kindle, sales of the e-reader in fact accelerated. Amazon's sales of e-books quickly eclipsed those of hardcover and paperback books. By the end of 2011, Amazon was selling over 1 million products in the Kindle family per week. The brand's success had paved the way for the company to extend it into the red-hot tablet market. Kindle Fire became Amazon's most successful new product launch ever and was the most popular gift and top best seller for the 2011 holiday season. With Kindle, Amazon has established a classic power brand with many growth opportunities.[32]

The enormous success of Kindle gives Amazon another brand on which to build in the marketplace.

Source: Kristoffer Tripplaar/Alamy

These brands all created their own associations and image and tapped into markets completely different from those that currently existed for other brands sold by the company. Thus, introducing a new product as a brand extension can have significant and potentially hidden costs in terms of the lost opportunities of creating a new brand franchise. The extension's brand positioning may be less flexible, too, given that it has to live up to the parent brand's promise and image. The positioning of a new brand, in contrast, could be introduced and updated in the most competitively advantageous way possible.

UNDERSTANDING HOW CONSUMERS EVALUATE BRAND EXTENSIONS

What determines whether a brand extension is able to capitalize on potential advantages and avoid, or at least minimize, potential disadvantages? Figure 12-5 displays some examples of successful and unsuccessful brand extensions through the years. Note how even leading marketing companies have sometimes failed despite their best intentions when launching a brand extension.

This section examines how consumers evaluate brand extensions and develops some ideas to help marketing managers better forecast and improve the odds for success of a brand extension.[33]

Successful Category Extensions	Unsuccessful Category Extensions
Dove shampoo and conditioner	Campbell's tomato sauce
Vaseline Intensive Care skin lotion	LifeSavers chewing gum
Hershey chocolate milk	Cracker Jack cereal
Jell-O Pudding Pops	Harley-Davidson wine coolers
Visa traveler's checks	Hidden Valley Ranch frozen entrees
Sunkist orange soda	Ben-Gay aspirin
Colgate toothbrushes	Kleenex diapers
Mars ice cream bars	Clorox laundry detergent
Arm and Hammer toothpaste	Levi's Tailored Classics suits
Bic disposable lighters	Nautilus athletic shoes
Honda lawn mowers	Domino's fruit-flavored bubble gum
Mr. Clean Auto Dry car wash system	Smucker's ketchup
Fendi watches	Fruit of the Loom laundry detergent
Porsche coffee makers	Coors Rocky Mountain Spring Water
Jeep strollers	Cadbury soap

FIGURE 12-5

Examples of Category Extensions

Managerial Assumptions

To analyze potential consumer response to a brand extension, let's start with a baseline case in which consumers are evaluating the brand extension based only on what they already know about the parent brand and the extension category, and before any advertising, promotion, or detailed product information is available. This baseline case provides the cleanest test of the extension concept itself, and it gives managers guidance about whether to proceed with an extension concept and, if so, what type of marketing program they might need.

Under these baseline conditions, we can expect consumers to use their existing brand knowledge, as well as what they know about the extension category, to try to infer what the extension product might be like. For these inferences to result in favorable evaluations of an extension, four basic conditions must generally hold true:

1. *Consumers have some awareness of and positive associations about the parent brand in memory.* Unless they have positive associations about the parent brand, consumers are unlikely to form favorable expectations of an extension.
2. *At least some of these positive associations will be evoked by the brand extension.* A number of different factors will determine which parent brand associations are evoked, but in general, consumers are likely to infer associations similar in strength, favorability, and uniqueness to the parent brand when they see the brand extension as similar or close in fit to the parent.
3. *Negative associations are not transferred from the parent brand.* Ideally, any negative associations that do exist for the parent brand will be left behind and not play a prominent role in consumers' evaluation of the extension.
4. *Negative associations are not created by the brand extension.* Finally, any parent-brand attributes or benefits that consumers view positively—or at least neutrally—must not be seen as negative for the extension. Consumers must also not infer any new attribute or benefit associations that did not characterize the parent brand but which they see as a potential drawback to the extension.

If any assumption does not hold true, problems can follow. Now we'll examine some factors that influence the validity of these assumptions and consider in more detail how a brand extension, in turn, affects brand equity.

Brand Extensions and Brand Equity

An extension's ultimate success will depend on its ability to both achieve some of its own brand equity in the new category and contribute to the equity of the parent brand.

Creating Extension Equity. For the brand extension to create equity, it must have a sufficiently high level of awareness and achieve necessary and desired points-of-parity and points-of-difference. Brand awareness will depend primarily on the marketing program and resources devoted to spreading the word about the extension. As Chapter 11 described, it will also obviously depend on the type of branding strategy adopted: The more prominently we use an existing brand that has already achieved a certain level of awareness and image to brand an extension, the easier it should be to create awareness of and an image for the extension in memory.

Initially, whether we can create a positive image for an extension will depend on three consumer-related factors:

1. How *salient* parent brand associations are in the minds of consumers in the extension context; that is, what information comes to mind about the parent brand when consumers think of the proposed extension, and the strength of those associations.
2. How *favorable* any inferred associations are in the extension context; that is, whether this information suggests the type of product or service the brand extension would be, and whether consumers view these associations as good or bad in the extension context.
3. How *unique* any inferred associations are in the extension category; that is, how these perceptions compare with those about competitors.

As with any brand, successful brand extensions must achieve desired points-of-parity and points-of-difference. Without powerful points-of-difference, the brand risks becoming an undistinguished "me-too" entry, vulnerable to well-positioned competitors.[34] Tauber refers to "competitive leverage" as the set of advantages that a brand conveys to an extended product in the new category, that is, "when the consumer, by simply knowing the brand, can think of important ways that they perceive that the new brand extension would be better than competing brands in the category."[35] This appeared to be the case with the UK launch of the Dettol Easy Mop disposable mop system, an extension of Reckitt-Benckiser's Dettol household cleaner brand, which leveraged the familiar Dettol brand in outselling other entrants into the category.[36]

At the same time, marketers must also establish any required points-of-parity. The more dissimilar the extension product is to the parent brand, the more likely that points-of-parity will become a positioning priority, and the more important it is to make sure that category POPs are sufficiently well established. Consumers might have a clear understanding of the extension's

The Nivea brand has been carefully expanded across a wide range of skin care and personal care products.
Source: Kay Nietfeld/dpa/picture-alliance/Newscom

intended point-of-difference because it uses an existing brand name. What they often need re-assurance about, however—and what should often be the focus of the marketing program—is whether the extension also has the necessary points-of-parity.

For example, Nivea became a leader in the skin cream category by creating strong points-of-difference on the benefits of "gentle," "mild," "caring," and "protective," which consumers value in many categories. Through skillful product development and marketing, the Nivea brand was successfully expanded across a wide variety of skin care and personal care product categories. When it leveraged its brand equity into categories such as deodorants, shampoos, and cosmetics, Nivea found it necessary to establish category points-of-parity before it could promote its points-of-difference. These were of little value unless consumers believed its deodorant was strong enough, its shampoo would produce beautiful enough hair, and its cosmetics would be colorful enough. Once points-of-parity were established, Nivea's core brand associations could be introduced as compelling points-of-difference.

Contributing to Parent Brand Equity. To contribute to parent brand equity, an extension must strengthen or add favorable and unique associations to the parent brand and not diminish the strength, favorability, or uniqueness of any existing associations. The effects of an extension on consumer brand knowledge will depend on four factors:

1. How *compelling* the evidence is about the corresponding attribute or benefit association in the extension context—that is, how attention-getting and unambiguous or easily interpretable the information is. Strong evidence is attention-getting and unambiguous. Weak evidence may be ignored or discounted.
2. How *relevant* or diagnostic the extension evidence is for the attribute or benefit for the parent brand, that is, how much consumers see evidence on product performance or imagery in one category as predictive of product performance or imagery for the brand in other categories. Evidence will affect parent brand evaluations only if consumers feel extension performance is indicative of the parent brand in some way.
3. How *consistent* the extension evidence is with the corresponding parent brand associations. Consistent extension evidence is less likely to change the evaluation of existing parent brand associations. Inconsistent extension evidence creates the potential for change, with the direction and extent of change depending on the relative strength and favorability of the evidence. Note, however, that consumers may discount or ignore highly inconsistent extension evidence if they don't view it as relevant.[37]
4. How *strongly* existing attribute or benefit associations are held in consumer memory for the parent brand, that is, how easy an association might be to change.

Feedback effects that change brand knowledge are thus most likely when consumers view information about the extension as equally revealing about the parent brand, and when they hold only a weak and inconsistent association between the parent brand and that information.[38] Note that negative feedback effects are not restricted to product-related performance associations. As we saw earlier, if a brand has a favorable prestige image association, then consumers may disapprove or even resent a vertical extension (a new version of the product at a lower price). Michelin is a premium brand that has extended carefully.

MICHELIN

From its travel roots, Michelin, famous for the safety and dependability for its tires, has extended its brand into a variety of different categories. The company has long published guidebooks, the Red Guides to hotels and restaurants and the Green Guides for tourism. It has also published a series of road maps for locales and regions all over the world. More recently, a new division called Michelin Lifestyle began to sell additional licensed merchandise in four distinct areas: (1) tire accessories, such as foot pumps, floor mats, and windshield wipers; (2) "high-specification lifestyle products," such as bicycle helmets, scuba suits, and golf balls; (3) clothing and accessories featuring Michelin's brand mascot Bibendum; and (4) safety products developed with other companies, including ear plugs, safety goggles, and gloves. Michelin intended these brand extensions to "enhance the value of our brand and add emotional-type values, not just functionality, and reach out to...a new generation that doesn't yet associate with us." Still, Michelin Lifestyle management was careful not to stretch the brand too far by moving into "fragrances and other things that have some legitimacy for a lifestyle brand. There still has to be an authentic Michelin reason for everything."[39]

Michelin has expanded its brand carefully to strengthen its image and reach new customers.

Source: Michelin North America, Inc.

Vertical Brand Extensions

We've seen that brand extensions can expand market coverage and bring new consumers into the brand franchise. Vertical brand extensions, which extend the brand up into more premium market segments or down into more value-conscious segments, are a common means of attracting new groups of consumers. The central logic here is that the equity of the parent brand can be transferred in either direction to appeal to consumers who otherwise would not consider it.

Pros and Cons.   Vertical extensions can confer a number of advantages. An upward extension can improve brand image, because a premium version of a brand often brings positive associations with it. Extensions in either direction can offer consumers variety, revitalize the parent brand, and permit further extensions in a given direction.

Yet vertical extensions are also susceptible to many of the disadvantages of brand extensions. A vertical extension to a new price point, whether higher or lower, can confuse or frustrate consumers who have learned to expect a certain price range from a brand. Consumers may reject the extension and the parent brand's image will suffer. For prestige brands in particular, firms must often maintain a balance between availability and scarcity such that people always aspire to be a customer and do not feel excluded.

Even a successful downward extension has the possibility of harming the parent's brand image by introducing associations common to lower-priced brands, such as inferior quality or reduced service. Interestingly, however, research has shown that higher-quality extensions are likely to improve evaluations of the parent brand more than lower-quality extensions might harm it.[40]

One of the biggest risk factors of a vertical extension, particularly a downward one, is that it will succeed but cannibalize sales of a parent brand. It may bring new consumers to the brand franchise, but it may also bring a greater number of existing customers of the parent brand.

For example, when it held 70 percent global market share with its Kodak Gold brand, Kodak launched the discount Kodak Funtime brand to compete with the threat of lower-priced Fuji film. Cannibalization of the Kodak Gold brand soon followed, and Kodak found itself in a price war with Fuji that ultimately led to a significant decline in Kodak Gold market share. While the parent brand name "gives you the credibility to quickly gain share in the lower-end market," cannibalization is a likely outcome because "if you've already persuaded people that only the best products are sold under your brand, then they'll readily buy the least expensive item with that brand name."[41]

Examples.   Despite the problems inherent in vertical extensions, many companies have succeeded in extending their brands to enter new markets across a range of price points. In fashion, the Armani brand has extended from high-end Giorgio Armani and Giorgio Armani Privé, to mid-range luxury with Emporio Armani, to affordable luxury with Armani Jeans and Armani Exchange.

As part of a plan to upgrade, Holiday Inn Worldwide broke its domestic hotels into five separate chains to tap into five different benefit segments: the upscale Crowne Plaza, the traditional Holiday Inn, the budget Holiday Inn Express, and the business-oriented Holiday Inn Select (although soon to be phased-out) and Holiday Inn Hotel & Suites. Different branded chains received different marketing programs and emphasis. A $100 million global ad campaign themed "Stay You" was launched in 2010 as part of the $1 billion brand refresh undertaken for the flagship Holiday Inn brand.[42]

In each case for Holiday Inn, a clear differentiation existed between brands, minimizing the potential for brand overlap and accompanying consumer confusion and brand cannibalization. Each extension also lived up to the core promise of the parent brand, thus reducing the possibility that any would hurt the parent's image.

Naming Strategies.   Firms often adopt sub-branding strategies to distinguish their lower-priced entries. US Airways introduced US Airways Shuttle as an inexpensive short-haul carrier to compete with no-frills Southwest Airlines in the lucrative Eastern corridor market. Such extension introductions clearly must be handled carefully; typically, the parent brand plays a secondary role.

An even more difficult vertical extension is an upward brand stretch. In general, it is difficult to change people's impressions of the brand enough to justify a significant upward extension. Concern about the unwillingness of consumers to update their brand knowledge was what led Honda, Toyota, and Nissan to introduce their luxury car models as separate nameplates (Acura, Lexus, and Infiniti, respectively). As it turns out, product improvements to the upper ends of their brand lines since the introduction of these new car nameplates may have made it easier to bridge the gap into the luxury market with their brands. When it later elected to move downmarket, Toyota developed the Scion brand in part to avoid reducing the strength of the Toyota image.

At the same time, it is possible to use certain brand modifiers to signal a noticeable, although presumably not dramatic, quality improvement—for example, Ultra Dry Pampers, Extra Strength Tylenol, or PowerPro Dustbuster Plus. These indirect extensions, or "super-brands," may be less risky than direct extensions when moving a master brand up-market.[43]

To avoid the potential difficulties associated with vertical extensions, however, companies sometimes elect to use new and different brand names to expand vertically. The Gap has employed a three-tier approach, using the Banana Republic brand to command a 40 percent price premium that the Gap would likely never attain on its own and launching the Old Navy brand to offer 40 percent discounts.

By developing unique brand names, companies pursuing vertical expansion can avoid a negative transfer of equity from a "lower" brand to a "higher" brand, but they sacrifice some ability to transfer positive associations. Yet when the parent brand makes no secret of its ownership of the vertical brands, as is the case with both the Gap and Toyota, some associations may be transferred because the parent acts as a "shadow endorser" of the new brand.[44]

Branding Brief 12-3 illustrates how Levi has been able to expand its market coverage and attract new consumers through vertical extensions into discount jeans.

EVALUATING BRAND EXTENSION OPPORTUNITIES

Academic research and industry experience have revealed a number of principles governing successful brand extensions. Marketers must consider their strategies carefully by systematically following the steps listed in Figure 12-6 and using managerial judgment and marketing research to help make *each* of these decisions.

Define Actual and Desired Consumer Knowledge about the Brand

It's critical for marketers to fully understand the depth and breadth of awareness of the parent brand, and the strength, favorability, and uniqueness of its associations. Moreover, marketers

BRANDING BRIEF 12-3

Levi Extends Its Brand

Levi Strauss & Co. is an iconic U.S. brand, best known for the distinctive red tab on the back pocket of its jeans. Founded in 1853 by Bavarian immigrant Levi Strauss, the company grew to one of the world's largest apparel companies, with more than $6 billion in revenue and cachet as the cool jeans teens aspired to wear. During the late 1990s, though, Levi faced declining sales and growing debt. Its long tradition of producing durable jeans became a liability for its fashion image, and the firm remained private despite pressure to take all or part of it public to pay down debt.

For years, market power had been shifting away from suppliers like Levi and toward retailers. Mass merchants were selling about one-third of all jeans in the United States, and their share of the market was growing. The advent of discount stores made many consumers more price-sensitive. In 1999, Levi Strauss brought in a new CEO, Philip Marineau, from PepsiCo. Marineau favored increased segmentation as a way to boost sales, so Levi adopted a segmentation strategy to convince different types of retailers (department stores, specialty chains, upscale boutiques, and mass merchants) to carry its products.

Under the segmentation strategy, Levi's brands ranged from a relatively inexpensive discount line to $150-and-up vintage designs. Levi already sold to J.C. Penney Co. and Sears, Roebuck and Co., and those choices had alienated some major retail customers who preferred the brand to remain exclusive and slightly more upscale. Despite management concerns about potential reputation damage, Levi created the Signature by Levi Strauss & Co. brand to sell at mass merchants and began selling to Walmart in 2003.

Signature, positioned as a premium mass brand, carried new labels and styles manufactured from less-expensive fabric. The Levi Strauss & Co. name appeared in cursive; gone were the red tab and traditional Levi pocket stitching and logo. At that time, Levi priced Signature jeans at $23—more than other mass brands but below its $29 regular brand.

Initially, the segmentation strategy created rough spots for other Levi brands. As Levi's executives struggled to appease Walmart and find the right price point for mass retailers, other parts of the business suffered. Orders from department stores slipped and sales of regular Levi's, which had finally steadied leading up to the launch of the Signature brand, resumed their decline. Furthermore, a new high-fashion line called Type 1 failed.

In 2006, however, Walmart's price-chopping move ultimately proved effective and Signature jeans began to sell more quickly. The company also added lines of Signature baby clothing, bags and wallets, and men's khaki pants, selling to other mass retailers such as Kmart and Meijer.

Around the same time, Levi attempted to expand into premium segments, selling premium lines such as Levi's Capital E to Bloomingdales and Barney's New York. The upward stretch has proven to be more challenging. Levi recently consolidated several premium sub-brands under just two names: Made & Crafted, a premium denim line featuring better fabrics and fit,

Levi Strauss has concentrated in recent years on introducing new products into new channels to bolster its sagging jeans sales.

Source: AP Photo/Wilfredo Lee

and Levi's Vintage Clothing, offering reproductions of items from the brand's historical archives.

The biggest launch, however, was another discount brand, dENiZEN from Levi's, first introduced into Asia in 2010. The name was chosen because it means "inhabitant" or someone belonging to a community of family and friends. After being launched in China, India, Mexico, Pakistan, Singapore, and South Korea, dENiZEN from Levi's was introduced into the U.S. market, initially sold exclusively at Target for $17.99–$29.99.

Sources: www.levi.com; Sandra O'Loughlin, "Levi Strauss Seeing Green with Signature Blues," *Brandweek*, 25 July 2005; "In Bow to Retailer's New Clout, Levi Strauss Makes Alterations," *Wall Street Journal*, 17 June 2004; Robert Guy Matthews, "Levi Strauss Bow-wows a Page from Shakespeare," *Wall Street Journal*, 14 January 2005; Jacques Chevron, "Tacit Messages: A Lesson from Levi's," *Brandweek*, 6 February 2006; "Strauss & Co.; On the Record: Phil Marineau," *San Francisco Chronicle*, 6 March 2006; Rachel Dodes, "Levi's Shoots for the High-End Hipster," *Wall Street Journal*, 14 April 2010; Purvita Chatterjee, "Levi's Takes on Private Labels with Denizen," *The Hindu Business Line*, 23 May 2011; "Levi's Launches Denizen Jeans in U.S.," www.marketplace.com, 20 July 2011; www.levistrauss.com.

1. Define actual and desired consumer knowledge about the brand (e.g., create mental map and identify key sources of equity).

2. Identify possible extension candidates on basis of parent brand associations and overall similarity or fit of extension to the parent brand.

3. Evaluate the potential of the extension candidate to create equity according to the three-factor model:
   • Salience of parent brand associations
   • Favorability of inferred extension associations
   • Uniqueness of inferred extension associations

4. Evaluate extension candidate feedback effects according to the four-factor model:
   • How compelling the extension evidence is
   • How relevant the extension evidence is
   • How consistent the extension evidence is
   • How strong the extension evidence is

5. Consider possible competitive advantages as perceived by consumers and possible reactions initiated by competitors.

6. Design marketing campaign to maximize the likelihood of success and potential positive feedback effects.

7. Evaluate extension success and effects on parent brand equity.

FIGURE 12-6

Steps in Successfully Introducing Brand Extensions

must know what is to be the basis of positioning and core benefits satisfied by the brand. Profiling actual and desired brand knowledge structures helps identify possible brand extensions as well as guide decisions that contribute to their success. In evaluating an extension, a company must understand where it would like to take the brand in the long run. Because the introduction of an extension can change brand meaning, it can affect consumer response to all subsequent marketing activity as well (see Chapter 13).

Identify Possible Extension Candidates

Chapter 11 described a number of consumer, firm, and competitor criteria for choosing which products and markets a firm should enter. With respect to consumer factors, marketers should consider parent brand associations—especially as they relate to brand positioning and core benefits—and product categories that might seem to fit with that brand image in the minds of consumers.[45] Although consumers are generally better able to react to an extension concept than to suggest one, it still may be instructive to ask consumers what products the brand should consider offering if it were to introduce a new product. Brainstorming is another way to generate category extension candidates, along with consumer research.

One or more associations can often serve as the basis of fit. Beecham marketed Lucozade in Britain for years as a glucose drink to combat dehydration and other maladies of sick children. By introducing new flavor formulas, packaging formats, and so forth, Beecham was able to capitalize on the association of the brand as a "fluid replenisher" to transform its meaning to "a healthy sports drink for people of all ages." Reinforced by ads featuring the famous British Olympic decathlete Daley Thompson, sales and profits for the brand increased dramatically. Thus, by recognizing that Lucozade did not have to be just a pharmaceutical product but could be repositioned through brand extensions and other marketing activity as a healthy and nutritious drink, Beecham was able to credibly transform the brand.[46]

Evaluate the Potential of the Extension Candidate

In forecasting the success of a proposed brand extension, marketers should assess—through judgment and research—the likelihood that the extension will realize the advantages and avoid the disadvantages of brand extensions, as summarized in Figures 12-2 and 12-4. As with any new product, analysis of the 3 Cs—consumer, corporate, and competitive factors—as well as category factors can be useful.

Consumer Factors.   To evaluate the potential of a proposed brand extension, we assess its ability to achieve its own brand equity, as well as the likelihood that it can affect the parent brand's existing brand equity. First, marketers must forecast the strength, favorability, and uniqueness of *all* associations to the brand extension. In other words, what will be the salience, favorability, or uniqueness of parent brand associations in the proposed extension context? Similarly, what will be the strength, favorability, and uniqueness of any other inferred associations? The three-factor model of extension evaluations and the four-factor model of extension feedback effects can provide guidance in studying consumer reactions.

To narrow down the list of possible extensions, we often need consumer research (see Chapter 10 for a review). We can ask consumers directly for their brand permission ("How well does the proposed extension fit with the parent brand?" or "Would you expect such a new product from the parent brand?"). We can even ask what products they believe are currently attached to the brand: If a majority of consumers believe a proposed extension product is already being sold under the brand, there would seem to be little risk in introducing it, at least based on initial consumer reaction.

To understand consumers' perceptions of a proposed extension, we can use open-ended associations ("What comes into your mind when you think of the brand extension?" or "What are your first impressions on hearing that the parent brand is introducing the extension?"), as well as ratings scales based on reactions to concept statements. An interesting new statistical approach uses Bayesian factor analysis to separate brand and category effects to better assess brand fit.[47]

Common pitfalls include failing to take all consumers' brand knowledge structures into account. Often marketers mistakenly focus on one or perhaps a few brand associations as a potential basis of fit and ignore other, possibly more important, brand associations in the process.

BIC

By emphasizing inexpensive, disposable products, the French company Société Bic was able to create markets for nonrefillable ballpoint pens in the late 1950s, disposable cigarette lighters in the early 1970s, and disposable razors in the early 1980s. It unsuccessfully tried the same strategy in marketing Bic perfumes in the United States and Europe in 1989. The perfumes—two for women ("Nuit" and "Jour") and two for men ("Bic for Men" and "Bic Sport for Men")—were packaged in quarter-ounce glass spray bottles that looked like fat cigarette lighters and sold for $5 each. The products were displayed on racks in plastic packages at checkout counters throughout Bic's extensive distribution channels, which included 100,000 or so drugstores, supermarkets, and other mass merchandisers. At the time, a Bic spokeswoman described the new products as extensions of the Bic heritage—"high quality at affordable prices, convenient to purchase, and convenient to use."[48] The brand extension was launched with a $20 million advertising and promotion campaign containing images of stylish people enjoying themselves with the perfume and using the tag line "Paris in Your Pocket." Nevertheless, Bic was unable to overcome its lack of cachet and negative image associations; failing to achieve a critical point-of-parity, the extension fell short.

Although Bic has loyal consumer followings for its disposable, pens, razors and lighters, its attempt to introduce a portable fragrance collection was a failure.
Source: BIC

Another major mistake in evaluating brand extensions is overlooking how literal consumers can be in evaluating brand extensions. Although consumers ultimately care about benefits, they often notice and evaluate attributes—especially concrete ones—in reacting to an extension. Brand managers, though, tend to focus on perceived benefits in predicting consumer reactions, and, as a result, they may overlook some potentially damaging attribute associations.

When Hershey's introduced strawberry syrup, Smuckers retaliated with a chocolate syrup.

Source: Keri Miksza

Corporate and Competitive Factors. Marketers must take not only a consumer perspective in evaluating a proposed brand extension, but also a broader corporate and competitive perspective. How effectively are the corporate assets leveraged in the extension setting? How relevant are existing marketing programs, perceived benefits, and target customers to the extension? What are the competitive advantages to the extension as consumers perceive them, and possible reactions initiated by competitors as a result?

One of the biggest mistakes marketers make in launching extensions is failing to properly account for competitors' actions and reactions.[49] Too many extension products and too strongly entrenched competition can put a strain on company resources. Arm & Hammer's brand extension program met major resistance in categories such as deodorants when existing competitors fought back.

Brand counterextensions—whereby a competing brand in the extension category chooses to launch its own extension into the parent brand's category—can pose a significant threat. The introduction of Hershey's strawberry syrup was followed by Smucker's chocolate syrup; Dixie paper plates was followed by Chinet paper cups. A successful extension can reduce the perceived fit between categories, making it easier for a brand to counterattack.[50]

Category Factors. Marketers must determine the optimal product line strategy for their brand. To do so, they need a clear understanding of the market and the cost interdependencies between products.[51] This in turn means examining the percentage of sales and profits contributed by each item in the product line and its ability to withstand competition and address consumer needs.

A product line is too short if the manager can increase long-term profits by adding items; the line is too long if the manager can increase profits by dropping items.[52] Increasing the length of the product line by adding new variants or items typically expands market coverage and therefore market share, but it also increases costs. From a branding perspective, longer product lines may decrease the consistency of the associated brand image if all items use the same brand.

Reddy, Holak, and Bhat studied the determinants of line extension success using data on 75 line extensions of 34 cigarette brands over a 20-year period.[53] Their major findings indicate that:

- Line extensions of strong brands are more successful than extensions of weak brands.
- Line extensions of symbolic brands enjoy greater market success than those of less symbolic brands.
- Line extensions that receive strong advertising and promotional support are more successful than those extensions that receive meager support.
- Line extensions entering earlier into a product subcategory are more successful than extensions entering later, but only if they are extensions of strong brands.
- Firm size and marketing competencies also play a part in an extension's success.
- Earlier line extensions have helped in the market expansion of the parent brand.
- Incremental sales generated by line extensions may more than compensate for the loss in sales due to cannibalization.

Despite the pitfalls of line extensions and the many considerations necessary to properly manage extensions, the allure of line extensions for companies remains strong, primarily due to the cost and risk incurred in launching an entirely new brand. One report showed that line extensions take half as long to develop, cost far less to market, and enjoy twice the success rate of major new brand launches.[54]

Design Marketing Programs to Launch Extension

Too often companies use extensions as a shortcut means of introducing a new product and pay insufficient attention to developing a branding and marketing strategy that will maximize the equity of the brand extension as well as enhance the equity of the parent brand. As is the case with a new brand, building brand equity for a brand extension requires choosing brand elements, designing the optimal marketing program to launch the extension, and leveraging secondary associations.

Choosing Brand Elements.   By definition, brand extensions retain one or more elements from an existing brand. They do not have to leverage only the brand name but can use other brand elements too. For example, Heinz and Campbell Soup have implemented package designs that distinguish different line extensions or brand types but reveal their common origin at the same time.[55]

Sometimes packaging is such a critical component of brand equity that it is hard to imagine an extension without it. Brand managers are in a real dilemma in such cases, because if they choose the same type of packaging, they run the risk that the extension will not be well distinguished. If they use different packaging, they may leave a key source of brand equity behind.

A brand extension can retain or modify one or more brand elements from the parent brand as well as adopt its own brand elements. In creating new brand elements for an extension, marketers should follow the same guidelines of memorability, meaningfulness, likeability, protectability, adaptability, and transferability that we described in Chapter 4 for the development of any brand.

New brand elements are often necessary to help distinguish the brand extension and build awareness and image. As Chapter 11 noted, the relative prominence of existing parent brand elements and new extension brand elements will dictate the strength of transfer from the parent brand to the extension, as well as the feedback from the extension to the parent brand.

Designing Optimal Marketing Program.   The marketing program for a brand extension must consider the same guidelines in building brand equity that we described in Chapters 5 and 6. Consumer perceptions of value must guide pricing decisions, distribution strategies must blend push and pull considerations, and the firm must integrate marketing communications by mixing and matching communication options.

When it comes to positioning, the less similar the extension is to the parent brand, the more important it typically is to establish necessary and competitive points-of-parity. The points-of-difference for a category extension in many cases directly follow from the points-of-difference for the parent brand, and consumers readily perceive them. Thus, when Nivea extended into

Cannibalization can be a major problem for brands like Budweiser that have many different but related sub-brands.
Source: Keri Miksza

shampoos and conditioners, deodorants, and cosmetics and other beauty products, its key "gentleness" point-of-difference transferred relatively easily. With line extensions, on the other hand, marketers have to create a new association that can serve as an additional point-of-difference and help distinguish the extension from the parent brand too.

For line extensions, consumers must also understand how the new product relates to existing products in order to minimize possible cannibalization or confusion. For example, when Anheuser-Busch first launched Bud Select, the low-carb beer with no aftertaste was positioned as an "upscale, white-collar brew." The emphasis on no aftertaste, however, drew an implicit comparison that cast other Anheuser-Busch products in a dim light and caused some consumers to abandon their usual Bud or Bud Light in favor of the new brand. As a result, nearly all of Bud Select's 1.3 percent share of supermarket sales earned in the month after its launch came at the expense of other Anheuser-Busch beers, which lost a share point during the same period.[56]

Leveraging Secondary Brand Associations.   Brand extensions will often leverage the same secondary associations as the parent brand, although competing in the extension category may require some additional fortification like linking to other entities. A brand extension differs in that, by definition, there is always some leveraging of another brand or company. The extent to which these other associations become linked to the extension, however, depends on the branding strategy the firm adopts and how it brands the extension. As we've seen, the more common the brand elements and the more prominence they receive, the more likely it is that parent brand associations will transfer.

Evaluate Extension Success and Effects on Parent Brand Equity

The final step in evaluating brand extension opportunities is to assess the extent to which an extension is able to achieve its own equity as well as contribute to the equity of the parent brand. To help measure its success, we can use brand tracking based on the customer-based brand equity model or other key measures of consumer response, centered on both the extension and the parent brand as a whole. Brand Focus 12.0 contains a simple checklist and describes a more detailed scorecard to help in evaluating brand extension opportunities.

EXTENSION GUIDELINES BASED ON ACADEMIC RESEARCH

Now we turn to some specific guidance about brand extensions. Fortunately, much academic research has focused on this strategy. We summarize some of the important conclusions in Figure 12-7 and describe them in detail in this section.

1. ***Successful brand extensions occur when the parent brand has favorable associations and consumers perceive a fit between the parent brand and the extension product.*** To better understand the process by which consumers evaluate a brand extension, many academic researchers have adopted a "categorization" perspective. Categorization research has its roots in psychological research, showing that people do not deliberately and individually evaluate each new stimulus to which they are exposed. Instead, they usually evaluate a stimulus in terms of whether they can classify it as a member of a previously defined mental category.

   We could argue that consumers use their categorical knowledge of brands and products to simplify, structure, and interpret their marketing environment.[57] For example, consumers may see brands as categories that over time have acquired a number of specific attributes based on their individual members.[58] As Method has expanded its range of cleaning

1. Successful brand extensions occur when the parent brand is seen as having favorable associations and there is a perception of fit between the parent brand and the extension product.

2. There are many bases of fit: product-related attributes and benefits as well as non-product-related attributes and benefits related to common usage situations or user types.

3. Depending on consumer knowledge of the product categories, perceptions of fit may be based on technical or manufacturing commonalities or more surface considerations such as necessary or situational complementarity.

4. High-quality brands stretch farther than average-quality brands, although both types of brands have boundaries.

5. A brand that is seen as prototypical of a product category can be difficult to extend outside the category.

6. Concrete attribute associations tend to be more difficult to extend than abstract benefit associations.

7. Consumers may transfer associations that are positive in the original product class but become negative in the extension context.

8. Consumers may infer negative associations about an extension, perhaps even based on other inferred positive associations.

9. It can be difficult to extend into a product class that is seen as easy to make.

10. A successful extension can not only contribute to the parent brand image but also enable a brand to be extended even farther.

11. An unsuccessful extension hurts the parent brand only when there is a strong basis of fit between the two.

12. An unsuccessful extension does not prevent a firm from backtracking and introducing a more similar extension.

13. Vertical extensions can be difficult and often require sub-branding strategies.

14. The most effective advertising strategy for an extension is one that emphasizes information about the extension (rather than reminders about the parent brand).

15. Individual differences can affect how consumers make an extension decision, and will moderate extension effects.

16. Cultural differences across markets can influence extension success.

FIGURE 12-7

Brand Extension Guidelines Based on Academic Research

products, consumers might develop stronger brand associations to "modern designs" and "environmentally friendliness."

In this categorization perspective, if consumers saw a brand extension as closely related or similar to the brand category, they could easily transfer their existing attitude about the parent brand to the extension. If they were not as sure about the similarity, they might evaluate the extension in a more detailed, piecemeal fashion. In this case, the strength, favorability, and uniqueness of salient brand associations would determine how they viewed the extension.[59]

Thus, a categorization view considers consumers' evaluations of brand extensions to be a two-step process. First, consumers determine whether there is a match between what they know about the parent brand and what they believe to be true about the extension. Then, if the match is good, consumers might transfer their existing brand attitudes to the extension.

Consistent with these notions, Aaker and Keller collected consumer reactions to 20 proposed extensions from six well-known brands and found that both a perception of fit between the original and extension product categories and a perception of high quality for the parent brand led to more favorable extension evaluations.[60]

A number of subsequent studies have explored the generalizability of these findings to markets outside the United States. Based on a comprehensive analysis of 131 brand extensions from seven such replication studies around the world, Bottomly and Holden concluded that this basic model clearly generalized, although cross-cultural differences influenced the relative importance attached to the model components.[61]

Thus, in general, brand extensions are more likely to be favorably evaluated by consumers if they see some bases of fit or congruity between the proposed extension and parent brand.[62] A lack of perceived fit may doom a potentially successful brand extension. Interestingly, moderately incongruent extensions can evoke more favorable extension evaluations than highly congruent extensions under certain specialized situations, such as when consumers are highly involved and the extension is otherwise undifferentiated from competitors.[63]

2. *There are many bases of fit: both product-related and non-product-related attributes and benefits may influence extension fit.* Any association about the parent brand that consumers hold in memory may serve as a potential basis of fit. Most academic researchers assume consumers' judgments of similarity are a function of salient shared associations between the parent brand and the extension product category. Specifically, the more common and the fewer distinctive associations that exist, the greater the perception of overall similarity, whether based on product- or non-product-related attributes and benefits.[64] Consumers may also use attributes for a prototypical brand or a particular exemplar as the standard of reference for the extension category and form their perceptions of fit with the parent brand on that basis.

To demonstrate how fit does not have to be based on product-related associations alone, Park, Milberg, and Lawson have distinguished between fit based on "product-feature similarity" (as described earlier) and "brand-concept consistency."[65] They define *brand concepts* as the brand-unique image associations that arise from a particular combination of attributes, benefits, and the marketing efforts used to translate these attributes into higher-order meanings (such as high status). *Brand-concept consistency* measures how well the brand concept accommodates the extension product. The important point these researchers make is that different types of brand concepts from the same original product category may extend into the same category with varying degrees of success, even when product-feature similarity is high.

Park and his coauthors further distinguish between *function-oriented brands*, whose dominant associations relate to product performance (like Timex watches), and *prestige-oriented brands*, whose dominant associations relate to consumers' expression of self-concepts or images (like Rolex watches). Experimentally, they showed that the Rolex brand could more easily extend into categories such as grandfather clocks, bracelets, and rings than the Timex brand; however, Timex could more easily extend into categories such as stopwatches, batteries, and calculators. In the former case, high brand-concept consistency for Rolex overcame a lack of product-feature similarity; in the latter case, product-feature similarity favored a function-oriented brand such as Timex.

Broniarczyk and Alba provide another compelling demonstration of the importance of recognizing salient brand associations. A brand that may not even be as favorably evaluated as a competing brand in its category may be more successfully extended into certain categories, depending on the particular parent brand associations involved. For example, although Close-Up toothpaste was not as well liked by their sample as Crest, a proposed Close-Up breath mint extension was evaluated more favorably than one from Crest. But a proposed Crest toothbrush extension was evaluated more favorably than one from Close-Up.[66]

Broniarczyk and Alba also showed that a perceived lack of fit between the parent brand's product category and the proposed extension category could be overcome if key parent brand associations were salient and relevant in the extension category. For example, Froot Loops cereal—which has strong brand associations to "sweet," "flavor," and "kids"—was better able to extend to dissimilar product categories such as lollipops and popsicles than to similar product categories such as waffles and hot cereal, because of the relevance of its brand associations in the dissimilar extension category. The reverse was true for Cheerios cereal, however, which had a "healthy grain" association that was relevant only in similar extension product categories.

Thus, extension fit is more than just the number of common and distinctive brand associations between the parent brand and the extension product category.[67] These research studies and others demonstrate the importance of taking a broader perspective of categorization and fit. For example, Bridges, Keller, and Sood refer to "category coherence." Coherent categories are those whose members "hang together" and "make sense." According to these authors, to understand the rationale for a grouping of products in a brand line, a consumer needs "explanatory links" that tie the products together and summarize their relationship. The physically dissimilar toy, bath care, and car seat products in the Fisher-Price product line can be united by the link "products for children."[68]

Researchers have also explored other, more specific, aspects of fit. Boush provides experimental data about the robustness and context sensitivity of fit judgments.[69] Similarity judgments between pairs of product categories were found to be asymmetrical, and brand name associations could reverse the direction of asymmetry. For example, more subjects agreed with the statement "*Time* magazine is like *Time* books" than with the statement, "*Time* books are like *Time* magazine," but without the brand names (just using "books" and "magazines"), the preferences were reversed. Smith and Andrews surveyed industrial goods marketers and found that the relationship between fit and new product evaluations was not direct; it was mediated and influenced by customers' confidence that a firm could provide a proposed new product.[70]

3. *Depending on their knowledge of the product categories, consumers may perceive fit based on technical or manufacturing commonalities, or on surface considerations such as necessary or situational complementarity.* Consumers can also base fit on considerations other than attributes or benefits. Taking a demand-side and supply-side perspective of consumer perceptions, Aaker and Keller showed that perceived fit between the parent brand and the extension product could be related to the economic notions of substitutability and complementarity in product use (from a demand-side perspective), as well as to the firm's perceived grasp of the skills and assets necessary to make the extension product (from a supply-side perspective).

Thus, Honda's perceived expertise in making motors for lawn mowers and cars may help perceptions of fit for any other machinery with small motors that Honda might want to introduce. Similarly, expertise with small disposable products offers numerous opportunities for Bic. On the other hand, some extension examples have little manufacturing compatibility but greater usage complementarity, such as Colgate's extension from toothpaste to toothbrushes or Duracell's extension from batteries to flashlights.

These perceptions of fit, however, may depend on how much consumers know about the product categories. As Muthukrishnan and Weitz demonstrated, "expert" consumers are more likely to use technical or manufacturing commonalities to judge fit, considering similarity in terms of technology, design and fabrication, and the materials and components used in the manufacturing process. Less knowledgeable "novice" consumers, on the other hand, are more likely to use superficial, perceptual considerations such as common package,

Honda's positive reputation for small motors has been an asset when it moved into categories that use similar types of machinery such as lawnmowers.

Source: American Honda Motor Co., Inc.

shape, color, size, and usage.[71] They may see a basis of fit between tennis racquets and tennis shoes rather than between tennis racquets and golf clubs, despite the fact that the latter actually share more manufacturing commonalities. The effects for more knowledgeable consumers were reversed, because they recognized the technical synergies in manufacturing tennis racquets and golf clubs.

Zhang and Sood showed a similar pattern of knowledge effects based on age. Children—who have less brand knowledge than adults—were more likely to evaluate extensions on the basis of surface cues (such as brand name linguistic characteristics of an extension, for example whether a brand name rhymed or not) while adults were more likely to use deep cues (like category similarity between the parent brand and extension category).[72]

4. *High-quality brands stretch farther than average-quality brands, although both types have boundaries.* Consumers often see high-quality brands as more credible, expert, and trustworthy. As a result, even if they believe a relatively distant extension does not really fit with the brand, they may be more willing to give a high-quality brand the benefit of the doubt than a brand they see as average in quality.[73]

Thus, one important benefit of building a strong brand is that it can extend more easily into more diverse categories.[74] Fedorikhin, Park, and Thomson found that if consumers had a high degree of attachment with a brand, they were willing to pay more for an extension, recommend it to others, and forgive any mishaps.[75] Similarly, Yeung and Wyer showed that if a brand evokes a strong positive emotional reaction, consumers are likely to be less influenced by the fit of the extension.[76]

Regardless, all brands have boundaries, as a number of observers have persuasively argued by pointing out ridiculous, and even comical, hypothetical brand extension possibilities. As Tauber once noted, few consumers would want Jell-O shoelaces or Tide frozen entrees!

5. *A brand that consumers see as prototypical for a product category can be difficult to extend outside the category.* As a caveat to the conclusion above, if consumers see a brand as exemplifying a category too strongly, it may be difficult for them to think of it in any other way. Numerous examples exist of category leaders that have failed in introducing brand extensions.[77]

Bayer, a brand synonymous with aspirin, ran into a stumbling block introducing the Bayer Select line of specialized nonaspirin painkillers.[78] Chiquita was unsuccessful in its attempt to move beyond its strong "banana" association with a frozen juice bar extension.[79] Country Time could not overcome its "lemonade" association to introduce an apple cider. Perhaps the most extreme examples are brands that lost their trademark distinctiveness and became a generic term for the category, such as Thermos and Kleenex. To illustrate the difficulty a prototypical brand may have in extending, consider the experiences of Clorox.

CLOROX

Clorox is a well-known brand whose name is virtually synonymous with bleach. In 1988, Clorox took on consumer goods giants Procter & Gamble and Unilever by introducing the first bleach with detergent. After pouring $225 million into the development and distribution of its detergent products over three years, Clorox was able to achieve only a 3 percent market share. Despite being beaten to market, P&G subsequently introduced Tide with Bleach and was able to achieve a 17 percent share. Reluctantly, Clorox chose to exit the market. Its failure can certainly be attributed in part to the fact that consumers could think of Clorox only in a very limited sense as a bleach product. In a combined "laundry detergent with bleach" product, too, they see laundry detergent as the primary ingredient and bleach as secondary. As a result, in this market we might expect a laundry detergent extension such as Tide with Bleach to have an advantage over a bleach extension such as Clorox. On the other hand, Clorox has successfully extended its brand into household cleaning products like toilet bowl cleaners, where the bleach ingredient is seen as more relevant.[80]

Although Clorox is a leader in bleach, the initial success of its detergent with bleach product faded away when Procter & Gamble introduced Tide detergent with bleach.
Source: Keri Miksza

The relationship between primary and secondary ingredients Clorox may have encountered might also explain why Aunt Jemima was successful in introducing a pancake syrup extension from its well-liked pancake mix product, but syrup maker Log Cabin was less successful in introducing a pancake mix extension: pancake mix is seen as a more dominant ingredient than pancake syrup in breakfast pancakes.

6. ***Concrete attribute associations tend to be more difficult to extend than abstract benefit associations.*** The limits to market leaders' extension boundaries may be more rigid because many market leaders have strong concrete product attribute associations. These may even be reinforced by their names, like Liquid Paper, Cheez Whiz, and Shredded Wheat.[81] La-Z-Boy, for example, has struggled some to expand its strong usage imagery outside the narrow product line of recliners.

Concrete attribute associations thus may not transfer as broadly to extension categories as more abstract attribute associations.[82] For example, the Aaker and Keller study showed that consumers dismissed a hypothetical Heineken popcorn extension as potentially tasting bad or like beer, and a hypothetical Crest chewing gum extension as tasting unappealing or like toothpaste. In each case, consumers inferred a concrete attribute association for an extension that was technically feasible, even though common sense might have suggested that, logically, a manufacturer would not likely introduce a product with such an attribute.

More abstract associations, on the other hand, may be more relevant across a wide set of categories because of their intangible nature. For example, Aaker and Keller also showed that the Vuarnet brand had a remarkable ability to transfer to a disparate set of product categories, such as sportswear, watches, wallets, and even skis. In these cases, complementarity may have led consumers to infer that the extension would have the "stylish" attribute associated with the Vuarnet name, and they valued such an association in the different contexts.

We should note several caveats, however. First, parent brands' concrete attributes *can* transfer to some product categories.[83] A concrete attribute that is highly valued in the extension category because it creates a distinctive taste, ingredient, or component can often make the extension successful. According to Farquhar and Herr, such extensions might include Tylenol sinus medication, Oreo cookies and cream ice cream, and Arm & Hammer carpet deodorizer.[84]

Second, abstract associations may not always transfer easily. This second caveat emerged from a study conducted by Bridges, Keller, and Sood, who examined the relative transferability of product-related brand information when it was represented either as an abstract brand association or as a concrete brand association. For example, one such comparison contrasted the relative transferability of a watch brand characterized by dominant concrete attribute associations such as "water-resistant quartz movements, a time-keeping mechanism encased in shockproof steel covers, and shatterproof crystal," with that of a brand characterized by dominant abstract attribute associations such as "durable."

Although these authors expected the abstract brand representation to fare better, they found that, for several reasons, the two types of brand images extended equally well into a dissimilar product category—handbags. Perhaps the most important reason was that consumers did not believe the abstract benefit would have the same meaning in the extension category (durability does not necessarily "transfer" because durability for a watch is not the same as durability for a handbag).[85]

Finally, Joiner and Loken, in a demonstration of the "inclusion effect" in a brand extension setting, showed that consumers often generalized possession of an attribute from a specific category (like Sony televisions) to a more general category (say, all Sony products) more readily than they generalized the attribute from the specific category (Sony televisions) to another specific category (Sony bicycles). The effect was greater the more the specific extension category was typical of the general category (Sony cameras are more typical than Sony bicycles).[86]

7. *Consumers may transfer associations that are positive in the original product class but become negative in the extension context.* Because they have different motivations or use the product differently in the extension category, consumers may not value a brand association as highly as the original product. For example, when Campbell test-marketed a tomato sauce with the Campbell's name, it flopped. Apparently, Campbell's strong associations to soup signaled to consumers that the new product would be watery. To give the product more credibility, Campbell changed the name to the Italian-sounding "Prego," and the product has gone on to be a long-term success.

8. *Consumers may infer negative associations about an extension, perhaps even based on other inferred positive associations.* Even if consumers transfer positive associations from the parent brand to the extension, they may still infer other negative associations. For example, the Bridges, Keller, and Sood study showed that consumers who thought a proposed handbag extension from a hypothetical maker of durable watches also would be durable also assumed it would not be fashionable, helping to contribute to low extension evaluations.[87]

9. ***It can be difficult to extend into a product class that consumers see as easy to make.*** Consumers may dismiss some seemingly appropriate extensions if they see the product as comparatively easy to make and brand differences are hard to come by. Then a high-quality brand may seem incongruous; alternatively, consumers may feel the extension will attempt to command an unreasonable price premium and be too expensive.

For example, Aaker and Keller showed that hypothetical extensions such as Heineken popcorn, Vidal Sassoon perfume, Crest shaving cream, and Häagen-Dazs cottage cheese received relatively poor marks from experimental subjects in part because all brands in the extension category were seen as being about the same in quality, suggesting that the proposed brand extension was unlikely to be superior to existing products.

When consumers see the extension category as difficult to make, on the other hand, such that brands can vary a great deal in quality, an extension has a greater opportunity to differentiate itself, although consumers may also be less sure what the exact quality level of the extension will be.[88]

10. ***A successful extension can not only contribute to the parent brand image but also enable a brand to extend even farther.*** An extension can help the image of the parent brand by improving the strength, favorability, or uniqueness of its associations.[89] For example, Keller and Aaker, as well as Swaminathan, Fox, and Reddy, showed that when consumers did not already have strongly held attitudes, the successful introduction of a brand extension improved their choice and evaluations of a parent brand they originally perceived to be of only average quality.

If an extension changes the image and meaning of the brand, subsequent extensions that otherwise might not have seemed appropriate to consumers may make more sense and appear to be a better fit. Keller and Aaker showed that by taking little steps, that is, by introducing a series of closely related but increasingly distant extensions, marketers may insert brands into product categories that would have been much more difficult, or perhaps even impossible, to enter directly.[90]

A successful extension thus helps brands grow in three important ways:

1. By establishing a new market for the brand,
2. By strengthening existing markets for the brand, and
3. By opening up the possibility of additional new markets for the brand to subsequently enter.

For example, when Toyota launched the successful Prius hybrid gasoline–electric car, it not only cast a positive halo on the Toyota corporate brand as a whole as innovative and environmentally concerned, but it also paved the way for the introduction of a whole family of four different Prius models.

Similarly, when Apple introduced the iPod and iTunes digital music systems, they quickly became the market leader, representing one of the company's most successful new products ever. It also provided a halo effect that significantly boosted sales for the company's existing computer and software products. Finally, it made it easier for the company to introduce the iPhone smartphone and perhaps even the iPad tablet computer.

Different factors affect the success of multiple extensions. Boush and Loken found that consumers evaluated far extensions from a "broad" brand more favorably than from a "narrow" brand.[91] Dacin and Smith have shown that if the perceived quality levels of different members of a brand portfolio are more uniform, then consumers tend to make higher, more confident evaluations of a proposed new extension.[92] They also showed that a firm that had demonstrated little variance in quality across a diverse set of product categories was better able to overcome perceptions of poor extension fit. It is as if consumers in this case think, "Whatever this company does, it tends to do well."

In an empirical study of 95 brands in 11 nondurable consumer goods categories, Sullivan found that, in terms of stages of the product category life cycle, early-entering brand extensions did not perform as well, on average, as either early-entering new-name products or late-entering brand extensions.[93]

Shine, Park, and Wyer demonstrate an interesting brand synergy effect of multiple extensions. The simultaneous introduction of two brand extensions (e.g., two digital cameras) had an effect on consumer evaluations of the extensions independent of their similarity or fit to the parent brand (e.g., Xerox). Consumers appear to view a related set of products from a single manufacturer as inherently appealing.[94] Mao and Krishnan point out that consumers may form their perceptions of extension fit very differently when a brand operates in multiple product domains.[95]

11. ***An unsuccessful extension hurts the parent brand only when there is a strong basis of fit between the two.*** The general rule of thumb emerging from academic research and industry experience is that an unsuccessful brand extension can damage the parent brand only when there is a high degree of similarity or fit—for example, in the case of a failed line extension in the same category.

Roedder John and Loken found that perceptions of quality for a parent brand in the health and beauty aids area decreased with the hypothetical introduction of a lower-quality extension in a similar product category (shampoo). Quality perceptions of the parent brand were unaffected, however, when the proposed extension was in a dissimilar product category (facial tissue).[96]

Similarly, Keller and Aaker, as well as Romeo, found that unsuccessful extensions in dissimilar product categories did not affect evaluations of the parent brand.[97] When the brand extension is further removed, it seems easier for consumers to compartmentalize the brand's products and disregard its performance in what is seen as an unrelated product category.

Additional research reinforces and amplifies this conclusion. Roedder John, Loken, and Joiner found that dilution effects were less likely to be present with flagship products; they occurred with line extensions but were not always evident for more dissimilar category extensions.[98]

Gürhan-Canli and Maheswaran extended the results of these studies by considering the moderating effect of consumer motivation and extension typicality.[99] In high-motivation conditions, they found that incongruent extensions were scrutinized in detail and led to the modification of family brand evaluations, regardless of the typicality of the extensions. In low-motivation conditions, however, brand evaluations were more extreme in the context of high (than low) typicality. Because consumers considered the less typical extension an exception, it had reduced impact.

Consistent with these high-motivation findings, Milberg and colleagues found that negative feedback effects were present when (1) consumers perceived extensions as belonging to product categories dissimilar from those associated with the family brand, and (2) extension attribute information was inconsistent with image beliefs that consumers associated with the family brand.[100]

In terms of individual differences, Lane and Jacobson found some evidence of a negative reciprocal impact from brand extensions, especially for high-need-for-cognition subjects, but did not explore extension similarity differences.[101] Kirmani, Sood, and Bridges found dilution effects with owners of prestige-image automobiles when low-priced extensions were introduced, but not with owners of nonprestige automobiles or nonowners of either automobile.[102]

Finally, Morrin examined the impact of brand extensions on the strength of parent brand associations in memory. Two computer-based studies revealed that exposing consumers to brand extension information strengthened rather than weakened parent brand associations in memory, particularly for parent brands that were dominant in their original product category. Higher fit also resulted in greater facilitation, but only for nondominant parent brands. Moreover, the advertised introduction of an extension did not improve memory of the parent brand as much as the same level of advertising directly promoting the parent.[103]

12. ***An unsuccessful extension does not prevent a firm from backtracking and introducing a more similar extension.*** The Keller and Aaker study also showed that unsuccessful extensions do not necessarily prevent a company from retrenching and later introducing a more similar extension. The failure of Levi's Tailored Classics is instructive in that regard.

LEVI'S TAILORED CLASSICS

In the early 1980s, Levi Strauss attempted to introduce a Tailored Classics line of men's suits, targeted to independent-thinking "clotheshorses," dubbed "Classic Individualists." Although the suit was not supposed to need tailoring, to allow for the better fit necessary for these demanding consumers, Levi designed the suit slacks and coat to be sold as separates. It chose to price these wool suits quite competitively and to distribute them through its existing department store accounts, instead of the specialty stores where the classic individualist traditionally shopped. Despite a determined marketing effort, the product failed to achieve its desired sales goals. There were problems with the chosen target market, distribution channels, and product design, but perhaps the most fundamental problem was the lack of fit between the Levi's informal, rugged, outdoor image and the image the company sought from its suits. Despite the ultimate withdrawal of the product, Levi Strauss later was able to execute one of the most successful apparel launches ever—Dockers pants—an extension much closer in fit and more strongly sub-branded.[104]

As these experiences with brand extensions illustrate, failure does not doom a firm *never* to be able to introduce any extensions—certainly not for a brand with as much equity as Levi. An unsuccessful extension does, however, create a "perceptual boundary" of sorts, in that it reveals the limits of the brand in the minds of consumers.

13. ***Vertical extensions can be difficult and often require sub-branding strategies.*** Some academic research has investigated vertical extension. In an empirical study of the U.S. mountain bicycle industry, Randall, Ulrich, and Reibstein found that brand price premium was positively correlated with the quality of the lowest-quality model in the product line for the lower-quality segments of the market; for the upper-quality segments of the market, brand price premium was also significantly positively correlated with the quality of the highest-quality model in the product line. They concluded that these results suggest managers wishing to maximize the equity of their brands should offer only high-quality products, although overall profit maximization could dictate a different strategy.[105]

Hamilton and Chernev show that upscale extensions increase the price image of a brand and downscale extensions decrease its price image when consumers are browsing or just looking around, but that does not necessarily apply when consumers are actively looking to make a purchase. In the latter case, the effects can even be reversed: upscale extensions may actually decrease price image and downscale extensions increase it if consumers have an explicit buying goal.[106]

Kirmani, Sood, and Bridges examined the "ownership effect"—whereby owners have more favorable responses than nonowners to brand extensions—in the context of brand line stretches. They found that the ownership effect occurred for upward and downward stretches of nonprestige brands (like Acura) and for upward stretches of prestige brands (like Calvin Klein and BMW). For downward stretches of prestige brands, however, the ownership effect did not occur because of owners' desires to maintain brand exclusivity. In this situation, a sub-branding strategy protected owners' parent brand attitudes from dilution.[107]

14. ***The most effective advertising strategy for an extension is one that emphasizes information about the extension (rather than reminders about the parent brand).*** A number of studies have shown that the information provided about brand extensions, by triggering selective retrieval from memory, may frame the consumer decision process and affect extension evaluations. In general, the most effective strategy appears to be one that recognizes the type of information already salient for the brand in the minds of consumers when they first consider the proposed extension, and that highlights additional information they would otherwise overlook or misinterpret.

Aaker and Keller found that elaborating briefly on specific extension attributes about which consumers were uncertain or concerned led to more favorable evaluations. Bridges, Keller, and Sood—as well as Klink and Smith—found that providing information could improve perceptions of fit when consumers perceived low fit between the brand and the extension, either by reinforcing an overlooked basis of fit or by addressing a distracting negative association.[108]

Lane found that repeating an ad that evoked primarily benefit brand associations could overcome negative perceptions of a highly incongruent brand extension. Moreover, for moderately incongruent brand extensions, even ads that evoked peripheral brand associations (say, via brand packaging or character) could improve negative extension perceptions with sufficient repetition.[109]

Research has also explored several other aspects of extension marketing programs. Sood and Keller found that "branding effects" in terms of inferences based on parent brand knowledge operated both in the absence and presence of product experience with an extension, although they were less pronounced or, in the case of an unambiguous negative experience, even nonexistent.[110]

In considering the effects of retailer displays, Buchanan, Simmons, and Bickart found that evaluations of a high-equity brand could be diminished by an unfamiliar competitive brand when (1) a mixed display structure led consumers to believe the competitive brand was relevant and useful for judging the high-equity brand, (2) the precedence given to one brand over another in the display made expectations about brand differences or similarities more evident to consumers, and (3) the unfamiliar competitive brand disconfirmed these expectations.[111]

15. *Individual differences can affect how consumers make an extension decision and will moderate extension effects.* Consumers vary in their short-term or long-term motivation, ability, and opportunity to evaluate an extension in a number of important ways. Researchers have shown how these differences can affect extension fit and evaluations, as follows.

Monga and John demonstrate that one important individual difference in extension evaluations is whether consumers are analytical or holistic thinkers. *Analytic thinkers* focus more on comparing specific attributes or benefits of the parent brand and extension; *holistic thinkers* focus more on comparing overall attitudes and judgments of the parent brand and extension. Analytical and holistic thinkers both gave prestige brands permission to extend widely, but holistic thinkers gave functional brands much greater permission to extend than analytical thinkers.[112]

Similarly, Yorkston, Nunes, and Matta show that consumers known as *incremental theorists*, who believe the personality traits of a brand are malleable, are more accepting of brand extensions than consumers known as *entity theorists*, who believe a brand's traits are fixed.[113]

Another important individual difference relates to *self-construal*, or how people view and make sense of life and their life.[114] A person with an *independent self-construal* is more concerned with the uniqueness of individuals; a person with an *interdependent self-construal* is more concerned with relationships between and among individuals.

In a branding context, Ahluwalia posited that a consumer with an interdependent self-construal should be better able to uncover the possible relationships among a brand extension and its parent brand and thus have higher perceptions of extension fit and favorability. In her study, these effects were observed as long as consumers with interdependent self-construal were sufficiently motivated.[115]

Similarly, Puligadda, Ross, and Grewal argue that *brand-schematic* consumers are more likely than others to process or organize information according to their brand knowledge. *Brand-aschematic* consumers, on the other hand, use other information such as product characteristics or attributes as a frame of reference. Brand schematic consumers were shown to be more likely to see the similarity in a brand extension concept.[116]

Another important individual difference between consumers is what academics call *regulatory focus*. This deals with motivation and how people go about pursuing their goals. Individuals with a *prevention focus* are concerned with negative outcomes and avoiding losses via safety, security, responsibility, and so on. Individuals with a *promotion focus* are concerned with positive outcomes, seeking gains and pleasure and avoiding missed opportunities.[117]

Yeo and Park showed that consumers who are focused on prevention tend to judge dissimilar extensions less favorably than consumers who focus on promotion, due to their different interpretations of risk.[118] Relatedly, Chang, Lin, and Chang showed that promotion-focused consumers are more likely to focus abstractly on the overlap in benefits in judging an extension, whereas prevention-focused consumers are more likely to focus concretely on sheer category similarity.[119]

Temporal factors can affect extension evaluations. Barone, Miniard, and Romeo experimentally demonstrated that positive mood led consumers to think more positively of extensions they viewed as moderately similar to a brand they valuated favorably (as opposed to very similar or dissimilar).[120]

16. *Cultural differences across markets can influence extension success.* Building in part on branding research on individual differences, much recent research has explored how different cultures respond differently to brand extensions. Monga and John, as well as Ng and Houston, have shown that consumers from Eastern cultures (such as China) have a more holistic style of thinking and perceive higher levels of extension fit than do consumers from Western cultures (like the United States) who have a more analytical style of thinking.[121]

Dilution effects for a typical or similar extension that fails also can vary by culture and consumer motivation: Consumers from Eastern cultures exhibit significantly greater dilution when their motivation is high; consumers from Western cultures exhibit significantly greater dilution when their motivation is low.[122]

Additionally, Torelli and Ahluwalia show that cultural congruency can aid culturally consistent brand extensions over and beyond the effects of perceived fit. They note that a cultural congruent brand extension might be something like Sony electric car; a culturally incongruent car might be something like Sony cappuccino-macchiato maker. According to the research, beyond the inherent levels of fit that any electronic manufacturer might enjoy with an electric car, Sony would be expected to get an extra boost in fit and evaluations because of its Japanese country of origin and Japan's strong association with electronics.[123]

REVIEW

Brand extensions occur when a firm uses an established brand name to introduce a new product. We can distinguish them by whether the new product is being introduced in a product category currently served by the parent brand (a line extension) or in a completely different product category (a category extension). Brand extensions can come in all forms. They offer many potential benefits but also can pose many problems.

The basic assumptions behind brand extensions are that consumers have some awareness of and positive associations about the parent brand in memory, and that the brand extension will evoke at least some of these. Moreover, marketers assume that negative associations will not be transferred from the parent brand or created by the brand extension.

The extension's ability to establish its own equity will depend on the salience of consumers' associations with the parent brand in the extension context and the favorability and uniqueness of any associations they infer. The extension's ability to contribute to parent brand equity will depend on how compelling is the evidence about the corresponding attribute or benefit association in the extension context, how relevant or diagnostic the extension evidence is about the attribute or benefit for the parent brand, and how strong consumers' existing attribute or benefit associations are for the parent brand.

To evaluate brand extension opportunities, marketers need to carefully consider brand extension strategies by applying managerial judgment and consumer research to the following steps: Define actual and desired consumer knowledge about the brand, identify possible extension candidates, evaluate the potential of extension candidates, design marketing programs to launch extensions, and evaluate extension success and effects on parent brand equity. Finally, a number of important research findings deal with factors affecting the acceptance of a brand extension, as well as the nature of feedback to the parent brand.

DISCUSSION QUESTIONS

1. Pick a brand extension. Use the models presented in the chapter to evaluate its ability to achieve its own equity as well as contribute to the equity of a parent brand. If you were the manager of that brand, what would you do differently?
2. Do you think Virgin's brand is overextended? What are the arguments for or against?
3. How successful do you predict these recently proposed extensions will be? Why?
   a. Mont Blanc (famous for pens): fragrances and other accessories (watches, cufflinks, sunglasses, and pocket knives)
   b. Evian (famous for water): high-end spas
   c. Starbucks (famous for coffee): film production and promotion
   d. Trump (famous for hotels and casinos): vodka and mortgage services

4. Consider the following brands, and discuss the extendability of each:
   a. Harley-Davidson
   b. Red Bull
   c. Tommy Hilfiger
   d. Whole Foods
   e. Netflix
   f. U.S. Marines
   g. Grey Goose Vodka
   h. Victoria's Secret
   i. BlackBerry
   j. Las Vegas
   k. Kate Spade

5. There are four fake brand extensions among the following list; the other six were marketed at one point. Can you identify the four fakes?[124]
   a. Ben-Gay Aspirin: Pain Relief That Comes with a Warm Glow
   b. Burberry Baby Stroller: For Discriminating Newborns
   c. Smith & Wesson Mountain Bikes: Ride without Fear
   d. Atlantic City Playing Cards: Talcum-Coated for Easy Shuffling
   e. Pond's Toothpaste: Reduces the Appearance of Fine Wines
   f. Slim Jim Beef-Flavored Throat Lozenges: For Meat Lovers Who Like to Sing Karaoke
   g. Frito-Lay Lemonade: A Tangy, Crunchy Thirst Quencher
   h. Cosmo Yoghurt: Spoon It Up, Slim Down Those Thighs
   i. Richard Simmons Sneakers: Shake Your Cute Little Booty to the Oldies
   j. Madonna Condoms: For Men Who Are Packing

BRAND FOCUS 12.0

Scoring Brand Extensions

When identifying and evaluating brand extensions, it is helpful to have a summary tool to judge their viability. The following checklist can provide some guidance:

1. Does the parent brand have strong equity?

2. Is there a strong basis of extension fit?

3. Will the extension have necessary points-of-parity and points-of-difference?

4. How can marketing programs enhance extension equity?

5. What implications will the extension have on parent brand equity and profitability?

6. How should feedback effects best be managed?

It's also useful to employ more systematic analysis of proposed extensions. The Brand Extendibility Scorecard is designed to help marketers conduct thoughtful, thorough analysis of brand extensions. Like any marketing tool or framework, however, it serves as a means to an end and is designed to inform decision making, not to provide black-and-white "go or no-go" decisions.

Figure 12-8 contains the Brand Extendibility Scorecard. Three of its four main criteria follow the classic "3 Cs" perspectives—the consumer, company, and competitive point of view—to judge brand positioning. The fourth criterion is unique to the Scorecard and measures brand equity feedback.

Within each criterion, there are two major factors and one minor factor. Major factors are scored on a 10-point scale, minor factors on a 5-point scale. Maximum points are awarded if the extension candidate is clearly ideal on that factor, using either company or industry measures.

When we are scoring extensions, relative performance is important as absolute performance. Ranking extension candidates by their scores can provide a clear sense of priority, but we may also want to set cutoff points to guide decisions about potential extensions, perhaps by first scoring recent successful and unsuccessful extensions for the brand and even for competitors. This step also allows the marketing team to become more familiar with the scorecard.

Allocate points according to how well the new product concept rates on the specific dimensions in the following areas:

Consumer Perspectives: Desirability

10 pts. _____ Product category appeal (size, growth potential)

10 pts. _____ Equity transfer (perceived brand fit)

5 pts. _____ Perceived consumer target fit

Company Perspectives: Deliverability

10 pts. _____ Asset leverage (product technology, organizational skills, marketing effectiveness via channels and communications)

10 pts. _____ Profit potential

5 pts. _____ Launch feasibility

Competitive Perspectives: Differentiability

10 pts. _____ Comparative appeal (many advantages, few disadvantages)

10 pts. _____ Competitive response (likelihood, immunity or invulnerability from)

5 pts. _____ Legal/regulatory/institutional barriers

Brand Perspectives: Equity Feedback

10 pts. _____ Strengthens parent brand equity

10 pts. _____ Facilitates additional brand extension opportunities

5 pts. _____ Improves asset base

TOTAL _____ pts

FIGURE 12-8
Brand Extendibility Scorecard

Notes

1. For a more comprehensive treatment, see Glen Urban and John Hauser, *Design and Marketing of New Products*, 2nd ed. (Upper Saddle River, NJ: Prentice Hall, 1993).

2. Peter Farquhar, "Managing Brand Equity," *Marketing Research* 1 (September 1989): 24–33.

3. Mark Dolliver, "Brand Extensions Set the Pace in 2009," *Adweek*, 22 March 2010.

4. "IRI Names Top New Products of 2010," www.symphonyiri.com, 22 March 2010.

5. Sheridan Prasso, "The Unlikely King of Yogurt," *Fortune*, 12 December 2011; Christopher Steiner, "The $700 Million Yogurt Startup," *Forbes*, 8 September 2011; Stuart Elliott, "Chobani, Greek Yogurt Leader, Lets Its Fans Tell the Story," *New York Times*, 16 February 2011.

6. J. J. Colao, "Here's the Beef," *Forbes*, 19 December 2011, 104–108; David A. Kaplan, "Shake Shack's New Adventure," *Fortune*, 7 November 2011, 45–46.

7. Byung-Do Kim and Mary W. Sullivan, "The Effect of Parent Brand Experience on Line Extension Trial and Repeat Purchase," *Marketing Letters* 9, no. 2 (1998): 181–193.

8. Henry J. Claycamp and Lucien E. Liddy, "Prediction of New Product Performance: An Analytical Approach," *Journal of Marketing Research* (November 1969): 414–420.

9. Kevin Lane Keller and David A. Aaker, "The Effects of Sequential Introduction of Brand Extensions," *Journal of Marketing Research* 29 (February 1992): 35–50; John Milewicz and Paul Herbig, "Evaluating the Brand Extension Decision Using a Model of Reputation Building," *Journal of Product & Brand Management* 3, no. 1 (1994): 39–47.

10. See also Jonlee Andrews, "Rethinking the Effect of Perceived Fit on Customers' Evaluations of New Products," *Journal of the Academy of Marketing Science* 23, no. 1 (1995): 4–14.

11. David B. Montgomery, "New Product Distribution: An Analysis of Supermarket Buyer Decisions," *Journal of Marketing Research* 12, no. 3 (1978): 255–264.

12. Tülin Erdem and Baohong Sun, "An Empirical Investigation of the Spillover Effects of Advertising and Sales Promotions in Umbrella Branding," *Journal of Marketing Research* 39 (November 2002): 408–420.

13. Mary W. Sullivan, "Brand Extensions: When to Use Them," *Management Science* 38 (June 1992): 793–806.

14. Daniel C. Smith, "Brand Extension and Advertising Efficiency: What Can and Cannot Be Expected," *Journal of Advertising Research* (November/December 1992):

11–20. See also Daniel C. Smith and C. Whan Park, "The Effects of Brand Extensions on Market Share and Advertising Efficiency," *Journal of Marketing Research* 29 (August 1992): 296–313.

15. Jack Neff, "Speichert Looks for Big Growth Bets as First CMO," *Advertising Age*, 21 February 2011; Jack Neff, "Zigging Where Others Zagged, L'Oréal Focuses on U.S.—to Beautiful Effect," *Advertising Age*, 7 November 2011; "L'Oréal Shifts Marketing Model," *WARC*, 25 October 2010; "Why L'Oréal's Jean-Paul Agon Believes He Is on the Winning Team," *Knowledge@Wharton*, 30 March 2005.

16. Theodore Levitt, "Marketing Myopia," *Harvard Business Review* (July–August 1960): 45–46.

17. "Gartner Says Worldwide Enterprise Software Market Grew 8.5 Percent in 2010 to Reach $245 Billion," www.gartner.com, 5 May 2011.

18. Keller and Aaker, "Effects of Sequential Introduction of Brand Extensions."

19. Naomi Aoki, "Beyond the Bag," *Boston Globe*, 26 September 2004, E1; Hoag Levins, "Bogged Down in Marketing Success: Ocean Spray Wades into New York," *Advertising Age*, 9 October 2008; Jon Chesto, "Ocean Spray CEO Is on a Mission to 'Juice Up' the Company's Equity," *Patriot Ledger*, 9 May 2009.

20. Gregory L. White, "GM Revitalizes Luxury Brand with Its New Cadillac Lineup," *Wall Street Journal*, 23 January 2003; Mae Anderson, "Call It a Comeback—How Old Brands Become New," *Associated Press*, 10 January 2012; Auto Editors of Consumer Guide, "Cadillac Escalade," http://auto.howstuffworks.com/2000-2008-cadillac3.htm, accessed 4 February 2012.

21. James Thomson, "Brand with Bucks: Australia's Most Valuable Brands," *Smart Company*, 11 March 2009; Shahnaz Mahmud, "Billabong Launches 'I Surf Because' Customer Acquisition Effort," *Direct Marketing News*, 30 July 2010; "Billabong to Buy Nixon," www.allbusiness.com, 1 February 2006.

22. Barry Schwartz, *The Paradox of Choice: Why More Is Less* (New York: Ecco, 2004).

23. Laura Shanahan, "Designated Shopper," *Brandweek*, 26 March 2001, 46.

24. Ibid.

25. Ira Teinowitz and Jennifer Lawrence, "Brand Proliferation Attacked," *Advertising Age*, 10 May 1993, 1, 48.

26. Berner, "There Goes the Rainbow Nut Crunch."

27. B. G. Yovovich, "Hit and Run: Cadillac's Costly Mistake," *Adweek's Marketing Week*, 8 August 1988, 24.

28. Mary W. Sullivan, "Measuring Image Spillovers in Umbrella-Branded Products," *Journal of Business* 63, no. 3 (1990): 309–329; Andreas Cremer and Tom Lavell, "Audi 1980s Scare May Mean Lost Generation for Toyota Sales," *Bloomberg BusinessWeek*, 4 February 2010; John Holusha, "A Hard Sell for Audi," *New York Times*, 24 July 1988.

29. Maureen Morrin, "The Impact of Brand Extensions on Parent Brand Memory Structures and Retrieval Processes," *Journal of Marketing Research* 36, no. 4 (1999): 517–525.

30. Alessandra Galloni, "Inside Out: At Gucci, Mr. Polet's New Design Upends Rules for High Fashion," *Wall Street Journal*, 9 August 2005, A1; www.interbrand.com/en/best-global-brands/Best-Global-Brands-2011.aspx.

31. Jessica Wohl, "Target Hopes Exclusive Designer Deals Boost Sales," *Reuters*, 2 August 2011.

32. Joseph Galante and Ira Boudway, "Amazon Doubles Down on the Kindle," *Bloomberg BusinessWeek*, 2 August 2010; Brad Stone, "The Omnivore," *Bloomberg BusinessWeek*, 3 October 2011; Jennifer Van Grove, "Kindle Fire Leads Android in Taking a Bite out of iPad Market Share, www.venturebeat.com, 27 January 2012.

33. For some reviews of the brand extension literature, see Sandor Czellar, "Consumer Attitude Toward Brand Extensions: An Integrative Model and Research Propositions," *International Journal of Research in Marketing* 20 (2003): 97–115; Barbara Loken, Rohini Ahluwalia, and Michael J. Houston, eds., *Brands and Brand Management: Contemporary Research Perspectives* (New York: Psychology Press, 2010); Franziska Volkner and Henrik Sattler, "Drivers of Brand Extension Success," *Journal of Marketing* 70 (April 2006): 18–34

34. Kalpesh Kaushik Desai, Wayne D. Hoyer, and Rajendra Srivastava, "Evaluation of Brand Extension Relative to the Extension Category Competition: The Role of Attribute Inheritance from Parent Brand and Extension Category," working paper, State University of New York at Buffalo, 1996.

35. Edward M. Tauber, "Brand Leverage: Strategy for Growth in a Cost-Control World," *Journal of Advertising Research* (August/September 1988): 26–30.

36. Laura Cohn, "Why It Pays to Reinvent the Mop," *BusinessWeek*, 24 January 2005.

37. Barbara Loken and Deborah Roedder John, "Diluting Brand Beliefs. When Do Brand Extensions Have a Negative Impact?" *Journal of Marketing* 57, no. 7 (1993): 71–84.

38. For another conceptual point of view, see Abishek Dwivedi, Bill Merrilees, and Arthur Sweeney, "Brand Extension Feedback Effects: A Holistic Framework," *Journal of Brand Management* 17, no. 5: 328–342.

39. Dale Buss, "Making Tracks Beyond Tires," *Brandweek*, 15 September 2003, 16; http://www.michelintravel.com; "Michelin Introduces a Unique, Worldwide Services Offer Designed to Ensure Travelers a Successful Trip," *PRNewswire*, 17 March 2010.

40. Timothy B. Heath, Devon DelVecchio, and Michael S. McCarthy, "The Asymmetric Effects of Extending Brands to Lower and Higher Quality," *Journal of Marketing* 75 (July 2011): 3–20.

41. Claudia H. Deutsch, "Name Brands Embrace Some Less-Well-Off Kinfolk," *New York Times*, 24 June 2005, C7.

42. "Holiday Inn Launches $100 Million Global Advertising Campaign," *PRNewswire*, 30 April 2010.

43. Farquhar, Han, Herr, and Ijiri, "Strategies for Leveraging Master Brands."

44. David A. Aaker, "Should You Take Your Brand Where the Action Is?" *Harvard Business Review*, September–October 1997, 135.

45. Gillian Oakenfull, Edward Blair, Betsy Gelb, and Peter Dacin, "Measuring Brand Meaning," *Journal of Advertising Research* (September–October 2000): 43–53.

46. John M. Murphy, *Brand Strategy* (New York: Prentice Hall, 1990).

47. Rajeev Batra, Peter Lenk, and Michel Wedel, "Brand Extension Strategy Planning: Empirical Estimation of Brand-Category Personality Fit and Atypicality," *Journal of Marketing Research* 48 (April 2010): 335–347.

48. Andrea Rothman, "France's Bic Bets U.S. Consumers Will Go for Perfume on the Cheap," *Wall Street Journal*, 12 January 1989, B6; Deborah Wise, "Bic Counts on a New Age for Spray Perfume," *New York Times*, 17 October 1988; David A. Aaker, *Managing Brand Equity* (New York: Free Press, 1991).

49. Sandra J. Milberg, Francisca Sinn, and Ronald C. Goodstein, "Consumer Reactions to Brand Extensions in a Competitive Context: Does Fit Still Matter?," *Journal of Consumer Research* 37 (October 2010): 543–553.

50. Piyush Kumar, "Brand Counterextensions: The Impact of Extension Success Versus Failure," *Journal of Marketing Research* 42 (May 2005): 183–194. See also Piyush Kumar, "The Impact of Cobranding on Customer Evaluation of Brand Counterextensions," *Journal of Marketing* 69 (July 2005): 1–18.

51. Glen L. Urban and Steven H. Star, *Advanced Marketing Strategy: Phenomena, Analysis, and Decisions* (Englewood Cliffs, NJ: Prentice Hall, 1991).

52. Kotler and Keller, *Marketing Management.*

53. Srinivas K. Reddy, Susan L. Holak, and Subodh Bhat, "To Extend or Not to Extend: Success Determinants of Line Extensions," *Journal of Marketing Research* 31 (May 1994): 243–262. For some conceptual discussion, see Kalpesh Kaushik Desai and Wayne D. Hoyer, "Line Extensions: A Categorization and an Information Processing Perspective," in *Advances in Consumer Research*, Vol. 20 (Provo, UT: Association for Consumer Research, 1993), 599–606.

54. Jack Neff, "Small Ball: Marketers Rely on Line Extensions," *Advertising Age*, 11 April 2005, 10.

55. Murphy, *Brand Strategy.*

56. Jim Arndorfer, "Bud Select Cannibalizes Sales of Sibling Brands," *Advertising Age*, 11 April 2005, 3.

57. Mita Sujan, "Nature and Structure of Product Categories," working paper, Pennsylvania State University, 1990; Joan Myers-Levy and Alice M. Tybout, "Schema Congruity as a Basis for Product Evaluation," *Journal of Consumer Research* 16 (June 1989): 39–54.

58. Deborah Roedder John and Barbara Loken, "Diluting Brand Equity: The Impact of Brand Extensions," *Journal of Marketing* (July 1993): 71–84.

59. David Boush and Barbara Loken, "A Process Tracing Study of Brand Extension Evaluations," *Journal of Marketing Research* 28 (February 1991): 16–28; Cathy L. Hartman, Linda L. Price, and Calvin P. Duncan, "Consumer Evaluation of Franchise Extension Products: A Categorization Processing Perspective," *Advances in Consumer Research*, Vol. 17 (Provo, UT: Association for Consumer Research, 1990), 120–126.

60. David A. Aaker and Kevin Lane Keller, "Consumer Evaluations of Brand Extensions," *Journal of Marketing* 54 (January 1990): 27–41.

61. Paul A. Bottomley and Stephen J. S. Holden, "Do We Really Know How Consumers Evaluate Brand Extensions? Empirical Generalizations Based on Secondary Analysis of Eight Studies," *Journal of Marketing Research* 38 (November 2001): 494–500. See also Jörg Hensler, Csilla Horváth, Marko Sarstedt, and Lorenz Zimmerman, "A Cross-Cultural Comparison of Brand Extensions Success Factors: A Meta-Study," *Journal of Brand Management* 18, no. 1 (2010): 5–20.

62. David Boush, Shannon Shipp, Barbara Loken, Ezra Gencturk, et al., "Affect Generalization to Similar and Dissimilar Line Extensions," *Psychology and Marketing* 4 (Fall 1987): 225–241.

63. Specifically, applying Mandler's congruity theory, Meyers-Levy and her colleagues showed that products associated with moderately incongruent brand names could be preferred over ones that were associated with either congruent or extremely incongruent brand names. They interpreted this finding in terms of the ability of moderately incongruent brand extensions to elicit more processing from consumers that could be satisfactorily resolved (assuming consumers could identify a meaningful relationship between the brand name and the product). See Joan Meyers-Levy, Therese A. Louie, and Mary T. Curren, "How Does the Congruity of Brand Names Affect Evaluations of Brand Name Extensions?" *Journal of Applied Psychology* 79, no. 1 (1994): 46–53. See also Eyal Maoz and Alice M. Tybout, "The Moderating Role of Involvement and Differentiation in the Evaluation of Brand Extensions," *Journal of Consumer Psychology* 12, no. 2 (2002): 119–131; Hyeong Min Kim, "Evaluations of Moderately Typical Products: The Role of Within-Versus Cross-Manufacturer Comparison," *Journal of Consumer Psychology* 16, no. 1 (2006): 70–78.

64. Deborah MacInnis and Kent Nakamoto, "Cognitive Associations and Product Category Comparisons: The Role of Knowledge Structures and Context," working paper, University of Arizona, 1990.

65. C. Whan Park, Sandra Milberg, and Robert Lawson, "Evaluation of Brand Extensions: The Role of Product Level Similarity and Brand Concept Consistency," *Journal of Consumer Research* 18 (September 1991): 185–193.

66. Susan M. Broniarczyk and Joseph W. Alba, "The Importance of the Brand in Brand Extension," *Journal of Marketing Research* 31 (May 1994): 214–228. Incidentally, although a Crest toothbrush was not available at the time that this study was conducted, one was later in fact introduced as Crest Complete.

67. Tammo H. A. Bijmolt, Michel Wedel, Rik G. M. Pieters, and Wayne S. DeSarbo, "Judgments of Brand Similarity," *International Journal of Research in Marketing* 15 (1998): 249–268.

68. Sheri Bridges, Kevin Lane Keller, and Sanjay Sood, "Explanatory Links and the Perceived Fit of Brand Extensions: The Role of Dominant Parent Brand Associations and Communication Strategies," *Journal of Advertising* 29, no. 4 (2000): 1–11.

69. David M. Boush, "Brand Name Effects on Interproduct Similarity Judgments," *Marketing Letters* 8, no. 4 (1997): 419–427.

70. Daniel C. Smith and Jonlee Andrews, "Rethinking the Effect of Perceived Fit on Customers' Evaluations of New Products," *Journal of the Academy of Marketing Science* 23, no. 1 (1995): 4–14.

71. A. V. Muthukrishnan and Barton A. Weitz, "Role of Product Knowledge in Brand Extensions," in *Advances in Consumer Research*, Vol. 18, eds. Rebecca H. Holman and Michael R. Solomon (Provo, UT: Association for Consumer Research, 1990), 407–413. See also Broniarczyk and Alba, "Importance of the Brand."

72. Shi Zhang and Sanjay Sood, "'Deep' and 'Surface' Cues: Brand Extension Evaluations by Children and Adults," *Journal of Consumer Research* 29 (June 2002): 129–141.

73. Keller and Aaker, "Effects of Sequential Introduction of Brand Extensions," Susan M. Broniarczyk and Andrew D. Gershoff, "The Reciprocal Effects of Brand Equity and Trivial Attributes," *Journal of Marketing Research* 40 (May 2003): 161–175.

74. See also Arvind Rangaswamy, Raymond Burke, and Terence A. Oliva, "Brand Equity and the Extendibility of Brand Names," *International Journal of Research in Marketing* 10 (1993): 61–75. See also Zeynep Gürhan-Canli, "The Effect of Expected Variability of Product Quality and Attribute Uniqueness on Family Brand Evaluations," *Journal of Consumer Research* 30 (June 2003): 105–114.

75. Alexander Fedorikhin, C. Whan Park, and Matthew Thomson, "Beyond Fit and Attitude: The Effect of Emotional Attachment on Consumer Responses to Brand Extensions," *Journal of Consumer Psychology* 18 (2008): 281–291.

76. Catherine W. M. Yeung and Robert S. Wyer Jr., "Does Loving a Brand Mean Loving Its Products? The Role of Brand-Elicited Affect in Brand Extension Evaluations," *Journal of Marketing Research* 42 (November 2005): 495–506.

77. See, for example, Peter H. Farquhar and Paul M. Herr, "The Dual Structure of Brand Associations," in *Brand Equity and Advertising: Advertising's Role in Building Strong Brands*, eds. David A. Aaker and Alexander L. Biel (Hillsdale, NJ: Lawrence Erlbaum Associates, 1993), 263–277.

78. Ian M. Lewis, "Brand Equity or Why the Board of Directors Needs Marketing Research," paper presented at the ARF Fifth Annual Advertising and Promotion Workshop, 1 February 1993.

79. Stephen Phillips, "Chiquita May Be a Little Too Ripe," *BusinessWeek*, 30 April 1990, 100.

80. Robert D. Hof, "A Washout for Clorox?" *BusinessWeek*, 9 July 1990, 32–33; Alicia Swasy, "P&G and Clorox Wade into Battle over the Bleaches," *Wall Street Journal*, 16 January 1989, 5; Maria Shao, "A Bright Idea That Clorox Wishes It Never Had," *BusinessWeek*, 24 June 1991, 118–119.

81. Peter H. Farquhar, Julia Y. Han, Paul M. Herr, and Yuji Ijiri, "Strategies for Leveraging Master Brands," *Marketing Research* (September 1992): 32–43.

82. Alokparna Basu Monga and Deborah Roedder John, "What Makes Brands Elastic? The Influence of Brand Concept and Styles of Thinking on Brand Extension Evaluation," *Journal of Marketing Research* 74 (May 2010): 80–92; Tom Meyvis and Chris Janiszewski, "When Are Broader Brands Stronger Brands? An Accessibility Perspective on the Success of Brand Extensions," *Journal of Consumer Research* 31 (September 2004): 346–357; Stijn M. J. Van Osselaer and Joseph W. Alba, "Locus of Equity and Brand Extensions," *Journal of Consumer Research* 29 (March 2003): 539–550; Henrik Hagtvedt and Vanessa M. Patrick, "The Broad Embrace of Luxury: Hedonic Potential as a Driver of Brand Extendibility," *Journal of Consumer Psychology* 19 (2009): 608–618.

83. Paul M. Herr, Peter H. Farquhar, and Russell H. Fazio, "Impact of Dominance and Relatedness on Brand Extensions," *Journal of Consumer Psychology* 5, no. 2 (1996): 135–159.

84. Farquhar, Han, Herr, and Ijiri, "Strategies for Leveraging Master Brands."

85. Bridges, Keller, and Sood, "Explanatory Links."

86. Christopher Joiner and Barbara Loken, "The Inclusion Effect and Category-Based Induction: Theory and Application to Brand Categories," *Journal of Consumer Psychology* 7, no. 2 (1998): 101–129.

87. Bridges, Keller, and Sood, "Explanatory Links and the Perceived Fit of Brand Extensions."

88. Frank Kardes and Chris Allen, "Perceived Variability and Inferences about Brand Extensions," in *Advances in Consumer Research*, Vol. 18, eds. Rebecca H. Holman and Michael R. Solomon (Provo, UT: Association for Consumer Research, 1990), 392–398; Babu John Mariadoss, Raj Echambadi, Mark J. Arnold, and Vishal Bindroo, "An Examination of the Effects of Perceived Difficulty of Manufacturing the Extension Product on Brand Extension Attitudes," *Journal of the Academy of Marketing Science* 38 (2010): 704–719.

89. Vanitha Swaminathan, Richard J. Fox, and Srinivas K. Reddy, "The Impact of Brand Extension Introduction on Choice," *Journal of Marketing* 65 (October 2001): 1–15; Subramanian Balachander and Sanjay Ghose, "Reciprocal Spillover Effects: A Strategic Benefit of Brand Extensions," *Journal of Marketing* 67 (January 2003): 4–13.

90. See also Sandy D. Jap, "An Examination of the Effects of Multiple Brand Extensions on the Brand Concept," in *Advances in Consumer Research*, Vol. 20 (Provo, UT: Association for Consumer Research, 1993), 607–611.

91. Boush and Loken, "Process Tracing Study."

92. Peter Dacin and Daniel C. Smith, "The Effect of Brand Portfolio Characteristics on Consumer Evaluations of Brand Extensions," *Journal of Marketing Research* 31 (May 1994): 229–242. See also Boush and Loken, "Process Tracing Study"; and Niraj Dawar, "Extensions of Broad Brands: The Role of Retrieval in Evaluations of Fit," *Journal of Consumer Psychology* 5, no. 2 (1996): 189–207.

93. Mary W. Sullivan, "Brand Extensions: When to Use Them," *Management Science* 38, no. 6 (1992): 793–806; Patrick DeGraba and Mary W. Sullivan, "Spillover Effects, Cost Savings, R&D and the Use of Brand Extensions," *International Journal of Industrial Organization* 13 (1995): 229–248.

94. Byung Chul Shine, Jongwon Park, and Robert S. Wyer Jr., "Brand Synergy Effects in Multiple Brand Extensions," *Journal of Marketing Research* 44 (November 2007): 663–670.

95. Huifang Mao and H. Shanker Krishnan, "Effects of Prototype and Exemplar Fit on Brand Extension Evaluations: A Two-Process Contingency Model," *Journal of Consumer Research* 33 (June 2006): 41–49. See also Ujwal Kayande, John H. Roberts, Gary L. Lilien, and Duncan K. H. Fong, "Mapping the Bounds of Incoherence: How Far Can You Go and How Does It Affect Your Brand?," *Marketing Science* 26 (July–August 2007): 504–513.

96. Deborah Roedder John and Barbara Loken, "Diluting Brand Beliefs: When Do Brand Extensions Have a Negative Impact?" *Journal of Marketing* 57 (Summer 1993): 71.

97. Jean B. Romeo, "The Effect of Negative Information on the Evaluation of Brand Extensions and the Family Brand," in *Advances in Consumer Research*, Vol. 18, eds. Rebecca H. Holman and Michael R. Solomon (Provo, UT: Association for Consumer Research, 1990), 399–406.

98. Deborah Roedder John, Barbara Loken, and Christopher Joiner, "The Negative Impact of Extensions: Can Flagship Products Be Diluted?," *Journal of Marketing* 62 (January 1998): 19–32.

99. Zeynep Gürhan-Canli and Durairaj Maheswaran, "The Effects of Extensions on Brand Name Dilution and Enhancement," *Journal of Marketing Research* 35, no. 11 (1998): 464–473.

100. Sandra J. Milberg, C. W. Park, and Michael S. McCarthy, "Managing Negative Feedback Effects Associated with Brand Extensions: The Impact of Alternative Branding Strategies," *Journal of Consumer Psychology* 6, no. 2 (1997): 119–140.

101. Vicki R. Lane and Robert Jacobson, "Stock Market Reactions to Brand Extension Announcements: The Effects of Brand Attitude and Familiarity," *Journal of Marketing* 59, no. 1 (1995): 63–77.

102. Amna Kirmani, Sanjay Sood, and Sheri Bridges, "The Ownership Effect in Consumer Responses to Brand Line Stretches," *Journal of Marketing* 63, no. 1 (1999): 88–101.

103. Maureen Morrin, "The Impact of Brand Extensions on Parent Brand Memory Structures and Retrieval Processes," *Journal of Marketing Research* 36, no. 4 (1999): 517–525.

104. David A. Aaker, *Managing Brand Equity* (New York: Free Press, 1991; Jean-Noel Kapferer, *Strategic Brand Management*, 2nd ed. (New York: Free Press, 2005); *Not By Jeans Alone* video, PBS *Enterprise*, 1983.

105. Taylor Randall, Karl Ulrich, and David Reibstein, "Brand Equity and Vertical Product Line Extent," *Marketing Science* 17, no. 4 (1998): 356–379.

106. Ryan Hamilton and Alexander Chernev, "The Impact of Product Line Extensions and Consumer Goals on the Formation of Price Image," *Journal of Marketing Research* 47 (February 2010): 51–62.

107. Kirmani, Sood, and Bridges, "The Ownership Effect."

108. Bridges, Keller, and Sood, "Explanatory Links." Richard R. Klink and Daniel C. Smith, "Threats to the External Validity of Brand Extension Research," *Journal of Marketing Research* 38 (August 2001): 326–335.

109. Vicki R. Lane, "The Impact of Ad Repetition and Ad Content on Consumer Perceptions of Incongruent Extensions," *Journal of Marketing* 64, no. 4 (2000): 80–91.

110. Sanjay Sood and Kevin Lane Keller, "The Effects of Product Experience and Branding Strategies on Parent Brand Evaluations and Brand Equity Dilution," *Journal of Marketing Research* (2012, in press).

111. Lauranne Buchanan, Carolyn J. Simmons, and Barbara A. Bickart, "Brand Equity Dilution: Retailer Display and Context Brand Effects," *Journal of Marketing Research* 36, no. 8 (1999): 345–355.

112. Alokparna Basu Monga and Deborah Roedder John, "What Makes Brands Elastic? The Influence of Brand Concept and Styles of Thinking on Brand Extension Evaluation," *Journal of Marketing Research* 74 (May 2010): 80–92. See also Hakkyun Kim and Deborah Roedder John, "Consumer Response to Brand Extensions: Construal Level as a Moderator of the Importance of Perceived Fit," *Journal of Consumer Psychology* 18, no. 2 (2008): 116–126.

113. Eric A. Yorkston, Joseph C. Nunes, and Shashi Matta, "The Malleable Brand: The Role of Implicit Theories in Evaluating Brand Extensions," *Journal of Marketing* 74 (January 2010): 80–93.

114. Hazel R. Markis and Shinobu Kitayama, "Culture and the Self: Implications for Cognition, Emotion, and Motivation," *Psychological Review* 98 (April 1991): 224–253; Angela Y. Lee, Jennifer L. Aaker, and Wendi L. Gardner, "The Pleasures and Pains of Distinct Self-Construals: The Role of Interdependence in Regulatory Focus," *Journal of Personality and Social Psychology* 78 (June 2000): 1122–1134; Angela Y. Lee, Punam Anand Keller, and Brian Sternthal, "Value from Regulatory Construal Fit," *Journal of Consumer Research* 36 (February 2010): 735–747.

115. Rohini Ahluwalia, "How Far Can a Brand Stretch? Understanding the Role of Self-Construal," *Journal of Marketing Research* 45 (June 2008): 337–350.

116. Sanjay Puligadda, William T. Ross Jr., and Radeep Grewal, "Individual Differences in Brand Schematicity," *Journal of Marketing Research* 49 (February 2012): 115–130.

117. Edward T. Higgins, "Beyond Pleasure and Pain," *American Psychologist* 52 (December 1997): 1280–1300; Edward T. Higgins, "How Self-Regulation Creates Distinct Values: The Case of Promotion and Prevention Decision Making," *Journal of Consumer Psychology* 12, no. 3 (2002): 177–191.

118. Junsang Yeo and Jongwon Park, "Effects of Parent-Extension Similarity and Self Regulatory Focus on Evaluations of Brand Extensions," *Journal of Consumer Psychology* 16, no. 3 (2006): 272–282.

119. Chung-Chau Chang, Bo-Chi Lin, and Shin-Shin Chang, "The Relative Advantages of Benefit Overlap Versus Category Similarity in Brand Extension

Evaluation: The Moderating Role of Self-Regulatory Focus," *Marketing Letters* 22 (November 2011): 391–404.

120. Michael J. Barone, Paul W. Miniard, and Jean B. Romeo, "The Influence of Positive Mood on Brand Extension Evaluations," *Journal of Consumer Research* 26 (December 2000): 386–400.

121. Alokparna Basu Monga and Deborah Roedder John (2007), "Cultural Differences in Brand Extension Evaluation: The Influence of Analytic versus Holistic Thinking," *Journal of Consumer Research* 33 (March 2007): 529–536; Sharon Ng and Michael Houston, "Exemplars or Beliefs? The Impact of Self-View on the Nature and Relative Influence of Brand Associations," *Journal of Consumer Research* 32 (March 2006): 519–529.

122. Sharon Ng, "Cultural Orientation and Brand Dilution: Impact of Motivation Level and Extension Typicality," *Journal of Marketing Research* 47 (February 2010): 186–198.

123. Carlos J. Torelli and Rohini Ahluwalia, "Extending Culturally Symbolic Brands: A Blessing or Curse?," *Journal of Consumer Research* 38 (February 2012): 933–947.

124. The fakes are Burberry Baby Stroller, Atlantic City Playing Cards, Slim Jim Beef Jerky Throat Lozenges, Richard Simmons Sneakers.

Managing Brands Over Time

13

Learning Objectives

After reading this chapter, you should be able to

1. Understand the important considerations in brand reinforcement.
2. Describe the range of brand revitalization options to a company.
3. Outline the various strategies to improve brand awareness and brand image.
4. Define the key steps in managing a brand crisis.

Some companies like Barnes & Noble have found it difficult to maintain market leadership in the face of strong competitors and other countervailing forces.
Source: AP Photo/Amy Sancetta, File

Preview

One of the obvious challenges in managing brands is constant change in the marketing environment. Shifts in consumer behavior, competitive strategies, government regulations, technological advances and other areas can profoundly affect the fortunes of a brand. Besides these external forces, the firm's own strategic focus may force minor or major adjustments in the way it markets its brands. Effective brand management thus requires proactive strategies designed to at least maintain—if not actually enhance—customer-based brand equity in the face of all these different forces.

Consider the fate of these four brands: Myspace, Yahoo!, Blockbuster, and Barnes & Noble. In the mid-2000s, each enjoyed a strong market position, if not outright leadership. In just a few short years, however, each was struggling for survival as Facebook, Google, Netflix, and Amazon, respectively, raced past them to establish market superiority. Although there are many explanations, the way these brands were managed certainly contributed to the outcomes.

This chapter considers how to best manage brands over time. Any marketing action a firm takes today can change consumers' brand awareness or brand image and have an indirect effect on the success of *future* marketing activities (see Figure 13-1). For example, the frequent use of temporary price decreases as sales promotions may create or strengthen a "discount" association to the brand, with potentially adverse implications on customer loyalty and responses to future price changes or non-price-oriented marketing communication efforts.[1]

Unfortunately, marketers may have a particularly difficult time trying to anticipate future consumer response: if the new knowledge structures that will influence future consumer response don't exist until the short-term marketing actions actually occur, how can they realistically simulate future consumer response to permit accurate predictions?

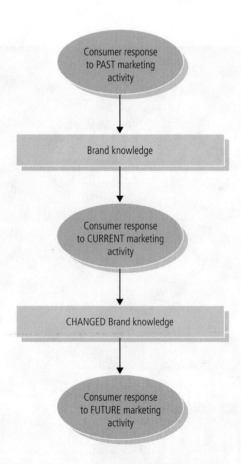

FIGURE 13-1

Understanding the Long-Term Effects of Marketing Actions on Brand Equity

The main assertion of this chapter is that marketers must actively manage brand equity over time by reinforcing the brand meaning and, if necessary, by making adjustments to the marketing program to identify new sources of brand equity. In considering these two topics, we'll look at a number of different brand reinforcement issues and brand revitalization strategies. The Brand Focus 13.0 at the end of the chapter considers how to deal with a marketing crisis, with specific emphasis on Johnson & Johnson's experiences with the Tylenol brand through the years.

REINFORCING BRANDS

How should we reinforce brand equity over time? How can marketers make sure consumers have knowledge structures that support brand equity for their brands? Generally, we reinforce brand equity by marketing actions that consistently convey the meaning of the brand to consumers in terms of brand awareness and brand image. As we have discussed before, questions marketers should consider are as follows:

- *What products does the brand represent, what benefits does it supply, and what needs does it satisfy?* Nutri-Grain has expanded from cereals into granola bars and other products, cementing its reputation as "makers of healthy breakfast and snack foods."
- *How does the brand make those products superior? What strong, favorable, and unique brand associations exist in the minds of consumers?* Through product development and the successful introduction of brand extensions, Black & Decker is now seen as offering "innovative designs" in its small appliance products.

Both these issues—brand meaning in terms of products, benefits, and needs as well as in terms of product differentiation—depend on the firm's general approach to product development, branding strategies, and other strategic concerns, as we discussed in Chapters 11 and 12. This section reviews some other important considerations for brand reinforcement, including the advantages of maintaining brand consistency, the importance of protecting sources of brand equity, and trade-offs between fortifying and leveraging brands.

If there is one rule for modern branding, however, it is that brands can never stand still. Brands must be constantly moving forward. A vivid example is the way Coldplay chose to launch their latest album.

COLDPLAY

Having sold 55 million albums in their careers, British rock band Coldplay might find the release of a new album to be nothing special. After all, their fourth album *Viva la Vida or Death and All His Friends* sold 2.8 million units in the United States alone, and their U.S. tour grossed more than $126 million. When launching their fifth album, *Mylo Xyloto*, however, Chris Martin, lead singer and frontman for the band, noted how aggressively they had to approach the release. "Because of the speed of media and entertainment, with every album you have to think like a new act," noted Martin, "just because they liked *A Rush of Blood to the Head* doesn't mean they're gonna like this one. So we start again." Before even launching a worldwide tour in 2012 that was scheduled to last over a year, the band had made 60 appearances of various sorts in 2011 to help promote the album: a video shoot in South Africa; a live-streamed *Amex Unstaged* launch show in Madrid shot by famed video and film director Anton Corbijn; a student union gig in Norwich, UK; guest spots on a host of U.S. talk shows; an acoustic show in a church in Hackney, East London; and headlining performances at the *Q* Music Awards and *X Factor* finale back in the UK. Performances of new songs appeared on YouTube and elsewhere. The band also released several singles online prior to the worldwide album release on October 24, 2011, all part of a viral campaign to generate fan interest and involvement. Leaving nothing to chance paid off for the band. *Mylo Xyloto* went to #1 in album sales in 17 countries, and most venues for the world tour sold out in minutes. The band did not stand still with respect to their world tour, either. In a concert first, each concertgoer received a RF-driven Xyloband flashing wristband that changed colors for different songs after receiving a signal.[2]

Despite being one of the most successful bands in the world, Coldplay took nothing for granted in launching their *Mylo Xyloto* album.
Source: AP Photo/John Marshall JME

Maintaining Brand Consistency

Without question, the most important consideration in reinforcing brands is consistency in the nature and amount of marketing support the brand receives. Brand consistency is critical to maintaining the strength and favorability of brand associations. Brands with shrinking research and development and marketing communication budgets run the risk of becoming technologically disadvantaged—or even obsolete—as well as out-of-date, irrelevant, or forgotten.

Market Leaders and Failures.   Inadequate marketing support is an especially dangerous strategy when combined with price increases. An example of failure to adequately support a brand occurred in the kitchen and bath fixtures market.

DELTA

Delta Faucet, the first company to advertise faucets on television in the 1970s, was the market leader in the 1980s with more than 30 percent market share. Beginning in the 1990s, however, two major factors contributed to a decline in market share. First, whereas Delta had built a strong business model based on the loyalty of professional plumbers, the advent of hardware superstores and online shopping empowered consumers to make their own choices and repairs. Second, Delta's support for its brand through innovation and advertising diminished during this time. These factors combined to give rival Moen an opportunity to gain market share, and by 2005 each company held 25 percent of the U.S. faucet market. That same year, Delta countered by raising its advertising budget 60 percent and conducting thousands of interviews and other forms of consumer research to feed R&D efforts.[3]

Even a cursory examination of the brands that have maintained market leadership for the last 50 or 100 years or so testifies to the advantages of staying consistent. Brands such as Disney, McDonald's, Mercedes Benz, and others have been remarkably true to their strategies once they achieved a preeminent market leadership position.

Perhaps an even more compelling demonstration of the benefits of consistency is the fortunes of brands that have constantly repositioned or changed ad agencies. Consider how Michelob's constant repositioning coincided with a steady sales decline.

MICHELOB

A brand that failed to turn around sales while enduring numerous repositionings is Michelob, an upscale, superpremium beer with a distinctive teardrop bottle designed in part to stand out in smoky bars and restaurants. In the 1970s, Michelob ran ads featuring successful young professionals that confidently proclaimed, "Where You're Going, It's Michelob." Moving away from the strong user imagery of that campaign, the next one focused on leisure situations and trumpeted, "Weekends Were Made for Michelob." Later, to bolster sagging sales, the ad theme switched to "Put a Little Weekend in Your Week." In the mid-1980s, the firm launched yet another campaign—featuring laid-back rock music and stylish shots of beautiful people—that proclaimed "The Night Belongs to Michelob." None of these campaigns could stop a sales slide from a peak of 8.1 million barrels in 1980 to 1.8 million in 1998. Leaving no stone unturned, the next ad campaign, "Some Days Are Better Than Others," explained to consumers that "A Special Day Requires a Special Beer," which later became "Some Days Were Made for Michelob." Pity the poor consumer! After so many different messages, people could hardly be blamed if they wondered exactly when they were supposed to drink the beer. Meanwhile, sales performance continued to suffer. The 2000s saw the brand concentrate on its Michelob Ultra extension, although the company did try to go after younger, import-drinking consumers in 2002 with hip, sexy ads. By the end of the decade, the brand had decided to return to its 100 percent malt roots—one of the defining characteristics of the exploding craft beer category—to chase after quality-conscious consumers, in yet another repositioning.[4]

Michelob has been repositioned so many times through the years, consumers could hardly be blamed for not knowing when (and why) they should drink the beer.

Source: AP Photo/PRNewsFoto/Anheuser-Busch

Consistency and Change.   Being consistent does not mean, however, that marketers should avoid making any changes in the marketing program. On the contrary, managing brand equity with consistency may require making numerous tactical shifts and changes in order to maintain the strategic thrust and direction of the brand. The most effective tactics for a particular brand at any one time can certainly vary. Prices may move up or down, product features may be added or dropped, ad campaigns may employ different creative strategies and slogans, and different brand extensions may be introduced or withdrawn to create the same desired knowledge structures in consumers' minds.

Nevertheless, the strategic positioning of many leading brands has been kept remarkably uniform over time by the retention of key elements of the marketing program and the preservation of the brand meaning. In fact, many brands have kept a key creative element in their marketing communication programs over the years and, as a result, have effectively created some "advertising equity." For example, Jack Daniels bourbon whiskey has stuck with rural scenes of its Tennessee home and the slogan "Charcoal Mellowed Drop by Drop" for literally decades.

As The Science of Branding 13-1 describes, brands sometimes return to their roots to remind existing or lapsed customers or to attract new ones. Such efforts to refresh awareness obviously can make sense. At the same time, marketers should be sure that these old advertising elements or marketing appeals have enduring meaning with older consumers but are also relevant to younger consumers. They should examine the entire marketing program to determine which elements are making a strong contribution to brand equity and must therefore be protected.

THE SCIENCE OF BRANDING 13-1

Brand Flashbacks

Older, heritage brands can reach into their past in different ways to develop successful new marketing campaigns. One way is to revisit well-known and loved past ad campaigns, perhaps giving them a twist and updating them in the process.

Dubbed *retro-branding* or *retro-advertising* by some marketing pundits, the tactic is a means to tie in with past advertising that was, and perhaps could still be, a key source of brand equity. Demonstrating the latent value of past advertising is the return of such advertising icons as Colonel Sanders for KFC, who reappeared in new advertising and packaging focused on the restaurant's Southern roots, albeit with a thinner face and a red apron instead of the classic three-piece suit.

Retro-branding can activate and strengthen brand associations that would be virtually impossible to recreate with new advertising today. In some cases, a key point-of-difference for the brand may just turn out to be heritage or nostalgia rather than any product-related difference. Heritage can be a powerful point-of-difference—at least as long as it conveys expertise, longevity, and experience and not just age!

Anniversaries and milestones of longevity can be excellent opportunities to launch a campaign to celebrate. Marketers should focus as much on the future of the brand as on its past, of course, perhaps emphasizing how all that the brand has gone through will benefit its customers in the future. L.L. Bean's 100th anniversary celebration in 2012 was intended to do just that. The main thrust of the campaign was to celebrate exploring the outdoors. To generate interest, the company engaged in a number of activities:

- It introduced a special-edition boot that closely replicated the first pair sold by founder Leon Leonwood Bean as well as other limited-edition offerings, including a $7,500 wooden canoe, a $149 Soule Coastal Duck Call, and a 20-gauge shotgun for $15,000.

Kraft Macaroni and Cheese Dinner used nostalgic reminders to target parents in addition to their kids.
Source: AP Images/Matt York

- L.L. Bean's Outdoor Discovery School guides traveled the country with the larger-than-life L.L. Bean Bootmobile to encourage people to get out of their homes and get back to nature.

Protecting Sources of Brand Equity

Consistency thus guides strategic direction and does not necessarily prescribe the particular tactics of the supporting marketing program for the brand at any one point in time. Unless some change in either consumer behavior, competition, or the company makes the strategic positioning of the brand less powerful, there is likely little need to deviate from a successful positioning.

Although brands should always look for potentially powerful new sources of brand equity, a top priority is to preserve and defend those that already exist, as illustrated by this classic episode with Intel.

INTEL

While the launch of the "Intel Inside" program in the early 1990s is a classic example of how to successfully introduce an ingredient brand, Intel did also encounter a public relations disaster with the "floating decimal" problem found by a Virginia researcher in its Pentium microprocessors in 1994. Although a flaw in the chip at the time resulted in miscalculations only in extremely unusual and exceedingly rare

- The company committed up to a million dollars in a year-long partnership with the National Park Foundation. Every time a consumer used social media to share outdoors experiences through online comments, photographs, stories, and video, the company donated $1 to the National Park Foundation's program for kids.

Nostalgia can play a valuable role for many brands. Oreo cookies and Keds tennis shoes have run nostalgia-focused campaigns targeting adults who presumably stopped using the product long ago. Kellogg's Frosted Flakes reminded an older audience that the cereal had "The Taste Adults Have Grown to Love." Later ads for the brand tug on the heartstrings of dads by suggesting, "Share What You Love With Who You Love."

Research shows that nostalgic advertising can positively influence consumers. One empirical study confirmed that intentionally nostalgic advertisements yielded favorable attitudes toward the advertisement and the brand. Another study identified a potential source of nostalgic purchase behavior, called "intergenerational influence," or the influence of a parent's purchase behavior and brand attitudes on a child's behavior and attitudes.

Some brands attempt to make the case that their enduring appeal is still relevant for lapsed users today. Kraft Macaroni and Cheese Dinner, long sold to parents as a meal favorite for children, turned the tables on grown-ups to remind them, "You Know You Love It." A $50 million campaign featuring TV, print and online ads, billboards, a Web site (www.youknowyouloveit.com), and social media communications on Facebook and Twitter supported the entire product line.

Heritage appeals do not necessarily have to use advertising though, as Pabst Blue Ribbon (PBR) beer shows. The brand was born in 1882, when the Pabst Brewing Company began tying silk ribbons to bottles of its Select beer. The company became one of the major U.S. beer brands and remained so through 1977, when sales peaked at 18 million barrels. As competition from Budweiser and Miller increased, however, the PBR brand suffered as a consequence of price cuts, quality problems, and ownership changes.

After years of decline, sales of PBR suddenly spiked in the Portland, Oregon area in 2001. Management investigated and discovered that young trendsetters were adopting the beer as a "blue-collar, Americana" alternative to the big brands and craft beers favored by their parents. Rather than using above-the-line advertising, which it had not done since the 1970s, Pabst sought to capitalize on this market through word-of-mouth, on-premise promotions, and event sponsorships, primarily of local bands and concerts, and licensed merchandise aimed at "hipsters."

By letting the brand's image be created as much by consumers as by the company itself and by keeping it local, hip, and organic, Pabst increased sales over the next nine years. With the Metropoulos family as new owners, other Pabst brands became candidates for revitalization—including Schlitz, Schaefer, Stroh's, and Falstaff. A total of 5 of the top 10 brands—from 1973!

Sources: Bruce Horovitz, "Southern Finger-Lickin' Roots Help KFC Revamp," *USA Today*, 20 April 2005, 3B; Darrel D. Muehling and David E. Sprott, "The Power of Reflection: An Empirical Examination of Nostalgia Advertising Effects," *Journal of Advertising* 33 (Fall 2004): 25; Elizabeth S. Moore, William L. Wilkie, and Richard J. Lutz, "Passing the Torch: Intergenerational Influences as a Source of Brand Equity." *Journal of Marketing* 66 (April 2002): 17–37; Stephen Brown, Robert V. Kozinets, and John F. Sherry Jr., "Teaching Old Brands New Tricks: Retro Branding and the Revival of Brand Meaning," *Journal of Marketing* 67 (July 2003): 19–33; Katherine E. Loveland, Dirk Smeesters, and Naomi Mandel, "Still Preoccupied with 1995: The Need to Belong and Preference for Nostalgiac Products," *Journal of Consumer Research* 37 (October 2010): 393–408; Jenn Abelson, "L.L. Bean Marks 100 Years with 'Bootmobile'," *Boston Globe*, 19 January 2012; Stuart Elliott, "Kraft Hope to Encourage Adults to Revert to a Childhood Favorite," *New York Times*, 26 May 2010; Jeremy Mullman, "Schlitz Tries to Revive '50s Heyday," *Advertising Age*, 17 April 2006, 8; Ann Cortissoz, "Not Your Father's Beer: Your Grandfather's," *Boston Globe*, 20 October 2004, F1; Matt Schwartz, "Can This Stay Cool? A Jet-Setting Family Takes Over a Blue Collar Brand," *Bloomberg BusinessWeek*, 20 September 2010; E.J. Schultz, "A Tiger at 60: How Kellogg's Tony Is Changing for a New Age," *Advertising Age*, 29 August 2011.

instances, once the problem became public, Intel endured an agonizing six-week period as the focus of media scrutiny and criticism. Intel was probably at fault—as company executives later admitted—for not telling consumers and proposing remedies more quickly. Two key sources of brand equity for Intel microprocessors like the Pentium—emphasized throughout the company's marketing program—are "power" and "safety." Although consumers primarily thought of safety in terms of upgradability, the potential for financial risk or other problems from a flawed chip certainly should have created a sense of urgency within Intel to protect one of its prize sources of brand equity. Eventually, Intel capitulated and offered a replacement chip. Perhaps not surprisingly, only a very small percentage of consumers (an estimated 1–3 percent) actually requested it, suggesting that it was Intel's stubbornness to act and not the defect per se that rankled many consumers. Although it was a painful episode, Intel maintains it learned a lot about how to manage its brand in the process.[5]

Ideally, the key sources of brand equity are of enduring value. Unfortunately, marketers can easily overlook that value as they attempt to expand the meaning of their brands and add new product-related or non-product-related brand associations. The next section considers these types of trade-offs.

Fortifying versus Leveraging

Chapters 4–7 described a number of different ways to raise brand awareness and create strong, favorable, and unique brand associations in consumer memory to build customer-based brand equity. In managing brand equity, marketers face tradeoffs between activities that fortify brand equity and those that leverage or capitalize on existing brand equity to reap some financial benefit.

Marketers can design marketing programs that mainly try to capitalize on or maximize brand awareness and image—for example, by reducing advertising expenses, seeking increasingly higher price premiums, or introducing numerous brand extensions. The more marketers pursue this strategy, however, the easier it is to neglect and perhaps diminish the brand and its sources of equity. Without its sources of brand equity, the brand itself may not continue to yield such valuable benefits. Just as failure to properly maintain a car eventually affects its performance, so too can neglecting a brand, for whatever reason, catch up with marketers.

WONDER BREAD

Wonder Bread was introduced as America's first sliced bread in the 1930s and, in its familiar blue, red, and yellow packaging, was a staple in many homes for decades since. After a series of ownership changes increased the company's focus on cost-cutting, however, Wonder Bread ceased advertising in the 1970s. Later, as consumer tastes shifted toward multigrain breads, Wonder Bread's corporate owners balked at the expense and time required to produce it. Although a new owner resurrected the brand's advertising campaign in 1996, the brand had effectively lost "two generations [of customers]" and struggled to recover, eventually filing for bankruptcy in 2004. The owners, Interstate Bakeries, took five years to fully emerge from the bankruptcy. Having done so, they initiated a series of actions and investments to help restore Wonder Bread to its previous stature. They reformulated the Wonder Classic and Wonder Classic Sandwich bread varieties to include more calcium and vitamin D. They also introduced Wonder Smartwhite—a new bread with the taste and soft texture of white bread, but with the fiber of 100 percent whole wheat. The company launched its first national advertising campaign for Wonder Bread in years, sending the message, "One thing you don't have to wonder about? The goodness of new Wonder."[6]

Once an iconic brand, Wonder Bread found its market position eroding after years of neglect until new owners launched new products and programs.

Source: Kristoffer Tripplaar/Alamy

Fine-Tuning the Supporting Marketing Program

Marketers are more likely to change the specific tactics and supporting marketing program for the brand than its basic positioning and strategic direction. They should make such changes, however, only when it's clear the marketing program and tactics are no longer making the desired contributions to maintaining or strengthening brand equity.

The way brand meaning is reinforced may depend on the nature of brand associations. We next look at specific considerations in terms of product-related performance and non-product-related imagery associations.

Product-Related Performance Associations. For brands whose core associations are primarily product-related performance attributes or benefits, innovation in product design, manufacturing, and merchandising is especially critical to maintaining or enhancing brand equity. Consider how Timex has evolved through the years to maintain its market position.

TIMEX

Timex has had a fascinating journey through time as it has dealt with a wave of competitors and changes in the marketing environment through the years. The origins of the brand stretch back into the nineteenth century, but its modern history began post–World War II with the launch of its popular line of inexpensive, durable wristwatches. Buoyed by "torture test" product demonstration ads and the clever slogan, "Takes a Licking and Keeps on Ticking," the brand became the market leader by the end of the 1950s. In subsequent years, after Timex watched brands such as Casio and Swatch gain significant market share by emphasizing digital technology and fashion (respectively) in their watches, it made a number of innovative marketing changes. Within a short period of time, Timex introduced Indiglo glow-in-the dark technology, showcased popular new models such as the Ironman in mass media advertising, and launched new Timex stores to showcase its products. The company also expanded its brand portfolio by buying the Guess and Monet watch brands to distribute through upscale department stores. These innovations in product design and merchandising significantly revived the brand's fortunes. In recent years, however, the growth of smartphones and other hand-held mobile devices that can tell time have posed yet more challenges. Once again, Timex responded by increasing the functionality of its watches. Beyond telling time, its new watches boast GPS technology and health-rate monitors and other wellness features.[7]

Constant innovation—such as the introduction of GPS into its Ironman line of watches—has helped Timex to maintain market leadership through the years.

Source: Timex Corporation

For companies in categories as diverse as toys and entertainment products, personal care products, and insurance, innovation is critical to success. For example, Progressive has become one of the most successful auto insurers, in part due to consistent innovations in service. A pioneer in direct sales of insurance online, the firm was the first to offer prospective customers the ability to instantly compare price quotes from up to three other insurers. Other Progressive innovations include an accident "concierge service" through which its representatives handle all aspects of the claims and repair process for its customers, and online policy management that lets customers make payments and change coverage at any time. See Branding Brief 13-1 for a summary of how Gillette has built equity in its razor and blades categories through innovation.

Failure to innovate can have dire consequences. Smith Corona, after struggling to sell its typewriters and word processors in a booming personal computer market, finally filed for bankruptcy. As one industry expert observed, "Smith Corona never realized they were in the document business, not the typewriter business. If they had understood that, they would have moved into software."[8] Guitar Hero was once touted as the first game franchise of the twenty-first century, but oversaturation and an inability to introduce engaging new products led its owner Activision to shutter the division after lackluster 2010 holiday sales.[9]

Product innovations are therefore critical for performance-based brands whose sources of equity reside primarily in product-related associations. In some cases, product advances may include brand extensions based on a new or improved product ingredient or feature. In fact, in many categories, a strong family sub-brand has emerged from product innovations associated with brand extensions (such as Wilson Hammer wide-body tennis racquets). In other cases, product innovations may center on existing brands. For example, General Mills' "Big G" cereal division historically strived to improve at least a third of its nearly two dozen brand lines each year.

At the same time, it is important not to change products too much, especially if the brand meaning for consumers is wrapped up in the product design or makeup. Recall the strong consumer resistance encountered by New Coke, described in Chapter 1. In making product changes to a brand, marketers want to reassure loyal consumers that it is a better product, but not necessarily a *different* one. The timing of the announcement and the introduction of a product improvement are also important: if the brand improvement is announced too soon, consumers may stop buying existing products; if too late, competitors may already have taken advantage of the market opportunity with their own introductions.

Non-Product-Related Imagery Associations.   For brands whose core associations are primarily non-product-related attributes and symbolic or experiential benefits, relevance in user and usage imagery is especially critical. Because of their intangible nature, non-product-related

Although once hugely popular—Annie Leunghe shown here had the highest score on Guitar Hero 3 for a female— the Guitar Hero brand eventually suffered from a lack of engaging new products to attract and retain users.
Source: ZUMA Press/ Newscom

BRANDING BRIEF 13-1

Razor-Sharp Branding at Gillette

Acquired by Procter & Gamble in 2005, Gillette is one of the strongest brands in the world, with roughly two-thirds of the U.S. blade and razor market and even more in Europe and Latin America. In fact, more than 70 percent of Gillette's sales and profits come from overseas operations in 200 countries. Moreover, its 10 percent profit margin is substantially higher than for other brands found at most packaged-goods companies. How has Gillette been so successful for so long? The marketing and branding practices that have supported the brand through the years provide a number of useful lessons.

Fundamentally, Gillette continually innovates to produce a demonstrably superior product. Gillette's credo is to "increase spending in 'growth drivers'—R&D, plant and equipment, and advertising—at least as fast as revenues go up." As Gillette's former CEO Alfred Zeien proclaimed, "Good products come out of market research. Great products come from R&D." Gillette typically spends more than 2 percent of its annual sales on R&D, double the average at many consumer products companies.

Gillette also backs its products with strong advertising and promotional support. TV ads have used champion athletes such as Roger Federer, Tiger Woods, Thierry Henry, Derek Jeter, and others with the now-familiar tag line, "The Best a Man Can Get." Skillful marketing thus creates both strong performance and imagery associations. Figure 13-2 summarizes Gillette's product innovations during the last 30 years. Here we highlight a few of the key developments over the last decade or so.

When it launched the Mach3 in 1998, Gillette considered it to be the most important new product in its history and invested more than $750 million in research and development and manufacturing expenses, securing 35 patents in the process. The major advancement of the Mach3 was the triple blade, each part of which was designed to shave progressively closer. The product was highly anticipated and generated more than 500 million media impressions before the advertising campaign began. During the launch year, Gillette set a marketing budget of $300 million globally and $100 million in the United States. The Mach3, which cost 35 percent more than the Sensor Excel, captured a stunning 35 percent of the razor market within two weeks of its launch date and surpassed the $1 billion sales mark only 15 months after its debut.

As successful as Mach3 was, Gillette's women's version of the product was perhaps an even more impressive achievement. Gillette spent $300 million on research and development for Venus, its first razor designed solely for women. Based on extensive consumer research and market testing, Venus was a marked departure from previous women's razor designs, which had essentially been colored or repackaged versions of men's razors. After research revealed that women change their grip on a razor about 30 times during each shaving session, Gillette designed the Venus with a wide, sculpted

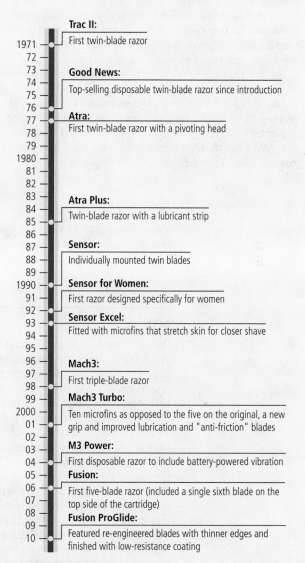

FIGURE 13-2
Gillette Razor Brand History

rubberized handle offering superior grip and control, and an oval-shaped blade in a storage case that could stick to shower walls. Research also indicated that women were reluctant to leave the shower in order to replace a dull blade, so the case was made to hold spare blade cartridges. Gillette spent $150 million on marketing for the highly successful worldwide Venus launch.

In 2004, it upgraded the Mach3 by introducing the M3 Power, the first disposable razor to feature a battery-powered vibration option, which allowed for a closer shave. A Venus version, called Venus Vibrance, soon followed. In its next major launch in 2006, Gillette introduced the six-bladed Fusion and

Fusion Power razors. Gillette had spent $1.2 billion on R&D since introducing the Mach3 and then spent more than $1 billion to market the product to the world's 3.2 billion males. The payoff? A four-pack of Fusion cartridges cost double the Mach3's original price. The Fusion ProGlide, Gillette's most expensive razor ever, followed a few years later. As Chapter 5 noted, the new sub-brand was successfully launched with a strong marketing campaign.

As its brand history clearly shows, much of Gillette's success results from its having relentlessly innovated and stayed relevant. The company has also carefully branded new products. Major introductions receive totally new sub-brand names (Sensor, Mach3, and Fusion), while minor improvements are given modifiers (Sensor Excel, Mach3 Turbo, and Fusion ProGlide).

Sources: Linda Grant, "Gillette Knows Shaving—and How to Turn Out Hot New Products," *Fortune*, 14 October 1996, 207–210; William C. Symonds, "Gillette's Edge," *BusinessWeek*, 19 January 1998; Chris Reidy, "The Unveiling of a New Venus," *Boston Globe*, 3 November 2000; Naomi Aoki, "Gillette Hopes to Create a Buzz with Vibrating Women's Razor," *Boston Globe*, 17 December 2004; A.G. Lafley, "It Was a No-Brainer," *Fortune*, 21 February 2005, 96; Editorial, "Gillette Spends Smart on Fusion," *Advertising Age*, 26 September 2005, 24; "Gillette Launches New Global Brand Marketing Campaign," *PRNewswire*, 1 July 2009; Jack Neff, "Gillette Fusion ProGlide," *Advertising Age*, 15 November 2010.

associations may be easier to change, for example, through a major new advertising campaign that communicates a different type of user or usage situation. MTV is a brand that has worked hard to stay relevant with young consumers.

MTV

Over the course of 30-plus years, MTV has built a powerful youth-oriented brand that spans the globe. When the all-music channel debuted in 1981, few dreamed it would attain such a prominent place in popular culture. Few also imagined that MTV would attract as many international viewers as it did—it is seen today in 592 million households in 161 countries and 33 languages. Domestically and abroad, MTV developed programming and content that consistently resonated with viewers over the years. It attracted loyal U.S. followers in the early 1980s and in each of its international broadcast regions in the 1990s and early 2000s. The channel built more than just its own brand equity. Throughout the years, MTV served as a star-making vehicle for pop artists and on-air talent. Experts credited the channel with changing the course of music and television, and in some cases even with having an impact upon sociopolitical events, including the collapse of the Eastern Bloc communist regime, the 2004 and 2008 Presidential elections, and the aftermath of September 11 and Hurricane Katrina. MTV's rise to cultural prominence was not achieved without difficulty. The channel endured a lengthy stretch of flat U.S. ratings in the mid-1990s as music tastes shifted and it lost touch with its core audience. However, MTV managed successfully to reinvent itself and establish a following from a new core audience by embracing "long-form" programming, starting with the run-away success of *Real World* and *Road Rules*. The channel even dropped the "music television" tagline from its logo in early 2010 in recognition of its new focus. Company president Van Toffler said at the time that MTV had evolved away from playing as many music videos as possible to including more "genre shows" such as *Jersey Shore, Teen Mom,* and *16 and Pregnant.* The shift in programming contributed to MTV's highest annual increase in ratings since 1999 and the explosion of teen pop. Toffler noted: "We really evolved in youth and pop culture and music, and we just speak to purely the 12–34 audience." The first decade of the new century had brought a new era of growth for MTV. In 1999, Viacom formed MTV Networks to offer its advertisers a full spectrum of demographic groups. MTV Networks included sister channels such as VH1, Nickelodeon, Nick at Nite, Comedy Central, and Spike TV. MTV also had expanded globally during this time—over 150 locally programmed and operated MTV channels now exist—to become the largest global media brand in the world. With the youngest member of Generation X turning 33 in 2012, however, MTV has moved on and now has set its sights squarely on the millennial generation, transforming programming and marketing in the process. Social media, original short-form programming, and a slew of digital content now play a key role in MTV's plans to engage this younger generation. Through the years, one thing has always been true: MTV has stayed focused on its central challenge of remaining current and relevant within the fickle world of popular culture.[10]

MTV evolved from a music video station hosted by VJs in the 1980s (on the top) to a long-form programming network focusing on youth culture as with its popular reality series like *Jersey Shore* (on the bottom).

Sources: Mark Weiss/WireImage/Getty Images; John Kessler/MTV/PictureGroup via AP Images

Nevertheless, ill-conceived or too-frequent repositionings can blur the image of a brand and confuse or perhaps even alienate consumers. It is particularly dangerous to flip-flop between product-related performance and non-product-related imagery associations because of the fundamentally different marketing and advertising approaches each entails. Heineken has sometimes been accused of flip-flopping too much between product-focused advertising ("It's All About the Beer") and more user-focused advertising ("Give Yourself a Good Name").

Significant repositionings may be dangerous for other reasons too. Brand images can be extremely sticky, and once strong associations have formed, they may be difficult to change. Consumers may choose to ignore or simply be unable to remember the new positioning when strong, but different, brand associations already exist in memory.[11] Club Med has attempted for years to transcend its image as a vacation romp for swingers to attract a broader cross-section of people.

For dramatic repositioning strategies to work, marketers must present convincing new brand claims in a compelling fashion. One classic example of a brand that successfully shifted from a primarily non-product-related image to a primarily product-related image is BMW, the quintessential "yuppie" vehicle of the 1980s. The brand's sales dropped almost in half from 1986 to 1991 as new Japanese competition emerged and a backlash to the "Greed Decade" set in. Convinced that high status was no longer a sufficiently desirable and sustainable position, marketing switched the focus to BMW's product developments and improvements, such as its responsive driving and leading-edge engineering. The brand was also able to add a strong safety message—but in a very BMW kind of way. Volvo's emphasis on safety, for instance, was about how the design and construction of the car would protect occupants if the car was hit. BMW's safety message was that the car handled so well, you just wouldn't get hit! These performance-focused efforts, showcased in creative ads, helped diminish the "yuppie" association, and by 1995 sales had approached their earlier peak.[12]

Summary.   Reinforcing brand equity requires consistency in the amount and nature of the supporting marketing program for the brand. Although the specific tactics may change, marketers should preserve and amplify the key sources of equity for the brand where appropriate. Product innovation and relevance are paramount in maintaining continuity and expanding the meaning of the brand.

At the end of every day, week, month, quarter, and year, marketers should ask themselves, What we have done to innovate our brand and its marketing and make them more relevant? A weak answer can have adverse consequences. One-time industry icons Nokia and Blackberry have both desperately struggled in recent years to catch up as the smartphone market has gone through remarkable technological and marketing transformations.[13] On a more positive note, Branding Brief 13-2 describes how the British brand Burberry remade itself in the world of fashion. Next, we consider what to do when brands find themselves in situations in which more drastic brand actions are needed.

REVITALIZING BRANDS

In virtually every product category are examples of once prominent and admired brands that have fallen on hard times or even completely disappeared. Nevertheless, a number of brands have managed to make impressive comebacks in recent years, as marketers have breathed new life into their customer franchises.[14] Boston Market, Altoids, Bally, and Ovaltine are among them. Consider Lacoste's comeback story.

LACOSTE

Lacoste, founded in France in 1933, became a style icon for its tennis-themed sportswear and is credited with selling the first polo shirt, the famed "alligator shirt" featuring an animal—actually, a crocodile—as the logo. During the 1980s, when it was owned by cereal maker General Mills, Lacoste failed to keep up with fashion trends and saw sales drop. In response, the company cut prices and sold to discounters like Walmart and Kmart, which further damaged the brand's image. Lacoste continued to suffer from slow sales until 2002, when Robert Siegel, a former Levi's executive credited with helping to create Dockers, was brought in to oversee the relaunch of the brand in the United States. Under Siegel, Lacoste stopped selling to non-luxury retailers, prohibiting sales to places like T.J. Maxx and a number of Macy's department stores. The company regenerated its fading fashion lines by introducing tighter-fitting shirts for women and opening own-brand boutiques in fashionable shopping areas to showcase its new look. Having established a strong foundation, its marketers now needed to sell a broader portfolio than just the polo shirt with which the brand is often strongly associated and which provides 30–40 percent of U.S. sales. To broaden its sales footprint in the marketplace, Lacoste introduced a new sub-brand,

Lacoste Live, targeting a younger, more contemporary customer. Working with U.S. tennis star Andy Roddick, it introduced a seven-style signature collection of performance apparel featuring polos, jackets, tennis shorts, track pants, and track jackets. Lacoste also expanded its collaboration with independent designers and top specialty retailers.[15]

To attract new customers, Lacoste introduced a collection of performance apparel in collaboration with American tennis champion Andy Roddick.

Source: Gerry Maceda/ZUMA Press/Newscom

For a successful turnaround, brands sometimes have to return to their roots to recapture lost sources of equity. In other cases, the brand meaning has had to fundamentally change to recapture market leadership. Regardless of approach, brands on the comeback trail must make more "revolutionary" than "evolutionary" changes to reinforce brand meaning.

Often, the first place to look in turning around the fortunes of a brand is the original sources of brand equity. In profiling brand knowledge structures to guide repositioning, marketers need to accurately and completely characterize the breadth and depth of brand awareness; the strength, favorability, and uniqueness of brand associations and brand responses held in consumer memory; and the nature of consumer–brand relationships. A comprehensive brand equity measurement system as outlined in Chapter 8 should help reveal the current status of these sources of brand equity. If not, or to provide additional insight, a special brand audit may be necessary.

Of particular importance is the extent to which key brand associations are still adequately functioning as points-of-difference or points-of-parity to properly position the brand. Are positive associations losing their strength or uniqueness? Have negative associations become linked to the brand, for example, because of some change in the marketing environment?

Marketers must next decide whether to retain the same positioning or create a new one and, if the latter, which positioning to adopt. The positioning considerations outlined in Chapter 3 can provide useful insights as to the desirability, deliverability, and differentiability of different possible positions based on consumer, company, and competitive considerations.

Sometimes the positioning is still appropriate, but the marketing program is the source of the problem because it is failing to deliver on it. In these instances, a back-to-basics strategy may make sense. Branding Brief 13-3 describes how Harley-Davidson rode a back-to-basics strategy to icon status.

BRANDING BRIEF 13-2

Remaking Burberry's Image

Burberry, founded in 1856 by 21-year-old Thomas Burberry, was a veritable "fashion disaster" in the mid-1990s. It was known to many as a stodgy throwback brand making raincoats for the middle-aged, "far off the radar screens of the fashion world." Yet within a span of several years, with the help of contemporary designs and updated marketing, the brand shrugged off its staid image and became fashionable again. The company instituted a new motto—"Never stop designing"—that encapsulated its new approach to establishing and maintaining relevance with the fickle fashion consumer.

One of Burberry's first moves to freshen the brand was to leverage its classic beige-check plaid in a series of accessories that quickly became bestsellers, including handbags, scarves, and headbands. Another was rejuvenating the check itself by using different colors, patterns, sizes, and materials. Burberry was careful to maintain a balance between the contemporary and the traditional, since tradition still resonated with modern consumers. It also sought to leverage other iconic imagery, such as the trench coat and the Prorsum horse insignia. The use of these brand icons reflected management's belief that "the core ethos and aesthetics of the brand were relevant today because of Thomas Burberry's ingenuity and creativity."

Another key to Burberry's turnaround was refreshing its advertising. The company hired famed fashion photographer Mario Testino to shoot a spread featuring edgy supermodels, such as Kate Moss, wearing iconic Burberry raincoats. The ads were credited with bringing a "rebellious, streetwise image to the brand." The company gave its retail stores a makeover as well in order to match the contemporary feel of the new designs.

Together, these different efforts turned the company's fortunes around—but almost too well. One of the challenges in any brand revitalization is sustaining momentum, and Burberry was no exception. After peaking in 2002 with a successful IPO, the brand began to suffer from overexposure and a slew of counterfeit products. Following a holiday sales slump in 2004, the company knew it had to set a different course.

One of the more remarkable brand revitalizations in recent years was accomplished by Burberry, which significantly upgraded its fashion image.
Source: Facundo Arrizabalaga/EPA/Newscom

A number of marketing changes were implemented. The trademark tan/black/white/red Burberry plaid was dialed down and made more discreet, appearing on only 10% of the brand's different items. More emphasis was placed on high-margin accessories—non-apparel accounts for one-third of revenue—and high-end fashions. The pricey Prorsum collections made up only 5 percent of the brand's sales, but they became the label's fashion flag-bearer and source of creative credibility.

Benefiting from vibrant emerging markets such as China, a constantly updated new product pipeline, and one of the most advanced digital strategies of any luxury brand, Burberry found itself in 2011 with annual revenues over $2 billion, far exceeding financial forecasts.

Sources: Sally Beatty, "Plotting Plaid's Future," *Wall Street Journal*, 9 September 2004, B1; Mark Tungate, "Fashion Statement," *Marketing*, 27 July 2005, 28; Sharon Wright, "The Tough New Yorker Who Transformed a UK Institution Gets Her Reward," *The Express*, 5 August 2004, 17; Kate Norton, "Burberry, Plaid in Check, Is Hot Again," *Bloomberg BusinessWeek*, 16 April 2007; Kathy Gordon, "Global Demand Buoys Burberry," *Wall Street Journal*, 13 July 2011; Nancy Hass, "Earning Her Stripes," *Wall Street Journal*, 9 September 2010.

In other cases, however, the old positioning is just no longer viable and reinvention is necessary. Mountain Dew completely overhauled its brand image to become a soft drink powerhouse. As Branding Brief 13-4 illustrates, it is often easiest to revive a brand that has simply been forgotten.

Revitalization strategies obviously run along a continuum, with pure back-to-basics at one end and pure reinvention at the other. Many campaigns combine elements of both.

BRANDING BRIEF 13-3

Harley-Davidson Motor Company

Harley-Davidson is one of the few companies in the world that can claim a legion of fans so dedicated to the brand that some of them get tattoos of the logo. Even more impressive is the fact that the company attracted such a loyal customer base with a minimum of advertising. Founded in 1903 in Milwaukee, Wisconsin, it has twice narrowly escaped bankruptcy and is today one of the most recognized brands in the world.

In recovering from its financial downfalls, Harley-Davidson realized its product needed to better live up to the brand promise. Quality problems plagued the product line in the 1970s. Although consumers loved what the brand repre-

One of the most successful and helpful brand communities is with the Harley Owners Group whose numbers exceed one million.
Source: AP Photo/The Sentinel-Record, Mara Kuhn

sented, they hated the constant need for repairs. The joke was that you needed to have two Harleys because one was always in the shop!

Harley's back-to-basics approach to revitalization centered on improving factories and production process to achieve higher levels of quality. The company also dialed up marketing efforts to better sell its products. Establishing a broader access point with consumers to make the brand relevant to more people, Harley was able to attract a diverse customer base that went way beyond the traditional biker image. The company also changed the way it went to market.

Before the 1980s, Harley-Davidson relied almost exclusively on word-of-mouth endorsements and the image of its user group to sell its motorcycles. In 1983, the company established an owners' club, the Harley Owners Group (HOG), which sponsors bike rallies, charity rides, and other motorcycle events. Every Harley owner becomes a member for free by signing up at the www.hog.com Web site. In its first year, HOG had 33,000 members. Now, it has more than one million in 1,400 chapters throughout the world.

In the early 1980s, Harley-Davidson began a licensing program to protect its trademarks and promote the brand. Early efforts primarily supported the riding experience with products like T-shirts, jewelry, small leather goods, and other products appealing to riders. Currently, the primary target for licensed products is existing customers through the Harley dealer network. To attract new customers, though, Harley-Davidson has licensed children's clothing, toys, games, and many other items aimed at children and sold beyond the dealer network. In the world of licensing, Harley-Davidson is considered an "evergreen" brand and earns the company tens of millions in revenue annually.

Motorcycle riding gear has been around almost as long as motorcycles. As business grew, Harley-Davidson created Harley-Davidson MotorClothes to produce traditional riding gear along with men's and women's casual sportswear and accessories to reach an ever-expanding and diverse customer base of riders and non-riders. Harley MotorClothes is a key facet of the company's General Merchandise division, whose revenues nearly doubled from $151 million in 2000 to $274 million in 2011.

Harley-Davidson continues to promote its brand with grassroots marketing efforts. Many employees and executives at the company own Harleys and often ride them with customers, making traditional advertising almost unnecessary. As ever, Harley's highly visible contingent of riders provides invaluable promotions and endorsements free of cost. Many other marketers seek to borrow the Harley cachet and use the bikes in their ads, giving the company free product placement.

One of the newest growth areas is women. For women and smaller riders, Harley offers Sportster motorcycles that are built low to the ground with narrower seats, softer clutches, and adjustable handlebars and windshields. Several times a year Harley dealers hold garage parties for women to help them learn about their bikes. Five hundred such events in March 2010 attracted 27,000 women, almost half of whom were at a Harley dealer for the first time, leading to 3,000 new bikes sold. After making up only 2 percent of Harley owners in 1995, women now represent about 12 percent of sales.

Sources: Bill Tucker, Terry Keenan, and Daryn Kagan, "In the Money," *CNNfn*, 20 January 2000; "Harley-Davidson Extends MDI Entertainment License for Lotteries' Hottest Brand," *Business Wire*, 1 May 2001; Glenn Rifkin, "How Harley-Davidson Revs Its Brand," *Strategy & Business*, Fourth Quarter 1997; Joseph Weber, "He Really Got Harley Roaring," *BusinessWeek*, 21 March 2005, 70; Rick Barrett, "From the Executive Suite to the Saddle," *Chicago Tribune*, 1 August 2004, CN3; Clifford Krauss, "Harley Woos Female Bikers," *New York Times*, 25 July 2007; Mark Clothier, "Why Harley Is Showing Its Feminine Side," *Bloomberg BusinessWeek*, 30 September 2010; Richard D'Aveni, "How Harley Fell Into the Commoditization Trap," *Forbes*, 17 March 2010; "Harley Motorcycle Sales Up in 2011," *Classic American Iron*, 25 January 2012.

BRANDING BRIEF 13-4

A New Morning for Mountain Dew

Mountain Dew was launched in 1969. PepsiCo initially marketed it with a rural folksy image, exemplified by the countrified tag line "Yahoo Mountain Dew! It'll Tickle Your Innards." Since then, the drink has far outgrown its provincial roots, though an unsuccessful attempt to bring urban teenagers to the brand in the early 1980s by advertising on MTV left it on the brink of deletion. The company decided to switch its ad focus to outdoors action scenes, and by the late 1980s, Mountain Dew had begun to show signs of life again.

The brand really hit its stride in the 1990s, experiencing phenomenal double-digit growth. Mountain Dew was the fastest-growing major U.S. soft drink for much of the decade, rising to a market share of 7.2 percent in 2000 from a mere 2.7 percent back in 1980. Growth was fueled by some edgy advertising from PepsiCo's long-time ad agency BBDO that was funny and fast-paced, featuring a rotating group of guys—the Dew dudes—engaged in action sports such as skydiving, skateboarding, and snowboarding to up-tempo music. The tag line "Do the Dew," was a strong call to action, and the ads were a high-energy blast of adrenalin.

The next decade saw much product expansion, introduction of nontraditional marketing, and a pioneering digital strategy. In 2000, PepsiCo launched Mountain Dew Code Red, the brand's first line extension since Diet Mountain Dew debuted in 1988. The bright red cherry-flavored drink was supported by a national advertising campaign that employed grassroots marketing as well as high-profile media buys. The launch was an unqualified success.

To better connect with its core teen audience, Mountain Dew increased its sponsorship of the Mix Tape street basketball tour and the Dew Action Sports Tour. The company also launched the Dew U loyalty program, in which drinkers exchanged codes printed under bottle caps for a variety of goods available on the Dew U Internet site.

In 2005, Mountain Dew launched another brand extension, a highly caffeinated energy drink called MDX aimed at the

estimated 180 million video game players, by introducing it as the official soft drink of the E3 Electronics Entertainment Expo. Prior to the launch, the company invited gamers to "beta-test" the product in order to refine the recipe and name.

All these actions helped Mountain Dew remain the number-four carbonated U.S. beverage in terms of sales throughout the decade. A logo change on the packaging occurred in 2008, as the company chose the simpler "Mtn Dew." An even bigger change was a viral marketing experiment in crowdsourcing that put customers into the actual product development process. The initial "Dewmocracy" campaign began in 2007 and included an online game in which players designed a new drink.

The follow-up Dewmocracy campaign in 2009 raised the stakes. Mountain Dew marketers put the bulk of their marketing budget online to allow consumers to select three new flavors to be distributed nationwide. The campaign began with 50 contest winners receiving home-tasting kits of seven potential flavors. They were instructed to share their tasting experiences via video on YouTube. Next, consumers helped pick the colors, names, packaging, and even the ad agency! Enormous buzz followed—much of it generated by the actual product users, as intended.

Sources: Theresa Howard, "Being True to Dew," *Brandweek,* 24 April 2000; Greg Johnson, "Mountain Dew Hits New Heights to Help Pepsi Grab a New Generation," *Los Angeles Times,* 6 October 1999; Michael J. McCarthy, "Mountain Dew Goes Urban to Revamp Country Image," *Wall Street Journal,* 19 April 1989; "Top-10 U.S. Soft Drink Companies and Brands for 2000," *Beverage Digest,* 15 February 2001; Kate MacArthur, "Mountain Dew Gives Gamers More Caffeine," *Advertising Age,* 26 September 2005, 6; Gregg Bennett, Mauricio Ferreora, Jaedeock Lee, and Fritz Polie, "The Role of Involvement in Sports and Sports Spectatorship in Sponsor's Brand Use: The Case of Mountain Dew and Action Sports Sponsorship," *Sports Marketing Quarterly,* 18 (March 2009): 14–24; Natalie Zmuda, "Why Mtn Dew Let Skater Dudes Take Control of Its Marketing," *Advertising Age,* 22 February 2010.

Finally, note that *market* failures, in which insufficient consumers are attracted to a brand, are typically much less damaging than *product* failures, in which the brand fundamentally fails to live up to its consumer promise. In the latter case, strong, negative associations may be difficult to overcome. With market failures, a relaunch can sometimes prove successful.

FEBREZE

When P&G introduced Febreze household odor eliminators, it adopted the classic problem–solution pattern that characterizes much of its brand advertising. But there was one flaw—people didn't think they had a problem! They had become accustomed to odors from cigarettes, pets, and cooking, no matter what others might say. When the problem–solution ads fell flat, P&G's marketers conducted in-depth research, prompting a relaunch that focused on Febreze as a finishing touch and a way to celebrate that a room was really clean. The new positioning connected, and sales exploded. With revenues now exceeding a billion dollars, Febreze has been successfully extended into air fresheners, candles, and laundry detergents.[16]

With an understanding of the current and desired brand knowledge structures in hand, we can again look to the customer-based brand equity framework for guidance about how to best refresh old sources of brand equity or create new ones to achieve the intended positioning. According to the model, we have two strategic options:

1. Expand the depth or breadth of brand awareness, or both, by improving consumer recall and recognition of the brand during purchase or consumption settings.
2. Improve the strength, favorability, and uniqueness of the brand associations making up the brand image. This may require programs directed at existing or new brand associations.

By enhancing brand salience and brand meaning in these ways, we can achieve more favorable responses and greater brand resonance.

Tactically, we can refurbish lost sources of brand equity and establish new ones in the same three ways we create sources of brand equity to start with: by changing brand elements, changing the supporting marketing program, or leveraging new secondary associations. Next, we consider several alternative strategies to achieve these goals.

Expanding Brand Awareness

With a fading brand, often *depth* of awareness is not the problem—consumers can still recognize or recall the brand under certain circumstances. Rather, the *breadth* of brand awareness is the stumbling block—consumers tend to think of the brand only in very narrow ways. As we suggested in Chapter 3, one powerful means of building brand equity is to increase the breadth of brand awareness, making sure consumers don't overlook the brand.

Assuming a brand has a reasonable level of consumer awareness and a positive brand image, perhaps the most appropriate starting point is to increase usage. This approach often does not require difficult and costly changes in brand image or positioning, but rather relatively easier changes in brand salience and awareness.

We can increase usage either by increasing the level or the quantity of consumption (how *much* consumers use the brand), or by increasing the frequency of consumption (how *often* they use it). It is probably easier to increase the number of times a consumer uses the product than to actually change the amount he or she uses at any one time. (A possible exception is impulse-purchase products like soft drinks and snacks, whose usage increases when the product is more available.) Increasing frequency of use is particularly attractive for category leaders with large market share; it requires either identifying new opportunities to use the brand in the same basic way or identifying completely new and different ways to use it. Let's look at both approaches.

Identifying Additional or New Usage Opportunities.   To identify additional or new opportunities for consumers to use the brand more—albeit in the same basic way—marketers should design a marketing program to include both of the following:

- Communications about the appropriateness and advantages of using the brand more frequently in existing situations or in new situations
- Reminders to consumers to actually use the brand as close as possible in time to those situations for which it could be used

For many brands, increasing usage may be as simple as improving top-of-mind awareness through reminder advertising (as V8 vegetable juice did with its classic "Wow! I Could Have Had a V8" ad campaign). In other cases, more creative retrieval cues may be necessary. Consumers often adopt "functional fixedness" with a brand, which makes it easy to ignore in nontraditional consumption settings.

For example, consumers see some brands as appropriate only for special occasions. An effective strategy here may be to redefine what it means for something to be "special." Chivas Regal ran a print ad campaign for its Blended Scotch with the theme "What are you saving the Chivas for?" The ads included headlines such as "Sometimes life begins when the baby-sitter arrives," "Your Scotch and soda is only as good as your Scotch and soda," and "If you think people might think you order Chivas to show off, maybe you're thinking too much." For campaigns like this to work, however, the brand has to retain its "premium" brand association—a key source of equity—while convincing consumers to adopt broader usage habits at the same time.

Another opportunity to increase frequency of use occurs when consumers' *perceptions* of their usage differ from the reality. For many products with relatively short life spans, consumers may fail to buy replacements soon enough or often enough.[17] Here are two possible solutions:

- Tie the act of replacing the product to a certain holiday, event, or time of year. For example, several brands, such as Oral-B toothbrushes, have run promotions tied in with the springtime switch to daylight saving time.
- Provide consumers with better information about either (1) when they first used the product or need to replace it, or (2) the current level of product performance. For example, batteries offer built-in gauges that show how much power they have left, and toothbrushes and razors have color indicators to indicate when they have worn out.

Finally, perhaps the simplest way to increase usage occurs when it is at less than the optimal or recommended level. Here, we want to persuade consumers of the merits of more regular usage and overcome any potential hurdles to increased usage, such as by making product designs and packaging more convenient and easier to use.

Identifying New and Completely Different Ways to Use the Brand.   The second approach to increasing frequency of use is to identify completely new and different applications. Food product companies have long advertised new recipes that use their branded products in entirely different ways. Perhaps the classic example of finding creative new applications is Arm & Hammer baking soda, whose deodorizing and cleaning properties have led to a number of new uses.

Other brands have taken a page from Arm & Hammer's book: Clorox has run ads stressing the many benefits of its bleach, such as how it eliminates kitchen odors; Wrigley's chewing gum advertising touts it as a substitute for smoking; and Tums promotes its antacid's benefits as a calcium supplement. Coach managed to expand usage and increase frequency for both the brand and the category, even in recessionary times.

COACH

Coach has played a key role over the past decade in getting U.S. women to buy more handbags; most now make three new purchases annually. Coach's strategy was to fill "usage voids"—situations where existing bag options were not appropriate—with a plethora of different bag options for almost every occasion, including evening bags, backpacks, satchels, totes, briefcases, coin purses, and duffels. Rather than owning a small number of bags suitable for a limited number of uses, women were encouraged to treat handbags as "the shoes of the 21st century: a way to frequently update wardrobes with different styles without shelling out for new clothes." When the recession of 2008 challenged many providers of luxury fashion accessories, who began to introduce steep discounts, Coach was an exception. The company maintained prices on its regular product lines and instead introduced new low-priced items. Coach always conducts much research, and here it engaged with consumers to confirm two facts: First, the new products would not cheapen or damage its image. Second, the resulting decreases in margin would be more than offset by increases in volume. Through renegotiated deals with suppliers, new sources of leather, fabric, and hardware, and other steps, the company assured itself the handbags could have the proper designs at the necessary price points. Thus, the youthful and somewhat eclectic

Coach's introduction of the youthful Poppy line at a lower price point helped the company weather a tough recession.
Source: Ross Hailey/MCT/Newscom

Poppy line was launched with an average price of $260, about 20 percent less than the typical Coach purse. The percentage of sales of low-priced handbags increased from about one-third to one-half of sales as a result of the shift in consumer willingness to pay. Handbags make up almost two-thirds of Coach sales.[18]

New usage applications may require more than just new ad campaigns or merchandising approaches. Sometimes they can arise from new packaging. For example, Arm & Hammer introduced a "Fridge-Freezer Pack" (with "freshflo vents") for its natural baking soda that was specially designed to better freshen and deodorize refrigerators and freezers.

Improving Brand Image

Although changes in brand awareness are probably the easiest means of creating new sources of brand equity, more fundamental changes are often necessary. We may need to create a new marketing program to improve the strength, favorability, and uniqueness of brand associations making up the brand image. As part of this repositioning—or recommitment to the existing positioning—we may need to bolster any positive associations that have faded, neutralize any negative associations that have been created, and create additional positive associations. These repositioning decisions require us to clearly specify the target market and the nature of the competition to set the competitive frame of reference.

Identifying the Target Market.   Marketers often focus on taking action with one or more of four key target market segments as part of a brand revitalization strategy:

1. Retaining vulnerable customers
2. Recapturing lost customers
3. Identifying neglected segments
4. Attracting new customers

There is a clear hierarchy in these strategic targeting options. In an attempt to turn sales around, some firms mistakenly focus initially on the fourth one, chasing after new customers. This is the riskiest option. If it fails, two bad things can happen: the firm may fail to attract any new customers, but even worse, it may lose existing ones.

When Talbots, seller of women's suits, blouses, and dresses in roughly 580 predominately suburban locations, ran into sales troubles after the 2008 recession, it decided to expand its target market. Bold jewelry and metallic suits appeared next to classic pearls and seasonal sweaters in an attempt to reach a younger audience than its traditional over-35-year-old woman. The result was a disaster that confused existing customers as well as hoped-for new prospects, and sales plunged. Asia's leading chain of low-priced casual wear, Uniqlo, ran into the exact same predicament when stores began to stock too many fashion-forward items at the expense of popular basics.[19]

To avoid this double whammy and steady the course in the face of a sales decline, it is often best to try to halt the erosion first and ensure that no more customers are lost in the short run before chasing after new ones. Some of the same marketing efforts to retain existing customers can also help recapture lost customers who are no longer using the brand. This may mean simply reminding consumers of the virtues of a brand they have forgotten about or begun to take for granted. Recall how the New Coke debacle described in Chapter 1—although not intended to do so—accomplished just that, in a roundabout way. Kellogg's Corn Flakes once ran a successful ad campaign with the slogan "Try Them Again for the First Time."

The third approach—segmenting on the basis of demographic variables or other means and identifying neglected segments—is the next-most viable brand revitalization option. Of course, the final strategic targeting option for revitalizing a fading brand is simply to more or less abandon the consumer group that supported it in the past to target a completely new market segment.

Many firms have reached out to new customer groups to build brand equity. The Home Shopping Network (HSN) found success in going after fashion-oriented power shoppers by dumping a slew of unknown brands with me-too products to make the cable channel more designer-friendly to celebrities such as Badgley Mischka, Sean "Diddy" Combs, Stefani Greenfield, and Serena Williams.[20]

Market segments the firm currently serves with other products may represent potential growth targets for the brand. Effectively targeting these segments, however, typically requires some changes or variations in the marketing program, especially in advertising and other communications, and the decision whether to do so ultimately depends on the outcome of a cost–benefit analysis.

Attracting a new market segment can be deceptively difficult. Brands such as Gillette, Harley-Davidson, and ESPN have worked hard for years to find the right blend of products and advertising to make their masculine-image brands relevant and attractive to women. Creating marketing programs to appeal to women has become a priority of makers of products from cars to computers.

Marketers have also introduced programs targeted to different racial and ethnic groups, age groups, and income groups. These cultural market segments may require different messages, creative strategies, and media. They can be fickle, however, as Tommy Hilfiger discovered, forcing the brand to implement a back-to-basics revitalization strategy.

TOMMY HILFIGER

One of the hottest fashion brands in the 1990s—when its worldwide sales peaked at $2 billion—Tommy Hilfiger was overexposed and struggling to stay relevant by the early 2000s. Other labels such as Phat Farm, FUBU, Sean John, and Ecko had drawn customers away by better executing the young urban, hip-hop style on which Hilfiger had built its 1990s success. Bloomingdale's reduced the number of Hilfiger boutiques from 23 to 1, and Hilfiger closed all but 7 of its 44 own-brand specialty shops in 2003. To recover, the firm essentially cut all ties with the style that had made it popular—oversized apparel, even more oversized logos, and an edgy urban aura—even going so far as to remove the stylized U.S. flag logo from many of its clothing products. Hilfiger struck out in a new direction with classic preppy styles more closely associated with the brand's original roots, although perhaps with a twist. One set of styles was inspired by the sun and surf, for instance. An exclusive distribution deal with Macy's in 2008 allowed the company to focus its marketing efforts, and by 2010, the brand was being sold in 1,000 retail locations in 65 countries. Hilfiger tailored its offerings in many of these markets. For example, German consumers preferred darker colors, whereas Spanish consumers wanted lighter and brighter shades. In many overseas markets such as China, India, and parts of Europe, the brand was seen as high status. All these revitalizing efforts were validated when the Hilfiger brand was purchased for $3 billion by Phillips-Van Heusen.[21]

A step out of fashion at times over the last decade, Tommy Hilfiger worked hard to restore the luster to its brand with updated new styles and marketing.

Source: Urman Lionel/SIPA/Newscom

Repositioning the Brand.   Regardless of the type of target market segment, repositioning the brand sometimes requires us to establish more compelling points-of-difference. At other times, we need to reposition a brand to establish a point-of-parity on some key image dimension.

A common problem for marketers of established, mature brands is to make them more contemporary by creating relevant usage situations, a more contemporary user profile, or a more modern brand personality. Heritage brands that have been around for years may be seen as trustworthy but also boring, uninteresting, and not that likable.

Updating a brand may require some combination of new products, new advertising, new promotions, and new packaging. Reaching its 100th birthday in 2013, Clorox is a heritage brand that must periodically take steps to update itself. To reach young parents on the go, it developed the myStain smartphone app dedicated to stain removal. Family-oriented images, such as photos of kids' faces covered with spaghetti sauce, were included to make the app more accessible and fun. Many solutions offered convenient alternatives to Clorox products, such as seltzer water as a stain treatment in a restaurant.[22]

Changing Brand Elements. Often we must change one or more brand elements either to convey new information or to signal that the brand has taken on new meaning because the product or some other aspect of the marketing program has changed. The brand name is typically the most important brand element, and it's often the most difficult to change. Nevertheless, we can drop names or combine them into initials to reflect shifts in marketing strategy or to ease pronounceability and recall. Shortened names or initials can also minimize potentially negative product associations.

For example, Federal Express chose to officially shorten its name to FedEx and introduce a new logo to acknowledge what consumers were actually calling the brand.[23] In an attempt to convey a healthier image, Kentucky Fried Chicken abbreviated its name to the initials KFC. The company also introduced a new logo incorporating the character of Colonel Sanders as a means of maintaining tradition but also modernizing its appeal. When the company began to emphasize grilled chicken and sandwiches in its national advertising over the traditional bone-in fried offerings though, some franchisees actually sued, saying the brand had strayed too far from its roots.[24]

It is easier to change other brand elements, and we may need to, especially if they play an important awareness or image function. Chapter 4 described how to modify and update packaging, logos, and characters over time. We noted there that changes generally should be moderate and evolutionary, and marketers must take great care to preserve the most salient aspects of the brand elements.

ADJUSTMENTS TO THE BRAND PORTFOLIO

Managing brand equity and the brand portfolio requires taking a long-term view and carefully considering the role of different brands in the portfolio and their relationships over time. Sometimes a brand refresh just requires cleaning up the brand architecture.

When P&G saw sales slump for its $3-billion-in-revenue Pantene hair care brand during the recession of 2008, the company engaged in a massive research and development process to improve and revamp the product line. Extensive consumer testing and technologies typically employed for medical and space research were used to examine how different ingredients interacted with various hair types to develop new and improved products. P&G reduced the number of its shampoos, conditioners, and styling aids by one-third and reorganized and color-coded the entire product line around four specific hair types: color-treated, curly, fine, and medium-to-thick.[25]

Migration Strategies

The ***brand migration strategy*** helps consumers understand how various brands in the portfolio can satisfy their needs as they change over time, or as the products and brands themselves change over time. Managing brand transitions is especially important in rapidly changing, technologically intensive markets. Ideally, brands will be organized in consumers' minds so they know at least implicitly how they can switch among them as their needs or desires change.

A corporate or family branding strategy in which brands are ordered in a logical manner could provide the hierarchical structure in consumers' minds to facilitate brand migration. Car companies are quite sensitive to this issue, and brands such as BMW—with its 3-, 5- and 7-series numbering systems to denote increasingly higher levels of quality—are good examples. Chrysler designated Plymouth as its "starter" car line and expected Plymouth owners to trade up later to higher-priced Chrysler models.

Acquiring New Customers

All firms face trade-offs between attracting new customers and retaining existing ones. In mature markets, trial is generally less important than building loyalty and retaining existing customers.

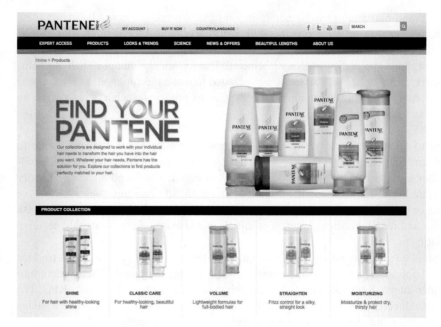

In response to a sales slump, P&G revamped its Pantene product line with new technology and a simplified branding strategy.

Source: The Procter & Gamble Company

Nevertheless, some customers inevitably leave the brand franchise—even if only from natural causes. Thus firms must proactively develop strategies to attract new customers, especially younger ones. The marketing challenge here, however, often lies in making a brand seem relevant to vastly different generations and cohort groups or lifestyles. The challenge is greater when the brand has a strong personality or user image associations that tie it to one particular consumer group.

Unfortunately, even as younger consumers age, there is no guarantee they will have the same attitudes and behaviors as the older consumers who preceded them. In 2011, the first wave of post–World War II baby boomers celebrated their 65th birthdays and officially entered the senior citizen market. Many experts forecast that this group will insist companies embrace their own unique values in marketing products and services. As one demographic expert says, "Nothing could be further from the truth than saying boomers will be like their parents."

The response to the challenge of marketing across generations and cohort groups has taken all forms. Some marketers have attempted to cut loose from the past, as Tommy Hilfiger did by renouncing the urban styles it had come to embody in the 1990s. Other brands have attempted to develop more inclusive marketing strategies to encompass both new and old customers. For example, Brooks Brothers has worked hard to upgrade its merchandise mix, renovate its fleet of stores, expand the franchise into overseas markets, and introduce its first designer label, Black Fleece, to retain the loyalty of older customers but attract new, younger customers at the same time. The company also engaged in an exclusive partnership with Nordstrom to sell a selected set of its more contemporary offerings.[26]

Retiring Brands

Because of dramatic or adverse changes in the marketing environment, some brands are just not worth saving. Their sources of brand equity may have essentially dried up, or, even worse, damaging and difficult-to-change new associations may have been created. At some point, the size of the brand franchise—no matter how loyal—fails to justify support. In the face of such adversity, decisive management actions are necessary to properly retire or milk the brand.

Several options are possible. A first step in retrenching a fading brand is to reduce the number of its product types (package sizes or variations). Such actions reduce the cost of supporting the brand and allow it to put its best foot forward so it can more easily hit profit targets. If a sufficiently large and loyal enough customer base exists, eliminating marketing support can be a means to milk or harvest profits from these cash cows.

An *orphan brand* is a once-popular brand with diminished equity that a parent company allows to decline by withdrawing marketing support. Typically, these orphan brands have a

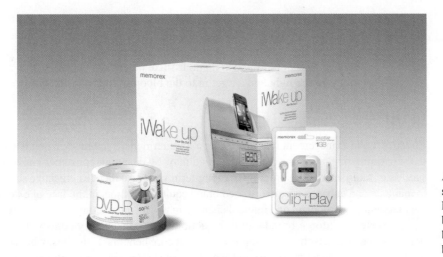

As proof there can be some marketplace life left in seemingly dead brands, Memorex has been reinvented as a broader technology brand.

Source: AP Photo/PRNewsFoto/Memorex

customer base too small to warrant advertising and promotional expenditures. The Polaroid camera is an example. After filing for bankruptcy in 2001, the brand was purchased by a private equity firm. A 2003 market research study indicated the brand name itself was still a powerful asset, so the Polaroid name soon appeared on electronic devices much more sophisticated than its outmoded instant camera, such as TVs and DVDs. These items, which achieved distribution in Walmart and Target, generated a reported $300 million in annual sales, proving that the orphan Polaroid still had some life in it.[27]

With the right marketing approach, it is possible to bring a jettisoned brand back to life. As another example, 3M spinoff Imation purchased Memorex, famous for its audio cassettes and "Is It Live, or Is It Memorex?" ads, for $330 million in 2006. Although that tagline had been dropped over 30 years ago, consumers surveys found awareness for the brand still exceeded 95 percent. Targeting mothers aged 28–40 who liked technology the family could use together, Memorex was relaunched to brand iPod accessories, digital photo frames, DVD and MP3 players, karaoke machines, and TVs at retailers such as Walmart and Target.[28]

When the brand is beyond repair, marketers have to take more drastic measures, such as consolidating it into a stronger brand. Procter & Gamble merged White Cloud and Charmin toilet paper, eliminating the White Cloud line. It also merged Solo and Bold detergents. With shelf space at a premium, brand consolidation has become increasingly necessary to create a stronger brand, cut costs, and focus marketing efforts.[29]

Finally, a permanent solution is to discontinue the product altogether. The marketplace is littered with brands that either failed to establish an adequate level of brand equity or saw their sources of brand equity disappear because of changes in the marketing environment. Companies sometimes spin off their orphan brands when sales drop too far, as Campbell did with Vlasic pickles and Swanson frozen dinners. Similarly, American Home Products spun off Chef Boyardee, Bumble Bee tuna, and Pam cooking spray. Other companies sell the orphan, as Procter & Gamble did by selling its Oxydol laundry detergent to Redox Brands.

Harvard professor Nancy Koehn explains that old brands retain some value because consumers often remember them from childhood. "There's at least an unconscious link," says Koehn.[30] Perhaps this fact helps explain the success of a Web site called www.hometownfavorites.com, which offers hundreds of exotic orphan brands such as Brer Rabbit Molasses and My-T-Fine Pudding. As long as orphan brands remain popular with a core audience, it seems that companies are willing to sell them.[31]

Obsoleting Existing Products.   How do you decide which brands to attempt to revitalize (or at least milk) and which ones to discontinue? Beecham chose to abandon such dying brands as 5-Day deodorant pads, Rose Milk skin care lotion, and Serutan laxative, but it attempted to resurrect Aqua Velva aftershave, Geritol iron and vitamin supplement, and Brylcreem hair styling products. The decision to retire a brand depends on a number of factors.

Fundamentally, the issue is the existing and latent equity of the brand. As the former head of consumer packaged-goods giant Unilever commented in explaining his company's decision to review about 75 percent of its brands and lines of businesses for possible sell-offs, "If businesses aren't creating value, we shouldn't be in them. It's like having a nice garden that gets weeds. You have to clean it up, so the light and air get in to the blooms which are likely to grow the best."[32]

REVIEW

Effective brand management requires taking a long-term view and recognizing that any changes in the supporting marketing program for a brand may, by changing consumer knowledge, affect the success of future marketing programs. A long-term view also dictates proactive strategies designed to maintain and enhance customer-based brand equity over time, in the face of external changes in the marketing environment and internal changes in a firm's marketing goals and programs.

Marketers reinforce brand equity by actions that consistently convey the meaning of the brand—what products the brand represents, what core benefits it supplies, what needs it satisfies, how it makes products superior, and which strong, favorable, and unique brand associations should exist in consumers' minds. The most important consideration in reinforcing brands is consistency in the nature and amount of marketing support. Consistency does not mean marketers should avoid making any changes in the marketing program; in fact, many tactical changes may be necessary to maintain the brand's strategic thrust and direction. Unless there is some change in the marketing environment or shift in strategic direction, however, there is little need to deviate from a successful positioning. The critical points-of-parity and points-of-difference that represent sources of brand equity should then be vigorously preserved and defended.

The strategy for reinforcing brand meaning depends on the nature of the brand association. For brands whose core associations are primarily product-related attributes and functional benefits, innovation in product design, manufacturing, and merchandising is especially critical to maintaining or enhancing brand equity. For brands whose core associations are primarily non-product-related attributes and symbolic or experiential benefits, relevance in user and usage imagery is especially critical to maintaining or enhancing brand equity.

In managing brand equity, managers have to make trade-offs between those marketing activities that fortify the brand and reinforce its meaning, and those that attempt to leverage or borrow from its existing brand equity to reap some financial benefit. At some point, failure to fortify the brand will diminish brand awareness and weaken brand image. Without these sources of brand equity, the brand itself may not continue to yield valuable benefits. Figure 13-3 summarizes brand reinforcement strategies.

Revitalizing a brand requires marketers to either recapture lost sources of brand equity or establish new ones. According to the CBBE framework, two general approaches are possible: (1) Expand the depth or breadth (or both) of brand awareness by improving brand recall and recognition by consumers during purchase or consumption settings; and (2) improve the strength, favorability, and uniqueness of brand associations making up the brand image. This latter approach may require programs directed at existing or new brand associations.

With a fading brand, the depth of brand awareness is often not a problem as much as the breadth; that is, consumers tend to think of the brand in very narrow ways. Although changing brand awareness is probably the easiest means of creating new sources of brand equity, we may often have to create a new marketing program to improve the strength, favorability, and uniqueness of brand associations.

As part of this repositioning, target markets should be analyzed carefully. It is often best to first retain new customers and then try to attract lapsed users or neglected segments before attempting to attract wholly different segments. The challenge in all these efforts to modify the brand image is not to destroy the equity that already exists. Figure 13-4 summarizes brand revitalization strategies.

Managers must also consider the role of different brands in the portfolio and their relationships over time. In particular, a brand migration strategy should ensure that consumers understand how various brands in the portfolio can satisfy their needs as they change or as the products and brands themselves change over time. Strategies exist to retire those brands whose sources of brand equity have essentially dried up or that have acquired damaging and difficult-to-change associations.

If a brand encounters a crisis, being swift and sincere are of paramount importance. Companies that come across as unresponsive or uncaring with their customers inevitably encounter problems.

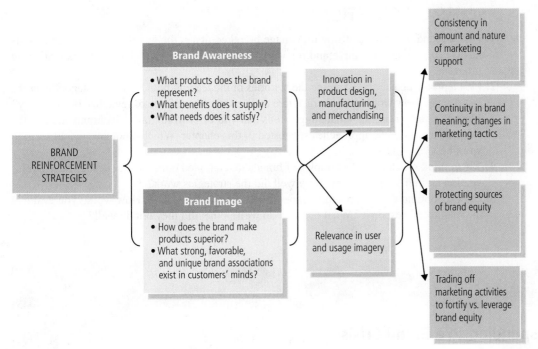

FIGURE 13-3 Brand Reinforcement Strategies

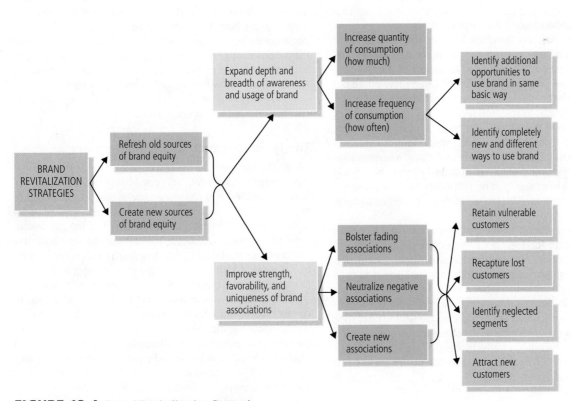

FIGURE 13-4 Brand Revitalization Strategies

DISCUSSION QUESTIONS

1. Pick a brand. Assess its efforts to manage brand equity in the last five years. What actions has it taken to be innovative and relevant? Can you suggest any changes to its marketing program?

2. Pick a product category. Examine the histories of the leading brands in that category over the last decade. How would you characterize their efforts to reinforce or revitalize brand equity?

3. Identify a fading brand. What suggestions can you offer to revitalize its brand equity? Try to apply the different approaches suggested in this chapter. Which strategies would seem to work best?

4. Try to think of additional examples of brands that adopted either a back-to-basics or a reinvention revitalization strategy. How well did the strategies work?

5. Choose a brand that has recently experienced a marketing crisis. How would you evaluate the marketers' response? What did they do well? What did they not do well?

BRAND FOCUS 13.0

Responding to a Brand Crisis

Tylenol has been a true marketing success story.[33] Originally introduced by McNeil Laboratories as a liquid alternative to aspirin for children, Tylenol achieved nonprescription status when McNeil was bought by Johnson & Johnson (J&J) in 1959. J&J's initial marketing plan promoted a tablet form of the product for physicians to prescribe as a substitute for aspirin when allergic reactions occurred. Tylenol consists of acetaminophen, a drug as effective as aspirin in the relief of pain and fever but without the stomach irritation that often accompanies aspirin use.

Backed by this selective physician push, sales for the brand grew slowly but steadily over the course of the next 15 years. By 1974, sales reached $50 million, or 10 percent of the analgesic market. In defending its turf from Bristol-Myers's low-priced but heavily promoted entry Datril, J&J recognized the value of advertising Tylenol directly to consumers.

Thanks also to the successful introduction of a line extension, Extra-Strength Tylenol in tablet and capsule form, the brand's market share had risen to 37 percent of the pain reliever market by 1982. As the largest single brand in the history of health and beauty aids, Tylenol was used by 100 million U.S. consumers. It contributed 8 percent to J&J's sales but almost twice that percentage in net profits.

Advertising support for the brand was heavy. A $40 million media campaign for 1982 used two different messages. The "hospital campaign" employed testimonials from people who had been given Tylenol in the hospital and had grown to trust it. The ad concluded with the tag line, "Trust Tylenol—hospitals do." The "hidden camera" campaign showed subjects who had been unobtrusively filmed while describing the symptoms of their headache, trying Extra-Strength Tylenol as a solution, and vowing to use it again based on its effectiveness. These ads concluded with the tag line, "Tylenol . . . the most potent pain reliever you can buy without a prescription."

The Tylenol Product Tampering Crisis

All this success came crashing to the ground in the first week of October 1982, with the news that seven people had died in the Chicago area after taking Extra-Strength Tylenol capsules that turned out to contain cyanide poison. Although it quickly became evident that the problem was restricted to that area of the country and had almost certainly been the work of some deranged person outside the company, consumer confidence was severely shaken.

Most marketing experts believed the damage to the brand's reputation was irreparable and that Tylenol would never fully recover. Well-known advertising guru Jerry Della Femina was quoted in the *New York Times* as saying, "On one day, every single human being in the country thought that Tylenol might kill them. I don't think there are enough advertising dollars, enough marketing men, to change that. . . . You'll not see the name Tylenol in any form within a year." Tylenol's comeback from these seemingly insurmountable odds has become a classic example of how best to handle a marketing crisis.

The Tylenol Product Tampering Recovery

Within the first week of the crisis, J&J issued a worldwide alert to the medical community, set up a 24-hour toll-free telephone number, recalled and analyzed sample batches of the product, briefed the Food and Drug Administration, and offered a $100,000 reward to apprehend the culprit of the tampering. During the week of October 5, the company began a voluntary withdrawal of the brand by repurchasing 31 million bottles with a retail value of $100 million. It stopped advertising, and all communications with the public were in the form of press releases.

To monitor consumer response to the crisis, J&J started to conduct weekly tracking surveys with 1,000 consumer respondents. Ultimately, the company spent a total of $1.5 million for marketing research in the fourth quarter of 1982. The following week of October 12, it introduced a capsule exchange offer, promoted in half-page press announcements in 150 major markets across the country, that invited the public to mail in bottles of capsules and receive tablets in exchange. Although well intentioned, this offer met with poor consumer response.

During the week of October 24, J&J made its return to TV advertising with the goals of convincing Tylenol users they could continue to trust the safety of Tylenol products and encouraging the use of the tablet form until tamper-resistant packaging was available. The spokesperson for the ad was Dr. Thomas N. Gates, the company's medical director, whose deep, reassuring voice exuded confidence and control. Looking calmly straight into the camera, he stated:

> You're all aware of the recent tragic events in which Extra-Strength Tylenol capsules were criminally tampered with in limited areas after they left our factories. This act damages all of us—you the American public because you have made Tylenol a trusted part of your healthcare and we who make Tylenol because we've worked hard to earn that trust. We will now work even harder to keep it. We have voluntarily withdrawn all Tylenol capsules from the shelf. We will reintroduce capsules in tamper-resistant containers as quickly as possible. Until then, we urge all Tylenol capsule users to use the tablet form and we have offered to replace your capsules with tablets. Tylenol has had the trust of the medical profession and 100 million Americans for over 20 years. We value that trust too much to let any individual tamper with it. We want you to continue to trust Tylenol.

The heavy media schedule for this ad ensured that 85 percent of the market viewed it at least four times during this week.

On November 11, 1982, six weeks after the poisonings and after intense behind-the-scenes activity, the chairman of J&J held a live teleconference with 600 news reporters throughout the United States to announce the return of Tylenol capsules to the market in a new, triple-sealed package that was regarded as virtually tamperproof. To get consumers to try the new packaging, the company undertook the largest program of couponing in commercial history.

On November 28, 1982, 60 million coupons offering a free Tylenol product (valued up to $2.50) were distributed in Sunday newspapers nationwide. Twenty million more coupons were distributed the following Sunday. By the end of December, 30 percent of the coupons had been redeemed. J&J also engaged in a number of activities to enlist the support of retailers in the form of trade promotions, sales calls, and so forth.

Convinced that market conditions were now stable enough to commence regular advertising, J&J's ad agency developed three ad executions using the testimony of loyal Tylenol users with the goal of convincing consumers that they could continue to use Tylenol with confidence. The first ad execution contained excerpts of consumers' reaction to the tampering incident, the second ad brought back a Tylenol supporter from an ad campaign run before the tampering incident to reassert her trust in Tylenol, and the third ad used the testimony of a Tylenol user who reasoned that she could still trust the product because hospitals still used it. The recall scores for two of the commercials were among the highest ever recorded by ASI, a well-known marketing research firm that conducted the ad testing for J&J. The return to advertising was accompanied by additional coupon promotional offers to consumers.

Incredibly, by February 1983, sales for Tylenol had almost fully returned to the lofty pretampering sales levels the brand had enjoyed six months earlier. Clearly, J&J's skillful handling of an extremely difficult situation was a major factor in the brand's comeback. Another important factor, however, was the equity of the brand and its strong and valuable "trust" association built up over the years prior to the incident. The feelings of trust the brand engendered helped speed its recovery, a fact certainly evident to J&J (note how often the word *trust* appears in the initial Gates ad—five times).

Johnson & Johnson and McNeil Consumer Healthcare's remarkable recovery from the brink of disaster allowed the company to reap the benefits of market leadership. A $1 billion brand, Tylenol was successfully extended into cough and cold remedies, nighttime pain relievers, and children's versions. The next-largest pain reliever competitor had only half the market share.

The tide began to turn in the 1990s, however, as the possibility of liver damage and even death from taking more than the recommended dosage of Tylenol was found. Some analysts felt J&J should have been more forthcoming about the possible product dangers in its labeling. This health issue persisted over the next two decades as research continued to uncover consumers' lack of understanding of proper dosing and dangers of side effects. The government continued to weigh its regulatory options.

Tylenol's Quality Control Crises

Concerns about dosage were exacerbated by a series of disastrous quality-control scandals and problems. During 2009 to 2011, the brand came under a flood of negative publicity and harsh criticism from government regulators. Unlike the tampering incidents, these wounds were self-inflicted, and although no deaths occurred, the care, comfort, and confidence of Tylenol customers was at stake, making Johnson & Johnson's actions—or inactions in some cases—highly troubling.

The problems seemed to arise in cutbacks in quality control and compliance at some of McNeil Consumer Healthcare's manufacturing facilities. Cost-cutting and a change in oversight procedures let several defective products fall through the cracks, while errors in judgment after the fact only compounded the problems.

In one of the first incidents, J&J recalled two dozen varieties of its Children's Tylenol in 2009 because of possible bacterial contamination at one of its manufacturing facilities. Additional problems emerged in the same plant the following year, and government regulators expressed their displeasure at the company's lack of progress in dealing with the problem.

In January 2010, J&J recalled several hundred batches of Tylenol, Motrin, Benadryl, and St. Joseph's Aspirin, 20 months after it reportedly first began to receive consumer complaints about moldy-smelling bottles that made some people feel ill. The FDA faulted the company for not conducting a timely, comprehensive investigation; not quickly identifying the source of the problem; and not notifying authorities of the problem, all of which prolonged consumer vulnerability.

The culprit was the breakdown of a chemical used to treat wood pallets that transported and stored product packaging in a Las Piedras, Puerto Rico facility. A few months later, in April 2010, J&J also recalled millions of bottles of Tylenol, Benadryl, Zyrtec, and Motrin because excessively high levels of an active drug, metal specks, or ingredients that had failed testing requirements led to possible safety violations. Ever-higher levels of scrutiny of the company followed, revealing that back in 2009, McNeil Consumer Healthcare had hired private contractors to buy scores of bottles of defective Motrin in a stealth recall. Because there was no actual safety risk, the company maintained that a formal recall was not necessary. Once again, federal regulators disagreed with its handling of a problem.

These unprecedented quality-control miscues cost the company $1 billion in sales and, perhaps more importantly, the trust, respect, and admiration of the public it had worked so hard to preserve back in 1982. After much criticism contrasting his handling of the quality control problems with the product tampering crisis, CEO William Weldon stepped down in April 2012.

Crisis Marketing Guidelines

Not all brands have handled their crises as well as Johnson & Johnson did the tampering incident, or as poorly as it did its quality-control problems. Another brand sharply criticized for its crisis response was Exxon. Although this company spent millions of dollars advertising its gasoline and crafting its brand image over the years, it essentially ignored the need to market its corporate identity and image.

This decision came back to haunt the company in the weeks following March 24, 1989, the day the tanker *Exxon Valdez* hit a reef in Prince William Sound, spilling some 11,000,000 gallons of oil into the waters off the Alaska shoreline. The spill wreaked devastation on the fish and wildlife of some 1,300 previously unspoiled square miles. Top Exxon officials declined to comment publicly for almost a week afterward, and the public statements they eventually made sometimes appeared to contradict information from other sources (for instance, regarding the severity of the spill) or blamed other parties, such as the U.S. Coast Guard, for the slow clean-up efforts.

Exxon received withering negative press and was the source of countless jokes on late-night talk shows. In frustration and anger, some customers cut up their Exxon credit cards. On April 3, fully 10 days after the accident, Exxon's chairman released a full-page open letter to the public expressing the company's concern and justifying its efforts to address the situation.[34]

Brands as diverse as Wendy's restaurants, Firestone tires, Tyco diversified holdings, and Vioxx painkiller have all experienced a potentially crippling brand crisis. Marketing managers must assume that at some point in time, a similar incident will occur. In general, the better they have established brand equity and a strong corporate image—especially credibility and trustworthiness—the more likely their firm can weather the storm.

Careful preparation and a well-managed crisis management program are also critical, however. Most experts would agree that the Exxon incident is a good example of how *not* to handle a brand crisis. As Johnson & Johnson's nearly flawless handling of the Tylenol product tampering incident suggests, the two keys to effectively managing a crisis are that the firm's response should be swift *and* that it should be sincere.[35] Marketers do not necessarily have to admit they are wrong in any way, just that they are concerned and will as quickly and thoroughly find out what has happened, keeping the customer's best interests in mind. Brands that drag their heels in recognizing and responding to a crisis inevitably encounter problems.

Swiftness.   The longer it takes a firm to respond to a marketing crisis, the more likely that customers will form negative impressions based on unfavorable media coverage or word-of-mouth. Perhaps worse, they may decide they do not really like the brand after all and permanently switch to alternatives.

For example, Perrier was forced to halt production worldwide and recall all existing bottles in February 1994 when traces of benzene, a known carcinogen, were found in excessive quantities in the bottled water. Over the next few weeks, several explanations were offered about how the contamination occurred, creating confusion and skepticism. Perhaps even more damaging, the product was off the shelves until May.

Despite an expensive relaunch featuring ads and promotions, Perrier struggled to regain lost market share, and a full year later its sales were still less than half what they once had been. One reason is that while the product was unavailable, consumers and retailers found satisfactory substitutes such as Saratoga and San Pellegrino. With its key "purity" association tarnished (the brand had been advertised as the "Earth's First Soft Drink" and "It's Perfect. It's Perrier."), the brand had no other compelling points-of-difference over these competitors.[36]

Finally, compounding the problems arising from the marketing crisis, Perrier was developing an increasingly stodgy image of appealing to the over-45 consumer rather than those under 25. Eventually, the company was taken over by Nestlé SA.

Sincerity.   Swift actions must also come across as sincere. Public acknowledgment of the severity of the impact on consumers and willingness to take whatever steps are necessary and feasible to solve the crisis reduce the chance that consumers will form negative attributions for the firm's behavior.

For example, although Gerber had established a strong image of trust with consumers, baby food is a product category characterized by an extremely high level of involvement and need for reassurance. When consumers reported finding shards of glass in some jars of its baby food, Gerber tried to reassure the public that there were no problems in its manufacturing plants but adamantly refused to have its baby food withdrawn from grocery stores. Some consumers clearly found Gerber's response unsatisfactory, because its market share slumped from 66 percent to 52 percent within a couple of months. As one company official admits, "Not pulling our baby food off the shelf gave the appearance that we aren't a caring company."[37]

Brand crises are difficult to manage because, despite a firm's best efforts, these situations are hard to control. To some extent, the firm is at the mercy of public sentiment and media coverage, which it can attempt to direct and influence but which sometimes take on a life of their own. Swift and sincere words and actions go a long way toward defusing the situation.

Notes

1. Leonard M. Lodish and Carl F. Mela, "If Brands Are Built Over Years, Why Are They Managed Over Quarters?," *Harvard Business Review* 85 (July–August 2007): 104–112.

2. Craig McLean, "Q Live: Coldplay," *Q*, March 2012, 123–125; Ben Sisario, "Chris Martin of Coldplay Asks: What Would Bruce Do?," *New York Times*, 13 October 2011; Ray Waddell, "Coldplay: The Billboard Cover Story," *Billboard*, 12 August 2011.

3. J. K. Wall, "Delta Opens Faucet on Marketing with New Ads," *USA Today*, 4 May 2005, 6B; Brooke Capps, "Delta Faucet Co. Names Y&L AOR," *Advertising Age*, 1 February 2007; Bridget A. Otto, "Interior News & Notes: Street of Dreams News; High-Tech Bathroom," *The Oregonian*, 23 August 2011.

4. Kevin Goldman, "Michelob Tries to Rebottle Its Old Success," *Wall Street Journal,* 28 September 1995, B8; James B. Arndorfer, "Low-Carb Beer Buzz Starts to Lose Steam," *Advertising Age*, 23 August 2004, 6; Jeremiah McWilliams, "Anheuser-Busch's Michelob Goes Back to All Malt," *St. Louis Post-Dispatch*, 8 February 2007.

5. Andy Grove, "My Biggest Mistake," *INC*, May 1998; John Markoff, "Chip Error Continuing to Dog Officials at Intel," *New York Times*, 6 December 1994; "Intel Agrees to Replace Faulty Pentium Chip," *NPR All Things Considered*, 20 December 1994.

6. "America's Best Selling Brand of Bread Introduces Wonder Smartwhite," *PRNewswire*, 29 March 2010; Suzanna Stagemeyer, "Interstate Bakeries Emerges from Bankruptcy," *Kansas City Business Journal*, 3 February 2009; Robert Klara, "White Bread Good for You? Sorta Makes You Wonder," *Adweek*, 28 March 2010.

7. Chris Roush, "At Timex, They're Positively Glowing," *BusinessWeek*, 12 July 1993, 141; Natalie Zmuda, "Timex Retools to Address Needs Beyond Time-Telling," *Advertising Age*, 23 May 2011; Barry Janoff, "Timex Runs (26.2 Miles) on Time, *Adweek*, 12 October 2008.

8. Jonathan Auerbach, "Smith Corona Seeks Protection of Chapter 11," *Wall Street Journal*, 6 July 1995, A4.

9. "Guitar Hero: What Went Wrong?," www.cnn.com, 10 February 2011; "The Music Dies for One Popular Guitar Hero Video Game," www.cnn.com, 9 February 2011.

10. Robert Sam Anson, "Birth of an MTV Nation," *Vanity Fair*, November 2000, 206–248; Thomas S. Mulligan and Sallie Hofmeister, "Once Again, Redstone Shakes Up Viacom." *Los Angeles Times*, 6 September 2006; Breeanna Hare, "Who Killed the Music Video Star?," www.cnn.com, 16 March 2010; Stuart Elliott, "MTV Strives to Keep Up with Young Viewers," *New York Times*, 30 January 2011; Meg James, "MTV Remakes Itself for the Millennial Generation," *Los Angeles Times*, 2 October 2011; www.mtv.com, accessed February 29, 2012.

11. Susan Heckler, Kevin Lane Keller, and Michael J. Houston, "The Effects of Brand Name Suggestiveness on Advertising Recall," *Journal of Marketing* 62 (January 1998): 48–57.

12. Raymond Serafin, "BMW: From Yuppie-Mobile to Smart Car of the '90s," *Advertising Age*, 3 October 1994, S2.

13. Matthew Lynn, "The Fallen King of Finland," *Bloomberg BusinessWeek*, 20 September 2010; Diane Brady and Hugo Miller, "Failure to Communicate," *Bloomberg BusinessWeek*, 11 October 2010; Elizabeth Woyke, "BlackBerry Battles back," *Forbes*, 28 February 2011.

14. Larry Light and Joan Kiddon, *Six Rules for Brand Revitalization* (Upper Saddle River, NJ: Pearson Education, 2009).

15. Greg Lindsay, "The Alligator's New Look," *Business 2.0*, April 2006, 68–69; Georgina Safe, "Crocodile Rocks a Comeback," *The Australian*, 28 July 2006; David Lipke, "Birkhold Outlines Lacoste Strategy," *Women's Wear Daily*, 12 February 2010; David Lipke, "Lacoste Launching Brand for Younger Customer," *Women's Wear Daily*, 12 July 2010; David Lipke, "Andy Roddick to Launch Signature Line with Lacoste," *Women's Wear Daily*, 2 June 2011.

16. Charles Duhigg, "How Companies Learn Your Secrets," *New York Times*, 16 February 2012; Ellen Byron, "Febreze Joins P&G's $1 Billion Club," *Wall Street Journal*, 9 March 2011; Karl Greenburg, "P&G: Febreze Makes Scents That Make Happiness," *Marketing Daily*, 10 July 2011.

17. John D. Cripps, "Heuristics and Biases in Timing the Replacement of Durable Products," *Journal of Consumer Research* 21 (September 1994): 304–318.

18. Ellen Byron, "How Coach Won a Rich Purse by Inventing New Uses for Bags," *Wall Street Journal*, 17 November 2004, A1; Kevin Lamiman, "Coach, Inc." *Better Investing*, October 2010; Susan Berfield, "Coach's Poppy Line Is Luxury for Recessionary Times," *Bloomberg BusinessWeek*, 18 June 2009.

19. Jenn Abelson, "A Makeover for Talbots," *Boston Globe*, 11 December 2011; Ashley Lutz, "How Talbots Got the Girl—and Lost the Woman," *Bloomberg BusinessWeek*, 20 June 2011; Sean Gregory, "Can Michelle Obama Save Fashion Retailing?," *Time*, 6 May 2009; Naoko Fujimura and Shunichi Ozasa, "Asia's Top Clothier Is Back to Basics," *Bloomberg BusinessWeek*, 10 January 2011.

20. Susan Berfield, "The New Star of Sellavision," *Bloomberg BusinessWeek*, 24 May 2010.

21. Tracie Rozhon, "Reinventing Tommy: More Surf, Less Logo," *New York Times*, 16 March 2003, 1; Michael Barbaro, "Macy's and Hilfiger Strike Exclusive Deal," *New York Times*, 26 October 2007; Ali McConnon, "Tommy Hilfiger's Upscale Move to Macy's," *Bloomberg BusinessWeek*, 22 October 2008; Michael J. de la Merced, "Why Phillips-Van Heusen Is Buying Tommy Hilfiger," *New York Times*, 15 March 2010; "'Keep the Heritage of the Brand Intact': Tommy Hilfiger on Weathering the Ups and

Downs of Retail Fashion," *Knowledge @ Wharton*, 17 March 2010.

22. Christine Birkner, "Mama's Got the Magic of Mobile, Too," *Marketing News*, 15 September 2011.

23. Tim Triplett, "Generic Fear to Xerox Is Brand Equity to FedEx," *Marketing News*, 15 August 1994, 12–13.

24. Burt Helm, "At KFC, a Battle Among the Chicken-Hearted," *Bloomberg BusinessWeek*, 16 August 2010.

25. Mark Clothier, "A Root-to-End Makeover for Pantene," *Bloomberg BusinessWeek*, 24 May 2010.

26. Jean E. Palmieri, "Man in the News: I, Claudio," *Menswear*, April 2011.

27. Peter Lattman, "Rebound," *Forbes*, 28 March 2005, 58.

28. Michael Arndt, "Night of the Living Dead Brands," *Bloomberg BusinessWeek*, 12 April 2010.

29. Jennifer Reingold, "Darwin Goes Shopping," *Financial World*, 1 September 1993, 44.

30. Nancy F. Koehn, *Brand New: How Entrepreneurs Earned Consumers' Trust from Wedgwood to Dell* (Boston: Harvard Business School Press, 2001).

31. Betsy McKay, "Why Coke Indulges (the Few) Fans of Tab," *Wall Street Journal*, 13 April 2001, B1; Devon Spurgeon, "Aurora Bet It Could Win by Fostering Neglected Foods," *Wall Street Journal*, 13 April 2001, B1; Jim Hopkins, "Partners Turn Decrepit Detergent into Boffo Start-Up," *USA Today*, 20 June 2001, 6B; Matthew Swibel, "Spin Cycle," *Forbes*, 2 April 2001, 118.

32. Tara Parker-Pope, "Unilever Plans a Long-Overdue Pruning," *Wall Street Journal*, 3 September 1996, A13.

33. The section on Tylenol is based on a series of articles and papers: John A. Deighton, "Features of Good Integration: Two Cases and Some Generalizations," in *Integrated Communications: The Search for Synergy in Communication Voices*, eds. J. Moore and E. Thorsen (Hillsdale, NJ: Lawrence Erlbaum Associations, 1996); O. C. Ferrell and Linda Ferrell, "Tylenol Continues Its Battle for Success," Daniel Funds Ethics Initiative, University of New Mexico, 2011; Mina Kimes, "Why J&J's Headache Won't Go Away," *Fortune*, 6 September 2010; Parija Kavilanz, "Johnson & Johnson CEO: 'We Made a Mistake'," www.cnnmoney.com, 30 September 2010; Jonathon D. Rockoff and Joann S. Lublin, "J&J CEO Weldon Is Out," *Wall Street Journal*, 22 February 2012.

34. Nancy Langford and Steven A. Greyser, "Exxon: Communications after Valdez," Case 9-593-014 (Boston: Harvard Business School, 1995).

35. For some relevant academic literature, see Michelle L. Roehm and Alice M. Tybout, "When Will a Brand Scandal Spill Over, and How Should Competitors Respond?," *Journal of Marketing Research* 43 (August 2006): 366–373.

36. Stephen A. Greyser and Norman Klein, "The Perrier Recall: A Source of Trouble," Case 9-590-104 (Boston: Harvard Business School, 1990); Stephen A. Greyser and Norman Klein, "The Perrier Relaunch," Case Supplement 9-590-130 (Boston: Harvard Business School, 1990).

37. Ronald Alsop, "Enduring Brands Hold Their Allure by Sticking Close to Their Roots," *Wall Street Journal Centennial Edition*, 1989.

Managing Brands Over Geographic Boundaries and Market Segments

14

Learning Objectives

After reading this chapter, you should be able to

1. Understand the rationale for developing a global brand.
2. Outline the main advantages and disadvantages of developing a standardized global marketing program.
3. Define the strategic steps in developing a global brand positioning.
4. Describe some of the unique characteristics of brand building in developing markets like India and China.

A global marketing pioneer, KFC is now setting its sights on market leadership in China.

Source: Zheng Xianzhang/TAO Images Limited/Alamy

Preview

In earlier chapters, we've considered how and why marketers (1) create brand portfolios to satisfy different market segments and (2) develop brand migration strategies to attract new and retain existing customers. This chapter looks at managing brand equity in different types of market segments. We'll pay particular attention to international issues and global branding strategies.

Specifically, we begin by considering brand management issues over regional, demographic, and cultural market segments. Next, after reviewing the basic rationale for taking brands into new international markets, we consider the broader issues in developing a global brand strategy and look at some of the pros and cons of developing a standardized global marketing program.

In the remainder of the chapter, we concentrate on specific strategic and tactical issues in building global customer-based brand equity, organized around the concept of the "Ten Commandments of Global Branding." To illustrate these guidelines, we'll rely on global brand pioneers such as Coca-Cola, Nestlé, and Procter & Gamble. Brand Focus 14.0 addresses branding issues in the exploding Chinese market.[1]

REGIONAL MARKET SEGMENTS

Regionalization seems to run counter to globalization. Marketers are interested in regional marketing today, however, because mass markets are splintering, computerized sales data from supermarket scanners can reveal regional pockets of sales strengths and weaknesses, and marketing communications make possible more focused targeting of consumer groups defined along virtually any lines.

A regionalization strategy can make a brand more relevant and appealing to any one individual. One study of retail stores found that a localization strategy could boost sales by one to three percentage points, and just 10–15 percent of inventory needed to be customized to get as much as 90 percent of the benefit. Tapping into several trends, Macy's has made its brand simultaneously more local and more national.[2]

MACY'S

Macy's celebrated its 150th anniversary in 2008, a milestone for any brand. Acquisitions, notably of the May Co. for over $11 billion, created a strong national chain of 825 stores, all under the iconic Macy's brand name. At the same time, Macy's recognizes the value of tailoring merchandise to suit local and regional tastes. With a strategy dubbed "My Macy's," the goal is to have 15 percent of merchandise in stores reflect local preferences, a high percentage given the 1.5–4 million different items typically stocked in each store. Using database technology, Macy's can determine the volume, type, and color of sweaters to sell in different stores, for example, and when to replenish inventory. For Bellevue, Washington, whose local Asian population has grown from 4 percent to 23 percent over a 20-year period, the local Macy's added more small and extra-small sizes. The company also needed to double the size of its sock department at the store, which store staff attributed to the forgetfulness of outsiders coming to visit Microsoft's nearby offices. With a sizable African American customer base interested in men's fashions, the Cumberland Mall store in Atlanta doubled the space devoted to men's hats. Combined with a number of other marketing initiatives, Macy's has outperformed its competition in recent years. In January 2012, after a stellar holiday season, CEO Terry Lundgren observed, "We clearly saw the tangible progress of our My Macy's localization, omnichannel integration of stores, online and mobile, and 'MAGIC Selling' [a customer engagement training program], which have been driving our business over the past two years."[3]

Macy's is adjusting its merchandise assortments to reflect local tastes, like expanding its hat department in hat-loving parts of Atlanta.

Source: David Walter Banks/The New York Times/Redux Pictures

Different battles are now being fought between brands in different regions of the country. Anheuser-Busch and Miller Brewing have waged a fierce battle in Texas for years, where nearly 1 in 10 beers sold in the United States is consumed. Anheuser-Busch made sizable inroads during this time through special ad campaigns, displays, and sales strategies. As one observer noted, "Texans believe it's a whole different country down here. They don't want you to just slap an armadillo in a TV spot."[4]

Regionalization can have downsides. Marketing efficiency may suffer and costs may rise with regional marketing. Moreover, regional campaigns may force local producers to become more competitive or blur a brand's national identity. The upside, however, is that marketing can have a stronger impact.

OTHER DEMOGRAPHIC AND CULTURAL SEGMENTS

Any market segment—however we define it—may be a candidate for a specialized marketing and branding program. For example, demographic dimensions such as age, income, gender, and race—as well as psychographic considerations—often are related to more fundamental differences in shopping behaviors or attitudes about brands. These differences can often serve as the rationale for a separate branding and marketing program. The decision ultimately rests on the costs and benefits of customized marketing efforts versus those of a less targeted focus.

For example, Chapter 13 described how important it is for marketers to consider age segments, and how younger consumers can be brought into the consumer franchise. Because of increased consumer mobility, better communication via social media and mobile phones, and expanding transnational entertainment options, lifestyles are fast becoming more similar *across* countries within sociodemographic segments, than they are *within* countries across sociodemographic segments. A teenager in Paris may have more in common with a teenager in London, New York, Sydney, or almost any other major city in the world than with his or her own parents. This younger generation may be more easily influenced by trends and broad cultural movements fueled by worldwide exposure to movies, television, and other media than ever before. One result is that brands able to tap into the global sensibilities of the youth market may be better prepared to adopt a standardized branding program and marketing strategy. Unilever uses a standard approach to market its Axe Body Spray globally based on sex appeal.

Marketers are also considering how various ethnic, racial, or cultural groups may require different marketing programs. In 2010, Hispanics accounted for 50.5 million of the 308 million people in the United States and about $1 trillion in annual purchasing power.[5] Established television networks such as Univision and Telemundo and targeted radio, newspapers, and magazines help marketers reach Hispanics with ads. Active online, the Hispanic market also has a higher smartphone penetration than the general population.[6]

Various firms have created specialized marketing programs with different products, advertising, promotions, and so on to better reach and persuade this market. Olive Garden Italian Restaurant chain spends 10 percent of its $150 million overall ad budget on Hispanic market television. Southwest Airlines communicates in "Spanglish"—a mixture of Spanish and English—in some ads. JC Penney's Hispanic team is made up of marketing, merchandising, planning, real estate, and store operations. The company may stock smaller sizes in stores with larger Hispanic customer bases and observe Mexican holidays (Mother's Day is on a different day than in the United States, for instance).[7]

The Asian population is also growing faster than the total population and is comparatively younger and better educated. Asian buying power is expected to grow by 42 percent in the coming years, from $544 billion in 2010 to $775 billion in 2015.[8] Bank of America prospered by targeting Asians in San Francisco with separate TV campaigns aimed at Chinese, Korean, and Vietnamese customers. Branding Brief 14-1 describes marketing efforts to build brand equity with African Americans.

Marketing critics say that some consumers may not like being targeted on the basis of their being different, since that only reinforces their image as outsiders or a minority. Moreover, consumers not in the targeted segment may feel alienated or distanced from the company and brand as a result.[9] Companies like Ford, McDonald's and Procter & Gamble that sell to a broad range of consumers are embracing diverse racial and ethnic markets in a natural, organic way, and they are seeing sales spikes among minority groups. In a different strategy, Burger King and Home Depot consolidated all their advertising with their general market agencies, believing there was no need to have separate agencies specializing in targeting particular minority groups; these consumers were being adequately included in their deliberately inclusive general market campaigns.[10]

RATIONALE FOR GOING INTERNATIONAL

A number of well-known global brands have derived much of their sales and profits from non-domestic markets for decades, including Coca-Cola, Shell, Bayer, Rolex, Marlboro, Pampers, and Mercedes-Benz, to name a few. Apple computers, L'Oréal cosmetics, and Nescafé instant coffee have become fixtures on the global landscape. Their successes are among the forces that have encouraged many firms to market their brands internationally, including the following:

• Perception of slow growth and increased competition in domestic markets
• Belief in enhanced overseas growth and profit opportunities
• Desire to reduce costs from economies of scale
• Need to diversify risk
• Recognition of global mobility of customers

In more product categories, the ability to establish a global profile is becoming a prerequisite for success. For example, in luxury goods such as jewelry, watches, and handbags, where the addressable market is a relatively small percentage of the global market, a global profile is necessary to grow profitably. Ideally, the marketing program for a global brand consists of one product formulation, one package design, one advertising program, one pricing schedule, one distribution plan, and so on that would prove the most effective and efficient option for every country in which the brand was sold. Unfortunately, such a uniformly optimal strategy is rarely possible. Consider how the Oreo brand has evolved globally.

BRANDING BRIEF 14-1

Marketing to African Americans

Census and marketing surveys have revealed that African Americans represent almost 13 percent of the U.S. population, and their buying power will rise from $957 billion to $1.2 trillion—an increase of 25 percent—from 2010 to 2015. Although much marketing has targeted baby boomers, millennials, Hispanics, and other demographic and psychographic groups, many critics argue that firms have not effectively targeted the African American market. African Americans occupy every income, education, and geographic segment; 2.4 million affluent households (17 percent of the total) account for 45 percent of total African American buying power.

Because almost all African Americans speak English as their first language and watch much network television, many companies rely on general marketing campaigns to reach them. But unique attitudes and behaviors distinguish this audience. Black media executives such as Thomas Burrell, founder and chairman emeritus of Burrell Advertising in Chicago, the largest black-owned agency in the United States, says: "Black people aren't dark-skinned white people. We have different preferences and customs, and we require special effort." Many observers note the important role of religion, church, and family. As a result of their historical experiences, African Americans are often thought to exhibit a strong togetherness and pride in their heritage. They are also seen as style leaders who set fashion trends, especially among younger people.

African Americans spend a disproportionate amount of their income on apparel, footwear, and home electronics. They are more likely to spend money on luxury items such as cruise-ship vacations, new cars, and designer clothes. Many companies have capitalized on these purchasing preferences.

- Recognizing that African Americans often prefer larger helpings of sugar, cream, or nondairy creamer in their coffee, CoffeeMate began marketing to African Americans more specifically through black radio, magazines, and billboards, with a corresponding increase in sales.

- Recognizing that African Americans account for 30 percent of total U.S. hair care expenditures, L'Oréal made separate acquisitions of Soft Sheen Products and Carson Products to target that multi-billion-dollar market.

- Recognizing that Coke "over-indexes" or is comparatively bought more often in single-parent-family African American households, Coca-Cola targets African American moms in their role as gatekeeper.

African American consumers make a disproportionate amount of purchases of menthol cigarettes, certain types of

Some marketers have found great success in targeting African Americans with their products, as L'Oréal did with Soft Sheen.

Source: Terrence Jennings/Sipa Press/Newscom

hard liquors—brandy, scotch, cognac—and malt liquor beers. Alcohol and tobacco companies were among the first to specifically target this group, although these strategies have been somewhat controversial. Given that African Americans are prone to certain health risks, such as hypertension and cardiovascular disease, food and drug advertising often also specifically target them. Ads for St. Joseph Aspirin highlighted the fact that the product contains the dosage recommended by the Association of Black Cardiologists.

The challenge for building brand equity among African Americans is to create relevant marketing programs and communication campaigns that accurately portray brand personality and user and usage imagery and avoid fostering stereotypes, offending sensibilities, or lumping market segments together. The president of one black-owned agency says the formula for marketing to blacks consists of relevance, recognition, and respect. As with global brand programs in general, marketers should blend standardization and customization as appropriate.

Sources: Based on material from Marlene L. Rossman, *Multicultural Marketing: Selling to a Diverse America* (New York: AMACOM, 1994); and Barbara Lloyd, *Capitalizing on the American Dream: Marketing to America's Ethnic Minorities*, Stanford Business School independent study, 1990; Richard C. Morais, "The Color of Beauty," *Forbes*, 27 November 2000, 170–176; Marcia Pledger, "There's No Debating One Thing: Hair Care Is a Healthy Business," *Cleveland Plain Dealer*, 27 October 2009; "Buying Power Among African Americans to Reach $1.1 Trillion by 2012, *Reuters*, 6 February 2008; Mike Beirne, "Has This Group Been Left Behind?" *Brandweek*, 14 March 2005; Natalie Zmuda, "How Coke Is Targeting Black Consumers: Q&A with Yolanda White, Assistant VP of African-American Marketing," *Advertising Age*, 1 July 2009; Vernellia R. Randall, "Targeting of African Americans," www.academic.udayton.edu, 2004.

OREO

In launching its Oreo brand of cookies worldwide, Kraft chose to adopt a consistent global positioning, "Milk's Favorite Cookie." Although not necessarily highly relevant in all countries, it did reinforce generally desirable associations like nurturing, caring, and health. To help ensure global understanding, Kraft created a brand book with a CD in an Oreo-shaped box that summarized brand management fundamentals—what needed to be common across countries, what could be changed, and what could not. In time, differences emerged across markets. In China, the original cookie is less sweet than in the United States and has different fillings, such as green tea ice cream, grape–peach, mango–orange, and raspberry–strawberry. In an example of reverse innovation, Kraft has actually successfully introduced some of these Oreo flavors into other countries. Oreo is also making a big push in India, where it is just entering the market and facing stiff competition from major local brands there, such as Parle, Britannia, and Sunfeast. Launch ads reflected Oreo's updated global positioning based on moments of togetherness and featured a father and son in the "twist, lick, dunk" ritual. Social media has Indian parents sign an "Oreo Togetherness Pledge" promising to spend more quality time with their children. An Oreo Togetherness Bus roams the country providing a platform for parents and children to catch fun family moments. Thanks to international marketing acumen, Oreo now is a $2 billion global brand for Kraft, with 23 million members in its Facebook community.[11]

Adapting its iconic Oreo cookie to reflect local tastes and culture, Kraft has found much success in developing markets like China and India.

Source: AP Photo/Imaginechina

Next, let's consider the advantages and disadvantages of creating globally standardized marketing programs for brands.

ADVANTAGES OF GLOBAL MARKETING PROGRAMS

A number of potential advantages attach to a global marketing program (see Figure 14-1).[12] In general, the less it varies from country to country, the more these advantages will be realized.

Economies of Scale in Production and Distribution

From a supply-side or cost perspective, the primary advantages of a global marketing program are the manufacturing efficiencies and lower costs that derive from higher volumes in production and distribution. The more that strong experience curve effects exist—driving down the cost of making and marketing a product with increases in production—the more economies of scale in production and distribution from a standardized global marketing program will prevail.

Economies of scale in production and distribution
Lower marketing costs
Power and scope
Consistency in brand image
Ability to leverage good ideas quickly and efficiently
Uniformity of marketing practices

FIGURE 14-1

Advantages of Global
Marketing Programs

Lower Marketing Costs

Another set of cost advantages arises from uniformity in packaging, advertising, promotion, and other marketing communication activities. The more uniform, the greater the potential savings. A global corporate branding strategy such as Sony's is perhaps the most efficient means of spreading marketing costs across both products and countries. Branding experts maintain that using one name can save a business tens of millions of dollars a year in marketing costs.[13]

As Chapter 13 noted, L'Oréal has pursued an aggressive global growth strategy, prompting one business writer to christen the company "the United Nations of beauty." Its Maybelline line is the best-selling brand in many Asian markets, while eastern Europeans prefer L'Oréal's French brands, and African immigrants in Europe go for the U.S. brand Dark and Lovely. L'Oréal ensures its business remains sound on a local level by establishing national divisions. Because Brazilian women traditionally bought their cosmetics from door-to-door sales reps, the company introduced personal beauty advisers at department stores there. As the one-time head of L'Oréal's head of luxury products said, "You have to be local and as strong as the best locals but backed by an international image and strategy."[14]

Power and Scope

A global brand profile can communicate credibility.[15] Consumers may believe that selling in many diverse markets is an indication that a manufacturer has gained much expertise and acceptance, meaning the product is high quality and convenient to use. An admired global brand can also signal social status and prestige.[16] Avis assures its customers that they can receive the same high-quality car rental service anywhere in the world, further reinforcing a key benefit promise embodied in its slogan, "We Try Harder."

Consistency in Brand Image

Maintaining a common marketing platform all over the world helps maintain the consistency of brand and company image; this is particularly important where customers move often or media exposure transmits images across national boundaries. Gillette sells "functional superiority" and "an appreciation of human character and aspirations" with its razors and blades brands worldwide. Services often desire to convey a uniform image due to consumer movements. For example, American Express communicates the prestige and utility of its card worldwide.

Ability to Leverage Good Ideas Quickly and Efficiently

One global marketer notes that globalization can increase sustainability and "facilitate continued development of core competencies with the organization . . . in manufacturing, in R&D, in marketing and sales, and in less talked about areas such as competitive intelligence . . . all of which enhance the company's ability to compete."[17] Not having to develop strictly local versions speeds a brand's market entry. Marketers can leverage good ideas across markets as long as the right knowledge transfer systems are put into place. IBM has a Web-based communications tool that provides instant multimedia interaction to connect marketers. MasterCard's corporate marketing group helps facilitate information and best practices across the organization.[18]

Uniformity of Marketing Practices

Finally, a standardized global marketing program may simplify coordination and provide greater control of communications in different countries. By keeping the core of the marketing program constant, marketers can pay greater attention to making refinements across markets and over time to improve its effectiveness. Chapter 3 described the rationale for the MasterCard "Priceless" campaign. Here is how it became a global blockbuster.

MASTERCARD

MasterCard quickly evolved its successful "Priceless" campaign, launched in 1996, into a "worldwide platform." By 1998, the tagline, "The best things in life are free. For everything else, there's MasterCard" was in use in over 30 countries. Some ads' premises were universal enough to work as is, with only language translation, such as the "Zipper" ad, in which the priceless moment is a man realizing his zipper is down before anyone else does. In other cases, a locally relevant premise was used instead, with the same tagline. "Every culture has those meaningful moments, which is why we've been able to globalize the campaign," stated a creative director for McCann Erickson, which developed the campaign. Sponsorships for sports with international appeal, such as World Cup soccer and Formula 1 racing, also increased the campaign's ability to connect with a worldwide audience. The campaign was credited with lifting brand awareness in a number of nations, driving card sales, and enabling MasterCard to take market share from Visa. Over 15 years later, the campaign is still running strong.[19]

DISADVANTAGES OF GLOBAL MARKETING PROGRAMS

Perhaps the most compelling disadvantage of standardized global marketing programs is that they often ignore fundamental differences of various kinds across countries and cultures (see Figure 14-2). Critics claim that designing one program for all possible markets results in unimaginative and ineffective strategies geared to the lowest common denominator. Possible differences across countries come in a host of forms, as we discuss next.

Differences in Consumer Needs, Wants, and Usage Patterns for Products

Differences in cultural values, economic development, and other factors across nationalities lead customers to behave very differently. For example, the per capita consumption of alcoholic beverages varies dramatically from country to country: in liters consumed per capita annually, the Czech Republic (8.51) and Ireland (7.04) drink the most beer; France (8.14) and Portugal (6.65) drink the most wine; and South Korea (9.57) and Russia (6.88) drink the most distilled spirits.[20]

Product strategies that work in one country may not work in another. Tupperware, which makes the bulk of its annual sales overseas—57 percent from emerging markets—needed to adjust its products to satisfy different consumer behavior. In India, a plastic container paired with a spoon becomes a "masala keeper" for spices. In Korea, stain-resistant canisters are ideal for kimchi fermentation. Larger boxes work as safe, airtight "kimono keepers" in Japan. In France, its more expensive cookware line does much better than in the United States, where customers buy more plastic containers. Tupperware parties in France feature cooking lessons more than selling. India has followed suit, introducing the stylish Ultimo line of kitchenware.[21]

Differences in Consumer Response to Branding Elements

Linguistic differences across countries can twist or change the meaning of a brand name. Sound systems that differ across dialects can make a word problematic in one country but not another. Cultural context is key. Customers may actually respond well to a name with potentially problematic associations. The questions are how widespread the association is, how immediate it is, and how problematic it actually would be.

Well-known brand consultancy Lexicon employs linguists to help make these assessments for clients.[22] The agency has uncovered names that would have been a sexual insult in

FIGURE 14-2

Disadvantages of Global
Marketing Programs

Differences in consumer needs, wants, and usage patterns for products
Differences in consumer response to branding elements
Differences in consumer response to marketing mix elements
Differences in brand and product development and the competitive
environment
Differences in the legal environment
Differences in marketing institutions
Differences in administrative procedures

Tupperware emphasizes different products and marketing strategies in different parts of the world.

Sources: Tupperware party in Indonesia. Courtesy of Tupperware Brands

Colombian Spanish, been sacrilegious in Hindi, conveyed impotence in Japanese, and translated as "prostitute" in Hebrew. GM went ahead and used the LaCrosse model name for its Buick line in Canada so it could leverage its U.S. advertising, even though the word was slang for masturbation in French-speaking Quebec. The hope was that its more formal English meaning as a well-known sport would dominate there.[23]

Differences in Consumer Responses to Marketing Mix Elements

Consumers in different parts of the world feel differently about marketing activity.[24] U.S. consumers tend to be fairly cynical toward advertising, whereas Japanese view it much more positively. Differences also exist in advertising style: Japanese ads tend to be softer and more abstract in tone, whereas U.S. ads are often richer in product information.

Price sensitivity, promotion responsiveness, sponsorship support, and other activities all may differ by country, and these differences can motivate differences in consumer behavior and decision making. In a comparative study of brand purchase intentions, U.S. consumers were twice as likely to be affected by their product beliefs and attitudes toward the brand itself, whereas Koreans were eight times more likely to be influenced by social normative beliefs and what they felt others would think about the purchase.[25]

Finding a brand name without some kind of negative connotations in a particular language can be challenging, as Buick LaCrosse found in Canada.

Source: AP Photo/Carlos Osorio

Brand Strength Rank	USA 2011	UK 2011	Germany 2009	France 2009	Brazil 2011	China 2011
1	United States	Google	Germany	France	Rede Globo	Chun Jie Wan Hui
2	Pixar	United Kingdom	Google	IKEA	Copa do Mundo	Q-Zone
3	Disney	Microsoft	IKEA	Arte	Fantástico	KFC
4	Google	Dyson	Die Olympischen Spiele	Canal +	SBT	Colgate
5	Discovery Channel	eBay	adidas	Google	Globo Repórter	QQ
6	U.S. Marines	Apple	eBay	Coca-Cola	Jornal Nacional	Baidu
7	Microsoft	Nintendo Wii	Windows	M6	Rede Record	China Mobile
8	National Geographic	Facebook	LEGO	Häagen-Dazs	Nestlé	Xin Wen Lian Bo
9	DreamWorks (SKG)	IKEA	BMW	Nutella	Coca-Cola	Apple (Computer)
10	Facebook	Channel 4	Aldi	Nintendo Wii	Brastemp	Nokia

Differences in Brand and Product Development and the Competitive Environment

Products may be at different stages of their life cycle in different countries. Moreover, the perceptions and positions of particular brands may also differ considerably across countries. Figure 14-3 shows the results of a comprehensive study of leading brands (of all kinds, including people and country brands) in different parts of the world according to the BrandAsset Valuator measurement technique (see Brand Focus 9.0). Relatively few brands appear on all the lists, suggesting that, if nothing else, consumer perceptions of even top brands can vary significantly by geographic region.

The nature of competition may also differ. Europeans tend to see more competitors because shipping products across borders is easy. Germany's *Mittelstand*—small and mid-sized companies with fewer than 500 people—employ more than 70 percent of German workers and contribute roughly half of the country's GDP. They are especially formidable competitors. Blending high technology with a focus on quality, they weathered the recession well in Europe's largest market (82 million people).[26]

Differences in the Legal Environment

One of the challenges in developing a global ad campaign is the maze of constantly changing legal restrictions from country to country. At one time, laws in Venezuela, Canada, and Australia stipulated that commercials had to be physically produced in the native country. Canada banned prescription drug advertising on television. Poland required commercial lyrics to be sung in Polish. Sweden prohibited advertising to children. Malaysia did not allow lawyers or law firms to advertise. Advertising restrictions have been placed on the use of children in commercials in Austria, comparative ads in Singapore, and product placement on public television channels in Germany. Although some of these laws have been challenged or are being relaxed, numerous legal differences still exist.

Differences in Marketing Institutions

Channels of distribution, retail practices, media availability, and media costs all may vary significantly from country to country, making implementation of the same marketing strategy difficult. Foreign companies struggled for years to break into Japan's rigid distribution system that locks out many foreign goods. The penetration of cable television, cell phones, supermarkets, and so on may also vary considerably, especially in developing countries.

Differences in Administrative Procedures

In practice, it may be difficult to achieve the control necessary to implement a standardized global marketing program. Local offices may resist having their autonomy threatened. Local managers may suffer from the "not invented here" syndrome and raise objections—rightly or wrongly—that the global marketing program misses some key dimension of the local market. Local managers who feel their autonomy has been reduced may lose motivation and feel doomed to failure.

GLOBAL BRAND STRATEGY

With that background, let's turn to some basic strategic issues in global branding. The contention of this chapter is that in building brand equity, we often must create different marketing programs to satisfy different market segments. Therefore we must:

1. Identify differences in consumer behavior—how consumers purchase and use *products* and what they know and feel about *brands*—in each market.
2. Adjust the branding program accordingly through the choice of brand elements, the nature of the actual marketing program and activities, and the leveraging of secondary associations.

Note that the third way to build global brand equity, leveraging secondary brand associations, is probably the most likely to require change across countries because the entities linked to a brand may take on very different meanings in different countries. For example, U.S. companies such as Coca-Cola, Levi Strauss, and Nike traditionally gained an important source of equity in going overseas by virtue of their U.S. heritage, which is not as much of an issue or asset in their domestic market. Harley-Davidson has aggressively marketed its classic U.S. image—customized for different cultures—to generate about 30 percent of its sales from abroad.[27] Brands large and small can try to tap into their geographical roots. Gosling's Black Seal Bermuda black rum uses its Caribbean heritage and its trademarked ingredient in the "dark and stormy" cocktail in its efforts to build a global brand.[28]

Understanding how consumers actually form their impressions of country of origin and update their brand knowledge can be challenging.[29] The design, manufacture, assembly, distribution, and marketing of products often involve several countries. Apple's iPhone is designed and owned by a U.S. company and assembled and shipped from China from parts produced largely in several Asian and European countries.[30]

Global Brand Equity

As we explained in Chapter 3, to build brand resonance, marketers must (1) establish breadth and depth of brand awareness; (2) create points-of-parity and points-of-difference; (3) elicit positive, accessible brand responses; and (4) forge intense, active brand relationships. Achieving these four steps, in turn, requires establishing six core brand building blocks: brand salience, brand performance, brand imagery, brand judgments, brand feelings, and brand resonance. In each and every market in which marketers sell the brand, they must consider how to achieve these steps and create these building blocks. Some of the issues that come into play are discussed in the following subsections.

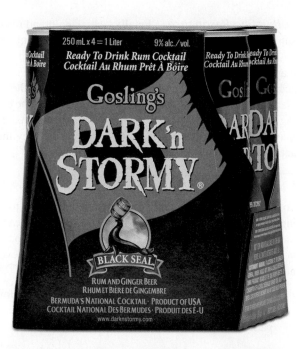

Black Seal Rum leverages its Bermuda heritage to build its brand equity in overseas markets.

Source: AP Photo/ PRNewsFoto/Gosling's Rum of Bermuda

Creating Brand Salience.   It is rare that a product will roll out in new markets the same way it did in the home market. Often, product introductions in the domestic market are sequential, stretched out over a longer period of time than the nearly simultaneous introductions that occur overseas.

NIVEA

Nivea's flagship product in its European home market has been its category leader, Nivea Creme. Although the company had introduced other skin care and personal care products, Nivea Creme had the most history and heritage and reflected many core brand values. In Asia, however, for cultural and climate reasons, the creme product was less well received, and the facial skin care sub-brand, Nivea Visage, and creme line extension, Nivea Soft, were of greater strategic and marketing importance. Because these two product brands have slightly different images than the Creme brand, an important issue was the impact on consumers' collective impressions of Nivea. A strong initial emphasis on Nivea for Men in North America raised similar questions.

Different orders of introduction can profoundly affect consumer perceptions about what products the brand offers, the benefits supplied, and the needs satisfied. Thus, we need to examine the breadth and depth of recall to ensure that the proper brand salience and meaning exist.

Crafting Brand Image.   If the product does not vary appreciably across markets, basic brand performance associations may not need to be that different. Brand imagery associations, on the other hand, may be quite different, and one challenge in global marketing is to meaningfully refine the brand image across diverse markets. History and heritage, which may be rich and a strong competitive advantage in the home market, may be virtually nonexistent in a new market. A desirable brand personality in one market may be less desirable in another. Nike's competitive, aggressive user imagery proved a detriment in its introduction into European markets in the early 1990s. The company achieved greater success when it dialed down its image somewhat and emphasized team concepts more.

Eliciting Brand Responses.   Brand judgments must be positive in new markets—consumers must find the brand to be of good quality, credible, worthy of consideration, and superior. Crafting the right brand image will help accomplish these outcomes. One of the challenges in global marketing, however, is creating the proper balance and type of emotional responses and brand feelings. Blending inner (enduring and private) and outer (immediate experiential) emotions can be difficult, given cultural differences across markets.

Cultivating Resonance.   Finally, achieving brand resonance in new markets means that consumers must have sufficient opportunities and incentives to buy and use the product, interact with other consumers and the company itself, and actively learn and experience the brand and its marketing. Clearly, interactive, online marketing can be advantageous here, as long as it can be accessible and relevant anywhere in the world. Nevertheless, digital efforts cannot completely replace grassroots marketing efforts that help connect the consumer with the brand. Simply exporting marketing programs, even with some adjustments, may be insufficient because consumers may be too much at "arm's length." As a result, they may not be able to develop the intense, active loyalty that characterizes brand resonance.

Global Brand Positioning

To best capture differences in consumer behavior, and to guide our efforts in revising the marketing program, we must revisit the brand positioning in each market. Recall that brand positioning means creating mental maps, defining core brand associations, identifying points-of-parity and points-of-difference, and crafting a band mantra. In developing a global brand positioning, we need to answer three key sets of questions:

1. How valid is the mental map in the new market? How appropriate is the positioning? What is the existing level of awareness? How valuable are the core brand associations, points-of-parity, and points-of-difference?

2. What changes should we make to the positioning? Do we need to create any new associations? Should we *not* recreate any existing associations? Should we modify any existing associations?

3. How should we create this new mental map? Can we still use the same marketing activities? What changes should we make? What new marketing activities are necessary?

Because the brand is often at an earlier stage of development when going abroad, we often must first establish awareness and key points-of-parity. Then we can consider additional competitive considerations. In effect, we need to define a hierarchy of brand associations in the global context that defines which associations we want consumers in all countries to hold, and which we want consumers only in certain countries to have. We have to determine how to create these associations in different markets to account for different consumer perceptions, tastes, and environments. Thus, we must be attuned to similarities and differences across markets.

As this discussion suggests, although firms are increasingly adopting an international marketing perspective to capitalize on market opportunities, a number of possible pitfalls exist. Before providing some specific tactical guidelines as to how to build global customer-based brand equity, we first turn to two fundamentally important contrasts in global branding: standardization versus customization, and developing versus developed markets.

STANDARDIZATION VERSUS CUSTOMIZATION

The most fundamental issue in developing a global marketing program is the extent to which the marketing program should be standardized across countries, because this decision has such a deep impact on marketing structure and processes. Perhaps the biggest proponent of standardization was the legendary Harvard professor Ted Levitt.

In a controversial 1983 article, Levitt argued that companies needed to learn to operate as if the world were one large market, ignoring superficial regional and national differences.[31] According to Levitt, because the world was shrinking—due to leaps in technology, communication, and so forth—well-managed companies should shift their emphasis from customizing items to offering globally standardized products that are advanced, functional, reliable, and low-priced for all. Levitt's strong position elicited an equally strong response. One ad executive commented, "There are about two products that lend themselves to global marketing—and one of them is Coca-Cola." Other critics pointed out that even Coca-Cola did not standardize its marketing—as Branding Brief 14-2 illustrates—and noted the lack of standardization in other leading global brands, such as McDonald's and Marlboro.

The experiences of these top marketers have been shared by others who found out—in many cases, the hard way—that differences in consumer behavior still prevail across countries. Many firms have been forced to tailor products and marketing programs to different national markets as a result. In short, it's difficult to identify any one company applying the global marketing concept in the strict sense—by selling the same brand exactly the same way everywhere.

Standardization *and* Customization

Increasingly, marketers are blending global objectives with local or regional concerns. From these perspectives, transferring products across borders may mean consistent positioning for the brand, but not necessarily the same brand name and marketing program in each market. Similarly, packaging may have the same overall look but be tailored as required to fit the local populace and market needs. For example, Danone's kids' yogurts are sold under a variety of names—Danonino, Danoontje, Danimals—in over 120 countries, while a general manager leads a central team that coordinates and oversees the local marketing efforts.[32]

In short, centralized marketing strategies that preserve local customs and traditions can be a boon for products sold in more than one country—even in diverse cultures. Fortunately, firms have improved their capabilities to tailor products and programs to local conditions. Flexible manufacturing technology has decreased the concentration of activities, and advances in information systems and telecommunications have allowed increased coordination.

Domino's Pizza tried to maintain the same delivery system everywhere but had to adapt the model to local customs in launching its brand overseas. In Britain, customers thought anybody

BRANDING BRIEF 14-2

Coca-Cola Becomes the Quintessential Global Brand

The most recognized brand name in the world got its start in an Atlanta pharmacy, where it sold for five cents a glass. The name Coca-Cola was registered as a trademark on January 31, 1893. The drink soon became a national phenomenon; by 1895, the company had established syrup plants in Chicago, Dallas, and Los Angeles.

In the 1920s, Coca-Cola pursued aggressive global branding, finding such creative placements for its logo as on dogsleds in Canada and on the walls of bullfighting arenas in Spain. Its popularity throughout the world was fueled by colorful and persuasive advertising that cemented its image as the "All-American" beverage. When the Vietnam War tarnished the U.S. iconography, Coca-Cola developed more globally aware advertising. In 1971, it ran its legendary "I'd like to buy the world a Coke" television spot, in which a crowd

Coca-Cola's global portfolio includes firmly entrenched local brands such as Thums Up in India.

Source: Jeffrey Blacker/Alamy

of children sang the song from atop a hill in Italy. Coca-Cola's early moves into formerly restricted markets, such as China in 1978 and the Soviet Union in 1979, bolstered its image as a global company. By 1988, Coca-Cola was voted the best known and most admired brand in the world.

Despite—or perhaps as a result of—this immense scope, Coca-Cola did not institute a uniform marketing program in each of its global markets. Rather, the company often tailored the flavor, packaging, price, and advertising to match tastes in specific markets. For example, Coke's famous "Mean Joe" Green TV ad from the United States—in which the weary football star reluctantly accepts a Coke from an admiring young fan and then unexpectedly tosses the kid his jersey in appreciation—was replicated in a number of different regions using

the same format but substituting famous athletes from those regions (ads in South America used the Argentine soccer star Maradona, while those in Asia used the Thai soccer star Niat).

Local managers were assigned responsibility for sales and distribution programs of Coke products, to reflect the marked differences in consumer behavior across countries. Perhaps the most consistently standardized element of Coca-Cola is its product appearance. Coke essentially keeps the same basic look and packaging of the product everywhere (except in countries where laws dictate use of the local language). The company simultaneously stresses that the brand be *relevant* and *well positioned* against the competition. To keep it relevant, Coca-Cola uses different advertising agencies in different countries in order to make the brand feel local.

knocking on the door was rude; in Kuwait, the delivery was just as likely to be made to a limousine as to a house; and in Japan, houses were not numbered sequentially, making finding a particular address difficult.

Although Heineken is seen as an everyday brand in the Netherlands, it is considered a "top-shelf" brand almost everywhere else. A case of the beer costs almost twice as much in the United States as the most popular U.S. brand, Budweiser.[33] For a long time, Heineken's slogan in the United Kingdom and other countries—"Heineken Refreshes the Parts Other Beers Can't Reach"—was different from its U.S. positioning.

As these examples suggest, top brands adapt their marketing programs in different parts of the world. We next review the four major elements of a marketing program—product, communications, distribution, and pricing strategies—in terms of adaptation issues.

Product Strategy. One reason so many companies ran into trouble initially going overseas is that they unknowingly—or perhaps even deliberately—overlooked differences in consumer behavior. Because of the relative expense and sometimes unsophisticated nature of the marketing

For example, in Australia, the advertising appeals to the same "classic, original" ideals but in a very Australian fashion which reflects their active lifestyles and fun-loving, irreverent attitude. Moreover, the marketing mix is designed in each country to stress that Coke is positioned positively on attributes relative to local competitive products. Hence, although Coke looks similar across the globe, its specific image may be very different, depending on what is considered "relevant" in each country. The advantage is that Coke becomes entwined with the cultural fabric of the country, just as it has in the United States. Over time this yields an advantage with younger generations, who don't even think of Coke as an imported brand. Coca-Cola recounts the example of a Japanese family visiting the United States for the first time. The young son, upon passing a vending machine, joyfully exclaimed to his parents, "Look, they have Coke here too!"

In 1999, Coca-Cola's new global marketing mantra became "Think Local. Act Local"—an important twist on its old mantra, "Think Global. Act Local." Intended to get Coca-Cola back to the basics, the strategy meant hiring more local staff and allowing field managers to tailor marketing to their regions. The results of this hyperlocal focus were missed sales targets and local advertising that, in some cases, did not fit with the carefully crafted Coke image, such as an Italian ad featuring skinny-dippers running along a beach. The company scrapped the "Think Local. Act Local" mantra in favor of a hybrid strategy, in which a global marketing network of local executives took direction from Coke's Atlanta headquarters, with some room for interpretation at the local level.

Today, Coca-Cola conducts business with more than 400 brands in over 200 countries. About three-quarters of its revenues come from outside the United States. For example, while Coca-Cola sells Coke to a growing group of consumers in Asia, it also sells local brands there, such as the hugely successful Georgia iced coffee in Japan, which actually outsells Coke, as well as new drinks, such as Nagomi green tea and the honey-and-grapefruit drink Hachimitsu. In China, the company introduced Tian Yu Di ("heaven and earth"), a fruit juice and tea, and Yangguang ("sunshine") lemon tea, plus other flavors. In India, a big seller for Coca-Cola is Thums Up, an indigenous variant it bought in 1993. It also sells Maaza fruit-based drinks there. The company finds its Coke brand trailing Pepsi in India, in part due to the fact that Coke was withdrawn from the market from 1977 to 1993. Its combination of local and global brands enables Coca-Cola to exploit the benefits of global branding and global trends in tastes while tapping into traditional domestic markets at the same time.

As much as Coke has accomplished globally, many opportunities still remain. Per capita consumption of Coke is much lower in India and China than in the United States, Europe, and Latin America. Africa has even more potential. Annual per capita consumption in Kenya is 39 servings, a far cry from Mexico, which consumes more Coke than any other country at 665 servings a year. Success in Africa requires literally a street-by-street campaign with mom-and-pop stores everywhere. Most Cokes are sold in returnable glass bottles there, which are refilled as many as 70 times each before being recycled. Returnable bottles help keep prices down—the consumer literally pays for just the liquid in the bottle—allowing the company to reach what it calls "economically diverse" customers.

Sources: Duane D. Stanford, "Coke's Last Round," *Bloomberg BusinessWeek*, 1 November 2010; Mehul Srivastava, "For India's Consumers, Pepsi Is the Real Thing, *Bloomberg BusinessWeek*, 20 September 2010; "Coke Profit Fails to Meet Expectations," *New York Times*, 20 April 2010; "The Story of Coca-Cola," www.coca-cola.com; Betsy McKay, "Coca-Cola Restructuring Effort Has Yet to Prove Effective," *Asian Wall Street Journal*, 2 March 2001; Kate MacArthur, "Coke Commits $400M to Fix It," *Advertising Age*, 15 November 2004; Theresa Howard, "Coca-Cola Hopes Taking New Path Leads to Success," *USA Today*, 6 March 2001, 6B; Michael Flagg, "Coca-Cola Adopts Local-Drinks Strategy in Asia," *Wall Street Journal*, 30 July 2001.

research industry in smaller markets, many companies chose to forgo basic consumer research and put products on the shelf to see what would happen. As a result, they sometimes became aware of consumer differences only after the fact. To avoid these types of mistakes, marketers may need to conduct research into local markets.

In many cases, however, marketing research reveals that product differences are not justified for certain countries. At one time, Palmolive soap was sold globally with 22 different fragrances, 17 packages, nine shapes, and numerous positionings. After conducting marketing analyses to reap the benefits of global marketing, the company chose to employ just seven fragrances, one core packaging design, and three main shapes, all executed around two related positionings (one for developing markets and one for developed markets).[34] Branding Brief 14-3 describes how UPS has successfully adapted its service for the European market.

From a corporate perspective, one obvious solution to the trade-off between global and local brands is to sell both types of brands as part of the brand portfolio in a category. Even companies that have succeeded with global brands maintain that standardized international marketing programs work with only some products, in some places, and at some times, and will never totally replace brands and ads with local appeal.[35] Thus, despite the trend toward globalization, it seems that there will always be opportunities for good local brands.

BRANDING BRIEF 14-3

UPS's European Express

After first entering the European market in 1976, United Parcel Service of America (UPS) spent $1 billion between 1987 and 1997 to buy 16 delivery businesses, put brown uniforms on 25,000 Europeans, and spray its brown paint on 10,000 delivery trucks in the process of becoming the largest delivery company in Europe. To achieve that goal, UPS had to overcome a number of obstacles along the way.

French drivers were outraged that they could not have wine with lunch; British drivers protested when their dogs were banned from delivery trucks; Spaniards were dismayed when they realized the brown UPS trucks resembled the local hearses; and Germans were shocked when brown shirts were required for the first time since 1945. UPS ultimately allowed a degree of local interpretation while standing firm on some issues of company policy, such as brown trucks and uniforms and alcohol-free drivers.

UPS has made leadership in package delivery and logistics a priority in Europe.
Source: Greg Balfour Evans/Alamy

Although UPS operations were basically the same, the company faced problems that were less common or even non-existent in the United States at that time: truck restrictions on weekends and holidays, low bridges and tunnels, widely varying weight regulations, terrible traffic, and, in some places, limited highway systems, primitive airports, and curfews. In addition, the standard of service in Europe in the 1990s was typically well below what U.S. consumers were accustomed to. Another issue was that express delivery was not yet as popular in Europe as it was in the States. As one industry analyst observed then, "Europeans are not as time-sensitive as the Americans are."

The spread of services and service-related jobs in Europe over the prior two decades had been hampered by a reluctance there to part with traditional ways of doing business, such as state-owned monopolies and rigid work practices. Workers resisted part-time work and had stronger employment protection and higher nonwage costs than workers in the United States. As a result, Manpower Inc. virtually created the temporary-help business in Europe and was able to derive more than 40 percent of its worldwide revenues there.

To improve its share of European business, UPS spent an estimated $1.1 billion between 1995 and 2000 upgrading its European operations by purchasing vehicles, aircraft, buildings, and logistics systems. Consequently, export shipping in Europe via UPS rose at a compound annual rate of 22 percent between 1996 and 2002. Since then, UPS has continued to invest in its European business, acquiring package delivery companies

Stolica and Lynx in Poland and the U.K., respectively, in 2005; building a modern new $135 million automated package sorting hub at Cologne/Bonn airport to double processing capacity; and introducing three daily time-definite delivery options to provide customers the greatest shipping flexibility.

The 2012 acquisition of Dutch-based TNT Express for almost $7 billion increased UPS's European small-parcel revenue to $60 billion in annual sales and its market share to 20 percent. It also expanded the company's aircraft and vehicle fleet infrastructure to help it move more deeply into the Asia-Pacific region and better compete with DHL and FedEx.

All these investments have paid off. Now the world's largest package delivery company and a global leader in supply chain management, UPS serves 60 European countries and territories from its Cologne/Bonn, Germany hub, with a staff of 43,000 employees and a delivery fleet of 8,800 package cars, vans, tractors, and motorcycles. The company has experienced years of strong export volume growth in Europe.

Sources: Dana Milbank, "Can Europe Deliver?" *Wall Street Journal,* 30 September 1994, R15; William Echikson, "The Continent Is Still a Tough Neighborhood for UPS," *BusinessWeek,* 29 September 1997; "Q&A: Nick Basford, Vice-President of Marketing, UPS Europe," *Marketing Week,* 7 September 2011; Matthew Young, "UPS Strikes Deal to Purchase TNT Express, Substantially Expanding European Parcel Market Share," www.morningstar.com, 20 March 2012; UPS Annual Reports, 2002, 2005, 2010; www.ups.com.

Communication Strategy.   Advertising is one area of marketing communications in which many firms face challenges internationally. Although the brand positioning may be the same in different countries, creative strategies in advertising may have to differ to some degree. One highly successful recent global brand campaign promoted Johnnie Walker Scotch.

JOHNNIE WALKER

The top Scotch brand of Diageo—the largest multinational wine and spirits company—has its roots in nineteenth-century Scotland. In 1908, the brand itself was launched, including the iconic logo of a cane-wielding man clad in boots and a top hat striding forward, in honor of the founder John, or "Johnnie," Walker. Every type of Johnnie Walker Scotch has a label color to denote type and quality and signify usage occasion. More recently, at about the turn of the century, the brand experienced a downturn, and sales dropped almost 10 percent. A new ad agency determined that the brand needed to better establish its "World Cup–level" icon status. The insight to achieve that goal was that a new generation of men shared a common desire to move forward and improve themselves in some way. Renowned ad agency BBH reversed the logo image so the "Striding Man" would be moving from left to right, to signify personal progress. With a slogan, "Keep Walking," a campaign was launched in 120 countries via 30 TV ads, 150 print ads, radio ads, Web sites, sponsorships, internal awards, and a cause program to support the brand's purpose. A five-minute film, *The Man Who Walked Around the World*, featured actor Robert Carlyle cleverly outlining Johnnie Walker's brand history in one continuous, flowing shot. The global brand concept was creatively applied in different markets to make it locally recognizable and relevant. In Africa, a key target for brand growth, Johnnie Walker is put forth as a symbol of personal success. Billboards and magazine ads there feature champion Ethiopian runner Haile Gebrselassie "running for gold."[36]

Diageo used its "Keep Walking" marketing campaign all over the world to support its Johnnie Walker brand.

Source: AP Photo/Andrew Milligan/PA Wire

Different countries can be more or less receptive to different creative styles. For example, humor is more common in U.S. and UK ads than, say, in German ads. European countries such as France and Italy are more tolerant of sex appeal and nudity in advertising.[37] The penetration of satellite and cable TV has expanded broadcast media options, making it easier to simultaneously air the same TV commercial in many different countries. U.S. cable networks such as CNN, MTV, and the Cartoon Network, and other networks such as Sky TV in Commonwealth countries and Star TV in Asia have increased advertisers' global reach.

In terms of print, *Fortune, Time, Newsweek,* and other magazines have printed foreign editions in English for years. Other publishers have also added local-language editions by licensing

Like many magazine publications, *Rolling Stone* produces local-language editions for overseas markets like China.

Source: Dong Ng/EyePress News/Newscom

their trademarks to local companies, entering into joint ventures, or creating wholly owned subsidiaries. *Rolling Stone* has 20 international editions outside the United States; *Maxim* has 27 overseas editions; and *Elle* has 42 editions targeting the same demographic group but tailored to the country where each is published.

Each country has its own unique media challenges and opportunities. When Colgate-Palmolive decided to further penetrate the market of the 630 million or so people who lived in rural India, the company had to overcome the fact that more than half of all Indian villagers are illiterate and only one-third live in households with television sets. Its solution was to create half-hour infomercials carried through the countryside in video vans.[38] To sell Tampax tampons in Mexico, Procter & Gamble created in-home informational gatherings or "bonding sessions" akin to Tupperware parties led by company-designated counselors. Although about 70 percent of women in the United States, Canada, and Western Europe used tampons, just 2 percent of women in most of Latin America did. To overcome cultural inhibitors, P&G developed its unorthodox approach.[39]

Sponsorship programs have a long tradition in many countries outside the United States because of a historical lack of advertising media there. Increasingly, marketers can execute sponsorship on a global basis. Entertainment and sports sponsorships can be an especially effective way to reach a younger audience.

Distribution Strategy.   Channels present challenges to many firms because there are few global retailers, especially supermarkets and grocery stores, although some progress has been made with Germany's Aldi and France's Carrefour. Established British retailers Sainsbury, Tesco, and Marks and Spencer have all struggled to enter the U.S. market. The common English language may actually have been a barrier—assumptions were made about consumers that didn't hold true on the other side of the Atlantic. In developing its Fresh & Easy store concept for California, Tesco found that U.S. shoppers liked to pick up and touch their fruit and vegetables and stock up with more frozen food than their British customers.[40]

Lacking many global retail powerhouses, companies often differ in their approach to distribution, and the results can be dramatic. Coca-Cola's intensive deployment of vending machines in Japan was a key to success in that market. From 1981 to 1993, Coca-Cola invested over

$3 billion internationally in infrastructure and marketing. PepsiCo, on the other hand, sold off some of its bottling investments during this time. Despite investing in expensive ad campaigns and diversifying into restaurants and snack foods, PepsiCo saw its global fortunes sag relative to Coca-Cola and has renewed its efforts in the years since.

As in domestic markets, firms will often want to blend push and pull strategies internationally to build brand equity. Sometimes companies mistakenly adapt strategies that were critical factors to success, only to discover that they erode the brand's competitive advantage.

DELL

Dell Computer initially abandoned its direct distribution strategy in Europe and instead decided to establish a traditional retailer network through existing channels. The end result was a paltry 2.5 percent market share, and the company lost money for the first time ever in 1994. Ignoring critics who claimed that a direct distribution model would never work in Europe, Dell revamped its direct approach and relaunched its personal computer line with a new management team to execute the direct model the company had pioneered in the United States. Between 1999 and 2004, Dell's sales in Europe grew at an average rate of 19 percent annually, substantially outpacing other competitors in the industry. Later in the decade, however, sales slumped as the PC market stagnated all over the world. Dell now must reinvent its product strategy in Europe and elsewhere, much as it did its distribution strategy so many years before.[41]

Pricing Strategy.   When it comes to designing a global pricing strategy, the value-pricing principle from Chapter 5 still generally applies. Marketers need to understand in each country what consumer perceptions of the value of the brand are, their willingness to pay, and their elasticities with respect to price changes. Sometimes differences in these considerations permit differences in pricing strategies. Brands such as Levi's, Heineken, and Perrier have been able to command a much higher price outside their domestic market because in other countries they have a distinctly different brand image—and thus sources of brand equity—that consumers value. Differences in distribution structures, competitive positions, and tax and exchange rates also may justify price differences.

But setting drastically different prices across countries can be difficult.[42] Pressures for international price alignment have arisen, in part because of the increasing numbers of legitimate imports and exports and the ability of retailers and suppliers to exploit price differences through "gray imports" across borders. This problem is especially acute in Europe, where price differences are often large (prices of identical car models may vary by 30–40 percent) and ample opportunity exists to ship or shop across national boundaries.

Hermann Simon, a German expert on pricing, recommends creating an international "price corridor" that takes into account both the inherent differences between countries and alignment pressures. Specifically, the corridor is calculated by company headquarters and its country subsidiaries by considering market data for the individual countries, price elasticities in the countries, parallel imports resulting from price differentials, currency exchange rates, costs in countries and arbitrage costs between them, and data on competition and distribution. No country is then allowed to set its price outside the corridor: countries with lower prices have to raise them, and countries with higher prices have to lower them. Another possible strategy suggested by Simon is to introduce different brands in high-price, high-income countries and in low-price, low-income countries, depending on the relative cost trade-offs of standardization versus customization.[43]

In Asia, many U.S. brands command hefty premiums over inferior home-grown competitors because consumers in these countries strongly associate the United States with high-quality consumer products. In assessing the viability of Asian markets, marketers look at average income but also consider the distribution of incomes, because the consumer population is so large. For example, although the average annual income in India may be less than $1,000, some 300 million people can still afford the same types of products that might be sold to middle-class Europeans. In China, Gillette introduced Oral-B toothbrushes at 90 cents even though locally produced toothbrushes sold at 19 cents. Gillette's reasoning was that even if it only gained 10 percent of the Chinese market, it still would sell more toothbrushes there than it is currently selling in the U.S. market.

DEVELOPING VERSUS DEVELOPED MARKETS

Perhaps the most basic distinction we make between the countries that global brands enter is whether they are developing or have developed markets. Some of the most important developing markets are captured by the acronym BRICS (for Brazil, Russia, India, China, and South Africa). To that list, many marketing experts would add Indonesia. Some experts also refer to the five Rs of currency in developing markets: the Brazilian real, the Russian ruble, the Indian rupee, the Chinese renminbi, and the Indonesian rupiah.[44] These countries are considered *developing* in that they do not yet have the infrastructure, institutions, and other features that characterize more fully developed economies in North America and Western Europe, for example. Yet they are among the largest and fastest-growing and have received much attention from companies all over the world.

Differences in consumer behavior, marketing infrastructure, competitive frame of reference, and so on are so profoundly different among developing markets, though, that distinct marketing programs are often needed for each. Often the product category itself may not be well developed, so the marketing program must operate at a very fundamental level. Consider how these firms successfully attacked the Indian market.

WINNING IN INDIA

Although some global brands have struggled entering the Indian market, others have succeeded by better understanding Indian consumers and tailoring their offerings accordingly. Hyundai became India's second-largest carmaker by offering small, affordable, and fuel-efficient cars such as the $7,000 Santro. Nokia earned 58 percent market share by selling models specially made for the Indian market, such as its 1100 phone, which features a flashlight. Pepsi earned 24 percent market share in part because it was the first Western cola to feature Indian megacelebrities as spokespeople, including cricketer Sachin Tendulkar and actor Shahrukh Khan. LG outpaced competitors Whirlpool and Haier to $1 billion in annual sales by offering refrigerators and air conditioners that stood up better to the temperature extremes and power surges that characterize rural India. As the Indian market continues to grow and mature, catering to local tastes will become even more important for global brands seeking to compete there.[45]

Heinz drew 20 percent of its corporate revenues from emerging markets in 2011—versus less than 5 percent just a few years before that—with a target of 30 percent by 2015. The company adheres to a "Three As" model for its emerging markets strategy and even put it on the cover of its annual report:[46]

1. *Applicability*—Product must suit local culture. Heinz ketchup has a slightly sweet taste in the United States, but in certain European countries, it is available in hot, Mexican, and curry flavors. In the Philippines, it includes bananas as an ingredient. Ketchup usage varies by country, too. In Greece, it is poured on pasta, eggs, and cuts of meat. Koreans put ketchup on pizza.
2. *Availability*—Product must be sold in channels that are relevant to the local population. In Indonesia, two-thirds of people buy food in tiny grocery stores or open-air markets, so Heinz must be there.
3. *Affordability*—Product can't be priced out of the target market's range. To meet consumer budget constraints in emerging markets, Heinz employs different packaging sizes or recipes. In Indonesia, it sells billions of small packets of soy sauce for 3 cents apiece.

Firms are organizing themselves differently to address the opportunities presented by developing markets. With over half its sales coming from developing markets, Unilever reorganized into eight regional clusters, six of which were wholly or mainly made up of developing markets. When Kraft Foods broke into two companies, one focused primarily on the United States and slower-growing food categories, the other on developing markets and its faster-growing global snack business.[47]

Procter & Gamble's CEO has talked about shifting the company's "center of gravity" toward Asia and Africa, where it is experiencing growth by targeting the "$2 a day" consumer based on average income. It is attempting to persuade half the men in India who use barbers to embrace at-home grooming, for instance. The "Women Against Lazy Stubble" campaign stresses the benefit

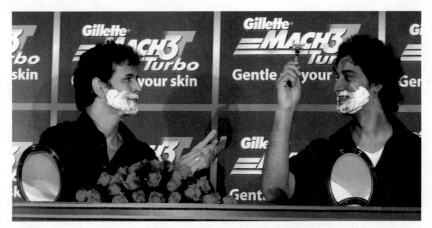

Procter & Gamble emphasizes developing markets in its marketing, for example using well-known Bollywood actors in India to promote its Gillette razors.

Source: STR/EPA/Newscom

of being clean-shaven. In Africa, the company is focusing on communicating to women the benefits of Western feminine hygiene products. In-depth consumer research is generating important insights into these markets, such as that low-income consumers do not always want the simplest products and are every bit as aspirational in their own way as more well-to-do consumers.[48]

Different income segments exist in developing markets. Although many marketers have successfully tapped into the high end of the income spectrum with luxury goods or by focusing on the growing middle class, opportunities also abound at the broader base of the income pyramid. One useful distinction has been made between: (1) low income ($3–5 a day; 1.4 billion people), (2) subsistence ($1–3 a day; 1.6 billion people); and (3) extreme poverty (below $1 a day; 1 billion people).[49]

BUILDING GLOBAL CUSTOMER-BASED BRAND EQUITY

In designing and implementing a global brand marketing program, marketers want to realize the advantages while suffering as few of the disadvantages as possible.[50] This section explores in more detail how to tactically build strong global brands, relying on the "Ten Commandments of Global Branding" (see Figure 14-4).

1. Understand Similarities and Differences in the Global Branding Landscape

The first—and most fundamental—guideline is to recognize that international markets can vary in terms of brand development, consumer behavior, marketing infrastructure, competitive activity, legal restrictions, and so on. Virtually every top global brand and company adjusts its marketing program in some way across some markets but holds the parameters fixed in other markets.

The best examples of global brands often retain a thematic consistency and alter specific elements of the marketing mix in accordance with consumer behavior and the competitive situation in each country. Snuggle fabric softener offers an example of effectively custom-tailoring the marketing mix.

1. Understand similarities and differences in the global branding landscape.
2. Don't take shortcuts in brand building.
3. Establish marketing infrastructure.
4. Embrace integrated marketing communications.
5. Cultivate brand partnerships.
6. Balance standardization and customization.
7. Balance global and local control.
8. Establish operable guidelines.
9. Implement a global brand equity measurement system.
10. Leverage brand elements.

FIGURE 14-4

Ten Commandments of Global Branding

SNUGGLE

Unilever launched the fabric-softener product in Germany in 1970 as an economy brand in a category dominated by Procter & Gamble. To counteract negative quality inferences associated with low price, Unilever emphasized softness as the product's key point-of-difference, naming it *Kuschelweich*, which means "enfolded in softness," and displaying a teddy bear on the package. When the product was launched in France, Unilever kept the brand positioning of economy and softness but changed the name to *Cajoline*, meaning softness, and gave the teddy bear center stage in advertising. Success in France led to global expansion, and in each case the brand name was changed to connote softness in the local language while the advertising featuring the teddy bear remained virtually identical across global markets. By the 1990s, Unilever was marketing the fabric softener around the globe with over a dozen brand names, including *Coccolino* in Italy and *Mimosin* in Spain, all with the same product positioning and advertising support. More important, the fabric softener was generally the number-one or number-two brand in each market. Although Snuggle is still a strong market leader, Unilever sold the brand to Sun Products in 2008 to streamline its product portfolio.[51]

The success of Snuggle reflects the importance of understanding similarities and differences in the branding landscape. Although marketers typically strive to keep the same brand name across markets, in this case, the need for a common name was reduced since people generally don't buy fabric softener away from home. On the other hand, a common consumer desire for softness that transcended country boundaries was effectively communicated by a teddy bear as the main character in a global ad campaign.

2. Don't Take Shortcuts in Brand Building

In terms of building global customer-based brand equity, many of the basic tactics we discussed in Part II of the text still apply. In particular, we must create brand awareness and a positive brand image in each country in which the brand is sold. The means may differ from country to country, or the actual sources of brand equity themselves may vary. Nevertheless, it is critically important to have sufficient levels of brand awareness and strong, favorable, and unique brand associations to provide sources of brand equity in each country. VW has struggled to gain a strong foothold in the U.S. market because, unlike its Asian import competitors, it has been less willing to modify its designs for U.S. buyers. Although it has ambitious goals for global auto supremacy, one industry analyst noted, "They need to spend much more time understanding the U.S. consumer."[52]

Building a brand in new markets must be done from the bottom up. Strategically, that means concentrating on building awareness first, before the brand image. Tactically, or operationally, it means determining how to best create sources of brand equity in new markets. Distribution, communication, and pricing strategies may not be appropriate in any two markets even if the same overall brand image is desired in both. If the brand is at an earlier stage of development, rather than alter it or the advertising to conform to local tastes, marketers will try to influence local behavior to fit the established uses of the brand. Consumer education then accompanies brand development efforts.

KELLOGG

When Kellogg first introduced its corn flakes into the Brazilian market in 1962, cereal was eaten as a dry snack—the way U.S. consumers eat potato chips—because many Brazilians did not eat breakfast at all. As a result, the ads there centered on the family and breakfast table—much more so than in the United States. As in other Latin American countries where big breakfasts have not been part of the meal tradition, Kellogg's task was to inform consumers of the "proper" way to eat cereal with cold milk in the morning. Similarly, Kellogg had to educate French consumers that corn flakes were meant to be eaten with cold instead of warm milk. Initial advertising showed milk being poured from transparent glass pitchers used for cold milk, rather than opaque porcelain jugs used for warm milk. A challenge to Kellogg in increasing the relatively low per capita consumption of ready-to-eat breakfast cereals in Asia was the low consumption of milk products and the positive distaste with which drinking milk was held in many Asian countries. Because cereal consumption and habits vary widely across countries, Kellogg learned to build the brand from the bottom up in each market.[53]

Kellogg's had to educate consumers about cereals in many international markets where breakfast habits were very different.
Source: dbimages/Alamy

This guideline suggests the need for patience, and the possibility of backtracking on brand development, to engage in a set of marketing programs and activities that the brand has long since moved beyond in its original markets. Marketers sometimes fail to realize that in their own country, they are building on a foundation of perhaps decades of carefully compiled associations in customers' minds. Although the period needed to build the brand in new markets may be compressed, it will still take some time.

The temptation—and often the mistake—is to export the current marketing program because it seems to work. Although that may be the case, the fact that a marketing program can meet with acceptance or even some success doesn't mean it is the best way to build strong, sustainable global brand equity. An important key to success is to understand each consumer, recognize what he or she knows or could value about the brand, and tailor marketing programs to his or her desires.

Observing that many large companies simply diluted formulas to make less expensive products, Hindustan Lever, an Indian subsidiary of Unilever, made a substantial commitment to R&D and innovation to better serve the Indian market. These efforts resulted in completely new products that were both affordable and uniquely suited to India's rural poor, including a high-quality combination soap and shampoo, and that were backed by successful new sales and marketing tactics specifically developed to reach remote and highly dispersed populations. Hindustan Lever trained 50,000 to go door-to-door in India to educate consumers there and sell soap, toothpaste, and other products.[54]

3. Establish Marketing Infrastructure

A critical success factor for many global brands is their manufacturing, distribution, and logistical advantages. These brands have created the appropriate marketing infrastructure, from scratch if necessary, and adapted to capitalize on the existing marketing infrastructure in other countries. We noted above that channels especially vary in their stages of development. Chain grocers have a 50 percent share in China, 40 percent in Russia, but only 15 percent in India.[55] Concerned about poor refrigeration in European stores, Häagen-Dazs ended up supplying thousands of free freezers to retailers across the continent.[56]

Companies go to great lengths to ensure consistency in product quality across markets. McDonald's gets over 90 percent of its raw materials from local suppliers and will even expend resources to create the necessary inputs if they are not locally available. Hence, investing to improve potato farms in Russia is standard practice because French fries are one of McDonald's core products and a key source of brand equity. More often, however, companies have to adapt production and distribution operations, invest in foreign partners, or both in order to succeed abroad. General Motors's success in Brazil in the 1990s after years of mediocre performance came about in part because of its concerted efforts to develop a lean manufacturing program and a sound dealership strategy to create the proper marketing infrastructure.[57]

4. Embrace Integrated Marketing Communications

A number of top global firms have introduced extensive integrated marketing communications programs. Overseas markets don't have the same advertising opportunities as the expansive, well-developed U.S. media market. As a result, U.S.-based marketers have had to embrace other forms of communication in those markets—such as sponsorship, promotions, public relations, merchandising activity, and so on—to a much greater extent.

To help make the quintessentially Vermont brand Ben & Jerry's more locally relevant in Britain, the company ran a contest to create the "quintessential British ice cream flavor." Finalists covered the gamut of the British cultural spectrum and included references to royalty (Cream Victoria and Queen Yum Mum), rock and roll (John Lemon and Ruby Chewsday), literature (Grape Expectations and Agatha Crispie), and Scottish heritage (Nessie's Nectar and Choc Ness Monster). Other finalists included Minty Python, Cashew Grant, and James Bomb. The winning flavor, Cool Britannia, was a play on the popular British military anthem *Rule Britannia* and consisted of vanilla ice cream, English strawberries, and chocolate-covered Scottish shortbread.[58]

Consider how DHL employed a wide range of communication options to strengthen its global brand.

DHL

DHL, part of Deutsche Post DHL, has positioned itself as "The Logistics Company for the World." The pillars of this brand positioning are unrivaled speed, efficiency, and strong customer service. The "International Specialists" campaign emphasizes the company's expertise in local delivery, customs clearance, express shipping, and customer care. The U.S. campaign included a mix of digital, elevator video, airport, and print advertising across the nation and ran in prominent daily newspapers and business magazines. The campaign is also running in global media across 42 key markets, translated into 25 local languages on 280 TV stations. The TV ads featured the classic anthem, *Ain't No Mountain High Enough*, sung by rising British star Dionne Bromfield. A social media digital component invited users to upload their own version of the song in a YouTube contest. The campaign was not entirely externally focused. An internal brand engagement initiative required all DHL employees to complete a course that would help their customers grow their business. During the campaign launch, DHL was also the Official Logistics Partner for Rugby World Cup 2011.[59]

---

5. Cultivate Brand Partnerships

Most global brands have marketing partners of some form in their international markets, ranging from joint venture partners, licensees or franchisees, and distributors, to ad agencies and other marketing support people. One common reason for establishing brand partnerships is to gain access to distribution. For example, Guinness has very strategically used partnerships to develop markets or provide expertise it lacked. Joint venture partners, such as with Moet Hennessey, have provided access to distribution abroad that otherwise would have been hard to achieve within the same time constraints. These partnerships were crucial for Guinness as it expanded operations into the developing markets that provide almost half its profits. Similarly, Lipton increased its sales by 500 percent in the first four years of partnering with PepsiCo to distribute its product. Lipton added the power of its brand to the ready-to-drink iced tea market, while PepsiCo added its contacts in global distribution.

Barwise and Robertson identify three alternative ways to enter a new global market:[60]

1. By exporting existing brands of the firm into the new market (introducing a "geographic extension")
2. By acquiring existing brands already sold in the new market but not owned by the firm
3. By creating some form of brand alliance with another firm (joint ventures, partnerships, or licensing agreements)

They also identify three key criteria—speed, control, and investment—by which to judge the different entry strategies.

According to Barwise and Robertson, there are trade-offs among the three criteria such that no strategy dominates. For example, the major problem with geographic extensions is speed. Because most firms don't have the necessary financial resources and marketing experience to roll out products to a large number of countries simultaneously, global expansion can be a slow, market-by-market process. Brand acquisitions, on the other hand, can be expensive and often more difficult to control than typically assumed. Brand alliances may offer even less control, although they are generally much less costly.

The choice of entry strategy depends in part on how the resources and objectives of the firm match up with each strategy's costs and benefits. Procter & Gamble would enter new markets in categories in which it excels (diapers, detergents, and sanitary pads), building its infrastructure and then bringing in other categories such as personal care or health care. Heineken's sequential strategy was slightly different. The company first entered a new market by exporting to build brand awareness and image. If the market response was deemed satisfactory, the company licensed its brands to a local brewer in hopes of expanding volume. If that relationship were successful, Heineken might then take an equity stake or forge a joint venture, piggybacking sales of its high-priced brand with an established local brand.[61] As a result, Heineken is the world's third-largest brewer in volume, selling in more than 170 countries with a product portfolio of over 250 brands. With brewing operations in about 70 countries and export activities all over the world, Heineken is the most international brewery group in the world.[62]

Companies are sometimes legally required to partner with a local company, as in many Middle Eastern countries, or when entering certain markets, such as insurance and telecoms in India. In other cases, companies elect to establish a joint venture with a corporate partner as a fast and convenient way to enter complex foreign markets. Fuji Xerox, initially formed to give Xerox a foothold in Japan, has been a highly successful joint venture that dominated the Japanese office equipment market for years and has even outperformed Xerox's U.S. parent company. Joint ventures have been popular in Japan, where convoluted distribution systems, tightly knit supplier relationships, and close business–government cooperation have long encouraged foreign companies to link up with knowledgeable local partners.[63]

Finally, some mergers or acquisitions result from a desire to command a higher global profile. U.S. baby food maker Gerber agreed to be acquired by Swiss drug maker Sandoz in part because it needed to establish a stronger presence in Europe and Asia, where Sandoz has a solid base. Sandoz later merged with Ciba-Geigy and now is part of the Novartis group of companies.[64]

As these examples illustrate, different entry strategies have been adopted by different firms, by the same firm in different countries, or even in combination by one firm in the same country. Entry strategies can also evolve over time. Through its licensee Coca-Cola Amatil, Coca-Cola not only sells its global brands such as Coke, Fanta, and Sprite in Australia; it also sells local brands it has acquired such as Lift, Deep Spring, and Mount Franklin. One of Coca-Cola's objectives with these acquisitions is to slowly migrate demand from some of the local brands to global brands, thus capitalizing on economies of scale. Branding Brief 14-4 describes how global brand powerhouse Nestlé has entered new markets.

6. Balance Standardization and Customization

As we discussed in detail above, one implication of similarities and differences across international markets is that marketers need to blend local and global elements in their marketing programs. The challenge, of course, is to get the right balance—to know which elements to customize or adapt and which to standardize.

Some of the factors often suggested in favor of a more standardized global marketing program include the following:

- Common customer needs
- Global customers and channels
- Favorable trade policies and common regulations
- Compatible technical standards
- Transferable marketing skills

BRANDING BRIEF 14-4

Managing Global Nestlé Brands

For about 15 years starting in 1984, Nestlé spent more than $30 billion on acquisitions in different countries, including such major brands as Carnation dairy (and other) products (United States), Perrier (France) and San Pellegrino (Italy) mineral water, Stouffer's frozen foods (United States), Rowntree confectionery (United Kingdom), Ralston Purina pet food (United States), and Buitoni-Perugina pasta and chocolate (Italy). Thus, major acquisitions yielded valuable economies of scale to Nestlé in developed markets.

In less-developed markets, however, the company adopted a different strategy. Its entry strategy there was to manipulate ingredients or processing technology for local conditions and then apply the appropriate brand name—existing brands like Nescafé coffee, in some cases, and new brands, such as Bear brand condensed milk in Asia, in others. Nestlé strove to get into markets first and was patient; it negotiated for more than a decade to enter China. To limit risks and simplify its efforts in new markets, the company attacked with a handful of labels selected from a set of strategic brand groups. Then it concentrated its advertising and marketing money on just two or three brands.

Nestlé attempts to balance global and local control in managing its brands. Some decisions, such as branding, follow strict corporate guidelines. The company has six *strategic corporate brands*—Nestlé, Nescafé, Nestea, Maggi, Buitoni, and Purina. There are 70 different *strategic international brands*, including Nesquik line of chocolate milk products as well as product brands Kit Kat, Friskies, and Perrier. Eighty-three *strategic regional brands* include Aquarel and Contrex. Finally, there are a host of *local brands* that are only important to particular countries.

Nestlé had used a decentralized management approach, in which most decisions—apart from decisions about the worldwide and corporate brands—were primarily decided by the local managers. In 1997, following many acquisitions, a new CEO determined that Nestlé needed more formal central and regional control. The company consolidated factory management by region and combined oversight of similar products into strategic business units. Still, local managers retained the decision-making power necessary to adapt products to local tastes. For example, Nestlé continued to make 200 different varieties of its Nescafé instant coffee, each tuned to local palates.

Nestlé's more centralized management approach enabled the company to focus on growing its core brands at each level. From 1999 to 2003, organic growth (excluding acquisitions) was 5.1 percent, almost double competitor Unilever's organic growth rate of 2.7 percent. The rest of the decade saw Nestlé enjoy even more above-average market performance. Despite tough economic conditions, the company experienced organic growth of approximately 7.5 percent in 2011.

Sources: Carla Rapoport, "Nestlé's Brand Building Machine," *Fortune,* 19 September 1994, 147–156; "Daring, Defying, to Grow," *The Economist,* 7 August 2004, 55; Laura MacInnis, "Nestlé Outshines Peers, Expects Stronger 2010," *Reuters,* 19 February 2010; "Full Year 2011: 7.5% Organic Growth," www.nestle.com, 16 February 2012; Jean-Nöel Kapferer, *The New Strategic Brand Management: Advanced Insights and Strategic Thinking,* 5th ed. (London: Kogan-Page, 2012).

What types of products are difficult to sell through standardized global marketing programs? Many experts note that foods and beverages with years of tradition and entrenched customer preferences and tastes can be particularly difficult to sell in a standardized global fashion. Unilever has found that preferences for cleaning products such as detergents and soaps are more common across countries than preferences for food products.

High-end products can also benefit from standardization because high quality or prestige often can be marketed similarly across countries. Italian coffee maker illycafé maintained a "one brand, one blend" strategy across the globe for years, offering only a single blend of espresso made of 100 percent Arabica beans. As Andrea Illy, CEO of his family's business, stated, "Our marketing strategy focuses on building quality consumer perceptions—no promotions, just differentiating ourselves from the competition by offering top quality, consistency, and an image of excellence."[65]

The following are likely candidates for global campaigns that retain a similar marketing strategy worldwide:

- *High-technology products with strong functional images:* Examples are televisions, watches, computers, digital cameras, and automobiles. Such products tend to be universally understood and are not typically part of the cultural heritage. Taiwan's HTC has employed its "quietly brilliant" brand positioning and "YOU" brand campaign to reinforce its reputation as one of the world's most innovative smartphone providers.[66]
- *High-image products with strong associations to fashionability, sensuality, wealth, or status:* Examples are cosmetics, clothes, jewelry, and liquor. Such products can appeal to the same type of market worldwide.

- *Services and business-to-business products that emphasize corporate images in their global marketing campaigns:* Examples are airlines and banks.
- *Retailers that sell to upper-class individuals or that specialize in a salient but unfulfilled need:* By offering a wide variety of toys at affordable prices, Toys'R'Us transformed the European toy market, getting Europeans to buy toys for children at any time of the year, not just Christmas, and forcing competitors to level prices across countries.[67]
- *Brands positioned primarily on the basis of their country of origin:* An example is Australia's Foster's beer, which ran the "How to Speak Australian" ad campaign for years in the United States.
- *Products that do not need customization or other special products to be able to function properly:* ITT Corporation found that stand-alone products such as heart pacemakers could easily be sold the same way worldwide, but that integrated products such as telecommunications equipment have to be tailored to function within local phone systems.[68]

7. Balance Global and Local Control

Building brand equity in a global context must be a carefully designed and implemented process. A key decision in developing a global marketing program is choosing the most appropriate organizational structure for managing global brands. In general, there are three main approaches to organizing for a global marketing effort:

1. Centralization at home office or headquarters
2. Decentralization of decision making to local foreign markets
3. Some combination of centralization and decentralization

In general, firms tend to adopt a combination of centralization and decentralization to better balance local adaptation and global standardization.[69] Some firms such as GE, Intel, and AstraZeneca have adopted a T-shaped country organization that localizes customer-facing operations to allow for fast, detailed marketing actions while at the same distributing back-end activities (manufacturing, product development, R&D) across countries.[70]

In many, if not most, markets, the cost savings of standardization may not outweigh the revenue potential from tailoring programs to different groups of consumers.[71] Each aspect of the marketing program is a candidate for globalization. Which elements of the marketing program should we standardize, and to what degree?[72] Cost and revenue should be the primary considerations in deciding which elements of the marketing program will be adapted for which country.

Riesenbeck and Freeling advocate a mixed strategy, standardizing the "core aspects" of the brand (those that provide its main competitive edge) but allowing local adaptation of "secondary aspects." According to their approach, branding, positioning, and product formulation are more likely to be standardized, and advertising and pricing less so; distribution is most often localized.[73]

Many global companies divide their markets into five or so regions, for example, Europe, Asia, Latin America, North America, and Africa/Middle East. A key theme is the need to balance global and local control. Coca-Cola, for example, distinguishes between local marketing activities that would appear to dilute brand equity and those that are not as effective as desired. Headquarters would stop the first from occurring but would not stop the latter, leaving the activity's appropriateness to the local manager's judgment but also holding him or her responsible for its success. Similarly, Levi Strauss has balanced global and local control with a "thermometer" model. Marketing elements below the "freezing point" are fixed: "brand soul" (akin to brand essence or mantra) and logos are standardized worldwide. Above the freezing point, product quality, pricing, advertising, distribution, and promotions are all fluid, meaning each international division can handle the marketing mix elements in any way that it feels is appropriate for its region.

Firms often centralize advertising, consolidating their worldwide ad accounts and shifting most or all of their advertising billings to agencies with extensive global networks, to reduce costs and increase efficiency and control. Nevertheless, Braun's and Levi Strauss's regional managers have been able to bar a global campaign from their area. Unilever's regional managers who seek to substitute their own campaigns must produce research showing that the global plan is inappropriate. Coca-Cola and Procter & Gamble have taken the middle ground, developing a global communications program but testing and fine-tuning it in meetings with regional managers.[74]

8. Establish Operable Guidelines

Brand definitions and guidelines must be established, communicated, and properly enforced so marketers in different regions have a good understanding of what they are and are not expected to do. The goal is for everyone within the organization to understand the brand's meaning and be able to translate it to satisfy local consumer preferences. Brand definition and communication often revolve around two related issues. First, some sort of document, such as a brand charter, should detail what the brand is and what it is not. Second, the product line should reflect only those products consistent with the brand definition.

Coca-Cola has a strategy document that clearly articulates the company's strategy and how the brand positioning is manifested in various aspects of the marketing mix elements. This document sets out the parameters for the brand and therefore determines how much is left to chance. Similarly, McDonald's operating manual imposes rigorous worldwide controls (for example, the 19 steps to cook and bag french fries).

COLGATE-PALMOLIVE

Colgate-Palmolive has been a highly successful global marketer for years because of its tight focus on marketing strategies and objectives. Colgate's "bundle books" contain, down to the smallest details, everything that Colgate knows about any given brand—and that a country or regional manager needs to know. They describe how to effectively market a particular product, including the product attributes, formulas, ingredient sourcing information, market research, pricing positions, graphics, and even advertising, public relations, and point-of-sales materials. With a bundle book, a manager in any one of the more than 200 countries and territories where Colgate sells its products can project the brand exactly like every one of her or his counterparts. As one executive noted, "As the smallest among our major competitors, we are trying to make sure that we maximize our resources. By having tightly controlled brands, we can leverage across borders rapidly."[75]

Colgate has learned how to successfully market in countries all over the world, such as by selling its products in small sachets in village shops all over India.
Source: REUTERS/Pawan Kumar

As an example of deriving product strategy from a brand definition, consider Disney. Everyone at the company is exposed to the Disney brand mantra, "fun family entertainment" (see Branding Brief 2-3). To establish global guidelines, Disney's centralized marketing group worked with members of the consumer products group for months to assign virtually every possible product to one of three categories:

- Acceptable to license without permission (like T-shirts)
- Not permissible to ever license (such as toilet paper)
- Requires validation from headquarters to license (about 20 categories, including air fresheners)

Internationally, Disney has noticed that the "gray areas" grow larger and more numerous. The company also has been trying to identify product groups that may be more amenable to localizing than others. For example, movies cannot be tailored for the European market because it is difficult to determine what will be attractive to those consumers. On the other hand, certain items may sell well in Germany but not in Japan.

Finally, for all this planning to work, there must be effective lines of communication. Coca-Cola stresses the importance of having people on the ground who can effectively manage the brand in concert with headquarters in Atlanta. To facilitate coordination, much training occurs at company headquarters; a sophisticated communication system is in place; and global databases are available. The goal of this heavily integrated information system is to facilitate the local manager's ability to tap into what constitutes "relevance" in any particular country and then communicate those ideals to headquarters.

9. Implement a Global Brand Equity Measurement System

As the guidelines in Chapter 8 suggest, a global brand equity measurement system is a set of research procedures designed to provide timely, accurate, and actionable information for marketers on brands, so they can make the best possible tactical decisions in the short run and strategic decisions in the long run in all relevant markets. As part of this system, a global brand equity management system defines the brand equity charter in a global context, outlining how to interpret the brand positioning and resulting marketing program in different markets, as suggested by the previous global branding commandment.[76] With the global brand strategy template in place, brand tracking can assess progress, especially in terms of creating the desired positioning, eliciting the proper responses, and developing brand resonance.

LEVI STRAUSS

Levi Strauss & Co. continually monitors its brand equity among consumers in most of its key markets around the world. The company developed "Brand Value Propositions" for each of its major brands. These are a set of enduring strategies that define each brand and differentiate it from competition. They succinctly list the brand's global positioning (including frame of reference and point-of-difference), its global character, and its global "building blocks" or desired state regarding consumer wants and needs. The Brand Value Propositions drive all brand strategies and actions and provide a globally consistent platform for regionally relevant product and marketing execution. In tracking each brand's equity, via ongoing consumer surveys, Levi Strauss & Co. monitors the consumer's perceptions and interactions with its brands; the impact its clothes, retail distribution, marketing, and other touchpoints are having on consumers; and whether the results of its efforts are in line with its Brand Value Propositions. Through these efforts, Levi Strauss & Co. is able to tailor brand strategies to ensure each brand is meeting consumer needs while being true to its essence.

The challenge is that the marketing research infrastructure may be lacking in many countries. When DuPont set out to implement a global tracking system for its various brands, its efforts were hampered by a level of sophistication among local marketing research companies that varied considerably for the 40 primary countries in which it operated. Now marketing research firms are creating global networks of companies that help overcome this problem.

10. Leverage Brand Elements

Proper design and implementation of brand elements can often be critical to the successful building of global brand equity. As Figure 4-2 showed, a number of brands have encountered resistance because of difficulty in translating their name, packaging, slogans, or other brand elements to another culture. The Science of Branding 14-1 describes some cultural differences in brand name memorability and recall.

In general, nonverbal brand elements such as logos, symbols, and characters are more likely to directly transfer well—at least as long as their meaning is visually clear—than verbal brand elements that may need to be translated into another language. Nonverbal brand elements are

THE SCIENCE OF BRANDING 14-1

Brand Recall and Language

Given the linguistic differences between cultures whose languages do not share a common root, perhaps it is not surprising that some brand names are more likely to be recalled in one culture than another. A series of studies addressing this issue found significant differences in the ways Chinese- and English-speaking consumers processed brand names. In one study, Chinese speakers were more likely to recall brand names in written rather than spoken recall, whereas English speakers were more likely to recall the names in spoken rather than written recall; this suggests that mental representations of verbal information are coded mainly visually among Chinese and in a phonological manner among English speakers. Results for bilinguals depend on their proficiency with the languages.

Another study showed that more positive brand attributes resulted when peripheral features of a brand name ("script" aspects, such as the type of font employed, or "sound" aspects, such as the way the name is pronounced) matched the associations or meaning of the brand: Chinese native speakers were affected primarily by script matching, whereas English native speakers' attitudes were primarily affected by sound matching. The researchers interpreted these results in terms of structural differences between logographic systems (such as Chinese, where characters stand for concepts and not sounds) and alphabetic systems (such as English, where the writing of a word is a close cue to its pronunciation) and their resulting visual and phonological representations in memory.

A related study investigated perceptions of brand names translated into Chinese. There are three possible types of translation for names. The first is phonetic: Chinese characters are used that sound most like the English word. The second is semantic: Chinese characters are chosen that approximate the meaning of the English word. The third is phono-semantic: a translation is formed that shares similarities in meaning and sound with the English original. It is common for products in China to use "bilingual" packaging that carries the brand

name both in logographic form (Chinese characters) and in the English alphabet. Typically, a package will emphasize one name over the other by making it appear larger on the package. The study found that consumers preferred phonetic translations if a hypothetical product emphasized the English name, while they favored phono-semantic and semantic translations equally regardless of which name was emphasized.

A different study demonstrated that "classifiers," a grammatical feature present in Chinese but not English, affected perceived similarity among objects and the way words are clustered upon recall. Chinese speakers were more likely to cluster names according to classifiers than English speakers, suggesting that judicious selection of classifiers could influence the way consumers perceive a brand. The study also showed that for Chinese speakers, images in hypothetical advertisements that corresponded with a classifier present in the ad copy were preferable to images that had no correspondence.

Sources: Bernd H. Schmitt, Yigang Pan, and Nader T. Tavassoli, "Language and Consumer Memory: The Impact of Linguistic Differences between Chinese and English," *Journal of Consumer Research* 21, no. 12 (1994): 419–431; Nader T. Tavassoli and Yih Hwai Lee, "The Differential Effect of Auditory and Visual Advertising Elements with Chinese and English," *Journal of Marketing Research* 40 (November 2003): 468–480; Yigang Pan and Bernd H. Schmitt, "Language and Brand Attitudes: Impact of Script and Sound Matching in Chinese and English," *Journal of Consumer Psychology* 5, no. 3 (1996): 263–277; Shi Zhang, Bernd H. Schmitt, and Hillary Haley, "Language and Culture: Linguistic Effects on Consumer Behavior in International Marketing Research," in *Handbook of Research in International Marketing*, ed. Subhash C. Jain (Northampton, MA: Edward Elgar, 2003), 228–242; Shi Zhang and Bernd H. Schmitt, "Activating Sound and Meaning: The Role of Language Proficiency in Bilingual Consumer Environments," *Journal of Consumer Research* 31 (June 2004): 220–228; Bernd H. Schmitt and Shi Zhang, "Selecting the Right Brand Name: An Examination of Tacit and Explicit Linguistic Knowledge in Name Translations," *Journal of Brand Management*, 2012, in press.

more likely to be helpful in creating brand awareness than brand image, however, which may require more explicit meaning and direct statements. If the meaning of a brand element is visually clear, it can be an invaluable source of brand equity worldwide. As the old saying goes, "A picture is worth a thousand words," so it is not surprising that the right brand logo, symbol, or character can have a huge impact on global marketing effectiveness.

The image of Ronald McDonald clearly communicates McDonald's association with kids without the need for words. Similarly, Mr. Peanut, the Apple logo, and the M&M characters need no translation. The Nike swoosh connotes sports, Coke's contour bottle connotes refreshment, and the Mercedes star connotes status and prestige worldwide. Perhaps the most compelling example of the importance of brand symbols is the Marlboro man.

MARLBORO

In the 1950s, Marlboro's brand slogan was "Mild as May." In repositioning the brand, Philip Morris created the Marlboro man, a cowboy who was almost always depicted somewhere in the western United States among magnificent scenery deemed "Marlboro country." By 1975, Marlboro had become the best-selling cigarette in the United States. By 2010, it controlled 43 percent of the U.S. market, more than the next 13 brands combined. But the appeal of the Marlboro man extends far beyond the United States. Indeed, the cowboy imagery attracts consumers from all over the world, in part by capturing an image that is uniquely American. Today the Marlboro man appears in over 180 countries, and Marlboro is the biggest-selling brand in the United States, France, Germany, Mexico, and nine other major global markets. The brand is consistently ranked as one of the world's most valuable, due in large part to the widespread appeal of its brand character and personality.[77]

Even nonverbal elements, however, can encounter translation problems. For example, certain colors have strong cultural meaning. Marketing campaigns using various shades of green in advertising, packaging, and other marketing programs ran into trouble in Malaysia, where these colors symbolize death and disease.[78]

Because of a desire to standardize globally, however, many firms have attempted to create more uniform brand elements. Pursuing a global branding strategy, Mars chose to replace its Treets and Bonitos brands with the M&M's brand worldwide and changed the name of its third-largest U.K. brand—Marathon—to the Snickers name used in the rest of Europe and the United States.[79] To create a stronger global brand, PepsiCo pulled together its dozens of company-owned brands of potato chips sold under different names and began to market them all abroad under a more uniform Lay's logo. The company also boosted advertising and improved quality to enhance the brand image at the same time.[80]

REVIEW

Increasingly, marketers must properly define and implement a global branding strategy. Some advantages of a global marketing program are economies of scale in production and distribution, lower marketing costs, communication of power and scope, consistency in brand image, an ability to leverage good ideas quickly and efficiently, and uniformity of marketing practices and thus greater competitiveness. The more standardized the marketing program, in general, the more the firm can actually realize these different advantages.

At the same time, the primary disadvantages of a standardized global marketing program are that it may ignore important differences across countries in various areas: consumer needs, wants, and usage patterns for products; consumer response to marketing mix elements; product development and the competitive environment; the legal environment; marketing institutions; and administrative procedures.

In developing a global marketing program, marketers attempt to obtain as many of these advantages as possible while minimizing any possible disadvantages. Building global customer-based brand equity means creating brand awareness and a positive brand image in each country in which the brand is sold.

Increasingly, marketers are blending global objectives with local or regional concerns. The means by which brand equity is built may differ from country to country, or the actual sources of brand equity themselves may vary across countries in terms of specific attribute or benefit associations. Nevertheless, there must be sufficient levels of brand awareness and strong, favorable, and unique brand associations in each country in which the brand is sold to provide sources of brand equity.

Some of the biggest differences in global marketing occur between developed and developing or emerging markets. Because of the extremely low incomes and differences in consumer behavior in developing markets, marketers must fundamentally rethink every aspect of their marketing program.

1. *Understand similarities and differences in the global branding landscape.*
   - Have you tried to find as many commonalities as possible across markets?
   - Have you identified what is unique about different markets?
   - Have you examined all aspects of the marketing environment (e.g., stages of brand development, consumer behavior, marketing infrastructure, competitive activity, legal restrictions)?
   - Have you reconciled these similarities and differences in the most cost-effective and brand-building manner possible?
2. *Don't take shortcuts in brand building.*
   - Have you ensured that the brand is being built from the bottom up strategically by creating brand awareness first before crafting the brand image?
   - Have you ensured that the brand is being built from the bottom up tactically by determining the appropriate marketing programs and activity for the brand in each market given the particular strategic goals?
3. *Establish marketing infrastructure.*
   - Have you created the appropriate marketing infrastructure—in terms of manufacturing, distribution, and logistics—from scratch if necessary?
   - Have you adapted to capitalize on the existing marketing infrastructure in other countries?
4. *Embrace integrated marketing communications.*
   - Have you considered nontraditional forms of communication that go beyond conventional advertising?
   - Have you ensured that all communications are integrated in each market and are consistent with the brand's desired positioning and heritage?
5. *Cultivate brand partnerships.*
   - Have you formed partnerships with global and local partners to improve possible deficiencies in your marketing programs?
   - Have you ensured that all partnerships avoid compromising the brand promise and do not harm brand equity in any way?
6. *Balance standardization and customization.*
   - Have you been careful to retain elements of marketing programs that are relevant and add value to the brand across all markets?
   - Have you sought to find local adaptations and additions that complement and supplement these global elements to achieve greater local appeal?
7. *Balance global and local control.*
   - Have you established clear managerial guidelines as to principles and actions that all global managers must adhere to?
   - Have you carefully delineated the areas in which local managers are given discretion and autonomy in their decision making?
8. *Establish operable guidelines.*
   - Have you explicated brand management guidelines in a clear and concise fashion in a document to be used by all global marketers?
   - Have you established means of seamless communication between headquarters and local and regional marketing organizations?
9. *Implement a global brand equity measurement system.*
   - Do you conduct brand audits when appropriate in overseas markets?
   - Have you devised a brand tracking system to provide timely, accurate, and actionable information on brands in relevant markets?
   - Have you established a global brand equity management system with brand equity charters, brand equity reports, and brand equity overseers?
10. *Leverage brand elements.*
    - Have you checked the relevance of brand elements in global markets?
    - Have you established visual brand identities that transfer across market boundaries?

FIGURE 14-5

Self-Evaluation Ratings for the 10 Commandments of Global Branding

In general, in entering a new market of any kind, it is necessary to identify differences in consumer behavior (how consumers purchase and use products and what they know and feel about brands) and adjust the branding program accordingly (through the choice of brand elements, nature of the supporting marketing program, and leverage of secondary associations).

Figure 14-5 lists the "Ten Commandments of Global Branding" along with a series of questions that can be asked to help guide effective global brand management.

DISCUSSION QUESTIONS

1. Pick a brand marketed in more than one country. Assess the extent to which the brand is marketed on a standardized versus customized basis.
2. How aware are you of the country of origin of different products you own? For which products do you care about the country of origin? Why? For those imported brands that you view positively, find out and critique how they are marketed in their home country.
3. Pick a product category. Consider the strategies of market leaders in different countries. How are they the same and how are they different?
4. Pick a product category. How are different leading brands targeting different demographic market segments?
5. Contrast Coca-Cola's and McDonald's global branding strategies. How are they similar and how are they different? Why are they so well respected?

BRAND FOCUS 14.0

China Global Brand Ambitions

Growth at Home

China, the world's most populous country with more than 1.3 billion people, was essentially closed to the West during the period between the Communist overthrow of the government in 1949 until gradual economic reforms began in 1978, culminating with China's admission into the World Trade Organization in 2001. Since reforms began, China has industrialized at a remarkable rate and is now the world's second-largest economy, a manufacturing giant boasting a record $100 billion trade surplus in 2011.[81]

The statistics of China's production are staggering: it is the world's largest garment exporter by a large margin, it is also the world's largest manufacturer of consumer electronics, and it manufactures 80 percent of the clocks sold in the world, 50 percent of all cameras, and 60 percent of all bicycles. The primary reason for China's manufacturing prowess is its remarkably cheap labor pool. Manufacturing wages in southern China average 60 cents an hour, 95 percent lower than U.S. averages.[82]

China's economic boom has created a wealth of opportunity for the country's citizens and companies, as well as an attractive consumer base for foreign companies seeking growth. The following sections will illustrate the successes and difficulties that characterize modern China.

A Growing Consumer Class

China's rise to a global economic superpower enriched many of its citizens; more than a million are now millionaires.[83] With this newfound wealth came an interest in consuming conspicuously, which precipitated a windfall for foreign luxury-goods manufacturers. With a rapidly expanding middle class, China went from consuming 1 percent of the world's luxury goods in 2001 to a projected 20 percent in 2015, making the country the world's largest luxury market. Roughly half these luxuries are being bought on the mainland, the other half abroad.[84] China's vast population of only children—called "Little Emperors" for the way many are doted on by their parents—are expected to drive demand for luxury goods for years to come.[85]

Luxury brands have flocked to China to try to cash in. L'Oréal purchased the country's most popular cosmetics brand, Yue Sai,

and bought bargain brand Mininurse, with an enviable distribution network of more than 250,000 small stores. L'Oréal also invested in a 32,000-square-foot laboratory in Pudong to develop products specific to the Chinese market and containing local ingredients such as ginkgo leaf and ginseng. One of the company's big challenges in China was educating consumers about the benefits of different cosmetic products. "In other countries, women learn how to use cosmetics from the mom," said Paolo Gasparrini, president of L'Oréal China. "That's not the case in China. We have to substitute [for the] mom." Still, L'Oréal experienced double-digit sales increases for 11 years, approaching $1.6 billion in sales in 2011.[86]

Despite the fortunate wealthy few, vast numbers of urban and especially rural poor have been left behind. Rural workers earn half the average salary of urban factory workers, often not enough to send their children to school. Consequently, rural Chinese are migrating to cities in search of better-paying jobs, increasing urban congestion and unemployment rates. By 2010, an estimated 50 percent of the population lived in cities, aggravating these problems.[87] Despite the concerns generated by this wealth polarization, China's consumer class still harbors enough purchasing power to attract foreign brands, as the next section describes.

Foreign Interest

Ever since China began relaxing its trade policy in 1978, foreign companies have eagerly sought the Chinese consumer's *yuan* (Chinese for dollar). Coca-Cola was one of the first Western brands in China, entering in 1979. Through an investment of more than $1 billion in a series of joint venture bottling plants, Coke gradually expanded its presence there. Over the years, it became far more successful than Jianlibao, China's biggest domestic soft drinks player, which saw its market share fall dramatically. With a goal of making China its biggest market by 2020, Coca-Cola announced at the end of 2011 that it would invest an additional $4 billion over a three-year period in new plants and existing operations such as bottling lines, warehouses, and coolers, raising its total investment there to $7 billion for 2009–2014. By December 2011, the company had

41 bottling plants in China and employed more than 48,000 people.[88] Other foreign companies have also achieved considerable success in China, notably KFC.

KFC

China accounts for over a third of international profits for Yum Brands, which owns KFC and Pizza Hut. KFC has been a global pioneer in many markets. Since it first opened a restaurant on the edge of Beijing's Tiananmen Square in 1987, the chain has experienced virtually uninterrupted growth, approaching 5,000 restaurants with an ultimate goal of 15,000. Local touches to the menu beyond Colonel Sanders's secret fried chicken recipe include spicy chicken, soy milk drinks, egg tarts, fried dough sticks, wraps with local spices, fish and shrimp burgers on fresh buns, and rice gruel with preserved or "thousand-year-old" egg. The company introduces 50 new products a year. Spiciness varies depending on the region—more in Sichuan and Hunan, less in Shanghai. KFC China established its own distribution system with warehouses and trucks to ensure the rapid response needed for a fast-changing menu. To ensure higher levels of customer service, the vast majority of KFC outlets are company owned. All these changes paid off. In 2011, KFC revenue in China surpassed U.S. earnings, with an expectation that it will double within five years.[89]

Some faded foreign brands have managed to remake their images in China. Howard Johnson operates four- and five-star hotels there complete with marble floors, which have enabled the company to successfully position itself as an upscale chain. But fierce competition in many markets has made it hard for some companies to sustain their success. Motorola, recognizing the enormous potential of the Chinese market early, entered in the late 1980s and worked extensively with government leaders to develop wireless telecommunications infrastructure and related skilled manufacturing, becoming the largest foreign investor in China's electronics industry. Yet it found its market leadership besieged by a wave of local competitors in the 2000s. By 2006, consumers had hundreds of models to choose from, and young urban users typically changed phones every eight months. When Motorola failed to introduce a worthy successor to the Razr, competitors Samsung and Nokia pounced. Motorola's market share plummeted, reinforcing the intense nature of competition in China.[90]

Competition comes not just from international brands. The next section highlights the growing number of local Chinese brands competing with, and at times beating, the foreign competition.

Emerging Local Leaders

Many Chinese consumer electronics and consumer packaged-goods brands are the market leaders at home. Haier, China's number-one appliance maker, is a multibillion manufacturing giant based in Qingdao. Gome and Suning are China's top electronics retailers, each with over 1,000 stores, $2 billion in sales, and "the kind of high-plateau brand recognition that Best Buy enjoys in the U.S."[91] Foreign brewers were forced to regroup after early forays into China were confounded by the cheaper and better-distributed market leaders Tsingtao

and Snow (partially owned by SAB Miller), as well as a host of other, smaller local beers. Zhangyu and Great Wall are top-10 selling wines worldwide whose sales are based almost entirely in China.[92] The Internet is another area where Chinese brands often rule at home.

CHINESE INTERNET BRANDS

With over 500 million Internet users by 2012, China had the largest online population in the world. But U.S. Internet giants Facebook, Google, eBay and others have all struggled to gain a foothold there in the face of strong local competition. Google famously withdrew from mainland China to Hong Kong in March 2010 after a censorship dispute with the Chinese government. Although the government exerts much control over local online services, portals Sina.com and Sohu.com, video Web sites Youku.com and Tudou.com, and search engine Baidu have reported growing traffic and revenues. The widespread appeal of Tencent's popular instant messaging service QQ and related suite of products has made it China's largest Internet company, with its cute penguin mascot as the brand symbol. Chinese users chat, game, watch movies, and top up their prepaid mobile phones with their QQ service—to the tune of $3 billion in revenue in 2010. Baidu followed Google's U.S. lead but added features to make the search engine work more effectively in China. Better able to parse sentences in Chinese, and with 11 links to other services, including a Wikipedia-like encyclopedia, the service has been seen as better at understanding the Chinese users' tastes. Alibaba Group has the world's largest online business-to-business trading platform for small and medium-sized businesses.[93]

One reason for their success is that local brands possess superior distribution networks built from the ground up, enabling them to reach millions of consumers not served by the multinationals, which initially targeted only major Chinese cities. Many local brands are outspending their foreign rivals on advertising. Of the top 10 advertisers in China in 2004, half were Chinese brands, spending a combined $1.5 billion.[94]

Perhaps no brand typifies Chinese brands' ability to win on their own turf better than Lenovo (formerly Legend), a Chinese PC manufacturer. Lenovo was started in 1984 and initially struggled to keep pace with foreign brands. As recently as 1997, it was losing money and market share to brands like IBM, HP, and Compaq. But within two years, it had turned its financial fortunes around with the help of low prices, government contracts, and a vast distribution network, growing more than 100 percent between 1998 and 1999 and grabbing 15 percent market share, about twice that of its closest rival. It protected and grew its market leadership in China, which enabled it to purchase IBM's PC division in 2005. In early 2006, it began selling low-priced PCs bearing the Lenovo name in the United States. In 2012, Lenovo still commanded over a third of China's giant PC market, while also passing Dell to become the world's second largest PC maker behind HP.[95] Its global ambitions illustrate the latest brand trend to emerge in China, that of local brands growing globally. This trend is the topic of the next section.

Locals Going Global

Due to its high-profile acquisition of IBM's PC unit, Lenovo is likely the best-known Chinese company seeking to build its brands abroad. Observers predict that many other brands will likewise follow in the footsteps of Korea's Samsung, LG, and Hyundai as Asian brands that rose from obscurity to global prominence in a matter of decades.

To better compete in overseas markets, appliance maker Haier increased its R&D spending to 4 percent of revenues. "In the past, we tried to design our products in Qingdao and sell them to the U.S. and Japan," explained CEO Zhang Ruimin. "They didn't meet overseas consumers' needs and didn't sell well."[96] By 2004, Haier had 22 factories overseas, and distribution at Walmart, Sears, and Best Buy helped its foreign revenues rise to $1.3 billion, or 13 percent of total revenues.

Athletic clothing and equipment maker Li-Ning sought to build its international profile by outfitting many Chinese athletes for the 2004 Athens and 2008 Beijing Olympics, and by acquiring the rights to use NBA players and logos in its marketing.[97] Other Chinese brands to set out for foreign soil include electronics firm TCL, cell phone manufacturer China Kejian, networking equipment maker Huawei, and Tsingtao beer.

These moves abroad are, in part, simply a function of the pressures facing large firms searching for sources of revenue growth beyond an increasingly competitive domestic market. Another cause is official encouragement from the Chinese government, which dictated that between 30 and 50 state firms should be built into "national champions" or "globally competitive" companies by 2010[98] and therefore exhorted Chinese companies "to set up overseas operations, acquire foreign assets, and transform themselves into multinational corporations."[99] A related reason is global brand recognition as a source of national pride. One Chinese industrialist had a slogan printed on the wall of one of his factories that captured this source of Chinese companies' global aspirations: "One who earns money in China is a winner; one who earns money overseas is a hero."[100]

Yet the path to global brand leadership remains fraught with complications. As of 2011, no Chinese brand could be considered a truly global brand powerhouse. In fact, one advertising executive working in China argued that "Chinese companies are light years away" from exporting their brands successfully.[101] Put plainly, Chinese companies were behind the curve when it came to branding compared to global competitors, a fact Haier CEO Zhang readily acknowledged, saying "[Chinese companies] started brand development very late, so we have to catch up in a very short period of time."[102]

Companies that did have an international presence, such as Haier and Lenovo, were priced as entry-level bargains, like their Korean predecessors. To shortcut their way to brand recognition and respect, some Chinese firms began bidding for foreign brands, as Lenovo did with IBM. Others, like Haier, invest more heavily in R&D to bolster their images through innovation. Despite the difficulties, one consultant remained optimistic about Chinese brands one day taking their place as global brand leaders:

> Market shares will go up and down. Some Chinese companies will lose. It's a learning process. But there is no doubt that world-class Chinese brands will emerge.[103]

Notes

1. For a more detailed discussion of branding in Asia, see Pierre Xiao Lu, *Elite China: Luxury Consumer Behavior in China* (Singapore: John Wiley & Sons, 2008); Martin Roll, *Asian Brand Strategy: How Asia Builds Strong Brands* (London: Palgrave Macmillan, 2005); and Paul Temporal, *Branding in Asia: The Creation, Development, and Management of Asian Brands for the Global Market* (New York: John Wiley & Sons, 2001).

2. Vanessa O'Connell, "Reversing Field, Macy's Goes Local," *Wall Street Journal*, 21 April 2008.

3. Vanessa O'Connell, "Reversing Field"; Stephanie Clifford, "Atlanta Hats? Seattle Socks? Macy's Goes Local," *New York Times*, 1 October 2010; "Macy's Q4 Earnings Up on Strong Holiday Performance," www.mrktplace.com, 12 February 2012.

4. Michael J. McCarthy, "In Texas Beer Brawl, Anheuser and Miller Aren't Pulling Punches," *Wall Street Journal*, 5 December 1996, A1, A12.

5. Sam Fahmy, "Despite Recession, Hispanic and Asian Buying Power Is Expected to Surge, According to Annual UGA Selig Center Multicultural Economy Study," www.terry.uga.edu, 4 November 2010.

6. "Hispanic Fact Pack," 2011 edition, a supplement to *Advertising Age*, 25 July 2011.

7. Edward Lewine and Malia Wollan, "Latin Lovers," *Fast Company*, July/August 2011.

8. Sam Fahmy, "Despite Recession, Hispanic and Asian Buying Power Is Expected to Surge, According to Annual UGA Selig Center Multicultural Economy Study," www.terry.uga.edu, 4 November 2010.

9. Jennifer L. Aaker, Anne M. Brumbaugh, and Sonya A. Grier, "Nontarget Markets and Viewer Distinctiveness: The Impact of Target Marketing on Advertising Attitudes," *Journal of Consumer Psychology* 9, no. 3 (2000): 127–140; Sonya A. Grier and Rohit Deshpande, "Social Dimensions of Consumer Distinctiveness: The Influence of Social Status on Group Identity and Advertising Persuasion," *Journal of Marketing Research* 38 (May 2001): 216–224.

10. Jim Edwards, "Minority Majority," *Adweek Next*, 27 September 2010.

11. Rohit Nautiyal, "Cookie Time," *The Financial Express*, 28 June 2011; Patti Waldmeir, "Oreo Takes the Biscuit for Its China Reinvention," *Financial Times*, 7 March 2012.

12. Shaoming Zou and S. Tamer Cavusgil, "The GMS: A Broad Conceptualization of Global Marketing Strategy and Its Effect on Firm Performance," *Journal of Marketing* 66 (October 2002): 40–56.

13. David Kiley, "One World, One Car, One Name," *Bloomberg BusinessWeek*, 13 March 2008.

14. Richard C. Morais, "The Color of Beauty," *Forbes*, 27 November 2000, 170–176; Gail Edmondson, "L'Oréal:

The Beauty of Global Branding," *BusinessWeek*, 28 June 1999, 24; Christian Passariello, "To L'Oréal, Brazil's Women Need New Style of Shopping," *Wall Street Journal*, 21 January 2011.

15. Dana L. Alden, Jan-Benedict E. M. Steenkamp, and Rajeev Batra, "Brand Positioning Through Advertising in Asia, North America, and Europe: The Role of Global Consumer Culture," *Journal of Marketing* 63 (January 1999): 75–87.

16. Rakeev Batra, Venkatram Ramaswamy, Dana L. Alden, Jan-Benedict E. M. Steenkap, and S. Ramachander, "Effects of Brand Local and Nonlocal Origin on Consumer Attitudes in Developing Countries," *Journal of Consumer Psychology* 9, no. 2 (2000): 83–95; Jan-Benedict, E. M. Steenkamp, Rajeev Batra, and Dana L. Alden, "How Perceived Globalness Creates Brand Value," *Journal of International Business Studies* 34 (2003): 53–65.

17. Ian M. Lewis, "Key Issues in Globalizing Brands: Why There Aren't Any Global OTC Medicine Brands," talk presented at the Third Annual Advertising and Promotion Workshop, Advertising Research Foundation, 5–6 February 1991.

18. Corporate Executive Board, "Overcoming Executional Challenges in Global Brand Management," Marketing Leadership Council, Case Book, March 2001; Bernard L. Simonin and Segül Özsomer, "Knowledge Processes and Learning Outcomes in MNCs: An Empirical Investigation of the Role Of HRM Practices in Foreign Subsidiaries," *Human Resource Management* 48 (July–August 2009): 505–530.

19. Terry Lefton, "The Global Exchange of Pricelessness," *Brandweek*, 30 November 1998; Alex Brownsell, "MasterCard Revamps 'Priceless' Campaign With City Rewards Scheme," *Marketing*, 27 September 2011; "MasterCard at 40," Special Advertising Section, *Advertising Age*, 26 June 2006.

20. World Health Organization report, www.wh.int, accessed 24 March 2012.

21. Caroline Hsu, "Beyond the Burbs," *U.S. News & World Report*, 20 October 2003; Diane Brady, "In France, Vive la Tupperware," *Bloomberg BusinessWeek*, 9 May 2012.

22. Emma Jacobs, "No Faux Pas in Any Language," *Financial Times*, 17 February 2012.

23. Steve Mertl, "Buick LaCrosse's French Slang Meaning Latest Example of Pitfalls of Car Names," *The Canadian Press*, 1 October 2009.

24. For example, see Niraj Dawar and Philip Parker, "Marketing Universals: Consumers' Use of Brand Name, Price, Physical Appearance, and Retailer Reputation as Signals of Quality," *Journal of Marketing* 58 (April 1994): 81–95; and Ayşegül Özsomer, "The Interplay Between Global and Local Brands: A Closer Look at Perceived Brand Globalness and Local Iconness," *Journal of International Marketing*, 2012, in press.

25. Choi Lee and Robert T. Green, "Cross-Cultural Examination of the Fishbein Behavioral Intentions Model," *Journal of International Business Studies* (Second Quarter 1991): 289–305.

26. Gabi Thesing, Jana Randow, and Aaron Kirchfield, "Germany's Growth: New Rules and Old Companies," *Bloomberg BusinessWeek*, 4 October 2010.

27. Randy D. McBee, "Harley-Davidson's Future," *International Journal of Motorcycle Studies* 7 (Fall 2011).

28. David Whitford, "Promoting the Spirit of Bermuda," *Fortune*, 2 May 2011.

29. Vanitha Swaminathan, Karen Page, and Zeynep Gürhan-Canli, "My Brand or Our Brand: Individual- and Group-Based Brand Relationships and Self-Construal Effects on Brand Evaluations," *Journal of Consumer Research* 34 (August 2007): 248–259.

30. Andrew Batson, "Not Really 'Made in China'," *Wall Street Journal*, 15 December 2010; Note that Apple has also received some criticism for its labor practices in its contract manufacturing, see Kevin Drew, "Apple Chief Visits iPhone Factory in China," *New York Times*, 29 March 2012.

31. Theodore Levitt, "The Globalization of Markets," *Harvard Business Review* (May–June 1983): 92–102.

32. Frank van den Driest, "Danone: Serving Up Servant Leadership," allaboutbranding.com, March 2006; www.danone.com, accessed 24 March 2012.

33. Julia Flynn, "Heineken's Battle to Stay Top Bottle," *Business Week*, 1 August 1994, 60–62.

34. Maureen Marston, "Transferring Equity Across Borders," paper presented at the ARF Fourth Annual Advertising and Promotion Workshop, 12–13 February 1992.

35. Joanne Lipman, "Marketers Turn Sour on Global Sales Pitch Harvard Guru Makes," *Wall Street Journal*, 12 May 1988, 1.

36. Marc de Swaan Arons and Frank van den Driest, "Johnnie Walker's Global 'Progress'," *The Global Brand CEO: Building the Ultimate Marketing Machine* (New York: Airstream International, 2010); "Keep on Walking," *The Economist*, 1 October 2011; David Kiefaber, "A Stroll Through History with Johnnie Walker," *Adweek*, 7 August 2009.

37. Martin S. Roth, "The Effects of Culture and Socioeconomics on the Performance of Global Brand Image Strategies," *Journal of Marketing Research* 32 (May 1995): 163–175.

38. Miriam Jordan, "In Rural India, Video Vans Sell Toothpaste and Shampoo," *Wall Street Journal*, 10 January 1996, B1, B5.

39. Emily Nelson and Miriam Jordan, "Seeking New Markets for Tampons, P&G Faces Cultural Barrier, "*Wall Street Journal,* 8 December 2000, A1, A8.

40. "Tesco's Problem with Fresh & Easy – Why Is It So Hard for Retailers to Cross the Pond?" www.perishablepundit.com, 9 September 2011.

41. "Technology's Mr. Predictable," *The Economist,* 24 September 2005; Joe Fay, "Dell Dives as Western Europe PC Market Stagnates," *PC Builder*, 6 May 2009; Jack Schofield, "European PC Market Slumps 11 Percent, Says Gartner," *ZDNet UK*, 14 November 2011.

42. Hermann Simon, "Pricing Problems in a Global Setting," *Marketing News*, 9 October 1995, 4.

43. See also, Robert J. Dolan and Hermann Simon, *Power Pricing: How Managing Price Transforms the Bottom Line* (New York: Free Press, 1996).

44. Ruben Farzad, "The BRIC Debate: Drop Russia, Add Indonesia?," *Bloomberg BusinessWeek*, 18 November 2010.

45. Om Malik, "The New Land of Opportunity," *Business 2.0* (July 2004): 72; Cris Prystay, "Branding Gains Respect in Emerging Markets," *Wall Street Journal*, 3 January 2006; Manjeet Kripalani, "Finally, Coke Gets It Right," *BusinessWeek*, 10 February 2003, 47. For a number of case studies, see Kevin Lane Keller, M. G. Parameswaran, and Isaac Jacob, *Strategic Brand Management* (Indian adaptation) (Pearson India, 2011).

46. Gabriella Stern, "Heinz Aims to Export Taste for Ketchup," *Wall Street Journal*, 20 November 1992, B1; Bill Johnson, "The CEO of Heinz on Powering Growth in Emerging Markets," *Harvard Business Review*, October 2011.

47. Jack Neff, "Consumer Power Shifts to Developing Markets," *Advertising Age*, 17 October 2011.

48. Lauren Coleman-Lochner, "Procter & Gamble Needs to Shave More Indians," *Bloomberg BusinessWeek*, 13 June 2011; Jennifer Reingold, "Can P&G Make Money in Places Where People Earn $2 a Day?," *Fortune*, 17 January 2011.

49. V. Kasturi Rangan, Michael Chu, and Djordjija Petkoski, "Segmenting the Base of the Pyramid," *Harvard Business Review* (June 2011): 113–117.

50. For more information on global marketing and branding strategies, see George S. Yip, *Total Global Strategy* (Englewood Cliffs, NJ: Prentice Hall, 1996); Johny K. Johansson, *Global Marketing: Foreign Entry, Local Marketing, and Global Management*, 5th ed. (Burr Ridge, IL: McGraw-Hill-Irwin, 2009); Nigel Hollis, *The Global Brand: How to Create and Develop Lasting Brand Value in the World Market* (New York: Palgrave Macmillan, 2010).

51. Asihish Banerjee, "Global Campaigns Don't Work; Multinationals Do," *Advertising Age*, 18 April 1994, 23; Jorge A. Monjaras, "Unilever Launches Snuggle in Mexico," *Advertising Age*, 24 February 2003; Jack Neff, "Unilever Sells Detergent Brands," *Advertising Age*, 28 July 2008.

52. Alex Taylor III, "VW's Grand Plan," *Fortune*, 18 October 2010.

53. Julie Skur Hill and Joseph M. Winski, "Goodbye Global Ads," *Advertising Age*, 16 November 1987, 22; www.kellogghistory.com; Gemma Charles, "Kellogg Looks at Altering Its Global Marketing Strategy," *The Economic Times*, 26 January 2011.

54. Vijay Govindarajan and Christopher Trimble, "Serving the Needs of the Poor—For Profit," *Across the Board*, December 2001; V. Kasturi Rangan, Michael Chu, and Djordjija Petkoski, "Segmenting the Base of the Pyramid," *Harvard Business Review* (June 2011): 113–117.

55. Bill Johnson, "The CEO of Heinz on Powering Growth in Emerging Markets," *Harvard Business Review* (October 2011).

56. Mark Maremont, "They're All Screaming for Häagen-Dazs," *BusinessWeek*, 4 October 1991, 121.

57. Peter Fritsch and Gregory L. White, "Even Rivals Concede GM Has Deftly Steered Road to Success in Brazil," *Wall Street Journal*, 25 February 1999, A1, A8.

58. William Wells, "Global Advertisers Should Pay Heed to Contextual Variations," *Marketing News*, 13 February 1987, 18.

59. Shiela Shayon, "DHL Launches Global Campaign with Fashion, Music and Flair," www.brandchannel.com, 14 September 2011; "DHL Wins Stevie Award for Global Advertising Campaign," 11 November 2011; "DHL's Global Brand Campaign," www.dp-dhl.com.

60. Patrick Barwise and Thomas Robertson, "Brand Portfolios," *European Management Journal* 10, no. 3 (September 1992): 277–285.

61. Flynn, "Heineken's Battle."

62. "Michael De Carvalho—On the Rise of the Heineken Empire," *Business Today*, Fall 2011.

63. David P. Hamilton, "United It Stands. Fuji Xerox Is a Rarity in World Business: A Joint Venture That Works," *Wall Street Journal*, 26 September 1996, R19.

64. Richard Gibson, "Gerber Missed the Boat in Quest to Go Global, So It Turned to Sandoz," *Wall Street Journal*, 24 May 1994, A1, A4.

65. Amy Barone, "Illycafe Andrea Illy," *Advertising Age*, 9 December 1996; "Why Coffee Aficionados Choose illy Coffee," www.prlog.org, 21 October 2009.

66. Bruce Einhorn, "A Former No-Name from Taiwan Builds a Global Brand," *Bloomberg BusinessWeek*, 1 November 2010.

67. "Toys"R"Us, Inc. Expands Presence in Europe with Market Entry into Poland," *Business Wire*, 26 October 2011.

68. George Anders, "Ad Agencies and Big Concerns Debate World Brands' Value," *Wall Street Journal*, 14 June 1984, 33.

69. For an in-depth examination of how Kimberly-Clark implements its global brand management strategy, see Tandadzo Matanda and Michael T. Ewing, "The Process of Global Brand Strategy Development and Regional Implementation," *International Journal of Research in Marketing* 29 (March 2012): 5–12.

70. Nirmalya Kumar and Phanish Puranam, "Have You Restructured For Global Success?," *Harvard Business Review* (October 2011): 123–128.

71. Hubert Gatignon and Piet Vanden Abeele, "To Standardize or Not to Standardize: Marketing Mix Effectiveness in Europe," MSI Report 95–109 (Cambridge, MA: Marketing Science Institute, 1995).

72. John A. Quelch and Edward J. Hoff, "Customizing Global Marketing," *Harvard Business Review* (May–June 1986): 59–68; John Quelch and Katherine Jocz, *All Business Is Local: Why Place Matters More Than Ever in a Global Virtual World* (New York: Portfolio/Penguin, 2012).

73. Hajo Riesenbeck and Anthony Freeling, "How Global Are Global Brands?" *McKinsey Quarterly* no. 4, 3–18, as referenced in Barwise and Robertson, "Brand Portfolios." See also Dennis M. Sandler and David Shani, "Brand Globally but Advertise Locally? An Empirical Investigation," *Journal of Product & Brand Management* 2, no. 2 (1993): 59–71; Gatignon and Vanden Abeele, "To Standardize or Not to Standardize"; Saeed Samiee and Kendall Roth, "The Influence of Global Marketing Standardization on Performance," *Journal of Marketing* 56 (April 1992): 1–17; and David M. Szymanski, Sundar G. Bharadwaj, and P. Rajan Varadarajan, "Standardization versus Adaptation of International Marketing Strategy:

An Empirical Investigation," *Journal of Marketing* 57 (October 1993): 1–17.

74. Ken Wells, "Global Campaigns, After Many Missteps, Finally Pay Dividends," *Wall Street Journal*, 27 August 1992, A1.

75. Sharen Kindel, "A Brush with Success: Colgate-Palmolive Company," *Hemisphere*, September 1996, 15; Stephen Kindel, "The Bundle Book: At Reuben Mark's Colgate, Attention to Small Details Creates Large Profits," *Financial World* 5 (January 1993): 34–35.

76. For an examination of brand equity measures across the Chinese and American markets, see Don Lehmann, Kevin Lane Keller, and John Farley, "The Structure of Survey-Based Brand Metrics," in special issue, "Branding in the Global Marketplace," of *Journal of International Marketing* 16 (December 2008): 29–56.

77. Chris Burritt, "The Popularity Issue: Cigarette: Marlboro," *Bloomberg BusinessWeek*, 16 August 2010; www.pmi.com, accessed March 29, 2012.

78. George E. Belch and Michael Belch, *Advertising and Promotion Management: An Integrated Marketing Communications Perspective*, 9th ed. (New York, McGraw-Hill Irwin, 2012).

79. Barwise and Robertson, "Brand Portfolios."

80. Robert Frank, "Potato Chips to Go Global—Or So Pepsi Bets," *Wall Street Journal*, 30 November 1995, B1.

81. "China's Trade Surplus May Be Gone in Two Years, Adviser Says," *Bloomberg BusinessWeek*, 21 November 2011.

82. David Barboza, "As China's Wages Rise, Export Prices Could Follow," *New York Times*, 7 June 2010.

83. Frederik Balfour, "China's Millionaires Leap Past 1 Million on Growth, Savings," www.bloomberg.com, 1 June 2011.

84. "Chinese Snap Up Luxury Goods," *China Daily*, 7 February 2012; Yuval Atsmon, Vinay Dixit, and Cathy Wu, "Tapping China's Luxury-Goods Market," *McKinsey Quarterly*, April 2011.

85. Clay Chandler, "Little Emperors," *Fortune*, 4 October 2004, 138.

86. Sheridan Prasso, "Battle for the Face of China," *Fortune*, 12 December 2005, 156; Wu Yiyao, "L'Oreal Sales Top $1.59B in China," *China Daily USA*, 29 February 2012.

87. "China's Mainland Population Grows to 1.3397 Billion in 2010: Census Data," www.news.xinhuanet.com, 28 April 2011.

88. Leslie Chang, "Cracking China's Market," *Wall Street Journal*, 9 January 2003, B1; Ma Zhenhuan, "Coca-Cola Unbottles New China Plan," *China Daily*, 24 March 2012.

89. David E. Bell and Mary L. Shelman, "KFC's Radical Approach to China," *Harvard Business Review*

(November 2011): 137–142; Patti Waldmeir, "Oreo Takes the Biscuit for Its China Reinvention," *Financial Times*, 7 March 2012; Bruce Shreiner, "Yum Brands Earnings: Q4 Profits Rise 30 Percent Due to Overseas Growth, Pizza Hut Sales Turnaround," *Huffington Post*, 6 February 2012; Lisa Baertlein and Nandita Bose, "Yum Eyes Young India to Help Mirror China Profits," *China Beverage News*, 2 March 2012.

90. Bruce Einhorn and Roger O. Crockett, "Motorola's Cell Phone Stumble in China," *Bloomberg BusinessWeek*, 28 August 2008; Sharon Gaudin, "Google Acquisition of Motorola Stalled as China Extends Probe," *Computerworld*, 21 March 2012.

91. Dexter Roberts, "China's Power Brands," *BusinessWeek*, 8 November 2004; Mark Lee and Michael Wei, "Gome Eyes 15% Sales Growth," *China Daily*, 30 August 2011.

92. Jennifer Cirillo, "Chinese Brands on the Rise," *Beverage World*, October 2010.

93. Joe McDonald, "China's Number of Web Users Rises to 513 Million," *Associated Press*, 15 January 2012; Lara Farrar, "Winners and Losers of Google's China Search Pullout," www.cnn.com, 24 March 2010; Tania Branigan, "Google Angers China by Shifting Service to Hong Kong," *The Guardian*, 23 March 2010; Bruce Einhorn and Brad Stone, "March of the Penguins," *Bloomberg BusinessWeek*, 8 August 2011; Bruce Einhorn and Brad Stone, "How Baidu Won China," *Bloomberg BusinessWeek*, 15 November 2010.

94. Frederik Balfour, "Ad Agencies Unchained," *BusinessWeek*, 25 April 2005, 50.

95. Dexter Roberts, "How a Legend Lives Up to Its Name," *BusinessWeek*, 15 February 1999; Lee Chyen Yee and Huang Yuntao, "Lenovo Beats Q3 Net Forecasts by Raising Market Share," *Reuters*, 9 February 2012.

96. Roberts, "China's Power Brands."

97. Deborah L. Vence, "*Not* Taking Care of Business," *Marketing News*, 15 March 2005, 19; Laurie Burkitt, "Chinese Sports-Apparel Maker Takes on Adidas, Nike," *Wall Street Journal*, 28 September 2010.

98. "The Struggle of the Champions," *The Economist*, 8 January 2005, 59.

99. David Barboza, "Name Goods in China but Brand X Elsewhere," *New York Times*, 29 June 2005.

100. David Barboza, "Some Assembly Needed: China as Asia's Factory," *New York Times*, 9 February 2006, C1.

101. Roberts, "China's Power Brands."

102. Gerry Khermouch, "Breaking into the Name Game," *BusinessWeek*, 7 April 2003, 54.

103. Roberts, "China's Power Brands."

Closing Observations

Learning Objectives

After reading this chapter, you should be able to

1. Understand the six future brand imperatives.
2. Identify the ten criteria for the brand report card.
3. Outline the seven deadly sins of brand management.

Strategic brand management needs to be a well thought out, carefully conducted process, helped by tools such as The Brand Report Card.

Source: Robyn Mackenzie/ Shutterstock

Preview

This final chapter provides some closing observations concerning strategic brand management. First, we'll briefly review the CBBE framework. Next, we highlight managerial guidelines and key themes that emerged in previous chapters and summarize some success factors for branding. Toward that goal, we'll present the brand report card to help brand managers understand and rate their brands' performance on key branding dimensions, as well as the seven deadly sins of brand management. We'll conclude by considering specific applications of branding in different types of industries in Brand Focus 15.0.

STRATEGIC BRAND MANAGEMENT GUIDELINES

Summary of Customer-Based Brand Equity Framework

Strategic brand management includes the design and implementation of marketing programs and activities to build, measure, and manage brand equity. Before we review some guidelines for strategic brand management, let's briefly summarize—one last time!—the customer-based brand equity framework.

The rationale behind the framework is to recognize the importance of the customer in the creation and management of brand equity. As one top marketing executive put it: "Consumers own brands, and your brand is what consumers will permit you to have." Consistent with this view, we defined customer-based brand equity in Chapter 2 as the differential effect that consumers' brand knowledge has on their response to the marketing of that brand. A brand has positive customer-based brand equity if customers react more favorably to a product and the way it is marketed when the brand is identified, than when the product carries a fictitious name or no name.

The basic premise of customer-based brand equity is thus that the power of a brand lies in the minds and hearts of consumers, and what they've experienced, learned, and felt about the brand over time. More formally, we described brand knowledge in Chapter 2 in terms of an associative network memory model, in which the brand is like a node in memory with a variety of different types of associations linked to it. As summarized in Figure 15-1, brand knowledge has two components: brand awareness and brand image.

Brand awareness is related to the strength of the brand node or trace in memory, as reflected by consumers' ability to recall or recognize the brand under different conditions. Brand awareness has depth and breadth. Depth describes the likelihood that consumers can recognize or recall the brand. Breadth describes the variety of purchase and consumption situations in which the brand comes to mind.

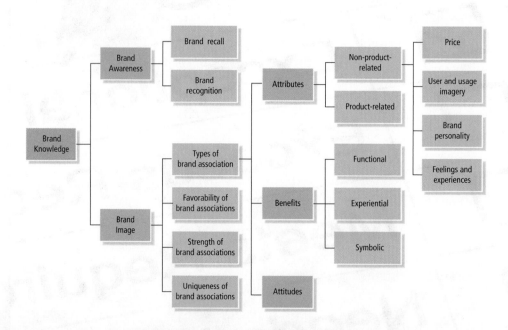

FIGURE 15-1

Summary of
Brand Knowledge

Brand image is consumer perceptions of and preferences for a brand, measured by the various types of brand associations held in memory. Although brand associations come in many forms, we can usefully distinguish between product-related or performance-related versus non-product-related or imagery-related attributes. A useful distinction with benefits is between functional (intrinsic product advantages), symbolic (extrinsic product advantages), or experiential (product consumption advantages) benefits. Some of these attribute and benefit associations may be more rational or cognitive in nature; others more emotional or affective.

Sources of Brand Equity.

Customer-based brand equity occurs when the consumer has a high level of awareness and familiarity with the brand and holds some strong, favorable, and unique brand associations in memory. In some cases, brand awareness alone is sufficient to result in more favorable consumer response, for example, in low-involvement decision settings in which consumers lack motivation or ability and are willing to base their choices merely on familiar brands. In other cases, the strength, favorability, and uniqueness of the brand associations help determine the differential response making up the brand equity. The dimensions of brand associations depend on three factors:

1. *Strength:* The strength of a brand association is a function of both the amount, or quantity, of processing that information initially receives, and the nature, or quality, of the processing. The more deeply a person thinks about brand information and relates it to existing brand knowledge, the stronger the resulting brand associations. The personal relevance of the information and the consistency with which the consumer sees it over time both strengthen the association.

2. *Favorability:* Favorable associations for a brand are those that are desirable to customers, successfully delivered by the product, and conveyed by the supporting marketing program. They can relate to the product or to intangible, non-product-related aspects like usage or user imagery. However, consumers will not deem all brand associations important or view them all favorably, nor will they value them equally across different purchase or consumption situations.

3. *Uniqueness:* To create the differential response that leads to customer-based brand equity, marketers need to associate unique, meaningful points-of-difference to the brand that provide a competitive advantage and a "reason why" consumers should buy it. For other brand associations, however, being comparable or roughly equal in favorability to competing associations might be enough. The brand's associations function as points-of-parity in consumers' minds to establish category membership and negate potential points-of-difference for competitors. In other words, they are designed to provide "no reason why not" to choose the brand.

Figure 15-2 summarizes these broad conceptual guidelines for creating desired brand knowledge structures.

1. **Depth of brand awareness:** Determined by the ease of brand recognition and recall.
2. **Breadth of brand awareness:** Determined by the number of purchase and consumption situations for which the brand comes to mind.
3. **Strong brand associations:** Created by marketing programs that convey relevant information to consumers in a consistent fashion at any one point in time, as well as over time.
4. **Favorable brand associations:** Created when marketing programs effectively deliver product-related and non-product-related benefits that are desired by consumers.
5. **Unique brand associations:** Strong and favorable, create points of difference that distinguish the brand from other brands. Brand associations that are not unique, however, can create valuable points-of-parity to establish necessary category associations or to neutralize competitive points-of-difference.

FIGURE 15-2

Determinants of Desired Brand Knowledge Structures

Outcomes of Brand Equity.   Assuming we can create a positive brand image, with marketing programs that register the brand in memory and link it to strong, favorable, and unique associations, we can realize a number of benefits for the brand, as follows:

- Improved perceptions of product performance
- Greater customer loyalty
- Less vulnerability to competitive marketing actions
- Less vulnerability to marketing crises
- Higher margins
- More inelastic consumer response to price increases
- More elastic consumer response to price decreases
- Greater trade cooperation and support
- Increased marketing communication effectiveness
- Possible licensing opportunities
- Additional brand extension opportunities

Tactical Guidelines

Chapter 1 highlighted the chief ingredients of the CBBE framework in terms of how to build, measure, and manage brand equity. The specific themes and recommendations we developed in subsequent chapters are as follows.

Building Brand Equity.   Tactically, we can build brand equity in three major ways: (1) through the initial choice of the brand elements making up the brand, (2) through marketing activities and the design of the marketing program, and (3) through the leverage of secondary associations that link the brand to other entities like a company, geographic region, other brand, person, or event. Guidelines emerged in Chapters 4–7 for each of these approaches, as summarized in Figures 15-3 and 15-4.

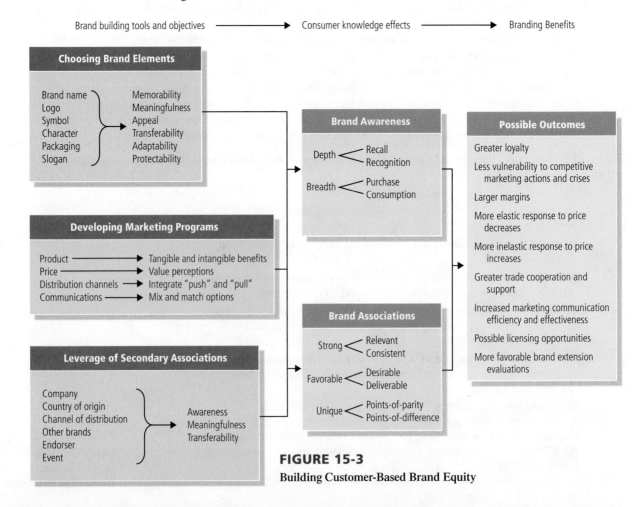

FIGURE 15-3

Building Customer-Based Brand Equity

1. Mix and match brand elements—brand names, logos, symbols, characters, slogans, jingles, and packages—by choosing different brand elements to achieve different objectives and by designing brand elements to be as mutually reinforcing as possible.

2. Ensure a high level of perceived quality and create a rich brand image by linking tangible and intangible product-related and non-product-related associations to the brand.

3. Adopt value-based pricing strategies to set prices and guide discount pricing policies over time that reflect consumers' perceptions of value and willingness to pay a premium.

4. Consider a range of direct and indirect distribution options and blend brand-building push strategies for retailers and other channel members with brand-building pull strategies for consumers.

5. Mix marketing communication options by choosing a broad set of communication options based on their differential ability to affect brand awareness and create, maintain, or strengthen favorable and unique brand associations. Match marketing communication options by ensuring consistency and directly reinforcing some communication options with other communication options.

6. Leverage secondary associations to compensate for otherwise missing dimensions of the marketing program by linking the brand to other entities such as companies, channels of distribution, other brands, characters, spokespeople or other endorsers, or events that reinforce and augment the brand image.

FIGURE 15-4
Guidelines for Building Brand Equity

Themes.   A dominant theme across many of these different ways to build brand equity is the importance of complementarity and consistency. Ensuring ***complementarity*** means choosing different brand elements and supporting marketing activities so that the potential contribution to brand equity of one compensates for the shortcomings of others. For example, some brand elements may primarily enhance awareness through a memorable brand logo, whereas others may facilitate the linkage of brand associations with a meaningful brand name or a clever slogan. Similarly, an ad campaign might create a certain point-of-difference association, whereas a retail promotion creates a vital point-of-parity association. Finally, we can link certain other entities to the brand to leverage secondary associations, provide other sources of brand equity, or further reinforce existing associations.

Thus, it is important to put into place a varied set of brand elements and marketing activities and programs in order to create the desired level of awareness and type of image that leads to brand equity. At the same time, a high degree of ***consistency*** across these elements helps create the highest level of awareness and the strongest and most favorable associations possible. Consistency ensures that diverse brand and marketing mix elements share a common core meaning, perhaps by conveying the same information, such as a benefit association that is reinforced by a highly integrated, well-branded marketing communications program.

Measuring Brand Equity.   We can gauge brand equity indirectly by measuring its potential sources, and directly by measuring its possible outcomes. This means measuring aspects of brand awareness and brand image leading to the differential customer response that creates brand equity: breadth and depth of brand awareness; the strength, favorability, and uniqueness of brand associations; the valence of brand responses; and the nature of brand relationships. Measuring outcomes requires us to estimate the various benefits from creating these sources of brand equity. The brand value chain depicts this relationship more broadly by considering how marketing activity affects these sources of brand equity, and how the resulting outcomes influence the investment community, as well as how various filters or multipliers intervene between the stages.

Marketers need to properly design and implement a ***brand equity measurement system***, a set of research procedures designed to provide timely, accurate, and actionable information for

1. Formalize the firm's view of brand equity into a document, the brand equity charter, that provides relevant branding guidelines to marketing managers.
2. Conduct brand inventories to profile how all of the products sold by a company are branded and marketed and conduct brand exploratories to understand what consumers think and feel about a brand as part of periodic brand audits to assess the health of brands, understand their sources of brand equity, and suggest ways to improve and leverage that equity.
3. Conduct consumer tracking studies on a routine basis to provide current information as to how brands are performing with respect to the key sources and outcomes of brand equity as identified by the brand audit.
4. Assemble results of tracking survey and other relevant outcome measures into a brand equity report to be distributed on a regular basis to provide descriptive information as to what is happening with a brand as well as diagnostic information as to why it is happening.
5. Establish a person or department to oversee the implementation of the brand equity charter and brand equity reports to make sure that, as much as possible, product and marketing actions across divisions and geographic boundaries are done in a way that reflects the spirit of the charter and the substance of the report so as to maximize the long-term equity of the brand.

FIGURE 15-5

Guidelines for Measuring Brand Equity

marketers about their brands. Implementing a brand equity measurement system has three steps: (1) conducting brand audits, (2) designing brand tracking studies, and (3) establishing a brand equity management system.

Guidelines for each of these areas are summarized in Figure 15-5.

Themes. The dominant theme in measuring brand equity is the need to employ a full complement of research techniques and processes that capture as much as possible the richness and complexity of brand equity. We need multiple techniques and measures to tap into all the various sources and outcomes of brand equity, to help interpret brand equity research, and to ensure that we get actionable information at the right time.

Managing Brand Equity. Finally, managing brand equity requires taking a broad, long-term perspective of brands. A broad view of brand equity is critically important, especially when firms are selling multiple products and brands in multiple markets. Here, brand hierarchies must define common and distinct brand elements among various nested products. New product and brand extension strategies also must ensure that we have optimal brand and product portfolios. Finally, we need to manage these brands and products effectively over geographic boundaries and target market segments by creating brand awareness and a positive brand image in each market in which the brand is sold.

We need a long-term view of brand equity because changes in current marketing programs and activities and in the marketing environment can affect consumers' brand knowledge structures and thus their response to future marketing programs and activities. Managing brands over time requires reinforcing the brand meaning and adjusting the branding program as needed. For brands whose equity has eroded over time, we rely on a number of revitalization strategies.

Figures 15-6 and 15-7 highlight some important guidelines for managing brand equity.

Themes. The dominant themes in managing brand equity are the importance of maintaining balance in marketing activities and of making moderate levels of change in the marketing program over time. Without some modifications of the marketing program, a brand runs the risk of becoming obsolete or irrelevant to consumers. At the same time, dramatic shifts back and forth in brand strategies can confuse or alienate consumers. Thus, a consistent thread of meaning—which consumers can recognize—should run through the marketing program and reflect the key sources of equity for the brand and its core brand associations.

1. Define Brand Hierarchy

    A. *Principle of Simplicity:* Employ as few levels as possible.

    B. *Principle of Clarity:* Logic and relationship of all brand elements employed must be obvious and transparent.

    C. *Principle of Relevance:* Create abstract associations relevant to as many products as possible.

    D. *Principle of Differentiation:* Differentiate individual products and brands.

    E. *Principle of Growth:* Investments in market penetration or expansion vs. product development should be made according to ROI opportunities.

    F. *Principle of Survival:* Brand extensions must achieve brand equity in their categories.

    G. *Principle of Synergy:* Brand extensions should enhance the equity of the parent brand.

    H. *Principle of Prominence:* Adjust prominence to affect perceptions of product distance.

    I. *Principle of Commonality:* Link common products through shared brand elements.

2. Define Brand–Product Matrix

    A. *Brand Extensions:* Establish new equity and enhance existing equity.

    B. *Brand Portfolio:* Maximize coverage and minimize overlap.

3. Enhance Brand Equity over Time

    A. *Brand Reinforcement:* Innovation in product design, manufacturing, and merchandising. Relevance in user and usage imagery.

    B. *Brand Revitalization:* "Back to basics" strategy. "Reinvention" strategy.

4. Establish Brand Equity over Market Segments

    A. *Identify Differences in Consumer Behavior:* How they purchase and use products. What they know and feel about different brands.

    B. *Adjust Branding Program:* Choice of brand elements. Nature of supporting marketing program. Leverage of secondary association.

FIGURE 15-6

Managing Customer-Based Brand Equity

1. Define the brand hierarchy in terms of the number of levels to use and the relative prominence that brands at different levels will receive when combined to brand any one product.

2. Create brand associations relevant to as many brands nested at the level below in the hierarchy as possible but sharply differentiate brands at the same level of the hierarchy.

3. Introduce brand extensions that complement the product mix of the firm, leverage parent brand associations, and enhance parent brand equity.

4. Clearly establish the roles of brands in the brand portfolio, adding, deleting, and modifying brands as necessary.

5. Reinforce brand equity over time through marketing actions that consistently convey the meaning of the brand in terms of what products the brand represents, what benefits it supplies, what needs it satisfies, and why it is superior to competitive brands.

6. Enhance brand equity over time through innovation in product design, manufacturing, and merchandising and continued relevance in user and usage imagery.

7. Identify differences in consumer behavior in different market segments and adjust the branding program accordingly on a cost-benefit basis.

FIGURE 15-7

Guidelines for Managing Brand Equity

WHAT MAKES A STRONG BRAND?

To create a strong brand and maximize brand equity, marketing managers must:

- Understand brand meaning and market appropriate products and services in an appropriate manner.
- Properly position the brand.
- Provide superior delivery of desired benefits.
- Employ a full range of complementary brand elements, supporting marketing activities, and secondary associations.
- Embrace integrated marketing communications and communicate with a consistent voice.
- Measure consumer perceptions of value and develop a pricing strategy accordingly.
- Establish credibility and appropriate brand personality and imagery.
- Maintain innovation and relevance for the brand.
- Strategically design and implement a brand architecture strategy.
- Implement a brand equity management system to ensure that marketing actions properly reflect the brand equity concept.

Branding Brief 15-1 provides more detail on these requirements for successful brand management in the form of the brand report card.[1]

On the flip side of the coin, what common branding mistakes prevent firms from creating strong, powerful brands? The seven deadly sins of brand management include the following (see Figure 15-8):[2]

1. *Failure to fully understand the meaning of the brand:* Given that consumers "own" brands, it is critical to understand what they think and feel about them and then plan and implement marketing programs accordingly. Too often, managers convince themselves of the validity of marketing actions—for example, a new brand extension, ad campaign, or price hike—based on a mistaken belief about what consumers know or what marketers would like them to know about the brand. Managers often ignore the full range of associations—both tangible and intangible—that may characterize the brand.
2. *Failure to live up to the brand promise:* A brand should be a promise and a commitment to consumers, but too often that promise is broken. A common mistake is to set brand expectations too high and then fail to live up to them in the marketing program. By overpromising and not delivering, a firm is worse off in many ways than if it had not set expectations at all.
3. *Failure to adequately support the brand:* Creating and maintaining brand knowledge structures requires marketing investments. Too often, managers want to get something for nothing by building brand equity without providing proper marketing support or, once brand equity has been built, by expecting the brand to remain strong despite the lack of further investments.
4. *Failure to be patient with the brand:* Brand equity must be carefully and patiently built from the ground up. A firm foundation requires that consumers have the proper depth and breadth of awareness and strong, favorable, and unique associations in memory. Managers should avoid taking shortcuts that bypass more basic branding considerations—such as achieving the necessary level of brand awareness—to concentrate on flashier aspects of brand building related to its image.

> 1. Failure to fully understand the meaning of the brand
> 2. Failure to live up to the brand promise
> 3. Failure to adequately support the brand
> 4. Failure to be patient with the brand
> 5. Failure to adequately control the brand
> 6. Failure to properly balance consistency and change with the brand
> 7. Failure to understand the complexity of brand equity measurement and management

FIGURE 15-8

Seven Deadly Sins of
Brand Management

BRANDING BRIEF 15-1

The Brand Report Card

The brand report card can reveal how well you are managing your brand. Rate your brand on a scale of 1 to 10 (1 = extremely poor; 10 = extremely good) for each of the characteristics below. Create a similar report card for your major competitors. Compare and contrast the results with all the relevant participants in the management of your brand. Doing so should help you identify where you excel, pinpoint areas that need improvement, and learn more about how your particular brand is configured. Be brutally honest in answering the questions—approach them as an outsider and from a consumer perspective.

Score

1. _____ **Managers understand what the brand means to consumers.**
   - Have you created detailed, research-driven mental maps of your target customers?
   - Have you attempted to define a brand mantra?
   - Have you outlined customer-driven boundaries for brand extensions and guidelines for marketing programs?

2. _____ **The brand is properly positioned.**
   - Have you established category, competitive, and correlational points-of-parity?
   - Have you established desirable, deliverable, and differentiated points-of-difference?

3. _____ **Customers receive superior delivery of the benefits they value most.**
   - Have you attempted to uncover unmet consumer needs and wants?
   - Do you relentlessly focus on maximizing your customers' product and service experiences?

4. _____ **The brand takes advantage of the full repertoire of branding and marketing activities available to build brand equity.**
   - Have you strategically chosen and designed your brand name, logo, symbol, slogan packaging, signage, and other brand elements to build brand awareness and image?
   - Have you implemented integrated push and pull strategies that target intermediaries and end customers, respectively?

5. _____ **Marketing and communications efforts are seamlessly integrated (or as close to it as humanly possible). The brand communicates with one voice.**
   - Have you considered all the alternative ways to create brand awareness and link brand associations?
   - Have you ensured that common meaning is contained throughout your marketing communication program?

- Have you capitalized on the unique capabilities of each communication option?
- Have you been careful to preserve important brand values in your communications over time?

6. _____ **The brand's pricing strategy is based on consumer perceptions of value.**
   - Have you estimated the added value perceived by customers?
   - Have you optimized price, cost, and quality to meet or exceed consumer expectations?

7. _____ **The brand uses appropriate imagery to support its personality.**
   - Have you established credibility by ensuring that the brand and the people behind it are seen as expert, trustworthy, and likable?
   - Have you established appropriate user and usage imagery?
   - Have you crafted the right brand personality?

8. _____ **The brand is innovative and relevant.**
   - Have you invested in product and marketing improvements that provide improved benefits and better solutions for your customers?
   - Have you stayed up-to-date and in touch with your customers?

9. _____ **For a multiproduct, multibrand company, the brand architecture is strategically sound.**
   - For the brand hierarchy, are associations at the highest levels relevant to as many products as possible at the next lower levels and are brands well differentiated at any one level?
   - For the brand portfolio, do the brands maximize market coverage while minimizing their overlap at the same time?

10. _____ **The company has in place a system to monitor brand equity and performance.**
    - Have you created a brand charter that defines the meaning and equity of the brand and how it should be treated?
    - Do you conduct periodic brand audits to assess the health of your brands and to set strategic direction?
    - Do you conduct routine tracking studies to evaluate current marketing performance?
    - Do you regularly distribute brand equity reports that summarize all brand-relevant research and information to assist marketing decision making?
    - Have you assigned people within the organization the responsibility of monitoring and preserving brand equity?

5. *Failure to adequately control the brand:* All employees of the firm must understand brand equity, and the firm's actions must reflect a broader corporate perspective as well as a more specific product perspective. Firms sometimes make decisions haphazardly, without a true understanding of the current and desired brand equity or recognition of the impact these decisions have on other brands or brand-related activities.

6. *Failure to properly balance consistency and change with the brand:* Managing a brand necessitates striking the delicate, but crucial, balance between maintaining continuity in marketing activities and keeping the product or image of a brand up-to-date. If managers do not make adjustments in their marketing program to reflect changes in the marketing environment, they can be left behind. Or they may make so many changes that the brand becomes a moving target without any meaning to consumers.

7. *Failure to understand the complexity of brand equity measurement and management:* Effective brand management requires discipline, creativity, focus, and the ability to make hundreds of decisions in the best possible manner. Sometimes marketers oversimplify the process and try to equate success in branding with taking one particular action or approach. Brand equity is not optimized as a result.

One of the most skilled brand-builders is Procter & Gamble. Branding Brief 15-2 describes some of the ways it has changed its marketing processes and philosophy in recent years to reflect new marketing realities.

FUTURE BRAND PRIORITIES

Our journey to better understand strategic brand management is about over, but it's worth considering a few final questions. How will branding change in the coming years? What are the biggest branding challenges? What will make a successful "twenty-first-century brand?"

The importance of branding seems unlikely to change for one critical reason: Consumers will continue to value the functions brands provide. In an increasingly complex world, well-managed brands can simplify, communicate, reassure, and provide important meaning to consumers.[3] Brands have survived for centuries because they serve a very fundamental purpose. At their best, they allow consumers to reduce risk and gain greater satisfaction in their lives. Strong brands can make consumers' lives a little—or sometimes even a lot—better. The role and functions of brands are so fundamentally pervasive and valued by consumers, it is difficult to see their *potential* importance diminishing.

However, managing brands to achieve that potential is as challenging as ever.[4] The marketing environment always changes, but the pace of change has greatly accelerated in the past decade. Consumers are increasingly diverse, enlightened, and empowered. Virtually every market has experienced heightened competition as a result of the entrance of global firms, private labels, and megabrands from related categories. Rapidly changing technology has profoundly affected how consumers live and shop and how marketers learn about consumer needs and wants and manage their brands. Finally, serious environmental, community, and social concerns exist all over the world.

As a result, the rules of the branding game have changed.[5] Marketers are rethinking—and sometimes fundamentally altering—their branding policies and practices. Using the principles reflected in the brand report card and avoiding the seven deadly sins of brand management reviewed earlier should help in the pursuit of brand management. Building on prior concepts and examples from the book, this final section highlights six branding imperatives to help managers navigate the challenges of brand management in the years to come, as summarized in Figure 15-9.[6]

1. Fully and Accurately Factor the Consumer into the Branding Equation

One of the most important rules of branding is, "The consumer owns the brand." The power of consumer perceptions and beliefs to make or break brands has been demonstrated time and again in the lab and in the real world. From the New Coke debacle to the modern challenges Detroit automakers face in convincing consumers of the quality of their vehicles, consumer sovereignty rules.

In turn, successful brands create mental structures and knowledge in consumers' minds that cause them to favor the brand. From a managerial perspective, a consumer voice must be incorporated in every branding decision. To illustrate, consider brand architecture decisions. Managers frequently err in naming new products by taking an internal company perspective

1. **Fully and Accurately Factor the Consumer into the Branding Equation**
   Focus on the consumer and recognize what they know and don't know about brands and what they want and don't want from brands. Engage in "participation marketing" in the process.
2. **Go Beyond Product Performance and Rational Benefits**
   Craft well-designed products and services that provide a full set of rational and emotional benefits.
3. **Make the Whole of the Marketing Program Greater than the Sum of the Parts**
   Develop fully integrated channel and communication strategies that optimally blend their strengths and weaknesses.
4. **Understand Where You Can Take a Brand (and How)**
   Design and implement a new product development and brand architecture strategy that maximizes long-term growth across product offerings, customer segments, and geographical markets.
5. **Do the "Right Thing" with Brands**
   Embrace corporate social responsibility and manage brands for the long-run.
6. **Take a Big Picture View of Branding Effects. Know What Is Working (and Why)**
   Justify brand investments and achieve deeper understanding of the power of brands.

FIGURE 15-9

Future Brand Imperatives

and arriving at overly complicated solutions with many different layers and levels of branding. Consumers then try to simplify the branding, or worse, they may move to a competitor with a straightforward, more easily grasped set of offerings. Part of the appeal of Colgate Total has undoubtedly been that its name suggests a very simple solution to navigating the toothpaste aisle, a section of the store consumers often find bewildering.

In naming products and services—and in developing marketing programs and activities to build those brands—managers must fully incorporate a consumer point of view. This requires illuminating consumer research and a sharp marketing mind-set to properly interpret and act on the findings. The best marketers use consumer insights to skillfully manage customers and

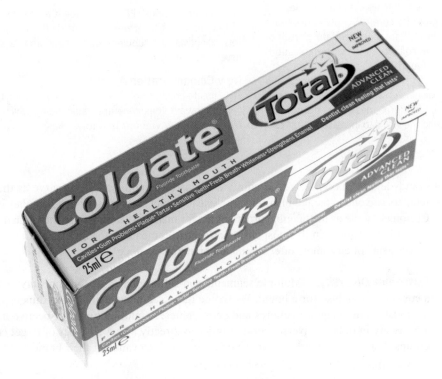

The success of Colgate Total may be due in part to the fact that it offers a simple solution to a surprisingly difficult category in which to buy.

Source: Martin Lee/ Mediablitzimages (uk) Limited/Alamy

Reinvigorating Branding at Procter & Gamble

Procter & Gamble has been a leader in marketing for much of its 160-plus years of existence and has been referred to as "the single greatest marketing company in the world." Already the world's largest consumer packaged-goods company, P&G became even larger with the $57 billion acquisition of Gillette in 2005. After struggling briefly at the turn of the twenty-first century, the company regained its reputation as the flag-bearer of marketing innovation and excellence under the direction of CEO A. G. Lafley, appointed in 2000. During Lafley's decade-long tenure, aided by famed CMO Jim Stengel, P&G boldly reasserted its leadership, in part by following these four key strategies.

Renewed Emphasis on R&D
In the first decade of the twenty-first century, one of the fastest-growing major corporations in revenue and profit was Procter & Gamble. Fueling its growth were successful new products such as Swiffer mop, a battery-powered Crest Spin-Brush toothbrush, Mr. Clean Magic Eraser, and Actonel (a prescription medication for osteoporosis). Many of these new products reflected innovation in what then CEO Lafley called "the core"—core markets, categories, brands, technologies, and capabilities.

To reinforce its innovation, P&G also placed a renewed emphasis on design by appointing its first-ever chief design officer in 2001 and installing a top design officer in each of its global business units. Lafley emphasized the importance of design in combination with innovation, saying, "When we consciously involved design at the front end—such as with Crest Whitestrips . . . and our whole line of Swiffer quick-clean products— we generated more trial, more repurchase, and more sales."

To more effectively grow its core, P&G also adopted a "connect and develop" model that emphasized the pursuit of outside innovation. The firm collaborates with organizations and individuals around the world, searching for proven technologies, packages, and products it can improve, scale up, and market on its own or in partnership with other companies. It has strong relationships with external designers, distributing product development around the world to increase what it calls

Procter & Gamble's new approach to R&D has produced innovative winners like Swiffer.
Source: L. Cohen/WireImage/Getty Images

"consumer sensing." P&G has made it a goal for 50 percent of new products to come from outside its labs—from inventors, scientists, and suppliers whose new-product ideas can be developed in-house.

New Communication Approaches
P&G has been shifting its ad budget away from TV advertising and toward "media-neutral" advertising, which determines media spending without bias toward any particular medium

---

brands and to maximize brand equity *and* customer equity. Brands serve as the "bait" that retailers and other channel intermediaries use to attract customers from whom they extract value. Customers serve as the tangible profit engine for marketers to monetize their brand value.

However, for even the most customer-centric companies, the increasing diversity and "empowerment" of customers offer significant branding challenges.

Customer Diversity. Multiple segments and sub-segments of consumers typically make up a customer franchise for a brand. We define these segments using many dimensions; some of the most challenging are cultures and geographies. A multicultural perspective in branding is a necessity in today's diverse world in order to directly affect all types of target consumers or groups. It also helps marketers focus on the *overall* relevance of their brand and how they can effectively adapt it to all segments in their target market.

based on precedent. In place of big television buys, P&G has pioneered the use of less obtrusive marketing techniques such as Vocalpoint, a word-of-mouth marketing program that enlists 600,000 mothers, among others, to promote its brands by giving positive testimonials, samples, and coupons to friends and neighbors.

P&G still values the power of TV ads, but it also taps into the power of the Internet at the same time. Among the more successful of the 30-second ads (estimated to cost over $2.5 million) to run during the 2010 Super Bowl was one for Old Spice Body Wash that targeted women as well as men. The tongue-in-cheek ad featured rugged ex-NFL football player Isaiah Mustafa as "The Man Your Man Could Smell Like." In one seamless take, Mustafa confidently strikes a variety of romantic poses while passing from a bathroom shower to a boat to a white horse. Uploaded onto YouTube and other social networking sites, the ad was viewed over 10 million additional times. Old Spice's Facebook page included a Web application called "My Perpetual Love," which featured Mustafa offering men the opportunity to be "more like him" by e-mailing and tweeting their sweethearts virtual love notes.

New Research Approaches

P&G conducts approximately 10,000 consumer research projects each year, spending more than $100 million annually. The company significantly changed its research practice after Lafley became CEO by using qualitative observational research techniques to unlock consumer insights instead of relying heavily on quantitative analysis. Lafley referred to ethnographic research as the "best way to create value," stating, "If you want to understand how a lion hunts, don't go to the zoo. Go to the jungle." In keeping with this view, Lafley required that the top 50 managers at P&G visit with consumers either in their homes or on shopping trips at least once per quarter.

New Branding Philosophy

While it did launch successful new brands such as Swiffer, P&G began pursuing a strategy with less inherent risk: leveraging existing assets by investing in well-known "power brands." The company now has 22 brands with more than $1 billion in annual sales and 19 with more than $500 million. In some cases, like Mr. Clean, it went as far as resurrecting a brand and turning it into a power brand with innovative new products. P&G often seeks to leverage its power brands with vertical extensions into higher-margin categories, as it did with Crest Whitestrips and Mr. Clean AutoDry Car Wash System, which retail for about $25 each.

P&G has broadened the meaning of its power brands in more than just a product sense. Lafley's successor Bob McDonald has made "brand purpose" a key component of the company's marketing strategies, noting: "Consumers have a higher expectation of brands and want to know what they are doing for the world. But it has to be authentic with a genuine desire to do it." With Downy fabric softener's "Touch of Comfort" cause program, for example, the company donates 5 cents from purchases of specially marked products to Quilts for Kids, an organization that works with volunteers to make and distribute custom-sewn quilts to children in hospitals.

Sources: A. G. Lafley Interview, "Fast Talk," *Fast Company*, June 2004, 51; Robert Berner, "P&G Has Rivals in a Wringer," *BusinessWeek*, 4 October 2004, 74; Mark Ritson, "P&G's Tactics Point to Marketing's Way Ahead," *Marketing*, 13 April 2005, 19; Bob Garfield, "The Chaos Scenario," *Advertising Age*, 4 April 2005, 1; Nirmalya Kumar, "Kill a Brand, Keep a Customer," *Harvard Business Review* (December 2003): 86.; www.pgconnectdevelop.com; A. G. Lafley and Ram Charan, *The Game Changer: How You Can Drive Revenue and Profit Growth Through Innovation* (New York: Crown Business, 2009); Robert Berner, "How P&G Pampers New Thinking," *BusinessWeek*, 14 April 2008, 73–74; Steve Hamm, "Speed Demons," *BusinessWeek*, 27 March 2006, 69–76; Larry Huston and Nabil Sakkab, "Connect and Develop: Inside Procter & Gamble's New Model for Innovation," *Harvard Business Review* (March 2006): 58–66; Geoff Colvin, "Lafley and Immelt: In Search of Billions," *Fortune*, 11 December 2006, 70–72; Rajat Gupta and Jim Wendler, "Leading Change: An Interview with the CEO of P&G," *McKinsey Quarterly* (July 2005); Dan Sewall, "Old Spice Rolls Out New Ads," *Associated Press*, 1 July 2010; Adam Tschorn, "Old Spice Ad Connects Women to Male Brand with a Wink," *Los Angeles Times*, 6 March 2010; MaryLou Costa, "P&G Marketing Boss Urges Brands to Move Beyond Traditional Advertising," *MarketingWeek*, 24 June 2010; Elaine Wong, "P&G Shows Its Softer Side With Downy Cause Effort," *Brandweek*, 1 February 2010, 6; Elaine Wang, "P&G Throws Values Into Value Equation," *Brandweek*, 9 March 2009, 5.

In recognition of customer diversity and increasing segmentation, marketing pundits have introduced concepts such as permission marketing, one-to-one marketing, and brand journalism (defined below). These concepts all reinforce the fact that any brand franchise has multiple constituents we need to understand and address in the marketplace.

We need to apply these concepts with care, however. Brand journalism, for example, suggests that—just as journalists tell many facets of a story to capture the interests of diverse groups of readers—marketers should communicate different messages to different market segments. However, this concept may overstate the case for highly distinctive branding segmentation and differentiation. For strong brands, the common core of the brand promise is found in virtually all aspects of the marketing program. Ritz-Carlton's brand mantra of "ladies and gentlemen serving ladies and gentlemen" affects how the hotel chain delivers service to *all* its guests as they come into contact with the brand.

Customer Empowerment.   Much has been made of the newly empowered consumer. One of the driving factors behind this trend is the greater transparency that now prevails in the marketing environment. The emergence of the Internet and social media—as well as the expansion and pervasiveness of traditional media—have given consumers the ability, for better or worse, to seek information and arrive at what they feel is "the truth" about products, services, and brands like never before. By merely being observant or proactive, consumers can find out and judge how well a product or service works or what a company is doing (or not doing) to the environment or their local community. Information and opinions can now travel around the world in mere minutes. Marketers must anticipate that any actions they take or claims they make will be scrutinized, deemed truthful or not, and shared with others almost instantaneously.

With this new transparency, consumers can undoubtedly be more actively involved in the fortunes of brands than ever before. But the reality is that only *some of the consumers* want to get involved with *some of the brands* they use and, even then, only *some of the time*. For consumers who do choose to become engaged at a deeper level, marketers must do everything they can to encourage them with social media and other marketing tools. But many consumers will choose *not* to do so, and it is crucially important to understand how to best market a brand given such diversity in consumer propensities, interests, and activity levels.

Moreover, even consumers who choose to become more engaged with a brand have undefined, ambiguous, or even conflicting preferences. They may need guidance and assistance in forming and conveying their preferences to firms. "Participation marketing" may then be a more appropriate concept for marketers to employ, because marketers and consumers need to work together to find out how the firm can best satisfy consumer goals. In participation marketing, consumers and firms freely exchange information to arrive at mutually beneficial solutions.[7] A highly successful premium brand, King Arthur Flour, has created a loyal online brand community by recognizing that baking is an activity consumers want to learn about and discuss with other consumers and company experts.

2. Go Beyond Product Performance and Rational Benefits

At the heart of a great brand is a great product or service. This is even more true in today's highly transparent world. Many firms make the design aspects of products and services an increasingly crucial component of their value proposition, including adept marketers such as Apple, Nike, Ritz Carlton, Singapore Airlines, and Samsung. Developing better-designed products and services, however, requires a clear, comprehensive, up-to-date understanding of consumers and how they purchase and use products and services and think and feel about brands.

King Arthur Flour has built a loyal online brand community among consumers highly involved with baking.

Source: Courtesy of King Arthur Flour

Procter & Gamble revamped the marketing of Pampers after it was repositioned as "caring for baby's development."
Source: AP Photo/Amy Sancetta

Product design encompasses not only how a product works, but also how it looks, feels, and even sounds and smells. Similarly, service design is a function of all sensory aspects that consumers encounter and experience with a brand. Designing products and services that can more efficiently and effectively deliver the full range of category benefits is still of paramount importance and provides a powerful means to gain competitive advantage. This is true even in many mature categories, as illustrated by Procter & Gamble's recent success with brands such as Tide, Gillette, and Venus.

Great product and service design comes from keen consumer insight and inspired, creative solutions. A well-designed brand offers advantages in product and service performance, and in the imagery that creates significant functional *and* psychological benefits. Emotional benefits will be most impactful, in particular, when they are directly linked to a functional benefit.

Consider Procter & Gamble's successful repositioning of its Pampers brand. The disposable diaper had been positioned for years on the basis of dryness and absorbency via classic product comparison advertising. As a result of insights gained from consumer research, the company leveraged those functional product benefits to create a powerful emotional benefit. It based the new Pampers positioning on consumers' beliefs that: (1) a dry baby sleeps better and (2) a well-rested baby will play and learn more the next day. In other words, to parents, the functional benefit "dryness" leads directly to the emotional benefit of "caring for your baby." The new positioning thus celebrated Pampers as "caring for baby's development"—the emotional payoff from the brand's rational product benefits.

Design considerations will increasingly drive the innovation pipeline. Competitive advantages and brand strength will come from having better-designed products and services than competitors, providing a wider range of compelling consumer benefits as a result.

3. Make the Whole of the Marketing Program Greater Than the Sum of the Parts

The diversity of means to communicate about and sell products and services to consumers has grown exponentially in recent years. Major shifts in media viewing habits have emerged due to a number of factors: the fragmentation of TV viewership; the growing use of DVRs, video gaming, and Internet broadband; the increasing use of mobile phones; the explosion of online blogs and social communities; and the greater importance of events, experience, and buzz marketing.

These developments have fundamentally affected how companies communicate about their products and services. Firms now have a host of ways to distribute and sell their products online or offline, directly or indirectly. Marketers are embracing different types of personal and mass media and combining online interactive communications, "real world" experiential communications, and traditional mass media communications. They are also merging "push" and "pull" distribution strategies to maximize coverage and impact, selling directly via the mail, the Internet, telephones and cell phones, and company stores, while also selling indirectly via wholesalers and retailers.

The challenge for top brands is assembling the best set of channel and communication options to maximize sales in the short run and brand equity in the long run. The art and science of integrated marketing is to optimally design and implement any one channel or communication activity so that it creates not only *direct* effects, but also *indirect* effects that increase the impact of other channel or communication options. A breathtaking TV ad may change a viewer's opinions of a brand, but it may also make that viewer more likely to visit the brand's Web site or respond more favorably to a later brand promotion.

As a result of the increasingly diverse communications options available to companies today, consumers have different channel and communications histories and, as a result, very different levels of brand knowledge. This creates a challenge—and an opportunity—for the wise brand marketer. Ideally, a channel or communication option or activity would be versatile enough to work effectively regardless of consumer history or past experience. Indeed, one advantage of a well-designed Web site is that, because of its interactivity, it can successfully communicate and sell to consumers regardless of their personal shopping or communications history.

For example, Nike's amazing marketing success is partly due to its combination of a broad range of distribution channels with an extensive online and offline communication program, as relevant to the world's elite athletes looking to excel in their sport as it is to the average person who just wants to incorporate Nike into everyday recreational life.

Social Media.   As more consumers spend more time on the Internet, it is crucial to use online, interactive communications to affect consumers directly at all stages of the consumer decision funnel and thus to reinforce offline marketing efforts. An online, interactive communications programs typically includes some or all of the following: a well-designed Web site (with customer-generated content and feedback); e-mails; banner, rich media, or other forms of electronic ads; search advertising; and social media. Of these, the newest and most challenging component is social media.

Social media programs—encompassing online communities, forums, blogs (including Sugar, Gawker, and others) and a presence on Web sites such as Facebook, Twitter, and YouTube—provide an effective means to creative active engagement and involvement with consumers. By offering the right online information, experiences, and platforms for brands, marketers can help consumers learn from each other about a brand as well as express their brand loyalty and observe that of others. However, engaging and involving consumers brings potential dangers as well, such as subversive behavior by a small group of consumers or undeservedly negative feedback. Undesirable branding effects can occur with or without a social media campaign, of course, although being online and providing a positive point of view may help counterbalance or even overcome them. Adopting a "thick-skin" stance online is imperative, given that a caustic comment or unpleasant review is only one consumer click away and some negativity is to be expected and tolerated.

Fortunately, an increasingly robust and detailed set of online metrics exist by which marketers can track the nature, extent, and valence of public sentiment. By monitoring online buzz and activities in this way, marketers can more effectively assess and determine the proper response to any potentially damaging online or even offline episode. When Accenture was debating what to do with its corporate spokesperson, Tiger Woods, after his sex scandal, the company closely followed the buzz online. An upset and outraged public was an important consideration when the firm decided to drop its long-time endorser.

Accenture closely monitored online buzz to help inform its decision to drop long-time spokesperson Tiger Woods.
Source: JC Salas/Icon SMI CCU/ Newscom

4. Understand Where You Can Take a Brand (and How)

For long-term financial prosperity, the successful launch of new products and services and the entry of existing products and services into new markets and customer segments are of paramount importance. From a branding standpoint, growth requires a well-thought-out and well-implemented brand architecture strategy that clarifies three key issues: (1) the potential of a brand in terms of the breadth of its "market footprint"; (2) the types of product and service extensions that would allow a brand to achieve that potential; and (3) the brand elements, positioning, and images that identify and are associated with all the offerings of a brand in different markets and to different consumers.

Brand Potential. A good brand architecture defines brand "boundaries": what products or services the brand could represent, what benefits it could supply, and what needs it could satisfy. It provides "guardrails" for appropriate—and inappropriate—line and category extensions. It clarifies the meaning and promise of the brand to consumers and helps consumers choose the right version of the product or service for themselves.

Understanding the brand promise and how it should best be translated and adapted to different products and markets is challenging, but critical. Every product or service sharing the brand name should deliver on the unique brand promise. If you can replace the specific brand in any of its marketing with a competitive brand, and its marketing would still essentially make sense and "work" with consumers, then the marketing is probably not aligned sharply enough with the brand promise and meaning.

By adhering to the brand promise and growing the brand carefully through little steps, marketers can cover a lot of ground. For example, as Chapter 11 described, when Crayola

When Crayola redefined itself as "colorful arts and crafts for kids," the boundaries of the brand expanded considerably.

Source: Crayola LLC

transformed its brand from essentially "crayons only" to all kinds of "colorful arts and crafts for kids," a whole new product world opened up. Markers, clay, paint, chalk, and many other new products all helped the brand deliver its promise and achieve its potential in a meaningful way.

Brand Extensions.   The vast majority of new products are extensions, and the vast majority of new products fail. In other words, too many brand extensions fail. Why? They are not creating sufficient relevance and differentiation in their new product or service categories. An increasingly competitive marketplace will be even more unforgiving to poorly positioned and marketed extensions in the years to come. To succeed, marketers must be rigorous and disciplined in analyzing and developing brand extensions.

We've looked at some of the academic research on brand extensions. Based on this and other inputs, Brand Focus 12.0 presented a scorecard with criteria for evaluating a proposed brand extension. The specifications there are intended to offer a starting point; particular items or the weights applied to them can be adjusted to the specific marketing context. The key point is that, by adopting some type of formal model or scorecard, we can apply systematic thinking to judging the merits of a proposed extension and increase its likelihood of success.

Brand Elements.   The third aspect in a brand architecture strategy encompasses the name, look, and other branding elements applied to new products. A key concept here is the proper use of sub-branding. By combining new brand elements with existing parent brand elements, we can use sub-branding effectively to signal the intended similarity or fit of a new extension with its parent brand. Consumers are very literal. For example, putting the parent brand name before a new, individual name makes it more like the parent brand than putting it second. Marriott's Courtyard is seen as much more of a Marriott hotel than Courtyard by Marriott by virtue of having the corporate name first.

A good sub-branding strategy can facilitate access to associations and attitudes to the company or family brand as a whole, while allowing for the creation of new brand beliefs to position the extension in the new category. Moreover, sub-branding can also help protect or shield the parent brand from any negative feedback that might be associated with an extension. In a carefully researched study, the sudden acceleration problems experienced by the Audi 5000 a number of years ago were found to significantly hurt the sales of its sibling Audi 4000, but they had a much less pronounced effect on sales of the Audi Quattro in part because of its more distinctive sub-branding.

To realize the benefits of association, however, sub-branding typically requires significant investments and disciplined and consistent marketing to establish the proper brand meanings with consumers. Without such financial commitments, marketers may be well advised to adopt the simplest brand hierarchy possible, such as using the company or family brand name with product descriptors.[8]

5. Do the "Right Thing" with Brands

Increased media coverage of business has brought greater transparency and awareness of companies' internal and external actions and statements. Many consumers believe companies should help benefit local communities, society as a whole, and the broader natural environment. At the same time, heightened scrutiny from the investment community has caused many companies to adopt an overly myopic short-term planning horizon for their brands. Brand marketers need to address both these marketplace realities.

Cause Marketing. Brand marketers must embrace social responsibility and ethically and morally proper behavior at all times. In particular, they need to find win–win solutions with cause marketing programs and other activities that allow them to enhance the welfare of consumers, society, or the environment while still profitably running their businesses. Effective cause marketing programs can accomplish a number of objectives for a brand: build brand awareness, enhance brand image, establish brand credibility, evoke brand feelings, create a sense of brand community, and elicit brand engagement.

A classic example of a successful cause marketing program is supplied by Tesco, a leading U.K. retailer.[9] Its "Tesco for Schools and Clubs" program dovetails well with its overall corporate brand positioning of "Every Little Bit Helps." Customers receive one voucher for every £10 spent, which they can donate to any school of their choice or any registered amateur club catering for children under the age of 18. In 2009, the company gave away 540,000 items worth £13.4 million. Tesco also gives vouchers for inkjet cartridges that are recycled and old working phones that are donated.

Protecting Brand Equity. Doing the right things with brands sometimes means doing something even simpler and more straight-forward: protecting and respecting the brand promise and meaning to consumers. Pepsi's recent packaging redesigns for Gatorade, Pepsi, and especially Tropicana, for example, were all criticized to varying degrees as not being faithful to the equity of those brands. When Tropicana dropped the familiar straw-in-the-orange image on the front of its packaging, negative public feedback forced the company to revert to its original packaging.

Overexposing, overextending, overmodernizing, overdiscounting—there are many ways to take advantage of a brand. The best and most widely admired marketers treat their brands with understanding and respect and a clear sense of commercial and social purpose. They take their brands on a well-mapped-out journey that allows them to profitably grow while preserving close bonds with consumers and benefits to society as a whole. Disney launched an internal brand mantra of "fun family entertainment" to help employees judge whether any marketing or other action was "on brand." The worry was not that any single decision would be fatal or even damaging to the brand, but that a number of little concessions and compromises would eventually add up to significantly erode the equity of the Disney brand.

The "Tesco for Schools and Clubs" program has been a huge win-win for the U.K. retail supermarket giant, raising millions of pounds for important causes and reinforcing the brand positioning at the same time.
Source: Carolyn Jenkins/ Alamy

6. Take a Big Picture View of Branding Effects. Know What Is Working (and Why)

Justifying Brand Investments.   Increasingly, marketers have had to do more with less in their marketing budgets and persuasively justify all marketing expenditures. One challenge in achieving brand accountability is that brand marketing activities are intended to have long-term, broad, and varied effects. Any particular marketing activity may increase the breadth or depth of brand awareness; establish or strengthen performance-related or imagery-related brand associations; elicit positive judgments or feelings; create stronger ties or bonds with the brand; initiate brand-related actions such as search, word-of-mouth, and purchase; or many or even all the above. And its effects may be enduring as well as short-term.

Marketers must adopt comprehensive, cohesive, and actionable models to help them develop ROI insights and interpretations. As an example, three linked, interlocking models in Chapters 2 and 3 that marketers can use in brand planning, tracking, and measurement are:

1. The *brand positioning model* describes how to establish competitive advantages via points-of-difference (associations unique to the brand that are also strongly held and favorably evaluated by consumers) and points-of-parity (associations shared with other brands that are designed to negate competitors' points-of-difference, overcome perceived vulnerabilities of the brand, or establish category credentials).

2. The *brand resonance model* considers how intense, active loyalty relationships are created with customers. The basic premise is that building a strong brand requires a series of steps as part of a "branding ladder" and a set of logically constructed "brand building blocks." Brand resonance occurs when consumers feels completely "in synch" with the brand. The second level of the model is where the output from the brand positioning model appears, in terms of which points-of-parity and points-of-difference are to be created with which performance and/or imagery associations.

3. The *brand value chain model* describes how to trace the value creation process to better understand the financial impact of marketing expenditures and investments. The model examines four different stages in the value creation process for a brand. It considers how marketing activities affect the customer mind-set—as measured by all the building blocks in the brand resonance model—which, in turn, creates various marketplace outcomes and ultimately shareholder value.

The specific components of these three models are not as important as their purpose and scope. The models can both assist planning and measurement, and they can capture a full range of marketing activities for any type of brand. In particular, by tracing the effects of marketing activities through the customer mind-set, and on to various marketplace outcomes such as price premiums, loyalty, sales, market share and profitability, marketers can gain a clearer picture of how well their marketing is doing and why.

Achieving Deeper Brand Understanding.   Branding is clearly a complex marketing endeavor. To better grasp all its dimensions, we adopt a multidisciplinary view to interpret branding effects and more completely understand brands, the value they have created, and how they should be managed as a result. We can develop marketing guidelines for branding from a variety of different perspectives, including economic, psychological, and sociological.

Fundamentally, marketing should help create or enhance the equity and value of a brand to all its various constituents. The stronger the brand, the more power brand marketers have with distributors and retailers, and the easier it is to implement marketplace programs to capitalize on brand equity. Extracting proper price premiums that reflect the value of the brand—and not over- or underpricing—is one of the most critical financial considerations for branding.

Finding the Branding Sweet Spot

Given their substantial intangible value, brands are likely to remain a top priority for organizations. The branding area continues to receive intense research attention, as researchers tackle old problems and address new challenges in important ways. Successful branding in the twenty-first century requires new areas of emphasis and new skills as described in the preceding six imperatives. We conclude by discussing one broad theme that cuts across all six: achieving balance in managing brands by finding the branding "sweet spot."

Brand Balance.   To find the branding sweet spot, managers must reconcile trade-offs in brand management and strike the balance between simplicity and complexity in all brand decision-making and activity. Trade-offs are pervasive in marketing a brand—short-run sales versus long-run brand equity, global control vs. local customization, retaining vs. acquiring customers, to name just a few.

The art and science of modern brand marketing is to fully understand and creatively address these significant branding trade-offs. To do so, companies have employed a variety of strategies: breakthrough product or service innovations, improved business models, expanded or leveraged resources, enhanced or embellished marketing, perceptual framing to overcome misperceptions, or just sheer creativity and inspiration.

For example, the trade-off between sales-generating and brand-building activities requires that marketing communications affect both the short run (sales) and the long run (brand building). Firms have addressed this in different ways: California's "Got milk?" campaign entertained consumers and sold milk; P&G's Ivory promotional campaign challenged consumers to find one of the few bars that was weighted to sink in the bathtub, reinforcing the key attribute of floating; the BMW film series, *The Hire* developed equity building communications by highlighting BMW performance aspects in short videos created by leading filmmakers.

Another trade-off focuses on points-of-difference and points-of-parity. To be effectively positioned, the brand must have points-of-difference (PODs) where it excels, and at least points-of-parity versus competitors where it may be seen as inferior. Volvo and Quicken approached this challenge by developing unique PODs (safety and ease of use, respectively), as well as parity with competitors on key points (for Volvo, style; for Quicken, performance). When the first Apple computer launched, it was so easy to use the market thought it must not be powerful. Apple reframed that negative perception by redefining the idea of power: power is not what is inside the computer, but what you can do with it.

In developing solutions to achieve balance in branding, it is important: (1) not to oversimplify branding so that all the richness is stripped away but, at the same time; (2) not to overcomplicate branding such that marketers and other employees are overwhelmed by the complexity. The optimal branding approach recognizes that many different aspects of branding matter; the imperatives we've discussed above point the way to the most critical.

New Capabilities for Brand Marketers.   We'll make one final observation, based on the need to better reconcile marketing trade-offs in branding: the talents and abilities of brand managers have necessarily evolved. Marketers require more skills in their toolkits than were necessary only 10 years ago.

Today's brand marketers must know all the usual marketing fundamentals but also embellish those skills in important ways. For example, they must at least have cultural skills to understand the diversity of the new consumer; fluency in working with design techniques and designers; IT and Internet skills to understand Web-related marketing activities; an appreciation of new branding models and formal qualitative and quantitative measurement methods; and creativity to devise holistic solutions. These are challenging requirements, but also very exciting opportunities as marketers adopt higher standards in brand management excellence.

REVIEW

The challenges and complexities of the modern marketplace make efficient and effective marketing an imperative. The businesses that win in the twenty-first century will be those whose marketers successfully build, measure, and manage brand equity. This final chapter reviewed some of the important guidelines put forth in this text to help in that endeavor.

Effective brand management requires consistent application of these guidelines across all aspects of the marketing program. Nevertheless, to some extent, rules are made to be broken, and the guidelines can be only a point of departure in the challenging process of creating a world-class brand. Each branding situation and application is unique and requires careful scrutiny and analysis about how best to apply, or perhaps in some cases ignore, these various recommendations and guidelines. Smart marketers will capitalize on every tool at their disposal—and devise new ones—in their relentless pursuit of brand preeminence.

DISCUSSION QUESTIONS

1. What do you think makes a strong brand? Can you add any criteria to the list provided?
2. Consider the deadly sins of brand management. Do you see anything missing from the list of seven in Figure 15-8?
3. Pick one of the special applications of branding and choose a representative brand within that category. How well do the five guidelines for that category apply? Can you think of others not listed?
4. What do you see as the future of branding? How will the roles of brands change? What different strategies might emerge for building, measuring, and managing brand equity in the coming years? What do you see as the biggest challenges?
5. Consider the trade-offs involved with achieving marketing balance. Can you identify a company that has excelled in achieving balance on various trade-offs?

BRAND FOCUS 15.0

Special Applications

In Chapter 1, we deliberately defined **product** as encompassing not only physical goods but also services, retail stores, people, organizations, places, and ideas. While the themes and guidelines for building, measuring, and managing brand equity that we've presented are appropriate for virtually all types of products, here we'll consider in greater detail some specific issues for some less conventional types of products—online brands, industrial and business-to-business products, high-technology products, services, retailers, and small businesses.

Online

Creating a brand online brings a special set of challenges. Many of the guidelines for business-to-business, high-tech, retailing, and small businesses identified below will apply, but a few others are worth reinforcing (as summarized in Figure 15-10).

Don't forget the brand-building basics. Remember brand-building basics such as establishing points-of-parity (convenience, price, and variety) and points-of-difference (customer service, credibility, and personality). As we noted in earlier chapters, one mistake of many failed dot-com brands was being impatient to build their brands and failing to build from the bottom up.

In research undertaken to understand *online service quality*, defined as the extent to which a Web site facilitates efficient and effective shopping, purchasing, and delivery, one study identified 11 dimensions of perceived e-service quality: access,

ease of navigation, efficiency, flexibility, reliability, personalization, security/privacy, responsiveness, assurance/trust, site aesthetics, and price knowledge.[10] Land's End became a top-selling company online by treating its Internet operations as a digital translation of its successful catalog, ensuring that merchandise was presented properly and excellent customer service prevailed.

Create strong brand identity. Given that consumers aren't physically confronted by brands online as they are in a store, brand awareness and recall are critical. Choosing the best URL and devising an effective search term strategy are therefore critical. Keep the basic brand element criteria in mind, perhaps with greater emphasis on brand recall as an objective (1-800-FLOWERS took its brand directly to the Web). A simple but evocative name can also be useful, like BabyCenter.com, an information and commerce Web site providing content on pregnancy and babies, an interactive community for parents and parents-to-be, and a store featuring thousands of baby products and supplies.

Generate strong consumer pull. An important lesson for online brands was the need to create demand off-line in order to drive consumers online. Online marketers must introduce the best possible integrated marketing communication program, using sampling and other trial devices as well as social media; public relations; sponsorships; and television, radio, and print advertising.

Selectively choose brand partnerships. Brand partnerships that satisfy brand-building and profit criteria can drive traffic, signal credibility, and help enhance image. In Australia, Seniors Club Online, which caters to consumers aged 60-plus with various entertainment and promotional offers, partnered with *Reader's Digest* magazine to offer free issues.[11]

Maximize relationship marketing. Finally, to leverage the advantages of customization and interactivity, marketers must engage in one-to-one, participatory, experiential, and other forms of relationship marketing. Creating a strong online brand community between the consumer and the brand, as well as with other consumers, through blogs, online contests, and social media can help achieve brand resonance. Online brands can offer much potentially relevant customer information; for example,

---

1. Don't forget the brand-building basics.
2. Create strong brand identity.
3. Generate strong consumer pull.
4. Selectively choose brand partnerships.
5. Maximize relationship marketing.

FIGURE 15-10 Additional Guidelines for Online Brands

1. Adopt a corporate or family branding strategy and create a well-defined brand hierarchy.
2. Link non-product-related imagery associations.
3. Employ a full range of marketing communication options.
4. Leverage equity of other companies that are customers.
5. Segment markets carefully and develop tailored branding and marketing programs.

FIGURE 15-11

Additional Guidelines for Industrial Products

Amazon provides professional and customer reviews, purchase circles and overall sales rankings, text samples, and personalized recommendations.

Industrial and Business-to-Business Products

Industrial goods and business-to-business marketing sometimes call for different branding practices.[12] Here are some basic branding guidelines (see Figure 15-11).

Adopt a corporate or family branding strategy and create a well-defined brand hierarchy. Because companies selling industrial goods often carry a large and complex number of product lines and variations, marketers should devise a logical and well-organized brand hierarchy. Given the breadth and complexity of their product mix, companies selling industrial goods—like GE, Hewlett-Packard, IBM, ABB, BASF, and John Deere—are more likely to emphasize corporate or family brands. Thus, a particularly effective branding strategy for industrial goods is to create sub-brands by combining a well-known and respected corporate name with descriptive product modifiers.

Link non-product-related imagery associations. Programs to build brand equity for industrial goods can be different from those for consumer goods because, given the nature of the organizational buying process, product-related associations may play a relatively more important role than non-product-related associations. Industrial brands often emphasize functionality and cost–benefit comparisons. Nevertheless, even non-performance-related associations can be useful for forming other perceptions of the firm, such as prestige or the type of companies that use its products.

Corporate or family brands must convey credibility and possess favorable overall associations. Corporate credibility is often a primary risk reduction heuristic adopted by industrial buyers. For years, one of the key sources of brand equity for IBM was the perception that "you'll never get fired for buying IBM." Once that special cachet faded, the brand found itself in a much more competitive situation. Creating a feeling of security for industrial buyers can thus be an important source of brand equity. Many industrial firms distinguish themselves on the basis of the customer service they provide, in addition to the quality of their products.

Employ a full range of marketing communication options. Another difference between industrial and consumer products is the way they are sold (see Figure 15-12). Industrial marketing communications tend to convey more detailed product information in a more direct or face-to-face manner. Thus, personal selling plays an important role. At the same time, other communication options can enhance awareness or the formation of brand associations. One effective industrial marketing communication approach is to combine direct hard-sell messages with indirect image-related messages that convey who and what the company is all about.

Leverage equity of other companies that are customers. Industrial brands can leverage secondary associations differently;

Media advertising (TV, radio, newspaper, magazines)

Trade journal advertising

Directories

Direct mail

Brochures and sales literature

Audiovisual presentation tapes

Giveaways

Sponsorship or event marketing

Exhibitions, trade shows, and conventions

Publicity or public relations

FIGURE 15-12 Alternative Communication Options: Business-to-Business Market

for example, identifying other companies that are customers for their products or services conveys credibility. The challenge in advertising that fact, however, is ensuring these other companies don't distract from the message about the advertised company and its brands.

Segment customers carefully and develop tailored branding and marketing programs. Finally, as for any brand, understand how different customer segments view products and brands. For industrial goods, different customer segments such as engineers, accountants, and purchasing managers may exist within as well as across organizations and have different associations that serve as sources of brand equity. It may be particularly important to achieve points-of-parity with these different constituencies, so that key points-of-difference can come into play.

Marketing programs must reflect the role of individuals in the buying center, or the process-initiator, influencer, purchaser, user, and so on. Some individuals within the organization may be more concerned with developing a deep relationship with the company and therefore place greater value on trustworthiness and corporate credibility; others may seek merely to make transactions and therefore place greater value on product performance and expertise.

High-Tech Products

One special category of physical goods, in both consumer and industrial markets, is technologically intensive or high-tech products. The distinguishing feature of high-tech products is that they change rapidly over time because of innovations and R&D breakthroughs. Technology isn't limited to computer-related products: it has played an important role in the branding and marketing of products as diverse as razor blades for Gillette and athletic shoes for Nike.

1. Establish brand awareness and a rich brand image.
2. Create corporate credibility associations.
3. Leverage secondary associations of quality.
4. Avoid overbranding products.
5. Selectively introduce new products as new brands and clearly identify the nature of brand extensions.

FIGURE 15-13

Additional Guidelines for High-Tech Products

The short product life cycles for high-tech products have several significant branding implications (see Figure 15-13 for specific guidelines).

Establish brand awareness and a rich brand image. Many high-tech companies have learned the hard way the importance of branding their products and not relying on product specifications alone to drive their sales. It's typically not true that "if you build a great product, they will come." You need well-designed and well-funded marketing programs to create brand awareness and a strong brand image. Non-product-related associations concerning brand personality or other imagery may be important, especially in distinguishing near-parity products.

Create corporate credibility associations. One implication of rapid product turnover is the need to create a corporate or family brand with strong credibility associations. Because of the often complex nature of high-tech products and the continual introduction of new products or modifications of existing products, consumer perceptions of the expertise and trustworthiness of the firm are particularly important. In a high-tech setting, trustworthiness also relates to consumers' perceptions of the firm's longevity and staying power. For technology companies, the president or CEO often is a key component of the brand and performs an important brand-building and communication function, in some cases as an advocate of the technology. Consider the late Steve Jobs, for example.

Leverage secondary associations of quality. Lacking the ability to judge the quality of high-tech products, consumers may use brand reputation as a means to reduce risk. This means secondary associations may better communicate product quality, such as third-party endorsements from top companies, leading consumer magazines, or industry experts. To garner these endorsements, however, products need to achieve demonstrable differences in product performance, suggesting the importance of innovative product development over time.

Avoid overbranding products. One mistake high-tech firms often make is to "overbrand" products by using too many ingredient and endorser brands. In a kind of "NASCAR effect," so many brands and logos are present for all the different product ingredients that the consumer can be overwhelmed or confused, and no individual brand element adds much value.

Selectively introduce new products as new brands, and clearly identify brand extensions. Short product life cycles in high-tech industries make well-designed brand portfolios and hierarchies even more important. With new products continually emerging, it would be prohibitively expensive to brand them with new names in each case. Typically, names for new products include modifiers from existing products—for example, alphabetical (Microsoft Windows XP), numerical (Microsoft Xbox 360), time-based (Microsoft Exchange Server 2010), or other schemes. A new name for a new product signals a major departure that is significantly different from prior versions.

Thus, family brands are an important means of grouping products. Marketers must clearly distinguish individual items or products within those brand families, however, and define brand migration strategies that reflect product introduction strategies and consumer market trends. When high-tech firms continually introduce totally new sub-brands, it grows difficult for consumers to develop product or brand loyalty to any one brand.

Services

We noted in Chapter 1 that the level of sophistication in service branding has greatly increased in recent years, as suggested by the following guidelines (see Figure 15-14).

Maximize service quality by recognizing the myriad ways to affect consumer service perceptions. It is challenging to develop brands for intangible services. Consumers may have difficulty forming their quality evaluations and may therefore base them on considerations other than their own service experience.

Researchers have identified a number of dimensions of service quality:[13]

- *Tangibles:* Physical facilities, equipment, and appearance of personnel
- *Reliability:* Ability to perform the promised service right the first time (standardized facilities and operations)

1. Maximize service quality by recognizing the myriad ways to affect consumer service perceptions.
2. Employ a full range of brand elements to enhance brand recall and signal more tangible aspects of the brand.
3. Create and communicate strong organizational associations.
4. Design corporate communication programs that augment consumers' service encounters and experiences.
5. Establish a brand hierarchy by creating distinct family brands or individual brands as well as meaningful ingredient brands.

FIGURE 15-14

Additional Guidelines for Services

- *Responsiveness:* Willingness to help customers and provide customer service
- *Competence:* Knowledge and skill of employees
- *Trustworthiness:* Believability and honesty (ability to convey trust and confidence)
- *Empathy:* Caring, individualized attention
- *Courtesy:* Friendliness of customer contact
- *Communication:* Keeping customers informed in language they can understand and listening to what they say

Thus, service quality perceptions depend on a number of specific associations that vary in how directly they relate to the actual service experience.[14]

Employ a full range of brand elements to enhance brand recall and signal more tangible aspects of the brand. Because consumers often make service decisions away from the actual service location itself (say, at home or at work), brand recall, preferably aided by an easy-to-remember and easy-to-pronounce brand name, becomes critically important. Product packaging is not really relevant, although the physical facilities of the service provider—primary and secondary signage, environmental design and reception area, apparel, collateral material—serve as external "packaging" for the service.

Other brand elements—logos, symbols, characters, and slogans—must pick up the slack and complement the brand name to build awareness and image. These elements can help make the service and some of its key benefits more tangible—for example, the "friendly skies" of United, the "good hands" of Allstate, and the "bullish" nature of Merrill Lynch. All aspects of the service delivery process can be branded, which is why Allied Moving Lines is concerned about the appearance of its drivers and laborers, why UPS has developed such strong equity with the brown color of its trucks, and why Doubletree hotels offer warm, fresh-baked cookies to symbolize the company's caring and friendliness.

Create and communicate strong organizational associations. Organizational associations are particularly important in creating perceptions of service quality. Relevant associations are company credibility and the perceived expertise, trustworthiness, and likability of the people who make up the organization and provide the service.

Design communication programs that augment consumers' service encounters and experiences. Service firms must design marketing communications so consumers learn more about the brand than what they glean from service encounters alone. Advertising, direct mail, and online communications are particularly effective at helping develop the brand personality.

The communication programs should be fully integrated and evolve over time. Citigroup walked away from a strong credibility position for its retail brand when it dropped its "Citi Never Sleeps" ad campaign, although it later returned to it during some tough economic times.

Establish a brand hierarchy by creating distinct family brands or individual brands as well as meaningful ingredient brands. Finally, services also must consider developing a brand hierarchy and brand portfolio that allow them to position and target different market segments on the basis of price and quality. Such vertical extensions often require sub-branding strategies that combine the corporate name with an individual brand name or modifier. Delta Airlines brands its business class service as Business Elite, its frequent flier program as SkyMiles, and its short-haul East Coast flights as Delta Shuttle. Hilton Hotel introduced Hilton Garden Inns to target budget-conscious business travelers and compete with the popular Courtyard by Marriott chain.

Retailers

Chapters 5 and 7 reviewed how retailers and other channel intermediaries can affect the brand equity of the products they sell, as well as creating their own brand equity, by establishing awareness and associations to their product assortment (breadth and depth), pricing and credit policy, and quality of service. Walmart has made itself a top U.S. retail brand by becoming the low-price, high-value provider of a host of everyday consumer products. Following are several guidelines relevant for building brand equity for a retailer (see Figure 15-15).

Create a brand hierarchy by branding the store as a whole, as well as individual departments, classes of service, or any other noteworthy aspects of the retail service or shopping experience. Establishing a brand hierarchy helps create synergies in brand development, including for retailers. Walmart introduced Sam's Club to tap into the growing discount or warehouse retail market. Similarly, individual departments can take on unique sets of associations that appeal to a particular target market. Nordstrom has a number of clothing departments, each designed with distinct images and positions, such as t.b.d. for the latest women's trends, BP for teen girls, and Encore for plus-size women. The retailer may brand these departments or even use them as "ingredient brands," designed and supported by a national manufacturer (like Polo shops in major department stores, which sell only that Ralph Lauren brand).

Enhance manufacturer's brand equity. Retailers should exploit as much as possible the brand equity of the manufacturer brands they sell, by communicating and demonstrating their points-of-difference and other strong, favorable, and unique

1. Create a brand hierarchy by branding the store as a whole, as well as individual departments, classes of service, or any other aspects of the retail service or shopping experience.
2. Enhance manufacturers' brand equity by communicating and demonstrating their points-of-difference and other strong, favorable, and unique brand associations.
3. Establish brand equity at all levels of the brand hierarchy by offering added value in the selection, purchase, or delivery of product offerings.
4. Create multichannel shopping experiences.
5. Avoid overbranding.

FIGURE 15-15

Additional Guidelines for Retailers

1. Emphasize building one or two strong brands.
2. Focus the marketing program on one or two key associations.
3. Employ a well-integrated set of brand elements that enhances both brand awareness and brand image.
4. Design creative brand-building push campaigns and consumer-involving pull campaigns that capture attention and generate demand.
5. Leverage as many secondary associations as possible.

FIGURE 15-16

Additional Guidelines for Small Business

brand associations. By cooperating with and perhaps even enhancing manufacturers' push strategies, retailers should be able to sell products at higher prices and margins.

Establish brand equity at all levels of the brand hierarchy by offering added value in the selection, purchase, or delivery of product offerings. Retailers must create their own strong, favorable, and unique associations that go beyond the products they sell. Victoria's Secret has gained popularity as a provider of stylish feminine clothing. Costco has created a strong discount association. To communicate these broader associations, image campaigns often focus on the advantages to consumers of shopping at and buying from the stores in general, rather than on promotions for specific sale items. For example, Ace Hardware advertises itself as the helpful hardware place.

Create multichannel shopping experiences. Retailers are selling their wares in a variety of channels, such as physical stores, catalogs, and online Web sites. Office Depot recognized the importance of supplementing its 800-plus stores with a strong online and catalog presence. By offering service and convenience—and by not cutting its prices—Office Depot has been able to maintain its market leadership. Regardless of the channel, consumers must have rewarding shopping experiences in searching, choosing, paying for, and receiving products. In some case, these experiences may turn out to be valuable points-of-difference, or at least necessary points-of-parity, with respect to competitors.

Avoid overbranding. Finally, if a retailer is selling its own private labels, it is important not to employ too many brands. Retailers are particularly susceptible to "bottom-up branding," in which each department creates its own set of brands. Nordstrom found itself supporting scores of various brands across its different departments, sometimes with little connection among them. Recall from Chapter 5 that one advantage of store brands, however, is that they often represent associations that transfer across categories. The more an abstract association like value or fashionability is desirable and deliverable across categories, the more likely that the marketer can gain efficiencies by concentrating on a few major brands.

Small Businesses

Building brands is a challenge for small businesses because of their limited resources and budgets. They usually do not have the luxury of making mistakes and must design and implement marketing programs much more carefully.[15] Nevertheless, many entrepreneurs have built their brands into powerhouses essentially from scratch.

Online footwear retailer Zappos, founded by Tony Hsieh, has become a top brand in a little over a decade because of its relentless customer focus and strong corporate culture.

With free shipping and returns, 24/7 customer service, and fast turnaround on a wide selection of 200,000 styles of shoes from 1,200 makers, Zappos finds that three-fourths of its purchases during any one day are from repeat customers. Bought by Amazon in 2009 for a reported $850 million but still run separately, the company now also sells clothing, handbags, and accessories.[16]

Because there are usually limited resources behind a small-business brand, marketing focus and consistency are critically important. Creativity is also paramount for finding new ways to market ideas about products to consumers. Figure 15-16 displays some specific branding guidelines for small businesses.

Emphasize building one or two strong brands. Given fewer resources, strategically it may be necessary to emphasize building one or two strong brands. A corporate branding strategy can be an efficient means to build brand equity, although the focus may just be on a major family brand. For example, Intuit concentrated its marketing efforts on building the Quicken brand name of software.

Focus the marketing program on one or two key associations. Small businesses often must rely on only one or two key associations as points-of-difference, consistently reinforcing them across the marketing program and over time. Former Navy SEAL Alden Mills created the Perfect Pushup, adding rotation to the classic U-shaped push-up stands to provide more natural movement and engage more muscles while going easy on the joints. Sales-generating print ads, direct-response TV ads, and a Web site hammered home the founder's exemplary Navy SEAL credentials and the significant fitness benefits of the product's unique design.[17]

Employ a well-integrated set of brand elements. Tactically, it is important for small businesses to maximize the contribution of each of the three main ways to build brand equity. First, a distinctive, well-integrated set of brand elements will enhance both brand awareness and brand image, as suggested by Smartfood popcorn. The company introduced its first product without any advertising, using a unique package that served as a strong visual symbol on the shelf and an extensive sampling program that encouraged trial. Proper names or family names that often characterize small businesses can provide distinctiveness, but if they lack pronounceability, meaningfulness, memorability, and other branding considerations, founders should explore other brand names and brand elements.

Design creative brand-building push campaigns and consumer-involving pull campaigns that capture attention and generate demand. Small businesses must design creative push and pull programs that capture the attention of consumers and other channel members alike. Clearly, this is a sizable challenge on a limited budget. Unfortunately, without a strong pull campaign creating product interest, retailers may not feel enough motivation to stock and support the brand. Conversely, without a strong push campaign that convinces retailers of the merits of the product, the brand may fail to achieve adequate support or even be stocked at all. Thus, creative and cost-effective push and pull marketing programs must increase the visibility of the brand and get both consumers and retailers talking about it.

Because small businesses often must rely on word-of-mouth to create strong, favorable, and unique brand associations, public relations and low-cost promotions and sponsorship can be inexpensive means to enhance brand awareness and brand image. Noah Alper, cofounder of Noah's Bagels, reached out to the Jewish community and transplanted New Yorkers in Northern California through well-publicized events and appearances that promoted the "authentic" nature of the bagel chain. Marketers of the PowerBar, a nutrient-rich, low-fat energy bar,

used selective sponsorship of top marathon runners, cyclists, and tennis players and events like the Boston Marathon to raise awareness and improve image. Selective distribution that targets opinion leaders can also be a cost-effective means to implement a push strategy. Perrier bottled water and Paul Mitchell and Nexus shampoo were initially introduced to a carefully selected set of outlets before broadening distribution.

Leverage as many secondary associations as possible. Finally, another way for small businesses to build brand equity is to leverage as many secondary associations as possible. Consider any entity with potentially relevant associations— a highly regarded location, a well-known set of customers or any prestigious awards—especially those that help signal quality or credibility. Along those lines, to make the company appear "bigger" than it really is, a well-designed Web site can be invaluable.

Notes

1. Based on Kevin Lane Keller, "The Brand Report Card," *Harvard Business Review* (January/February 2000): 147–157.
2. Based on Kevin Lane Keller, "The Brand Report Card."
3. Allen P. Adamson, *Brand Simple* (New York: Palgrave Macmillan, 2006); Francis J. III Kelly and Barry Silverstein, *The Breakaway Brand* (New York: McGraw-Hill, 2005).
4. John Gerzema and Ed Lebar, *The Brand Bubble* (New York: Jossey-Bass, 2008).
5. For some practical tools, see Mark Sherrington, *Added Value: The Alchemy of Brand-Led Growth* (Hampshire, UK: Palgrave Macmillan, 2003); David Taylor, *The Brand Gym*, 2nd ed. (Chichester, UK: John Wiley & Sons, 2010).
6. For some in-depth reviews, see Tim Calkins and Alice M. Tybout, *Kellogg on Branding* (New York: John Wiley & Sons, 2001); Rita Clifton and John Simmon, eds., *The Economist on Branding*, 2nd ed. (New York: Bloomberg Press, 2009); Barbara Loken, Rohini Ahluwalia, and Michael J. Houston, eds., *Brands and Brand Management: Contemporary Research Perspectives* (New York: Taylor & Francis, 2010).
7. For some provocative discussion, see Deborah J. Macinnis, C. Whan Park, and Joseph R. Priester, eds., *Handbook of Brand Relationships* (Armonk, NY: M. E. Sharpe, 2009).
8. Mary Jo Hatch and Majken Schultz, *Taking Brand Initiative* (San Francisco: Jossey-Bass, 2008).
9. www.tescoforschoolsandclubs.co.uk.
10. Valarie A. Zeithaml, Parsu Parasuraman, and Arvind Malhotra, "Understanding e-Service Quality," presentation made at MSI Board of Trustees Meeting, "Marketing Knowledge in the Age of e-Commerce," November 2000; William Boulding, Ajay Kalra, and Richard Staelin, "A Dynamic Process Model of Service Quality: From Expectations to Behavioral Intentions," *Journal of Marketing Research* (February

1993): 7–27; Joel E. Collier and Carol C. Bienstock, "Measuring Service Quality in E-Retailing," *Journal of Service Research* (February 2006): 260–275.
11. http://www.partnershipmarketing.com/readers-digest-partners-with-seniors-club-online/.
12. Kevin Lane Keller and Frederick E. Webster, Jr., "A Roadmap for Branding in Industrial Markets," *Journal of Brand Management* 11 (May 2004): 388–402. See also Mark S. Glynn and Arch G. Woodside, eds., "Business-to-Business Brand Management: Theory, Research, and Executive Case Study Exercises," in *Advances in Business Marketing & Purchasing* series, Vol. 15 (Bingley, UK: Emerald Group Publishing, 2009); Philip Kotler and Waldemar Pfoertsch, *B2B Brand Management* (Berlin, Germany: Springer, 2006).
13. A. Parasuraman, Valarie A. Zeithaml, and Leonard L. Berry, "A Conceptual Model of Service Quality and Its Implications for Future Research," *Journal of Marketing* (Fall 1985): 41–50; Michael K. Brady and J. Joseph Cronin Jr., "Some New Thoughts on Conceptualizing Perceived Service Quality: A Hierarchical Approach," *Journal of Marketing* 65 (July 2001): 34–49.
14. Leonard L. Berry, A. Parasuraman, and Valarie A. Zeithaml, "Ten Lessons for Improving Service Quality," MSI Report 93–104 (Cambridge, MA: Marketing Science Institute, 1993).
15. Adam Morgan, *Eating the Big Fish*, 2nd ed. (Hoboken, NJ: John Wiley & Sons, 2009).
16. Helen Coster, "A Step Ahead," *Forbes*, 2 June 2008, 78–80; Paula Andruss, "Delivering Wow Through Service," *Marketing News*, 15 October 2008, 10; Jeffrey M. O'Brien, Zappos Knows How to Kick It," *Fortune*, 2 February 2009, 55–60; Brian Morrissey, "Amazon to Buy Zappos," *Adweek*, 22 July 2009; Christopher Palmeri, "Now for Sale, the Zappos Culture," *Bloomberg BusinessWeek*, 11 January 2010, 57.
17. "How I Did It: Alden Mills of Perfect Fitness," *Inc.*, September 2009.

Epilogue

When asked how he beat Jimmy Conners in the 1980 Master's tournament after losing to him in their previous 16 matches, Vitas Gerulaitis quipped:

"Nobody…but *nobody*…beats Vitas Gerulaitis 17 times in a row."

I guess you have to draw the line somewhere.

May all your brands be winners.

Index

as confusing/frustrating, 413
consumer evaluation of, 420–424
consumer variety-seeking, 409
creating extension equity, 421–422
defining, 405
dilution effects, 441
dilution of brand meaning, 418
diminish category identification, 416
disadvantages of, 413–419
efficiencies of, 409
examples of, 420
failure of, 415
feedback benefits of, 410–412
future priorities, 536
gaining distribution and trial, 408
image of parent brand, 418
for increased competition, 28
increased market coverage, 411
line extension, 399
managerial assumptions, 420–422
marketing programs and, 408
new brands and, 418–419
new customers to franchise, 411
new product acceptance, 408–409
new products and, 404–407
parent brand equity, 422
parent brand image, 411
perceived risk, 408
promotional expenditures, 409
retailer resistance to, 414
revitalizing the brand, 412
scoring, 442–443
subsequent extensions, 412
vertical brand extensions, 423–424
Brand extensions, evaluation of,
424–430
brand elements, 429–430
consumer factors, 427
corporate/competitive factors, 428
define actual/desired consumer
knowledge, 424–426
evaluate potential of candidate,
426–429
identify extension candidates, 426
leveraging secondary brand associations, 430
marketing programs for launch,
429–430
parent brand equity, 430
Brand feelings, 90–91
brand tracking survey, 274
corporate societal marketing, 396
excitement, 92
fun, 91
security, 92
self-respect, 92
social approval, 92

summary, 92
warmth, 91
Brand functions, 67
Brand growth, 363
Brand hierarchy, 32, 370–380, 525
corporate/company brand level,
370–371
decisions of, 374
design of, 372–380
desired awareness and image,
376–377
family brand level, 371–372
individual brand level, 372
modifier level, 372
number of levels of, 374–376
product descriptor, 372
Brand history, 88
Brand identity, 79, 140. *See also*
Brand elements
Brand image, 44, 48–51, 358, 521
brand extensions and, 408, 411
brand tracking survey, 274
consistency in, 487
corporate societal marketing, 396
favorability of, 50
global brand, 492
improving of, 469–471
strength of, 48–51
uniqueness of, 50–51
Brand imagery, 85–87
Brand inventory, 266–267, 288
rationale for, 267
Brand investments, 538
Brand journalism, 531
Brand judgments, 89–90, 273
brand considerations, 90
brand credibility, 89
brand quality, 89
brand superiority, 90
Brand knowledge, 233–234. *See also*
Secondary brand associations
cause marketing program and, 234
guidelines for, 521
strong brand and, 43–45
summary of, 520
transfer of, 234
Brand knowledge structure (BKS),
347
Brand leadership, 23–24
Brand licensing, 343
Brand line, 359
Brand line campaigns, 388
Brand loyalty, 7, 52, 94, 96
Brand management. *See also* Strategic
brand management
brand priorities, 528–539
changing brand elements, 469–471

consistency and change, 453
customer-centered, 108
establishment of standards, 35
expanding brand awareness,
467–469
fortifying vs. leveraging, 456
improving brand image, 469–471
maintaining consistency, 452–453
managerial assumptions, 420–422
market leaders and failures,
452–453
marketing programs and, 456–462
new/additional usage opportunities,
467–469
product-related performance associations, 457–458
protecting brand equity, 454–455
reinforcing brands, 451–462
repositioning, 470–471
revitalizing brands, 462–471
Rolex example, 287–293
seven deadly sins of, 526–528
Brand mantras
communicate, simplify, inspire, 68
core brand associations, 268
defining and establishing, 65–68
designing of, 66–68
implementing of, 68
Brand marketers, 539
Brand marketing programs
brand elements, 31
integrating/supporting the brand, 31
leveraging secondary associations,
31–32
planning and implementing, 30–31
positioning and, 270–271
standardization vs. customization,
493–499
Brand meaning, 79, 85–87, 410–411,
418
Brand mix, 359
Brand name, 2–3, 119–126
brand associations and, 122–124
brand awareness and, 120–122
differentiated, distinctive, and
unique, 121–122
familiarity and meaningfulness, 121
linguistic characteristics, 123–124
naming guidelines, 120–124
naming mistakes, 124–125
naming procedures, 124–126
pronunciation and spelling of,
120–121
trademark issues of, 144–145
Brand partnerships, 504–505
Brand performance, 32, 83–85, 88–89,
273–274, 457–458